Cognition

seventh edition

Cognition

7e

exploring the science of the mind

Daniel Reisberg

REED COLLEGE

W. W. Norton & Company
New York · London

W. W. Norton & Company has been independent since its founding in 1923, when William Warder Norton and Mary D. Herter Norton first published lectures delivered at the People's Institute, the adult education division of New York City's Cooper Union. The firm soon expanded its program beyond the Institute, publishing books by celebrated academics from America and abroad. By midcentury, the two major pillars of Norton's publishing program—trade books and college texts—were firmly established. In the 1950s, the Norton family transferred control of the company to its employees, and today—with a staff of four hundred and a comparable number of trade, college, and professional titles published each year—W. W. Norton & Company stands as the largest and oldest publishing house owned wholly by its employees.

Editor: Ken Barton
Project Editor: David Bradley
Assistant Editor: Eve Sanoussi
Editorial Assistant: Katie Pak
Manuscript Editor: Alice Vigliani
Managing Editor, College: Marian Johnson
Managing Editor, College Digital Media: Kim Yi
Production Managers: Ashley Horna and Jane Searle
Media Editors: Scott Sugarman and Kaitlin Coats
Associate Media Editor: Victoria Reuter
Assistant Media Editors: Alex Trivilino and Allison Nicole Smith
Marketing Manager: Ashley Sherwood
Design Director: Rubina Yeh
Art Director: Jillian Burr
Designer: Lisa Buckley
Photo Editor: Ted Szczepanski
Photo Researcher: Lynn Gadson
Permissions Manager: Megan Schindel
Composition/Illustrations: GraphicWorld
Manufacturing: LSC Communications—Willard

Permission to use copyrighted material is included in the credits section of this book, which begins on page C1.

Library of Congress Cataloging-in-Publication Data

Names: Reisberg, Daniel.
Title: Cognition : exploring the science of the mind / Daniel Reisberg, Reed
  College.
Description: Seventh Edition. | New York : W. W. Norton & Company, [2018] |
  Revised edition of the author's Cognition, [2016]o | Includes
  bibliographical references and index.
Identifiers: LCCN 2018022174 | **ISBN 9780393665017** (hardcover)
Subjects: LCSH: Cognitive psychology.
Classification: LCC BF201 .R45 2018 | DDC 153—dc23 LC record available at https://lccn.loc.
gov/2018022174

W. W. Norton & Company, Inc., 500 Fifth Avenue, New York, NY 10110
wwnorton.com
W. W. Norton & Company Ltd., 15 Carlisle Street, London W1D 3BS

4 5 6 7 8 9 0

With love
— always —
for the family that
enriches every
aspect of my life.

Brief Contents

Contents

Preface

I was a college sophomore when I took my first course in cognitive psychology. I was excited about the material then, and, many years later, the excitement hasn't faded. Part of the reason lies in the fact that cognitive psychologists are pursuing fabulous questions, questions that have intrigued humanity for thousands of years: Why do we think the things we think? Why do we believe the things we believe? What is "knowledge," and how *secure* (how complete, how accurate) is our knowledge of the world around us?

Other questions asked by cognitive psychologists concern more immediate, personal, issues: How can I help myself to remember more of the material that I'm studying in my classes? Is there some better way to solve the problems I encounter? Why is it that my roommate can study with music on, but I can't?

And sometimes the questions have important consequences for our social or political institutions: If an eyewitness reports what he saw at a crime, should we trust him? If a newspaper raises questions about a candidate's integrity, how will voters react?

Of course, we want more than interesting questions—we also want *answers* to these questions, and this is another reason I find cognitive psychology so exciting. In the last half-century or so, the field has made extraordinary progress on many fronts, providing us with a rich understanding of the nature of memory, the processes of thought, and the content of knowledge. There are many things still to be discovered—that's part of the fun. Even so, we already have a lot to say about all of the questions just posed and many more as well. We can speak to the specific questions and to the general, to the theoretical issues and to the practical. Our research has uncovered principles useful for improving the process of education, and we have made discoveries of considerable importance for the criminal justice system. What I've learned as a cognitive psychologist has changed how I think about my own memory; it's changed how I make decisions; it's changed how I draw conclusions when I'm thinking about events in my life.

On top of all this, I'm also excited about the *connections* that cognitive psychology makes possible. In the academic world, intellectual disciplines are often isolated from one another, sometimes working on closely related problems without even realizing it. In the last decades, though, cognitive psychology has forged rich connections with its neighboring disciplines, and in this book we'll touch on topics in philosophy, neuroscience, law and criminal justice, economics, linguistics, politics, computer science, and medicine. These connections bring obvious benefits, since insights and information can be traded back and forth between the domains. But these connections also highlight the importance of the material we'll be examining, since the connections make it clear that the issues before us are of interest to a wide range of scholars. This provides a strong signal that we're working on questions of considerable power and scope.

I've tried in this text to convey all this excitement. I've done my best to describe the questions being asked within my field, the substantial answers we can provide for these questions, and, finally, some indications of how cognitive psychology is (and has to be) interwoven with other intellectual endeavors.

I've also had other goals in writing this text. In my own teaching, I try to maintain a balance among many different elements: the nuts and bolts of how our science proceeds, the data provided by the science, the practical implications of our research findings, and the theoretical framework that holds all of these pieces together. I've tried to find the same balance in this text. Perhaps most important, though, I try, both in my teaching and throughout this book, to "tell a good story," one that conveys how the various pieces of our field fit together into a coherent package. Of course, I want the evidence for our claims to be in view, so that readers can see how our field tests its hypotheses and why our claims must be taken seriously. But I've also put a strong emphasis on the flow of ideas—how new theories lead to new experiments, and how those experiments can lead to new theory.

The notion of "telling a good story" also emerges in another way: I've always been impressed by the ways in which the different parts of cognitive psychology are interlocked. Our claims about attention, for example, have immediate implications for how we can theorize about memory; our theories of object recognition are linked to our proposals for how knowledge is stored in the mind. Linkages like these are intellectually satisfying, because they ensure that the pieces of the puzzle really do fit together. But, in addition, these linkages make the material within cognitive psychology easier to learn, and easier to remember. Indeed, if I were to emphasize one crucial fact about memory, it would be that memory is best when the memorizer perceives the organization and interconnections within the material being learned. (We'll discuss this point further in Chapter 6.) With an eye on this point, I've therefore made sure to highlight the interconnections among various topics, so that readers can appreciate the beauty of our field and can also be helped in their learning by the orderly nature of our theorizing.

I've tried to help readers in other ways, too. First, I've tried throughout the book to make the prose approachable. I want my audience to gain a sophisticated understanding of the material in this text, but I don't want readers to struggle with the ideas.

Second, I've taken various steps that I hope will foster an "alliance" with readers. My strategy here grows out of the fact that, like most teachers, I value the questions I receive from students and the discussions I have with them. In the classroom, this allows a two-way flow of information that unmistakably improves the educational process. Of course, a two-way flow isn't possible in a textbook, but I've offered what I hope is a good approximation: Often, the questions I hear from students, and the discussions I have with them, focus on the relevance of the course material to students' own lives, or relevance to the world outside of academics. I've tried to capture that dynamic, and to present my answers to these student questions, in the essay at the end of each chapter (I'll say more about these essays in a moment). These essays appear under the banner **Cognitive Psychology and Education**, and—as the label suggests—the essays will help readers understand how the materials covered in that chapter matter for (and might change!) the readers' own learning. In addition, I've written a separate series of essays (available online), titled **Cognitive Psychology and the Law**, to explore how each chapter's materials matter in another arena—the enormously important domain of the justice system. I hope that both types of essays—**Education and Law**—help readers see that all of this material is indeed relevant to their lives, and perhaps as exciting for them as it is for me.

Have I met all of these goals? You, the readers, will need to be the judges of this. I would love to hear from you about what I've done well in the book and what I could have done better; what I've covered (but should have omitted) and what I've left out. I'll do my best to respond to every comment. You can reach me via email (reisberg@reed.edu); I've been delighted to get comments from readers about previous editions, and I hope for more emails with this edition.

An Outline of the Seventh Edition

The book's 14 chapters are designed to cover the major topics within cognitive psychology. The chapters in Part 1 lay the foundation. Chapter 1 provides the conceptual and historical background for the subsequent chapters. In addition, this chapter seeks to convey the extraordinary scope of the field and why, therefore, research on cognition is so important. The chapter also highlights the relationship between theory and evidence in cognitive psychology, and it discusses the logic on which this field is built.

Chapter 2 then offers a brief introduction to the study of the brain. Most of cognitive psychology is concerned with the functions that our brains make possible, and not the brain itself. Nonetheless, our understanding of cognition has certainly been enhanced by the study of the brain, and throughout this book we'll use biological evidence as one means of evaluating our theories. Chapter 2 is designed to make this evidence fully accessible to the reader—by providing a quick survey of the research tools used in studying the brain, an overview of the brain's anatomy, and also an example of how we can use brain evidence as a source of insight into cognitive phenomena.

Part 2 of the book considers the broad issue of how we gain information from the world. Chapter 3 covers visual perception. At the outset, this chapter links to the previous (neuroscience) chapter with descriptions of the eyeball and the basic mechanisms of early visual processing. In this context, the chapter introduces the crucial concept of parallel processing and the prospect of mutual influence among separate neural mechanisms. From this base, the chapter builds toward a discussion of the perceiver's *activity* in shaping and organizing the visual world, and explores this point by discussing the rich topics of perceptual constancy and perceptual illusions.

Chapter 4 discusses how we recognize the objects that surround us. This seems a straightforward matter—what could be easier than recognizing a telephone, or a coffee cup, or the letter *Q*? As we'll see, however, recognition is surprisingly complex, and discussion of this complexity allows me to amplify key themes introduced in earlier chapters: how *active* people are in organizing and interpreting the information they receive from the world; the degree to which people *supplement* the information by relying on prior experience; and the ways in which this knowledge can be built into a *network*.

Chapter 5 then considers what it means to "pay attention." The first half of the chapter is concerned largely with selective attention—cases in which you seek to focus on a target while ignoring distractors. The second half of the chapter is concerned with divided attention ("multi-tasking")—that is, cases in which you seek to focus on more than one target, or more than one task, at the same time. Here, too, we'll see that seemingly simple processes turn out to be more complicated than one might suppose.

Part 3 turns to the broad topic of memory. Chapters 6, 7, and 8 start with a discussion of how information is "entered" into long-term storage, but then turn to the complex interdependence between how information is first learned and how that same information is subsequently retrieved. A recurrent theme in this section is that learning that's effective for one sort of task, one sort of use, may be quite ineffective for other uses. This theme is examined in several contexts, and leads to a discussion of research on unconscious memories—so-called memory without awareness. These chapters also offer a broad assessment of human memory: How accurate are our memories? How complete? How long-lasting? These issues are pursued both with regard to theoretical treatments of memory and also with regard to the practical consequences of memory research, including the application of this research to the assessment, in the courtroom, of eyewitness testimony.

The book's Part 4 is about knowledge. Earlier chapters show over and over that humans are, in many ways, guided in their thinking and experiences by what they already know—that is, the broad pattern of knowledge they bring to each new experience. This invites the questions posed by Chapters 9, 10, and 11: What is knowledge? How is it represented in the mind? Chapter 9 tackles the question of how "concepts," the building blocks of our knowledge, are represented in the mind. Chapters 10 and 11 focus on two special types of knowledge. Chapter 10 examines our knowledge about language; Chapter 11 considers visual knowledge and examines what is known about mental imagery.

The chapters in Part 5 are concerned with the topic of thinking. Chapter 12 examines how each of us draws conclusions from evidence—including cases in which we are trying to be careful and deliberate in our judgments, and also cases of informal judgments of the sort we often make in our everyday lives. The chapter then turns to the question of how we reason from our beliefs—how we check on whether our beliefs are correct, and how we draw conclusions, based on things we already believe. The chapter also considers the practical issue of how errors in thinking can be diminished through education.

Chapter 13 is also about thinking, but with a different perspective: This chapter considers some of the ways people differ from one another in their ability to solve problems, in their creativity, and in their intelligence. The chapter also addresses the often heated, often misunderstood debate about how different groups—especially American Whites and African Americans—might (or might not) differ in their intellectual capacities.

The final chapter in the book does double service. First, it pulls together many of the strands of contemporary research relevant to the topic of consciousness—what consciousness is, and what consciousness is for. In addition, most readers will reach this chapter at the end of a full semester's work, a point at which they are well served by a review of the topics already covered and ill served by the introduction of much new material. Therefore, this chapter draws many of its themes and evidence from previous chapters, and in that fashion it serves as a review of points that appear earlier in the book. Chapter 14 also highlights the fact that we're using these materials to approach some of the greatest questions ever asked about the mind, and, in that way, this chapter should help to convey some of the power of the material we've been discussing throughout the book.

New in the Seventh Edition

What's new in this edition? Every chapter contains new material, in most cases because readers specifically requested the new content! Chapter 1, for example, now includes discussion of how the field of cognitive psychology emerged in the 1950s and 1960s. Chapter 4 includes coverage of recent work on how people differ from one another in their level of face-recognition skill. Chapter 5 discusses what it is that people pay attention to, with a quick summary of research on how men and women differ in what they focus on, and how different cultures seem to differ in what they focus on. Chapter 8 discusses a somewhat controversial and certainly dramatic study showing that college students can be led to a false memory of a time they committed a felony (an armed assault) while in high school; this chapter also now includes coverage of the social nature of remembering. Chapter 10 now discusses the topics of *prosody* and *pragmatics*. Chapter 12 discusses the important difference between "opt-in" and "opt-out" procedures for social policy, and Chapter 14 now includes discussion of (both the myths and the reality of) subliminal perception.

In this edition, I've also added three entirely new features. First, my students are always curious to learn how cognitive psychology research can be applied to issues and concerns that arise in everyday life. I've therefore added a **Cognition Outside the Lab** essay to every chapter. For example, in Chapter 4, in discussing how word recognition proceeds, I've tackled the question of how the choice of font can influence readers (sometimes in good ways and sometimes not). In

Chapter 7, I've written about cryptoplagiarism, a pattern in which you can steal another person's ideas without realizing it!

Second, I have always believed that, as someone teaching cognitive psychology, I need to respect the practical lessons of my field. As one example, research suggests that students' understanding and memory are improved if they pause and reflect on materials they've just heard in a lecture or just read in a book. "What did I just hear? What were the main points? Which bits were new, and which bits had I thought about before?" Guided by that research, I've added **Test Yourself** questions throughout the book. These questions are then echoed at the end of the chapter, with the aim of encouraging readers to do another round of reflection. All these questions are designed to be easy and straightforward—but should, our research tells us, be genuinely helpful for readers.

Third, the topics covered in this book have many implications, and I hope readers will find it both fun and useful to think about some of these implications. On this basis, every chapter also ends with a couple of **Think About It** questions, inviting readers to extend the chapter's lessons into new territory. For example, at the end of Chapter 3, I invite readers to think about how research on *attention* might help us understand what happens in the focused exercise of meditation (including Buddhist meditation). The question at the end of Chapter 7 invites readers to think through how we might explain the eerie sensation of déjà vu. A question at the end of Chapter 8 explores how your memory is worse than a video recorder, and also how it's better than a video recorder.

Other Special Features

In addition, I have (of course) held on to features that were newly added in the previous edition—including an art program that showcases the many points of contact between cognitive psychology and cognitive neuroscience, and the **"What if . . ."** section that launches each chapter. The "What if . . ." material serves several aims. First, the mental capacities described in each chapter (the ability to recognize objects, the ability to pay attention, and so on) are crucial for our day-to-day functioning, and to help readers understand this point, most of the "What if . . ." sections explore what someone's life is like if they *lack* the relevant capacity. Second, the "What if . . ." sections are rooted in concrete, human stories; they talk about specific individuals who lack these capacities. I hope these stories will be inviting and thought-provoking for readers, motivating them to engage the material in a richer way. And, third, most of the "What if . . ." sections involve people who have lost the relevant capacity through some sort of brain damage. These sections therefore provide another avenue through which to highlight the linkage between cognitive psychology and cognitive neuroscience.

This edition also includes explicit coverage of **Research Methods**. As in the previous edition, this material is covered in an appendix, so that it's easily accessible to all readers, but set to the side to accommodate readers (or instructors) who prefer to focus on the book's substantive content. The appendix is divided into separate essays for each chapter, so that the appendix can be used on a chapter-by-chapter basis. This organization will help readers see, for each chapter, how the research described in the chapter unfolds, and it will simultaneously provide a context for each methods essay so that readers can see why the methods are so important.

The appendix is surely no substitute for a research methods course, but nonetheless it's sequenced in a manner that builds toward a broad understanding of how the scientific method plays out in our field. An early essay, for example, works through the question of what a "testable hypothesis" is, and why this is so important; another essay works through the power of random assignment; another discusses how we deal with confounds. In all cases, my hope is that the appendix will guide readers toward a sophisticated understanding of why our research is as it is, and why, therefore, our research is so persuasive.

I have already mentioned the end-of-chapter essays on **Cognitive Psychology and Education**, which show students how cognitive psychology is connected to their own learning. Readers often seek "take-home messages" from the material that will, in a direct way, benefit them. We are, after all, talking about memory, and students obviously are engaged in an endeavor of putting lots of new information—information they're learning in their courses—into their memories. We're talking about attention, and students often struggle with the chore of keeping themselves "on task" and "on target." In light of these points, the end-of-chapter essays build a bridge between the content in the chapter and the concerns that fill students' lives. This will, I hope, make the material more useful for students, and also make it clear just how important an enterprise cognitive psychology is.

There are also essays in the ebook on **Cognitive Psychology and the Law**. Here, I've drawn on my own experience in working with law enforcement and the criminal justice system. In this work, I'm called on to help juries understand how an eyewitness might be certain in his recollection, but *mistaken*. I also work with police officers to help them elicit as much information from a witness as possible, without leading the witness in any way. Based on this experience, the online essays discuss how the material in each chapter might be useful for the legal system. These essays will, I hope, be immediately interesting for readers, and will also make it obvious why it's crucial that the science be done carefully and well—so that we bring only high-quality information into the legal system.

I've also included **Demonstrations** in the ebook to accompany the book's description of key concepts in the field. Many of these demos are miniature versions of experimental procedures, allowing students to see for themselves what these experiments involve, and also allowing them to see just how powerful many of our effects are. Readers who want to run the demos for themselves as they read along certainly can; instructors who want to run the demos within their classrooms (as I sometimes do) are certainly encouraged to do so. Instructors who want to use the demos in discussion sections, aside from the main course, can do that as well. In truth, I suspect that some demos will work better in one of these venues, and that other demos will work better in others; but, in all cases, I hope the Demonstrations help bring the material to life—putting students directly in contact with both our experimental methods and our experimental results.

As in previous editions, this version of *Cognition* also comes with various supplementary materials, some aimed at students, and some aimed at instructors.

For Students

ZAPS Cognition Labs. Every copy of the text comes packaged with free access to ZAPS Cognition Labs, an updated revision of Norton's popular online psychology labs. Crafted specifically to support cognitive psychology courses, this version helps students learn about core psychological phenomena. Each lab (one or two per chapter) begins with a brief introduction that relates the topic to students' lives. Students then engage in a hands-on experience that, for most labs, produces data based on their individual responses. The theories behind the concepts are then explained alongside the data the student has generated. Also, an assessment component lets students confirm that they understand the concepts central to each lab. Finally, this edition of *Cognition* is accompanied by five new ZAPS labs: Encoding Specificity, Mental Rotation 3D, Memory Span, Operation Span, and Selective Attention.

Ebook. Every print copy of the text comes packaged with free access to the ebook. The ebook can also be purchased separately at a fraction of the price of the printed version. The ebook has several advantages over the print text. First, the ebook includes *Demonstrations*—quick, pen-and-paper mini experiments—designed to show students what key experiments involve and how powerful many of the effects are. Second, the ebook includes the *Cognitive Psychology and the Law* essays, described above. In addition, the ebook can be viewed on any device—laptop, tablet, phone, public computer—and will stay synced between devices. The ebook is therefore a perfect solution for students who want to learn in more convenient settings—and pay less for doing so.

For Instructors

All instructor resources for this edition of *Cognition* can be accessed via the "Instructor Resources" tile at the following URL: **https://digital.wwnorton .com/cognition7**.

Interactive Instructor's Guide (IIG). This online repository of teaching assets offers material for every chapter that both veteran and novice instructors of the course will find helpful. Searchable by chapter or asset class, the IIG provides multiple resources for teaching: links to online video clips (selected and annotated by the author), teaching suggestions, and other class activities and exercises. It also includes all of the Education, Law, and Research Methods essays described above, as well as discussion questions to support the Education and Law essays. The demonstrations from the ebook can also be found here. This repository of lecture and teaching materials functions both as a course prep tool and as a means of tracking the latest ideas in teaching the cognitive psychology course.

I'm especially excited about the online video clips. Students love videos and probably spend more time than they should surfing the Internet (and YouTube in particular) for fun clips. As it turns out, though, YouTube contains far more than cute-kittens movies; it also contains intriguing, powerful material directly relevant to the topics in this text. The IIG therefore provides a listing of carefully selected online videos to accompany each of the chapters. (A dozen of these videos are newly added for the seventh edition!) The annotated list describes each clip, and gives information about timing, in ways that should make these videos easy to use in the classroom. I use them in my own teaching, and my students love them. But let me also make a request: I'm sure there are other videos available that I haven't seen yet. I'll therefore be grateful to any readers who help me broaden this set, so that we can make this resource even better.

Test Bank. The test bank features over 900 questions, including multiple-choice and short-answer questions for each chapter. I have personally vetted each question, and all questions have been updated according to Norton's assessment guidelines to make it easy for instructors to construct quizzes and exams that are meaningful and diagnostic. All questions are classified according to learning objective, text section, difficulty, and question type. This Norton test bank is available with ExamView Test Generator software, allowing instructors to create, administer, and manage assessments. The intuitive test-making wizard makes it easy to create customized exams. Other features include the ability to create paper exams with algorithmically generated variables and to export files directly to your LMS.

Lecture PowerPoints. These text-focused PowerPoints follow the chapter outlines, include figures from the text, and feature instructor-only notes.

Art Slides. All the figures, photos, and tables from the text are offered as JPEGs, both separately and embedded in a PowerPoint for each chapter. All text art is enhanced for optimal viewing when projected in large classrooms.

Coursepack (Blackboard, Canvas, Angel, Moodle, and other LMS systems). Available at no cost to professors or students, Norton coursepacks for online, hybrid, or lecture courses are available in a variety of formats. With a simple download from the instructor's website, an adopter can bring high-quality Norton digital media into a new or existing online course (no extra student passwords required), and it's theirs to keep. Instructors can edit assignments at the question level and set up custom grading policies to assess student understanding. In addition to the instructor resources listed above, the coursepack includes additional chapter quizzes, flashcards, chapter outlines, chapter summaries, all of the Education, Law, and Research Methods essays described above, and additional questions on the essays.

Acknowledgments

Finally, let me turn to the happiest of chores—thanking all of those who have contributed to this book. I begin with those who helped with the previous editions: Bob Crowder (Yale University) and Bob Logie (University of Aberdeen) both read the entire text of the first edition, and the book was unmistakably improved by their insights. Other colleagues read, and helped me enormously with, specific chapters: Enriqueta Canseco-Gonzalez (Reed College), Rich Carlson (Pennsylvania State University), Henry Gleitman (University of Pennsylvania), Lila Gleitman (University of Pennsylvania), Peter Graf

(University of British Columbia), John Henderson (Michigan State University), Jim Hoffman (University of Delaware), Frank Keil (Cornell University), Mike McCloskey (Johns Hopkins University), Hal Pashler (UCSD), Steve Pinker (MIT), and Paul Rozin (University of Pennsylvania).

The second edition was markedly strengthened by the input and commentary provided by Martin Conway (University of Bristol), Kathleen Eberhard (Notre Dame University), Howard Egeth (Johns Hopkins University), Bill Gehring (University of Michigan), Steve Palmer (University of California, Berkeley), Henry Roediger (Washington University), and Eldar Shafir (Princeton University).

In the third edition, I was again fortunate to have the advice, criticism, and insights provided by a number of colleagues who, together, made the book better than it otherwise could have been, and I'd like to thank Rich Carlson (Penn State), Richard Catrambone (Georgia Tech), Randall Engle (Georgia Tech), Bill Gehring and Ellen Hamilton (University of Michigan), Nancy Kim (Rochester Institute of Technology), Steve Luck (University of Iowa), Michael Miller (University of California, Santa Barbara), Evan Palmer, Melinda Kunar, and Jeremy Wolfe (Harvard University), Chris Shunn (University of Pittsburgh), and Daniel Simons (University of Illinois).

A number of colleagues also provided their insights and counsel for the fourth edition. I'm therefore delighted to thank Ed Awh (University of Oregon), Glen Bodner (University of Calgary), William Gehring (University of Michigan), Katherine Gibbs (University of California, Davis), Eliot Hazeltine (University of Iowa), William Hockley (Wilfrid Laurier University), James Hoffman (University of Delaware), Helene Intraub (University of Delaware), Vikram Jaswal (University of Virginia), Karsten Loepelmann (University of Alberta), Penny Pexman (University of Calgary), and Christy Porter (College of William and Mary).

Then, even more people to thank for their help with the fifth edition: Karin M. Butler (University of New Mexico), Mark A. Casteel (Penn State University, York), Alan Castel (University of California, Los Angeles), Robert Crutcher (University of Dayton), Kara D. Federmeier (University of Illinois, Urbana-Champaign), Jonathan Flombaum (Johns Hopkins University), Katherine Gibbs (University of California, Davis), Arturo E. Hernandez (University of Houston), James Hoeffner (University of Michigan), Timothy Jay (Massachusetts College of Liberal Arts), Timothy Justus (Pitzer College), Janet Nicol (University of Arizona), Robyn T. Oliver (Roosevelt University), Raymond Phinney (Wheaton College, and his comments were especially thoughtful!), Brad Postle (University of Wisconsin, Madison), Erik D. Reichle (University of Pittsburgh), Eric Ruthruff (University of New Mexico), Dave Sobel (Brown University), Martin van den Berg (California State University, Chico), and Daniel R. VanHorn (North Central College).

For the sixth edition: Michael Dodd (University of Nebraska, Lincoln), James Enns (University of British Columbia), E. Christina Ford (Penn State University), Danielle Gagne (Alfred University), Marc Howard (Boston University), B. Brian Kuhlman (Boise State University), Guy Lacroix (Carleton University), Ken Manktelow (University of Wolverhampton), Aidan Moran (University College Dublin, Ireland), Joshua New (Barnard College), Janet Nicol (University of

Arizona), Mohammed K. Shakeel (Kent State University), David Somers (Boston University), and Stefan Van der Stigchel (Utrecht University).

And now, happily, for the current edition: Alan Castel (UCLA), Jim Hoelzle (Marquette University), Nate Kornell (Williams College), Catherine Middle-brooks (UCLA), Stefanie Sharman (Deakin University), Erin Sparck (UCLA), and Cara Laney Thede (The College of Idaho).

I also want to thank the people at Norton. I've had a succession of terrific editors, and I'm grateful to Ken Barton, Sheri Snavely, Aaron Javsicas, and Jon Durbin for their support and fabulous guidance over the years. There's no question that the book is stronger, clearer, and *better* because of their input and advice.

I also want to thank David Bradley for doing a fabulous job of keeping this project on track, and also Eve Sanoussi and Katie Pak for their extraordinary work in helping me bring out a book of the highest quality. (I should also thank them for putting up with my gruff impatience when things don't work quite as we all hoped.) I'm also delighted with the design that Rubina Yeh, Jillian Burr, and Lisa Buckley created; Ted Szczepanski has been great in dealing with my sometimes-zany requests for photographs. Thanks in advance to Ashley Sherwood and the Norton sales team; I am, of course, deeply grateful for all you do. Thanks also to the crew that has produced the ZAPS, the Internet presence, and the various supplements for this book.

And I once again get to celebrate the pleasure of working with Alice Vigliani as manuscript editor. Alice is, of course, a terrific editor, but, in addition, she's efficient and *fun* to work with. As I've said before: If she tends her peonies with the same skill that she devotes to her editing, her garden must be marvelous indeed.

Finally, it brings me joy to reiterate with love the words I said in the previous edition: In countless ways, Friderike makes all of this possible and worthwhile. She forgives me the endless hours at the computer, tolerates the tension when I'm feeling overwhelmed by deadlines, and is always ready to read my pages and offer thoughtful, careful, instructive insights. My gratitude to, and love for, her are boundless.

Daniel Reisberg
Portland, Oregon

The Foundations of Cognitive Psychology

What is cognitive psychology? In Chapter 1, we'll define this discipline and offer a sketch of what this field can teach us — through its theories and its practical applications. We'll also provide a brief history to explain why cognitive psychology has taken the form that it has.

Chapter 2 has a different focus. At many points in this book, we'll draw insights from the field of *cognitive neuroscience* — the effort toward understanding our mental functioning through close study of the brain and nervous system. To make sure this biological evidence is useful, though, we need to provide some background, and that's the main purpose of Chapter 2. There, we'll offer a rough mapping of what's where in the brain, and we'll describe the functioning of many of the brain's parts. We'll also discuss *what it means* to describe the functioning of this or that brain region, because, as we will see, each of the brain's parts is highly specialized in what it does. As a result, mental achievements such as reading, remembering, or deciding depend on the coordinated functioning of many different brain regions, with each contributing its own small bit to the overall achievement.

chapter 1

The Science of the Mind

Almost everything you do, and everything you feel or say, depends on your *cognition*—what you know, what you remember, and what you think. As a result, the book you're now reading—a textbook on cognition—describes the foundation for virtually every aspect of who you are.

As illustrations of this theme, in a few pages we'll consider the way in which your ability to cope with grief depends on how your memory functions. We'll also discuss the role that memory plays in shaping your self-image—and, therefore, your self-esteem. As another example, we'll discuss a case in which your understanding of a simple story depends on the background knowledge that you supply. Examples like these make it clear that cognition matters in an extraordinary range of circumstances, and it's on this basis that our focus in this book is on the intellectual foundation of almost every aspect of human experience.

The Scope of Cognitive Psychology

When the field of cognitive psychology was first launched, it was broadly focused on the *scientific study of knowledge*, and this focus led immediately to a series of questions: How is knowledge acquired? How is knowledge retained so that it's available when needed? How is knowledge used—whether as a basis for making decisions or as a means of solving problems?

These are great questions, and it's easy to see that answering them might be quite useful. For example, imagine that you're studying for next Wednesday's exam, but for some reason the material just won't "stick" in your memory. You find yourself wishing, therefore, for a better strategy to use in studying and memorizing. What would that strategy be? Is it possible to have a "better memory"?

As a different case, let's say that while you're studying, your friend is moving around in the room, and you find this quite distracting. Why can't you just shut out your friend's motion? Why don't you have better control over your attention and your ability to concentrate?

Here's one more example: You're looking at your favorite Internet news site, and you're horrified to learn how many people have decided to vote for candidate X. How do people decide whom to vote for? For that matter, how do people decide what college to attend, or which car to buy, or even what to have for dinner? And how can we help people make *better* decisions—so that, for example, they choose healthier foods, or vote for the candidate who (in your view) is preferable?

preview of chapter themes

- The chapter begins with a description of the *scope* of cognitive psychology. The domain of this field includes activities that are obviously "intellectual" (such as remembering, paying attention, or making judgments) but also a much broader range of activities that depend on these intellectual achievements.

- What form should a "science of the mind" take? We discuss the difficulties in trying to study the mind by means of direct observation. But we also explore why we must study the mental world if we're to understand behavior; the reason is that our behavior depends in crucial ways on how we *perceive* and *understand* the world around us.

- Combining these themes, we come to the view that we must study the mental world *indirectly*. But as we will see, the method for doing this is the method used by most sciences.

Before we're through, we'll consider evidence pertinent to all of these questions. Let's note, though, that in these examples, things aren't going as you might have wished: You remember less than you want to; you can't ignore a distraction; the voters make a choice you don't like. What about the other side of the picture? What about the remarkable intellectual feats that humans achieve—brilliant deductions or creative solutions to complex problems? In this text, we'll also discuss these cases and explore how people manage to accomplish the great things they do.

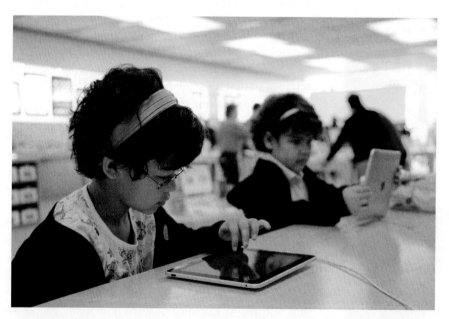

CELEBRATING HUMAN ACHIEVEMENTS

Many of the text's examples involve *failures* or *limitations* in our cognition. But we also need to explain the incredible intellectual achievements of our species—the complex problems we've solved and the extraordinary devices we've invented.

The Broad Role for Memory

The questions we've mentioned so far might make it sound like cognitive psychology is concerned just with your functioning as an intellectual—your ability to remember, or to pay attention, or to think through options when making a choice. As we've said, though, the relevance of cognitive psychology is much broader—thanks to the fact that a huge range of your actions, thoughts, and feelings *depend on your cognition.* As one way to convey this point, let's ask: When we investigate how memory functions, what's at stake? Or, to turn this around, what aspects of your life depend on memory?

You obviously rely on memory when you're taking an exam—memory for what you learned during the term. Likewise, you rely on memory when you're at the supermarket and trying to remember the cheesecake recipe so that you can buy the right ingredients. You also rely on memory when you're reminiscing about childhood. But what else draws on memory?

Consider this simple story (adapted from Charniak, 1972):

> Betsy wanted to bring Jacob a present. She shook her piggy bank. It made no sound. She went to look for her mother.

This four-sentence tale is easy to understand, but *only because you provided important bits of background.* For example, you weren't at all puzzled about why Betsy was interested in her piggy bank; you weren't puzzled, specifically, about why the story's first sentence led naturally to the second. This is because you already knew (a) that the things one gives as presents are often things bought for the occasion (rather than things already owned), (b) that buying things requires money, and (c) that money is sometimes stored in piggy banks. Without these facts, you would have wondered why a desire to give a gift would lead someone to her piggy bank. (Surely you didn't think Betsy intended to give the piggy bank itself as the present!) Likewise, you immediately understood why Betsy *shook* her piggy bank. You didn't suppose that she was shaking it in frustration or trying to find out if it would make a good percussion instrument. Instead, you understood that she was trying to determine its contents. But you knew this fact only because you already knew (d) that Betsy was a child (because few adults keep their money in piggy banks), (e) that children don't keep track of how much money is in their banks, and (f) that piggy banks are made out of opaque material (and so a child can't simply look into the bank to see what's inside). Without these facts, Betsy's shaking of the bank would make no sense. Similarly, you understood what it meant that the bank made no sound. That's because you know (g) that it's usually coins (not bills) that are kept in piggy banks, and (h) that coins make noise when they're shaken. If you didn't know these facts, you might have interpreted the bank's silence, when it was shaken, as good news, indicating perhaps that the bank was jammed full of $20 bills—an inference that would have led you to a very different expectation for how the story would unfold from there.

A SIMPLE STORY

What is involved in your understanding of this simple story? Betsy wanted to bring Jacob a present. She shook her piggy bank. It made no sound. She went to look for her mother.

TRYING TO FOCUS

Often, you want to focus on just one thing, and you want to shut out the other sights and sounds that are making it hard for you to concentrate. What steps should you take to promote this focus and to avoid distraction?

Of course, there's nothing special about the "Betsy and Jacob" story, and we'd uncover a similar reliance on background knowledge if we explored how you understand some other narrative, or follow a conversation, or comprehend a TV show. Our suggestion, in other words, is that many (perhaps all) of your encounters with the world depend on your supplementing your experience with knowledge that you bring to the situation. And perhaps this *has* to be true. After all, if you didn't supply the relevant bits of background, then anyone telling the "Betsy and Jacob" story would need to spell out all the connections and all the assumptions. That is, the story would have to include all the facts that, *with* memory, are supplied by you. As a result, the story would have to be much longer, and the telling of it much slower. The same would be true for every story you hear, every conversation you participate in. Memory is thus crucial for each of these activities.

Amnesia and Memory Loss

Here is a different sort of example: In Chapter 7, we will consider cases of clinical *amnesia*—cases in which someone, because of brain damage, has lost the ability to remember certain materials. These cases are fascinating at many levels and provide key insights into what memory is *for*. Without memory, what is disrupted?

H.M. was in his mid-20s when he had brain surgery intended to control his severe epilepsy. The surgery was, in a narrow sense, a success, and H.M.'s epilepsy was brought under control. But this gain came at an enormous cost, because H.M. essentially lost the ability to form new memories. He survived for more than 50 years after the operation, and for all those years he had little trouble remembering events *prior to* the surgery. But H.M. seemed completely unable to recall any event that occurred *after* his operation. If asked who the president is, or about recent events, he reported facts and events that were current at the time of the surgery. If asked questions about last week, or even an hour ago, he recalled nothing.

This memory loss had massive consequences for H.M.'s life, and some of the consequences are surprising. For example, he had an uncle he was very fond of, and he occasionally asked his hospital visitors how his uncle was doing. Unfortunately, the uncle died sometime after H.M.'s surgery, and H.M. was told this sad news. The information came as a horrible shock, but because of his amnesia, H.M. soon forgot about it.

Sometime later, because he'd *forgotten* about his uncle's death, H.M. again asked how his uncle was doing and was again told of the death. But with no memory of having heard this news before, he was once more hearing it "for the first time," with the shock and grief every bit as strong as it was initially. Indeed, each time he heard this news, he was hearing it "for the first time." With no memory, he had no opportunity to live with the news, to adjust to it. As a result, his grief could not subside. Without memory, H.M. had no way to come to terms with his uncle's death.

H.M.'S BRAIN

When H.M. died in 2008, the world learned his full name — Henry Molaison. Throughout his life, H.M. had cooperated with researchers in many studies of his memory loss. Even after his death, H.M. is contributing to science: His brain (shown here) was frozen and has now been sliced into sections for detailed anatomical study. Unfortunately, though, there has been debate over who "owns" H.M.'s brain and how we might interpret some observations about his brain (see, for example, Dittrich, 2016).

A different glimpse of memory function comes from some of H.M.'s comments about what it felt like to be in his situation. Let's start here with the notion that for those of us without amnesia, numerous memories support our conception of who we are: We know whether we deserve praise for our good deeds or blame for our transgressions because we remember those good deeds and transgressions. We know whether we've kept our promises or achieved our goals because, again, we have the relevant memories. None of this is true for people who suffer from amnesia, and H.M. sometimes commented that in important ways, he didn't know who he was. He didn't know if he should be proud of his accomplishments or ashamed of his crimes; he didn't know if he'd been clever or stupid, honorable or dishonest, industrious or lazy. In a sense, then, without a memory, there is no self. (For broader discussion, see Conway & Pleydell-Pearce, 2000; Hilts, 1995.)

What, then, is the scope of cognitive psychology? As we mentioned earlier, this field is sometimes defined as the scientific study of the acquisition, retention, and use of knowledge. We've now seen, though, that "knowledge" (and hence the study of how we gain and use knowledge) is relevant to a huge range of concerns. Our self-concept, it seems, depends on our knowledge (and, in particular, on our memory for various episodes in our past). Our

TEST YOURSELF

1. Why is memory crucial for behaviors and mental operations that don't in any direct or explicit way ask you "to remember"?
2. What aspects of H.M.'s life were disrupted as a result of his amnesia?

emotional adjustments to the world rely on our memories. Even our ability to understand a simple story — or, presumably, our ability to understand any experience — depends on our supplementing that experience with some knowledge.

The suggestion, then, is that cognitive psychology can help us understand capacities relevant to virtually every moment of our lives. Activities that don't appear to be intellectual would collapse without the support of our cognitive functioning. The same is true whether we're considering our physical movements through the world, our social lives, our emotions, or any other domain. This is the scope of cognitive psychology and, in a real sense, the scope of this book.

The Cognitive Revolution

The enterprise that we now call "cognitive psychology" is a bit more than 50 years old, and the emergence of this field was in some ways dramatic. Indeed, the science of psychology went through a succession of changes in the 1950s and 1960s that are often referred to as psychology's "cognitive revolution." This "revolution" involved a new style of research, aimed initially at questions we've already met: questions about memory, decision making, and so on. But this new type of research, and its new approach to theorizing, soon influenced other domains, with the result that the cognitive revolution dramatically changed the intellectual map of our field.

The cognitive revolution centered on two key ideas. One idea is that the science of psychology cannot study the mental world directly. A second idea is that the science of psychology *must* study the mental world if we're going to understand behavior. As a path toward understanding these ideas, let's look at two earlier traditions in psychology that offered a rather different perspective. Let's emphasize, though, that our purpose here is not to describe the full history of modern cognitive psychology. That history is rich and interesting, but our goal is a narrow one — to explain why the cognitive revolution's themes were as they were. (For readers interested in the history, see Bartlett, 1932; Benjamin, 2008; Broadbent, 1958; Malone, 2009; Mandler, 2011.)

The Limits of Introspection

In the late 19th century, Wilhelm Wundt (1832–1920) and his student Edward Bradford Titchener (1867–1927) launched a new research enterprise, and according to many scholars it was their work that eventually led to the modern field of experimental psychology. In Wundt's and Titchener's view, psychology needed to focus largely on the study of conscious mental events — feelings, thoughts, perceptions, and recollections. But how should these events be studied? These early researchers started with the fact that there is no way for you to experience my thoughts, or I yours. The only person who can experience or observe your thoughts is you. Wundt, Titchener, and their colleagues

WILHELM WUNDT

Wilhelm Wundt (1832–1920) is shown here sitting and surrounded by his colleagues and students. Wundt is often regarded as the "father of experimental psychology."

concluded, therefore, that the only way to study thoughts is through **introspection**, or "looking within," to observe and record the content of our own mental lives and the sequence of our own experiences.

Wundt and Titchener insisted, though, that this introspection could not be casual. Instead, introspectors had to be meticulously trained: They were given a vocabulary to describe what they observed; they were taught to be as careful and as complete as possible; and above all, they were trained simply to report on their experiences, with a minimum of interpretation.

This style of research was enormously influential for several years, but psychologists gradually became disenchanted with it, and it's easy to see why. As one concern, these investigators soon had to acknowledge that some thoughts are *un*conscious, which meant that introspection was limited as a research tool. After all, by its very nature introspection is the study of conscious experiences, so of course it can tell us nothing about unconscious events.

Indeed, we now know that unconscious thought plays a huge part in our mental lives. For example, what is your middle name? Most likely, the moment you read this question, the name "popped" into your thoughts without any effort. But, in fact, there's good reason to think that this simple bit of remembering requires a complex series of steps. These steps take place outside of awareness; and so, if we rely on introspection as our means of studying mental events, we have no way of examining these processes.

But there's another, deeper problem with introspection. In order for any science to proceed, there must be some way to test its claims; otherwise, we have no means of separating correct assertions from false ones, accurate descriptions of the world from fictions. Along with this requirement, science needs some way of resolving disagreements. If you claim that Earth has one moon and I insist that it has two, we need some way of determining who is right. Otherwise, our "science" will become a matter of opinion, not fact.

With introspection, this testability of claims is often unattainable. To see why, imagine that I insist my headaches are worse than yours. How could we ever test my claim? It might be true that I describe my headaches in extreme terms: I talk about them being "agonizing" and "excruciating." But that might indicate only that I like to use extravagant descriptions; those words might reveal my tendency to exaggerate (or to complain), not the actual severity of my headaches. Similarly, it might be true that I need bed rest whenever one of my headaches strikes. Does that mean my headaches are truly intolerable? It might mean instead that I'm self-indulgent and rest even when I feel mild pain. Perhaps our headaches are identical, but you're stoic about yours and I'm not.

How, therefore, should we test my claim about my headaches? What we need is some way of directly comparing my headaches to yours, and that would require transplanting one of my headaches into your experience, or vice versa. Then one of us could make the appropriate comparison. But (setting aside science fiction or fantasy) there's no way to do this, leaving us, in the end, unable to determine whether my headache reports are distorted or accurate. We're left, in other words, with the brute fact that our only information about my headaches is what comes through the filter of my description, and we have no way to know how (or whether) that filter is coloring the evidence.

For purposes of science, this is unacceptable. Ultimately, we do want to understand conscious experience, and so, in later chapters, we will consider introspective reports. For example, we'll talk about the subjective feeling of "familiarity" and the conscious experience of mental imagery; in Chapter 14, we'll talk about consciousness itself. In these settings, though, we'll rely on introspection as a source of observations *that need to be explained*. We won't rely on introspective data as a means of evaluating our hypotheses — because, usually, we can't. If we want to test hypotheses, we need data we can rely on, and, among other requirements, this means data that aren't dependent on a particular point of view or a particular descriptive style. Scientists generally achieve this objectivity by making sure the raw data are out in plain view, so that you can inspect my evidence, and I can inspect yours. In that way, we can be certain that neither of us is distorting or misreporting the facts. And that is precisely what we cannot do with introspection.

The Years of Behaviorism

Historically, the concerns just described led many psychologists to abandon introspection as a research tool. Psychology couldn't be a science, they argued, if it relied on this method. Instead, psychology needed objective data, and that meant data out in the open for all to observe.

What sorts of data does this allow? First, an organism's *behaviors* are observable in the right way: You can watch my actions, and so can anyone else who is appropriately positioned. Therefore, data concerned with behavior are objective data and thus grist for the scientific mill. Likewise, *stimuli* in the world are in the same "objective" category: These are measurable, recordable, physical events.

In addition, you can arrange to record the stimuli I experience day after day after day and also the behaviors I produce each day. This means that you can record how the pattern of my behavior changes over time and with the accumulation of experience. In other words, my *learning history* can be objectively recorded and scientifically studied.

In contrast, my *beliefs, wishes, goals, preferences, hopes,* and *expectations* cannot be directly observed, cannot be objectively recorded. These "mentalistic" notions can be observed only via introspection; and introspection, we've suggested, has little value as a scientific tool. Therefore, a scientific psychology needs to avoid these invisible internal entities.

This perspective led to the **behaviorist** movement, a movement that dominated psychology in America for the first half of the 20th century. The movement

JOHN B. WATSON

John B. Watson (1878–1958) was a prominent and persuasive advocate for the behaviorist movement. Given his focus on learning and learning histories, it's not surprising that Watson was intrigued by babies' behavior and learning. Here, he tests the grasp reflex displayed by human infants.

was in many ways successful and uncovered a range of principles concerned with how behavior changes in response to various stimuli (including the stimuli we call "rewards" and "punishments"). By the late 1950s, however, psychologists were convinced that a lot of our behavior could not be explained in these terms. The reason, basically, is that the ways people act, and the ways they feel, are guided by how they *understand* or *interpret* the situation, and not by the objective situation itself. Therefore, if we follow the behaviorists' instruction and focus only on the objective situation, we will often misunderstand why people are doing what they're doing and make the wrong predictions about how they'll behave in the future. To put this point another way, the behaviorist perspective demands that we not talk about mental entities such as beliefs, memories, and so on, because these things cannot be studied directly and so cannot be studied scientifically. Yet it seems that these subjective entities play a pivotal role in guiding behavior, and so we *must* consider them if we want to understand behavior.

Evidence pertinent to these assertions is threaded throughout the chapters of this book. Over and over, we'll find it necessary to mention people's perceptions and strategies and understanding, as we explain why (and how) they perform various tasks and accomplish various goals. Indeed, we've already seen an example of this pattern. Imagine that we present the "Betsy and Jacob" story to people and then ask various questions: Why did Betsy shake her piggy bank? Why did she go to look for her mother? People's responses will surely reflect their understanding of the story, which in turn depends on far more than the physical stimulus—that is, the 29 syllables of the story itself. If we want to predict someone's responses to these questions, therefore, we'll need to refer to the stimulus (the story itself) *and also* to the person's knowledge and understanding of this stimulus.

Here's a different example that makes the same general point. Imagine you're sitting in the dining hall. A friend produces this physical stimulus: "Pass the salt, please," and you immediately produce a bit of salt-passing behavior. In this exchange, there is a physical stimulus (the words your friend uttered) and an easily defined response (your passing of the salt), and so this simple event seems fine from the behaviorists' perspective—the elements are out in the open, for all to observe, and can be objectively recorded. But note that the event would have unfolded in the same way if your friend had offered a different stimulus. "Could I have the salt?" would have done the trick. Ditto for "Salt, please!" or "Hmm, this sure needs salt!" If your friend is both loquacious and obnoxious, the utterance might have been: "Excuse me, but after briefly contemplating the gustatory qualities of these comestibles, I have discerned that their sensory qualities would be enhanced by the addition of a number of sodium and chloride ions, delivered in roughly equal proportions and in crystalline form; could you aid me in this endeavor?" You might giggle (or snarl) at your friend, but you would still pass the salt.

Now let's work on the science of salt-passing behavior. When is this behavior produced? We've just seen that the behavior is evoked by a number of different stimuli, and so we would surely want to ask: What do these stimuli have in common? If we can answer that question, we're on our way to understanding why these stimuli all have the same effect.

The problem, though, is that if we focus on the observable, objective aspects of these stimuli, they actually have little in common. After all, the sounds being produced in that long statement about sodium and chloride ions are rather different from the sounds in the utterance "Salt, please!" And in many circumstances, *similar* sounds would not lead to salt-passing behavior. Imagine that your friend says, "Salt the pass" or "Sass the palt." These are acoustically similar to "Pass the salt" but wouldn't have the same impact. Or imagine that your friend says, "She has only a small part in the play. All she gets to say is 'Pass the salt, please.'" In this case, the right syllables were uttered, but you wouldn't pass the salt in response.

It seems, then, that our science of salt passing won't get very far if we insist on talking only about the physical stimulus. Stimuli that are physically different from each other ("Salt, please" and the bit about ions) have similar effects. Stimuli that are physically similar to each other ("Pass the salt" and "Sass the palt") have different effects. Physical similarity, therefore, is not what unites the various stimuli that evoke salt passing.

It's clear, though, that the various stimuli that evoke salt passing do have something in common: *They all mean the same thing.* Sometimes this meaning derives from the words themselves ("Please pass the salt"). In other cases, the meaning depends on certain pragmatic rules. (For example, you understand that the question "Could you pass the salt?" isn't a question about arm strength, although, interpreted literally, it might be understood that way.) In all cases, though, it seems plain that to predict your behavior in the dining hall, we need to ask what these stimuli *mean to you.* This seems an extraordinarily simple point, but it is a point, echoed by countless other examples, that indicates the impossibility of a complete behaviorist psychology.[1]

The Intellectual Foundations of the Cognitive Revolution

One might think, then, that we're caught in a trap. On one side, it seems that the way people act is shaped by how they *perceive* the situation, how they *understand* the stimuli, and so on. If we want to explain behavior, then, we have no choice. We need to talk about the mental world. But, on the other side, the only direct means of studying the mental world is introspection, and introspection is scientifically unworkable. Therefore: We need to study the mental world, but we can't.

There is, however, a solution to this impasse, and it was suggested years ago by the philosopher Immanuel Kant (1724–1804). To use Kant's **transcendental method,** you begin with the observable facts and then work backward from

PASSING THE SALT

If a friend requests the salt, your response will depend on how you understand your friend's words. This is a simple point, echoed in example after example, but it is the reason why a rigid behaviorist perspective cannot explain your behavior.

---

1. The behaviorists themselves quickly realized this point. As a result, modern behaviorism has abandoned the radical rejection of mentalistic terms; indeed, it's hard to draw a line between modern behaviorism and a field called "animal cognition," a field that often uses mentalistic language! The behaviorism being criticized here is a historically defined behaviorism, and it's this perspective that, in large measure, gave birth to modern cognitive psychology.

these observations. In essence, you ask: How could these observations have come about? What must be the underlying *causes* that led to these *effects*?

This method, sometimes called "inference to best explanation," is at the heart of most modern science. Physicists, for example, routinely use this method to study objects or events that cannot be observed directly. To take just one case, no physicist has ever observed an electron, but this hasn't stopped physicists from learning a great deal about electrons. How do the physicists proceed? Even though electrons themselves aren't observable, their presence often leads to observable results—in essence, *visible effects* from an *invisible cause*. For example, electrons leave observable tracks in cloud chambers, and they can produce momentary fluctuations in a magnetic field. Physicists can then use these observations in the same way a police detective uses clues—asking what the "crime" must have been like if it left this and that clue. (A size 11 footprint? That probably tells us what size feet the criminal has, even though no one saw his feet. A smell of tobacco smoke? That suggests the criminal was a smoker. And so on.) In the same way, physicists observe the clues that electrons leave behind, and from this information they form hypotheses about what electrons must be like in order to have produced those effects.

Of course, physicists (and other scientists) have a huge advantage over a police detective. If the detective has insufficient evidence, she can't arrange for the crime to happen again in order to produce more evidence. (She can't say to the robber, "Please visit the bank again, but this time don't wear a mask.") Scientists, in contrast, can arrange for a repeat of the "crime" they're seeking to explain—they can arrange for new experiments, with new measures. Better still, they can set the stage in advance, to maximize the likelihood that the "culprit" (in our example, the electron) will leave useful clues behind. They can, for example, add new recording devices to the situation, or they can place various obstacles in the electron's path. In this way, scientists can gather more and more data, including data crucial for testing the predictions of a particular theory. This prospect—of reproducing experiments and varying the experiments to test hypotheses—is what gives science its power. It's what enables scientists to assert that their hypotheses have been rigorously tested, and it's what gives scientists assurance that their theories are correct.

Psychologists work in the same fashion—and the notion that we *could* work in this fashion was one of the great contributions of the cognitive revolution. The idea is this: We know that we need to study mental processes; that's what we learned from the limitations of classical behaviorism. But we also know that mental processes cannot be observed directly; we learned that from the downfall of introspection. Our path forward, therefore, is to study mental processes *indirectly*, relying on the fact that these processes, themselves invisible, have visible consequences: measurable delays in producing a response, performances that can be assessed for accuracy, errors that can be scrutinized and categorized. By examining these (and other) effects produced by mental processes, we can develop—and *test*—hypotheses about what the mental processes must have been. In this way, we use Kant's method, just as

IMMANUEL KANT

Philosopher Immanuel Kant (1724-1804) made major contributions to many fields, and his transcendental method enabled him to ask what qualities of the mind make experience possible.

physicists (or biologists or chemists or astronomers) do, to develop a science that does not rest on direct observation.

The Path from Behaviorism to the Cognitive Revolution

In setting after setting, cognitive psychologists have applied the Kantian logic to explain how people remember, make decisions, pay attention, or solve problems. In each case, we begin with a particular performance—say, a problem that someone solved—and then hypothesize a series of unseen mental events that made the performance possible. But we don't stop there. We also ask whether some other, perhaps simpler, sequence of events might explain the data. In other words, we do more than ask how the data came about; we seek the *best* way to think about the data.

This pattern of theorizing has become the norm in psychology—a powerful indication that the cognitive revolution did indeed change the entire field. But what triggered the revolution? What happened in the 1950s and 1960s that propelled psychology forward in this way? It turns out that multiple forces were in play.

One contribution came from within the behaviorist movement itself. We've discussed concerns about classical behaviorism, and some of those concerns were voiced early on by Edward Tolman (1886-1959)—a researcher who can be counted both as a behaviorist and as one of the forerunners of cognitive psychology. Prior to Tolman, most behaviorists argued that learning could be understood simply as a *change in behavior*. Tolman argued, however, that learning involved something more abstract: the acquisition of new knowledge.

In one of Tolman's studies, rats were placed in a maze day after day. For the initial 10 days, no food was available anywhere in the maze, and the rats wandered around with no pattern to their behavior. Across these days, therefore, there was no change in behavior—and so, according to the conventional view, no learning. But, in fact, there was learning, because *the rats were learning the layout of the maze*. That became clear on the 11th day of testing, when food was introduced into the maze in a particular location. The next day, the rats, placed back in the maze, ran immediately to that location. Indeed, their behavior was essentially identical to the behavior of rats who had had many days of training with food in the maze (Tolman, 1948; Gleitman, 1963).

What happened here? Across the initial 10 days, rats were acquiring what Tolman called a "cognitive map" of the maze. In the early days of the procedure, however, the rats had no motivation to use this knowledge. On Days 11 and 12, though, the rats gained a reason to use what they knew, and at that point they revealed their knowledge. The key point, though, is that—even for rats—we need to talk about (invisible) mental processes (e.g., the formation of cognitive maps) if we want to explain behavior.

A different spur to the cognitive revolution also arose out of behaviorism— but this time from a strong *critique* of behaviorism. B.F. Skinner (1904–1990) was an influential American behaviorist, and in 1957 he applied his style of

ULRIC NEISSER

Many intellectual developments led to the cognitive revolution. A huge boost, though, came from Ulric Neisser's book, *Cognitive Psychology* (1967). Neisser's influence was so large that many scholars refer to him as the "father of cognitive psychology."

analysis to humans' ability to learn and use language, arguing that language use could be understood in terms of behaviors and rewards (Skinner, 1957). Two years later, the linguist Noam Chomsky (1928–) published a ferocious rebuttal to Skinner's proposal, and convinced many psychologists that an entirely different approach was needed for explaining language learning and language use, and perhaps for other achievements as well.

European Roots of the Cognitive Revolution

Research psychology in the United States was, we've said, dominated by the behaviorist movement for many years. The influence of behaviorism was not as strong, however, in Europe, and several strands of European research fed into and strengthened the cognitive revolution. In Chapter 3, we will describe some of the theorizing that grew out of the Gestalt psychology movement, an important movement based in Berlin in the early decades of the 20th century. (Many of the Gestaltists fled to the United States in the years leading up to World War II and became influential figures in their new home.) Overall, the Gestalt psychologists argued that behaviors, ideas, and perceptions are organized in a way that could not be understood through a part-by-part, element-by-element, analysis of the world. Instead, they claimed, the elements take on meaning only as part of the whole—and therefore psychology needed to understand the nature of the "whole." This position had many implications, including an emphasis on the role of the perceiver in organizing his or her experience. As we will see, this notion—that perceivers shape their own experience—is a central theme for modern cognitive psychology.

Another crucial figure was British psychologist Frederic Bartlett (1886–1969). Although he was working in a very different tradition from the Gestalt psychologists, Bartlett also emphasized the ways in which each of us shapes and organizes our experience. Bartlett claimed that people spontaneously fit their experiences into a mental framework, or "schema," and rely on this schema both to interpret the experience as it happens and to aid memory later on. We'll say more about Bartlett's work (found primarily in his book *Remembering,* published in 1932) in Chapter 8.

Computers and the Cognitive Revolution

Tolman, Chomsky, the Gestaltists, and Bartlett disagreed on many points. Even so, a common theme ran through their theorizing: These scholars all agreed that we could not explain humans' (or even rats') behavior unless we explain what is going on within the mind—whether our emphasis is on cognitive maps, schemata, or some other form of knowledge. But, in explaining this knowledge and how the knowledge is put to use, where should we begin? What sorts of processes or mechanisms might we propose?

Here we meet another crucial stream that fed into the cognitive revolution, because in the 1950s a new approach to psychological explanation became available and turned out to be immensely fruitful. This new approach was

FREDERIC BARTLETT

Frederic Bartlett was the first professor of experimental psychology at the University of Cambridge. He is best known for his studies of memory and the notion that people spontaneously fit their experiences into a "schema," and they rely on the schema both to guide their understanding and (later) to guide their memory.

suggested by the rapid developments in electronic information processing, including developments in computer technology. It soon became clear that computers were capable of immensely efficient information storage and retrieval ("memory"), as well as performance that seemed to involve decision making and problem solving. Indeed, some computer scientists proposed that computers would soon be genuinely intelligent—and the field of "artificial intelligence" was launched and made rapid progress (e.g., Newell & Simon, 1959).

Psychologists were intrigued by these proposals and began to explore the possibility that the human mind followed processes and procedures similar to those used in computers. As a result, psychological data were soon being explained in terms of "buffers" and "gates" and "central processors," terms borrowed from computer technology (e.g., Miller, 1956; Miller, Galanter, & Pribram, 1960). This approach was evident, for example, in the work of another British psychologist, Donald Broadbent (1926–1993). He was one of the earliest researchers to use the language of computer science in explaining human cognition. His work emphasized a succession of practical issues, including the mechanisms through which people focus their attention when working in complex environments, and his book *Perception and Communication* (1958) framed discussions of attention for many years.

This computer-based vocabulary allowed a new style of theorizing. Given a particular performance, say, in paying attention or on some memory task, one could hypothesize a series of information-processing events that made the performance possible. As we will see, hypotheses cast in these terms led psychologists to predict a broad range of new observations, and in this way both organized the available information and led to many new discoveries.

TEST YOURSELF

3. Why is introspection limited as a source of scientific evidence?
4. Why do modern psychologists agree that we *have to* refer to mental states (what you believe, what you perceive, what you understand) in order to explain behavior?
5. Describe at least one historical development that laid the groundwork for the cognitive revolution.

Research in Cognitive Psychology: The Diversity of Methods

Over the last half-century, cognitive psychologists have continued to frame many hypotheses in these computer-based terms. But we've also developed other options for theorizing. For example, before we're done in this book, we'll also discuss hypotheses framed in terms of the strategies a person is relying on, or the inferences she is making. No matter what the form of the hypothesis, though, the next steps are crucial. First, we derive new predictions from the hypothesis, along the lines of "If this is the mechanism behind the original findings, then things should work differently in *this* circumstance or *that* one." Then, we gather new data to test those predictions. If the data fit with the predictions, this outcome confirms the hypothesis. If the data don't line up with the predictions, a new hypothesis is needed.

But what methods do we use, and what sorts of data do we collect? The answer, in brief, is that we use *diverse* methods and collect many types of data. In other words, what unites cognitive psychology is not an allegiance to any particular procedure in the laboratory. Instead, what unites the field is the logic that underlies our research, no matter what method we use.

(We discuss this logic more fully in the appendix for this textbook. The appendix contains a series of modules, with each module exploring an aspect of research methodology directly related to one of the book's chapters.)

What sorts of data do we use? In some settings, we ask how well people perform a particular task. For example, in tests of memory we might ask *how complete* someone's memory is (does the person remember all of the objects in view in a picture?) and also *how accurate* the memory is (does the person perhaps remember seeing a banana when, in truth, no banana was in view?). We can also ask how performance changes if we change the "input" (how well does the person remember a story, rather than a picture?), and we can change the person's circumstances (how is memory changed if the person is happy, or afraid, when hearing the story?). We can also manipulate the person's plans or strategies (what happens if we teach the person some sort of memorization technique?), and we can compare different people (children vs. adults; novices at a task vs. experts; people with normal vision vs. people who have been blind since birth).

A different approach relies on measurements of *speed*. The idea here is that mental operations are fast but do take a measurable amount of time, and by examining the **response time (RT)**—that is, how long someone needs to make a particular response—we can often gain important insights into what's going on in the mind. For example, imagine that we ask you: "Yes or no: Do cats have whiskers?" And then: "Yes or no: Do cats have heads?" Both questions are absurdly easy, so there's no point in asking whether you're accurate in your responses—it's a sure bet that you will be. We can, however, measure your response times to questions like these, often with intriguing results. For example, if you're forming a mental picture of a cat when you're asked these questions, you'll be faster for the "heads" question than the "whiskers" question. If you think about cats without forming a mental picture, the pattern reverses—you'll be faster for the "whiskers" question. In Chapter 11, we'll use results like these to test hypotheses about how information—and mental pictures in particular—are represented and analyzed in your mind.

We can also gain insights from observations focused on the brain and nervous system. Over the last few decades, cognitive psychology has formed a productive partnership with the field of **cognitive neuroscience**, the effort toward understanding humans' mental functioning through close study of the brain and nervous system. But here, too, numerous forms of evidence are available. We'll say more about these points in the next chapter, but for now let's note that we can learn a lot by studying people with damaged brains and also people with healthy brains. Information about damaged brains comes from the field of **clinical neuropsychology**, the study of brain function that uses, as its main data source, cases in which damage or illness has disrupted the working of some brain structure. We've already mentioned H.M., a man whose memory was massively disrupted as an unexpected consequence of surgery. As a different example, in Chapter 12 we'll consider cases in which someone's ability to make ordinary decisions (Coke or Pepsi? Wear the blue sweater or the green one?) is disrupted if brain centers involved in *emotion* are disrupted; observations like these provide crucial information about the role of emotion in decision making.

Information about healthy brains comes from **neuroimaging techniques**, which enable us, with some methods, to scrutinize the precise structure of the brain and, with other methods, to track the moment-by-moment pattern of activation within someone's brain. We'll see in Chapter 7, for example, that different patterns of brain activation during learning lead to different types of memory, and we'll use this fact as we ask what the types of memory are.

There's no reason for you, as a reader, to memorize this catalogue of different types of evidence. That's because we'll encounter each of these forms of data again and again in this text. Our point for now is simply to highlight the fact that there are multiple tools with which we can test, and eventually confirm, various claims. Indeed, relying on these tools, cognitive psychology has learned a tremendous amount about the mind. Our research has brought us powerful new theories and enormously useful results. Let's dive in and start exploring what the science of the mind has taught us.

TEST YOURSELF

6. Describe at least three types of evidence that cognitive psychologists routinely rely on.

APPLYING COGNITIVE PSYCHOLOGY

Research in cognitive psychology can help us understand deep theoretical issues, such as what it means to be rational or what the function of consciousness might be. But our research also has broad practical implications, and so our studies often provide lessons for how we should conduct our daily lives.

Some of the practical lessons from cognitive psychology are obvious. For example, research on memory can help students who are trying to learn new materials in the classroom; studies of how people draw conclusions can help people to draw smarter, more defensible conclusions. Following these leads, each chapter in this text ends with an essay that explores how the material in that chapter can be applied to an issue that's important for *education*. This emphasis is rooted, in part, in the fact that most readers of this book will be college students, using the book in the context of one of their courses. I hope, therefore, that the Cognitive Psychology and Education essays are directly useful for these readers! Concretely, the essay at the end of Chapter 4, for example, will teach you how to speed-read (but will also explain the limitations of speed-reading). The essay at the end of Chapter 6 will offer suggestions for how to study and retain the material you're hoping to learn.

Let's emphasize, though, that research in cognitive psychology also has implications for other domains. For example, think about the criminal justice system and what happens in a criminal investigation. Eyewitnesses provide evidence, based on what they paid attention to during a crime and what they remember. Police officers question the witnesses, trying to get the most out of what each witness recalls—but without leading the witness in any way. Then, the police try to deduce, from the evidence, who the perpetrator was.

Later, during the trial, jurors listen to evidence and make a judgment about the defendant's innocence or guilt.

Cast in these terms, it should be obvious that an understanding of *attention*, *memory*, *reasoning*, and *judgment* (to name just a few processes) is directly relevant to what happens in the legal system. On this basis, therefore, I've also written essays that focus on the interplay between cognitive psychology and the law. The essay for Chapter 3, for example, uses what we know about visual perception to ask what we can expect witnesses to see. The essay for Chapter 7 explores a research-based procedure for helping witnesses to recall more of what they've observed. If you're curious to see these Cognitive Psychology and the Law essays, you can find them online in the ebook, available at http://digital.wwnorton.com/cognition7.

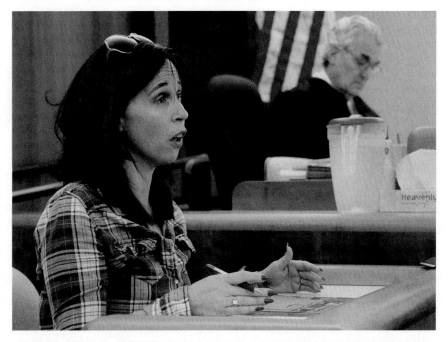

COGNITIVE PSYCHOLOGY AND THE CRIMINAL JUSTICE SYSTEM

Eyewitnesses in the courtroom rely on what they *remember* about key events, and what they remember depends crucially on what they *perceived* and *paid attention to*. Therefore, our understanding of memory, perception, and attention can help the justice system in its evaluation of witness evidence.

chapter review

SUMMARY

- Cognitive psychology is concerned with how people remember, pay attention, and think. The importance of all these issues arises partly from the fact that most of what we do, say, and feel is guided by things we already know. One example is our comprehension of a simple story, which turns out to be heavily influenced by the knowledge we supply.

- Cognitive psychology emerged as a separate discipline in the late 1950s, and its powerful impact on the wider field of psychology has led many academics to speak of this emergence as the cognitive revolution. One predecessor of cognitive psychology was the 19th-century movement that emphasized introspection as the main research tool for psychology. But psychologists soon became disenchanted with this movement for several reasons: Introspection cannot inform us about unconscious mental events; and even with conscious events, claims rooted in introspection are often untestable because there is no way for an independent observer to check the accuracy or completeness of an introspective report.

- The behaviorist movement rejected introspection as a method, insisting instead that psychology speak only of mechanisms and processes that are objective and out in the open for all to observe. However, evidence suggests that our thinking, behavior, and feelings are often shaped by our perception or understanding of the events we experience. This is problematic for the behaviorists: Perception and understanding are exactly the sorts of mental processes that the behaviorists regarded as subjective and not open to scientific study.

- In order to study mental events, psychologists have turned to a method in which one focuses on observable events but then asks what (invisible) events must have taken place in order to make these (visible) effects possible.

- Many factors contributed to the emergence of cognitive psychology in the 1950s and 1960s. Tolman's research demonstrated that even in rats, learning involved the acquisition of new knowledge and not just a change in behavior. Chomsky argued powerfully that a behaviorist analysis was inadequate as an explanation for language learning and language use. Gestalt psychologists emphasized the role of the perceiver in organizing his or her experience. Bartlett's research showed that people spontaneously fit their experiences into a mental framework, or schema.

- Early theorizing in cognitive psychology often borrowed ideas from computer science, including early work on artificial intelligence.

- Cognitive psychologists rely on a diverse set of methods and collect many types of data. Included are measures of the quality of someone's performance, measures of response speed, and, in some cases, methods that allow us to probe the underlying biology.

KEY TERMS

introspection (p. 9)
behaviorist theory (p. 11)
transcendental method (p. 13)
response time (RT) (p. 18)

cognitive neuroscience (p. 18)
clinical neuropsychology (p. 18)
neuroimaging techniques (p. 19)

TEST YOURSELF AGAIN

1. Why is memory crucial for behaviors and mental operations that don't in any direct or explicit way ask you "to remember"?

2. What aspects of H.M.'s life were disrupted as a result of his amnesia?

3. Why is introspection limited as a source of scientific evidence?

4. Why do modern psychologists agree that we *have to* refer to mental states (what you believe, what you perceive, what you understand) in order to explain behavior?

5. Describe at least one historical development that laid the groundwork for the cognitive revolution.

6. Describe at least three types of evidence that cognitive psychologists routinely rely on.

THINK ABOUT IT

1. The chapter argues that in a wide range of settings, our behaviors and our emotions depend on what we know, believe, and remember. Can you come up with examples of your own that illustrate this reliance on cognition in a circumstance that doesn't seem, on the surface, to be one that involves "intellectual activity"?

2. Some critics of Darwin's theory of evolution via natural selection argue this way: "Darwin's claims can never be tested, because of course no one was around to observe directly the processes of evolution that Darwin proposed." Why is this assertion misguided, resting on a false notion of how science proceeds?

eBOOK DEMONSTRATIONS & ESSAYS

Go to http://digital.wwnorton.com/cognition7 for the online demonstrations and essays relevant to this chapter. These can be found in the ebook.

Online Applying Cognitive Psychology and the Law Essays

- Cognitive Psychology and the Law: Improving the Criminal Justice System

ZAPS COGNITION LABS

Go to http://digital.wwnorton.com/cognition7 to experience interactive online psychology labs relevant to this chapter.

chapter **2**

The Neural Basis for Cognition

what if...

Throughout this text, we'll be examining ordinary achievements. A friend asks: "Where'd you grow up?" and you immediately answer. You're meeting a friend at the airport, and you instantly recognize her the moment she steps into view. An instructor says, "Listen carefully," and you have no trouble focusing your attention.

Ordinary or not, achievements like these are crucial for you, and your life would be massively disrupted if you couldn't draw information from memory, or recognize the objects you encounter, or choose where you'll point your attention. As a way of dramatizing this point, we'll begin each chapter by asking: What would happen to someone if one of these fundamental capacities *didn't work* as it normally does? What if . . . ?

The disorder known as Capgras syndrome (Capgras & Reboul-Lachaux, 1923) is relatively rare, but it can result from various injuries to the brain (Ellis & De Pauw, 1994) and is sometimes found in people with Alzheimer's syndrome (Harwood, Barker, Ownby, & Duara, 1999). Someone with this syndrome is fully able to recognize the people in her world — her husband, her parents, her friends — but is utterly convinced that these people are not who they appear to be. The real husband or the real son, the afflicted person insists, has been kidnapped (or worse). The person now in view, therefore, must be a fraud of some sort, impersonating the (allegedly) absent person.

Imagine what it's like to have this disorder. You turn to your father and exclaim, "You look like my father, sound like him, and act like him. But I can tell that you're not my father! *Who are you?*"

Often, a person with Capgras syndrome insists that there are slight differences between the "impostor" and the person he (or she) has supposedly replaced — subtle changes in personality or appearance. Of course, no one else detects these (nonexistent) differences, which can lead to paranoid suspicions about why a loved one has been taken away and why no one else will acknowledge the replacement. In the extreme, these suspicions can lead a Capgras sufferer to desperate steps. In some cases, patients suffering from this syndrome have murdered the supposed impostor in an attempt to end the charade and relocate the "genuine" character. In one case, a Capgras patient was convinced his father had been replaced by a robot and so

preview of chapter themes

- We begin by exploring the example of Capgras syndrome to illustrate how seemingly simple achievements actually depend on many parts of the brain. We also highlight the ways that the study of the brain can illuminate questions about the mind.

- We then survey the brain's anatomy, emphasizing the function carried out by each region. Identification of these functions is supported by neuroimaging data, which can assess the activity levels in different areas, and by studies of the effects of brain damage.

- We then take a closer look at the various parts of the cerebral cortex—the most important part of the brain for cognitive functioning. These parts include the motor areas, the sensory areas, and the so-called association cortex.

- Finally, we turn to the individual cells that make up the brain—the neurons and glia—and discuss the basic principles of how these cells function.

decapitated him in order to look for the batteries and microfilm in his head (Blount, 1986).

What is going on here? The answer lies in the fact that facial recognition involves two separate systems in the brain. One system leads to a cognitive appraisal ("I know what my father looks like, and I can perceive that you closely resemble him"), and the other to a more global, emotional appraisal ("You look familiar to me and also trigger a warm response in me"). When these two appraisals agree, the result is a confident recognition ("You obviously are my father"). In Capgras syndrome, though, the emotional processing is disrupted, leading to an intellectual identification without a familiarity response (Ellis & Lewis, 2001; Ellis & Young, 1990; Ramachandran & Blakeslee, 1998): "You resemble my father but trigger no sense of familiarity, so you must be someone else." The result? Confusion and, at times, bizarre speculation about why a loved one has been kidnapped and replaced—and a level of paranoia that can, as we have seen, lead to homicide.

Explaining Capgras Syndrome

We began this chapter with a description of Capgras syndrome, and we've offered an account of the mental processes that characterize this disorder. Specifically, we've suggested that someone with this syndrome is able to recognize a loved one's face, but with no feeling of familiarity. Is this the right way to think about Capgras syndrome?

One line of evidence comes from neuroimaging techniques that enable researchers to take high-quality, three-dimensional "pictures" of living brains without in any way disturbing the brains' owners. We'll have more to say about neuroimaging later; but first, what do these techniques tell us about Capgras syndrome?

The Neural Basis for Capgras Syndrome

Some types of neuroimaging provide portraits of the physical makeup of the brain: What's where? How are structures shaped or connected to each other? Are there structures present (such as tumors) that shouldn't be there, or structures that are missing (because of disease or birth defects)? This information about structure was gained in older studies from positron emission tomography (more commonly referred to as a PET scan). More recent studies usually rely on magnetic resonance imaging (MRI; see **Figure 2.1**). These scans suggest a link between Capgras syndrome and abnormalities in several brain areas, indicating that our account of the syndrome will need to consider several elements (Edelstyn & Oyebode, 1999; also see O'Connor, Walbridge, Sandson, & Alexander, 1996).

FIGURE 2.1 NEUROIMAGING

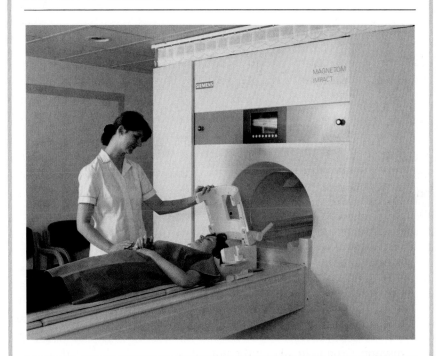

Scanners like this one are used for both MRI and fMRI scans. MRI scans tell us about the structure of the brain; fMRI scans tell us which portions of the brain are especially active during the scan. An fMRI scan usually results in color images, with each hue indicating a particular activity level.

FIGURE 2.2   THE LOBES OF THE HUMAN BRAIN

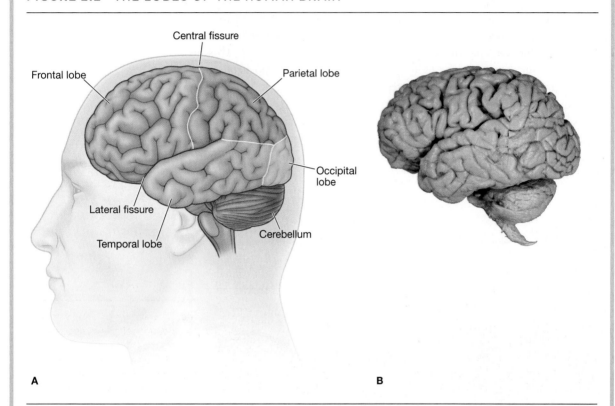

Panel A identifies the various lobes and some of the brain's prominent features. Actual brains, however, are uniformly colored, as shown in the photograph in Panel B. The four lobes of the forebrain surround (and hide from view) the midbrain and most of the hindbrain. (The cerebellum is the only part of the hindbrain that is visible in the figure, and, in fact, the temporal lobe has been pushed upward a bit in the left panel to make the cerebellum more visible.) This side view shows the left cerebral hemisphere; the structures on the right side of the brain are similar. However the two halves of the brain have somewhat different functions, and so the results of brain injury depend on which half is damaged. The symptoms of Capgras syndrome, for example, result from damage to specific sites on the right side of the frontal and temporal lobes.

One site of damage in Capgras patients is in the temporal lobe (see **Figure 2.2**), particularly on the right side of the head. This damage probably disrupts circuits involving the **amygdala**, an almond-shaped structure that—in the intact brain—seems to serve as an "emotional evaluator," helping an organism detect stimuli associated with threat or danger (see **Figure 2.3**). The amygdala is also important for detecting positive stimuli— indicators of safety or of available rewards. With *damaged* amygdalae, therefore, people with Capgras syndrome won't experience the warm sense of feeling good (and safe and secure) when looking at a loved one's familiar

FIGURE 2.3 THE AMYGDALA AS AN "EMOTIONAL EVALUATOR"

The area shown in yellow marks the location of the amygdala. In this image, the yellow is a reflection of increased activity created by a fear memory—the memory of receiving an electric shock.

face. This lack of an emotional response is probably why these faces don't feel familiar to them, and is fully in line with the two-systems hypothesis we've already sketched.

Patients with Capgras syndrome also have brain abnormalities in the frontal lobe, specifically in the right **prefrontal cortex**. What is this area's normal function? To find out, we turn to a different neuroimaging technique, functional magnetic resonance imaging (fMRI), which enables us to track moment-by-moment activity levels in different sites in a living brain. (We'll say more about fMRI in a later section.) This technique allows us to answer such questions as: When a person is reading, which brain regions are particularly active? How about when a person is listening to music? With data like these, we can ask which tasks make heavy use of a brain area, and from that base we can draw conclusions about that brain area's function.

Studies make it clear that the prefrontal cortex is especially active when a person is doing tasks that require planning or careful analysis. Conversely, this area is less active when someone is *dreaming*. Plausibly, this latter pattern reflects the absence of careful analysis of the dream material, which helps explain why dreams are often illogical or bizarre.

Related, consider fMRI scans of patients suffering from schizophrenia (e.g., Silbersweig et al., 1995). Neuroimaging reveals diminished activity in the frontal lobes whenever these patients are experiencing hallucinations. One interpretation is that the diminished activity reflects a decreased ability to distinguish internal events (thoughts) from external ones (voices) or to distinguish imagined events from real ones (cf. Glisky, Polster, & Routhieaux, 1995).

How is all of this relevant to Capgras syndrome? With damage to the frontal lobe, Capgras patients may be less able to keep track of what is real and what is not, what is sensible and what is not. As a result, weird beliefs can emerge unchecked, including delusions (about robots and the like) that you or I would find totally bizarre.

What Do We Learn from Capgras Syndrome?

Other lines of evidence add to our understanding of Capgras syndrome (e.g., Ellis & Lewis, 2001; Ramachandran & Blakeslee, 1998). Some of the evidence comes from the psychology laboratory and confirms the suggestion that recognition of all stimuli (not just faces) involves two separate mechanisms—one that hinges on factual knowledge, and one that's more "emotional" and tied to the warm sense of familiarity (see Chapter 7).

Note, then, that our understanding of Capgras syndrome depends on a combination of evidence drawn from cognitive psychology and from cognitive neuroscience. We use both perspectives to test (and, ultimately, to confirm) the hypothesis we've offered. In addition, just as both perspectives can illuminate Capgras syndrome, both *can be illuminated by* the syndrome. That is, we can use Capgras syndrome (and other biological evidence) to illuminate broader issues about the nature of the brain and of the mind.

For example, Capgras syndrome suggests that the amygdala plays a crucial role in supporting the feeling of familiarity. Other evidence suggests that the amygdala also helps people remember the emotional events of their lives (e.g., Buchanan & Adolphs, 2004). Still other evidence indicates that the amygdala plays a role in decision making (e.g., Bechara, Damasio, & Damasio, 2003), especially for decisions that rest on emotional evaluations of one's options. Facts like these tell us a lot about the various functions that make cognition possible and, more specifically, tell us that our theorizing needs to include a broadly useful "emotional evaluator," involved in many cognitive processes. Moreover, Capgras syndrome tells us that this emotional evaluator works in a fashion separate from the evaluation of factual information, and this observation gives us a way to think about occasions in which your evaluation of the facts points toward one conclusion, while an emotional evaluation points toward a different conclusion. These are valuable clues as we try to understand the processes that support ordinary remembering or decision making. (For more on the role of emotion in decision making, see Chapter 12.)

What does Capgras syndrome teach us about the brain itself? One lesson involves the fact that many different parts of the brain are needed for even the simplest achievement. In order to recognize your father, for example, one part of your brain needs to store the factual memory of what he looks like. Another part of the brain is responsible for analyzing the visual input you receive when looking at a face. Yet another brain area has the job of comparing this now-analyzed input to the factual information provided from memory, to determine whether there's a match. Another site provides the emotional evaluation of the input. A different site presumably assembles the data from all these other sites—and registers the fact that the face being inspected does match the factual recollection of your father's face, and also produces a warm sense of familiarity.

Usually, all these brain areas work together, allowing the recognition of your father's face to go smoothly forward. If they don't work together—that is, if coordination among these areas is disrupted—yet another area works to make sure you offer reasonable hypotheses about this disconnect, and not zany ones. (In other words, if your father looks less familiar to you on some occasion, you're likely to explain this by saying, "I guess he must have gotten new glasses" rather than "I bet he's been replaced by a robot.")

Unmistakably, this apparently easy task—seeing your father and recognizing who he is—requires multiple brain areas. The same is true of most tasks, and in this way Capgras syndrome illustrates this crucial aspect of brain function.

TEST YOURSELF

1. What are the symptoms of Capgras syndrome, and why do they suggest a two-part explanation for how you recognize faces?

The Study of the Brain

In order to discuss Capgras syndrome, we needed to refer to different brain areas and had to rely on several different research techniques. In this way, the syndrome also illustrates another point—that this is a domain in which we need some technical foundations before we can develop our theories. Let's start building those foundations.

The human brain weighs (on average) a bit more than 3 pounds (roughly 1.4 kg), with male brains weighing about 10% more than female brains (Hartmann, Ramseier, Gudat, Mihatsch, & Polasek, 1994). The brain is roughly the size of a small melon, yet this compact structure has been estimated to contain 86 billion nerve cells (Azevedo et al., 2009). Each of these cells is connected to 10,000 or so others—for a total of roughly 860 trillion connections. The brain also contains a huge number of *glial cells*, and we'll have more to say about all of these individual cells later on in the chapter. For now, though, how should we begin our study of this densely packed, incredibly complex organ?

One place to start is with a simple fact we've already met: that different parts of the brain perform different jobs. Scientists have known this fact about the brain for many years, thanks to clinical evidence showing that the symptoms produced by brain damage depend heavily on the location of the damage. In 1848, for example, a horrible construction accident caused Phineas Gage to suffer damage in the frontmost part of his brain

FIGURE 2.4 PHINEAS GAGE

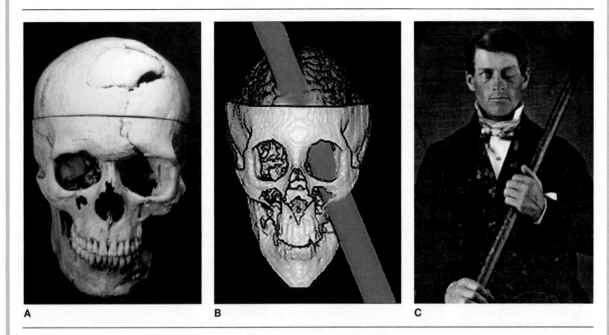

A   B   C

Phineas Gage was working as a construction foreman when some blasting powder misfired and launched a piece of iron into his cheek and through the front part of his brain. Remarkably, Gage survived and continued to live a fairly normal life, but his pattern of intellectual and emotional impairments provide valuable cues about the function of the brain's frontal lobes. Panel A is a photo of Gage's skull; the drawing in Panel B depicts the iron bar's path as it blasted through his head. Panel C is an actual photograph of Gage, and he's holding the bar that went through his brain!

(see **Figure 2.4**), and this damage led to severe personality and emotional problems. In 1861, physician Paul Broca noted that damage in a different location, on the left side of the brain, led to a disruption of language skills. In 1911, Édouard Claparède (1911/1951) reported his observations with patients who suffered from profound memory loss produced by damage in still another part of the brain.

Clearly, therefore, we need to understand brain functioning with reference to brain anatomy. Where was the damage that Gage suffered? Where was the damage in Broca's patients or Claparède's? In this section, we fill in some basics of brain anatomy.

Hindbrain, Midbrain, Forebrain

The human brain is divided into three main structures: the hindbrain, the midbrain, and the forebrain. The **hindbrain** is located at the very top of the spinal cord and includes structures crucial for controlling key life

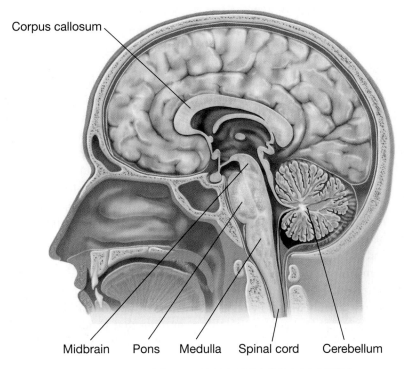

Corpus callosum

Midbrain   Pons   Medulla   Spinal cord   Cerebellum

GROSS ANATOMY OF A BRAIN SHOWING BRAIN STEM

The pons and medulla are part of the hindbrain. The medulla controls vital functions such as breathing and heart rate. The pons (Latin for "bridge") is the main connection between the cerebellum and the rest of the brain.

functions. It's here, for example, that the rhythm of heartbeats and the rhythm of breathing are regulated. The hindbrain also plays an essential role in maintaining the body's overall tone. Specifically, the hindbrain helps maintain the body's posture and balance; it also helps control the brain's level of alertness.

The largest area of the hindbrain is the **cerebellum**. For many years, investigators believed this structure's main role was in the coordination of bodily movements and balance. Research indicates, however, that the cerebellum plays various other roles and that damage to this organ can cause problems in spatial reasoning, in discriminating sounds, and in integrating the input received from various sensory systems (Bower & Parsons, 2003).

The **midbrain** has several functions. It plays an important part in coordinating movements, including the precise movements of the eyes as they explore the visual world. Also in the midbrain are circuits that relay auditory information from the ears to the areas in the forebrain where this information is processed and interpreted. Still other structures in the midbrain help to regulate the experience of pain.

For our purposes, though, the most interesting brain region (and, in humans, the largest region) is the **forebrain**. Drawings of the brain (like the one shown in Figure 2.2) show little other than the forebrain, because this structure surrounds (and so hides from view) the entire midbrain and most of the hindbrain. Of course, only the outer surface of the forebrain—the **cortex**—is visible in such pictures. In general, the word "cortex" (from the Latin word for "tree bark") refers to an organ's outer surface, and many organs each have their own cortex; what's visible in the drawing, then, is the *cerebral* cortex.

The cortex is just a thin covering on the outer surface of the forebrain; on average, it's a mere 3 mm thick. Nonetheless, there's a great deal of cortical tissue; by some estimates, the cortex makes up 80% of the human brain. This considerable volume is made possible by the fact that the cerebral cortex, thin as it is, consists of a large sheet of tissue. If stretched out flat, it would cover more than 300 square inches, or roughly 2,000 cm². (For comparison, this is an area roughly 20% greater than the area covered by an extra-large—18 inch, or 46 cm—pizza.) But the cortex isn't stretched flat; instead, it's crumpled up and jammed into the limited space inside the skull. It's this crumpling that produces the brain's most obvious visual feature—the wrinkles, or **convolutions**, that cover the brain's outer surface.

Some of the "valleys" between the wrinkles are actually deep grooves that divide the brain into different sections. The deepest groove is the **longitudinal fissure**, running from the front of the brain to the back, which separates the left **cerebral hemisphere** from the right. Other fissures divide the cortex in each hemisphere into four lobes (again, look back at Figure 2.2), and these are named after the bones that cover them—bones that, as a group, make up the skull. The **frontal lobes** form the front of the brain, right behind the forehead. The **central fissure** divides the frontal lobes on each side of the brain from the **parietal lobes**, the brain's topmost part. The bottom edge of the frontal lobes is marked by the **lateral fissure**, and below it are the **temporal lobes**. Finally, at the very back of the brain, connected to the parietal and temporal lobes, are the **occipital lobes**.

Subcortical Structures

Hidden from view, underneath the cortex, are several **subcortical structures**. One of these structures, the **thalamus**, acts as a relay station for nearly all the sensory information going to the cortex. Directly underneath the thalamus is the **hypothalamus**, a structure that plays a crucial role in controlling behaviors that serve specific biological needs—behaviors that include eating, drinking, and sexual activity.

Surrounding the thalamus and hypothalamus is another set of structures that form the **limbic system**. Included here is the amygdala, and close by is the **hippocampus**, both located underneath the cortex in the temporal lobe (plurals: amygdalae and hippocampi; see **Figure 2.5**). These structures

FIGURE 2.5   THE LIMBIC SYSTEM AND THE HIPPOCAMPUS

Cingulate cortex

Fornix

Thalamus

Mamillary body

Hypothalamus

Amygdala

Hippocampus

Color is used in this drawing to help you visualize the arrangement of these brain structures. Imagine that the cortex is semitransparent, allowing you to look into the brain to see the (subcortical) structures highlighted here. The limbic system includes a number of subcortical structures that play a crucial role in learning and memory and in emotional processing.

are essential for learning and memory, and the patient H.M., discussed in Chapter 1, developed his profound amnesia after surgeons removed large portions of these structures—strong confirmation of their role in the formation of new memories.

We mentioned earlier that the amygdala plays a key role in emotional processing, and this role is reflected in many findings. For example, presentation of frightful faces causes high levels of activity in the amygdala (Williams et al., 2006). Likewise, people ordinarily show more complete, longer-lasting memories for emotional events, compared to similar but emotionally flat events. This memory advantage for emotional events is especially pronounced in people who showed greater activation in the amygdala while they were witnessing the event in the first place. Conversely, the memory advantage for emotional events is diminished (and may not be observed at all) in people who (through sickness or injury) have suffered damage to the amygdalae.

Lateralization

Virtually all parts of the brain come in pairs, and so there is a hippocampus on the left side of the brain and another on the right, a left-side amygdala and a right-side one. The same is true for the cerebral cortex itself: There is a temporal cortex (i.e., a cortex of the temporal lobe) in the left hemisphere and another in the right, a left occipital cortex and a right one, and so on. In all cases, cortical and subcortical, the left and right structures in each pair have roughly the same shape and the same pattern of connections to other brain areas. Even so, there are differences in function between the left-side and right-side structures, with each left-hemisphere structure playing a somewhat different role from the corresponding right-hemisphere structure.

Let's remember, though, that the two halves of the brain work together—the functioning of one side is closely integrated with that of the other side. This integration is made possible by the **commissures**, thick bundles of fibers that carry information back and forth between the two hemispheres. The largest commissure is the **corpus callosum**, but several other structures also make sure that the two brain halves work as partners in almost all mental tasks.

In certain cases, though, there are medical reasons to sever the corpus callosum and some of the other commissures. (For many years, this surgery was a last resort for extreme cases of epilepsy.) The person is then said to be a "split-brain patient"—still having both brain halves, but with communication between the halves severely limited. Research with these patients has taught us a great deal about the specialized function of the brain's two hemispheres. It has provided evidence, for example, that many aspects of language processing are lodged in the left hemisphere, while the right hemisphere seems crucial for a number of tasks involving spatial judgment (see **Figure 2.6**).

However, it's important not to overstate the contrast between the two brain halves, and it's misleading to claim (as some people do) that we need to silence our "left-brain thinking" in order to be more creative, or that intuitions grow out of "right-brain thinking." These claims do begin with a kernel of truth, because some elements of creativity depend on specialized processing in the right hemisphere (see, e.g., Kounios & Beeman, 2015). Even so, whether we're examining creativity or any other capacity, the two halves of the brain have to work together, with each hemisphere making its own contribution to the overall performance. Therefore, "shutting down" or "silencing" one hemisphere, even if that were biologically possible, wouldn't allow you new achievements, because the many complex, sophisticated skills we each display (including creativity, intuition, and more) depend on the whole brain. In other words, our hemispheres are not cerebral competitors, each trying to impose its style of thinking on the other. Instead, the hemispheres pool their specialized capacities to produce a seamlessly integrated, single mental self.

TEST YOURSELF

2. What is the cerebral cortex?

3. What are the four major lobes of the forebrain?

4. Identify some of the functions of the hippocampus, the amygdala, and the corpus callosum.

FIGURE 2.6 STUDYING SPLIT-BRAIN PATIENTS

In this experiment, the patient is shown two pictures, one of a spoon and one of a fork (Panel A). If asked what he sees, his verbal response is controlled by the left hemisphere, which has seen only the fork (because it's in the right visual field. However, if asked to pick up the object shown in the picture, the patient—reaching with his left hand—picks up the spoon (Panel B). That happens because the left hand is controlled by the right hemisphere, and this hemisphere receives visual information from the left-hand side of the visual world.

Sources of Evidence about the Brain

How can we learn about these various structures—and many others that we haven't named? Cognitive neuroscience relies on many types of evidence to study the brain and nervous system. Let's look at some of the options.

Data from Neuropsychology

We've already encountered one form of evidence—the study of individuals who have suffered brain damage through accident, disease, or birth defect. The study of these cases generally falls within the domain of *neuropsychology*: the study of the brain's structures and how they relate to brain function. Within neuropsychology, the specialty of *clinical neuropsychology* seeks (among other goals) to understand the functioning of intact, undamaged brains by means of careful scrutiny of cases involving brain damage.

Data drawn from clinical neuropsychology will be important throughout this text. For now, though, we'll emphasize that the symptoms resulting from brain damage depend on the site of the damage. A **lesion** (a specific area of damage) in the hippocampus produces memory problems but not language disorders; a lesion in the occipital cortex produces problems in vision but spares the other sensory modalities. Likewise, the consequences of brain lesions depend on which hemisphere is damaged. Damage to the left side of the frontal lobe, for example, is likely to produce a disruption of language use; damage to the right side of the frontal lobe generally doesn't have this effect. In obvious ways, then, these patterns confirm the claim that different brain areas perform different functions. In addition, these patterns provide a rich source of data that help us develop and test hypotheses about those functions.

Data from Neuroimaging

Further insights come from **neuroimaging techniques**. There are several types of neuroimaging, but they all produce precise, three-dimensional pictures of a living brain. Some neuroimaging procedures provide *structural* imaging, generating a detailed portrait of the shapes, sizes, and positions of the brain's components. Other procedures provide *functional* imaging, which tells us about activity levels throughout the brain.

For many years, **computerized axial tomography (CT scans)** was the primary tool for structural imaging, and **positron emission tomography (PET scans)** was used to study the brain's activity. CT scans rely on X-rays and so—in essence—provide a three-dimensional X-ray picture of the brain. PET scans, in contrast, start by introducing a tracer substance such as glucose into the patient's body; the molecules of this tracer have been tagged with a low dose of radioactivity, and the scan keeps track of this radioactivity, allowing us to tell which tissues are using more of the glucose (the body's main fuel) and which ones are using less.

For each type of scan, the primary data (X-rays or radioactive emissions) are collected by a bank of detectors placed around the person's head. A computer then compares the signals received by each of the detectors and uses this information to construct a three-dimensional map of the brain—a map of structures from a CT scan, and a map showing activity levels from a PET scan.

More recent studies have turned to two newer techniques, introduced earlier in the chapter. **Magnetic resonance imaging (MRI scans)** relies on the magnetic properties of the atoms that make up the brain tissue, and it yields fabulously detailed pictures of the brain. MRI scans provide structural images, but a closely related technique, **functional magnetic resonance imaging (fMRI scans)**, provides functional imaging. The fMRI scans measure the oxygen content in blood flowing through each region of the brain; this turns out to be an accurate index of the level of neural activity in that region. In this way, fMRI scans offer an incredibly precise picture of the brain's moment-by-moment activities.

The results of structural imaging (CT or MRI scans) are relatively stable, changing only if the person's brain structure changes (because of an injury, perhaps, or the growth of a tumor). The results of PET or fMRI scans, in contrast, are highly variable, because the results depend on what task the person is performing. We can therefore use these latter techniques to explore brain function—using fMRI scans, for example, to determine which brain sites are

VISUAL STIMULATION

EYES CLOSED   EYES OPEN   COMPLEX SCENE

UCLA SCHOOL OF MEDICINE

especially activated when someone is making a moral judgment or trying to solve a logic problem. In this way, the neuroimaging data can provide crucial information about how these activities are made possible by specific patterns of functioning within the brain.

Data from Electrical Recording

Neuroscientists have another technique in their toolkit: electrical recording of the brain's activity. To explain this point, though, we need to say a bit about how the brain functions. As mentioned earlier, the brain contains billions of nerve cells—called "neurons"—and it is the neurons that do the brain's main work. (We'll say more about these cells later in the chapter.) Neurons vary in their functioning, but for the most part they communicate with one another via chemical signals called "neurotransmitters." Once a neuron is "activated," it releases the transmitter, and this chemical can then activate (or, in some cases, *de*-activate) other, adjacent neurons. The adjacent neurons "receive" this chemical signal and, in turn, send their own signal onward to other neurons.

Let's be clear, though, that the process we just described is communication *between* neurons: One neuron releases the transmitter substance, and this activates (or de-activates) another neuron. But there's also communication *within* each neuron. The reason, basically, is that neurons have an "input" end and an "output" end. The "input" end is the portion of the neuron that's most sensitive to neurotransmitters; this is where the signal from other neurons is received. The "output" end is the portion that releases neurotransmitters, sending the

A   B   C

MAGNETIC RESONANCE IMAGING

Magnetic resonance imaging produces magnificently detailed pictures of the brain. Panel A shows an "axial view"—a "slice" of the brain viewed from the top of the head (the front of the head is at the top of the image). Clearly visible is the longitudinal fissure, which divides the left cerebral hemisphere from the right. Panel B, a "coronal view," shows a slice of the brain viewed from the front. Again, the separation of the two hemispheres is clearly visible, as are some of the commissures linking the two brain halves. Panel C, a "sagittal view," shows a slice of the brain viewed from the side. Here, many of the structures in the limbic system (see Figure 2.5) are easily seen.

signal on to other neurons. These two ends can sometimes be far apart. (For example, some neurons in the body run from the base of the spine down to the toes; for these cells, the input and output ends might be a full meter apart.) The question, then, is how neurons get a signal from one end of the cell to the other.

The answer involves an electrical pulse, made possible by a flow of charged atoms (ions) in and out of the neuron (again, we'll say more about this process later in the chapter). The amount of electrical current involved in this ion flow is tiny; but many millions of neurons are active at the same time, and the current generated by all of them together is strong enough to be detected by sensitive electrodes placed on the surface of the scalp. This is the basis for *electroencephalography*—a recording of voltage changes occurring at the scalp that reflect activity in the brain underneath. This procedure generates an **electroencephalogram (EEG)**—a recording of the brain's electrical activity.

Often, EEGs are used to study broad rhythms in the brain's activity. For example, an *alpha rhythm* (with the activity level rising and falling seven to ten times per second) can usually be detected in the brain of someone who is awake but calm and relaxed; a *delta rhythm* (with the activity rising and falling roughly one to four times per second) is observed when someone is deeply asleep. A much faster *gamma rhythm* (between 30 and 80 cycles per second) has received a lot of research attention, with a suggestion that this rhythm plays a key role in creating conscious awareness (e.g., Crick & Koch, 1990; Dehaene, 2014).

Sometimes, though, we want to know about the electrical activity in the brain over a shorter period—for example, when the brain is responding to a specific input or a particular stimulus. In this case, we measure changes in the EEG in the brief periods just before, during, and after the event. These changes are referred to as **event-related potentials** (see **Figure 2.7**).

FIGURE 2.7 RECORDING THE BRAIN'S ELECTRICAL ACTIVITY

A

B

C

To record the brain's electrical signals, researchers generally use a cap that has electrodes attached to it. The procedure is easy and entirely safe—it can even be used to measure brain signals in a baby (Panel A). In some procedures, researchers measure recurrent rhythms in the brain's activity, including rhythms that distinguish the stages of sleep (Panel B). In other procedures, they measure brain activity produced in response to a single event—such as the presentation of a well-defined stimulus (Panel C).

The Power of Combining Techniques

Each of the research tools we've described has strengths and weaknesses. CT scans and MRI data tell us about the shape and size of brain structures, but they tell nothing about the activity levels within these structures. PET scans and fMRI studies do tell us about brain activity, and they can locate the activity rather precisely (within a millimeter or two). But these techniques are less precise about *when* the activity took place. For example, fMRI data summarize the brain's activity over a period of several seconds and cannot indicate when exactly, within this time window, the activity took place. EEG data give more precise information about timing but are much weaker in indicating *where* the activity took place.

Researchers deal with these limitations by means of a strategy commonly used in science: We seek data from multiple sources, so that the strengths of one technique can make up for the shortcomings of another. As a result, some studies combine EEG recordings with fMRI scans, with the EEGs telling us when certain events took place in the brain, and the scans telling us where the activity took place. Likewise, some studies combine fMRI scans with CT data, so that findings about brain activation can be linked to a detailed portrait of the person's brain anatomy.

Researchers also face another complication: the fact that many of the techniques described so far provide *correlational data*. To understand the concern here, let's look at an example. A brain area called the **fusiform face area (FFA)** is especially active whenever a face is being perceived (see **Figure 2.8**)—and so there is a correlation between a mental activity (perceiving a face) and a pattern of brain activity. Does this mean the FFA is needed for face perception? A different possibility is that the FFA activation may just be a by-product of face perception and doesn't play a crucial role. As an analogy, think about the fact that a car's speedometer becomes "more activated" (i.e., shows a higher value) whenever the car goes faster. That doesn't mean that the speedometer *causes* the speed or *is necessary* for the speed. The car would go just as fast and would, for many purposes, perform just as well if the speedometer were removed. The speedometer's state, in other words, is correlated with the car's speed but in no sense causes (or promotes, or is needed for) the car's speed.

In the same way, neuroimaging data can tell us that a brain area's activity is correlated with a particular function, but we need other data to determine whether the brain site plays a role in *causing* (or supporting, or allowing) that function. In many cases, those other data come from the study of brain lesions. If damage to a brain site disrupts a particular function, it's an indication that the site does play some role in supporting that function. (And, in fact, the FFA does play an important role in face recognition.)

Also helpful here is a technique called **transcranial magnetic stimulation (TMS)**. This technique creates a series of strong magnetic pulses at a specific location on the scalp, and these pulses activate the neurons directly underneath this scalp area (Helmuth, 2001). TMS can thus be used as a means of

FIGURE 2.8 BRAIN ACTIVITY AND AWARENESS

Panel A shows an fMRI scan of a subject looking at faces. Activation levels are high in the fusiform face area (FFA), an area that is apparently more responsive to faces than to other visual stimuli. Panel B shows a scan of the same subject looking at pictures of places; now, activity levels are high in the parahippocampal place area (PPA). Panel C compares the activity in these two areas when the subject has a picture of a face in front of one eye and a picture of a house in front of the other eye. When the viewer's perception shifts from the house to the face, activation increases in the FFA. When the viewer's perception shifts from the face to the house, PPA activation increases. In this way, the activation level reflects what the subject is aware of, and not just the pattern of incoming stimulation.

(AFTER TONG, NAKAYAMA, VAUGHAN, & KANWISHER, 1998)

asking what happens if we stimulate certain neurons. In addition, because this stimulation *disrupts* the ordinary function of these neurons, it produces a (temporary) lesion—allowing us to identify, in essence, what functions are compromised when a particular bit of brain tissue is briefly "turned off." In these ways, the results of a TMS procedure can provide crucial information about the functional role of that brain area.

Localization of Function

Drawing on the techniques we have described, neuroscientists have learned a great deal about the function of specific brain structures. This type of research effort is referred to as the **localization of function,** an effort (to put it crudely) aimed at figuring out what's happening where within the brain.

Localization data are useful in many ways. For example, think back to the discussion of Capgras syndrome earlier in this chapter. Brain scans told us that people with this syndrome have damaged amygdalae, but how is this damage related to the symptoms of the syndrome? More broadly, what problems does a damaged amygdala create? To tackle these questions, we rely on localization of function—in particular, on data showing that the amygdala is involved in many tasks involving emotional appraisal. This combination of points helped us to build (and test) our claims about this syndrome and, in general, claims about the role of emotion within the ordinary experience of "familiarity."

As a different illustration, consider the experience of calling up a "mental picture" before the "mind's eye." We'll have more to say about this experience in Chapter 11, but we can already ask: How much does this experience have in common with ordinary seeing—that is, the processes that unfold when we place a real picture before someone's eyes? As it turns out, localization data reveal enormous overlap between the brain structures needed for these two activities (visualizing and actual vision), telling us immediately that these activities do have a great deal in common (see **Figure 2.9**). So, again, we build on localization—this time to identify how exactly two mental activities are related to each other.

The Cerebral Cortex

As we've noted, the largest portion of the human brain is the cerebral cortex—the thin layer of tissue covering the cerebrum. This is the region in which an enormous amount of information processing takes place, and so, for many topics, it is the brain region of greatest interest for cognitive psychologists.

The cortex includes many distinct regions, each with its own function, but these regions are traditionally divided into three categories. *Motor areas* contain brain tissue crucial for organizing and controlling bodily movements. *Sensory areas* contain tissue essential for organizing and analyzing the information received from the senses. *Association areas* support many functions, including the essential (but not well-defined) human activity we call "thinking."

Motor Areas

Certain regions of the cerebral cortex serve as the "departure points" for signals leaving the cortex and controlling muscle movement. Other areas are the "arrival points" for information coming from the eyes, ears, and

TEST YOURSELF

5. What is the difference between *structural imaging* of the brain and *functional imaging*? What techniques are used for each?
6. What do we gain from *combining* different methods in studying the brain?
7. What is meant by the phrase "localization of function"?

FIGURE 2.9 A PORTRAIT OF THE BRAIN AT WORK

These fMRI images show different "slices" through the living brain, revealing levels of activity in different brain sites. Regions that are more active are shown in yellow, orange, and red; lower activity levels are indicated in blue. The first column shows brain activity while a person is making judgments about simple pictures. The second column shows brain activity while the person is making the same sorts of judgments about "mental pictures," visualized before the "mind's eye."

other sense organs. In both cases, these areas are called "primary projection areas," with the departure points known as the **primary motor projection areas** and the arrival points contained in regions known as the **primary sensory projection areas**.

Evidence for the motor projection area comes from studies in which investigators apply mild electrical current to this area in anesthetized animals. This stimulation often produces specific movements, so that current applied to one site causes a movement of the left front leg, while current applied to a different site causes the ears to prick up. These movements show a pattern of **contralateral control**, with stimulation to the left hemisphere leading to movements on the right side of the body, and vice versa.

Why are these areas called "projection areas"? The term is borrowed from mathematics and from the discipline of map making, because these areas seem to form "maps" of the external world, with particular positions on the cortex corresponding to particular parts of the body or particular locations in space. In the human brain, the map that constitutes the motor projection area is located on a strip of tissue toward the rear of the frontal lobe, and the pattern of mapping is illustrated in **Figure 2.10**. In this illustration, a drawing of a person has been overlaid on a depiction of the brain, with each part of the little person positioned on top of the brain area that controls its movement. The figure shows that areas of the body that we can move with great precision (e.g., fingers and lips) have a lot of cortical area devoted to them; areas of the body over which we have less control (e.g., the shoulder and the back) receive less cortical coverage.

Sensory Areas

Information arriving from the skin senses (your sense of touch or your sense of temperature) is projected to a region in the parietal lobe, just behind the motor projection area. This is labeled the "somatosensory" area in Figure 2.10. If a patient's brain is stimulated in this region (with electrical current or touch), the patient will typically report a tingling sensation in a specific part of the body. Figure 2.10 also shows the region (in the temporal lobes) that functions as the primary projection area for hearing (the "auditory" area). If the brain is directly stimulated here, the patient will hear clicks, buzzes, and hums. An area in the occipital lobes is the primary projection area for vision; stimulation here causes the patient to see flashes of light or visual patterns.

The sensory projection areas differ from each other in important ways, but they also have features in common—and they're features that parallel the attributes of the motor projection area. First, each of these areas provides a "map" of the sensory environment. In the somatosensory area, each part of the body's surface is represented by its own region on the cortex; areas of the body that are near to each other are typically represented by similarly nearby areas in the brain. In the visual area, each region of visual space has its own cortical representation, and adjacent areas of visual space are usually represented by adjacent brain sites. In the auditory projection area, different

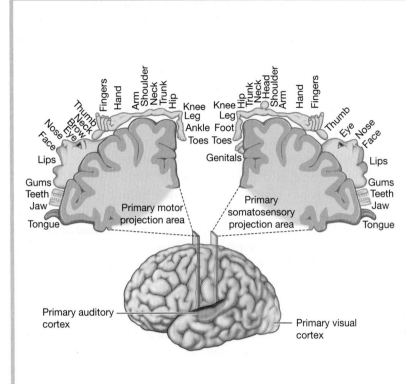

FIGURE 2.10 THE PRIMARY PROJECTION AREAS

The primary motor projection area is located at the rearmost edge of the frontal lobe, and each region within this projection area controls the motion of a specific body part, as illustrated on the top left. The primary somatosensory projection area, receiving information from the skin, is at the forward edge of the parietal lobe; each region within this area receives input from a specific body part. The primary projection areas for vision and hearing are located in the occipital and temporal lobes, respectively. These two areas are also organized systematically. For example, in the visual projection area, adjacent areas of the brain receive visual inputs that come from adjacent areas in visual space.

frequencies of sound have their own cortical sites, and adjacent brain sites are responsive to adjacent frequencies.

Second, in each of these sensory maps, the assignment of cortical space is governed by function, not by anatomical proportions. In the parietal lobes, parts of the body that aren't very discriminating with regard to touch—even if they're physically large—get relatively little cortical area. Other, more sensitive areas of the body (the lips, tongue, and fingers) get much more space. In the occipital lobes, more cortical surface is devoted to the fovea, the part of the eyeball that is most sensitive to detail. (For more on the fovea, see Chapter 3.) And in the auditory areas, some frequencies of sound get more cerebral coverage than others. It's surely no coincidence that these "advantaged" frequencies are those essential for the perception of speech.

Finally, we also find evidence here of contralateral connections. The somatosensory area in the left hemisphere, for example, receives its main input from the right side of the body; the corresponding area in the right hemisphere receives its input from the left side of the body. Likewise for the visual projection areas, although here the projection is not contralateral with regard to body parts. Instead, it's contralateral with regard to physical space. Specifically, the visual projection area in the right hemisphere receives information from both the left eye and the right, but the information it receives corresponds to the left half of visual space (i.e., all of the things

THE SENSORY HOMUNCULUS

An artist's rendition of what a man would look like if his appearance were proportional to the area allotted by the somatosensory cortex to his various body parts.

TEST YOURSELF

8. What is a projection area in the brain? What's the role of the motor projection area? The sensory projection area?
9. What does it mean to say that the brain relies on "contralateral" connections?

visible to your left when you're looking straight ahead). The reverse is true for the visual area in the left hemisphere. It receives information from both eyes, but from only the right half of visual space. The pattern of contralateral organization is also evident—although not as clear-cut—for the auditory cortex, with roughly 60% of the nerve fibers from each ear sending their information to the opposite side of the brain.

Association Areas

The areas described so far, both motor and sensory, make up only a small part of the human cerebral cortex—roughly 25%. The remaining cortical areas are traditionally referred to as the **association cortex**. This terminology is falling out of use, however, partly because this large volume of brain tissue can be subdivided further on both functional and anatomical grounds. These subdivisions are perhaps best revealed by the diversity of symptoms that result if the cortex is damaged in one or another specific location. For example, some lesions in the frontal lobe produce **apraxias,** disturbances in the initiation or organization of voluntary action. Other lesions (generally in the occipital cortex, or in the rearmost part of the parietal lobe) lead to **agnosias,** disruptions in the ability to identify familiar objects. Agnosias usually affect one modality only—so a patient with visual agnosia, for example, can recognize a fork by touching it but not by looking at it. A patient with auditory agnosia, by contrast, might be unable to identify familiar voices but might still recognize the face of the person speaking.

Still other lesions (usually in the parietal lobe) produce **neglect syndrome,** in which the individual seems to ignore half of the visual world. A patient afflicted with this syndrome will shave only half of his face and eat food from only half of his plate. If asked to read the word "parties," he will read "ties," and so on.

Damage in other areas causes still other symptoms. We mentioned earlier that lesions in areas near the lateral fissure (the deep groove that separates the frontal and temporal lobes) can result in disruption to language capacities, a problem referred to as **aphasia.**

Finally, damage to the frontmost part of the frontal lobe, the prefrontal area, causes problems in planning and implementing strategies. In some cases, patients with damage here show problems in inhibiting their own behaviors, relying on habit even in situations for which habit is inappropriate. Frontal lobe damage can also (as we mentioned in our discussion of Capgras syndrome) lead to a variety of confusions, such as whether a remembered episode actually happened or was simply imagined.

We'll discuss more about these diagnostic categories—aphasia, agnosia, neglect, and more—in upcoming chapters, where we'll consider these disorders in the context of other things that are known about object recognition, attention, and so on. Our point for the moment, though, is simple: These clinical patterns make it clear that the so-called association cortex contains many subregions, each specialized for a particular function, but with all of the subregions working together in virtually all aspects of our daily lives.

Brain Cells

Our brief tour so far has described some of the large-scale structures in the brain. For many purposes, though, we need to zoom in for a closer look, in order to see how the brain's functions are actually carried out.

Neurons and Glia

We've already mentioned that the human brain contains many billions of **neurons** and a comparable number of **glia.** The glia perform many functions. They help to guide the development of the nervous system in the fetus and young infant; they support repairs if the nervous system is damaged; they also control the flow of nutrients to the neurons. Specialized glial cells also provide a layer of electrical insulation surrounding parts of some neurons; this insulation dramatically increases the speed with which neurons can send their signals. (We'll return to this point in a moment.) Finally, some research suggests the glia may also constitute their own signaling system within the brain, separate from the information flow provided by the neurons (e.g., Bullock et al, 2005; Gallo & Chitajullu, 2001).

There is no question, though, that the main flow of information through the brain—from the sense organs inward, from one part of the brain to the others, and then from the brain outward—is made possible by the neurons. Neurons come in many shapes and sizes (see **Figure 2.11**), but in general, neurons have three major parts. The **cell body** is the portion of the cell that contains the neuron's nucleus and all the elements needed for the normal metabolic activities of the cell. The **dendrites** are usually the

---

FIGURE 2.11   NEURONS

A   B   C

Panel A shows neurons from the spinal cord (stained in red); Panel B shows neurons from the cerebellum; Panel C shows neurons from the cerebral cortex.

"input" side of the neuron, receiving signals from many other neurons. In most neurons, the dendrites are heavily branched, like a thick and tangled bush. The **axon** is the "output" side of the neuron; it sends neural impulses to other neurons (see **Figure 2.12**). Axons can vary enormously in length—the giraffe, for example, has neurons with axons that run the full length of its neck.

FIGURE 2.12   REGIONS OF THE NEURON

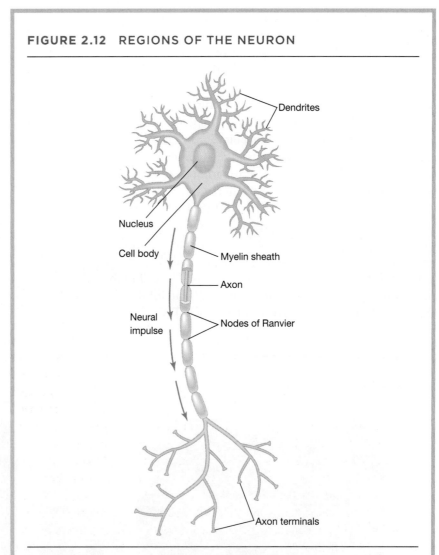

Dendrites

Nucleus

Cell body

Myelin sheath

Axon

Neural impulse

Nodes of Ranvier

Axon terminals

Most neurons have three identifiable regions. The *dendrites* are the part of the neuron that usually detects incoming signals. The *cell body* contains the metabolic machinery that sustains the cell. The *axon* is the part of the neuron that transmits a signal to another location. When the cell fires, neurotransmitters are released from the terminal endings at the tip of the axon. The myelin sheath is created by glial cells that wrap around the axons of many neurons. The gaps in between the myelin cells are called the nodes of Ranvier.

Of the many drugs that influence the brain, one is readily available and often consumed: alcohol. Alcohol influences the entire brain, and even at low levels of intoxication we can detect alcohol's effects—for example, with measures of motor skills or response time.

Alcohol's effects are more visible, though, in some functions than in others, and so someone who's quite intoxicated can perform many activities at a fairly normal level. However, alcohol has a strong impact on activities that depend on the brain's prefrontal cortex. This is the brain region that's essential for the mind's *executive function*—the system that allows you to control your thoughts and behaviors. (We'll say more about executive function in upcoming chapters.) As a result, alcohol undercuts your ability to resist temptation or to overcome habit. Impairments in executive function also erode your ability to make thoughtful decisions and draw sensible conclusions.

In addition, alcohol can produce impairments in memory, including "alcoholic blackouts." So-called fragmentary blackouts, in which the person remembers some bits of an experience but not others, are actually quite common. In one study, college students were asked: "Have you ever awoken after a night of drinking not able to remember things that you did or places where you went?" More than half of the students indicated that, yes, this had happened to them at some point; 40% reported they'd had a blackout within the previous year.

How drunk do you have to be in order to experience a blackout? Many authorities point to a blood alcohol level of 0.25 (roughly nine or ten drinks for someone of average weight), but other factors also matter. For example, blackouts are more common if you become drunk rapidly—as when you drink on an empty stomach, or when you gulp alcohol rather than sipping it.

Let's combine these points about blackouts, though, with our earlier observation about alcohol's uneven effects. It's possible for someone to be quite drunk, and therefore suffer an alcoholic blackout, even if the person seemed alert and coherent during the drunken episode. To see some of the serious problems this can cause, consider a pattern that often emerges in cases involving allegations of sexual assault. Victims of assault sometimes report that they have little or no memory of the sexual encounter; they therefore assume they were barely conscious during the event and surely incapable of giving consent. But is this assumption correct?

The answer is complex. If someone was drunk enough to end up with a blackout, then that person was probably impaired to a degree that would interfere with decision making—and so the person could not have given legitimate, meaningful consent. But, even so, the person might have been functioning in a way that seemed mostly normal (able to converse, to move around) and may even have expressed consent in words or actions.

In this situation, then, the complainant is correct in saying that he or she couldn't have given (and therefore didn't give) meaningful consent, but the accused person can legitimately say that he or she perceived that there was consent. We can debate how best to judge these situations, but surely the best path forward is to avoid this sort of circumstance—by drinking only in safe settings or by keeping a strict limit on your drinking.

The Synapse

We've mentioned that communication from one neuron to the next is generally made possible by a chemical signal: When a neuron has been sufficiently stimulated, it releases a minute quantity of a **neurotransmitter**. The molecules of this substance drift across the tiny gap between neurons and latch on to the dendrites of the adjacent cell. If the dendrites receive enough of this substance, the next neuron will "fire," and so the signal will be sent along to other neurons.

Notice, then, that neurons usually don't touch each other directly. Instead, at the end of the axon there is a gap separating each neuron from the next. This entire site—the end of the axon, plus the gap, plus the receiving membrane of the next neuron—is called a **synapse**. The space between the neurons is the *synaptic gap*. The bit of the neuron that releases the transmitter into this gap is the **presynaptic membrane**, and the bit of the neuron on the other side of the gap, affected by the transmitters, is the **postsynaptic membrane**.

When the neurotransmitters arrive at the postsynaptic membrane, they cause changes in this membrane that enable certain ions to flow into and out of the postsynaptic cell (see **Figure 2.13**). If these ionic flows are relatively small, then the postsynaptic cell quickly recovers and the ions are transported back to where they were initially. But if the ionic flows are large enough, they trigger a response in the postsynaptic cell. In formal terms, if the incoming signal reaches the postsynaptic cell's **threshold**, then the cell fires. That is, it produces an **action potential**—a signal that moves down its axon, which in turn causes the release of neurotransmitters at the next synapse, potentially causing the next cell to fire.

In some neurons, the action potential moves down the axon at a relatively slow speed. For other neurons, specialized glial cells are wrapped around the axon, creating a layer of insulation called the **myelin sheath** (see Figure 2.12). Because of the myelin, ions can flow in or out of the axon only at the gaps between the myelin cells. As a result, the signal traveling down the axon has to "jump" from gap to gap, and this greatly increases the speed at which the signal is transmitted. For neurons without myelin, the signal travels at speeds below 10 m/s; for "myelinated" neurons, the speed can be ten times faster.

Overall, let's emphasize four points about this sequence of events. First, let's note once again that neurons depend on two different forms of information flow. Communication from one neuron to the next is (for most neurons) mediated by a chemical signal. In contrast, communication from one end of the neuron to the other (usually from the dendrites down the length of the axon) is made possible by an electrical signal, created by the flow of ions in and out of the cell.

Second, the postsynaptic neuron's initial response can vary in size; the incoming signal can cause a small ionic flow or a large one. Crucially, though, once these inputs reach the postsynaptic neuron's firing threshold, there's no variability in the response—either a signal is sent down the axon or it is not. If the signal is sent, it is always of the same magnitude, a fact referred to as

FIGURE 2.13 SCHEMATIC VIEW OF SYNAPTIC TRANSMISSION

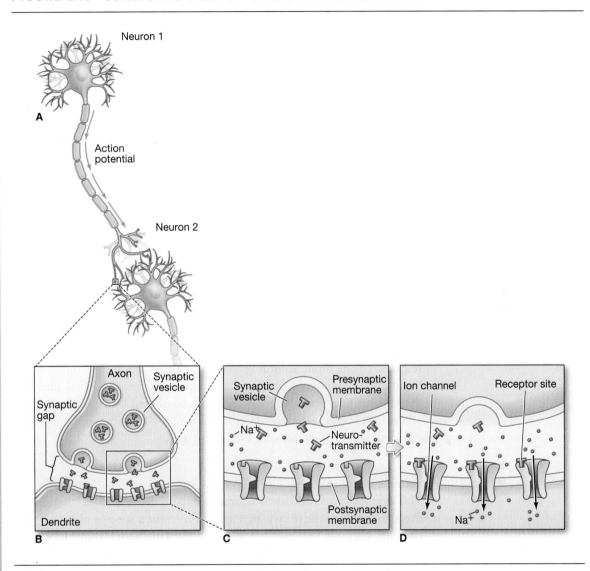

(Panel A) Neuron 1 transmits a message across the synaptic gap to Neuron 2. The neurotransmitters are initially stored in structures called "synaptic vesicles" (Panel B). When a signal travels down the axon, the vesicles are stimulated and some of them burst (Panel C), ejecting neurotransmitter molecules into the synaptic gap and toward the postsynaptic membrane (Panel D). Neurotransmitter molecules settle on receptor sites, ion channels open, and sodium (Na+) floods in.

the **all-or-none law**. Just as pounding on a car horn won't make the horn any louder, a stronger stimulus won't produce a stronger action potential. A neuron either fires or it doesn't; there's no in-between.

This does not mean, however, that neurons always send exactly the same information. A neuron can fire many times per second or only occasionally. A neuron can fire just once and then stop, or it can keep firing for an extended span. But, even so, each individual response by the neuron is always the same size.

Third, we should also note that the brain relies on many different neurotransmitters. By some counts, a hundred transmitters have been catalogued so far, and this diversity enables the brain to send a variety of different messages. Some transmitters have the effect of stimulating subsequent neurons; some do the opposite and *inhibit* other neurons. Some transmitters play an essential role in learning and memory; others play a key role in regulating the level of arousal in the brain; still others influence motivation and emotion.

Fourth, let's be clear about the central role of the synapse. The synaptic gap is actually quite small—roughly 20 to 30 nanometers across. (For contrast's sake, the diameter of a human hair is roughly 80,000 nanometers.) Even so, transmission across this gap slows down the neuronal signal, but this is a tiny price to pay for the advantages created by this mode of signaling: Each neuron receives information from (i.e., has synapses with) many other neurons, and this allows the "receiving" neuron to integrate information from many sources. This pattern of many neurons feeding into one also makes it possible for a neuron to "compare" signals and to adjust its response to one input according to the signal arriving from a different input. In addition, communication at the synapse is *adjustable*. This means that the strength of a synaptic connection can be altered by experience, and this adjustment is crucial for the process of *learning*—the storage of new knowledge and new skills within the nervous system.

Coding

This discussion of individual neurons leads to a further question: How do these microscopic nerve cells manage to represent a specific idea or a specific content? Let's say that right now you're thinking about your favorite song. How is this information represented by neurons? The issue here is referred to as **coding**, and there are many options for what the neurons' "code" might be (Gallistel, 2017). As one option, we might imagine that a specific group of neurons somehow represents "favorite song," so that whenever you're thinking about the song, it's precisely these neurons that are activated. Or, as a different option, the song might be represented by a broad *pattern* of neuronal activity. If so, "favorite song" might be represented in the brain by something like "Neuron X firing strongly while Neuron Y is firing weakly and Neuron Z is not firing at all" (and so on for thousands of other neurons). Note that within this scheme the same neurons might be involved in the representation of other sounds, but with different patterns. So—to continue our example—Neuron X might also be involved in the representation of the sound of a car

TEST YOURSELF

10. What are glia? What are dendrites? What is an axon? What is a synapse?

11. What does it mean to say that neurons rely on two different forms of information flow, one chemical and one electrical?

engine, but for this sound it might be part of a pattern that includes Neurons Q, R, and S also firing strongly, and Neuron Y not firing at all.

As it turns out, the brain uses both forms of coding. For example, in Chapter 4 we'll see that some neurons really are associated with a particular content. In fact, researchers documented a cell in one of the people they tested that fired whenever a picture of Jennifer Aniston was in view, and didn't fire in response to pictures of other faces. Another cell (in a different person's brain) fired whenever a picture of the Sydney Opera House was shown, but didn't fire when other buildings were in view (Quiroga, Reddy, Kreiman, Koch, & Fried, 2005)! These do seem to be cases in which an idea (in particular, a certain visual image) is represented by specific neurons in the brain.

In other cases, evidence suggests that ideas and memories are represented in the brain through widespread patterns of activity. This sort of "pattern coding" is, for example, certainly involved in the neural mechanisms through which you plan, and then carry out, particular motions—like reaching out to turn a book page or lifting your foot to step over an obstacle (Georgopoulos, 1990, 1995). We'll return to pattern coding in Chapter 9, when we discuss the notion of a *distributed representation*.

Moving On

We have now described the brain's basic anatomy and have also taken a brief look at the brain's microscopic parts—the individual neurons. But how do all of these elements, large and small, function in ways that enable us to think, remember, learn, speak, or feel? As a step toward tackling this issue, the next chapter takes a closer look at the portions of the nervous system that allow us to *see*. We'll use the visual system as our example for two important reasons. First, vision is the modality through which humans acquire a huge amount of information, whether by reading or simply by viewing the world around us. If we understand vision, therefore, we understand the processes that bring us much of our knowledge. Second, investigators have made enormous progress in mapping out the neural "wiring" of the visual system, offering a detailed and sophisticated portrait of how this system operates. As a result, an examination of vision provides an excellent illustration of how the study of the brain can proceed and what it can teach us.

TEST YOURSELF

12. How is information coded, or represented, in the brain?

COGNITIVE PSYCHOLOGY AND EDUCATION

food supplements and cognition

Various businesses try to sell you training programs or food supplements that (they claim) will improve your memory, help you think more clearly, and so on. Evidence suggests, though, that the currently offered training programs may provide little benefit. These programs do improve performance on the specific exercises contained within the training itself, but they have no impact on any tasks beyond these exercises. In other words, the programs don't seem to help with the sorts of mental challenges you encounter in day-to-day functioning (Simons et al., 2016).

What about food supplements? Most of these supplements have not been tested in any systematic way, and so there's little (and often no) solid evidence to support the claims sometimes made for these products. One supplement, though, has been rigorously tested: *Ginkgo biloba*, an extract derived from a tree of the same name and advertised as capable of enhancing memory. Is *Ginkgo biloba* effective? To answer that question, let's begin with the fact that for its normal functioning, the brain requires an excellent blood flow and, with that, a lot of oxygen and a lot of nutrients. Indeed, it's estimated that the brain, constituting roughly 2% of your body weight, consumes 15% percent of your body's energy supply.

It's not surprising, therefore, that the brain's operations are impaired if some change in your health interferes with the flow of oxygen or nutrients. If (for example) you're ill, or not eating enough, or not getting enough sleep, these conditions affect virtually all aspects of your biological functioning. However, since the brain is so demanding of nutrients and oxygen, it's one of the first organs to suffer if the supply of these necessities is compromised. This is why poor nutrition or poor health almost inevitably undermines your ability to think, to remember, or to pay attention.

Within this context, it's important that *Ginkgo biloba* can improve blood circulation and reduce some sorts of bodily inflammation. Because of these effects, *Ginkgo* can be helpful for people who have circulatory problems or who are at risk for nerve damage, and one group that may benefit is patients with Alzheimer's disease. Evidence suggests that *Ginkgo* helps these patients remember more and think more clearly, but this isn't because *Ginkgo* is making these patients "smarter" in any direct way. Instead, the *Ginkgo* is broadly improving the patients' blood circulation and the health status of their nerve cells, allowing these cells to do their work.

What about healthy people—those not suffering from bodily inflammations or damage to their brain cells? Here, the evidence is mixed, but most studies have observed no benefit from this food supplement. Apparently, *Ginkgo*'s effects, if they exist at all in healthy adults, are so small that they're difficult to detect.

Are there other steps that *will* improve the mental functioning of healthy young adults? Answers here have to be tentative, because new "smart pills" and "smart foods" are being proposed all the time, and each one has to be tested before we can know its effects. For now, though, we've already indicated part of a positive answer: Good nutrition, plenty of sleep, and adequate exercise will keep your blood supply in good condition, and this will help your brain to do its job. In addition, there may be something else you can do. The brain needs "fuel" to do its work, and the body's fuel comes from the sugar *glucose*. You can protect yourself, therefore, by making sure that your

GINKGO BILOBA

A variety of food supplements derived from the ginkgo tree are alleged to improve cognitive functioning. Current understanding, though, suggests that the benefits of *Ginkgo biloba* are indirect: This supplement improves functioning because it can improve blood circulation and can help the body to fight some forms of inflammation.

brain has all the glucose it needs. This isn't a recommendation to jettison all other aspects of your diet and eat nothing but chocolate bars. In fact, most of the glucose your body needs doesn't come from sugary foods; instead, most comes from the breakdown of carbohydrates—from the grains, dairy products, fruits, and vegetables you eat. For this reason, it might be a good idea to have a slice of bread and a glass of milk just before taking an exam or walking into a particularly challenging class. These steps will help make sure that you're not caught by a glucose shortfall that could interfere with your brain's functioning.

Also, be careful not to ingest *too much* sugar. If you eat a big candy bar just before an exam, you might get an upward spike in your blood glucose followed by a sudden drop, and these abrupt changes can produce problems of their own.

Overall, then, it seems that food supplements tested so far offer no "fast track" toward better cognition. *Ginkgo biloba* is helpful, but mostly for special populations. A high-carb snack may help, but it will be of little value if you're already adequately nourished. Therefore, on all these grounds, the best path toward better cognition seems to be the one that common sense would already recommend—eating a balanced diet, getting a good night's sleep, and paying careful attention during your studies.

For more on this topic . . .

Allen, A. L., & Strand, N. K. (2015). Cognitive enhancement and beyond: Recommendations from the Bioethics Commission. *Trends in Cognitive Sciences, 19*, 549–555.

Gold, P. E., Cahill, L., & Wenk, G. L. (2002). *Ginkgo biloba:* A cognitive enhancer? *Psychological Science in the Public Interest, 3*, 2–11.

Husain, M., & Mehta, M. A. (2011). Cognitive enhancement by drugs in health and disease. *Trends in Cognitive Sciences, 15*, 28–36.

Masicampo, E., & Baumeister, R. (2008). Toward a physiology of dual-process reasoning and judgment: Lemonade, willpower, and expensive rule-based analysis. *Psychological Science, 19*, 255–260.

McDaniel, M. A., Maier, S. F., & Einstein, G. O. (2002). "Brain-specific" nutrients: A memory cure? *Psychological Science in the Public Interest, 3*, 12–38.

Stough, C., & Pase, M. P. (2015). Improving cognition in the elderly with nutritional supplements. *Current Directions in Psychological Sciences, 24*, 177–183.

chapter review

SUMMARY

- The brain is divided into several different structures, but of particular importance for cognitive psychology is the forebrain. In the forebrain, each cerebral hemisphere is divided into the frontal lobe, parietal lobe, temporal lobe, and occipital lobe. In understanding these brain areas, one important source of evidence comes from studies of brain damage, enabling us to examine what sorts of symptoms result from lesions in specific brain locations. This has allowed a localization of function, an effort that is also supported by neuroimaging research, which shows that the pattern of activation in the brain depends on the particular task being performed.

- Different parts of the brain perform different jobs; but for virtually any mental process, different brain areas must work together in a closely integrated way. When this integration is lost (as it is, for example, in Capgras syndrome), bizarre symptoms can result.

- The primary motor projection areas are the departure points in the brain for nerve cells that initiate muscle movement. The primary sensory projection areas are the main points of arrival in the brain for information from the eyes, ears, and other sense organs. These projection areas generally show a pattern of contralateral control, with tissue in the left hemisphere sending or receiving its main signals from the right side of the body, and vice versa. Each projection area provides a map of the environment or the relevant body part, but the assignment of space in this map is governed by function, not by anatomical proportions.

- Most of the forebrain's cortex has traditionally been referred to as the association cortex, but this area is subdivided into specialized regions. This subdivision is reflected in the varying consequences of brain damage, with lesions in the occipital lobes leading to visual agnosia, damage in the temporal lobes leading to aphasia, and so on. Damage to the prefrontal area causes many different problems, but these are generally in the forming and implementing of strategies.

- The brain's functioning depends on neurons and glia. The glia perform many functions, but the main flow of information is carried by the neurons. Communication from one end of the neuron to the other is electrical and is governed by the flow of ions in and out of the cell. Communication from one neuron to the next is generally chemical, with a neuron releasing neurotransmitters that affect neurons on the other side of the synapse.

KEY TERMS

amygdala (p. 28)
prefrontal cortex (p. 29)
hindbrain (p. 32)
cerebellum (p. 33)
midbrain (p. 33)
forebrain (p. 34)
cortex (p. 34)
convolutions (p. 34)

longitudinal fissure (p. 34)
cerebral hemisphere (p. 34)
frontal lobes (p. 34)
central fissure (p. 34)
parietal lobes p. 34)
lateral fissure (p. 34)
temporal lobes (p. 34)
occipital lobes (p. 34)

TEST YOURSELF AGAIN

1. What are the symptoms of Capgras syndrome, and why do they suggest a two-part explanation for how people recognize faces?

2. What is the cerebral cortex?

3. What are the four major lobes of the forebrain?

4. Identify some of the functions of the hippocampus, the amygdala, and the corpus callosum.

5. What is the difference between *structural imaging* of the brain and *functional imaging*? What techniques are used for each?

6. What do we gain from *combining* different methods in studying the brain?

7. What is meant by the phrase "localization of function"?

8. What is a projection area in the brain? What's the role of the motor projection area? The sensory projection area?

9. What does it mean to say that the brain relies on "contralateral" connections?

10. What are glia? What are dendrites? What is an axon? What is a synapse?

11. What does it mean to say that neurons rely on two different forms of information flow, one chemical and one electrical?

12. How is information coded, or represented, in the brain?

THINK ABOUT IT

1. People often claim that humans only use 10% of their brains. Does anything in this chapter help us in evaluating this claim?

2. People claim that you need to "liberate your right brain" in order to be creative. What's true about this claim? What's false about this claim?

e eBOOK DEMONSTRATIONS & ESSAYS

Go to http://digital.wwnorton.com/cognition7 for the online demonstrations and essays relevant to this chapter. These can be found in the ebook.

Online Demonstrations

- Demonstration 2.1: Brain Anatomy
- Demonstration 2.2: The Speed of Neural Transmission
- Demonstration 2.3: "Acuity" in the Somatosensory System

Online Applying Cognitive Psychology and the Law Essays

- Cognitive Psychology and the Law: Improving the Criminal Justice System

ZAPS COGNITION LABS

Go to http://digital.wwnorton.com/cognition7 to experience interactive online psychology labs relevant to this chapter.

Learning about the World around Us

I n setting after setting, you rely on your knowledge and beliefs. But where does knowledge come from? The answer, usually, is *experience*, but this invites another question: What is it that makes experience possible? Tackling this issue will force us to examine mental processes that turn out to be surprisingly complex.

In Chapter 3, we'll ask how visual perception operates — and, therefore, how you manage to perceive the world around you. We'll start with events in the eyeball and then move to how you organize and interpret the visual information you receive. We'll also consider the ways in which you can *mis*interpret this information, so that you're vulnerable to illusions.

Chapter 4 takes a further step and asks how you manage to recognize and categorize the objects that you see. We'll start with a simple case: how you recognize printed letters. We'll then turn to the recognition of more complex (three-dimensional) objects.

In both chapters, we'll discuss the active role that you play in shaping your experience. We'll see, for example, that your perceptual apparatus doesn't just "pick up" the information that's available to you. You don't, in other words, just open your eyes and let the information "flow in." Instead, we'll discuss the ways in which you supplement and interpret the information you receive. In Chapter 3, we'll see that this activity begins very early in the sequence of biological events that support visual perception. In Chapter 4, these ideas will lead us to a mechanism made up of very simple components, but shaped by a broad pattern of knowledge.

Chapter 5 then turns to the study of attention. As we'll see, paying attention is a complex achievement involving many elements. We'll discuss how the mechanisms of attention can sometimes limit what people achieve — and so part of what's at stake in Chapter 5 is the question of what people ultimately can or cannot accomplish, and whether there may be ways to escape these apparent limits on human performance.

chapter **3** | Visual Perception

what if... You look around the world and instantly, effortlessly, recognize the objects that surround you — words on this page, objects in the room where you're sitting, things you can view out the window. Perception, in other words, seems fast, easy, and automatic. But even so, there is complexity here, and your ability to perceive the world depends on many separate and individually complicated processes.

Consider the disorder *akinetopsia* (Zeki, 1991). This condition is rare, and much of what we know comes from a single patient — L.M. — who developed this disorder because of a blood clot in her brain, at age 43. L.M. was completely unable to perceive motion — even though other aspects of her vision (e.g., her ability to recognize objects, to see color, or to discern detail in a visual pattern) seemed normal.

Because of her akinetopsia, L.M. can detect that an object *now* is in a position different from its position a moment ago, but she reports seeing "nothing in between." As a way of capturing this experience, think about what you see when you're looking at really slow movement. If, for example, you stare at the hour hand on a clock as it creeps around the clock face, you cannot discern its motion. But you can easily see the hand is now pointing, say, at the 4, and if you come back a while later, you can see that it's closer to the 5. In this way, you can *infer* motion from the change in position, but you can't *perceive* the motion. This is your experience with very slow movement; L.M., suffering from akinetopsia, has the same experience with *all* movement.

What's it like to have this disorder? L.M. complained, as one concern, that it was hard to cross the street because she couldn't tell which of the cars in view were moving and which ones were parked. (She eventually learned to estimate the position and movement of traffic by listening to cars' *sounds* as they approached, even though she couldn't see their movement.)

Other problems caused by akinetopsia are more surprising. For example, L.M. complained about difficulties in following conversations, because she was essentially blind to the speaker's lip movement or changing facial expressions. She also felt insecure in social settings. If more than two people were moving around in a room, she felt anxious because "people were suddenly here or there, but [she had] not seen them moving" (Zihl, von Cramon, & Mai, 1983, p. 315). Or, as a different example: She had trouble in everyday activities like pouring a cup of

- We explore vision—humans' dominant sensory modality. We discuss the mechanisms through which the visual system detects patterns in the incoming light, but we also showcase the *activity* of the visual system in interpreting and shaping the incoming information.

- We also highlight the ways in which perception of one aspect of the input is shaped by perception of other

aspects—so that the detection of simple features depends on how the overall form is organized, and the perception of size depends on the perceived distance of the target object.

- We emphasize that the interpretation of the visual input is usually accurate—but the same mechanisms can lead to illusions, and the study of those illusions can often illuminate the processes through which perception functions.

coffee. She couldn't see the fluid level's gradual rise as she poured, so she didn't know when to stop pouring. For her, "the fluid appeared to be frozen, like a glacier" (Zihl et al., 1983, p. 315; also Schenk, Ellison, Rice, & Milner, 2005; Zihl, von Cramon, Mai, & Schmid, 1991).

We will have more to say about cases of disordered perception later in the chapter. For now, though, let's note the specificity of this disorder—a disruption of movement perception, with other aspects of perception still intact. Let's also highlight the important point that each of us is, in countless ways, dependent on our perceptual contact with the world. That point demands that we ask: What makes this perception possible?

The Visual System

You receive information about the world through various sensory modalities: You hear the sound of the approaching train, you smell the freshly baked bread, you feel the tap on your shoulder. Researchers have made impressive progress in studying all of these modalities, and students interested in, say, hearing or the sense of smell will find a course in (or a book about) sensation and perception to be fascinating.

There's no question, though, that for humans vision is the dominant sense. This is reflected in how much brain area is devoted to vision compared to any of the other senses. It's also reflected in many aspects of our behavior. For example, if visual information conflicts with information received from other senses, you usually place your trust in vision. This is the basis for ventriloquism, in which you see the dummy's mouth moving while the sounds themselves are coming from the dummy's master. Vision wins out in this contest, and so you experience the illusion that the voice is coming from the dummy.

The Photoreceptors

How does vision operate? The process begins, of course, with light. Light is produced by many objects in our surroundings—the sun, lamps, candles—and then reflects off other objects. In most cases, it's this reflected light—reflected from this book page or from a friend's face—that launches the processes of visual perception. Some of this light hits the front surface of the eyeball, passes through the **cornea** and the **lens**, and then hits the **retina**, the light-sensitive tissue that lines the back of the eyeball (see **Figure 3.1**). The cornea and lens focus the incoming light, just as a camera lens might, so that a sharp image is cast onto the retina. Adjustments in this process can take place because the lens is surrounded by a band of muscle. When the muscle tightens, the lens bulges somewhat, creating the proper shape for focusing the images cast by nearby objects. When the muscle relaxes, the lens returns to a flatter shape, allowing the proper focus for objects farther away.

On the retina, there are two types of **photoreceptors**—specialized neural cells that respond directly to the incoming light. One type, the **rods**, are sensitive to very low levels of light and so play an essential role whenever you're moving around in semidarkness or trying to view a fairly dim

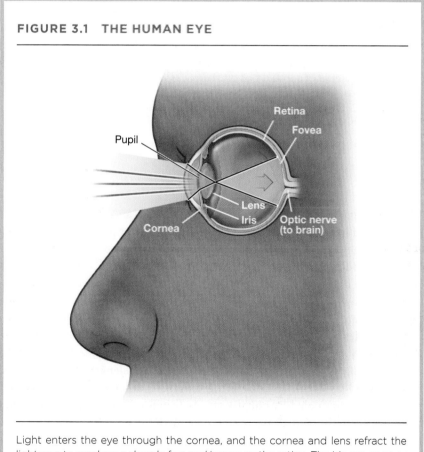

FIGURE 3.1 THE HUMAN EYE

Light enters the eye through the cornea, and the cornea and lens refract the light rays to produce a sharply focused image on the retina. The iris can open or close to control the amount of light that reaches the retina. The retina is made up of three main layers: the rods and cones, which are the photoreceptors; the bipolar cells; and the ganglion cells, whose axons make up the optic nerve.

FIGURE 3.2   RODS AND CONES

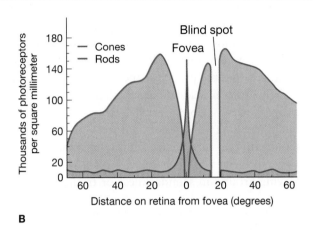

A   B

(Panel A) Rods and cones are the light-sensitive cells at the back of the retina that launch the neural process of vision. In this (colorized) photo, cones appear green; rods appear brown. (Panel B) Distribution of photoreceptors. Cones are most frequent at the fovea, and the number of cones drops off sharply as we move away from the fovea. In contrast, there are no rods at all on the fovea. There are neither rods nor cones at the retina's blind spot—the position at which the neural fibers that make up the optic nerve exit the eyeball. Because this position is filled with these fibers, there's no space for any rods or cones.

stimulus. But the rods are also color-blind: They can distinguish different intensities of light (and in that way contribute to your perception of brightness), but they provide no means of discriminating one hue from another (see **Figure 3.2**).

Cones, in contrast, are less sensitive than rods and so need more incoming light to operate at all. But cones are sensitive to color differences. More precisely, there are three different types of cones, each having its own pattern of sensitivities to different wavelengths (see **Figure 3.3**). You perceive color, therefore, by comparing the outputs from these three cone types. Strong firing from only the cones that prefer short wavelengths, for example, accompanied by weak (or no) firing from the other cone types, signals purple. Blue is signaled by equally strong firing from the cones that prefer short wavelengths and those that prefer medium wavelengths, with only modest firing by cones that prefer long wavelengths. And so on, with other patterns of firing, across the three cone types, corresponding to different perceived hues.

Cones have another function: They enable you to discern fine detail. The ability to see fine detail is referred to as **acuity,** and acuity is much higher for

FIGURE 3.3 WAVELENGTHS OF LIGHT

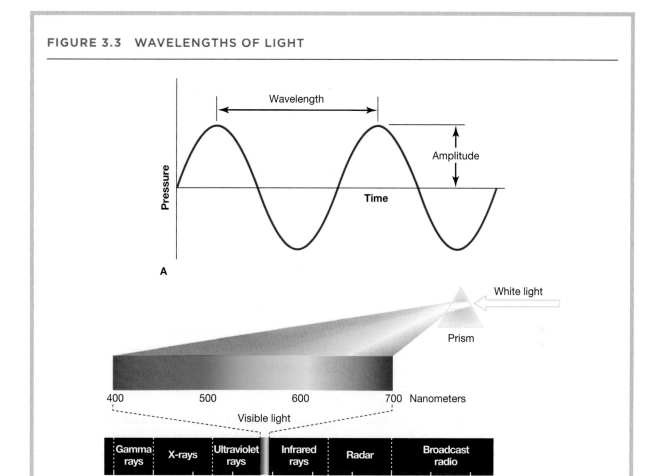

The physics of light are complex, but for many purposes light can be thought of as a wave (Panel A), and the shape of the wave can be described in terms of its amplitude and its wavelength (i.e., the distance from "crest" to "crest"). The wavelengths our visual system can sense are only a tiny part of the broader electromagnetic spectrum (Panel B). Light with a wavelength longer than 750 nanometers is invisible to us, although we feel these longer infrared waves as heat. Ultraviolet light, which has a wavelength shorter than 360 nanometers, is also invisible to us. That leaves the narrow band of wavelengths between 750 and 360 nanometers — the so-called visible spectrum. Within this spectrum, we usually see wavelengths close to 400 nanometers as violet, those close to 700 nanometers as red, and those in between as the rest of the colors in the rainbow.

the cones than it is for the rods. This explains why you point your eyes toward a target whenever you want to perceive it in detail. What you're actually doing is positioning your eyes so that the image of the target falls onto the **fovea,** the very center of the retina. Here, cones far outnumber rods (and, in fact, the center of the fovea has no rods at all). As a result, this is the region of the retina with the greatest acuity.

In portions of the retina more distant from the fovea (i.e., portions of the retina in the so-called visual periphery), the rods predominate; well out into the periphery, there are no cones at all. This distribution of photoreceptors explains why you're better able to see very dim lights out of the corner of your eyes. Psychologists have understood this point for at least a century, but the key observation here has a much longer history. Sailors and astronomers have known for hundreds of years that when looking at a barely visible star, it's best not to look directly at the star's location. By looking slightly away from the star, they ensured that the star's image would fall outside of the fovea and onto a region of the retina dense with the more light-sensitive rods.

Lateral Inhibition

Rods and cones do not report directly to the cortex. Instead, the photoreceptors stimulate **bipolar cells**, which in turn excite **ganglion cells**. The ganglion cells are spread uniformly across the entire retina, but all of their axons converge to form the bundle of nerve fibers that we call the **optic nerve**. This is the nerve tract that leaves the eyeball and carries information to various sites in the brain. The information is sent first to a way station in the thalamus called the **lateral geniculate nucleus (LGN)**; from there, information is transmitted to the primary projection area for vision, in the occipital lobe.

Let's be clear, though, that the optic nerve is not just a cable that conducts signals from one site to another. Instead, the cells that link retina to brain are already analyzing the visual input. One example lies in the phenomenon of **lateral inhibition**, a pattern in which cells, when stimulated, inhibit the activity of neighboring cells. To see why this is important, consider two cells, each receiving stimulation from a brightly lit area (see **Figure 3.4**). One cell (Cell B in the figure) is receiving its stimulation from the middle of the lit area. It is intensely stimulated, but so are its neighbors (including Cell A and Cell C). As a result, all of these cells are active, and therefore each one is trying to inhibit its neighbors. The upshot is that the activity level of Cell B is *increased* by the stimulation but *decreased* by the lateral inhibition it's receiving from Cells A and C. This combination leads to only a moderate level of activity in Cell B.

In contrast, another cell (Cell C in the figure) is receiving its stimulation from the edge of the lit area. It is intensely stimulated, and so are its neighbors *on one side*. Therefore, this cell will receive inhibition from one side but not from the other (in the figure: inhibition from Cell B but *not* from Cell D), so it will be less inhibited than Cell B (which is receiving inhibition from both sides). Thus, Cells B and C initially receive the same input, but C is less inhibited than B and so will end up firing more strongly than B.

FIGURE 3.4 LATERAL INHIBITION

Cell B receives strong inhibition from all its neighbors, because its neighbors are intensely stimulated. Cell C, in contrast, receives inhibition only from one side (because its neighbor on the other side, Cell D, is only moderately stimulated). As a result, Cells B and C start with the same input, but Cell C, receiving less inhibition, sends a stronger signal to the brain, emphasizing the edge in the stimulus. The same logic applies to Cells D and E, and it explains why Cell D sends a weaker signal to the brain. Note, by the way, that the spikes per second numbers, shown in the figure, are hypothetical and intended only to illustrate lateral inhibition's effects.

Notice that the pattern of lateral inhibition highlights a surface's edges, because the response of cells detecting the edge of the surface (such as Cell C) will be stronger than that of cells detecting the middle of the surface (such as Cell B). For that matter, by *increasing* the response by Cell C and *decreasing* the response by Cell D, lateral inhibition actually exaggerates the contrast at the edge—a process called **edge enhancement**. This process is of enormous

FIGURE 3.5   MACH BANDS

Edge enhancement, produced by lateral inhibition, helps us to perceive the outline that defines an object's shape. But the same process can produce illusions—including the Mach bands. Each vertical strip in this figure is of uniform light intensity, but the strips don't appear uniform. For each strip, contrast makes the left edge (next to its darker neighbor) look brighter than the rest, while the right edge (next to its lighter neighbor) looks darker. To see that the differences are illusions, try placing a thin object (such as a toothpick or a straightened paper clip) on top of the boundary between strips. With the strips separated in this manner, the illusion disappears.

TEST YOURSELF

1. What are the differences between rods and cones? What traits do these cells *share*?
2. What is lateral inhibition? How does it contribute to edge perception?

importance, because it's obviously highlighting the information that defines an object's shape—information essential for figuring out what the object *is*. And let's emphasize that this edge enhancement occurs at a very early stage of the visual processing. In other words, the information sent to the brain isn't a mere copy of the incoming stimulation; instead, the steps of interpretation and analysis begin immediately, in the eyeball. (For a demonstration of an *illusion* caused by this edge enhancement—the so-called **Mach bands**—see **Figure 3.5**.)

Visual Coding

In Chapter 2, we introduced the idea of coding in the nervous system. This term refers to the relationship between activity in the nervous system and the stimulus (or idea or operation) that is somehow represented by that activity. In the study of perception, we can ask: What's the code through which neurons (or groups of neurons) manage to represent the shapes, colors, sizes, and movements that you perceive?

Single Neurons and Single-Cell Recording

Part of what we know about the visual system—actually, part of what we know about the entire brain—comes from a technique called **single-cell recording**. As the name implies, this is a procedure through which investigators can record, moment by moment, the pattern of electrical changes within a single neuron.

We mentioned in Chapter 2 that when a neuron fires, each response is the same size; this is the *all-or-none law*. But neurons can vary in *how often* they fire, and when investigators record the activity of a single neuron, what they're usually interested in is the cell's firing rate, measured in "spikes per second." The investigator can then vary the circumstances (either in the external world or elsewhere in the nervous system) in order to learn what makes the cell fire more and what makes it fire less. In this way, we can figure out what job the neuron does within the broad context of the entire nervous system.

The technique of single-cell recording has been used with enormous success in the study of vision. In a typical procedure, the animal being studied is first immobilized. Then, electrodes are placed just outside a neuron in the animal's optic nerve or brain. Next, a computer screen is placed in front of the animal's eyes, and various patterns are flashed on the screen: circles, lines at various angles, or squares of various sizes at various positions. Researchers can then ask: Which patterns cause that neuron to fire? To what visual inputs does that cell respond?

By analogy, we know that a smoke detector is a smoke detector because it "fires" (i.e., makes noise) when smoke is on the scene. We know that a motion detector is a motion detector because it "fires" when something moves nearby. But what kind of detector is a given neuron? Is it responsive to any light in any position within the field of view? In that case, we might call it a "light detector." Or is it perhaps responsive only to certain shapes at certain positions (and therefore is a "shape detector")? With this logic, we can map out precisely what the cell responds to—what kind of detector it is. More formally, this procedure allows us to define the cell's **receptive field**—that is, the size and shape of the area in the visual world to which that cell responds.

Multiple Types of Receptive Fields

In 1981, the neurophysiologists David Hubel and Torsten Wiesel were awarded the Nobel Prize for their exploration of the mammalian visual system (e.g., Hubel & Wiesel, 1959, 1968). They documented the existence of specialized neurons within the brain, each of which has a different type of receptive field, a different kind of visual trigger. For example, some neurons seem to function as "dot detectors." These cells fire at their maximum

TORSTEN WIESEL AND DAVID HUBEL

Much of what we know about the visual system is based on the pioneering work done by David Hubel and Torsten Wiesel. This pair of researchers won the 1981 Nobel Prize for their discoveries. (They shared the Nobel with Roger Sperry for his independent research on the cerebral hemispheres.)

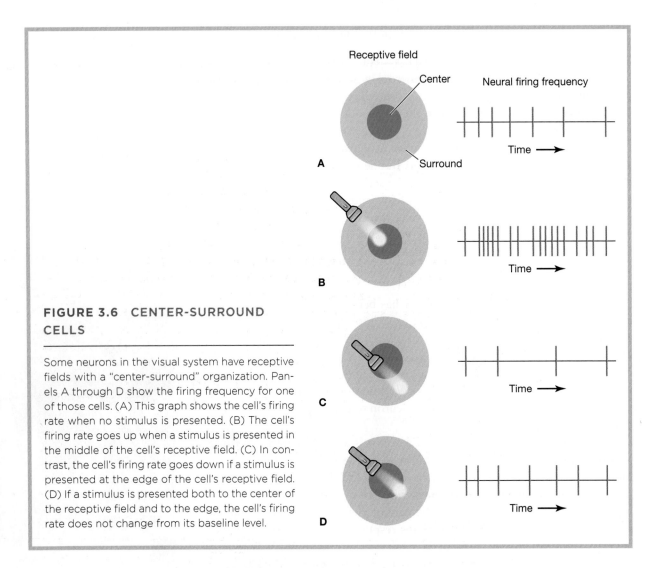

FIGURE 3.6 CENTER-SURROUND CELLS

Some neurons in the visual system have receptive fields with a "center-surround" organization. Panels A through D show the firing frequency for one of those cells. (A) This graph shows the cell's firing rate when no stimulus is presented. (B) The cell's firing rate goes up when a stimulus is presented in the middle of the cell's receptive field. (C) In contrast, the cell's firing rate goes down if a stimulus is presented at the edge of the cell's receptive field. (D) If a stimulus is presented both to the center of the receptive field and to the edge, the cell's firing rate does not change from its baseline level.

rate when light is presented in a small, roughly circular area in a specific position within the field of view. Presentations of light just outside of this area cause the cell to fire at *less* than its usual "resting" rate, so the input must be precisely positioned to make this cell fire. **Figure 3.6** depicts such a receptive field.

These cells are often called **center-surround cells**, to mark the fact that light presented to the central region of the receptive field has one influence, while light presented to the surrounding ring has the opposite influence. If both the center and the surround are strongly stimulated, the cell will fire neither more nor less than usual. For this cell, a strong uniform stimulus is equivalent to no stimulus at all.

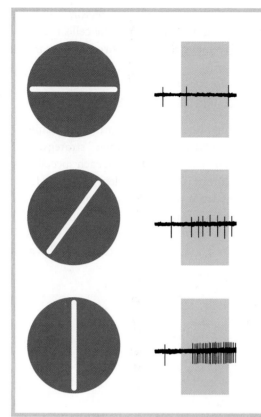

FIGURE 3.7 ORIENTATION-SPECIFIC VISUAL FIELDS

Some cells in the visual system fire only when the input contains a line segment at a certain orientation. For example, one cell might fire very little in response to a horizontal line, fire only occasionally in response to a diagonal, and fire at its maximum rate only when a vertical line is present. In this figure, the circles show the stimulus that was presented. The right side shows records of neural firing. Each vertical stroke represents a firing by the cell; the left–right position reflects the passage of time.   (AFTER HUBEL, 1963)

Other cells fire at their maximum only when a stimulus containing an edge of just the right orientation appears within their receptive fields. These cells, therefore, can be thought of as "edge detectors." Some of these cells fire at their maximum rate when a horizontal edge is presented; others, when a vertical edge is in view; still others fire at their maximum to orientations in between horizontal and vertical. Note, though, that in each case, these orientations merely define the cells' "preference," because these cells are not oblivious to edges of other orientations. If a cell's preference is for, say, horizontal edges, then the cell will still respond to other orientations— but less strongly than it does for horizontals. Specifically, the farther the edge is from the cell's preferred orientation, the weaker the firing will be, and edges sharply different from the cell's preferred orientation (e.g., a vertical edge for a cell that prefers horizontal) will elicit virtually no response (see **Figure 3.7**).

Other cells, elsewhere in the visual cortex, have receptive fields that are more specific. Some cells fire maximally only if an angle of a particular size appears in their receptive fields; others fire maximally in response to corners and notches. Still other cells appear to be "movement detectors" and fire strongly if a stimulus moves, say, from right to left across the cell's receptive field. Other cells favor left-to-right movement, and so on through the various possible directions of movement.

Parallel Processing in the Visual System

This proliferation of cell types highlights another important principle—namely, that the visual system relies on a "divide and conquer" strategy, with different types of cells, located in different areas of the cortex, each specializing in a particular kind of analysis. This pattern is plainly evident in **Area V1,** the site on the occipital lobe where axons from the LGN first reach the cortex (see **Figure 3.8**). In this brain area, some cells fire to (say) horizontals in *this* position in the visual world, others to horizontals in *that* position, others to verticals in specific positions, and so on. The full ensemble of cells in this area

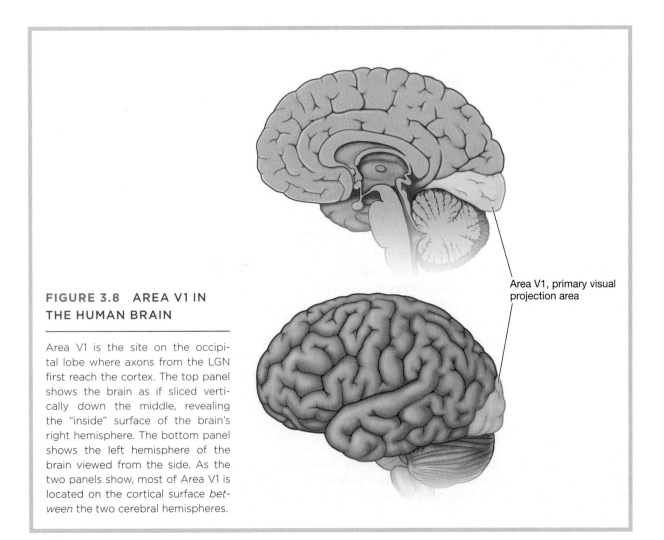

Area V1, primary visual projection area

FIGURE 3.8 AREA V1 IN THE HUMAN BRAIN

Area V1 is the site on the occipital lobe where axons from the LGN first reach the cortex. The top panel shows the brain as if sliced vertically down the middle, revealing the "inside" surface of the brain's right hemisphere. The bottom panel shows the left hemisphere of the brain viewed from the side. As the two panels show, most of Area V1 is located on the cortical surface *between* the two cerebral hemispheres.

provides a detector for every possible stimulus, making certain that no matter what the input is or where it's located, some cell will respond to it.

The pattern of specialization is also evident when we consider other brain areas. **Figure 3.9**, for example, reflects one summary of the brain areas known to be involved in vision. The details of the figure aren't crucial, but it is noteworthy that some of these areas (V1, V2, V3, V4, PO, and MT) are in the occipital cortex; other areas are in the parietal cortex; others are in the temporal cortex. (We'll have more to say in a moment about these areas outside of the occipital cortex.) Most important, each area seems to have its own function. Neurons in Area MT, for example, are acutely sensitive to direction and speed of movement. (This area is the brain region that has suffered damage in cases involving akinetopsia.) Cells in Area V4 fire most strongly when the input is of a certain color and a certain shape.

Let's also emphasize that all of these specialized areas are active at the same time, so that (for example) cells in Area MT are detecting movement in the visual input at the same time that cells in Area V4 are detecting shapes. In other words, the visual system relies on **parallel processing**—a system in

FIGURE 3.9   THE VISUAL PROCESSING PATHWAYS

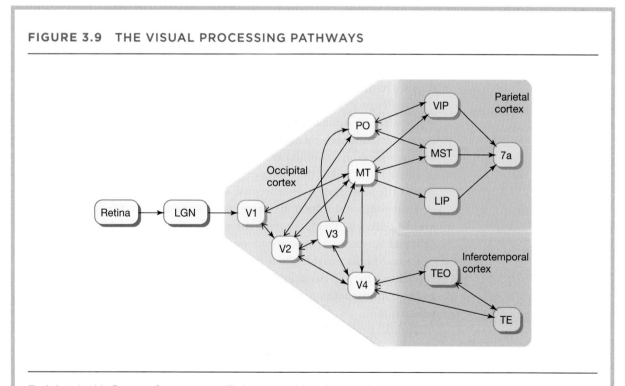

Each box in this figure refers to a specific location within the visual system. Notice that vision depends on many brain sites, each performing a specialized type of analysis. Note also that the flow of information is complex, so there's no strict sequence of "this step" of analysis followed by "that step." Instead, everything happens at once, with a great deal of back-and-forth communication among the various elements.

which many different steps (in this case, different kinds of analysis) are going on simultaneously. (Parallel processing is usually contrasted with **serial processing**, in which steps are carried out one at a time—i.e., in a series.)

One advantage of this simultaneous processing is speed: Brain areas trying to discern the shape of the incoming stimulus don't need to wait until the motion analysis or the color analysis is complete. Instead, all of the analyses go forward immediately when the input appears before the eyes, with no waiting time.

Another advantage of parallel processing is the possibility of mutual influence among multiple systems. To see why this matters, consider the fact that sometimes your interpretation of an object's motion depends on your understanding of the object's three-dimensional shape. This suggests that it might be best if the perception of shape happened first. That way, you could use the results of this processing step as a guide to later analyses. In other cases, though, the relationship between shape and motion is reversed. In these cases, your interpretation of an object's three-dimensional shape depends on your understanding of its motion. To allow for this possibility, it might be best if the perception of motion happened first, so that it could guide the subsequent analysis of shape.

How does the brain deal with these contradictory demands? Parallel processing provides the answer. Since both sorts of analysis go on simultaneously, each type of analysis can be informed by the other. Put differently, neither the shape-analyzing system nor the motion-analyzing system gets priority. Instead, the two systems work concurrently and "negotiate" a solution that satisfies both systems (Van Essen & DeYoe, 1995).

Parallel processing is easy to document throughout the visual system. As we've seen, the retina contains two types of specialized receptors (rods and cones) each doing its own job (e.g., the rods detecting stimuli in the periphery of your vision and stimuli presented at low light levels, and the cones detecting hues and detail at the center of your vision). Both types of receptors function at the same time—another case of parallel processing.

Likewise, within the optic nerve itself, there are two types of cells, **P cells** and **M cells**. The P cells provide the main input for the LGN's **parvocellular cells** and appear to be specialized for spatial analysis and the detailed analysis of form. M cells provide the input for the LGN's **magnocellular cells** and are specialized for the detection of motion and the perception of depth.[1] And, again, both of these systems are functioning at the same time—more parallel processing.

Parallel processing remains in evidence when we move beyond the occipital cortex. As **Figure 3.10** shows, some of the activation from the occipital

---

1. The names here refer to the relative sizes of the relevant cells: *parvo* derives from the Latin word for "small," and *magno* from the word for "large." To remember the function of these two types of cells, many students think of the P cells as specialized roughly for the perception of *pattern* and M cells as specialized for the perception of *motion*. These descriptions are crude, but they're easy to remember.

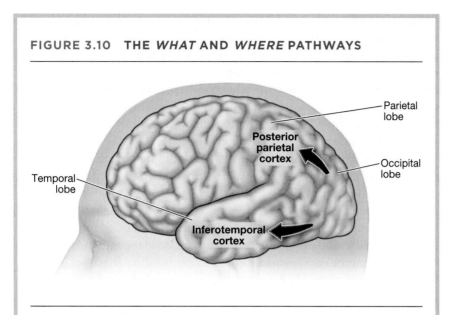

FIGURE 3.10 THE *WHAT* AND *WHERE* PATHWAYS

Parietal lobe

Posterior parietal cortex

Occipital lobe

Temporal lobe

Inferotemporal cortex

Information from the primary visual cortex at the back of the head is transmitted to the inferotemporal cortex (the so-called *what* system) and to the posterior parietal cortex (the *where* system). The term "inferotemporal" refers to the lower part of the temporal lobe. The term "posterior parietal cortex" refers to the rearmost portion of this cortex.

lobe is passed along to the cortex of the temporal lobe. This pathway, often called the **what** system, plays a major role in the identification of visual objects, telling you whether the object is a cat, an apple, or whatever. At the same time, activation from the occipital lobe is also passed along a second pathway, leading to the parietal cortex, in what is often called the **where** system. This system seems to guide your action based on your perception of where an object is located—above or below you, to your right or to your left. (See Goodale & Milner, 2004; Humphreys & Riddoch, 2014; Ungerleider & Haxby, 1994; Ungerleider & Mishkin, 1982. For some complications, though, see Borst, Thompson, & Kosslyn, 2011; de Haan & Cowey, 2011.)

The contrasting roles of these two systems can be revealed in many ways, including through studies of brain damage. Patients with lesions in the *what* system show visual agnosia—an inability to recognize visually presented objects, including such common things as a cup or a pencil. However, these patients show little disorder in recognizing visual orientation or in reaching. The reverse pattern occurs with patients who have suffered lesions in the *where* system: They have difficulty in reaching, but no problem in object identification (Damasio, Tranel, & Damasio, 1989; Farah, 1990; Goodale, 1995; Newcombe, Ratcliff, & Damasio, 1987).

Still other data echo this broad theme of parallel processing among separate systems. For example, we noted earlier that different brain areas are critical for the perception of color, motion, and form. If this is right, then someone who has suffered damage in just one of these areas might show problems in the perception of color but not the perception of motion or form, or problems in the perception of motion but not the perception of form or color. These predictions are correct. As we mentioned at the chapter's start, some patients suffer damage to the motion system and so develop akinetopsia (Zihl et al., 1983). For such patients, the world is described as a succession of static photographs. They're unable to report the speed or direction of a moving object; as one patient put it, "When I'm looking at the car first, it seems far away. But then when I want to cross the road, suddenly the car is very near" (Zihl et al., 1983, p. 315).

Other patients suffer a specific loss of color vision through damage to the central nervous system, even though their perception of form and motion remains normal (Damasio, 1985; Gazzaniga, Ivry, & Mangun, 2014; Meadows, 1974). To them, the entire world is clothed only in "dirty shades of gray."[2]

Cases like these provide dramatic confirmation of the separateness of our visual system's various elements and the ways in which the visual system is vulnerable to very specific forms of damage. (For further evidence with neurologically intact participants, see Bundesen, Kyllingsbaek, & Larsen, 2003.)

Putting the Pieces Back Together

Let's emphasize once again, therefore, that even the simplest of our intellectual achievements depends on an array of different, highly specialized brain areas all working together in parallel. This was evident in Chapter 2 in our consideration of Capgras syndrome, and the same pattern has emerged in our description of the visual system. Here, too, many brain areas must work together: the *what* system and the *where* system, areas specialized for the detection of movement and areas specialized for the identification of simple forms.

We have identified the advantages that come from this division of labor and the parallel processing it allows. But the division of labor also creates a problem: If multiple brain areas contribute to an overall task, how is their functioning coordinated? When you see an athlete make an astonishing jump, the jump itself is registered by motion-sensitive neurons, but your recognition of the athlete depends on shape-sensitive neurons. How are the pieces put back together? When you reach for a coffee cup but stop midway because you see that the cup is empty, the reach itself is guided by the *where* system; the fact that the cup is empty is registered by the *what* system. How are these two streams of processing coordinated?

Investigators refer to this broad issue as the **binding problem**—the task of reuniting the various elements of a scene, elements that are initially addressed by different systems in different parts of the brain. And obviously

---

2. This is different from ordinary color blindness, which is usually present from birth and results from abnormalities that are outside the brain itself—for example, abnormalities in the photoreceptors.

this problem is solved. What you perceive is not an unordered catalogue of sensory elements. Instead, you perceive a coherent, integrated perceptual world. Apparently, this is a case in which the various pieces of Humpty Dumpty are reassembled to form an organized whole.

Visual Maps and Firing Synchrony

Look around you. Your visual system registers whiteness and blueness and brownness; it also registers a small cylindrical shape (your coffee cup), a medium-sized rectangle (this book page), and a much larger rectangle (your desk). How do you put these pieces together so that you see that it's the coffee cup, and not the book page, that's blue; the desktop, and not the cup, that's brown?

There is debate about how the visual system solves this problem, but we can identify three elements that contribute to the solution. One element is *spatial position*. The part of the brain registering the cup's shape is separate from the parts registering its color or its motion; nonetheless, these various brain areas all have something in common. They each keep track of where the target is—where the cylindrical shape was located, and where the blue-ness was; where the motion was detected, and where things were still. As a result, the reassembling of these pieces can be done with reference to position. In essence, you can overlay the map of *which forms are where* on top of the map of *which colors are where* to get the right colors with the right forms, and likewise for the map showing *which motion patterns are where*.

Information about spatial position is, of course, useful for its own sake: You have a compelling reason to care whether the tiger is close to you or far away, or whether the bus is on your side of the street or the other. But in addition, location information apparently provides a frame of reference used to solve the binding problem. Given this double function, we shouldn't be surprised that spatial position is a major organizing theme in all the various brain areas concerned with vision, with each area seeming to provide its own map of the visual world.

Spatial position, however, is not the whole story. Evidence also suggests that the brain uses special *rhythms* to identify which sensory elements belong with which. Imagine two groups of neurons in the visual cortex. One group of neurons fires maximally whenever a vertical line is in view; another group fires maximally whenever a stimulus is in view moving from a high position to a low one. Let's also imagine that right now a vertical line is presented and it is moving downward; as a result, both groups of neurons are firing strongly. How does the brain encode the fact that these attributes are bound together, different aspects of a single object? There is evidence that the visual system marks this fact by means of **neural synchrony**: If the neurons detecting a vertical line are firing in synchrony with those signaling movement, then these attributes are registered as belonging to the same object. If they aren't in synchrony, then the features aren't bound together (Buzsáki & Draguhn, 2004; Csibra, Davis, Spratling, & Johnson, 2000; Elliott & Müller, 2000; Fries, Reynolds, Rorie, & Desimone, 2001).

What causes this synchrony? How do the neurons become synchronized in the first place? Here, another factor appears to be important: *attention*. We'll have more to say about attention in Chapter 5, but for now let's note that attention plays a key role in binding together the separate features of a stimulus. (For a classic statement of this argument, see Treisman & Gelade, 1980; Treisman, Sykes, & Gelade, 1977. For more recent views, see Quinlan, 2003; Rensink, 2012; and also Chapter 5.)

Evidence for attention's role comes from many sources, including the fact that when we overload someone's attention, she is likely to make **conjunction errors**. This means that she's likely to correctly detect the features present in a visual display, but then to make mistakes about how the features are bound together (or *conjoined*). Thus, for example, someone shown a blue *H* and a red *T* might report seeing a blue *T* and a red *H*—an error in binding.

Similarly, individuals who suffer from severe attention deficits (because of brain damage in the parietal cortex) are particularly impaired in tasks that require them to judge how features are conjoined to form complex objects (e.g., Robertson, Treisman, Friedman-Hill, & Grabowecky, 1997). Finally, studies suggest that synchronized neural firing occurs in an animal's brain when the animal is attending to a specific stimulus but does not occur in neurons activated by an unattended stimulus (e.g., Buschman & Miller, 2007; Saalmann, Pigarev, & Vidyasagar, 2007; Womelsdorf et al., 2007). All of these results point toward the claim that attention is crucial for the binding problem and, moreover, that attention is linked to the neural synchrony that seems to unite a stimulus's features.

Notice, then, that there are several ways in which information is represented in the brain. In Chapter 2, we noted that the brain uses different chemical signals (i.e., different neurotransmitters) to transmit different types of information. We now see that there is information reflected in *which* cells are firing, *how often* they are firing, whether the cells are firing in *synchrony* with other cells, and the *rhythm* in which they are firing. Plainly, this is a system of considerable complexity!

Form Perception

So far in this chapter, we've been discussing how visual perception begins: with the detection of simple attributes in the stimulus—its color, its motion, and its catalogue of features. But this detection is just the start of the process, because the visual system still has to assemble these features into recognizable wholes. We've mentioned the binding problem as part of this "assembly"—but binding isn't the whole story. This point is reflected in the fact that our perception of the visual world is organized in ways that the stimulus input is not—a point documented early in the 20th century by a group called the "Gestalt psychologists."[3] The Gestaltists argued that the organization is

---

3. *Gestalt* is the German word for "shape" or "form." The Gestalt psychology movement was committed to the view that theories about perception and thought need to emphasize the organization of patterns, not just focus on a pattern's elements.

contributed by the perceiver; this is why, they claimed, the perceptual whole is often different from the sum of its parts. Some years later, Jerome Bruner (1973) voiced related claims and coined the phrase "beyond the information given" to describe some of the ways our perception of a stimulus differs from (and goes beyond) the stimulus itself.

For example, consider the form shown in the top of **Figure 3.11**: the **Necker cube**. This drawing is an example of a **reversible (or ambiguous) figure**—so-called because people perceive it first one way and then another. Specifically, this form can be perceived as a drawing of a cube viewed from above (in which case it's similar to the cube marked A in the figure); it can also be perceived as a cube viewed from below (in which case it's similar to the cube marked B). Let's be clear, though, that this isn't an "illusion," because neither of these interpretations is "wrong," and the drawing itself (and, therefore, the information reaching your eyes) is fully compatible with either interpretation. Put differently, the drawing shown in Figure 3.11 is entirely neutral with regard to the shape's configuration in depth; the lines on the page don't specify which is the "proper" interpretation. Your perception of the cube, however, is not neutral. Instead, you perceive the cube as having one configuration or the other—similar either to Cube A or to Cube B. Your perception goes beyond the information given in the drawing, by specifying an arrangement in depth.

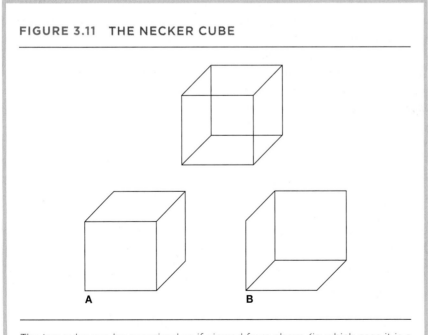

FIGURE 3.11   THE NECKER CUBE

A   B

The top cube can be perceived as if viewed from above (in which case it is a transparent version of Cube A) or as if viewed from below (in which case it is a transparent version of Cube B).

FIGURE 3.12 AMBIGUOUS FIGURES

A   B

Some stimuli easily lend themselves to reinterpretation. The figure in Panel A, for example, is perceived by many to be a white vase or candlestick on a black background; others see it as two black faces shown in profile. A similar bistable form is visible in the Canadian flag (Panel B).

The same point can be made for many other stimuli. **Figure 3.12A** (after Rubin, 1915, 1921) can be perceived either as a vase centered in the picture or as two profiles facing each other. The drawing by itself is compatible with either of these perceptions, and so, once again, the drawing is neutral with regard to perceptual organization. In particular, it is neutral with regard to **figure/ground organization**, the determination of what is the figure (the depicted object, displayed against a background) and what is the ground. Your perception of this drawing, however, isn't neutral about this point. Instead, your perception somehow specifies that you're looking at the vase and not the profiles, or that you're looking at the profiles and not the vase.

Figure/ground ambiguity is also detectable in the Canadian flag (**Figure 3.12B**). Since 1965, the centerpiece of Canada's flag has been a red maple leaf. Many observers, however, note that a different organization is possible, at least for part of the flag. On their view, the flag depicts two profiles, shown in white against a red backdrop. Each profile has a large nose, an open mouth, and a prominent brow ridge, and the profiles are looking downward, toward the flag's center.

In all these examples, then, your perception contains information—about how the form is arranged in depth, or about which part of the form is figure and which is ground—that is not contained within the stimulus itself. Apparently, this is information contributed by you, the perceiver.

The Gestalt Principles

With figures like the Necker cube or the vase/profiles, your role in shaping the perception seems undeniable. In fact, if you stare at either of these figures, your perception flips back and forth—first you see the figure one way, then another, then back to the first way. But the stimulus itself isn't changing, and so the information that's reaching your eyes is constant. Any changes in perception, therefore, are caused by *you* and not by some change in the stimulus.

One might argue, though, that reversible figures are special—carefully designed to support multiple interpretations. On this basis, perhaps you play a smaller role when perceiving other, more "natural" stimuli.

This position is plausible—but wrong, because many stimuli (and not just the reversible figures) are ambiguous and in need of interpretation. We often don't detect this ambiguity, but that's because the interpretation happens so quickly that we don't notice it. Consider, for example, the scene shown in **Figure 3.13**. It's almost certain that you perceive segments B and E as being

---

FIGURE 3.13   THE ROLE OF INTERPRETATION IN PERCEIVING AN ORDINARY SCENE

A

B

Consider the still life (Panel A) and an overlay designating five different segments of the scene (Panel B). For this picture to be perceived correctly, the perceptual system must first decide what goes with what—for example, that Segment B and Segment E are different bits of the same object (even though they're separated by Segment D) and that Segment B and Segment A are different objects (even though they're adjacent and the same color).

united, forming a complete apple, but notice that this information isn't provided by the stimulus; instead, it's your interpretation. (If we simply go with the information in the figure, it's possible that segments B and E are parts of entirely different fruits, with the "gap" between the two fruits hidden from view by the banana.) It's also likely that you perceive the banana as entirely banana-shaped and therefore continuing downward out of your view, into the bowl, where it eventually ends with the sort of point that's normal for a banana. In the same way, surely you perceive the horizontal stripes in the background as continuous and merely hidden from view by the pitcher. (You'd be surprised if we removed the pitcher and revealed a pitcher-shaped gap in the stripes.) But, of course, the stimulus doesn't in any way "guarantee" the banana's shape or the continuity of the stripes; these points are, again, just your interpretation.

Even with this ordinary scene, therefore, your perception goes "beyond the information given"—and so the unity of the two apple slices and the continuity of the stripes is "in the eye of the beholder," not in the stimulus itself. Of course, you don't feel like you're "interpreting" this picture or extrapolating beyond what's on the page. But your role becomes clear the moment we start cataloguing the differences between your perception and the information that's truly present in the photograph.

Let's emphasize, though, that your interpretation of the stimulus isn't careless or capricious. Instead, you're guided by a few straightforward principles that the Gestalt psychologists catalogued many years ago—and so they're routinely referred to as the **Gestalt principles**. For example, your perception is guided by *proximity* and *similarity*: If, within the visual scene, you see elements that are close to each other, or elements that resemble each other, you assume these elements are parts of the same object (**Figure 3.14**). You also tend to assume that contours are smooth, not jagged, and you avoid

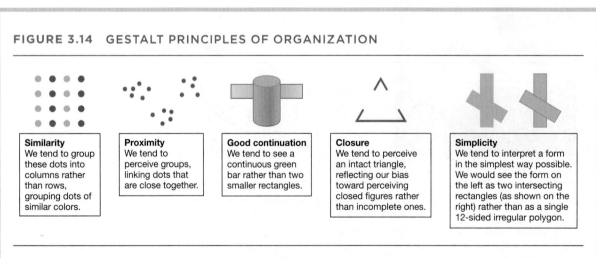

FIGURE 3.14   GESTALT PRINCIPLES OF ORGANIZATION

Similarity
We tend to group these dots into columns rather than rows, grouping dots of similar colors.

Proximity
We tend to perceive groups, linking dots that are close together.

Good continuation
We tend to see a continuous green bar rather than two smaller rectangles.

Closure
We tend to perceive an intact triangle, reflecting our bias toward perceiving closed figures rather than incomplete ones.

Simplicity
We tend to interpret a form in the simplest way possible. We would see the form on the left as two intersecting rectangles (as shown on the right) rather than as a single 12-sided irregular polygon.

As Figure 3.13 illustrated, your ordinary perception of the world requires you to make decisions about what goes with what—which elements are part of the same object, and which elements belong to different objects. Your decisions are guided by a few simple principles, catalogued many years ago by the Gestalt psychologists.

interpretations that involve coincidences. (For a modern perspective on these principles and Gestalt psychology in general, see Wagemans, Elder, Kubovy et al., 2012; Wagemans, Feldman, Gephstein et al., 2010.)

These perceptual principles are quite straightforward, but they're essential if your perceptual apparatus is going to make sense of the often ambiguous, often incomplete information provided by your senses. In addition, it's worth mentioning that everyone's perceptions are guided by the same principles, and that's why you generally perceive the world in the same way that other people do. Each of us imposes our own interpretation on the perceptual input, but we all tend to impose the *same* interpretation because we're all governed by the same rules.

Organization and Features

We've now considered two broad topics—the detection of simple attributes in the stimulus, and then the ways in which you *organize* those attributes. In thinking about these topics, you might want to think about them as separate steps. First, you collect information about the stimulus, so that you know (for example) what corners or angles or curves are in view—the **visual features** contained within the input. Then, once you've gathered the "raw data," you interpret this information. That's when you "go beyond the information given"—deciding how the form is laid out in depth (as in Figure 3.11), deciding what is figure and what is ground (Figure 3.12A or B), and so on.

The idea, then, is that perception might be divided (roughly) into an "information gathering" step followed by an "interpretation" step. This view, however, is *wrong*, and, in fact, it's easy to show that in many settings, your interpretation of the input happens *before* you start cataloguing the input's basic features, not after. Consider **Figure 3.15**. Initially, these shapes seem to

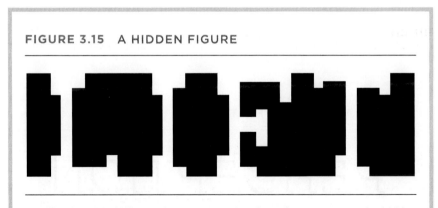

FIGURE 3.15 A HIDDEN FIGURE

Initially, these dark shapes have no meaning, but after a moment the hidden figure becomes clearly visible. Notice, therefore, that at the start the figure seems not to contain the features needed to identify the various letters. Once the figure is reorganized, with the white parts (not the dark parts) making up the figure, the features are easily detected. Apparently, the analysis of features depends how the figure is first organized by the viewer.

have no meaning, but after a moment most people discover the word hidden in the figure. That is, people find a way to reorganize the figure so that the familiar letters come into view. But let's be clear about what this means. At the start, the form seems not to contain the features needed to identify the *L*, the *I*, and so on. Once the form is reorganized, though, it does contain these features, and the letters are immediately recognized. In other words, with one organization, the features are absent; with another, they're plainly present. It would seem, then, that the features themselves depend on how the form is organized by the viewer—and so the features are as much "in the eye of the beholder" as they are in the figure itself.

As a different example, you have no difficulty reading the word printed in **Figure 3.16**, although most of the features needed for this recognition are absent. You easily "provide" the missing features, though, thanks to the fact that you interpret the black marks in the figure as shadows cast by solid letters. Given this interpretation and the extrapolation it involves, you can easily "fill in" the missing features and read the word.

How should we think about all of this? On one hand, your perception of a form surely has to start with the stimulus itself and must in some ways be governed by what's in that stimulus. (After all, no matter how you try to interpret Figure 3.16, it won't look to you like a photograph of Queen Elizabeth—the basic features of the queen are just not present, and your perception respects this obvious fact.) This suggests that the features must be in place *before* an interpretation is offered, because the features govern the interpretation. But, on the other hand, Figures 3.15 and 3.16 suggest that the opposite is the case: that the features you find in an input depend on how the figure is interpreted. Therefore, it's the interpretation, not the features, that must be first.

The solution to this puzzle, however, is easy, and builds on ideas that we've already met: Many aspects of the brain's functioning depend on parallel processing, with different brain areas all doing their work at the same time. In addition, the various brain areas all influence one another, so that what's going on in one brain region is shaped by what's going on elsewhere. In this

---

FIGURE 3.16 MISSING FEATURES

People have no trouble reading this word, even though most of the features needed for recognition are absent from the stimulus. People easily "supply" the missing features, illustrating once again that the analysis of features depends on how the overall figure has been interpreted and organized.

way, the brain areas that analyze a pattern's basic features do their work at the same time as the brain areas that analyze the pattern's large-scale configuration, and these brain areas interact so that the perception of the features is guided by the configuration, and analysis of the configuration is guided by the features. In other words, neither type of processing "goes first." Neither has priority. Instead, they work together, with the result that the perception that is achieved makes sense at both the large-scale and fine-grained levels.

Constancy

We've now seen many indications of the perceiver's role in "going beyond the information given" in the stimulus itself. This theme is also evident in another aspect of perception: the achievement of **perceptual constancy**. This term refers to the fact that we perceive the constant properties of objects in the world (their sizes, shapes, and so on) even though the sensory information we receive about these attributes changes whenever our viewing circumstances change.

To illustrate this point, consider the perception of size. If you happen to be far away from the object you're viewing, then the image cast onto your retinas by that object will be relatively small. If you approach the object, then the image size will increase. This change in image size is a simple consequence of physics, but you're not fooled by this variation. Instead, you manage to achieve **size constancy**—you correctly perceive the sizes of objects despite the changes in retinal-image size created by changes in viewing distance.

Similarly, if you view a door straight on, the retinal image will be rectangular; but if you view the same door from an angle, the retinal image will have a different shape (see **Figure 3.17**). Still, you achieve **shape constancy**—that is, you correctly perceive the shapes of objects despite changes in the retinal image created by shifts in your viewing angle. You also achieve **brightness constancy**—you correctly perceive the brightness of objects whether they're illuminated by dim light or strong sun.

TEST YOURSELF

6. What evidence tells us that perception goes beyond (includes more information than) the stimulus input?

7. What are the Gestalt principles, and how do they influence visual perception?

8. What evidence is there that the perception of an overall form depends on the detection of features? What evidence is there that the detection of features depends on the overall form?

FIGURE 3.17 SHAPE CONSTANCY

If you change your viewing angle, the shape of the retinal image cast by a target changes. In this figure, the door viewed straight on casts a rectangular image on your retina; the door viewed from an angle casts a trapezoidal image. Nonetheless, you generally achieve shape constancy.

Unconscious Inference

How do you achieve each of these forms of constancy? One hypothesis focuses on relationships within the retinal image. In judging size, for example, you generally see objects against some background, and this can provide a basis for comparison with the target object. To see how this works, imagine that you're looking at a dog sitting on the kitchen floor. Let's say the dog is half as tall as the nearby chair and hides eight of the kitchen's floor tiles from view. If you take several steps back from the dog, none of these relationships change, even though the sizes of all the retinal images are reduced. Size constancy, therefore, might be achieved by focusing not on the images themselves but on these unchanging relationships (see **Figure 3.18**).

Relationships do contribute to size constancy, and that's why you're better able to judge size when comparison objects are in view or when the target you're judging sits on a surface that has a uniform visual texture (like the floor tiles in the example). But these relationships don't tell the whole story. Size constancy is achieved even when the visual scene offers no basis for comparison (if, for example, the object to be judged is the only object in view), provided that other cues signal the *distance* of the target object (Harvey & Leibowitz, 1967; Holway & Boring, 1947).

How does your visual system use this distance information? More than a century ago, the German physicist Hermann von Helmholtz developed an influential hypothesis regarding this question. Helmholtz started with the fact that there's a simple inverse relationship between distance and retinal image size: If an object doubles its distance from the viewer, the size of its image is reduced by half. If an object triples its distance, the size of its

---

FIGURE 3.18 AN INVARIANT RELATIONSHIP THAT PROVIDES INFORMATION ABOUT SIZE

One proposal is that you achieve size constancy by focusing on *relationships* in the visual scene. For example, the dog sitting nearby on the kitchen floor (Panel A) is half as tall as the chair and hides eight of the kitchen's floor tiles from view. If you take several steps back from the dog (Panel B), none of these relationships change, even though the sizes of all the retinal images are reduced. By focusing on the relationships, then, you can see that the dog's size hasn't changed.

A

B

image is reduced to a third of its initial size. This relationship is guaranteed to hold true because of the principles of optics, and the relationship makes it possible for perceivers to achieve size constancy by means of a simple calculation. Of course, Helmholtz knew that we don't run through a conscious calculation every time we perceive an object's size, but he believed we're calculating nonetheless—and so he referred to the process as an **unconscious inference** (Helmholtz, 1909).

What is the calculation that enables someone to perceive size correctly? It's multiplication: the size of the image on the retina, multiplied by the distance between you and the object. (We'll have more to say about how you know this distance in a later section.) As an example, imagine an object that, at a distance of 10 ft, casts an image on the retina that's 4 mm across. Because of straightforward principles of optics, the same object, at a distance of 20 ft, casts an image of 2 mm. In both cases, the product—10×4 or 20×2—is the same. If, therefore, your size estimate depends on that product, your size estimate won't be thrown off by viewing distance—and that's exactly what we want (see **Figure 3.19**).

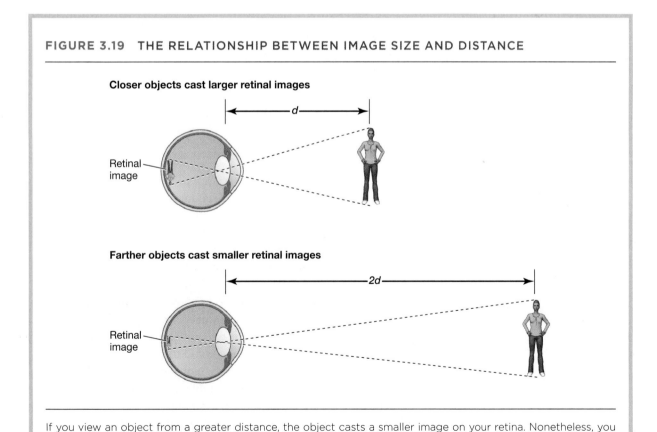

FIGURE 3.19   THE RELATIONSHIP BETWEEN IMAGE SIZE AND DISTANCE

Closer objects cast larger retinal images

Retinal image

d

Farther objects cast smaller retinal images

Retinal image

2d

If you view an object from a greater distance, the object casts a smaller image on your retina. Nonetheless, you generally achieve size constancy—perceiving the object's actual size. Helmholtz proposed that you achieve constancy through an unconscious inference—essentially multiplying the image size by the distance.

What's the evidence that size constancy does depend on this sort of inference? In many experiments, researchers have shown participants an object and, without changing the object's retinal image, have changed the apparent distance of the object. (There are many ways to do this—lenses that change how the eye has to focus to bring the object into sharp view, or mirrors that change how the two eyes have to angle inward so that the object's image is centered on both foveas.) If people are—as Helmholtz proposed—using distance information to judge size, then these manipulations should affect size perception. Any manipulation that makes an object seem farther away (without changing retinal image size) should make that object seem bigger (because, in essence, the perceiver would be "multiplying" by a larger number). Any manipulation that makes the object seem closer should make it look smaller. And, in fact, these predictions are correct—a powerful confirmation that people do use distance to judge size.

A similar proposal explains how people achieve shape constancy. Here, you take the slant of the surface into account and make appropriate adjustments—again, an unconscious inference—in your interpretation of the retinal image's shape. Likewise for brightness constancy: Perceivers are sensitive to how a surface is oriented relative to the available light sources, and they take this information into account in estimating how much light is reaching the surface. Then, they use this assessment of lighting to judge the surface's brightness (e.g., whether it's black or gray or white). In all these cases, therefore, it appears that the perceptual system does draw some sort of unconscious inference, taking viewing circumstances into account in a way that enables you to perceive the constant properties of the visual world.

Illusions

This process of taking information into account—whether it's distance (in order to judge size), viewing angle (to judge shape), or illumination (to judge brightness)—is crucial for achieving constancy. More than that, it's another indication that you don't just "receive" visual information; instead, you *interpret* it. The interpretation is an essential part of your perception and generally helps you perceive the world correctly.

The role of the interpretation becomes especially clear, however, in circumstances in which you *misinterpret* the information available to you and end up misperceiving the world. Consider the two tabletops shown in **Figure 3.20**. The table on the left looks quite a bit longer and thinner than the one on the right; a tablecloth that fits one table surely won't fit the other. Objectively, though, the parallelogram depicting the left tabletop is exactly the same shape as the one depicting the right tabletop. If you were to cut out the shape on the page depicting the left tabletop, rotate it, and slide it onto the right tabletop, they'd be an exact match. (Not convinced? Just lay another piece of paper on top of the page, trace the left tabletop, and then move your tracing onto the right tabletop.)

FIGURE 3.20 TWO TABLETOPS

These two tabletops seem to have very different shapes and sizes. However, this contrast is an illusion—and the shapes drawn here (the two parallelograms depicting the tabletops) are identical in shape and size. The illusion is caused by the same mechanisms that, in most circumstances, allow you to achieve constancy.

Why do people misperceive these shapes? The answer involves the normal mechanisms of shape constancy. Cues to depth in this figure cause you to perceive the figure as a drawing of three-dimensional objects, each viewed from a particular angle. This leads you—quite automatically—to adjust for the (apparent) viewing angles in order to perceive the two tabletops, and it's this adjustment that causes the illusion. Notice, then, that this illusion about shape is caused by a misperception of depth: You misperceive the depth relationships in the drawing and then take this faulty information into account in interpreting the shapes. (For a related illusion, see **Figure 3.21**.)

FIGURE 3.21 THE MONSTER ILLUSION

The two monsters appear rather different in size. But, again, this is an illusion, because the two drawings are exactly the same size. The illusion is created by the distance cues in the picture, which make the monster on the right appear to be farther away. This (mis)perception of distance leads to a (mis)perception of size.

FIGURE 3.22 A BRIGHTNESS ILLUSION

The central square (third row, third column) appears much brighter than the square marked by the arrow. Once again, though, this is an illusion. If you don't believe it, use your fingers or pieces of paper to cover everything in the figure except for these two squares.

TEST YOURSELF

9. What does it mean to say that size constancy may depend on an unconscious inference? An inference about what?

10. How do the ordinary mechanisms of constancy lead to visual illusions?

A different example is shown in **Figure 3.22**. It seems obvious to most viewers that the center square in this checkerboard (third row, third column) is a brighter shade than the square indicated by the arrow. But, in truth, the shade of gray shown on the page is identical for these two squares. What has happened here? The answer again involves the normal processes of perception. First, the mechanisms of lateral inhibition (described earlier) play a role here in producing a *contrast effect*: The central square in this figure is surrounded by dark squares, and the contrast makes the central square look brighter. The square marked at the edge of the checkerboard, however, is surrounded by white squares; here, contrast makes the marked square look darker.

But, in addition, the visual system also detects that the central square is in the shadow cast by the cylinder. Your vision compensates for this fact—again, an example of unconscious inference that takes the shadow into account in judging brightness—and therefore powerfully magnifies the illusion.

The Perception of Depth

In discussing constancy, we said that perceivers take distance, slant, and illumination into account in judging size, shape, and brightness. But to do this, they need to know what the distance is (how far away is the target object?), what the viewing angle is ("Am I looking at the shape straight on or at an angle?"), and what the illumination is. Otherwise, they'd have no way to take these factors into account and, therefore, no way to achieve constancy.

Let's pursue this issue by asking how people judge *distance*. We've just said that distance perception is crucial for size constancy, but, of course, information about where things are in your world is also valuable for its own sake. If you want to walk down a hallway without bumping into obstacles, you need to know which obstacles are close to you and which ones are far off. If you wish to caress a loved one, you need to know where he or she is;

otherwise, you're likely to swat empty space when you reach out with your caress or (worse) poke him or her in the eye. Plainly, then, you need to know where objects in your world are located.

Binocular Cues

The perception of distance depends on various **distance cues**—features of the stimulus that indicate an object's position. One cue comes from the fact that your eyes look out on the world from slightly different positions; as a result, each eye has a slightly different view. This difference between the two eyes' views is called **binocular disparity**, and it provides important information about distance relationships in the world.

Binocular disparity can lead to the perception of depth even when no other distance cues are present. For example, the bottom panels of **Figure 3.23** show the views that each eye would receive while looking at a pair of nearby objects. If we present each of these views to the appropriate eye (e.g., by drawing the views on two cards and placing one card in front of each eye), we can obtain a striking impression of depth.

Monocular Cues

Binocular disparity is a powerful determinant of perceived depth. But we can also perceive depth with one eye closed; plainly, then, there are also depth cues that depend only on what each eye sees by itself. These are the **monocular distance cues.**

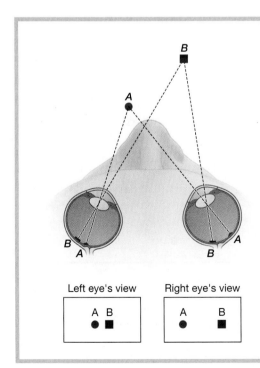

Left eye's view   Right eye's view

FIGURE 3.23   BINOCULAR DISPARITY

Your two eyes look out on the world from slightly different positions, and therefore they get slightly different views. The visual system uses this difference in views as a cue to distance. This figure shows what the left eye's and right eye's views would be in looking at objects A and B.

One monocular cue depends on the adjustment that the eye must make in order to see the world clearly. We mentioned earlier that in each eye, muscles adjust the shape of the lens to produce a sharply focused image on the retina. The amount of adjustment depends on how far away the viewed object is—there's a lot of adjustment for nearby objects, less for those a few steps away, and virtually no adjustment at all for objects more than a few meters away. It turns out that perceivers are sensitive to the amount of adjustment and use it as a cue indicating how far away the object is.

Other monocular cues have been exploited by artists for centuries to create an impression of depth on a flat surface—that is, within a picture—and that's why these cues are called **pictorial cues**. In each case, these cues rely on straightforward principles of physics. For example, imagine a situation in which a man is trying to admire a sports car, but a mailbox is in the way (see **Figure 3.24A**). In this case, the mailbox will inevitably block the view simply because light can't travel through an opaque object. This fact about the physical world provides a cue you can use in judging distance. The cue is known as **interposition**—the blocking of your view of one object by some other object. In **Figure 3.24B**, interposition tells the man that the mailbox is closer than the car.

In the same way, distant objects produce a smaller retinal image than do nearby objects of the same size; this is a fact about optics. But this physical fact again provides perceptual information you can use. In particular, it's the

FIGURE 3.24   INTERPOSITION AS A DEPTH CUE

A   B

This man is looking at the sports car, but the mailbox blocks part of his view (Panel A). Here's how the scene looks from the man's point of view (Panel B). Because the mailbox blocks the view, the man gets a simple but powerful cue that the mailbox must be closer to him than the sports car is.

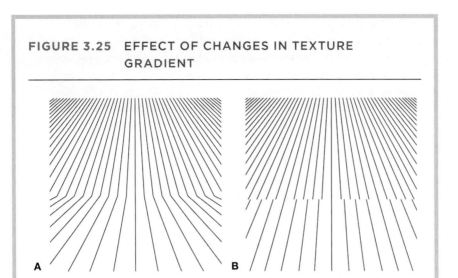

FIGURE 3.25   EFFECT OF CHANGES IN TEXTURE GRADIENT

A   B

Changes in texture provide important information about spatial arrangements in the world. Examples here show (Panel A) an upward tilt and (Panel B) a sudden drop.

basis for the cue of **linear perspective**, the name for the pattern in which parallel lines seem to converge as they get farther and farther from the viewer.

A related cue is provided by texture gradients. Consider what meets your eye when you look at cobblestones on a street or patterns of sand on a beach. The retinal projection of the sand or cobblestones shows a pattern of continuous change in which the elements of the texture grow smaller and smaller as they become more distant. This pattern of change by itself can reveal the spatial layout of the relevant surfaces. If, in addition, there are discontinuities in these textures, they can tell you even more about how the surfaces are laid out (see **Figure 3.25**; Gibson, 1950, 1966).

The Perception of Depth through Motion

Whenever you move your head, the images projected by objects in your view move across your retinas. For reasons of geometry, the projected images of nearby objects move more than those of distant ones, and this pattern of motion in the retinal images gives you another distance cue, called **motion parallax** (Helmholtz, 1909).

A different cue relies on the fact that the pattern of stimulation across the entire visual field changes as you move forward. This change in the visual input—termed **optic flow**—provides another type of information about depth and plays a large role in the coordination of bodily movements (Gibson, 1950, 1979).

We obviously move around in a three-dimensional world. For centuries, though, people have been trying to create an *illusion* of 3-D with displays that are actually flat. Painters during the Renaissance, for example, developed great skill in the use of the "pictorial cues" (including visual perspective) to create a sense of depth on a flat canvas. In the extreme, the art technique of trompe l'oeil (French for "deceive the eye") could leave people truly puzzled about whether an object was painted or actually present. Panel C in the figure on the following page shows a modern version — created by a talented sidewalk artist.

A different technique relies on binocular ("two-eyed") vision. Consider the Holmes stereoscope (invented by a man whose son went on to be a Supreme Court Justice for thirty years!). This wooden device (Panel A in the figure below) allows the presentation of a pair of pictures, one to each eye. The two pictures show the same scene but viewed from slightly different vantage points, and these "stereoviews" produce a compelling sense of depth.

The same principle — and your capacity for "stereovision" — is used with the "virtual reality" (VR) accessory that works with many smartphones. The accessory, often made of cardboard, places a lens in front of each eye so that you'll be comfortable pointing your eyes straight ahead (as if you were looking at something far away), even though you're actually looking at an image just an inch or so away. With this

A   **B**

CLASSICAL USES OF BINOCULAR DISPARITY

Binocular disparity was the principle behind the stereoscope (Panel A), a device popular in the 19th century that presented a slightly different photograph to each eye, creating a vivid sense of depth. The ViewMaster (Panel B), a popular children's toy, works in exactly the same way. The photos on the wheel are actually in pairs — and so, at any rotation, the left eye views one photo in the pair (the one at 9 o'clock on the wheel) and the right eye views a slightly different photo (the one at 3 o'clock), one that shows the same scene from a slightly different angle. Again, the result is a powerful sense of depth.

C

D

MODERN SIMULATIONS OF 3-D

Panel C shows a chalk drawing on a flat (and entirely undamaged) sidewalk. By manipulating pictorial cues, though, the artist creates a compelling illusion of depth—with a car collapsed into a pit that in truth isn't there at all. Panel D shows one of the devices used to turn a smartphone into a "virtual reality" viewer.

setup, your phone displays two views of the same scene (one view to each eye), viewed from slightly different angles. Your eyes "fuse" these inputs into a single image, but that doesn't mean you ignore the differences between the inputs. Instead, your visual system is solving the geometric puzzle posed by the two inputs. In other words, your brain manages to figure out how the scene must have been arranged in order to produce these two different views, and it's the end product of this computation that you experience as a three-dimensional scene.

Three-D movies work the same way. There are actually *two separate movies* projected onto the theater's screen. In some cases, the movies were recorded from slightly different positions; in other cases, the two perspectives were computer generated. In either situation, the separate movies are projected through filters that polarize the light and

viewers wear eyeglasses that contain corresponding filters. The eyeglass filters "pass" light that's polarized in a way that matches the filter, and block light that's polarized differently. As a result, each eye sees only one of the projected movies — and, again, viewers fuse the images but use the binocular disparity to produce the experience of depth.

If you've enjoyed a 3-D movie or a smartphone VR system, you've seen that the sense of depth is quite compelling. But these systems don't work for everyone. Some people have a strong pattern of "ocular dominance," which means that they rely on one eye far more than on the other. For these people, binocular disparity (which depends on combining the inputs from both eyes) loses its force. However, these people can still draw depth information from other (monocular or motion-based) cues, and so they can enjoy the same movies as anyone else.

The Role of Redundancy

One might think that the various distance cues all end up providing the same information—each one tells you which objects are close by and which ones are distant. On that basis, it might be efficient for the visual system to focus on just one or two cues and ignore the others. The fact is, however, that you use all these cues, as well as several others we haven't described (e.g., see **Figure 3.26**).

Why is our visual system influenced by so many cues, especially since these cues do, in fact, often provide redundant information? It's because different distance cues become important in different circumstances. For example, binocular disparity is a powerful cue, but it's informative only when objects are relatively close by. (For targets farther than 30 ft away, the two eyes receive virtually the same image.) Likewise, motion parallax tells you a great deal about the spatial layout of your world, but only if you're moving. Texture gradients are informative only if there's a suitably uniform texture in view. So while these various cues are often redundant, each type of cue can provide information when the others cannot. By being sensitive to them all, you're able to judge distance in nearly any situation you encounter. This turns out to be a consistent theme of perception—with multiple cues to distance, multiple cues to illumination, multiple paths through which to detect motion, and so on. The result is a system that sometimes seems inelegant and inefficient, but it's one that guarantees flexibility and versatility.

TEST YOURSELF

11. What are the monocular cues to distance?

12. Why is it helpful that people rely on several different cues in judging distance?

FIGURE 3.26 MONOCULAR CLUES TO DEPTH: LIGHT AND SHADOW

A

B

In this chapter, we've covered only a subset of the cues to distance that are used by our visual system. Another cue is provided by the shadows "attached" to an object. In Panel A, most viewers will say that the figure contains six "bulges" in a smiley-face configuration (two eyes, a nose, a mouth). In Panel B, the same figure has been turned upside-down. Now, the bulges appear to be "dents," and the other circles that appeared concave in the Panel A view now look like bulges. The reason is the location of the shadows. When the shadow is at the bottom, the object looks convex—a point that makes sense because in our day-to-day lives light almost always comes from above us, not below.

COGNITIVE PSYCHOLOGY AND EDUCATION

an "educated eye"

In the courtroom, eyewitnesses are often asked to describe what they saw at a crime scene, and asked if they can identify the person who committed the crime. Judges and juries generally rely on this testimony and accept the witness's report as an accurate description of how things unfolded. Judges and juries are, however, especially likely to accept the witness's report as accurate *if the witness is a police officer.* In support of this position, some attorneys argue that police officers have "educated eyes," with the result that police can (for example) recognize faces that they viewed only briefly or at a considerable distance. In one trial, a police officer even claimed that thanks to years of working a late-night shift, he'd improved his ability to see in the dark.

Related ideas arise in other settings. In Chapter 4, we'll discuss programs that teach you how to "speed-read," but for now let's just note that some of these programs make a strong claim in their advertising: They claim that they train your eyes so that you can "see more in a single glance."

At one level, these claims are nonsensical. How much you can see "in a single glance" is limited by your visual acuity, and acuity is limited by the optical properties of the eyeball and the functional properties of the photoreceptors. To see more "in a single glance," we'd need to give you a new cornea, a new lens, and a new retina—and, of course, no speed-reading program offers that sort of transplant surgery. Likewise, your ability to see in the dark is constrained by the biological properties of the eye (including the structure of the photoreceptors and the chemical principles that govern the photoreceptors' response to light). No experience, and no training, is going to change these properties.

At a different level, though, it *is* possible to have an "educated eye"—or, more precisely, to be more observant and more discerning than other people. For example, when looking at a complex, fast-moving crime scene, police officers are more likely to focus their attention on details that will matter for the investigation—and so will likely see (and remember) more of the perpetrator's actions (although, ironically, this means they'll see *less* of what's happening elsewhere in the scene). In the same way, referees and umpires in professional sports know exactly what to focus on during a game. (Did the player's knee touch the ground before he fumbled the ball? Did the basketball player drag her pivot foot or not?) As a result, they'll see things that ordinary observers would miss.

These advantages (for police officers or for referees) may seem obvious, but the advantages are closely tied to points raised in the chapter. You are able to see detail only for visual inputs landing on your foveas; what lands on your foveas depends on where exactly you're pointing your eyes; and movements of the eyes (pointing them first *here* and then *there*) turn out to be relatively slow. As a result, knowledge about where to look has an immense impact on what you'll be able to see.

It's also true that experience can help you to see certain *patterns* that you'd otherwise miss. In some cases, the experience helps you to stop looking at a visual input on a feature-by-feature basis, but instead to take a more "global" perspective so that you look at the pattern overall. Expert chess players, for example, seem to perceive a chess board in terms of the patterns in place (patterns indicating an upcoming attack, or patterns revealing the opponent's overall strategy), and this perspective helps them to plan their own moves. (For more on chess experts, see Chapter 13.) Or, as a very different example, consider the dog experts who serve as judges at the Westminster Kennel Club Dog Show. Evidence suggests that these experts are sensitive to each dog's overall form, and not just the shape of the front legs, the chest, the ears, and so on, with the result that they can make more discerning assessments than an ordinary dog-lover could.

KNOWING WHERE TO LOOK

Referees in football games know exactly where to look in order to pick up the information they need in making their judgments. Did the player tap both feet on the ground before going out of bounds? Did the player's knee touch the ground before he fumbled the ball? Referees seem to have an "educated eye," but, in reality, their advantage comes from how (and where) they focus their attention.

Experience can also help you to see (or hear or feel) certain *combinations* that are especially important or informative. One prominent example involves experienced firefighters who sometimes have an eerie ability to judge when a floor is about to collapse—allowing these professionals to evacuate a building in time, saving their lives and others'. What explains this perception? The answer may be a combination of feeling an especially high temperature *and* hearing relative quiet—a combination that signals a ferocious fire burning underneath them, hidden under the floor that they're standing on.

In short, then, people *can* have "educated eyes" (or ears or noses or palates). This "education" can't change the basic biological properties of your sense organs. But knowledge and experience can certainly help you to see things that others overlook, to detect patterns that are largely invisible to other people, and to pick up on combinations that can—in some settings—save your life.

For more on this topic . . .

Biederman, I., & Shiffrar, M. M. (1987). Sexing day-old chicks: A case study and expert systems analysis of a difficult perceptual learning task. *Journal of Experimental Psychology: Learning, Memory & Cognition*, *13*, 640–645.

Diamond, R., & Carey, S. (1986). Why faces are and are not special: An effect of expertise. *Journal of Experimental Psychology: General*, *115*, 107–117.

Klein, R. (2013). *Seeing what others don't*. New York, NY: Public Affairs.

Vredeveldt, A., Knol, J. W., & van Kopen, P. J. (2017). Observing offenders: Incident reports by surveillance detectives, uniformed police, and civilians. *Legal and Criminological Psychology*, *22*, 150–163.

chapter review

SUMMARY

- One brain area that has been mapped in considerable detail is the visual system. This system takes its main input from the rods and cones on the retina. Then, information is sent via the optic nerve to the brain. An important point is that cells in the optic nerve do much more than transmit information; they also begin the analysis of the visual input. This is reflected in the phenomenon of lateral inhibition, which leads to edge enhancement.

- Part of what we know about the brain comes from single-cell recording, which can record the electrical activity of an individual neuron. In the visual system, this recording has allowed researchers to map the receptive fields for many cells. The mapping has provided evidence for a high degree of specialization among the various parts of the visual system, with some parts specialized for the perception of motion, others for the perception of color, and so on. The various areas function in parallel, and this parallel processing allows great speed. It also allows mutual influence among multiple systems.

- Parallel processing begins in the optic nerve and continues throughout the visual system. For example, the *what* system (in the temporal lobe) appears to be specialized for the identification of visual objects; the *where* system (in the parietal lobe) seems to identify where an object is located.

- The reliance on parallel processing creates a problem of reuniting the various elements of a scene so that these elements are perceived in an integrated way. This is the binding problem. One key in solving this problem lies in the fact that different brain systems are organized in terms of maps, so that spatial position can be used as a framework for reuniting the separately analyzed aspects of the visual scene.

- Visual perception requires more than the "pickup" of features. Those features must be organized into wholes—a process apparently governed by the so-called Gestalt principles. The visual system also must interpret the input, a point that is especially evident with reversible figures. Crucially, though, these interpretive steps aren't separate from, and occurring after, the pickup of elementary features, because the features themselves are shaped by the perceiver's organization of the input.

- The active nature of perception is also evident in perceptual constancy. We achieve constancy through a process of unconscious inference, taking one aspect of the input (e.g., the distance to the target) into account in interpreting another aspect (e.g., the target's size). This process is usually quite accurate, but it can produce illusions.

- The perception of distance relies on many cues—some dependent on binocular vision, and some on monocular vision. The diversity of cues lets us perceive distance in a wide range of circumstances.

KEY TERMS

cornea (p. 65)
lens (p. 65)
retina (p. 65)
photoreceptors (p. 65)

rods (p. 65)
cones (p. 66)
acuity (p. 66)
fovea (p. 67)

TEST YOURSELF AGAIN

1. What are the differences between rods and cones? What traits do these cells *share*?

2. What is lateral inhibition? How does it contribute to edge perception?

3. How do researchers use single-cell recording to reveal a cell's receptive field?

4. What are the advantages of parallel processing in the visual system? What are the disadvantages?

5. How is firing synchrony relevant to the solution of the binding problem?

6. What evidence tells us that perception goes beyond (i.e., includes more information than) the stimulus input?

7. What are the Gestalt principles, and how do they influence visual perception?

8. What evidence is there that the perception of an overall form depends on the detection of features? What evidence is there that the detection of features depends on the overall form?

9. What does it mean to say that size constancy may depend on an unconscious inference? An inference about what?

10. How do the ordinary mechanisms of constancy lead to visual illusions?

11. What are the monocular cues to distance?

12. Why is it helpful that people rely on several different cues in judging distance?

THINK ABOUT IT

1. The chapter emphasizes the *active nature* of perception—and the idea that we don't just "pick up" information from the environment; instead, we *interpret* and *supplement* that information. What examples of this pattern can you think of—either from the chapter or from your own experience?

2. Chapter 2 argued that the functioning of the brain depends on the coordination of many specialized operations. How does that claim, about the brain in general, fit with the discussion of visual perception in this chapter?

eBOOK DEMONSTRATIONS & ESSAYS

Go to http://digital.wwnorton.com/cognition7 for the online demonstrations and essays relevant to this chapter. These can be found in the ebook.

Online Demonstrations

- Demonstration 3.1: Foveation
- Demonstration 3.2: Eye Movements
- Demonstration 3.3: The Blind Spot and the Active Nature of Vision
- Demonstration 3.4: A Brightness Illusion
- Demonstration 3.5: A Size Illusion and a Motion Illusion

ZAPS COGNITION LABS

Go to http://digital.wwnorton.com/cognition7 to experience interactive online psychology labs relevant to this chapter.

chapter **4** Recognizing Objects

what if... In Chapter 3, we discussed some of the steps involved in visual perception—steps allowing you to see that the object in front of you is, let's say, brown, large, and moving. But you don't leave things there; you also *recognize* objects and can identify what they are (perhaps: a UPS truck). This sort of recognition is usually easy for you, so you have no difficulty in recognizing the vast array of objects in your world—trucks, squirrels, shoes, frying pans, and more. But, easy or not, recognition relies on processes that are surprisingly sophisticated, and your life would be massively disrupted if you couldn't manage this (seemingly simple) achievement.

We mentioned in Chapter 2 that certain types of brain damage produce a disorder called "agnosia." In some cases, patients suffer from apperceptive agnosia—they seem able to see an object's shape and color and position, but they can't put these elements together to perceive the entire object. For example, one patient—identified as D.F.—suffered from brain damage in the sites shown in **Figure 4.1.** D.F. was asked to copy drawings that were in plain view (**Figure 4.2A**). The resulting attempts are shown in **Figure 4.2B**. The limit here is not some problem in drawing ability. **Figure 4.2C** shows what happened when D.F. was asked to draw various forms *from memory*. Plainly, D.F. can draw; the problem instead is in her ability to see and assemble the various elements that she sees.

Other patients suffer from associative agnosia. They can see but cannot link what they see to their basic visual knowledge. One remarkable example comes from a case described by neurologist Oliver Sacks:

> "What is this?" I asked, holding up a glove.
> "May I examine it?" he asked, and, taking it from me, he proceeded to examine it. "A continuous surface," he announced at last, "infolded in itself. It appears to have"—he hesitated—"five outpouchings, if this is the word."
> "Yes," I said cautiously. ". . .Now tell me what it is."
> "A container of some sort?"
> "Yes," I said, "and what would it contain?"
> "It would contain its contents!" said Dr. P., with a laugh. "There are many possibilities. It could be a change purse, for example, for coins of five sizes. It could . . ." (Sacks, 1985, p. 14)

- Recognition of visual inputs begins with features, but it's not just the features that matter. How easily people recognize a pattern also depends on how frequently or recently they have viewed the pattern and on whether the pattern is well formed (such as letter sequences with "normal" spelling patterns).

- We explain these findings in terms of a feature net — a network of detectors, each of which is "primed" according to how often or how recently it has fired. The network relies on distributed knowledge to make inferences, and this process gives up some accuracy in order to gain efficiency.

- The feature net can be extended to other domains, including the recognition of three-dimensional objects. However, the recognition of faces requires a different sort of model, sensitive to configurations rather than to parts.

- Finally, we consider top-down influences on recognition. The existence of these influences tells us that object recognition is not a self-contained process. Instead, knowledge external to object recognition is imported into and clearly shapes the process.

FIGURE 4.1 D.F.'S LESIONS

A Lesions in subject D.F.

B Location of LOC in neurologically intact subjects

Panel A shows the location of the brain damage in D.F. Panel B shows the areas in the lateral occipital complex (LOC) that are especially activated when neurologically healthy people are recognizing objects.

FIGURE 4.2 DRAWINGS FROM PATIENT D.F.

Line-drawing models	Drawn from the models	Drawn from memory

A   B   C

Patients who suffer from apperceptive agnosia can see, but they can't organize the elements they see in order to perceive an entire object. This deficit was evident when patient D.F. was asked to copy the drawings shown in Panel A. Her attempts are shown in Panel B. The problem is not in her drawing ability, because D.F.'s performance was much better (as shown in Panel C) when she was asked to draw the same forms from memory, rather than from a model.

Dr. P. obviously can see, and he uses his (considerable) intelligence to figure out what he is seeing. Nonetheless, his agnosia profoundly disrupts his life. Sacks describes one incident in which Dr. P. failed to put on his shoe, because he didn't recognize it as a shoe. (In fact, Sacks notes that at one point Dr. P. was confused about which object was his shoe and which was his foot.) Then, at the end of their time together, Sacks reports that Dr. P. "reached out his hand and took hold of his wife's head, tried to lift it off, to put it on. He had apparently mistaken his wife for a hat!" (p. 11).

As these examples make clear, object recognition may not be a glamorous skill, but it is one that we all rely on for even our most ordinary interactions with the world. What are the processes that make object recognition possible?

Recognition: Some Early Considerations

You're obviously able to recognize a huge number of different patterns—different objects (cats, cups, coats), various actions (crawling, climbing, clapping), and different sorts of situations (crises, comedies). You can also recognize many variations of each of these things. You recognize cats standing up and cats sitting down, cats running and cats asleep. And the same is true for recognition of most other patterns in your recognition repertoire.

You also recognize objects even when the available information is incomplete. For example, you can still recognize a cat if only its head and one paw are visible behind a tree. You recognize a chair even when someone is sitting on it, even though the person blocks much of the chair from view.

All of this is true for print as well. You can recognize tens of thousands of words, and you can recognize them whether the words are printed in large type or small, *italics* or straight letters, UPPER CASE or lower. You can even recognize handwritten words, for which the variation from one to the next is huge.

These variations in the "stimulus input" provide our first indication that object recognition involves some complexity. Another indication comes from the fact that your recognition of various objects, print or otherwise, is influenced by the *context* in which you encounter those objects. Consider **Figure 4.3**. The middle character is the same in both words, but the character looks more like an *H* in the word on the left and more like an *A* in the word on the right. With this, you easily read the word on the left as "THE" and not "TAE" and the word on the right as "CAT" and not "CHT."

Of course, object recognition is powerfully influenced by the stimulus itself—that is, by the features that are in view. Processes directly shaped by the stimulus are sometimes called "data driven" but are more commonly said

FIGURE 4.3 CONTEXT INFLUENCES PERCEPTION

You are likely to easily read this sequence as "THE CAT," recognizing the middle symbol as an *H* in one case and as an *A* in the other.   (AFTER SELFRIDGE, 1955)

to involve **bottom-up processing**. The effect of context, however, reminds us that recognition is also influenced by one's knowledge and expectations. As a result, your reading of Figure 4.3 is guided by your knowledge that "THE" and "CAT" are common words but that "TAE" and "CHT" are not. This sort of influence—relying on your knowledge—is sometimes called "concept-driven," and processes shaped by knowledge are said to involve **top-down processing**.

What mechanism underlies both the top-down and bottom-up influences? In the next section, we'll consider a classic proposal for what the mechanism might be. We'll then build on this base as we discuss more recent elaborations of this proposal.

The Importance of Features

Common sense suggests that many objects can be recognized by virtue of their parts. You recognize an elephant because you see the trunk, the thick legs, the large body. You know a lollipop is a lollipop because you see the circle shape on top of the straight stick. But how do you recognize the parts themselves? How, for example, do you recognize the trunk on the elephant or the circle in the lollipop? The answer may be simple: Perhaps you recognize the parts by looking at *their* parts—such as the arcs that make up the circle in the lollipop, or the (roughly) parallel lines that identify the elephant's trunk.

To put this more generally, recognition might begin with the identification of visual features in the input pattern—the vertical lines, curves, diagonals, and so on. With these features appropriately catalogued, you can start assembling the larger units. If you detect a horizontal together with a vertical, you know you're looking at a right angle; if you've detected four right angles, you know you're looking at a square.

This broad proposal lines up well with the neuroscience evidence we discussed in Chapter 3. There, we saw that specialized cells in the visual system do seem to act as feature detectors, firing (producing an action potential) whenever the relevant input (i.e., the appropriate feature) is in view. Also, we've already noted that people can recognize many variations on the objects they encounter—cats in different positions, *A*'s in different fonts or different handwritings. An emphasis on features, though, might help with this point. The various *A*'s, for example, differ from one another in overall shape, but they do have certain things in common: two inwardly sloping lines and a horizontal crossbar. Focusing on features, therefore, might allow us to concentrate on elements shared by the various *A*'s and so might allow us to recognize *A*'s despite their apparent diversity.

The importance of features is also evident in data from **visual search tasks**—tasks in which participants are asked to examine a display and to judge whether a particular target is present in the display or not. This search is remarkably efficient when someone is searching for a target defined by a simple feature—for example, finding a vertical segment in a field of horizontals or a green shape in a field of red shapes. But people are generally slower

THE VARIABILITY OF STIMULI WE RECOGNIZE

We recognize cats from the side or the front, whether we see them close up or far away.

FIGURE 4.4   VISUAL SEARCH

In Panel A, you can immediately spot the vertical, distinguished from the other shapes by just one feature. Likewise, in Panel B, you can immediately spot the lone green bar in the field of reds. But in Panel C, it takes longer to find the one red vertical, because now you need to search for a combination of features—not just for red or vertical, but for the one form that has both of these attributes.

in searching for a target defined as a *combination* of features (see **Figure 4.4**). This is just what we would expect if feature analysis is an early step in your analysis of the visual world—and separate from the step in which you combine the features you've detected.

Further support for these claims comes from studies of brain damage. At the start of the chapter, we mentioned *apperceptive agnosia*—a disorder that involves an inability to assemble the various aspects of an input into an organized whole. A related disorder, **integrative agnosia**, derives from damage to the parietal lobe. Patients with this disorder appear relatively normal in tasks requiring them simply to detect features in a display, but they are markedly impaired in tasks that require them to judge how the features are bound together to form complex objects. (See, for example, Behrmann, Peterson, Moscovitch, & Suzuki, 2006; Humphreys & Riddoch, 2014; Robertson, Treisman, Friedman-Hill, & Grabowecky, 1997. For related results, in which *transcranial magnetic stimulation* was used to disrupt portions of the brain in healthy individuals, see Ashbridge, Walsh, & Cowey, 1997.)

Word Recognition

Several lines of evidence, therefore, indicate that object recognition does begin with the detection of simple features. Then, once this detection has occurred, separate mechanisms are needed to put the features together, assembling them into complete objects. But how does this assembly proceed, so that we end up seeing not just the features but whole words—or Chihuahuas, or fire hydrants? In tackling this question, it will be helpful to fill in some more facts that we can then use as a guide to our theory building.

TEST YOURSELF

1. What is the difference between "bottom-up" and "top-down" processing?
2. What is the evidence that features play a special role in object recognition?

Factors Influencing Recognition

In many studies, participants have been shown stimuli for just a brief duration—perhaps 20 or 30 ms (milliseconds). Older research did this by means of a **tachistoscope**, a device designed to present stimuli for precisely controlled amounts of time. More modern research uses computers, but the brief displays are still called "tachistoscopic presentations."

Each stimulus is followed by a post-stimulus **mask**—often, a random pattern of lines and curves, or a random jumble of letters such as "XJDKEL." The mask interrupts any continued processing that participants might try to do for the stimulus just presented. In this way, researchers can be certain that a stimulus presented for (say) 20 ms is visible for exactly 20 ms and no longer.

Can people recognize these briefly visible stimuli? The answer depends on many factors, including how *familiar* a stimulus is. If the stimulus is a word, we can measure familiarity by counting how often that word appears in print, and these counts are an excellent predictor of tachistoscopic recognition. In one early experiment, Jacoby and Dallas (1981) showed participants words that were either very frequent (appearing at least 50 times in every million printed words) or infrequent (occurring only 1 to 5 times per million words of print). Participants viewed these words for 35 ms, followed by a mask. Under these circumstances, they recognized almost twice as many of the frequent words (see **Figure 4.5A**).

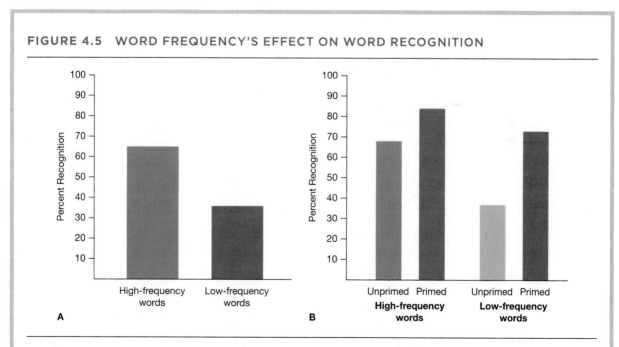

FIGURE 4.5 WORD FREQUENCY'S EFFECT ON WORD RECOGNITION

In one study, recognition was much more likely for words appearing often in print, in comparison to words appearing only rarely—an effect of frequency (Panel A). Similarly, words that had been viewed recently were more often recognized, an effect of recency that in this case creates a benefit called "repetition priming" (Panel B).

(AFTER JACOBY & DALLAS, 1981)

Another factor influencing recognition is recency of view. If participants view a word and then, a little later, view it again, they will recognize the word more readily the second time around. The first exposure **primes** the participant for the second exposure; more specifically, this is a case of **repetition priming**.

As an example, participants in one study read a list of words aloud. The participants were then shown a series of words in a tachistoscope. Some of these words were from the earlier list and so had been primed; others were unprimed. For words that were high in frequency, 68% of the unprimed words were recognized, compared to 84% of the primed words. For words low in frequency, 37% of the unprimed words were recognized, compared to 73% of the primed words (see **Figure 4.5B**; Jacoby & Dallas, 1981).

The Word-Superiority Effect

Figure 4.3 suggests that the recognition of a letter depends on its context—and so an ambiguous letter is read as an *A* in one setting but an *H* in another setting. But context also has another effect: Even when a letter is properly printed and quite unambiguous, it's *easier to recognize* if it appears within a word than if it appears in isolation.

This result might seem paradoxical, because here we have a setting in which it seems easier to do "more work" rather than "less"—and so you're more accurate in recognizing all the letters that make up a word (maybe a total of five or six letters) than you are in recognizing just one letter on its own. Paradoxical or not, this pattern is easy to demonstrate, and the advantage for perceiving letters-in-context is called the **word-superiority effect (WSE)**.

The WSE is demonstrated with a "two-alternative, forced-choice" procedure. For example, in some trials we might present a single letter—let's say *K*—followed by a post-stimulus mask, and follow that with a question: "Which of these was in the display: an *E* or a *K*?" In other trials, we might present a word—let's say "DARK"—followed by a mask, followed by a question: "Which of these was in the display: an *E* or a *K*?"

Note that participants have a 50-50 chance of guessing correctly in either of these situations, and so any contribution from guessing is the same for the letters as it is for the words. Also, for the word stimulus, both of the letters we've asked about are plausible endings for the stimulus; either ending would create a common word ("DARE" or "DARK"). Therefore, participants who saw only part of the display (perhaps "DAR") couldn't use their knowledge of the language to figure out the display's final letter. In order to choose between *E* and *K*, therefore, participants really need to have seen the relevant letter—and that is exactly what we want.

In this procedure, accuracy rates are reliably higher in the word condition. Apparently, recognizing an entire word is easier than recognizing isolated letters (see **Figure 4.6**; Johnston & McClelland, 1973; Reicher, 1969; Rumelhart & Siple, 1974; Wheeler, 1970).

FIGURE 4.6   THE WORD-SUPERIORITY EFFECT

The word-superiority effect is usually demonstrated with a two-alternative forced-choice procedure (which means that a participant can get a score of 50% just by guessing randomly). Performance is much better if the target letter is shown in context—within an entire word—than if it is shown on its own.

(AFTER JOHNSTON & McCLELLAND, 1973)

Degree of Well-Formedness

As it turns out, though, the term "word-superiority effect" may be misleading, because we don't need *words* to produce the pattern evident in Figure 4.6. We get a similar effect if we present participants with letter strings like "FIKE" or "LAFE." These letter strings are not English words and they're not familiar, but they *look like* English strings and (related) are easy to pronounce. And, crucially, strings like these produce a context effect, with the result that letters in these contexts are easier to identify than letters alone.

This effect occurs, though, only if the context is of the right sort. There's no context benefit if we present a string like "HZYE" or "SBNE." An *E* presented within these strings will *not* show the word-superiority effect—that is, it won't be recognized more readily than an *E* presented in isolation.

A parallel set of findings emerge if, instead of asking participants to detect specific letters, we ask them to report all of what they have seen. A letter string like "HZYE" is extremely hard to recognize if presented briefly. With a stimulus like this and, say, a 30-ms exposure, participants may report that they only saw a flash and no letters at all; at best, they may report a letter or two. But with the same 30-ms exposure, participants will generally recognize (and be able to report) strings like "FIKE" or "LAFE," although they do even better if the stimuli presented are actual, familiar words.

How should we think about these findings? One approach emphasizes the statistically defined regularities in English spelling. Specifically, we can work through a dictionary, counting how often (for example) the letter combination "FI" occurs, or the combination "LA," or "HZ." We can do the same for three-letter sequences ("FIK," "LAF," and so on). These counts will give us a tally that reveals which letter combinations are more probable in English spelling and which are less probable. We can then use this tally to evaluate new strings—asking, for any string, whether its letter sequences are high-probability ones (occurring often) or low-probability (occurring rarely).

These statistical measures allow us to evaluate how "well formed" a letter string is—that is, how well the letter sequence conforms to the usual spelling patterns of English—and **well-formedness** is a good predictor of word recognition: The more English-like the string is, the easier it will be to recognize that string, and also the greater the context benefit the string will produce. This well-documented pattern has been known for more than a century (see, e.g., Cattell, 1885) and has been replicated in many studies (Gibson, Bishop, Schiff, & Smith, 1964; Miller, Bruner, & Postman, 1954).

Making Errors

Let's recap some important points. First, it seems that a letter will be easier to recognize if it appears in a well-formed sequence, but not if it appears in a random sequence. Second, well-formed strings are, overall, easier to perceive than ill-formed strings; this advantage remains even if the well-formed strings are made-up ones that you've never seen before (strings like "HAKE" or "COTER"). All of these facts suggest that you somehow are using your knowledge of spelling patterns when you look at, and recognize, the words you encounter—and so you have an easier time with letter strings that conform to these patterns, compared to strings that do not.

The influence of spelling patterns is also evident in the mistakes you make. With brief exposures, word recognition is good but not perfect, and the errors that occur are systematic: There's a strong tendency to misread less-common letter sequences as if they were more-common patterns. So, for example, "TPUM" is likely to be misread as "TRUM" or even "DRUM." But the reverse errors are rare: "DRUM" is unlikely to be misread as "TRUM" or "TPUM."

These errors can sometimes be quite large—so that someone shown "TPUM" might instead perceive "TRUMPET." But, large or small, the errors show the pattern described: Misspelled words, partial words, or nonwords are read in a way that brings them into line with normal spelling. In effect, people perceive the input as being more regular than it actually is. Once again, therefore, our recognition seems to be guided by (or, in this case, misguided by) some knowledge of spelling patterns.

Feature Nets and Word Recognition

What lies behind this broad pattern of evidence? What are the processes inside of us that lead to the findings we've described? Psychologists' understanding of these points grows out of a theory published many years ago (Selfridge, 1959). Let's start with that theory, and then use it as our base as we look at more modern work. (For a glimpse of some of the modern research, including work that links theorizing to neuroscience, see Carreiras, Armstrong, Perea, & Frost, 2014.)

TEST YOURSELF

3. What is repetition priming, and how is it demonstrated?
4. What procedure demonstrates the word-superiority effect?
5. What's the evidence that word perception is somehow governed by the rules of ordinary spelling?

Font

You encounter printed material in a variety of formats and in a wide range of fonts. You also come across hand-written material, and of course people differ enormously in their handwriting. Despite all this variety, you're able to read almost everything you see—somehow rising above the variations from one bit to the next.

These variations do matter, however. Some people's handwriting is an almost impenetrable scrawl; some fonts are difficult to decipher. Even if we step away from these extremes and only consider cases in which you can figure out what's on the page, poor handwriting or an obscure font can make your reading less fluent. How this drop in fluency matters, though, depends on the circumstances.

In one study, college students read a passage printed either in a clear font (**Times New Roman**) or in a difficult font (*Italicized Juice ITC*). Students in both groups were then asked to rate the *intelligence* of the author who'd written the passage (Oppenheimer, 2006). Students who read the less clear font rated the author as less intelligent; apparently, they had noticed that their reading wasn't fluent but didn't realize the problem was in the font. Instead, they decided that the lack of fluency was the author's fault: They decided that the author hadn't been clear enough in composing the passage, and therefore was less intelligent!

Another experiment, though, showed an *advantage* for a (slightly) obscure font (Diemond-Yauman, Oppenheimer, & Vaughan, 2011). College students were asked to read made-up facts about space aliens—for example, that the Norgletti are 2 ft tall and eat flower petals. Half of the students read these facts in a clear font (**Arial printed in pure black**), and half read the facts in less clear font (e.g., Bodoni MT, printed in 60% grayscale). When tested later, participants who'd seen the fluent print remembered 73% of the facts; participants who'd seen the less fluent print recalled 86% of the facts. What was going on here? We'll see in Chapter 6 that memory is promoted by active engagement with the to-be-remembered materials, and it seems that the somewhat obscure font promoted that sort of engagement— and so created what (in Chapter 6) we'll refer to as "desirable difficulty" in the learning process.

What about other aspects of formatting? We've discussed the individual features that you use in recognizing letters, but it turns out that you're also sensitive to a word's overall *shape*. This is one of the reasons WHY IT IS MORE DIFFICULT TO READ CAPITALIZED TEXT. Capitalized words all have the same rectangular shape; gone are the portions of the letter that hang belong the line— the so-called descenders, like the bottom tail on a *g* or a *j*. Also gone are the portions of the letters that stick up (ascenders), like the top of an *h* or an *l*, or the dot over an *i*. Your reading slows down when these features aren't available, so it's slower IF YOU READ BLOCK CAPITALS compared to the normal pattern of print.

Are there practical lessons here? In some cases, you might prefer the look of block capitals; but if so, be aware that this format slows reading a bit. In choosing a font, you should probably avoid the obscure styles (unless you *want* less-fluent reading!), but notice that a moderately challenging font can actually help readers to process and remember what you've written.

The Design of a Feature Net

Imagine that we want to design a system that will recognize the word "CLOCK" whenever it is in view. How might our "CLOCK" detector work? One option is to "wire" this detector to a *C*-detector, an *L*-detector, an *O*-detector, and so on. Then, whenever these letter detectors are activated, this would activate the word detector. But what activates the letter detectors? Maybe the *L*-detector is "wired" to a horizontal-line detector and also a vertical-line detector, as shown in **Figure 4.7**. When these feature detectors are activated, this activates the letter detector.

The idea is that there could be a network of detectors, organized in layers. The "bottom" layer is concerned with features, and that is why networks of this sort are often called **feature nets**. As we move "upward" in the network, each subsequent layer is concerned with larger-scale objects; using the term we introduced earlier, the flow of information would be *bottom-up*—from the lower levels toward the upper levels.

But what does it mean to "activate" a detector? At any point in time, each detector in the network has a particular **activation level**, which reflects the status of the detector at that moment—roughly, how energized the detector is. When a detector receives some input, its activation level increases. A strong input will increase the activation level by a lot, and so will a series of weaker inputs. In either case, the activation level will eventually reach the detector's **response threshold**, and at that point the detector will *fire*—that is, send its signal to the other detectors to which it is connected.

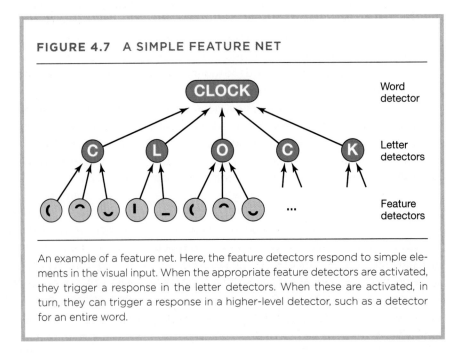

FIGURE 4.7 A SIMPLE FEATURE NET

An example of a feature net. Here, the feature detectors respond to simple elements in the visual input. When the appropriate feature detectors are activated, they trigger a response in the letter detectors. When these are activated, in turn, they can trigger a response in a higher-level detector, such as a detector for an entire word.

These points parallel our description of neurons in Chapter 2, and that's no accident. If the feature net is to be a serious candidate for how humans recognize patterns, then it has to use the same sorts of building blocks that the brain does. However, let's be careful not to overstate this point: No one is suggesting that detectors are neurons or even large groups of neurons. Instead, detectors probably involve complex assemblies of neural tissue. Nonetheless, it's plainly attractive that the hypothesized detectors in the feature net function in a way that's biologically sensible.

Within the net, some detectors will be easier to activate than others — that is, some will require a strong input to make them fire, while others will fire even with a weak input. This difference is created in part by how activated each detector is to begin with. If the detector is moderately activated at the start, then only a little input is needed to raise the activation level to threshold, and so it will be easy to make this detector fire. If a detector is not at all activated at the start, then a strong input is needed to bring the detector to threshold, and so it will be more difficult to make this detector fire.

What determines a detector's starting activation level? As one factor, detectors that have fired recently will have a higher activation level (think of it as a "warm-up" effect). In addition, detectors that have fired frequently in the past will have a higher activation level (think of it as an "exercise" effect). Overall, then, activation level is dependent on principles of **recency** and **frequency**.

We now can put these mechanisms to work. Why are frequent words in the language easier to recognize than rare words? Frequent words, by definition, appear often in the things you read. Therefore, the detectors needed for recognizing these words have been frequently used, so they have relatively high levels of activation. Thus, even a weak signal (e.g., a brief or dim presentation of the word) will bring these detectors to their response threshold and will be enough to make them fire. As a result, the word will be recognized even with a degraded input.

Repetition priming is explained in similar terms. Presenting a word once will cause the relevant detectors to fire. Once they've fired, activation levels will be temporarily lifted (because of recency of use). Therefore, only a weak signal will be needed to make the detectors fire again. As a result, the word will be more easily recognized the second time around.

The Feature Net and Well-Formedness

The net we've described so far cannot, however, explain all of the data. Consider the effects of well-formedness — for instance, the fact that people are able to read letter strings like "PIRT" or "HICE" even when those strings are presented very briefly (or dimly or in low contrast), but not strings like "ITPR" or "HCEI." How can we explain this finding? One option is to add another layer to the net, a layer filled with detectors for *letter combinations*.

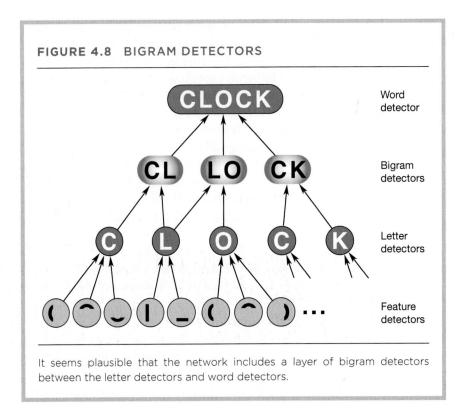

FIGURE 4.8   BIGRAM DETECTORS

Word detector

Bigram detectors

Letter detectors

Feature detectors

It seems plausible that the network includes a layer of bigram detectors between the letter detectors and word detectors.

Thus, in **Figure 4.8,** we've added a layer of **bigram detectors**—detectors of letter pairs. These detectors, like all the rest, will be triggered by lower-level detectors and send their output to higher-level detectors. And just like any other detector, each bigram detector will start out with a certain activation level, influenced by the frequency with which the detector has fired in the past and by the recency with which it has fired.

This turns out to be all the theory we need. You have never seen the sequence "HICE" before, but you have seen the letter pair *HI* (in "HIT," "HIGH," or "HILL") and the pair *CE* ("FACE," "MICE," "JUICE"). The detectors for these letter pairs, therefore, have high activation levels at the start, so they don't need much additional input to reach their threshold. As a result, these detectors will fire with only weak input. That will make the corresponding letter combinations easy to recognize, facilitating the recognition of strings like "HICE." None of this is true for "IJPV" or "RSFK." Because none of these letter combinations are familiar, these strings will receive no benefits from priming. As a result, a strong input will be needed to bring the relevant detectors to threshold, and so these strings will be recognized only with difficulty. (For more on bigram detectors and how they work, see Grainger, Rey, & Dufau, 2008; Grainger & Whitney, 2004; Whitney, 2001. For some complications, see Rayner & Pollatsek, 2011.)

Recovery from Confusion

Imagine that we present the word "CORN" for just 20 ms. In this setting, the visual system has only a limited opportunity to analyze the input, so it's possible that you'll miss some of the input's features. For example, let's imagine that the second letter in this word—the O—is hard to see, so that only the bottom curve is detected.

This partial information invites confusion. If all you know is "the second letter had a bottom curve," then perhaps this letter was an O, or perhaps it was a U, or a Q, or maybe an S. **Figure 4.9** shows how this would play out in terms of the network. We've already said that you detected the bottom curve, and that means the "bottom-curve detector" is activated. This detector, in turn, provides input to the O-detector and also to the detectors for U,

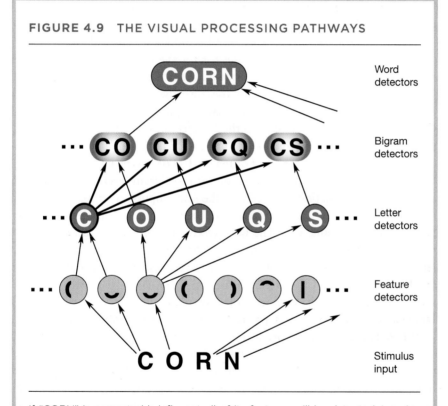

FIGURE 4.9   THE VISUAL PROCESSING PATHWAYS

If "CORN" is presented briefly, not all of its features will be detected. Imagine that only the bottom curve of the O is detected, not the O's top or sides. This will (weakly) activate the O-detector, but it will also activate the detectors of various other letters having a bottom curve, including U, Q, and S. This will, in turn, send weak activation to the appropriate bigram detectors. The CO-detector, however, is well primed and so is likely to respond even though it is receiving only a weak input. The other bigram detectors (for CQ or CS) are less well primed and so will not respond to this weak input. Therefore, "CORN" will be correctly perceived, despite the confusion at the letter level caused by the weak signal.

Q, and *S*, and so activation in this *feature* detector causes activation in all of these *letter* detectors.

Of course, each of these letter detectors is wired so that it can also receive input from other feature detectors. (And so usually the *O*-detector also gets input from detectors for left curves, right curves, and top curves.) We've already said, though, that with this brief input these other features weren't detected this time around. As a result, the *O*-detector will only be weakly activated (because it's not getting its usual full input), and the same is true for the detectors for *U*, *Q*, and *S*.

In this situation, therefore, the network has partial information at the feature level (because only one of the *O*'s features was detected), and this leads to confusion at the letter level: Too many letter detectors are firing (because the now-activated bottom-curve detector is wired to all of them). And, roughly speaking, all of these letter detectors are firing in a fashion that signals uncertainty, because they're each receiving input from only *one* of their usual feature detectors.

The confusion continues in the information sent upward from the letter level to the bigram level. The detector for the *CO* bigram will receive a strong signal from the *C*-detector (because the *C* was clearly visible) but only a weak signal from the *O*-detector (because the *O* wasn't clearly visible). The *CU*-detector will get roughly the same input—a strong signal from the *C*-detector and a weak signal from the *U*-detector. Likewise for the *CQ*- and *CS*-detectors. In other words, we can imagine that the signal being sent from the letter detectors is "maybe *CO* or maybe *CU* or maybe *CQ* or maybe *CS*."

The confusion is, however, sorted out at the bigram level. All four bigram detectors in this situation are receiving the same input—a strong signal from one of their letters and a weak signal from the other. But the four detectors don't all respond in the same way. The *CO*-detector is well primed (because this is a frequent pattern), so the activation it's receiving will probably be enough to fire this (primed) detector. The *CU*-detector is less primed (because this is a less frequent pattern); the *CQ*- and *CS*-detectors, if they even exist, are not primed at all. The input to these latter detectors is therefore unlikely to activate them—because, again, they're less well primed and so won't respond to this weak input.

What will be the result of all this? The network was "under-stimulated" at the feature level (with only a subset of the input's features detected) and therefore confused at the letter level (with too many detectors firing). But then, at the bigram level, it's only the *CO*-detector that fires, because at this level it is the detector (because of priming) most likely to respond to the weak input. Thus, in a totally automatic fashion, the network recovers from its own confusion and, in this case, avoids an error.

Ambiguous Inputs

Look again at Figure 4.3. The second character is exactly the same as the fifth, but the left-hand string is perceived as "THE" (and the character is identified as an *H*) and the right-hand string is perceived as "CAT" (and the character as an *A*).

What's going on here? In the string on the left, the initial *T* is clearly in view, and so presumably the *T*-detector will fire strongly in response. The next character in the display will probably trigger some of the features normally associated with an *A* and some normally associated with an *H*. This will cause the *A*-detector to fire, but only weakly (because only some of the *A*'s features are present), and likewise for the *H*-detector. At the letter level, then, there will be uncertainty about what this character is.

What happens next, though, follows a by-now familiar logic: With only weak activation of the *A*- and *H*-detectors, only a moderate signal will be sent upward to the *TH*- and *TA*-detectors. Likewise, it seems plausible that only a moderate signal will be sent to the *THE*- and *TAE*-detectors at the word level. But, of course, the *THE*-detector is enormously well primed; if there is a *TAE*-detector, it would be barely primed, since this is a string that's rarely encountered. Thus, the *THE*- and *TAE*-detectors might be receiving similar input, but this input is sufficient only for the (well-primed) *THE*-detector, so only it will respond. In this way, the net will recognize the ambiguous pattern as "THE," not "TAE." (The same logic applies, of course, to the ambiguous pattern on the right, perceived as "CAT," not "CHT.")

A similar explanation will handle the word-superiority effect (see, e.g., Rumelhart & Siple, 1974). To take a simple case, imagine that we present the letter *A* in the context "AT." If the presentation is brief enough, participants may see very little of the *A*, perhaps just the horizontal crossbar. This wouldn't be enough to distinguish among *A*, *F*, or *H*, and so all these letter detectors would fire weakly. If this were all the information the participants had, they'd be stuck. But let's imagine that the participants did perceive the second letter in the display, the *T*. It seems likely that the *AT* bigram is much better primed than the *FT* or *HT* bigrams. (That's because you often encounter words like "CAT" or "BOAT"; words like "SOFT" or "HEFT" are used less frequently.) Therefore, the weak firing of the *A*-detector would be enough to fire the *AT* bigram detector, while the weak firing for the *F* and *H* might not trigger their bigram detectors. In this way, a "choice" would be made at the bigram level that the input was "AT" and not something else. Once this bigram has been detected, answering the question "Was there an *A* or an *F* in the display?" is easy. In this way, the letter will be better detected in context than in isolation. This isn't because context enables you to see more; instead, context allows you to make better use of what you see.

Recognition Errors

There is, however, a downside to all this. Imagine that we present the string "CQRN" to participants. If the presentation is brief enough, the participants will register only a subset of the string's features. Let's imagine that they register only the bottom bit of the string's second letter. This detection of the bottom curve will weakly activate the *Q*-detector and also the

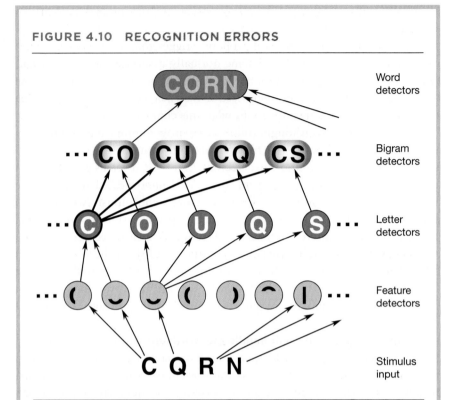

FIGURE 4.10 RECOGNITION ERRORS

If "CQRN" is presented briefly, not all of its features will be detected. Perhaps only the bottom curve of the Q is detected, and this will weakly activate various other letters having a bottom curve, including O, U, and S. However, the same situation would result from a brief presentation of "CORN" (as shown in Figure 4.9); therefore, by the logic we have already discussed, this stimulus is likely to be misperceived as "CORN."

U-detector and the *O*-detector. The resulting pattern of network activation is shown in **Figure 4.10**.

Of course, the pattern of activation here is exactly the same as it was in Figure 4.9. In both cases, perceivers have seen the features for the *C, R,* and *N* and have only seen the second letter's bottom curve. And we've already walked through the network's response to this feature pattern: This configuration will lead to confusion at the letter level, but the confusion will get sorted out at the bigram level, with the (primed) *CO*-detector responding to this input and other (less well primed) detectors *not* responding. As a result, the stimulus will be (mis)identified as "CORN." In the situation described in Figure 4.9, the stimulus actually was "CORN," and so the dynamic built into the net aids performance, allowing the network to recover from its initial confusion. In the case we're considering now (with

"CQRN" as the stimulus), the exact same dynamic causes the network to misread the stimulus.

This example helps us understand how recognition errors occur and why those errors tend to make the input look more regular than it really is. The basic idea is that the network is biased, favoring frequent letter combinations over infrequent ones. In effect, the network operates on the basis of "when in doubt, assume that the input falls into the frequent pattern." The reason, of course, is simply that the detectors for the frequent pattern are well primed—and therefore easier to trigger.

Let's emphasize, though, that the bias built into the network *facilitates* perception if the input is, in fact, a frequent word, and these (by definition) are the words you encounter most of the time. The bias will pull the network toward errors if the input happens to have an unusual spelling pattern, but (by definition) these inputs are less common in your experience. Hence, the network's bias helps perception more often than it hurts.

Distributed Knowledge

We've now seen many indications that the network's functioning is guided by knowledge of spelling patterns. This is evident in the fact that letter strings are easier to recognize if they conform to normal spelling. The same point is evident in the fact that letter strings provide a context benefit (the WSE) only if they conform to normal spelling. Even more evidence comes from the fact that when errors occur, they "shift" the perception toward patterns of normal spelling.

To explain these results, we've suggested that the network "knows" (for example) that *CO* is a common bigram in English, while *CF* is not, and also "knows" that *THE* is a common sequence but *TAE* is not. The network seems to rely on this "knowledge" in "choosing" its "interpretation" of unclear or ambiguous inputs. Similarly, the network seems to "expect" certain patterns and not others, and is more efficient when the input lines up with those "expectations."

Obviously, we've wrapped quotations around several of these words to emphasize that the sense in which the net "knows" facts about spelling, or the sense in which it "expects" things or makes "interpretations," is a little peculiar. In reality, knowledge about spelling patterns isn't explicitly stored anywhere in the network. Nowhere within the net is there a sentence like "*CO* is a common bigram in English; *CF* is not." Instead, this memory (if we even want to call it that) is manifest only in the fact that the *CO*-detector happens to be more primed than the *CF*-detector. The *CO*-detector doesn't "know" anything about this advantage, nor does the *CF*-detector know anything about its disadvantage. Each one simply does its job, and in the course of doing their jobs, sometimes a "competition" will take place between these detectors. (This sort of competition was illustrated in

Figures 4.9 and 4.10.) When these competitions occur, they'll be "decided" by activation levels: The better-primed detector will be more likely to respond and therefore will be more likely to influence subsequent events. That's the entire mechanism through which these "knowledge effects" arise. That's how "expectations" or "inferences" emerge — as a direct consequence of the activation levels.

To put this into technical terms, the network's "knowledge" is not **locally represented** anywhere; it isn't stored in a particular location or built into a specific process. As a result, we cannot look just at the level of priming in the CO-detector and conclude that this detector represents a frequently seen bigram. Nor can we look at the *CF*-detector and conclude that it represents a rarely seen bigram. Instead, we need to look at the *relationship* between these priming levels, and we also need to look at how this relationship will lead to one detector being more influential than the other. In this way, the knowledge about bigram frequencies is contained within the network via a **distributed representation**; it's knowledge, in other words, that's represented by a pattern of activations that's distributed across the network and detectable only if we consider how the entire network functions.

What may be most remarkable about the feature net, then, lies in how much can be accomplished with a distributed representation, and thus with simple, mechanical elements correctly connected to one another. The net appears to make inferences and to know the rules of English spelling. But the actual mechanics of the net involve neither inferences nor knowledge (at least, not in any conventional sense). You and I can see how the inferences unfold by taking a bird's-eye view and considering how all the detectors work together as a system. But nothing in the net's functioning depends on the bird's-eye view. Instead, the activity of each detector is locally determined — influenced by just those detectors feeding into it. When all these detectors work together, though, the result is a process that acts as if it knows the rules. But the rules themselves play no role in guiding the network's moment-by-moment activities.

Efficiency versus Accuracy

One other point about the network needs emphasis: The network does make mistakes, misreading some inputs and misinterpreting some patterns. As we've seen, though, these errors are produced by exactly the same mechanisms that are responsible for the network's main advantages — its ability to deal with ambiguous inputs, for example, or to recover from confusion. Perhaps, therefore, we should view the errors as the price you pay in order to gain the benefits associated with the net: If you want a mechanism that's able to deal with unclear or partial inputs, you have to live with the fact that sometimes the mechanism will make errors.

But do you really need to pay this price? After all, outside of the lab you're unlikely to encounter fast-paced tachistoscopic inputs. Instead, you see stimuli that are out in view for long periods of time, stimuli that you can inspect at your leisure. Why, therefore, don't you take the moment to scrutinize these inputs so that you can rely on fewer inferences and assumptions, and in that way gain a higher level of accuracy in recognizing the objects you encounter?

The answer is straightforward. To maximize accuracy, you could, in principle, scrutinize every character on the page. That way, if a character were missing or misprinted, you would be sure to detect it. But the cost associated with this strategy would be intolerable. Reading would be unspeakably slow (partly because the speed with which you move your eyes is relatively slow—no more than four or five eye movements per second). In contrast, it's possible to make inferences about a page with remarkable speed, and this leads readers to adopt the obvious strategy: They read some of the letters and make inferences about the rest. And for the most part, those inferences are safe—thanks to the simple fact that our language (like most aspects of our world) contains some redundncies, so that one doesn't need every lettr to identify what a wrd is; oftn the missng letter is perfctly predctable from the contxt, virtually guaranteeing that inferences will be correct.

TEST YOURSELF

6. How does a feature net explain the word-frequency effect?
7. How does a feature net explain the types of *errors* people make in recognizing words?
8. What are the benefits, and what are the costs, associated with the feature net's functioning?

Descendants of the Feature Net

We mentioned early on that we were discussing the "classic" version of the feature net. This discussion has enabled us to bring a number of themes into view—including the trade-off between efficiency and accuracy and the idea of distributed knowledge built into a network's functioning.

Over the years, though, researchers have offered improvements on this basic conceptualization, and in the next sections we'll consider three of their proposals. All three preserve the idea of a network of interconnected detectors, but all three extend this idea in important ways. We'll look first at a proposal that highlights the role of *inhibitory* connections among detectors. Then we'll turn to a proposal that applies the network idea to the recognition of complex three-dimensional objects. Finally, we'll consider a proposal that rests on the idea that your ability to recognize objects may depend on your viewing perspective when you encounter those objects.

The McClelland and Rumelhart Model

In the network proposal we've considered so far, activation of one detector serves to activate other detectors. Other models involve a mechanism through which detectors can *inhibit* one another, so that the activation of one detector can *decrease* the activation in other detectors.

FIGURE 4.11   AN ALTERNATIVE CONCEPTION OF THE FEATURE NETWORK

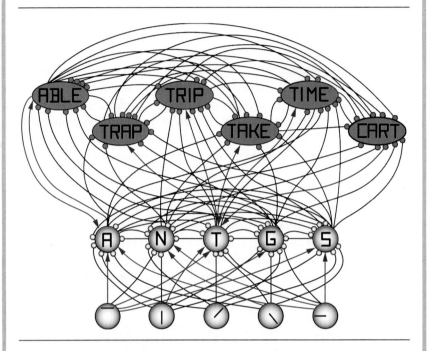

The McClelland and Rumelhart (1981) pattern-recognition model includes both excitatory connections (indicated by red arrows) and inhibitory connections (indicated by connections with dots). Connections within a specific level are also possible—so that, for example, activation of the "TRIP" detector will inhibit the detectors for "TRAP," "TAKE," and "TIME."

One highly influential model of this sort was proposed by McClelland and Rumelhart (1981); a portion of their model is illustrated in **Figure 4.11**. This network, like the one we've been discussing, is better able to identify well-formed strings than irregular strings; this net is also more efficient in identifying characters in context as opposed to characters in isolation. However, several attributes of this net make it possible to accomplish all this without bigram detectors.

In Figure 4.11, **excitatory connections**—connections that allow one detector to activate its neighbors—are shown as red arrows; for example, detection of a *T* serves to "excite" the "TRIP" detector. Other connections are *inhibitory*, and so (for example) detection of a *G* deactivates, or inhibits, the "TRIP" detector. These **inhibitory connections** are shown in the figure with dots. In addition, this model allows for more complicated signaling than we've used so far. In our discussion, we have assumed that lower-level detectors trigger upper-level detectors, but not the reverse. The flow of information, it seemed, was a one-way street. In the McClelland and Rumelhart model, though, higher-level detectors (word detectors) can influence lower-level detectors, and detectors at any level can also influence other detectors at the same level (e.g., letter detectors can inhibit other letter detectors; word detectors can inhibit other word detectors).

To see how this would work, let's say that the word "TRIP" is briefly shown, allowing a viewer to see enough features to identify only the *R*, *I*, and *P*. Detectors for these letters will therefore fire, in turn activating the detector for "TRIP." Activation of this word detector will inhibit the firing of other word detectors (e.g., detectors for "TRAP" and "TAKE"), so that these other words are less likely to arise as distractions or competitors with the target word.

At the same time, activation of the "TRIP" detector will also excite the detectors for its component letters—that is, detectors for *T*, *R*, *I*, and *P*. The *R*-, *I*-, and *P*-detectors, we've assumed, were already firing, so this extra activation "from above" has little impact. But the *T*-detector wasn't firing before. The relevant features were on the scene but in a degraded form (thanks to the brief presentation), and this weak input was insufficient to trigger an unprimed detector. But once the excitation from the "TRIP" detector primes the *T*-detector, it's more likely to fire, even with a weak input.

In effect, then, activation of the word detector for "TRIP" implies that this is a context in which a *T* is quite likely. The network therefore responds to this suggestion by "preparing itself" for a *T*. Once the network is suitably prepared (by the appropriate priming), detection of this letter is facilitated. In this way, the detection of a letter sequence (the word "TRIP") makes the network more sensitive to elements that are likely to occur within that sequence. That is exactly what we need in order for the network to be responsive to the regularities of spelling patterns.

Let's also note that the two-way communication that's in play here fits well with how the nervous system operates: Neurons in the eyeballs send activation to the brain but also *receive* activation from the brain; neurons in the lateral geniculate nucleus (LGN) send activation to the visual cortex but also receive activation from the cortex. Facts like these make it clear that visual processing is not a one-way process, with information flowing simply from the eyes toward the brain. Instead, signaling occurs in both an ascending (toward the brain) and a descending (away from the brain) direction, just as the McClelland and Rumelhart model claims.

Recognition by Components

The McClelland and Rumelhart model—like the feature net we started with—was designed initially as an account of how people recognize *printed language*. But, of course, we recognize many objects other than print, including the three-dimensional objects that fill our world—chairs and lamps and cars and trees. Can these objects also be recognized by a feature network? The answer turns out to be yes.

Consider a network theory known as the **recognition by components (RBC) model** (Hummel & Biederman, 1992; Hummel, 2013). This model

FIGURE 4.12　GEONS

Panel A shows five different geons; Panel B shows how these geons can be assembled into objects. The numbers in Panel B identify the specific geons—for example, a bucket contains Geon 5 top-connected to Geon 3.

includes several important innovations, one of which is the inclusion of an intermediate level of detectors, sensitive to **geons** (short for "geometric ions"). The idea is that geons might serve as the basic building blocks of all the objects we recognize—geons are, in essence, the alphabet from which all objects are constructed.

Geons are simple shapes, such as cylinders, cones, and blocks (see **Figure 4.12A**), and according to Biederman (1987, 1990), we only need 30 or so different geons to describe every object in the world, just as 26 letters are all we need to spell all the words of English. These geons can be combined in various ways—in a top-of relation, or a side-connected relation, and so on—to create all the objects we perceive (see **Figure 4.12B**).

The RBC model, like the other networks we've been discussing, uses a hierarchy of detectors. The lowest-level detectors are feature detectors, which respond to edges, curves, angles, and so on. These detectors in turn activate the geon detectors. Higher levels of detectors are then sensitive to combinations of geons. More precisely, geons are assembled into complex arrangements called "geon assemblies," which explicitly represent the relations between geons (e.g., top-of or side-connected). These assemblies, finally, activate the *object model*, a representation of the complete, recognized object.

The presence of the geon and geon-assembly levels within this hierarchy offers several advantages. For one, geons can be identified from virtually any angle of view. As a result, recognition based on geons is **viewpoint-independent**. Thus, no matter what your position is relative to a cat, you'll be able to identify its geons and identify the cat. Moreover, it seems that most objects can be recognized from just a few geons. As a consequence, geon-based models like RBC can recognize an object even if many of the object's geons are hidden from view.

Recognition via Multiple Views

A number of researchers have offered a different approach to object recognition (Hayward & Williams, 2000; Tarr, 1995; Tarr & Bülthoff, 1998; Vuong & Tarr, 2004; Wallis & Bülthoff, 1999). They propose that people have stored in memory a number of different views of each object they can recognize: an image of what a cat looks like when viewed head-on, an image of what it looks like from the left, and so on. According to this perspective, you'll recognize Felix as a cat only if you can match your current view of Felix with one of these remembered views. But the number of views in memory is limited—maybe a half dozen or so—and so, in many cases, your current view won't line up with any of the available images. In that situation, you'll need to "rotate" the current view to bring it into alignment with one of the views in memory, and this mental rotation will cause a slight delay in the recognition.

The key, then, is that recognition sometimes requires mental rotation, and as a result it will be slower from some viewpoints than from others. In other words, the speed of recognition will be **viewpoint-dependent**, and a growing body of data confirms this claim. We've already noted that you can recognize objects from many different angles, and your recognition is generally fast. However, data indicate that recognition is faster from some angles than others, in a way that's consistent with this multiple-views proposal.

According to this perspective, how exactly does viewpoint-dependent recognition proceed? One proposal resembles the network models we've been discussing (Riesenhuber & Poggio, 1999, 2002; Tarr, 1999). In this proposal, there is a hierarchy of detectors, with each successive layer within the network concerned with more complex aspects of the whole. Thus, low-level detectors respond to lines at certain orientations; higher-level detectors respond to corners and notches. At the top of the hierarchy are detectors that respond to the sight of whole objects. It is important, though, that these detectors each represent what the object looks like from a particular vantage point, and so the detectors fire when there is a match to one of these view-tuned representations.

These representations are probably supported by tissue in the inferotemporal cortex, near the terminus of the *what* pathway (see Figure 3.10). Recording from cells in this area has shown that many neurons here seem object-specific—that is, they fire preferentially when a certain type of object is on the scene. (For an example of just how specific these cells can be in their

FIGURE 4.13   THE JENNIFER ANISTON CELL

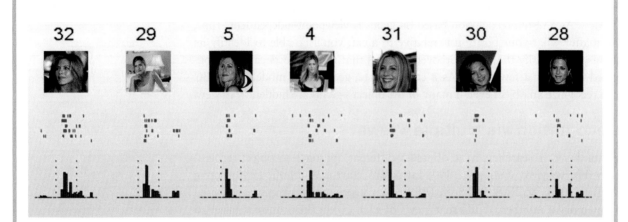

Researchers in one study were able to do single-cell recording within the brains of people who were undergoing surgical treatment for epilepsy. The researchers located cells that fired strongly whenever a picture of Jennifer Aniston was in view — whether the picture showed her close up (picture 32) or far away (picture 29), with long hair (picture 32) or shorter (picture 5). These cells are largely viewpoint-independent; other cells, though, are viewpoint-dependent.

TEST YOURSELF

9. How does the McClelland and Rumelhart model differ from the older, "classical" version of the feature net?

10. On what issues is there disagreement between the recognition by components (RBC) proposal and the recognition via multiple views proposal? On what issues is there agreement?

"preferred" target, see **Figure 4.13**.) Crucially, though, many of these neurons are view-tuned: They fire most strongly to a particular view of the target object. This is just what one might expect with the multiple-views proposal (Peissig & Tarr, 2007).

However, there has been lively debate between advocates of the RBC approach (with its claim that recognition is largely viewpoint-independent) and the multiple-views approach (with its argument that recognition is viewpoint-dependent). And this may be a case in which both sides are right — with some brain tissue being sensitive to viewpoint, and some brain tissue not being sensitive (see **Figure 4.14**). Moreover, the perceiver's *task* may be crucial. Some neuroscience data suggest that categorization tasks ("Is this a cup?") may rely on viewpoint-independent processing in the brain, while identification tasks ("Is this the cup I showed you before?") may rely on viewpoint-dependent processing (Milivojevic, 2012).

In addition, other approaches to object recognition are being explored (e.g., Hayward, 2012; Hummel, 2013; Peissig & Tarr, 2007; Ullman, 2007). Obviously, there is disagreement in this domain. Even so, let's be clear that all of the available proposals involve the sort of hierarchical network we've been discussing. In other words, no matter how the debate about object recognition turns out, it looks like we're going to need a network model along the lines we've considered.

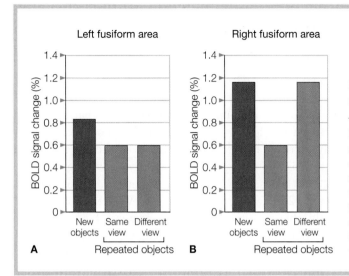

FIGURE 4.14 VIEWPOINT INDEPENDENCE

Is object recognition viewpoint-dependent? Some aspects of object recognition may be viewpoint-dependent while other aspects are not. Here, researchers documented viewpoint independence in the left occipital cortex (Panel A), and so the activity in the fusiform area was the same even when an object was viewed from a novel perspective. However, as we see in Panel B, other data show viewpoint dependence in the right occipital cortex.

Face Recognition

We began our discussion of network models with a focus on how people recognize letters and words. We've now extended our reach and considered how a network might support the recognition of three-dimensional objects. But there's one type of recognition that seems to demand a different approach: the recognition of *faces*.

Faces Are Special

As we described at the start of this chapter, damage to the visual system can produce a disorder known as agnosia—an inability to recognize certain stimuli—and one type of agnosia specifically involves the perception of faces. People who suffer from **prosopagnosia** generally have normal vision. Indeed, they can look at a photograph and correctly say whether the photo shows a face or something else; they can generally say whether a face is a man's or a woman's, and whether it belongs to someone young or someone old. But they can't recognize individual faces—not even of their own parents or children, whether from photographs or "live." They can't recognize the faces of famous performers or politicians. In fact, they can't recognize *themselves* (and so they sometimes think they're looking through a window at a stranger when they're actually looking at themselves in a mirror).

Often, this condition is the result of brain damage, but in some people it appears to be present from birth, without any detectable brain damage (e.g., Duchaine & Nakayama, 2006). Whatever its origin, prosopagnosia seems to imply the existence of special neural structures involved almost exclusively in the recognition and discrimination of faces. Presumably, prosopagnosia results from some problem or limitation in the functioning of this brain tissue. (See Behrman & Avidan, 2005; Burton, Young, Bruce, Johnston, & Ellis, 1991; Busigny, Graf, Mayer, & Rossion, 2010; Damasio, Tranel, & Damasio, 1990; De Renzi, Faglioni, Grossi, & Nichelli, 1991. For a related condition, involving an inability to recognize *voices*, see Shilowich & Biederman, 2016.)

The special nature of face recognition is also suggested by a pattern that is the *opposite* of prosopagnosia. Some people seem to be "super-recognizers" and are magnificently accurate in face recognition, even though they have no special advantage in other perceptual or memory tasks (e.g., Bobak, Hancock, & Bate, 2015; Davis, Lander, Evans, & Jansari, 2016; Russell, Duchaine, & Nakayama, 2009; Tree, Horry, Riley, & Wilmer, 2017). These people are consistently able to remember (and recognize) faces that they viewed only briefly at some distant point in the past, and they're also more successful in tasks that require "face matching"—that is, judging whether two different views of a face actually show the same person.

There are certainly advantages to being a super-recognizer, but also some disadvantages. On the plus side, being able to remember faces is obviously a benefit for a politician or a sales person; super-recognizers also seem to be much more accurate as eyewitnesses (e.g., in selecting a culprit from a police lineup). In fact, London's police force now has a special unit of super-recognizers involved in many aspects of crime investigation (Keefe, 2016). On the downside, being a super-recognizer can produce some social awkwardness. Imagine approaching someone and cheerfully announcing, "I know you! You used to work at the grocery store on Main Street." The other person (who, let's say, did work in that grocery eight years earlier) might find this puzzling, perhaps creepy, and maybe even alarming.

What about the rest of us—people who are neither prosopagnosic nor super-recognizers? It turns out that people differ widely in their ability to remember and recognize faces (Bindemann, Brown, Koyas, & Russ, 2012; DeGutis, Wilmer, Mercado, & Cohan, 2013; Wilmer, 2017). These differences, from person to person, are easy to measure, and there are online face memory tests that can help you find out whether you're someone who has trouble recognizing faces. (If you're curious, point your browser at the Cambridge Face Memory Test.)

In all people, though, face recognition seems to involve processes different from those used for other forms of recognition. For example, we've mentioned the debate about whether recognition of houses, or teacups, or automobiles is viewpoint-dependent. There is no question about this issue, however, when we're considering faces: Face recognition is strongly dependent on orientation, and so it shows a powerful **inversion effect**. In one study, four categories of stimuli were considered—right-side-up faces, upside-down faces, right-side-up pictures of common objects other than faces, and upside-down pictures of common objects. As **Figure 4.15** shows, performance suffered for all of the upside-down (i.e., inverted) stimuli. However, this effect was much larger for faces than for other kinds of

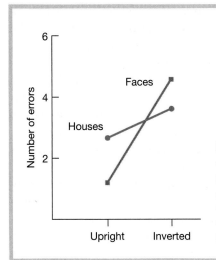

FIGURE 4.15 FACES AND THE INVERSION EFFECT

People's memory for faces is quite good, when compared with memory for other pictures (in this case, pictures of houses). However, performance is very much disrupted when the pictures of faces are inverted. Performance with houses is also worse with inverted pictures, but the effect of inversion is much smaller. (AFTER YIN, 1969)

stimuli (Bruyer, 2001; Yin, 1969). Moreover, with non-faces, the (relatively small) effect of inversion becomes even smaller with practice; with faces, the effect of inversion remains in place even after practice (McKone, Kanwisher, & Duchaine, 2007).

The role of orientation in face recognition can also be illustrated informally. **Figure 4.16** shows two upside-down photographs of former British prime minister Margaret Thatcher (from Thompson, 1980). You can probably tell that something is odd about them, but now try turning the book upside down so that the faces are right side up. As you can see, the difference

FIGURE 4.16 PERCEPTION OF UPSIDE-DOWN FACES

The left-hand picture looks somewhat odd, but the two pictures still look relatively similar to each other. Now, try turning the book upside down (so that the faces are upright). In this position, the left-hand face (now on the right) looks ghoulish, and the two pictures look very different from each other. Our perception of upside-down faces is apparently quite different from our perception of upright faces.

(AFTER THOMPSON, 1980)

between the faces is striking, and yet this fiendish contrast is largely lost when the faces are upside down. (Also see Rhodes, Brake, & Atkinson, 1993; Valentine, 1988.)

Plainly, then, face recognition is strongly dependent on orientation in ways that other forms of object recognition are not. Once again, though, we need to acknowledge an ongoing debate. According to some authors, the recognition of faces really is in a category by itself, distinct from all other forms of recognition (e.g., Kanwisher, McDermott, & Chun, 1997). Other authors, however, offer a different perspective: They agree that face recognition is special but argue that certain other types of recognition, in addition to faces, are special in the same way. As one line of evidence, they argue that prosopagnosia isn't just a disorder of face recognition. In one case, for example, a prosopagnosic bird-watcher lost not only the ability to recognize faces but also the ability to distinguish the different types of warblers (Bornstein, 1963; Bornstein, Sroka, & Munitz, 1969). Another patient with prosopagnosia lost the ability to tell cars apart; she can locate her car in a parking lot only by reading all the license plates until she finds her own (Damasio, Damasio, & Van Hoesen, 1982).

Likewise, in Chapter 2, we mentioned neuroimaging data showing that a particular brain site—the fusiform face area (FFA)—is specifically responsive to faces. (See, e.g., Kanwisher & Yovel, 2006. For a description of other brain areas involved in face recognition, see Gainotti & Marra, 2011.) One study, however, suggests that tasks requiring subtle distinctions among birds, or among cars, can also produce high levels of activation in this brain area (Gauthier, Skudlarski, Gore, & Anderson, 2000; also Bukach, Gauthier, & Tarr, 2006). This finding suggests that the neural tissue "specialized" for faces isn't used *only* for faces. (For more on this debate, see, on the one side, Grill-Spector, Knouf, & Kanwisher, 2004; McKone et al., 2007; Weiner & Grill-Spector, 2013. On the other side, see McGugin, Gatenby, Gore, & Gauthier, 2012; Richler & Gauthier, 2014; Stein, Reeder, & Peeler, 2016; Wallis, 2013; Zhao, Bülthoff, & Bülthoff, 2016.)

What should we make of all this? There's no question that humans have a specialized recognition system that's crucial for face recognition. This system certainly involves the FFA in the brain, and damage to this system can cause prosopagnosia. What's controversial is how exactly we should describe this system. According to some authors, the system is truly a *face* recognition system and will be used for other stimuli only if those stimuli happen to be "face-like" (see Kanwisher & Yovel, 2006). According to other authors, this specialized system needs to be defined more broadly: It is used whenever you are trying to recognize specific individuals within a highly familiar category (e.g., Gauthier et al., 2000). The recognition of faces certainly has these traits (e.g., you distinguish Fred from George from Jacob within the familiar category of "faces"), but other forms of recognition may have the same traits (e.g., if a bird-watcher is distinguishing different types within the familiar category of "warblers").

So far, the data don't provide a clear resolution of this debate; both sides of the argument have powerful evidence supporting their view. But let's focus on the key point of agreement: Face recognition is achieved by a process that's different from the process described earlier in this chapter. We need to ask, therefore, how face recognition proceeds.

Holistic Recognition

The networks we've been considering so far all begin with an analysis of a pattern's *parts* (e.g., features, geons); the networks then assemble those parts into larger wholes. Face recognition, in contrast, seems not to depend on an inventory of a face's parts; instead, this process seems to depend on **holistic perception** of the face. In other words, face recognition depends on the face's overall configuration—the spacing of the eyes relative to the length of the nose, the height of the forehead relative to the width of the face, and so on. (For more on face recognition, see Bruce & Young, 1986; Duchaine & Nakayama, 2006; Hayward, Crookes, Chu, Favelle, & Rhodes, 2016.)

Of course, a face's features still matter in this holistic process. The key, however, is that the features can't be considered one by one, apart from the context of the face. Instead, the features matter because of the relationships they create. It's the relationships, not the features on their own, that guide face recognition. (See Fitousi, 2013; Rakover, 2013; Rhodes,

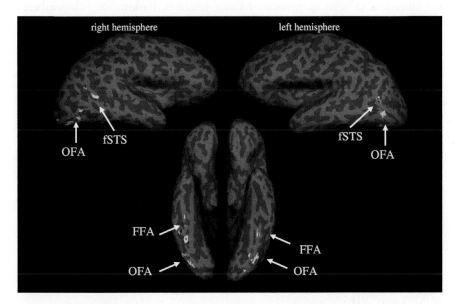

BRAIN AREAS CRUCIAL FOR FACE PERCEPTION

Several brain sites seem to be especially activated when people are looking at faces. These sites include the fusiform face area (FFA), the occipital face area (OFA), and the superior temporal sulcus (fSTS).

2012; Wang, Li, Fang, Tian, & Liu, 2012, but also see Richler & Gauthier, 2014. For more on holistic perception of facial *movement,* see Zhao & Bülthoff, 2017.)

Some of the evidence for this holistic processing comes from the *composite effect* in face recognition. In an early demonstration of this effect, Young, Hellawell, and Hay (1987) combined the top half of one face with the bottom half of another, and participants were asked to identify just the top half. This task is difficult if the two halves are properly aligned. In this setting, participants seemed unable to focus only on the top half; instead, they saw the top of the face as part of the whole (see **Figure 4.17A**). Thus, in the figure, it's difficult to see that the top half of the face is Hugh Jackman (shown in normal view in **Figure 4.17C**). This task is relatively easy, though, if the halves are misaligned (as in **Figure 4.17B**). Now, the stimulus itself breaks up the configuration, making it possible to view the top half on its own. (For related results, see Amishav & Kimchi, 2010; but also see Murphy, Gray, & Cook, 2017. For evidence that the *strength* of holistic processing is predictive of face-recognition accuracy, see Richler, Cheung, & Gauthier, 2011. For a complication, though, see Rezlescu, Susilo, Wilmer, & Caramazza, 2017.)

More work is needed to specify how the brain detects and interprets the relationships that define each face. Also, our theorizing will need to take some complications into account—including the fact that the recognition processes used for *familiar* faces may be different from the processes used for faces you've seen only once or twice (Burton, Jenkins, & Schweinberg, 2011; Burton, Schweinberger, Jenkins, & Kaufmann, 2015; Young & Burton, 2017). Evidence suggests that in recognizing familiar faces, you rely more heavily on the relationships among the *internal* features of the face; for unfamiliar faces, you may be more influenced by the face's *outer parts* such as the hair and the overall shape of the head (Campbell et al., 1999).

Moreover, psychologists have known for years that people are more accurate in recognizing faces of people from their own racial background (e.g., Caucasians looking at other Caucasians, or Asians looking at other Asians) than they are when trying to recognize people of other races (e.g., Meissner & Brigham, 2001). In fact, some people seem entirely prosopagnosic when viewing faces of people from other groups, even though they have no difficulty recognizing faces of people from their own group (Wan et al., 2017). These points may suggest that people rely on different mechanisms for, say, "same-race" and "cross-race" face perception, and this point, too, must be accommodated in our theorizing. (For recent discussions, see Horry, Cheong, & Brewer, 2015; Wan, Crookes, Reynolds, Irons, & McKone, 2015.)

Obviously, there is still work to do in explaining how we recognize our friends and family—not to mention how we manage to remember and recognize someone we've seen only once before. We know that face recognition relies on processes different from those discussed earlier in the chapter, and we know that these processes rely on the configuration of the face, rather than

FIGURE 4.17 THE COMPOSITE EFFECT IN FACE RECOGNITION

Participants were asked to identify the top half of composite faces like those in Panels A and B. This task was much harder if the halves were properly aligned (as in Panel A), and easier if the halves weren't aligned (as in Panel B). With the aligned faces, participants have a difficult time focusing on just the face's top (and so have a hard time recognizing Hugh Jackman — shown in Panel C). Instead, they view the face as a whole, and this context changes their perception of Jackman's features, making it harder to recognize him. (The bottom of the composite face belongs to Justin Timberlake, shown in Panel D.)

TEST YOURSELF

11. What's the evidence that face recognition is different from other forms of object recognition?

12. What's the evidence that face recognition depends on the face's configuration, rather than the features one by one?

its individual features. More research is needed, though, to fill in the details of this holistic processing. (For examples of other research on memory for faces, see Jones & Bartlett, 2009; Kanwisher, 2006; Michel, Rossion, Han, Chung, & Caldara, 2006; Rhodes, 2012. For discussion of how these issues play out in the *justice system*, with evidence coming from eyewitness identifications, see Reisberg, 2014.)

Top-Down Influences on Object Recognition

We've now discussed one important limitation of feature nets. These nets can, as we've seen, accomplish a great deal, and they're crucial for the recognition of print, three-dimensional objects in the visual environment, and probably sounds as well. But there are some targets—faces, and perhaps others—for which recognition depends on configurations rather than individual features.

It turns out, though, that there is another limit on feature nets, even if we're focusing on the targets for which a feature net *is* useful—print, common objects, and so on. Even in this domain, feature nets must be supplemented with additional mechanisms. This requirement doesn't undermine the importance of the feature net idea; feature nets are definitely needed as part of our theoretical account. The key word, however, is "part," because we need to place feature nets within a larger theoretical frame.

The Benefits of Larger Contexts

Earlier in the chapter, we saw that letter recognition is improved by context. For example, the letter *V* is easier to recognize in the context "VASE," or even the nonsense context "VIMP," than it is if presented alone. These are examples of "top-down" effects—effects driven by your knowledge and expectations. And these particular top-down effects, based on spelling patterns, are easily accommodated by the network: As we have discussed, priming (from recency and frequency of use) guarantees that detectors that have often been used in the past will be easier to activate in the future. In this way, the network "learns" which patterns are common and which are not, and it is more receptive to inputs that follow the usual patterns.

Other top-down effects, however, require a different type of explanation. Consider the fact that words are easier to recognize if you see them as part of a sentence than if you see them in isolation. There have been many formal demonstrations of this effect (e.g., Rueckl & Oden, 1986; Spellman, Holyoak, & Morrison, 2001; Tulving & Gold, 1963; Tulving, Mandler, & Baumal, 1964), but for our purposes an informal example will work. Imagine that we tell research participants, "I'm about to show you a word very briefly on a computer screen; the word is the name of something that you can eat." If we forced the participants to guess the word at this point, they would be unlikely to name the target word. (There are, after all, many things you can eat, so the chances are slim of guessing just the right one.) But if we briefly show the word "CELERY," we're likely to observe a large priming effect; that is, participants are more likely to recognize "CELERY" with this cue than they would have been without the cue.

Think about what this priming involves. First, the person needs to understand each of the words in the instruction. If she didn't understand the word "eat" (e.g., if she mistakenly thought we had said, "something that you can beat"), we wouldn't get the priming. Second, the person must understand the relations among the words in the instruction. For example, if she mistakenly thought we had said, "something that can eat you," we would expect a very different sort of priming. Third, the person has to know some facts about the world—namely, the kinds of things that can be eaten; without this knowledge, we would expect no priming.

Obviously, then, this instance of priming relies on a broad range of knowledge, and there is nothing special about this example. We could observe similar priming effects if we tell someone that the word about to be shown is the name of a historical figure or that the word is related to the Star Wars movies. In each case, the instruction would facilitate perception, with the implication that in order to explain these various priming effects, we'll need to hook up our object-recognition system to a much broader library of information.

Here's a different example, this time involving what you *hear*. Participants in one study listened to a low-quality recording of a conversation. Some participants were told they were listening to an interview with a job candidate; others were told they were listening to an interview with a suspect in a criminal case (Lange, Thomas, Dana, & Dawes, 2011). This difference in context had a powerful effect on what the participants heard. For example, the audio contained the sentence "I got scared when I saw what it'd done to him." Participants who thought they were listening to a criminal often mis-heard this statement and were sure they had heard ". . . when I saw what I'd done to him."

Where does all of this bring us? Examples like we're considering here tell us that we cannot view object recognition as a self-contained process. Instead, knowledge that is external to object recognition (e.g., knowledge about what is edible, or about the sorts of things a criminal might say) is imported into and influences the process. In other words, these examples (unlike the ones we considered earlier in the chapter) don't depend just on the specific stimuli you've encountered recently or frequently. Instead, what's crucial for this sort of priming is what you know coming into the experiment—knowledge derived from a wide range of life experiences.

We have, therefore, reached an important juncture. We've tried in this chapter to examine object recognition apart from other cognitive processes, considering how a separate object-recognition module might function, with the module then handing its product (the object it had recognized) on to subsequent processes. We have described how a significant piece of object

TEST YOURSELF

13. What's the evidence that word recognition (or object recognition in general) is influenced by processes separate from what has been seen recently or frequently?

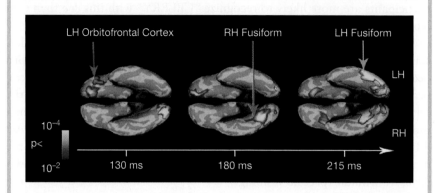

When viewers had only a very brief glimpse of a target object, brain activity indicating top-down processing was evident in the front part of the brain (the orbitofrontal cortex) 130 ms after the target came into view. Roughly 50 ms later (and so 180 ms after the target came into view), brain activity increased further back in the brain (in the right hemisphere's fusiform area), indicating successful recognition. This pattern was not evident when object recognition was easy (because of a longer presentation of the target). Sensibly, top-down processing plays a larger role when bottom-up processing is somehow limited or inadequate.

recognition might proceed, but in the end we have run up against a problem—namely, top-down priming that draws on knowledge from outside of object recognition itself. (For neuroscience evidence that word and object recognition interacts with other sorts of information, see Carreiras et al., 2014; also **Figure 4.18**.) This sort of priming depends on what is in memory and on how that knowledge is accessed and used, and so we can't tackle this sort of priming until we've said more about memory, knowledge, and thought. We therefore must leave object recognition for now in order to fill in other pieces of the puzzle. We'll have more to say about object recognition in later chapters, once we have some additional theoretical machinery in place.

COGNITIVE PSYCHOLOGY AND EDUCATION

speed-reading

Students often wish they could read more quickly, and, in fact, it's easy to teach people how to speed-read. It's important to understand, however, how speed-reading works, because this will help you see when speed-reading is a good idea—and when it's a terrible strategy.

As the chapter describes, in normal reading there's no need to look at every word on the page. Printed material (like language in general) follows predictable patterns, and so, having read a few words, you're often able to guess what the next words will be. And without realizing you're doing it, you're already exploiting this predictability. In reading this (or any) page, your eyes skip over many of the words, and you rely on rapid inference to fill in what you've skipped.

The same process is central for speed-reading. Courses that teach you how to speed-read actually encourage you to skip more, as you move down the page, and to rely more on inference. As a result, speed-reading isn't really "reading faster"; it is instead "reading *less* and inferring more."

How does this process work? First, before you speed-read some text, you need to lay the groundwork for the inference process—so that you'll make the inferences efficiently and accurately. Therefore, before you speed-read a text, you should flip through it quickly. Look at the figures and the figure captions. If there's a summary at the end or a preview at the beginning, read them. These steps will give you a broad sense of what the material is about, preparing you to make rapid—and sensible—inferences about the material.

Second, you need to make sure you do rely on inference, rather than word-by-word scrutiny of the page. To do this, read for a while holding an index card just under the line you're reading, or using your finger to slide along the line of print to indicate what you're reading at that moment. These

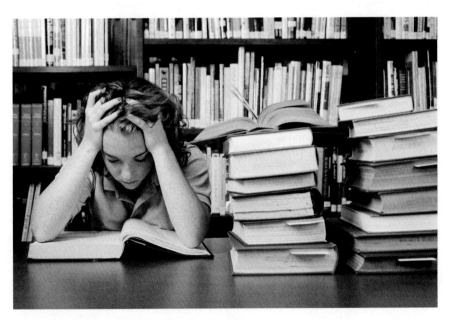

WHEN SHOULD YOU SPEED-READ?

Students are often assigned an enormous amount of reading, so strategies for speed-reading can be extremely helpful. But it's important to understand *why* speed-reading works as it does; knowing this will help you decide when speed-reading is appropriate and when it's unwise.

procedures establish a physical marker that helps you keep track of where your eyes are pointing as you move from word to word.

This use of a pointer will become easy and automatic after a little practice, and once it does, you're ready for the key step. Rather than using the marker to *follow* your eye position, use the marker to *lead* your eyes. Specifically, try moving the index card or your finger a bit more quickly than you have so far, and try to move your eyes to "keep up" with this marker.

Of course, if you suddenly realize that you don't have a clue what's on the page, then you've been going too fast. Just move quickly enough so that you have to hustle along to keep up with your pointer. Don't move so quickly that you lose track of what you're reading.

This procedure will feel awkward at first, but it will become easier with practice, and you'll gradually learn to move the pointer faster and faster. As a result, you'll increase your reading speed by 30%, 40%, or more. But let's be clear about what's going on here: You're simply shifting the balance between how much input you're taking in and how much you're filling in the gaps with sophisticated guesswork. Often, this is a fine strategy. Many of the things you read are highly predictable, so your inferences about the skipped words are likely to be correct. In settings like these, you might as well use the faster process of making inferences, rather than the slower process of looking at individual words.

But speed-reading is a bad bet if the material is hard to understand. In that case, you won't be able to figure out the skipped words via inference, so speed-reading will hurt you. Speed-reading is also a poor choice if you're trying to appreciate an author's style. If, for example, you speed-read Shakespeare's *Romeo and Juliet*, you probably will be able to make inferences about the plot, but you won't be able to make inferences about the specific words you're skipping over; you won't be able to make inferences about the language Shakespeare actually used. And, of course, if you miss the language of Shakespeare and miss the poetry, you've missed the point.

Speed-reading will enable you to zoom through many assignments. But don't speed-read material that's technical, filled with details that you'll need, or beautiful for its language. In those cases, you need to pay attention to the words on the page and not rely on your own inferences.

For more on this topic . . .

Rayner, K., Schotter, E.R., Masson, M.E.J., Potter, M.C., & Treiman, R. (2016). So much to read, so little time: How do we read, and can speed reading help? *Psychological Science in the Public Interest, 17,* 4–34.

chapter review

SUMMARY

● We easily recognize a wide range of objects in a wide range of circumstances. Our recognition is significantly influenced by context, which can determine how or whether we recognize an object. To study these achievements, investigators have often focused on the recognition of printed language, using this case to study how object recognition in general might proceed.

● Many investigators have proposed that recognition begins with the identification of features in the input pattern. Key evidence for this claim comes from neuroscience studies showing that the detection of features is separate from the processes needed to assemble these features into more complex wholes.

● To study word recognition, investigators often use tachistoscopic presentations. In these studies, words that appear frequently in the language are easier to identify than words that don't appear frequently, and so are words that have been recently viewed—an effect known as repetition priming. The data also show a pattern known as the "word-superiority effect"; this refers to the fact that letters are more readily perceived if they appear in the context of a word than if they appear in isolation. In addition, well-formed nonwords are more readily perceived than letter strings that do not conform to the rules of normal spelling. Another reliable pattern is that recognition errors, when they occur, are quite systematic, with the input typically perceived as being more regular than it actually is. These findings, taken together, indicate that recognition is influenced by the regularities that exist in our environment (e.g., the regularities of spelling patterns).

● We can understand these results in terms of a network of detectors. Each detector collects input and fires when the input reaches a threshold level. A network of these detectors can accomplish a great deal; for example, it can interpret ambiguous inputs, recover from its own errors, and make inferences about barely viewed stimuli.

● The feature net seems to "know" the rules of spelling and "expects" the input to conform to these rules. However, this knowledge is distributed across the entire network and emerges only through the network's parallel processing. This setup leads to enormous efficiency in our interactions with the world because it enables us to recognize patterns and objects with relatively little input and under diverse circumstances. But these gains come at the cost of occasional error. This trade-off may be necessary, though, if we are to cope with the informational complexity of our world.

● A feature net can be implemented in different ways—with or without inhibitory connections, for example. With some adjustments (e.g., the addition of geon detectors), the net can also recognize three-dimensional objects. However, some stimuli—for example, faces—probably are not recognized through a feature net but, instead, require a different sort of recognition system, one that is sensitive to relationships and configurations within the stimulus input.

● The feature net also needs to be supplemented to accommodate top-down influences on object recognition. These influences can be detected in the benefits of larger contexts in facilitating recognition and in forms of priming that are concept-driven rather than data-driven. These other forms of priming call for an interactive model that merges bottom-up and top-down processes.

KEY TERMS

bottom-up processing (p. 111)
top-down processing (p. 111)
visual search task (p. 111)
integrative agnosia (p. 112)
tachistoscope (p. 113)
mask (p. 113)
priming (p. 114)
repetition priming (p. 114)
word-superiority effect (WSE) (p. 114)
well-formedness (p. 116)
feature nets (p. 118)
activation level (p. 118)
response threshold (p. 118)
recency (p. 119)

frequency (p. 119)
bigram detectors (p. 120)
local representation (p. 126)
distributed representation (p. 126)
excitatory connections (p. 128)
inhibitory connections (p. 128)
recognition by components (RBC) model (p. 129)
geons (p. 130)
viewpoint-independent recognition (p. 131)
viewpoint-dependent recognition (p. 131)
prosopagnosia (p. 133)
inversion effect (p. 134)
holistic perception (p. 137)

TEST YOURSELF AGAIN

1. What is the difference between "bottom-up" and "top-down" processing?

2. What is the evidence that features play a special role in object recognition?

3. What is repetition priming, and how is it demonstrated?

4. What procedure demonstrates the word-superiority effect?

5. What's the evidence that word perception is somehow governed by the rules of ordinary spelling?

6. How does a feature net explain the word-frequency effect?

7. How does a feature net explain the types of *errors* people make in recognizing words?

8. What are the benefits, and what are the costs, associated with the feature net's functioning?

9. How does the McClelland and Rumelhart model differ from the older, "classical" version of the feature net?

10. On what issues is there disagreement between the recognition by components (RBC) proposal and the recognition via multiple views proposal? On what issues is there agreement?

11. What's the evidence that face recognition is different from other forms of object recognition?

12. What's the evidence that face recognition depends on the face's configuration, rather than the features one by one?

13. What's the evidence that word recognition (or object recognition in general) is influenced by processes separate from what has been seen recently or frequently?

THINK ABOUT IT

1. Imagine that you were designing a mechanism that would recognize *items of clothing* (shirts, pants, jackets, belts). Would some sort of feature net be possible? If so, what would the net involve?

2. Imagine that you were designing a mechanism that would recognize different *smells* (roses, cinnamon, freshly mown grass, car exhaust). Do you think some sort of feature net would be possible? If so, what would the net involve?

e eBOOK DEMONSTRATIONS & ESSAYS

Go to http://digital.wwnorton.com/cognition7 for the online demonstrations and essays relevant to this chapter. These can be found in the ebook.

Online Demonstrations

- Demonstration 4.1: Features and Feature Combination
- Demonstration 4.2: The Broad Influence of the Rules of Spelling
- Demonstration 4.3: Inferences in Reading

Online Applying Cognitive Psychology and the Law Essays

- Cognitive Psychology and the Law: Cross-Race Identification

ZAPS COGNITION LABS

Go to http://digital.wwnorton.com/cognition7 to experience interactive online psychology labs relevant to this chapter.

Paying Attention

what if... Right now, you're paying attention to this page, reading these words. But you could, if you chose, pay attention to the other people in the room, or your plans for the weekend, or even the feel of the floor under your feet.

What would your life be like if you couldn't control your attention in this way? Every one of us has, of course, had the maddening experience of being distracted when we're trying to concentrate. For example, there you are on the bus, trying to read your book. You have no interest in the conversation going on in the seats behind you, but you seem unable to shut it out, and so you make no progress in your book.

The frustration in this experience is surely fueled by the fact that usually you *can* control your attention, so it's especially irritating when you can't focus in the way you want to. The life challenge is much worse, though, for people who suffer from *attention deficit disorder.* This disorder is often associated with *hyperactivity*—and hence the abbreviation *ADHD*. People with ADHD are often overwhelmed by the flood of information that's available to them, and they're unable to focus on their chosen target.

The diagnosis of ADHD can range from relatively mild to quite severe, and we'll have more to say about ADHD later in the chapter. Nothing in this range, though, approaches a much more extreme disruption in attention termed "unilateral neglect syndrome." This pattern is generally the result of damage to the parietal cortex, and patients with this syndrome ignore all inputs coming from one side of the body. A patient with neglect syndrome will, for example, eat food from only one side of the plate, wash only half of his or her face, and fail to locate sought-for objects if they're on the neglected side (see Logie, 2012; Sieroff, Pollatsek, & Posner, 1988). Someone with this disorder cannot safely drive a car and, as a pedestrian, is likely to trip over unnoticed obstacles.

This syndrome typically results from damage to the *right* parietal lobe, and so the neglect is for the *left* side of space. (Remember the brain's contralateral organization; see Chapter 2.) Neglect patients will therefore read only the right half of words shown to them—they'll read "threat" as "eat," "parties" as "ties." If asked to draw a clock, they'll probably remember that the numbers from 1 to 12 need to be included, but they'll jam all the numbers into the clock's right side.

All these observations remind us just how crucial the ability to pay attention is—so that you can focus on the things you want to focus

- Multiple mechanisms are involved in the seemingly simple act of paying attention, because people must take various steps to facilitate the processing of desired inputs. Without these steps, their ability to pick up information from the world is dramatically reduced.

- Many of the steps necessary for perception have a "cost": They require the commitment of mental resources. These resources are limited in availability, which is part of the reason you usually can't pay attention to two inputs at once—doing so would require more resources than you have.

- Divided attention (the attempt to do two things at once) can also be understood in terms of resources. You can perform two activities at the same time only if the activities don't require more resources than you have available.

- Some of the mental resources you use are specialized, which means they're required only for tasks of a certain sort. Other resources are more general, needed for a wide range of tasks. However, the resource demand of a task can be diminished through practice.

- We emphasize that attention is best understood not as a process or mechanism but as an *achievement*. Like most achievements, paying attention involves many elements, all of which help you to be aware of the stimuli you're interested in and not be pulled off track by irrelevant distractors.

on and not be pulled off track by distraction. But what is "attention"? As we'll see in this chapter, the ability to pay attention involves many independent elements.

Selective Attention

William James (1842–1910) is one of the historical giants of the field of psychology, and he is often quoted in the modern literature. One of his most famous quotes provides a starting point for this chapter. Roughly 125 years ago, James wrote:

> Everyone knows what attention is. It is the taking possession by the mind, in clear and vivid form, of one out of what seem several simultaneously possible objects or trains of thought. Focalization, concentration, of consciousness are of its essence. It implies withdrawal from some things in order to deal effectively with others, and is a condition which has a real opposite in the confused, dazed, scatterbrained state which in French is called distraction. . . . (James, 1890, pp. 403–404)

In this quote, James is describing what modern psychologists call **selective attention**—that is, the skill through which a person focuses on one input or one task while ignoring other stimuli that are also on the scene. But what does this skill involve? What steps do you need to take in order to achieve the focus that James described, and why is it that the focus "implies withdrawal from some things in order to deal effectively with others"?

Dichotic Listening

Early studies of attention used a setup called **dichotic listening**: Participants wore headphones and heard one input in the left ear and a different input in the right ear. The participants were instructed to pay attention to one of these inputs—the **attended channel**—and to ignore the message in the other ear—the **unattended channel**.

FIGURE 5.1   THE INVISIBLE GORILLA

In this procedure, participants are instructed to keep track of the ballplayers in the white shirts. Intent on their task, participants are oblivious to what the black-shirted players are doing, and—remarkably—they fail to see the person in the gorilla suit strolling through the scene.   (FIGURE PROVIDED BY DANIEL J. SIMONS.)

To make sure participants were paying attention, investigators gave them a task called **shadowing:** Participants were required to repeat back what they were hearing, word for word, so that they were echoing the attended channel. Their shadowing performance was generally close to perfect, and they were able to echo almost 100% of what they heard. At the same time, they heard remarkably little from the unattended channel. If asked, after a minute or so of shadowing, to report what the unattended message was about, they had no idea (e.g., Cherry, 1953). They couldn't even tell if the unattended channel contained a coherent message or random words. In fact, in one study, participants shadowed speech in the attended channel, while in the unattended channel they heard a text in Czech, read with English pronunciation. The individual sounds, therefore (the vowels, the consonants), resembled English, but the message itself was (for an English speaker) gibberish. After a minute of shadowing, only 4 of 30 participants detected the peculiar character of the unattended message (Treisman, 1964).

We can observe a similar pattern with *visual* inputs. Participants in one study viewed a video that has now gone viral on the Internet and is widely known as the "invisible gorilla" video. In this video, a team of players in white shirts is passing a basketball back and forth; people watching the video are urged to count how many times the ball is passed from one player to another. Interwoven with these players (and visible in the video) is another team, wearing black shirts, also passing a ball back and forth; viewers are instructed to ignore these players.

Viewers have no difficulty with this task, but, while doing it, they usually don't see another event that appears on the screen right in front of their eyes. Specifically, they fail to notice when someone wearing a gorilla costume walks through the middle of the game, pausing briefly to thump his chest before exiting. (See **Figure 5.1**; Neisser & Becklen, 1975; Simons & Chabris, 1999; also see Jenkins, Lavie, & Driver, 2005.)

Even so, people are not altogether oblivious to the unattended channel. In selective listening experiments, research participants easily and accurately report whether the unattended channel contained human speech, musical instruments, or silence. If the unattended channel did contain speech, participants can report whether the speaker was male or female, had a high or low voice, or was speaking loudly or softly. (For reviews of this early work, see Broadbent, 1958; Kahneman, 1973.) Apparently, then, *physical attributes* of the unattended channel are heard, even though participants are generally clueless about the unattended channel's semantic content.

In one study, however, participants were asked to shadow one passage while ignoring a second passage. Embedded within the unattended channel was a series of names, and roughly one third of the participants did hear their own name when it was spoken—even though (just like in other studies) they heard almost nothing else from the unattended input (Moray, 1959).

And it's not just names that can "catch" your attention. Mention of a recently seen movie, or of a favorite restaurant, will often be noticed in the unattended channel. More broadly, words with some personal importance are often noticed, even though the rest of the unattended channel is perceived only as an undifferentiated blur (Conway, Cowan, & Bunting, 2001; Wood & Cowan, 1995).

Inhibiting Distractors

How can we put all these research results together? How can we explain both the general insensitivity to the unattended channel and also the cases in which the unattended channel "leaks through"?

One option focuses on what you do with the *unattended* input. The proposal is that you somehow block processing of the inputs you're not interested in, much as a sentry blocks the path of unwanted guests but stands back and does nothing when legitimate guests are in view, allowing them to pass through the gate unimpeded. This sort of proposal was central for early theories of attention, which suggested that people erect a **filter** that shields them from potential distractors. Desired information (the attended channel) is not filtered out and so goes on to receive further processing (Broadbent, 1958).

But what does it mean to "filter" something out? The key lies in the nervous system's ability to *inhibit* certain responses, and evidence suggests that you do rely on this ability to avoid certain forms of distraction. This inhibition, however, is rather specific, operating on a distractor-by-distractor basis. In other words, you might have the ability to inhibit your response to *this* distractor and the same for *that* distractor, but these abilities are of little value if some new, unexpected distractor comes along. In that case, you need to develop a new skill aimed at blocking the new intruder. (See Cunningham & Egeth, 2016; Fenske, Raymond, Kessler, Westoby, & Tipper, 2005; Frings & Wühr, 2014; Jacoby, Lindsay, & Hessels, 2003; Tsushima, Sasaki, & Watanabe, 2006; Wyatt & Machado, 2013. For a glimpse of brain mechanisms that support this inhibition, see Payne & Sekuler, 2014.)

THE COCKTAIL PARTY EFFECT

We have all experienced some version of the so-called cocktail party effect. There you are at a party, deep in conversation. Other conversations are going on, but somehow you're able to "tune them out." All you hear is the single conversation you're attending to, plus a buzz of background noise. But now imagine that someone a few steps away from you mentions the name of a close friend of yours. Your attention is immediately caught, and you find yourself listening to that other conversation and (momentarily) oblivious to the conversation you had been engaged in. This experience, easily observed outside the laboratory, matches the pattern of experimental data.

The ability to ignore certain distractors—to shut them out—therefore needs to be part of our theory. Other evidence, though, indicates that this isn't the whole story. That's because you not only inhibit the processing of distractors, you also *promote* the processing of *desired* stimuli.

Inattentional Blindness

We saw in Chapters 3 and 4 that perception involves a lot of activity, as you organize and interpret the incoming stimulus information. It seems plausible that this activity would require some initiative and some resources from you—and evidence suggests that it does.

In one experiment, participants were told that they would see large "+" shapes on a computer screen, presented for 200 ms (milliseconds), followed by a pattern mask. (The mask was just a meaningless jumble on the screen, designed to disrupt any further processing.) If the horizontal bar of the "+" was longer than the vertical, participants were supposed to press one button; if the vertical bar was longer, they had to press a different button. As a complication, participants weren't allowed to look directly at the "+." Instead, they fixated on (i.e., pointed their eyes at) a mark in the center of the computer screen—a **fixation target**—and the "+" shapes were shown just off to one side (see **Figure 5.2**).

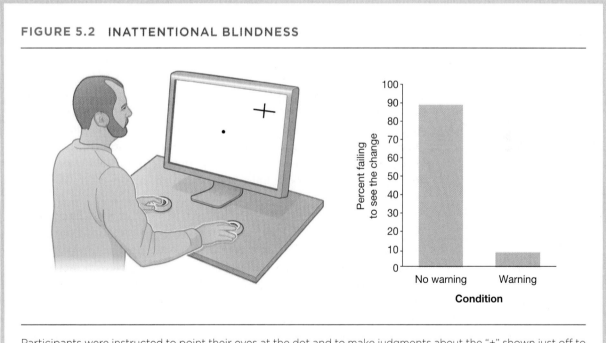

FIGURE 5.2 INATTENTIONAL BLINDNESS

Participants were instructed to point their eyes at the dot and to make judgments about the "+" shown just off to the side. However, the dot itself briefly changed to another shape. If participants weren't warned about this (and so weren't paying attention to the dot), they failed to detect this change—even though they had been pointing their eyes right at the dot the whole time.   (AFTER MACK & ROCK, 1998)

INATTENTIONAL BLINDNESS OUTSIDE THE LAB

Inattentional blindness is usually demonstrated in the laboratory, but it has a number of real-world counterparts. Most people, for example, have experienced the peculiar situation in which they can't find the mayonnaise in the refrigerator (or the ketchup or the salad dressing) even though they're staring right at the bottle. This happens because they're so absorbed in other thoughts that they become blind to an otherwise salient stimulus.

For the first three trials of the procedure, events proceeded just as the participants expected, and the task was relatively easy. On Trial 4, though, things were slightly different: While the target "+" was on the screen, the fixation target disappeared and was replaced by one of three shapes—a triangle, a rectangle, or a cross. Then, the entire configuration (the "+" target and this new shape) was replaced by the mask.

Immediately after the trial, participants were asked: Was there anything different on this trial? Was anything present, or anything changed, that wasn't there on previous trials? Remarkably, 89% of the participants reported that there was no change; they had failed to see anything other than the (attended) "+." To probe the participants further, the researchers told them (correctly) that during the previous trial the fixation target had momentarily disappeared and had been replaced by a shape. The participants were then asked what that shape had been, and were given the choices of a triangle, a rectangle, or a cross (one of which, of course, was the right answer). The responses to this question were essentially random. Even when probed in this way, participants seemed not to have seen the shape directly in front of their eyes (Mack & Rock, 1998; also see Mack, 2003).

This pattern has been named **inattentional blindness** (Mack & Rock, 1998; also Mack, 2003)—a pattern in which people fail to see a prominent stimulus, even though they're staring straight at it. In a similar effect, called "inattentional deafness," participants regularly fail to *hear* prominent stimuli if they aren't expecting them (Dalton & Fraenkel, 2012). In other studies, participants fail to *feel* stimuli if the inputs are unexpected; this is "inattentional numbness" (Murphy & Dalton, 2016).

What's going on here? Are participants truly blind (or deaf or numb) in response to these various inputs? As an alternative, some researchers propose that participants in these experiments did see (or hear or feel) the targets but, a moment later, couldn't *remember* what they'd just experienced (e.g., Wolfe, 1999; also Schnuerch, Kreiz, Gibbons, & Memmert, 2016). For purposes of theory, this distinction is crucial, but for now let's emphasize what the two proposals have in common: By either account, your normal ability to see what's around you, and to make use of what you see, is dramatically diminished in the absence of attention.

Think about how these effects matter outside of the laboratory. Chabris and Simons (2010), for example, call attention to reports of traffic accidents in which a driver says, "I never saw the bicyclist! He came out of nowhere! But then—suddenly—there he was, right in front of me." Drew, Võ, and Wolfe (2013) showed that experienced radiologists often miss obvious anomalies in a patient's CT scan, even when looking right at the anomaly. (For similar concerns, related to inattentional blindness in eyewitnesses to crimes, see Jaeger, Levin, & Porter, 2017.) Or, as a more mundane example, you go to the refrigerator to find the mayonnaise (or the ketchup or the juice) and don't see it, even though it's right in front of you.

In these cases, we lament the neglectful driver and the careless radiologist, and your inability to find the mayo may cause you to worry that you're losing your mind (as well as your condiments). The reality, though, is that these cases of failing-to-see are entirely normal. Perception requires more than "merely" having a stimulus in front of your eyes. Perception requires some work.

Change Blindness

The active nature of perception is also evident in studies of **change blindness**—observers' inability to detect changes in scenes they're looking directly at. In some experiments, participants are shown pairs of pictures separated by a brief blank interval (e.g., Rensink, O'Regan, & Clark, 1997). The pictures in each pair are identical except for one aspect—an "extra" engine shown on the airplane in one picture and not in the other; a man wearing a hat in one picture but not wearing one in the other; and so on (see **Figure 5.3**).

FIGURE 5.3   CHANGE BLINDNESS

In some change-blindness demonstrations, participants see one picture, then a second, then the first again, then the second, and must spot the difference between the two pictures. Here, we've displayed the pictures side by side, rather than putting them in alternation. Can you find the differences? For most people, it takes a surprising amount of time and effort to locate the differences—even though some of the differences are large. Apparently, having a stimulus directly in front of your eyes is no guarantee that you will perceive the stimulus.

FIGURE 5.4
CHANGE
BLINDNESS

In this video, every time there was a shift in camera angle, there was a change in the scene—so that the woman in the red sweater abruptly gained a scarf, the plates that had been red were suddenly white, and so on. When viewers watched the video, though, they noticed none of these changes.

Participants know that their task is to detect any changes in the pictures, but even so, the task is difficult. If the change involves something central to the scene, participants may need to look back and forth between the pictures as many as a dozen times before they detect the change. If the change involves some peripheral aspect of the scene, as many as 25 alternations may be required.

A related pattern can be documented when participants watch videos. In one study, observers watched a movie of two women having a conversation. The camera first focused on one woman, then the other, just as it would in an ordinary TV show or movie. The crucial element of this experiment, though, was that certain aspects of the scene changed every time the camera angle changed. For example, from one camera angle, participants could plainly see the red plates on the table between the women. When the camera shifted to a different position, though, the plates' color had changed to white. In another shift, one of the women gained a prominent scarf that she didn't have on a fraction of a second earlier (see **Figure 5.4**). Most observers, however, noticed none of these changes (Levin & Simons, 1997; Shore & Klein, 2000; Simons & Rensink, 2005).

Incredibly, the same pattern can be documented with live (i.e., not filmed) events. In a remarkable study, an investigator (let's call him "Leon") approached pedestrians on a college campus and asked for directions to a certain building. During the conversation, two men carrying a door approached and deliberately walked *between* Leon and the research participant. As a result, Leon was momentarily hidden (by the door) from the participant's view, and in that moment Leon traded places with one of the men carrying the door. A second later, therefore, Leon was able to walk away, unseen, while the new fellow (who had been carrying the door) stayed behind and continued the conversation with the participant.

Roughly half of the participants failed to notice this switch. They continued the conversation as though nothing had happened—even though Leon and his replacement were wearing different clothes and had easily distinguishable voices. When asked whether anything odd had happened in this event, many participants commented only that it was rude that the guys carrying the door had walked right through their conversation. (See Simons & Ambinder, 2005; Chabris & Simons, 2010; also see Most et al., 2001; Rensink, 2002; Seegmiller, Watson, & Strayer, 2011. For similar effects with auditory stimuli, see Gregg & Samuel, 2008; Vitevitch, 2003.)

Early versus Late Selection

It's clear, then, that people are often oblivious to stimuli directly in front of their eyes—whether the stimuli are simple displays on a computer screen, photographs, videos, or real-life events. (Similarly, people are sometimes oblivious to prominent sounds in the environment.) As we've said, though, there are two ways to think about these results. First, the studies may reveal genuine limits on *perception*, so that participants literally don't see (or hear) these stimuli; or, second, the studies may reveal limits on *memory*, so that participants do see (or hear) the stimuli but immediately forget what they've just experienced.

Which proposal is correct? One approach to this question hinges on *when* the perceiver selects the desired input and (correspondingly) when the perceiver stops processing the *un*attended input. According to the **early selection hypothesis,** the attended input is privileged from the start, so that the unattended input receives little analysis and therefore is never perceived. According to the **late selection hypothesis,** all inputs receive relatively complete analysis, and selection occurs after the analysis is finished. Perhaps the selection occurs just before the stimuli reach consciousness, so that we become aware only of the attended input. Or perhaps the selection occurs later still—so that all inputs make it (briefly) into consciousness, but then the selection occurs so that only the attended input is remembered.

Each hypothesis captures part of the truth. On the one side, there are cases in which people seem unaware of distractors but are influenced by them anyway— so that the (apparently unnoticed) distractors guide the interpretation of the attended stimuli (e.g., Moore & Egeth, 1997; see **Figure 5.5**). This seems to be a case of *late selection:* The distractors are perceived (so that they do have

FIGURE 5.5   UNCONSCIOUS PERCEPTION

A   B   C

One study, apparently showing late selection, found that participants perceived (and were influenced) by background stimuli even though the participants did not *consciously* perceive these stimuli. The participants were shown a series of images, each containing a pair of horizontal lines; their task was to decide which line was longer. For the first three trials, the background dots in the display were arranged randomly (Panel A). For the fourth trial, the dots were arranged as shown in Panel B, roughly reproducing the configuration of the Müller-Lyer illusion; Panel C shows the standard form of this illusion. Participants in this study didn't perceive the "fins" consciously, but they were influenced by them—judging the top horizontal line in Panel B to be longer, fully in accord with the usual misperception of this illusion.

1. What information do people reliably pick up from the *attended* channel? What do they pick up from the *unattended* channel?

2. How is inattentional blindness demonstrated? What situations outside of the laboratory seem to reflect inattentional blindness?

3. What evidence seems to confirm early selection? What evidence seems to confirm late selection?

an influence) but are selected out before they make it to consciousness. On the other side, though, we can also find evidence for *early selection*, with attended inputs being privileged from the start and distractor stimuli falling out of the stream of processing at a very early stage. Relevant evidence comes, for example, from studies that record the brain's electrical activity in the milliseconds after a stimulus has arrived. These studies confirm that the brain activity for attended inputs is distinguishable from that for unattended inputs just 80 ms or so after the stimulus presentation—a time interval in which early sensory processing is still under way (Hillyard, Vogel, & Luck, 1998; see **Figure 5.6**).

Other evidence suggests that attention can influence activity levels in the lateral geniculate nucleus, or LGN (Kastner, Schneider, & Wunderlich, 2006; McAlonan, Cavanaugh & Wurtz, 2008; Moore & Zirnsak, 2017; Vanduffel, Tootell, & Orban, 2000). In this case, attention is changing the flow of signals within the nervous system even before the signals reach the brain. (For more on how attention influences processing in the visual cortex, see Carrasco, Ling, & Read, 2004; Carrasco, Penpeci-Talgar, & Eckstein, 2000; McAdams & Reid, 2005; Reynolds, Pasternak, & Desimone, 2000; also see O'Connor, Fukui, Pinsk, & Kastner, 2002; Yantis, 2008.)

Selection via Priming

Whether selection is early or late, it's clear that people often fail to see stimuli that are directly in front of them, in plain view. But what is the obstacle here? Why *don't* people perceive these stimuli?

In Chapter 4, we proposed that recognition requires a network of detectors, and we argued that these detectors fire most readily if they're suitably primed. In some cases, the priming is produced by your visual experience—specifically, whether each detector has been used recently or frequently in the past. But we suggested that priming can also come from another source: your expectations about what the stimulus will be.

The proposal, then, is that you can literally prepare yourself for perceiving by priming the relevant detectors. In other words, you somehow reach into the network and deliberately activate just those detectors that, you believe, will soon be needed. Then, once primed in this way, those detectors will be on "high alert" and ready to fire.

Let's also suppose that this priming isn't "free." Instead, you need to spend some effort or allocate some resources in order to do the priming, and these resources are in limited supply. As a result, there's a limit on just how much priming you can do.

We'll need to flesh out this proposal in several ways, but even so, we can already use it to explain some of the findings we've already met. Why don't participants notice the shapes in the inattentional blindness studies? The answer lies in the fact that they don't expect any stimulus to appear, so they have no reason to prepare for any stimulus. As a result, when the stimulus is presented, it falls on unprepared (unprimed, unresponsive) detectors. The

FIGURE 5.6   EVIDENCE FOR EARLY SELECTION

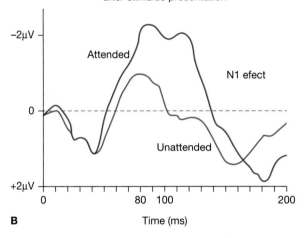

Electrical activity in the brain in the interval just
after stimulus presentation

Participants were instructed to pay attention to the targets arriving in one
ear, but to ignore targets in the other ear (Panel A; dots indicate which of the
input signals were actually targets). During this task, researchers monitored
the electrical activity in the participants' brains, with special focus on a brain
wave termed the "N1" (so-called because the wave reflects a negative voltage
roughly 100 ms after the target). As Panel B shows, the N1 effect was different
for the attended and unattended inputs within 80 ms of the target's arrival—
indicating that the attended and unattended inputs were processed differently from a very early stage.   (FROM HILLYARD ET. AL. "ELECTRIC SIGNS OF SELECTIVE
ATTENTION IN THE HUMAN BRAIN," *SCIENCE* 182 © 1973 AAAS. REPRINTED WITH PERMISSION.)

detectors therefore don't respond to the stimulus, so the participants end up
not perceiving it.

What about selective listening? In this case, you've been instructed to
ignore the unattended input, so you have no reason to devote any resources
to this input. Hence, the detectors needed for the distractor message
are unprimed, and this makes it difficult to hear the distractor. But why

does attention sometimes "leak," so that you do hear some aspects of the unattended input? Think about what will happen if your name is spoken on the unattended channel. The detectors for this stimulus are already primed, but this isn't because at that moment you're expecting to hear your name. Instead, the detectors for your name are primed simply because this is a stimulus you've often encountered in the past. Thanks to this prior exposure, the activation level of these detectors is already high; you don't need to prime them further. So they will fire even if your attention is elsewhere.

Two Types of Priming

The idea before us, in short, has three elements. First, perception is vastly facilitated by the *priming* of relevant detectors. Second, the priming is sometimes stimulus-driven—that is, produced by the stimuli you've encountered (recently or frequently) in the past. This is **repetition priming**—priming produced by a prior encounter with the stimulus. This type of priming takes no effort on your part and requires no resources, and it's this sort of priming that enables you to hear your name on the unattended channel. But third, a different sort of priming is also possible. This priming is expectation-driven and under your control. In this form of priming, you deliberately prime detectors for inputs you think are upcoming, so that you're ready for those inputs when they arrive. You don't do this priming for inputs you have no interest in, and you *can't* do this priming for inputs you can't anticipate.

Can we test these claims? In a classic series of studies, Posner and Snyder (1975) gave participants a straightforward task: A pair of letters was shown on a computer screen, and participants had to decide, as swiftly as they could, whether the letters were the same or different. So someone might see "AA" and answer "same" or might see "AB" and answer "different."

Before each pair, participants saw a warning signal. In the neutral condition, the warning signal was a plus sign ("+"). This signal notified participants that the stimuli were about to arrive but provided no other information. In a different condition, the warning signal was a letter that actually matched the stimuli to come. So someone might see the warning signal "G" followed by the pair "GG." In this case, the warning signal served to prime the participants for the stimuli. In a third condition, though, the warning signal was misleading. It was again a letter, but a different letter from the stimuli to come. Participants might see "H" followed by the pair "GG." Let's consider these three conditions *neutral*, *primed*, and *misled*.

In this simple task, accuracy rates are very high, but Posner and Snyder also recorded how *quickly* people responded. By comparing these response times (RTs) in the *primed* and *neutral* conditions, we can ask what benefit there is from the prime. Likewise, by comparing RTs in the *misled* and *neutral* conditions, we can ask what cost there is, if any, from being misled.

Before we turn to the results, there's a complication: Posner and Snyder ran this procedure in two different versions. In one version, the warning signal was an excellent predictor of the upcoming stimuli. For example, if the warning signal was an *A*, there was an 80% chance that the upcoming stimulus pair would contain *A*'s. In Posner and Snyder's terms, the warning signal provided a "high validity" prime. In a different version of the procedure, the warning signal was a poor predictor of the upcoming stimuli. For example, if the warning signal was an *A*, there was only a 20% chance that the upcoming pair would contain *A*'s. This was the "low validity" condition (see **Table 5.1**).

Let's consider the low-validity condition first, and let's focus on those few occasions in which the prime did match the subsequent stimuli. That is, we're focusing on 20% of the trials and ignoring the other 80% for the moment. In this condition, the participant can't use the prime as a basis for predicting the stimuli because the prime is a poor indicator of things to come. Therefore, the prime should not lead to any specific expectations. Nonetheless, we do expect faster RTs in the *primed* condition than in the *neutral* condition. Why? Thanks to the prime, the relevant detectors have just fired, so the detectors should still be warmed up. When the target stimuli arrive, therefore, the detectors should fire more readily, allowing a faster response.

TABLE 5.1   DESIGN OF POSNER AND SNYDER'S EXPERIMENT

	TYPICAL SEQUENCE			Provides Repetition Priming?	Provides Basis for Expectation?
	Type of Trial	Warning Signal	Test Stimuli		
Low-validity Condition	Neutral	+	AA	No	No
	Primed	G	GG	Yes	No
	Misled	H	GG	No	No
High-validity Condition	Neutral	+	AA	No	No
	Primed	G	GG	Yes	Prime leads to correct expectation
	Misled	H	GG	No	Prime leads to incorrect expectation

In the low-validity condition, misled trials occurred four times as often as primed trials (80% vs. 20%). Therefore, participants had no reason to trust the primes and, correspondingly, no reason to generate an expectation based on the primes. In the high-validity condition, the arrangement was reversed: Now, *primed* trials occurred four times as often as *misled* trials. Therefore, participants had good reason to trust the primes and good reason to generate an expectation based on the prime.

(AFTER POSNER & SNYDER, 1975)

The results bear this out. RTs were reliably faster (by roughly 30 ms) in the *primed* condition than in the *neutral* condition (see **Figure 5.7**, left side; the figure shows the *differences* between conditions). Apparently, detectors can be primed by mere exposure to a stimulus, even in the absence of expectations, and so this priming is truly stimulus-based.

What about the *misled* condition? With a low-validity prime, misleading the participants had no effect: Performance in the *misled* condition was the same as performance in the *neutral* condition. Priming the "wrong" detector, it seems, takes nothing away from the other detectors—including the detectors actually needed for that trial. This fits with our discussion in Chapter 4: Each of the various detectors works independently of the others, and so priming one detector obviously influences the functioning of that specific detector but neither helps nor hinders the other detectors.

FIGURE 5.7   THE EFFECTS OF PRIMING ON STIMULUS PROCESSING

As one way of assessing the Posner and Snyder (1975) results, we can subtract the response times for the *neutral* condition from those for the *primed* condition; in this way, we measure the benefits of priming. Likewise, we can subtract the response times for the *neutral* condition from those for the *misled* condition; in this way, we measure the costs of being misled. In these terms, the low-validity condition shows a small benefit (from repetition priming) but zero cost from being misled. The high-validity condition, in contrast, shows a larger benefit—but also a substantial cost. The results shown here reflect trials with a 300 ms interval between the warning signal and the test stimuli. Results were somewhat different at other intervals.

Let's look next at the high-validity primes. In this condition, people might see, for example, a "J" as the warning signal and then the stimulus pair "JJ." Presentation of the prime itself will fire the *J*-detectors, and this should, once again, "warm up" these detectors, just as the low-validity primes did. As a result, we expect a stimulus-driven benefit from the prime. However, the high-validity primes may also have another influence: High-validity primes are excellent predictors of the stimulus to come. Participants are told this at the outset, and they have lots of opportunity to see that it's true. High-validity primes will therefore produce a warm-up effect *and also* an expectation effect, whereas low-validity primes produce only the warm-up. On this basis, we should expect the high-validity primes to help participants more than low-validity primes—and that's exactly what the data show (Figure 5.7, right side). The combination of warm-up and expectations leads to faster responses than warm-up alone. From the participants' point of view, it pays to know what the upcoming stimulus might be.

Explaining the Costs and Benefits

The data make it clear, then, that we need to distinguish two types of primes. One type is stimulus-based—produced merely by presentation of the priming stimulus, with no role for expectations. The other type is expectation-based and is created only when the participant believes the prime allows a prediction of what's to come.

These types of primes can be distinguished in various ways, including the biological mechanisms that support them (see **Figure 5.8**; Corbetta & Shulman, 2002; Hahn, Ross, & Stein, 2006; but also Moore & Zirnsak, 2017) and also a difference in what they "cost." Stimulus-based priming

FIGURE 5.8 BIOLOGICAL MECHANISMS FOR THE TWO TYPES OF PRIMING

Brain sites shown in black have been identified in various studies as involved in expectation-based (sometimes called "goal directed") attention; sites shown in blue have been implicated in "stimulus-driven" attention. Sites shown in gray have been identified as involved in both types of attention.

appears to be "free" — we can prime one detector without taking anything away from other detectors. (We saw this in the low-validity condition, in the fact that the *misled* trials led to responses just as fast as those in the *neutral* trials.) Expectation-based priming, in contrast, does have a cost, and we see this in an aspect of Figure 5.7 that we've not yet mentioned: With high-validity primes, responses in the *misled* condition were slower than responses in the *neutral* condition. That is, misleading the participants actually hurt their performance. As a concrete example, *F*-detection was slower if *G* was primed, compared to *F*-detection when the prime was simply the neutral warning signal ("+"). In broader terms, it seems that priming the "wrong" detector takes something away from the other detectors, and so participants are worse off when they're misled than when they receive no prime at all.

What produces this cost? As an analogy, let's say that you have just $50 to spend on groceries. You can spend more on ice cream if you wish, but if you do, you'll have less to spend on other foods. Any increase in the ice cream allotment, in other words, must be covered by a decrease somewhere else. This trade-off arises, though, only because of the limited budget. If you had unlimited funds, you could spend more on ice cream and still have enough money for everything else.

Expectation-based priming shows the same pattern. If the *Q*-detector is primed, this takes something away from the other detectors. Getting prepared for one target seems to make people less prepared for other targets. But we just said that this sort of pattern implies a limited "budget." If an unlimited supply of activation were available, you could prime the *Q*-detector and leave the other detectors just as they were. And that is the point: Expectation-based priming, by virtue of revealing costs when misled, reveals the presence of a **limited-capacity system**.

We can now put the pieces together. Ultimately, we need to explain the facts of selective attention, including the fact that while listening to one message you hear little content from other messages. To explain this, we've proposed that perceiving involves some work, and this work requires some limited **mental resources** — some process or capacity needed for performance, but in limited supply. That's why you can't listen to two messages at the same time; doing so would require more resources than you have. And now, finally, we're seeing evidence for those limited resources: The Posner and Snyder research (and many other results) reveals the workings of a limited-capacity system, just as our hypothesis demands.

Spatial Attention

The Posner and Snyder study shows that expectations about an upcoming stimulus can influence the processing of that stimulus. But what exactly is the nature of these expectations? How precise or vague are they?

As one way of framing this issue, imagine that participants in a study are told, "The next stimulus will be a *T*." In this case, they know exactly what to

TEST YOURSELF

4. What are the differences between the way that stimulus-based priming functions and the way that expectation-based priming functions?

5. Why is there a "cost" associated with being misled by expectation-based priming?

get ready for. But now imagine that participants are told, "The next stimulus will be a letter" or "The next stimulus will be on the left side of the screen." Will these cues allow participants to prepare themselves?

These issues have been examined in studies of **spatial attention**—that is, the mechanism through which someone focuses on a particular position in space. In one early study, Posner, Snyder, and Davidson (1980) required their participants simply to detect letter presentations; the task was just to press a button as soon as a letter appeared. Participants kept their eyes pointed at a central fixation mark, and letters could appear either to the left or to the right of this mark.

For some trials, a neutral warning signal was presented, so that participants knew a trial was about to start but had no information about stimulus location. For other trials, an arrow was used as the warning signal. Sometimes the arrow pointed left, sometimes right; and the arrow was generally an accurate predictor of the location of the stimulus-to-come. If the arrow pointed right, the stimulus would be on the right side of the computer screen. (In the terms we used earlier, this was a high-validity cue.) On 20% of the trials, however, the arrow misled participants about location.

The results show a familiar pattern (Posner et al., 1980). With high-validity priming, the data show a benefit from cues that correctly signal where the upcoming target will appear. The differences between conditions aren't large, but keep the task in mind: All participants had to do was detect the input. Even with the simplest of tasks, it pays to be prepared (see **Figure 5.9**).

What about the trials in which participants were misled? RTs in this condition were about 12% slower than those in the neutral condition. Once again, therefore, we're seeing evidence of a limited-capacity system. In order to devote more attention to (say) the left position, you have to devote *less*

FIGURE 5.9 SPATIAL ATTENTION

In the Posner et al. (1980) study, participants simply had to press a button as soon as they saw the target. If the target appeared in the expected location, participants detected it a bit more quickly. If, however, participants were misled about the target's position (so that the target appeared in an unexpected location), their responses were slower than when the participants had no expectations at all.

attention to the right. If the stimulus then shows up on the right, you're less prepared for it—which is the cost of being misled.

Attention as a Spotlight

Studies of spatial attention suggest that visual attention can be compared to a spotlight beam that can "shine" anywhere in the visual field. The "beam" marks the region of space for which you are prepared, so inputs within the beam are processed more efficiently. The beam can be wide or narrowly focused (see **Figure 5.10**) and can be moved about at will as you explore (i.e., attend to) various aspects of the visual field.

FIGURE 5.10 ADJUSTING THE "BEAM" OF ATTENTION

Charles Allan Gilbert's painting *All Is Vanity* can be perceived either as a woman at her dressing table or as a human skull. As you shift from one of these perceptions to the other, you need to adjust the spotlight beam of attention—to a narrow beam to see details (e.g., to see the woman) or to a wider beam to see the whole scene (e.g., to see the skull).

Let's emphasize, though, that the spotlight idea refers to movements of *attention*, not movements of the eyes. Of course, eye movements do play an important role in your selection of information from the world: If you want to learn more about something, you generally look at it. (For more on how you move your eyes to explore a scene, see Henderson, 2013; Moore & Zirnsak, 2017.) Even so, movements of the eyes can be separated from movements of attention, and it's attention, not the eyes, that's moving around in the Posner et al. (1980) study. We know this because of the timing of the effects. Eye movements are surprisingly slow, requiring 180 to 200 ms. But the benefits of primes can be detected within the first 150 ms after the priming stimulus is presented. Therefore, the benefits of attention occur *prior to* any eye movement, so they cannot be a consequence of eye movements.

But what does it mean to "move attention"? The spotlight beam is just a metaphor, so we need to ask what's really going on in the brain to produce these effects. The answer involves a network of sites in the frontal cortex and the parietal cortex. According to one proposal (Posner & Rothbart, 2007; see **Figure 5.11**), one cluster of sites (the *orienting* system) is needed to disengage attention from one target, shift attention to a new target, and then

FIGURE 5.11 MANY BRAIN SITES ARE CRUCIAL FOR ATTENTION

Many brain sites are important for controlling attention. Some sites play a pivotal role in *alerting* the brain, so that it is ready for an upcoming event. Other sites play a key role in *orienting* attention, so that you're focused on this position or that, on one target or another. Still other sites are crucial for controlling the brain's *executive* function—a function we'll discuss later in the chapter. (AFTER POSNER & ROTHBART, 2007) engage attention on the new target. A second set of sites (the *alerting* system) is responsible for maintaining an alert state in the brain. A third set of sites (the *executive* system) controls voluntary actions.

These points echo a theme we first met in Chapter 2. There, we argued that cognitive capacities depend on the coordinated activity of multiple brain regions, with each region providing a specialized process necessary for the overall achievement. As a result, a problem in *any* of these regions can disrupt the overall capacity, and if there are problems in *several* regions, the disruption can be substantial.

As an illustration of this interplay between brain sites and symptoms, consider a disorder we mentioned earlier—ADHD. (We'll have more to say about ADHD later in the chapter.) **Table 5.2** summarizes one proposal about this disorder. Symptoms of ADHD are listed in the left column; the right column identifies brain areas that may be the main source of each symptom. This proposal is not the only way to think about ADHD, but it illustrates the complex, many-part relationship between overall function (in this case, the ability to pay attention) and brain anatomy. (For more on ADHD, see Barkley, Murphy, & Fischer, 2008; Brown, 2005; Seli, Smallwood, Cheyne, & Smilek, 2015; Zillmer, Spiers, & Culbertson, 2008.)

In addition, the sites listed in Table 5.2 can be understood roughly as forming the "control system" for attention. Entirely different sites (including

TABLE 5.2   ATTENTION-DEFICIT/HYPERACTIVITY DISORDER SYMPTOMS, COGNITIVE PROCESSES, AND NEURAL NETWORKS

Symptom Domains and Cognitive Processes	Relevant Brain Site
Problems in the "Alerting" system	
Has difficulty sustaining attention	Right frontal cortex
Fails to finish	Right posterior parietal
Avoids sustained efforts	Locus ceruleus
Problems in the "Orienting" system	
Is distracted by stimuli	Bilateral parietal
Does not appear to listen	Superior colliculus
Fails to pay close attention	Thalamus
Problems in the "Executive" system	
Blurts out answers	Anterior cingulate
Interrupts or intrudes	Left lateral frontal
Cannot wait	Basal ganglia

Earlier in the chapter, we mentioned the disorder known as ADHD. The table summarizes one influential proposal about this disorder, linking the symptoms of ADHD to the three broad processes (*alerting, orienting,* and *executive*) described in the text, and then linking these processes to relevant brain areas (Swanson et al., 2000; for a somewhat different proposal, though, see Barkley, Murphy, & Fischer, 2008).

FIGURE 5.12 SELECTIVE ATTENTION ACTIVATES THE VISUAL CORTEX

The brain sites that *control* attention are separate from the brain sites that do the actual analysis of the input. Thus, the intention to attend to, say, stimuli on the left is implemented through the many brain sites shown in Figure 5.11. However, these sites collectively activate a different set of sites—in the visual cortex—to promote the actual processing of the incoming stimulus. Shown here are activity levels in one participant (measured through fMRI scans) overlaid on a structural image of the brain (obtained through MRI scans). Keep in mind that because of the brain's contralateral organization, the intention to pay attention to the left side of space requires activation in the right hemisphere (Panel A); the intention to pay attention to the right requires activation in the left (Panel B).

the visual areas in the occipital cortex) do the actual analysis of the incoming information (see **Figure 5.12**). In other words, neural connections from the areas listed in the table carry signals to the brain regions that do the work of analyzing the input. These control signals can amplify (or, in some cases, inhibit) the activity in these other areas and, in this way, they can promote the processing of inputs you're interested in, and undermine the processing of distractors. (See Corbetta & Shulman, 2002; Hampshire, Duncan, & Owen, 2007; Hon, Epstein, Owen, & Duncan, 2006; Hung, Driver, & Walsh, 2005; Miller & Cohen, 2001.)

Thus, there is no spotlight beam. Instead, certain neural mechanisms enable you to adjust your sensitivity to certain inputs. This is, of course, entirely in line with the proposal we're developing—namely, that a large part of "paying attention" involves priming. For stimuli you don't care about, you don't bother to prime yourself, and so those stimuli fall on unprepared (and unresponsive) detectors. For stimuli you do care about, you do your best to anticipate the input, and you use these anticipations to prime the relevant processing channel. This increases your sensitivity to the desired input, which is just what you want. (For further discussion of the "spotlight" idea, see Cave, 2013; Rensink, 2012; Wright & Ward, 2008; but also Awh & Pashler, 2000; Morawetz, Holz, Baudewig, Treue, & Dechent, 2007.)

Where Do We "Shine" the "Beam"?

So far, we've been discussing *how* people pay attention, but we can also ask *what people pay attention to*. Where do people "shine" the "spotlight beam"? The answer has several parts. As a start, you pay attention to elements of the input that are visually prominent (Parkhurst, Law, & Niebur, 2002) and also to elements that you think are interesting or important. Decisions about what's important, though, depend on the context. For example, **Figure 5.13** shows classic data recording a viewer's eye movements while inspecting a picture (Yarbus, 1967). The target picture is shown in the top left. Each of the other panels shows a three-minute recording of the viewer's eye movements;

FIGURE 5.13 EYE MOVEMENTS AND VISION

1 Free examination.

2 Estimate material circumstances of the family.

3 Give the ages of the people.

4 Surmise what the family had been doing before the arrival of the unexpected visitor.

5 Remember the clothes worn by the people.

6 Remember positions of people and objects in the room.

7 Estimate how long the visitor had been away from the family.

Participants were shown the picture in the top left. Each of the other panels shows a three-minute recording of one viewer's eye movements while inspecting the picture. The labels for each panel summarize the viewer's goal while looking at the picture. Plainly, the pattern of the movements depended on what the viewer was trying to learn.

---

plainly, the pattern of movements depended on what the viewer was trying to learn about the picture.

In addition, your *beliefs* about the scene play an important role. You're unlikely to focus, for example, on elements of a scene that are entirely predictable, because you'll gain no information from inspecting things that are already obvious (Brewer & Treyens, 1981; Friedman, 1979; Võ & Henderson, 2009). But you're also unlikely to focus on aspects of the scene that are totally unexpected. If, for example, you're walking through a forest, you won't be on the lookout for a stapler sitting on the ground, and so you may fail to notice the stapler (unless it's a bright color, or directly in your path, or some such). This point provides part of the basis for inattentional blindness (pp. 155–156) and also leads to a pattern called the "ultra-rare item effect" (Mitroff & Biggs, 2014). The term refers to a pattern in which rare items are often overlooked; as the authors of one paper put it, "If you don't find it often, you often don't find it" (Evans, Birdwell, & Wolfe, 2013; for a troubling consequence of this pattern, see **Figure 5.14**).

As another complication, people differ in what they pay attention to (e.g., Castelhano & Henderson, 2008), although some differences aren't surprising. For example, in looking at a scene, women are more likely than men to focus on how the people within the scene are dressed; men are more likely to focus on what the people look like (including their body shapes; Powers, Andriks, & Loftus, 1979).

Perhaps more surprising are differences from one *culture* to the next in how people pay attention. The underlying idea here is that people in the West (the United States, Canada, most of Europe) live in "individualistic" cultures that emphasize the achievements and qualities of the single person; therefore, in thinking about the world, Westerners are likely to focus on individual people, individual objects, and their attributes. In contrast, people in East Asia have traditionally lived in "collectivist" cultures that emphasize the ways in which all people are linked to, and shaped by, the people around them. East Asians are therefore encouraged to think more holistically, with a focus on the context and how people and

FIGURE 5.14 IF YOU DON'T FIND IT OFTEN . . .

Data both in the laboratory and in real-world settings tell us that people often overlook targets if the targets happen to be quite rare. As one group of authors put it, "If you don't find it often, you often don't find it." This pattern has troubling implications for the security inspections routinely conducted at airports: The inspectors will see troubling items only rarely and, as a result, are likely to overlook those troubling items.

objects are related to one another. (See Nisbett, 2003; Nisbett, Peng, Choi, & Norenzayan, 2001; also Tardif et al., 2017. For a broad review, see Heine, 2015.)

This linkage between culture and cognition isn't rigid, and so people in any culture can stray from these patterns. Even so, researchers have documented many manifestations of these differences from one culture to the next—including differences in how people pay attention. In one study, researchers tracked participants' eye movements while the participants were watching animated scenes on a computer screen (Masuda et al., 2008). In the initial second of viewing, there was little difference between the eye movements of American participants and Japanese participants: Both groups spent 90% of the time looking at the target person, located centrally in the display. But in the second and third seconds of viewing, the groups differed. The Americans continued to spend 90% of their time looking directly at the central figure (and so spent only 10% of their time looking at the faces of people visible in the scene's background); Japanese participants, in contrast, spent between 20% and 30% of their time looking at the faces in the background. This difference in viewing time was reflected in the participants' judgments about the scene. When asked to make a judgment about the target person's emotional state, American participants weren't influenced by the emotional expressions of the people standing in the background, but Japanese participants were.

In another study, American and East Asian students were tested in a change-blindness procedure. They viewed one picture, then a second, then the first again, and this alternation continued until the participants spotted the difference between the two pictures. For some pairs of pictures, the difference involved an attribute of a central object in the scene (e.g., the color of a truck changed from one picture to the next). For these pictures, Americans and East Asians performed equivalently, needing a bit more than 9 seconds to spot the change. For other pairs of pictures, the difference involved the context (e.g., a pattern of the clouds in the background of the scene). For these pictures, the East Asians were notably faster than the Americans in detecting the change. (See Masuda & Nisbett, 2006. For other data, exploring when Westerners have a performance advantage and when East Asians have the advantage, see Amer, Ngo, & Hasher, 2016; Boduroglu, Shah, & Nisbett, 2010.)

Finally, let's acknowledge that sometimes you choose what to pay attention to—a pattern called **endogenous control of attention**. But sometimes an element of the scene "seizes" your attention whether you like it or not, and this pattern is called **exogenous control of attention**. Exogenous control is of intense interest to theorists, and it's also important for pragmatic reasons. For example, people who design ambulance sirens or warning signals in an airplane cockpit want to make sure these stimuli cannot be ignored. In the same way, advertisers do all they can to ensure that their product name or logo will grab your attention even if you're

FIGURE 5.15 EXOGENOUS CONTROL OF ATTENTION

Public health officials would like the health warning shown here to seize your attention, so that you can't overlook it. The tobacco industry, however, might have a different preference.

intensely focused on something else (e.g., the competitor's product; also see **Figure 5.15**).

Attending to Objects or Attending to Positions

A related question is also concerned with the "target" of the attention "spotlight." To understand the issue, think about how an actual spotlight works. If a spotlight shines on a donut, then part of the beam will fall on the donut's hole and will illuminate part of the plate underneath the donut. Similarly, if the beam isn't aimed quite accurately, it may also illuminate the plate just to the left of the donut. The region illuminated by the beam, in other words, is defined purely in spatial terms: a circle of light at a particular position. That circle may or may not line up with the boundaries of the object you're shining the beam on.

Is this how attention works—so that you pay attention to whatever falls in a certain region of space? If this is the case, you might at times end up paying attention to part of this object, part of that. An alternative is that you pay attention to *objects* rather than to *positions in space*. To continue the example, the target of your attention might be the donut itself rather than

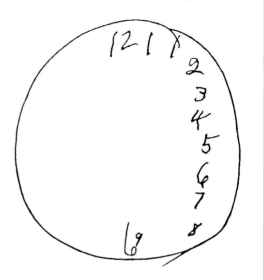

its location. In that case, the plate just to the left and the bit of plate visible through the donut's hole might be close to your focus, but they aren't part of the attended object and so aren't attended.

Which is the correct view of attention? Do you pay attention to regions in space, no matter what objects (or parts of objects) fall in that region? Or do you pay attention to objects? It turns out that each view captures part of the truth.

One line of evidence comes from the study of people we mentioned at the chapter's start – people who suffer from **unilateral neglect syndrome** (see **Figure 5.16**). Taken at face value, the symptoms shown by these patients seem to support a space-based account of attention: The afflicted patient seems insensitive to all objects within a region that's defined spatially—namely, everything to the left of his or her current focus. If an object falls half within the region and half outside of it, then the spatial boundary is what matters, not the object's boundaries. This is clear, for example, in how these patients read words (likely to read "BOTHER" as "HER" or "CARROT" as "ROT")—responding only to the word's right half, apparently oblivious to the word's overall boundaries.

Other evidence, however, demands further theory. In one study, patients with neglect syndrome had to respond to targets that appeared within a barbell-shaped frame (see **Figure 5.17**). Not surprisingly, they were much more sensitive to the targets appearing within the red circle (on the right) and missed many of the targets appearing in the blue circle (on the left); this result confirms the patients' diagnosis. What's crucial, though, is what happened next. While the patients watched, the barbell frame was slowly spun around,

FIGURE 5.17 SPACE-BASED OR OBJECT-BASED ATTENTION

Patient initially sees:

As the patient watches:

Patient now sees:

Patients with unilateral neglect syndrome were much more sensitive to targets appearing within the red circle (on the right) and missed many of the targets appearing within the blue circle (on the left); this observation confirms their clinical diagnosis. Then, as the patients watched, the barbell-shaped frame rotated, so that now the red circle was on the left and the blue circle was on the right. After this rotation, participants were still more sensitive to targets in the red circle (now on the left), apparently focusing on this attended object even though it had moved into their "neglected" side.

so that the red circle, previously on the right, was now on the left and the blue circle, previously on the left, was now on the right.

If the patients consistently neglect a region of space, they should now be more sensitive to the (right-side) blue circle. But here's a different possibility: Perhaps these patients have a powerful bias to attend to the right side, and so initially they attend to the red circle. Once they have "locked in" to this circle, however, it's the object, not the position in space, that defines their focus of attention. According to this view, if the barbell rotates, they will continue attending to the red circle (this is, after all, the focus of their attention), even though it now appears on their "neglected" side. This prediction turns out to be correct: When the barbell rotates, the patients' focus of attention seems to rotate with it (Behrmann & Tipper, 1999).

To describe these patients, therefore, we need a two-part account. First, the symptoms of neglect syndrome plainly reveal a spatially defined bias: These patients neglect half of space. But, second, once attention is directed toward a target, it's the target itself that defines the focus of attention; if the target moves, the focus moves with it. In this way, the focus of attention is object-based, not space-based. (For more on these issues, see Chen & Cave, 2006; Logie & Della Salla, 2005; Richard, Lee, & Vecera, 2008.)

And it's not just people with brain damage who show this complex pattern. People with intact brains also show a mix of space-based and object-based attention. We've already seen evidence for the spatial base: The Posner et al. (1980) study and many results like it show that participants can focus on a particular region of space *in preparation for* a stimulus. In this situation, the stimulus has not yet appeared; there is no object to focus on. Therefore, the attention must be spatially defined.

In other cases, though, attention is heavily influenced by object boundaries. For example, in some studies, participants have been shown displays with *visually superimposed* stimuli (e.g., Becklen & Cervone, 1983; Neisser & Becklen, 1975). Participants can usually pay attention to one of these stimuli and ignore the other. This selection cannot be space-based (because both stimuli are in the same place) and so must be object-based.

This two-part account is also supported by neuroscience evidence. Various studies have examined the pattern of brain activation when participants are attending to a particular position in space, and the pattern of activation when participants are attending to a particular object. These data suggest that the tasks involve different brain circuits—with one set of circuits (the *dorsal attention system*), near the top of the head, being primarily concerned with spatial attention, and a different set of circuits (the *ventral attention system*) being crucial for nonspatial tasks (Cave, 2013; Cohen, 2012; Corbetta & Shulman, 2011). Once again, therefore, our description of attention needs to include a mix of object-based and space-based mechanisms.

Perceiving and the Limits on Cognitive Capacity: An Interim Summary

Let's pause to review. In some circumstances, you seem to *inhibit* the processing of unwanted inputs. This inhibitory process is quite specific (the inhibition blocks the processing of a particular well-defined input) and certainly benefits from practice.

More broadly, though, various mechanisms *facilitate* the processing of *desired* inputs. The key here is priming. You're primed for some stimuli because you've encountered them often in the past, with the result that you're more likely to process (and therefore more likely to notice) these stimuli if you encounter them again. In other cases, the priming depends on your ability to anticipate what the upcoming stimulus will be. If you can predict what the stimulus will likely be, you can prime the relevant processing pathway so that you're ready for the stimulus when it arrives. The priming will make you more responsive to the anticipated input if it does arrive, and this gives the anticipated input an advantage relative to other inputs. That advantage is what you want—so that you end up perceiving the desired input (the one you've prepared yourself for) but don't perceive the inputs you're hoping to ignore (because they fall on unprimed detectors).

The argument, then, is that your ability to pay attention depends to a large extent on your ability to anticipate the upcoming stimulus. This anticipation, in turn, depends on many factors. You'll have a much easier time anticipating (and so an easier time paying attention to) materials that you understand as opposed to materials that you don't understand. Likewise, when a stimulus sequence is just beginning, you have little basis for anticipation, so your only option may be to focus on the position in space that holds the sequence. Once the sequence begins, though, you get a sense of how it's progressing, and this lets you sharpen your anticipations (shifting to object-based attention, rather than space-based)—which, again, makes you more sensitive to the attended input and more resistant to distractors.

Putting all these points together, perhaps it's best not to think of the term "attention" as referring to a particular process or a particular mechanism. Instead, it's better to think of attention (as one research group put it) as an *effect* rather than as a *cause* (Krauzlis, Bollimunta, Arcizet, & Wang, 2014). In other words, the term "attention" doesn't refer to some mechanism in the brain that produces a certain outcome. It's better to think of attention as itself an outcome—a byproduct of many other mechanisms.

As a related perspective, it may be helpful to think of paying attention, not as a process or mechanism, but as an *achievement*—something that you're able to do. Like many other achievements (e.g., doing well in school, staying healthy), paying attention involves many elements, and the exact set of elements needed will vary from one occasion to the next. In all cases, though, multiple steps are needed to ensure that you end up being aware of the stimuli you're interested in, and not getting pulled off track by irrelevant inputs.

TEST YOURSELF

6. In what ways does the notion of a spotlight beam accurately reflect how spatial attention functions?

7. In what ways does the notion of a spotlight beam differ from the way spatial attention functions?

8. When you first start paying attention to an input, your attention seems to be space-based. Once you've learned a bit about the input, though, your attention seems to be object-based. How does this pattern fit with the idea that you pay attention by *anticipating* the input?

Divided Attention

So far in this chapter, we've emphasized situations in which you're trying to focus on a single input. If other tasks and other stimuli were on the scene, they were mere distractors. Sometimes, though, your goal is different: You want to "multitask"—that is, deal with multiple tasks, or multiple inputs, all at the same time. What can we say about this sort of situation—a situation involving **divided attention**?

Sometimes divided attention is easy. Almost anyone can walk and sing simultaneously; many people like to knit while they're holding a conversation or listening to a lecture. It's much harder, though, to do calculus homework while listening to a lecture; and trying to get your assigned reading done while watching TV is surely a bad bet. What lies behind this pattern? Why are some combinations difficult while others are easy?

CAESAR THE MULTITASKER

Some writers complain about the hectic pace of life today and view it as a sad fact about the pressured reality of the modern world. But were things different in earlier times? More than 2,000 years ago, Julius Caesar was praised for his ability to multitask. (The term is new, but the capacity is not.) According to the Roman historian Suetonius, Caesar could write, dictate letters, and read at the same time. Even on the most important subjects, he could dictate four letters at once—and if he had nothing else to do, as many as seven letters at once. From a modern perspective, though, we can ask: Is any of this plausible? Perhaps it is—some people do seem especially skilled at multitasking (Just & Buchweitz, 2017; Redick et al., 2016), and maybe Caesar was one of those special people!

Our first step toward answering these questions is already in view. We've proposed that perceiving requires resources that are in limited supply; the same is presumably true for other tasks—remembering, reasoning, problem solving. They, too, require resources, and without these resources the processes cannot go forward. What are the resources? The answer includes a mix of things: certain mechanisms that do specific jobs, certain types of memory that hold on to information while you're working on it, energy supplies to keep the mental machinery going, and more. No matter what the resources are, though, a task will be possible only if you have the needed resources—just as a dressmaker can produce a dress only if he has the raw materials, the tools, the time needed, the energy to run the sewing machine, and so on.

All of this leads to a proposal: You can perform concurrent tasks only if you have the resources needed for both. If the two tasks, when combined, require more resources than you've got, then divided attention will fail.

The Specificity of Resources

Imagine that you're hoping to read a novel while listening to an academic lecture. These tasks are different, but both involve the use of language, and so it seems likely that these tasks will have overlapping resource requirements. As a result, if you try to do the tasks at the same time, they're likely to *compete* for resources—and therefore this sort of multitasking will be difficult.

Now, think about two very different tasks, such as *knitting* and listening to a lecture. These tasks are unlikely to interfere with each other. Even if all your language-related resources are in use for the lecture, this won't matter for knitting, because it's not a language-based task.

More broadly, the prediction here is that divided attention will be easier if the simultaneous tasks are very different from each other, because different tasks are likely to have distinct resource requirements. Resources consumed by Task 1 won't be needed for Task 2, so it doesn't matter for Task 2 that these resources are tied up in another endeavor.

Is this the pattern found in the research data? In an early study by Allport, Antonis, and Reynolds (1972), participants heard a list of words presented through headphones into one ear, and their task was to shadow (i.e., repeat back) these words. At the same time, they were also presented with a second list. No immediate response was required to the second list, but later on, memory was tested for these items. In one condition, the second list (the memory items) consisted of words presented into the other ear, so the participants were hearing (and shadowing) a list of words in one ear while simultaneously hearing the memory list in the other. In another condition, the memory items were presented visually. That is, while the participants were shadowing one list of words, they were also seeing a different list of words on a screen before them. Finally, in a third condition, the memory items consisted of pictures, also presented on a screen.

These three conditions had the same requirements—shadowing one list while memorizing another. But the first condition (hear words + hear words) involved very similar tasks; the second condition (hear words + see words) involved less similar tasks; the third condition (hear words + see pictures), even less similar tasks. On the logic we've discussed, we should expect the most interference in the first condition and the least interference in the third. And that is what the data showed (see **Figure 5.18**).

The Generality of Resources

Similarity among tasks, however, is not the whole story. If it were, then we'd observe less and less interference as we consider tasks further and further apart. Eventually, we'd find tasks so different from each other that we'd observe *no* interference at all between them. But that's not the pattern of the evidence.

Consider the common practice of talking on a cell phone while driving. When you're on the phone, the main stimulus information comes into your ear, and your primary response is by talking. In driving, the main stimulation comes into your eyes, and your primary response involves control of your hands on the steering wheel and your feet on the pedals. For the phone conversation, you're relying on language skills. For driving, you need spatial skills. Overall, it looks like there's little overlap in the specific demands of these two tasks, and so little chance that the tasks will compete for resources.

Data show, however, that driving and cell-phone use do interfere with each other. This is reflected, for example, in the fact that phone use has been implicated in many automobile accidents (Lamble, Kauranen, Laakso, & Summala, 1999). Even with a hands-free phone, drivers engaged in cell-phone conversations are more likely to be involved in accidents, more likely to overlook traffic signals, and slower to hit the brakes when they need to.

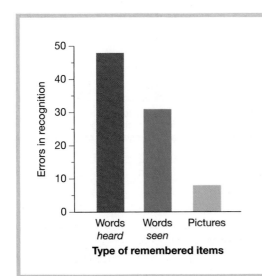

FIGURE 5.18   DIVIDED ATTENTION AMONG DISTINCT TASKS

Participants perform poorly if they are trying to shadow one list of words while *hearing* other words. They do somewhat better if shadowing while *seeing* other words. They do better still if shadowing while seeing *pictures*. In general, the greater the difference between two tasks, the easier it will be to combine the tasks.   (AFTER ALLPORT, ANTONIS, & REYNOLDS, 1972)

(See Kunar, Carter, Cohen, & Horowitz, 2008; Levy & Pashler, 2008; Sanbonmatsu, Strayer, Biondi, Behrends, & Moore, 2016; Stothart, Mitchum, & Yehnert, 2015; Strayer & Drews, 2007; Strayer, Drews, & Johnston, 2003. For some encouraging data, though, on why phone-related accidents don't occur even more often, see Garrison & Williams, 2013; Medeiros-Ward, Watson, & Strayer, 2015.)

As a practical matter, therefore, talking on the phone while driving is a bad idea. In fact, some people estimate that the danger caused by driving while on the phone is comparable to (and perhaps greater than) the risk of driving while drunk. But, on the theoretical side, notice that the interference observed between driving and talking is interference between two hugely distinctive activities—a point that provides important information about the nature of the resource competition involved, and therefore the nature of mental resources.

Before moving on, we should mention that the data pattern is different if the driver is talking to a *passenger* in the car rather than using the phone. Conversations with passengers seem to cause little interference with driving (Drews, Pasupathi, & Strayer, 2008; see **Figure 5.19**), and the reason is simple. If the traffic becomes complicated or the driver has to perform some

FIGURE 5.19   CELL PHONE USE AND DRIVING

Many studies show that driving performance is impaired when the driver is on the phone (whether hand-held or hands-free). While on the phone, drivers are more likely to miss a red light (Panel A) and are slower in responding to a red light (Panel B). Disruption is not observed, however, if the driver is conversing with a passenger rather than on the phone (Panel C). That's because the passenger is likely to adjust her conversation to accommodate changes in driving—such as not speaking while the driver is navigating an obstruction.

(AFTER STRAYER & JOHNSTON, 2001)

tricky maneuver, the passenger can see this—either by looking out of the car's window or by noticing the driver's tension and focus. In these cases, passengers helpfully slow down their side of the conversation, which takes the load off of the driver, enabling the driver to focus on the road (Gaspar et al., 2014; Hyman, Boss, Wise, McKenzie, & Caggiano, 2010; Nasar, Hecht, & Wener, 2008).

Executive Control

The evidence is clear, then, that tasks as different as driving and talking compete with each other for some mental resource. But what is this resource, which is apparently needed for both verbal tasks and spatial ones, tasks with visual inputs and tasks with auditory inputs?

Evidence suggests that *multiple* resources may be relevant. Some authors describe resources that serve (roughly) as an energy supply, drawn on by all tasks (Eysenck, 1982; Kahneman, 1973; Lavie, 2001, 2005; Lavie, Lin, Zokaei, & Thoma, 2009; MacDonald & Lavie, 2008; Murphy, Groeger, & Greene, 2016). According to this perspective, tasks vary in the "load" they put on you, and the greater the load, the greater the interference with other tasks. In one study, drivers were asked to estimate whether their vehicle would fit between two parked cars (Murphy & Greene, 2016). When the judgment was difficult, participants were less likely to notice an unexpected pedestrian at the side of the road. In other words, higher perceptual load (from the driving task) increased inattentional blindness. (Also see Murphy & Greene, 2017.)

Other authors describe mental resources as "mental tools" rather than as some sort of mental "energy supply." (See Allport, 1989; Baddeley, 1986; Bourke & Duncan, 2005; Dehaene, Sergent, & Changeux, 2003; Johnson-Laird, 1988; Just, Carpenter, & Hemphill, 1996; Norman & Shallice, 1986; Ruthruff, Johnston, & Remington, 2009; Vergaujwe, Barrouillet, & Camos, 2010. For an alternative perspective on these resources, see Franconeri, 2013; Franconeri, Alvarez, & Cavanagh, 2013.) One of these tools is especially important, and it involves the mind's **executive control**. This term refers to the mechanisms that allow you to control your own thoughts, and these mechanisms have multiple functions. Executive control helps keep your current goals in mind, so that these goals (and not habit) will guide your actions. The executive also ensures that your mental steps are organized into the right sequence—one that will move you toward your goals. And if your current operations aren't moving you toward your goal, executive control allows you to shift plans, or change strategy. (For discussion of how the executive operates and how the brain tissue enables executive function, see Brown, Reynolds, & Braver, 2007; Duncan et al., 2008; Gilbert & Shallice, 2002; Kane, Conway, Hambrick, & Engle, 2007; Miller & Cohen, 2001; Miyake & Friedman, 2012; Shipstead, Harrison, & Engle, 2015; Stuss & Alexander, 2007; Unsworth & Engle, 2007; Vandierendonck, Liefooghe, & Verbruggen, 2010.)

CELL-PHONE DANGERS FOR PEDESTRIANS

It's not just driving that's disrupted by cell-phone use. Compared to pedestrians who aren't using a phone, pedestrians engaged in phone conversations tend to walk more slowly and more erratically, and are less likely to check traffic before they cross a street. They're also less likely to notice things along their path. In one study, researchers observed pedestrians walking across a public square (Hyman, Boss, Wise, McKenzie, & Caggiano, 2010). If the pedestrian was walking with a friend (and so engaged in a "live" conversation), there was a 71% chance the pedestrian would notice the unicycling clown just off the pedestrian's path. But if the pedestrian was on the phone (i.e., engaging in a telephonic conversation), the person had only a 25% chance of detecting the clown.

Executive control can only handle one task at a time, and this point obviously puts limits on your ability to multitask—that is, to divide your attention. But executive control is also important when you're trying to do just a single task. Evidence comes from studies of people who have suffered damage to the prefrontal cortex (PFC), a brain area right behind the eyes that seems crucial for executive control. People with this damage (including Phineas Gage, whom we met in Chapter 2) can lead relatively normal lives, because in their day-to-day behavior they can often rely on habit or can simply respond to prominent cues in their environment. With appropriate tests, though, we can reveal the disruption that results from frontal lobe damage. In one commonly used task, patients with frontal lesions are asked to sort a deck of cards into two piles. At the start, the patients have to sort the cards according to color; later, they need to switch strategies and sort according to the shapes shown on the cards. The patients have enormous difficulty in making this shift and continue to sort by color, even though the experimenter tells them again and again that they're placing the cards on the wrong piles (Goldman-Rakic, 1998). This is referred to as a **perseveration error**, a tendency to produce the same response over and over even when it's plain that the task requires a change in the response.

These patients also show a pattern of **goal neglect**—failing to organize their behavior in a way that moves them toward their goals. For example, when one patient was asked to copy **Figure 5.20A**, the patient produced the drawing shown in **Figure 5.20B**. The copy preserves features of the

---

FIGURE 5.20   GOAL NEGLECT

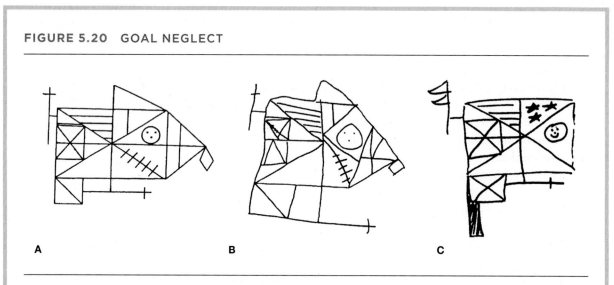

Patients who had suffered damage to the prefrontal cortex were asked to copy the drawing in Panel A. One patient's attempt is shown in Panel B; the drawing is reasonably accurate but seems to have been drawn with no overall plan—for example, the large rectangle in the original, and the main diagonals, were created piecemeal rather than being used to organize the drawing. Another patient's attempt is shown in Panel C; this patient started to re-create the drawing but then got swept up in her own artistic impulses.

original, but close inspection reveals that the patient drew the copy with no particular plan in mind. The large rectangle that defines the shape was never drawn, and the diagonal lines that organize the figure were drawn in a piecemeal fashion. Many details are correctly reproduced but weren't drawn in any sort of order; instead, these details were added whenever they happened to catch the patient's attention (Kimberg, D'Esposito, & Farah, 1998). Another patient, asked to copy the same figure, produced the drawing shown in **Figure 5.20C**. This patient started to draw the figure in a normal way, but then she got swept up in her own artistic impulses, adding stars and a smiley face (Kimberg et al., 1998). (For more on executive control, see Aron, 2008; Courtney, Petit, Maisog, Ungerleider, & Haxby, 1998; Duncan et al., 2008; Gilbert & Shallice, 2002; Huey, Krueger, & Grafman, 2006; Kane & Engle, 2003; Kimberg et al., 1998; Logie & Della Salla, 2005; Ranganath & Blumenfeld, 2005; Stuss & Levine, 2002; also Chapter 13.)

Divided Attention: An Interim Summary

Our consideration of *selective* attention drove us toward a several-part account, with one mechanism serving to block out unwanted distractors and other mechanisms promoting the processing of interesting stimuli. Now, in our discussion of *divided* attention, we again need several elements in our theory. Interference between tasks is increased if the tasks are similar to each other, presumably because similar tasks overlap in their processing requirements and make competing demands on mental resources that are specialized for that sort of task.

But interference can also be observed with tasks that are entirely different from each other—such as driving and talking on a cell phone. Therefore, our account needs to include resources that are general enough in their use that they're drawn on by almost any task. We've identified several of these general resources: an energy supply needed for mental tasks, executive control, and others as well. No matter what the resource, though, the key principle will be the same: Tasks will interfere with each other if their combined demand for a resource is greater than the amount available—that is, if the demand exceeds the supply.

Practice

For a skilled driver, talking on a cell phone while driving is easy as long as the driving is straightforward and the conversation is simple. Things fall apart, though, the moment the conversation becomes complex or the driving becomes challenging. Engaged in deep conversation, the driver misses a turn; while maneuvering through an intersection, the driver suddenly stops talking.

The situation is different, though, for a *novice* driver. For someone who's just learning to drive, driving is difficult all by itself, even on a straight road with no traffic. If we ask the novice to do anything else at the same

TEST YOURSELF

9. Why is it easier to divide attention between very different activities (e.g., knitting while listening to a lecture) than it is to divide attention between more similar activities?

10. What is executive control, and why does it create limits on your ability to divide your attention between two simultaneous tasks?

At the start of this chapter, we refer to common experiences like this one: You're trying to read a book—perhaps an assignment for one of your courses. You're in a public place, though, and two people nearby are having a conversation. You have no interest in their conversation and really need to get through your reading assignment. Even so, you find yourself unable to ignore their conversation, so your reading doesn't get done. What's going on here? Why can't you control what you're paying attention to?

Think about the mechanisms that allow you to pay attention. When you're reading or listening to something, you do what you can to anticipate the upcoming input, and that anticipation lets you prime the relevant detectors so that they'll be ready when the input arrives. As a result, the input falls onto "prepared" detectors and so you're more sensitive to the input—more likely to notice it, more likely to process it.

In contrast, you won't try to anticipate inputs you don't care about. With no anticipation, the input falls on unprepared detectors—and so the detectors are less sensitive to the input. In other words, you've done nothing to make yourself sensitive to these inputs, and so you're relatively *insensitive* to them, just as you wish.

Now think about the situation with which we began. Perhaps you're trying to read something challenging. You'll therefore have some difficulty anticipating how the passage will unfold—what words or phrases will be coming up. Therefore, you'll have little basis for priming the soon-to-be-needed detectors, and so you won't be especially sensitive to the input when it arrives.

What about the conversation you're overhearing and hoping to ignore? Maybe it's unfolding according to a familiar script—for example, the people behind you on the bus, or on the other side of the room, are discussing romance or a popular movie. In this setting, with almost no thought you'll easily anticipate where this distractor conversation is going, and the anticipation will prime the relevant nodes in your mind, making you more sensitive to the input—the opposite of what you want.

Part of our explanation, then, lies in ease-of-anticipation. That's why you'll probably avoid distraction if the material you're trying to read *is* something you can anticipate (and so prime yourself for) and if the irrelevant conversation involves content you can't easily anticipate. In the extreme, imagine that the irrelevant conversation is in some foreign language that you don't speak; here, because there's no basis for anticipation, the distraction will be minimal.

However, we need another element in our explanation. Most people aren't distracted if they try to read while music is playing in the room or if there are traffic noises in the background. Why don't these (potential) distractors cause problems? Here, the key is resource competition. Reading a book and hearing a conversation both involve language, so these activities draw on the same mental resources and compete for those resources. But reading a book and hearing music (especially instrumental music) draw on different mental resources, so those activities don't compete for resources.

time—whether it's talking on a cell phone or even listening to the radio—we put the driver (and other cars) at substantial risk. Why is this? Why are things so different after practice?

Practice Diminishes Resource Demand

We've already said that mental tasks require resources, with the particular resources required being dependent on the nature of the task. Let's now add another claim: As a task becomes more practiced, it requires *fewer* resources, or perhaps it requires *less frequent* use of these resources.

This decrease in a task's resource demand may be inevitable, given the function of some resources. Consider executive control. We've mentioned that this control plays little role if you can rely on habit or routine in performing a task. (That's why Phineas Gage was able to live a mostly normal life, despite his brain damage.) But early in practice, when a task is new, you haven't formed any relevant habits yet, so you have no habits to fall back on. As a result, executive control is needed all the time. Once you've done the task over and over, though, you do acquire a repertoire of suitable habits, and so the demand for executive control decreases.

How will this matter? We've already said that tasks interfere with each other if their combined resource demand is greater than the amount of resources available. Interference is less likely, therefore, if the "cognitive cost" of a task is low. In that case, you'll have an easier time accommodating the task within your "resource budget." And we've now added the idea that the resource demand (the "cost") will be lower after practice than before. Therefore, it's no surprise that practice makes divided attention easier—enabling the skilled driver to continue chatting with her passenger as they cruise down the highway, even though this combination is hopelessly difficult for the novice driver.

Automaticity

With practice in a task, then, the need for executive control is diminished, and we've mentioned one benefit of this: Your control mechanisms are available for other chores, allowing you to divide your attention in ways that would have been impossible before practice. Let's be clear, though, that this gain comes at a price. With sufficient practice, task performance can go forward with *no* executive control, and so the performance is essentially *not controlled*. This can create a setting in which the performance acts as a "mental reflex," going forward, once triggered, whether you like it or not.

Psychologists use the term **automaticity** to describe tasks that are well practiced and involve little (or no) control. (For a classic statement, see Shiffrin & Schneider, 1977; also Moors, 2016; Moors & De Houwer, 2006.) The often-mentioned example is an effect known as **Stroop interference**. In the classic demonstration of this effect, study participants are shown a series of words and asked to name aloud the color of the ink used for each word. The trick, though, is that the words themselves are color names. So people might see the word "BLUE" printed in green ink and would have to say "green" out loud, and so on (see **Figure 5.21**; Stroop, 1935).

This task turns out to be extremely difficult. There's a strong tendency to read the printed words themselves rather than to name the ink color, and people make many mistakes in this task. Presumably, this reflects the fact that word recognition, especially for college-age adults, is enormously well practiced and therefore can proceed automatically. (For more on these issues, including debate about what exactly automaticity involves, see Besner et al., 2016; Durgin, 2000; Engle & Kane, 2004; Jacoby et al., 2003; Kane & Engle, 2003; Labuschagne & Besner, 2015; Moors, 2016.)

Where Are the Limits?

As we near the end of our discussion of attention, it may be useful again to summarize where we are. Two simple ideas are key: First, tasks require resources, and second, you can't "spend" more resources than you have.

FIGURE 5.21 STROOP INTERFERENCE

Column A	Column B
ZYP	RED
QLEKF	BLACK
SUWRG	YELLOW
XCIDB	BLUE
WOPR	RED
ZYP	GREEN
QLEKF	YELLOW
XCIDB	BLACK
SUWRG	BLUE
WOPR	BLACK

As rapidly as you can, name out loud the colors of the *ink* in Column A. (You'll say, "black, green" and so on.) Next, do the same for Column B—again, naming out loud the colors of the ink. You'll probably find it much easier to do this for Column A, because in Column B you experience interference from the automatic habit of reading the words.

These claims are central for almost everything we've said about selective and divided attention.

As we've seen, though, there are different types of resources, and the exact resource demand of a task depends on several factors. The nature of the task matters, of course, so that the resources required by a verbal task (e.g., reading) are different from those required by a spatial task (e.g., remembering a shape). The novelty of the task and the amount of flexibility the task requires also matter. Connected to this, *practice* matters, with well-practiced tasks requiring fewer resources.

What, then, sets the limits on divided attention? When can you do two tasks at the same time, and when not? The answer varies, case by case. If two tasks make competing demands on task-specific resources, the result will be interference. If two tasks make competing demands on task-general resources (the energy supply or executive control), again the result will be interference. Also, it will be especially difficult to combine tasks that involve similar stimuli—tasks that both involve printed text, for example, or that both involve speech. The problem here is that these stimuli can "blur together," with a danger that you'll lose track of which elements belong in which input ("Was it the man who said 'yes,' or was it the woman?"; "Was the red dog in the top picture or the bottom one?"). This sort of "crosstalk" (leakage of bits of one input into the other input) can compromise your performance.

In short, it seems again like we need a multipart theory of attention, with performance being limited by different factors at different times. This perspective draws us back to a claim we've made several times in this chapter: Attention cannot be thought of as a skill or a mechanism. Instead, attention is an achievement—an achievement of performing multiple activities simultaneously or an achievement of successfully avoiding distraction when you want to focus on a single task. And this achievement rests on an intricate base, so that many elements contribute to your ability to attend.

Finally, we have discussed various limits on human performance—that is, limits on how much you can do at any one time. How rigid are these limits? We've discussed the improvements in divided attention that are made possible by practice, but are there boundaries on what practice can accomplish? Can you gain new mental resources or find new ways to accomplish a task in order to avoid the bottleneck created by some limited resource? Some evidence indicates that the answer may be yes; if so, many of the claims made in this chapter must be understood as claims about what is *usual*, not about what is *possible*. (See Hirst, Spelke, Reaves, Caharack, & Neisser, 1980; Spelke, Hirst, & Neisser, 1976. For a neuroscience perspective, see Just & Buchweitz, 2017.) With this, some traditions in the world—Buddhist meditation traditions, for example—claim it's possible to *train* attention so that one has better control over one's mental life. How do these claims fit into the framework we've developed in this chapter? These are issues in need of exploration, and, in truth, what's at stake here is a question about the boundaries on human potential, making these issues of deep interest for future researchers to pursue.

TEST YOURSELF

11. Why does practice decrease the resource demand of a task?
12. Why does practice create a situation in which you can lose control over your own mental steps?

ADHD

When students learn about attention, they often have questions about *failures* of attention: "Why can't I focus when I need to?"; "Why am I so distracted by my roommate moving around the room when I'm studying?"; "Why can some people listen to music while they're reading, but I can't?"

One question comes up more than any other: "I [or "my friend" or "my brother] was diagnosed with ADHD. What's that all about?" This question refers to a common diagnosis: attention-deficit/hyperactivity disorder. The disorder is characterized by a number of problems, including impulsivity, constant fidgeting, and difficulty in keeping attention focused on a task. People with ADHD hop from activity to activity and have trouble organizing or completing projects. They sometimes have trouble following a conversation and are easily distracted by an unimportant sight or sound. Even their own thoughts can distract them—and so they can be pulled off track by their own daydreams.

The causes of ADHD are still unclear. Contributing factors that have been mentioned include encephalitis, genetic influences, food allergies, high lead concentrations in the environment, and more. The uncertainty about this point comes from many sources, including some ambiguity in the diagnosis of ADHD. There's no question that there's a genuine disorder, but diagnosis is complicated by the fact that the disorder can vary widely in its severity. Some people have relatively mild symptoms; others are massively disrupted, and this variation can make diagnosis difficult.

In addition, some critics argue that in many cases the ADHD diagnosis is just a handy label for children who are particularly active or who don't easily adjust to a school routine or a crowded classroom. Indeed, some critics suggest that ADHD is often just a convenient categorization for physicians or school counselors who don't know how else to think about an especially energetic child.

In cases in which the diagnosis is warranted, though, what does it involve? As we describe in the chapter, there are many steps involved in "paying attention," and some of those steps involve inhibition—so that we don't follow every stray thought, or every cue in the environment, wherever it may lead. For most of us, this is no problem, and we easily inhibit our responses to most distractors. We're thrown off track only by especially intrusive distractors—such as a loud noise or a stimulus that has special meaning for us.

Some researchers propose, though, that people with ADHD have less effective inhibitory circuits in their brains, making them more vulnerable to momentary impulses and chance distractions. This is what leads to their scattered thoughts, their difficulty in schoolwork, and so on.

What can be done to help people with ADHD? One of the common treatments is Ritalin, a drug that is a powerful stimulant. It seems ironic that we'd give a stimulant to people who are already described as too active and too energetic, but the evidence suggests that Ritalin is effective in treating actual cases of ADHD—plausibly because the drug activates the inhibitory circuits within the brain, helping the person to guard against wayward impulses.

However, we probably shouldn't rely on Ritalin as the sole treatment for ADHD. One reason is the risk of overdiagnosis—it's worrisome that this drug may be routinely given to people, including young children, who don't actually have ADHD. Also, there are concerns about the long-term effects and possible side effects of Ritalin, and this certainly motivates us to seek other forms of treatment. (Common side effects include weight loss, insomnia, anxiety, and slower growth during childhood.) Some of the promising alternatives involve restructuring of the environment. If people with ADHD are vulnerable to distraction, we can help them by the simple step of reducing the sources of distraction in their surroundings. Likewise, if people with ADHD are influenced by whatever cues they detect, we can surround them with helpful cues—reminders of what they're supposed to be doing and the tasks they're supposed to be working on. These simple interventions do seem to be helpful, especially with adults diagnosed with ADHD.

Overall, then, our description of ADHD requires multiple parts. Researchers have considered a diverse set of causes, and there may be a diverse set of psychological mechanisms involved in the disorder. (See pp. 168.) The diagnosis probably is overused, but the diagnosis is surely genuine in many cases, and the problems involved in ADHD are real and serious. Medication can help, but we've noted the concern about side effects of the medication. Environmental interventions can also help and may, in fact, be the best bet for the long term, especially given the important fact that in most cases the symptoms of ADHD diminish as the years go by.

For more on this topic . . .

Barkley, R. A. (2004). Adolescents with ADHD: An overview of empirically based treatments. *Journal of Psychiatric Practice, 10,* 39–56.

Barkley, R. A. (2008). *ADHD in adults: What the science says.* New York, NY: Guilford.

Zillmer, E. A., Spiers, M. V., & Culbertson, W. C. (2008). *Principles of neuropsychology.* Belmont, CA: Wadsworth.

chapter review

SUMMARY

- People are often oblivious to unattended inputs; they usually cannot tell if an unattended auditory input was coherent prose or random words, and they often do not detect unattended visual inputs, even though such inputs are right in front of their eyes. However, some aspects of the unattended inputs are detected. For example, people can report on the pitch of the unattended sound and whether it contained human speech or some other sort of noise. Sometimes they can also detect stimuli that are especially meaningful; some people, for example, hear their own name if it is spoken on the unattended channel.

- These results suggest that perception may require the commitment of mental resources, with some of these resources helping to prime the detectors needed for perception. This proposal is supported by studies of inattentional blindness—that is, studies showing that perception is markedly impaired if the perceiver commits no resources to the incoming stimulus information. The proposal is also supported by results showing that participants perceive more efficiently when they can anticipate the upcoming stimulus (and so can prime the relevant detectors). In many cases, the anticipation is spatial—if, for example, participants know that a stimulus is about to arrive at a particular location. This priming, however, seems to draw on a limited-capacity system, with the result that priming one stimulus or one position takes away resources that might be spent on priming some other stimulus.

- The ability to pay attention to certain regions of space has caused many researchers to compare attention to a spotlight beam, with the idea that stimuli falling "within the beam" are processed more efficiently than stimuli that fall "outside the beam." However, this spotlight analogy is potentially misleading. In many circumstances, people do seem to devote attention to identifiable regions of space, no matter what falls within those regions. In other circumstances, attention seems to be object-based, not space-based, and so people pay attention to specific objects, not specific positions.

- Perceiving seems to require the commitment of resources, and so do most other mental activities. This observation suggests an explanation for the limits on divided attention: It is possible to perform two tasks simultaneously only if the two tasks do not in combination demand more resources than are available. Some of the relevant mental resources, including executive control, are task-general, being required in a wide variety of mental activities. Other mental resources are task-specific, being required only for tasks of a certain type.

- Divided attention is influenced by practice, with the result that it is often easier to divide attention between familiar tasks than between unfamiliar tasks. In the extreme, practice may produce automaticity, in which a task seems to require virtually no mental resources but is also difficult to control. One proposal is that automaticity results from the fact that decisions are no longer needed for a well-practiced routine; instead, one can simply run off the entire routine, doing on this occasion just what one did on prior occasions.

KEY TERMS

selective attention (p. 150)
dichotic listening (p. 150)
attended channel (p. 150)
unattended channel (p. 150)
shadowing (p. 151)
filter (p. 152)
fixation target (p. 153)
inattentional blindness (p. 154)
change blindness (p. 155)
early selection hypothesis (p. 157)
late selection hypothesis (p. 157)
repetition priming (p. 160)

limited-capacity system (p. 164)
mental resources (p. 164)
spatial attention (p. 165)
endogenous control of attention (p. 172)
exogenous control of attention (p. 172)
unilateral neglect syndrome (p. 174)
divided attention (p. 177)
executive control (p. 181)
perseveration error (p. 182)
goal neglect (p. 182)
automaticity (p. 185)
Stroop interference (p. 185)

TEST YOURSELF AGAIN

1. What information do people reliably pick up from the *attended* channel? What do they pick up from the *unattended* channel?

2. How is inattentional blindness demonstrated? What situations outside of the laboratory seem to reflect inattentional blindness?

3. What evidence seems to confirm early selection? What evidence seems to confirm late selection?

4. What are the differences between the way that stimulus-based priming functions and the way that expectation-based priming functions?

5. Why is there a "cost" associated with being misled by expectation-based priming?

6. In what ways does the notion of a spotlight beam accurately reflect how spatial attention functions?

7. In what ways does the notion of a spotlight beam differ from the way spatial attention functions?

8. When you first start paying attention to an input, your attention seems to be space-based. Once you've learned a bit about the input, though, your attention seems to be object-based. How does this pattern fit with the idea that you pay attention by *anticipating* the input?

9. Why is it easier to divide attention between very different activities (e.g., knitting while listening to a lecture) than it is to divide attention between more similar activities?

10. What is executive control, and why does it create limits on your ability to divide your attention between two simultaneous tasks?

11. Why does practice decrease the resource demand of a task?

12. Why does practice create a situation in which you can lose control over your own mental steps?

THINK ABOUT IT

1. It's easy to keep your attention focused on materials that you *understand*. But if you try to focus on difficult material, your mind is likely to wander. Does the chapter help you in understanding why that is? Explain your response.

2. People claim that some forms of meditation training (including Buddhist meditation) can help those who do it become better at paying attention—staying focused and not suffering from distraction. Does the chapter help you in understanding why that might be? Explain your response.

ⓔ eBOOK DEMONSTRATIONS & ESSAYS

Go to http://digital.wwnorton.com/cognition7 for the online demonstrations and essays relevant to this chapter. These can be found in the ebook.

Online Demonstrations

- Demonstration 5.1: Shadowing
- Demonstration 5.2: Color-Changing Card Trick
- Demonstration 5.3: The Control of Eye Movements
- Demonstration 5.4: Automaticity and the Stroop Effect

Online Applying Cognitive Psychology and the Law Essays

- Cognitive Psychology and the Law: Guiding the Formulation of New Laws

ZAPS COGNITION LABS

Go to http://digital.wwnorton.com/cognition7 to experience interactive online psychology labs relevant to this chapter.

part 3

Memory

As you move through life, you encounter new facts, gain new skills, and have new experiences. And you're often *changed* by all of this, so that later on you know things and can do things that you couldn't know or do before. How do these changes happen? How do you get new information into your memory, and then how do you retrieve this information when you need it? And how much trust can you put in this process? Why, for example, do people sometimes *not* remember things (including important things)? And why are memories sometimes *wrong* — so that in some cases you remember an event one way, but a friend who was present at the same event remembers things differently?

We'll tackle all these issues in this section, and they will lead us to theoretical claims and practical applications. We'll offer suggestions, for example, about how students should study their class materials to maximize retention, and also what students can do later on so that they'll retain things they learned at some earlier point.

In our discussion, several themes will emerge again and again. One theme concerns the active nature of learning, and we'll discuss the fact that passive exposure to information, with no intellectual engagement, leads to poor memory. From this base, we'll consider why some forms of engagement with to-be-learned material lead to especially good memory but other forms do not.

A second theme concerns the role of memory connections. In Chapter 6, we'll see that learning involves the creation of connections, and the more connections formed, the better the learning. In Chapter 7, we'll argue that these connections can serve as "retrieval paths" — paths that, you hope, will lead you from your memory search's starting point to the information you're trying to recall. As we'll see, this idea has clear implications for when you will remember a previous event and when you won't.

Chapter 8 then explores a different aspect of the connections idea: Memory connections can actually be a source of memory errors. We'll ask what this means for memory accuracy overall, and we'll discuss what you can do to minimize error and to improve the completeness and accuracy of your memory.

chapter **6**

The Acquisition of Memories and the Working-Memory System

what if... Clive Wearing is an accomplished musician and a scholar of Renaissance music. When he was 47 years old, however, his brain was horribly damaged by a Herpes virus, and he now has profound amnesia. He is still articulate and intelligent, able to participate in an ongoing conversation, and still able to play music (beautifully) and conduct. But ever since the viral infection, he's been unable to form new memories. He can't recall any of the experiences he's had in the thirty years since he suffered the brain damage. He can't even remember events that happened just moments ago, with a bizarre result: Every few minutes, Wearing realizes he can't recall anything from a few seconds back, and so he concludes that he must have just woken up. He grabs his diary and writes "8:31 a.m. Now I am really, completely awake." A short while later, though, he again realizes he can't recall the last seconds, so he decides that *now* he has just woken up. He picks up his diary to record this event and immediately sees his previous entry. Puzzled, he crosses it out and replaces it with "9:06 a.m. Now I am perfectly, overwhelmingly awake." But then the process repeats, and so this entry, too, gets scribbled out and a new entry reads "9:34 a.m.: Now I am superlatively, actually awake."

Despite this massive disruption, Wearing's love for his wife, Deborah, has not in any way been diminished by his amnesia. But here, too, the memory loss has powerful effects. Each time Deborah enters his room — even if she's been away just a few minutes — he races to embrace her as though it's been countless lonely months since they last met. If asked directly, he has no recollection of her previous visits — including a visit that might have happened just minutes earlier.

We met a different case of amnesia in Chapter 1 — the famous patient H.M. He, too, was unable to recall his immediate past — and the many, deep problems this produced included an odd sort of disorientation: If you were smiling at him, was it because you'd just said something funny? Or because he'd said something embarrassing? Or had you been smiling all along? As H.M. put it, "Right now, I'm wondering. Have I done or said anything amiss? You see, at this moment, everything looks clear to me, but what happened just before? That's what worries me" (Milner, 1970, p. 37; also see Corkin, 2013).

Cases like these remind us how profoundly our memories shape our everyday lives. But these cases also raise many questions: Why is it that

A

B

CLIVE WEARING

Clive Wearing (shown here with his wife) developed profound amnesia as a result of viral encephalitis, and now he seems to have only a moment-to-moment consciousness. With no memory at all of what he was doing just seconds ago, he is often convinced he just woke up, and he repeatedly writes in his diary, "Now perfectly awake (1st time)." On the diary page shown here, he has recorded his thought, at 5:42 a.m., as his "1st act" because he has no memory of any prior activity. Soon after, though, he seems to realize again that he has no memory of any earlier events, and so he scribbles out the entry and now records that his bath is his "1st act." The sequence repeats over and over, with Wearing never recalling what he did before his current activity, and so he records act after act as his "first."

- We begin the chapter with a discussion of the broad architecture of memory. We then turn to a closer examination of one component of this architecture: working memory.

- We emphasize the active nature of working memory—activity that is especially evident when we discuss working memory's "central executive," a mental resource that serves to order, organize, and control our mental lives.

- The active nature of memory is also evident in the process of *rehearsal*. Rehearsal is effective only if the person engages the materials in some way; this is reflected,

for example, in the contrast between deep processing (which leads to excellent memory) and mere maintenance rehearsal (which produces basically no memory benefit).

- Activity during learning appears to establish *memory connections*, which can serve as retrieval routes when it comes time to remember the target material. For complex material, the best way to establish these connections is to seek to understand the material; the better the understanding, the better the memory will be.

Wearing still remembers who his wife is? How is it possible that even with his amnesia, Wearing remains such a talented musician? Why does H.M. still remember his young adult years, even though he can't remember what he said just five minutes earlier? We'll tackle questions like these in this chapter and the next two.

Acquisition, Storage, and Retrieval

How does new information—whether it's a friend's phone number or a fact you hope to memorize for the bio exam—become established in memory? Are there ways to learn that are particularly effective? Then, once information is in storage, how do you locate it and "reactivate" it later? And why does search through memory sometimes fail—so that, for example, you forget the name of that great restaurant downtown (but then remember the name when you're midway through a mediocre dinner someplace else)?

In tackling these questions, there's a logical way to organize our inquiry. Before there can be a memory, you need to gain, or "acquire," some new information. Therefore, **acquisition**—the process of gaining information and placing it into memory—should be our first topic. Then, once you've acquired this information, you need to hold it in memory until the information is needed. We refer to this as the **storage** phase. Finally, you *remember*. In other words, you somehow locate the information in the vast warehouse that is memory and you bring it into active use; this is called **retrieval**.

This organization seems logical; it fits, for example, with the way most "electronic memories" (e.g., computers) work. Information ("input") is provided to a computer (the acquisition phase). The information then resides in some dormant form, generally on the hard drive or perhaps in the cloud (the storage phase). Finally, the information can be brought back from this dormant form, often via a search process that hunts through the disk (the retrieval phase). And there's nothing special about the computer comparison here; "low-tech" information storage works the same way. Think about a file drawer—information is acquired (i.e., filed), rests in this or that folder, and then is retrieved.

Guided by this framework, we'll begin our inquiry by focusing on the acquisition of new memories, leaving discussion of storage and retrieval for later. As it turns out, though, we'll soon find reasons for challenging this overall approach to memory. In discussing acquisition, for example, we might wish to ask: What is good learning? What guarantees that material is firmly recorded in memory? As we'll see, evidence indicates that what counts as "good learning" depends on how the memory is to be used later on, so that good preparation for one kind of use may be poor preparation for a different kind of use. Claims about acquisition, therefore, must be interwoven with claims about retrieval. These interconnections between acquisition and retrieval will be the central theme of Chapter 7.

In the same way, we can't separate claims about memory acquisition from claims about memory storage. This is because *how you learn* (acquisition) depends *on what you already know* (information in storage). We'll explore this important relationship in both this chapter and Chapter 8.

We begin, though, in this chapter, by describing the acquisition process. Our approach will be roughly historical. We'll start with a simple model, emphasizing data collected largely in the 1970s. We'll then use this as the framework for examining more recent research, adding refinements to the model as we proceed.

TEST YOURSELF

1. Define the terms "acquisition," "storage," and "retrieval."

The Route into Memory

For many years, theorizing in cognitive psychology focused on the process through which information was perceived and then moved into memory storage—that is, on the process of information acquisition. One early proposal was offered by Waugh and Norman (1965). Later refinements were added by Atkinson and Shiffrin (1968), and their version of the proposal came to be known as the **modal model**. **Figure 6.1** provides a simplified depiction of this model.

Updating the Modal Model

According to the modal model, when information first arrives, it is stored briefly in **sensory memory**. This form of memory holds on to the input in "raw" sensory form—an *iconic memory* for visual inputs and an *echoic memory* for auditory inputs. A process of selection and interpretation then moves the information into **short-term memory**—the place where you hold information while you're working on it. Some of the information is then transferred into *long-term memory*, a much larger and more permanent storage place.

This proposal captures some important truths, but it needs to be updated in several ways. First, the idea of "sensory memory" plays a much smaller role in modern theorizing, so modern discussions of perception (like our

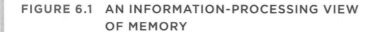

FIGURE 6.1   AN INFORMATION-PROCESSING VIEW OF MEMORY

Diagrams like this one depict the flow of information hypothesized by the modal model. The model captures many important truths but must be updated in important ways. Current theorizing, for example, emphasizes that short-term memory (now called "working memory") is not a place serving as a "loading dock" outside of long-term memory. Instead, working memory is best understood as an activity, in ways described in the chapter.

discussion in Chapters 2 and 3) often make no mention of this memory. (For a recent assessment of visual sensory memory, though, see Cappiello & Zhang, 2016.) Second, modern proposals use the term **working memory** rather than "short-term memory," to emphasize the function of this memory. Ideas or thoughts in this memory are currently activated, currently being thought about, and so they're the ideas you're currently *working on*. **Long-term memory (LTM)**, in contrast, is the vast repository that contains all of your knowledge and all of your beliefs—most of which you aren't thinking about (i.e., aren't working on) at this moment.

The modal model also needs updating in another way. Pictures like the one in Figure 6.1 suggest that working memory is a *storage place*, sometimes described as the "loading dock" just outside of the long-term memory "warehouse." The idea is that information has to "pass through" working memory on the way into longer-term storage. Likewise, the picture implies that memory retrieval involves the "movement" of information out of storage and back into working memory.

In contrast, contemporary theorists don't think of working memory as a "place" at all. Instead, working memory is (as we will see) simply the name we give to a *status*. Therefore, when we say that ideas are "in working memory," we simply mean that these ideas are currently activated and being worked on by a specific set of operations.

W R T O
Y D S A
L M R E

ICONIC MEMORY

In a classic experiment (Sperling, 1960), participants viewed a grid like this one for just 50 ms. If asked to report all of the letters, participants could report just three or four of them. In a second condition, participants saw the grid and then immediately afterward heard a cue signaling which row they had to report. No matter which row they were asked about, participants could recall most of the row's letters. It seems, therefore, that participants could remember the entire display (in iconic memory) for a brief time, and could "read off" the contents of any row when appropriately cued. The limitation in the report-all condition, then, came from the fact that iconic memory faded away before the participants could report on all of it.

We'll have more to say about this modern perspective before we're through. It's important to emphasize, though, that contemporary thinking also preserves some key ideas from the modal model, including its claims about how working memory and long-term memory differ from each other. Let's identify those differences.

First, working memory is limited in size; long-term memory is enormous. In fact, long-term memory has to be enormous, because it contains all of your knowledge—including specific knowledge (e.g., how many siblings you have) and more general themes (e.g., that water is wet, that Dublin is in Ireland, that unicorns don't exist). Long-term memory also contains all of your "episodic" knowledge—that is, your knowledge about events, including events early in your life as well as more recent experiences.

Second, getting information into working memory is easy. If you think about a particular idea or some other type of content, then you're "working on" that idea or content, and so this information—by definition—is now in your working memory. In contrast, we'll see later in the chapter that getting information into long-term memory often involves some work.

Third, getting information out of working memory is also easy. Since (by definition) this memory holds the ideas you're thinking about right now, the information is already available to you. Finding information in long-term memory, in contrast, can sometimes be difficult and slow—and in some settings can fail completely.

Fourth, the contents of working memory are quite fragile. Working memory, we emphasize, contains the ideas you're thinking about right now. If your thoughts shift to a new topic, therefore, the new ideas will enter working memory, pushing out what was there a moment ago. Long-term memory, in contrast, isn't linked to your current thoughts, so it's much less fragile—information remains in storage whether you're thinking about it right now or not.

We can make all these claims more concrete by looking at some classic research findings. These findings come from a task that's quite artificial (i.e., not the sort of memorizing you do every day) but also quite informative.

Working Memory and Long-Term Memory: One Memory or Two?

In many studies, researchers have asked participants to listen to a series of words, such as "bicycle, artichoke, radio, chair, palace." In a typical experiment, the list might contain 30 words and be presented at a rate of one word per second. Immediately after the last word is read, the participants must repeat back as many words as they can. They are free to report the words in any order they choose, which is why this task is called a **free recall** procedure. People usually remember 12 to 15 words in this test, in a consistent pattern. They're very likely to remember the first few words on the list, something known as the **primacy effect**, and they're also likely to remember the last few words on the list, a **recency effect**. The resulting pattern is a U-shaped

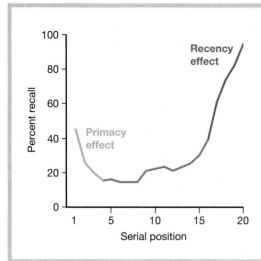

FIGURE 6.2 PRIMACY AND RECENCY EFFECTS IN FREE RECALL

Research participants in this study heard a list of 20 common words presented at a rate of one word per second. Immediately after hearing the list, participants were asked to write down as many of the words on the list as they could recall. The results show that position in the series strongly affected recall—participants had better recall for words at the beginning of the list (the primacy effect) and for words at the end of the list (the recency effect), compared to words in the middle of the list.

curve describing the relation between positions within the series—or **serial position**—and the likelihood of recall (see **Figure 6.2**; Baddeley & Hitch, 1977; Deese & Kaufman, 1957; Glanzer & Cunitz, 1966; Murdock, 1962; Postman & Phillips, 1965).

Explaining the Recency Effect

What produces this pattern? We've already said that working memory contains the material someone is *working on* at just that moment. In other words, this memory contains whatever the person is currently thinking about; and during the list presentation, the participants are thinking about the words they're hearing. Therefore, it's these words that are in working memory. This memory, however, is limited in size, capable of holding only five or six words. Consequently, as participants try to keep up with the list presentation, they'll be placing the words *just heard* into working memory, and this action will bump the previous words out of working memory. As a result, as participants proceed through the list, their working memories will, at each moment, contain only the half dozen words that arrived most recently. Any words that arrived earlier than these will have been pushed out by later arrivals.

Of course, the last few words on the list don't get bumped out of working memory, because no further input arrives to displace them. Therefore, when the list presentation ends, those last few words stay in place. Moreover, our hypothesis is that materials in working memory are readily available—easily and quickly retrieved. When the time comes for recall, then, working memory's contents (the list's last few words) are accurately and completely recalled.

The key idea, then, is that the list's last few words are still in working memory when the list ends (because nothing has arrived to push out these items), and we know that working memory's contents are easy to retrieve. This is the source of the recency effect.

Explaining the Primacy Effect

The primacy effect has a different source. We've suggested that it takes some work to get information into long-term memory (LTM), and it seems likely that this work requires some time and attention. So let's examine how participants allocate their attention to the list items. As participants hear the list, they do their best to be good memorizers, and so when they hear the first word, they repeat it over and over to themselves ("bicycle, bicycle, bicycle")—a process known as **memory rehearsal**. When the second word arrives, they rehearse it, too ("bicycle, artichoke, bicycle, artichoke"). Likewise for the third ("bicycle, artichoke, radio, bicycle, artichoke, radio"), and so on through the list. Note, though, that the first few items on the list are privileged. For a brief moment, "bicycle" is the only word participants have to worry about, so it has 100% of their attention; no other word receives this privilege. When "artichoke" arrives a moment later, participants divide their attention between the first two words, so "artichoke" gets only 50% of their attention—less than "bicycle" got, but still a large share of the participants' efforts. When "radio" arrives, it has to compete with "bicycle" and "artichoke" for the participants' time, and so it receives only 33% of their attention.

Words arriving later in the list receive even less attention. Once six or seven words have been presented, the participants need to divide their attention among all these words, which means that each one receives only a small fraction of the participants' focus. As a result, words later in the list are rehearsed fewer times than words early in the list—a fact that can be confirmed simply by asking participants to rehearse out loud (Rundus, 1971).

This view of things leads immediately to our explanation of the primacy effect—that is, the observed memory advantage for the early list items. These early words didn't have to share attention with other words (because the other words hadn't arrived yet), so more time and more rehearsal were devoted to them than to any others. This means that the early words have a greater chance of being transferred into LTM—and so a greater chance of being recalled after a delay. That's what shows up in these classic data as the primacy effect.

Testing Claims about Primacy and Recency

This account of the serial-position curve leads to many predictions. First, we're claiming the recency portion of the curve is coming from working memory, while other items on the list are being recalled from LTM. Therefore, manipulations of working memory should affect recall of the recency items but not items earlier in the list. To see how this works, consider a modification of our procedure. In the standard setup, we allow participants to recite what they remember immediately after the list's end. But instead, we can delay recall by asking participants to perform some other task before they report the list items—for example, we can ask them to count backward by threes, starting from 201. They do this for just 30 seconds, and then they try to recall the list.

We've hypothesized that at the end of the list working memory still contains the last few items heard from the list. But the task of counting backward will itself require working memory (e.g., to keep track of where you are in the counting sequence). Therefore, this chore will *displace* working memory's current contents; that is, it will bump the last few list items out of working memory. As a result, these items won't benefit from the swift and easy retrieval that working memory allows, and, of course, that retrieval was the presumed source of the recency effect. On this basis, the simple chore of counting backward, even if only for a few seconds, will eliminate the recency effect. In contrast, the counting backward should have no impact on recall of the items earlier in the list: These items are (by hypothesis) being recalled from long-term memory, not working memory, and there's no reason to think the counting task will interfere with LTM. (That's because LTM, unlike working memory, isn't dependent on current activity.)

Figure 6.3 shows that these predictions are correct. An activity interpolated, or inserted, between the list and recall essentially eliminates the recency effect, but it has no influence elsewhere in the list (Baddeley & Hitch, 1977; Glanzer & Cunitz, 1966; Postman & Phillips, 1965). In contrast, merely delaying the recall for a few seconds after the list's end, with no interpolated activity, has no impact. In this case, participants can continue rehearsing the last few items during the delay and so can maintain them in working memory. With no new materials coming in, nothing pushes the recency items out of working memory, and so, even with a delay, a normal recency effect is observed.

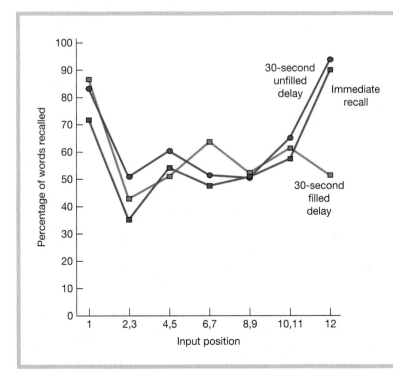

FIGURE 6.3 THE IMPACT OF INTERPOLATED ACTIVITY ON THE RECENCY EFFECT

With immediate recall (the red line in the figure), or if recall is delayed by 30 seconds with no activity during the delay (the purple line), a strong recency effect is detected. In contrast, if participants spend 30 seconds on some other activity between hearing the list and the subsequent memory test (the blue line), the recency effect is eliminated. This interpolated activity has no impact on the pre-recency portion of the curve (i.e., the portion of the curve other than the last few positions).

FIGURE 6.4 RATE OF LIST PRESENTATION AND THE SERIAL-POSITION EFFECT

Presenting the to-be-remembered materials at a slower rate improves pre-recency performance but has no effect on recency. The slow presentation rate in this case was 9 seconds per item; the faster rate was 3 seconds per item.

We'd expect a different outcome, though, if we manipulate long-term memory rather than working memory. In this case, the manipulation should affect all performance *except* for recency (which, again, is dependent on working memory, not LTM). For example, what happens if we slow down the presentation of the list? Now, participants will have more time to spend on all of the list items, increasing the likelihood of transfer into more permanent storage. This should improve recall for all items coming from LTM. Working memory, in contrast, is limited by its size, not by ease of entry or ease of access. Therefore, the slower list presentation should have no influence on working-memory performance. Research results confirm these claims: Slowing the list presentation improves retention of all the pre-recency items but does not improve the recency effect (see **Figure 6.4**).

Other variables that influence long-term memory have similar effects. Using more familiar or more common words, for example, would be expected to ease entry into long-term memory and does improve pre-recency retention, but it has no effect on recency (Sumby, 1963).

It seems, therefore, that the recency and pre-recency portions of the curve are influenced by distinct sets of factors and obey different principles. Apparently, then, these two portions of the curve are the products of different mechanisms, just as our theory proposed. In addition, fMRI scans suggest that memory for early items on a list depends on brain areas (in and around the hippocampus) that are associated with long-term memory; memory for later items on the list do not show this pattern (Talmi, Grady, Goshen-Gottstein, & Moscovitch, 2005; also Eichenbaum, 2017; see **Figure 6.5**). This provides further confirmation for our memory model.

TEST YOURSELF

2. List the four ways in which (either in the modal model or in more recent views) working memory is different from long-term storage.

3. How is the primacy effect usually explained? How is the recency effect usually explained?

FIGURE 6.5 BRAIN REGIONS SUPPORTING WORKING MEMORY AND LONG-TERM MEMORY

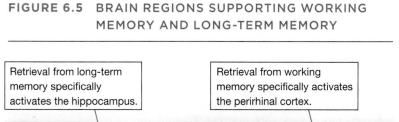

Retrieval from long-term memory specifically activates the hippocampus.

Retrieval from working memory specifically activates the perirhinal cortex.

We can confirm the distinction between working memory and long-term memory with fMRI scans. These scans suggest that memory for early items on a list depends on brain areas (in and around the hippocampus) that are associated with long-term memory; memory for later items on the list do not show this pattern. (TALMI, GRADY, GOSHEN-GOTTSTEIN, & MOSCOVITCH, 2005)

A Closer Look at Working Memory

Earlier, we counted four fundamental differences between working memory and LTM—the *size* of these two stores, the *ease of entry*, the *ease of retrieval*, and the fact that working memory is dependent on current activity (and therefore *fragile*) while LTM is not. These are all points proposed by the modal model and preserved in current thinking. As we've said, though, investigators' understanding of working memory has developed over the years. Let's examine the newer conception in more detail.

The Function of Working Memory

Virtually all mental activities require the coordination of several pieces of information. Sometimes the relevant bits come into view one by one, so that you need to hold on to the early-arrivers until the rest of the information is available, and only then weave all the bits together. Alternatively, sometimes the relevant bits are all in view at the same time—but you still need to hold on to them together, so that you can think about the relations and combinations. In either case, you'll end up with multiple ideas in your thoughts, all activated simultaneously, and thus several bits of information in the status we describe as "in working memory." (For more on how you manage to focus on these various bits, see Oberauer & Hein, 2012.)

Framing things in this way makes it clear how important working memory is: You use it whenever you have multiple ideas in your mind, multiple elements that you're trying to combine or compare. Let's now add that people differ in the "holding capacity" of their working memories. Some people are able to hold on to (and work with) more elements, and some with fewer. How does this matter? To find out, we first need a way of *measuring* working memory's capacity, to determine if your memory capacity is above average, below, or somewhere in between. The procedure for obtaining this measurement, however, has changed over the years; looking at this change will help clarify what working memory *is*, and what working memory *is for*.

Digit Span

For many years, the holding capacity of working memory was measured with a **digit-span task**. In this task, research participants hear a series of digits read to them (e.g., "8, 3, 4") and must immediately repeat them back. If they do so successfully, they're given a slightly longer list (e.g., "9, 2, 4, 0"). If they can repeat this one without error, they're given a still longer list ("3, 1, 2, 8, 5"), and so on. The procedure continues until the participant starts to make errors—something that usually happens when the list contains more than seven or eight items. The number of digits the person can echo back without errors is referred to as that person's digit span.

Procedures such as this imply that working memory's capacity is typically around seven items—at least five and probably not more than nine. These estimates have traditionally been summarized by the statement that this memory holds **"7 plus-or-minus 2"** items (Chi, 1976; Dempster, 1981; Miller, 1956; Watkins, 1977).

However, we immediately need a refinement of these measurements. If working memory can hold 7 plus-or-minus 2 items, what exactly is an "item"? Can people remember seven sentences as easily as seven words? Seven letters as easily as seven equations? In a classic paper, George Miller (one of the founders of the field of cognitive psychology) proposed that working memory holds 7 plus-or-minus 2 **chunks** (Miller, 1956). The term "chunk" doesn't sound scientific or technical, and that's useful because this informal terminology reminds us that a chunk doesn't hold a fixed quantity of information. Instead, Miller proposed, working memory holds 7 plus-or-minus 2 packages, and what those packages contain is largely up to the individual person.

The flexibility in how people "chunk" input can easily be seen in the span test. Imagine that we test someone's "letter span" rather than their "digit span," using the procedure already described. So the person might hear

"R, L" and have to repeat this sequence back, and then "F, C, H," and so on. Eventually, let's imagine that the person hears a much longer list, perhaps one starting "H, O, P, T, R, A, S, L, U. . . ." If the person thinks of these as individual letters, she'll only remember 7 of them, more or less. But she might reorganize the list into "chunks" and, in particular, think of the letters as forming syllables ("HOP, TRA, SLU, . . ."). In this case, she'll still remember 7 plus-or-minus 2 items, but the items are *syllables*, and by remembering the syllables she'll be able to report back at least a dozen letters and probably more.

How far can this process be extended? Chase and Ericsson (1982; Ericsson, 2003) studied a remarkable individual who happens to be a fan of track events. When he hears numbers, he thinks of them as finishing times for races. The sequence "3, 4, 9, 2," for example, becomes "3 minutes and 49.2 seconds, near world-record mile time." In this way, four digits become one chunk of information. This person can then retain 7 finishing times (7 chunks) in memory, and this can involve 20 or 30 digits! Better still, these chunks can be grouped into larger chunks, and these into even larger chunks. For example, finishing times for individual racers can be chunked together into heats within a track meet, so that, now, 4 or 5 finishing times (more than a dozen digits) become one chunk. With strategies like this and a lot of practice, this person has increased his apparent memory span from the "normal" 7 digits to 79 digits.

However, let's be clear that what has changed through practice is merely this person's chunking strategy, not the capacity of working memory itself. This is evident in the fact that when tested with sequences of letters, rather than numbers, so that he can't use his chunking strategy, this individual's memory span is a normal size—just 6 consonants. Thus, the 7-chunk limit is still in place for this man, even though (with numbers) he's able to make extraordinary use of these 7 slots.

Operation Span

Chunking provides one complication in our measurement of working memory's capacity. Another—and deeper—complication grows out of the very nature of working memory. Early theorizing about working memory, as we said, was guided by the modal model, and this model implies that working memory is something like a box in which information is stored or a location in which information can be displayed. The traditional digit-span test fits well with this idea. If working memory is like a box, then it's sensible to ask how much "space" there is in the box: How many slots, or spaces, are there in it? This is precisely what the digit span measures, on the idea that each digit (or each chunk) is placed in its own slot.

We've suggested, though, that the modern conception of working memory is more dynamic—so that working memory is best thought of as a *status* (something like "currently activated") rather than a *place*. (See, e.g.,

FIGURE 6.6 IS WORKING MEMORY A "PLACE"?

- Verbal and numbers
- Objects
- Spatial
- Problem solving

Modern theorists argue that working memory is not a place at all, but is instead the name we give for a certain set of mental activities. Consistent with this modern view, there's no specific location within the brain that serves as working memory. Instead, working memory is associated with a wide range of brain sites, as shown here.   (AFTER CABEZA & NYBERG, 2000)

Christophel, Klink, Spitzer, Roelfsema, & Haynes, 2017; also **Figure 6.6.**) On this basis, perhaps we need to rethink how we measure this memory's capacity—seeking a measure that reflects working memory's active operation.

Modern researchers therefore measure this memory's capacity in terms of **operation span**, a measure of working memory when it is "working." There are several ways to measure operation span, with the types differing in what "operation" they use (e.g., Bleckley, Foster, & Engle, 2015; Chow & Conway, 2015). One type is *reading span*. To measure this span, a research participant might be asked to read aloud a series of sentences, like these:

Due to his gross inadequacies, his position as director was terminated abruptly.

It is possible, of course, that life did not arise on Earth at all.

Immediately after reading the sentences, the participant is asked to recall each sentence's final word—in this case, "abruptly" and "all." If she can do this with these two sentences, she's asked to do the same task with a group of three sentences, and then with four, and so on, until the limit on

FIGURE 6.7 DYNAMIC MEASURES OF WORKING MEMORY

$(7 \times 7) + 1 = 50$; dog
$(10/2) + 6 = 10$; gas
$(4 \times 2) + 1 = 9$; nose
$(3/1) + 1 = 5$; beat
$(5/5) + 1 = 2$; tree

Operation span can be measured in several different ways. In one procedure, participants must announce whether each of these "equations" is true or false, and then recall the words appended to each equation. If participants can do this with two equations, we ask them to do three; if they can do that, we ask them to try four. By finding out how far they can go, we measure their working-memory capacity.

her performance is located. This limit defines the person's **working-memory capacity**, or **WMC**. (However there are other ways to measure operation span—see **Figure 6.7**.)

Let's think about what this task involves: storing materials (the ending words) for later use in the recall test, while simultaneously working with other materials (the full sentences). This juggling of processes, as the participant moves from one part of the task to the next, is exactly what working memory must do in day-to-day life. Therefore, performance in this test is likely to reflect the efficiency with which working memory will operate in more natural settings.

Is operation span a valid measure—that is, does it measure what it's supposed to? Our hypothesis is that someone with a higher operation span has a larger working memory. If this is right, then someone with a higher span should have an advantage in tasks that make heavy use of this memory. Which tasks are these? They're tasks that require you to keep multiple ideas active at the same time, so that you can coordinate and integrate various bits of information. So here's our prediction: People with a larger span (i.e., a greater WMC) should do better in tasks that require the coordination of different pieces of information.

Consistent with this claim, people with a greater WMC do have an advantage in many settings—in tests of reasoning, assessments of reading comprehension, standardized academic tests (including the verbal SAT), tasks that require multitasking, and more. (See, e.g., Ackerman, Beier, & Boyle, 2002; Butler, Arrington, & Weywadt, 2011; Daneman & Hannon, 2001; Engle & Kane, 2004; Gathercole & Pickering, 2000; Gray, Chabris, & Braver, 2003; Redick et al., 2016; Salthouse & Pink, 2008. For some complications, see

Chow & Conway, 2015; Harrison, Shipstead, & Engle, 2015; Kanerva & Kalakoski, 2016; Mella, Fagot, Lecert, & de Ribaupierre, 2015.)

These results convey several messages. First, the correlations between WMC and performance provide indications about when it's helpful to have a larger working memory, which in turn helps us understand when and how working memory is used. Second, the link between WMC and measures of intellectual performance provide an intriguing hint about what we're measuring with tests (like the SAT) that seek to measure "intelligence." We'll return to this issue in Chapter 13 when we discuss the nature of intelligence. Third, it's important that the various correlations are observed with the more active measure of working memory (operation span) but not with the more traditional (and more static) span measure. This point confirms the advantage of the more dynamic measures and strengthens the idea that we're now thinking about working memory in the right way: not as a passive storage box, but instead as a highly active information processor.

The Rehearsal Loop

Working memory's active nature is also evident in another way: in the actual structure of this memory. The key here is that working memory is not a single entity but is instead, a *system* built of several components (Baddeley, 1986, 1992, 2012; Baddeley & Hitch, 1974; also see Logie & Cowan, 2015). At the center of the **working-memory system** is a set of processes we discussed in Chapter 5: the executive control processes that govern the selection and sequence of thoughts. In discussions of working memory, these processes have been playfully called the "central executive," as if there were a tiny agent embedded in your mind, running your mental operations. Of course, there is no agent, and the central executive is just a name we give to the set of mechanisms that do run the show.

The central executive is needed for the "work" in working memory; if you have to plan a response or make a decision, these steps require the executive. But in many settings, you need less than this from working memory. Specifically, there are settings in which you need to keep ideas in mind, not because you're analyzing them right now but because you're likely to need them *soon*. In this case, you don't need the executive. Instead, you can rely on the executive's "helpers," leaving the executive free to work on more difficult matters.

Let's focus on one of working memory's most important helpers, the **articulatory rehearsal loop**. To see how the loop functions, try reading the next few sentences while holding on to these numbers: "1, 4, 6, 3." Got them? Now read on. You're probably repeating the numbers over and over to yourself, rehearsing them with your inner voice. But this takes very little effort, so you can continue reading while doing this rehearsal. Nonetheless, the moment you need to recall the numbers (what were they?), they're available to you.

In this setting, the four numbers were maintained by working memory's rehearsal loop, and with the numbers thus out of the way, the central executive could focus on the processes needed for reading. That is the advantage of this system: With mere storage handled by the helpers, the executive is available for other, more demanding tasks.

To describe this sequence of events, researchers would say that you used **subvocalization**—silent speech—to launch the rehearsal loop. This production by the "inner voice" produced a representation of the target numbers in the **phonological buffer**, a passive storage system used for holding a representation (essentially an "internal echo") of recently heard or self-produced sounds. In other words, you created an auditory image in the "inner ear." This image started to fade away after a second or two, but you then subvocalized the numbers once again to create a new image, sustaining the material in this buffer. (For a glimpse of the biological basis for the "inner voice" and "inner ear," see **Figure 6.8**.)

FIGURE 6.8 BRAIN ACTIVITY AND WORKING-MEMORY REHEARSAL

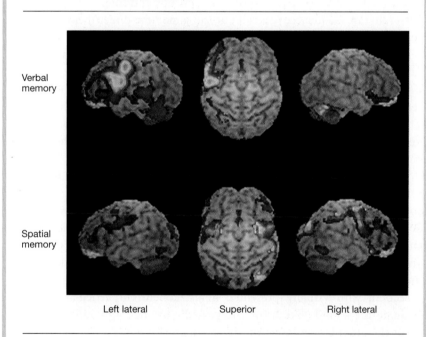

| | Left lateral | Superior | Right lateral |

Verbal memory

Spatial memory

Color is used here as an indication of increased brain activity (measured in this case by positron emission tomography). When research participants are doing a verbal memory task (and using the articulatory loop), activation increases in areas ordinarily used for language production and perception. A very different pattern is observed when participants are doing a task requiring memory for spatial position. Notice, then, that the "inner voice" and "inner ear" aren't casual metaphors; instead, they involve mechanisms that are ordinarily used for overt speech and actual hearing.

(AFTER JONIDES, LACEY, & NEE, 2005; ALSO SEE JONIDES ET AL., 2008)

Many lines of evidence confirm this proposal. For example, when people are storing information in working memory, they often make "sound-alike" errors: Having heard "F," they'll report back "S." When trying to remember the name "Tina," they'll slip and recall "Deena." The problem isn't that people mis-hear the inputs at the start; similar sound-alike confusions emerge if the inputs are presented visually. So, having *seen* "F," people are likely to report back "S"; they aren't likely in this situation to report back the similar-looking "E."

What produces this pattern? The cause lies in the fact that for this task people are relying on the rehearsal loop, which involves a mechanism (the "inner ear") that stores the memory items as (internal representations of) sounds. It's no surprise, therefore, that errors, when they occur, are shaped by this mode of storage.

As a test of this claim, we can ask people to take the span test while simultaneously saying "Tah-Tah-Tah" over and over, out loud. This **concurrent articulation** task obviously requires the mechanisms for speech production. Therefore, those mechanisms are not available for other use, including subvocalization. (If you're directing your lips and tongue to produce the "Tah-Tah-Tah" sequence, you can't at the same time direct them to produce the sequence needed for the subvocalized materials.)

How does this constraint matter? First, note that our original span test measured the *combined capacities* of the central executive and the loop. That is, when people take a standard span test (as opposed to the more modern measure of *operation span*), they store some of the to-be-remembered items in the loop and other items via the central executive. (This is a poor use of the executive, underutilizing its talents, but that's okay here because the standard span task doesn't require anything beyond mere storage.)

With concurrent articulation, though, the loop isn't available for use, so we're now measuring the capacity of working memory without the rehearsal loop. We should predict, therefore, that concurrent articulation, even though it's extremely easy, should cut memory span drastically. This prediction turns out to be correct. Span is ordinarily about seven items; with concurrent articulation, it drops by roughly a third—to four or five items (Chincotta & Underwood, 1997; see **Figure 6.9**).

Second, with visually presented items, concurrent articulation should eliminate the sound-alike errors. Repeatedly saying "Tah-Tah-Tah" blocks use of the articulatory loop, and it's in this loop, we've proposed, that the sound-alike errors arise. This prediction, too, is correct: With concurrent articulation and visual presentation of the items, sound-alike errors are largely eliminated.

The Working-Memory System

As we have mentioned, your working memory contains the thoughts and ideas you're working on right now, and often this means you're trying to keep multiple ideas in working memory all at the same time. That can cause

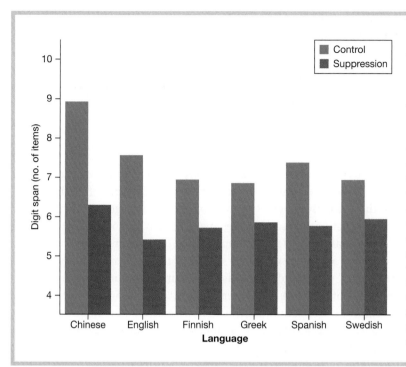

FIGURE 6.9 THE EFFECT OF CONCURRENT ARTICULATION ON SPAN

In the Control condition, participants were given a normal digit-span test. In the Suppression condition, participants were required to do concurrent articulation while taking the test. Concurrent articulation is easy, but it blocks use of the articulatory loop and consistently decreases memory span, from roughly seven items to five or so. And, plainly, this use of the articulatory loop is not an occasional strategy; instead, it can be found in a wide range of countries and languages. (AFTER CHINCOTTA & UNDERWOOD, 1997)

difficulties, because working memory only has a small capacity. That's why working memory's helpers are so important, because they substantially increase working memory's capacity.

Against this backdrop, it's not surprising that the working-memory system relies on other helpers in addition to the rehearsal loop. For example, the system also relies on the *visuospatial buffer*, used for storing visual materials such as mental images, in much the same way that the rehearsal loop stores speech-based materials. (We'll have more to say about mental images in Chapter 11.) Baddeley (the researcher who launched the idea of a working-memory system) has also proposed another component of the system: the *episodic buffer*. This component is proposed as a mechanism that helps the executive organize information into a chronological sequence—so that, for example, you can keep track of a story you've just heard or a film clip you've just seen (e.g., Baddeley, 2000, 2012; Baddeley & Wilson, 2002; Baddeley, Eysenck, & Anderson, 2009). The role of this component is evident in patients with profound amnesia who seem unable to put new information into long-term storage, but who still can recall the flow of narrative in a story they just heard. This short-term recall, it seems, relies on the episodic buffer—an aspect of working memory that's unaffected by the amnesia.

In addition, other helpers can be documented in some groups of people. Consider people who have been deaf since birth and communicate via sign language. We wouldn't expect these individuals to rely on an "inner voice" and an "inner ear"—and they don't. People who have been deaf since birth rely on a different helper for working memory: They use an "inner hand" (and covert sign language) rather than an "inner voice" (and covert speech). As a result, they are disrupted if they're asked to wiggle their fingers during a memory task (similar to a hearing person saying "Tah-Tah-Tah"), and they also tend to make "same hand-shape" errors in working memory (similar to the sound-alike errors made by the hearing population).

The Central Executive

What can we say about the main player within the working-memory system—the central executive? In our discussion of attention (in Chapter 5), we argued that executive control processes are needed to govern the sequence of thoughts and actions; these processes enable you to set goals, make plans for reaching those goals, and select the steps needed for implementing those plans. Executive control also helps whenever you want to rise above habit or routine, in order to "tune" your words or deeds to the current circumstances.

For purposes of the current chapter, though, let's emphasize that the same processes control the selection of ideas that are active at any moment in time. And, of course, these active ideas (again, by definition) constitute the contents of working memory. It's inevitable, then, that we would link executive control with this type of memory.

With all these points in view, we're ready to move on. We've now updated the modal model (Figure 6.1) in important ways, and in particular we've abandoned the notion of a relatively passive *short-term memory* serving largely as storage container. We've shifted to a dynamic conception of *working memory*, with the proposal that this term is merely the name for an organized set of activities—especially the complex activities of the central executive together with its various helpers.

But let's also emphasize that in this modern conception, just as in the modal model, working memory is quite fragile. Each shift in attention brings new information into working memory, and the newly arriving material displaces earlier items. Storage in this memory, therefore, is temporary. Obviously, then, we also need some sort of enduring memory storage, so that we can remember things that happened an hour, or a day, or even years ago. Let's turn, therefore, to the functioning of long-term memory.

TEST YOURSELF

4. What does it mean to say that working memory holds seven (plus-or-minus two) "chunks"? What is a chunk?

5. What evidence suggests that operation span is a better measure of working memory than the more standard digit-span measure?

6. How does the rehearsal loop manage to hold on to information with only occasional involvement by the central executive?

Entering Long-Term Storage: The Need for Engagement

We've already seen an important clue regarding how information gets established in long-term storage: In discussing the primacy effect, we suggested that the more an item is rehearsed, the more likely you are to remember that item later. To pursue this point, though, we need to ask what exactly rehearsal is and how it might work to promote memory.

Two Types of Rehearsal

The term "rehearsal" doesn't mean much beyond "thinking about." In other words, when a research participant rehearses an item on a memory list, she's simply thinking about that item—perhaps once, perhaps over and over; perhaps mechanically, or perhaps with close attention to what the item means. Therefore, there's considerable variety within the activities that count as rehearsal, and psychologists find it useful to sort this variety into two broad types.

As one option, people can engage in **maintenance rehearsal**, in which they simply focus on the to-be-remembered items themselves, with little thought about what the items mean or how they relate to one another. This is a rote, mechanical process, recycling items in working memory by repeating them over and over. In contrast, **relational**, or **elaborative, rehearsal** involves thinking about what the to-be-remembered items mean and how they're related to one another and to other things you already know.

Relational rehearsal is vastly superior to maintenance rehearsal for establishing information in memory. In fact, in many settings maintenance rehearsal provides no long-term benefit at all. As an informal demonstration of this point, consider the following experience (although, for a formal demonstration of this point, see Craik & Watkins, 1973). You're watching your favorite reality show on TV. The announcer says, "To vote for Contestant #4, text 4 to 21523 from your mobile phone!" You reach into your pocket for your phone but realize you left it in the other room. So you recite the number to yourself while scurrying for your phone, but then, just before you dial, you see that you've got a text message. You pause, read the message, and then you're ready to dial, but . . . you don't have a clue what the number was.

What went wrong? You certainly heard the number, and you rehearsed it a couple of times while moving to grab your phone. But despite these rehearsals, the brief interruption from reading the text message seems to have erased the number from your memory. However, this isn't ultra-rapid forgetting. Instead, you never established the number in memory in the first place, because in this setting you relied only on maintenance rehearsal. That kept the number in your thoughts while you were moving across the room, but it did nothing to establish the number in long-term storage. And when you try to dial the number after reading the text message, it's long-term storage that you need.

The idea, then, is that if you think about something only in a mindless and mechanical way, the item won't be established in your long-term memory. Similarly, long-lasting memories aren't created simply by *repeated exposures* to the items to be remembered. If you encounter an item over and over but, at each encounter, barely think about it (or think about it only in a mechanical way), then this, too, won't produce a long-term memory. As a demonstration, consider the ordinary penny. Adults in the United States have probably seen pennies tens of thousands of times. Adults in other countries have seen their own coins just as often. If sheer exposure is what counts for memory, people should remember perfectly what these coins look like.

WE DON'T REMEMBER THINGS WE DON'T PAY ATTENTION TO

To promote public safety, many buildings have fire extinguishers and automatic defibrillators positioned in obvious and easily accessible locations. But in a moment of need, will people in the building remember where this safety equipment is located? Will they even remember that the safety equipment is conveniently available? Research suggests they may not. Occupants of the building have passed by the safety equipment again and again—but have had no reason to notice the equipment. As a result, they're unlikely to remember where the equipment is located. (After Castel, Vendetti, & Holyoak, 2012)

But, of course, most people have little reason to pay attention to the penny. Pennies are a different color from the other coins, so they can be identified at a glance without further scrutiny. And, if it's scrutiny that matters for memory—or, more broadly, *if we remember what we pay attention to and think about*—then memory for the coin should be quite poor.

The evidence on this point is clear: People's memory for the penny is remarkably bad. For example, most people know that Lincoln's head is on the "heads" side, but which way is he facing? Is it his right cheek that's visible or his left? What other markings are on the coin? Most people do very badly with these questions; their answers to the "Which way is he facing?" question are close to random (Nickerson & Adams, 1979). And performance is similar for people in other countries remembering their own coins. (Also see Bekerian & Baddeley, 1980; Rinck, 1999, for a much more consequential example.)

As a related example, consider the logo that identifies Apple products—the iPhone, the iPad, or one of the Apple computers. Odds are good that you've seen this logo hundreds and perhaps thousands of time, but you've probably had no reason to pay attention to its appearance. The prediction, then, is that your memory for the logo will be quite poor—and this prediction is correct. In one study, only 1 of 85 participants was able to draw the logo correctly—with the bite on the proper side, the stem tilted the right way, and the dimple properly placed in the logo's bottom (Blake, Nazarian, & Castel, 2015; see **Figure 6.10**). And—surprisingly—people who use an Apple computer (and therefore see the logo every time they turn on the machine) perform at a level not much better than people who use a PC.

The Need for Active Encoding

Apparently, it takes some work to get information into long-term memory. Merely having an item in front of your eyes isn't enough—even if the item is there over and over and over. Likewise, repeatedly thinking about an item doesn't, by itself, establish a memory. That's evident in the fact that maintenance rehearsal seems ineffective at promoting memory.

FIGURE 6.10 MEMORY FOR AN OFTEN-VIEWED LOGO

Most people have seen the Apple logo countless times, but they've had no reason to pay attention to its features. As a result, they have poor memories for the features. Test yourself. Can you find the correct version among the options displayed here?

(THE ANSWER IS AT THE END OF THE CHAPTER.)

Further support for these claims comes from studies of brain activity during learning. In several procedures, researchers have used fMRI recording to keep track of the moment-by-moment brain activity in participants who were studying a list of words (Brewer, Zhao, Desmond, Glover, & Gabrieli, 1998; Wagner, Koutstaal, & Schacter, 1999; Wagner et al., 1998; also see Levy, Kuhl, & Wagner, 2010). Later, the participants were able to remember some of the words they had learned, but not others, which allowed the investigators to return to their initial recordings and compare brain activity *during the learning process* for words that were later remembered and words that were later forgotten. **Figure 6.11** shows the results, with a clear difference, during the initial encoding, between these two types of words. Greater levels of brain

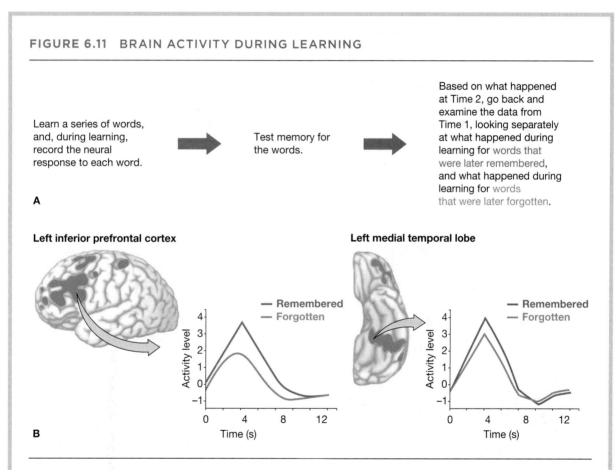

FIGURE 6.11 BRAIN ACTIVITY DURING LEARNING

Learn a series of words, and, during learning, record the neural response to each word.

Test memory for the words.

Based on what happened at Time 2, go back and examine the data from Time 1, looking separately at what happened during learning for words that were later remembered, and what happened during learning for words that were later forgotten.

A

Left inferior prefrontal cortex

Left medial temporal lobe

— Remembered
— Forgotten

Activity level

Time (s)

B

(Panel A) Participants in this study were given a series of words to memorize, and their brain activity was recorded during this initial presentation. These brain scans were then divided into two types: those showing brain activity during the encoding of words that were remembered in the subsequent test, and those showing activity during encoding of words that were forgotten in the test. (Panel B) As the figure shows, activity levels during encoding were higher for the later-remembered words than they were for the later-forgotten words. This finding confirms that whether a word is forgotten or not depends on participants' mental activity when they encountered the word in the first place.

activity (especially in the hippocampus and regions of the prefrontal cortex) were reliably associated with greater probabilities of retention later on.

These fMRI results are telling us, once again, that learning is not a passive process. Instead, activity is needed to lodge information into long-term memory, and, apparently, higher levels of this activity lead to better memory. But this raises some new questions: What is this activity? What does it accomplish? And if—as it seems—*maintenance* rehearsal is a poor way to memorize, what type of rehearsal is more effective?

Incidental Learning, Intentional Learning, and Depth of Processing

Consider a student taking a course in college. The student knows that her memory for the course materials will be tested later (e.g., in the final exam). And presumably she'll take various steps to help herself remember: She may read through her notes again and again; she may discuss the material with friends; she may try outlining the material. Will these various techniques work—so that she'll have a complete and accurate memory when the exam takes place? And notice that the student is taking these steps in the context of wanting to memorize; she wants to do well on the exam! How does this motivation influence performance? In other words, how does the intention to memorize influence how or how well material is learned?

In an early experiment, participants in one condition heard a list of 24 words; their task was to remember as many as they could. This is **intentional learning**—learning that is deliberate, with an expectation that memory will be tested later. Other groups of participants heard the same 24 words but had no idea that their memories would be tested. This allows us to examine the impact of **incidental learning**—that is, learning in the absence of any intention to learn. One of the incidental-learning groups was asked simply, for each word, whether the word contained the letter *e*. A different incidental-learning group was asked to look at each word and to report how many letters it contained. Another group was asked to consider each word and to rate how *pleasant* it seemed.

Later, all the participants were tested—and asked to recall as many of the words as they could. (The test was as expected for the intentional-learning group, but it was a surprise for the other groups.) The results are shown in **Figure 6.12A** (Hyde & Jenkins, 1969). Performance was relatively poor for the "Find the *e*" and "Count the letters" groups but appreciably better for the "How pleasant?" group. What's striking, though, is that the "How pleasant?" group, with no intention to memorize, performed just as well as the intentional-learning ("Learn these!") group. The suggestion, then, is that the intention to learn doesn't add very much; memory can be just as good without this intention, provided that you approach the materials in the right way.

This broad pattern has been reproduced in many other experiments (to name just a few: Bobrow & Bower, 1969; Craik & Lockhart, 1972; Hyde & Jenkins, 1973; Jacoby, 1978; Lockhart, Craik, & Jacoby, 1976; Parkin, 1984;

Slamecka & Graf, 1978). As one example, consider a study by Craik and Tulving (1975). Their participants were led to do incidental learning (i.e., they didn't know their memories would be tested). For some of the words shown, the participants did **shallow processing**—that is, they engaged the material in a superficial way. Specifically, they had to say whether the word was printed in CAPITAL letters or not. (Other examples of shallow processing would be decisions about whether the words are printed in red or in green, high or low on the screen, etc.) For other words, the participants had to do a moderate level of processing: They had to judge whether each word shown *rhymed* with a particular cue word. Finally, for other words, participants had to do **deep processing**. This is processing that requires some thought about what the words *mean*; specifically, Craik and Tulving asked whether each word shown would fit into a particular sentence.

The results are shown in **Figure 6.12B**. Plainly, there is a huge effect of **level of processing**, with deeper processing (i.e., more attention to meaning) leading to better memory. In addition, Craik and Tulving (and many other researchers) have confirmed the Hyde and Jenkins finding that the intention

TEST YOURSELF

7. What is the difference between maintenance rehearsal and relational (or elaborative) rehearsal?

8. What does it mean to say, "It doesn't matter if you *intend* to memorize; all that matters for memory is how exactly you engage the material you encounter"?

9. What is deep processing, and what impact does it have on memory?

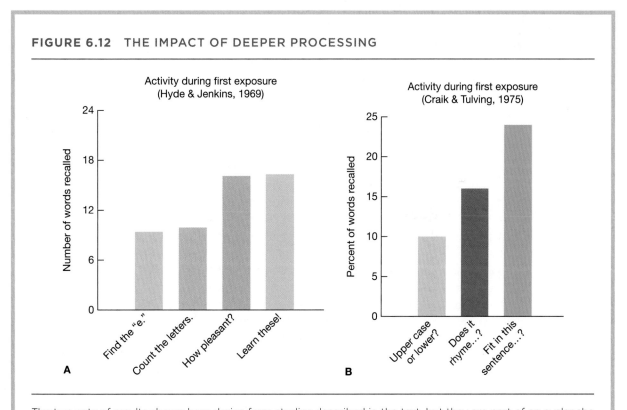

FIGURE 6.12   THE IMPACT OF DEEPER PROCESSING

The two sets of results shown here derive from studies described in the text, but they are part of an avalanche of data confirming the broad pattern: Shallow processing leads to poor memory. Deeper processing (paying attention to meaning) leads to much better memory. And what matters seems to be the level of engagement; the specific intention to learn (because participants know their memory will be tested later on) contributes little.

Gender Differences?

Most of this book focuses on principles that apply to all people—young or old, sociable or shy, smart or slow. But, of course, people differ in many ways, leading us to ask: Are there differences in how people remember? As one aspect of this issue, do men and women differ in their memories?

Let's emphasize at the start that there's no overall difference between the genders in memory accuracy, or quantity of information retained, or susceptibility to outside influences that might pull memory off track. (See Chapter 8 for more on the influences on memory.) If we take a closer look, though, we do find some differences (e.g., Herlitz & Rehnman, 2014)—with some studies suggesting an advantage for women in remembering verbal materials, and other studies suggesting an advantage for men in remembering spatial arrangement.

Other differences in what the genders remember are the consequence of cultural factors. Bear in mind that people tend to remember what they paid attention to, and don't remember things they didn't attend. From this base, it's not surprising that after viewing an event, women are more likely than men to recall the clothing people were wearing or their jewelry. Men, in contrast, are more likely than women to recall the people's body shapes. (Also see Chapter 5, pp. 170–173.) There is even some indication that women may have better face memory—but only when remembering the faces of other women. All these differences probably reflect the "attention priorities" that Western culture encourages for men and women, priorities that derive from the conventional roles assumed (for better or worse) for each gender.

Some results also suggest that women may have better memory for day-to-day events, especially emotional events; but this, too, might be a difference in attention rather than a true difference in memory. Women are, in Western culture, encouraged to pay attention to social dynamics and in many settings are encouraged to be more emotionally responsive and more emotionally sensitive than men. It may be these points that color how women pay attention to and think about an event—and ultimately how they remember the event.

It seems likely, then, that most of these differences (none of them profound) are a direct reflection of cultural bias. Even so, the differences do underscore some important messages. First, with regard to their cognition, men and women are much more similar to each other than they are different. Second, it's crucial to bear in mind that what you remember *now* is dependent on what you paid attention to *earlier.* Therefore, if people differ in what they focus on, they'll remember different things later on.

to learn adds little. That is, memory performance is roughly the same in conditions in which participants do shallow processing *with* an intention to memorize, and in conditions in which they do shallow processing *without* this intention. Likewise, the outcome is the same whether people do deep processing *with* the intention to memorize or *without.* In study after study, what matters is how people approach the material they're seeing or hearing.

It's that approach—that manner of engagement—that determines whether memory will be excellent or poor later on. The intention to learn seems, by itself, not to matter.

The Role of Meaning and Memory Connections

The message so far seems clear: If you want to remember the sentences you're reading in this text, or the materials you're learning in the training sessions at your job, you should pay attention to what these materials mean. That is, you should try to do deep processing. And if you do deep processing, it won't matter if you're trying hard to memorize the materials (intentional learning) or merely paying attention to the meaning because you find the material interesting, with no plan for memorizing (incidental learning).

But what lies behind these effects? Why does attention to meaning lead to good recall? Let's start with a broad proposal; we'll then fill in the evidence for this proposal.

Connections Promote Retrieval

Perhaps surprisingly, the benefits of deep processing may not lie in the learning process itself. Instead, deep processing may influence subsequent events. More precisely, attention to meaning may help you by facilitating *retrieval* of the memory later on. To understand this point, consider what happens whenever a library acquires a new book. On its way into the collection, the new book must be catalogued and shelved appropriately. These steps happen when the book arrives, but the cataloguing doesn't literally influence the arrival of the book into the building. The moment the book is delivered, it's physically in the library, catalogued or not, and the book doesn't become "more firmly" or "more strongly" in the library because of the cataloguing.

Even so, the cataloguing is crucial. If the book were merely tossed on a random shelf somewhere, with no entry in the catalogue, users might never be able to find it. Without a catalogue entry, users of the library might not even realize that the book was in the building. Notice, then, that cataloguing happens at the time of arrival, but the benefit of cataloguing isn't for the arrival itself. (If the librarians all went on strike, so that no books were being catalogued, books would continue to arrive, magazines would still be delivered, and so on. Again: The *arrival* doesn't depend on cataloguing.) Instead, the benefit of cataloguing is for events that happen after the book's arrival—cataloguing makes it possible (and maybe makes it *easy*) to find the book later on.

The same is true for the vast library that is your memory (cf. Miller & Springer, 1973). The task of learning is not merely a matter of placing information into long-term storage. Learning also needs to establish some appropriate indexing; it must pave a path to the newly acquired information, so that this information can be retrieved at some future point. Thus, one of

WHY DO MEMORY CONNECTIONS HELP?

When books arrive in a library, the librarians must catalogue them. This doesn't facilitate the "entry" of books into the library, because the books are in the building whether they're catalogued or not. But cataloguing makes the books much easier to find later on. Memory connections may serve the same function: The connections don't "bring" material into memory, but they do make the material "findable" in long-term storage later.

the main chores of memory acquisition is to lay the groundwork for memory retrieval.

But what is it that facilitates memory retrieval? There are, in fact, several ways to search through memory, but a great deal depends on memory *connections*. Connections allow one memory to trigger another, and then that memory to trigger another, so that you're "led," connection by connection, to the sought-after information. In some cases, the connections link one of the items you're trying to remember to some of the other items; if so, finding the first will lead you to the others. In other settings, the connections might link some aspect of the context-of-learning to the target information, so that when you think again about the context ("I recognize this room—this is where I was last week"), you'll be led to other ideas ("Oh, yeah, I read the funny story in this room"). In all cases, though, this triggering will happen only if the relevant connections are in place—and establishing those connections is a large part of what happens during learning.

This line of reasoning has many implications, and we can use those implications as a basis for testing whether this proposal is correct. But right at the start, it should be clear why, according to this account, deep processing (i.e., attention to meaning) promotes memory. The key is that attention to meaning involves thinking about relationships: "What words are related in meaning to the word I'm now considering? What words have *contrasting* meaning? What is the relationship between the start of this story and the way the story turned out?" Points like these are likely to be prominent when you're thinking about what some word (or sentence or event) means, and these points will help you to find (or, perhaps, to *create*) connections among your various ideas. It's these connections, we're proposing, that really matter for memory.

Elaborate Encoding Promotes Retrieval

Notice, though, that on this account, attention to meaning is not the only way to improve memory. Other strategies should also be helpful, provided that they help you to establish memory connections. As an example, consider another classic study by Craik and Tulving (1975). Participants were shown a word and then shown a sentence with one word left out. Their task was to decide whether the word fit into the sentence. For example, they might see the word "chicken" and then the sentence "She cooked the _____." The appropriate response would be yes, because the word does fit in this sentence. After a series of these trials, there was a surprise memory test, with participants asked to remember all the words they had seen.

But there was an additional element in this experiment. Some of the sentences shown to participants were simple, while others were more elaborate. For example, a more complex sentence might be: "The great bird swooped down and carried off the struggling _____." Sentences like this one produced a large memory benefit—words were much more likely to be remembered if they appeared with these rich, elaborate sentences than if they had appeared in the simpler sentences (see **Figure 6.13**).

Apparently, then, deep *and elaborate* processing leads to better recall than deep processing on its own. Why? The answer hinges on memory connections. Maybe the "great bird swooped" sentence calls to mind a barnyard scene with the hawk carrying away a chicken. Or maybe it calls to mind

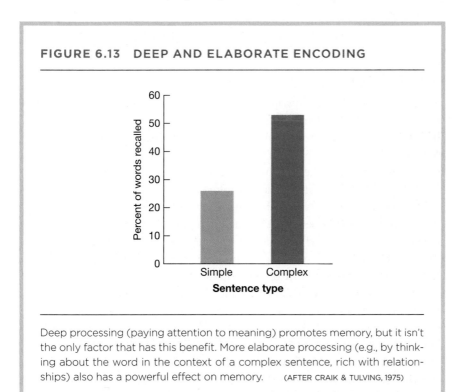

FIGURE 6.13   DEEP AND ELABORATE ENCODING

Deep processing (paying attention to meaning) promotes memory, but it isn't the only factor that has this benefit. More elaborate processing (e.g., by thinking about the word in the context of a complex sentence, rich with relationships) also has a powerful effect on memory.   (AFTER CRAIK & TULVING, 1975)

10. What does it mean to say, "The creation of memory connections often occurs at the time of learning, but the main benefit of those connections comes later, at the time of memory retrieval"?

11. In what ways is deep and elaborate processing superior to deep processing on its own?

thoughts about predator-prey relationships. One way or another, the richness of the sentence offers the potential for many connections as it calls other thoughts to mind, each of which can be connected to the target sentence. These connections, in turn, provide potential **retrieval paths**—paths that can, in effect, guide your thoughts toward the content to be remembered. All of this seems less likely for the simpler sentences, which will evoke fewer connections and so establish a narrower set of retrieval paths. Consequently, words associated with these sentences are less likely to be recalled later on.

Organizing and Memorizing

Sometimes, we've said, memory connections link the to-be-remembered material to other information already in memory. In other cases, the connections link one aspect of the to-be-remembered material to another aspect of the same material. Such a connection ensures that if any part of the material is recalled, then all will be recalled.

In all settings, though, the connections are important, and that leads us to ask how people go about discovering (or creating) these connections. More than 70 years ago, a psychologist named George Katona argued that the key lies in *organization* (Katona, 1940). Katona's argument was that the processes of organization and memorization are inseparable: You memorize well when you discover the order within the material. Conversely, if you find (or impose) an organization on the material, you will easily remember it. These suggestions are fully compatible with the conception we're developing here, since what organization provides is memory connections.

Mnemonics

MNEMOSYNE

Strategies that are used to improve memory are known as mnemonic strategies, or mnemonics. The term derives from the name of the goddess of memory in Greek mythology—Mnemosyne.

For thousands of years, people have longed for "better" memories and, guided by this desire, people in the ancient world devised various techniques to improve memory—techniques known as **mnemonic strategies**. In fact, many of the mnemonics still in use date back to ancient Greece. (It's therefore appropriate that these techniques are named in honor of Mnemosyne, the goddess of memory in Greek mythology.)

How do mnemonics work? In general, these strategies provide some way of organizing the to-be-remembered material. For example, one broad class of mnemonic, often used for memorizing sequences of words, links the *first letters* of the words into some meaningful structure. Thus, children rely on ROY G. BIV to memorize the sequence of colors in the rainbow (*red, orange, yellow* . . .), and they learn the lines in music's treble clef via "Every Good Boy Deserves Fudge" or ". . . Does Fine" (the lines indicate the musical notes *E, G, B, D,* and *F*). Biology students use a sentence like "King Philip Crossed the Ocean to Find Gold and Silver" (or: ". . . to Find Good Spaghetti") to memorize the sequence of taxonomic categories: *kingdom, phylum, class, order, family, genus,* and *species.*

Other mnemonics involve the use of mental imagery, relying on "mental pictures" to link the to-be-remembered items to one another. (We'll have much more to say about "mental pictures" in Chapter 11.) For example, imagine a student trying to memorize a list of word pairs. For the pair *eagle-train*, the student might imagine the eagle winging back to its nest with a locomotive in its beak. Classic research evidence indicates that images like this can be enormously helpful. It's important, though, that the images show the objects in some sort of relationship or interaction—again highlighting the role of organization. It doesn't help just to form a picture of an eagle and a train sitting side-by-side (Wollen, Weber, & Lowry, 1972; for another example of a mnemonic, see **Figure 6.14**).

A different type of mnemonic provides an external "skeleton" for the to-be-remembered materials, and mental imagery can be useful here, too. Imagine that you want to remember a list of largely unrelated items—perhaps

FIGURE 6.14   MNEMONIC STRATEGIES

With a bit of creativity, you can make up mnemonics for memorizing all sorts of things. For example, can you name all ten of the Canadian provinces? Perhaps there is a great mnemonic available, but in the meantime, this will do. It's a complicated mnemonic but unified by the theme of the early-morning meal: "**B**reakfast **C**ooks **A**lways **S**ell **M**ore **O**melets. **Q**uiche **N**ever **B**ought; **N**ever **S**old. **P**erhaps **E**ggs **I**n **N**ew **F**orms?" (You're on your own for remembering the three northern territories.)

the entries on your shopping list, or a list of questions you want to ask your adviser. For this purpose, you might rely on one of the so-called **peg-word systems**. These systems begin with a well-organized structure, such as this one:

One is a bun.

Two is a shoe.

Three is a tree.

Four is a door.

Five is a hive.

Six are sticks.

Seven is heaven.

Eight is a gate.

Nine is a line.

Ten is a hen.

This rhyme provides ten "peg words" ("bun," "shoe," etc.), and in memorizing something you can "hang" the materials to be remembered on these "pegs." Let's imagine that you want to remember the list of topics you need to discuss with your adviser. If you want to discuss your unhappiness with chemistry class, you might form an association between chemistry and the first peg, "bun." You might picture a hamburger bun floating in an Erlenmeyer flask. If you also want to discuss your plans for after graduation, you might form an association between some aspect of those plans and the next peg, "shoe." (You could think about how you plan to pay your way after college by selling shoes.) Then, when meeting with your adviser, all you have to do is think through that silly rhyme again. When you think of "one is a bun," it's highly likely that the image of the flask (and therefore of chemistry lab) will come to mind. With "two is a shoe," you'll be reminded of your job plans. And so on.

Hundreds of variations on these techniques—the first-letter mnemonics, visualization strategies, peg-word systems—are available. Some variations are taught in self-help books (you've probably seen the ads—"How to Improve Your Memory!"); some are taught as part of corporate management training. But all the variations use the same basic scheme. To remember a list with no apparent organization, you impose an organization on it by using a tightly organized skeleton or scaffold. And, crucially, these systems all work. They help you remember individual items, and they also help you remember those items in a specific sequence. **Figure 6.15** shows some of the data from one early study; many other studies confirm this pattern (e.g., Bower, 1970, 1972; Bower & Reitman, 1972; Christen & Bjork, 1976; Higbee, 1977; Roediger, 1980; Ross & Lawrence, 1968; Yates, 1966). All of this strengthens our central claim: Mnemonics work because they impose an organization on the materials you're trying to memorize. And, consistently and powerfully, organizing improves recall.

Given the power of mnemonics, students are well advised to use these strategies in their studies. In fact, for many topics there are online databases

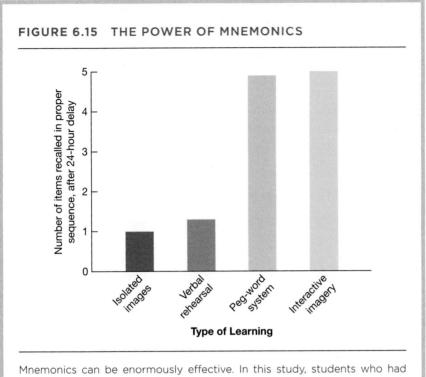

FIGURE 6.15   THE POWER OF MNEMONICS

Mnemonics can be enormously effective. In this study, students who had relied on peg words or interactive imagery vastly outperformed students who'd used other memorizing strategies.   (AFTER ROEDIGER, 1980)

containing thousands of useful mnemonics—helping medical students to memorize symptom lists, chemistry students to memorize the periodic table, neuroscientists to remember the brain's anatomy, and more.

Bear in mind, though, that there's a downside to the use of mnemonics in educational settings. When using a mnemonic, you typically focus on just one aspect of the material you're trying to memorize—for example, just the first letter of the word to be remembered—and so you may cut short your effort toward understanding this material, and likewise your effort toward finding multiple connections between the material and other things you know.

To put this point differently, mnemonic use involves a trade-off. If you focus on just one or two memory connections, you'll spend little time thinking about other possible connections, including those that might help you understand the material. This trade-off will be fine if you don't care very much about the meaning of the material. (Do you care why, in taxonomy, "order" is a subset of "class," rather than the other way around?) But the trade-off is troubling if you're trying to memorize material that is meaningful. In this case, you'd be better served by a memory strategy that seeks out *multiple* connections between the material you're trying to learn and things you already know. This effort toward multiple links will help you in two ways. First, it will foster your understanding of the material to be remembered, and so will lead to better, richer, deeper learning. Second, it will help you retrieve this information later. We've already suggested that memory connections serve as retrieval paths, and the more paths there are, the easier it will be to find the target material later.

For these reasons, mnemonic use may not be the best approach in many situations. Still, the fact remains that mnemonics are immensely useful in some settings (What were those rainbow colors?), and this confirms our initial point: Organization promotes memory.

Understanding and Memorizing

So far, we've said a lot about how people memorize simple stimulus materials—lists of randomly selected words, or colors that have to be learned in the right sequence. In our day-to-day lives, however, we typically want to remember more meaningful, more complicated, material. We want to remember the episodes we experience, the details of rich scenes we've observed, or the many-step arguments we've read in a book. Do the same memory principles apply to these cases?

The answer is clearly yes (although we'll have more to say about this issue in Chapter 8). In other words, your memory for events, or pictures, or complex bodies of knowledge is enormously dependent on your being able to organize the material to be remembered. With these more complicated materials, though, we've suggested that your best bet for organization isn't some arbitrary skeleton like those used in mnemonics. Instead, the best organization of these complex materials is generally dependent on understanding. That is, you remember best what you understand best.

There are many ways to show that this is true. For example, we can give people a sentence or paragraph to read and test their comprehension by asking questions about the material. Sometime later, we can test their memory. The results are clear: The better the participants' understanding of a sentence or a paragraph, if questioned immediately after viewing the material, the greater the likelihood that they will remember the material after a delay (for classic data on this topic, see Bransford, 1979).

Likewise, consider the material you're learning right now in the courses you're taking. Will you remember this material 5 years from now, or 10, or 20? The answer depends on how well you understand the material, and one measure of understanding is the grade you earn in a course. With full and rich understanding, you're likely to earn an A; with poor understanding, your grade is likely to be lower. This leads to a prediction: If understanding is (as we've proposed) important for memory, then the higher someone's grade in a course, the more likely that person is to remember the course contents, even years later. This is exactly what the data show, with A students remembering the material quite well, and C students remembering much less (Conway, Cohen, & Stanhope, 1992).

The relationship between understanding and memory can also be demonstrated in another way: by *manipulating* whether people understand the material or not. For example, in an early experiment by Bransford and Johnson (1972, p. 722), participants read this passage:

> The procedure is actually quite simple. First you arrange items into different groups. Of course one pile may be sufficient depending on how much there is to do. If you have to go somewhere else due to lack of facilities that is the next step; otherwise you are pretty well set. It is important not to overdo things. That is, it is better to do too few things at once than too many. In the short run, this may not seem important but complications can easily arise. A mistake can be expensive as well. At first, the whole procedure will seem complicated. Soon, however, it will become just another facet of life. It is difficult to foresee any end to the necessity for this task in the immediate future, but then, one never can tell. After the procedure is completed one arranges the materials into different groups again. Then they can be put into their appropriate places. Eventually they will be used once more and the whole cycle will then have to be repeated. However, that is part of life.

You're probably puzzled by the passage, and so are most research participants. The story is easy to understand, though, if we give it a title: "Doing the Laundry." In the experiment, some participants were given the title before reading the passage; others were not. Participants in the first group easily understood the passage and were able to remember it after a delay. Participants in the second group, reading the same words, weren't confronting a meaningful passage and did poorly on the memory test. (For related data, see Bransford & Franks, 1971; Sulin & Dooling, 1974. For another example, see **Figure 6.16**.)

FIGURE 6.16 MEMORY FOR DIGITS

$$1\ 4\ 9\ 1\ 6\ 2\ 5\ 3\ 6\ 4\ 9\ 6\ 4\ 8\ 1$$

Examine this series of digits for a moment, and then turn away from the page and try to recall all 15 in their proper sequence. The chances are good that you will fail in this task—perhaps remembering the first few and the last few digits, but not the entire list. Things will go differently, though, if you discover the pattern within the list. Now, you'll easily be able to remember the full sequence. What is the pattern? Try thinking of the series this way: 1, 4, 9, 16, 25, 36. . . . Here, as always, organizing and understanding aid memory.

FIGURE 6.17 COMPREHENSION ALSO AIDS MEMORY FOR PICTURES

People who perceive this picture as a pattern of meaningless blotches are unlikely to remember the picture. People who perceive the "hidden" form do remember the picture. (AFTER WISEMAN & NEISSER, 1974)

TEST YOURSELF

12. Why do mnemonics help memory? What are the limitations involved in mnemonic use?
13. What's the evidence that there's a clear linkage between how well you understand material when you first meet it, and how fully you'll recall that information later on?

Similar effects can be documented with nonverbal materials. Consider the picture shown in **Figure 6.17**. At first it looks like a bunch of meaningless blotches; with some study, though, you may discover a familiar object. Wiseman and Neisser (1974) tested people's memory for this picture. Consistent with what we've seen so far, their memory was good if they understood the picture—and bad otherwise. (Also see Bower, Karlin, & Dueck, 1975; Mandler & Ritchey, 1977; Rubin & Kontis, 1983.)

The Study of Memory Acquisition

This chapter has largely been about memory acquisition. How do we acquire new memories? How is new information, new knowledge, established in long-term memory? In more pragmatic terms, what is the best, most effective way to learn? We now have answers to these questions, but our discussion has indicated that we need to place these questions into a broader context—with attention on the substantial contribution from the memorizer, and also a consideration of the interconnections among acquisition, retrieval, and storage.

The Contribution of the Memorizer

Over and over, we've seen that memory depends on *connections* among ideas, connections fostered by the steps you take in your effort toward organizing and understanding the materials you encounter. Hand in hand with this, it appears that memories are not established by sheer contact with the items you're hoping to remember. If you're merely exposed to the items without giving them any thought, then subsequent recall of those items will be poor.

These points draw attention to the huge role played by the memorizer. If, for example, we wish to predict whether this or that event will be recalled, it isn't enough to know that someone was exposed to the event. Instead, we need to ask what the person was *doing* during the event. Did she only do maintenance rehearsal, or did she engage the material in some other way? If the latter, how did she think about the material? Did she pay attention to the appearance of the words or to their meaning? If she thought about meaning, was she able to understand the material? These considerations are crucial for predicting the success of memory.

The contribution of the memorizer is also evident in another way. We've argued that learning depends on making connections, but connections to what? If you want to connect the to-be-remembered material to other knowledge, to other memories, then you need to have that other knowledge—you need to have other (potentially relevant) memories that you can "hook" the new material on to.

This point helps us understand why sports fans have an easy time learning new facts about sports, and why car mechanics can easily learn new facts about cars, and why memory experts easily memorize new information about memory. In each situation, the person enters the learning situation with a considerable advantage—a rich framework that the new materials can be woven into. But, conversely, if someone enters a learning situation with little relevant background, then there's no framework, nothing to connect to, and learning will be more difficult. Plainly, then, if we want to predict someone's success in memorizing, we need to consider what other knowledge the individual brings into the situation.

The Links among Acquisition, Retrieval, and Storage

These points lead us to another important theme. The emphasis in this chapter has been on memory acquisition, but we've now seen that claims about acquisition cannot be separated from claims about storage and retrieval. For example, why is memory acquisition improved by organization? We've suggested that organization provides retrieval paths, making the memories "findable" later on, and this is a claim about retrieval. Therefore, our claims about acquisition are intertwined with claims about retrieval.

TEST YOURSELF

14. Explain why memorizing involves a contribution from the memorizer, both in terms of what the memorizer *does* while memorizing, and also in terms of what the memorizer *knows* prior to the memorizing.

Likewise, we just noted that your ability to learn new material depends, in part, on your having a framework of prior knowledge to which the new materials can be tied. In this way, claims about memory acquisition need to be coordinated with claims about the nature of what is already in storage.

These interactions among acquisition, knowledge, and retrieval are crucial for our theorizing. But the interactions also have important implications for learning, for forgetting, and for memory accuracy. The next two chapters explore some of those implications.

how should i study?

Throughout your life, you encounter information that you hope to remember later—whether you're a student taking courses or an employee in training for a new job. In these and many other settings, what helpful lessons can you draw from memory research?

For a start, bear in mind that the *intention to memorize*, on its own, has no effect. Therefore, you don't need any special "memorizing steps." Instead, you should focus on making sure you *understand* the material, because if you do, you're likely to remember it.

As a specific strategy, it's useful to spend a moment after a class, or after you've done a reading assignment, to quiz yourself about what you've just learned. You might ask questions like these: "What are the new ideas here?"; "Do these new ideas fit with other things I know?"; "Do I know what evidence or arguments support the claims here?" Answering questions like these will help you find meaningful connections within the material you're learning, and between this material and other information already in your memory. In the same spirit, it's often useful to rephrase material you encounter, putting it into your own words. Doing this will force you to think about what the words mean—again, a good thing for memory.

Surveys suggest, however, that most students rely on study strategies that are much more passive than this—in fact, far *too* passive. Most students try to learn materials by simply rereading the textbook or reading over their notes several times. The problem with these strategies should be obvious: As the chapter explains, memories are produced by active engagement with materials, not by passive exposure.

As a related point, it's often useful to study with a friend—so that he or she can explain topics to you, and you can do the same in return. This step has several advantages. In explaining things, you're forced into a more active role. Working with a friend is also likely to enhance your understanding, because each of you can help the other to understand bits you're having trouble with. You'll also benefit from hearing your friend's perspective on the materials. This additional perspective offers the possibility of creating new connections among ideas, making the information easier to recall later on.

Memory will also be best if you spread your studying out across multiple occasions—using *spaced learning* (e.g., spreading out your learning across several days) rather than *massed learning* (essentially, "cramming" all at once). It also helps to vary your focus while studying—working on your history assignment for a while, then shifting to math, then over to the novel your English professor assigned, and then back to history. There are several reasons for this, including the fact that spaced learning and a changing focus will make it likely that you'll bring a somewhat different perspective to the material each time you turn to it. This new perspective will let you see connections you didn't see before; and—again—these new connections provide retrieval paths that can promote recall.

Spaced learning also has another advantage. With this form of learning, some time will pass between the episodes of learning. (Imagine, for example, that you study your sociology text for a while on Tuesday night and then return to it on Thursday, so that two days go by between these study sessions.) This situation allows some amount of forgetting to take place, and that's actually helpful because now each episode of learning will have to take a bit more effort, a bit more thought. This stands in contrast to massed learning, in which your second and third passes through the material may only be separated by a few minutes. In this setting, the second and third passes may feel easy enough so that you zoom through them, with little engagement in the material.

Note an ironic point here: Spaced learning may be more difficult (because of the forgetting in between sessions), but this difficulty leads to better learning overall. Researchers refer to this as "desirable difficulty"—difficulty that may feel obnoxious when you're slogging through the material you hope to learn but that is nonetheless beneficial, because it leaves you with more complete, more long-lasting memory.

What about mnemonic strategies, such as a peg-word system? These are enormously helpful—but often at a cost. When you're first learning something new, focusing on a mnemonic can divert your time and attention away from efforts at understanding the material, and so you'll end up understanding the material less well. You'll also be left with only the one or two retrieval paths that the mnemonic provides, not the multiple paths created by comprehension. In some circumstances these drawbacks aren't serious—and so, for example, mnemonics are often useful for memorizing dates, place names, or particular bits of terminology. But for richer, more meaningful material, mnemonics may hurt you more than they help.

Mnemonics can be more helpful, though, *after* you've understood the new material. Imagine that you've thoughtfully constructed a many-step argument or a complex derivation of a mathematical formula. Now, imagine that you hope to re-create the argument or the derivation later on—perhaps for an oral presentation or on an exam. In this situation, you've already achieved a level of mastery, and you don't want to lose what you've gained. Here, a mnemonic (like the peg-word system) might be quite helpful, allowing you to remember the full argument or derivation in its proper sequence.

MEANINGFUL CONNECTIONS

What sort of connections will help you to remember? The answer is that almost any connection can be helpful. Here's a silly—but useful—example. Students learning about the nervous system have to learn that *efferent* fibers carry information *away* from the brain and central nervous system, while *afferent* fibers carry information *inward*. How to keep these terms straight? It may be helpful to notice that efferent fibers carry information *exiting* the nervous system, while afferent fibers provide information *arriving* in the nervous system. And, as a bonus, the same connections will help you remember that you can have an *effect* on the world (an influence outward, from you), but that the world can also *affect* you (an influence coming inward, toward you).

Finally, let's emphasize that there's more to say about these issues. Our discussion here (like Chapter 6 itself) focuses on the "input" side of memory—getting information into storage, so that it's available for use later on. There are also steps you can take that will help you to locate information in the vast warehouse of your memory, and still other steps that you can take to avoid forgetting materials you've already learned. Discussion of those steps, however, depends on materials we'll cover in Chapters 7 and 8.

For more on this topic . . .

Brown, P. C., Roediger, H. L., & McDaniel, M. A. (2014). *Make it stick: The science of successful learning.* New York, NY: Belknap Press.

McCabe, J. A., Redick, T. S., & Engle, R. W. (2016). Brain-training pessimism, but applied memory optimism. *Psychological Science in the Public Interest, 17,* 187–191.

Putnam, A. L., Sungkhasettee, V. W., & Roediger, H. L. (2016). Optimizing learning in college: Tips from cognitive psychology. *Perspective on Psychological Science, 11*(5), 652–660.

chapter review

SUMMARY

● It is convenient to think of memorizing as having separate stages. First, one acquires new information (acquisition). Next, the information remains in storage until it is needed. Finally, the information is retrieved. However, this separation among the stages may be misleading. For example, in order to memorize new information, you form connections between this information and things you already know. In this way, the acquisition stage is intertwined with the retrieval of information already in storage.

● Information that is currently being considered is held in working memory; information that isn't currently active but is nonetheless in storage is in long-term memory. The distinction between these two forms of memory has traditionally been described in terms of the modal model and has been examined in many studies of the serial-position curve. The primacy portion of this curve reflects items that have had extra opportunity to reach long-term memory; the recency portion of this curve reflects the accurate retrieval of items currently in working memory.

● Psychologists' conception of working memory has evolved in important ways in the last few decades. Crucially, psychologists no longer think of working memory as a "storage container" or even as a "place." Instead, working memory is a status—and so we say items are "in working memory" when they're being actively thought about. This activity is governed by working memory's central executive. For mere storage, the executive often relies on low-level assistants, including the articulatory rehearsal loop and the visuospatial buffer, which work as mental scratch pads. The activity inherent in this overall system is reflected in the flexible way material can be chunked in working memory. The activity is also reflected in current measures of working memory, via operation span.

● Maintenance rehearsal serves to keep information in working memory and requires little effort, but it has little impact on subsequent recall. To maximize your chances of recall, elaborative rehearsal is needed, in which you seek connections within the material to be remembered or connections between the material to be remembered and things you already know.

● In many cases, elaborative processing takes the form of attention to meaning. This attention to meaning is called "deep processing," in contrast to attention to sounds or visual form, which is considered "shallow processing." Many studies have shown that deep processing leads to good memory performance later on, even if the deep processing occurred with no intention of memorizing the target material. In fact, the intention to learn has no direct effect on performance; what matters instead is how someone engages or thinks about the material to be remembered.

● Deep processing has beneficial effects by creating effective retrieval paths that can be used later on. Retrieval paths depend on connections linking one memory to another; each connection provides a path potentially leading to a target memory. Mnemonic strategies rely on the same mechanism and focus on the creation of specific memory connections, often tying the to-be-remembered material to a frame (e.g., a strongly structured poem).

● Perhaps the best way to form memory connections is to understand the material to be remembered. In understanding, you form many connections within the material to be remembered, as well as between this material and other knowledge. With all these retrieval paths, it becomes easy to locate this material in memory. Consistent with these suggestions, studies have shown a close correspondence between the ability to understand some material and the ability to recall that material later on. This pattern has been demonstrated with stories, visual patterns, number series, and many other stimuli.

KEY TERMS

acquisition (p. 197)
storage (p. 197)
retrieval (p. 197)
modal model (p. 198)
sensory memory (p. 198)
short-term memory (p. 198)
working memory (p. 199)
long-term memory (LTM) (p. 199)
free recall (p. 200)
primacy effect (p. 200)
recency effect (p. 200)
serial position (p. 201)
memory rehearsal (p. 202)
digit-span task (p. 206)
"7 plus-or-minus 2" (p. 206)
chunks (p. 206)
operation span (p. 208)

working-memory capacity (WMC) (p. 209)
working-memory system (p. 210)
articulatory rehearsal loop (p. 210)
subvocalization (p. 211)
phonological buffer (p. 211)
concurrent articulation (p. 212)
maintenance rehearsal (p. 215)
relational (or elaborative) rehearsal (p. 215)
intentional learning (p. 218)
incidental learning (p. 218)
shallow processing (p. 219)
deep processing (p. 219)
level of processing (p. 219)
retrieval paths (p. 224)
mnemonic strategies (p. 224)
peg-word systems (p. 226)

TEST YOURSELF AGAIN

1. Define the terms "acquisition," "storage" and "retrieval."

2. List the four ways in which (either in the modal model or in more recent views) working memory is different from long-term storage.

3. How is the primacy effect usually explained? How is the recency effect usually explained?

4. What does it mean to say that working memory holds seven (plus-or-minus two) "chunks"? What is a chunk?

5. What evidence suggests that operation span is a better measure of working memory than the more standard digit-span measure?

6. How does the rehearsal loop manage to hold on to information with only occasional involvement by the central executive?

7. What is the difference between maintenance rehearsal and relational (or elaborative) rehearsal?

8. What does it mean to say, "It doesn't matter if you *intend* to memorize; all that matters for memory is how exactly you engage the material you encounter"?

9. What is deep processing, and what impact does it have on memory?

10. What does it mean to say, "The creation of memory connections often occurs at the time of learning, but the main benefit of those connections comes later, at the time of memory retrieval"?

11. In what ways is deep and elaborate processing superior to deep processing on its own?

12. Why do mnemonics help memory? What are the limitations of mnemonic use?

13. What's the evidence that there's a clear linkage between how well you understand material when you first meet it, and how fully you'll recall that information later on?

14. Explain why memorizing involves a contribution from the memorizer, both in terms of what the memorizer *does* while memorizing, and also in terms of what the memorizer *knows* prior to the memorizing.

THINK ABOUT IT

1. Imagine that, based on what you've read in this chapter, you were asked to write a "training pamphlet" advising students how to study more effectively, so that they would remember what they studied more fully and more accurately. What would you write in the pamphlet?

e eBOOK DEMONSTRATIONS & ESSAYS

Go to http://digital.wwnorton.com/cognition7 for the online demonstrations and essays relevant to this chapter. These can be found in the ebook.

Online Demonstrations

- Demonstration 6.1: Primacy and Recency Effects
- Demonstration 6.2: Chunking
- Demonstration 6.3: The Effects of Unattended Exposure
- Demonstration 6.4: Depth of Processing
- Demonstration 6.5: The Articulatory Rehearsal Loop
- Demonstration 6.6: Sound-Based Coding

Online Applying Cognitive Psychology and the Law Essays

- Cognitive Psychology and the Law: The Video-Recorder View

ZAPS COGNITION LABS

Go to http://digital.wwnorton.com/cognition7 to experience interactive online psychology labs relevant to this chapter.

Answer: Actually, *none* of the images shown in Figure 6.10 depict the Apple logo. The bottom-middle image has the bite and the dimple in the right positions, but it shows the stem pointing the wrong way. The bottom-left image shows the stem and bite correctly, but it's missing the dimple!

chapter 7 | Interconnections between Acquisition and Retrieval

what if... The man known as H.M. was in his mid-20s when he had brain surgery intended to control his epilepsy. (We first met H.M. in Chapter 1; we also mentioned him briefly in Chapters 2 and 6.) This surgery did achieve its aim, and H.M.'s seizures were reduced. But the surgery had an unexpected and horrible consequence: H.M. lost the ability to form new memories. If asked what he did last week, or yesterday, or even an hour ago, H.M. had no idea. He couldn't recognize the faces of medical staff he'd seen day after day. He could read and reread a book yet never realize he'd read the same book many times before.

A related pattern of memory loss occurs among patients who suffer from Korsakoff's syndrome. We'll say more about this syndrome later in the chapter, but for now let's highlight a paradox. These patients, like H.M., are profoundly amnesic; they're completely unable to recall the events of their own lives. But these patients (again, like H.M.) have "unconscious" memories—memories that they don't know they have.

We reveal these unconscious memories if we test Korsakoff's patients *indirectly*. For example, if we ask them, "Which of these melodies did you hear an hour ago?" they'll answer randomly—confirming their amnesia. But if we ask them, "Which of these melodies do you prefer?" they're likely to choose the ones that, in fact, they heard an hour ago—indicating that they do somehow remember (and are influenced by) the earlier experience. If we ask them, "Have you ever seen a puzzle like this one before?" they'll say no. But if we ask them to solve the puzzle, their speed will be much faster the second time—even though they insist it's the *first* time they've seen the puzzle. Their speed will be even faster the third time they solve the puzzle and the fourth, although again and again they'll claim they're seeing the puzzle for the very first time. Likewise, they'll fail if we ask them, "I showed you some words a few minutes ago; can you tell me which of those words began 'CHE . . .'?" But, alternatively, we can ask them, "What's the first word that comes to mind that starts 'CHE . . .'?" With this question, they're likely to respond with the word they'd seen earlier—a word that they ostensibly could not remember.

- Learning does not simply place information in memory; instead, learning prepares you to retrieve the information in a particular way. As a result, learning that is good preparation for one sort of retrieval may be inadequate for other sorts of retrieval.

- In general, retrieval is more likely to succeed if your perspective is the same during learning and during retrieval, just as we would expect if learning establishes retrieval paths that help you later when you "travel" the same path in your effort toward locating the target material.

- Some experiences seem to produce unconscious memories. Consideration of these "implicit memory" effects will help us understand the various ways in which memory influences you and will also help us see where the feeling of familiarity comes from.

- Finally, an examination of amnesia confirms a central theme of the chapter—namely, that we cannot speak of "good" or "bad" memory in general. Instead, we need to evaluate memory by considering how, and for what purposes, the memory will be used.

These observations strongly suggest that there must be different types of memory—including a type that's massively disrupted in these amnesic patients, yet one that is apparently intact (also see **Figure 7.1**). But how many types of memory are there? How does each one function? Is it possible that processes or strategies that create one type of memory might be less useful for some other type? These questions will be central in this chapter.

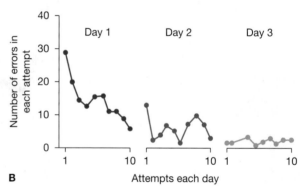

B

Attempts each day

FIGURE 7.1 MIRROR DRAWING

(Panel A) In a mirror-drawing task, participants must draw a precisely defined shape—they might be asked, for example, to trace a line between the inner and outer star. The trick, though, is that the participants can see the figure (and their own hand) only in the mirror. (Panel B) Performance is usually poor at first but gradually gets better. Remarkably, the same pattern of improvement is observed with amnesic patients, even though on each attempt they insist that they're performing this task for the very first time.

A

Learning as Preparation for Retrieval

Putting information into long-term memory helps you only if you can retrieve that information later on. Otherwise, it would be like putting money into a savings account without the option of ever making withdrawals, or writing books that could never be read. But let's emphasize that there are different ways to retrieve information from memory. You can try to *recall* the information ("What was the name of your tenth-grade homeroom teacher?") or to *recognize* it ("Was the name perhaps Miller?"). If you try to recall the information, a variety of cues may or may not be available (you might be told, as a hint, that the name began with an *M* or rhymes with "tiller").

In Chapter 6, we largely ignored these variations in retrieval. We talked as if material was well established in memory or was not, with little regard for how the material would be retrieved from memory. There's reason to believe, however, that we can't ignore these variations in retrieval, and in this chapter we'll examine the interaction between how a bit of information was learned and how it is retrieved later.

Crucial Role of Retrieval Paths

In Chapter 6, we argued that when you're learning, you're making connections between the newly acquired material and other information already in your memory. These connections make the new knowledge "findable" later on. Specifically, the connections serve as *retrieval paths*: When you want to locate information in memory, you travel on those paths, moving from one memory to the next until you reach the target material.

These claims have an important implication. To see this, bear in mind that retrieval paths—like any paths—have a starting point and an ending point: The path leads you from Point A to Point B. That's useful if you want to move from A to B, but what if you're trying to reach B from somewhere else? What if you're trying to reach Point B, but at the moment you happen to be nowhere close to Point A? In that case, the path linking A and B may not help you.

As an analogy, imagine that you're trying to reach Chicago from somewhere to the west. For this purpose, what you need is some highway coming in from the west. It won't help that you've constructed a wonderful road coming into Chicago from the *east*. That road might be valuable in other circumstances, but it's not the path you need to get from where you are right now to where you're heading.

Do retrieval paths in memory work the same way? If so, we might find cases in which your learning is excellent preparation for one sort of retrieval but useless for other types of retrieval—as if you've built a road coming in from one direction but now need a road from another direction. Do the research data show this pattern?

Context-Dependent Learning

Consider classic studies on **context-dependent learning** (Eich, 1980; Overton, 1985). In one such study, Godden and Baddeley (1975) asked scuba divers to learn various materials. Some of the divers learned the material while sitting on dry land; others learned it while underwater, hearing the material via a special communication set. Within each group, half of the divers were then tested while above water, and half were tested below (see **Figure 7.2**).

Underwater, the world has a different look, feel, and sound, and this context could easily influence what thoughts come to mind for the divers in the study. Imagine, for example, that a diver is feeling cold while underwater. This context will probably lead him to think "cold-related" thoughts, so those thoughts will be in his mind during the learning episode. In this situation, the diver is likely to form memory connections between these thoughts and the materials he's trying to learn.

Let's now imagine that this diver is back underwater at the time of the memory test. Most likely he'll again feel cold, which may once more lead him to "cold-related" thoughts. These thoughts, in turn, are now connected (we've proposed) to the target materials, and that gives us what we want: The cold triggers certain thoughts, and because of the connections formed during learning, those thoughts can trigger the target memories.

Of course, if the diver is tested for the same memory materials *on land*, he might have other links, other memory connections, that will lead to the target memories. Even so, on land the diver will be at a disadvantage because the "cold-related" thoughts aren't triggered—so there will be no benefit from the memory connections that are now in place, linking those thoughts to the sought-after memories.

FIGURE 7.2   THE DESIGN OF A CONTEXT-DEPENDENT LEARNING EXPERIMENT

Half of the participants (deep-sea divers) learned the test material while underwater; half learned while on land. Then, within each group, half were tested while underwater; half were tested on land. We expect a retrieval advantage if the learning and test circumstances match. Therefore, we expect better performance in the top left and bottom right cells.

		Test while	
		On land	**Underwater**
Learn while	**On land**	Learning and test circumstances match	*CHANGE* of circumstances between learning and test
	Underwater	*CHANGE* of circumstances between learning and test	Learning and test circumstances match

By this logic, we should expect that divers who learn material while underwater will remember the material best if they're again underwater at the time of the test. This setting will enable them to use the connections they established earlier. In terms of our previous analogy, they've built certain highways, and we've put the divers into a situation in which they can use what they've built. And the opposite is true for divers who learned while on land; they should do best if tested on land. And that is exactly what the data show (see **Figure 7.3**).

Similar results have been obtained in other studies, including those designed to mimic the learning situation of a college student. In one experiment, research participants read a two-page article similar to the sorts of readings they might encounter in their college courses. Half the participants read the article in a quiet setting; half read it in noisy circumstances. When later given a short-answer test, those who read the article in quiet did best if tested in quiet—67% correct answers, compared to 54% correct if tested in a noisy environment. Those who read the article in a noisy environment did better if tested in a noisy environment—62% correct, compared to 46%. (See Grant et al., 1998; also see Balch, Bowman, & Mohler, 1992; Cann & Ross, 1989; Schab, 1990; Smith, 1985; Smith & Vela, 2001.)

In another study, Smith, Glenberg, and Bjork (1978) reported the same pattern if learning and testing took place in different *rooms*—with the rooms varying in appearance, sounds, and scent. In this study, though, there was an important twist: In one version of the procedure, the participants learned materials in one room and were tested in a different room. Just before testing, however, the participants were urged to think about the room in which they had learned—what it looked like and how it made them feel. When tested, these participants performed as well as those for whom there was no room change (Smith, 1979). What matters, therefore, is not the *physical* context

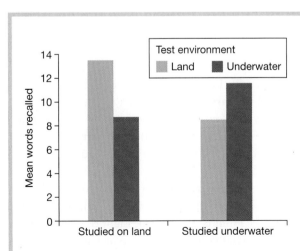

FIGURE 7.3 CONTEXT-DEPENDENT LEARNING

Scuba divers learned materials either while on land or while underwater. Then, they were tested while on land or underwater. Performance was best if the divers' circumstances at the time of test were matched to those in place during learning.   (AFTER GODDEN & BADDELEY, 1975)

TEST YOURSELF

1. What does context-dependent learning tell us about the nature of retrieval paths?

2. In what ways is a retrieval path like an "ordinary" path (e.g., a path or highway leading to a particular city)?

but the *psychological* context—a result that's consistent with our account of this effect. As a result, you can get the benefits of context-dependent learning through a strategy of **context reinstatement**—re-creating the thoughts and feelings of the learning episode even if you're in a very different place at the time of recall. That's because what matters for memory retrieval is the mental context, not the physical environment itself.

Encoding Specificity

The results we've been describing also illuminate a further point: what it is that's stored in memory. Let's go back to the scuba-diving experiment. The divers in this study didn't just remember the words they'd learned; apparently, they also remembered something about the context in which the learning took place. Otherwise, the data in Figure 7.3 (and related findings) make no sense: If the context left no trace in memory, there'd be no way for a *return* to the context to influence the divers later.

Here's one way to think about this point, still relying on our analogy. Your memory contains both the information you were focusing on during learning, *and* the highways you've now built, leading toward that information. These highways—the memory connections—can of course influence your search for the target information; that's what we've been emphasizing so far. But the connections can do more: They can also change the *meaning* of what is remembered, because in many settings "memory plus *this* set of connections" has a different meaning from "memory plus *that* set of connections." This change in meaning, in turn, can have profound consequences for how you remember the past.

In one of the early experiments exploring this point, participants read target words (e.g., "piano") in one of two contexts: "The man lifted the piano" or "The man tuned the piano." In each case, the sentence led the participants to think about the target word in a particular way, and it was this thought that was encoded into memory. In other words, what was placed in memory wasn't just the word "piano." Instead, what was recorded in memory was the idea of "piano as something heavy" or "piano as musical instrument."

This difference in memory content became clear when participants were later asked to recall the target words. If they had earlier seen the "lifted" sentence, they were likely to recall the target word if given the cue "something heavy." The hint "something with a nice sound" was much less effective. But if participants had seen the "tuned" sentence, the result reversed: Now, the "nice sound" hint was effective, but the "heavy" hint wasn't (Barclay, Bransford, Franks, McCarrell, & Nitsch, 1974). In both cases, the cue was effective only if it was congruent with what was stored in memory.

Other experiments show a similar pattern, traditionally called **encoding specificity** (Tulving, 1983; also see Hunt & Ellis, 1974; Light & Carter-Sobell, 1970). This label reminds us that what you encode (i.e., place into memory) is indeed specific—not just the physical stimulus as you encountered it, but the stimulus together with its context. Then, if you later encounter the stimulus *in some other context*, you ask yourself, "Does this match anything I learned previously?" and you correctly answer no. And we emphasize that this "no" response is indeed correct. It's as if you had learned the word "other" and were later asked whether you'd been shown the word "the." In fact, "the" does appear as part of "other"—because the letters *t h e* do appear within "other." But it's the whole that people learn, not the parts. Therefore, if you've seen "other," it makes sense to deny that you've seen "the"—or, for that matter, "he" or "her"—even though all these letter combinations are contained within "other."

Learning a list of words works in the same way. The word "piano" was contained in what the research participants learned, just as "the" is contained in "other." What was learned, however, wasn't just this word. Instead, what was learned was the broader, integrated experience: the word as the perceiver understood it. Therefore, "piano as musical instrument" *isn't* what participants learned if they saw the "lifted" sentence, so they were correct in asserting that this item wasn't on the earlier list (also see **Figure 7.4**).

TEST YOURSELF

3. What is encoding specificity? How is it demonstrated?

FIGURE 7.4
REMEMBERING
"RE-CREATES" AN
EARLIER EXPERIENCE

The text argues that what goes into your memory is a record of the material you've encountered *and also* a record of the connections you established during learning. On this basis, it makes sense that the brain areas activated when you're remembering a target overlap considerably with the brain areas that were activated when you first encountered the target. Here, the top panels show brain activation while viewing one picture (A) or another picture (C) or while hearing a particular sound (E). The bottom panels show brain activation while *remembering* the same targets. (AFTER WHEELER, PETERSON, & BUCKNER, 2000)

The Memory Network

In Chapter 6, we introduced the idea that memory acquisition—and, more broadly, *learning*—involves the creation (or strengthening) of memory connections. In this chapter, we've returned to the idea of memory connections, building on the idea that these connections serve as retrieval paths guiding you toward the information you seek. But what are these connections? How do they work? And who (or what?) is traveling on these "paths"?

According to many theorists, memory is best thought of as a vast *network* of ideas. In later chapters, we'll consider how exactly these ideas are represented (as pictures? as words? in some more abstract format?). For now, let's just think of these representations as **nodes** within the network, just like the knots in a fisherman's net. (In fact, the word "node" is derived from the Latin word for knot, *nodus*.) These nodes are tied to each other via connections we'll call **associations** or **associative links**. Some people find it helpful to think of the nodes as being like light bulbs that can be turned on by incoming electricity, and to imagine the associative links as wires that carry the electricity.

Spreading Activation

Theorists speak of a node becoming *activated* when it has received a strong enough input signal. Then, once a node has been activated, it can activate other nodes: Energy will spread out from the just-activated node via its associations, and this will activate the nodes connected to the just-activated node.

To put all of this more precisely, nodes receive activation from their neighbors, and as more and more activation arrives at a particular node, the **activation level** for that node increases. Eventually, the activation level will reach the node's **response threshold**. Once this happens, we say that the node *fires*. This firing has several effects, including the fact that the node will now itself be a source of activation, sending energy to its neighbors and activating them. In addition, firing of the node will draw attention to that node; this is what it means to "find" a node within the network.

Activation levels below the response threshold, so-called **subthreshold activation**, also play an important role. Activation is assumed to accumulate, so that two subthreshold inputs may add together, in a process of **summation**, and bring the node to threshold. Likewise, if a node has been partially activated recently, it is in effect already "warmed up," so that even a weak input will now be sufficient to bring it to threshold.

These claims mesh well with points we raised in Chapter 2, when we considered how neurons communicate with one another. Neurons receive activation from other neurons; once a neuron reaches its threshold, it fires, sending activation to other neurons. All of this is precisely parallel to the suggestions we're describing here.

Our current discussion also parallels claims offered in Chapter 4, when we described how a network of detectors might function in object recognition. In other words, the network linking *memories* to each other will resemble the networks we've described linking *detectors* to each other (e.g., Figures 4.9 and 4.10). Detectors, like memory nodes, receive their activation from other detectors; they can accumulate activation from different inputs, and once activated to threshold levels, they fire.

Returning to long-term storage, however, the key idea is that activation travels from node to node via associative links. As each node becomes activated and fires, it serves as a source for further activation, spreading onward through the network. This process, known as **spreading activation**, enables us to deal with a key question: How does one navigate through the maze of associations? If you start a search at one node, how do you decide where to go from there? The answer is that in most cases you don't "choose" at all. Instead, activation spreads out from its starting point in all directions simultaneously, flowing through whatever connections are in place.

Retrieval Cues

This sketch of the memory network leaves a great deal unspecified, but even so it allows us to explain some well-established results. For example, why do hints help you to remember? Why, for example, do you draw a blank if asked, "What's the capital of South Dakota?" but then remember if given the cue "Is it perhaps a man's name?" Here's one likely explanation. Mention of South Dakota will activate nodes in memory that represent your knowledge about this state. Activation will then spread outward from these nodes, eventually reaching nodes that represent the capital city's name. It's possible, though, that there's only a weak connection between the SOUTH DAKOTA nodes and the nodes representing PIERRE. Maybe you're not very familiar with South Dakota, or maybe you haven't thought about this state's capital for some time. In either case, this weak connection will do a poor job of carrying the activation, with the result that only a trickle of activation will flow into the PIERRE nodes, and so these nodes won't reach threshold and won't be "found."

Things will go differently, though, if a hint is available. If you're told, "South Dakota's capital is also a man's name," this will activate the MAN'S NAME node. As a result, activation will spread out from this source at the same time that activation is spreading out from the SOUTH DAKOTA nodes. Therefore, the nodes for PIERRE will now receive activation from two sources simultaneously, and this will probably be enough to lift the nodes' activation

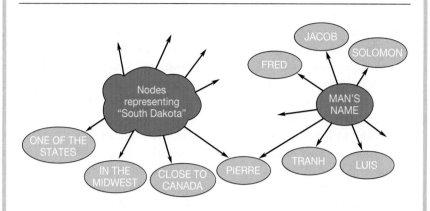

FIGURE 7.5   ACTIVATION OF A NODE FROM TWO SOURCES

A participant is asked, "What is the capital of South Dakota?" This activates the SOUTH DAKOTA nodes, and activation spreads from there to all of the associated nodes. However, it's possible that the connection between SOUTH DAKOTA and PIERRE is weak, so PIERRE may not receive enough activation to reach threshold. Things will go differently, though, if the participant is also given the hint "South Dakota's capital is also a man's name." Now, the PIERRE node will receive activation from two sources: the SOUTH DAKOTA nodes and the MAN'S NAME node. With this double input, it's more likely that the PIERRE node will reach threshold. This is why the hint ("man's name") makes the memory search easier.

to threshold levels. In this way, question-plus-hint accomplishes more than the question by itself (see **Figure 7.5**).

Semantic Priming

The explanation we've just offered rests on a key assumption—namely, the *summation of subthreshold activation*. In other words, we relied on the idea that the insufficient activation received from one source can add to the insufficient activation received from another source. Either source of activation on its own wouldn't be enough, but the two can combine to activate the target nodes.

Can we document this summation more directly? In a **lexical-decision task**, research participants are shown a series of letter sequences on a computer screen. Some of the sequences spell words; other sequences aren't words (e.g., "blar, plome"). The participants' task is to hit a "yes" button if the sequence spells a word and a "no" button otherwise. Presumably, they perform this task by "looking up" these letter strings in their "mental dictionary," and they base their response on whether or not they find the string in the dictionary. We can therefore use the participants' speed of response in this task as an index of how quickly they can locate the word in their memories.

In a series of classic studies, Meyer and Schvaneveldt (1971; Meyer, Schvaneveldt, & Ruddy, 1974) presented participants with *pairs* of letter strings, and participants had to respond "yes" if both strings were words and "no" otherwise. For example, participants would say "yes" in response to "chair, bread" but "no" in response to "house, fime." Also, if both strings were words, sometimes the words were semantically related in an obvious way (e.g., "nurse, doctor") and sometimes they weren't ("cake, shoe"). Of interest was how this relationship between the words would influence performance.

Consider a trial in which participants see a related pair, like "bread, butter." To choose a response, they first need to "look up" the word "bread" in memory. This means they'll search for, and presumably activate, the relevant node, and in this way they'll decide that, yes, this string is a legitimate word. Then, they're ready for the second word. But in this sequence, the node for BREAD (the first word in the pair) has just been activated. This will, we've hypothesized, trigger a spread of activation outward from this node, bringing activation to other, nearby nodes. These nearby nodes will surely include BUTTER, since the association between "bread" and "butter" is a strong one. Therefore, once the BREAD node (from the first word) is activated, some activation should also spread to the BUTTER node.

From this base, think about what happens when a participant turns her attention to the second word in the pair. To select a response, she must locate "butter" in memory. If she finds this word (i.e., finds the relevant node), then she knows that this string, too, is a word, and she can hit the "yes" button. But the process of activating the BUTTER node has already begun, thanks to the (subthreshold) activation this node just received from BREAD. This should accelerate the process of bringing this node to threshold (since it's already partway there), and so it will require less time to activate. As a result, we expect quicker responses to "butter" in this context, compared to a context in which "butter" was preceded by some unrelated word.

Our prediction, therefore, is that trials with related words will produce **semantic priming**. The term "priming" indicates that a specific prior event (in this case, presentation of the first word in the pair) will produce a state of readiness (and, therefore, faster responding) later on. There are various forms of priming (in Chapter 4, we discussed *repetition* priming). In the procedure we're considering here, the priming results from the fact that the two words in the pair are related in meaning — therefore, this is *semantic* priming.

The results confirm these predictions. Participants' lexical-decision responses were faster by almost 100 ms if the stimulus words were related

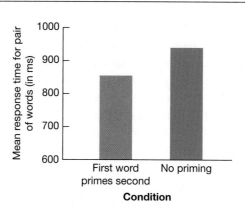

FIGURE 7.6 SEMANTIC PRIMING

Mean response time for pair of words (in ms)

1000
900
800
700
600

First word primes second   No priming

Condition

Participants were given a lexical-decision task involving pairs of words. In some pairs, the words were semantically related (and so the first word in the pair primed the second); in other pairs, the words were unrelated (and so there was no priming). Responses to the second word were reliably faster if the word had been primed—providing clear evidence of the importance of subthreshold activation.

(AFTER MEYER & SCHVANEVELDT, 1971)

(see **Figure 7.6**), just as we would expect on the model we're developing. (For other relevant studies, including some alternative conceptions of priming, see Hutchison, 2003; Lucas, 2000.)

Before moving on, though, we should mention that this process of spreading activation—with one node activating nearby nodes—is not the whole story for memory search. As one complication, people have some degree of control over the *starting points* for their memory searches, relying on the processes of reasoning (Chapter 12) and the mechanisms of executive control (Chapters 5 and 6). In addition, evidence suggests that once the spreading activation has begun, people have the option of "shutting down" some of this spread if they're convinced that the wrong nodes are being activated (e.g., Anderson & Bell, 2001; Johnson & Anderson, 2004). Even so, spreading activation is a crucial mechanism. It plays a central role in retrieval, and it helps us understand why memory connections are so important and so helpful.

Different Forms of Memory Testing

Let's pause to review. In Chapter 6, we argued that learning involves the creation or strengthening of connections. This is why memory is promoted by understanding (because understanding consists, in large part, of seeing

TEST YOURSELF

4. What is subthreshold activation of a memory node? What role does subthreshold activation play in explaining why retrieval hints are often helpful?

5. How does semantic priming illustrate the effectiveness of subthreshold activation?

how new material is connected to other things you know). We also proposed that these connections later serve as retrieval paths, guiding your search through the vast warehouse that is memory. In this chapter, we've explored an important implication of this idea: that (like all paths) the paths through memory have both a starting point and an end point. Therefore, retrieval paths will be helpful only if you're at the appropriate starting point; this, we've proposed, is the basis for the advantage produced by *context reinstatement*. And, finally, we've now started to lay out what these paths really are: connections that carry activation from one memory to another.

This theoretical base also helps us with another issue: the impact of different forms of memory testing. Both in the laboratory and in day-to-day life, you often try to **recall** information from memory. This means that you're presented with a retrieval cue that broadly identifies the information you seek, and then you need to come up with the information on your own: "What was the name of that great restaurant your parents took us to?"; "Can you remember the words to that song?"; "Where were you last Saturday?"

In other circumstances, you draw information from your memory via **recognition**. This term refers to cases in which information is presented to you, and you must decide whether it's the sought-after information: "Is this the man who robbed you?"; "I'm sure I'll recognize the street when we get there"; "If you let me taste that wine, I'll tell you if it's the same one we had last time."

These two modes of retrieval — recall and recognition — are fundamentally different from each other. Recall requires memory search because you have to come up with the sought-after item on your own; you need to locate that item within memory. As a result, recall depends heavily on the memory connections we've been emphasizing so far. Recognition, in contrast, often depends on a sense of familiarity. Imagine, for example, that you're taking a recognition test, and the fifth word on the test is "butler." In response to this word, you might find yourself thinking, "I don't recall seeing this word on the list, but this word feels really familiar, so I guess I must have seen it recently. Therefore, it must have been on the list." In this case, you don't have **source memory**; that is, you don't have any recollection of the *source* of your current knowledge. But you do have a strong sense of **familiarity**, and you're willing to make an inference about where that familiarity came from. In other words, you attribute the familiarity to the earlier encounter, and thanks to this **attribution** you'll probably respond "yes" on the recognition test.

Familiarity and Source Memory

We need to be clear about our terms here, because source memory is actually a type of recall. Let's say, for example, that you hear a song on the radio and say, "I know I've heard this song before because it feels familiar *and*

I remember where I heard it." In this setting, you're able to remember the source of your familiarity, and that means you're recalling when and where you encountered the song. On this basis, we don't need any new theory to talk about source memory, because we can use the same theory that we'd use for other forms of recall. Hearing the song was the retrieval cue that launched a search through memory, a search that allowed you to identify the setting in which you last encountered the song. That search (like any search) was dependent on memory connections, and would be explained by the spreading activation process that we've already described.

But what about familiarity? What does this sort of remembering involve? As a start, let's be clear that familiarity is truly distinct from source memory. This is evident in the fact that the two types of memory are independent of each other—it's possible for an event to be familiar without any source memory, and it's possible for you to have source memory without any familiarity. This independence is evident when you're watching a movie and realize that one of the actors is familiar, but (sometimes with considerable frustration, and despite a lot of effort) you can't recall where you've seen that actor before. Or you're walking down the street, see a familiar face, and find yourself asking, "Where do I know that woman from? Does she work at the grocery store I shop in? Is she the driver of the bus I often take?" You're at a loss to answer these questions; all you know is that the face is familiar.

In cases like these, you can't "place" the memory; you can't identify the episode in which the face was last encountered. But you're certain the face is familiar, even though you don't know why—a clear example of familiarity without source memory.

The inverse case is less common, but it too can be demonstrated. For example, in Chapter 2 we discussed Capgras syndrome. Someone with this syndrome might have detailed, accurate memories of what friends and family members look like, and probably remembers where and when these other people were last encountered. Even so, when these other people are in view they seem hauntingly unfamiliar. In this setting, there is source memory without familiarity. (For further evidence—and a patient who, after surgery, has intact source memory but disrupted familiarity—see Bowles et al., 2007; also see Yonelinas & Jacoby, 2012.)

We can also document the difference between source memory and familiarity in another way. In many studies, (neurologically intact) participants have been asked, during a recognition test, to make a **"remember/know" distinction.** This involves pressing one button (to indicate "remember") if they actually recall the episode of encountering a particular item, and pressing a different button ("know") if they don't recall the encounter but just have a broad feeling that the item must have been on the earlier list. With one response, participants are indicating that they have a source memory; with the other, they're indicating an *absence* of source memory. Basically, a participant using the "know" response is saying, "This item seems familiar,

"FAMILIAR . . . BUT *WHERE DO I KNOW HIM FROM?!?*"

The photos here show successful TV or film actors. The odds are good that for some of them you'll immediately know their faces as familiar but won't be sure why. You know you've seen these actors in some movie or show, but which one? (We provide the actors' names at the chapter's end.)

so I know it was on the earlier list even though I don't remember the experience of seeing it" (Gardiner, 1988; Hicks & Marsh, 1999; Jacoby, Jones, & Dolan, 1998).

Researchers can use fMRI scans to monitor participants' brain activity while they're taking these memory tests, and the scans indicate that "remember" and "know" judgments depend on different brain areas. The scans show heightened activity in the hippocampus when participants indicate that they "remember" a particular test item, suggesting that this brain structure is crucial for source memory. In contrast, "know" responses are associated with activity in a different area — the anterior parahippocampus, with the implication that this brain site is crucial for familiarity. (See Aggleton & Brown, 2006; Diana, Yonelinas, & Ranganath, 2007; Dobbins, Foley, Wagner, & Schacter, 2002; Eldridge, Knowlton, Furmanski, Bookheimer, & Engel, 2000; Montaldi, Spencer, Roberts, & Mayes, 2006; Wagner, Shannon, Kahn, & Buckner, 2005. Also see Rugg & Curran, 2007; Rugg & Yonelinas, 2003.)

Familiarity and source memory can also be distinguished during learning. If certain brain areas (e.g., the rhinal cortex) are especially active during learning, then the stimulus is likely to seem familiar later on. In contrast, if other brain areas (e.g., the hippocampal region) are particularly active during learning, there's a high probability that the person will indicate source memory for that stimulus when tested later (see **Figure 7.7**). (See, e.g., Davachi & Dobbins, 2008; Davachi, Mitchell, & Wagner, 2003; Ranganath et al., 2003.)

We still need to ask, though, what's going on in these various brain areas to create the relevant memories. Activity in the hippocampus is probably helping to create the memory connections we've been discussing all along, and it's these connections, we've suggested, that promote source memory. But

TEST YOURSELF

6. Define "recognition" and "recall."
7. What evidence indicates that source memory and familiarity are distinct from each other?

FIGURE 7.7 FAMILIARITY VERSUS SOURCE MEMORY

Subsequent familiarity effects

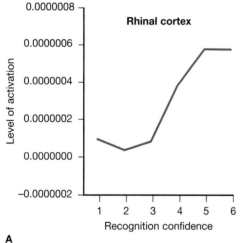

If the rhinal cortex was especially activated during encoding, then the stimulus was likely to seem familiar when viewed later on.

Subsequent recollection effects

If the hippocampus was especially activated during encoding, then later on the participant was likely to recollect having seen that stimulus.

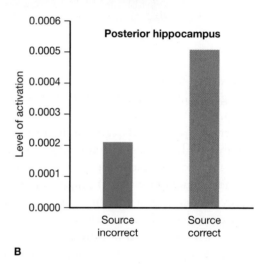

A

B

In this study, researchers tracked participants' brain activity during encoding and then analyzed the data according to what happened later, when the time came for retrieval.   (AFTER RANGANATH ET AL., 2003)

what about familiarity? What "record" does it leave in memory? The answer to this question leads us to a very different sort of memory.

Implicit Memory

How can we find out if someone remembers a previous event? The obvious path is to ask her—"How did the job interview go?"; "Have you ever seen *Casablanca*?"; "Is this the book you told me about?" But at the start of this chapter, we talked about a different approach: We can expose someone to an event, and then later re-expose her to the same event and assess whether her response on the second encounter is different from the first. Specifically, we can ask whether the first encounter somehow *primed* the person—got her ready—for the second exposure. If so, it would seem that the person must retain some record of the first encounter—she must have some sort of memory.

Memory without Awareness

In a number of studies, participants have been asked to read through a list of words, with no indication that their memories would be tested later on. (They might be told that they're merely checking the list for spelling errors.) Then, sometime later, the participants are given a lexical-decision task: They are shown a series of letter strings and, for each, must indicate (by pressing one button or another) whether the string is a word or not. Some of the letter strings in the lexical-decision task are duplicates of the words seen in the first part of the experiment (i.e., they were on the list participants had checked for spelling), enabling us to ask whether the first exposure somehow primed the participants for the second encounter.

In these experiments, lexical decisions are quicker if the person has recently seen the test word; that is, lexical decision shows the pattern that in Chapter 4 we called "repetition priming" (e.g., Oliphant, 1983). Remarkably, this priming is observed even when participants have no recollection for having encountered the stimulus words before. To demonstrate this, we can show participants a list of words and then test them in two different ways. One test assesses memory directly, using a standard recognition procedure: "Which of these words were on the list I showed you earlier?" The other test is indirect and relies on lexical decision: "Which of these letter strings form real words?" In this procedure, the two tests will yield different results. At a sufficient delay, the direct memory test is likely to show that the participants have completely forgotten the words presented earlier; their recognition performance is essentially random. According to the lexical-decision results, however, the participants still remember the words—and so they show a strong priming effect. In this situation, then, participants are influenced by a specific past experience that they seem (consciously) not to remember at all—a pattern that some researchers refer to as "memory without awareness."

A different example draws on a task called **word-stem completion**. In this task, participants are given three or four letters and must produce a word with this beginning. If, for example, they're given *cla-*, then "clam" or "clatter" would be acceptable responses, and the question of interest for us is which of these responses the participants produce. It turns out that people are more likely to offer a specific word if they've encountered it recently; once again, this priming effect is observed even if participants, when tested directly, show no conscious memory of their recent encounter with that word (Graf, Mandler, & Haden, 1982).

Results like these lead psychologists to distinguish two types of memory. **Explicit memories** are those usually revealed by **direct memory testing**—testing that urges participants to remember the past. Recall is a direct memory test; so is a standard recognition test. **Implicit memories**, however, are typically revealed by **indirect memory testing** and are often manifested as priming effects. In this form of testing, participants' current behavior is demonstrably influenced by a prior event, but they may be unaware of this. Lexical decision, word-stem completion, and many other tasks provide indirect means of assessing memory. (See, for example, Mulligan & Besken, 2013; for a different perspective on these data, though, see Cabeza & Moscovitch, 2012.)

How exactly is implicit memory different from explicit memory? We'll say more about this question before we're done; but first we need to say more about how implicit memory *feels* from the rememberer's point of view. This will lead us back into our discussion of familiarity and source memory.

False Fame

In a classic research study, Jacoby, Kelley, Brown, and Jasechko (1989) presented participants with a list of names to read out loud. The participants were told nothing about a memory test; they thought the experiment was concerned with how they pronounced the names. Some time later, during the second step of the procedure, the participants were shown a new list of names and asked to rate each person on this list according to how famous each one was. The list included some real, very famous people; some real but not-so-famous people; and some fictitious names that the experimenters had invented. Crucially, the fictitious names were of two types: Some had occurred on the prior ("pronunciation") list, and some were simply new names. A comparison between those two types will indicate how the prior familiarization (during the pronunciation task) influenced the participants' judgments of fame.

For some participants, the "famous" list was presented right after the "pronunciation" list; for other participants, there was a 24-hour delay between these two steps. To see how this delay matters, imagine that you're a participant in the immediate-testing condition: When you see one of the fictitious-but-familiar names, you might decide, "This name sounds familiar, but that's because I just saw it on the previous list." In this situation, you have a feeling that the (familiar) name is distinctive, but you also know *why* it's distinctive—because you remember your earlier encounter with the name. In other words, you have both a sense of familiarity *and* a source memory, so there's nothing here to persuade you that the name belongs to someone famous, and you respond accordingly. But now imagine that you're a participant in the other condition, with the 24-hour delay. Because of the delay, you may not recall the earlier episode of seeing the name in the pronunciation task. But the broad sense of familiarity remains anyway, so in this setting you might say, "This name rings a bell, and I have no idea why. I guess this must be a famous person." And this is, in fact, the pattern of the data: When the two lists are presented one day apart, participants are likely to rate the made-up names as being famous.

Apparently, the participants in this study noted (correctly) that some of the names did "ring a bell" and so did trigger a certain feeling of familiarity.

The false judgments of fame, however, come from the way the participants *interpreted* this feeling and what conclusions they drew from it. Basically, participants in the 24-hour-delay condition forgot the real source of the familiarity (appearance on a recently viewed list) and instead filled in a bogus source ("Maybe I saw this person in a movie?"). And it's easy to see why they made this misattribution. After all, the experiment was described to them as being about fame, and other names on the list were actually those of famous people. From the participants' point of view, therefore, it was reasonable to infer in this setting that any name that "rings a bell" belongs to a famous person.

We need to be clear, though, that this misattribution is possible only because the feeling of familiarity produced by these names was relatively vague, and therefore open to interpretation. The suggestion, then, is that implicit memories may leave people with only a broad sense that a stimulus is somehow distinctive—that it "rings a bell" or "strikes a chord." What happens after this depends on how they interpret that feeling.

Implicit Memory and the "Illusion of Truth"

How broad is this potential for *mis*interpreting an implicit memory? Participants in one study heard a series of statements and had to judge how interesting each statement was (Begg, Anas, & Farinacci, 1992). As an example, one sentence was "The average person in Switzerland eats about 25 pounds of cheese each year." (This is false; the average in 1992, when the experiment was done, was closer to 18 pounds.) Another was "Henry Ford forgot to put a reverse gear in his first automobile." (This is true.)

After hearing these sentences, the participants were presented with some more sentences, but now they had to judge the credibility of these sentences, rating them on a scale from *certainly true* to *certainly false*. However, some of the sentences in this "truth test" were repeats from the earlier presentation, and the question of interest is how sentence credibility is influenced by sentence familiarity.

The result was a propagandist's dream: Sentences heard before were more likely to be accepted as true; that is, familiarity increased credibility. (See Begg, Armour, & Kerr, 1985; Brown & Halliday, 1990; Fiedler, Walther, Armbruster, Fay, & Naumann, 1996; Moons, Mackie, & Garcia-Marques, 2009; Unkelbach, 2007.) This effect was found even when participants were warned in advance not to believe the sentences in the first list. In one procedure, participants were told that half of the statements had been made by men and half by women. The women's statements, they were told, were always true; the men's, always false. (Half the participants were told the reverse.) Then, participants rated how interesting the sentences were, with each sentence attributed to either a man or a woman: for example, "Frank Foster says that house mice can run an average of 4 miles per hour" or "Gail Logan says that crocodiles sleep with their eyes open." Later, participants were presented with more sentences and had to judge their truth, with these new sentences including the earlier assertions about mice, crocodiles, and so forth.

Let's focus on the sentences initially identified as being false—in our example, Frank's claim about mice. If someone explicitly remembers this sentence ("Oh yes—Frank said such and such"), then he should judge the assertion to be false ("After all, the experimenter said that the men's statements were all lies"). But what about someone who lacks this explicit memory? This person will have no conscious recall of the episode in which he last encountered this sentence (i.e., will have no source memory), and so he won't know whether the assertion came from a man or a woman. He therefore can't use the source as a basis for judging the truthfulness of the sentence. But he might still have an implicit memory for the sentence left over from the earlier exposure ("Gee, that statement rings a bell"), and this might increase his sense of the statement's credibility ("I'm sure I've heard that somewhere before; I guess it must be true"). This is exactly the pattern of the data: Statements plainly identified as false when they were first heard still created the so-called **illusion of truth**; that is, these statements were subsequently judged to be more credible than sentences never heard before.

The relevance of this result to the political arena or to advertising should be clear. A newspaper headline might inquire, "Is Mayor Wilson a crook?" Or the headline might declare, "Known criminal claims Wilson is a crook!" In either case, the assertion that Wilson is a crook would become familiar. The Begg et al. data indicate that this familiarity will, by itself, increase the likelihood that you'll later believe in Wilson's dishonesty. This will be true even if the paper merely raised the question; it will be true even if the allegation came from a disreputable source. Malicious innuendo does, in fact, produce nasty effects. (For related findings, see Ecker, Lewandowsky, Chang, & Pillai, 2014.)

Attributing Implicit Memory to the Wrong Source

Apparently, implicit memory can influence us (and, perhaps, *bias* us) in the political arena. Other evidence suggests that implicit memory can influence us in the marketplace—and can, for example, guide our choices when we're shopping (e.g., Northup & Mulligan, 2013, 2014). Yet another example involves the justice system, and it's an example with troubling implications. In an early study by Brown, Deffenbacher, and Sturgill (1977), research participants witnessed a staged crime. Two or three days later, they were shown "mug shots" of individuals who supposedly had participated in the crime. But as it turns out, the people in these photos were different from the actual "criminals"—no mug shots were shown for the truly "guilty" individuals. Finally, after four or five more days, the participants were shown a lineup and asked to select the individuals seen in Step 1—namely, the original crime (see **Figure 7.8**).

FIGURE 7.8 A PHOTO LINEUP

Middletown Police Department   Lineup ID: 24601   20 Mar 2009

1 _____ 2 _____ 3 _____

4 _____ 5 _____ 6 _____

FOR OFFICIAL USE ONLY

On TV, crime victims view a live lineup, but it's far more common in the United States for the victim (or witness) to see a "photo lineup" like this one. Unfortunately, victims sometimes pick the wrong person, and this error is more likely to occur if the suspect is familiar to the victim for some reason other than the crime. The error is unlikely, though, if the face is *very* familiar, because in that case the witness will have both a feeling of familiarity and an accurate source memory. ("Number Two looks familiar, but that's because I see him at the gym all the time.")

The data in this study show a pattern known as **source confusion**. The participants correctly realized that one of the faces in the lineup looked familiar, but they were confused about the source of the familiarity. They falsely believed they had seen the person's face in the original "crime," when, in truth, they'd seen that face only in a subsequent photograph. In fact, the likelihood of this error was quite high, with 29% of the participants (falsely) selecting from the lineup an individual they had seen only in the mug shots. (Also see Davis, Loftus, Vanous, & Cucciare, 2008; Kersten & Earles, 2017. For examples of similar errors that interfere with real-life criminal investigations, see Garrett, 2011. For a broader discussion of eyewitness errors, see Reisberg, 2014.)

TEST YOURSELF

8. What is the difference between implicit and explicit memory? Which of these is said to be "memory without awareness"?
9. What is the role of implicit memory in explaining the false fame effect?

In 1970, (former Beatle) George Harrison released the song "My Sweet Lord." It turned out that the song is virtually identical to one released years before that—"He's So Fine," by the Chiffons—and in 1976 Harrison was found guilty of copyright infringement. (You can find both recordings on YouTube, and you'll instantly see that they're essentially the same song.) In his conclusion to the court proceedings, the judge wrote, "Did Harrison deliberately use the music of 'He's So Fine'? I do not believe he did so deliberately. Nevertheless, it is clear that 'My Sweet Lord' is the very same song as 'He's So Fine.' . . . This is, under the law, infringement of copyright, and is no less so even though subconsciously accomplished" (*Bright Tunes Music Corp. v. Harrisongs Music, Ltd.*, 420 F. Supp. 177—Dist. Court, SD New York 1976).

How can we understand the judge's remarks? Can there be "subconscious" plagiarism? The answer is yes, and the pattern at issue is sometimes referred to as "cryptoplagiarism"—inadvertent copying that is entirely unwitting and uncontrollable, and usually copying that comes with the strong sense that you're the inventor of the idea, even though you've taken the idea from someone else.

In one early study, participants sat in groups and were asked to generate words in particular categories—for example, names of sports or musical instruments (Brown & Murphy, 1989; also Marsh, Ward, & Landau, 1999). Later, the same participants were asked to recall the words they (and not others in the group) had generated, and also to generate new entries in the same category. In this setting, participants often "borrowed" others' contributions—sometimes (mis)remembering others' words as though they had themselves produced them, sometimes offering words as "new"

when, in fact, they'd been mentioned by some one else in the initial session.

This pattern fits well with the chapter's discussion of implicit memory. The participants in this study (and others) have lost their explicit memory of the earlier episode in which they encountered someone else's ideas. Even so, an implicit memory remains and emerges as a priming effect. With certain words primed in memory, participants are more likely to produce those words when asked—with no realization that their production has been influenced by priming.

Likewise, imagine talking with a friend about your options for an upcoming writing assignment. Your friend suggests a topic, but after a moment's thought you reject the suggestion, convinced that the topic is too challenging. A few days later, though, you're again trying to choose a topic, and (thanks to the priming) your friend's suggestion comes to mind. As a result of the earlier conversation with your friend, you've had some "warm-up" in considering this topic, so your thinking now is a bit more fluent—and you decide that the topic isn't so challenging. As a result, you go forward with the topic. You may, however, have no explicit memory of the initial conversation with your friend—and you may not realize either that the idea "came to you" because of a priming effect *or* that the idea seemed workable because of the "warm-up" provided by the earlier conversation. The outcome: You'll present the idea as though it's entirely your own, giving your friend none of the credit she deserves.

We'll never know if this is what happened with George Harrison. Even so, the judge's conclusion in that case seems entirely plausible, and there's no question that inadvertent, unconscious plagiarism is a real phenomenon.

Theoretical Treatments of Implicit Memory

One message coming from these studies is that people are often better at remembering *that* something is familiar than they are at remembering *why* it is familiar. This explains why it's possible to have a sense of familiarity without source memory ("I've seen her somewhere before, but I can't figure out where!") and also why it's possible to be *correct* in judging familiarity but *mistaken* in judging source.

In addition, let's emphasize that in many of these studies participants are being influenced by memories they aren't aware of. In some cases, participants realize that a stimulus is somehow familiar, but they have no memory of the encounter that produced the familiarity. In other cases, they don't even have a sense of familiarity for the target stimulus; nonetheless, they're influenced by their previous encounter with the stimulus. For example, experiments show that participants often *prefer* a previously presented stimulus over a novel stimulus, even though they have no sense of familiarity with either stimulus. In such cases, people have no idea that their preference is being guided by memory (Murphy, 2001; also Montoy, Horton, Vevea, Citkowicz, & Lauber, 2017).

It does seem, then, that the phrase "memory without awareness" is appropriate, and it does make sense to describe these memories as *implicit* memories. But how can we explain this form of unconscious "remembering"?

Processing Fluency

Our discussion so far—here and in Chapters 4 and 5—has laid the foundation for a proposal about implicit memory. Let's build the argument in steps.

When a stimulus arrives in front of your eyes, it triggers certain detectors, and these trigger other detectors, and these still others, until you recognize the object. ("Oh, it's my stuffed bear, Blueberry.") We can think of this sequence as involving a "flow" of activation that moves from detector to detector. We could, if we wished, keep track of this flow and in this way identify the "path" that the activation traveled through the network. Let's refer to this path as a **processing pathway**—the sequence of detectors, and the connections *between* detectors, that the activation flows through in recognizing a specific stimulus.

In the same way, we've proposed in this chapter that *remembering* often involves the activation of a node, and this node triggers other, nearby, nodes so that they become activated; they trigger still other nodes, leading eventually to the information you seek in memory. So here, too, we can speak of a processing pathway—the sequence of nodes, and connections between nodes, that the activation flows through during memory retrieval.

We've also said the use of a processing pathway *strengthens* that pathway. This is because the baseline activation level of nodes or detectors increases if the nodes or detectors have been used frequently in the past, or if they've been used recently. Likewise, connections (between detectors or nodes) grow stronger with use. For example, by thinking about the link between, say, "Jacob" and "Boston," you can strengthen the connection between the corresponding nodes, and this will help you remember that your friend Jacob comes from Boston.

Now, let's put the pieces together. Use of a processing pathway strengthens the pathway. As a result, the pathway will be a bit more efficient, a bit faster, the next time you use it. Theorists describe this fact by saying that use of a pathway increases the pathway's **processing fluency**—that is, the speed and ease with which the pathway will carry activation.

In many cases, this is all the theory we need to explain implicit memory effects. Consider implicit memory's effect on lexical decision. In this procedure, you first are shown a list of words, including the word "bubble." Then, we ask you to do the lexical-decision task, and we find that you're faster for words (like "bubble") that had been included in the earlier list. This increase in speed provides evidence for implicit memory, and the explanation is straightforward. When we show you "bubble" early in the experiment, you read the word, and this involves activation flowing through the appropriate processing pathway for this word. This warms up the pathway, and as a result the path's functioning will be more fluent the next time you use it. Of course, when "bubble" shows up later as part of the lexical-decision task, it's handled by the same (now more fluent) pathway, and so the word is processed more rapidly—exactly the outcome that we're trying to explain.

For other implicit-memory effects, though, we need a further assumption—namely, that people are *sensitive* to the degree of processing fluency. That is, just as people can tell whether they've lifted a heavy carton or a lightweight one, or whether they've answered an easy question ("What's 2 + 2?") or a harder one ("What's 17 × 19?"), people also have a broad sense of when they have perceived easily and when they have perceived only by expending more effort. They likewise know when a sequence of thoughts was particularly fluent and when the sequence was labored.

This fluency, however, is perceived in an odd way. For example, when a stimulus is easy to perceive, you don't experience something like "That stimulus sure was easy to recognize!" Instead, you merely register a vague sense of specialness. You feel that the stimulus "rings a bell." No matter how it is described, though, this sense of specialness has a simple cause—namely, the detection of fluency, created by practice.

There's one complication, however. What makes a stimulus feel "special" may not be fluency itself. Instead, people seem sensitive to *changes* in fluency (e.g., they notice if it's a little harder to recognize a face this time than it was in the past). People also seem to notice *discrepancies* between how easy (or hard) it was to carry out some mental step and how easy (or hard) they expected it to be (Wanke & Hansen, 2015; Whittlesea, 2002). In other words, a stimulus is registered as distinctive, or "rings a bell," when people detect a change or a discrepancy between experience and expectations.

To see how this matters, imagine that a friend unexpectedly gets a haircut (or gets new eyeglasses, or adds or removes some facial hair). When you see your friend, you realize immediately that *something* has changed, but you're not sure what. You're likely to ask puzzled questions ("Are those new glasses?") and get a scornful answer. ("No, you've seen these glasses a hundred times over the last year.") Eventually your friend tells you what the change is—pointing out that you failed to notice that he'd shaved off his mustache (or some such).

What's going on here? You obviously can still recognize your friend, but your recognition is less fluent than in the past because of the change in your friend's appearance, and you notice this change—but then are at a loss to explain it (see **Figure 7.9**).

On all of these grounds, we need another step in our hypothesis, but it's a step we've already introduced: When a stimulus feels special (because of a change in fluency, or a discrepancy between the fluency expected and the fluency experienced), you often want to know why. Thus the vague feeling of specialness (again, produced by fluency) can trigger an attribution process, as you ask, "Why did that stimulus stand out?"

In many circumstances, you'll answer this question correctly, and so the specialness will be (accurately) interpreted as *familiarity* and attributed to the correct source. ("That woman seems distinctive, and I know why: It's the woman I saw yesterday in the dentist's office.") Often, you make this attribution because you have the relevant source memory—and this memory guides you in deciding why a stimulus (a face, a song, a smell) seems to stand out. In other cases, you make a reasonable inference, perhaps guided by the context. ("I don't remember where I heard this joke before, but it's the sort of joke that Conor is always telling, so I bet it's one of his and that's why the joke is familiar.") In other situations, though, things don't go so smoothly, and

FIGURE 7.9 CHANGES IN APPEARANCE

The text emphasizes our sensitivity to increases in fluency, but we can also detect decreases. In viewing a picture of a well-known actor, for example, you might notice immediately that something is new in his appearance, but you might be unsure about what exactly the change involves. In this setting, the change in appearance disrupts your well-practiced steps of perceiving for an otherwise familiar face, so the perception is *less* fluent than in the past. This lack of fluency is what gives you the "something is new" feeling. But then the attribution step fails: You can't identify what produced this feeling (so you end up offering various weak hypotheses, such as "Is that a new haircut?" when, in fact, it's the mustache and goatee that are new). This case provides the mirror image of the cases we've been considering, in which familiarity leads to an increase in fluency, so that something "rings a bell" but you can't say why. In the picture shown here, you probably recognize Denzel Washington, and you probably also realize that something is "off" in the picture. Can you figure out what it is? (We've actually made several changes to Denzel's appearance; can you spot them all?)

so—as we have seen—people sometimes misinterpret their own processing fluency, falling prey to the errors and illusions we have been discussing.

The Nature of Familiarity

All of these points provide us—at last—with a proposal for what "familiarity" is, and the proposal is surprisingly complex. You might think that familiarity is simply a feeling that's produced more or less directly when you encounter a stimulus you've met before. But the research findings described in the last few sections point toward a different proposal—namely, that "familiarity" is more like a *conclusion that you draw* rather than a *feeling triggered by a stimulus*. Specifically, the evidence suggests that a stimulus will seem familiar whenever the following list of requirements is met: First, you have encountered the stimulus before. Second, because of that prior encounter (and the "practice" it provided), your processing of that stimulus is now faster and more efficient; there is, in other words, an increase in processing fluency. Third, you detect that increased fluency, and this leads you to register the stimulus as somehow distinctive or special. Fourth, you try to figure out *why* the stimulus seems special, and you reach a particular conclusion—namely, that the stimulus has this distinctive quality *because* it's a stimulus you've met before in some prior episode (see **Figure 7.10**).

FIGURE 7.10   THE CHAIN OF EVENTS LEADING TO THE SENSE OF "FAMILIARITY"

The Steps Leading to a Judgment of Familiarity

Exposure to a stimulus → Practice in perceiving → Fluency → Stimulus registered as "special" → Attribution of fluency, perhaps attribution to a specific prior event → "Familiarity"

The Creation of an Illusion of Familiarity

Manipulation of stimulus presentation designed to make perceiving easier → Fluency → Stimulus registered as "special" → Attribution of fluency, perhaps attribution to a specific prior event → "Familiarity"

In the top line, practice in perceiving leads to fluency, and if the person attributes the fluency to some specific prior event, the stimulus will "feel familiar." The bottom line, however, indicates that fluency can be created in other ways: by presenting the stimulus more clearly or for a longer exposure. Once this fluency is detected, though, it can lead to steps identical to those in the top row. In this way, an "illusion of familiarity" can be created.

Let's be clear, though, that none of these steps happens consciously—you're not aware of seeking an interpretation or trying to explain why a stimulus feels distinctive. All you experience consciously is the end product of all these steps: the sense that a stimulus feels familiar. Moreover, this conclusion about a stimulus isn't one you draw capriciously; instead, you're likely to arrive at this conclusion and decide a stimulus is familiar only when you have supporting information. Thus, imagine that you encounter a stimulus that "rings a bell." As we mentioned before, you're likely to decide the stimulus is familiar if you also have an (explicit) source memory, so that you can recall where and when you last encountered that stimulus. You're also more likely to decide a stimulus is familiar if the surrounding circumstances support it. For example, if you're asked, "Which of these words were on the list you saw earlier?" the question itself gives you a cue that some of the words were recently encountered, and so you're more likely to attribute fluency to that encounter.

The fact remains, though, that judgments like these sometimes go astray, which is why we need this complicated theory. We've considered several cases in which a stimulus is objectively familiar (you've seen it recently) but doesn't *feel* familiar—just as our theory predicts. In these cases, you detect the fluency but attribute it to some other source. ("That melody is lovely" rather than "The melody is familiar.") In other words, you go through all of the steps shown in the top of Figure 7.10 except for the last two: You don't attribute the fluency to a specific prior event, and so you don't experience a sense of familiarity.

We can also find the opposite sort of case—in which a stimulus is not familiar (i.e., you've *not* seen it recently) but feels familiar anyhow—and this, too, fits with the theory. This sort of *illusion of familiarity* can be produced if the processing of a completely novel stimulus is more fluent than you expected—perhaps because (without telling you) we've sharpened the focus of a computer display or presented the stimulus for a few milliseconds longer than other stimuli you're inspecting (Jacoby & Whitehouse, 1989; Whittlesea, 2002; Whittlesea, Jacoby, & Girard, 1990). Cases like these can lead to the situation shown in the bottom half of Figure 7.10. And as our theory predicts, these situations do produce an illusion: Your processing of the stimulus is unexpectedly fluent; you seek an attribution for this fluency, and you're fooled into thinking the stimulus is familiar—so you say you've seen the stimulus before, when in fact you haven't. This illusion is a powerful confirmation that the sense of familiarity does rest on processes like the ones we've described. (For more on fluency, see Besken & Mulligan, 2014; Griffin, Gonzalez, Koehler, & Gilovich, 2012; Hertwig, Herzog, Schooler, & Reimer, 2008; Lanska, Olds, & Westerman, 2013; Oppenheimer, 2008; Tsai & Thomas, 2011. For a glimpse of what fluency amounts to in the nervous system, see Knowlton & Foerde, 2008.)

The Hierarchy of Memory Types

Clearly, we're often influenced by the past without being aware of that influence. We often respond differently to familiar stimuli than we do to novel stimuli, even if we have no subjective feeling of familiarity. On this basis, it seems that our conscious recollection seriously underestimates what's in our memories, and research has documented many ways in which unconscious memories influence what we do, think, and feel.

In addition, the data are telling us that there are two different kinds of memory: one type ("explicit") is conscious and deliberate, the other ("implicit") is typically unconscious and automatic. These two broad categories can be further subdivided, as shown in **Figure 7.11**. Explicit memories can be subdivided into episodic memories (memory for specific events) and semantic memory (more general knowledge). Implicit memory is often divided into four subcategories, as shown in the figure. Our emphasis here has been on one of the subtypes—priming—largely because of its role in producing the feeling of familiarity. However, the other subtypes of implicit memory are also important and can be distinguished from priming both in terms of their functioning (i.e., they follow somewhat different rules) and in terms of their biological underpinnings.

Some of the best evidence for these distinctions, though, comes from the clinic, not the laboratory. In other words, we can learn a great deal about

TEST YOURSELF

10. What is processing fluency, and how does it influence us?
11. In what sense is familiarity more like *a conclusion that you draw*, rather than *a feeling triggered by a stimulus*?

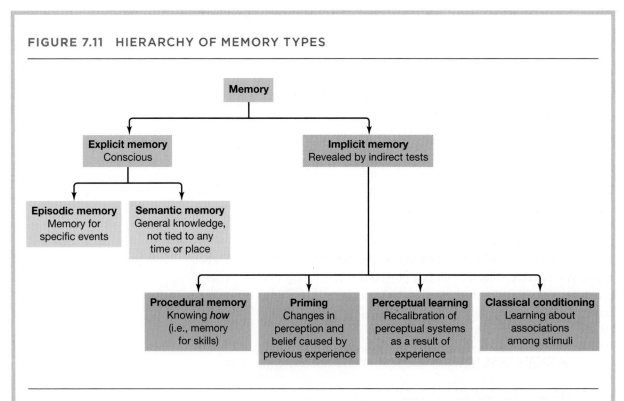

FIGURE 7.11   HIERARCHY OF MEMORY TYPES

In our discussion, we've distinguished two types of memory—explicit and implicit. However, there are reasons to believe that each of these categories must be subdivided further, as shown here. Evidence for these subdivisions includes functional evidence (the various types of memory follow different rules) and biological evidence (the types depend on different aspects of brain functioning).

these various types of memory by considering individuals who have suffered different forms of brain damage. Let's look at some of that evidence.

Amnesia

As we have already mentioned, a variety of injuries or illnesses can lead to a loss of memory, or **amnesia**. Some forms of amnesia are *retrograde*, meaning that they disrupt memory for things learned *prior to* the event that initiated the amnesia (see **Figure 7.12**). **Retrograde amnesia** is often caused by blows to the head; the afflicted person is unable to recall events that occurred just before the blow. Other forms of amnesia have the reverse effect, causing disruption of memory for experiences *after* the onset of amnesia; these are cases of **anterograde amnesia**. (Many cases of amnesia involve both retrograde and anterograde memory loss.)

Disrupted Episodic Memory, but Spared Semantic Memory

Studies of amnesia can teach us many things. For example, do we need all the distinctions shown in Figure 7.11? Consider the case of Clive Wearing, whom we met in the opening to Chapter 6. (You can find more detail about Wearing's case in an extraordinary book by his wife—see Wearing, 2011.) Wearing's episodic memory is massively disrupted, but his memory for generic information, as well as his deep love for his wife, seem to be entirely intact. Other patients show the reverse pattern—disrupted semantic memory but preserved episodic knowledge. One patient, for example, suffered damage (from encephalitis) to the front portion of her temporal lobes. As a consequence, she lost her memory of many common words, important historical events, famous people, and even the fundamental traits of animate and inanimate objects. "However, when asked about her wedding and honeymoon, her father's illness and death, or other specific past episodes,

FIGURE 7.12 RETROGRADE AND ANTEROGRADE AMNESIA

Moment of brain injury

Time

Period for which retrograde amnesia disrupts memory

Period for which anterograde amnesia disrupts memory

Retrograde amnesia disrupts memory for experiences *before* the injury, accident, or disease that triggered the amnesia. Anterograde amnesia disrupts memory for experiences *after* the injury or disease. Some patients suffer from both retrograde and anterograde amnesia.

she readily produced detailed and accurate recollections" (Schacter, 1996, p. 152; also see Cabeza & Nyberg, 2000). (For more on amnesia, see Brown, 2002; Clark & Maguire, 2016; Kopelman & Kapur, 2001; Nadel & Moscovitch, 2001; Riccio, Millin, & Gisquet-Verrier, 2003.)

These cases (and other evidence too; see **Figure 7.13**) provide the *double dissociation* that demands a distinction between episodic and semantic memory. It's observations like these that force us to the various distinctions shown in Figure 7.11. (For evidence, though, that episodic and semantic memory are intertwined in important ways, see McRae & Jones, 2012.)

Anterograde Amnesia

We've already mentioned the patient known as H.M. His memory loss was the result of brain surgery in 1953, and over the next 55 years (until his death in 2008) H.M. participated in a vast number of studies. Some people suggest he

---

FIGURE 7.13   SEMANTIC MEMORY WITHOUT EPISODIC MEMORY

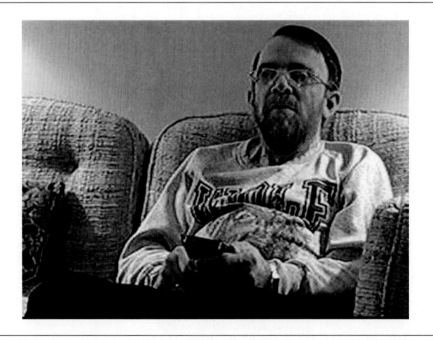

Kent Cochrane—known for years as "Patient K.C."—died in 2014. In 1981, at age 30, he skidded off the road on his motorcycle and suffered substantial brain damage. The damage caused severe disruption of Cochrane's episodic memory, but it left his semantic memory intact. As a result, he could still report on the events of his life, but these reports were entirely devoid of autobiographical quality. In other words, he could remember the bare facts of, say, what happened at his brother's wedding, but the memory was totally impersonal, with no recall of context or emotion. He also knew that during his childhood his family had fled their home because a train had derailed nearby, spilling toxic chemicals. But, again, he simply knew this as factual material—the sort of information you might pick up from a reference book—and he had no recall of his own experiences during the event.

---

was the most-studied individual in the entire history of psychology (which is one of the reasons we've returned to his case several times). In fact, the data gathering continued after H.M.'s death—with careful postmortem scrutiny of his brain. (For a review of H.M.'s case, see Corkin, 2013; Milner, 1966, 1970; also O'Kane, Kensinger, & Corkin, 2004; Skotko et al., 2004; Skotko, Rubin, & Tupler, 2008.)

After his surgery, H.M. was still able to recall events that took place *before* the surgery—and so his amnesia was largely anterograde, not retrograde. But the amnesia was severe. Episodes he had experienced after the surgery, people he had met, stories he had heard—all seemed to leave no lasting record, as though nothing new could get into his long-term storage.

H.M. could hold a mostly normal conversation (because his working memory was still intact), but his deficit became instantly clear if the conversation was interrupted. If you spoke with him for a while, then left the room and came back 3 or 4 minutes later, he seemed to have totally forgotten that the earlier conversation ever took place. If the earlier conversation was your first meeting with H.M., he would, after the interruption, be certain he was now meeting you for the very first time.

A similar amnesia has been found in patients who have been longtime alcoholics. The problem isn't the alcohol itself; the problem instead is that alcoholics tend to have inadequate diets, getting most of their nutrition from whatever they're drinking. It turns out, though, that most alcoholic beverages are missing several key nutrients, including vitamin B1 (thiamine). As a result, longtime alcoholics are vulnerable to problems caused by thiamine deficiency, including the disorder known as **Korsakoff's syndrome** (Rao, Larkin, & Derr, 1986; Ritchie, 1985).

Patients suffering from Korsakoff's syndrome seem similar to H.M. in many ways. They typically have no problem remembering events that took place before the onset of alcoholism. They can also maintain current topics in mind as long as there's no interruption. New information, though, if displaced from the mind, seems to be lost forever. Korsakoff's patients who have been in the hospital for decades will casually mention that they arrived only a week ago; if

Hippocampus
missing

A Anterior

Hippocampus
intact

B Posterior

H.M.'S BRAIN

For many years, researchers thought that surgery had left H.M. with no hippocampus at all. These MRI scans of his brain show that the surgery did destroy the anterior portion of the hippocampus (the portion closer to the front of the head; Panel A) but not the posterior portion (closer to the rear of the head; Panel B).

asked the name of the current president or events in the news, they unhesitatingly give answers appropriate for two or three decades earlier, whenever the disorder began (Marslen-Wilson & Teuber, 1975; Seltzer & Benson, 1974).

Anterograde Amnesia: What Kind of Memory Is Disrupted?

At the chapter's beginning, we alluded to other evidence that complicates this portrait of anterograde amnesia, and it's evidence that brings us back to the distinction between implicit and explicit memory. As it turns out, some of this evidence has been available for a long time. In 1911, the Swiss psychologist Édouard Claparède (1911/1951) reported the following incident. He was introduced to a young woman suffering from Korsakoff's amnesia, and he reached out to shake her hand. However, Claparède had secretly positioned a pin in his own hand so that when they clasped hands the patient received a painful pinprick. (Modern investigators would regard this experiment as a cruel violation of a patient's rights, but ethical standards were much, much lower in 1911.) The next day, Claparède returned and reached out to shake hands with the patient. Not surprisingly, she gave no indication that she recognized Claparède or remembered anything about the prior encounter. (This confirms the diagnosis of amnesia.) But just before their hands touched, the patient abruptly pulled back and refused to shake hands with Claparède. He asked her why, and after some confusion the patient said vaguely, "Sometimes pins are hidden in people's hands."

What was going on here? On the one side, this patient seemed to have no memory of the prior encounter with Claparède. She certainly didn't mention it in explaining her refusal to shake hands, and when questioned closely about the earlier encounter, she showed no knowledge of it. But, on the other side, she obviously remembered something about the painful pinprick she'd gotten the previous day. We see this clearly in her behavior.

A related pattern occurs with other Korsakoff's patients. In one of the early demonstrations of this point, researchers used a deck of cards like those used in popular trivia games. Each card contained a question and some possible answers, in a multiple-choice format (Schacter, Tulving, & Wang, 1981). The experimenter showed each card to a Korsakoff's patient, and if the patient didn't know the answer, he was told it. Then, outside of the patient's view, the card was replaced in the deck, guaranteeing that the same question would come up again in a few minutes.

When the question did come up again, the patients in this study were likely to get it right—and so apparently had learned the answer in the previous encounter. Consistent with their diagnosis, though, the patients had no recollection of the learning: They were unable to explain *why* their answers were correct. They didn't say, "I know this bit of trivia because the same question came up just five minutes ago." Instead, patients were likely to say things like "I read about it somewhere" or "My sister once told me about it."

Many studies show similar results. In setting after setting, Korsakoff's patients are unable to recall episodes they've experienced; they seem to have no explicit memory. But if they're tested indirectly, we see clear indications of memory—and so these patients seem to have intact implicit memories. (See, e.g., Cohen & Squire, 1980; Graf & Schacter, 1985; Moscovitch, 1982; Schacter, 1996; Schacter & Tulving, 1982; Squire & McKee, 1993.) In fact, in many tests of implicit memory, amnesic patients seem indistinguishable from ordinary individuals.

Can There Be Explicit Memory without Implicit?

We can also find patients with the reverse pattern—intact explicit memory, but impaired implicit. One study compared a patient who had suffered brain damage to the hippocampus but not the amygdala with a second patient who had the opposite pattern: damage to the amygdala but not the hippocampus (Bechara et al., 1995). These patients were exposed to a series of trials in which a particular stimulus (a blue light) was reliably followed by a loud boat horn, while other stimuli (green, yellow, or red lights) were not followed by the horn. Later on, the patients were exposed to the blue light on its own, and their bodily arousal was measured; would they show a fright reaction in response to this stimulus? In addition, the patients were asked directly, "Which color was followed by the horn?"

The patient with damage to the hippocampus did show a fear reaction to the blue light—assessed via the *skin conductance response (SCR)*, a measure of bodily arousal. As a result, his data on this measure look just like results for control participants (i.e., people without brain damage; see **Figure 7.14**).

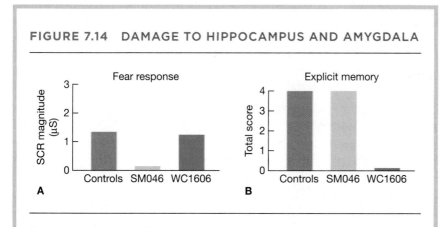

FIGURE 7.14   DAMAGE TO HIPPOCAMPUS AND AMYGDALA

Panel A shows results for a test probing implicit memory via a fear response; Panel B shows results for a test probing explicit memory. Patient SM046 had suffered damage to the amygdala and shows little evidence of implicit memory (i.e., no fear response—indexed by the *skin conductance response*, or SCR) but a normal level of explicit memory. Patient WC1606 had suffered damage to the hippocampus and shows the opposite pattern: massively disrupted explicit memory but a normal fear response.   (AFTER BECHARA ET AL., 1995)

However, when asked directly, this patient couldn't recall which of the lights had been associated with the boat horn.

In contrast, the patient with damage to the amygdala showed the opposite pattern. She was able to report that just one of the lights had been associated with the horn and that the light's color had been blue—demonstrating fully intact explicit memory. When presented with the blue light, however, she showed no fear response.

Optimal Learning

Before closing this chapter, let's put these amnesia findings into the broader context of the chapter's main themes. Throughout the chapter, we've suggested that we cannot make claims about learning or memory acquisition without some reference to how the learning will be used later on. For example, whether it's better to learn underwater or on land depends on where you will be tested. Whether it's better to learn while listening to jazz or while sitting in a quiet room depends on the acoustic background of the memory test environment.

These ideas are echoed in the neuropsychology data. Specifically, it would be misleading to say that brain damage (whether from Korsakoff's syndrome or some other source) ruins someone's ability to create new memories. Instead, brain damage is likely to disrupt some types of learning but not others, and how this matters for the person depends on how the newly learned material will be accessed. Thus, someone who suffers hippocampal damage will probably appear normal on an indirect memory test but seem amnesic on a direct test, while someone who suffers amygdala damage will probably show the reverse pattern.

All these points are enormously important for our theorizing about memory, but they also have a practical implication. Right now, you are reading this material and presumably want to remember it later on. You're also encountering new material in other settings (perhaps in other classes you're taking), and surely you want to remember that as well. How should you study all of this information if you want the best chances of retaining it for later use?

At one level, the message from this chapter might be that the ideal form of learning would be one that's "in tune with" the approach to the material that you'll need later. If you're going to be tested explicitly, you want to learn the material in a way that prepares you for that form of retrieval. If you'll be tested underwater or while listening to music, then, again, you want to learn the material in a way that prepares you for that context and the mental perspective it produces. If you'll need source memory, then you want one type of preparation; if you'll need familiarity, you might want a different type of preparation.

The problem, though, is that during learning, you often don't know how you'll be approaching the material later—what the retrieval environment will be, whether you'll need the information implicitly or explicitly, and so on. As a result, maybe the best strategy in learning would be to use *multiple perspectives*. To revisit our earlier analogy, imagine that you know at some point in the future you'll want to reach Chicago, but you don't know yet whether you'll be approaching the city from the north, the south, or the west. In that case, your best bet might be to build multiple highways, so that you can reach your goal from any direction. Memory works the same way. If you initially think about a topic in different ways and in relation to many other ideas, then you'll establish many paths leading to the target material—and so you'll be able to access that material from many different perspectives. The practical message from this chapter, then, is that this multiperspective approach may provide the optimal learning strategy.

TEST YOURSELF

12. Define "retrograde" and "anterograde" amnesia.
13. What type(s) of memory are disrupted in patients suffering from Korsakoff's syndrome?

COGNITIVE PSYCHOLOGY AND EDUCATION

familiarity can be treacherous

Sometimes you see a picture of someone and immediately say, "Gee—she looks familiar!" This seems like a simple and direct reaction to the picture, but the chapter describes how complicated familiarity really is. Indeed, the chapter makes it clear that we can't think of familiarity just as a "feeling" somehow triggered by a stimulus. Instead, familiarity seems more like a *conclusion* that you draw at the end of a many-step process. As a result of these complexities, *errors* about familiarity are possible: cases in which a stimulus feels familiar even though it's not, or cases in which you correctly realize that the stimulus is familiar but then make a mistake about *why* it's familiar.

These points highlight the dangers, for students, of relying on familiarity. As one illustration, consider the advice that people sometimes give for taking a multiple-choice test. They tell you, "Go with your first inclination" or "Choose the answer that feels familiar." In some cases these strategies will help, because sometimes the correct answer will indeed feel familiar. But in other cases these strategies can lead you astray, because the answer you're considering may seem familiar *for a bad reason*. What if your professor once said, "One of the common mistakes people make is to believe . . ." and then talked about the claim summarized in the answer you're now considering? Alternatively, what if the answer seems familiar because it *resembles* the correct answer but is, in some crucial way, different from the correct answer (and therefore mistaken)? In either of these cases, your sense of familiarity might lead you to a wrong answer.

Even worse, one study familiarized people with phrases like "the record for tallest pine tree." Because of this exposure, these people were later *more likely to accept as true* a longer phrase, such as "the record for tallest pine tree is 350 feet." Why? Because they realized that (at least) part of the sentence was familiar and therefore drew the reasonable inference that they must have

FAMILIARITY CAN BE TREACHEROUS

"Option C rings a bell. . . ." Often, in taking a multiple-choice test, students will realize they don't know the answer to a question but, even so, one of the answer options seems somehow familiar. For reasons described in the chapter, though, this sense of familiarity is an unreliable guide in choosing a response.

encountered the entire sentence at some previous point. The danger here should be obvious: On a multiple-choice test, *part* of an incorrect option may be an exact duplicate of some phrase in your reading; if so, relying on familiarity will get you into trouble! (And, by the way, this claim about pines is false; the tallest pine tree—a sugar pine—is only about 273 feet tall.)

As a different concern, think back to the end-of-chapter essay for Chapter 6. There, we noted that one of the most common study strategies used by students is to read and reread their notes, or read and reread the textbook. This strategy turns out not to help memory very much, and other strategies are demonstrably better. But, in addition, the rereading strategy can actually *hurt you*. Thanks to the rereading, you become more and more familiar with the materials, which makes it easy to interpret this familiarity as *mastery*. But this is a mistake, and because of the mistake, familiarity can sometimes lead students to think they've mastered material when they haven't, causing them to end their study efforts too soon.

What can you do to avoid all these dangers? You'll do a much better job of assessing your own mastery if, rather than relying on familiarity, you give yourself some sort of quiz (perhaps one you find in the textbook, or one that a friend creates for you). More broadly, it's valuable to be alert to the various complexities associated with familiarity. After all, you don't want to ignore familiarity, because sometimes it's all you've got. If you really don't know the answer to a multiple-choice question but option B seems somehow familiar, then choosing B may be your only path forward. But given the difficulties we've mentioned here, it may be best to regard familiarity just as a weak clue about the past and not as a guaranteed indicator. That attitude may encourage the sort of caution that will allow you to use familiarity without being betrayed by it.

For more on this topic . . .

Brown, P. C., Roediger, H. L., & McDaniel, M. A. (2014). *Make it stick: The science of successful learning.* New York, NY: Belknap Press.

Jacoby, L., & Hollingshead, A. (1990). Reading student essays may be hazardous to your spelling: Effects of reading incorrectly and correctly spelled words. *Canadian Journal of Psychology, 44,* 345–358.

Preston, J., & Wegner, D. M. (2007). The Eureka error: Inadvertent plagiarism by misattributions of effort. *Journal of Personality and Social Psychology, 92,* 575–584.

Stark, L.-J., Perfect, T., & Newstead, S. (2008). The effects of repeated idea elaboration on unconscious plagiarism. *Memory & Cognition, 36,* 65–73.

Swire, B., Ecker, U. K. H., & Lewandowsky, S. (2017). The role of familiarity in correcting inaccurate information. *Journal of Experimental Psychology: Learning, Memory & Cognition, 43,* 1948–1961.

chapter review

SUMMARY

- In general, the chances that someone will remember an earlier event are greatest if the physical and mental circumstances in place during memory retrieval match those in place during learning. This is reflected in the phenomenon of context-dependent learning.

- A similar pattern is reflected in the phenomenon of "encoding specificity." This term refers to the idea that people usually learn more than the specific material to be remembered itself; they also learn that material within its associated context.

- All these results arise from the fact that learning establishes connections among memories, and these connections serve as retrieval paths. Like any path, these lead from some starting point to some target. To use a given path, therefore, you must return to the appropriate starting point. In the same way, if there is a connection between two memories, then activating the first memory is likely to call the second to mind. But if the first memory isn't activated, this connection, no matter how well established, will not help in locating the second memory—just as a large highway approaching Chicago from the south won't be helpful if you're trying to reach Chicago from the north.

- This emphasis on memory connections fits well with a conceptualization of memory as a vast network, with individual nodes joined to one another via connections or associations. An individual node becomes activated when it receives enough of an input signal to raise its activation level to its response threshold. Once activated, the node sends activation out through its connections to all the nodes connected to it.

- Hints are effective because the target node can receive activation from two sources simultaneously—from nodes representing the main cue or question, and also from nodes representing the hint.

- Activating one node does seem to prime nearby nodes through the process of spreading activation. This is evident in studies of semantic priming in lexical-decision tasks.

- Some learning strategies are effective as preparation for some sorts of memory tests but ineffective for other sorts of tests. Some strategies, for example, are effective at establishing source memory rather than familiarity; other strategies do the reverse.

- Different forms of learning also play a role in producing implicit and explicit memories. Implicit memories are those that influence you even when you have no awareness that you're being influenced by a previous event. In many cases, implicit-memory effects take the form of priming—for example, in a lexical decision task or word-stem completion. But implicit memories can also influence you in other ways, producing a number of memory-based illusions.

- Implicit memory can be understood as the consequence of increased processing fluency, produced by experience in a particular task with a particular stimulus. The fluency is sometimes detected and registered as a sense of "specialness" attached to a stimulus. Often, this specialness is attributed to some cause, but this attribution can be inaccurate.

- Implicit memory is also important in understanding the pattern of symptoms in anterograde amnesia. Amnesic patients perform badly on tests requiring explicit memory and may not even recall events that happened just minutes earlier. However, they often perform at near-normal levels on tests involving implicit memory. This disparity underscores the fact that we cannot speak in general about good and bad memories, good and poor learning. Instead, learning and memory must be matched to a particular task and a particular form of test; learning and memory that are excellent for some tasks may be poor for others.

KEY TERMS

context-dependent learning (p. 242)
context reinstatement (p. 244)
encoding specificity (p. 244)
nodes (p. 246)
associations (or associative links) (p. 246)
activation level (p. 246)
response threshold (p. 246)
subthreshold activation (p. 246)
summation (p. 246)
spreading activation (p. 247)
lexical-decision task (p. 248)
semantic priming (p. 249)
recall (p. 251)
recognition (p. 251)
source memory (p. 251)
familiarity (p. 251)

attribution (p. 251)
"remember/know" distinction (p. 252)
word-stem completion (p. 255)
explicit memory (p. 255)
direct memory testing (p. 255)
implicit memory (p. 255)
indirect memory testing (p. 256)
illusion of truth (p. 258)
source confusion (p. 259)
processing pathway (p. 261)
processing fluency (p. 262)
amnesia (p. 267)
retrograde amnesia (p. 267)
anterograde amnesia (p. 267)
Korsakoff's syndrome (p. 269)

TEST YOURSELF AGAIN

1. What does context-dependent learning tell us about the nature of retrieval paths?

2. In what ways is a retrieval path like an "ordinary" path (e.g., a path or highway leading to a particular city)?

3. What is encoding specificity? How is it demonstrated?

4. What is subthreshold activation of a memory node? What role does subthreshold activation play in the explanation of why retrieval hints are often helpful?

5. How does semantic priming illustrate the effectiveness of subthreshold activation?

6. Define "recognition" and "recall."

7. What evidence indicates that source memory and familiarity are distinct from each other?

8. What is the difference between implicit and explicit memory? Which of these is said to be "memory without awareness"?

9. What is the role of implicit memory in explaining the false fame effect?

10. What is processing fluency, and how does it influence us?

11. In what sense is familiarity more like *a conclusion that you draw*, rather than *a feeling triggered by a stimulus*?

12. Define "retrograde" and "anterograde" amnesia.

13. What type(s) of memory are disrupted in patients suffering from Korsakoff's syndrome?

THINK ABOUT IT

1. Some people describe the eerie sensation of "déjà vu"—a feeling in which a place or face seems familiar, even though they're quite certain they've never been in this place, or seen this face, before. Can you generate a hypothesis about the roots of déjà vu, drawing on the material in the chapter?

ⓔ eBOOK DEMONSTRATIONS & ESSAYS

Go to http://digital.wwnorton.com/cognition7 for the online demonstrations and essays relevant to this chapter. These can be found in the ebook.

Online Demonstrations

- Demonstration 7.1: Retrieval Paths and Connections
- Demonstration 7.2: Encoding Specificity
- Demonstration 7.3: Spreading Activation in Memory Search
- Demonstration 7.4: Semantic Priming
- Demonstration 7.5: Priming From Implicit Memory

Online Applying Cognitive Psychology and the Law Essays

- Cognitive Psychology and the Law: Unconscious Transference

ZAPS COGNITION LABS

Go to http://digital.wwnorton.com/cognition7 to experience interactive online psychology labs relevant to this chapter.

The performers who appear on p. 253 are (*left to right*). Michael K. Williams, Margo Martindale, Adam Rodriguez, Judy Greer, and Adina Porter.

Remembering Complex Events

what if... What were you doing on March 23, 2009? What did you have for lunch that day? What was the weather like? These seem like odd questions; why should you remember these details from almost a decade ago? But imagine if you *could* remember those details — and similar details for every other day in your life. In other words, what would life be like if you had a "super memory" — so that, essentially, you never forgot anything?

Researchers have identified a small number of people who have *hyperthymesia*, also called "highly superior autobiographical recall" (HSAM). These people seem able to remember every single day of their lives, over a span of many years. One of these individuals claims that she can recall every day of her life over the last four decades. "Starting on February 5, 1980, I remember everything. That was a Tuesday."

If asked about a randomly selected date — say, February 10, 2012 — these individuals can recall exactly where they were that day, what time they woke up, and what shoes they wore. Their performance is just as good if they're asked about October 8, 2008, or December 19, 2007. And when checked, their memories turn out to be uniformly accurate.

These individuals are remarkable in how much they remember, but they seem quite normal in other ways. For example, their extraordinary memory capacity hasn't made them amazing geniuses or incredible scholars. Even though they have an exceptional capacity for remembering their own lives, they have no advantage in remembering other sorts of content or performing other mental tasks. This point has been documented with careful testing, but it is also evident in the fact that researchers weren't aware such people existed until just a few years ago (e.g., Parker, Cahill, & McGaugh, 2006). Apparently, these individuals, even with their incredible memory capacity, are ordinary enough in other ways so that we didn't spot them until recently (McGaugh & LePort, 2014.)

Humans have been trying for centuries to improve their memories, but it seems that a "perfect" memory may provide less of an advantage than you might think. We'll return to this point, and what it implies about memory functioning, later in the chapter.

- Outside the lab, you often try to remember materials that are related in some way to other things you know or have experienced. Over and over, we will see that this other knowledge—the knowledge you bring to a situation—helps you to remember by promoting retrieval, but it can also promote error.

- The memory errors produced by prior knowledge tend to be quite systematic: You often recall the past as more "normal," more in line with your expectations, than it actually was.

- Even acknowledging the memory errors, our overall assessment of memory can be quite positive. This is because memories are accurate most of the time, and the errors that do occur can be understood as the by-products of mechanisms that generally serve you well.

- Finally, we will consider three factors that play an important role in shaping memory outside of the laboratory: *involvement with an event*, *emotion*, and the *passage of time*. These factors require some additional principles as part of our overall theory, but they also confirm the power of more general principles—principles hinging, for example, on the role of memory connections.

Memory Errors, Memory Gaps

Where did you spend last summer? What country did you grow up in? Where were you five minutes ago? These are easy questions, and you effortlessly retrieve this information from memory the moment you need it. If we want to understand how memory functions, therefore, we need to understand how you locate these bits of information (and thousands of others just like them) so readily.

But we also need to account for some other observations. Sometimes, when you try to remember an episode, you draw a blank. On other occasions, you recall something, but with no certainty that you're correct: "I think her nickname was Dink, but I'm not sure." And sometimes, when you do recall a past episode, it turns out that your memory is mistaken. Perhaps a few details of the event were different from the way you recall them. Or perhaps your memory is completely wrong, misrepresenting large elements of the original episode. Worse, in some cases you can remember entire events that never happened at all! In this chapter, we'll consider how, and how often, these errors arise. Let's start with some examples.

Memory Errors: Some Initial Examples

In 1992, an El Al cargo plane lost power in two of its engines just after taking off from Amsterdam's Schiphol Airport. The pilot attempted to return the plane to the airport but couldn't make it. A few minutes later, the plane crashed into an 11-story apartment building in Amsterdam's Bijlmermeer neighborhood. The building collapsed and burst into flames; 43 people were killed, including the plane's entire crew.

Ten months later, researchers questioned 193 Dutch people about the crash, asking them in particular, "Did you see the television film of the moment the plane hit the apartment building?" More than half of the participants (107 of them) reported seeing the film, even though there was no such film. No camera had recorded the crash; no film (or any reenactment) was shown on television. The participants seemed to be remembering something that never took place (Crombag, Wagenaar, & van Koppen, 1996).

In a follow-up study, investigators surveyed another 93 people about the plane crash. These people were also asked whether they'd seen the (non-existent) TV film, and then they were asked detailed questions about exactly what they had seen in the film: Was the plane burning when it crashed, or did it catch fire a moment later? In the film, did they see the plane come down vertically with no forward speed, or did it hit the building while still moving horizontally at a considerable speed?

Two thirds of these participants reported seeing the film, and most of them were able to provide details about what they had seen. When asked about the plane's speed, for example, only 23% said that they couldn't remember. The others gave various responses, presumably based on their "memory" of the (nonexistent) film.

Other studies have produced similar results. There was no video footage of the car crash in which Princess Diana was killed, but 44% of the British participants in one study recalled seeing the footage (Ost, Vrij, Costall, & Bull, 2002). More than a third of the participants questioned about a nightclub bombing in Bali recalled seeing a (nonexistent) video, and nearly all these participants reported details about what they'd seen in the video (Wilson & French, 2006).

It turns out that more persistent questioning can lead some of these people to admit they actually don't remember seeing the video. Even with persistent questioning, though, many participants continue to insist that they did see the video—and they offer additional information about exactly what they saw in the film (e.g., Patihis & Loftus, 2015; Smeets et al., 2006). Also, in all these studies, let's emphasize that participants are thinking back to an emotional and much-discussed event; the researchers aren't asking them to recall a minor occurrence.

Is memory more accurate when the questions come after a shorter delay? In a study by Brewer and Treyens (1981), participants were asked to wait briefly in the experimenter's office prior to the procedure's start. After 35 seconds, participants were taken out of this office and told that there actually was no experimental procedure. Instead, the study was concerned with their memory for the room in which they'd just been sitting.

Participants' descriptions of the office were powerfully influenced by their prior beliefs. Surely, most participants would expect an academic office to contain shelves filled with books. In this particular office, though, no books

TEST YOURSELF

1. What is the evidence that in some circumstances many people will misremember significant events they have experienced?

2. What is the evidence that in some circumstances people will even misremember *recent* events?

FIGURE 8.1 THE OFFICE USED IN THE BREWER AND TREYENS STUDY

No books were in view in this office, but many participants, biased by their expectations of what should be in an academic office, remembered seeing books.

(AFTER BREWER & TREYENS, 1981)

were in view (see **Figure 8.1**). Even so, almost one third of the participants (9 of 30) reported seeing books in the office. Their recall, in other words, was governed by their expectations, not by reality.

How could this happen? How could so many Dutch participants be wrong in their recall of the plane crash? How could intelligent, alert college students fail to remember what they'd seen in an office just moments earlier?

Memory Errors: A Hypothesis

In Chapters 6 and 7, we emphasized the importance of memory connections that link each bit of knowledge in your memory to other bits. Sometimes these connections tie together similar episodes, so that a trip to the beach ends up connected in memory to your recollection of other trips. Sometimes the connections tie an episode to certain ideas—ideas, perhaps, that were part of your *understanding* of the episode, or ideas that were triggered by some element within the episode.

It's not just separate episodes and ideas that are linked in this way. Even for a single episode, the elements of the episode are stored separately from one another and are linked by connections. In fact, the storage is "modality-specific," with the bits representing what you *saw* stored in brain areas devoted to visual processing, the bits representing what you *heard* stored in brain areas specialized for auditory processing, and so on (e.g., Nyberg, Habib, McIntosh, & Tulving, 2000; Wheeler, Peterson, & Buckner, 2000; also see Chapter 7, Figure 7.4, p. 245).

With all these connections in place—element to element, episode to episode, episode to related ideas—information ends up stored in memory in a system that resembles a vast spider web, with each bit of information connected by many threads to other bits elsewhere in the web. This was the idea that in Chapter 7 we described as a huge *network* of interconnected *nodes*.

However, within this network there are no boundaries keeping the elements of one episode separate from elements of other episodes. The episodes, in other words, aren't stored in separate "files," each distinct from the others. What is it, therefore, that holds together the various bits within each episode? To a large extent, it's simply the density of connections. There are many connections linking the various aspects of your "trip to the beach" to one another; there are fewer connections linking this event to other events.

As we've discussed, these connections play a crucial role in memory retrieval. Imagine that you're trying to recall the restaurant you ate at during your beach trip. You'll start by activating nodes in memory that represent some aspect of the trip—perhaps your memory of the rainy weather. Activation will then flow outward from there, through the connections you've established, and this will energize nodes representing other aspects of the trip. The flow of activation can then continue from there, eventually reaching the nodes you seek. In this way, the connections serve as *retrieval paths*, guiding your search through memory.

Obviously, then, memory connections are a good thing; without them, you might never locate the information you're seeking. But the connections can also create problems. As you add more and more links between the bits of *this* episode and the bits of *that* episode, you're gradually knitting these two episodes together. As a result, you may lose track of the "boundary" between the episodes. More precisely, you're likely to lose track of which bits of information were contained within which event. In this way, you become vulnerable to what we might think of as "transplant" errors, in which a bit of information encountered in one context is transplanted into another context.

In the same way, as your memory for an episode becomes more and more interwoven with other thoughts you've had about the event, it will become difficult to keep track of which elements are linked to the episode because they were actually *part of* the episode itself, and which are linked merely because they were *associated with* the episode in your thoughts. This, too, can produce transplant errors, in which elements that were part of your thinking get misremembered as if they were actually part of the original experience.

Understanding Both Helps and Hurts Memory

It seems, then, that memory connections both help and hurt recollection. They *help* because the connections, serving as retrieval paths, enable you to locate information in memory. But connections can *hurt* because they sometimes make it difficult to see where the remembered episode stops and other, related knowledge begins. As a result, the connections encourage **intrusion errors**—errors in which other knowledge intrudes into the remembered event.

To see how these points play out, consider an early study by Owens, Bower, and Black (1979). In this study, half of the participants read the following passage:

Nancy arrived at the cocktail party. She looked around the room to see who was there. She went to talk with her professor. She felt she had to talk to him but was a little nervous about just what to say. A group of people started to play charades. Nancy went over and had some refreshments. The hors d'oeuvres were good, but she wasn't interested in talking to the rest of the people at the party. After a while she decided she'd had enough and left the party.

Other participants read the same passage, but with a prologue that set the stage:

Nancy woke up feeling sick again, and she wondered if she really was pregnant. How would she tell the professor she had been seeing? And the money was another problem.

All participants were then given a recall test in which they were asked to remember the sentences as exactly as they could. **Table 8.1** shows the results—the participants who had read the prologue (the Theme condition) recalled much more of the original story (i.e., they remembered the propositions actually contained within the story). This is what we should expect, based on the claims made in Chapter 6: The prologue provided a meaningful context for the remainder of the story, and this helped understanding. Understanding, in turn, promoted recall.

At the same time, the story's prologue also led participants to include elements in their recall that weren't mentioned in the original episode. In fact, participants who had seen the prologue made *four times* as many intrusion errors as did participants who hadn't seen the prologue. For example, they might include in their recall something like "The professor had gotten Nancy pregnant." This idea isn't part of the story but is certainly implied, so will probably be part of participants' understanding of the story. It's then this understanding (including the imported element) that is remembered.

TABLE 8.1   NUMBER OF PROPOSITIONS REMEMBERED BY PARTICIPANTS

STUDIED PROPOSITIONS (THOSE IN STORY)		INFERRED PROPOSITIONS (THOSE NOT IN STORY)	
Theme Condition	Neutral Condition	Theme Condition	Neutral Condition
29.2	20.2	15.2	3.7

In the Theme condition, a brief prologue set the theme for the passage that was to be remembered.   (AFTER OWENS ET AL., 1979)

The DRM Procedure

Similar effects, with memory connections both *helping* and *hurting* memory, can be demonstrated with simple word lists. For example, in many experiments, participants have been presented with lists like this one: "bed, rest, awake, tired, dream, wake, snooze, blanket, doze, slumber, snore, nap, peace, yawn, drowsy." Immediately after hearing this list, participants are asked to recall as many of the words as they can.

As you surely noticed, the words in this list are all associated with sleep, and the presence of this theme helps memory: The list words are easy to remember. It turns out, though, that the word "sleep" is not itself included in the list. Nonetheless, research participants spontaneously make the connection between the list words and this associated word, and this connection almost always leads to a memory error. When the time comes for recall, participants are extremely likely to recall that they heard "sleep." In fact, they're just as likely to recall "sleep" as they are to recall the actual words on the list (see **Figure 8.2**). When asked how confident they are in their memories, participants are just as confident in their (false) recall of "sleep" as they are in their (correct) memory of genuine list words (Gallo, 2010; for earlier and classic papers in this arena, see Deese, 1957; Roediger & McDermott, 1995, 2000).

This experiment (and many others like it) uses the **DRM procedure**, a bit of terminology that honors the investigators who developed it (James Deese, Henry Roediger III, and Kathleen McDermott). The procedure yields many errors even if participants are put on their guard before the procedure begins—that is, told about the nature of the lists and the frequency with which they produce errors (Gallo, Roberts, & Seamon, 1997; McDermott &

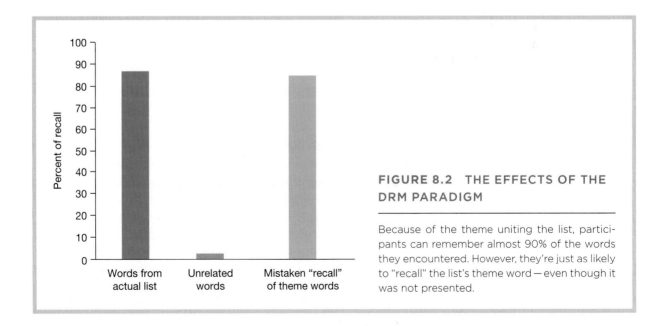

FIGURE 8.2   THE EFFECTS OF THE DRM PARADIGM

Because of the theme uniting the list, participants can remember almost 90% of the words they encountered. However, they're just as likely to "recall" the list's theme word—even though it was not presented.

Roediger, 1998). Apparently, the mechanisms leading to these errors are so automatic that people can't inhibit them.

Schematic Knowledge

Imagine that you go to a restaurant with a friend. This setting is familiar for you, and you have some commonsense knowledge about what normally happens here. You'll be seated; someone will bring menus; you'll order, then eat; eventually, you'll pay and leave. Knowledge like this is often referred to with the Greek word **schema** (plural: *schemata*). Schemata summarize the broad pattern of what's normal in a situation—and so your kitchen schema tells you that a kitchen is likely to have a stove but no piano; your dentist's office schema tells you that there are likely to be magazines in the waiting room, that you'll probably get a new toothbrush when you leave, and so on.

Schemata help you in many ways. In a restaurant, for example, you're not puzzled when someone keeps filling your water glass or when someone else drops by to ask, "How is everything?" Your schema tells you that these are normal occurrences in a restaurant, and you instantly understand how they fit into the broader framework.

Schemata also help when the time comes to *recall* how an event unfolded. This is because there are often gaps in your recollection—either because you didn't notice certain things in the first place, or because you've gradually forgotten some aspects of the experience. (We'll say more about forgetting later in the chapter.) In either case, you can rely on your schemata to fill in these gaps. So, in thinking back to your dinner at Chez Pierre, you might not remember anything about the menus. Nonetheless, you can be reasonably sure that there were menus and that they were given to you early on and taken away after you placed your order. On this basis, you're likely to include menus within your "recall" of the dinner, even if you have no memory of seeing the menus for this particular meal. In other words, you'll supplement what you actually remember with a plausible reconstruction based on your schematic knowledge. And in most cases this after-the-fact reconstruction will be correct, since schemata do, after all, describe what happens most of the time.

Evidence for Schematic Knowledge

Clearly, then, schematic knowledge helps you, by guiding your understanding and enabling you to reconstruct things you can't remember. But schematic knowledge can sometimes hurt you, by promoting errors in perception and memory. Moreover, the *types* of errors produced by schemata are quite predictable. As an example, imagine that you visit a dentist's office, and this one happens not to have any magazines in the waiting room. It's likely that you'll forget this detail after a while, so what will happen when you later try to recall your trip to the dentist? Odds are good that you'll rely on schematic knowledge and "remember" that there were magazines (since, after all, there usually are some scattered around a waiting room). In this way, your recollection will make this dentist's office seem more typical, more ordinary, than it actually was.

Here's the same point in more general terms. We've already said that schemata tell you what's typical in a setting. Therefore, if you rely on schematic knowledge to fill gaps in your recollection, you'll fill those gaps with *what's normally in place* in that sort of situation. As a result, any reliance on schemata will make the world seem more "normal" than it really is and will make the past seem more "regular" than it actually was.

This tendency toward "regularizing" the past has been documented in many settings. The classic demonstration, however, comes from studies published long ago by British psychologist Frederick Bartlett. Bartlett presented his participants with a story taken from the folklore of Native Americans (Bartlett, 1932). When tested later, the participants did reasonably well in recalling the gist of the story, but they made many errors in recalling the particulars. The pattern of errors, though, was quite systematic: The details omitted tended to be ones that made little sense to Bartlett's British participants. Likewise, aspects of the story that were unfamiliar were often changed into aspects that were more familiar; steps of the story that seemed inexplicable were supplemented to make the story seem more logical.

Overall, then, the participants' memories seem to have "cleaned up" the story they had read—making it more coherent (from their perspective), more sensible. This is exactly what we would expect if the memory errors derived from the participants' attempts to understand the story and, with that, their efforts toward fitting the story into a schematic frame. Elements that fit within the frame remained in their memories (or could be reconstructed later). Elements that didn't fit dropped out of memory or were changed.

In the same spirit, consider the Brewer and Treyens study mentioned at the start of this chapter—the study in which participants remembered seeing shelves full of books, even though there were none. This error was produced by schematic knowledge. During the event itself (while the participants were sitting in the office), schematic knowledge told the participants that academic offices usually contain many books, and this knowledge biased what the participants paid attention to. (If you're already certain that the shelves contain books, why should you spend time looking at the shelves? This would only confirm something you already know—see Vo & Henderson, 2009.) Then, when the time came to recall the office, participants used their schema to reconstruct what the office *must have* contained—a desk, a chair, and of course lots of books. In this way, the memory for the actual office was eclipsed by generic knowledge about what a "normal" academic office contains.

Likewise, think back to the misremembered plane crash and the related studies of people remembering videos of other prominent events, even though there were no videos of these events. Here, too, the memory errors distort reality by making the past seem more regular, more typical, than it really was. After all, people often hear about major news events via a television broadcast or Internet coverage, and these reports usually include vivid video footage. So here, too, the past as remembered seems to have been assimilated

TEST YOURSELF

3. What is the evidence that your *understanding* of an episode can produce intrusion errors?
4. What is the DRM procedure, and what results does this procedure produce?
5. What is schematic knowledge, and what evidence tells us that schematic knowledge can help us—and also can undermine memory accuracy?

into the pattern of the ordinary. The event as it unfolded was unusual, but the event *as remembered* becomes typical of its kind—just as we would expect if understanding and remembering were guided by our knowledge of the way things generally unfold.

The Cost of Memory Errors

There's clearly a "good news, bad news" quality to our discussion so far. On the positive side, memory connections serve as retrieval paths, allowing you to locate information in storage. The connections also enrich your understanding, because they tie each of your memories into a context provided by other things you know. In addition, links to schematic knowledge enable you to supplement your perception and recollection with well-informed (and usually accurate) inference.

On the negative side, though, the same connections can undermine memory accuracy, and memory errors are troubling. As we've discussed in other contexts, you rely on memory in many aspects of life, and it's unsettling that the memories you rely on may be *wrong*—misrepresenting how the past unfolded.

Eyewitness Errors

In fact, we can easily find circumstances in which memory errors are large in scale (not just concerned with minor details in the episode) and deeply consequential. For example, errors in eyewitness testimony (e.g., identifying the wrong person as the culprit or misreporting how an event unfolded) can potentially send an innocent person to jail and allow a guilty person to go free.

How often do eyewitnesses make mistakes? One answer comes from U.S. court cases in which DNA evidence, not available at the time of the trial, shows that the courts had convicted people who were, in truth, not guilty. There are now more than 350 of these exonerations, and the exonerees had (on average) spent more than a dozen years in jail for crimes they didn't commit. Many of them were on death row, awaiting execution.

When closely examined, these cases yield a clear message. Some of these men and women were convicted because of dishonest informants; some because analyses of forensic evidence had been botched. But by far the most common concern is eyewitness errors. In fact, according to most analyses, eyewitness errors account for at least three quarters of these false convictions—more than all other causes combined (e.g., Garrett, 2011; Reisberg, 2014).

Cases like these make it plain that memory errors, including misidentifications, are profoundly important. We're therefore led to ask: Are there ways to avoid these errors? Or are there ways to *detect* the errors, so that we can decide which memories are correct and which ones are not?

EXONERATION OF THE INNOCENT

Guy Miles spent more than 18 years in prison for an armed robbery he did not commit. He is one of the hundreds of people who were convicted in U.S. courts but then proven innocent by DNA evidence. Mistaken eyewitness evidence accounts for more of these false convictions than all other causes combined. Note in addition that these false convictions typically involve a "double error"—with someone innocent doing time in jail, and the guilty person walking around free.

Planting False Memories

An enormous number of studies have examined eyewitness memory—the sort of memory that police rely on when investigating crimes. In one of the earliest procedures, Loftus and Palmer (1974) showed participants a series of pictures depicting an automobile collision. Later, participants were asked questions about the collision, but the questions were phrased in different ways for different groups. Some participants were asked, for example, "How fast were the cars going when they hit each other?" A different group was asked, "How fast were the cars going when they smashed into each other?" The differences among these questions were slight, but had a substantial influence: Participants in the "hit" group estimated the speed to have been 34 miles per hour; those in the "smashed" group estimated 41 miles per hour—20% higher (see **Figure 8.3**).

But what is critical comes next: One week later, the participants were asked in a perfectly neutral way whether they had seen any broken glass in the pictures. Participants who had initially been asked the "hit" question tended to remember (correctly) that no glass was visible; participants who had been asked the "smashed" question, though, often made this error. It

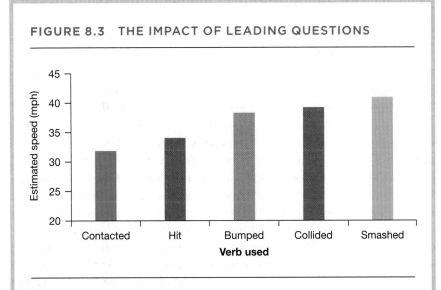

FIGURE 8.3   THE IMPACT OF LEADING QUESTIONS

Witnesses who were asked how fast cars were going when they "hit" each other reported (on average) a speed of 34 miles per hour. Other witnesses, asked how fast the cars were going when they "smashed" into each other, gave estimates 20% higher. When all participants were later asked whether they'd seen broken glass at the scene, participants who'd been asked the "smashed" question were more likely to say yes—even though there was no broken glass.   (AFTER LOFTUS & PALMER, 1974) seems, therefore, that the change of just one word within the initial question can have a significant effect—in this case, more than doubling the likelihood of memory error.

In other studies, participants have been asked questions that contain overt misinformation about an event. For example, they might be asked, "How fast was the car going when it raced by the barn?" when, in truth, no barn was in view. In still other studies, participants are exposed to descriptions of the target event allegedly written by "other witnesses." They might be told, for example, "Here's how someone else recalled the crime; does this match what you recall?" Of course, the "other witness" descriptions contained some misinformation, enabling researchers to determine if participants "pick up" the false leads (e.g., Paterson & Kemp, 2006; also Edelson, Sharon, Dolan, & Dudai, 2011). In other studies, researchers ask questions that require the participants themselves to *make up* some bit of misinformation. For example, participants could be asked, "In the video, was the man bleeding from his knee or from his elbow after the fall?" Even though it was clear in the video that the man wasn't bleeding at all, participants are forced to choose one of the two options (e.g., Chrobak & Zaragoza, 2008; Zaragoza, Payment, Ackil, Drivdahl, & Beck, 2001).

These procedures differ in important ways, but they are all variations on the same theme. In each case, the participant experiences an event and then is exposed to a misleading suggestion about how the event unfolded. Then some time is allowed to pass. At the end of this interval, the partici-pant's memory is tested. And in each of these variations, the outcome is the same: A substantial number of participants—in some studies, more than one third—end up incorporating the false suggestion into their memory of the original event.

Of course, some attempts at manipulating memory are more success-ful, some less so. It's easier, for example, to plant *plausible* memories rather than implausible ones. (However, memories for implausible events can also be planted—see Hyman, 2000; Mazzoni, Loftus, & Kirsch, 2001; Pezdek, Blandon-Gitlin, & Gabbay, 2006; Scoboria, Mazzoni, Kirsch, & Jimenez, 2006; Thomas & Loftus, 2002.) Errors are also more likely if the post-event information *supplements* what the person remembers, in comparison to *con-tradicting* what the person would otherwise remember. It's apparently easier, therefore, to "add to" a memory than it is to "replace" a memory (Chrobak & Zaragoza, 2013). False memories are also more easily planted if the research participants don't just *hear* about the false event but, instead, are urged to *imagine* how the suggested event unfolded. In one study, participants were given a list of possible childhood events (going to the emergency room late at night; winning a stuffed animal at a carnival; getting in trouble for calling 911) and were asked to "picture each event as clearly and completely" as they could. This simple exercise was enough to increase participants' confidence that the event had really occurred (Garry, Manning, Loftus, & Serman, 1996; also Mazzoni & Memon, 2003; Sharman & Barnier, 2008; Shidlovski, Schul, & Mayo, 2014).

Even acknowledging these variations, though, let's emphasize the consistency of the findings. We can use subtle procedures (with slightly leading questions) to plant false information in someone's memory, or we can use a more blatant procedure (demanding that the person make up the bogus facts). We can use pictures, movies, or live events as the to-be-remembered materials. In all cases, it's remarkably easy to alter someone's memory, with the result that the past as the person remembers it can differ markedly from the past as it really was. This is a widespread pattern, with numerous implications for how we think about the past and how we think about our *reliance* on our own memories. (For more on research in this domain, see Carpenter & Schacter, 2017; Cochran, Greenspan, Bogart, & Loftus, 2016; Frenda, Nichols, & Loftus, 2011; Laney, 2012; Loftus, 2017; Rich & Zaragoza, 2016. For research documenting similar memory errors in *children,* see, e.g., Bruck & Ceci, 1999, 2009; Reisberg, 2014.)

Are There Limits on the Misinformation Effect?

The studies just described reflect the **misinformation effect**—a term referring to memory errors that result from misinformation received after an event was experienced. What sorts of memory errors can be planted in this way?

We've mentioned studies in which participants remember broken glass when really there was none or remember a barn when there was no barn in view. Similar procedures have altered how *people* are remembered—and so, with just a few "suggestions" from the experimenter, participants remember clean-shaven men as bearded, young people as old, and fat people as thin (e.g., Christiaansen, Sweeney, & Ochalek, 1983; Frenda et al., 2011).

It's remarkably easy to produce these errors—with just one word ("hit" vs. "smashed") being enough to alter an individual's recollection. What happens, though, if we ramp up our efforts to plant false memories? Can we create larger-scale errors? In one study, college students were told that the investigators were trying to learn how different people remember the same experience. The students were then given a list of events that (they were told) had been reported by their parents; the students were asked to recall these events as well as they could, so that the investigators could compare the students' recall with their parents' (Hyman, Husband, & Billings, 1995).

Some of the events on the list actually had been reported by the participants' parents. Other events were bogus—made up by the experimenters. One of the bogus events was an overnight hospitalization for a high fever; in a different experiment, the bogus event was attending a wedding reception and accidentally spilling a bowlful of punch on the bride's family.

The college students were easily able to remember the genuine events (i.e., the events actually reported by their parents). In an initial interview, more than 80% of these events were recalled, but none of the students recalled the bogus events. However, repeated attempts at recall changed this pattern. By a third interview, 25% of the participants were able to remember the embarrassment of spilling the punch, and many were able to supply the details of this (entirely

FIGURE 8.4 THE BALLOON RIDE THAT NEVER WAS

A   B

In this study, participants were shown a faked photo (Panel B) created from a real childhood snapshot (Panel A). With this prompt, many participants were led to a vivid, detailed recollection of the balloon ride—even though it never occurred!

fictitious) episode. Other studies have shown similar results. Participants have been led to recall details of particular birthday parties that, in truth, they never had (Hyman et al., 1995); or an incident of being lost in a shopping mall even though this event never took place; or a (fictitious) event in which they were the victim of a vicious animal attack (Loftus, 2003, 2004; also see, e.g., Chrobak & Zaragoza, 2008; Geraerts et al., 2009; Laney & Loftus, 2010).

Errors Encouraged through "Evidence"

Other researchers have taken a further step and provided participants with "evidence" in support of the bogus memory. In one procedure, researchers obtained a real childhood snapshot of the participant (see **Figure 8.4A** for an example) and, with a few clicks of a computer mouse, created a fictitious picture like the one shown in **Figure 8.4B**. With this prompt, many participants were led to a vivid, detailed recollection of the hot-air balloon ride—even though it never occurred (Wade, Garry, Read, & Lindsay, 2002). Another study used an *unaltered* photo showing the participants' second-grade class (see **Figure 8.5** for an example). This was apparently enough to persuade participants that the experimenters really did have information about their childhood. Therefore, when the experimenters "reminded" the participants about an episode of their childhood misbehavior, the participants took this reminder seriously. The result: Almost 80% were able to "recall"

FIGURE 8.5 PHOTOGRAPHS CAN ENCOURAGE MEMORY ERRORS

In one study, participants were "reminded" of a (fictitious) stunt they'd pulled while in the second grade. Participants were much more likely to "remember" the stunt (and so more likely to develop a false memory) if the experimenter showed them a copy of their actual second-grade class photo. Apparently, the photo convinced the participants that the experimenter really did know what had happened, and this made the experimenter's (false) suggestion much more persuasive.   (LINDSAY ET AL., 2004)

the episode, often in detail, even though it had never happened (Lindsay, Hagen, Read, Wade, & Garry, 2004).

False Memories, False Confessions

It is clear that people can sometimes remember entire events that never took place. They sometimes remember emotional episodes (like being lost in a shopping mall) that never happened. They can remember their own transgressions (spilling the punch bowl, misbehaving in the second grade), even though these misdeeds never occurred.

One study pushed things still further, using a broad mix of techniques to encourage false memories (Shaw & Porter, 2015). The interviewer repeatedly asked participants to recall an event that (supposedly) she had learned about from their parents. She assured participants that she had detailed information about the (fictitious) event, and she applied social pressure with comments like "Most people are able to retrieve lost memories if they try

A substantial number of people have vivid, elaborate memories for an episode in which they were abducted by space aliens. They report the aliens' medical examination of their human captive; in some cases, they describe being impregnated by the aliens. Some people regard these reports as proof that our planet has been visited by extraterrestrials. Most scientists, however, regard these reports as false—as "memories" for an event that never happened. On this interpretation, the abduction reports illustrate how *wrong* our memories can sometimes be.

TEST YOURSELF

6. What is the misinformation effect? Describe three different procedures that can produce this effect.

7. Some people insist that our memories are consistently accurate in remembering the gist, or overall content, of an event; when we make memory errors, they claim, we make mistakes only about the details within an event. What evidence allows us to *reject* this claim?

hard enough." She offered smiles and encouraging nods whenever participants showed signs of remembering the (bogus) target events. If participants couldn't recall the target events, she showed signs of disappointment and said things like "That's ok. Many people can't recall certain events at first because they haven't thought about them for such a long time." She also encouraged participants to use a memory retrieval technique (guided imagery) that is known to foster false memories.

With these (and other) factors in play, Shaw and Porter persuaded many of their participants that just a few years earlier the participants had committed a crime that led to police contact. In fact, many participants seemed able to remember an episode in which they had assaulted another person with a weapon and had then been detained by the police. This felony never happened, but many participants "recalled" it anyhow. Their memories were in some cases vivid and rich with detail, and on many measures indistinguishable from memories known to be accurate.

Let's be clear, though, that this study used many forms of influence and encouragement. It takes a lot to pull memory this far off track! There has also been debate over just how many of the participants in this study truly developed false memories. Even so, the results show that it's possible for a large number of people to have memories that are emotionally powerful, deeply consequential, and utterly false. (For discussion of Shaw and Porter's study, see Wade, Garry, & Pezdek, 2017. Also see Brewin & Andrews, 2017, and then in response, Becker-Blease & Freyd, 2017; Lindsay & Hyman, 2017; McNally, 2017; Nash, Wade, Garry, Loftus, & Ost, 2017; Otgaar, Merckelbach, Jelicic, & Smeets, 2017; and Scoboria & Mazzoni, 2017.)

Psychology students sometimes get teased by their peers: "Why are you taking Psych courses? It's all a matter of common sense!" The same sentiment can arise when psychologists testify in court cases, with the goal of helping judges and juries understand how memory functions—and how someone's memory can be mistaken. Some judges, however, refuse this testimony. In support of this refusal, they note that expert testimony is allowed only if it will be helpful in deciding the case, and the testimony won't be helpful if it simply covers points that judge and jury already know. In legal jargon, the testimony is permitted only if it covers topics "beyond the ken of the average juror."

How should we think about these notions? Are psychology's claims about memory simply a confirmation of common sense? Each of us, of course, has had a lifetime of experience working with and relying on our memories; that experience has surely taught us a lot about how memory functions. Even so, it's easy to find widespread beliefs about memory that are incorrect. Often, these beliefs start with a kernel of truth but understate the actual facts. For example, everyone knows that memories are sometimes inaccurate; people talk about their memories "playing tricks" on them. However, most people are astonished to learn how common memory errors are and how large the errors can sometimes be. Therefore, in relying on common sense, people (including judges and juries) probably trust memory more than they should.

For example, in one study, college students were surveyed about their perceptions of various risks (Wilson & Brekke, 1994). These students were largely unconcerned about the risk of someone biasing their memory with leading questions; they regarded this risk as roughly equivalent to the risk of someday being kidnapped by space aliens. In contrast, though, studies make it plain that just a word or two of leading can produce memory errors in roughly one third of the people questioned. Surely, the danger of extraterrestrial abduction is much lower than this.

Other commonsense beliefs are flatly wrong. For example, some people have the view that certain types of events are essentially immune to forgetting. They speak about those events as somehow "burned into the brain" and say things like "I'll never forget the events of 9/11" or ". . . the day I got married" or ". . . what he looked like when he pulled the trigger." However, the "burned into the brain" idea is wrong, and investigators can often document large-scale errors in these singular, significant memories.

Additional examples are easy to find. These include the widely held view that someone's degree of certainty is a good index of whether his or her memory is accurate (this is true only in a narrow set of circumstances); the common belief that our memories function just as a video recorder functions (not at all true); or the belief that hypnosis can allow someone to recover long-lost memories (utterly false).

In fact, let's note an irony here. Commonsense beliefs about memory (or about psychology in general) are sometimes sensible and sometimes not. If scientific research corrects a mistaken commonsense belief, then obviously we've learned something. But if the research turns out to *confirm* common sense, then here too we've learned something—because we've learned that this is one of the times when common sense is on track. On that basis, we shouldn't scoff at results that "merely" confirm common sense, because these results can be just as informative as results that truly surprise us.

Avoiding Memory Errors

Evidence is clear that people do make mistakes—at times, large mistakes—in remembering the past. But people usually *don't* make mistakes. In other words, you generally can trust your memory, because more often than not your recollection is detailed, long-lasting, and *correct*.

This mixed pattern, though, demands a question: Is there some way to figure out when you've made a memory mistake and when you haven't? Is there a way to decide which memories you can rely on and which ones you can't?

Memory Confidence

In evaluating memories, people rely heavily on expressions of *certainty* or *confidence*. Specifically, people tend to trust memories that are expressed with confidence. ("I distinctly remember her yellow jacket; I'm sure of it.") They're more cautious about memories that are hesitant. ("I think she was wearing yellow, but I'm not certain.") We can see these patterns when people are evaluating their own memories (e.g., when deciding whether to take action or not, based on a bit of recollection); we see the same patterns when people are evaluating memories they hear from someone else (e.g., when juries are deciding whether they can rely on an eyewitness's testimony).

Evidence suggests, though, that a person's degree of certainty is an uneven indicator of whether a memory is trustworthy. On the positive side, there are circumstances in which certainty and memory accuracy are highly correlated (e.g., Wixted, Mickes, Clark, Gronlund, & Roediger, 2015; Wixted & Wells, 2017). On the negative side, though, we can easily find exceptions to this pattern—including memories that are expressed with total certainty ("I'll never forget that day; I remember it as though it were yesterday") but that turn out to be entirely mistaken. In fact, we can find circumstances in which there's no correspondence at all between how certain someone says she is, in recalling the past, and how accurate that recollection is likely to be. As a result, if we try to categorize memories as correct or incorrect based on someone's confidence, we'll often get it wrong. (For some of the evidence, see Busey, Tunnicliff, Loftus, & Loftus, 2000; Hirst et al., 2009; Neisser & Harsch, 1992; Reisberg, 2014; Wells & Quinlivan, 2009.)

How can this be? One reason is that a person's confidence in a memory is often influenced by factors that have no impact on memory accuracy. When these factors are present, confidence can shift (sometimes upward, sometimes downward) with no change in the accuracy level, with the result that any connection between confidence and accuracy can be strained or even shattered.

Participants in one study witnessed a (simulated) crime and later were asked if they could identify the culprit from a group of pictures. Some of the participants were then given feedback—"Good, you identified the suspect"; others weren't. The feedback couldn't possibly influence the accuracy of the identification, because the feedback arrived only after the identification had occurred. But the feedback did have a large impact on how confident participants said

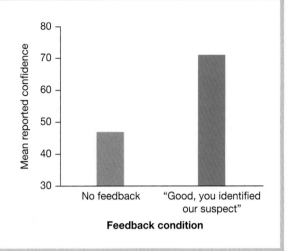

FIGURE 8.6 CONFIDENCE MALLEABILITY

In one study, participants first tried to identify a culprit from a police lineup and then indicated (on a scale of 0 to 100) how confident they had been in their selection. Some participants received no feedback about their choice; others received feedback after making their selection but before indicating their confidence level. The feedback couldn't possibly influence accuracy (because the selection had already been made), but it dramatically increased confidence.   (AFTER WELLS & BRADFIELD, 1998)

they'd been when making their lineup selection (see **Figure 8.6**), and so, with confidence inflated but accuracy unchanged, the linkage between confidence and accuracy was essentially eliminated. (Wells & Bradfield, 1998; also see Douglas, Neuschatz, Imrich, & Wilkinson, 2010; Semmler & Brewer, 2006; Wells, Olson, & Charman, 2002, 2003; Wright & Skagerberg, 2007.)

Similarly, think about what happens if someone is asked to report on an event over and over. The repetitions don't change the memory content—and so the accuracy of the report won't change much from one repetition to the next. However, with each repetition, the recall becomes easier and more fluent, and this ease of recall seems to make people more confident that their memory is correct. So here, too, accuracy is unchanged but confidence is inflated—and thus there's a gradual erosion, with each repetition, of the correspondence between accuracy and confidence. (For more on the disconnection between accuracy and confidence, see, e.g., Bradfield Douglas & Pavletic, 2012; Charman, Wells, & Joy, 2011.)

In many settings, therefore, we cannot count on confidence as a means of separating accurate memories from inaccurate ones. In addition, other findings tell us that memory errors can be just as emotional, just as vivid, as accurate memories (e.g., McNally et al., 2004). In fact, research overall suggests that there simply are no indicators that can reliably guide us in deciding which memories to trust and which ones not to trust. For now, it seems that memory errors, when they occur, may often be undetectable.

Forgetting

We've been discussing the errors people sometimes make in recalling the past, but of course there's another way your memory can let you down: Sometimes you *forget*. You try to recall what was on the shopping list, or the name of

TEST YOURSELF

8. What factors seem to *undermine* the relationship between your degree of certainty in a memory and the likelihood that the memory is accurate?

an acquaintance, or what happened last week, and you simply draw a blank. Why does this happen? Are there things you can do to diminish forgetting?

The Causes of Forgetting

Let's start with one of the more prominent examples of "forgetting"—which turns out not to be forgetting at all. Imagine meeting someone at a party, being told his name, and moments later realizing you don't have a clue what his name is—even though you just heard it. This common (and embarrassing) experience is not the result of ultra-rapid forgetting. Instead, it stems from a failure in acquisition. You were exposed to the name but barely paid attention to it and, as a result, never learned it in the first place.

What about "real" cases of forgetting—cases in which you once knew the information but no longer do? For these cases, one of the best predictors of forgetting (not surprisingly) is the passage of time. Psychologists use the term **retention interval** to refer to the amount of time that elapses between the initial learning and the subsequent retrieval; as this interval grows, you're likely to forget more and more of the earlier event (see **Figure 8.7**).

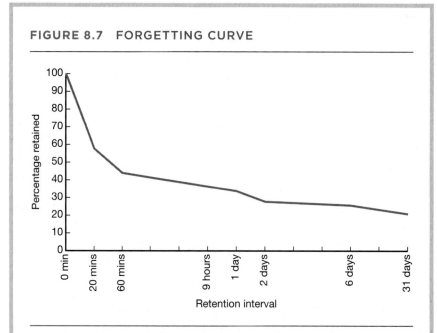

FIGURE 8.7 FORGETTING CURVE

The figure shows retention after various intervals since learning. The data shown here are from classic work by Hermann Ebbinghaus, so the pattern is often referred to as an "Ebbinghaus forgetting curve." The actual speed of forgetting (i.e., how "steep" the "drop-off" is) depends on how well learned the material was at the start. Across most situations, though, the pattern is the same—with the forgetting being rapid at first but then slowing down. Mathematically, this pattern is best described by an equation framed in terms of "exponential decay."

One explanation for this pattern comes from the **decay theory of forgetting**, which proposes rather directly that memories fade or erode with the passage of time. Maybe this is because the relevant brain cells die off. Or maybe the connections among memories need to be constantly refreshed—and if they're not refreshed, the connections gradually weaken.

A different possibility is that new learning somehow interferes with older learning. This view is referred to as **interference theory**. According to this view, the passage of time isn't the direct cause of forgetting. Instead, the passage of time creates the opportunity for new learning, and it is the new learning that disrupts the older memories.

A third hypothesis blames **retrieval failure**. The idea here is that the "forgotten memory" is still in long-term storage, but the person trying to retrieve the memory simply cannot locate it. This proposal rests on the notion that retrieval from memory is far from guaranteed, and we argued in Chapter 7 that retrieval is more likely if your perspective at the time of retrieval matches the perspective in place at the time of learning. If we now assume that your perspective is likely to change as time goes by, we can make a prediction about forgetting: The greater the retention interval, the greater the likelihood that your perspective has changed, and therefore the greater the likelihood of retrieval failure.

Which of these hypotheses is correct? It turns out that they all are. Memories do decay with the passage of time (e.g., Altmann & Schunn, 2012; Wixted, 2004; also Hardt, Nader, & Nadel, 2013; Sadeh, Ozubko, Winocur, & Moscovitch, 2016), so any theorizing about forgetting must include this factor. But there's also no question that a great deal of "forgetting" is retrieval failure. This point is evident whenever you're initially unable to remember some bit of information, but then, a while later, you do recall that information. Because the information was eventually retrieved, we know that it wasn't "erased" from memory through either decay or interference. Your initial failure to recall the information, then, must be counted as an example of retrieval failure.

Sometimes retrieval failure is *partial*: You can recall some aspects of the desired content, but not all. An example comes from the maddening circumstance in which you're trying to think of a word but simply can't come up with it. The word is, people say, on the "tip of their tongue," and following this lead, psychologists refer to this as the **TOT phenomenon**. People experiencing this state can often recall the starting letter of the sought-after word and approximately what it sounds like. So, for example, a person might remember "it's something like *Sanskrit*" in trying to remember "scrimshaw" or "something like *secant*" in trying to remember "sextant" (Brown, 1991; Brown & McNeill, 1966; Harley & Brown, 1998; James & Burke, 2000; Schwartz & Metcalfe, 2011).

What about interference? In one early study, Baddeley and Hitch (1977) asked rugby players to recall the names of the other teams they had played against over the course of a season. The key here is that not all players made it to all games (because of illness, injuries, or schedule conflicts). This fact allows us to compare players for whom "two games back" means two weeks ago, to players for whom "two games back" means four weeks ago. In this way, we can look at the effects of retention interval (two weeks vs. four) with the number of intervening games held constant. Likewise, we can compare players for whom the game a month ago was "three games back" to players for whom a month ago means "one game back." Now, we have the retention interval held constant, and we can look at the effects of intervening events. In this setting, Baddeley and Hitch reported that the mere passage of time accounts for very little; what really matters is the number of intervening events (see **Figure 8.8**). This is just what we would expect if interference, and not decay, is the major contributor to forgetting.

But *why* does memory interference occur? Why can't the newly acquired information coexist with older memories? The answer has several parts, but one element is linked to issues we've already discussed: In many cases, newly arriving information gets interwoven with older information, producing a risk of confusion about which bits are old (i.e., the event you're trying to remember) and which bits are new (i.e., information that you picked up after the event). In addition, in some cases, new information seems literally to replace old information—much as you no longer save the rough draft of one

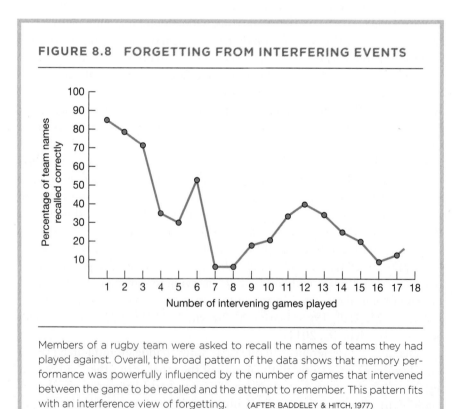

FIGURE 8.8   FORGETTING FROM INTERFERING EVENTS

Members of a rugby team were asked to recall the names of teams they had played against. Overall, the broad pattern of the data shows that memory performance was powerfully influenced by the number of games that intervened between the game to be recalled and the attempt to remember. This pattern fits with an interference view of forgetting.   (AFTER BADDELEY & HITCH, 1977) of your papers once the final draft is done. In this situation, the new information isn't woven into the older memory; instead, it erases it.

Undoing Forgetting

Is there any way to *undo* forgetting and to recover seemingly lost memories? One option, often discussed, is hypnosis. The idea is that under hypnosis a person can "return" to an earlier event and remember virtually everything about the event, including aspects the person didn't even notice (much less think about) at the time.

The reality, however, is otherwise. Hypnotized participants often do give detailed reports of the target event, but not because they remember more; instead, they're just willing to *say* more in order to comply with the hypnotist's instructions. As a result, their "memories" are a mix of recollection, guesses, and inferences—and, of course, the hypnotized individual cannot tell which of these are which (Lynn, Neuschatz, Fite, & Rhue, 2001; Mazzoni & Lynn, 2007; Spiegel, 1995).

On the positive side, though, there are procedures that do seem to diminish forgetting, including the so-called cognitive interview. This procedure was

A Drawings done by hypnotized adult told that he was 6 years old

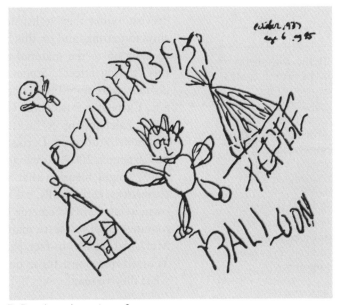

B Drawings done at age 6

HYPNOTIC AGE REGRESSION

In one study, participants were asked to draw a picture while mentally "regressed" to age 6. At first glance, their drawings (see Panel A for an example) looked remarkably childlike. But when compared to the participants' own drawings made at that age (see Panel B for an example), it's clear that the hypnotized adults' drawings were much more sophisticated. They represent an adult's conception of what a childish drawing is, rather than being the real thing.

designed to help police in their investigations and, specifically, is aimed at maximizing the quantity and accuracy of information obtained from eye-witnesses to crimes (Fisher & Schreiber, 2007; Memon, Meissner, & Fraser, 2010). The cognitive interview has several elements, including an effort toward *context reinstatement*—steps that put witnesses back into the mind-set they were in at the time of the crime. (For more on context reinstatement, see Chapter 7.) In addition, the cognitive interview builds on the simple fact that retrieval of memories from long-term storage is more likely if a suitable cue is provided. The interview therefore offers a diverse set of retrieval cues with the idea that the more cues provided, the greater the chance of finding one that triggers the target memory.

The cognitive interview is quite successful, both in the laboratory and in real crime investigations, producing more complete recollection without compromising accuracy. This success adds to the argument that much of what we call "forgetting" can be attributed to retrieval failure, and can be undone simply by providing more support for retrieval.

Also, rather than *undoing* forgetting, perhaps we can *avoid* forgetting. The key here is simply to "revisit" a memory periodically. Each "visit" seems to refresh the memory, with the result that forgetting is much less likely. Re-searchers have examined this effect in several contexts, including one that's pragmatically quite important: Students often have to take exams, and con-fronting the material on an exam is, of course, an occasion in which students "revisit" what they've learned. These revisits, we've just suggested, should slow forgetting, and on this basis, taking an exam can actually help students to hang on to the material they've learned. Several studies have confirmed this "testing effect": Students have better long-term retention for materi-als they were tested on, compared to materials they weren't tested on. (See, e.g., Carpenter, Pashler, & Cepeda, 2009; Halamish & Bjork, 2011; Healy, Jones, Lalchandani, & Tack, 2017; Karpicke, 2012; Karpicke & Blunt, 2011; McDaniel, Anderson, Derbish, & Morrisette, 2007; Pashler, Rohrer, Cepeda, & Carpenter, 2007; Rowland, 2014.)

We might mention that similar effects can be observed if students *test themselves* periodically, taking little quizzes that they've created on their own. Related effects emerge if students are occasionally asked questions that require a brief revisit to materials they've encountered (Brown, Roediger, & McDaniel, 2014). In fact, that's the reason why this textbook includes Test Yourself questions; those questions will actually help readers to remember what they've read!

Memory: An Overall Assessment

We've now seen that people sometimes recall with confidence events that never took place, and sometimes forget information they'd hoped to remem-ber. But we've also mentioned the positive side of things: how much people *can* recall, and the key fact that your memory is accurate far more often than not. Most of the time, it seems, you do recall the past as it truly was.

TEST YOURSELF

9. Explain the mecha-nisms hypothesized by each of the three major theories of forgetting: decay, interference, and retrieval failure.

10. What techniques or procedures seem *in*effective as a means of "un-doing" forget-ting? What techniques or procedures seem to diminish or avoid forgetting?

Perhaps most important, we've also suggested that memory's "failings" may simply be the price you pay in order to gain crucial advantages. For example, we've argued that memory errors arise because the various episodes in your memory are densely interconnected with one another; it's these interconnections that allow elements to be transplanted from one remembered episode to another. But we've also noted that these connections have a purpose: They're the retrieval paths that make memory search possible. Therefore, to avoid the errors, you would need to restrict the connections; but if you did that, you would lose the ability to locate your own memories within long-term storage.

The memory connections that lead to error also help you in other ways. Our environment, after all, is in many ways predictable, and it's enormously useful for you to exploit that predictability. There's little point, for example, in scrutinizing a kitchen to make sure there's a stove in the room, because in the vast majority of cases there is. So why take the time to confirm the obvious? Likewise, there's little point in taking special note that, yes, this restaurant does have menus and, yes, people in the restaurant are eating and not having their cars repaired. These, too, are obvious points, and it would be a waste of effort to give them special notice.

On these grounds, reliance on schematic knowledge is a good thing. Schemata guide your attention to what's informative in a situation, rather than what's self-evident (e.g., Gordon, 2006), and they guide your inferences at the time of recall. If this use of schemata sometimes leads you astray, that's a small price to pay for the gain in efficiency that schemata allow. (For similar points, see Chapter 4.)

In the same way, the blurring together of episodes may be a blessing, not a problem. Think, for example, about all the times when you've been with a particular friend. These episodes are related to one another in an obvious way, and so they're likely to become interconnected in your memory. This will cause difficulties if you want to remember which episode is which and whether you had a particular conversation in this episode or in that one. But rather than lamenting this, maybe we should *celebrate* what's going on here. Because of the "interference," all the episodes will merge together in your memory, so that what resides in memory is one integrated package, containing all of your knowledge about your friend. As a result, rather than complaining about memory confusion, we should rejoice over the memory *integration* and "cross-referencing."

In all of these ways, then, our overall assessment of memory can be rather upbeat. We have, to be sure, discussed a range of memory errors, but these errors are in most cases a side product of mechanisms that otherwise help you—to locate your memories within storage, to be efficient in your contact with the world, and to form general knowledge. Thus, even with the errors, even with forgetting, it seems that human memory functions in a way that serves us extraordinarily well. (For more on the benefits produced by memory's apparent limitations, see Howe, 2011; Nørby, 2015; Schacter, Guerin, & St. Jacques, 2011.)

TEST YOURSELF

11. Explain why the mechanisms that produce memory *errors* may actually be mechanisms that help us in important ways.

Autobiographical Memory

Most of the evidence in Chapters 6 and 7 was concerned with memory for simple stimuli—such as word lists or short sentences. In this chapter, we've considered memories for more complex materials, and this has drawn our attention to the ways in which your knowledge (whether knowledge of a general sort or knowledge about related episodes) can both improve memory and also interfere with it.

In making these points, we've considered memories in which the research participant was actually involved in the remembered episode, and not just an external witness (e.g., the false memory that he committed a felony). We've also looked at studies that involved memories for emotional events (e.g., the plane crash discussed at the chapter's start) and memory over the very long term (e.g., memories for childhood events "planted" in adult participants).

Do these three factors—involvement in the remembered event, emotion, and long delay—affect how or how well someone remembers? These factors are surely relevant to the sorts of remembering people do outside the laboratory, and all three are central for **autobiographical memory**. This is the memory that each of us has for the episodes and events of our lives, and this sort of memory plays a central role in shaping how each of us thinks about ourselves and, therefore, how we behave. (For more on the importance of autobiographical memory, see Baddeley, Aggleton, & Conway, 2002; Prebble, Addis, & Tippett, 2013; Steiner, Thomsen, & Pillemer, 2017. For more on the distinction between the types of memory, including *biological* differences between autobiographical memory and "lab memory," see Cabeza & St. Jacques, 2007; Hodges & Graham, 2001; Kopelman & Kapur, 2001; Tulving, 1993, 2002.)

Let's explore how the three factors we've mentioned, each seemingly central for autobiographical memory, influence what we remember.

Memory and the Self

Having some involvement in an event (as opposed to passively witnessing it) turns out to have a large effect on memory, because, overall, information relevant to the self is better remembered than information that's not self-relevant—a pattern known as the "self-reference effect" (e.g., Symons & Johnson, 1997; Westmacott & Moscovitch, 2003). This effect emerges in many forms, including an advantage in remembering adjectives that apply to you relative to adjectives that don't, better memory for names of places you have visited relative to names of places you've never been, and so on (see **Figure 8.9**).

But here, too, we can find memory errors, in part because your "memory" for your own life is (just like other memories) a mix of genuine recall and some amount of schema-based reconstruction. For example, consider the fact that most adults believe they've been reasonably consistent, reasonably stable, over their lifetimes. They believe, in other words, that they've always been pretty much the same as they are now. This idea of consistency is part of their **self-schema**—the set of interwoven beliefs and memories that constitute

FIGURE 8.9   SELF-REFERENCING AND THE BRAIN

MPFC activated during self-referential condition.

You are more likely to remember words that refer to *you,* in comparison to words in other categories. Here, participants were asked to judge adjectives in three conditions: answering questions like "Does this word describe the president?" or "Is this word printed in capital letters?" or "Does this word describe you?" Data from fMRI recordings showed a distinctive pattern of processing when the words were "self-referential." Specifically, self-referential processing is associated with activity in the medial prefrontal cortex (MPFC). This extra processing is part of the reason why self-referential words are better remembered.   (AFTER KELLEY ET AL., 2002)

people's knowledge about themselves. When the time comes to remember the past, therefore, people will rely to some extent on this belief in their own consistency, so they'll reconstruct their history in a biased way—one that maximizes the (apparent) stability of their lives. As a result, people often misremember their past attitudes and past romantic relationships, unwittingly distorting their personal history in a way that makes the past look more like the present than it really was. (See Conway & Ross, 1984; Holmberg & Homes, 1994. For related results, see Levine, 1997; Marcus, 1986; McFarland & Buehler, 2012; Ochsner & Schacter, 2000; Ross & Wilson, 2003.)

It's also true that most of us would like to have a positive view of ourselves, including a positive view of how we've acted in the past. This, too, can shape memory. As one illustration, Bahrick, Hall, and Berger (1996) asked college students to recall their high school grades as accurately as they could, and the data showed a clear pattern of self-service. When students forgot a good grade, their (self-serving) reconstruction led them to the (correct) belief that the grade must have been a good one; consistent with this, 89% of the A's were correctly remembered. But when students forgot a poor grade, reconstruction led them to the (false) belief that the grade must have been okay; as a result, only 29% of the D's were correctly recalled. (For other mechanisms through which motivation can color autobiographical recall, see Conway & Holmes, 2004; Conway & Pleydell-Pearce, 2000; Molden & Higgins, 2012.)

Memory and Emotion

Another factor important for autobiographical memory is *emotion*. Many of your life experiences are of course emotional, making you feel happy, or sad, or angry, or afraid, and in general emotion helps you to remember. One reason is emotion's impact on memory **consolidation**—the process through which memories are biologically "cemented in place." (See Hardt, Einarsson, & Nader, 2010; Wang & Morris, 2010; although also see Dewar, Cowan, & Della Sala, 2010.)

Whenever you experience an event or gain new knowledge, your memory for this new content is initially fragile and is likely represented in the brain via a pattern of neural activation. Over the next few hours, though, various biological processes stabilize this memory and put it into a more enduring form. This process—consolidation—takes place "behind the scenes," without you thinking about it, but it's crucial. If the consolidation is interrupted for some reason (e.g., because of extreme fatigue or injury), no memory is established and recall later will be impossible. (That's because there's no information in memory for you to retrieve; you can't read text off a blank page!)

A number of factors can promote consolidation. For example, evidence is increasing that key steps of consolidation take place while you're asleep—and so a good night's rest actually helps you, later on, to remember things you learned while awake the day before. (See Ackermann & Rasch, 2014; Giuditta, 2014; Rasch & Born, 2013; Tononi & Cirelli, 2013; Zillmer, Spiers, & Culbertson, 2008.)

Also, there's no question that emotion enhances consolidation. Specifically, emotional events trigger a response in the amygdala, and the amygdala in turn increases activity in the hippocampus. The hippocampus is, as we've seen, crucial for getting memories established. (See Chapter 7; for reviews of emotion's biological effects on memory, see Buchanan, 2007; Hoschedidt, Dongaonkar, Payne, & Nadel, 2010; Joels, Fernandez, & Roosendaal, 2011; Kensinger, 2007; LaBar, 2007; LaBar & Cabeza, 2006; Yonelinas & Ritchey, 2015. For a complication, though, see **Figure 8.10**.)

Emotion also shapes memory through other mechanisms. An event that's emotional is likely to be important to you, virtually guaranteeing that you'll pay close attention as the event unfolds, and we know that attention and thoughtful processing help memory. Moreover, you tend to mull over emotional events in the minutes (or hours) following the event, and this is tantamount to memory rehearsal. For all these reasons, it's not surprising that emotional events are well remembered (Reisberg & Heuer, 2004; Talmi, 2013).

FIGURE 8.10 INDIVIDUAL DIFFERENCES IN EPISODIC MEMORY

BB EE KB

BK HG NL

CC JL SC

Group

Researchers have made enormous progress in explaining the brain mechanisms that support memory. One complication, though, is that the brain mechanisms may differ from one individual to the next. This figure shows data from nine different people (and then an average of the nine) engaged in a task requiring the retrieval of episodic memories. As you can see, the pattern of brain activation differs somewhat from person to person.

(AFTER MILLER ET AL., 2002)

Let's note, though, that emotion doesn't just influence *how well* you remember; it also influences *what* you remember. Specifically, in many settings, emotion seems to produce a "narrowing" of attention, so that all of your attention will be focused on just a few aspects of the scene (Easterbrook, 1959). This narrowing helps guarantee that these attended aspects will be firmly placed into memory, but it also implies that the rest of the event, excluded from the narrowed focus, won't be remembered later (e.g., Gable & Harmon-Jones, 2008; Reisberg & Heuer, 2004; Steblay, 1992).

What exactly you'll focus on, though, may depend on the specific emotion. Different emotions lead you to set different *goals*: If you're afraid, your goal is to escape; if you're angry, your goal is to deal with the person or issue that's made you angry; if you're happy, your goal may be to relax and enjoy! In each case, you're more likely to pay attention to aspects of the scene directly relevant to your goal, and this will color how you remember the emotional event. (See Fredrickson, 2000; Harmon-Jones, Gable, & Price, 2013; Huntsinger, 2012, 2013; Kaplan, Van Damme, & Levine, 2012; Levine & Edelstein, 2009.)

Flashbulb Memories

One group of emotional memories seems special. These are the so-called **flashbulb memories**—memories of extraordinary clarity, typically for highly emotional events, retained despite the passage of many years. When Brown and Kulik (1977) introduced the term "flashbulb memory," they pointed to the memories people had of the moment in 1963 when they first heard that President Kennedy had been assassinated. In the Brown and Kulik study, people interviewed more than a decade after that event remembered it "as though it were yesterday," and many participants were certain they'd never forget that awful day. Moreover, participants' recollection was quite detailed—with people remembering where they were at the time, what they were doing, and whom they were with. Indeed, many participants were able to recall the clothing worn by people around them, the exact words uttered, and the like.

Many other events have also produced flashbulb memories. For example, most Americans can clearly recall where they were when they heard about the attack on the World Trade Center in 2001; many people vividly remember what they were doing in 2009 when they heard that Michael Jackson had died; many Italians have clear memories of their country's victory in the 2006 World Cup; and so on. (See Pillemer, 1984; Rubin & Kozin, 1984; also see Weaver, 1993; Winograd & Neisser, 1993.)

Remarkably, though, these vivid, high-confidence memories can contain substantial errors. Thus, when people say, "I'll never forget that day . . ." they're sometimes *wrong*. For example, Hirst et al. (2009) interviewed more than 3,000 people soon after the September 11 attack on the World Trade Center, asking how they first heard about the attack; who brought them the news; and what they were doing at the time. When these individuals were re-interviewed a year later, however, more than a third (37%) provided a substantially different account. Even so, the participants were strongly confident in their recollection (rating their degree of certainty, on a 1-to-5 scale, at an average of 4.4). The outcome was the same for participants interviewed three years after the attack—with 43% offering different accounts from those they had given initially. (For similar data, see Neisser & Harsch, 1992; also Hirst & Phelps, 2016; Rubin & Talarico, 2007; Schmidt, 2012; Talarico & Rubin, 2003.)

Other data, though, tell a different story, suggesting that some flashbulb memories are entirely accurate. Why should this be? Why are some flashbulb events remembered well, while others aren't? The answer involves several factors, including how, how often, and with whom someone discusses the flashbulb event. In many cases, this discussion may encourage people to "polish" their reports—so that they're offering their audience a "better," more interesting narrative. After a few occasions of telling and re-telling this version of the

FLASHBULB MEMORIES

People often have especially clear and long-lasting memories for events like first hearing about Princess Diana's death in 1997, the attack on the World Trade Center in September 2001, or the news of Michael Jackson's death in 2009. These memories—called "flashbulb memories"—are vivid and compelling, but they are not always accurate.

event, the new version may replace the original memory. (For more on these issues, see Conway et al., 1994; Hirst et al., 2009; Luminet & Curci, 2009; Neisser, Winograd, & Weldon, 1991; Palmer, Schreiber, & Fox, 1991; Tinti, Schmidt, Sotgiu, Testa, & Curci, 2009; Tinti, Schmidt, Testa, & Levine, 2014.)

Notice, then, that an understanding of flashbulb memories requires us to pay attention to the *social aspects* of remembering. In many cases, people "share" memories with one another (and so, for example, I tell you about my vacation, and you tell me about yours). Likewise, in the aftermath of an important event, people often compare their recollections. ("Did you see how he ran when the alarm sounded!?") In all cases, people are likely to alter their accounts in various ways, to allow for a better conversation. They may, for example, leave out mundane bits, or add bits to make their account more interesting or to impress their listeners. These new points about how the event is described will, in turn, often alter the way the event is later remembered.

In addition, people sometimes "pick up" new information in these conversations—if, for example, someone who was present for the same event noticed a detail that you missed. Often, this new information will be absorbed into other witnesses' memory—a pattern sometimes referred to as "co-witness contamination." Let's note, though, that sometimes another person who witnessed the event will make a *mistake* in recalling what happened, and, after conversation, other witnesses may absorb this mistaken bit into their own recollection (Hope, Gabbert, & Fraser, 2013). In this way, conversations after an event can sometimes have a positive impact on the accuracy and content of a person's eventual report, and sometimes a negative impact.

For all these reasons, then, it seems that "remembering" is not an activity shaped only by the person who holds the memory, and exploring this point will be an important focus for future research. (For early discussion of this broad issue, see Bartlett, 1932. For more recent discussion, see Choi, Kensinger, & Rajaram, 2017; Gabbert & Hope, 2013; Roediger & Abel, 2015.)

Returning to flashbulb memories, though, let's not lose track of the fact that the accuracy of these memories is uneven. Some flashbulb memories are marvelously accurate; others are filled with error. Therefore, the commonsense idea that these memories are somehow "burned into the brain," and thus always reliable, is surely mistaken. In addition, let's emphasize that from the point of view of the person who has a flashbulb memory, there's no detectable difference between an accurate flashbulb memory and an inaccurate one: Either one will be recalled with great detail and enormous confidence. In each case, the memory can be intensely emotional. Apparently, memory errors can occur even in the midst of our strongest, most vivid recollections.

Traumatic Memories

Flashbulb memories usually concern events that were strongly emotional. Sadly, though, we can also find cases in which people experience truly extreme emotion, and this leads us to ask: How are *traumatic* events remembered? If someone has witnessed wartime atrocities, can we count on the accuracy of their testimony in a war-crimes trial? If someone suffers through the horrors of a sexual assault, will the painful memory eventually fade?

Evidence suggests that most traumatic events are well remembered for many years. In fact, victims of atrocities often seem plagued by a cruel enhancement of memory, leaving them with extra-vivid and long-lived recollections of the terrible event (e.g., Alexander et al., 2005; Goodman et al., 2003; Peace & Porter, 2004; Porter & Peace, 2007; Thomsen & Berntsen, 2009). As a result, people who have experienced trauma sometimes complain about having "too much" memory and wish they remembered *less*.

This enhanced memory can be understood in terms of a mechanism we've already discussed: consolidation. This process is promoted by the conditions that accompany bodily arousal, including the extreme arousal typically present in a traumatic event (Buchanan & Adolphs, 2004; Hamann, 2001; McGaugh, 2015). But this doesn't mean that traumatic events are always well remembered. There are, in fact, cases in which people who've suffered through extreme events have little or no recall of their experience (e.g., Arrigo & Pezdek, 1997). We can also sometimes document substantial errors in someone's recall of a traumatic event (Paz-Alonso & Goodman, 2008).

What factors are producing this mixed pattern? In some cases, traumatic events are accompanied by sleep deprivation, head injuries, or substance abuse, each of which can disrupt memory (McNally, 2003). In other cases, the memory-promoting effects of arousal are offset by the complex memory effects of *stress*. The key here is that the experience of stress sets off a cascade of biological reactions. These reactions produce changes throughout the body, and the changes are generally beneficial, helping the organism to survive the stressful event. However, the stress-produced changes are disruptive to some biological functions, and this can lead to a variety of problems (including medical problems caused by stress).

How does the mix of stress reactions influence memory? The answer is complicated. Stress experienced at the time of an event seems to enhance memory for materials directly relevant to the source of the stress, but has the opposite effect—undermining memory—for other aspects of the event (Shields, Sazma, McCullough, & Yonelinas, 2017). Also, stress experienced during memory *retrieval* interferes with memory, especially if the target information was itself emotionally charged.

How does all this play out in situations away from the laboratory? One line of evidence comes from a study of soldiers who were undergoing survival training. As part of their training, the soldiers were deprived of sleep and food, and they went through a highly realistic simulation of a prisoner-of-war interrogation. One day later, the soldiers were asked to identify the interrogator from a lineup. Despite the extensive (40-minute) face-to-face encounter with the interrogator and the relatively short (one-day) retention interval, many soldiers picked the wrong person from the lineup. Soldiers who had experienced a moderate-stress interrogation picked the wrong person from a live lineup 38% of the time; soldiers who had experienced a high-stress interrogation (one that included a physical confrontation) picked the wrong person 56% of the time if tested with a live lineup, and 68% of the time if tested with a photographic lineup. (See Morgan et al., 2004; also see Deffenbacher, Bornstein, Penrod, & McCorty, 2004; Hope, Lewinski, Dixon, Blocksidge, & Gabbert, 2012; Valentine & Messout, 2008.)

Repression and "Recovered" Memories

Some authors argue in addition that people defend themselves against extremely painful memories by pushing these memories out of awareness. Some writers suggest that the painful memories are "repressed"; others use the term "dissociation" to describe this self-protective mechanism. No matter what terms we use, the idea is that these painful memories (including, in many cases, memories for childhood abuse) won't be consciously available but will still exist in a person's long-term storage and in suitable circumstances can be "recovered"—that is, made conscious again. (See, for discussion, Belli, 2012; Freyd, 1996, 1998; Terr, 1991, 1994.)

Most memory researchers, however, are skeptical about this proposal. As one consideration, painful events—including events that seem likely candidates for repression—seem typically to be well remembered, and this is the opposite of what we would expect if a self-protective mechanism was in place. In addition, some of the abuse memories reported as "recovered" may, in fact, have been remembered all along, and so they provide no evidence of repression or dissociation. In these cases, the memories had appeared to be "lost" because the person refused to discuss these memories for many years; "recovery" of these memories simply reflects the fact that the person is at last willing to talk about them. This sort of "recovery" can be extremely consequential—emotionally and legally—but doesn't tell us anything about how memory works.

Sometimes, though, memories do seem to be genuinely lost for a while and then recovered. But this pattern may not reveal the operation (and, eventually, the "lifting") of repression or dissociation. Instead, this pattern may be the result of retrieval failure—a mechanism that can "hide" memories for periods of time, only to have them reemerge once a suitable retrieval cue is available. Here, too, the recovery may be of enormous importance for the person who is finally remembering the long-lost episodes; but again, this merely confirms the role of an already-documented memory mechanism, with no need for theorizing about repression.

In addition, we need to acknowledge the possibility that at least some recovered memories may, in fact, be false memories. After all, we know that false memories occur and that they're more likely when someone is recalling the distant past than when one is trying to remember recent events. It's also relevant that many recovered memories emerge only with the assistance of a therapist who is genuinely convinced that a client's psychological problems stem from long-forgotten episodes of childhood abuse. Even if therapists scrupulously avoid leading questions, their expectations might still lead them to shape their clients' memory in other ways—for example, by giving signs of interest or concern if the clients hit on the "right" line of exploration, by spending more time on topics related to the alleged memories, and so on. In these ways, the climate within a therapeutic session could guide the client toward finding exactly the "memories" the therapist expects to find.

Overall, then, the idea of a self-protective mechanism "hiding" painful memories from view is highly controversial. Some psychologists (often, those working in a mental health specialty) insist that they routinely observe this sort of self-protection, and other psychologists (generally, memory researchers) reject the idea that memories can be hidden in this way. It does seem clear, however, that at least some of these now-voiced memories are accurate and provide evidence for terrible crimes. As in all cases, though, the veracity of recollection cannot be taken for granted. This warning is important in evaluating any memory, but especially so for anyone wrestling with traumatic recollection. (For discussions of this difficult—and sometimes angrily debated—issue, see, among others, Belli, 2012; Brewin &Andrews, 2014, 2016; Dalenberg et al., 2012; Geraerts et al., 2009; Giesbrecht, Lynn, Lilienfeld, & Merckelbach, 2008; Kihlstrom, 2006; Küpper, Benoid, Dalgleish, & Anderson, 2014; Loftus, 2017; Ost, 2013; Patihis, Lilienfeld, Ho, & Loftus, 2014; Pezdek & Blandon-Gitlin, 2017.)

Long, Long-Term Remembering

In the laboratory, a researcher might ask you to recall a word list you read just minutes ago or a film you saw a week ago. Away from the lab, however, people routinely try to remember events from years—perhaps decades—back.

We've mentioned that these longer *retention intervals* are generally associated with a greater amount of forgetting. But, impressively, memories from long ago can sometimes turn out to be entirely accurate.

In an early study, Bahrick, Bahrick, and Wittlinger (1975; also Bahrick, 1984; Bahrick & Hall, 1991) tracked down the graduates of a particular high school—people who had graduated in the previous year, and the year before, and the year before that, and ultimately, people who had graduated 50 years earlier. These alumni were shown photographs from their own year's high school yearbook, and for each photo they were given a group of names and had to choose the name of the person shown in the picture. The data for this "name-matching" task show remarkably little forgetting; performance was approximately 90% correct if tested 3 months after graduation, the same after 7 years, and the same after 14 years. In some versions of the test, performance was still excellent after 34 years (see **Figure 8.11**).

FIGURE 8.11 MEMORY OVER THE VERY LONG TERM

When people were tested for how well they remembered names and faces of their high school classmates, their memory was remarkably long-lasting. In the name-matching task, participants were given a group of names and had to choose the right one. In the picture-cueing task, participants had to come up with the names on their own. In both tasks, the data show a sharp drop-off after 47 years, but it is unclear whether this reflects an erosion of memory or a more general drop-off in performance caused by the normal process of aging. (AFTER BAHRICK, BAHRICK, & WITTLINGER, 1975)

As a different example, what about the material you're learning right now? Five years from now, will you still remember what you've learned? How about a decade from now? Conway, Cohen, and Stanhope (1991, 1992) explored these questions, testing students' retention of a cognitive psychology course taken years earlier. The results echo the pattern we've already seen. Some forgetting of names and specific concepts was observed during the first 3 years after the course. After the third year, however, performance stabilized, so that students tested after 10 years still remembered a fair amount—in fact, just as much as students tested after 3 years (see **Figure 8.12**).

In an earlier section, we argued that the retention interval is crucial for memory and that memory gets worse as times goes by. The data now in front of us, though, indicate that *how much* the interval matters—that is, how quickly memories "fade"—may depend on how well established the memories were in the first place. The high school students in the Bahrick et al. study had seen their classmates day after day, for (perhaps) several years. They therefore knew their classmates' names very, very well—and this is why the passage of time had only a slight impact on their memories for the names. Likewise, students in the Conway et al. study had apparently learned their psychology quite well—and so they retained what they'd learned for a very long time. In fact, we first met this study in Chapter 6, when we mentioned that students' *grades* in the course were good predictors of how much the students would still remember many years after the course was done. Here, too, the better the original learning, the slower the forgetting.

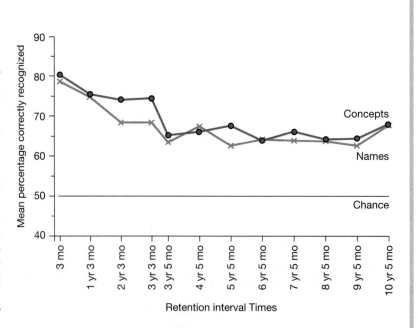

FIGURE 8.12 LONG-TERM RETENTION OF COURSE MATERIALS

Participants in this study were quizzed about material they had learned in a college course taken as recently as three months ago or as far back as a decade ago. The data showed some forgetting, but then performance leveled off; memory seemed remarkably stable from three years onward. Note that in a recognition task, memory is probed with "familiar-or-not" questions, so someone with no memory, responding at random, would get 50% right just by chance.

(AFTER CONWAY, COHEN, & STANHOPE, 1991)

We can maintain our claim, therefore, that the passage of time is the enemy of memory: Longer retention intervals produce lower levels of recall. However, if the material is very well learned at the start, and also if you periodically "revisit" the material, you can dramatically diminish the impact of the passing years.

How General Are the Principles of Memory?

There is certainly more to be said about autobiographical memory. For example, it can't be surprising that people tend to remember significant turning points in their lives and often use these turning points as a means of organizing their autobiographical recall (Enz & Talarico, 2015; Rubin & Umanath, 2015). Perhaps related, there are also memory patterns associated with someone's *age*. Specifically, most people recall very little from the early years of childhood (before age 3 or so; e.g., Akers et al., 2014; Bauer, 2007; Hayne, 2004; Howe, Courage, & Rooksby, 2009; Morrison & Conway, 2010). In contrast, people generally have clear and detailed memories of their late adolescence and early adulthood, a pattern known as the "reminiscence bump." (See **Figure 8.13**; Conway & Haque, 1999; Conway, Wang, Hanyu, & Haque 2005; Dickson, Pillemer, & Bruehl, 2011; Koppel & Rubin, 2016; Rathbone, Moulin, & Conway, 2008; Rathbone, O'Connor, & Moulin, 2017.) As a result, for many Americans, the last years of high school

TEST YOURSELF

12. What is memory consolidation?
13. What is a flashbulb memory? Are flashbulb memories distinctive in how *accurate* they seem to be?

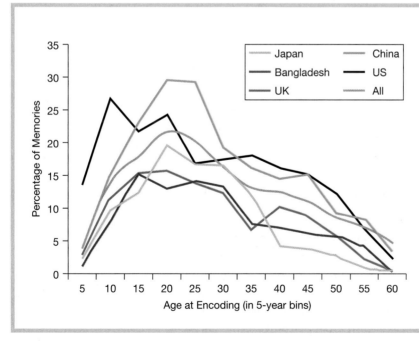

FIGURE 8.13 THE LIFESPAN RETRIEVAL CURVE

Most people have few memories of their early childhood (roughly from birth to age 3 or 4); this pattern is referred to as "childhood amnesia." In contrast, the period from age 10 to 30 is well remembered, producing a pattern called the "reminiscence bump." This "bump" has been observed in multiple studies and in diverse cultures; events from this time in young adulthood are often remembered in more detail (although perhaps less *accurately*) than more recent events.

and the years they spend in college are likely to be the most memorable periods of their lives.

But in terms of the broader themes of this chapter, where does our brief survey of autobiographical memory leave us? In many ways, this form of memory is similar to other sorts of remembering. Autobiographical memories can last for years and years, but so can memories that don't refer directly to your own life. Autobiographical remembering is far more likely if the person occasionally revisits the target memories; these rehearsals dramatically reduce forgetting. But the same is true in non-autobiographical remembering.

Autobiographical memory is also open to error, just as other forms of remembering are. We saw this in cases of flashbulb memories that turn out to be false. We've also seen that misinformation and leading questions can plant false autobiographical memories—about birthday parties that never happened and trips to the hospital that never took place (also see Brown & Marsh, 2008). Misinformation can even reshape memories for traumatic events, just as it can alter memories for trivial episodes in the laboratory (Morgan, Southwick, Steffan, Hazlett, & Loftus, 2013; Paz-Alonso & Goodman, 2008).

These facts strengthen a claim that has been emerging in our discussion over the last three chapters: Certain principles seem to apply to memory in general, no matter what is being remembered. All memories depend on connections. The connections promote retrieval. The connections also facilitate interference, because they allow one memory to blur into another. The connections can fade with the passage of time, producing memory gaps, and the gaps are likely to be filled via reconstruction based on generic knowledge. All these things seem to be true whether we're talking about relatively recent memories or memories from long ago, emotional memories or memories of calm events, memories for complex episodes or memories for simple word lists.

But this doesn't mean that all principles of memory apply to all types of remembering. As we saw in Chapter 7, the rules that govern implicit memory may be different from those that govern explicit memory. And as we've now seen, some of the factors that play a large role in shaping autobiographical remembering (e.g., the role of emotion) may be irrelevant to other sorts of memory.

In the end, therefore, our overall theory of memory is going to need more than one level of description. We'll need some principles that apply to only certain types of memory (e.g., principles specifically aimed at emotional remembering). But we'll also need broader principles, reflecting the fact that some themes apply to memory of all sorts (e.g., the importance of memory connections). As the last three chapters have shown, these more general principles have moved us forward considerably in our understanding of memory in many different domains and have enabled us to illuminate many aspects of learning, of memory retrieval, and of the sources of memory error.

remembering for the long term

Sometimes you need to recall things after a short delay—a friend tells you her address and you drive to her apartment an hour later, or you study for a quiz that you'll take tomorrow morning. Sometimes, however, you want to remember things over a much longer time span—perhaps trying to recall things you learned months or years ago. This longer-term retention is certainly important in educational settings. Facts that you learn in high school may be crucial for your professional work later in life. Likewise, facts that you learn in your first year at college, or in your first year in a job, may be crucial in your third or fourth year. How, therefore, can we help people to remember things for the very long term?

The chapter has suggested a two-part answer to this question. First, you're more likely to hang on to material that you learned very well in the first place. The chapter mentions one study in which people tried to recall the material they'd learned in a college course a decade earlier. In that study, students' *grades* in the course were good predictors of how much the students would remember years after the course was done—and so, apparently, the better the original learning, the slower the forgetting.

But long-term retention also depends on another factor—whether you occasionally "revisit" the material you've learned. Even a brief refresher can help enormously. In one study, students were quizzed on little factoids they had most likely learned at some prior point in their lives (Berger, Hall, & Bahrick, 1999)—for example, "Who was the first astronaut to walk on the moon?"; "Who wrote the fable about the fox and the grapes?" In many cases, the students knew these little facts but couldn't recall them at that moment. In that situation, the students were given a quick reminder. The correct answer was shown to them for 5 seconds, with the simple instruction that they should look at the answer because they would need it later on.

Nine days after this reminder, participants were able to recall roughly half the answers. This obviously wasn't perfect performance, but it was an enormous return (an improvement from 0% to 50%) from a very small investment (5 seconds of "study time"). And it's likely that a *second* reminder a few days later, again lasting just 5 seconds, would have lifted their performance still further and allowed the participants to recall the items after an even longer delay.

One suggestion, then, is that testing yourself (perhaps with flashcards—with a cue on one side and an answer on the other) can be quite useful. Flashcards are often a poor way to *learn* material, because (as we've seen) learning requires thoughtful and meaningful engagement with the materials you're trying to memorize, and running through a stack of flash cards probably won't promote that thoughtful engagement. But using flashcards may be an

AIDS FOR STUDENTS?

Memory research provides powerful lessons for students hoping to retain what they are learning in their courses.

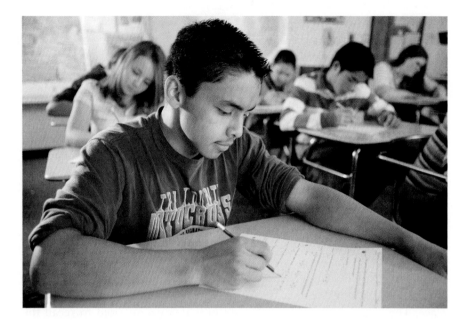

excellent way to review material that is already learned—and so a way to avoid forgetting this material.

Other, more substantial, forms of testing can also be valuable. Think about what happens each time you take a vocabulary quiz in your Spanish class. A question like "What's the Spanish word for 'bed'?" gives you practice in retrieving the word, and that practice promotes fluency in retrieval. In addition, seeing the word (*cama*) can itself refresh the memory, promoting retention.

The key idea here is the "testing effect." This term refers to a consistent pattern in which students who have taken a test have better retention later on, in comparison to students who didn't take the initial test. (See, e.g., Carpenter, Pashler, & Cepeda, 2009; Glass & Sinha, 2013; Halamish & Bjork, 2011; Karpicke, 2012; McDermott, Agarwal, D'Antonio, Roediger, & McDaniel, 2014; Pyc & Rawson, 2012.) This pattern has been documented with students of various ages (including high school and college students) and with different sorts of material.

The implications for students should be clear. It really does pay to go back periodically and review what you've learned—including material you learned earlier this academic year as well as material from previous years. The review doesn't have to be lengthy or intense; in the first study described here, just a 5-second exposure was enough to decrease forgetting dramatically.

Finally, you shouldn't complain if a teacher insists on giving frequent quizzes. Of course, quizzes can be a nuisance, but they serve two functions. First, they can help you assess your learning, so that you can judge whether—perhaps—you need to adjust your study strategies. Second, the quizzes actually help you retain what you've learned—for days, and probably months, and perhaps even decades after you've learned it.

For more on this topic . . .

Brown, P. C., Roediger, H. L., & McDaniel, M. A. (2014). *Make it stick: The science of successful learning.* New York, NY: Belknap Press.

Putnam, A. L., Nestojko, J. F., & Roediger, H. L. (2016). Improving student learning: Two strategies to make it stick. In J. C. Horvath, J. Lodge, & J. A. C. Hattie (Eds.), *From the laboratory to the classroom: Translating the science of learning for teachers* (pp. 94–121). Oxford, UK: Routledge.

Putnam, A. L., Sungkhasettee, V., & Roediger, H. L. (2016). Optimizing learning in college: Tips from cognitive psychology. *Perspectives on Psychological Science, 11*(5), 652–660.

chapter review

SUMMARY

- Memory is usually accurate, but errors do occur and can be quite significant. In general, these errors are produced by the connections that link memories to one another and link memories for specific episodes to other, more general knowledge. These connections help you because they serve as retrieval paths. But the connections can also "knit" separate memories together, making it difficult to keep track of which elements belong in which memory.

- Some memory errors arise from your understanding of an episode. The understanding promotes memory for the episode's gist but also encourages memory errors. A similar pattern emerges in the DRM procedure, in which a word related to other words on a list is (incorrectly) recalled as being part of the list. Closely related effects arise from schematic knowledge. This knowledge helps you understand an episode, but at the same time a reliance on schematic knowledge can lead you to remember an episode as being more "regular," more "normal," than it actually was.

- Memory errors can also arise through the misinformation effect, in which people are exposed to some (false) suggestion about a previous event. Such suggestions can easily change the details of how an event is remembered and can, in some cases, plant memories for entire episodes that never occurred at all.

- People seem genuinely unable to distinguish their accurate memories from their inaccurate ones. This is because false memories can be recalled with just as much detail, emotion, and confidence as historically accurate memories. The absence of a connection between memory accuracy and memory confidence contrasts with the commonsense belief that you should rely on someone's degree of certainty in assessing their memory. The problem in this commonsense belief lies in the fact that confidence is influenced by factors (such as feedback) that have no impact on accuracy, and this influence undermines the linkage between accuracy and confidence.

- While memory errors are easily documented, cases of accurate remembering can also be observed, and they are probably more numerous than cases involving memory error. Memory errors are more likely, though, in recalling distant events rather than recent ones. One reason is decay of the relevant memories; another reason is retrieval failure. Retrieval failure can be either complete or partial; the tip-of-the-tongue pattern provides a clear example of partial retrieval failure. Perhaps the most important source of forgetting, though, is interference.

- People have sought various ways of undoing forgetting, including hypnosis and certain drugs. These approaches, however, seem ineffective. Forgetting can be diminished, though, through procedures that provide a rich variety of retrieval cues, and it can be avoided through occasional revisits to the target material.

- Although memory errors are troubling, they may be the price you pay in order to obtain other advantages. For example, many errors result from the dense network of connections that link your various memories. These connections sometimes make it difficult to recall which elements occurred in which setting, but the same connections serve as retrieval paths—and without those connections, you might have great difficulty in locating your memories in long-term storage.

- Autobiographical memory is influenced by the same principles as any other form of memory, but it is also shaped by its own set of factors. For example, episodes connected to the self are, in general, better remembered—a pattern known as the "self-reference effect."

- Autobiographical memories are often emotional, and this has multiple effects on memory. Emotion seems to promote memory consolidation, but it may also produce a pattern of memory narrowing. Some emotional events give rise to very clear, long-lasting flashbulb memories. Despite their subjective clarity, these memories can contain errors and in some cases can be entirely inaccurate. At the extreme of emotion, trauma has mixed effects on memory. Some traumatic events are not remembered, but most traumatic events seem to be remembered for a long time and in great detail.

● Some events can be recalled even after many years have passed. In some cases, this is because the knowledge was learned very well in the first place. In other cases, occasional rehearsals preserve a memory for a very long time.

KEY TERMS

intrusion errors (p. 283)
DRM procedure (p. 285)
schema (plural: *schemata*) (p. 286)
misinformation effect (p. 291)
retention interval (p. 298)
decay theory of forgetting (p. 299)
interference theory (p. 299)

retrieval failure (p. 299)
TOT phenomenon (p. 299)
autobiographical memory (p. 304)
self-schema (p. 304)
consolidation (p. 306)
flashbulb memories (p. 308)

TEST YOURSELF AGAIN

1. What is the evidence that in some circumstances many people will misremember significant events they have experienced?

2. What is the evidence that in some circumstances people will even misremember *recent* events?

3. What is the evidence that your *understanding* of an episode can produce intrusion errors?

4. What is the DRM procedure, and what results does this procedure produce?

5. What is schematic knowledge, and what evidence tells us that schematic knowledge can help us—and also can undermine memory accuracy?

6. What is the misinformation effect? Describe three different procedures that can produce this effect.

7. Some people insist that our memories are consistently accurate in remembering the gist, or overall content, of an event; when we make memory errors, they claim, we make mistakes only about the details within an event. What evidence allows us to *reject* this claim?

8. What factors seem to *undermine* the relationship between your degree of certainty in a memory and the likelihood that the memory is accurate?

9. Explain the mechanisms hypothesized by each of the three major theories of forgetting: decay, interference, and retrieval failure.

10. What techniques or procedures seem *ineffective* as a means of "un-doing" forgetting? What techniques or procedures seem to diminish or avoid forgetting?

11. Explain why the mechanisms that produce memory *errors* may actually be mechanisms that help us in important ways.

12. What is memory consolidation?

13. What is a flashbulb memory? Are flashbulb memories distinctive in how *accurate* they seem to be?

THINK ABOUT IT

1. People sometimes compare the human eye to a camera, and compare human memory to a video recorder (like TiVo or the video recorder on your smartphone). Ironically, though, there are important ways in which your memory is *worse* than a video recorder, and also important ways in which it's far *better* than a video recorder. Describe both versions of this comparison—the ways in which video recorders are superior, and the ways in which your memory is superior.

🄴 eBOOK DEMONSTRATIONS & ESSAYS

Go to http://digital.wwnorton.com/cognition7 for the online demonstrations and essays relevant to this chapter. These can be found in the ebook.

Online Demonstrations

* Demonstration 8.1: Associations and Memory Error
* Demonstration 8.2: Memory Accuracy and Confidence
* Demonstration 8.3: The Tip-of-the-Tongue Effect
* Demonstration 8.4: Childhood Amnesia

Online Applying Cognitive Psychology and the Law Essays

* Cognitive Psychology and the Law: Jurors' Memory

ZAPS COGNITION LABS

Go to http://digital.wwnorton.com/cognition7 to experience interactive online psychology labs relevant to this chapter.

Knowledge

In Parts 2 and 3, we saw case after case in which your interactions with the world are guided by knowledge. In perceiving, for example, you make inferences guided by knowledge about the world's regular patterns. In attending, you anticipate inputs guided by your knowledge about what's likely to occur. In learning, you connect new information to things you already know.

But what is knowledge? How is it represented in your mind? How do you locate knowledge in memory when you need it? We've already taken some steps toward answering these questions—by arguing that knowledge is represented in the mind by means of a network of interconnected nodes. In this section, we'll expand this proposal in important ways. In Chapter 9, we'll describe the basic building blocks of knowledge—individual concepts—and consider several hypotheses about how concepts are represented in the mind. Because each hypothesis captures a part of the truth, we'll be driven toward a several-part theory that combines the various views. We'll also see that knowledge about individual concepts depends on linkages to other, related concepts. For example, you can't know what a "dog" is without also understanding what an "animal" is, what a "living thing" is, and so on. As a result, connections among ideas will be crucial here, just as they were in previous chapters.

Chapters 10 and 11 then focus on two special types of knowledge: knowledge about language and knowledge about visual images. In Chapter 10, we'll see that your knowledge of language is highly creative, allowing you to produce new words and new sentences that no one has ever used before. But at the same time, the creativity is constrained, so there are some words and sequences of words that are considered unacceptable by virtually any language-user. In order to understand this pattern of "constrained creativity," we'll consider the possibility that language knowledge involves abstract rules that are, in some way, honored by every user of the language.

In Chapter 11, we'll see that mental images involve representations that are distinct from those involved in other forms of knowledge, but we'll also consider some of the ways in which memory for visual appearances is governed by the same principles as other forms of knowledge.

Concepts and Generic Knowledge

what if... In Chapter 8, we mentioned people who have superior autobiographical recall. It's remarkable how much these individuals can remember — but some people, it turns out, remember even more. One might say that these people have "perfect memories," but this terminology would be misleading.

We begin with a work of fiction. In a wonderful short story titled "Funes the Memorious," the Argentine writer Jorge Luis Borges describes a character — Funes — who never forgets anything. But rather than being proud of this capacity, Funes is immensely distressed by his memorial prowess: "My memory, sir, is like a garbage heap" (p. 152).

Among other problems, Funes complains that he's incapable of thinking in general terms. He remembers so much about how individuals *differ* that he has a hard time focusing on what they might *have in common*: "Not only was it difficult for him to comprehend that the generic symbol *dog* embraces so many unlike individuals of diverse size and form; it bothered him that the dog at 3:14 (seen from the side) should have the same name as the dog at 3:15 (seen from the front)" (Borges, 1964, p. 153).

Funes is a fictional character, but consider the actual case of Solomon Shereshevsky (Luria, 1968). Shereshevsky, like Funes, never forgot anything. After hearing a lengthy speech, he could repeat it back word for word. If shown a complex mathematical formula (even one that had no meaning for him), he could reproduce it perfectly months later. He effortlessly memorized poems written in languages he didn't understand. And Shereshevsky's flawless retention wasn't the result of some deliberate trick or strategy. Just the opposite: Shereshevsky seemed to have no choice about his level of recall.

Like Funes, Shereshevsky wasn't well served by his extraordinary memory. He was so alert to the literal form of his experiences that he couldn't remember their deeper implications. Similarly, he had difficulty recognizing faces because he was so alert to the *changes* in a face from one view to the next. And, like Funes, Shereshevsky was often distracted by the detail of his own recollections, so he found it difficult to think in abstract terms.

There are, of course, settings in which you do want to remember the specific episodes of your life. You want to recall what you saw at a crime scene, holding to the side (as best you can) the information you picked up later in your conversation with the police. You hope to remember

- Basic concepts—like "chair" and "dog"—are the building blocks of all knowledge. However, attempts at *defining* these concepts usually fail because we easily find exceptions to any definition that might be proposed.

- This leads to a suggestion that knowledge of these concepts is cast in terms of *probabilities*—so that a creature that has wings and feathers, and that flies and lays eggs, is *probably* a bird.

- Many results are consistent with this probabilistic idea and show that the more a test case resembles the "prototype" for a category, the more likely people are to judge the case as being in that category.

- Other results, however, indicate that conceptual knowledge includes other beliefs—beliefs that link a concept to other concepts and also specify why the concept is as it is.

- These beliefs may be represented in the mind as propositions encoded in a network structure. Alternatively, they may be represented in a distributed form in a connectionist network.

- We are driven, therefore, to a multipart theory of concepts. Your conceptual knowledge likely includes a prototype for each category and also a set of remembered exemplars. But you also seem to have a broad set of beliefs about each concept—beliefs that provide a "theory" for why the concept takes the form it does, and you use this theory in a wide range of judgments about the concept.

what you read in your textbook, trying to ignore the (possibly bogus) information you heard from your roommate. Funes and Shereshevsky obviously excel in this type of memory, but their limitations remind us that there are also disadvantages for this type of particularized recall. In many settings, you want to set aside the details of this or that episode and, instead, weave your experiences together so that you can pool information received from various sources. This allows you to create a more complete, more integrated type of knowledge—one that allows you to think about dogs in general rather than focusing on *this* view of *that* dog; or one that helps you remember what your friend's face generally looks like rather than what she looked like, say, yesterday at 1:42 in the afternoon. This more general type of knowledge is surely drawn from your day-to-day experience, but it is somehow abstracted away from that experience. What is this more general type of knowledge?

Understanding Concepts

Imagine that a friend approaches you and boasts that he knows what a "spoon" is or what a "shoe" is. You'd probably be impressed by your friend's foolishness, not by his knowledge. After all, concepts like these are so ordinary, so straightforward, that there seems to be nothing special about knowing—and being able to think about—these simple ideas.

However, ordinary concepts like these are the building blocks out of which all knowledge is created, and as we've seen in previous chapters, you depend on your knowledge in many aspects of day-to-day functioning. Thus, you know what to pay attention to in a restaurant because you understand the basic concept of "restaurant." You're able to understand a simple story about a child checking her piggy bank because you understand the concepts of "money," "shopping," and so on.

The idea, then, is that you need concepts in order to have knowledge, and you need knowledge in order to function. In this way, your understanding of ideas like "spoon" and "shoe" might seem commonplace, but it is an ingredient without which cognition cannot proceed.

But what exactly does it mean to understand concepts like these? How is this knowledge represented in the mind? In this chapter, we'll begin with the hypothesis that understanding a concept is like knowing a dictionary definition—and so, if someone knows what a "house" is, or a "taxi," he or she can offer something like a definition for these terms—and likewise for all the other concepts in each person's knowledge base. As we'll see, though, this hypothesis quickly runs into problems, so we'll need to turn to a more complicated proposal.

Definitions: What Is a "Dog"?

You know perfectly well what a dog is. But what is it that you know? One possibility is that your knowledge is somehow akin to a dictionary definition—that is, what you know is something like: "A dog is a creature that (a) is an animal, (b) has four legs, (c) barks, (d) wags its tail." You could then use this definition in straightforward ways: When asked whether a candidate creature is a dog, you could use the definition as a checklist, scrutinizing the candidate for the various defining features. When told that "a dog is an animal," you would know that you hadn't learned anything new, because this information is already contained within the definition. If you were asked what dogs, cats, and horses have in common, you could scan your definition of each one looking for common elements.

This proposal is correct in some cases, and so, for example, you certainly know definitions for concepts like "triangle" and "even number." But what about more commonplace concepts? The concern here was brought to light by the 20th-century philosopher Ludwig Wittgenstein, who argued (e.g., Wittgenstein, 1953) that the simple terms we all use every day actually don't have definitions. For example, consider the word "game." You know this word and can use it sensibly, but what is a game? As an approach to this question, we could ask, for example, about the game of hide-and-seek. What makes hide-and-seek a "game"? Hide-and-seek (a) is an activity most often practiced by children, (b) is engaged in for fun, (c) has certain rules, (d) involves several people, (e) is in some ways competitive, and (f) is played during periods of leisure. All these are plausible attributes of games, and so we seem well on our way to defining "game." But are these attributes really part of the *definition* of "game"? What about the Olympic Games? The competitors in these games aren't children, and runners in marathon races don't look like they're having a lot of fun. Likewise, what about card games played by one person? These are played alone, without competition. For that matter, what about the case of professional golfers?

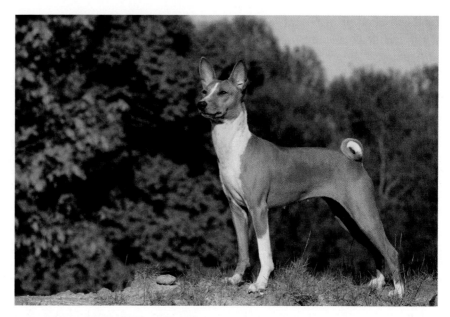

THE HUNT FOR DEFINITIONS

It is remarkably difficult to define even very familiar terms. For example, what is a "dog"? Most people include "has fur" in the definition, but what about the hairless Chihuahua? Many people include "communicates by barking" in the definition, but what about the Basenji (one of which is shown here)—a breed of dog that doesn't bark?

TEST YOURSELF

1. Consider the word "chair." Name some attributes that might plausibly be included in a definition for this word. But, then, can you describe objects that you would count as chairs even though they don't have one or more of these attributes?

2. What does it mean to say that there is a "family resemblance" among the various animals that we call "dogs"?

It seems that for each clause of the definition, we can find an exception—an activity that we call a "game" but that doesn't have the relevant characteristic. And the same is true for almost any concept. We might define "shoe" as an item of apparel made out of leather, designed to be worn on the foot. But what about wooden shoes? What about a shoe designed by a master shoemaker, intended only for display? What about a shoe filled with cement, which therefore can't be worn? Similarly, we might define "dog" in a way that includes four-leggedness, but what about a dog that has lost a limb in some accident? We might specify "communicates by barking" as part of the definition of dog, but what about the African Basenji, which has no bark?

Family Resemblance

It seems, then, we can't say things like "A dog is a creature that has fur and four legs and barks." That's because we easily find exceptions to this rule (a hairless Chihuahua; a three-legged dog; the barkless Basenji). But surely we *can* say, "Dogs *usually* are creatures that have fur, four legs, and bark, and a creature without these features is *unlikely to be* a dog." This probabilistic phrasing preserves what's good about definitions—the fact that they do name relevant features, shared by most members of the category. But this phrasing also allows a degree of uncertainty, some number of exceptions to the rule.

In a similar spirit, Wittgenstein proposed that members of a category have a **family resemblance** to one another. To understand this term, think about an actual family—your own, perhaps. There are probably no "defining features" for your family—features that every family member has. Nonetheless, there are features that are common in the family, and so, if we consider family members two or three at a time, we can usually find shared attributes. For example, you, your brother, and your mother might all have the family's beautiful red hair and the same wide lips; as a result, you three look alike to some extent. Your sister, however, doesn't have these features. But she's still recognizable as a member of the family because (like you and your father) she has the family's typical eye shape and the family's distinctive chin. In this way, the common features in the family depend on what "subgroup" you're considering—hair color shared for *these* family members; eye shape shared by *those* family members; and so on.

One way to think about this pattern is by imagining the "ideal" for each family—someone who has *all* of the family's features. (In our example, this would be a wide-lipped redhead with the right eye and chin shapes.) In many families, this person may not exist, so perhaps there's nobody who has every one of the family's distinctive features—and so no one who looks like the "perfect Jones" (or the "perfect Martinez" or the "perfect Goldberg"). Nonetheless, each member of the family shares at least some features with this ideal—and therefore has some features in common with other family members. This feature overlap is why the family members resemble one another, and it's how we manage to recognize these individuals as all belonging to the same family.

Wittgenstein proposed that ordinary categories like "dog" or "game" or "furniture" work in the same way. There may be no features that are shared by all dogs or all games. Even so, we can identify "characteristic features" for each category—features that many (perhaps most) category members have. These are the features that enable you to recognize that a dog is a dog, a game is a game, and so on.

There are several ways we might translate all these points into a psychological theory, but one influential translation was proposed by psychologist Eleanor Rosch in the mid-1970s (Rosch, 1973, 1978; Rosch & Mervis, 1975; Rosch, Mervis, Gray, Johnson, & Boyes-Braem, 1976). Let's look at her model.

Prototypes and Typicality Effects

One way to think about definitions is that they set the "boundaries" for a category. If a test case has certain attributes, then it's "inside" the boundaries. If a test case doesn't have the defining attributes, then it's "outside" the category. **Prototype theory**, in contrast, begins with a different tactic: Perhaps the best way to identify a category is to specify the "center" of the category, rather than the boundaries. Just as we spoke earlier about the "ideal" family member, perhaps the concept of "dog" is represented in the mind by some

TYPICALITY IN FAMILIES

In the Smith family, many (but not all) of the brothers have dark hair, so dark hair is typical for the family (i.e., is found in *many* family members) but doesn't define the family (i.e., is not found in *all* family members). Likewise, wearing glasses is typical for the family but not a defining feature; so is having a mustache and a big nose. Many concepts have the same character—with many features shared among the instances of the concept, but no features shared by all of the instances.

depiction of the "ideal" dog, and all judgments about dogs are made with reference to this ideal. Likewise for "bird" or "house" or any other concept in your repertoire—in each case, the concept is represented by the appropriate prototype.

In most cases, this "ideal"—the prototype—will be an average of the various category members you've encountered. So, for example, the prototype dog will be the average color of the dogs you've seen, the average size of the dogs you've seen, and so forth. (Notice, then, that different people, each with their own experiences, will have slightly different prototypes.) No matter what the specifics of the prototype, though, you'll use this "ideal" as the benchmark for your conceptual knowledge. Thus, whenever you use your conceptual knowledge, your reasoning is done with reference to the prototype.

Prototypes and Graded Membership

To make these ideas concrete, imagine that you're trying to decide whether a creature currently before your eyes is or is not a dog. In making this decision, you'll compare the creature with the prototype in your memory. If there's no similarity, the creature standing before you is probably not in the category; if there's considerable similarity, you draw the opposite conclusion.

This sounds plausible enough, but note an important implication. Membership in a category depends on resemblance to the prototype, and resemblance is a matter of degree. (After all, some dogs are likely to resemble the prototype closely, while others will have less in common with this ideal.) As a result, membership in the category isn't a simple "yes or no" decision;

CATEGORIES HAVE PROTOTYPES

As the text describes, people seem to have a prototype in their minds for a category like "dog." For many people, the German shepherd shown here is close to that prototype, and the other dogs depicted are more distant from the prototype.

instead, it's a matter of "more" or "less." In technical terms, we'd say that categories, on this view, have a **graded membership,** such that objects closer to the prototype are "better" members of the category than objects farther from the prototype. Basically, the idea is that some dogs are "doggier" than others, some books "bookier" than others, and so on for all the other categories you can think of.

Testing the Prototype Notion

This proposal—that mental categories have a graded membership—was tested in a series of experiments conducted years ago. For example, in classic studies using a **sentence verification task,** research participants were presented with a series of sentences, and their job was to indicate (by pressing the appropriate button) whether each sentence was true or false. In this procedure, participants' responses were slower for sentences like "A penguin is a bird" than for sentences like "A robin is a bird"; slower for "An Afghan hound is a dog" than for "A German shepherd is a dog" (Smith, Rips, & Shoben, 1974).

Why should this be? According to a prototype perspective, participants chose their response ("true" or "false") by comparing the thing mentioned (e.g., penguin) to their prototype for that category (i.e., their bird prototype). When there was close similarity between the test case and the prototype, participants could make their decisions quickly; in contrast, judgments about items distant from the prototype took more time. And given the results, it seems that penguins and Afghans are more distant from their respective prototypes than are robins and German shepherds.

Other early results can also be understood in these terms. For example, in a **production task** we simply ask people to name as many birds or dogs as they can. According to a prototype view, they'll do this task by first locating their bird or dog prototype in memory and then asking themselves what resembles this prototype. In essence, they'll start with the center of the category (the prototype) and work their way outward from there. So birds close to the prototype should be mentioned first; birds farther from the prototype, later on.

By this logic, the first birds mentioned in the production task should be the birds that yielded fast response times in the verification task; that's because what matters in both tasks is proximity to the prototype. Likewise, the birds mentioned later in production should have yielded slower response times in verification. This is exactly what happened (Mervis, Catlin, & Rosch, 1976).

In fact, this outcome sets the pattern of evidence for prototype theory. Over and over, in category after category, members of a category that are "privileged" on one task (e.g., they yield the fastest response times) turn out also to be privileged on other tasks (e.g., they're most likely to be mentioned). As another illustration of this pattern, consider the data from **rating tasks.** In these tasks, participants are given instructions like these: "We all know that some birds are 'birdier' than others, some dogs are 'doggier' than others, and so on. I'm going to present you with a list of birds or of dogs, and I want you to rate each one on the basis of how 'birdy' or 'doggy' it is" (Rosch, 1975; also Malt & Smith, 1984).

People are easily able to make these judgments, and quite consistently they rate items as being very "birdy" or "doggy" when these instances are close to the prototype (as determined in the other tasks). They rate items as being less "birdy" or "doggy" when these are farther from the prototype. This finding suggests that once again, people perform the task by comparing the test item to the prototype (see **Table 9.1**).

Basic-Level Categories

It does seem, then, that certain category members are "privileged," just as the prototype theory proposes. It turns out, also, that certain *types of category* are privileged—in their structure and the way they're used. For example, imagine

TABLE 9.1 PARTICIPANTS' TYPICALITY RATINGS FOR THE CATEGORY "FRUIT" AND THE CATEGORY "BIRD"

Fruit	Rating	Bird	Rating
Apple	6.25	Robin	6.89
Peach	5.81	Bluebird	6.42
Pear	5.25	Seagull	6.26
Grape	5.13	Swallow	6.16
Strawberry	5.00	Falcon	5.74
Lemon	4.86	Mockingbird	5.47
Blueberry	4.56	Starling	5.16
Watermelon	4.06	Owl	5.00
Raisin	3.75	Vulture	4.84
Fig	3.38	Sandpiper	4.47
Coconut	3.06	Chicken	3.95
Pomegranate	2.50	Flamingo	3.37
Avocado	2.38	Albatross	3.32
Pumpkin	2.31	Penguin	2.63
Olive	2.25	Bat	1.53

Ratings were made on a 7-point scale, with 7 corresponding to the highest typicality. Note also that the least "birdy" of the birds isn't (technically speaking) a bird at all!

(AFTER MALT & SMITH, 1984)

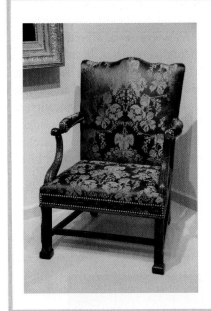

FIGURE 9.1 BASIC VERSUS SUPERORDINATE LABELING

What is this? The odds are good that you would answer, "It's a chair," using the basic-level description rather than the more general label ("It's a piece of furniture") or a more specific description ("It's an upholstered armchair")—even though these other descriptions would certainly be correct.

that we show you a picture like the one in **Figure 9.1** and ask, "What is this?" You're likely to say "a chair" and unlikely to offer a more specific response ("upholstered armchair") or a more general one ("an item of furniture"). Likewise, we might ask, "How do people get to work?" In responding, you're unlikely to say, "Some people drive Fords; some drive Toyotas." Instead, your answer is likely to use more general terms, such as "cars," "trains," and "buses."

In keeping with these observations, Rosch and others have argued that there is a "natural" level of categorization, neither too specific nor too general, that people tend to use in their conversations and their reasoning. The special status of this **basic-level categorization** can be demonstrated in many ways. Basic-level categories are usually represented in our language via a single word, while more specific categories are identified with a phrase. Thus, "chair" is a basic-level category, and so is "apple." The more specific (subordinate) categories of "lawn chair" or "kitchen chair" aren't basic level; neither is "Granny Smith apple" or "Golden Delicious apple."

We've already suggested that if you're asked to describe an object, you're likely to use the basic-level term. In addition, if asked to explain what members of a category have in common with one another, you have an easy time with basic-level categories ("What do all chairs have in common?") but some difficulty with more inclusive (superordinate) categories ("What does all furniture have in common?"). Moreover, children learning to talk often acquire basic-level terms earlier than either the more specific subcategories or the more general, more encompassing categories. In these (and other) ways, basic-level categories do seem to reflect a natural way to categorize the objects in our world. (For more on basic-level categories, see Corter & Gluck, 1992; Murphy, 2016; Pansky & Koriat, 2004; Rogers & Patterson, 2007; Rosch et al., 1976.)

TEST YOURSELF

3. Why is graded membership a consequence of representing the category in terms of a prototype?
4. What tasks show us that concept judgments often rely on prototypes and typicality?
5. Give an example of a basic-level category, and then name some of the subcategories within this basic-level grouping.

Exemplars

Let's return, though, to our main agenda. As we've seen, a broad range of tasks reflects the graded membership of mental categories. In other words, some members of the categories are "better" than others, and the better members are recognized more readily, mentioned more often, judged to be more typical, and so on. (For yet another way you're influenced by typicality, see **Figure 9.2**.) All of this fits well with the idea that conceptual knowledge is represented via a prototype and that we categorize by making comparisons to that prototype. It turns out, though, that your knowledge about "birds" and "fruits" and "shoes" and so on also includes another element.

FIGURE 9.2 TYPICALITY AND ATTRACTIVENESS

Typicality influences many judgments about category members, including attractiveness. Which of these pictures shows the most attractive-looking fish? Which one shows the least attractive-looking? In several studies, participants' ratings of attractiveness have been closely related to (other participants') ratings of typicality—so that people seem to find more-typical category members to be more attractive (e.g., Halberstadt & Rhodes, 2003).

Analogies from Remembered Exemplars

Imagine that we place a wooden object in front of you and ask, "Is this a chair?" According to the prototype view, you'll answer by calling up your chair prototype from memory and then comparing the candidate to that prototype. If the resemblance is great, you'll announce, "Yes, this is a chair."

But you might make this decision in a different way. You might notice that the object is very similar to an object in your Uncle Jerry's living room, and you know that Uncle Jerry's object is a chair. (After all, you've seen Uncle Jerry sitting in the thing, reading his newspaper; you've heard Jerry referring to the thing as "my chair," and so on.) These points allow an easy inference: If the new object resembles Jerry's, and if Jerry's object is a chair, then it's a safe bet that the new object is a chair too.

The idea here is that in some cases categorization relies on knowledge about specific category members (e.g., "Jerry's chair") rather than the prototype (e.g., the ideal chair). This process is referred to as **exemplar-based reasoning**, with an exemplar defined as a specific remembered instance—in essence, an example.

The exemplar-based approach is in many ways similar to the prototype view. According to each of these proposals, you categorize objects by comparing them to a mentally represented "standard." The difference between the views lies in what that standard is. For prototype theory, the standard is the prototype—an average representing the entire category; for exemplar theory, the standard is provided by whatever example of the category comes to mind (and different examples may come to mind on different occasions). In either case, the process is then the same. You assess the similarity between a candidate object and the standard. If the resemblance is great, you judge the candidate as being within the relevant category; if the resemblance is minimal, you seek some alternative categorization.

A Combination of Exemplars and Prototypes

There is, in fact, reason for you to rely on prototypes *and* on exemplars in your thinking about categories. Prototypes provide an economical representation of what's typical for a category, and there are many circumstances in which this quick summary is useful. But exemplars, for their part, provide information that's lost from the prototype—including information about the variability within the category.

To see how this matters, consider the fact that people routinely "tune" their concepts to match the circumstances. For example, they think about birds differently when considering Chinese birds than when thinking about American birds; they think about gifts differently when considering gifts for a student rather than gifts for a faculty member (Barsalou, 1988; Barsalou & Sewell, 1985). In fact, people can adjust their categories in fairly precise ways: not just "gift," but "gift for a 4-year-old" or "gift for a 4-year-old who recently broke her wrist" or "gift for a 4-year-old who likes sports but recently broke her wrist." This pliability in concepts is easy to understand if people are relying on exemplars; after all, different settings, or different perspectives, would trigger different memories and so bring different exemplars to mind.

It's useful, then, that conceptual knowledge includes prototypes *and* exemplars, because each has its own advantages. However, the mix of exemplar and prototype knowledge may vary from person to person and from concept to concept. One person might have extensive knowledge about individual horses, so she has many exemplars in memory; the same person might have only general information (a prototype, perhaps) about snowmobiles. Some other person might show the reverse pattern. And for all people, the pattern of knowledge might depend on the size of the category and how easily confused the category memories are with one another—with exemplars being used when the individuals are more distinct. (For further discussion, see Murphy, 2016; Rips, Smith, & Medin, 2012; Rouder & Ratcliff, 2006; Smith, Zakrzewski, Johnson, & Valleau, 2016; Vanpaemel & Storms, 2008. For discussion of the likely *neural basis* for exemplar storage, see Ashby & Rosedahl, 2017; also see **Figure 9.3**.)

Overall, though, it cannot be surprising that people can draw on either prototypes or exemplars when thinking about concepts. The reason is that the two types of information are used in essentially the same way. In either case, an object before your eyes triggers some representation in memory (either a representation of a specific instance, according to exemplar theory, or the prototype, according to prototype theory). In either case, you assess the

FIGURE 9.3 DISTINCTIONS WITHIN CATEGORIES

The chapter suggests that you have knowledge of both exemplars and prototypes. As a further complication, you also have special knowledge about distinctive individuals within a category. Thus, you know that Kermit has many frogly properties (he's green, he eats flies, he hops) but also has unusual properties that make him a rather unusual frog (since, after all, he can talk, he can sing, and he's in love with a pig).

resemblance between this conceptual knowledge, supplied by memory, and the novel object before you: "Does this object resemble my sister's couch?" If so, the object is a couch. "Does the object resemble my prototype for a soup bowl?" If so, it's probably a soup bowl.

Given these similarities, it seems plausible that we might merge the prototype and exemplar proposals, with each of us on any particular occasion relying on whichever sort of information (exemplar or prototype) comes to mind more readily.

The Difficulties with Categorizing via Resemblance

We're moving, it seems, toward a clear-cut set of claims. First, for most concepts, definitions are not available. Second, for many purposes, you don't need a definition and can rely instead on a mix of prototypes and exemplars. Third, **typicality**—the degree to which a particular object or situation or event is typical for its kind—plays a large role in people's thinking, with more-typical category members being "privileged" in many ways. Fourth, typicality is exactly what we would expect if category knowledge does, in fact, hinge on prototypes and exemplars.

This reasoning seems straightforward enough. However, some results don't fit into this picture, so the time has come to broaden our conception of concepts.

The Differences between Typicality and Categorization

If you decide that Mike is a bully, or that an event is a tragedy, or that a particular plant is a weed, it's usually because you've compared the "candidate" in each case to the relevant prototype or exemplar. In essence, you've asked yourself how much the candidate person (or event, or object) resembles a typical member of the target category. If the resemblance is strong, you decide the candidate is typical for the category, and likely a member of that category. If the resemblance is poor, you decide the candidate isn't at all typical, and its category status is (at best) uncertain.

The essential point, then, is that judgments of category membership *depend on* judgments of typicality, and so these two types of judgment will inevitably go hand in hand. This point certainly fits with the data we've seen so far, but it doesn't fit with some other results—results that show no linkage at all between judgments of category membership and judgments of typicality.

Armstrong, Gleitman, and Gleitman (1983) gave participants this peculiar instruction: "We all know that some numbers are even-er than others. What I want you to do is to rate each of the numbers on this list for how good an example it is for the category 'even number.'" Participants were then given a

TEST YOURSELF

6. What is *similar* in the processes of categorizing via a prototype and the processes of categorizing via an exemplar? What is *different* between these two types of processes?

list of numbers (4, 16, 32, and so on) and had to rate "how even" each number was. The participants thought this was a strange task but followed the instruction nonetheless—and, interestingly, were quite consistent with one another in their judgments (see **Table 9.2**).

Of course, participants responded differently (and correctly!) if asked in a direct way which numbers on the list were even and which were not. Apparently, then, participants could judge category membership as easily as they could judge typicality, but—importantly—these judgments were entirely independent of each other. Thus, for example, participants responded that 4 is a more typical even number than 7,534, but they knew this has nothing to do with the fact that both are unmistakably in the category "even number." Clearly, therefore, there's some basis for judging category membership that's separate from the assessment of typicality.

One might argue, though, that mathematical concepts like "even number" are somehow special, and so their status doesn't tell us much about other, more "ordinary" concepts. However, this suggestion is quickly rebutted, because other concepts show a similar distinction between category membership and typicality. For example, robins strike us as being closer to the typical bird than penguins are; even so, most of us are certain that both robins and penguins are birds. Likewise, Moby Dick was definitely not a typical whale, but he certainly was a whale; Abraham Lincoln wasn't a typical American, but he was an American. These informal observations, like the even-number result, drive a wedge between typicality and category membership—a wedge that doesn't fit with our theory so far.

TABLE 9.2   PARTICIPANTS' TYPICALITY RATINGS FOR
WELL-DEFINED CATEGORIES

EVEN NUMBER		ODD NUMBER	
Stimulus	Typicality Rating	Stimulus	Typicality Rating
4	5.9	3	5.4
8	5.5	7	5.1
10	5.3	23	4.6
18	4.4	57	4.4
34	3.6	501	3.5
106	3.1	447	3.3

Participants rated numbers on how typical they were for the category "even number." Ratings were on a scale from 0 to 7, with 7 meaning the item was (in the participants' view) very typical. Mathematically this is absurd: Either a number is even (divisible by 2 without a remainder) or it is not. Even so, participants rated some numbers as "evener" than others, and likewise rated some odd numbers as being "odder" than others.   (AFTER ARMSTRONG ET AL., 1983)

How are category judgments made when they *don't* rely on typicality? As an approach to this question, let's think through an example. Consider a lemon. Paint the lemon with red and white stripes. Is it still a lemon? Most people say that it is. Now, inject the lemon with sugar water, so it has a sweet taste. Then, run over the lemon with a truck, so that it's flat as a pancake. What have we got at this point? Do we have a striped, artificially sweet, flattened lemon? Or do we have a non-lemon? Most people still accept this poor, abused fruit as a lemon, but consider what this judgment involves. We've taken steps to make this object more and more distant from the prototype and also very different from any specific lemon you've ever encountered (and therefore very different from any remembered exemplars). But this seems not to shake your faith that the object remains a lemon. To be sure, we have a not-easily-recognized lemon, an exceptional lemon, but it's still a lemon. Apparently, something can be a lemon with virtually no resemblance to other lemons.

Related points emerge in research with children. In one early study, preschool children were asked what makes something a "coffeepot," a "raccoon," and so on (Keil, 1986). As a way of probing their beliefs, the children were asked whether it would be possible to turn a toaster into a coffeepot. Children realized that we'd have to widen the holes in the top of the toaster

CATEGORIZATION OUTSIDE OF TYPICALITY

Moby Dick was not a typical whale, but he unmistakably was a whale. Clearly, then, in some settings, typicality can be separated from category membership.

and fix things so that the water wouldn't leak out of the bottom. We'd also need to design a place to put the coffee grounds. But the children saw no obstacles to these manipulations and were quite certain that with these adjustments in place, we would have created a bona fide coffeepot.

Things were different, though, when the children were asked a parallel question—whether one could, with suitable adjustments, turn a skunk into a raccoon. The children understood that we could dye the skunk's fur, teach it to climb trees, and, in general, teach it to behave in a raccoon-like fashion. Even with these adjustments, the children steadfastly denied that we would have created a raccoon. A skunk that looks, sounds, and acts just like a raccoon might be a very peculiar skunk, but it would be a skunk nonetheless. (For other evidence suggesting that people reason differently about *naturally occurring items* like raccoons and *manufactured items* like coffeepots, see Caramazza & Shelton, 1998; Estes, 2003; German & Barrett, 2005; Levin, Takarae, Miner, & Keil, 2001. Also see "Different Profiles for Different Concepts" section on p. 347.)

What lies behind all these judgments? If people are asked why the abused lemon still counts as a lemon, they're likely to mention that it grew on a lemon tree, is genetically a lemon, and is still made up of (mostly) the "right stuff." It's these "deep" features that matter, not the lemon's current properties. And so, too, for raccoons: In the children's view, being a raccoon isn't merely a function of having the relevant features; instead, according to the children, the key to being a raccoon involves (among other things) having a raccoon mommy and a raccoon daddy. In this way, a raccoon, just like a lemon, is defined in ways that refer to deep properties and not to mere appearances.

Notice, though, that these claims about an object's deep properties depend on a web of other beliefs—beliefs that are, in each case, "tuned" to the category being considered. Thus, you're more likely to think that a creature is a raccoon if you're told that it has raccoons as parents, but this is true only because you have some ideas about how a creature comes to be a raccoon—ideas that are linked to your broader understanding of biological categories and inheritance. It's this understanding that tells you that parentage is relevant here. If this point isn't clear, consider as a contrasting case the steps you'd go through in deciding whether Judy really is a doctor. In this case, you're unlikely to worry about whether Judy has a doctor mommy and a doctor daddy, because your beliefs tell you, of course, that for this category parentage doesn't matter.

As a different example, think about the category "counterfeit money." A counterfeit bill, if skillfully produced, will have a nearly perfect resemblance to the prototype for legitimate money. Despite this resemblance, you understand that a counterfeit bill isn't in the category of legitimate money, so here, too, your categorization doesn't depend on typicality. Instead, your categorization depends on a web of other beliefs, including beliefs about circumstances of printing. A $20 bill is legitimate, you believe, only if it was printed with the approval of, and under the supervision of, the relevant government

A SPANIEL, NOT A WOLF, IN SHEEP'S CLOTHING?

Both of these creatures resemble the prototype for sheep, and both resemble many sheep exemplars you've seen (or perhaps read about). But are they really sheep?

agencies. And once again, these beliefs arise only because you have a broader understanding of what money is and how government regulations apply to monetary systems. In other words, you consider circumstances of printing only because your understanding tells you that the circumstances are relevant here, and you won't consider circumstances of printing in a wide range of other cases. If asked, for example, whether a copy of the Lord's Prayer is "counterfeit," your beliefs tell you that the Lord's Prayer is the Lord's Prayer no matter where (or by whom) it was printed. Instead, what's crucial for the prayer's "authenticity" is simply whether the words are the correct words.

The Complexity of Similarity

Let's pause to review. There's no question that judgments about categories are often influenced by typicality, and we'll need to account for this fact in our theorizing. Sometimes, though, category judgments are independent of typicality: You judge some candidates to be category members even though they don't resemble the prototype (think about Moby Dick or the abused lemon). You judge some candidates not to be in the category even though they do resemble the prototype (think about counterfeit money or the disguised skunk).

We need to ask, therefore, how you think about categories when you're not guided by typicality. The answer, it seems, is that you focus on attributes that you believe are essential for each category. Your judgments about what's essential, however, depend, on your *beliefs* about that category. Therefore, you consider parentage when thinking about a category (like skunk or raccoon) for which you believe biological inheritance is important. You consider circumstances of printing when you're concerned with a category (like counterfeit money) that's shaped by your beliefs about economic systems. And so on.

Is it possible, though, that we're pushed into these complexities only because we've been discussing oddball categories such as abused citrus fruits and transformed forest animals? The answer is no, because similar complexities emerge in less exotic cases. The reason is that the prototype and exemplar views both depend on judgments of *resemblance* (resemblance either to a prototype or to some remembered instance), and resemblance, in turn, is itself a complex notion.

How do you decide whether two objects resemble each other? The obvious suggestion is that objects resemble each other if they share properties, and the more properties shared, the greater the resemblance. Therefore, we can say there's some resemblance between an apple and a tennis ball because they share a shape (round) and a size (about 3 or 4 inches in diameter). The resemblance is limited, though, because there are many properties that these objects don't share (color, "furry" surface, and so on).

It turns out, though, that this idea of "resemblance from shared properties" won't work. To see why, consider plums and lawn mowers; how much do these two things resemble each other? Common sense says they don't resemble each other at all, but we'll reach the opposite conclusion if we simply count "shared properties" (Murphy & Medin, 1985). After all, both weigh less than a ton, both are found on Earth, both have a detectable odor, both are used by people, both can be dropped, both cost less than a thousand dollars, both are bigger than a grain of sand, both are unlikely birthday presents for your infant daughter, both contain carbon molecules, both cast a shadow on a sunny day. And on and on and on. With a little creativity, you could probably count thousands of properties shared by these two objects—but that doesn't change the basic assessment that there's not a close resemblance here. (For discussion, see Goldstone & Son, 2012; Goodman, 1972; Markman & Gentner, 2001; Medin, Goldstone, & Gentner, 1993.)

The solution to this puzzle, though, seems easy: Resemblance *does* depend on shared properties, but—more precisely—it depends on whether the objects share *important, essential* properties. On this basis, you regard plums and lawn mowers as different from each other because the features they share are trivial or inconsequential. But this idea leads to a question: How do you decide which features to ignore when assessing similarity and which features to consider? How do you decide, in comparing a plum and a lawn mower, which features are relevant and which ones aren't?

These questions bring us back to familiar territory, because your decisions about which features are important depend on your *beliefs about the concept in question*. Thus, in judging the resemblance between plums and lawn mowers, you were unimpressed that they share the feature "cost less than a thousand dollars." That's because you believe cost is irrelevant for these categories. (If a super-deluxe lawn mower cost a million dollars, it would still be a lawn mower, wouldn't it?) Likewise, you don't perceive plums to be similar to lawn mowers even though both weigh less than a ton, because you know this attribute, too, is irrelevant for these categories.

Overall, then, the idea is that prototype use depends on judgments of resemblance (i.e., resemblance between a candidate object and a prototype). Judgments of resemblance, in turn, depend on your being able to focus on the features that are essential, so that you're not misled by trivial features. And, finally, decisions about what's essential (cost or weight or whatever) vary from category to category, and vary in particular according to your beliefs about that category. Thus, *cost* isn't essential for plums and lawn mowers, but it is a central attribute for other categories (e.g., the category "luxury item"). Likewise, having a particular weight isn't essential for plums or lawn mowers, but it is prominent for other categories. (Does a sumo wrestler resemble a hippopotamus? Here you might be swayed by weight.)

The bottom line is that you're influenced by your background beliefs when considering oddball cases like the mutilated lemon. But you're also influenced by your beliefs in ordinary cases, including, we now see, any case in which you're relying on a judgment of resemblance.

Concepts as Theories

It seems clear, then, that our theorizing needs to include more than prototypes and exemplars. Several pieces of evidence point this way, including the fact that whenever you *use* a prototype or exemplar, you're relying on a judgment of resemblance, and resemblance, we've argued, depends on other knowledge—knowledge about which attributes to pay attention to and which ones to regard as trivial. But what is this other knowledge?

TEST YOURSELF

7. Give an example in which something is definitely a category member even though it has little resemblance to the prototype for the category.
8. In judging similarity, why is it not enough simply to count all of the properties that two objects have in common?

BLUE GNU

In judging resemblance or in categorizing an object, you focus on the features that you believe are important for an object of that type, and you ignore nonessential features. Imagine that you encounter a creature and wonder what it is. Perhaps you reason, "This creature reminds me of the animal I saw in the zoo yesterday. The sign at the zoo indicated that the animal was a gnu, so this must be one, too. Of course, the gnu in the zoo was a different color and slightly smaller. But I bet that doesn't matter. Despite the new blue hue, this is a zoo gnu, too." Notice that in drawing this conclusion you've decided that color isn't a critical feature, so you categorize despite the contrast on this dimension. But you know that color does matter for other categories—and so, for example, you know that something's off if a jeweler tries to sell you a green ruby or a red emerald. Thus, in case after case, the features that you consider depend on the specific category.

Explanatory Theories

In the cases we've discussed, your understanding of a concept seems to involve a network of beliefs linking the target concept to other concepts. To understand what counterfeit is, you need to know what money is, and probably what a government is, and what crime is. To understand what a raccoon is, you need to understand what parents are, and with that, you need to know some facts about life cycles, heredity, and the like.

Perhaps, therefore, we need to change our overall approach. We've been trying throughout this chapter to characterize concepts one by one, as though each concept could be characterized independently of other concepts. We talked about the prototype for bird, for example, without considering how this prototype is related to the animal prototype or the egg prototype. Maybe, though, we need a more holistic approach, one in which we put more emphasis on the interrelationships among concepts. This would enable us to include in our accounts the wide network of beliefs in which concepts seem to be embedded.

To see how this might play out, let's again consider the concept "raccoon." Your knowledge about this concept probably includes a raccoon prototype and some exemplars, and you rely on these representations in many settings. But your knowledge also includes your belief that raccoons are biological creatures (and therefore the offspring of adult raccoons) and your belief that raccoons are wild animals (and therefore usually not pets, usually living in the woods). These various beliefs may not be sophisticated, and they may sometimes be inaccurate, but nonetheless they provide you with a broad cause-and-effect understanding of why raccoons are as they are. (Various authors have suggested different proposals for how we should conceptualize this web of beliefs. See, e.g., Bang, Medin, & Atran, 2007; Keil, 1989, 2003; Lakoff, 1987; Markman & Gentner, 2001; Murphy, 2003; Rips et al., 2012.)

Guided by these considerations, many authors suggest that each of us has something we can think of as a "theory" about raccoons—what they are, how they act, why they are as they are—and likewise a "theory" about most of the other concepts we hold. The theories are less precise, less elaborate, than a scientist's theory, but they serve the same function. They provide a crucial knowledge base that we rely on in thinking about an object, event, or category; and they enable us to understand new facts we might encounter about the object or category.

The Function of Explanatory Theories

We've already suggested that implicit "theories" influence how you categorize things—that is, your decisions about whether a test case is or is not in a particular category. This was crucial in our discussion of the abused lemon, the transformed raccoon, and the counterfeit bill. Your "theory" for a concept was also crucial for our discussion of resemblance—guiding your decisions about which features matter in judging resemblance and which ones do not.

As a different example, imagine that you see someone at a party jump fully clothed into a pool. Odds are good that you would decide this person belongs in the category "drunk," but why? Jumping into a pool in this way surely isn't part of the *definition* of being drunk, and it's unlikely to be part of the *prototype* (Medin & Ortony, 1989). But each of us has certain beliefs about how drunks behave; we have, in essence, a "theory" of drunkenness. This theory enables us to think through what being drunk will cause someone to do, and on this basis we would decide that, yes, someone who jumped into the pool fully clothed probably was drunk.

You also draw on a "theory" when thinking about new possibilities for a category. For example, could an airplane fly if it were made of wood? What if it were ceramic? How about one made of whipped cream? You immediately reject this last option, because you know that a plane's function depends on its aerodynamic properties, and those depend on the plane's shape. Whipped cream wouldn't hold its shape, so it isn't a candidate for airplane construction. This is an easy conclusion to draw—but only because your "airplane" concept contains some ideas about why airplanes are as they are.

Your "theories" also affect how quickly you learn new concepts. Imagine that you're given a group of objects and must decide whether each belongs in Category A or Category B. Category A, you're told, includes objects that are metal, have a regular surface, are of medium size, and are easy to grasp. Category B, in contrast, includes objects that aren't made of metal, have irregular surfaces, and are small and hard to grasp. This sorting task would be difficult—unless we give you another piece of information: namely, that

A WOODEN AIRPLANE?

Could an airplane be made of wood? Made from ceramic? Made from whipped cream? You immediately reject the last possibility, because your "theory" about airplanes tells you that planes can fly only because of their wings' shape, and whipped cream wouldn't maintain this shape. Planes can, however, be made of wood—and this one (the famous *Spruce Goose*) was.

Category A includes objects that could serve as substitutes for a hammer. With this clue, you immediately draw on your other knowledge about hammers, including your understanding of what a hammer is and how it's used. This understanding enables you to see why Category A's features aren't an arbitrary hodgepodge; instead, the features form a coherent package. And once you see this point, learning the experimenter's task (distinguishing Category A from Category B) is easy. (See Medin, 1989; Wattenmaker, Dewey, Murphy, & Medin, 1986. For related findings, see Heit & Bott, 2000; Kaplan & Murphy, 2000; Rehder & Ross, 2001.)

Inferences Based on Theories

If you meet my pet, Milo, and decide that he's a dog, then you instantly know a great deal about Milo—the sorts of things he's likely to do (bark, beg for treats, chase cats) and the sorts of things he's unlikely to do (climb trees, play chess, hibernate all winter). Likewise, if you learn some new fact about Milo, you'll be able to make broad use of that knowledge—applying it to other creatures of his kind. If, for example, you learn that Milo is vulnerable to circovirus, you'll probably conclude that other dogs are also vulnerable to this virus.

These examples remind us of one of the reasons categorization is so important: Categorization enables you to apply your general knowledge (e.g., knowledge about dogs) to new cases you encounter (e.g., Milo). Conversely, categorization enables you to draw broad conclusions from your experience (so that things you learn about Milo can be applied to other dogs you meet). All this is possible, though, only because you realize that Milo *is a dog*; without this simple realization, you wouldn't be able to use your knowledge in this way. But how exactly does this use-of-knowledge proceed?

Early research indicated that inferences about categories were guided by typicality. In one study, participants, told a new fact about robins, were willing to infer that the new fact would also be true for ducks. If they were told a new fact about ducks, however, they wouldn't extrapolate to robins (Rips, 1975). Apparently, people were willing to make inferences from the typical case to the whole category, but not from an atypical case to the category. (For discussion of *why* people are more willing to draw conclusions from typical cases, see Murphy & Ross, 2005.)

However, your inferences are also guided by your broader set of beliefs, and so, once again, we find a role for the "theory" linked to each concept. For example, if told that gazelle's blood contains a certain enzyme, people are willing to conclude that lion's blood contains the same enzyme. However, if told that lion's blood contains the enzyme, people are less willing to conclude that gazelle's blood does too. What's going on here? People find it easy to believe the enzyme can be transmitted from gazelles to lions, because they can easily imagine that lions sometimes *eat* gazelles; people have a harder time imagining a mechanism that would transmit the enzyme in the reverse direction. Likewise, if told that grass contains a certain chemical, people are willing to believe that cows have the same chemical inside them. This makes

WHY IS CATEGORIZATION SO IMPORTANT?

If you decide that Milo is a dog, then you instantly know a great deal about him (e.g., that he's likely to bark and chase cats, unlikely to climb trees or play chess). In this way, categorization enables you to apply your general knowledge to new cases. And if you learn something new about Milo (e.g., that he's at risk for a particular virus), you're likely to assume the same is true for other dogs. In this way, categorization also enables you to draw broad conclusions from specific experiences.

perfect sense if people are thinking of the inference in terms of cause and effect, relying on their beliefs about how these concepts are related to each other (Medin, Coley, Storms, & Hayes, 2003; also see Heit, 2000; Heit & Feeney, 2005; Rehder & Hastie, 2004).

Different Profiles for Different Concepts

This proposal about "theories" and background knowledge has another implication: People may think about different concepts in different ways. For example, most people believe that *natural kinds* (groups of objects that exist naturally in the world, such as bushes or alligators or stones or mountains) are as they are because of forces of nature that are consistent across the years. As a result, the properties of these objects are relatively stable. Thus there are certain properties that a bush must have in order to survive as a bush; certain properties that a stone must have because of its chemical composition. Things are different, though, for *artifacts* (objects made by human beings). If we wished to make a table with 15 legs rather than 4, or one made of gold, we could do this. The design of tables is up to us; and the same is true for most artifacts.

This observation leads to the proposal that people will reason differently about natural kinds and artifacts—because they have different beliefs about why categories of either sort are as they are. We've already seen one result consistent with this idea: the finding that children agree that toasters could be turned into coffeepots but not that skunks could be turned into raccoons. Plainly, the children had different ideas about artifacts (like toasters) than they had about animate objects (like skunks). Other results confirm this pattern. In general, people tend to assume more stability and more homogeneity when reasoning about natural kinds than when reasoning about artifacts (Atran, 1990; Coley, Medin, & Atran, 1997; Rehder & Hastie, 2004).

The diversity of concepts, as well as the role of beliefs, is also evident in another context. Many concepts can be characterized in terms of their features (e.g., the features that most dogs have, the features that chairs usually have, and so on; after Markman & Rein, 2013). Other concepts, though, involve *goal-derived categories*, like "diet foods" or "exercise equipment" (Barsalou, 1983, 1985). Your understanding of concepts like these depends on your understanding of the goal (e.g., "losing weight") and some cause-and-effect beliefs about how a particular food might help you achieve that goal. Similar points apply to *relational categories* ("rivalry," "hunting") and *event categories* ("visits," "dates," "shopping trips"); here, too, you're influenced by a web of beliefs about how various elements (the predator and the prey; the shopper and the store) are related to each other.

Concepts and the Brain

The contrasts among different types of concepts are also reflected in neuroscience evidence. For example, fMRI scans show that different brain sites are activated when people are thinking about living things than when thinking about nonliving things (e.g., Chao, Weisberg, & Martin, 2002), and different sites are activated when people are thinking about manufactured objects such as tools rather than natural objects such as rocks (Gerlach, Law, & Paulson, 2002; Kellenbach et al., 2003).

These results suggest that different types of concepts are represented in different brain areas, and this point is confirmed by observations of people who have suffered brain damage. In some cases, these people lose the ability to name certain objects—a pattern termed **anomia**—or to answer simple questions about these objects ("Does a whale have legs?"). Often, the problem is specific to certain categories, such that some patients lose the ability to name living things but not nonliving things; other patients show the reverse pattern. (See Mahon & Caramazza, 2009; Mahon & Hickok, 2016. For broader discussion, see Peru & Avesani, 2008; Phillips, Noppeney, Humphreys, & Price, 2002; Rips et al., 2012; Warrington & Shallice, 1984.) Sometimes the disruption caused by brain damage is even more specific, with some patients losing the ability to answer questions about fruits and vegetables but still able to answer questions about other objects, living or nonliving (see **Figure 9.4**).

Why does the brain separate things in this way? One proposal emphasizes the idea that different types of information are essential for different concepts. In this view, the recognition of living things may depend on perceptual properties (especially visual properties) that allow us to identify horses or trees or other animate objects. In contrast, the recognition of nonliving things may depend on their functional properties (Warrington & McCarthy, 1983, 1987).

As an interesting complication, though, brain scans also show that *sensory* and *motor* areas in the brain are activated when people are thinking about certain concepts (Mahon & Caramazza, 2009; Mahon & Hickok, 2016;

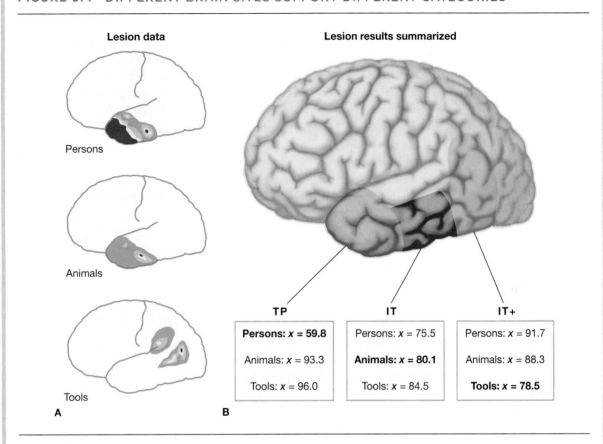

FIGURE 9.4   DIFFERENT BRAIN SITES SUPPORT DIFFERENT CATEGORIES

Lesion data

Persons

Animals

Tools

A

Lesion results summarized

TP	IT	IT+
Persons: $x = 59.8$	Persons: $x = 75.5$	Persons: $x = 91.7$
Animals: $x = 93.3$	**Animals: $x = 80.1$**	Animals: $x = 88.3$
Tools: $x = 96.0$	Tools: $x = 84.5$	**Tools: $x = 78.5$**

B

Brain damage often causes anomia—an inability to name common objects. But the specific loss depends on where exactly the brain damage has occurred. Panel A summarizes lesion data for patients who had difficulty naming persons (top), animals (middle), or tools (bottom). The colors indicate the percentage of patients with damage at each site: red, most patients; purple, few. Panel B offers a different summary of the data: Patients with damage in the brain's temporal pole (TP, shown in blue) had difficulty naming persons (only 59.8% correct) but were easily able to name animals and tools. Patients with damage in the inferotemporal region (IT, shown in red) had difficulty naming persons and animals but did somewhat better naming tools. Finally, patients with damage in the lateral occipital region (IT+) had difficulty naming tools but did reasonably well naming animals and persons.

(AFTER DAMASIO, GRABOWSKI, TRANEL, HICHWA, & DAMASIO, 1996)

McRae & Jones, 2012). For example, when someone is thinking about the concept "kick," we can observe activation in brain areas that (in other circumstances) control the movement of the legs; when someone is thinking about rainbows, we can detect activation in brain areas ordinarily involved in color vision. Findings like these suggest that conceptual knowledge is intertwined with knowledge about what particular objects look like (or sound like or feel like) and also with knowledge about how one might interact with the object.

Some theorists go a step further and argue for a position referred to as "embodied" or "grounded cognition." The proposal is that the body's sensory and action systems play an essential role in all our cognitive processes; it's inevitable, then, that our concepts will include representations of perceptual properties and motor sequences associated with each concept. (See Barsalou, 2008, 2016; Chrysikou, Csasanto, & Thompson-Schill, 2017; Pulvermüller, 2013. For a glimpse of the debate over this perspective, see Binder, 2016; Bottini, Bucur, & Crepaldi, 2016; Dove, 2016; Goldinger, Papesh, Barnhart, Hansen, & Hout, 2016; Leshinskaya & Caramazza, 2016; Reilly, Peele, Garcia, & Crutch, 2016. For a discussion of how this approach might handle *abstract* concepts, see Borghi et al., 2017.)

Even if we hold the embodied cognition proposal to the side, the data here fit well with a theme we've been developing throughout this chapter—namely, that conceptual knowledge has many elements. These include a prototype, exemplars, a theory, and (we now add) representations of perceptual properties and actions associated with the concept. Let's also emphasize that which of these elements you'll focus on likely depends on your needs at that moment. In other words, each of your concepts includes many types of information, but when you're using your conceptual knowledge, you call to mind just the subset of information that's needed for whatever task you're engaged in. (See Mahon & Hickok, 2016, especially pp. 949–950; also Yee & Thompson-Schill, 2016.)

The Knowledge Network

Overall, our theorizing is going to need some complexities, but, within this complexity, one idea has come up again and again: How you think about your concepts, how you use your concepts, and what your concepts *are,* are all shaped by a web of beliefs and background knowledge. But what does this "web of beliefs" involve?

Traveling through the Network to Retrieve Knowledge

In earlier chapters, we explored the idea that information in long-term memory is represented by means of a network, with associative links connecting nodes to one another. Let's now carry this proposal one step further. The associative links don't just tie together the various bits of knowledge; they also help *represent* the knowledge. For example, you know that George Washington was an American president. This simple idea can be represented as an associative link between a node representing WASHINGTON and a node representing PRESIDENT. In other words, the link itself is a constituent of the knowledge.

On this view, how do you retrieve knowledge from the network, so that you can use what you know? Presumably, the retrieval relies on processes we've described in other chapters—with activation spreading from one

TEST YOURSELF

9. Why is an (informal, usually unstated) "theory" needed in judging the resemblance between two objects?
10. What's different between your (informal, usually unstated) theory of artifacts and your theory of natural kinds?

node to the next. This spread of activation is quick but does take time, and the farther the activation must travel, the more time needed. This leads to a prediction—that you'll need less time to retrieve knowledge involving closely related ideas, and more time to retrieve knowledge about more distant ideas.

Collins and Quillian (1969) tested this prediction many years ago, using the *sentence verification task* described earlier in this chapter. Their participants were shown sentences such as "A robin is a bird" or "Cats have claws" or "Cats have hearts." Mixed together with these obviously true sentences were various false sentences (e.g., "A cat is a bird"), and in response to each sentence, participants had to hit a "true" or "false" button as quickly as they could.

Participants presumably perform this task by "traveling" through the network, seeking a connection between nodes. When the participant finds the connection from, say, the ROBIN node to the BIRDS node, this confirms that there's an associative path linking these nodes, which tells the participant that the sentence about these two concepts is true. This travel should require little time if the two nodes are directly linked by an association, as ROBIN and BIRDS probably are (see **Figure 9.5**). In this case, we'd expect participants to answer "true" rather quickly. The travel will require more time, however, if the two nodes are connected only indirectly (e.g., ROBIN and ANIMALS),

FIGURE 9.5   HYPOTHETICAL MEMORY STRUCTURE FOR KNOWLEDGE ABOUT ANIMALS

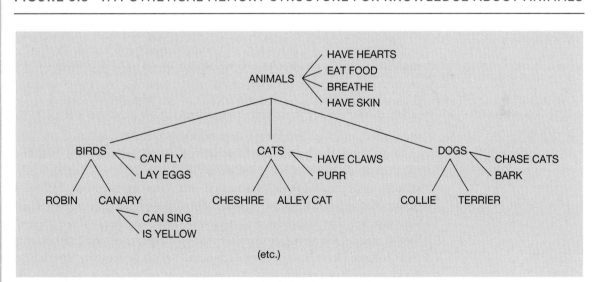

Collins and Quillian proposed that the memory system avoids redundant storage of connections between CATS and HAVE HEARTS, and between DOGS and HAVE HEARTS, and so on for all the other animals. Instead, HAVE HEARTS is stored as a property of all animals. To confirm that cats have hearts, therefore, you must traverse two links: from CATS to ANIMALS, and from ANIMALS to HAVE HEARTS.   (AFTER COLLINS & QUILLIAN, 1969)

so that we'd expect slower responses to sentences that require a "two-step" connection than to sentences that require a single connection.

Collins and Quillian also argued that there's no point in storing in memory the fact that cats have hearts *and* the fact that dogs have hearts *and* the fact that squirrels have hearts. Instead, they proposed, it would be more efficient just to store the fact that these various creatures are animals, and then the separate fact that animals have hearts. As a result, the property "has a heart" would be associated with the ANIMALS node rather than the nodes for each individual animal, and the same is true for all the other properties of animals, as shown in the figure. According to this logic, we should expect relatively slow responses to sentences like "Cats have hearts," since, to choose a response, a participant must locate the linkage from CAT to ANIMALS and then a second linkage from ANIMALS to HAVE HEARTS. We would expect a quicker response to "Cats have claws," because here there would be a direct connection between CAT and the node representing this property. (Why a direct connection? All cats have claws but some other animals don't, so this information couldn't be entered at the higher level.)

As **Figure 9.6** shows, these predictions are borne out. Responses to sentences like "A canary is a canary" take approximately 1 second (1,000 ms). This is presumably the time it takes just to read the sentence and to move your finger on the response button. Sentences like "A canary can sing" require an additional step of traversing one link in memory and yield slower responses. Sentences like "A canary can fly" require the traversing of two links, from CANARY to BIRDS and then from BIRDS to CAN FLY, so they are correspondingly slower.

More recent data, however, add some complications. For example, we saw earlier in the chapter that verifications are faster if a sentence involves creatures close to the prototype—so that responses are faster to, say, "A canary is a bird" than to "An ostrich is a bird." This difference isn't reflected in Figure 9.6, nor is it explained by the layout in Figure 9.5. Clearly, then, the Collins and Quillian view is incomplete.

In addition, the principle of "nonredundancy" proposed by Collins and Quillian doesn't always hold. For example, the property of "having feathers" should, on their view, be associated with the BIRDS node rather than (redundantly) with the ROBIN node, the PIGEON node, and so on. This fits with the fact that responses are relatively slow to sentences like "Sparrows have feathers." However, it turns out that participants respond rather quickly to a sentence like "Peacocks have feathers." This is because in observing peacocks, you often think about their prominent tail feathers (Conrad, 1972). Therefore, even though it is informationally redundant, a strong association between PEACOCK and HAVE FEATHERS is likely to be established.

Even with these complications, we can often predict the speed of knowledge access by counting the number of nodes participants must traverse in answering a question. This observation powerfully confirms the claim that associative links play a pivotal role in knowledge representation.

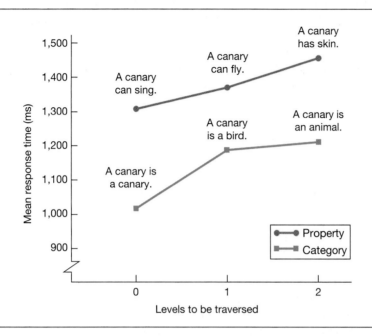

FIGURE 9.6 TIME NEEDED TO CONFIRM VARIOUS SEMANTIC FACTS

In a sentence verification task, participants' responses were fastest when the test required them to traverse zero links in memory ("A canary is a canary"), slower when the necessary ideas were separated by one link, and slower still if the ideas were separated by two links. Responses were also slower if participants had to take the additional step of traversing the link from a category label ("bird") to the node representing a property of the category (CAN FLY).

(AFTER COLLINS & QUILLIAN, 1969)

Propositional Networks

To represent the full fabric of your knowledge, however, we need more than simple associations. After all, we need somehow to represent the contrast between "Sam has a dog" and "Sam is a dog." If all we had is an association between SAM and DOG, we wouldn't be able to tell these two ideas apart.

One widely endorsed proposal solves this problem with a focus on **propositions,** defined as the smallest units of knowledge that can be either true or false (Anderson, 1976, 1980, 1993; Anderson & Bower, 1973). For example, "Children love candy" is a proposition, but "Children" is not; "Susan likes blue cars" is a proposition, but "blue cars" is not. Propositions are easily represented as sentences, but this is just a convenience. They can also be represented in various nonlinguistic forms, including a structure of nodes and linkages, and that's exactly what Anderson's model does.

Figure 9.7 provides an example. Here, each ellipse identifies a single proposition. Associations connect an ellipse to ideas that are the proposition's constituents, and the associations are labeled to specify the constituent's role within that proposition. This enables us to distinguish, say, the proposition "Dogs chase cats" (shown in the figure) from the proposition "Cats chase dogs" (not shown).

This model shares many claims with the network theorizing we discussed in earlier chapters. Nodes are connected by associative links. Some of these links are stronger than others. The strength of a link depends on how frequently and recently it has been used. Once a node is activated, the process of spreading activation causes nearby nodes to become activated as well. The model is distinctive, however, in its attempt to represent knowledge in terms of propositions, and the promise of this approach has attracted the support of many researchers. (For recent discussion, see Salvucci, 2017; for some alternative models, see Flusberg & McClelland, 2017; Kieras, 2017. For more on how this network can store information, see **Figure 9.8**.)

Distributed Processing

In the model just described, individual ideas are represented with **local representations**. Each node represents one idea so that when that node is activated, you're thinking about that idea, and when you're thinking about that idea, that node is activated. **Connectionist networks**, in contrast, take a different approach. They rely on **distributed representations**, in which each idea is represented, not by a certain set of nodes, but instead by a pattern of activation across the network. To take a simple case, the concept "birthday" might be represented by a pattern in which nodes B, F, H, N, P, and R are firing, whereas the concept "computer" might be represented by a pattern in which nodes C, G, H, M, O, and S are firing. Note that node H is part of both of these patterns and probably part of the pattern for other concepts as well. Therefore, we can't attach any meaning or interpretation to this node by itself; we can only learn what's being represented by looking at many nodes simultaneously to find out what pattern of activation exists across the entire network. (For more on local and distributed representations, see Chapter 4; also see the related discussion of neural coding in Chapter 2.)

This reliance on distributed representation has important consequences for how a connectionist network functions. Imagine being asked what sort of computer you use. For you to respond, the idea "computer" needs to trigger the idea "MacBook" (or "Toshiba" or whatever it is you have). In a distributed network, this means that the many nodes representing the concept "computer" have to manage collectively to activate the many nodes representing "MacBook." To continue our simple illustration, node C has to trigger node L at the same time that node G triggers node A, and so on, leading ultimately to the activation of the L-A-F-J-T-R combination that, let's say, represents "MacBook." In short, a network using distributed representations must use processes that are similarly distributed, so that one widespread activation pattern can evoke a different (but equally widespread) pattern.

You have concepts of *things* ("chair," "book," "kitchen"), concepts for *actions* ("running," "hiding," "dancing"), and concepts for *animals* ("cat," "cow," "dragon"). But you also have concepts that apply to *people*. You understand what a "nurse" is, and a "toddler," and a "nerd" or a "jock." You also have concepts for various religious, racial, and ethnic groups ("Jew," "Muslim," "African American," "Italian"), various political groups ("radical," "ultra-conservative"), and many others as well.

In many ways, concepts representing your ideas about groups of people have the same profile as any other concepts: It's difficult to find a rigid definition for most of these groups, because we can usually find individuals who are in the group even though they don't quite fit the definition. You also have a cluster of interwoven beliefs (a "theory") about these groups—beliefs that link your ideas about the group to many other ideas. You also have a prototype in mind for the group, but here we typically use a different term: You have a *stereotype* for the group.

How are stereotypes different from prototypes? Prototypes are a summary of your experience—and so your prototype for "dog" can be thought of as an average of all the dogs you've seen. Stereotypes, in contrast, are often acquired through social channels—with friends or family, or perhaps public figures, shaping your ideas about what "lawyers" are like, or "Canadians," or "Italians." In addition, stereotypes often include an emotional or evaluative dimension, with the result that there are groups you're afraid of, groups you respect, groups you sneer at.

Let's acknowledge, though, that stereotypes can serve the same cognitive function as prototypes. In both cases, these representations provide an efficient means of organizing large quantities of information (and so both serve the same function as *schemata*, which we described in Chapter 8). But, of course, a reliance on stereotypes can lead to a list of toxic problems—racism, sexism, homophobia, prejudice against anyone wearing a hijab, and more.

Many factors fuel these ugly tendencies, including the fact that people often act as if all members of the stereotyped group are alike. They assume, for example, that a tall African American individual is probably a talented basketball player, and that a Semitic-looking young man wearing a headscarf is probably a terrorist. These assumptions are, of course, indefensible because humans in any group differ from one another, and there's no justification for jumping to conclusions about someone just because you've decided he or she is a member of a particular group.

This kind of assumption, though, is widespread enough so that social psychologists give it a name: the *outgroup homogeneity effect*. This term refers to the fact that most people are convinced that their "ingroup" (the group they belong to) is remarkably varied, while "outgroups" (groups they don't belong to) are quite homogeneous. In other words, no matter who you count as "they" and who you count as "we," you're likely to agree that "*they* all think and act alike; *we*, however, are wonderfully diverse."

In combating prejudice, then, it's useful to realize that this assumption of homogeneity isn't just wrong; it can also have ugly consequences. There may be intellectual efficiency in thinking about women, or the elderly, or politicians as if these groups were uniform, but in doing so you fail to respect the differences from one person to the next—and may end up with beliefs, feelings, or actions that are impossible to justify and often deeply harmful.

In addition, the steps bringing this about must all occur simultaneously — in parallel — with each other, so that one entire representation can smoothly trigger the next. This is why connectionist models are said to involve **parallel distributed processing (PDP)**.

Many theorists argue that models of this sort make biological sense. We know that the brain relies on parallel processing, with ongoing activity in many regions simultaneously. We also know that the brain uses a "divide and conquer" strategy, with complex tasks being broken down into small components, and with separate brain areas working on each component.

In addition, PDP models are remarkably powerful, and computers relying on this sort of processing are often able to conquer problems that seemed insoluble with other approaches. As a related point, PDP models have an excellent capacity for detecting *patterns* in the input they receive, despite a range of variations in how the pattern is implemented. The models can therefore recognize a variety of different sentences as all having the same structure, and a variety of game positions as all inviting the same next move. As a result, these models are impressively able to generalize what they have "learned" to new, never-seen-before variations on the pattern. (For a broad view of what connectionism can accomplish, see Flusberg & McClelland, 2017.)

Learning as the Setting of Connection Weights

How do PDP models manage to detect patterns? How do these models "learn"? Recall that in any associative network, knowledge is represented by the associations themselves. To return to an earlier example, the knowledge that "George Washington was president" is represented via a link between the nodes representing "Washington" and those representing "president." When we first introduced this example, we phrased it in terms of local representations, with individual nodes having specific referents. The idea, however, is the same in a distributed system. What it means to know this fact about Washington is to have a pattern of connections among the many nodes that together represent "Washington" and the many nodes that together represent "president." Once these connections are in place, activation of either pattern will lead to the activation of the other.

Notice, then, that knowledge refers to a *potential* rather than to a *state*. If you know that Washington was a president, then the connections are in place so that if the "Washington" pattern of activations occurs, this will lead to the "president" pattern of activations. And this state of readiness will remain even if you happen not to be thinking about Washington right now. In this way, "knowing" something, in network terms, corresponds to how the activation will flow *if* there is activation on the scene. This is different from "thinking about" something, which corresponds to which nodes are active at a particular moment, with no comment about where that activation will spread next.

According to this view, "learning" involves adjustments of the connections among nodes, so that after learning, activation will flow in a way that can represent the newly gained knowledge. Technically, we would say that learning involves the adjustment of **connection weights** — the strength of the individual

TEST YOURSELF

11. What does it mean to say that knowledge can be represented via network connections?
12. What is a propositional network?
13. Why do distributed representations require distributed processing?

connections among nodes. Moreover, in this type of model, learning requires the adjustment of *many* connection weights. We need to adjust the connections, for example, so that the thousands of nodes representing "Washington" manage, together, to activate the thousands of nodes representing "president." In this way, learning, just like everything else in the connectionist scheme, is a distributed process involving thousands of changes across the network.

Concepts: Putting the Pieces Together

We have now covered a lot of ground—discussing both individual concepts and also how these concepts might be woven together, via the network, to form larger patterns of knowledge. We've also talked about how the network itself might be set up—with knowledge perhaps represented by propositions, or perhaps via a connectionist network. But where does all of this leave us?

You might think there's nothing glorious or complicated about knowing what a dog is, or a lemon, or a fish. Your use of these concepts is effortless, and so is your use of thousands of other concepts. No one over the age of 4 takes special pride in knowing what an odd number is, nor do people find it challenging to make the elementary sorts of judgments we've considered throughout this chapter.

As we've seen, though, human conceptual knowledge is impressively complex. At the very least, this knowledge contains several parts. We've suggested that people have a prototype for most of their concepts as well as a set of remembered exemplars, and use them for a range of judgments about the relevant category. People also seem to have a set of beliefs about each concept they hold, and these beliefs reflect the person's understanding of cause-and-effect relationships—for example, why drunks act as they do, or how enzymes found in gazelles might be transmitted to lions. These beliefs are woven into the broader network that manages to store all the information in your memory, and that network influences how you categorize items and also how you reason about the objects in your world.

Apparently, then, even our simplest concepts require a multifaceted representation in our minds, and at least part of this representation (the "theory") seems reasonably sophisticated. It is all this richness, presumably, that makes human conceptual knowledge extremely powerful and flexible—and so easy to use in a remarkable range of circumstances.

COGNITIVE PSYCHOLOGY AND EDUCATION

learning new concepts

In your studies, you encounter many new terms. For example, in this book (and in many others) you'll find **boldfaced terms** introducing new concepts, and often the book provides a helpful definition, perhaps in a glossary (as this book does). As the chapter argues, though, this mode of presentation doesn't line up all that well with the structure of human knowledge. The reason is that you don't have (or need) a definition for most of the concepts in your repertoire; in fact, for many concepts, a definition may not even exist. And even when you do know a definition, your use of the concept often relies on other information—including a prototype for that term as well as a set of exemplars.

In addition, your use of conceptual information depends on a broader fabric of knowledge, linking each concept to other things you know. This broader knowledge encompasses what we've called your "theory" about that concept—a theory that (among other things) explains why the concept's attributes are as they are. You use this theory in many ways; for example, we've argued that whenever you rely on a prototype, you're drawing conclusions based on the *resemblance* between the prototype and the new case you're thinking about, and that resemblance depends on your theory. Specifically, it's your theory that tells you which attributes to pay attention to in judging the resemblance, and which ones to ignore. (So if you're thinking about computers, for example, your "theory" about computers tells you that the *color* of the machine's case is irrelevant. In contrast, if you're identifying types of birds, your knowledge tells you that color is an important attribute.)

What does all of this imply for the *learning* of new concepts? First, let's be clear that in some technical domains, concepts do have firm definitions. (For example, in a statistics class, you learn the definition for the *mean* of a set of numbers, and that term is precisely defined.) More broadly, though, you should bear in mind that definitions tell you what's *generally* true of a concept, but rarely name attributes that are *always* in place. It's also important not to be fooled into thinking that knowing a definition is the same as understanding the concept. In fact, if you *only* know the definition, you may end up using the concept foolishly. (And so you might misidentify a hairless Chihuahua: "That couldn't be a dog—it doesn't have fur.")

What other information do you need, in addition to the definition? At the least, you should seek out *examples* of the new concept, because you'll often be able to draw analogies based on these examples. You also want to think about what these examples have in common; that will help you develop a *prototype* for the category.

In addition, many students (and many teachers) believe that when learning a new concept, it's best to view example after example, so that you really master the concept. Then, you can view example after example of the next concept, so that you'll learn that one too. But what if you're trying to learn about *related* concepts or categories? What if, for example, you're an art student trying to learn what distinguishes Picasso's artwork from the work of his contemporaries, or if you're a medical student learning how to distinguish the symptom patterns for various diseases? In these settings, it's best to hop back and forth with the examples—so that you examine a couple of instances of *this* concept, then a couple of instances of *that* one, then back to the first, and so on. This interweaving may *slow*

LEARNING NEW CONCEPTS

When learning to distinguish two categories, it's best to hop back and forth between the categories. To learn to distinguish Monet's art from van Gogh's, therefore, you might view a painting by Monet, then one by van Gogh, then another by Monet, and so on. This sequence will lead to better learning than a sequence of first viewing a large block of Monet's paintings and then a large block of van Gogh's. (The painting on top is Monet's *The Artist's Garden in Argenteuil*; the painting on the bottom is van Gogh's *Farmhouse in Provence*.)

down learning initially, but it will help you in the long run (leaving you with a sharper and longer-lasting understanding) because you'll learn both the attributes that are *shared* within a category and also the attributes that *distinguish* one category from another.

In viewing the examples, though, you also want to think about what makes them count as examples—what is it about them that puts them into the category? How are the examples different, and why are they all in the same category despite these differences? Why are other candidates, apparently similar to these examples, *not* in the category? Are some of the qualities of the examples predictable from other qualities? What caused these qualities to be as they are? These questions will help you to start building the network of beliefs that provide your theory about this concept. These beliefs will help you to understand and use the concept. But, as the chapter discusses, these beliefs are also *part of* the concept—providing the knowledge base that specifies, in your thoughts, what the concept is all about.

These various points put an extra burden on you and your teachers. It would be easier if the teacher could simply provide a crisp definition for you to memorize, and then you could go ahead and commit that definition to memory. But that's not what it means to learn a concept. Strict attention just to a definition will leave you with a conceptual representation that's not very useful, and certainly far less rich than you want.

For more on this topic . . .

Brown, P. C., Roediger, H. L., & McDaniel, M. A. (2014). *Make it stick: The science of successful learning.* New York, NY: Belknap Press.

Dorek, K., Brooks, L., Weaver, B., & Norman, G. (2012). Influence of familiar features on diagnosis: Instantiated features in an applied setting. *Journal of Experimental Psychology: Applied, 18,* 109–125.

Kim, N. S., & Ahn, W.-K. (2002). Clinical psychologists' theory-based representations of mental disorders predict their diagnostic reasoning and memory. *Journal of Experimental Psychology: General, 131,* 451–476.

chapter review

SUMMARY

- People cannot provide definitions for most of the concepts they use; this suggests that knowing a concept and being able to use it competently do not require knowing a definition. However, when trying to define a term, people mention properties that are in fact closely associated with the concept. One proposal, therefore, is that your knowledge specifies what is typical for each concept, rather than naming properties that are truly definitive for the concept. Concepts based on typicality will have a family resemblance structure, with different category members sharing features but with no features being shared by the entire group.

- Concepts may be represented in the mind via prototypes, with each prototype representing what is most typical for that category. This implies that categories will have graded membership, and many research results are consistent with this prediction. The results converge in identifying some category members as "better" members of the category. This is reflected in sentence verification tasks, production tasks, explicit judgments of typicality, and so on.

- In addition, basic-level categories seem to be the ones we learn earliest and use most often. Basic-level categories (e.g., "chair") are more homogeneous than their broader, superordinate categories ("furniture") and much broader than their subordinate categories ("armchair"). They are also usually represented by a single word.

- Typicality results can also be explained with a model that relies on specific category exemplars, and with category judgments being made by the drawing of analogies to these remembered exemplars. The exemplar model can explain your ability to view categories from a new perspective. Even so, prototypes provide an efficient summary of what is typical for the category. Perhaps it's not surprising, therefore, that your conceptual knowledge includes exemplars and prototypes.

- Sometimes categorization doesn't depend at all on whether the test case resembles a prototype or a category exemplar. This is evident with some abstract categories ("even number") and some weird cases (a mutilated lemon), but it's also evident with more mundane categories ("raccoon"). In these examples, categorization seems to depend on knowledge about a category's essential properties.

- Knowledge about essential properties is not just a supplement to categorization via resemblance. Instead, knowledge about essential properties may be a *prerequisite* for judgments of resemblance. With this knowledge, you're able to assess resemblance with regard to just those properties that truly matter for the category and not be misled by irrelevant or accidental properties.

- The properties that are essential for a category vary from one category to the next. The identification of these properties seems to depend on beliefs held about the category, including causal beliefs that specify why the category features are as they are. These beliefs can be thought of as forming implicit theories, and they describe the category not in isolation but in relation to various other concepts.

- Researchers have proposed that knowledge is stored within the same memory network that we've discussed in earlier chapters. Searching through this network seems to resemble travel in the sense that greater travel distances (more connections to be traversed) require more time.

- To store all of knowledge, the network may need more than simple associations. One proposal is that the network stores propositions, with different nodes each playing the appropriate role within the proposition.

- A different proposal is that knowledge is contained in memory via distributed representations. These representations require distributed processes, including the processes that adjust connection weights to allow the creation of new knowledge.

KEY TERMS

family resemblance (p. 329)
prototype theory (p. 329)
graded membership (p. 331)
sentence verification task (p. 331)
production task (p. 331)
rating task (p. 331)
basic-level categorization (p. 333)
exemplar-based reasoning (p. 335)

typicality (p. 337)
anomia (p. 348)
propositions (p. 353)
local representations (p. 354)
connectionist networks (p. 354)
distributed representations (p. 354)
parallel distributed processing (PDP) (p. 357)
connection weights (p. 357)

TEST YOURSELF AGAIN

1. Consider the word "chair." Name some attributes that might plausibly be included in a definition for this word. But, then, can you describe objects that you would count as chairs even though they don't have one or more of these attributes?

2. What does it mean to say that there is a family resemblance among the various animals that we call "dogs"?

3. Why is graded membership a consequence of representing the category in terms of a prototype?

4. What tasks show us that concept judgments often rely on prototypes and typicality?

5. Give an example of a basic-level category, and then name some of the subcategories within this basic-level grouping.

6. What is *similar* in the processes of categorizing via a prototype and the processes of categorizing via an exemplar? What is *different* between these two types of processes?

7. Give an example in which something is definitely a category member even though it has little resemblance to the prototype for the category.

8. In judging similarity, why is it not enough simply to count all of the properties that two objects have in common?

9. Why is an (informal, usually unstated) "theory" needed in judging the resemblance between two objects?

10. What's different between your (informal, usually unstated) theory of artifacts and your theory of natural kinds?

11. What does it mean to say that knowledge can be represented via network connections?

12. What is a propositional network?

13. Why do distributed representations require distributed processing?

THINK ABOUT IT

1. You easily understand the following sentence: "At most colleges and universities, a large number of students receive financial aid." But how do you manage to understand the sentence? How is the concept of "financial aid" represented in your mind? Do you have a prototype (perhaps for "student on financial aid")? Do you have some number of exemplars? A theory? Can you specify what the theory involves? What other concepts do you need to understand in order to understand "financial aid"?

e eBOOK DEMONSTRATIONS & ESSAYS

Go to http://digital.wwnorton.com/cognition7 for the online demonstrations and essays relevant to this chapter. These can be found in the ebook.

Online Demonstrations

- Demonstration 9.1: The Search for Definitions
- Demonstration 9.2: Assessing Typicality
- Demonstration 9.3: Basic-Level Categories

ZAPS COGNITION LABS

Go to http://digital.wwnorton.com/cognition7 to experience interactive online psychology labs relevant to this chapter.

chapter 10

Language

what if... On January 8, 2011, Congresswoman Gabby Giffords was meeting with citizens outside a grocery store near Tucson, Arizona. A man ran up to the crowd and began shooting. Six people were killed; Giffords was among the others who were wounded. A bullet had passed through her head, traveling the length of her brain's left side and causing extensive damage.

As a result of her brain injury, Giffords has suffered from many profound difficulties, including a massive disruption of her language capacity, and, among its many other implications, her case brought public attention to the disorder termed "aphasia"—a loss of the ability to produce and understand ordinary language.

In the years since the shooting, though, Giffords has shown a wonderful degree of recovery. Just five months after the injury, an aide announced that her ability to comprehend language had returned to a level that was "close to normal, if not normal." Her progress has been slower for language production. Consider an interview she gave in early 2014. Giffords had, on the third anniversary of her shooting, decided to celebrate life by skydiving. In a subsequent TV interview, she described the experience: "Oh, wonderful sky. Gorgeous mountain. Blue skies. I like a lot. A lot of fun. Peaceful, so peaceful."

Giffords's recovery is remarkable, but—sadly—not typical. The outcome for patients with aphasia is highly variable, and many recover far less of their language ability than Giffords has. Her case is typical, though, in other ways. Different brain areas control the comprehension and the production of speech, so it's common for one of these capacities to be spared while the other is damaged, and the prospects for recovery are generally better for language comprehension than for production. And like Giffords, many patients with aphasia retain the ability to *sing* even if they've lost the ability to *speak*—a clear indication that these seemingly similar activities are controlled by different processes.

Giffords also shares with other patients the profound frustration of aphasia. This condition is, after all, a disorder of *language*, not a disorder of *thought*. As a result, patients with aphasia can think normally but complain (often with great difficulty) that they feel "trapped" in their own heads, unable to express what they're thinking. They are sometimes forced to grunt and point in hopes of conveying their meaning; in other cases, their speech is so slurred that others cannot understand them,

- Language can be understood as having a hierarchical structure—with units at each level being assembled to form the larger units at the next level.

- At each level in the hierarchy, we can combine and recombine units, but the combinations seem to be governed by various types of rules. The rules provide an explanation of why some combinations of elements are rare and others seem prohibited outright. Within the boundaries created by these rules, though, language is *generative*, allowing any user of the language to create a virtually unlimited number of new forms (new sound combinations, new words, new phrases).

- A different set of principles describes how, moment by moment, people interpret the sentences they encounter; in this process, people are guided by many factors, including syntax, semantics, and contextual information.

- In interpreting sentences, people seem to use a "compile as you go" strategy, trying to figure out the role of each word the moment it arrives. This approach is efficient but can lead to error.

- Our extraordinary skill in using language is made possible in part by the fact that large portions of the brain are specialized for language use, making it clear that we are, in a literal sense, a "linguistic species."

- Finally, language surely influences our thoughts, but in an indirect fashion: Language is one of many ways to draw our attention to this or that aspect of the environment. This shapes our experience, which in turn shapes our cognition.

so they are caught in a situation of trying again and again to express themselves—but often without success.

To understand the extent of this frustration, bear in mind that we use language (whether it's the spoken language most of us use or the sign language of the deaf) to convey our ideas to one another, and our wishes and our needs. Without language, cooperative endeavors would be a thousand times more difficult—if possible at all. Without language, the acquisition of knowledge would be enormously impaired. Plainly, then, language capacity is crucial for us all, and in this chapter we'll consider the nature of this extraordinary and uniquely human skill.

The Organization of Language

Language use involves a special type of translation. I might, for example, want to tell you about a happy event in my life, and so I need to translate my ideas about the event into sounds that I can utter. You, in turn, detect those sounds and need to convert them into some sort of comprehension. How does this translation—from ideas to sounds, and then back to ideas—take place?

The answer lies in the fact that language relies on well-defined patterns— patterns in how individual words are used, patterns in how words are put together into phrases. I follow those patterns when I express my ideas, and the same patterns guide you in figuring out what I just said. In essence, then, we're both using the same "codebook," with the result that (most of the time) you can understand my messages, and I yours.

But where does this "codebook" come from? And what's in the codebook? More concretely, what are the patterns of English (or whatever language you speak) that—apparently—we all know and use? As a first step toward tackling these issues, let's note that language has a well-defined structure, as depicted in **Figure 10.1**. At the highest level of the structure (not shown in the figure) are the ideas intended by the speaker, or the ideas that the listener derives from the input. These ideas are typically expressed in **sentences**—coherent sequences of words that express the speaker's intended meaning. Sentences, in turn, are composed of phrases, which are composed of words. Words are composed of **morphemes**, the smallest language units that carry meaning. Some morphemes, like "umpire" or "talk," are units that can stand alone, and they usually refer to particular objects, ideas, or actions. Other morphemes get "bound" onto these "free" morphemes and add information crucial for interpretation. Examples of bound morphemes in Figure 10.1 are the past-tense morpheme "ed" and the plural morpheme "s." Then, finally, in spoken language, morphemes are conveyed by sounds called **phonemes**, defined as the smallest unit of sound that serves to distinguish words in a language.

Language is also organized in another way: Within each of these levels, people can combine and recombine the units to produce novel utterances—assembling phonemes into brand-new morphemes or assembling words into

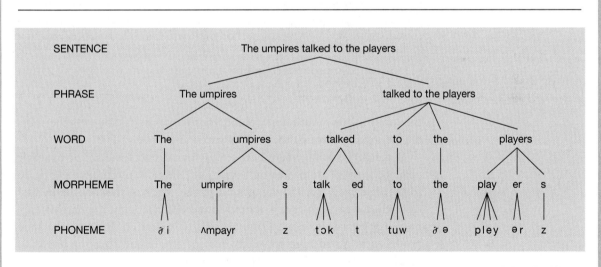

FIGURE 10.1   THE HIERARCHY OF LINGUISTIC UNITS

It is useful to think of language as having a hierarchical structure. At the top of the hierarchy, there are sentences. These are composed of phrases, which are themselves composed of words. The words are composed of morphemes, and when the morphemes are pronounced, the units of sound are called "phonemes." In describing phonemes, the symbols correspond to the actual sounds produced, independent of how these sounds are expressed in ordinary writing.

brand-new phrases. Crucially, though, not all combinations are possible—so that a new breakfast cereal, for example, might be called "Klof" but would probably seem strange to English speakers if it were called "Ngof." Likewise, someone might utter the novel sentence "I admired the lurking octopi" but almost certainly wouldn't say, "Octopi admired the I lurking." What lies behind these points? Why are some sequences acceptable—even if strange—while others seem awkward or even unacceptable? The answers to these questions are crucial for any understanding of what language *is*.

Phonology

Let's use the hierarchy in Figure 10.1 as a way to organize our examination of language. We'll start at the bottom of the hierarchy—with the sounds of speech.

The Production of Speech

In ordinary breathing, air flows quietly out of the lungs and up through the nose and mouth (see **Figure 10.2**). There will usually be some sort of sound, though, if this airflow is interrupted or altered, and this fact is crucial for vocal communication.

For example, within the larynx there are two flaps of muscular tissue called the "vocal folds." (These structures are also called the "vocal cords," although they're not cords at all.) These folds can be rapidly opened and closed, producing a buzzing sort of vibration known as **voicing**. You can feel this vibration by putting your palm on your throat while you produce a [z] sound. You'll feel no vibration, though, if you hiss like a snake, producing a sustained [s] sound. Try it! The [z] sound is voiced; the [s] is not.

You can also produce sound by narrowing the air passageway within the mouth itself. For example, hiss like a snake again and pay attention to your tongue's position. To produce this sound, you placed your tongue's tip near the roof of your mouth, just behind your teeth; the [s] sound is the sound of the air rushing through the narrow gap you created.

If the gap is somewhere else, a different sound results. For example, to produce the [sh] sound (as in "shoot" or "shine"), the tongue is positioned so that it creates a narrow gap a bit farther back in the mouth; air rushing through this gap causes the desired sound. Alternatively, the narrow gap can be more toward the front. Pronounce an [f] sound; in this case, the sound is produced by air rushing between your bottom lip and your top teeth.

These various aspects of speech production provide a basis for categorizing speech sounds. We can distinguish sounds, first, according to how the airflow is restricted; this is referred to as **manner of production**. Thus, air is allowed to move through the nose for some speech sounds but not others. Similarly, for some speech sounds, the flow of air is fully stopped for a moment (e.g., [p], [b], and [t]). For other sounds, the air passage is restricted, but air continues to flow (e.g., [f], [z], and [r]).

TEST YOURSELF

1. What are morphemes? What are phonemes?

FIGURE 10.2   THE HUMAN VOCAL TRACT

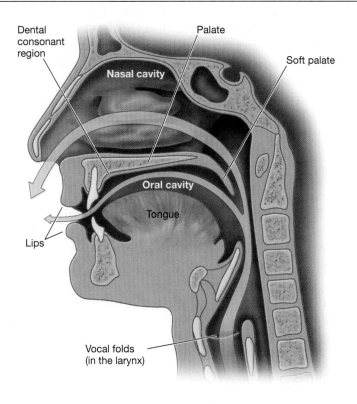

Speech is produced by airflow from the lungs that passes through the larynx and from there through the oral and nasal cavities. Different vowels are created by movements of the lips and tongue that change the size and shape of the oral cavity. Consonants are produced by movements that temporarily obstruct the airflow through the vocal tract.

Second, we can distinguish between sounds that are voiced—produced with the vocal folds vibrating—and those that are not. The sounds of [v], [z], and [n] (to name a few) are voiced; [f], [s], [t], and [k] are unvoiced. (You can confirm this by running the hand-on-throat test while producing each of these sounds.) Finally, sounds can be categorized according to where the airflow is restricted; this is referred to as **place of articulation**. For example, you close your lips to produce "bilabial" sounds like [p] and [b]; you place your top teeth close to your bottom lip to produce "labiodental" sounds like [f] and [v]; and you place your tongue just behind your upper teeth to produce "alveolar" sounds like [t] and [d].

This categorization scheme enables us to describe any speech sound in terms of a few simple features. For example, what are the features of a [p] sound?

First, we specify the manner of production: This sound is produced with air moving through the mouth (not the nose) and with a full interruption to the flow of air. Second, voicing: The [p] sound happens to be unvoiced. Third, place of articulation: The [p] sound is bilabial. These features are all we need to identify the [p], and if any of these features changes, so does the sound's identity.

In English, these features of sound production are combined and recombined to produce 40 or so different phonemes. Other languages use as few as a dozen phonemes; still others use many more. (For example, there are 141 different phonemes in the language of Khoisan, spoken by the Bushmen of Africa; Halle, 1990.) In all cases, though, the phonemes are created by simple combinations of the features just described.

The Complexity of Speech Perception

This description of speech sounds invites a simple proposal about speech *perception*. We've just said that each speech sound can be defined in terms of a small number of features. Perhaps, then, all a perceiver needs to do is detect these features, and with this done, the speech sounds are identified.

It turns out, though, that speech perception is more complicated. Consider **Figure 10.3**, which shows the moment-by-moment sound amplitudes produced by a speaker uttering a brief greeting. It's these amplitudes, in the form of air-pressure changes, that reach the ear, and so, in an important sense, the figure shows the pattern of input with which "real" speech perception begins.

Notice that within this stream of speech there are no markers to indicate where one phoneme ends and the next begins. Likewise, there are, for the most part, no gaps to indicate the boundaries between successive syllables

FIGURE 10.3   THE ACTUAL PATTERN OF SPEECH

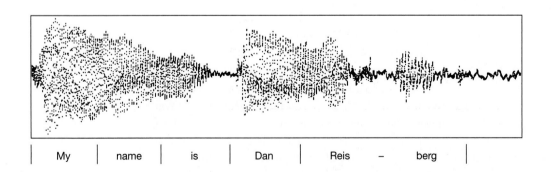

| My | name | is | Dan | Reis – berg |

Shown here are the moment-by-moment sound amplitudes produced by the author uttering a greeting. Notice that there is no gap between the sounds carrying the word "my" and the sounds carrying "name." Nor is there a gap between the sounds carrying "name" and the sounds carrying "is." Therefore, the listener needs to figure out where one sound stops and the next begins, a process known as "speech segmentation."

or successive words. Therefore, as your first step toward phoneme identification, you need to "slice" this stream into the appropriate segments—a step known as **speech segmentation**.

For many people, this pattern comes as a surprise. Most of us are convinced that there are brief pauses between words in the speech that we hear, and it's these pauses, we assume, that mark the word boundaries. But this perception turns out to be an illusion, and we are "hearing" pauses that aren't actually there. This is evident when we "hear" the pauses in the "wrong places" and segment the speech stream in a way the speaker didn't intend (see **Figure 10.4**). The illusion is also revealed when we physically measure the

---

FIGURE 10.4 AMBIGUITY IN SEGMENTATION

*"Boy, he must think we're pretty stupid
to fall for that again."*

Almost every child has heard the story of Chicken Little. No one believed this poor chicken when he announced, "The sky is falling!" It turns out, though, that the acoustic signal—the actual sounds produced—would have been the same if Chicken Little had exclaimed, "This guy is falling!" The difference between these utterances ("The sky . . ." vs. "This guy . . .") isn't in the input. Instead, the difference lies in how the listener segments the sounds.

speech stream (as we did in order to create Figure 10.3) or when we listen to speech we can't understand—for example, speech in a foreign language. In the latter circumstance, we lack the skill needed to segment the stream, so we're unable to "supply" the word boundaries. As a consequence, we hear what is really there: a continuous, uninterrupted flow of sound. That is why speech in a foreign language often sounds so fast.

Speech perception is further complicated by a phenomenon known as **coarticulation** (Liberman, 1970; also Daniloff & Hammarberg, 1973). This term refers to the fact that in producing speech, you don't utter one phoneme at a time. Instead, the phonemes overlap, so that while you're producing the [s] sound in "soup," for example, your mouth is getting ready to say the vowel. While uttering the vowel, you're already starting to move your tongue, lips, and teeth into position for producing the [p].

This overlap helps to make speech production faster and considerably more fluent. But the overlap also has consequences for the sounds produced, so that the [s] you produce while getting ready for one upcoming vowel is actually different from the [s] you produce while getting ready for a different vowel. As a result, we can't point to a specific acoustical pattern and say, "This is the pattern of an [s] sound." Instead, the acoustical pattern is different in different contexts. Speech perception therefore has to "read past" these context differences in order to identify the phonemes produced.

Aids to Speech Perception

The need for segmentation in a continuous speech stream, the variations caused by coarticulation, and also the variations from speaker to speaker all make speech perception rather complex. Nonetheless, you manage to perceive speech accurately and easily. How do you do it?

Part of the answer lies in the fact that the speech you encounter, day by day, is surprisingly limited in its range. Each of us knows tens of thousands of words, but most of these words are rarely used. In fact, we've known for many years that the 50 most commonly used words in English make up roughly half of the words you actually hear (Miller, 1951).

In addition, the perception of speech shares a crucial attribute with other types of perception: a reliance on knowledge and expectations that supplement the input and guide your interpretation. In other words, speech perception (like perception in other domains) weaves together "bottom-up" and "top-down" processes—processes that, on the one side, are driven by the input itself, and, on the other side, are driven by the broader pattern of what you know.

In perceiving speech, therefore, you don't rely just on the stimuli you receive (that's the bottom-up part). Instead, you supplement this input with other knowledge, guided by the context. This is evident, for example, in the **phonemic restoration effect**. To demonstrate this effect, researchers start by recording a bit of speech, and then they modify what they've recorded. For example, they might remove the [s] sound in the middle of "legislatures" and replace the [s] with a brief burst of noise. This now-degraded stimulus can then be presented to participants, embedded in a sentence such as

The state governors met with their respective legi*latures.

When asked about this stimulus, participants insist that they heard the complete word, "legislatures," accompanied by a burst of noise (Repp, 1992; Samuel, 1987, 1991). It seems, then, that they use the context to figure out what the word must have been, but then they insist that they actually heard the word. In fact, participants are often inaccurate if asked when exactly they heard the noise burst. They can't tell whether they heard the noise during the second syllable of "legislatures" (so that it blotted out the missing [s], forcing them to *infer* the missing sound) or at some other point (so that they were able to *hear* the missing [s] with no interference). Apparently, the top-down process literally changes what participants hear—leaving them with no way to distinguish what was heard from what was inferred.

How much does the context in which we hear a word help us? In a classic experiment, Pollack and Pickett (1964) recorded a number of naturally occurring conversations. From these recordings, they spliced out individual words and presented them in isolation to their research participants. With no context to guide them, participants were able to identify only half of the words. If restored to their original context, though, the same stimuli were easy to identify. Apparently, the benefits of context are considerable.

Categorical Perception

Speech perception also benefits from a pattern called **categorical perception.** This term refers to the fact that people are much better at hearing the differences *between* categories of sounds than they are at hearing the variations *within* a category of sounds. In other words, you're very sensitive to the differences between, say, a [g] sound and a [k], or the differences between a [d] and a [t]. But you're surprisingly insensitive to differences within each of these categories, so you have a hard time distinguishing, say, one [p] sound from another, somewhat different [p] sound. And, of course, this pattern is precisely what you want, because it enables you to hear the differences that matter without hearing (and being distracted by) inconsequential variations within the category.

Demonstrations of categorical perception generally rely on a series of stimuli, created by computer. The first stimulus in the series might be a [ba] sound. Another stimulus might be a [ba] that has been distorted a tiny bit, to make it a little bit closer to a [pa] sound. A third stimulus might be a [ba] that has been distorted a bit more, so that it's a notch closer to a [pa], and so on. In this way we create a series of stimuli, each slightly different from the one before, ranging from a clear [ba] sound at one extreme, through a series of "compromise" sounds, until we reach at the other extreme a clear [pa] sound.

CATEGORICAL PERCEPTION IN OTHER SPECIES

The pattern of categorical perception isn't limited to language—or to humans. A similar pattern, for example, with much greater sensitivity to between-category differences than to within-category variations, has been documented in the hearing of the chinchilla.

FIGURE 10.5   CATEGORICAL PERCEPTION

With computer speech, we can produce a variety of compromises between a [pa] and a [ba] sound, differing only in when the voicing begins (i.e., the voice-onset time, or VOT). Panel A shows a plausible hypothesis about how these sounds will be perceived: As the sound becomes less and less like an ordinary [ba], people should be less and less likely to perceive it as a [ba]. Panel B, however, shows the actual data: Research participants seem indifferent to small variations in the [ba] sound, and they categorize a sound with a 10 ms or 15 ms VOT in essentially the same way that they categorize a sound with a 0 VOT. The categorizations also show an abrupt categorical boundary between [pa] and [ba], although there is no corresponding abrupt change in the stimuli themselves.

(AFTER LISKER & ABRAMSON, 1970)

How do people perceive these various sounds? **Figure 10.5A** shows the pattern we might expect. After all, our stimuli are gradually shading from a clear [ba] to a clear [pa]. Therefore, as we move through the series, we might expect people to be less and less likely to identify each stimulus as a [ba], and correspondingly more and more likely to identify each as a [pa]. In the terms we used in Chapter 9, this would be a "graded-membership" pattern: Test cases close to the [ba] prototype should be reliably identified as [ba]; as we move away from this prototype, cases should be harder and harder to categorize.

However, the actual data, shown in **Figure 10.5B**, don't fit with this prediction. Even though the stimuli are gradually changing from one extreme to another, participants "hear" an abrupt shift, so that roughly half the stimuli are reliably categorized as [ba] and half are reliably categorized as [pa]. Moreover, participants seem indifferent to the differences *within* each category. Across the first dozen stimuli, the syllables are becoming less and less [ba]-like, but this is not reflected in how the listeners identify the sounds. Likewise, across the last dozen stimuli, the syllables are becoming more and more [pa]-like, but again, this trend has little effect. What listeners seem to hear is either a [pa] or a [ba], with no gradations inside of either category. (For early demonstrations, see Liberman, Harris, Hoffman, & Griffith, 1957; Lisker & Abrahmson, 1970; for reviews, see Handel, 1989; Yeni-Komshian, 1993.)

It seems, then, that your perceptual apparatus is "tuned" to provide just the information you need. After all, you want to know whether someone advised you to "take a path" or "take a bath." You certainly care whether a friend said, "You're the best" or "You're the pest." Plainly, the difference between [b] and [p] matters to you, and this difference is clearly marked in your perception. In contrast, you usually don't care how exactly the speaker pronounced "path" or "best"—that's not information that matters for getting the meaning of these utterances. And here too, your perception serves you well by largely ignoring these "subphonemic" variations. (For more on the broad issue of speech perception, see Mattys, 2012.)

Combining Phonemes

English relies on just a few dozen phonemes, but these sounds can be combined and recombined to produce thousands of different morphemes, which can themselves be combined to create word after word after word. As we mentioned earlier, though, there are rules governing these combinations, and users of the language reliably respect these rules. So, in English, certain sounds (such as the final sound in "going" or "flying") can occur at the end of a word but not at the beginning. Other combinations seem prohibited outright. For example, the sequence "tlof" seems anomalous to English speakers; no words in English contain the "tl" combination within a single syllable. (The combination can, however, occur at the boundary between syllables—as in "motley" or "sweetly.") These limits, however, are simply facts about English; they are not at all a limit on what human ears can hear or human tongues can produce, and other languages routinely use combinations that for English speakers seem unspeakable.

There are also rules governing the adjustments that occur when certain phonemes are uttered one after another. For example, consider the "s" ending that marks the English plural—as in "books," "cats," and "tapes." In these cases, the plural is pronounced as an [s]. In other contexts, though, the plural ending is pronounced differently. Say these words out loud: "bags," "duds," "pills." If you listen carefully, you'll realize that these words actually end with a [z] sound, not an [s] sound.

English speakers all seem to know the rule that governs this distinction. (The rule hinges on whether the base noun ends with a voiced or an unvoiced sound; for classic statements of this rule, see Chomsky & Halle, 1968; Halle, 1990.) Moreover, they obey this rule even with novel, made-up cases. For

TEST YOURSELF

2. Define "voicing," "manner of production," and "place of articulation."
3. What is speech segmentation, and why is it an important step in speech perception?
4. What is categorical perception?

In 1988, presidential candidate George H. W. Bush uttered the memorable instruction "Read my lips," and then he slowly enunciated "No . . . new . . . taxes." Bush intended the initial phrase to mean something like, "Note what I'm saying. You can count on it." Other speakers have picked up this idiom, and today many people use the words "read my lips" to emphasize their message.

Aside from this locution, though, what is lip-reading, and who uses it? People assume that lip-reading is a means of understanding speech based on visual cues, used when normal sound isn't available. Of course, the set of cues available to vision is limited, because many phonemes depend on movements or positions that are hidden inside of the mouth and throat. Even so, skilled lip-readers (relying on a mix of visual cues, context, and knowledge of the language) can glean much of the content of the speech that they see.

However, we need to set aside the idea that lip-reading is used only when the auditory signal is weak. Instead, lip-reading is an integral part of ordinary speech perception. Of course, you often don't *need* lip-reading; if you did, you'd never be able to use the telephone or understand an interview on the radio. But even so, you rely on lip-reading in many settings — even if the acoustic signal reaching your ears is perfectly clear.

Powerful evidence comes from the McGurk effect, first described in a 1976 paper entitled "Hearing Lips and Seeing Voices" (McGurk & MacDonald, 1976). In this effect, the audio track plainly conveys the sound of someone saying one sound (perhaps "ba"), but the carefully synchronized video shows someone uttering a different sound ("va"). If you listen to the recording with eyes closed, you consistently hear one sound; if you listen while watching the video, you

unmistakably hear the other sound. (Try it. There are many versions of this effect available on YouTube.) It seems, then, that you have no choice about using the lip cues, and when those cues are available to you, they can change what you "hear."

A different sort of evidence comes from settings in which the input is easy to hear, but difficult to understand. Consider the case of someone who's had a year or two of training in a new language — maybe someone who took two years of French in high school. This person now travels to Paris and is able to communicate well enough in face-to-face conversation, but she's hopelessly lost when trying to communicate in a phone call.

Can we document this pattern in the laboratory? In one study, participants tried to understand someone speaking in a language that the participants knew, but were not fluent in. (This is, of course, the situation of the French novice trying to get by in Paris.) In a second study, (English-speaking) participants tried to understand someone speaking English with a moderately strong foreign accent. In a third study, the participants heard material that was clearly spoken, with no unfamiliar accent, but was difficult to understand because the prose was quite dense. (They were listening to a complex excerpt from the writings of the philosopher Immanuel Kant.) In all cases, participants were able to "hear" more if they could both see and hear the speaker, in comparison to a condition in which there was no visual input.

You shouldn't be embarrassed, therefore, if you dread making a phone call in a language that's not your native tongue. Whether you're using your second language or your first, lip-reading is a normal part of speech perception, and at least part of what you "hear" is actually coming to you through your eyes.

example, I have one wug, and now I acquire another. Now, I have two . . . what? Without hesitation, people pronounce "wugs" using the [z] ending—in accord with the standard pattern. Even young children pronounce "wugs" with a [z], and so, it seems, they too have internalized—and obey—the relevant principles (Berko, 1958).

Morphemes and Words

A typical college graduate in the United States knows between 75,000 and 100,000 different words. These counts have been available for many years (e.g., Oldfield, 1963; Zechmeister, Chronis, Cull, D'Anna, & Healy, 1995), and there's no reason to think they're changing. For each word, the speaker knows the word's *sound* (the sequence of phonemes that make up the word) and its *orthography* (the sequence of letters that spell the word). The speaker also knows how to use the word within various phrases, governed by the rules of syntax (see **Figure 10.6**). Finally, speakers know the meaning of a word; they have a *semantic representation* for the word to go with the *phonological representation*.

Building New Words

Estimates of vocabulary size, however, need to be interpreted with caution, because the size of someone's vocabulary is subject to change. One reason is that new words are created all the time. For example, the world of computers has demanded many new terms—with the result that someone who wants to know something will often "google" it; many of us get information from "blogs"; and most of us are no longer fooled by the "phishing" we sometimes find in our "email." The terms "software" and "hardware" have been around for a while, but "spyware" and "malware" are relatively new.

FIGURE 10.6   KNOWING A WORD

---

(1)	* She can place the books on the table.
(2)	* She can place on the table.
(3)	* She can sleep the books on the table
(4)	She can sleep on the table.

Part of what it means to "know a word" is knowing how to use a word. For example, a verb like "place" requires an object—so that Sentence 1 (with an object) sounds fine, but Sentence 2 is anomalous. Other words have other requirements. "Sleep," for example, does not take an object—so Sentence 3 is anomalous, but Sentence 4 is fine.

Changes in social habits and in politics also lead to new vocabulary. It can't be surprising that slang terms come and go, but some additions to the language seem to last. Changes in diet, for example, have put words like "vegan," "localvore/locavore," and "paleo" into common use. The term "metrosexual" has been around for a couple of decades, and likewise "buzzword." It was only in 2012, though, that *Time* magazine listed "selfie" as one of the year's top ten buzzwords, and it was a 2016 vote in Great Britain that had people talking about "Brexit."

Often, these new words are created by combining or adjusting existing words (and so "Brexit" combines "Britain" and "exit;" "paleo" is a shortened form of "Paleolithic"). In addition, once these new entries are in the language, they can be combined with other elements—usually by adding the appropriate morphemes. Imagine that you've just heard the word "hack" for the first time. You know instantly that someone who does this activity is a "hacker" and that the activity itself is "hacking," and you understand someone who says, "I've been hacked."

Once again, therefore, note the **generativity** of language—that is, the capacity to create an endless series of new combinations, all built from the same set of fundamental units. Therefore, someone who "knows English" (or someone who knows *any* language) hasn't just memorized the vocabulary of the language and some set of phrases. Instead, people who "know English" know how to create new forms within the language: They know how to combine morphemes to create new words, know how to "adjust" phonemes when they're put together into novel combinations, and so on. This knowledge isn't conscious—and so most English speakers could not articulate the principles governing the sequence of morphemes within a word, or why they pronounce "wugs" with a [z] sound rather than an [s]. Nonetheless, speakers honor these principles with remarkable consistency in their day-by-day use of the language and in their day-to-day creation of novel words.

Syntax

The potential for producing new forms is even more remarkable when we consider the upper levels in the language hierarchy—the levels of *phrases* and *sentences*. This point becomes obvious when we ask: If you have 60,000 words in your vocabulary, or 80,000, how many sentences can you build from those words?

Sentences range in length from the very brief ("Go!" or "I do") to the absurdly long. Most sentences, though, contain 20 words or fewer. With this length limit, it has been estimated that there are 100,000,000,000,000,000,000 possible sentences in English (Pinker, 1994). If you could read these sentences at the insane rate of 1,000 per second, you'd still need over 30,000 *centuries* to read through this list! (In fact, this estimate may be too low. Decades before Pinker's work, Miller, Galanter, & Pribram, 1960, estimated that the number of possible sentences is actually 10^{30}—billions of times larger than the estimate we're using here.)

Once again, though, there are limits on which combinations (i.e., which sequences of words) are acceptable and which ones are not. For example, in English you could say, "The boy hit the ball" but not "The boy hit ball the." Likewise, you could say, "The moose squashed the car" but not "The moose squashed the" or just "Squashed the car." Virtually any speaker of the language would agree that these errant sequences have something wrong in them, but what exactly is the problem with these "bad" strings? The answer lies in the rules of **syntax**—rules that govern the structure of a phrase or sentence.

One might think that the rules of syntax depend on *meaning*, so that meaningful sequences are accepted as "sentences" while meaning*less* sequences are rejected as non-sentences. This suggestion, though, is wrong. As one concern, many non-sentences do seem meaningful, and no one's confused when Sesame Street's Cookie Monster insists "Me want cookie." Likewise, viewers understood the monster's wistful comment in the 1935 movie *Bride of Frankenstein*: "Alone, bad; friend, good."

In addition, consider these two sentences:

'Twas brillig, and the slithy toves did gyre and gimble in the wabe.

Colorless green ideas sleep furiously.

(The first of these is from Lewis Carroll's famous poem "Jabberwocky"; the second was penned by the linguist Noam Chomsky.) These sentences are, of course, without meaning: Colorless things aren't green; ideas don't sleep; toves

SYNTAX AND MORPHEMES IN "JABBERWOCKY"

In the poem "Jabberwocky," Lewis Carroll relies on proper syntax and appropriate use of morphemes to create gibberish that is wonderfully English-like. "He left it dead, and with its head / He went galumphing back."

YODA'S DIALECT

"Named must your fear be before banish it you can."

Yoda is, of course, a source of great wisdom, and this quotation is meaningful and maybe even insightful. Even so, the quotation is (at best) syntactically odd. Apparently, then, we need to distinguish whether a word string is meaningful from whether the string is well formed according to the rules of syntax.

aren't slithy. Nonetheless, speakers of English, after a moment's reflection, regard these sequences as grammatically acceptable in a way that "Furiously sleep ideas green colorless" is not. It seems, therefore, that we need principles of syntax that are separate from considerations of semantics or sensibility.

Phrase Structure

The rules of syntax take several forms, but they include rules that specify which elements must appear in a phrase and (for some languages) that govern the sequence of those elements. These **phrase-structure rules** also specify the overall organization of the sentence—and therefore determine how the various elements are linked to one another.

One way to depict phrase-structure rules is with a **tree structure** like the one shown in **Figure 10.7**. You can read the structure from top to bottom, and as you move from one level to the next, you can see that each element (e.g., a noun phrase or a verb phrase) has been "expanded" in a way that's strictly governed by the phrase-structure rules.

Prescriptive Rules, Descriptive Rules

We need to be clear, though, about what sorts of rules we're discussing. Let's begin with the fact that most of us were taught, at some stage of our education, how to talk and write "properly." We were taught never to say "ain't." Many

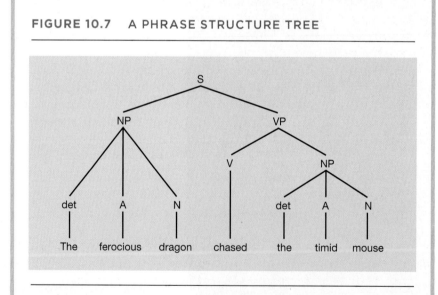

FIGURE 10.7   A PHRASE STRUCTURE TREE

The diagram shows that the overall sentence (S) consists of a noun phrase (NP) plus a verb phrase (VP). The noun phrase is composed of a determiner (det) followed by an adjective (A) and a noun (N). The verb phrase is composed of a verb (V) followed by a noun phrase (NP).

of us were scolded for writing in the passive voice or starting a sentence with "And." Warnings like these are the result of **prescriptive rules**—rules describing how something (in this case: language) is "supposed to be." Language that doesn't follow these rules, it's claimed, is "improper" or maybe even "bad."

You should, however, be skeptical about these prescriptive rules. After all, languages change with the passage of time, and what's "proper" in one period is often different from what seems right at other times. In the 1600s, for example, people used the pronouns "thou" and "ye," but those words are gone from modern usage. In more recent times, people just one generation back insisted it was wrong to end a sentence with a preposition; modern speakers think this prohibition is silly. Likewise, consider the split infinitive. Prominent writers of the 18th and 19th centuries (e.g., Ben Franklin, William Wordsworth, Henry James) commonly split their infinitives; grammarians of the early 20th century, in contrast, energetically condemned this construction. Now, in the 21st century, most English speakers seem entirely indifferent to whether their infinitives are split or not (and may not even know what a split infinitive *is*).

This pattern of change makes it difficult to justify prescriptive rules. Some people, for example, still insist that split infinitives are improper and must be avoided. This suggestion, however, seems to rest on the idea that the English spoken in, say, 1926 was proper and correct, and that the English spoken a few decades before or after this "Golden Age" is somehow inferior. It's hard to think of any basis for this claim, so it seems instead that this prescriptive rule reflects only the habits and preferences of a particular group at a particular time—and there's no reason why our usage should be governed by their preferences. In addition, it's not surprising that the groups that set these rules are usually groups with high prestige or social standing (Labov, 2007). When people strive to follow prescriptive rules, then, it's often because they hope to join (or, at least, be associated with) these elite groups.

Phrase-structure rules, in contrast, are not prescriptive; they are **descriptive rules**—that is, rules characterizing the language as it's ordinarily used by fluent speakers and listeners. There are, after all, strong regularities in the way English is used, and the rules we're discussing here describe these patterns. No value judgment is offered about whether these patterns constitute "proper" or "good" English. These patterns simply describe how English is structured—or perhaps we should say, *what English is*.

The Function of Phrase Structure

No one claims that language users are consciously aware of phrase-structure rules. Instead, the idea is that people have somehow internalized these rules and obey the rules in their use of, and judgments about, language.

For example, your intuitions about whether a sentence is well formed or not respect phrase-structure rules—and so, if a sequence of words lacks an element that should, according to the rules, be in place, you'll probably think there's a mistake in the sequence. Likewise, you'll balk at sequences of words that include elements that (according to the rules) shouldn't be there,

THE (SOMETIMES) PECULIAR NATURE OF PRESCRIPTIVE RULES

According to an often-repeated story, an editor had rearranged one of Winston Churchill's sentences to bring it into alignment with "proper" English. Specifically, the editor rewrote the sentence to avoid ending it in a preposition. In response, the prime minister, proud of his style, scribbled this note: "This is the sort of English up with which I will not put." (Often repeated or not, we note that there's debate about the historical roots of this story!)

or elements that should be in a different position within the string. These points allow us to explain why you think sequences like these need some sort of repair: "His argument emphasized in modern society" or "Susan appeared cat in the door."

Perhaps more important, phrase-structure rules help you *understand* the sentences you hear or read, because syntax in general specifies the relationships among the words in each sentence. For example, the NP + VP sequence typically divides a sentence into the "doer" (the NP) and some information about that doer (the VP). Likewise, the V + NP sequence usually indicates the action described by the sentence and then the recipient of that action. In this way, the phrase structure of a sentence provides an initial "road map" that's useful in understanding the sentence. For a simple example, it's syntax that tells us who's doing what when we hear "The boy chased the girl." Without syntax (e.g., if our sentences were merely lists of words, such as "boy, girl, chased"), we'd have no way to know who was the chaser and who (if anyone) was chaste. (Also see **Figure 10.8**.)

Sometimes, though, two different phrase structures can lead to the same sequence of words, and if you encounter one of these sequences, you may not know which structure was intended. How will this affect you? We've just suggested that phrase structures guide interpretation, and so, with multiple phrase structures available, there should be more than one way to interpret the sentence. This turns out to be correct—often, with comical consequences (see **Figure 10.9**).

Sentence Parsing

A sentence's phrase structure, we've said, conveys crucial information about who did what to whom. Once you know the phrase structure, therefore, you're well on your way to understanding the sentence. But how do you figure out the phrase structure in the first place? This would be an easy question if sentences were uniform in their structure: "The boy hit the ball. The girl drove the car. The elephant trampled the geraniums." But, of course,

TEST YOURSELF

6. What evidence tells us that the rules of syntax can be separated from considerations of whether or not a string of words has meaning?

7. What are phrase-structure rules, and what does it mean that these rules are "descriptive," not "prescriptive"?

A
```
The large tomato
made
a satisfying splat
when
it hit
the floor.
```

B
```
The
large tomato made
a satisfying
splat when it
hit the
floor.
```

FIGURE 10.8 PHRASE STRUCTURE ORGANIZATION AIDS THE READER

Panel A shows a sentence written so that the breaks between lines correspond to breaks between phrases; this makes reading easier because the sentence has been visually "pre-organized." In Panel B, the sentence has been rewritten so that the visual breaks don't correspond to the boundaries between phrases. Reading is now slower and more difficult.

FIGURE 10.9   PHRASE STRUCTURE AMBIGUITY

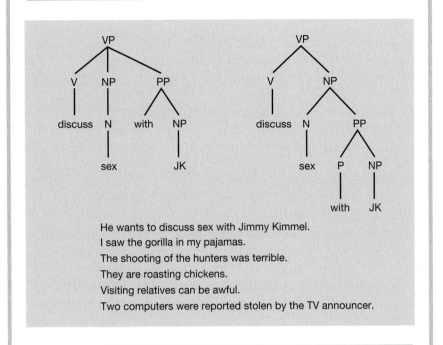

He wants to discuss sex with Jimmy Kimmel.
I saw the gorilla in my pajamas.
The shooting of the hunters was terrible.
They are roasting chickens.
Visiting relatives can be awful.
Two computers were reported stolen by the TV announcer.

Often, the words of a sentence are compatible with more than one phrase structure; in such cases, the sentence will be ambiguous. Therefore, you can understand the first sentence here either as describing *a discussion with Kimmel* or as describing *sex with Kimmel*; both analyses of the verb phrase are shown. Can you find both interpretations for the remaining sentences?

sentences are more variable than this, and this variation makes the identification of a sentence's phrase structure much more difficult.

How, therefore, do you **parse** a sentence—that is, figure out each word's syntactic role? It seems plausible that you'd wait until the sentence's end, and only then go to work on figuring out the structure. With this strategy, your comprehension might be slowed a little (because you're waiting for the sentence's end), but you'd avoid errors, because your interpretation could be guided by full information about the sentence's content.

It turns out, though, that people don't use this wait-for-all-the-information strategy. Instead, they parse sentences as they hear them, trying to figure out the role of each word the moment it arrives (e.g., Marcus, 2001; Savova, Roy, Schmidt, & Tenenbaum, 2007; Tanenhaus & Trueswell, 2006). This approach is efficient (since there's no waiting) but, as we'll see, can lead to errors.

NOAH'S ARC

Sometimes linguistic ambiguity involves the interpretation of a phrase's organization. Sometimes, though, the ambiguity involves the interpretation of a single word. Sometimes the ambiguity is evident in spoken language but not in written language.

Garden Paths

Even simple sentences can be ambiguous if you're open-minded (or perverse) enough:

> Mary had a little lamb. (But I was quite hungry, so I had the lamb and also a bowl of soup.)

> Time flies like an arrow. (But fruit flies, in contrast, like a banana.)

Temporary ambiguity is also common inside a sentence. More precisely, the early part of a sentence is often open to multiple interpretations, but then the later part of the sentence clears things up. Consider this example:

> The old man the ships.

In this sentence, most people read the initial three words as a noun phrase: "the old man." However, this interpretation leaves the sentence with no verb, so a different interpretation is needed, with the subject of the sentence being "the old" and with "man" being the verb. (Who mans the ships? It is the old, not the young. The old man the ships.) Likewise:

The secretary applauded for his efforts was soon promoted.

Here, people tend to read "applauded" as the sentence's main verb, but it isn't. Instead, this sentence is just a shorthand way of answering the question, "Which secretary was soon promoted?" (Answer: "The one who was applauded for his efforts.")

These examples are referred to as **garden-path sentences**: You're initially led to one interpretation (you are, as they say, "led down the garden path"), but this interpretation then turns out to be wrong. So you need to reject your first interpretation and find an alternative. Here are two more examples:

Fat people eat accumulates.

Because he ran the second mile went quickly.

Garden-path sentences highlight the risk attached to the strategy of interpreting a sentence as it arrives: The information you need in order to understand these sentences arrives only late in the sequence, and so, to avoid an interpretive dead end, you'd be better off remaining neutral about the sentence's meaning until you've gathered enough information. That way, you'd know that "the old man" couldn't be the sentence's subject, that "applauded" couldn't be the sentence's main verb, and so on. But this isn't what you do. Instead, you commit yourself fairly early to one interpretation and then try to "fit" subsequent words, as they arrive, into that interpretation. This strategy is often effective, but it does lead to the "double-take" reaction when late-arriving information forces you to abandon your initial interpretation (Grodner & Gibson, 2005).

Syntax as a Guide to Parsing

What is it that leads you down the garden path? Why do you initially choose one interpretation of a sentence, one parsing, rather than another? Many cues are relevant, because many types of information influence parsing. For one, people usually seek the simplest phrase structure that will accommodate the words heard so far. This strategy is fine if the sentence structure is indeed simple; the strategy produces problems, though, with more complex sentences. To see how this plays out, consider the earlier sentence, "The secretary applauded for his efforts was soon promoted." As you read "The secretary applauded," you had the option of interpreting this as a noun phrase plus the beginning of a separate clause modifying "secretary." This is the correct interpretation, and it's required by the way the sentence ends. However, you ignored this possibility, at least initially, and went instead with a simpler interpretation—of a noun phrase plus verb, with no idea of a separate embedded clause.

People also tend to assume that they'll be hearing (or reading) *active-voice* sentences rather than *passive-voice* sentences, so they generally interpret a sentence's initial noun phrase as the "doer" of the action and not the recipient. As it happens, most of the sentences you encounter are active, not passive, so this assumption is usually correct (for early research, see Hornby, 1974; Slobin, 1966; Svartik, 1966). However, this assumption can slow you down when you do encounter a passive sentence, and, of course, this assumption added to your difficulties with the "secretary" sentence: The embedded clause there is in the passive voice (the secretary was applauded by someone else); your tendency to assume active voice, therefore, works against the correct interpretation of this sentence.

Not surprisingly, parsing is also influenced by the function words that appear in a sentence and by the various morphemes that signal syntactic role (Bever, 1970). For example, people easily grasp the structure of "He gliply rivitched the flidget." That's because the "-ly" morpheme indicates that "glip" is an adverb; the "-ed" identifies "rivitch" as a verb; and "the" signals that "flidget" is a noun—all excellent cues to the sentence structure. This factor, too, is relevant to the "secretary" sentence, which included none of the helpful function words. Notice that we didn't say, "The secretary who was applauded . . ."; if we had said that, the chance of misunderstanding would have been greatly reduced.

With all these factors stacked against you, it's no wonder you were (temporarily) confused about "the secretary." Indeed, with all these factors in place, garden-path sentences can sometimes be enormously difficult to comprehend. For example, spend a moment puzzling over this (fully grammatical) sequence:

The horse raced past the barn fell.

(If you get stuck with this sentence, try adding the word "that" after "horse.")

Background Knowledge as a Guide to Parsing

Parsing is also guided by background knowledge, and in general, people try to parse sentences in a way that makes sense to them. So, for example, readers are unlikely to misread the headline *Drunk Gets Six Months in Violin Case* (Gibson, 2006; Pinker, 1994; Sedivy, Tanenhaus, Chambers, & Carlson, 1999). And this point, too, matters for the "secretary" sentence: Your background knowledge tells you that women secretaries are more common than men, and this added to your confusion in figuring out who was applauding and who was applauded.

How can we document these knowledge effects? Several studies have tracked how people move their eyes while reading, and these movements can tell us when the reading is going smoothly and when the reader is confused. Let's say, then, that we ask someone to read a garden-path

A The detectives examined by the reporter revealed the truth about the robbery.

B The evidence examined by the reporter revealed the truth about the robbery.

Readers are momentarily confused when they reach the "by the reporter" phrase in Sentence A. That is because they initially interpreted "examined" as the sentence's main verb. Readers aren't confused by Sentence B, though, because their background knowledge told them that "examined" couldn't be the main verb (because evidence is not capable of examining anything). Notice, though, that readers *won't* be confused if the sentences are presented as they are here—with a picture. In that case, the extralinguistic context guides interpretation and helps readers avoid the garden path.

sentence. The moment the person realizes he has misinterpreted the words so far, he'll backtrack and reread the sentence's start, and, with appropriate instruments, we can easily detect these backwards eye movements (MacDonald, Pearlmutter, & Seidenberg, 1994; Trueswell, Tanenhaus, & Garnsey, 1994).

Using this technique, investigators have examined the effects of *plausibility* on readers' interpretations of the words they're seeing. For example, participants might be shown a sentence beginning "The detectives examined . . . "; upon seeing this, the participants sensibly assume that "examined" is the sentence's main verb and are therefore puzzled when the sentence continues "by the reporter . . ." (see **Figure 10.10A**). We detect this puzzlement in their eye movements: They pause and look back at "examined," realizing that their initial interpretation was wrong. Then, after this recalculation, they press onward.

Things go differently, though, if the sentence begins "The evidence examined . . . " (see **Figure 10.10B**). Here, readers can draw on the fact that "evidence" can't examine anything, so "examined" can't be the sentence's main verb. As a result, they're not surprised when the sentence continues "by the reporter . . ." Their understanding of the world had already told them that

FIGURE 10.11 SEMANTIC AND SYNTACTIC PROCESSING

A Electrical activity in the brain after hearing a sentence that violates *semantic* expectations

B Electrical activity in the brain after hearing a sentence that violates *syntactic* expectations

Many types of information influence parsing. The figures here show patterns of electrical activity on the scalp (with different voltages represented by different colors). (Panel A) If the person hears a sentence that violates *semantic* expectations (e.g., a sentence like, "He drinks his coffee with cream and dog"), this triggers a brain wave termed the N400 (so-called because the wave involves a negative voltage roughly 400 ms after the trigger "dog" is encountered). (Panel B) If the person hears a sentence that violates *syntactic* expectations, though (e.g., a sentence like, "He prefers to solve problems herself"), a different brain wave is observed—the so-called left anterior negativity (LAN).

the first three words were the start of a passive sentence, not an active one. (Also see **Figures 10.11** and **10.12**.)

The Extralinguistic Context

We've now mentioned several strategies that you use in parsing the sentences you encounter. The role of these strategies is obvious when the strategies mislead you, as they do with garden-path sentences. Bear in mind, though, that the same strategies are used for *all* sentences and usually do lead to the correct parsing.

It turns out, however, that our catalogue of strategies isn't complete, because you also make use of another factor: the *context* in which you encounter sentences, including the conversational context. For example, the garden-path problem is much less likely to occur in the following setting:

FIGURE 10.12 N400 BRAIN WAVE

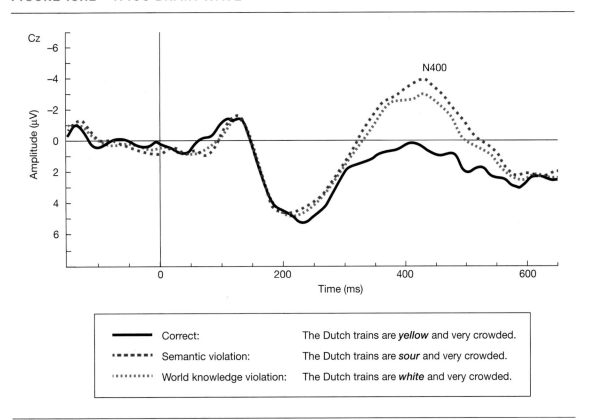

	Correct:	The Dutch trains are *yellow* and very crowded.
━━━━	Semantic violation:	The Dutch trains are *sour* and very crowded.
▪▪▪▪▪▪▪	World knowledge violation:	The Dutch trains are *white* and very crowded.

In parsing a sentence, you rely on your (nonlinguistic) knowledge about the world. This point is evident in a study of electrical activity in the brain while people were hearing different types of sentences. Some of the sentences were sensible and true ("The Dutch trains are yellow and very crowded"). Other sentences contained a semantic anomaly ("The Dutch trains are sour and very crowded"), and this peculiarity produced the N400 brain wave. The key, though, is that a virtually identical N400 was produced in a third condition in which sentences were perfectly sensible but false: "The Dutch trains are white and very crowded." (The falsity was immediately obvious to the Dutch participants in this study.) Apparently, world knowledge (including knowledge about train color) is a part of sentence processing from a very early stage.   (FIG. 1 FROM HAGOORT ET AL., "INTEGRATION OF WORD MEANING AND WORLD KNOWLEDGE IN LANGUAGE COMPREHENSION," *SCIENCE* 304 [APRIL 2004]: 438–441. © 2004 AAAS. REPRINTED WITH PERMISSION FROM AAAS.)

Jack: Which horse fell?

Kate: The horse raced past the barn fell.

Just as important is the **extralinguistic context**—the physical and social setting in which you encounter sentences. To see how this factor matters, consider the following sentence:

Put the apple on the towel into the box.

FIGURE 10.13   THE EXTRALINGUISTIC CONTEXT

"Put the apple on the towel into the box." Without the setting shown here, this sentence causes momentary confusion: The listener will initially think she's supposed to put the apple onto the towel and is then confused by the sentence's last three words. If, however, the sentence is spoken in a setting like the one shown in this picture, there's no confusion. Now, the listener immediately sees the ambiguity (which apple is being discussed?), counts on the speaker to provide clarification for this point, and so immediately understands "on the towel" as specification, not a destination.

At its start, this sentence seems to be an instruction to put an apple onto a towel; this interpretation must be abandoned, though, when the words "into the box" arrive. Now, you realize that the box is the apple's destination; "on the towel" is simply a specification of which apple is to be moved. (Which apple should be put into the box? The one that's on the towel.) In short, this is another garden-path sentence—initially inviting one analysis but eventually requiring another.

This confusion is avoided, however, if the sentence is spoken in the appropriate setting. Imagine that two apples are in view, as shown in **Figure 10.13**. In this context, a listener hearing the sentence's start ("Put the apple . . .") would immediately see the possibility for confusion (which apple is being referred to?) and so would expect the speaker to specify which one is to be moved. Therefore, when the phrase "on the towel" comes along, the listener immediately understands it (correctly) as the needed specification. There is no confusion and no garden path (Eberhard, Spivey-Knowlton, Sedivy, & Tanenhaus, 1995; Tanenhaus & Spivey-Knowlton, 1996).

Prosody

One other cue is also useful in parsing: the rise and fall of speech intonation and the pattern of pauses. These pitch and rhythm cues, together called **prosody**, can communicate a great deal of information. Prosody can, for example, reveal the mood of a speaker; it can also direct the listener's attention by specifying the focus or theme of a sentence (Jackendoff, 1972; also see Kraus & Slater, 2016). Consider the simple sentence "Sol sipped the soda." Now, imagine how you'd pronounce this sentence in response to each of these questions: "Was it Sue who sipped the soda?"; "Did Sol gulp the soda?"; or "Did

TEST YOURSELF

8. What's the evidence that *multiple factors* play a role in guiding how you parse a sentence?
9. What is a garden-path sentence?

Sol sip the soup?" You'd probably say the same words ("Sol sipped the soda") in response to each of these queries, but you'd adjust the prosody in order to highlight the information crucial for each question. (Try it. Imagine answering each question, and pay attention to how you shift your pronunciation.)

Prosody can also render unambiguous a sentence that would otherwise be entirely confusing (Beach, 1991). This is why *printed versions* of garden-path sentences, and ambiguous sentences in general, are more likely to puzzle you, because in print prosody provides no information. Imagine, therefore, that you *heard* the sentence "The horse raced past the barn fell." The speaker would probably pause momentarily between "horse" and "raced," and again between "barn" and "fell," making it likely that you'd understand the sentence with no problem.

As a different example, consider two objects you might buy for your home. One is a small box designed as a house for bluebirds. The other is a small box that can be used by any type of bird, and the box happens to be painted blue. In print, we'd call the first of these a "bluebird house," and the second a "blue birdhouse." But now, pronounce these phrases out loud, and you'll notice how prosody serves to distinguish these two structures.

Some aspects of prosody depend on the language being spoken, and even on someone's dialect within a language. Other prosodic cues—especially cues that signal the speaker's emotions and attitudes—seem to be shared across languages. This point was noted more than a century ago by Charles Darwin (1871) and has been amply confirmed in the years since then (e.g., Bacharowski, 1999; Pittham & Scherer, 1993).

TEST YOURSELF

10. What is prosody?
11. Why are printed versions of garden-path sentences more likely to puzzle you, compared to spoken versions of the same sentences?

Pragmatics

What does it mean to "know a language"—to "know English," for example? It should be clear by now that the answer has many parts. Any competent language user needs somehow to know (and obey) a rich set of rules about how (and whether) elements can be combined. Language users rely on a further set of principles whenever they perceive and understand linguistic inputs. Some of these principles are rooted in syntax; others depend on semantics (e.g., knowing that detectives can "examine" but evidence can't); still others depend on prosody or on the extralinguistic context. All these factors then seem to interact, so that your understanding of the sentences you hear (or see in print) is guided by all these principles at the same time.

These points, however, still *understate* the complexity of language use and, with that, the complexity of the knowledge someone must have in order to use a language. This point becomes clear when we consider language use at levels beyond the hierarchy shown in Figure 10.1—for example, when we consider language as it's used in ordinary conversation. As an illustration, consider the following bit of dialogue (after Pinker, 1994; also see Gernsbacher & Kaschak, 2013; Graesser & Forsyth, 2013; Zwaan, 2016):

Woman: I'm leaving you.

Man: Who is he?

You easily provide the soap-opera script that lies behind this exchange, but you do so by drawing on a fabric of additional knowledge—in this case, knowledge about the vicissitudes of romance. Likewise, in Chapter 1 we talked about the importance of background knowledge in your understanding of a simple story. (It was the story that began, "Betsy wanted to bring Jacob a present . . . ."). There, too, your understanding depended on you providing a range of facts about gift-giving, piggy banks, and more. Without those facts, the story would have been incomprehensible.

Your use of language also depends on your assumptions about how, in general, people communicate with each other—assumptions that involve the **pragmatics** of language use. For example, if someone asks, "Do you know the time?" you understand this as a request that you report the time—even though the question, understood literally, is a yes/no question about the extent of your temporal knowledge.

What do the pragmatics of language—that is, your knowledge of how language is ordinarily used—actually involve? Many years ago, philosopher Paul Grice described the conversational "rules" in terms of a series of maxims that speakers follow and listeners count on (Grice, 1989). The "maxim of relation," for example, says that speakers should say things that are relevant to the conversation. For example, imagine that someone asks, "What happened to the roast beef?" and gets a reply, "The dog sure looks happy." Here, your assumption of relevance will most likely lead you to infer that the dog must have stolen the meat. Likewise, the "maxim of quantity" specifies that a speaker shouldn't be more informative than is necessary. On this point, imagine that you ask someone, "What color are your eyes?" and he responds, "My left eye is blue." The extra detail here invites you to assume that the speaker specified "left eye" for a reason—and so you'll probably infer that the person's right eye is some other color. In these ways, listeners count on speakers to be cooperative and collaborative, and speakers proceed knowing that listeners make these assumptions. (For more on the collaborative nature of conversation and the assumptions that conversational partners make, see Andor, 2011; Clark, 1996; Davis & Friedman, 2007; Graesser, Millis, & Zwaan, 1997; Holtgraves, 2002; Noveck & Reboul, 2008; Noveck & Sperber, 2005).

The Biological Roots of Language

Each of us uses language all the time—to learn, to gossip, to instruct, to persuade, to warn, to express affection. We use this tool as easily as we breathe; we spend far more effort in choosing our clothes in the morning than we do in choosing the words we will speak. But these observations must not hide the facts that language is a remarkably complicated tool and that we are all exquisitely skilled in its use.

How is all of this possible? How is it that ordinary human beings—even ordinary two-and-a-half-year-olds—manage the extraordinary task of

TEST YOURSELF

12. "What happened to the roast beef?" "The dog sure looks happy." Explain what happened in this conversational exchange, and how the exchange will be understood.

mastering and fluently using language? According to many authors, the answer lies in the fact that humans are equipped with sophisticated neural machinery specialized for learning, and then using, language. Let's take a quick look at this machinery.

Aphasias

As we described at the chapter's start, damage to specific parts of the brain can cause a disruption of language known as **aphasia**. Damage to the brain's left frontal lobe, especially a region known as **Broca's area** (see **Figure 10.14**), usually produces a pattern of symptoms known as **nonfluent aphasia**. People with this disorder can understand language they hear but cannot write or speak. In extreme cases, a patient with this disorder cannot utter any words at all. In less severe cases, only a part of the patient's vocabulary is lost, but the patient's speech becomes labored and fragmented, and articulating each

FIGURE 10.14 BRAIN AREAS CRUCIAL FOR THE PERCEPTION AND PRODUCTION OF LANGUAGE

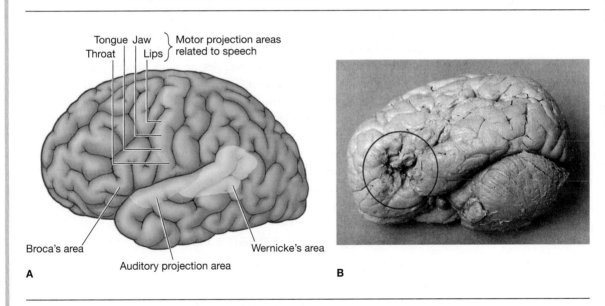

Panel A shows some of the many brain regions that are crucial in supporting the comprehension and production of language. For most individuals, most of these regions are in the left cerebral hemisphere (as shown here). Broca's area (named after the physician Paul Broca) is heavily involved in language production; Wernicke's area (named after the physician Karl Wernicke) plays a crucial role in language comprehension. Panel B shows a photograph of the actual brain of Broca's patient "Tan." Because of his brain damage, this patient was no longer able to say anything other than the syllable "Tan"—leading to the nickname that's often used for him. This pattern (along with observations gained through Tan's autopsy) led Broca to propose that a specific brain region is crucial for speech.

word requires special effort. One early study quoted a patient with aphasia as saying, "Here . . . head . . . operation . . . here . . . speech . . . none . . . talking . . . what . . . illness" (Luria, 1966, p. 406).

Different symptoms are associated with damage to a brain site known as **Wernicke's area** (again see Figure 10.14). Patients with this sort of damage usually suffer from a pattern known as **fluent aphasia**. These patients can talk freely, but they say very little. One patient, for example, uttered, "I was over the other one, and then after they had been in the department, I was in this one" (Geschwind, 1970, p. 904). Or another patient: "Oh, I'm taking the word the wrong way to say, all of the barbers here whenever they stop you it's going around and around, if you know what I mean, that is tying and tying for repucer, repuceration, well, we were trying the best that we could while another time it was with the beds over there the same thing" (Gardner, 1974, p. 68).

This distinction between fluent and nonfluent aphasia, however, captures the data only in the broadest sense. One reason lies in the fact that—as we've seen—language use involves the coordination of many different steps, many different processes. These include processes needed to "look up" word meanings in your "mental dictionary," processes needed to figure out the structural relationships within a sentence, processes needed to integrate information about a sentence's structure with the meanings of the words within the sentence, and so on. Each of these processes relies on its own set of brain pathways, so damage to those pathways disrupts the process. As a result, the language loss in aphasia can sometimes be quite specific, with impairment just to a specific processing step (Cabeza & Nyberg, 2000; Demonet, Wise, & Frackowiak, 1993; Martin, 2003).

Even with these complexities, the point here is that humans have a considerable amount of neural tissue that is specialized for language. Damage to this tissue can disrupt language understanding, language production, or both. In all cases, though, the data make it clear that our skill in using language rests in part on the fact that we have a lot of neural apparatus devoted to precisely this task.

The Biology of Language Learning

The biological roots of language also show up in another manner—in the way that language is learned. This learning occurs remarkably rapidly, and so, by the age of 3 or 4, almost every child is able to converse at a reasonable level. Moreover, this learning can proceed in an astonishingly wide range of environments. Children who talk a lot with adults learn language, and so do children who talk very little with adults. In fact, children learn language even if their communication with adults is strictly limited. Evidence on this last point comes from children who are born deaf and have no opportunity to learn sign language. (In some cases, this is because their caretakers don't know how to sign; in other cases, it's because their caretakers choose not to teach signing.) Even in these extreme cases, language emerges: Children

SIGN LANGUAGE

Across the globe, humans speak many different languages — English, Hindi, Mandarin, Quechua, to name just a few. Many humans, though, communicate through sign language. Actually, there are multiple sign languages, and so, for example, American Sign Language (ASL) is quite different from South African Sign Language or Danish Sign Language. In all cases, though, sign languages are truly languages, with all of the richness and complexity of oral languages. Indeed, sign languages show many of the fundamental properties of oral languages, and so (for example) they have complex grammars of their own.

in this situation *invent* their own gestural language (called "home sign") and teach the language to the people in their surroundings (Feldman, Goldin-Meadow, & Gleitman, 1978; Goldin-Meadow, 2003, 2017; Senghas, Román, & Mavillapalli, 2006).

How should we think about this? According to many psychologists, the answer lies in highly sophisticated learning capacities that have specifically evolved for language learning. Support for this claim comes from many sources, including observations of **specific-language impairment (SLI)**. Children with this disorder have normal intelligence and no problems with the muscle movements needed to produce language. Nonetheless, they are slow to learn language and, throughout their lives, have difficulty in understanding and producing many sentences. They are also impaired on tasks designed to test their linguistic knowledge. They have difficulty, for example, completing passages like this one: "I like to blife. Today I blife. Tomorrow I will blife. Yesterday I did the same thing. Yesterday I _____." Most 4-year-olds know that the answer is "Yesterday I blifed." But adults with SLI cannot do this task—apparently having failed to learn the simple rule of language involved in forming the past tense of regular verbs (Bishop & Norbury, 2008; Lai, Fisher, Hurst, Vargha-Khadem, & Monaco, 2001; van der Lely, 2005; van der Lely & Pinker, 2014).

Claims about SLI remain controversial, but many authors point to this disorder as evidence for brain mechanisms that are somehow specialized for language learning. Disruption to these mechanisms throws language off track but seems to leave other aspects of the brain's functioning undisturbed.

The Processes of Language Learning

Even with these biological contributions, there's no question that learning plays an essential role in the acquisition of language. After all, children who grow up in Paris learn to speak French; children who grow up in Beijing learn to speak Chinese. In this rather obvious way, language learning depends on the child's picking up information from her environment.

But what learning mechanisms are involved here? Part of the answer rests on the fact that children are exquisitely sensitive to patterns and regularities in what they hear, as though each child were an astute statistician, keeping track of the frequency-of-occurrence of this form or that. In one study, 8-month-old infants heard a 2-minute recording that sounded something like "bidakupadotigolabubidaku." These syllables were spoken in a monotonous tone, with no difference in stress from one syllable to the next and no pauses in between the syllables. But there was a pattern. The experimenters had decided in advance to designate the sequence "bidaku" as a word. Therefore, they arranged the sequences so that if the infant heard "bida," then "ku" was sure to follow. For other syllables, there was no such pattern. For instance, "daku" (the end of the nonsense word "bidaku") would sometimes be followed by "go," sometimes by "pa," and so on.

The babies reliably detected these patterns. In a subsequent test, babies showed no surprise if they heard the string "bidakubidakubidaku." From the babies' point of view, these were simply repetitions of a word they already knew. However, the babies showed surprise if they were presented with the string "dakupadakupadakupa." This wasn't a "word" they had heard before, although they had heard each of its syllables many times. It seems, then, that the babies had learned the "vocabulary" of this made-up language. They had detected the statistical pattern of which syllables followed which, despite their brief, passive exposure to these sounds and despite the absence of any supporting cues such as pauses or shifts in intonation (Aslin, Saffran, & Newport, 1998; Marcus, Vijayan, Rao, & Vishton, 1999; Saffran, 2003; Xu & Garcia, 2008).

In addition, children don't just detect patterns in the speech they hear. Children also seem to derive broad principles from what they hear. Consider, for example, how English-speaking children learn to form the past tense. Initially, they proceed in a word-by-word fashion, so they memorize that the past tense of "play" is "played," the past tense of "climb" is "climbed," and so on. By age 3 or so, however, children seem to realize that they don't have to memorize each word's past tense as a separate vocabulary item. Instead, they realize they can produce the past tense by manipulating morphemes—that is, by adding the "-ed" ending onto a word. This is, of course, an important discovery for children, because this principle allows them to generate the past tense for many new verbs, including verbs they've never encountered before.

However, children over-rely on this pattern, and their speech at this age contains **overregularization errors**: They say things like "Yesterday we goed" or "Yesterday I runned." The same thing happens with other morphemes, so that children of this age also overgeneralize their use of the plural ending— they say things like, "I have two foots" or "I lost three tooths" (Marcus et al., 1992). They also generalize the use of contractions; having heard "she isn't" and "you aren't," they say things like "I amn't."

It seems, then, that children (even young infants) are keenly sensitive to patterns in the language that they're learning, and they're able to figure out the (sometimes rather abstract) principles that govern these patterns. In addition, language learning relies on a theme that has been in view throughout this chapter: Language has many elements (syntax, semantics, phonology, prosody, etc.), and these elements interact in ordinary language use (so that you rely on a sentence's syntactic form to figure out its meaning; you rely on semantic cues in deciphering the syntax). In the same way, language learning also relies on all these elements in an interacting fashion. For example, children rely on prosody (the rise and fall of pitch, the pattern of timing) as clues to syntax, and adults speaking to children helpfully exaggerate these prosodic signals, easing the children's interpretive burden. Children also rely on their vocabulary, listening for words they already know as clues helping them to process more complex strings. Likewise, children rely on their knowledge of semantic relationships as a basis for figuring out syntax—a process known as **semantic bootstrapping** (Pinker, 1987). In this way, the very complexity of language is both a burden for the child (because there's so much to learn in "learning a language") and an aid (because the child can use each element as a source of information in trying to figure out the other elements).

Animal Language

We suggested earlier that humans are biologically prepared for language learning, and this claim has many implications. Among other points, can we locate the genes that underlie this preparation? Many researchers claim that we can, and they point to a gene called "FOXP2" as crucial; people who have a mutated form of this gene are markedly impaired in their language learning (e.g., Vargha-Khadem, Gadian, Copp, & Mishkin, 2005).

As a related point, if language learning is somehow tied to human genetics, then we might expect *not* to find language capacity in other species. Of course, many species do have sophisticated communication systems—including the songs and clicks of dolphins and whales, the dances of honeybees, and the various alarm calls of monkeys. These naturally occurring systems, however, are extremely limited—with small vocabularies and little (or perhaps nothing) that corresponds to the rules of syntax that are evident in human language. These systems will certainly not support the sort of *generativity* that is a prominent feature of human language—and so these other species don't have anything approaching our capacity to produce or understand an unending variety of new sentences.

Perhaps, though, these naturally occurring systems understate what animals can do. Perhaps animals can do more if only we help them a bit. To explore this issue, researchers have tried to train animals to use more sophisticated forms of communication. Some researchers have tried to train dolphins to communicate with humans; one project involved an African grey parrot; other projects have focused on primates—asking what a chimpanzee, gorilla, or bonobo might be capable of. The results from these studies are impressive, but it's notable that the greatest success involves animals that are quite similar to humans genetically (e.g., Savage-Rumbaugh & Lewin, 1994; Savage-Rumbaugh & Fields, 2000). For example, Kanzi, a male bonobo,

COMMUNICATION AMONG VERVET MONKEYS

Animals of many species communicate with one another. For example, Vervet monkeys give alarm calls when they spot a nearby predator. But they have distinct alarm calls for different types of predator—so their call when they see a leopard is different from their call when they see an eagle or a python. The fact remains, though, that no naturally occurring animal communication system comes close to human language in richness or complexity.

seems to understand icons on a keyboard as *symbols* that refer to other ideas, and he also has some mastery of syntax—so he responds differently and (usually) appropriately, using stuffed animals, to the instructions "Make the doggie bite the snake" or "Make the snake bite the doggie."

Kanzi's abilities, though, after an enormous amount of careful training, are way below those of the average 3- or 4-year-old human who has received no explicit language training. (For example, as impressive as Kanzi is, he hasn't mastered the distinction between present, past, and future tense, although every human child effortlessly learns this basic aspect of language.) Therefore, it seems that other species (especially those closely related to us) can learn the rudiments of language, but nothing in their performance undercuts the amazing differences between human language capacity and that in other organisms.

"Wolf Children"

Before moving on, we should address one last point—one that concerns the *limits* on our "biological preparation" for language. To put the matter simply, our human biology gives us a fabulous start on language learning, but to turn this "start" into "language capacity," we also need a communicative partner.

In 1920, villagers in India discovered a wolf mother in her den together with four cubs. Two were baby wolves, but the other two were human children, subsequently named Kamala and Amala. No one knows how they got

A MODERN WILD BOY

Ramu, a young boy discovered in India in 1976, appears to have been raised by wolves. He was deformed— apparently from lying in cramped positions, as in a den. He couldn't walk, and he drank by lapping with his tongue. His favorite food was raw meat, which he seemed to be able to smell at a distance. After he was found, he lived at the home for destitute children run by Mother Teresa in Lucknow, Uttar Pradesh. He learned to bathe and dress himself but never learned to speak. He continued to prefer raw meat and would often sneak out to prey upon fowl in the neighbor's chicken coop. Ramu died at the age of about 10 in February 1985.

there or why the wolf adopted them. Roger Brown (1958) tells us what these children were like:

> Kamala was about eight years old and Amala was only one and one-half. They were thoroughly wolfish in appearance and behavior: Hard callus had developed on their knees and palms from going on all fours. Their teeth were sharp edged. They moved their nostrils sniffing food. Eating and drinking were accomplished by lowering their mouths to the plate. They ate raw meat. . . . At night they prowled and sometimes howled. They shunned other children but followed the dog and cat. They slept rolled up together on the floor. . . . Amala died within a year but Kamala lived to be eighteen. . . . In time, Kamala learned to walk erect, to wear clothing, and even to speak a few words. (p. 100)

The outcome was similar for the 30 or so other wild children for whom researchers have evidence. When found, they were all shockingly animal-like. None could be rehabilitated to use language normally, although some (like Kamala) did learn to speak a few words.

Of course, the data from these wild children are difficult to interpret, partly because we don't know why the children were abandoned in the first place. (Is it possible that these children were abandoned because their human parents detected some birth defect? If so, these children may have been impaired in their functioning from the start.) Nonetheless, the consistency of these findings underscores an important point: Language learning may depend on both a human genome and a human environment.

Language and Thought

Virtually every human knows and uses a language. But it's also important that people speak *different* languages—for example, some of us speak English, others German, and still others Abkhaz or Choctaw or Kanuri or

TEST YOURSELF

13. What is aphasia?
14. What are overregularization errors?
15. What do we learn from the fact that so-called wolf-children never gain full language proficiency?

MYTHS ABOUT LANGUAGE AND THOUGHT

Many people believe that the native peoples of the far north (including the Inuit) have an enormous number of terms for various forms of snow and are correspondingly skilled in discriminating types of snow. It turns out, though, that the initial claim (the number of terms for snow) is wrong; the Inuit have roughly the same number of snow terms as do people living further south. In addition, if the Inuit people are more skilled in discriminating snow types, is this because of the language that they speak? Or is it because their day-to-day lives require that they stay alert to the differences among snow types? (AFTER ROBERSON, DAVIES, & DAVIDOFF, 2000)

Quanzhou. How do these differences matter? Is it possible that people who speak different languages end up being different in their thought processes?

Linguistic Relativity

The notion that language shapes thought is generally attributed to the anthropologist Benjamin Whorf and is often referred to as the "Whorfian hypothesis." Whorf (e.g., 1956) argued that the language you speak forces you into certain modes of thought. He claimed, therefore, that people who speak different languages inevitably *think* differently—a claim of **linguistic relativity**.

To test this claim, one line of work has examined how people perceive colors, building on the fact that some languages have many terms for colors (red, orange, mauve, puce, salmon, fawn, ocher, etc.) and others have few (see **Figure 10.15**). Do these differences among languages affect perception? Evidence suggests, in fact, that people who speak languages with a richer color vocabulary may perceive colors differently—making finer and more sharply defined distinctions (Özgen, 2004; Roberson, Davies, & Davidoff, 2000; Winawer et al., 2007).

Other studies have focused on other ways in which languages differ. Some languages, for example, emphasize absolute directions (terms like the English words "east" or "west" that are defined independently of which way the speaker is facing at the moment). Other languages emphasize relative directions (words like "right" or "left" that do depend on which way the speaker is facing). Research suggests that these language differences can lead to corresponding differences in how people remember—and perhaps how they perceive—position (Majid, Bowerman, Kita, Haun, & Levinson, 2004; Pederson et al., 1998).

Languages also differ in how they describe events. In English, we tend to use active-voice sentences that name the agent of the action, even if the action was accidental ("Sam made a mistake"). It sounds awkward or evasive to describe these events in other terms ("Mistakes were made"). In other languages, including Japanese or Spanish, it's common *not* to mention the agent for an accidental event, and this in turn can shape memory: After viewing videos of accidental events, Japanese and Spanish speakers are less likely than English speakers to remember the person who triggered the accident (Boroditsky, 2011).

How should we think about all these results? One possibility—in line with Whorf's original hypothesis—is that language has a direct impact on cognition, so that the categories recognized by your language become the categories used in your thought. In this view, language has a unique effect on cognition (because no other factor can shape cognition in this way), and because language's influence is unique, it is also irreversible: Once your language has led you to think in certain ways, you will forever think in those ways. From this perspective, therefore, there are literally some ideas that, say, a Japanese speaker can contemplate but that an English speaker cannot, and vice versa—and likewise, say, for a Hopi or a French speaker.

FIGURE 10.15 COLORS IN DIFFERENT LANGUAGES

English naming

Berinmo naming

The Berinmo people, living in Papua New Guinea, have only five words for describing colors, and so, for example, they use a single word ("nol") to describe colors that English speakers call "green" and colors we call "blue." (The letters and numbers in these panels refer to a system often used for classifying colors.) These differences, from one language to the next, have an impact on how people perceive and remember colors. This effect is best understood in terms of attention: Language can draw our attention to some aspect of the world and in this way can shape our experience and, therefore, our cognition. (AFTER ROBERSON, DAVIES, & DAVIDOFF, 2000)

A different possibility is more modest—and also more plausible: The language you hear guides what you pay attention to, and what you pay attention to shapes your thinking. In this view, language does have an influence, but the influence is indirect: The influence works *via* the mechanisms of attention. Why is this distinction (direct effect vs. indirect effect) important? The key is that other factors can also guide your attention, with the result that in many settings these factors will erase any impact that language might have. Put differently, the idea here is that your language might bias your attention in one way, but other factors will bias your attention in the opposite way—canceling out language's impact. On this basis, the effects of language on cognition might easily be reversible, and certainly not as fundamental as Whorf proposed.

To see how this point plays out, let's look at a concrete case. We've mentioned that when English speakers describe an event, our language usually requires that we name (and so pay attention to) the actor who caused the event; when a Spanish speaker describes the same event, her language doesn't have this requirement, and so it doesn't force her to think about the actor. In this way, the structure of each language influences what the person will pay attention to, and the data tell us that this difference in focus has consequences for thinking and for memory.

But we could, if we wished, simply give the Spanish speaker an instruction: "Pay attention to the actor." Or we could make sure that the actor is wearing a brightly colored coat, using a perceptual cue to guide attention. These simple steps can (and often do) offset the bias created by language.

The logic is similar for the effect of language on color perception. If you're a speaker of Berinmo (a language spoken in New Guinea), your language makes no distinction between "green" and "blue," so it never leads you to think about these as separate categories. If you're an English speaker, your language does make this distinction, and this can draw your attention to what all green objects have in common and what all blue objects have in common. If your attention is drawn to this point again and again, you'll gain familiarity with the distinction and eventually become better at making the distinction. Once more, therefore, language does matter—but it matters because of language's impact on attention.

Again, let's be clear on the argument here: If language directly and uniquely shapes thought, then the effects of language on cognition will be systematic and permanent. But the alternative is that it's your *experience* that shapes thought, and your experience depends on what you pay attention to, and (finally) language is just one of the many factors guiding what you pay attention to. On this basis, the effects of language may sometimes be large, but can be offset by a range of other influences. (For evidence, see Boroditsky, 2001; and then Chen, 2007, or January & Kako, 2007. Also see Li, Abarbanell, Gleitman, & Papafragou, 2011; Li & Gleitman, 2002.)

More than a half-century ago, Whorf argued for a strong claim—that the language people speak plays a unique role in shaping their thought and has a lifelong impact, determining what they can or cannot think, what ideas they can or cannot consider. There is an element of truth here, because language can and does shape cognition. But language's impact is neither profound nor permanent, and there is no reason to accept Whorf's ambitious proposal. (For more on these issues, see Gleitman & Papafragou, 2012; Hanako & Smith, 2005; Hermer-Vazquez, Spelke, & Katsnelson, 1999; Kay & Regier, 2007; Özgen & Davies, 2002; Papafragou, Li, Choi, & Han, 2007; Stapel & Semin, 2007.)

Bilingualism

There's one more—and intriguing—way that language is said to influence cognition. It comes from cases in which someone knows more than one language.

Children raised in bilingual homes generally learn both languages quickly and well (Kovelman, Shalinksy, Berens, & Petitto, 2008). Bilingual children do tend to have smaller vocabularies, compared to monolingual children, but this contrast is evident only at an early age, and bilingual children soon catch up on this dimension (Bialystok, Craik, Green, & Gollan, 2009).

These findings surprise many people, on the expectation that bilingual children would become confused—blurring together their languages and getting mixed up about which words and which rules belong in each language. But this confusion seems not to occur. In fact, children who are raised bilingually seem to develop skills that specifically help them avoid this sort of confusion—so that they develop a skill of (say) turning off their French-based habits in *this* setting so that they can speak uncompromised English, and then turning off their English-based habits in *that* setting so that they can speak fluent French. This skill obviously supports their language learning, but it may also help them in other settings. (See Bialystok et al., 2009; Calvo & Bialystok, 2013; Engel de Abreau, Cruz-Santos, Tourinho, Martion, & Bialystok, 2012; Hernández, Costa, & Humphreys, 2012; Hilchey & Klein, 2011; Kroll, Bobb, & Hoshino, 2014; Pelham & Abrams, 2014; Zelazo, 2006.) In Chapter 5 we introduced the idea of executive control, and the suggestion here is that being raised bilingually may encourage *better* executive control. As a result, bilinguals may be better at avoiding distraction, switching between competing tasks, or holding information in mind while working on some other task.

There has, however, been considerable debate about these findings, and not all experiments find a bilingual advantage in executive control. (See, e.g., Bialystok & Grundy, 2018; Costa, Hernández, Costa-Faidella, & Sebastián-Galés, 2009; de Bruin, Treccani, & Della Salla, 2015; Goldsmith & Morton, 2018; Von Bastian, Souza & Gade, 2016; Zhou & Kross, 2016.) There is some suggestion that this advantage only emerges with certain tasks or in certain age groups (perhaps in children, but not adults). There is also some indication that other forms of training can improve executive control—and so bilingualism may be just one way to achieve this goal. Obviously, further research is needed in this domain, especially since the alleged benefits of bilingualism have important implications—for public policy, for education, and for parenting. These implications become all the more intriguing when we bear in mind that roughly a fifth of the population in the United States speaks a language at home that is different from the English they use in other settings; the proportion is even higher in some states, including California, Texas, New Mexico, and Nevada (Shin & Kominski, 2010). These points aside, though, research on bilingualism provides one more (and perhaps a surprising) arena in which scholars continue to explore the ways in which language use may shape cognition.

TEST YOURSELF

16. What does it mean to say that language's effects on cognition are *indirect* and *reversible*?

writing

Students are often required to do a lot of writing—for example, in an essay exam or a term paper. Can cognitive psychology provide any help in this activity—specifically, helping you to write more clearly and more persuasively?

Research tells us that people usually have an easier time understanding active sentences than passive, and so (all things being equal) active sentences are preferable. We also know that people approach a sentence with certain parsing strategies, and that's part of the reason why sentences are clearer if the structure of the sentence is laid out early, with the details following, rather than the other way around. Some guidelines refer to this as an advantage for "right-branching sentences" rather than "left-branching sentences." The idea here is that the "branches" represent the syntactic and semantic complexity, and you want that complexity to arrive late, after the base structure is established.

By the same logic, lists are easier to understand if they arrive late in the sentence ("I went to the store with Juan, Fred, George, Sue, and Judy"), so that they can be fitted into the structure, rather than arriving early ("Juan, Fred, George, Sue, Judy, and I went to the store") *before* the structure.

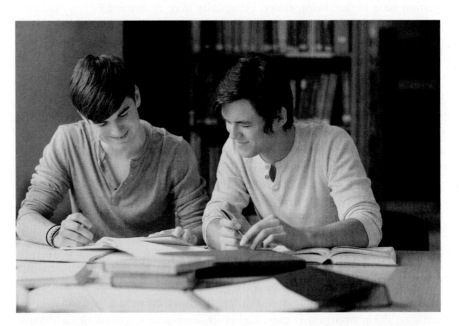

PEER EDITING

It is often useful to have a peer (a friend, perhaps) edit your prose (and you can then do the same for the friend's prose). These steps can lead to a large improvement in how clearly you write!

Readers are also helped by occasional words or phrases that signal the flow of ideas in the material they're reading. Sentences that begin "In contrast," or "Similarly," or "However," provide the reader with some advance warning about what's coming up and how it's related to the ideas covered so far. This warning, in turn, makes it easier for the reader to see how the new material fits into the framework established up to that point. The warning also requires the *writer* to think about these relationships, and often that encourages the writer to do some fine-tuning of the sequence of sentences!

In addition, it's important to remember that many people *speak* more clearly than they *write,* and it's interesting to ask why this is so. One reason is *prosody*—the pattern of pitch changes and pauses that we use in speaking. These cannot be reproduced in writing—although prosodic cues can sometimes be mimicked by the use of commas (to indicate pauses) or italics (to indicate emphasis). These aspects of print can certainly be overused, but they are in all cases important, and writers should probably pay more attention to them than they do—in order to gain in print some of the benefits that (in spoken language) are provided by prosody.

But how should you use these cues correctly? One option is to rely on the fact that as listeners and speakers we all know how to use prosodic cues, and we can exploit that knowledge when we write by means of a simple trick: reading your prose out loud. If you see a comma on the page but you're not inclined, as a speaker, to pause at that moment, then the comma is probably unnecessary. Conversely, if you find yourself pausing as you read aloud but there's no comma, then you may need one.

Another advantage of spoken communication, as opposed to written, is the prospect of immediate feedback. If you say something that isn't clear, your conversation partner may frown, look confused, or say something to indicate misunderstanding. What can take the place of this feedback when you're writing? As one option, it's almost always useful to have someone (a friend, perhaps) read over your drafts; this peer editing can often catch ambiguities, absence of clarity, or absence of flow that you might have missed on your own. Even without a peer editor, you can gain some of the same benefits from reading your own prose out loud. Some studies suggest that reading your own prose out loud helps you to gain some distance from it that you might not have with ordinary (silent) reading, so that you can, at least in a rough way, provide your own peer editing. As a related point, we know that people routinely *skip* words when they're reading (this was important in the Chapter 4 discussion of speed-reading). The skipping helps when you're reading, but it's a problem when you're editing your own prose (how can you edit words that you didn't even see?). It's important, therefore, that the skipping is less likely when you read the prose out loud—another advantage of reading aloud when you're checking on your own writing.

Finally, many people shift into a different style of expressing themselves when they're writing. Maybe they're convinced that they need some degree of formality in their written expression. Maybe they're anxious while writing, and this stiffens their prose. Or maybe they're trying to impress the reader, so they deliberately reach for more complex constructions and more obscure vocabulary. Whatever the reason for these shifts, they are often counterproductive and make your writing less clear, wordier, and stiffer than your ordinary (spoken) expression. Part of the cure here is to abandon the idea that complex and formal prose is better prose. And part of the cure lies in peer editing or reading aloud. In either case, the question to ask is this: Would you express these ideas more clearly, more simply, if you were *speaking* them rather than writing them? Often, this will lead you to better writing.

Will these simple suggestions improve every writer? Probably not. Will these suggestions take obscure, fractured prose and lift it to a level that makes you eligible for a Pulitzer Prize? Surely not. Even so, the suggestions offered here may well help you in some ways, and for anyone's writing, any source of improvement should be welcome!

For more on this topic . . .

Oppenheimer, D. M. (2006). Consequences of erudite vernacular utilized irrespective of necessity: Problems with using long words needlessly. *Applied Cognitive Psychology, 20*, 139-156.

chapter review

SUMMARY

- All speech is built up from a few dozen phonemes, although the selection of phonemes varies from language to language. Phonemes, in turn, are built up from a small number of production features, including voicing, place of articulation, and manner of production. Phonemes can be combined to form more complex sounds, but combinations are constrained by a number of rules.

- Speech perception is more than a matter of detecting the relevant features in the input sound stream. The perceiver needs to deal with speaker-to-speaker variation in how sounds are produced; she also needs to segment the stream of speech and cope with coarticulation. The process of speech perception is helped enormously by context, but we also have the impressive skill of categorical perception, which makes us keenly sensitive to differences between categories of speech sounds but insensitive to distinctions within each category.

- People know many thousands of words, and for each one they know the sound of the word, its syntactic role, and its semantic representation. Our understanding of words is also generative, enabling us to create limitless numbers of new words. Some new words are wholly made up (e.g., "geek"), but many new words are combinations of familiar morphemes.

- The rules of syntax govern whether a sequence of words is grammatical. One set of rules governs phrase structure, and the word groups identified by these rules do correspond to natural groupings of words. Phrase-structure rules also guide interpretation. Like all the rules discussed in this chapter, though, phrase-structure rules are descriptive, not prescriptive.

- To understand a sentence, a listener or reader needs to parse the sentence, determining each word's syntactic role. Evidence suggests that people parse a sentence as they see or hear each word, and this approach sometimes leads them into parsing errors that must be repaired later; this outcome is revealed by garden-path sentences. Parsing is guided by syntax, semantics, and the extralinguistic context.

- The biological roots of language are revealed in many ways. The study of aphasia makes it clear that some areas of the brain are specialized for learning and using language. The rapid learning of language also supports the biological basis for language.

- Processes of imitation and direct instruction play relatively small parts in language learning. This is evident in the fact that children produce many forms (often, overregularization errors) that no adult produces; these forms are obviously not the result of imitation. However, language learning is strongly influenced by children's remarkable sensitivity to patterns in the language they hear. Children can also use their understanding of one aspect of language (e.g., phonology or vocabulary) to help learn about other aspects (e.g., syntax).

- There has been considerable discussion about the ways in which thought might be shaped by the language one speaks. Language certainly guides and influences your thoughts, and the way a thought is formulated into words can have an effect on how you think about the thought's content. In addition, language can call your attention to a category or to a distinction, which makes it likely that you will have experience in thinking about the category or distinction. This experience, in turn, can promote fluency in these thoughts. However, these effects are not unique to language (because other factors can also draw your attention to the category), nor are they irreversible. As a result, there is no evidence that language can shape what you *can* think.

• Research shows that children raised in bilingual homes learn both languages as quickly and as well as monolingual children learning their single language. In fact, bilingual children seem to develop an impressive ability to switch between languages, and this ability may also help them in other settings that require executive control of mental processes.

KEY TERMS

sentences (p. 367)
morphemes (p. 367)
phonemes (p. 367)
voicing (p. 368)
manner of production (p. 368)
place of articulation (p. 369)
speech segmentation (p. 371)
coarticulation (p. 372)
phonemic restoration effect (p. 372)
categorical perception (p. 373)
generativity (p. 378)
syntax (p. 379)
phrase-structure rules (p. 380)
tree structure (p. 380)
prescriptive rules (p. 381)

descriptive rules (p. 381)
parse (p. 383)
garden-path sentences (p. 385)
extralinguistic context (p. 389)
prosody (p. 390)
pragmatics (p. 392)
aphasia (p.393)
Broca's area (p. 393)
nonfluent aphasia (p. 393)
Wernicke's area (p. 394)
fluent aphasia (p. 394)
specific-language impairment (SLI) (p. 395)
overregularization errors (p. 396)
semantic bootstrapping (p. 397)
linguistic relativity (p. 400)

TEST YOURSELF AGAIN

1. What are morphemes? What are phonemes?

2. Define "voicing," "manner of production," and "place of articulation."

3. What is speech segmentation, and why is it an important step in speech perception?

4. What is categorical perception?

5. Why is it difficult to give an exact count of the number of words in someone's vocabulary?

6. What evidence tells us that the rules of syntax can be separated from considerations of whether or not a string of words has meaning?

7. What are phrase-structure rules, and what does it mean that these rules are "descriptive," not "prescriptive"?

8. What's the evidence that *multiple factors* play a role in guiding how you parse a sentence?

9. What is a garden-path sentence?

10. What is prosody?

11. Why are printed versions of garden-path sentences more likely to puzzle you, compared to spoken versions of the same sentences?

12. "What happened to the roast beef?" "The dog sure looks happy." Explain what happened in this conversational exchange, and how the exchange will be understood.

13. What is aphasia?

14. What are overregularization errors?

15. What do we learn from the fact that so-called wolf-children never gain full language proficiency?

16. What does it mean to say that language's effects on cognition are *indirect* and *reversible*?

THINK ABOUT IT

1. There is no question that some languages capture, in a single word, ideas that in other languages can only be described with a long phrase. One example is the German word "Schadenfreude," which translates as "a feeling of joy that comes from learning about another person's troubles." Do you think this difference matters for cognition—so that people who know this word can think more efficiently, or more effectively, than people who don't know this word? If so, how is this different from the hypothesis offered years ago by Whorf?

▣ eBOOK DEMONSTRATIONS & ESSAYS

Go to http://digital.wwnorton.com/cognition7 for the online demonstrations and essays relevant to this chapter. These can be found in the ebook.

Online Demonstrations

- Demonstration 10.1: Phonemes and Subphonemes
- Demonstration 10.2: The Speed of Speech
- Demonstration 10.3: Coarticulation
- Demonstration 10.4: The Most Common Words
- Demonstration 10.5: Patterns in Language
- Demonstration 10.6: Ambiguity

Online Applying Cognitive Psychology and the Law Essays

- Cognitive Psychology and the Law: Jury Instructions

ZAPS COGNITION LABS

Go to http://digital.wwnorton.com/cognition7 to experience interactive online psychology labs relevant to this chapter.

Visual Knowledge

what if... Researchers use many approaches to study *dreams*. The most obvious path, though, is simply to ask people about the content of their dreams. For example, consider this exchange. E is the experimenter; S is the person reporting the dream, which was about a cancer clinic (Kerr, 1983, p. 276).

S: I was in a room that looked similar to my instant banker at work, but it was a big machine with lots of buttons, like a car machine.

E: Like an instant banker machine?

S: Right, at [name of bank]. And I don't know why I was there, but I guess there was a screen and there were other buttons you could push, you could look in and see how different cancer patients are doing.

E: Was this visual, could you see anything?

S: I couldn't, but I stood by the screen and I knew that *others* could see what was going on through all the little panels.

. . .

S: I guess I imagined the board with the buttons. Maybe because I imagined them in my mind, it was not that I could really see them with my eyes, but I know what that board looks like, and the only reason I know what it looks like is by touch, and I could remember where the buttons were without touching them on the boards.

. . .

E: Okay. Where did the events in this experience seem to be taking place? What were the settings?

S: It seemed to be a large room that was oblong in shape, and there seemed to be an X-ray machine's work. I felt like it was in an office building where I worked.

E: And you mentioned something before about the bank?

S: Uh huh, it looked like the bank where I do my instant banking (E: Okay.), except it was larger and more oblong.

E: And is that more like where you worked?

S: No, where I do work, the room is smaller, just large enough for that little instant banker machine.

. . . .

- In important ways, mental images are picture-like, representing in a direct way the spatial layout of the represented scene. It's not surprising, therefore, that there is considerable overlap between imagery and perception—in how each functions and in their neural bases.

- In addition to visual imagery, people use spatial imagery, which may be represented in the mind in terms of movements or perhaps in some abstract format.

- Although they are picture-like, images (visual or spatial) are not pictures; instead, images seem to be organized in a way that pictures are not.

- Even though images in working memory provide a distinctive form of representation, information about appearances in long-term memory may not be distinctive. In fact, long-term memory for sensory information seems to obey all the principles we described in earlier chapters for verbal or symbolic memories.

This dream report seems in most ways unremarkable—other people, describing their own dreams, offer reports that are similar. What is remarkable, though, is that this report was offered by someone who had been blind since birth.

The dreamer's blindness helps us understand some aspects of this report (e.g., she says that she only knew what the board looked like *by touch*). But how should we think about other aspects of the dream? How could she know "what that board *looks like*"? What was it, in the dream, that told her the room was large and oblong?

Of course, close reading of her account of the dream reveals the absence of truly "visual" properties: There are no mentions of colors or visible textures on surfaces. This pattern—an absence of visual descriptions—is typical for individuals who were blinded before the age of 5 or so (e.g., Kerr & Domhoff, 2004).

What would your mental life be like—in your dreams and while you're awake—if you had lost the sense of sight at an early age? More broadly, what does it mean for something to be "truly visual"? To work our way toward these issues, we'll start with the sort of visual imagery that most sighted people have all the time.

Visual Imagery

You have knowledge of many different types. For example, you know what a fish is, but you also know what a fish looks like and what fish smells like when it's cooking. You know what a guitar is, but you also know what one sounds like. Likewise, people describe their *thoughts* in a variety of ways: Sometimes, they claim, their thoughts seem to be formulated in words. Sometimes their thoughts seem more abstract—a sequence of ideas that lack any concrete form. But sometimes, people claim, their thoughts involve a sequence of *pictures* or *sounds* or other sensory impressions.

What can we say about this variety? How are sights or sounds or smells represented in the mind? In this chapter, we'll focus largely on *visual* knowledge and *visual* thoughts (and so, for now, our focus will be on sighted individuals, not the blind). As we proceed, therefore, you should keep an eye on how the questions we're asking might be applied to other forms of nonverbal knowledge.

The Mind's Eye

How many windows are there in your house or apartment? Who has a broader mouth, relative to the shape of her face: Taylor Swift or Beyoncé? For most people, questions like these seem to elicit "mental pictures." You know what Swift and Beyoncé look like, and you call a "picture" of each woman before your "mind's eye" in order to make the comparison. Likewise, you call to mind a "map" of your apartment and count the windows by inspecting this map. Many people even trace the map in the air when they're counting the windows, moving their finger around to follow the imagined map's contours.

Various practical problems also seem to evoke images. There you are in a store, trying on a new sweater. Will it look good with your blue pants? To decide, you'll probably try to visualize the blue of the pants, using your "mind's eye" to consider how they'll look with the sweater. Similarly, if a friend asks you, "Was David in class yesterday?" you might try to answer by visualizing what the room looked like during the class; is David "visible" in your image?

These examples illustrate the common, everyday use of visual images—as a basis for making decisions, as an aid to remembering. But surely there's no tiny eye somewhere deep in your brain; the phrase "mind's eye" therefore cannot be taken literally. Likewise, mental "pictures" cannot be actual pictures; with no eye deep inside the brain, who or what would inspect such pictures? In light of these puzzles, what *are* images?

Introspections about Images

People have written about imagery (and the "mind's eye") for hundreds of years. The first systematic research, though, was conducted in the late 1800s by Francis Galton, an important figure who made contributions as an inventor, explorer, statistician, and meteorologist. (Among his other achievements, Galton devised the first weather map, developed a system for analyzing fingerprints in criminal investigations, and invented the silent dog whistle. He also happened to be Charles Darwin's cousin.) Galton was particularly interested in how people differ from one another, and as part of his inquiry he explored the nature of visual imagery. His method was straightforward: He asked various people simply to describe their images and rate them for vividness (Galton, 1883). In other words, he asked his research participants to *introspect*, or "look within" (a method that we first met in Chapter 1), and to report on their own mental contents.

The **self-report data** that Galton obtained fit well with common sense. Many of his participants reported that they could "inspect" their images much as they would inspect a picture, and their descriptions made it clear that they were "viewing" their images from a certain position and a certain distance—just as they'd look at an actual scene from a specific viewing perspective. They also reported that they could "read off" from the image details of color and texture. All of this implies a mode of representation that is, in many ways, picture-like—and this is, of course, consistent with our informal manner of describing mental images as "pictures in the head," to be inspected with the "mind's eye."

There was, however, another side of these early data: Galton's participants differed widely from one another in their self-reports. Some described images of photographic clarity, rich in detail, almost as if they were *seeing* the imaged scene rather than visualizing it. Other participants, though, reported very sketchy images or no images at all. They were able to think about the scenes that Galton named for them, but they insisted that in no sense were they "seeing" these scenes. Their reports rarely included mention of color or size or viewing perspective; in fact, their reports were devoid of *any* visual qualities.

These observations suggest that people differ enormously in their imagery—so that some people are "visualizers" and others are not. Indeed, these observations invite the notion that some people may be *incapable* of forming visual images; but if so, what consequences does this notion have? Are there some tasks that visualizers can do that "nonvisualizers" cannot (or vice versa)?

Before we can answer these questions, we need to address a methodological concern raised by Galton's data, and it's one that might have occurred to you at the start of this chapter, when we talked about dreams in someone who was blind. When a blind person says a room "looked similar" to her bank machine, what does that mean? Surely this person intends something different from what a sighted person would mean when saying the same words. For that matter, blind people routinely talk about "watching TV" or "taking a look at something," and they know that a star "appears" as a small spot in the night sky (Kerr & Domhoff, 2004). These phrases are surely metaphorical when used by the blind, and obviously the subjective experience of someone blind "watching TV" is different from the experience of someone with full vision.

Points like these remind us that there's a "translation step" involved whenever people translate their subjective inner experience into a verbal report, and there's no guarantee that everyone translates in the same way. Returning to Galton's study, it's therefore possible that all of his participants had the *same* imagery skill but varied in how they described their experience (i.e., in how they translated the experience into words). Maybe some were cautious, so they kept their descriptions brief and undetailed; others were more extravagant and took pleasure in providing elaborate reports. In this way, Galton's data might reveal differences in how people *talk about* their imagery, not differences in imagery itself.

To address this concern, we need a more objective means of assessing imagery—one that doesn't rely on the subjectivity inherent in self-reports.

With this more objective approach, we could assess the differences, from one individual to the next, suggested by Galton's data. In fact, with this more objective approach, we could hope to find out exactly what images *are*. Let's look at the data, and then, from that base, we'll return to the intriguing differences in imagery experience from one person to the next. This framework will also allow us to address the puzzle we met at the chapter's start: the imagery experience of the blind.

TEST YOURSELF

1. What is the concern about "self-report" data, and Galton's data in particular?

Chronometric Studies of Imagery

Imagery researchers are keenly sensitive to the concerns we've just described, and so they rarely ask participants to *describe* their images. Instead, imagery experiments require people to *do something* with their images—usually, make a judgment based on the image. Researchers can then examine how fast people are in making these judgments, and these measurements can be used to test hypotheses. In other words, many such studies are **chronometric** ("time-measuring") **studies**.

Mental Images as "Picture-like"

Consider what would happen if you were asked to *write a paragraph* describing a cat. Most likely you'd mention the distinctive features of cats—their whiskers, their claws, and so on. Your paragraph probably wouldn't include the fact that cats have heads, since this is obvious and not worth mentioning. But now consider what would happen if we ask you to *draw a picture* of a cat. In this format, the cat's head would be rather prominent, simply because the head is relatively large and up front. Claws and whiskers might be less prominent, because these features are small and would take up little space in your drawing.

The point here is that the pattern of *what information is included*, as well as what information is prominent, depends on the mode of presentation. For a description, features that are prominent will be those that are distinctive and strongly associated with the object being described. For a *depiction*, in contrast, size and position will determine what's prominent and what's not.

Against this backdrop, we can ask what information is available in a visual image. Is it the pictorially prominent features, which would imply a depictive mode of representation, or is it the verbally prominent ones, implying a descriptive mode? In an early study by Kosslyn (1976), research participants were asked to form a series of mental images and to answer yes/no questions about each. For example, they were instructed to form a mental image of a cat and then asked: "Does the cat have a head? Does the cat have claws?" Participants responded to these questions quickly, but—crucially—responses to the head question were quicker than those to the claws question. This difference suggests that information readily available in the image follows the rules for pictures, not paragraphs. For comparison, though, a different group of participants was instructed merely to think about cats (with no mention of imagery). These participants, when asked the same questions, gave quicker responses about the claws than about the head—the reverse pattern of the first group. It seems, therefore, that people have the option of thinking about cats via imagery and also the option of thinking about cats without imagery; as the mode of representation changes, so does the pattern of information availability.

In a different experiment, participants were asked to memorize the fictional map shown in **Figure 11.1** and, in particular, to memorize the locations of the various landmarks: the well, the straw hut, and so on (Kosslyn, Ball, & Reiser, 1978). The experimenters made sure participants had the map

FIGURE 11.1   FICTIONAL ISLAND USED IN
IMAGE-SCANNING EXPERIMENTS

Participants in the study first memorized this map, including the various landmarks (the hut, the well, the patch of grass, and so on). They then formed a mental image of the map for the scanning procedure.

(AFTER KOSSLYN, 1983)

memorized by asking them to draw a replica of it from memory; once they could do this, the main experiment began. Participants were asked to form an image of the island and to point their "mind's eye" at a specific landmark—let's say, the well. Another landmark was then mentioned, perhaps the hut, and participants were asked to imagine a black speck moving in a straight line from the first landmark to the second. When the speck "reached" the target, participants pressed a button, stopping a clock. This action provided a measure of how long the participants needed to "scan" from the well to the hut. The same was done for the well and the tree, and the hut and the patch of grass, so that the researchers ended up with scanning times for each of the various pairs of landmarks.

Figure 11.2 shows the results. The data from this **image-scanning procedure** reveal that participants scan across their images at a constant rate, so that doubling the scanning "distance" doubles the time required for the scan, and tripling the distance triples the time required.

Similar results emerge if participants are given a task that requires them to "zoom in" on their images (e.g., a task that requires them to inspect the image for some small detail) or a task that requires them to "zoom out" (e.g., a task that requires a more global judgment). In these studies, response times are directly proportional to the amount of zoom required, suggesting once

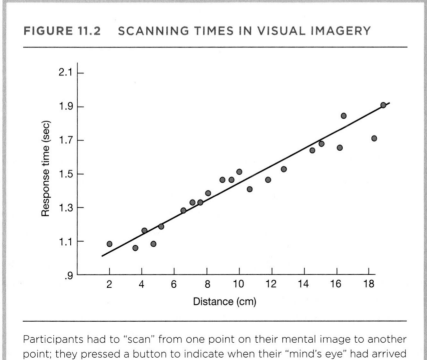

FIGURE 11.2   SCANNING TIMES IN VISUAL IMAGERY

Participants had to "scan" from one point on their mental image to another point; they pressed a button to indicate when their "mind's eye" had arrived at its destination. Response times were closely related to the "distance" participants had to scan across on the image.   (AFTER KOSSLYN, 1983)

FIGURE 11.3   ZOOMING IN ON MENTAL PICTURES

Just as it takes time to "scan across" a mental image, it also takes time to "zoom in" on one. As a result, participants respond slowly if they're instructed to imagine a mouse standing with an elephant and then are asked: "Does the mouse have whiskers?" To answer this question, participants need a bit of time (which we can measure) to zoom in on the mouse, in order to bring the whiskers "into view." Responses were faster if participants were initially asked to imagine the mouse standing next to a paper clip. For this image, participants started with a "close-up" view, so no zooming was needed to "see" the whiskers.

again that "travel" in the imaged world resembles travel in the actual world, at least with regard to timing (**Figure 11.3**).

Depictions versus Descriptions

Whether you're scanning across a mental image, therefore, or zooming in on one, "traveling" a greater "distance" requires more time. This is the same relationship we would observe if we asked research participants to move their eyes across an actual map (rather than an image of one) or literally to zoom in on a real picture. In these cases, too, traveling a greater distance would require more time. All of this points toward the similarity between mental images and actual out-in-the-world pictures.

More precisely, though, the data are telling us a great deal about the nature of mental images. According to these results, images represent a scene in a manner that preserves all of the distance relationships within that scene: Points close to one another in the scene are somehow "close" to one another in the image; points farther apart in the scene are somehow "farther apart" in the image. So, in a very real sense, the image preserves the spatial layout of the represented scene and, therefore, rather directly represents the *geometry* of the scene. In this way, images *depict* the scene rather than describing it; thus, they are much more similar to pictures or maps than they are to descriptions.

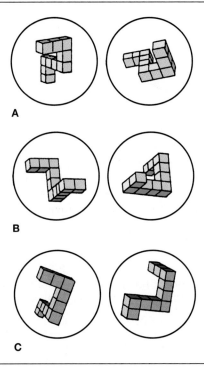
Mental Rotation

In a series of classic experiments by Shepard, Cooper, and Metzler, participants were asked to decide whether pairs like the one in **Figure 11.4A** showed two different shapes or just one shape viewed from two different perspectives (Cooper & Shepard, 1973; Shepard & Cooper, 1982; Shepard & Metzler, 1971). In other words, is it possible to "rotate" the form shown on the left in Figure 11.4A so that it will end up looking just like the form on the right? What about the two shapes shown in **Figure 11.4B** or the two in **11.4C**?

To perform this **mental rotation task**, participants seem first to imagine one of the forms rotating into alignment with the other. Then, once the forms are oriented in the same way, participants can make their judgment. This step of

Panel A shows data from stimulus pairs requiring mental rotation in two dimensions, so that the imaged forms stay within the imagined picture plane. Panel B shows data from pairs requiring an imagined rotation in depth. The data are similar, indicating that participants can imagine three-dimensional rotations as easily as they can imagine two-dimensional rotations.

(AFTER SHEPARD & METZLER, 1971)

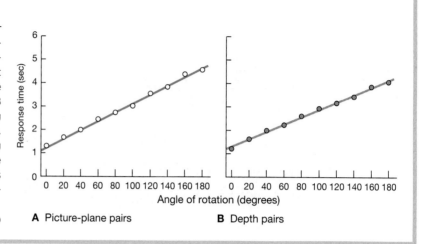

A Picture-plane pairs   **B** Depth pairs

imagined rotation takes some time, and the amount of time depends on how much rotation is needed. **Figure 11.5** shows the data pattern, with response times clearly influenced by how far apart the two forms were in their initial orientations. Once again, therefore, imagined "movement" resembles actual movement: The farther you have to imagine a form rotating, the longer the evaluation takes.

As a complication, notice that if you were to cut out the left-hand drawing in Figure 11.4A and spin it around while leaving it flat on the table, you could align it with the drawing on the right. The relevant rotation, therefore, is one that leaves the pictures within the two-dimensional plane in which they are drawn. In contrast, the two forms shown in Figure 11.4B are identical except for a rotation in depth. No matter how you spin the *picture* on the left, it won't line up with the picture on the right. You can align these forms, but only if you spin them around a vertical axis—in essence, lifting them off the page.

Can people imagine rotations in depth? It turns out that the accuracy level in these judgments is around 95%, and the data resemble those obtained with picture-plane rotation (compare Figures 11.5A and 11.5B). Apparently, then, participants can represent three-dimensional forms and three-dimensional movement in their images. In some circumstances, therefore, visual images are not mental pictures; they're more like mental sculptures. (For more on mental rotation, including differences between men and women in how well they do this task, see Boone & Hegarty, 2017; also see **Figure 11.6.**)

The Concern about Demand Character

In both mental rotation and mental scanning, then, the farther the imagined "travel," the longer it takes. We've interpreted these results as an indication of how images represent spatial layout—with points that are more distant in

FIGURE 11.6 BRAIN ACTIVITY IN MENTAL ROTATION

As the text describes, it takes more time to imagine something rotating, say, 80 degrees than it does to imagine it moving 40 degrees. Related data come from brain scans — with more brain activity needed for a 40-degree rotation than for no rotation at all, and even more activity needed for an 80-degree or a 120-degree rotation.

(AFTER CARPENTER ET AL., 1999)

the represented scene being somehow farther apart in the image. But there's another way one might try to interpret the data. Participants in these studies obviously know that movement through the world takes time and that moving a longer distance takes more time. Perhaps, therefore, the participants simply control the timing of their responses in order to re-create this "normal" pattern.

This proposal can be fleshed out in a variety of ways, but to phrase things strongly, maybe participants in these studies aren't imagining rotations or scanning across an image at all. Instead, maybe they're thinking, "The experimenter just asked me to scan a long way, and I'd like to make it look like I'm obeying. I know that a long scan takes a long time, so let me wait a moment before hitting the response button."

Why should participants act in this way? One reason is that research participants usually want to be helpful, and they do all they can to give the experimenter "good" data. As a result, they're very sensitive to the **demand character** of the experiment—that is, cues that might signal how they're "supposed to" behave in that situation. (For early discussion of how demand character might influence imagery experiments, see Intons-Peterson, 1983, 1999; Intons-Peterson & White, 1981).

A different possibility is that this sort of "simulation" is, in fact, what imagery is really all about. Perhaps whenever people try to "imagine" something, they draw on their knowledge about how an event in the world would actually unfold, and they do their best to simulate this event. In this case, a longer scan or a greater rotation requires more time, not because there really is some "travel" involved but because people know that these manipulations should take more time and do their best to simulate the process (Pylyshyn, 1981).

As it turns out, though, we can set aside these concerns, allowing us to maintain the claims we've already sketched—namely, that the scanning and rotation data are as they are, not through simulation but *because of how images*

IMAGERY AS "SIMULATION"

There is, of course, no "box" trapping this mime. Instead, the mime is simulating what would happen if he were trapped in a box. In the same way, researchers have asked whether study participants, guided by an experiment's demand character, are simply simulating (re-creating?) how they'd act if they were looking at a picture.

TEST YOURSELF

2. What is a chronometric study?
3. Why do image-scanning studies indicate that images *depict* a scene rather than *describing* the scene?
4. What does it mean to say that an experiment's results might be influenced by demand character?

represent spatial layout. Several lines of evidence support this claim, including (crucially) data we will turn to, later in the chapter, examining the neural bases for imagery. But we can also tackle concerns about demand character directly. In several studies, experimenters have asked participants to make judgments about spatial layout but have taken care never to mention that imagery might be relevant to the task (e.g., Finke & Pinker, 1982). This procedure avoids any suggestion to participants that they should simulate some sort of "mental travel." Even so, participants in these procedures spontaneously form images and scan across them, and their responses show the standard pattern: longer response times observed with longer scans. Apparently, this result emerges whenever participants are using visual imagery—whether the result is encouraged by the experimenters' instructions or not.

Imagery and Perception

If images are—as it seems—so much like pictures, then are the mental processes used to inspect images similar to those used to inspect stimuli? More broadly, what is the relation between imaging and perceiving?

In an early study by Segal and Fusella (1970, 1971), participants were asked to detect very faint signals—either dim visual stimuli or soft tones, and the participants did this in one of two conditions: either while forming a visual image before their "mind's eye" or while forming an auditory image before their "mind's ear." In this way, we have a 2 × 2 design: two types of signals to be detected, and two types of imagery.

Let's hypothesize that there's some overlap between imaging and perceiving—that is, there are mental processes that are involved in both activities. On this basis, we should expect interference if participants try to do both of these activities at once, on the idea that if these processes are occupied with imaging, then they're not available for perceiving, and vice versa. That interference is exactly what Segal and Fusella observed. They found that forming a visual image interferes with seeing and that forming an auditory image interferes with hearing (see **Figure 11.7**; also see Farah & Smith, 1983).

You'll notice in the figure that the effect here was relatively small and error rates were relatively low. These points remind us that images are not hallucinations, and people usually know their images *are* images. (For evidence, though, on how "hallucination-prone" individuals fare on tasks like this one, see Moseley, Smailes, Ellison, & Fernyhough, 2016.) Nonetheless, the pattern in these data is statistically reliable—confirming that there is interference, in line with the claims we're exploring.

Notice also that Segal and Fusella's participants were trying to visualize one thing while perceiving something entirely different. What happens if participants are contemplating a mental image *related to* the stimulus they're trying to perceive? Can visualizing a possible input "pave the way" for perception? Farah (1985) had participants visualize a form (either an *H* or a *T*). A moment later, either an *H* or a *T* was actually presented—but at a very low contrast, making the letter difficult to perceive. With this setup, perception was facilitated if participants had just been visualizing the target form, and the effect was quite specific: Visualizing an *H* made it easier to perceive an *H*; visualizing a *T* made it easier to perceive a *T*. This result provides further

---

FIGURE 11.7   CAN YOU VISUALIZE AND SEE AT THE SAME TIME?

	Percentage of Detections			Percentage of False Alarms	
	Visual signal	Auditory signal		Visual signal	Auditory signal
While visualizing	61%	67%	While visualizing	7.8%	3.7%
While maintaining an auditory image	63%	61%	While maintaining an auditory image	3.6%	6.7%
A			**B**		

(Panel A) Participants were less successful in detecting a weak visual signal if they were simultaneously maintaining a visual image than if they were maintaining an auditory image. (The effect is small but highly reliable.) The reverse is true with weak auditory signals: Participants were less successful in this detection if maintaining an auditory image than if visualizing. (Panel B) In addition, visual images often led to "false alarms" for participants trying to detect visual signals; auditory images led to false alarms for auditory signals.

(AFTER SEGAL & FUSELLA, 1970)

confirmation of the claim that visualizing and perceiving draw on similar mechanisms, so that one of these activities can prime the other. (Also see Heil, Rösler, & Hennighausen, 1993; McDermott & Roediger, 1994.)

More recent studies have explored another way in which imagery can prime perception. **Binocular rivalry** occurs when two different visual stimuli are presented, one to each eye—for example, green vertical stripes might be presented to your left eye and red horizontal stripes to your right eye. With this setup, your visual system is sometimes unable to combine the inputs, and you end up being aware of just one of the stimuli for a few moments, then aware of the other for a bit of time, then the first again. How this sequence plays out, though, can be shaped by visualization—and so, for example, if you visualize a specific pattern, the pattern is likely to dominate (to be perceived earlier and for more time) in a subsequent binocular-rivalry presentation. (See Pearson, 2014; Pearson, Clifford, & Tong, 2008; Pearson, Naselaris, Holmes, & Kosslyn, 2015; Pearson, Rademaker, & Tong, 2011. For yet another parallel between visualization and vision, see Laeng & Suluvedt, 2014.)

Visual Imagery and the Brain

The overlap between imaging and perceiving is also clear in biological evidence. As we discussed in Chapter 3, we know a great deal about the specific brain structures required for vision, and it turns out that many of the same structures are crucial for imagery. This can be documented in several ways, including procedures that rely on neuroimaging techniques (like PET or fMRI) that map moment-by-moment activity in the brain (see Figure 2.9 in Chapter 2). These techniques confirm that vision relies heavily on tissue located in the occipital cortex (and so these brain areas are highly activated whenever you're examining a visual stimulus). It turns out that activity levels are also high in these areas when participants are visualizing a stimulus before their "mind's eye" (Behrmann, 2000; Isha & Sagi, 1995; Kosslyn, 1994; Miyashita, 1995; Thompson & Kosslyn, 2000).

The biological parallels between imagery and perception can be documented even at a fine grain. Specifically, we know that different areas of the occipital cortex are involved in different aspects of visual perception—for example, Areas V1 and V2 in the cortex are involved in the earliest stages of visual perception, responding to specific low-level features of the input. It's striking, therefore, that the same brain areas are particularly active whenever participants are maintaining highly detailed images, and that the amount of brain tissue showing activation increases as participants imagine larger and larger objects (Behrmann, 2000; Kosslyn & Thompson, 2003; Pearson et al., 2015). In a similar way, certain areas in the brain are highly sensitive to motion in ordinary visual perception, and it turns out that the same brain areas are particularly activated when participants are asked to *imagine* movement patterns (Goebel, Khorram-Sefat, Muckli, Hacker, & Singer, 1998). Likewise, brain areas that are especially active during the perception of faces are also highly activated when people are imagining faces (O'Craven & Kanwisher, 2000; also see **Figure 11.8**).

TEST YOURSELF

5. What's the evidence that visual imagery relies on some of the same mental processes as actual vision?

FIGURE 11.8 IMAGERY FOR FACES AND PLACES IN THE BRAIN

The successive brain pictures in each row show different "slices" through the brain, moving from the front to the back. To analyze the data, researchers initially compared brain activity in two conditions: when participants were viewing *faces* and when they were viewing *places* (scenes). Next, the researchers compared brain activity in two more conditions: when the participants were *visualizing* faces or places. The row marked A shows brain sites that were more activated when participants were viewing *faces* than *places*; not surprisingly, activity levels are high in the fusiform face area (FFA). The row marked B shows brain sites that were more activated when participants were *visualizing faces* than when they were visualizing places. The key here is that rows A and B look rather similar: The pattern of brain activation is roughly the same in the perception and imagery conditions. The bottom two rows show the brain sites that were more activated when participants were viewing (row C) or visualizing (row D) *places*, with considerable activity in the parahippocampal place area (PPA). Again, the activity pattern is quite similar for the perception and imagery conditions.

In fact, these various parallels have led researchers to develop techniques for "decoding" patterns of brain activation in people who are holding visual images (e.g., Albers, Kok, Toni, Dijkerman, & de Lange, 2013; Kay, Naselaris, Prenger, & Gallant, 2008; Pearson, 2014; Schlegel et al., 2013; Thirion et al., 2006). This idea sounds like a science-fiction account of mind reading, but it's entirely real. Research participants are first shown various pictures, so that the researchers can document the pattern of brain activity associated with viewing each picture. The participants are then asked to create and maintain a visual image while the investigators record brain activity. The activity (an fMRI pattern) is then subjected to mathematical analysis, allowing computers to compare the activation patterns while *visualizing* with the activation patterns while *seeing*. With impressive accuracy, the comparison allows the researchers to figure out just what the participant was imagining at that moment—in essence, using brain data to read the participant's thoughts.

Visual Imagery and Brain Disruption

Further evidence comes from *transcranial magnetic stimulation* (TMS), a technique we first described in Chapter 2. TMS creates a series of strong magnetic pulses at a specific location on the scalp; this causes a (temporary!) disruption in the brain region directly below this scalp area (Helmuth, 2001). In this way, it's possible to disrupt Area V1 in an otherwise normal brain. (Area V1, recall, is the brain area where axons from the visual system first reach the occipital cortex; see Chapter 2.) Not surprisingly, using TMS in this way causes problems in vision, but it also causes parallel problems in visual imagery, providing a powerful argument that Area V1 is important both for the processing of visual information and for the creation of visual images (Kosslyn et al., 1999).

Still more evidence comes from studies of brain damage, and here, too, we find parallels between visual perception and visual imagery. For example, in some patients brain damage has disrupted the ability to perceive color; in most cases, these patients also lose the ability to imagine scenes in color. Likewise, patients who, because of brain damage, have lost the ability to perceive fine detail seem also to lose the ability to visualize fine detail; and so on. (See Farah, Soso, & Dasheiff, 1992; Kosslyn, 1994; however, we'll add some complications to this point later in the chapter.)

Brain damage also causes parallels in how people *pay attention* to visual inputs and to visual images. In one case, a patient had suffered a stroke and, as a result, had developed the "neglect syndrome" we described in Chapter 5. If this patient was shown a picture, he seemed to see only the right side of it; if asked to read a word, he read only the right half. The same pattern was evident in the patient's imagery. In one test, he was urged to visualize a familiar plaza in his city and to list the buildings "in view" in the image. If the patient imagined himself standing at the northern edge of the plaza, he listed all the buildings on the plaza's western side (i.e., on his right), but none on the eastern. If the patient imagined himself standing on the southern edge of the plaza, he listed all the sights on the plaza's eastern side, but none on the western. In both cases, he neglected half of the imaged scene, just as he did with perceived scenes (Bisiach & Luzzatti, 1978; Bisiach, Luzzatti, & Perani, 1979).

Spatial Images and Visual Images

We are building an impressive case for a close relationship between imagery and perception. Indeed, the evidence so far implies that we can truly speak of imagery as being *visual* imagery, drawing on the same mechanisms and

NEGLECT SYNDROME IN VISUAL IMAGERY

Because of brain damage, a patient had developed the pattern (first discussed in Chapter 2) of unilateral neglect—so he paid attention only to the right half of the visual world. He showed the same pattern in his visual images. When asked to imagine himself standing at the southern edge of the Piazza del Duomo and to describe all he could "see" in his image, he only listed buildings on the piazza's eastern side. When he imagined himself standing at the northern edge of the piazza, he only listed buildings on the western side. In both cases, he neglected the left half of the (visualized) piazza.

having many of the same traits as actual vision. Other results, however, add some complications.

Early in the chapter, we discussed dreams in people who have been blind since birth, and more broadly, many studies have examined imagery in the blind. These procedures need to be adapted in important ways—so that, for example, the stimuli to be imaged are initially presented as sculptures to be explored with the hands, rather than as pictures to be examined visually. Once this is done, however, experiments parallel to those we've described can be carried out with the blind—procedures examining how the blind scan across an image, for example, or how they imagine a form in rotation. What are the results? In tests involving mental scanning, blind individuals produce response times proportional to the "distance" traveled in the image—exactly the result we've already seen with sighted people. In tests requiring mental rotation, response times with blind research participants are proportional to the amount of "rotation" needed, just as with participants who have normal vision. In fact, in procedure after procedure, people blind since birth produce results just like those from people who can see. The blind, in other words, seem to have normal imagery. (For a sampling of the data, see Carpenter & Eisenberg, 1978; Giudice, Betty, & Loomis, 2011;

Kerr, 1983; Marmor & Zabeck, 1976; also see Jonides, Kahn, & Rozin, 1975; Paivio & Okovita, 1971; Zimler & Keenan, 1983. For a broad overview of imagery in the blind—including discussion of the important ways in which visually impaired individuals differ from one another—see Heller & Gentaz, 2014.)

What's going on here? It seems unlikely that people blind since birth are using a sense of what things "look like" to perform these tasks. Presumably, therefore, they have some other way of thinking about spatial layout and spatial relations. This "spatial imagery" might be represented in the mind in terms of a series of imagined movements, so that it's body imagery or motion imagery rather than visual imagery. Alternatively, perhaps spatial imagery isn't tied to any sensory modality but is instead part of our broader cognition about spatial arrangements and layout.

One way or another, though, it looks like we need to distinguish between *visual* and *spatial* imagery. Blind individuals presumably use spatial imagery to carry out the tasks we've been discussing in this chapter; it seems plausible that sighted people can use either visual or spatial imagery to carry out these tasks. (For a related distinction among several types of imagery, see Kosslyn & Thompson, 1999, 2003. For other data emphasizing the importance of the visual/spatial distinction, see Hegarty, 2004; Hegarty & Stull, 2012; Klauer & Zhao, 2004; Liesefeld & Zimmer, 2013.)

This distinction between visual and spatial imagery is confirmed by neuroscience evidence. For example, fMRI data tell us that the brain areas activated for visual tasks are different from those activated for spatial tasks (Thompson, Slotnick, Burrage, & Kosslyn, 2009). Likewise, we've already noted the cases in which brain damage seems to produce similar patterns of disruption in seeing and imaging. For example, patients who (because of brain damage) have lost their color vision also seem to lose the ability to imagine scenes in color; patients who have lost their ability to perceive motion also lose the ability to imagine movement. However, there are exceptions to this pattern—that is, cases in which brain damage causes problems in imagery but not in perception, or vice versa. (See, e.g., Bartolomeo et al., 1998; Behrmann, 2000; Goldenberg, Müllbacher, & Nowak, 1995; Logie & Della Salla, 2005; Servos & Goodale, 1995.) What should we make of this uneven pattern—with brain damage sometimes causing similar problems in imagery and in perception, and sometimes not? The answer lies in the fact that *visual* imagery relies on brain areas also needed for vision, with the result that damage to these areas disrupts both imagery and vision. *Spatial* imagery, in contrast, relies on different brain areas, and so damage to visual areas won't interfere with this form of imagery, and damage to brain sites needed for this imagery won't interfere with vision (see **Figure 11.9**).

Likewise, consider patient L.H. He suffered brain damage in an automobile accident and, afterward, had enormous difficulty in tasks requiring judgments about visual appearance—for example, judgments about *color* (Farah, Hammond, Levine, & Calvanio, 1988). In contrast, L.H. performed well on tasks like image scanning or mental rotation. More generally, he showed little disruption on tasks requiring spatial manipulations or memory for spatial positions. To make sense of L.H.'s profile, therefore, it seems once

FIGURE 11.9 BRAIN AREAS CRUCIAL FOR VISUAL AND SPATIAL TASKS

In one condition of this study, participants had to visualize a particular target in a particular location. In the other condition, participants had to imagine a rotation of a target. The authors refer to these conditions as Spatial Location and Spatial Transformation, but the distinction at issue parallels the distinction made in the text between visual and spatial tasks. The two types of tasks clearly relied on distinct brain regions, providing further evidence that we must distinguish between visual and spatial imagery. The blue areas in the figure indicate brain regions associated with the more "visual" task; the yellow areas indicate brain regions associated with the more "spatial" task.

6. What do we learn from the fact that some forms of brain damage have *similar* effects on a person's ability to see and the person's ability to perform many imagery tasks?

7. What do we learn from the fact that some forms of brain damage have *different* effects on a person's ability to see and the person's ability to perform many imagery tasks?

again crucial to distinguish between visual tasks (for which he's impaired) and spatial ones (for which he's not) and, correspondingly, between visual imagery and spatial imagery.

Individual Differences in Imagery

Various lines of evidence, therefore, suggest there are at least two types of imagery—one visual and one spatial—and, presumably, most people have the capacity for both types: They can "visualize" and they can "spatialize." But this invites a new question: When do people use one type of imagery, and when do they use the other?

To some extent, the answer depends on the task. For example, to think about *colors*, you need to imagine exactly what something *looks like*; it won't be enough just to think about shapes or spatial positions. In this case, therefore, you'll need visual imagery, not spatial. Or, as a reverse case, think about tasks that require complex navigation—perhaps navigation through a building or across an entire city. For tasks like these, visualizing the relevant layout may be difficult and would include a lot of detail irrelevant to the navigation. In this setting, spatial imagery, not visual, may be a better option (compare Hegarty & Stull, 2012).

In other cases, either form of imagery will get the job done. For an image-scanning task, for example, you can think about what a speck would *look like* as it zooms across an imagined scene, or you can think about what it would *feel like* to move your finger across the scene. In these cases, the choice between visual and spatial imagery will depend on other factors, including your preferences and perhaps the exact instructions you receive.

The choice between these forms of imagery will also be influenced by each individual's ability levels. Some people may be poor visualizers but good "spatializers," and they would surely rely on spatial imagery, not visual, in most tasks. For other people, this pattern might be reversed.

With this context, think back to Galton's data, mentioned early in this chapter. If we take those data at face value, they imply that people differ markedly in their conscious experience of imaging. People with vivid imagery report that their images are truly picture-like: in color, quite detailed, and with the depicted objects viewed from a particular distance and a particular viewing angle. People without vivid imagery, in contrast, say none of these things. Their images, they report, are not at all picture-like, and it's meaningless to ask them whether an image is in color or in black and white; their image, they say, simply isn't the sort of thing that could be in color or in black and white. Likewise, it's meaningless to ask whether their image is viewed from a particular distance or angle; their image is abstract in a way that makes these points inapplicable. In no sense, then, do these "non-imagers" feel like they're "seeing" with the "mind's eye." From their perspective, these figures of speech are (at best) loosely metaphorical. This stands in clear contrast to the reports offered by vivid imagers; for them, mental seeing really does seem like actual seeing.

Roughly 10% of the population will, in this way, "declare themselves entirely deficient in the power of seeing mental pictures" (Galton, 1883, p. 110).

If you're someone who experiences vivid visual imagery, you may find it bizarre that other people never have this experience. After all, "mental pictures" are probably a prominent aspect of your mental life, and you use imagery even when there's no need. For example, when reading a novel, you may form mental pictures of what the characters look like—and when you see the movie based on the book, you may be annoyed because the performers don't look like they "should"!

What would it be like, though, to lack this capacity? Maybe we can gain some understanding by considering people blind from birth—people with no vision and no capacity for visualization. Specifically, you might explore a remarkable series of YouTube videos starring Tommy Edison. With wonderful humor and a fabulous openness, Edison answers questions he's received about what it's like to be blind.

Some of the questions people send to Edison seem odd: Do blind people turn on the lights when they're home alone? (No.) Can he tell when people are staring at him? (No.) Would it bother him if he had a houseguest who walked around naked? (No, although he thinks the idea is strange, and he hopes they don't sit on the furniture.)

In answering other questions, though, Edison makes it clear that he has little understanding of the visual world. For example, he doesn't understand what *color* is all about. When people describe color to him, they might tell him that both the sky and ice are blue, and that's a puzzle for him. "Same color means two completely different things? I don't get it."

Edison can, however, imagine things. In one video, he's asked to imagine a soda bottle. "I think about the shape of it. . . . I think about the plastic; I think about the cap; those things on the bottom so it doesn't fall down—the five things there. . . ." He then explains, "I couldn't imagine a bottle of soda on the table because I'd have to be touching it to know it was there. I see the shape through my hands." Describing another object, he says, "Of course, I imagine it, but I just don't do it the way you do. . . . To 'visualize' something for me is to remember what it feels like."

Tommy Edison also understands the larger-scale spatial world. He's worked as a radio disk jockey—and so he commuted to the station and moved around the studio. These achievements required an accurate grasp of where things were relative to each other and relative to him, and he plainly had that spatial understanding.

Edison's spatial sense is also evident in his ability to *draw*. He does find it odd to "put a three-dimensional thing onto a flat piece of paper." Even so, he can draw objects—for example, a car—combining what he's learned from multiple experiences, all knit together by an overall sense of the parts' positions relative to one another. It's interesting that his drawings also preserve a "vantage" point: He draws the cat with two legs, "because, from where I'm sitting, that's all I can see of the kitty."

People with rich visual imagery probably can't understand what Edison's internal experience is like. Nonetheless, his descriptions powerfully remind us of how much can be achieved without vision or visualizing, and therefore may help us understand what these capacities provide for us. Above all, Edison's candid reports give us a wonderful portrait of experiences and a mental life different from the ones most of us enjoy. Visit him on YouTube!

As William James (1890) put it, they "have no visual images at all worthy of the name" (p. 57). Note the dates here; we've known for more than a century that some people lack the capacity for visualization. Even so, this pattern was largely unknown to medical doctors and not discussed at all in the medical literature; as a result, the pattern was described in 2015 as newly "discovered" (e.g., Zimmer, 2015, 2010) and given a new name: aphantasia. (Despite the media reports, the scholars who actually suggested this term certainly knew the relevant history, including Galton's important contribution; Zeman, Dewar, & Della Salla, 2015, 2016.)

What should we make of this? Do members of our species really differ in whether or not they're capable of experiencing visual images? To explore this issue, a number of studies have compared "vivid imagers" and "non-imagers" on tasks that depend on mental imagery, with the obvious prediction that people with vivid imagery will do better in these tasks. The key, though, is that when people describe their images as "vivid," they seem to be reporting how much their image experience is *like seeing*—their self-report, in other words, provides an assessment of *visual* imagery. To document the benefits of this imagery, therefore, we need to focus on tasks that truly require visual imagery (i.e., tasks that cannot be performed perfectly well with *spatial* imagery).

Consider, for example, tasks that require people to make a judgment about what an imagined object would look like—for example, what its color would look like or whether a small gap in the object would be "visible" in the image. People with vivid imagery do perform better on these tasks—presumably, because their vivid images enable them to "see" exactly what the imagined objects look like. (See, e.g., Cui, Jeter, Yang, Montague, & Eagleman, 2006; Finke & Kosslyn, 1980; Keogh & Pearson, 2011; Kozhevnikov, Kosslyn, & Shephard, 2005; McKelvie, 1995; Pearson, Rademaker, & Tong, 2011. For more on procedures that assess "color imagery," see Wantz, Borst, Mast, & Lobmaier, 2015.)

Imagery differences from one person to the next are also reflected in patterns of brain activation. In one study, participants self-reported how vivid their imagery was, rating specific images on a scale that ranged from "perfectly clear and vivid as normal vision" (a score of 1) to "no image; you just know you are thinking of the object" (a score of 5). Then, while in an fMRI scanner, the participants were instructed to visualize a specific scene (e.g., someone climbing up stairs). The results, shown in **Figure 11.10**, indicate a clear relationship between self-reported vividness and degree of activation in the brain's visual cortex (Cui, Jeter, Yang, Montague, & Eagleman, 2007).

How Does Vivid Imagery Matter?

It appears, then, that people really do differ in the nature of their imagery experience, and the differences seem quite large. Most people report detailed, colorful visual images and claim that these images are a routine part of their inner experience. Other people (including the author of this book!) insist they have no visual images—for example, they can't close their eyes and call to mind a picture of their best friend's face; they seem unable to call up an image

FIGURE 11.10   BRAIN ACTIVATION REFLECTS IMAGERY VIVIDNESS

(Panel A) Participants began to visualize when they heard the "go" signal and stopped when they heard the "stop" signal. The fMRI signal being measured focused on early visual cortex (Brodmann's areas 17 and 18); the relevant brain areas are highlighted in Panel B. In Panel C, *low* scores of self-reported vividness indicate vivid imagery; a score of 5 indicates a self-report that the person was experiencing no visual image at all.

of scenes that they've seen countless times. As we mentioned before, for them, concepts like "mental pictures" or the "mind's eye" are strained metaphors.

How do these differences in experience influence people outside the laboratory, away from experimenters' tasks? What can people "with imagery" do that people "without imagery" cannot? These are issues in need of further research, but evidence so far suggests that vivid imagery may have a range of consequences. One study indicated a link between imagery prowess and career choice, with visual imagers being more likely to succeed in the arts, while people with spatial imagery are better suited to careers in science or engineering (Kozhevnikov et al., 2005). Another, somewhat playful, study collected imagery vividness reports from scientists who study visual imagery; the data suggest that scientists' intuitions and hypotheses about imagery are shaped by their own (vivid or nonvivid) subjective experience of imagery (Reisberg, Pearson, & Kosslyn, 2003).

Visual imagery also seems to play a role in autobiographical memory, with "non-imagers" being less likely to feel as if they can "relive" their memories (Greenberg & Knowlton, 2014; also see Butler, Rice, Wooldridge, & Rubin, 2016). Perhaps related, severe amnesia can result from damage to brain regions that are crucial for long-term *visual* memory (Rubin & Greenberg, 1998; Rubin & Umanath, 2015).

There may also be a linkage between vivid visual imagery and some aspects of mental illness (Pearson et al., 2015). For example, people diagnosed with phobias sometimes experience troubling images—such as vivid images of snakes for someone with *ophidiophobia* (fear of snakes), or images of spiders for someone with *arachnophobia* (fear of spiders). It seems plausible that future therapies will embrace these findings, seeking somehow to disrupt or defuse these troubling images.

Let's emphasize, though, that more research is needed to explore the consequences of vivid imagery—or to explore the consequences of being a non-imager. In the meantime, the available data do suggest that this aspect of someone's inner experience may have far-reaching effects.

Eidetic Imagery

If you're someone with vivid imagery, you may have been surprised to hear that other individuals lack this capacity. In fact, you may find it difficult to conceptualize what it would be like to have no visual images. But the differences among people are just as striking if we consider variation in the opposite direction: people who have "super-skills" in imagery.

There is a lot of folklore associated with the idea of "photographic memory," but this term needs to be defined carefully. Some people have fabulously detailed, wonderfully long-lasting memories, but without any "photographic" quality. These people use careful rehearsal, or complex, well-practiced mnemonics, to remember facts and faces—and so they can recall the value of pi to a hundred decimal places, or the names of a hundred people they've just met. These memories, however, aren't in any way "visual," and imagery isn't necessary for these memorization strategies.

Other people, in contrast, do seem to have exquisitely detailed imagery that can truly be described as "photographic." Researchers refer to this type of imagery as **eidetic imagery**, and people with this skill are called "eidetikers." This form of imagery is sometimes found in people who have been diagnosed as autistic: They can briefly glance at a complex scene and then draw incredibly detailed reproductions of the scene, as though they really had taken a "photograph" when first viewing it. But similar capacities can be documented with no link to autism. For example, in one early study Stromeyer (1982) described a woman who could recall poetry written in a language she didn't understand, even years after she'd seen the poem; she was also able to recall complicated random dot patterns after viewing them only briefly. Similarly, Haber (1969; also Haber & Haber, 1988) showed a picture like the one in **Figure 11.11** to a 10-year-old eidetiker for just 30 seconds. After the picture was taken away, the boy was unexpectedly asked detail questions: "How many stripes were there on the cat's back? How many leaves on the front flower?" The child was able to give completely accurate answers, as though his memory had perfectly preserved the picture's content.

We know relatively little about this form of imagery. We do know that the capacity is rare. We know that some people who claim to have this capacity do not: They often do have fabulous memories, but they rely on mnemonics,

TEST YOURSELF

8. What evidence confirms that people do actually differ in the vividness of their visual images?
9. What is eidetic imagery?

FIGURE 11.11   EIDETIC IMAGERY

Eidetic imagery is vastly more detailed than ordinary imagery. In one study (Haber, 1969), a 10-year-old was shown a picture like this one for 30 seconds. After the picture was taken away, the boy was unexpectedly asked detail questions: "How many stripes were there on the cat's back? How many leaves on the front flower?" The child was able to give completely accurate answers, as though his memory had perfectly preserved the picture's content.

not on some special form of imagery. But beyond these obvious points, this remains a truly intriguing phenomenon in need of further research.

Images Are Not Pictures

Let's return to more "normal" (at least, more ordinary) forms of imagery. At many points in this chapter, we've referred to mental images (especially *visual* images) as "mental pictures," and that terminology does seem appropriate in many ways: Visual images do depict a scene in a way that seems quite pictorial. In other regards, though, this comparison may be misleading.

We've already mentioned that mental images can represent three-dimensional figures, and so they may be more like mental sculptures than

FIGURE 11.12   THE NECKER CUBE AND THE DUCK/RABBIT

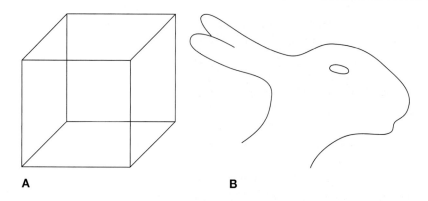

A   B

(Panel A) The cube can be perceived as if viewed from above or below. The drawing, in other words, is neutral with regard to interpretation. However, your *perception* of the drawing isn't neutral, and so you perceive the cube as having one interpretation or the other. (Panel B) This figure can be perceived either as a duck looking left or a rabbit looking right. The picture itself is ambiguous, specifying neither duck nor rabbit. When people view the picture, they can easily find both interpretations. When people view a mental image of this figure, however, the form seems to lose its ambiguity.

mental pictures. We've also distinguished visual images and spatial images, and we've seen that *some* images are like pictures to be explored with the mind's eye, and other images are not. But on top of these points, there's a further complication. To introduce this issue, let's review some points we raised in Chapter 3 and, with that, an example we met there. **Figure 11.12A** shows the figure known as the Necker cube (see also Figure 3.11). The drawing of this cube—the stimulus itself—is ambiguous: It can be understood as a depiction of a cube viewed from above or as a depiction of a cube viewed from below. The picture itself, in other words, doesn't specify which of these two cubes it shows, and so the picture is neutral with regard to interpretation— and fully compatible with either interpretation.

Unlike the picture, though, your *perception* of the cube is not neutral, is not indeterminate with regard to depth. Instead, at any moment in time you perceive the cube as having one arrangement in depth or another. Your perception, in other words, "goes beyond the information given" by specifying a configuration in depth, a specification that in this case supplements an ambiguous drawing in order to create an unambiguous perception.

As we discussed in Chapter 3, the configuration in depth is just one of the ways that perception goes beyond the information given in a stimulus. Your perception of a stimulus also specifies a figure/ground organization, the form's orientation (e.g., identifying the form's "top"), and so on. These specifications serve to organize the form and have a powerful impact on its subjective appearance—and with that, what the form is seen to resemble and what the form will evoke in memory.

The point, then, is that your **percepts** (i.e., your mental representations of the stimuli you're perceiving) are in some ways similar to pictures, but in other ways different. Like pictures, percepts are *depictions*, representing key aspects of the three-dimensional layout of the world. Percepts, in other words, are not descriptions of a stimulus; instead, percepts (just like pictures) show directly what a stimulus looks like. At the same time, percepts are in some ways different from pictures: They are *organized* depictions and therefore unambiguous in a way that pictures are not.

What about visual images? Are they like pictures—neutral with regard to organization and open to different interpretations? Or are they organized in the way percepts seem to be, and so, in a sense, already interpreted? One line of evidence comes from studies of ambiguous figures. Participants were first shown a series of practice stimuli to make sure that they understood what it meant to reinterpret an ambiguous figure (Chambers & Reisberg, 1985). They were then shown a drawing of one more ambiguous figure—the duck/rabbit, shown in **Figure 11.12B**. Then, after this figure had been removed from view, they were instructed to form a mental image of it and asked if they could reinterpret this image, just as they had reinterpreted the practice figures.

Across several experiments, not one of the participants succeeded in reinterpreting his or her images: They reliably failed to find the duck in a "rabbit image" or the rabbit in a "duck image." Is it possible that they didn't understand their task or didn't remember the figure? To rule out these possibilities, participants were given a blank piece of paper immediately after their failure at reinterpreting their image and were asked to draw the figure based on their image. Now, looking at their own drawings, all the participants were able to reinterpret the configuration in the appropriate way. In other words, we have 100% failure in reinterpreting these forms with images and 100% success a moment later with drawings.

Apparently, therefore, what participants "see" in their image (even if it's a *visual* image, not a spatial one) isn't a "picture"—neutral with regard to interpretation and open to new interpretations. Instead, images are inherently organized, just as percepts are. As such, images are entirely unambiguous and strongly resistant to reinterpretation. (For more on these issues, see Peterson, Kihlstrom, Rose, & Glisky, 1992; Thompson, Kosslyn, Hoffman, & Kooij, 2008. For a discussion on how image-based discovery is used in a real-world setting, see Verstijnen, Hennessey, van Leeuwen, Hamel, & Goldschmidt, 1998; Verstijnen, van Leeuwen, Goldschmidt, Hamel, & Hennessey, 1998.)

Images and Pictures: An Interim Summary

Images, both visual and spatial, provide a distinctive way of representing the world—and so *visualizing* a robot, for example, is quite different from thinking about the word "robot" or merely contemplating the idea "robot." As one key difference, images are, without question, like pictures in the fact that

"THE MIND'S EYE"

Hamlet: My father—methinks I see my father—
Horatio: Where, my lord?
Hamlet: In my mind's eye, Horatio.
(*Hamlet,* act 1, scene 2)
William Shakespeare is credited with popularizing the phrase "the mind's eye."

CHANGING A FRAME OF REFERENCE

In many professions—architecture, for example—designers visualize the early stages of their ideas with no need to sketch the designs on paper. Research suggests, though, that there may be limits on this image-based process and that some discoveries are much more likely if the designers put their ideas down on paper and then inspect the drawings. This is because the drawing, on its own, has no interpretive "reference frame," making it much easier for the designer to impose a new reference frame.

images show exactly what a form looks like. Visualizing a robot, therefore, will highlight the robot's appearance in your thoughts and make it much more likely that you'll be reminded of other forms having a similar appearance. Thinking about the robot without an image might not highlight appearance and so will probably call different ideas to mind.

Creating an image will also make some attributes of a form more prominent and others less so (e.g., the cat's head rather than its whiskers). This, too, can influence what further ideas the image calls to mind—and so, again, putting your thoughts into imagery can literally shape the flow and sequence of your ideas.

At the same time, we've highlighted ways in which images are *not* picture-like. Images, it seems, are inherently organized in a way that pictures are not, and this organization can influence the sequence of your thoughts—with your understanding of the image (e.g., where its "top" and "front" are; its figure/ground organization) guiding which discoveries will, and which will not, easily flow from the image.

Where does all this leave us? Images have a great deal in common with pictures, but they are also different from pictures. As a result, the common phrase "mental pictures" is misleading, and it would be more accurate to say that mental images are picture-like. We also need to keep track of the contrast between visual images and spatial images. As we have seen, this contrast shows up in many aspects of the data, and it must be part of our theorizing if we're going to explain what imagery is, how it is supported by the brain, and how it functions in shaping our thoughts.

TEST YOURSELF

10. Images are certainly picture-*like*, but what evidence points to a distinction between mental images and actual out-in-the-world pictures?

Long-Term Visual Memory

So far, our discussion has focused on "active" images—images that you're currently contemplating, images presumably held in working memory. What about visual information in long-term memory? For example, if you wish to form an image of an elephant, you need to draw on your knowledge of what an elephant looks like in order to create the active image. What is this knowledge, and how is it represented in long-term storage? Likewise, if you recognize a picture as familiar, this is probably because you've detected a "match" between it and some memory of an earlier-viewed picture. What is the nature of this memory?

Image Information in Long-Term Memory

In earlier chapters, we suggested that your various concepts—for example, your concept of "president" or "animal" or "Trafalgar Square"—are represented by some number of nodes in long-term memory. Perhaps we can adapt this proposal to account for long-term storage of visual information.

One possibility is that nodes in long-term memory represent entire, relatively complete pictures. In other words, to form a mental image of, say, an elephant, you would activate the ELEPHANT PICTURE nodes; to scrutinize an image of your father's face, you would activate the FATHER'S FACE nodes; and so on. However, evidence speaks against this idea (e.g., Kosslyn, 1980, 1983). Instead, images seem to be stored in memory in a piece-by-piece fashion. To form an image, therefore, you first have to activate the nodes specifying the "image frame," which depicts the form's global shape. Then, elaborations can be added to this frame, if you wish, to create a full and detailed image.

In support of this claim, images containing *more parts* take longer to create, just as we would expect if images are formed on a piece-by-piece basis (see **Figure 11.13**). In addition, images containing *more detail* take longer to create, in accord with this hypothesis. We also know that imagers have some degree of control over how complete and detailed their images will

FIGURE 11.13   COLUMNS OR ROWS?

This picture shows "three rows of dots." It also shows "four columns of dots." There is, in other words, no difference between a picture of rows of dots and a picture of columns of dots. There *is* a difference, however, between a mental image of "three rows of dots" and a mental image of "four columns of dots." The latter image takes longer to generate and is more difficult to maintain, presumably because it contains a larger number of units—four columns, rather than three rows.

be, so that (depending on the task, the imagers' preferences, etc.) images can be quite sketchy or quite elaborate (Reisberg, 1996). This variation is easily explained if imagers first create an image frame and only then add as much detail as they want. (For discussion of the neural basis for this frame-then-details sequence, see Pearson et al., 2015.)

We still need to ask, though, how the imager knows *how to* construct an image—what its form should be and what it should include. The relevant information is apparently drawn from **image files** in long-term memory, and one proposal is that these files contain something like a set of instructions, or a "recipe," for creating an image. By analogy, someone could instruct you in how to create a picture by uttering the appropriate sentences: "In the top left, place a circle. Underneath it, draw a line, angling down. . . ." Instructions like these would enable you to create a picture, but notice that there's nothing pictorial about the instructions themselves; they're sentences, not pictures. In the same way, the instructions within an image file allow you to create a representation that, as we've repeatedly seen, is picture-like in important ways. In long-term memory, however, this information may not be at all picture-like.

Verbal Coding of Visual Materials

The proposal before us, therefore, is that visual information is represented in long-term memory in a way that isn't itself "visual." Instead, visual information may be represented in long-term memory via propositions that provide a "recipe" to be used, when needed, for creating an image.

In some cases, though, visual information is represented in long-term storage in an even simpler format: a verbal label. This point is relevant to issues we met in Chapter 10, concerning the interplay between language and thought. Specifically, evidence tells us that individuals with large color vocabularies have better color memories, probably because they're remembering the verbal label for the color rather than the color itself, and it's easier to remember a word than it is to recall a tint.

A related point was made in a classic study by Carmichael, Hogan, and Walters (1932). Their research participants were shown pictures like those in the center column of **Figure 11.14**. Half of the participants were shown the top form and told, "This is a picture of eyeglasses." The other half were told, "This is a picture of a barbell." Later, the participants were asked to reproduce these pictures as carefully as they could, and those who had understood the picture as eyeglasses produced drawings that resembled eyeglasses; those who understood the picture as weights distorted their drawings appropriately. This is, again, what one would expect if the participants had memorized the description rather than the picture itself and were re-creating the picture on the basis of this description. (For a related finding, showing that how we perceive and remember *faces* is biased by verbal labels, see Eberhardt, Dasgupta, & Banaszynski, 2003.)

FIGURE 11.14 THE INFLUENCE OF VERBAL LABELS ON VISUAL MEMORY

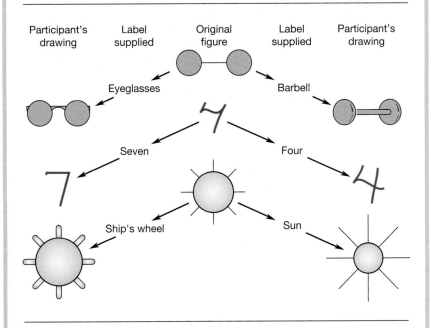

Participants were shown the figures in the middle column. If the top figure was presented with the label "eyeglasses," participants were later likely to reproduce the figure as shown on the left. If the figure was presented with the label "barbell," they were likely to reproduce it as shown on the right. (And so on for the other figures.) One interpretation of these data is that participants were remembering the verbal label and not the drawing itself.

(AFTER CARMICHAEL, HOGAN, & WALTERS, 1932)

A similar message emerges from tasks that require participants to reason about spatial position. In one study, participants were asked: "Which is farther north: Seattle or Montreal? Which is farther west: Reno, Nevada; or San Diego, California?" Many participants responded that Montreal is farther north and that San Diego is farther west, but both responses are wrong. Montreal, for example, is at roughly the same latitude as Portland, Oregon, a city almost 200 miles south of Seattle (Stevens & Coupe, 1978).

These errors arise because participants seem to be reasoning this way: "Montreal is in Canada; Seattle is in the United States. Canada is north of the United States. Therefore, Montreal must be farther north than Seattle." This kind of reasoning makes sense, since it will often bring you to the correct answer. (That's because most parts of Canada are indeed farther north

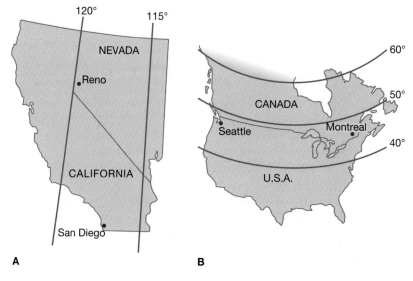

A   B

CONCEPTUAL MENTAL MAPS

Research participants tend to judge San Diego to be west of Reno and Montreal to be north of Seattle. But these judgments are wrong. (Panel A) A map of California and Nevada with lines of longitude shows that in fact San Diego is east of Reno. (Panel B) A map of the United States and southern Canada with lines of latitude shows that Seattle is slightly north of Montreal.

than most parts of the United States.) Even so, this reasoning will sometimes lead to error, and it does so in this case. (The logic is the same for the Reno/San Diego question.)

Of course, what is of interest here isn't the participants' knowledge about the longitude and latitude of these particular cities. What's important is that the sort of reasoning revealed in these studies hinges on propositional knowledge, not on any sort of mental images or maps. Apparently, at least some of our spatial knowledge relies on a symbolic/propositional code. (For more on reasoning about geography, see Friedman & Brown, 2000a, 2000b.)

Imagery Helps Memory

No matter how images are stored in long-term memory, however, it's clear that they influence memory in important ways and that, in general, imagery improves memory. For example, materials that evoke imagery are considerably easier to remember than materials that don't evoke imagery. This can be demonstrated in many ways, but the original demonstration involved a two-step procedure. First, participants were presented with a list of nouns and asked to rate each noun, on a scale from 1 to 7, for how readily it evoked an image (Paivio, 1969; Paivio, Yuille, & Madigan, 1968). Examples of words receiving high ratings were "church," with an average rating of 6.63, and "elephant," rated at 6.83. Words receiving lower ratings included "context" (2.13) and "virtue" (3.33).

As a second step, the researchers asked whether these imagery ratings, generated by one group of participants, could be used to predict memory performance with a new group of participants. The new participants were asked to memorize lists of words, and the data reliably indicated that these participants learned high-imagery words more readily than low-imagery words (Paivio, 1969; Paivio, Smythe, & Yuille, 1968).

As a related point, it's clear that memory can be enormously aided by the use of imagery mnemonics. In one study, some participants were asked to learn pairs of words by rehearsing each pair silently. Other participants were instructed to make up a sentence for each pair of words, linking the words in some sensible way. Still other participants were told to form a mental image for each pair of words, with the image combining the words in some interaction. The results showed poorest recall performance by the rehearsal group and intermediate performance by the group that generated the sentences. Both of these groups, though, did much worse than the imagery group (Bower & Winzenz, 1970; for further discussion of mnemonic techniques, see Chapter 6).

In order to be helpful, though, imagery mnemonics need to do more than depict the objects side by side. These mnemonics are helpful only if they show the objects to be remembered *interacting* in some way. (For the classic demonstration of this point, see Wollen, Weber, & Lowry, 1972.) This isn't surprising: As we saw in Chapter 6, memory is improved in general if you can find ways to organize the material; interacting images provide one way of achieving this organization.

Imagery can also help you memorize materials that aren't in any strict sense "visual"—including materials concerned with issues of *timing* and *sequence*. Let's say that you want to learn several facts about Marta, with some of the facts concerned with Marta's past and some with her future. Perhaps you want to remember that a week ago Marta was in a great mood, that two months ago she bought a new car, and that next month she'll be flying to London. To learn these various facts, you might imagine them arranged in a line—with past events off to the left and future events, in proper sequence, arrayed to the right.

Do people use this strategy? One study examined patients with neglect syndrome. As we mentioned in Chapter 5, these patients attend only to the right side of space and consistently overlook stimuli on their left. We then saw in this chapter (p. 426) that these patients show a corresponding pattern in their *imagery*, consistently overlooking objects that might be depicted on the left in an image. How will all of this matter if these patients are using the mnemonic strategy just described? If they're imagining events on a line, they'll probably overlook events on the left—that is, past events. And that's the pattern of the results: Patients with left spatial neglect have a harder time remembering *past* facts about Marta (in the example we sketched) and an easier time remembering future facts. As the study's authors put it, these patients seem to neglect the "left side" of time—just as we would expect if they're using the strategy we've outlined (Saj, Fuhrman, Vuilleumier, & Boroditsky, 2014).

Dual Coding

There's no question, then, that imagery improves memory. But what's the mechanism behind this effect? The answer has two parts. First, we've just suggested that imagery provides a way of organizing materials, and of course organization helps memory. But, second, imageable materials, such as high-imagery words, will probably be doubly represented in memory: The word itself will be remembered, and so will the corresponding picture. This pattern is referred to as **dual coding**, and it has a significant advantage: When the time comes to retrieve these memories, either record—the verbal or the image—will provide the information you seek. This gives you a double chance of locating the information you need, thereby easing the process of memory search.

Of course, framing things in this way builds on the idea that you have (at least) two types of information in long-term storage: memories that represent the content of symbolic (and perhaps verbal) materials, and memories that represent imagery-based materials. Paivio (1971), the source of the dual-coding proposal, argued that these two types of memory differ from each other in important ways—including the information that they contain and the ways they're accessed. Access to symbolic memories, he suggested, is easiest if the cue provided is a word, as in: "Do you know the word 'squirrel'?" Access to an image-based memory, in contrast, is easiest if one begins with a picture: "Do you recognize this pictured creature?"

Memory for Pictures

Paivio (1971) also proposed that there are two separate memory systems: one containing the symbolic memories, the other containing images. Many psychologists, however, are skeptical about this claim, arguing instead that there's just one long-term memory, holding both types of information (and perhaps other types as well). Within this single memory, each type of content does have its own traits, its own pattern of functioning. But even with these differences, the two types of information are contained in a unified memory—much as a single library building, with one indexing system and one set of rules, can hold both books and photographs, sound recordings as well as videos.

On this basis, we would expect the two types of memory to have many traits in common, thanks to the fact that both reside within a single memory system. This expectation turns out to be correct, and so many of the claims we made in Chapters 6, 7, and 8 apply with equal force to visual memories and verbal memories. Recall of both memory types, for example, is dependent on memory connections; priming effects can be observed with both types of memory; encoding specificity is observed in both domains; and so on.

Likewise, visual memory (like memory in general) is heavily influenced by schema-based, generic knowledge—knowledge about how events unfold in general. Chapter 8 described how these knowledge effects influence memory for sentences and stories, but similar effects can be demonstrated with pictures. In an early study, Friedman (1979) showed participants pictures of scenes such as a typical kitchen or a typical barnyard. The pictures also contained some unexpected objects—the kitchen picture, for example, included some items rarely found in a kitchen, such as a fireplace. Participants later took a recognition test in which they had to discriminate between pictures they'd actually seen and altered versions of these pictures in which something had been changed.

Participants' memories were plainly influenced by their broader knowledge of what "should be" included in these scenes. Thus, in some of the test pictures, one of the ordinary, expected objects in the scene had been changed—for example, participants might be shown a kitchen picture in which a different kind of stove appeared in place of the original stove, or one in which a radio replaced the toaster on the counter. Participants rarely noticed these changes and tended (incorrectly) to respond that this new picture was "old"—that is, had been seen before. This outcome is sensible on schema grounds: Both the original and the altered pictures were fully consistent with the kitchen schema, so both would be compatible with a schema-based memory.

However, participants almost always noticed changes to the unexpected objects in the scene. If the originally viewed kitchen had a fireplace and the test picture did not, participants consistently detected this alteration. Again, this outcome is predictable on schema grounds: The fireplace didn't fit with the kitchen schema and so was likely to be noted in memory. In fact, Friedman recorded participants' eye movements during the original presentations of the pictures. Her data showed that participants tended to look twice as long at the unexpected objects as they did at the expected ones; clearly, these objects did catch the participants' attention. (For more on schema guidance of eye movements, see Henderson & Hollingworth, 2003; Vo & Henderson, 2009.)

A different line of evidence also shows schema effects in picture memory. Recall our claim that in understanding a story, people place the story within a schematic frame. As we saw in Chapter 8, this can often lead to intrusion errors, as people import their own expectations and understanding into the story and, therefore, end up remembering the story as including more than it actually did.

A similar pattern can be demonstrated with picture memory, in a phenomenon known as **boundary extension**. (See Intraub & Bodamer, 1993; Intraub & Dickinson, 2008; Intraub, Gottesman, & Bills, 1998; Intraub, Hoffman, Wetherhold, & Stoehs, 2006. Also see Hale, Brown, & McDunn, 2016; McDunn, Siddiqui, & Brown, 2014.) That is, people remember a picture as including more than it actually did, in effect extending the

FIGURE 11.15
BOUNDARY EXTENSION
IN PICTURE MEMORY

Participants were initially shown the photograph at the top of this picture. The two panels below show the scene as drawn from memory by two different participants. They clearly recalled the scene as a wide-angle shot, revealing more of the background than the photograph actually did.

(AFTER INTRAUB & RICHARDSON, 1989)

boundaries of the remembered depiction. In one of the early demonstrations of this pattern, participants were shown the top panel in **Figure 11.15**, and then were later asked to sketch what they had seen (Intraub & Richardson, 1989). Two of the participants' drawings are shown at the bottom of Figure 11.15, and the boundary extension is clear: Participants remember the scene as less of a close-up view than it actually was, and they correspondingly remember the scene as containing more of the backdrop than it did. This effect is observed whether participants initially see a few pictures or many, whether they are tested immediately or after a delay, and even when they are explicitly warned about boundary extension and urged to avoid this effect.

Intraub has argued that this boundary extension arises from the way in which people perceive these pictures in the first place. People understand a picture, she claims, by means of a perceptual schema. This schema places the picture in a larger context, informing the perceiver about the real-world scene only partially revealed by the picture. Intraub suggests that this leads people to a series of expectations about what they might see if they could somehow look beyond the picture's edges, and these expectations become part of the experience of viewing the picture. It's then the *experience* that is remembered—and so your memory includes both the picture itself and also your understanding of what you'd see if you explored further, leading to the boundary extension that reliably emerges in the data.

It seems, therefore, that picture memory generally follows the same rules, and is influenced by the same factors, as memory for verbal materials. Schema effects can be found in both domains. Similarly, participants show primacy and recency effects when they learn a series of pictures (Tabachnick & Brotsky, 1976), just as they do when they learn a series of words (Chapter 6). Spread of activation can be demonstrated with nonverbal materials (Kroll & Potter, 1984), just as it can be with verbal materials (Chapter 9). In short, there's considerable commonality between picture memory and memory of other sorts, confirming our suggestion of a single memory system—a system that holds diverse contents but with a uniform set of operating principles.

The Diversity of Knowledge

When you're thinking about an image—that is, holding the image in working memory—there's no question that you're considering a distinctive form of mental representation. Images in working memory contain different information than other representations do; they make different information prominent; they require a set of operations (like scanning, or rotation, or zooming) that are irrelevant to other sorts of memory contents. Therefore, our theorizing about active images has to be different from our theorizing about other forms of representation.

The situation changes, however, when we turn to long-term memory and consider your long-term retention for what a circus clown looks like or your recollection of what an earlier-viewed picture contained. The *content* of these memories is different from, say, your memory for stories. But even so, the image-based memories seem to be stored in the same memory system as every other memory—and so they're influenced by exactly the same principles. In support of this claim, we can find many commonalities in the ways people remember diverse types of knowledge. We've mentioned some of these commonalities already, but let's add that memory for faces benefits from rehearsal (Sporer, 1988), just as memory for stories does. Memory for a series of tastes shows a primacy and recency effect, just like memory for words (Daniel & Katz, 2017). Similarly, a separation between *familiarity* and *source memory* (see Chapter 7) can be demonstrated for remembered music or remembered faces (Brigham & Cairns, 1988; Brown, Deffenbacher, & Sturgill, 1977), just as it can be for remembered words. And so on.

It appears, therefore, that there may just be one long-term memory, with a set of rules consistently applicable to all its diverse contents. However, we should attach a caution to this claim. In this chapter, we've focused on visual memories, and one might ask whether similar conclusions would emerge with other categories of knowledge. For example, do memories for smells benefit from rehearsal, show schema effects, and the like? Do memories for emotions or for pain benefit from deep processing? Do they show the effects we called (in Chapter 7) "implicit memory" effects? Relatively little research speaks to these issues.

On this basis, the claims about the singularity of long-term memory should remain tentative, and that is one of the reasons that throughout this chapter our agenda has been both substantive and methodological. We've

TEST YOURSELF

11. What evidence suggests that visual information is often stored in long-term memory via a representation that's not really "visual"?
12. What's the evidence that imagery can help you to memorize?

surveyed what is known about visual imagery and visual memory, but we've also tried to illustrate the questions that you might ask and the methods that you might use in exploring other types of knowledge—asking whether the content is distinctive in working memory and what evidence we'd need in order to propose a separate system within long-term memory. We've seen how things stand on these issues with regard to visual materials. However, the field awaits additional data before these issues can be resolved for other modalities.

using imagery

As we've discussed in the chapter, visual imagery can serve as a powerful aid to memory, so visualization is often helpful when you're trying to learn new materials. In other words, it's often useful to form "mental pictures" of the materials you're studying.

You should, however, be careful about how and when you rely on visualization. On the positive side, mental images certainly represent what something looks like, so imagery mnemonics can help a lot if you want to remember appearances—how a visualized scene looked and what it included. Images are also an excellent way of representing how things are *arranged*—both spatially and (as we discussed in the chapter) temporally. So images can help you to remember this information as well.

But there's also a downside. Let's say that you hope to remember the term "Korsakoff's syndrome" (a form of amnesia discussed in Chapter 7). You therefore form a mental picture of someone standing on a racecourse and coughing. Later, when trying to recall the term, you call this mental picture to mind, and after examining the picture (with your "mind's eye") you confidently announce, "I remember—the term is Race-cough syndrome" (or "Track-sick syndrome" or some such). These responses are consistent with the picture, but they're wrong—a point that reminds us that pictures (mental or otherwise) are often not specific enough to provide the information you need.

Likewise, in forming a mnemonic picture, you'll probably focus on what the to-be-remembered items look like, and this may distract you from thinking about what these items mean. Imagine that you want to remember that a hypothesis was offered by the important psychologist Henry Roediger. To remember this name, you might playfully convert it to "rod-digger" and form a mental picture of someone digging in the earth with a fishing rod. This will help you remember the name, but it will promote no insights into what Roediger's hypothesis was, or how it relates to other aspects of his theorizing, or to other things you know. Images, in other words, are excellent for remembering some things, but often what you need (or want) to remember goes beyond this.

These points aren't meant to warn you against using image-based mnemonics. In fact, let's again emphasize how effective these mnemonics are. However, it's important to understand why they work, because with that knowledge you can avoid using these mnemonics in circumstances in which they might not serve you well.

In the same way, imagery can be a powerful aid to problem solving and can sometimes be more helpful than an actual, out-in-the-world drawing. Images can, for example, represent movement and 3-D in ways that a drawing cannot. Mental images can also be more easily adjusted than a drawing (e.g., if you want to alter the size or position of one of the image's elements).

Sometimes, though, images are less helpful than a drawing. If the scene you're contemplating is complex, it may be difficult to maintain all of its elements in a mental image, so in this case a drawing would be better. In addition, the chapter argues that mental images are understood within a certain framework—one that indicates the imager's understanding of the image's figure/ground organization and its orientation in space. This framework helps the imager interpret the depicted form but can also limit what the imager will discover from a given mental picture. (This is, for example, why imagers routinely fail to find a "duck" in a "rabbit image" and vice versa, as described in the chapter.)

However, people can often escape these limits by drawing a picture based on their own mental image. The picture depicts the same form as the image; but because the picture isn't linked to a particular reference frame, it will often support new discoveries that the original image wouldn't. We can demonstrate this in the laboratory (e.g., in people discovering the duck in their own drawing of the duck/rabbit form, even though they couldn't make this discovery from their image). We can also demonstrate this in real-world settings (e.g., in architects who can't reconceptualize a building plan by scrutinizing their mental image of the plan, but who then make striking new discoveries once they draw out the plan on paper).

Overall, then, we can again see the benefits of understanding the limits of your own strategies. Once you understand those limits, you can find ways to make full use of these strategies to improve your problem-solving skills, your memory, and your comprehension of new materials—but without falling into traps created by the strategies' limits.

For more on this topic . . .

Rubin, D. C. (1997). *Memory in oral traditions: The cognitive psychology of epic, ballads, and counting-out rhymes.* New York, NY: Oxford University Press.

Thomas, A. K., & Loftus, E. F. (2002). Creating bizarre false memories through imagination. *Memory & Cognition, 30,* 423–431.

Verstijnen, I. M., van Leeuwen, C., Goldschmidt, G., Hamel, R., & Hennessey, J. M. (1998). Creative discovery in imagery and perception: Combining is relatively easy, restructuring takes a sketch. *Acta Psychologica, 99,* 177–200.

THE HAZARDS OF IMAGERY MNEMONICS?

To remember the name "Korsakoff," you might visualize someone near a racecourse who is *coughing*. This mnemonic may be effective . . . but may mislead you. Later, when you recall the image, you might decide the name was "Coursick" or "Racecold."

chapter review

SUMMARY

- People differ enormously in how they describe their imagery experience, particularly the vividness of that experience. However, concerns about how we should interpret these self-reports have led investigators to seek more objective ways of studying mental imagery.

- Chronometric studies indicate that the pattern of what information is more available and what is less available in an image closely matches the pattern of what is available in an actual picture. Likewise, the times needed to scan across an image, to zoom in on an image to examine detail, or to imagine the form rotating, all correspond closely to the times needed for these operations with actual pictures. These results emerge even when the experimenter makes no mention of imagery, ruling out an account of these data in terms of the experiment's demand character.

- In many settings, visual imagery seems to involve mechanisms that overlap with those used for visual perception. This is reflected in the fact that imaging one thing can make it difficult to perceive something else, or that imaging the appropriate target can prime a subsequent perception. Further evidence comes from neuroimaging and studies of brain damage; this evidence confirms the considerable overlap between the biological basis for imagery and that for perception.

- Not all imagery, however, is visual, so that we need to distinguish between *visual* and *spatial* imagery. This proposal is confirmed by studies of individuals with brain damage, some of whom seem to lose the capacity for visual imagery but retain their capacity for spatial imagery. This proposal may also help us understand the pattern of individual differences in imagery ability, with some individuals being particularly skilled in visual imagery and some in spatial.

- Just as some individuals seem to have little or no visual imagery, other individuals—called "eidetikers"—seem to have fabulously detailed, photographic imagery. There's no question that this astonishingly vivid imagery exists in some people, but the mechanisms behind it remain unknown.

- Even when imagery is visual, mental images are picture-like; they aren't actually pictures. Unlike pictures, mental images seem to be accompanied by a perceptual reference frame that guides the interpretation of the image and also influences what can be discovered about the image.

- To create a mental image, you draw on information stored in an image file in long-term memory. These image files can be thought of as "recipes" for the construction of a mental image, usually by first constructing a frame and then by elaborating the frame as needed. Also, at least some information about visual appearance or spatial arrangement is stored in long-term memory in terms of verbal labels or conceptual frameworks. For example, information about the locations of cities may be stored in terms of propositions ("Montreal is in Canada; Canada is north of the United States") rather than being stored in some sort of mental map.

- Imagery helps people to remember, so word lists are more readily recalled if the words are easily imaged; similarly, instructions to form images help people to memorize. These benefits may be the result of dual coding: storing information in both a verbal format and a format that encodes appearances; this approach doubles the chances of recalling the material later on.

- When you're using imagery to remember combinations of ideas, it is best to imagine the objects to be remembered interacting in some way.

- Memory for pictures can be accurate, but it follows most of the same rules as any other form of memory; for example, it is influenced by schematic knowledge.

● It is unclear what other categories of memory there might be. In each case, other kinds of memory are likely to have some properties that are distinctive and also many properties that are shared with memories of other sorts.

KEY TERMS

self-report data (p. 413)
chronometric studies (p. 415)
image-scanning procedure (p. 417)
mental rotation task (p. 419)
demand character (p. 421)

binocular rivalry (p. 424)
eidetic imagery (p. 434)
percepts (p. 437)
image files (p. 440)
dual coding (p. 444)
boundary extension (p. 445)

TEST YOURSELF AGAIN

1. What is the concern about "self-report" data, and Galton's data in particular?

2. What is a chronometric study?

3. Why do image-scanning studies indicate that images *depict* a scene rather than *describing* the scene?

4. What does it mean to say that an experiment's results might be influenced by demand character?

5. What's the evidence that visual imagery relies on some of the same mental processes as actual vision?

6. What do we learn from the fact that some forms of brain damage have *similar* effects on a person's ability to see and the person's ability to perform many imagery tasks?

7. What do we learn from the fact that some forms of brain damage have *different* effects on a person's ability to see and the person's ability to perform many imagery tasks?

8. What evidence confirms that people do actually differ in the vividness of their visual images?

9. What is eidetic imagery?

10. Images are certainly picture-*like,* but what evidence points to a distinction between mental images and actual out-in-the-world pictures?

11. What evidence suggests that visual information is often stored in long-term memory via a representation that's not really "visual"?

12. What's the evidence that imagery can help you to memorize?

THINK ABOUT IT

1. People differ markedly in their skill of recognizing previously viewed faces. (Want to know how you measure up? Point an Internet browser at the Cambridge Face Memory Test.) Is it plausible that these differences are linked to the person's skill in forming visual images? How might you test this?

2. Often, a movie is based on a popular book, and you sometimes hear people say things like this: "The movie was hard to watch because the main figure in the story didn't look at all like I'd imagined her, based on the book." Is it plausible that people who most often say this are the people with the clearest, most vivid imagery? How might you test this?

eBOOK DEMONSTRATIONS & ESSAYS

Go to http://digital.wwnorton.com/cognition7 for the online demonstrations and essays relevant to this chapter. These can be found in the ebook.

Online Demonstrations

- Demonstration 11.1: Imaged Synthesis
- Demonstration 11.2: Mnemonic Strategies
- Demonstration 11.3: Auditory Imagery

Online Applying Cognitive Psychology and the Law Essays

- Cognitive Psychology and the Law: Lineups

ZAPS COGNITION LABS

Go to http://digital.wwnorton.com/cognition7 to experience interactive online psychology labs relevant to this chapter.

Thinking

The capacity for *thought* is arguably what makes us human. And of course we rely on this capacity all the time. We draw conclusions; we make choices; we solve problems. But how do we achieve these things? How do we think? How *well* do we think? In this section, we'll see that human thinking is often flawed, and we'll encounter examples of bad judgment, improper reasoning, and highly inefficient problem solving. As we'll see, though, this poor performance is not the product of laziness or stupidity. The explanation lies instead in a theme that has already come up in our discussion: In a wide range of settings, humans rely on mental shortcuts — strategies that are efficient but that risk error. These shortcuts played an important part in Chapter 4, when we discussed object recognition, and in Chapter 8, when we discussed memory errors. Similar shortcuts will emerge in this section, and as we'll see, they play a central role in guiding human thought.

However, it's clear that in many circumstances people rise above these shortcuts and think carefully and well. This will drive us toward a multilayered conception of thinking, because we'll need to describe both the shortcuts that people use and also the more careful strategies that people often turn to. In addition, we'll need to tackle the obvious questions of *why* and *when* people rely on one sort of thinking or the other. What are the circumstances, or the reasons, that lead to efficient-but-risky thinking, and what are the triggers for slower-but-better thinking?

It's also important that people seem to differ in their thinking. Some people are wonderfully logical; others seem capricious. Some people are creative problem solvers; others are stymied by even simple problems. Some people seem fabulously intelligent; others seem less so. In this section, we'll examine these differences as well.

Finally, one other set of issues will arise in this section: How much of thought is conscious? Are there benefits associated with conscious thought, as opposed to unconscious thought? We will tackle these questions in the book's final chapter, but we'll do this largely by pulling together points we've made in earlier chapters. In this way, the final chapter will provide something of a review for the text at the same time that it explores a series of enormously important theoretical questions.

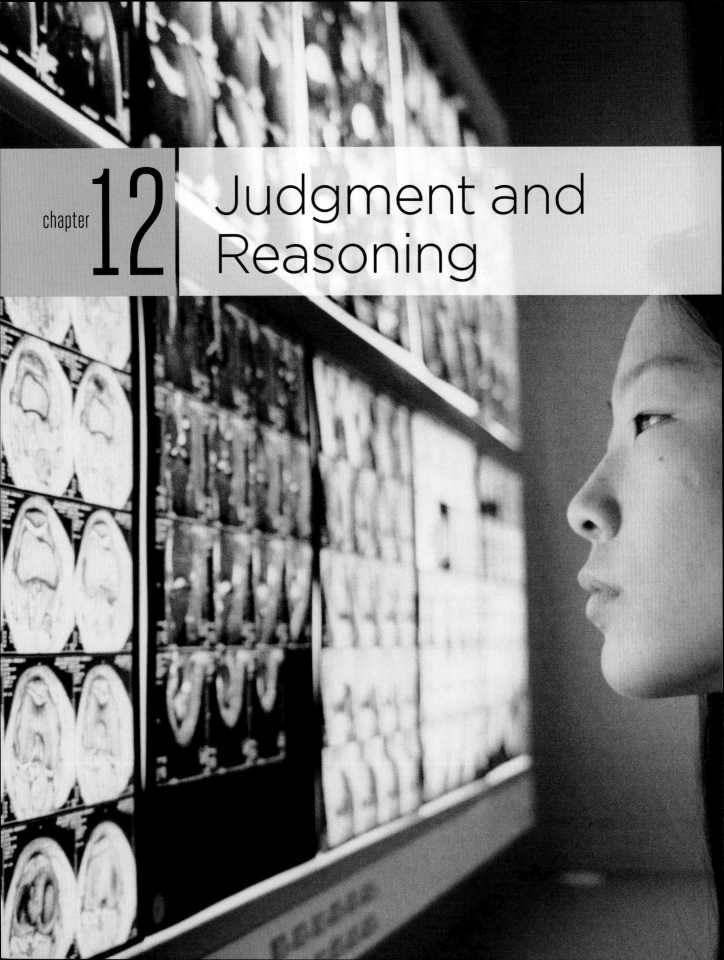

chapter 12 | Judgment and Reasoning

what if... The activity we call "thinking" involves many processes, and this simple point blocks us from asking in a general way: "What would happen if you lost the ability to think?" We can, however, ask what would happen if you lost *this* aspect of thinking or *that* aspect — and the answers are often surprising.

Many of us regard *emotion* as a force that disrupts thinking. We say things like "I was so angry I couldn't think straight" or "I knew I'd regret the choice, but at that moment I was listening more to my heart than to my head." These sentiments capture important truths, but they overstate the separation between "heart" and "head," because emotion turns out to play a huge role in our ordinary thinking. We see this if we ask: "What if someone loses *the capacity for ordinary emotion*?" Consider Elliot, a patient whose case is discussed in detail by Antonio Damasio (1994). Elliot had undergone surgery to remove a small brain tumor, and the surgery seemed to have little impact on his intellect; his IQ score was just as high after the operation as it was before. But after the operation, Elliot became hopelessly indecisive. In scheduling an appointment, he needed 30 minutes, staring at his calendar, to decide which of two days would be better for him. He'd spend an entire afternoon deciding whether to classify a set of records by "place" or by "date." He needed so much time to choose where he'd eat lunch that he was likely to miss lunchtime. In choosing a restaurant, he'd scrutinize each place's menu and he'd drive to each restaurant to see how busy it was — but he still couldn't decide where to eat. Even the simplest of decisions — whether to use a blue pen or a black one for office paperwork — was paralyzing for him.

Because of damage to a part of the brain called the "orbitofrontal cortex" (see **Figure 12.1**), Elliot seemed to have lost emotions; Damasio reports that he "never saw a tinge of emotion" in his hours of conversation with Elliot. When tested in the laboratory, Elliot showed no bodily response at all if shown pictures depicting tragedy or aggression; he didn't react to sexual images, or gruesome pictures of wounds, or any other image that for most people cause a powerful emotional response.

But why did Elliot's lack of emotion lead to paralysis in his decision making? Part of the answer lies in the fact that decisions often involve an element of risk ("Will this dinner taste as good as the menu description implies?"). To evaluate these risks, people rely heavily on emotion — and so, if thinking about the dinner fills you with joyful anticipation, you'll judge the

preview of chapter themes

- In a wide range of circumstances, people use cognitive shortcuts, or "heuristics," to make judgments. These heuristics are efficient and often lead to sensible conclusions, but sometimes they can lead to error.

- People use heuristics even when they're highly motivated to be accurate, and trained experts often rely on the same heuristics. Therefore, expert judgments are also vulnerable to error.

- In some circumstances, people step away from heuristic use ("Type 1" thinking) and rely instead on more sophisticated ("Type 2") forms of reasoning—and so they judge covariation accurately, are sensitive to base rates, and so on.

- Evidence suggests that Type 2 reasoning is likely to come into play only if the circumstances are right and only if the case being judged contains the appropriate triggers for this form of reasoning.

- The quality of people's thinking is also uneven within the broad domain of deduction. For example, people show a pattern of "confirmation bias" and so are more sensitive to, and more accepting of, evidence that supports their beliefs than they are of evidence that challenges their beliefs.

- Errors in logical reasoning follow patterns that suggest people are guided by principles other than those of logic. Contrary to the principles of formal logic, people's reasoning is heavily influenced by the *content* of what they're reasoning about.

- People seem not to base their decisions on utility calculations; this is evident in the fact that many factors (including a decision's frame) have a strong impact on decisions even though these factors don't change utilities in any way. People seem instead to make decisions that they feel they can justify, so they are influenced by factors that make one choice or another seem more compelling.

- Another factor influencing decision making is emotion. However, people are often inept in predicting their future emotions, with the result that they work hard to avoid regret that they wouldn't have felt anyhow, and they spend money for things that provide only short-term pleasure.

risk to be low (cf. Slovic & Peters, 2010). Or, as a contrasting case, if thinking about a terrorist attack fills you with dread, you'll likely judge the risk of an attack to be high. But these processes were unavailable for (never-emotional) Elliot, with disastrous consequences for his decision making.

There are, of course, occasions in which emotion can disrupt thinking. But, apparently, there are also occasions in which emotion *contributes* in important ways to your thinking. We'll need to address this contribution before we're through.

Judgment

The activity of "thinking" takes many forms, but one of the central forms is *judgment*—the process through which people draw conclusions from the evidence they encounter, often evidence provided by life experiences. But how—and how well—do people make judgments?

Experience is, of course, an extraordinary teacher, and so you're likely to believe the sports coach who, after many seasons, tells you which game strategies work and which ones don't. Likewise, you trust the police detective who asserts that over the years he's learned how to tell whether a suspect is lying. You welcome the advice of the hair stylist who says, "I can tell you from the hair I cut every day, this shampoo repairs split ends."

But we can also find cases in which people *don't* learn from experience: "He's getting married *again*? Why does he think this one will last longer than

FIGURE 12.1 ORBITOFRONTAL CORTEX

The area highlighted in green is the orbitofrontal cortex—the portion of the brain just behind the eyeballs. Many researchers argue that this brain region plays a crucial role in the processes through which we detect and interpret our emotions.

the last four?"; "It doesn't matter how many polite New Yorkers she meets; she's still convinced that everyone from that city is rude."

What's going on here? Why do people sometimes draw accurate conclusions from their experience, and sometimes not?

Attribute Substitution

Let's start with the *information* you use when drawing a conclusion from experience. Imagine that you're shopping for a car and trying to decide if European cars are reliable. Surely, you'd want to know how often these cars break down and need repair—how frequent are the problems? As a different case, imagine that you're trying to choose an efficient route for your morning drive to work. Here, too, the information you need concerns frequencies: When you've gone down 4th Avenue, how often were you late? How often were you late when you stayed on Front Street instead?

Examples like these remind us that a wide range of judgments begin with a **frequency estimate**—an assessment of how often various events have occurred in the past. For many of the judgments you make in day-to-day life, though, you don't have direct access to frequency information. You probably don't have instant access to a count of how many VW's break down, in comparison to how many Hondas. You probably don't have a detailed list of your various commute times. How, therefore, do you proceed in making your judgments?

Let's pursue the decision about commuting routes. In making your choice, you're likely to do a quick scan through memory, looking for relevant cases. If you can immediately think of three occasions when you got caught in a traffic snarl on 4th Avenue and can't think of similar occasions on Front Street, you'll probably decide that Front Street is the better bet. In contrast, if you can recall two horrible traffic jams on Front Street but only one on 4th Avenue, you'll draw the opposite conclusion.

The strategy you're using here is known as **attribute substitution**—a strategy in which you rely on easily assessed information as a proxy for the information you really need. In this judgment about traffic, the information you need is *frequency* (how often you've been late when you've taken one route or the other), but you don't have access to this information. As a substitute, you base your judgment on *availability*—how easily and how quickly you can come up with relevant examples. The logic is this: "Examples leap to mind? Must be a common, often-experienced event. A struggle to come up with examples? Must be a rare event."

This strategy—relying on *availability* as a substitute for *frequency*—is a form of attribute substitution known as the **availability heuristic** (Tversky & Kahneman, 1973). Here's a different type of attribute substitution: Imagine that you're applying for a job. You hope that the employer will examine your credentials carefully and make a thoughtful judgment about whether you'd be a good hire. It's likely, though, that the employer will rely on a faster, easier strategy. Specifically, he may barely glance at your résumé and, instead, ask himself how much you resemble other people he's hired who have worked out well. Do you have the same mannerisms or the same look as Joan, an employee that he's very happy with? If so, you're likely to get the job. Or do you remind him of Jane, an employee he had to fire after just two months? If so, you'll still be looking at the job ads tomorrow.

In this case, the person who's interviewing you needs to judge a *probability* (namely, the probability that you'd work out well if hired) and instead relies on *resemblance* to known cases. This substitution is referred to as the **representativeness heuristic**.

The Availability Heuristic

People rely on heuristics like availability and representativeness in a wide range of settings, and so, if we understand these strategies, we understand how a great deal of thinking proceeds. (See **Table 12.1** for a summary comparison of these two strategies.)

TABLE 12.1 DIFFERENT TYPES OF ATTRIBUTE SUBSTITUTION

You want to judge . . .	Instead you rely on . . .	This usually works because . . .	But this strategy can lead to error because . . .
Frequency of occurrence in the world	Availability in memory: How easily can you think of cases?	Events that are frequent in the world are likely to be more available in memory.	Many factors *other than* frequency in the world can influence availability from memory!
Probability of an event being in a category or having certain properties	Resemblance between that event and other events in the category	Many categories are homogeneous enough so that the category members do resemble one another.	Many categories are not homogeneous!

In general, the term **heuristic** describes an efficient strategy that usually leads to the right answer. The key word, however, is "usually," because heuristics allow errors; that's the price you pay in order to gain the efficiency. The availability and representativeness heuristics both fit this profile. In each case, you're relying on an attribute (availability or resemblance) that's easy to assess, and that's the source of the efficiency. And in each case, the attribute is correlated with the target dimension, so that it can serve as a reasonable proxy for the target: Events or objects that are frequent in the world are, in most cases, likely to be easily available in memory, so generally you'll be fine if you rely on availability as an index for frequency. And many categories are homogeneous enough so that members of the category do resemble one another; that's why you can often rely on resemblance as a way of judging probability of category membership.

Nonetheless, these strategies can lead to error. To take a simple case, ask yourself: "Are there more words in the dictionary beginning with the letter *R* ('rose,' 'rock,' 'rabbit') or more words with an *R* in the third position ('tarp,' 'bare,' 'throw')?" Most people insist that there are more words beginning with *R* (Tversky & Kahneman, 1973, 1974), but the reverse is true—by a margin of at least 2-to-1.

Why do people get this wrong? The answer lies in availability. If you search your memory for words starting with *R*, many will come to mind. (Try it: How many *R*-words can you name in 10 seconds?) But if you search your memory for words with an *R* in the third position, fewer will come up. (Again, try this for 10 seconds.) This difference, favoring the words beginning with *R*, arises because your memory is organized roughly like a dictionary, with words that share a starting sound all grouped together. As a result, it's easy to search memory using "starting letter" as your cue; a search based on "*R* in third position" is more difficult. In this way, the organization of memory creates a bias in what's easily available, and this bias in availability leads to an error in frequency judgment.

The Wide Range of Availability Effects

The *R*-word example isn't very interesting on its own—after all, how often do you need to make judgments about spelling patterns? But other examples are easy to find, including cases in which people are making judgments of some importance.

For example, people regularly overestimate the frequency of events that are, in actuality, quite rare (Lichtenstein, Slovic, Fischhoff, Layman, & Combs, 1978). This probably plays a part in people's willingness to buy lottery tickets; they overestimate the likelihood of winning. Likewise, physicians often overestimate the likelihood of a rare disease and, in the process, fail to pursue other, more appropriate, diagnoses (e.g., Elstein et al., 1986; Obrecht, Chapman, & Gelman, 2009).

What causes this pattern? There's little reason to spend time thinking about familiar events ("Oh, look—that airplane has wings!"), but you're likely to notice and think about rare events, especially rare *emotional* events ("How awful—that airplane crashed!"). As a result, rare events are likely to be well recorded in memory, and this will, in turn, make these events easily available to you. As a consequence, if you rely on the availability heuristic, you'll overestimate the frequency of these distinctive events and, correspondingly, overestimate the likelihood of similar events happening in the future.

Here's a different example. Participants in one study were asked to think about episodes in their lives in which they'd acted in an assertive manner (Schwarz et al., 1991; also see Raghubir & Menon, 2005). Half of the participants were asked to recall 6 episodes; half were asked to recall 12 episodes. Then, all the participants were asked some general questions, including how assertive overall they thought they were.

Participants had an easy time coming up with 6 episodes, and so, using the availability heuristic, they concluded, "Those cases came quickly to mind; therefore, there must be a large number of these episodes; therefore, I must be an assertive person." In contrast, participants who were asked for 12 episodes had some difficulty generating the longer list, so they concluded, "If these cases are so difficult to recall, I guess the episodes can't be typical for how I act."

Consistent with these suggestions, participants who were asked to recall fewer episodes judged themselves to be more assertive. Notice, ironically, that the participants who tried to recall more episodes actually ended up with more evidence in view for their own assertiveness. But it's not the quantity of evidence that matters. Instead, what matters is the ease of coming up with the episodes. Participants who were asked for a dozen episodes had a hard time with the task *because they'd been asked to do something difficult*—namely, to come up with a lot of cases. But the participants seemed not to realize this. They reacted only to the fact that the examples were difficult to generate, and using the availability heuristic, they concluded that being assertive was relatively infrequent in their past.

The Representativeness Heuristic

Similar points can be made about the representativeness heuristic. Just like availability, this strategy often leads to the correct conclusion. But here, too, the strategy can sometimes lead you astray.

How does the representativeness heuristic work? Let's start with the fact that many of the categories you encounter are relatively homogeneous. The category "birds," for example, is reasonably uniform with regard to the traits of *having wings, having feathers,* and so on. Virtually every member of the category has these traits, and so, in these regards, each member of the category resembles most of the others. Likewise, the category "motels" is

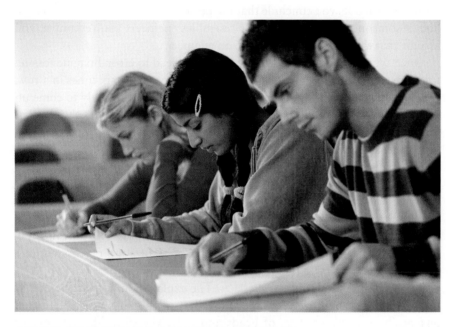

ABUSE OF THE AVAILABILITY HEURISTIC?

Imagine a diabolical college professor who wants to improve student evaluations of his teaching. A possible strategy is suggested by a study in which students were asked to list ways a particular course could be improved (Fox, 2006). Students were then asked for an overall rating of how good the course was. Students in one group were asked to list just two potential improvements to the course. These students had an easy time generating this short list, and guided by the availability heuristic, they seemed to reason this way: "It surely was easy to come up with possible improvements for the course. I guess, therefore, that the course must have many flaws and so isn't very good." As a result, they gave the course lower ratings than students who were asked to do a more difficult task—come up with ten potential improvements for the course. Students in the latter group ended up with much more evidence in their view for the course's problems, but that's not what mattered. Instead, these students seemed to be thinking: "It was hard to produce this list. I guess, therefore, the course doesn't have many flaws; if it did, I'd have had an easier time thinking of improvements. So, I'll give the course a high rating." Of course, no professor would ever think about exploiting this pattern to manipulate student evaluations. . . .

homogeneous with regard to traits like *has beds in each room, has a Bible in each room,* and *has an office,* and so, again, in these regards each member of the category resembles the others.

The representativeness heuristic capitalizes on this homogeneity. We expect each individual to resemble the other individuals in the category (i.e., we expect each individual to be *representative* of the category overall). As a result, we can use resemblance as a basis for judging the likelihood of category membership. So if a creature resembles other birds you've seen, you conclude that the creature probably is a bird. We first met this approach in Chapter 9, when we were discussing simple categories like "dog" and "fruit." But the same approach can be used more broadly—and this is the heart of the representativeness strategy. Thus, if a job candidate resembles successful hires you've made, you conclude that the person will probably be a successful hire; if someone you meet at a party resembles engineers you've known, you assume that the person is likely to be an engineer.

Once again, though, use of this heuristic can lead to error. Imagine tossing a coin over and over, and let's say that it lands "heads" up six times in a row. Many people believe that on the next toss the coin is more likely to come up tails. They reason that if the coin is fair, then any series of tosses should contain roughly equal numbers of heads and tails. If no tails have appeared for a while, then some are "overdue" to make up the balance.

This pattern of thinking is called the "gambler's fallacy." To see that it is a fallacy, bear in mind that a coin has no "memory," so the coin has no way of knowing how long it has been since the last tails. Therefore, the likelihood of a tail occurring on any particular toss must be independent of what happened on previous tosses; there's no way that the previous tosses could possibly influence the next one. As a result, the probability of a tail on toss number 7 is .50, just as it was on the first toss—and on every toss.

What produces the gambler's fallacy? The explanation lies in the assumption of category homogeneity. We know that in the long run, a fair coin will produce equal numbers of heads and tails. Therefore, the category of "all tosses" has this property. Our assumption of homogeneity, though, leads us to expect that any "representative" of the category will also have this property—that is, any sequence of tosses will also show the 50-50 split. But this isn't true: Some sequences of tosses are 75% heads; some are 5% heads. It's only when we combine these sequences that the 50-50 split emerges. (For a different perspective on the gambler's fallacy, see Farmer, Warren, & Hahn, 2017.)

Reasoning from a Single Case to the Entire Population

The assumption of homogeneity can also lead to a different error, one that's in view whenever people try to persuade each other with a "man who" argument. To understand this term (first proposed by Nisbett & Ross, 1980), imagine that you're shopping for a new cell phone. You've read various consumer magazines and decided, based on their test data, that you'll buy a Smacko brand phone. You report this to a friend, who is aghast. "Smacko?

You must be crazy. Why, I know a guy who bought a Smacko, and the case fell apart two weeks after he got it. Then, the wire for the headphones went. Then, the charger failed. How could you possibly buy a Smacko?"

What should you make of this argument? The consumer magazines tested many phones and reported that, say, 2% of all Smackos have repair problems. In your friend's "data," 100% of the Smackos (one out of one) broke. It seems silly to let this "sample of one" outweigh the much larger sample tested by the magazine, but even so your friend probably thinks he's offering a persuasive argument. What guides your friend's thinking? He must be assuming that the category will resemble the instance. Only in that case would reasoning from a single instance be appropriate. (For a classic demonstration of the "man who" pattern, see Hamill, Wilson, & Nisbett, 1980.)

If you listen to conversations around you, you'll regularly hear "man who" (or "woman who") arguments. "What do you mean, cigarette smoking causes cancer?! I have an aunt who smoked for 50 years, and she runs in marathons!" Often, these arguments seem persuasive. But they have force only by virtue of the representativeness heuristic and your assumption of category homogeneity.

TEST YOURSELF

1. What is attribute substitution?
2. In the availability heuristic, what is the information you need, and what attribute do you use as a substitute?
3. In the representativeness heuristic, what is the information you need, and what attribute do you use as a substitute?
4. What is a "man who" argument? Why are "man who" arguments often misleading?

Detecting Covariation

It cannot be surprising that people often rely on mental shortcuts. After all, you don't have unlimited time, and many of the judgments you make, day by day, are far from life-changing. It's unsettling, though, that people use the same shortcuts when making deeply consequential judgments. And to make things worse, the errors caused by the heuristics can trigger other sorts of errors, including errors in judgments of **covariation**. This term has a technical meaning, but for our purposes we can define it this way: X and Y "covary" if X tends to be on the scene whenever Y is, and if X tends to be absent whenever Y is absent. For example, exercise and stamina covary: People who do the first tend to have a lot of the second. Years of education and annual salary also covary (and so people with more education tend to earn more), but the covariation is weaker than that between exercise and stamina. Notice, then, that covariation can be strong or weak, and it can also be negative or positive. Exercise and stamina, for example, covary positively (as exercise increases, so does stamina). Exercise and risk of heart attacks covary negatively (because exercise strengthens the heart muscle, decreasing the risk).

Covariation is important for many reasons—including the fact that it's what you need to consider when checking on a belief about cause and effect. For example, do you feel better on days when you eat a good breakfast? If so, then the presence or absence of a good breakfast in the morning should covary with how you feel as the day wears on. Similarly: Are you more likely to fall in love with someone tall? Does your car start more easily if you pump the gas pedal? These, too, are questions that hinge on covariation, leading us to ask: How accurately do people judge covariation?

Illusions of Covariation

People routinely "detect" covariation even where there is none. For example, many people are convinced there's a relationship between someone's astrological sign (e.g., whether the person is a Libra or a Virgo) and their personality, yet no serious study has documented this covariation. Likewise, many people believe they can predict the weather by paying attention to their arthritis pain ("My knee always acts up when a storm is coming"). This belief, too, turns out to be groundless. Other examples concern social stereotypes (e.g., the idea that being "moody" covaries with gender), superstitions (e.g., the idea that Friday the 13th brings bad luck), and more. (For some of the evidence, see King & Koehler, 2000; Redelmeier & Tversky, 1996; Shaklee & Mims, 1982.)

What causes illusions like these? One reason, which we've known about for years, is centered on the *evidence* people consider when judging covariation: In making these judgments, people seem to consider only a subset of the facts, and it's a subset skewed by their prior expectations (Baron, 1988; Evans, 1989; Gilovich, 1991; Jennings, Amabile, & Ross, 1982). This virtually guarantees mistaken judgments, since even if the judgment process were 100% fair, a biased input would lead to a biased output.

Specifically, when judging covariation, your selection of evidence is likely to be guided by **confirmation bias**—a tendency to be more alert to evidence that *confirms* your beliefs rather than to evidence that might *challenge* them (Nisbett & Ross, 1980; Tweney, Doherty, & Mynatt, 1981). We'll have more to say about confirmation bias later, but for now let's note how confirmation bias can distort the assessment of covariation. Let's say, for example, that you have the belief that big dogs tend to be vicious. With this belief, you're more likely to notice big dogs that are, in fact, vicious and little dogs that are friendly. As a result, a biased sample of dogs is available to you, in the dogs you perceive and the dogs you remember. Therefore, if you try to estimate covariation between dog size and temperament, you'll get it wrong. This isn't because you're ignoring the facts. The problem instead lies in your "data"; if the data are biased, so will be your judgment.

Base Rates

Assessment of covariation can also be pulled off track by another problem: neglect of **base-rate information**—information about how frequently something occurs in general. Imagine that we're testing a new drug in the hope that it will cure the common cold. Here, we're trying to find out if taking the drug covaries with a better medical outcome, and let's say that our study tells us that 70% of patients taking the drug recover from their illness within 48 hours. This result is uninterpretable on its own, because we need the base rate: We need to know how often *in general* people recover from their colds in the same time span. If it turns out that the overall recovery rate within 48 hours is 70%, then our new drug is having no effect whatsoever.

Similarly, do good-luck charms help? Let's say that you wear your lucky socks whenever your favorite team plays, and the team has won 85% of its games. Here, too, we need to ask about base rates: How many games has your team won over the last few years? Perhaps the team has won 90% overall. In that case, your socks are actually a jinx.

Despite the importance of base rates, people often ignore them. In a classic study, Kahneman and Tversky (1973) asked participants this question: If someone is chosen at random from a group of 70 lawyers and 30 engineers, what is his profession likely to be? Participants understood perfectly well that in this setting the probability of the person being a lawyer is .70. Apparently, in some settings people are appropriately sensitive to base-rate information.

Other participants did a similar task, but they were given the same base rates *and also* brief descriptions of certain individuals. Based on this information, they were asked whether each individual was more likely to be a lawyer or an engineer. These descriptions provide **diagnostic information**—information about the particular case—and some of the descriptions had been crafted (based on common stereotypes) to suggest that the person was a lawyer; some suggested engineer; some were relatively neutral.

Participants understood the value of these descriptions and—as we've just seen—also seem to understand the value of base rates: They're responsive to base-rate information if this is the only information they have. When given both types of information, therefore, we should expect that the participants will combine these inputs as well as they can. If both the base rate and the diagnostic information favor the lawyer response, participants should offer this response with confidence. If the base rate indicates one response and the diagnostic information the other response, participants should temper their estimates accordingly.

However, this isn't what participants did. When provided with both types of information, they relied only on the descriptive information about the individual. In fact, when given both the base rate and diagnostic information, participants' responses were the same if the base rates were as already described (70 lawyers, 30 engineers) or if the base rates were reversed (30 lawyers, 70 engineers). This reversal had no impact on participants' judgments, confirming that they were indeed ignoring the base rates.

What produces this neglect of base rates? The answer, in part, is attribute substitution. When asked whether a particular person—Tom, let's say—is a lawyer or an engineer, people seem to turn this question about category membership into a question about resemblance. (In other words, they rely on the representativeness heuristic.) Therefore, to ask whether Tom *is* a lawyer, they ask themselves how much Tom *resembles* (their idea of) a lawyer. This substitution is (as we've discussed) often helpful, but the strategy provides no role for base rates—and this guarantees that people will routinely ignore base rates. Consistent with this claim, base-rate neglect is widespread and can be observed both in laboratory tasks and in many real-world judgments. (For some indications, though, of when people *do* take base rates into account, see Griffin et al., 2012; Klayman & Brown, 1993; Pennycook, Trippas, Handley, & Thompson, 2014.)

TEST YOURSELF

5. What is a base rate? Why is base-rate information important?

Dual-Process Models

We seem to be painting a grim portrait of human judgment, and we can document errors even among experts—financial managers making large investments (e.g., Hilton, 2003; Kahneman, 2011) and physicians diagnosing cancer (but ignoring base rates; Eddy, 1982; also see Koehler, Brenner, & Griffin, 2002). The errors occur even when people are strongly motivated to be careful, with clear instructions and financial rewards offered for good performance (Arkes, 1991; Gilovich, 1991; Hertwig & Ortmann, 2003).

Could it be, then, that human judgment is fundamentally flawed? If so, this might explain why people are so ready to believe in telepathy, astrology, and a variety of bogus cures (Gilovich, 1991; King & Koehler, 2000). In fact, maybe these points help us understand why warfare, racism, neglect of poverty, and environmental destruction are so widespread; maybe these problems are the inevitable outcome of people's inability to understand facts and to draw decent conclusions.

Before we make these claims, however, let's acknowledge another side to our story: Sometimes human judgment rises above the heuristics we've described so far. People often rely on availability in judging frequency, but sometimes they seek other (more accurate) bases for making their judgments (Oppenheimer, 2004; Schwarz, 1998; Winkielman & Schwarz, 2001). Likewise, people often rely on the representativeness heuristic, and so (among other concerns) they draw conclusions from "man who" stories. But in other settings people are keenly sensitive to sample size, and they draw no conclusions if their sample is small or possibly biased. (For an early statement of this point, see Nisbett, Krantz, Jepson, & Kunda, 1983; for more recent discussion, see Kahneman, 2011.) How can we make sense of this mixed pattern?

Ways of Thinking: Type 1, Type 2

A number of authors have proposed that people have two distinct ways of thinking. One type of thinking is fast and easy; the heuristics we've described fall into this category. The other type is slower and more effortful, but also more accurate.

Researchers have offered various versions of this **dual-process model**, and different theorists use different terminology (Evans, 2006, 2012a; Ferreira, Garcia-Marques, Sherman, & Sherman, 2006; Kahneman, 2011; Pretz, 2008; Shafir & LeBoeuf, 2002). We'll rely on rather neutral terms (initially proposed by Stanovich and West, 2000; Stanovich, 2012), so we'll use **Type 1** as the label for the fast, easy sort of thinking and **Type 2** as the label for the slower, more effortful thinking. (Also see **Figure 12.2**.)

When do people use one type of thinking or the other? One hypothesis is that people *choose* when to rely on each system; presumably, they shift to the more accurate Type 2 when making judgments that really matter. As we've seen, however, people rely on Type 1 heuristics even when incentives are offered for accuracy, even when making important professional judgments,

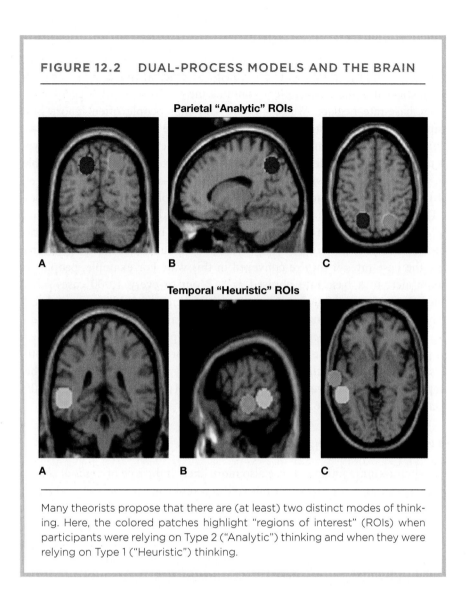

FIGURE 12.2 DUAL-PROCESS MODELS AND THE BRAIN

Parietal "Analytic" ROIs

A   B   C

Temporal "Heuristic" ROIs

A   B   C

Many theorists propose that there are (at least) two distinct modes of thinking. Here, the colored patches highlight "regions of interest" (ROIs) when participants were relying on Type 2 ("Analytic") thinking and when they were relying on Type 1 ("Heuristic") thinking.

even when making medical diagnoses that may literally be matters of life and death. Surely people would choose to use Type 2 in these cases if they could, yet they still rely on Type 1 and fall into error. On these grounds, it's difficult to argue that using Type 2 is a matter of deliberate choice.

Instead, evidence suggests that Type 2 is likely to come into play only if it's triggered by certain cues and only if the circumstances are right. We've suggested, for example, that Type 2 judgments are slower than Type 1, and on this basis it's not surprising that heuristic-based judgments (and, thus, heuristic-based *errors*) are more likely when judgments are made under time pressure (Finucane, Alhakami, Slovic, & Johnson, 2000). We've also said that Type 2 judgments require *effort*, so this form of thinking is more likely if the person can focus attention on the judgment being made (De Neys, 2006; Ferreira et al., 2006; for some complexity, though, see Chun & Kruglanski, 2006).

Triggers for Skilled Intuition

We need to be clear, though, that we cannot equate Type 1 thinking with "bad" or "sloppy" thinking, because fast-and-efficient thinking can be quite sophisticated if the environment contains the "right sort" of triggers. Consider base-rate neglect. We've already said that people often ignore base rates—and, as a result, misinterpret the evidence they encounter. But *sensitivity* to base rates can also be demonstrated, even in cases involving Type 1 thinking (e.g., Pennycook et al., 2014). This mixed pattern is attributable, in part, to how the base rates are presented. Base-rate neglect is more likely if the relevant information is cast in terms of probabilities or proportions: "There is a .01 chance that people like Mary will have this disease"; "Only 5% of the people in this group are lawyers." But base-rate information can also be conveyed in terms of *frequencies*, and it turns out that people often use the base rates if they're conveyed in this way. For example, people are more alert to a base rate phrased as "12 out of every 1,000 cases" than they are to the same information cast as a percentage (1.2%) or a probability (.012). (See Gigerenzer & Hoffrage, 1995; also Brase, 2008; Cosmides & Tooby, 1996.) It seems, then, that much depends on how the problem is presented, with some presentations being more "user friendly" than others. (For more on the circumstances in which Type 1 thinking can be rather sophisticated, see Gigerenzer & Gaissmaier, 2011; Kahneman & Klein, 2009; Oaksford & Hall, 2016.)

The Role for Chance

Fast-but-accurate judgments are also more likely if the role of *random chance* is conspicuous in a problem. If this role is prominent, people are more likely to realize that the "evidence" they're considering may just be a fluke or an accident, not an indication of a reliable pattern. With this, people are more likely to pay attention to the *quantity* of evidence, on the (sensible) idea that a larger set of observations is less vulnerable to chance fluctuations.

In one study, participants were asked about someone who evaluated a restaurant based on just one meal (Nisbett, Krantz, Jepson, & Kunda, 1983). This is, of course, a weak basis for judging the restaurant: If the diner had a great meal, maybe he was lucky and selected by chance the one entrée the chef knew how to cook. If the meal was lousy, maybe the diner happened to choose the weakest option on the menu. With an eye on these possibilities, we should be cautious in evaluating the diner's report, based on his limited experience of just one dinner.

In one condition of the study, participants were told that the diner chose his entrée by blindly dropping a pencil onto the menu. This cue helped the participants realize that a different sample, and perhaps different views of the restaurant, might have emerged if the pencil had fallen on a different selection. As a result, these participants were appropriately cautious about the diner's assessment based on just a single meal. (Also see Gigerenzer, 1991; Gigerenzer, Hell, & Blank, 1988; Tversky & Kahneman, 1982.)

Education

The quality of a person's thinking is also shaped by the background knowledge that she or he brings to a judgment; **Figure 12.3** provides an illustration of this pattern (after Nisbett et al., 1983). In addition, a person's quality of thinking is influenced by *education*. For example, Fong, Krantz, & Nisbett (1986) conducted a telephone survey of "opinions about sports," calling

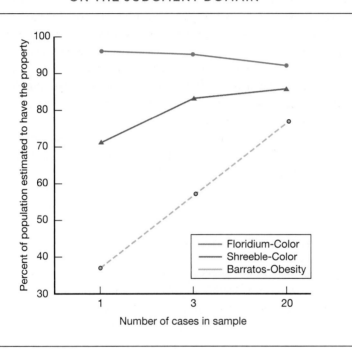

FIGURE 12.3   THE IMPACT OF SAMPLE SIZE DEPENDS ON THE JUDGMENT DOMAIN

Participants were told that they were visitors to an island and that they had viewed one native (from the Barratos tribe) and had observed that he was obese. They were then asked how likely they thought it was that all Barratos were obese. Other participants were asked whether they would draw a conclusion after seeing *three* Barratos, or *twenty*. Participants were also asked whether they would draw conclusions after observing the color of one Shreeble (a type of bird on the island) or three, or twenty. They were likewise asked whether they would draw conclusions after observing samples of a new mineral, Floridium. The data show that participants' willingness to draw conclusions depended heavily on the category — presumably, because the participants were guided by background knowledge that samples of minerals tend to resemble one another; that individual birds, however, can differ from one another; and certainly, that tribal members can differ from one another. As a result, with the more diverse groups, participants insisted on gaining more evidence before drawing any conclusions.   (AFTER NISBETT ET AL., 1983) students who were taking an undergraduate course in statistics. Half of the students were contacted during the first week of the semester; half were contacted during the last week.

In their course, these students had learned about the importance of sample size. They'd been reminded that accidents do happen, but that accidents don't keep happening over and over. Therefore, a pattern visible in a small sample of data might be the result of some accident, but a pattern evident in a large sample probably isn't. Consequently, large samples are more reliable, more trustworthy, than small samples.

This classroom training had a broad impact. In the phone interview (which was—as far as the students knew—not in any way connected to their course), one of the questions involved a comparison between how well a baseball player did in his first year and how well he did in the rest of his career. This is essentially a question about sample size (with the first year being just a sample of the player's overall performance). Did the students realize that sample size was relevant here? For those contacted early in the term, only 16% gave answers that showed any consideration of sample size. For those contacted later, the number of answers influenced by sample size more than doubled (to 37%).

It seems, then, that how well people think about evidence can be improved, and the improvement applies to problems in new domains and new contexts. Training in statistics, it appears, can have widespread benefits. (For more on education effects, see Ferreira et al., 2006; Gigerenzer, Gaissmaier, Kurz-Milcke, Schwartz, & Woloshin, 2008; Lehman & Nisbett, 1990.)

The Cognitive Reflection Test

Even with education, some people make judgment errors all the time, and part of the explanation is suggested by the Cognitive Reflection Test (CRT). This test includes just three questions (**Figure 12.4**), and for each one,

---

FIGURE 12.4   THE COGNITIVE REFLECTION TEST (CRT)

(1) A bat and a ball cost $1.10 in total. The bat costs $1.00 more than the ball. How much does the ball cost? _____ cents

(2) If it takes 5 machines 5 minutes to make 5 widgets, how long would it take 100 machines to make 100 widgets? _____ minutes

(3) In a lake, there is a patch of lily pads. Every day, the patch doubles in size. If it takes 48 days for the patch to cover the entire lake, how long would it take for the patch to cover half of the lake? _____ days

there is an obvious answer that turns out to be *wrong*. To do well on the test, therefore, you need to resist the obvious answer and instead spend a moment reflecting on the question; if you do, the correct answer is readily available.

Many people perform poorly on the CRT, even when we test students at elite universities (Frederick, 2005). People who do well on the CRT, in contrast, are people who in general are more likely to rely on Type 2 thinking—and therefore likely to avoid the errors we've described in this chapter. In fact, people with higher CRT scores tend to have better scientific understanding, show greater skepticism about paranormal abilities, and even seem more analytic in their moral decisions (Baron, Scott, Fincher, & Metz, 2015; Pennycook, Cheyne, Koehler, & Fugelsang, 2016; Travers, Rolison, & Feeney, 2016). Let's be clear, though, that no one is immune to the errors we've been discussing, but the risk of error does seem lower in people who score well on the CRT.

TEST YOURSELF

6. What are the differences between Type 1 and Type 2 thinking?
7. What are some of the factors that can, in some settings, encourage (or perhaps allow) Type 2 thinking?

Confirmation and Disconfirmation

In this chapter so far, we've been looking at a type of thinking that requires **induction**—the process through which you make forecasts about new cases, based on cases you've observed so far. Just as important, though, is **deduction**—a process in which you start with claims or assertions that you count as "given" and ask what follows from these premises. For example, perhaps you're already convinced that red wine gives you headaches or that relationships based on physical attraction rarely last. You might want to ask: What follows from this? What implications do these claims have for your other beliefs or actions?

Deduction has many functions, including the fact that it helps keep your beliefs in touch with reality. After all, if deduction leads you to a prediction based on your beliefs and the prediction turns out to be *wrong*, this indicates that something is off track in your beliefs—so that claims you thought were solidly established aren't so solid after all.

Does human reasoning respect this principle? If you encounter evidence confirming your beliefs, does this strengthen your convictions? If evidence challenging your beliefs should come your way, do you adjust?

Confirmation Bias

It seems sensible that in evaluating any belief, you'd want to take a balanced approach—considering evidence that supports the belief, and weighing that information against other evidence that might challenge the belief. And, in fact, evidence that challenges you is especially valuable; many authors argue that this type of evidence is more informative than evidence that seems to support you. (For the classic statement of this position, see Popper, 1934.)

"MY PARENTS DIED. THEIR PARENTS DIED. THEIR PARENTS DIED... IT RUNS IN THE FAMILY."

DRAWING CONCLUSIONS FROM EVIDENCE

We rely on induction in many settings. Sometimes we misread the pattern. Sometimes we detect the pattern but draw the wrong conclusions.

There's a substantial gap, however, between these suggestions about what people *should* do and what they actually do. Specifically, people routinely display a pattern we've already mentioned, *confirmation bias*: a greater sensitivity to confirming evidence and a tendency to neglect disconfirming evidence. Let's emphasize, however, that this is an "umbrella" term, because confirmation bias can take many different forms (see **Figure 12.5**). What all the forms have in common is the tendency to protect your beliefs from challenge. (See, among others, Gilovich, 1991; Kassin, Bogart, & Kerner, 2012; Schulz-Hardt, Frey, Lüthgens, & Moscovici, 2000; Stangor & McMillan, 1992.)

In an early demonstration of confirmation bias, Wason (1966, 1968) presented research participants with a series of numbers, such as "2, 4, 6." The participants were told that this trio of numbers conformed to a specific rule, and their task was to figure out the rule. Participants were allowed to propose their own trios of numbers ("Does '8, 10, 12' follow the rule?"), and in each case the experimenter responded appropriately ("Yes, it follows the rule" or "No, it doesn't"). Then, once participants were satisfied that they had discovered the rule, they announced their "discovery."

The rule was actually quite simple: The three numbers had to be in ascending order. For example, "1, 3, 5" follows the rule, but "6, 4, 2" does not, and neither does "10, 10, 10." Despite this simplicity, participants had difficulty discovering the rule, often requiring many minutes. This was largely due to the

FIGURE 12.5 CONFIRMATION BIAS

Confirmation bias takes many forms:

- First, when people are assessing a belief or a hypothesis, they're more likely to seek evidence that might confirm the belief than evidence that might disconfirm it.
- Second, when disconfirming evidence is made available to them, people often fail to use it in adjusting their beliefs.
- Third, when people encounter confirming evidence, they take it at face value; when they encounter disconfirming evidence, they reinterpret the evidence to diminish its impact.
- Fourth, people often show better memory for confirming evidence than for disconfirming evidence, and, if they do recall the latter, they remember it in a distorted form that robs the evidence of its force.
- Finally, people often fail to consider alternative hypotheses that might explain the available data just as well as their current hypothesis does.

"Confirmation bias" is a blanket term that refers to many specific effects. We've listed some of these effects here.

type of information they requested as they tried to evaluate their hypotheses: To an overwhelming extent, they sought to *confirm* the rules they had proposed; requests for disconfirmation were relatively rare. And it's noteworthy that those few participants who did seek out disconfirmation for their hypotheses were more likely to discover the rule. It seems, then, that confirmation bias was strongly present in this experiment and interfered with performance.

Reinterpreting Disconfirming Evidence

Here's a different manifestation of confirmation bias. When people encounter information consistent with their beliefs, they're likely to take the evidence at face value, accepting it without challenge or question. In contrast, when people encounter evidence that's inconsistent with their beliefs, they're often skeptical and scrutinize this new evidence, seeking flaws or ambiguities.

One study examined gamblers who bet on professional football games (Gilovich, 1983; see also Gilovich, 1991; Gilovich & Douglas, 1986). These people all believed they had good strategies for picking winning teams, and their faith in these strategies was undiminished by a series of losses. Why is this? It's because the gamblers didn't understand their losses as "losses." Instead, they remembered them as flukes or oddball coincidences: "I was right. New York was going to win if it hadn't been for that crazy injury to their running back"; "I was correct in picking St. Louis. They would have won except for that goofy bounce the ball took after the kickoff." In this way, winning bets were remembered as wins; losing bets were remembered as "near wins." No wonder, then, that the gamblers maintained their views despite the contrary evidence provided by their empty wallets.

Belief Perseverance

Even when disconfirming evidence is undeniable, people sometimes don't use it, leading to a phenomenon called **belief perseverance**. Participants in a classic study were asked to read a series of suicide notes; their task was to figure out which notes were authentic, collected by the police, and which were fake, written by other students as an exercise. As participants offered their judgments, they received feedback about how well they were doing—that is, how accurate they were in detecting the authentic notes. The trick, though, was that the feedback had nothing to do with the participants' actual judgments. By prearrangement, some participants were told that they were performing at a level well above average in this task; other participants were told the opposite—that they were performing at a level far below average (Ross, Lepper, & Hubbard, 1975; also Ross & Anderson, 1982).

Later on, participants were debriefed. They were told that the feedback they had received was bogus and had nothing to do with their performance. They were even shown the experimenter's instruction sheet, which had assigned them in advance to the *success* or *failure* group. They were then asked a variety of additional questions, including some for which they had to assess their own "social sensitivity." Specifically, they were asked to rate their actual ability, as they perceived it, in tasks like the suicide-note task.

Let's emphasize that participants were making these judgments about themselves after they'd been told clearly that the feedback they'd received was randomly determined and had no credibility whatsoever. Nonetheless, participants who had received the "above average" feedback continued to think of their social sensitivity as being above average, and likewise their ability to judge suicide notes. Those who had received the "below average" feedback showed the opposite pattern. All participants, in other words, persevered in their beliefs even when the basis for the belief had been completely discredited.

What is going on here? Imagine yourself as one of the participants, and let's say that we've told you that you're performing rather poorly at the suicide-note task. As you digest this new "information" about yourself, you'll probably wonder, "Could this be true? Am I less sensitive than I think I am?" To check on this possibility, you might search through your memory, looking for evidence that will help you evaluate this suggestion.

What sort of evidence will you seek? This is where confirmation bias comes into play. Because of this bias, chances are good that you'll check on the researcher's information by seeking other facts or other episodes in your memory that might confirm your lack of social perception. As a result, you'll soon have two sources of evidence for your social insensitivity: the (bogus)

Virtually all climate experts agree that climate change is real and to a large extent human-caused. And the consequences of climate change are already visible. The polar ice is melting. Wet areas are becoming wetter, and dry areas drier. The frequency of severe storms is increasing.

To educate the public about climate change, various groups offer a "balanced" presentation on this issue: They invite a pair of speakers, chosen so that the audience will hear opposing viewpoints. But this "balance" doesn't represent the distribution of expert views: The speaker on one side is representing the position held by more than 90% of the experts who have studied this issue. The speaker on the other side is drawn from the tiny group that holds a nonstandard view.

What will be the impact of this "balanced" presentation? A recent study was designed to model the situation. In one version of the procedure, participants were told directly how many critics had given positive reviews to a movie and how many had given negative reviews. In addition, some participants were given an apparently balanced presentation—an excerpt from the most positive review and an excerpt from the most negative one (Koehler, 2016).

In this study, the balanced presentation seemed to draw participants' attention away from the fact that a clear majority of the critics had loved the movie, and only a few hadn't. As a result, the balanced presentation made it more difficult for participants to distinguish movies that virtually all the critics agreed were good from movies for which there was little agreement.

Movie reviews, though, can be quite subjective, and perhaps the participants didn't trust the reviewers at all. A follow-up study used the same procedure, but focused on technical issues for which ordinary citizens have little basis for judgment. One of the test cases involved economists' views of the likely impact of a carbon tax; another case focused on "surge pricing" for taxicab drivers. Here, too, an apparently balanced presentation seemed to mislead participants. Even though they were plainly told how many experts agreed with each position, the balanced presentation caused participants to perceive less agreement among the experts than there actually was. The balanced presentation also made participants less likely to believe there was enough agreement among the experts to justify following the experts' advice.

Of course, sometimes experts are wrong. And sometimes the view expressed by a minority of the experts is correct. Even so, it does seem reasonable to take experts' advice more seriously when virtually all of them are on the same side of the issue. It seems, though, that a "balanced presentation" can pull people away from this reasonable perspective. Worse, this problem is amplified by the fact that the Internet makes it all too easy to find opposing opinions for almost any issue. "What do you mean, humans are causing climate change? Here's a blog in which the author argues . . ." Or "How can you say that ESP doesn't exist? I saw on FaceBook that . . ."

How to respond to these findings? We all need to be alert to where our information is coming from—and take information more seriously if the source is credible. We also need to be alert to evidence that tells us whether an assessment of the facts comes from the majority of relevant authorities or from a single (and perhaps idiosyncratic) writer. We need good information in forming our judgments, and we should be aware of the ways in which we're sometimes misled by poor-quality information!

HOW LOGICAL ARE WE?

Errors in logic are extraordinarily common—in adults and in children, and even when we are contemplating very simple logical arguments.

TEST YOURSELF

8. What is confirmation bias? What are some of the specific forms that confirmation bias can take?

9. What is the role of confirmation bias in producing belief perseverance?

feedback provided by the researcher, and the supporting information you came up with yourself, thanks to your (selective) memory search. So even if the researcher discredits the information he provided, you still have the information you provided yourself, and on this basis you might maintain your belief. (For discussion, see Nisbett & Ross, 1980; also Johnson & Seifert, 1994.)

Of course, in this experiment, participants could be led either to an enhanced estimate of their own social sensitivity or to a diminished estimate, depending on which false information they were given in the first place. Presumably, this is because the range of episodes in participants' memories is wide: In some previous episodes they've been sensitive, and in some they haven't been. Therefore, if they search through their memories seeking to confirm the hypothesis that they've been sensitive in the past, they'll find confirming evidence. If they search through memory seeking to confirm the opposite hypothesis, this too will be possible. In short, they can confirm either hypothesis via a suitably selective memory search. This outcome highlights the dangers built into a selective search of the evidence and, more broadly, the danger associated with confirmation bias.

Logic

In displaying confirmation bias, people sometimes seem to defy logic. "If my gambling strategy is good, then I'll win my next bet. But I lose the bet. Therefore, my strategy is good." How should we think about this? In general, do people fail to understand—or perhaps ignore—the rules of *logic*?

Reasoning about Syllogisms

Over the years, a number of theorists have proposed that human thought does follow the rules of logic, and so, when people make reasoning errors, the problem must lie elsewhere: carelessness, perhaps, or a misinterpretation

FIGURE 12.6 EXAMPLES OF CATEGORICAL SYLLOGISMS

All of the syllogisms shown here are valid—that is, if the two premises are true, then the conclusion must be true.

of the problem (Boole, 1854; Mill, 1874; Piaget, 1952). It turns out, however, that errors in logical reasoning happen all the time. If people are careless or misread problems, they do so rather frequently. This is evident, for example, in studies using **categorical syllogisms**—a type of logical argument that begins with two assertions (the problem's **premises**), each containing a statement about a category, as shown in **Figure 12.6**. The syllogism can then be completed with a conclusion that may or may not follow from these premises. The cases shown in the figure are all **valid syllogisms**—that is, the conclusion *does* follow from the premises stated. In contrast, here is an example of an **invalid syllogism**:

All P are M.

All S are M.

Therefore, all S are P.

To see that this is invalid, try translating it into concrete terms, such as "All plumbers are mortal" and "All secretaries are mortal." Both of these are surely true, but it doesn't follow from this that "All secretaries are plumbers."

Research participants who are asked to reason about syllogisms do remarkably poorly—a fact that the research has confirmed for many years. Chapman and Chapman (1959), for example, gave their participants a number of syllogisms, including the one just discussed, with premises of "All P are M," and "All S are M." The vast majority of participants endorsed the invalid conclusion "All S are P." Only 9% got this problem right. More recently, other studies, with other problems, have yielded similar data—with error rates regularly as high as 70% to 90%. (Khlemani & Johnson-Laird, 2012, provide a review.)

Belief Bias

Errors in logical reasoning are also quite *systematic*. For example, people often show a pattern called **belief bias**: If a syllogism's conclusion happens to be something people believe to be true anyhow, they're likely to judge the conclusion as following logically from the premises. Conversely, if the conclusion happens to be something they believe to be false, they're likely to reject the conclusion as invalid (Evans, 2012b; Trippas, Thompson, & Handley, 2017; Trippas, Verde, & Handley, 2014).

This strategy at first appears reasonable. Why wouldn't you endorse conclusions you believe to be true, based on the totality of your knowledge, and reject claims you believe to be false? Let's be clear, though, that there's a problem here: When people show the belief-bias pattern, they're failing to distinguish between good arguments (those that are truly persuasive) and bad ones. As a result, they'll endorse an illogical argument if it happens to lead to conclusions they like, and they'll reject a logical argument if it leads to conclusions they have doubts about.

The Four-Card Task

Similar conclusions derive from research on reasoning about **conditional statements**. These are statements of the "If X, then Y" format, with the first statement providing a *condition* under which the second statement is guaranteed to be true.

Often, psychologists study conditional reasoning with the **selection task** (sometimes called the **four-card task**). In this task, participants are shown four playing cards, as in **Figure 12.7** (after Wason, 1966, 1968). The participants are told that each card has a number on one side and a letter on the

---

FIGURE 12.7   THE FOUR-CARD TASK

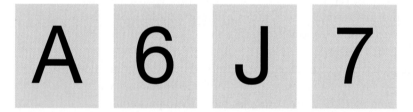

Which cards would you turn over to test this rule: "If a card has a vowel on one side, it must have an even number on the other side"? If we turn over the "A" card and find an even number, that's consistent with the rule. But if we turn it over and find an odd number, that's inconsistent. Therefore, by turning over the "A," we'll discover whether this card is consistent with the rule or not. In other words, there's something to be learned by turning over this card. What about the "J"? The rule makes no claims about what's on the flip side of a consonant card, so no matter what we find on the other side, it won't challenge the rule. Therefore, there's nothing to be learned by turning over this card; we already know (without flipping it over) that it's consistent with the rule. By similar reasoning, we'll learn nothing by turning over the "6"; no matter what we find, it satisfies the rule. Finally, if we turn over the "7" and a consonant is on the other side, this fits with the rule. If there's a vowel on the other side, this doesn't fit. Therefore, we do want to turn over this card, because there's a chance that we might find something informative.

other. Their task is to evaluate this rule: "If a card has a vowel on one side, it must have an even number on the other side." Which cards must be turned over to put this rule to the test?

In many studies, roughly a third of the participants turn over just the "A" card to check for an even number. In addition, many turn over both the "A" and the "6." However, just a handful of participants give the correct answer—turning over the "A" and the "7." Plainly, performance is atrocious in this problem, with more than 90% of participants giving wrong answers. (See the caption for Figure 12.7 for an explanation of the right answer.)

Performance is much better, though, with some variations of the four-card task. For example, Griggs and Cox (1982) asked their participants to test rules like this one: "If a person is drinking beer, then the person must be at least 21 years old." As in the other studies, participants were shown four cards and asked which cards they would need to turn over to test the rule (see **Figure 12.8**). In this version, participants did quite well: 73% (correctly) selected the card labeled "Drinking a beer" and also the card labeled "16 years of age." They did not select "Drinking a Coke" or "22 years of age."

It seems, then, that how well you think depends on what you're thinking about. The problems posed in Figures 12.7 and 12.8 have the same logical structure, but they yield very different performances. Researchers have offered a variety of explanations for this pattern, but the data don't allow us to determine which account is preferable. (For some of the options, see Almor & Sloman, 2000; Cheng, Holyoak, Nisbett, & Oliver, 1986; Cummins, 2004; Cummins & Allen, 1998; Gigerenzer & Hug, 1992; Girotto, 2004; Nisbett, 1993.)

Even with this unsettled issue, it's important to note the parallels between these points and our earlier discussion of how people make judgments about the evidence they encounter. In both domains (inductive judgments and deductive reasoning), it's easy to document errors in people's thinking.

FIGURE 12.8   AN EASIER VERSION OF THE FOUR-CARD TASK

| DRINKING A BEER | 22 YEARS OF AGE | DRINKING A COKE | 16 YEARS OF AGE |

Participants do reasonably well with this version of the four-card task. Here, each card shows a person's age on one side and what the person is drinking on the other side. The participants' task is to select the cards that would have to be turned over in order to test the following rule: "If a person is drinking beer, then the person must be over 21 years of age."

TEST YOURSELF

10. What is belief bias? Why is belief bias a problem in logical reasoning?

11. What is the four-card (or selection) task? How well do people perform in this task?

But in both domains we can also document higher-quality thinking, and this more-sophisticated thinking can be encouraged by the "right" circumstances. Specifically, in our discussion of judgment, we listed several factors that can trigger better thinking. Now, in our discussion of logic, we've seen that a problem's *content* can sometimes trigger more accurate reasoning. Thus, the quality of thinking is certainly uneven—but with the right triggers (and, it turns out, proper education), it can be improved.

Decision Making

We turn now to a different type of thinking: the thinking that underlies *choices*. Choices, big and small, fill your life, whether you're choosing what courses to take next semester, how to spend your next vacation, or whether to stay with your current partner. How do you make any of these decisions?

Costs and Benefits

Each of us has our own values—things we prize, or conversely, things we hope to avoid. Likewise, each of us has a series of goals—things we hope to accomplish, things we hope to see. The obvious suggestion, then, is that we use these values and goals in making decisions. In choosing courses for next semester, for example, you'll choose classes that are interesting (something you value) and also those that help fill the requirements for your major (one of your goals). In choosing a medical treatment, you hope to avoid pain and also to retain your physical capacities as long as possible.

To put this a bit more formally, each decision will have certain costs attached to it (consequences that will carry you farther from your goals) as well as benefits (consequences moving you toward your goals and providing things you value). In deciding, you weigh the costs against the benefits and seek a path that will minimize the former and maximize the latter. When you have several options, you choose the one that provides the best balance of benefits and costs.

Economists cast these ideas in terms of **utility maximization**. The word "utility" refers to the value that you place on a particular outcome—some people gain utility from eating in fancy restaurants; others gain utility from watching their savings accumulate in a bank account; still others, from giving their money to charity. No matter how you gain utility, the proposal is that you try to make decisions that will bring you as much utility as possible. (See von Neumann & Morgenstern, 1947; also see Baron, 1988; Speekenbrink & Shanks, 2012.)

Framing of Outcomes

It's remarkably easy, however, to find cases in which decisions are guided by principles that have little to do with utility maximization. Consider the problem posed in **Figure 12.9**. In this choice, a huge majority of people—72%—choose Program A, selecting the sure bet rather than the gamble (Tversky & Kahneman, 1987; also Willemsen, Böckenholt, & Johnson, 2011). Now consider the problem in **Figure 12.10**. Here, an enormous

FIGURE 12.9 THE DISEASE PROBLEM: POSITIVE FRAME

Imagine that the United States is preparing for the outbreak of an unusual disease, which is expected to kill 600 people. Two alternative programs to combat the disease have been proposed. Assume that the exact scientific estimates of the consequences of the programs are as follows:

If Program A is adopted, 200 people will be saved.

If Program B is adopted, there is a one-third probability that 600 people will be saved, and a two-thirds probability that no people will be saved.

Which program would you prefer? There is clearly no right answer to this question; one could defend selecting the "risky" choice (Program B) or the less rewarding but less risky choice (Program A). The clear majority of respondents, however, lean toward Program A, with 72% choosing it over Program B. Note that this problem is "positively" framed in terms of lives "saved." (FROM A. TVERSKY & D. KAHNEMAN. "THE FRAMING OF DECISIONS AND THE PSYCHOLOGY OF CHOICE," *SCIENCE* 211 © 1981 AAAS. REPRINTED WITH PERMISSION.)

FIGURE 12.10 THE DISEASE PROBLEM: NEGATIVE FRAME

Imagine that the United States is preparing for the outbreak of an unusual disease, which is expected to kill 600 people. Two alternative programs to combat the disease have been proposed. Assume that the exact scientific estimates of the consequences of the programs are as follows:

If Program A is adopted, 400 people will die.

If Program B is adopted, there is a one-third probability that nobody will die, and a two-thirds probability that 600 people will die.

Which program would you prefer? This problem is identical in content to the one shown in Figure 12.9: 400 dead out of 600 people is the same as 200 saved out of 600. Nonetheless, respondents react to the problem shown here rather differently than they do to the one in Figure 12.9. In the "lives saved" version, 72% choose Program A. In the "will die" version, 78% choose Program B. Essentially, by changing the phrasing we reverse the pattern of respondents' preferences. (FROM A. TVERSKY & D. KAHNEMAN. "THE FRAMING OF DECISIONS AND THE PSYCHOLOGY OF CHOICE," *SCIENCE* 211 © 1981 AAAS. REPRINTED WITH PERMISSION.)

majority—78%—choose Program B, preferring the gamble rather than the sure bet.

The puzzle lies in the fact that the two problems are objectively identical: 200 people saved out of 600 is the same as 400 dead out of 600. Nonetheless, the change in how the problem is phrased—that is, the **framing** of the decision—has an enormous impact, turning a 3-to-1 preference (72% to 28%) in one direction into a 4-to-1 preference (78% to 22%) in the opposite direction.

We should emphasize that there's nothing wrong with participants' individual choices. In either Figure 12.9 or Figure 12.10, there's no "right answer," and you can persuasively defend either the decision to avoid risk (by selecting Program A) or the decision to gamble (by choosing Program B). The problem lies in the contradiction created by choosing Program A in one context and Program B in the other context. In fact, if a single participant is given both frames on slightly different occasions, he's quite likely to contradict himself. For that matter, if you wanted to manipulate someone's evaluation of these programs (e.g., if you wanted to manipulate voters or shoppers), then framing effects provide an effective way to do this.

Related effects are easy to demonstrate. When participants are given the first problem in **Figure 12.11**, almost three quarters of them (72%) choose Option A—the sure gain of $100. Participants contemplating the second

---

FIGURE 12.11   FRAMING EFFECTS IN MONETARY CHOICES

Problem 1

Assume yourself richer by $300 than you are today. You have to choose between:
A. a sure gain of $100
B. 50% chance to gain $200 and 50% chance to gain nothing

Problem 2

Assume yourself richer by $500 than you are today. You have to choose between:
A. a sure loss of $100
B. 50% chance to lose nothing and 50% chance to lose $200

These two problems are identical. In both cases, the first option leaves you with $400, while the second option leaves you with an even chance between $300 and $500. Despite this identity, respondents prefer the first option in Problem 1 (72% select this option) and the second option in Problem 2 (64% select this option). Once again, by changing the frames we reverse the pattern of preferences.

problem generally choose Option B, with 64% going for this choice (Tversky & Kahneman, 1987). Note, though, that the problems are once again identical. Both pose the question of whether you'd rather end up with a certain $400 or with an even chance of ending up with either $300 or $500. Despite this equivalence, participants treat these problems very differently, preferring the sure thing in one case and the gamble in the other.

In fact, there's a reliable pattern in these data. If the frame casts a choice in terms of *losses*, decision makers tend to be **risk seeking**—that is, they prefer to gamble, presumably attracted by the idea that maybe they'll avoid the loss. So, for example, when the disease problem is cast in terms people dying (Figure 12.10), people choose Program B, apparently focused on the hope that, with this program, there may be no loss of life. Likewise, Problem 2 in Figure 12.11 casts the options in terms of financial losses, and this, too, triggers risk seeking: Here, people reliably choose the 50-50 gamble over the sure loss. (This pattern—a willingness to take risks—is especially strong when people contemplate *large* losses; Harinck, Van Dijk, Van Beest, & Mersmann, 2007; also see LeBoeuf & Shafir, 2012.)

In contrast, if the frame casts a choice in terms of gains, decision makers are likely to show **risk aversion**: They refuse to gamble, choosing instead to hold tight to what they already have. Thus, Figure 12.9 casts the disease problem in terms of gains (the number of people saved), and this leads people to prefer the risk-free choice (Program A) over the gamble offered by Program B. (And likewise for Problem 1 in Figure 12.11.)

Again, there's nothing wrong with either of these strategies by itself: If someone prefers to be risk seeking, this is fine; if someone prefers to be risk averse, this is okay too. The problem arises when people flip-flop between these strategies, depending on how the problem is framed.

Framing of Questions and Evidence

Related effects emerge with changes in how a *question* is framed. For example, imagine that you're on a jury in a messy divorce case; the parents are battling over who will get custody of their only child. The two parents have the attributes listed in **Figure 12.12**. To which parent will you award sole custody of the child?

Research participants who are asked this question tend to favor Parent B by a wide margin. After all, this parent does have a close relationship with the child and has a good income. Note, though, that we asked to which parent you would *award* custody. Results are different if we ask participants to which parent they would *deny* custody. In this case, 55% of the participants choose to deny custody to Parent B (and so, by default, end up awarding custody to Parent A). In other words, the decision is simply reversed: With the "award" question, most participants award custody to Parent B. With the "deny" question, the majority deny custody to Parent B—and so give custody to Parent A (Shafir, 1993; Shafir, Simonson, & Tversky, 1993).

FIGURE 12.12   THE INFLUENCE OF HOW A QUESTION IS FORMED

Imagine that you serve on the jury of an only-child sole-custody case following a relatively messy divorce. The facts of the case are complicated by ambiguous economic, social, and emotional considerations, and you decide to base your decision entirely on the following few observations. To which parent would you award sole custody of the child?

Parent A   average income
average health
average working hours
reasonable rapport with the child
relatively stable social life

Parent B   above-average income
very close relationship with the child
extremely active social life
lots of work-related travel
minor health problems

When asked the question shown here, 64% of the research participants decided to award sole custody to Parent B. Other participants, however, were asked a different question: "To which parent would you deny sole custody?" Asked this question, 55% of the participants chose to deny sole custody to Parent B (and so, by default, to award custody to Parent A). Thus, with the "award" question, a majority votes for granting custody to Parent B; with the "deny" question, a majority votes for granting custody to Parent A.

People are also influenced by how *evidence* is framed. For example, they rate a basketball player more highly if the player has made 75% of his free throws, compared to their ratings of a player who has missed 25% of his free throws. They're more likely to endorse a medical treatment with a "50% success rate" than one with a "50% failure rate." And so on. (See Levin & Gaeth, 1988; Levin, Schnittjer, & Thee, 1988; also Dunning & Parpal, 1989.)

Opt-In versus Opt-Out

A related pattern again hinges on how a decision is presented. Let's start with the fact that more than 100,000 people in the United States are waiting for medically necessary organ transplants. You can help these people—and save lives—by agreeing to be an organ donor. If so, then, in the event of your death, healthy organs from your body might help as many as 50 people.

In light of these facts, it's discouraging that relatively few Americans agree to be organ donors, and the reason may lie in the way the decision to donate is framed. In the United States, decisions about organ donation are "opt-in" decisions: The potential donor has to say explicitly that he or she wishes to be a donor; otherwise, the assumption is that the person will not be an organ donor. Other countries use the reverse system: Unless people say explicitly that they don't want to be donors ("opt-out"), the assumption is that they will be donors.

How much does this contrast matter? In Germany, which relies on an opt-in system like the one used in the United States, only 12% of German citizens have agreed to be organ donors. Neighboring Austria, with a reasonably similar culture, uses an opt-out system, and here 99% of the citizens agree to be donors (Johnson & Goldstein, 2003; Thaler, 2009).

Similar patterns have been observed with other decisions—for example, the decision to participate in "green energy" programs, or the step of signing up for a plan that will make an automatic monthly contribution to your pension fund (Sunstein, 2016). In each case, there's a sharp contrast between the number of people who say they're in favor of these programs and the number of people who actually participate. And, in each case, part of the reason for non-participation is the reliance on an opt-in system.

This pattern has broad implications for public policy, and some public figures suggest that governments should design programs that "nudge" people to sign up for green energy, to save for their retirement, and so on. (See Thaler & Sunstein, 2009; Sunstein, 2016; although, for discussion, see Burzzone, 2008; Randhawa, Brocklehurst, Pateman, & Kinsella, 2010.) But, in addition, the contrast between opt-in and opt-out decisions reminds us that our choices are governed not just by what's at stake, but also by how the decision is framed.

Maximizing Utility versus Seeing Reasons

In case after case, then, people are powerfully influenced by changes in how a decision is framed, even though, on most accounts, these changes have no impact on the utility you'd receive from the various options. To explain these findings, one possibility is that people are trying to use (something like) utility calculations when making decisions, but aren't very good at it. As a result, they're pulled off track by distractions, including how the decision is framed. A different possibility, though, is more radical. Perhaps we're not guided by utilities at all. Instead, suppose our goal is simply to make decisions that we feel good about, decisions that we think are reasonable and justified. This view of decision making is called **reason-based choice** (Shafir et al., 1993; also Redelmeier & Shafir, 1995). To see how this account plays out, let's go back to the divorce/custody case just described. Half of the participants in this study were asked to which parent they would *award* custody. These participants therefore asked themselves: "What would justify giving custody to one parent or another?" and this drew their attention to each parent's positive traits. As a result, they were swayed by Parent B's above-average income and close relationship with the child. Other

ENDOWMENT EFFECT

What produces the contrast between opt-in and opt-out decisions? Part of the answer is the "endowment effect"—the tendency to put a higher value on your current status and possessions simply because they are currently your own. In an early demonstration of this effect, one group of participants was given a coffee mug and then given the opportunity to sell it. A different group of participants was given cash and then the opportunity to buy the coffee mug. The first group set a value on the mug that was twice as high as the value set by the second group; apparently, the simple fact of already possessing the mug doubled its value. (See Kahneman, Knetsch, & Thaler, 1990; also see Carmon & Ariely, 2000; Morewedge & Giblin, 2015.)

participants were asked to which parent they would *deny* custody, and this led them to ask: "What would justify this denial?" This approach drew attention to the parents' negative attributes—especially, Parent B's heavy travel schedule and health problems.

In both cases, then, the participants relied on *justification* in making their decision. As it turns out, though, the shift in framing caused a change in the factors relevant to that justification, and this is why the shift in framing reversed the pattern of decisions. (For a different example, see **Figure 12.13.**)

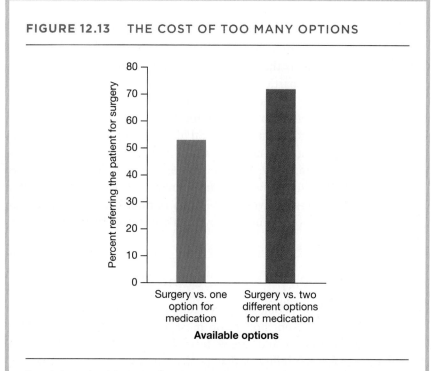

FIGURE 12.13   THE COST OF TOO MANY OPTIONS

Practicing physicians were given a description of a patient and were asked to choose a treatment. For one group of physicians, the choices offered were surgery and a specific medication. For a second group, the choices included surgery, the same medication, and a different medication. When doctors were choosing between one drug and surgery, many thought the drug was worth a try, and only 53% referred the patient for surgery. When the doctors had three choices, though, they found it difficult to justify choosing either drug over the other; each had its advantages and disadvantages. And, with no good reasons for choosing either drug, the physicians chose neither, and so most—72%—opted for surgery instead. This outcome makes little sense from a utility perspective, but it's easy to understand if we assume that the doctors were looking for *reasons* for their decisions, and took action only when they could justify the action.   (AFTER REDELMEIER & SHAFIR, 1995)

Emotion

Still another factor needs to be included in our theorizing, because people's decisions are powerfully influenced by *emotion*. (See, among others, Kahneman, 2003; Loewenstein, Weber, Hsee, & Welch, 2001; Medin, Schwartz, Blok, & Birnbaum, 1999; Slovic, Finucane, Peters, & MacGregor, 2002; Weber & Johnson, 2009.)

We mentioned the importance of emotion early in the chapter, when we saw that Elliot, unable to feel emotion, seems unable to make decisions. But what is the linkage between emotion and decision making? At the chapter's start, we pointed out that many decisions involve an element of risk. (Should you try out a new, experimental drug? Should we rely more on nuclear power? Should you sign up for the new professor's course, even though you don't know much about her?) In cases like these, we suggested, people seem to assess the risk in emotional terms. For example, they ask themselves how much dread they experience when thinking about a nuclear accident, and they use that dread as an indicator of risk (Fischhoff, Slovic, & Lichtenstein, 1978; Slovic et al., 2002; also Pachur, Hertwig, & Steinmann, 2012).

But there are also other ways that emotion can influence decisions. Here, we start with the fact that—of course—*memories* can cause a strong bodily reaction. In remembering a scary movie, for example, you again become tense and your palms might sweat. In remembering a romantic encounter, you again become aroused. In the same way, *anticipated events* can also produce bodily arousal, and Damasio (1994) suggests that you use these sensations—he calls them **somatic markers**—as a way of evaluating your options. So, in making a choice, you literally rely on your "gut feelings" to assess your options—an approach that pulls you toward options that trigger positive feelings and away from ones that trigger negative feelings.

We've mentioned that a particular region of the brain—the orbitofrontal cortex (at the base of the frontal lobe, just behind the eyeballs)—is crucial in your use of these somatic markers, because this is the brain region that enables you to interpret your emotions. When this region is damaged (as it was in Elliot, the case we met at the chapter's start), decision making is markedly impaired. (See Damasio, 1994; Naqvi, Shiv, & Bechara, 2006. Also see Coricelli, Dolan, & Sirigu, 2007; Dunn et al., 2010; Jones et al., 2012; also **Figure 12.14.**)

Predicting Emotions

Here's another way emotion shapes decision making: Many decisions depend on a *forecast* of future emotions. Imagine that you're choosing between two apartments you might rent for next year. One is cheaper and larger but faces a noisy street. Will you just get used to the noise, so that sooner or later it won't bother you? If so, then you should take the apartment. Or will the noise grow increasingly obnoxious as the weeks pass? If so, you should pay the extra money for the other apartment. Plainly, your decision here depends

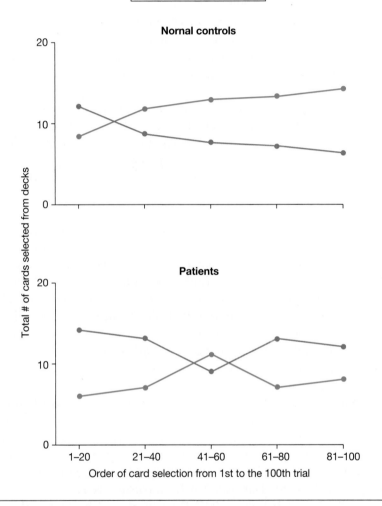

FIGURE 12.14   EMOTION AND DECISION MAKING

In this study, participants had to choose cards from one of two decks. One deck (the "disadvantageous" one) offered large payoffs but also large penalties; so, in the long run, it was better to choose from the other ("advantageous" deck), which provided smaller payoffs but also smaller penalties. "Normal control" participants—people with no brain damage—quickly learned about the decks and were soon making most of their choices from the advantageous deck (and so earned more overall). Participants with damage to the orbitofrontal cortex, in contrast, continued to favor the risky deck. Because of their brain damage, they were unable to use the somatic markers normally associated with risk—so they failed to heed the "gut feeling" that could have warned them against a dangerous choice.

on a prediction about the future—about how your likes and dislikes will change as time goes by.

Research suggests that **affective forecasting**—your predictions for your own emotions—is often inaccurate. In many studies, people have been asked how they would feel after a significant event; the events at issue include "breaking up with a romantic partner, losing an election, receiving a gift, learning they have a serious illness, failure to secure a promotion, scoring well on an exam," and so on (Gilbert & Ebert, 2002, p. 503; Kermer, Driver-Linn, Wilson, & Gilbert, 2006; see also **Figure 12.15**). People can usually predict whether their reaction will be positive or negative—and so they realize that scoring well on an exam will make them feel good and that a romantic breakup will make them feel bad. But people consistently overestimate how long these feelings will last—apparently underestimating their ability to adjust to changes in fortune, and also underestimating how easily they'll find excuses and rationalizations for their own mistakes. (For evidence, though, that people aren't awful all the time in predicting their own emotions, see Doré, Meksin, Mather, Hirst, & Ochsner, 2016.)

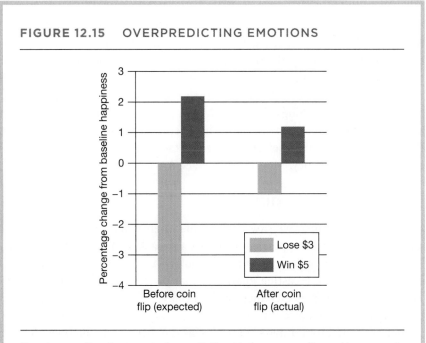

FIGURE 12.15   OVERPREDICTING EMOTIONS

People are often inaccurate in predicting their own emotions. Here, people sensibly predicted that they'd be unhappy if a gamble caused a $3 loss, but the sadness they actually experienced after the coin flip (right side of the figure) was much less than the sadness they'd predicted before the coin flip (left side of the figure). Likewise, people knew they'd be happy if they won $5, but the happiness they experienced was less than the happiness they'd predicted.   (AFTER KERMER ET AL., 2006)

off the mark.com
by Mark Parisi

offthemark.com

©2010 MARK PARISI DIST. BY UFS INC.

THE ROLE OF REGRET

In making decisions, people are powerfully motivated to avoid decisions they might regret later. It turns out, though, that when decisions work out badly, people generally experience far less regret over their choice than they'd anticipated.

As a related matter, people generally believe that their *current* feelings will last longer than they actually will—so they seem to be convinced that things that bother them now will continue to bother them in the future, and that things that please them now will continue to bring pleasure in the future. In both directions, people underestimate their own ability to adapt; as a result, they work to avoid things that they'd soon get used to anyhow and spend money for things that provide only short-term pleasure. (For the data, see Hsee & Hastie, 2005; Loewenstein & Schkade, 1999; Sevdalis & Harvey, 2007; Wilson, Wheatley, Meyers, Gilbert, & Axsom, 2000.)

Research on Happiness

Earlier in this chapter, we saw that people often make errors in judgment and reasoning. It now appears that people also lack skill in decision making. Framing effects leave them open to manipulation and self-contradiction, and errors in affective forecasting guarantee that people will often take steps to avoid regrets that in reality they wouldn't have felt, and pay for expensive toys that they'll soon lose interest in.

Some investigators draw strong conclusions from these findings. Maybe people really are incompetent in making decisions. Maybe they really don't know what will make them happy and might be better off if someone else made their choices for them. (See, e.g., Gilbert, 2006; Hsee, Hastie, & Chen, 2008; but for different views, see Kahneman, 2011; Keys & Schwartz, 2007; Weber & Johnson, 2009.)

These are strong claims, and they've been the subject of considerable debate. One author, for example, simply asserts that people are "predictably irrational" in their decision making and we're stuck with that (Ariely, 2009). Another author suggests that in general people are unable to move efficiently toward happiness; the best they can do is "stumble on happiness" (Gilbert, 2006). Yet another author notes that we all like to have choices but argues that having too many choices actually makes us less happy—a pattern he calls the "paradox of choice" (Schwartz, 2003).

Plainly, these are issues that demand scrutiny, with implications for how each of us lives and also, perhaps, implications that might guide government policies or business practices, helping people to become happy (Layrd, 2010; Thaler & Sunstein, 2009). In fact, the broad study of "subjective well-being"—what it is, what promotes it—has become an active and exciting area of research. In this way, the study of *how* people make decisions has led to important questions—and, perhaps, some helpful answers—regarding how they *should* make decisions. In the meantime, the research highlights some traps to avoid and suggests that each of us should be more careful in making the choices that shape our lives.

TEST YOURSELF

12. What does it mean to say that decision making is heavily influenced by how a decision is "framed"?
13. In what circumstances are people risk averse? When are they risk seeking?
14. What is affective forecasting, and how accurate are people in this type of forecasting?

COGNITIVE PSYCHOLOGY AND EDUCATION

making people smarter

This chapter documents the many errors people make in judgment, but it also offers encouragement: We can take certain steps to improve our judgments. Some of those steps involve changes in the decision-making environment—so that we can, for example, ensure that the evidence we consider has been converted to *frequencies* (e.g., "4 cases out of 100") rather than percentages ("4%") or proportions (".04"). This simple step, it seems, is enough to make judgments more accurate and to increase the likelihood that people will consider base rates when drawing conclusions.

Other steps, in contrast, involve *education*. As the chapter mentions, training students in *statistics* seems to improve their ability to think about evidence—including evidence that's obviously quantitative (e.g., a baseball player's batting average or someone's exam scores) and also evidence that's not, at first appearance, quantitative (e.g., thinking about how to interpret a dancer's audition or someone's job interview). The benefits of statistics training are large, with some studies showing error rates in subsequent reasoning essentially cut in half.

The key element in statistical training, however, is probably not in the mathematics per se. It is surely valuable to know the derivation of statistical equations or the procedure for using a statistics software package. For improvement of everyday judgment, however, the key involves the *perspective* that a statistics course encourages. This perspective helps you realize that certain observations (e.g., an audition or an interview) can be thought of as a *sample* of evidence, drawn from a larger pool of observations that potentially you could have made. The perspective also alerts you to the fact that a sample may not be representative of a broader population and that larger samples are more likely to be representative. For purposes of the statistics course itself, these are simple points; but being alert to these points can have striking and widespread consequences in your thinking about issues separate from the topics covered in the statistics class.

In fact, once we cast things in this way, it becomes clear that other forms of education can also have the same benefit. Many courses in psychology, for example, include coverage of methodological issues. These courses can highlight the fact that a single observation is just a sample and that a small sample sometimes cannot be trusted. These courses also cover topics that might reveal (and warn you against) confirmation bias or caution against the dangers of informally collected evidence. On this basis, it seems likely that other courses (not just statistics classes) can actually improve your everyday thinking—and, in fact, several studies confirm this optimistic conclusion.

Ironically, though, courses in the "hard sciences"—such as chemistry and physics—may not have these benefits. These courses are obviously of immense value for their own sake and will provide you with impressive and sophisticated skills. However, these courses may do little to improve your day-to-day reasoning. Why not? These courses do emphasize the process of testing hypotheses through the collection of evidence, as well as quantitative analysis of the evidence. But bear in mind that the data in, say, a chemistry course involve relatively homogeneous sets of observations: The weight of one carbon atom is the same as the weight of other carbon atoms; the temperature at which water boils (at a particular altitude) is the same on Tuesday as it is on Thursday. As a result, issues of *variability* in the data are less prominent in chemistry than in, say, psychology. (Compare how much *people* differ from one another to how much *benzene molecules* differ from one another.) This is a great strength for chemistry; it's one of the many reasons why chemistry has become such a sophisticated science. But this point means that chemists have to worry less than psychologists do about the variability within their sample, or whether their sample is of adequate size to compensate for the variability. As a result, chemistry courses often provide little practice in thinking about issues that are crucial when confronting the far messier data provided by day-to-day life.

In the same way, cause-and-effect sequences are often more straightforward in the "hard sciences" than they are in daily life: If a rock falls onto a surface, the impact depends simply on the mass of the rock and its velocity at the moment of collision. We don't need to ask what mood the rock was in, whether the surface was expecting the rock, or whether the rock was acting peculiarly on this occasion because it knew we were watching its behavior. But these latter factors are the sort of concerns that routinely crop up in the "messy" sciences—and in daily life. So here, too, the hard sciences gain enormous power from the "clean" nature of their data but, by the same token, don't provide practice in the skills of reasoning about these complications.

Which courses, therefore, should you take? Again, courses in chemistry and physics (and biology and mathematics) are important and will teach you sophisticated methods and fascinating content. They will provide you with skills that you probably can't gain in any other setting. But, for purposes of improving your day-to-day reasoning, you probably want to seek out courses that involve the *testing of hypotheses* through *quantitative evaluation* of *messy data*. These courses will include many of the offerings of your school's psychology department, and probably some of the offerings in sociology, anthropology, political science, and economics. These are the courses that may genuinely make you a better, more critical thinker about the evidence you're likely to encounter in your daily existence.

For more on this topic . . .

Fong, G., & Nisbett, R. (1991). Immediate and delayed transfer of training effects in statistical reasoning. *Journal of Experimental Psychology: General, 120,* 34–45.

Lehman, D. R., Lempert, R. O., & Nisbett, R. E. (1988). The effects of graduate training on reasoning: Formal discipline and thinking about everyday-life events. *American Psychologist, 43*(6), 431–442.

Lehman, D., & Nisbett, R. (1990). A longitudinal study of the effects of under-graduate training on reasoning. *Developmental Psychology, 26,* 952–960.

chapter review

SUMMARY

- Induction often relies on attribute substitution—so that, for example, people estimate frequency by relying on availability. Thus, they judge an observation to be frequent if they can easily think of many examples of that observation. The more available an observation is, the greater the frequency is judged to be.

- Judgments based on the availability heuristic are often accurate, but they do risk error. The risk derives from the fact that many factors influence availability, including the pattern of what's easily retrievable from memory and bias in what you notice in your experiences.

- People also use the representativeness heuristic, relying on the assumption that categories are relatively homogeneous, so that any case drawn from the category will be representative of the entire group. Because of this assumption, people expect a relatively small sample of evidence to have all the properties that are associated with the entire category; an example is the gambler's fallacy. Similarly, people seem insensitive to the importance of sample size, so they believe that a small sample of observations is just as informative as a large sample. In the extreme, people are willing to draw conclusions from just a single observation, as in "man who" arguments.

- People are likely to make errors in judging covariation. In particular, their beliefs and expectations sometimes lead them to perceive illusory covariations. The errors are often attributable to the fact that confirmation bias causes people to notice and remember a biased sample of the evidence, which leads to inaccurate covariation judgments.

- People often seem insensitive to base rates. Again, this can be demonstrated both in novices evaluating unfamiliar materials and in experts making judgments in their professional domains.

- Use of heuristics is widespread, and so are the corresponding errors. However, we can also find cases in which people rely on more sophisticated judgment strategies, and thus are alert to sample size and sample bias, and do consider base rates. This has led many theorists to propose dual-process models of thinking. One process (Type 1) relies on fast, effortless shortcuts; another process (Type 2) is slower and more effortful but is less likely to lead to error.

- Type 1 thinking is more likely when people are pressed for time or distracted. However, Type 1 thinking can be observed even in the absence of time pressure or distraction, and even when the matter being judged is both familiar and highly consequential.

- Better-quality thinking seems more likely when the data are described in terms of frequencies rather than probabilities and also when the data are easily coded in statistical terms (with *chance* playing a prominent role in shaping the sample). Type 2 thinking is also more likely if people bring to a situation background knowledge that helps them to code the data and to understand the cause-and-effect role of sample bias or base rates. Training in statistics also makes Type 2 thinking more likely, leading us to the optimistic view that judging is a *skill* that can be improved through suitable education.

- Reasoning often shows a pattern of confirmation bias. People tend to seek evidence that might confirm their beliefs rather than evidence that might challenge their beliefs. When evidence challenging a belief is in view, it tends to be underused or reinterpreted. One manifestation of confirmation bias is belief perseverance, a pattern in which people continue to believe a claim even after the basis for it has been thoroughly discredited.

- People's performance with logic problems such as categorical syllogisms or problems involving conditional statements is often quite poor. The errors aren't the product of carelessness and often derive from belief bias.

- How well people reason depends on what they're reasoning about. This is evident in the four-card task, in which some versions of the task yield reasonably good performance, even though other versions yield enormous numbers of errors.

- According to many economists, people make decisions by calculating the expected utility of each of their options. Evidence suggests, however, that decisions are often influenced by factors that have nothing to do with utility—for example, how the question is framed or how the possible outcomes are described. If the outcomes are described as potential gains, decision makers tend to be risk averse; if outcomes are described as potential losses, decision makers tend to be risk seeking.

- Some investigators have proposed that people's goal in making decisions is not to maximize utility but, instead, to make decisions that they think are reasonable or justified. When people cannot justify a decision, they sometimes decide *not* to decide.

- Decisions are also clearly influenced by emotion. This influence is evident in decision makers' efforts toward avoiding regret; it is also evident in decision makers' reliance on their own bodily sensations as a cue for evaluating various options. Decision makers are surprisingly inept, however, at predicting their own future reactions. This is true both for predictions of regret and for predictions of future enjoyment or future annoyance.

KEY TERMS

frequency estimate (p. 458)
attribute substitution (p. 458)
availability heuristic (p. 458)
representativeness heuristic (p. 458)
heuristic (p. 459)
covariation (p. 463)
confirmation bias (p. 464)
base-rate information (p. 464)
diagnostic information (p. 465)
dual-process model (p. 466)
Type 1 thinking (p. 466)
Type 2 thinking (p. 466)
induction (p. 471)
deduction (p. 471)
belief perseverance (p. 474)

categorical syllogisms (p. 477)
premises (p. 477)
valid syllogisms (p. 477)
invalid syllogisms (p. 477)
belief bias (p. 477)
conditional statements (p. 478)
selection task (p. 478)
four-card task (p. 478)
utility maximization (p. 480)
framing (p. 482)
risk seeking (p. 483)
risk aversion (p. 483)
reason-based choice (p. 485)
somatic markers (p. 487)
affective forecasting (p. 489)

TEST YOURSELF AGAIN

1. What is attribute substitution?

2. In the availability heuristic, what is the information you need, and what attribute do you use as a substitute?

3. In the representativeness heuristic, what is the information you need, and what attribute do you use as a substitute?

4. What is a "man who" argument? Why are "man who" arguments often misleading?

5. What is a base rate? Why is base-rate information important?

6. What are the differences between Type 1 and Type 2 thinking?

7. What are some of the factors that can, in some settings, encourage (or perhaps allow) Type 2 thinking?

8. What is confirmation bias? What are some of the specific forms that confirmation bias can take?

9. What is the role of confirmation bias in producing belief perseverance?

10. What is belief bias? Why is belief bias a problem in logical reasoning?

11. What is the four-card (or selection) task? How well do people perform in this task?

12. What does it mean to say that decision making is heavily influenced by how a decision is "framed"?

13. In what circumstances are people risk averse? When are they risk seeking?

14. What is affective forecasting, and how accurate are people in this type of forecasting?

THINK ABOUT IT

1. Science is usually concerned with *what is*. Scientists typically leave it to others (philosophers, social theorists, policy makers) to decide *what should be*. In the domain of decision making, though, many psychologists do make policy recommendations—for "opt-out" procedures rather than "opt-in," or for specific decision-making practices that (according to research) will make people happier. Should scientists take these steps? Or should the highly subjective realm of "what is valuable, what is desirable" be kept separate from the realm of objective scientific study?

eBOOK DEMONSTRATIONS & ESSAYS

Go to http://digital.wwnorton.com/cognition7 for the online demonstrations and essays relevant to this chapter. These can be found in the ebook.

Online Demonstrations

- Demonstration 12.1: Sample Size
- Demonstration 12.2: Relying on the Representativeness Heuristic
- Demonstration 12.3: Applying Base Rates
- Demonstration 12.4: Frequencies versus Percentages
- Demonstration 12.5: The Effect of Content on Reasoning
- Demonstration 12.6: Wealth versus Changes in Wealth
- Demonstration 12.7: Probabilities versus Decision Weights
- Demonstration 12.8: Framing Questions
- Demonstration 12.9: Mental Accounting
- Demonstration 12.10: Seeking Reasons

Online Applying Cognitive Psychology and the Law Essays

- Cognitive Psychology and the Law: Juries' Judgment
- Cognitive Psychology and the Law: Pretrial Publicity

ZAPS COGNITION LABS

Go to http://digital.wwnorton.com/cognition7 to experience interactive online psychology labs relevant to this chapter.

chapter **13**

Problem Solving and Intelligence

what if...

In many ways, humans are remarkably alike. We all have one nose, two arms, a liver with three lobes, and a heart with four chambers. We all have the same biochemistry, and to a large extent we all have the same brains — and so the structures inside your skull are virtually identical to the ones inside mine. It's no surprise, then, that throughout this book we've been able to discuss truths that apply to all of us — the ways in which we all pay attention, the ways in which we all learn and remember.

But people also differ — in their personalities, their values, and their cognition. We've occasionally mentioned these differences, but the time has come to focus on these differences directly — including differences in *intelligence.* After all, every one of us knows people who seem amazingly smart and also people who seem comparatively slow. What do these differences amount to? What is "intelligence"?

Researchers have developed various tests for measuring intelligence, and as we will see, there are powerful reasons to take these tests seriously — they do measure something important. But people with very *low* scores often have amazing abilities, and a consideration of these individuals can provide insights into what intelligence is and when intelligence is needed.

Consider Stephen Wiltshire. His IQ score has been measured at 52, way below the score of 70 often used as an indication of disability. But Stephen also is a gifted artist and has a near-perfect visual memory. He has been called the "Living Camera," and it's easy to see why: After a 30-minute helicopter ride over London, he was able to draw (from memory) an exquisitely detailed aerial view of the city. He's done the same for Rome, New York City, and Tokyo. The resulting drawings are so large (more than 15 ft across) and so precise that Stephen needs many days to finish each one. And, when carefully checked, the drawings turn out to be fabulously accurate, with an exact correspondence between his artwork and the actual view. Not only does Stephen create an error-free reproduction of building positions and sizes, he's even correct in drawing the number of windows in each building, the number of columns on each building's façade, and more. (For more on cases like this, see Treffert, 2014.)

People like Stephen are termed "autistic savants." This label refers to a condition in which someone with a mental disability nonetheless shows some remarkable talent. Scholars estimate that worldwide there may

preview of chapter themes

* Often, people solve problems by using heuristics. In other cases, people solve problems by drawing analogies based on problems they've solved in the past.

* Training can draw someone's attention to a problem's deep structure, promoting analogy use and helping the person divide a problem into subproblems. Experts also benefit from highly cross-referenced knowledge in their domain of expertise.

* Problem solving is often stymied by how the person approaches the problem, and that leads to questions about how people find new and creative approaches to problems.

* When closely examined, creative approaches seem to be the result of the same processes that are evident in "ordinary" problem solving—processes hinging on analogies, heuristics, and the like. As a result, we can say that the creative *product* is often extraordinary, but the creative *process* may not be.

* Measures of intelligence turn out to be reliable and valid, and so, if we know someone's score on an intelligence test,

we can predict that person's performance in a wide range of settings (both academic and otherwise).

* The data suggest that we can truly speak of "intelligence in general"—intelligence that applies to a wide range of tasks. General intelligence may be a result of mental speed or the result of better executive control, with some people being better able to control their own thoughts.

* Genetic and environmental factors both matter for intelligence, but, crucially, these factors interact in producing a person's level of intelligence.

* There has been much discussion about how *groups* differ in their average level of performance. For example, American Whites and American Blacks differ in the average scores for each group, and part of the explanation lies in the differing levels of nutrition, health care, and education available to large segments of these groups. In addition, social stereotypes play an enormous role in how individuals are trained and encouraged, as well as in the expectations individuals hold for their own performance.

only be 100 autistic savants at this level of talent, and the achievements of these individuals remain deeply puzzling to science. Even so, these cases are a compelling reminder that there can sometimes be a huge separation between being intelligent and having some incredible talent.

We'll return to the autistic savants later in the chapter. We begin, though, with a different way in which people differ — in their ability to solve problems. Why are some people skilled — and perhaps even *creative* — in their problem solving, while others are not? And, as a related matter, why are some problems so difficult, while others are easily dealt with?

General Problem-Solving Methods

People solve problems all the time. Some problems are pragmatic ("I want to go to the store, but Tom borrowed my car. How can I get there?"). Others are social ("I really want Amy to notice me; how should I arrange it?"). Others are academic ("I'm trying to prove this theorem. How can I do it, starting from these axioms?"). What these situations share, though, is the desire to figure out how to reach some goal — a configuration that defines what we call **problem solving**. How do people solve problems?

Problem Solving as Search

Researchers compare problem solving to a process of *search*, as though you were navigating through a maze, seeking a path toward your goal (see Newell & Simon, 1972; also Bassok & Novick, 2012; Mayer, 2012). To make this

FIGURE 13.1 THE HOBBITS AND ORCS PROBLEM

This problem has been used in studies of problem solving. Can you solve it?

point concrete, consider the Hobbits and Orcs problem in **Figure 13.1**. For this problem, you have choices for the various moves you can make (transporting creatures back and forth), but you're limited by the size of the boat and the requirement that Hobbits can never be outnumbered (lest they be eaten). This situation leaves you with a set of options shown graphically in **Figure 13.2**. The figure shows the moves available early in the solution and depicts the options as a tree, with each step leading to more branches. All the branches together form the **problem space**—that is, the set of all states that can be reached in solving the problem.

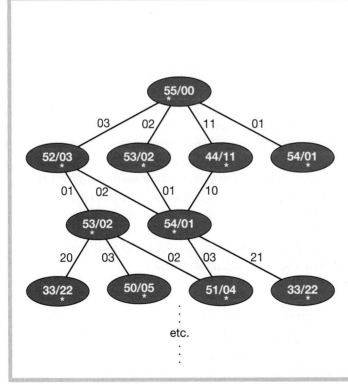

FIGURE 13.2 THE PROBLEM SPACE FOR HOBBITS AND ORCS

Each circle shows a possible problem state. The state 54/01, for example, indicates that five Hobbits and four Orcs are on the east bank; there are no Hobbits, but one Orc, on the west bank. The star shows the position of the boat. The numbers alongside each line indicate the number of creatures in the boat during each river crossing. The move 02, for example, transports no Hobbits, but two Orcs. The problem states shown here are all the "legal" states. (Other states and other moves would result in some of the Hobbits being eaten.) Thus, there are four legal moves one can make, starting from the initial state. From these, there are four possible moves one can make, but these lead to just two problem states (53/02 and 54/01). From these two states, there are four new states that can be reached, and so on. We have here illustrated the initial moves that can be made in solving this problem; the shortest path to the problem's solution involves 11 moves.

To solve this problem, one strategy would be to trace through the entire problem space, exploring each branch in turn. This would be like exploring every possible corridor in a maze, an approach that would guarantee that you'd eventually find the solution. For most problems, however, this approach would be hopeless. Consider the game of chess. In chess, which move is best at any point in the game depends on what your opponent will be able to do in response to your move, and then what you'll do next. To make sure you're choosing the best move, therefore, you need to think ahead through a few cycles of play, so that you can select as your current move the one that will lead to the best sequence.

Let's imagine, therefore, that you decide to look ahead just three cycles of play—three of your moves and three of your opponent's. Some calculation, however, tells us that for three cycles of chess play there are roughly 700 million possibilities for how the game could go; this number immediately rules out the option of considering every possibility. If you could evaluate 10 sequences per second, you'd still need more than 2 years, on a 24/7 schedule, to evaluate the full set of options for each move. And, of course, there's nothing special here about chess, because most real-life problems offer so many options that you couldn't possibly explore every one.

Plainly, then, you somehow need to narrow your search through a problem space, and, specifically, what you need is a problem-solving heuristic. As we've discussed in other chapters, heuristics are strategies that are efficient but at the cost of occasional errors. In the domain of problem solving, a heuristic is a strategy that narrows your search through the problem space—but (you hope) in a way that still leads to the problem's solution.

General Problem-Solving Heuristics

One commonly used heuristic is called the **hill-climbing strategy**. To understand this term, imagine that you're hiking through the woods and trying to figure out which trail leads to the mountaintop. You obviously need to climb uphill to reach the top, so whenever you come to a fork in the trail, you select the path that's going uphill. The problem-solving strategy works the same way: At each point, you choose the option that moves you in the direction of your goal.

This strategy is of limited use, however, because many problems require that you briefly move *away* from your goal; only then, from this new position, can the problem be solved. For instance, if you want Mingus to notice you more, it might help if you go away for a while; that way, he'll be more likely to notice you when you come back. You would never discover this ploy, though, if you relied on the hill-climbing strategy.

Even so, people often rely on this heuristic. As a result, they have difficulties whenever a problem requires them to "move backward in order to go forward." Often, at these points, people drop their current plan and seek some other solution to the problem: "This must be the wrong strategy; I'm going the wrong way." (See, e.g., Jeffries, Polson, Razran, & Atwood, 1977; Thomas, 1974.)

> I want to take my son to nursery school. What's the difference between what I have and what I want? One of distance. What changes distance? My automobile. My automobile won't work. What is needed to make it work? A new battery. What has new batteries? An auto repair shop.
>
> I want the repair shop to put in a new battery; but the shop doesn't know I need one. What is the difficulty? One of communication. What allows communication? A telephone . . .

One commonly used problem-solving heuristic is means-end analysis. In this strategy, you compare your current status to your desired status and ask: "What means do I have to make these more alike?" Among other benefits, this strategy helps you to break a problem into small subproblems.

(AFTER NEWELL & SIMON, 1972, P. 416)

Fortunately, people have other heuristics available to them. For example, people often rely on **means-end analysis.** In this strategy, you compare your current state to the goal state and you ask: "What means do I have to make these more alike?" **Figure 13.3** offers a commonsense example.

Pictures and Diagrams

People have other options in their mental toolkit. For example, it's often helpful to translate a problem into concrete terms, relying on a mental image or a picture. As an illustration, consider the problem in **Figure 13.4.** Most people try an algebraic solution to this problem (width of each volume

> Solomon is proud of his 26-volume encyclopedia, placed neatly, with the volumes in alphabetical order, on his bookshelf. Solomon doesn't realize, though, that there's a bookworm sitting on the front cover of the *A* volume. The bookworm begins chewing his way through the pages on the shortest possible path toward the back cover of the *Z* volume.
>
> Each volume is 3 inches thick (including pages and covers), so that the entire set of volumes requires 78 inches of bookshelf. The bookworm chews through the pages and covers at a steady rate of ¾ of an inch per month. How long will it take before the bookworm reaches the back cover of the *Z* volume?

FIGURE 13.4   THE BOOKWORM PROBLEM

People who try an algebraic solution to this problem often end up with the wrong answer.

TEST YOURSELF

1. What does it mean to say that a problem-solving heuristic allows you to trim the size of the problem space?
2. What is means-end analysis?

multiplied by the number of volumes, divided by the worm's eating rate) and end up with the wrong answer. People generally get this problem right, though, if they start by visualizing the arrangement. Now, they can see the actual positions of the worm's starting point and end point, and this usually takes them to the correct answer. (See **Figure 13.5**; also see Anderson, 1993; Anderson & Helstrup, 1993; Reed, 1993; Verstijnen, Hennessey, van Leeuwen, Hamel, & Goldschmidt, 1998.)

Drawing on Experience

Where do these points leave us with regard to the questions with which we began—and, in particular, the ways in which people differ from one another in their mental abilities? There's actually little difference from one person to the next in the use of strategies like hill climbing or means-end analysis—most people can and do use these strategies. People do differ, of course, in their drawing ability and in their imagery prowess (see Chapter 11), but these points are relevant only for some problems. Where, then, do the broader differences in problem-solving skill arise?

Problem Solving via Analogy

Often, a problem reminds you of other problems you've solved in the past, and so you can rely on your past experience in tackling the current challenge. In other words, you solve the current problem by means of an analogy with other, already solved, problems.

FIGURE 13.5 DIAGRAM FOR THE BOOKWORM PROBLEM

When the bookworm problem is illustrated, people solve it more easily. Notice that a worm starting on the front cover of the A volume wouldn't have to chew through volume A's pages in moving toward the Z volume. Likewise, at the end of the worm's travel, he would reach the back cover of the Z volume before penetrating that volume!

It's easy to show that analogies are helpful (Chan, Paletz, & Schunn, 2012; Donnelly & McDaniel, 1993; Gentner & Smith, 2012; Holyoak, 2012), but it's also plain that people under-use analogies. Consider the tumor problem (see **Figure 13.6A**). This problem is difficult, but people generally solve it if they use an analogy. Gick and Holyoak (1980) first had their participants read about a related situation (see **Figure 13.6B**) and then presented them with the tumor problem. When participants were encouraged to use this hint, 75% were able to solve the tumor problem. Without the hint, only 10% solved the problem.

FIGURE 13.6   THE TUMOR PROBLEM

Suppose you are a doctor faced with a patient who has a malignant tumor in his stomach. To operate on the patient is impossible, but unless the tumor is destroyed the patient will die. A kind of ray, at a sufficiently high intensity, can destroy the tumor. Unfortunately, at this intensity the healthy tissue that the rays pass through on the way to the tumor will also be destroyed. At lower intensities the rays are harmless to healthy tissue but will not affect the tumor. How can the rays be used to destroy the tumor without injuring the healthy tissue?

A

A dictator ruled a country from a strong fortress, and a rebel general, hoping to liberate the country, vowed to capture the fortress. The general knew that an attack by his entire army would capture the fortress, but he also knew that the dictator had planted mines on each of the many roads leading to the fortress. The mines were set so that small groups of soldiers could pass over them safely, since the dictator needed to move his own troops to and from the fortress. However, any large force would detonate the mines, blowing them up and also destroying the neighboring villages.

The general knew, therefore, that he couldn't just march his army up one of the roads to the fortress. Instead, he devised a simple plan. He divided his army into small groups and dispatched each group to the head of a different road. When all were ready, he gave the signal and each group marched up a different road to the fortress, with all the groups arriving at the fortress at the same time. In this way, the general captured the fortress and overthrew the dictator.

B

The tumor problem, designed by Duncker (1945) and presented in Panel A, has been studied extensively. Can you solve it? One solution is to aim multiple low-intensity rays at the tumor, each from a different angle. The rays will meet at the site of the tumor and so, at just that location, will sum to full strength. People are much more likely to solve this problem if they're encouraged to use the hint provided by the problem shown in Panel B.

Note, though, that Gick and Holyoak had another group of participants read the "general and fortress" story, but these participants weren't told that this story was relevant to the tumor problem. Only 30% of this group solved the tumor problem (see **Figure 13.7**). (Also see Kubricht, Lu, & Holyoak, 2017.)

Apparently, then, uninstructed use of analogies is rare, and one reason lies in how people search through memory when seeking an analogy. In solving the tumor problem, people seem to ask themselves: "What else do I know about tumors?" This search will help them remember other situations in which they thought about tumors, but it won't lead them to the "general and fortress" problem. This (potential) analogue will therefore lie dormant in memory and provide no help. (See, e.g., Bassok, 1996; Cummins, 1992; Hahn, Prat-Sala, Pothos, & Brumby, 2010; Wharton, Holyoak, Downing, & Lange, 1994.)

To locate helpful analogies in memory, you generally need to look beyond the superficial features of the problem and think instead about the principles governing the problem—focusing on what's sometimes called the problem's "deep structure." As a related point, you'll be able to use an analogy only if you figure out how to map the prior case onto the problem now being solved—only if you realize, for example, that converging groups of soldiers correspond to converging rays and that a fortress-to-be-captured corresponds to a tumor-to-be-destroyed. This **mapping** process can be difficult (Holyoak, 2012; Reed, 2017), and failures to figure out the mapping are another reason people regularly fail to find and use analogies.

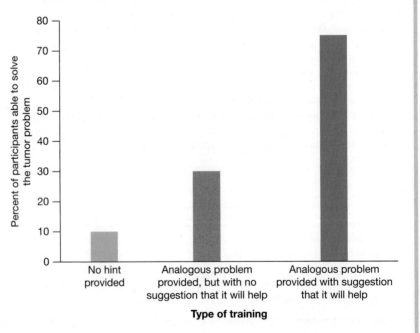

FIGURE 13.7 THE IMPORTANCE OF ANALOGIES IN SOLVING PROBLEMS

Participants rarely solved the tumor problem if they were given no hints. However, if they were given an analogous problem (the general and fortress) and encouraged to use this problem as a guide, most did solve the tumor problem. Surprisingly, though, participants often failed to make use of the analogy unless they were specifically encouraged to do so.

(AFTER GICK & HOLYOAK, 1980)

Strategies to Make Analogy Use More Likely

Perhaps, then, we have our first suggestion about why people differ in their problem-solving ability. Perhaps the people who are better problem solvers are those who make better use of analogies—plausibly, because they pay attention to a problem's deep structure rather than its superficial traits.

Consistent with these claims, it turns out that we can *improve* problem solving by encouraging people to pay attention to the problems' underlying dynamic. For example, Cummins (1992) instructed participants in one group to analyze a series of algebra problems one by one. Participants in a second group were asked to *compare* the problems to one another, describing what the problems had in common. The latter instruction forced participants to think about the problems' underlying structure; guided by this perspective, the participants were more likely, later on, to use the training problems as a basis for forming and using analogies. (Also see Catrambone, Craig, & Nersessian, 2006; Kurtz & Loewenstein, 2007; Lane & Schooler, 2004; Pedrone, Hummel, & Holyoak, 2001.)

Expert Problem Solvers

How far can we go with these points? Can we use these simple ideas to explain the difference between ordinary problem solvers and genuine experts? To some extent, we can.

We just suggested, for example, that it's helpful to think about problems in terms of their deep structure, and this is, it seems, the way experts think about problems. In one study, participants were asked to categorize simple physics problems (Chi, Feltovich, & Glaser, 1981). Novices tended to place together all the problems involving river currents, all the problems involving springs, and so on, in each case focusing on the surface form of the problem. In contrast, experts (Ph.D. students in physics) ignored these details of the problems and, instead, sorted according to the physical principles relevant to the problems' solution. (For more on expertise, see Ericsson & Towne, 2012.)

We've also claimed that attention to a problem's deep structure promotes analogy use, so if experts are more attentive to this structure, they should be more likely to use analogies—and they are (e.g., Bassok & Novick, 2012). Experts' reliance on analogies is evident both in the laboratory (e.g., Novick and Holyoak, 1991) and in real-world settings. Christensen and Schunn (2005) recorded work meetings of a group of engineers trying to create new products for the medical world. As the engineers discussed their options, analogy use was frequent—with an analogy being offered in the discussion every 5 minutes!

Setting Subgoals

Experts also have other advantages. For example, for many problems, it's helpful to break a problem into subproblems so that the overall problem can be solved part by part rather than all at once. This, too, is a technique that experts often use.

Classic evidence on this point comes from studies of chess experts (de Groot, 1965, 1966; also see Chase & Simon, 1973). The data show that these experts are particularly skilled in organizing a chess game—in seeing the structure of the game, understanding its parts, and perceiving how the parts are related to one another. This skill can be revealed in many ways, including how chess masters remember board positions. In one procedure, chess masters were able to remember the positions of 20 pieces after viewing the board for just 5 seconds; novices remembered many fewer (see **Figure 13.8**). In addition, there was a clear pattern to the experts' recollection: In recalling the layout of the board, the experts would place four or five pieces in their proper positions, then pause, then recall another group, then pause, and so on. In each case, the group of pieces was one that made "tactical sense"—for example, the pieces involved in a "forked" attack, a chain of mutually defending pieces, and the like. (For similar data with other forms of expertise, see Tuffiash, Roring, & Ericsson, 2007; also see Sala & Gobet, 2017.)

It seems, then, that the masters—experts in chess—memorize the board in terms of higher-order units, defined by their strategic function within the game. This perception of higher-order units helps to organize the experts' thinking. By focusing on the units and how they're related to one another, the experts keep track of broad strategies without getting bogged down in the details. Likewise, these units set subgoals for the experts. Having

FIGURE 13.8 EXPERTS REMEMBERING PATTERNS

  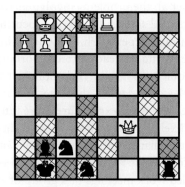

A Actual position

B Typical master player's performance

C Typical average player's performance

Experienced chess players who viewed the pattern in Panel A for 5 seconds were easily able to memorize it (Panel B); average players could not (Panel C), and performance from outright novices was even worse. This is because the experts were able to organize the pattern into meaningful chunks, thereby lightening their memory load. Cross-hatched squares indicate memory errors. (FIG. 8.15 FROM R. BOOTZIN, *PSYCHOLOGY TODAY: AN INTRODUCTION*, 4TH ED. © 1979 MCGRAW-HILL EDUCATION. REPRINTED WITH PERMISSION.)

perceived a group of pieces as a coordinated attack, an expert sets the subgoal of preparing for the attack. Having perceived another group of pieces as the early development of a pin (a situation in which a player cannot move without exposing a more valuable piece to an attack), the expert creates the subgoal of avoiding the pin.

It turns out, though, that experts also have other advantages, including the simple fact that they know much more about their domains of expertise than novices do. Experts also organize their knowledge more effectively than novices. In particular, studies indicate that experts' knowledge is heavily cross-referenced, so that each bit of information has associations to many other bits (e.g., Bédard & Chi, 1992; Bransford, Brown & Cocking, 1999; Reed, 2017). As a result, experts have better access to what they know.

It's clear, therefore, that there are multiple factors separating novices from experts, but these factors all hinge on the processes we've already discussed—with an emphasis on analogies, subproblems, and memory search. Apparently, then, we can use our theorizing so far to describe how people (in particular, novices and experts) differ from one another.

TEST YOURSELF

3. Why do people seem to under-use analogies in solving problems?
4. What are some of the advantages that expert problem solvers have, compared to those who are not experts?

Defining the Problem

Experts, we've said, define problems in their area of expertise in terms of the problems' underlying dynamic. As a result, the experts are more likely to break a problem into meaningful parts, more likely to realize what other problems are analogous to the current problem, and so more likely to benefit from analogies.

Clearly, then, there are better and worse ways to define a problem—ways that will lead to a solution and ways that will obstruct it. But what does it mean to "define" a problem? And what determines how people define the problems they encounter?

Ill-Defined and Well-Defined Problems

For many problems, the goal and the options for solving the problems are clearly stated at the start: Get all the Hobbits to the other side of the river, using the boat. Solve the math problem, using the axioms stated. Many problems, though, are rather different. For example, we all hope for peace in the world, but what will this goal involve? There will be no fighting, of course, but what other traits will the goal have? Will the nations currently on the map still be in place? How will disputes be settled? It's also unclear what steps should be tried in an effort toward reaching this goal. Would diplomatic negotiations work? Or would economic measures be more effective?

Problems like this one are said to be **ill-defined**, with no clear statement at the outset of how the goal should be characterized or what operations might serve to reach that goal. Other examples of ill-defined problems include "having a good time while on vacation" and "saving money for college" (Halpern, 1984; Kahney, 1986; Schraw, Dunkle, & Bendixen, 1995).

When confronting ill-defined problems, your best bet is often to create subgoals, because many ill-defined problems have reasonably well-defined parts, and by solving each of these you can move toward solving the overall problem. A different strategy is to add some structure to the problem by including extra constraints or extra assumptions. In this way, the problem becomes well-defined instead of ill-defined—perhaps with a narrower set of options in how you might approach it, but with a clearly specified goal state and, eventually, a manageable set of operations to try.

Functional Fixedness

Even for well-defined problems, there's usually more than one way to understand the problem. Consider the problem in **Figure 13.9**. To solve it, you need to cease thinking of the box as a container and instead think of it as a potential platform. Thus, your chances of solving the problem depend on how

FIGURE 13.9 THE CANDLE PROBLEM

You are given the objects shown: a candle, a book of matches, and a box of tacks. Your task is to find a way to attach the candle to the wall of the room, at eye level, so that it will burn properly and illuminate the room.

What makes this problem difficult is the tendency to think of the box of tacks as a box—that is, as a container. The problem is readily solved, though, once you think of the box as a potential platform. However, this approach is less likely if the box is presented initially *full of tacks*. This presentation emphasizes the usual function of the box (as a container), making it less likely that participants will think of an alternative function for it.

you represent the box in your thoughts, and we can show this by *encouraging* one representation or another. In a classic study, participants were given the equipment shown in Figure 13.9A: some matches, a box of tacks, and a candle. This configuration (implicitly) underscored the box's conventional function. As a result, the configuration increased **functional fixedness**—the tendency to be rigid in how one thinks about an object's function. With fixedness in place, the problem was rarely solved (Duncker, 1945; Fleck & Weisberg, 2004).

Other participants were given the same tools, but configured differently. They were given some matches, a pile of tacks, the box (now empty), and a candle. In this setting, the participants were less likely to think of the box as a container for the tacks, and so they were less likely to think of the box *as a container*. As a result, they were more likely to solve the problem (Duncker, 1945). (Also see **Figure 13.10**; for more on fixedness, see McCaffrey, 2012.)

FIGURE 13.10   THE TWO-STRING PROBLEM

You enter a room in which two strings are hanging from the ceiling and a pair of pliers is lying on a table. Your task is to tie the two strings together. Unfortunately, though, the strings are positioned far enough apart so that you can't grab one string and hold on to it while reaching for the other. How can you tie them together?

The two-string problem is difficult—because of functional fixedness. The trick here is not to think of the pliers in terms of their usual function—squeezing or pulling. Instead, the trick is to think of them as a weight. The solution to the puzzle is to tie the pliers to one string and push the pliers away from the other string. While this pendulum is in motion, go and grab the second string. Then, when the pendulum swings back toward you, grab it and you're all set.

"Thinking outside the Box"

A related obstacle derives from someone's **problem-solving set**—the collection of beliefs and assumptions a person makes about a problem. One often-discussed example involves the nine-dot problem (see **Figure 13.11**). People routinely fail to solve this problem, because—according to some interpretations—they (mistakenly) assume that the lines they draw need to stay inside the "square" defined by the dots. In fact, this problem is probably the source of the cliché "You need to think outside the box."

Ironically, though, this cliché may be misleading. In one study, participants were told explicitly that to solve the problem their lines would need to go outside the square. The hint provided little benefit, and most participants still failed to find the solution (Weisberg & Alba, 1981). Apparently, beliefs about "the box" aren't the obstacle. Even when we eliminate these beliefs, performance remains poor.

Nonetheless, the expression "think outside the box" does get the broad idea right, because to solve this problem people do need to jettison their initial approach. Specifically, most people assume that the lines they draw must begin and end on dots. People also have the idea that they'll need to maximize the number of dots "canceled" with each move; as a result, they seek solutions in which each line cancels a full row or column of dots. It turns out, though, that these assumptions are wrong; and so, guided by these

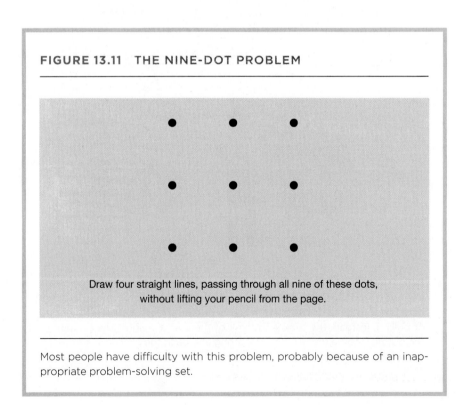

FIGURE 13.11   THE NINE-DOT PROBLEM

Draw four straight lines, passing through all nine of these dots, without lifting your pencil from the page.

Most people have difficulty with this problem, probably because of an inappropriate problem-solving set.

mistaken beliefs, people find this problem quite hard. (See Kershaw & Ohlsson, 2004; MacGregor, Ormerod, & Chronicle, 2001; also Öllinger, Jones, Faber, & Knoblich, 2013.)

In the nine-dot problem, people seem to be victims of their own problem-solving set; to find the solution, they need to change that set. This phrasing, however, makes it sound like a set is a bad thing, blocking the discovery of a solution. Let's emphasize, though, that sets also provide a benefit. This is because (as we mentioned earlier) most problems offer a huge number of options as you seek the solution—an enormous number of moves you might try or approaches you might consider. A problem-solving set helps you, therefore, by narrowing your options, which in turn eases the search for a solution. Thus, in solving the nine-dot problem, you didn't waste any time wondering whether you should try drawing the lines while holding the pencil between your toes or whether the problem was hard because you were sitting down while you worked on it instead of standing up. These are foolish ideas, so you brushed past them. But what identifies them as foolish? It's your problem-solving set, which tells you, among other things, which options are plausible, which ones are physically possible, and so on.

"Actually, I got some pretty good ideas when I was in the box."

THINKING OUTSIDE THE BOX

The expression "thinking outside the box" captures an important truth: Often, our problem solving is limited by unnecessary or misleading assumptions, and it's helpful to break free of those assumptions. However, the likely source of this expression (the nine-dot problem; see Figure 13.11) involves more than just thinking outside the box (i.e., the square formed by the dots).

5. Why are problem-solving sets often a problem? But why are problem-solving sets also useful?

6. What is functional fixedness?

In this way, a set can blind you to important options and thus be an obstacle. But a set can also blind you to a wide range of futile strategies, and this is a good thing: It enables you to focus, much more productively, on options that are likely to work out. Indeed, without a set, you might be so distracted by silly notions that even the simplest problem would become insoluble.

Creativity

There is no question, though, that efforts toward a problem solution are sometimes hindered by someone's set, and this observation points us toward another way in which people differ. Some people are remarkably flexible in their approaches to problems; they seem easily able to "think outside the box." Other people, in contrast, seem far too ready to rely on routine, so they're more vulnerable to the obstacles we've just described.

How should we think about these differences? Why do some people reliably produce novel and unexpected solutions, while other people offer only familiar solutions? This is, in effect, a question of why some people are *creative* and others aren't—a question that forces us to ask: What is creativity?

Case Studies of Creativity

One approach to this issue focuses on individuals who've been enormously creative—artists like Pablo Picasso and Johann Sebastian Bach, or scientists like Charles Darwin and Marie Curie. By studying these giants, perhaps we can draw hints about the nature of creativity when it arises, on a much smaller scale, in day-to-day life—when, for example, you find a creative way to begin a conversation or to repair a damaged friendship. As some researchers put it, we may be able to learn about "little-c creativity" (the everyday sort) by studying "Big-C Creativity" (the sort shown by people we count as scientific or artistic geniuses—Simonton & Damian, 2012).

Research suggests, in fact, that highly creative people like Bach and Curie tend to have certain things in common, and we can think of these elements as "prerequisites" for creativity (e.g., Hennessey & Amabile, 2010). These individuals, first of all, generally have great knowledge and skills in their domain. (This point can't be surprising: If you don't know a lot of chemistry, you can't be a creative chemist. If you're not a skilled storyteller, you can't be a great novelist.) Second, to be creative, you need certain personality traits: a willingness to take risks, a willingness to ignore criticism, an ability to tolerate ambiguous findings or situations, and an inclination not to "follow the crowd." Third, highly creative people tend to be motivated by the pleasure of their work rather than by the promise of external rewards. With this, highly creative people tend to work extremely hard on their endeavors and to produce a lot of their product, whether these products are poems, paintings, or scientific papers. Fourth, these highly creative people have generally been "in the right place at the right time"—that is, in environments that allowed them freedom, provided them with the appropriate supports, and offered them problems "ripe" for solution with the resources available.

Notice that these observations highlight the contribution of factors outside the person, as well as the person's own capacities and skills. The external environment, for example, is the source of crucial knowledge and resources, and it often defines the problem itself. This is why many authors have suggested that we need a systematic "sociocultural approach" to creativity—one that considers the social and historical context, as well as the processes unfolding inside the creative individual's mind (e.g., Sawyer, 2006).

We still need to ask, however: What does go on in a creative mind? If a person has all the prerequisites just listed, what happens next to produce the creative step forward? Actually, there is wide disagreement on these points (see Hennessey & Amabile, 2010; Mumford & Antes, 2007). It will be instructive, though, to examine a proposal offered years ago by Wallas (1926). His notion fits well with some commonsense ideas about creativity, and this is one of the reasons his framework continues to guide modern research. Nonetheless, the evidence forces us to question several of Wallas's claims.

The Moment of Illumination

According to Wallas, creative thought proceeds through four stages. In the first stage, **preparation**, the problem solver gathers information and does some work on the problem, but with little progress. In the second stage, **incubation**, the problem solver sets the problem aside and seems not to be working on it. Wallas argued, though, that the problem solver continues to work on the problem unconsciously during this stage, so actually the problem's solution is continuing to develop, unseen. This development leads to the third stage, **illumination**, in which a key insight or new idea emerges, paving the way for the fourth stage, **verification**, in which the person confirms that the new idea really does lead to a solution and works out the details.

Historical evidence suggests, however, that many creative discoveries don't include the steps Wallas described—or, if they do, they include these steps in a complex, back-and-forth sequence (Weisberg, 1986). Likewise, the moment of illumination celebrated in Wallas's proposal may be more myth than reality. When we examine creative discoveries in science or art, we usually find that the new ideas emerged, not from some glorious and abrupt leap forward, but instead from a succession of "mini-insights," each moving the process forward in some small way (Klein, 2013; Sawyer, 2006).

And when people do have the "Aha!" experience that, for Wallas, signified illumination, what does this involve? Metcalfe (1986; Metcalfe & Weibe, 1987) gave her participants a series of "insight problems" like those shown in **Figure 13.12A**. As participants worked on each problem, they rated their progress by using a judgment of "warmth" ("I'm getting warmer . . . , I'm getting warmer . . ."), and these ratings did capture the "moment of insight." Initially, the participants didn't have a clue how to proceed and gave warmth ratings of 1 or 2; then, abruptly, they saw a way forward, and at that instant their warmth ratings shot up to the top of the scale.

To understand this pattern, though, we need to look separately at those participants who subsequently announced the correct solution to the problem and those who announced an *incorrect* solution. Remarkably, the pattern is the same for both groups (see **Figure 13.12B**). In other words, some participants abruptly announced that they were getting "hot" and, moments later, solved the problem. Other participants made the same announcement and, moments later, slammed into a dead end.

It seems, therefore, that when you say "Aha!" it means only that you've discovered a new approach, one that you've not yet considered. This

FIGURE 13.12 INSIGHT PROBLEMS

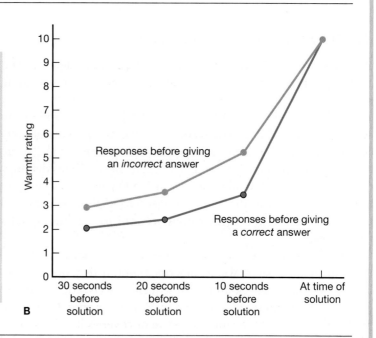

Problem 1

A stranger approached a museum curator and offered him an ancient bronze coin. The coin had an authentic appearance and was marked with the date 544 B.C. The curator had happily made acquisitions from suspicious sources before, but this time he promptly called the police and had the stranger arrested. Why?

Problem 2

A landscape gardener is given instructions to plant four special trees so that each one is exactly the same distance from each of the others. How should the trees be arranged?

As participants worked on these problems, they were asked to judge their progress by using an assessment of "warmth" ("I'm getting warmer . . . , I'm getting warmer . . . , I'm getting hot!"). To solve Problem 1, you need to realize that no one in the year 544 B.C. knew that it was 544 B.C.; that is, no one could have known that Christ would be born 544 years later. For Problem 2, the gardener needs to plant one of the trees at the top of a tall mound and then plant the other trees around the base of the mound, with the three together forming an equilateral triangle and with the fourth forming a triangle-based pyramid (i.e., a tetrahedron). (AFTER METCALFE, 1986) is important, because often a new approach is just what you need. But there's nothing magical about the "moment of illumination." This moment doesn't signal that you've at last discovered a path leading to the solution. Instead, it means only that you've discovered something new to try, with no guarantee that this "something new" will be helpful. (For more on procedures that can *promote* "Aha!" moments, see Patrick, Ahmed, Smy, Seeby & Sambrooks, 2015; also Patrick & Ahmed, 2014. For more on the insight process overall, see Bassok & Novick, 2012; Smith & Ward, 2012; van Steenburgh, Fleck, Beeman, & Kounios, 2012. For discussion of neural mechanisms underlying insight, see Kounios & Beeman, 2014, 2015, and also **Figure 13.13**. For an alternative view, though, see Chuderski & Jastrzębski, 2018.)

Incubation

What about Wallas's second stage, incubation? His claim here fits well with a common experience: You're working on a problem but getting nowhere with it. You give up and turn to other matters. Sometime later, when you're thinking about something altogether different, the problem's solution pops into your thoughts. What has happened? According to Wallas, your time away from the problem allowed incubation to proceed—unconscious work on the problem that allowed considerable progress.

FIGURE 13.13   NEURAL CORRELATES OF INSIGHT

Problems requiring insight involve a distinctive set of brain processes. In Panel A, the yellow *R* indicates the moment at which the research participant announced that he or she had figured out the problem solution, either for a problem requiring some insight (red line, keyed "I") or for a problem not requiring a special insight (blue line, keyed "NI"). To make the difference between these lines easily visible, the difference is shaded in yellow. The time axis shows the time relative to the participants' announcement that they'd found the problem's solution. The measure of "gamma power" is derived from EEG procedures, and it represents the square of the voltage measured in brain waves. Panel B shows the spatial focus of this distinctive brain process—called "gamma-band activity." The red dots in Panel B show where the EEG electrodes were placed.

Systematic studies, however, tell us that this pattern is (at best) unreliable. In these studies, participants are given a problem to solve. Some participants work on the problem continuously; some are interrupted for a while. The prediction, based on Wallas's proposal, is that we'll observe better performance in the latter group—the group that can benefit from incubation.

The data, however, are mixed. Some studies do show that time away from a problem helps in finding the problem's solution, but many studies find no effect at all. (See Baird et al., 2012; Dodds, Ward, & Smith, 2007, 2012; Gilhooly, Georgiou, Garrison, Reston, & Sirota, 2012; Hélie & Sun, 2010; Sio, Kotovsky, & Cagan, 2017.) The explanation for this mixed pattern isn't clear. Some researchers argue that incubation is disrupted if you're under pressure to solve the problem. Other authors focus on how you spend your time during the incubation period, with the suggestion that incubation takes place only if the circumstances allow your thoughts to "wander" during this period. (For reviews of this literature, see Baird et al., 2012; Gilhooly et al., 2012; Kounios & Beeman, 2015.)

Why should "mind wandering" be relevant here? Recall that in Chapter 9 we described the process of *spreading activation* through which one memory can activate related memories. It seems likely that when you're carefully working on a problem, you try to direct this flow of activation—and perhaps end up directing it in unproductive ways. When you simply allow your thoughts to wander, though, the activation can flow wherever the memory connections take it, and this may lead to new ideas being activated. (See Ash & Wiley, 2006; Bowden, Jung-Beeman, Fleck, & Kounios, 2005; Kounios & Beeman, 2015; Radel, Davaranche, Fournier, & Dietrick, 2015; Smith & Ward, 2012.) This process provides no guarantee that *helpful* or *productive* ideas will come to mind, only that *more* (and perhaps unanticipated) ideas will be activated. In this way, incubation is like illumination—a source of new possibilities that may or may not pay off.

Other authors, however, offer a more mundane explanation of incubation effects. They note that your early efforts with a problem may have been tiring or frustrating, and if so, the interruption simply provides an opportunity for the frustration or fatigue to dissipate. Likewise, your early efforts with a problem may have been dominated by a particular approach, a particular set. If you put the problem aside for a while, it's possible you'll forget about these earlier tactics, freeing you to explore other, more productive avenues. (See Smith & Blankenship, 1989, 1991; Storm, Angello, & Bjork, 2011; Storm & Patel, 2014; Vul & Pashler, 2007.)

For the moment, there is no consensus about which of these proposals is best, so it's unclear why time away from a problem sometimes helps and sometimes doesn't. To put the matter bluntly, sometimes when you're stymied by a problem, it does help to walk away from it for a while. But sometimes your best bet is just to keep plugging away, doggedly trying to move forward. For now, research provides less guidance than we'd like in choosing which of these is the better plan.

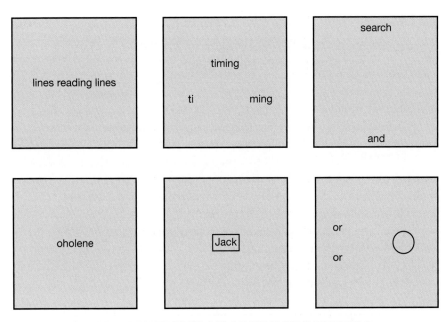

AN INCUBATION BENEFIT FROM SIMPLE FORGETTING

Shown here are the problems used in a study of incubation. Each panel refers to a familiar word or phrase; participants had to figure out what the word or phrase was. Clues were given for each problem, but for many of the problems the clues were designed to be misleading. Control participants had a minute to work on each puzzle; other participants worked on each puzzle for 30 seconds, then were interrupted, and later returned to the puzzle for an additional 30 seconds. This interruption did improve performance, so that problem solution was more likely for the incubation group. Crucially, though, the researchers tested participants' memory for the misleading clues, and they found that the incubation participants were less likely to remember the clues. The researchers argued that this forgetting is what created the incubation advantage: After the interruption, participants were no longer misled by the bad clues, and their performance improved accordingly. (The solutions to these puzzles appear at the end of the chapter.)   (AFTER SMITH & BLANKENSHIP, 1991)

The Nature of Creativity

Where does this discussion leave us with regard to our overarching question—the question of how people differ in their cognitive abilities? In discussing *expertise*, we saw that experts in a domain have a stack of advantages: a tendency to think about problems in terms of their structure rather than their surface form, a broad knowledge base deriving from their experience in a field, heavily cross-referenced memories, and so on. Now, in discussing *creativity*, we've seen a similar pattern: Highly creative people tend to have certain personality traits (e.g., a willingness to take risks), a lot of knowledge, intense motivation, and some amount of luck. But what mental processes do they rely on? When we examine Darwin's notebooks or Picasso's early sketches, we discover that these creative giants relied on analogies, hints, heuristics, and a lot of hard work, just as the rest of us do (Gruber, 1981; Sawyer, 2006; Weisberg, 1986). In some cases, creativity may even depend on blind trial and error (e.g., Klein, 2013; Simonton, 2011); with this sort of process, the great artist or great inventor is simply someone who's highly discriminating—and thus able to discern which of the randomly produced products actually have value.

Research also suggests that creative people may have advantages in how they search through memory. Some authors emphasize the skill of **convergent thinking**—an ability to spot ways in which seemingly distinct ideas might be interconnected. This ability is sometimes measured through the Remote Associates Test (Mednick, 1962; Mednick & Mednick, 1967; also Smith, Huber, & Vul, 2013; **Figure 13.14**). In this test, you're given a trio of words, and you need to find one more word that fits with each of the three. For example, you might be given the trio *cross, rain,* and *tie;* the correct answer is *bow* (as in *crossbow, rainbow,* and *bowtie*).

Other authors emphasize the skill of **divergent thinking**—an ability to move one's thoughts in novel, unanticipated directions. (See Guilford, 1967, 1979; also see Beaty, Silvia, Nusbaum, Jauk, & Benedek, 2014; Hass, 2017; Vartanian, Martindale, & Matthews, 2009; see **Figure 13.15**. For a related idea, see Zabelina, Saporta, & Beeman, 2016.) Here, there's no "right

FIGURE 13.15 CREATIVITY AS DIVERGENT THINKING

Tests of divergent thinking require you to think of new uses for simple objects or new ways to think about familiar ideas. How many different uses can you think of for a brick?

> As a paperweight.
> As the shadow-caster in a sundial (if positioned appropriately).
> As a means of writing messages on a sidewalk.
> As a stepladder (if you want to grab something just slightly out of reach).
> As a nutcracker.
> As a pendulum useful for solving the two-string problem.

Choose five names, at random, from the telephone directory. In how many different ways could these names be classified?

> According to the number of syllables.
> According to whether there is an even or odd number of vowels.
> According to whether their third letter is in the last third of the alphabet.
> According to whether they rhyme with things that are edible.

Guilford (1967, 1979) argued that creativity lies in the ability to take an idea in a new, unprecedented direction. Among its other items, his test of creativity asks people to think of new uses for a familiar object. Some possible responses are listed here.

answer." Instead, success in divergent thinking is reflected in an ability to come up with a large number of new ideas—ideas that can then be evaluated to see if they're of any value.

Overall, though, what is it that allowed Darwin or Picasso, Rachel Carson or Georgia O'Keeffe, to achieve their monumental creativity? Research provides no reason to think these giants possessed some special "creativity mechanism." (See DeHaan, 2011; Goldenberg, Mazursky, & Solomon, 1999; Klahr & Simon, 2001; Simonton, 2003, 2009; Simonton & Damian, 2012; Weisberg, 2006.) However, there is one way in which these individuals surely were distinctive. Many of us are smart or particularly skillful in memory search; many of us are willing to take risks and to ignore criticism; many of us live in a cultural setting that might support a new discovery. What distinguishes creative geniuses, though, is that they are the special people who have *all* of these ingredients—the right intellectual tools, the right personality characteristics, the good fortune to be living in the right context, and so on. It's a rare individual who has all of these elements, and it's probably the combination of all these elements that provides the recipe for extraordinary creativity.

TEST YOURSELF

7. Define each of the stages proposed by Wallas—preparation, incubation, illumination, and verification.
8. What does research tell us about whether incubation truly helps problem solving?
9. What does research tell us is really going on in the "Aha!" moment of illumination?

Intelligence

We all admire people who seem wonderfully intelligent, and we express concerns about (and try to help) those we consider intellectually dull. But what is "intelligence"? Is there a way to measure it? And should we be focused on *intelligence* (singular) or *intelligences* (plural)? In other words, is there such a thing as "intelligence-in-general," so that someone who has this resource will be better off in all mental endeavors? Or should we instead talk about different types of intelligence, so that someone might be "smart" in some domains but less so in others?

Measuring Intelligence

Scholars disagree about how the word "intelligence" should be defined. Remarkably, though, early efforts toward measuring intelligence proceeded without a clear definition. Instead, Alfred Binet (1857–1911) and his colleagues began with a simple idea—namely, that intelligence is a capacity that matters for many aspects of cognitive functioning. They therefore created a test that included a range of tasks: copying a drawing, repeating a string of digits, understanding a story, doing arithmetic, and so on. Performance was then assessed with a composite score, summing across these various tasks.

In its original form, the test score was computed as a ratio between someone's "mental age" (the level of development reflected in the test performance) and his or her chronological age. (The ratio was then multiplied by 100 to get the final score.) This ratio—or *quotient*—was the source of the test's name: The test evaluated a person's "intelligence quotient," or IQ.

Modern forms of the test no longer calculate this ratio, but they're still called "IQ tests." One commonly used test is the Wechsler Intelligence Scale for Children, or WISC (Wechsler, 2003). Similarly, adult intelligence is often evaluated with the Wechsler Adult Intelligence Scale, or WAIS. Like Binet's original test, though, these modern tests rely on numerous subtests. In the WAIS, for example, there are tests to assess general knowledge, vocabulary, and comprehension (see **Figure 13.16A**), and a perceptual-reasoning scale includes visual puzzles like the one shown in **Figure 13.16B**. Separate subtests assess working memory and speed of intellectual processing.

Other intelligence tests have different formats. The Raven's Progressive Matrices Test (**Figure 13.16C**; Raven & Raven, 2008) hinges entirely on a person's ability to analyze figures and detect patterns. This test presents the test taker with a series of grids (these are the "matrices"), and he or she must select an option that completes the pattern in each grid. This test is designed to minimize influence from verbal skills or background knowledge.

Reliability and Validity

Whenever we design a test—to assess intelligence, personality, or anything else—we need to determine whether the test is *reliable* and *valid*. **Reliability** refers to how consistent a measure is, and one aspect of reliability

FIGURE 13.16 INTELLIGENCE TEST ITEMS

- Vocabulary
  Presents a series of words of increasing difficulty; asks for a definition of each word: "What is a lute?" or "What does solitude mean?"
- Comprehension
  Asks the test-taker to explain why certain social practices are followed or the meaning of common proverbs: "What does it mean to say, 'Don't judge a book by its cover'?"
- Similarities
  Presents pairs of objects and asks how the items in each pair are alike: "In what ways are an airplane and a car alike?"
- Information
  Asks whether the test-taker knows various bits of information, with each bit being something that is widely known in our culture: "Who is the president of Russia?"

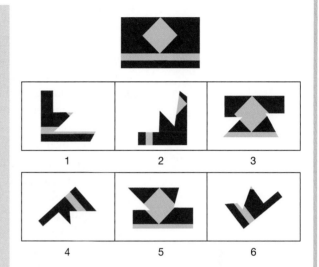

A Sample questions from verbal scale of the WAIS

B WAIS visual puzzle

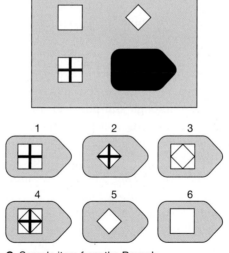

C Sample item from the Raven's Progressive Matrices

Panel A shows questions used in some of the subtests of the Wechsler Adult Intelligence Scale (WAIS). Panel B shows a sample item used in the perceptual-reasoning portion of the WAIS; the task is to assemble some of the parts to form the pattern shown. Panel C shows an easy item from the Raven's Progressive Matrices; the task is to identify the figure that completes the pattern. The test items get harder and harder as the test progresses.

is *consistency from one occasion to another*: If we give you a test, wait a while, and then give it again, do we get the same outcome? The issue here is **test-retest reliability**.

Intelligence tests have strong test-retest reliability. There is, for example, a high correlation between measurements of someone's IQ at age 6 and measurements of IQ when she's 18. For that matter, if we know someone's IQ at age 11, we can accurately predict what her IQ will be at age 80. (See, e.g., Deary, 2014; Deary, Pattie, & Starr, 2013; Plomin & Spinath, 2004.)

It's important, though, that IQ scores can change—especially if there's a substantial change in the person's environment. (We'll return to this point later in the chapter; also see Ramsden et al., 2011.) Nonetheless, if the environment is reasonably stable, the data show remarkable constancy in IQ scores, even over spans as long as 70 or 80 years.

What about the validity of the IQ test? In general, the term **validity** refers to whether a test actually measures what it is intended to measure, and one way to approach this issue is via an assessment of **predictive validity**. The logic behind this assessment is straightforward. If intelligence tests truly measure what they're supposed to, then someone's score on the test should enable us to predict how well that person will do in settings that require intelligence. And here, too, the results are impressive. For example, there's at least a .50 correlation between a person's IQ and measures of academic performance, such as grade-point average. (See Arneson, Sackett, & Beatty, 2011; Deary, 2012; Kuncel, Hezlett, & Ones, 2004; Strenze, 2007.)

IQ scores are also correlated with performance outside of the academic world. For example, an IQ score is a strong predictor of how someone will perform on the job, although—sensibly—the data indicate that IQ matters more for some jobs than for others (Sackett, Borneman, & Connelly, 2008; Schmidt & Hunter, 1998, 2004). Jobs of low complexity require relatively little intelligence, so the correlation between IQ and job performance is small (although still positive) for such jobs—for example, a correlation of .20 between IQ and performance on an assembly line. As jobs become more complex, intelligence matters more, so the correlation between IQ and performance gets stronger (Gottfredson, 1997). For example, we find correlations between .50 and .60 when we look at IQ scores and people's success as accountants or shop managers.

IQ scores are also correlated with other life outcomes. People with higher IQ's tend to end up with higher-prestige careers and are less likely to suffer various life problems (and so are less likely to end up in jail, less likely to become pregnant as teens, and more). Higher-IQ people even live longer—with various mechanisms contributing to this longevity. Among other considerations, higher-IQ individuals are less likely to die in automobile accidents (see **Table 13.1**) and less likely to have difficulty following doctors' instructions. (See Deary, Weiss, & Batty, 2010; Gottfredson, 2004; Kuncel et al., 2004; Lubinski, 2004; Murray, Pattie, Starr, & Deary, 2012.)

Let's emphasize, though, that no matter what the setting, IQ scores are never a perfect predictor of life outcomes. (Notice that all of these correlations

TABLE 13.1 THE RELATION BETWEEN IQ
AND HIGHWAY DEATHS

IQ	Death Rate per 100,000 Drivers
>115	51.3
100–115	51.5
85–99	92.2
80–84	146.7

From "The Practical Benefits of General Intelligence," by
C. Holden, 2003, *Science, 299*, pp. 192–193.

are appreciably less than +1.00.) This cannot be a surprise, however, because
of course other factors beyond intelligence matter in all of these domains.
For example, how well you'll do in school also depends on your motivation,
whether you stay healthy, whether your friends encourage you to study or
instead go to parties, and dozens of other factors. These points make it inevitable that intelligence levels won't be a perfect predictor of your academic
achievement. More bluntly, these points make it inevitable that some high-IQ
people will perform poorly in school, while some low-IQ people will excel.
(Clearly, therefore, an IQ score doesn't define your destiny.)

Even so, there's no question that there's a strong correlation between IQ
and many important life outcomes—academic or job performance, longevity,
and more. In fact, in many domains IQ is a better predictor of performance
than any other factor. It seems plain, then, that IQ tests do have impressive
predictive validity—with the clear implication that these tests are measuring
something interesting, important, and consequential.

General versus Specialized Intelligence

If—as it seems—IQ tests are measuring something important, what is
this "something"? This question is often framed in terms of two options.
One proposal is that the tests measure a singular ability that can apply to
any content. The idea is that your score on an IQ test reveals your *general*
intelligence, a capacity that provides an advantage on virtually any mental
task. (See Spearman, 1904, 1927; for more recent discussion, see Kaufman,
Kaufman, & Plucker, 2012.)

In contrast, some authors argue that there's no such thing as being intelligent in a general way. Instead, they claim, each person has a collection of
more specific talents—and so you might be "math smart" but not strong with
language, or "highly verbal" but not strong with tasks requiring visualization.
From this perspective, if we represent your capacities with a single number—an
IQ score—this is only a crude summary of what you can do, because it averages together the things you're good at and the things you're not.

Which proposal is correct? One way to find out relies on the fact that, as
we've said, many intelligence tests include numerous subtests. It's therefore

instructive to compare a person's score on each subtest with his or her scores on other subtests. In this way, we can ask: If someone does well on one portion of the test, is she likely to do well across the board? If someone does poorly on one subtest, will he do poorly on other subtests as well? If we observe these patterns, this would indicate that there is such a thing as intelligence-in-general, a cognitive capacity that shapes how well someone does no matter what the specific task might be.

More than a century ago, Charles Spearman developed a statistical procedure that enables us to pursue this issue in a precise, quantitative manner. The procedure is called **factor analysis,** and, as the name implies, this procedure looks for common factors—elements that contribute to multiple subtests and therefore link those subtests. Factor analysis confirms that there is a common element shared by all the components of the IQ test. (See Carroll, 1993; Deary, 2012; Johnson, Carothers, & Deary, 2008; Watkins, Wilson, Kotz, Carbone, & Babula, 2006.) Some subtests (e.g., comprehension of a simple story) depend heavily on this general factor; others (e.g., the ability to recall a string of digits) depend less on the factor. Nonetheless, this general factor matters across the board, and that's why scores on all the subtests end up correlated with one another.

Spearman named this common element **general intelligence,** usually abbreviated with the letter *g*. Spearman (1927) argued that people with a high level of *g* will have an advantage in virtually every intellectual endeavor. Conversely, if someone has a low level of *g*, that person will do poorly on a wide range of tasks.

A Hierarchical Model of Intelligence

The data tell us, though, that *g* isn't the whole story, because people also have more specialized skills. One of these skills involves aptitude for verbal tasks, so that performance on (say) a reading comprehension test depends on how much *g* a person has *and also* on the strength of these verbal skills. A second specialized ability involves quantitative or numerical aptitude, so performance on an arithmetic test depends on how much *g* a person has and also the strength of these skills.

Putting these pieces together, we can think of intellectual performance as having a hierarchical structure as shown in **Figure 13.17.** At the top of the hierarchy is *g*, contributing to all tasks. At the next level down are the abilities we just mentioned—linguistic and numerical—and several more, including spatial skill, an ability to handle fast-paced mental tasks, and an ability to learn new and unfamiliar materials. Then, at the next level are more specific capacities, each useful for a narrow and specialized set of tasks. (See Carroll, 1993; Flanagan, McGrew, & Ortiz, 2000; Johnson, Nijenhuis, & Bouchard, 2007; McGrew, 2009; Snow, 1994, 1996.)

This hierarchical conception leads to a prediction. If we choose tasks from two different categories—say, a verbal task and one requiring arithmetic—we should still find a correlation in performance, because no matter how different

FIGURE 13.17 A HIERARCHICAL MODEL OF INTELLIGENCE

Specialized abilities

Most modern researchers regard intelligence as having a hierarchical structure. General intelligence (*g*) is an ability called on by virtually all mental tasks. At the next level, linguistic, numerical, and spatial abilities are each called on by a range of tasks of a certain type; other abilities at this level include an ability to handle fast-paced tasks and also to memorize new material. At the next level down, more than 80 specialized abilities have been identified, each applicable to a certain type of task.

these tasks seem, they do have something in common: They both draw on *g*. If we choose tasks from the *same* category, though — say, two verbal tasks or two quantitative tasks — we should find a *higher* correlation because these tasks have two things in common: They both draw on *g*, and they both draw on the more specialized capacity needed for just that category. The data confirm both of these predictions — moderately strong correlations among all of the IQ test's subtests, and even stronger correlations among subtests in the same category.

It seems, then, that both of the broad hypotheses we introduced earlier are correct. There is some sort of general capacity that is useful for all mental endeavors, but there are also various forms of more specialized intelligence. Each person has some amount of the general capacity and draws on it in all tasks; this is why there's an overall consistency in each person's performance. At the same time, the consistency isn't perfect, because each task also requires more specialized abilities. Each of us has our own profile of strengths and weaknesses for these skills, with the result that there are things we do relatively well and things we do less well.

Fluid and Crystallized Intelligence

It's also important to distinguish between *fluid intelligence* and *crystallized intelligence* (Carroll, 2005; Horn, 1985; Horn & Blankson, 2005). **Fluid intelligence** involves the ability to deal with novel problems. It's the form of intelligence you need when you have no well-practiced routines you can bring to bear on a problem. **Crystallized intelligence**, in contrast, involves your acquired knowledge, including your verbal knowledge and your repertoire of skills—skills useful for dealing with problems similar to those already encountered.

Fluid and crystallized intelligence are highly correlated (e.g., if you have a lot of one, you're likely to have a lot of the other). Nonetheless, these two aspects of intelligence differ in important ways. Crystallized intelligence usually increases with age, but fluid intelligence reaches its peak in early adulthood and then declines across the lifespan (see **Figure 13.18**; Horn, 1985; Horn & Noll, 1994; Salthouse, 2004, 2012). Similarly, many factors—including alcohol consumption, fatigue, and depression—cause more impairment in tasks requiring fluid intelligence than in those dependent on crystallized intelligence (Duncan, 1994; Hunt, 1995). Therefore, someone who is tired will probably perform adequately on tests involving familiar routines and familiar facts. The same individual, however, may be markedly impaired if the test requires quick thinking or a novel approach—earmarks of fluid intelligence.

The Building Blocks of Intelligence

It's clear, then, that intelligence has many components. However, one component—g—is crucial, because this aspect of intelligence is relevant to virtually all mental activities. But what is g? What gives a person more g or less?

One proposal is simple. Mental processes are quick but do take time, and perhaps the people we consider intelligent are those who are especially fast

**FIGURE 13.18
INTELLIGENCE ACROSS
THE LIFESPAN**

Tests that involve crystallized intelligence (like tests of vocabulary) often show improvement in test scores across the lifespan, declining only when—at age 70 or so—the person's overall condition starts to deteriorate. In contrast, tests that involve fluid intelligence (like tests requiring speeded performance) peak at age 20 or so and decline thereafter. The "Z-scores" shown here are a common statistical measure used for comparing tests with disparate scoring schemes.

in these processes. This speed would enable them to perform intellectual tasks more quickly; it also would give them time for more steps in comparison with those of us who aren't so quick. (See Coyle, Pillow, Snyder, & Kochunov, 2011; Deary, 2012; Nettelbeck, 2003; Sheppard, 2008; Vernon, 1987.) As a variant of this proposal, some researchers argue that intelligence is created by faster processing, not throughout the brain, but in particular neural pathways—for example, the pathways linking temporal and parietal areas. (See Schubert, Hagemann & Frischkom, 2017; for a related idea, see **Figure 13.19.**)

Support for these ideas comes from measures of **inspection time**—the time a person needs to decide which of two lines is longer or which of two tones is higher. These measures correlate around –.30 with intelligence scores. (See Bates & Shieles, 2003; Danthiir, Roberts, Schulze, & Wilhelm, 2005; Deary & Derr, 2005; Ravenzwaaij, Brown, & Wagenmakers, 2011.) The correlation is negative because lower response times go with higher scores on intelligence tests.

A different proposal about *g* centers on the notion of *working-memory capacity* (WMC). We first met this notion in Chapter 6, where we saw that WMC is actually a measure of *executive control*—and so it is a measure of

FIGURE 13.19   THE P-FIT MODEL

What is it in the brain that makes intelligence possible? One view is the parieto-frontal integration theory (P-FIT), suggested by Jung & Haier (2007). Their theory identifies a network of brain sites that seem crucial for intellectual performance. Some of the sites are in the parietal lobe and are heavily involved in the control of attention. Other sites are in the frontal lobe and are essential for working memory. Still other important sites are crucial for language processing. (The dark circles in the figure indicate brain areas that are especially relevant in the left hemisphere; the light circles indicate brain areas that are relevant in both hemispheres. The numbers refer to a scheme—so-called Brodmann areas—commonly used for labeling brain regions.) The P-FIT conception emphasizes, though, that what really matters for intelligence is the integration of information from all of these sites—and, thus, the coordinated functioning of many cognitive components.

TEST YOURSELF

10. What does it mean to assess a measurement's reliability and its validity?

11. What evidence tells us that IQ tests do have predictive validity?

12. What's the evidence that something like *g* — or intelligence-in-general — exists?

13. What's the difference between fluid intelligence and crystallized intelligence?

14. What hypotheses have been proposed for the processes or characteristics that give someone a lot of *g*?

how well people can monitor and direct their own thought processes. We mentioned in the earlier chapter that people with a larger WMC do better on many intellectual tasks, including, we now add, tests specifically designed to measure *g*. (See Burgess, Braver, Conway, & Gray, 2011; Engel & Kane, 2004; Fukuda, Vogel, Mayr, & Awh, 2011; Jewsbury, Bowden, & Strauss, 2016; Redick et al., 2016.) Perhaps, therefore, the people we consider intelligent are those who literally have better control of their own thoughts, so they can coordinate their priorities in an appropriate way, override errant impulses, and in general proceed in a deliberate manner when making judgments or solving problems. (For debate on how exactly WMC contributes to intelligence, see Bleckley, Foster & Engle, 2015; Gonthier & Thomassin, 2015; Harrison, Shipstead, & Engle, 2015; Kanerva & Kalakoski, 2016; Redick et al., 2013.)

Intelligence beyond the IQ Test

We've now seen that IQ tests do measure something important, and we've gained important insights into what this "something" is. But, stepping away from what the IQ test *does* measure, we can also ask what it *doesn't* measure. Are there types of intelligence *not* included in conventional intelligence tests?

Practical Intelligence

Some people seem to be "street-smart"—that is, capable of sophisticated reasoning in day-to-day settings—even though they seem to lack the sort of analytical skill needed in a classroom. Psychologist Robert Sternberg has studied this sort of **practical intelligence**, with some of his research focused on whether *teaching* is more effective when instruction is matched to students' abilities (with different forms of instruction for students high in practical ability, students high in analytical ability, and students high in creative ability). Evidence suggests that "tuning" the curriculum in this way can be helpful. (See Grigorenko, Jarvin, & Sternberg, 2002; Sternberg & Grigorenko, 2004; also see Sternberg, Kaufman, & Grigorenko, 2008; Wagner, 2000. For concerns, though, see Gottfredson, 2003.)

Measures of Rationality

A different sort of complexity has been highlighted by Keith Stanovich. He reminds us that we all know people who are smart according to their test scores, but who nonetheless ignore facts, are overconfident in their judgment, are insensitive to inconsistencies in their views, and more. It's people like these who lead us to ask: "How could someone that smart be so stupid?"

In light of such cases (and much other evidence), Stanovich argues that we need separate measures of *intelligence* and *rationality* (Stanovich, 2009; Stanovich, West, & Toplak, 2016). He defines the latter term as the capacity for critically assessing information as it is gathered in the natural environment.

Other Types of Intelligence

Still other authors highlight a capacity they call **emotional intelligence**—the ability to understand one's own emotions and others', as well as the ability to control one's emotions when appropriate (Mayer, Roberts, & Barsade, 2008; Salovey & Mayer, 1990). Tests have been constructed to measure this capacity, and people who score well on these tests are judged to create a more positive atmosphere in the workplace and to have more leadership potential (Grewal & Salovey, 2005; Lopes, Salovey, Côté, & Beers, 2005). Likewise, college students who score well on these tests are rated by their friends as being more caring and more supportive; they're also less likely to experience conflict with peers (Brackett & Mayer, 2003; Mayer et al., 2008).

Perhaps the best-known challenge to IQ testing, however, comes from Howard Gardner's **theory of multiple intelligences**. Gardner (1983, 2006) argues for *eight* types of intelligence. Three of these are assessed in standard IQ tests: linguistic intelligence, logical-mathematical intelligence, and spatial intelligence. But Gardner also argues that we should acknowledge musical intelligence, bodily-kinesthetic intelligence (the ability to learn and create complex patterns of movement), interpersonal intelligence (the ability to understand other people), intrapersonal intelligence (the ability to understand ourselves), and naturalistic intelligence (the ability to understand patterns in nature).

Some of Gardner's evidence comes from the study of people with so-called **savant syndrome**—including people like Stephen Wiltshire, mentioned at the start of this chapter. These individuals are profoundly disabled, with IQ scores as low as 40 or 50, but each of them has a stunning level of specialized talent. Some are incredible artists (see **Figure 13.20**). Others are "calendar calculators,"

FIGURE 13.20 AN "AUTISTIC SAVANT"

We briefly discussed Stephen Wiltshire at the start of this chapter. According to standard intelligence tests, Wiltshire is profoundly disabled, but he has an extraordinary visual memory and is an astounding artist. After a few minutes in a helicopter flying over London, he was able to draw—from memory—a huge, incredibly detailed, highly accurate picture of what he'd seen.

able to answer immediately when asked questions like "What day of the week was March 19 in the year 1642?" Still others have remarkable musical skills and can effortlessly memorize lengthy musical works (Hill, 1978; Miller, 1999).

Apparently, then, it's possible to have extreme talent that is separate from intelligence as it's measured on IQ tests. But beyond this intriguing point, how should we think about Gardner's claims? First, his proposal reminds us that a broad range of human achievements are of enormous value, and surely we should celebrate the skill displayed by an artist at her canvas, a skilled dancer in the ballet, or an empathetic clergyman in a hospital room. These are certainly talents to be acknowledged and, as much as possible, nurtured and developed.

But let's also be clear that Gardner's conception shouldn't be understood as a challenge to conventional intelligence testing. IQ tests were never designed to measure all human talents—so it's no surprise that these tests tell us little about, say, musical intelligence or bodily-kinesthetic intelligence. These other talents are important, but that takes nothing away from the importance of the capacities measured by IQ tests—capacities that (as we've seen) are needed for many aspects of life.

Finally, there's room for debate about whether the capacities showcased by Gardner (or, for that matter, the capacity labeled "emotional intelligence") should be thought of as forms of intelligence. In ordinary conversation, we make a distinction between "intelligence" and "talent"—and so, for example, we mean something different if we talk about an "intelligent" athlete in contrast to a "talented" athlete. Likewise, various television shows seek performers with *talent* rather than performers with *intelligence*. Gardner's proposal invites us to step away from this distinction, and the motivation is clear: His use of the term "intelligence" does encourage us to give these other pursuits the esteem they surely deserve. At the same time, his terminology may lead us to ignore distinctions we might otherwise need. (For more on Gardner's claims, see Cowan & Carney, 2006; Deary, 2012; Thioux, Stark, Klaiman, & Shultz, 2006; Visser, Ashton, & Vernon, 2006; White 2008.)

TEST YOURSELF

15. What types of intelligence have been proposed that are separate from the capacities measured by the IQ test?

"BRITAIN'S GOT TALENT"

Many types of performance can reveal "talent," and so are eligible for the TV show *Britain's Got Talent*. Even so, most people make a distinction between "talent" and "intelligence," and Gardner's proposal for multiple intelligences deliberately blurs this distinction.

The Roots of Intelligence

Differences in intelligence, we've suggested, may be the result of variations in mental speed or in the functioning of executive control. But what causes those differences? Why does one person end up with a high level of intelligence, while other people end up with a lower level?

Discussions of these questions often frame the issue as if it were a choice between two alternatives—"nature versus nurture." In other words, should our explanation emphasize genetics and heredity, or should we focus on learning and the environment? This framing of the issue, however, is misleading: Both types of influence—one rooted in genetics, one rooted in experience—play an important role in shaping intelligence. Moreover, these influences aren't separate; instead, the two types of influence actually *depend* on each other.

We can see the impact of genetic influences on intelligence in the fact that people who resemble each other genetically also resemble each other in their IQ scores. This resemblance is in place even if the individuals grow up in different environments. For example, identical (i.e., monozygotic) twins tend to have highly similar IQ scores even if the twins are reared in different households. (See **Figure 13.21**; also see Bouchard, Lykken, McGue, Segal,

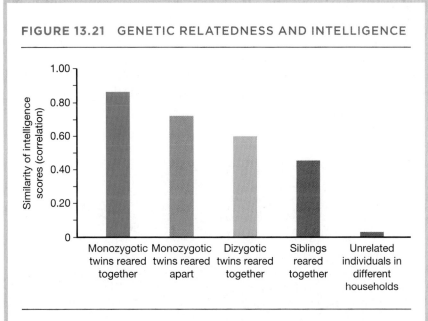

FIGURE 13.21 GENETIC RELATEDNESS AND INTELLIGENCE

Monozygotic twins share 100% of their DNA and tend to resemble each other in intelligence whether they were raised together or not. Dizygotic twins (with 50% overlap in their DNA) show less resemblance, although they resemble each other more than non-twin siblings or randomly selected (unrelated) individuals do.

& Tellegen, 1990; McGue, Bouchard, Iacono, & Lykken, 1993; Plomin & Spinath, 2004. For research examining which genes, and exactly which DNA patterns, contribute to individual differences in IQ, see Benyamin et al., 2013; Payton, 2009; Plomin et al., 2013; Rizzi & Posthuma, 2012.)

There's no question, though, that environmental factors also matter for intelligence. For example, we've known for many years that *living in poverty* impedes intellectual development, and the effect is cumulative: The longer the child remains in such an environment, the greater the harm. This point emerges in the data as a negative correlation between IQ and age. That is, the older the child (the longer she had been in the impoverished environment), the lower her IQ. (See Asher, 1935; Gordon, 1923; for more recent data, see Heckman, 2006. For discussion of *why* poverty undermines intellectual development, see Nisbett, 2009; Protzko, Aronson, & Blair, 2013.)

A related—and more optimistic—finding is that *improving* the environment can *increase* IQ. In one study, researchers focused on cases in which the government had removed children from their biological parents because of abuse or neglect (Duyme, Dumaret, & Tomkiewicz, 1999). The researchers compared the children's "pre-adoption IQ" (when the children were living in a high-risk environment) with their IQ in adolescence—after years of living with adoptive families. The data showed substantial improvements in the children's scores, thanks to this environmental change (see **Figure 13.22**). (Also see Diamond & Lee, 2011; Nisbett et al., 2012a, b; Protzko, Aronson, & Blair, 2013.)

The impact of environmental factors is also undeniable in another fact. Around the globe, scores on intelligence tests have been increasing over the last few decades, at a rate of approximately 3 points per decade. This pattern is known as the **Flynn effect**, after James Flynn (1984, 1987, 1999, 2009), the first researcher to document this effect. (See also Daley, Whaley, Sigman,

FIGURE 13.22 IQ IMPROVEMENT DUE TO ENVIRONMENTAL CHANGE

Researchers examined the IQ scores of children who were adopted out of horrible environments in which they had been abused or neglected. After the adoption (when the children were in better environments), the children's IQ scores were markedly higher—especially if the children were adopted into a family with higher socioeconomic status (SES). (AFTER DUYME, DUMARET, & TOMKIEWICZ, 1999)

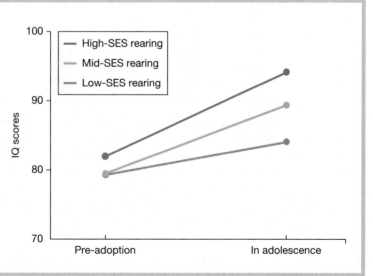

Espinosa, & Neumann, 2003; Kanaya, Scullin, & Ceci, 2003; Pietschnig & Voracek, 2015; Trahan, Stuebing, Fletcher, & Hiscock, 2014; Wai, Putallaz, & Makel, 2012.) This improvement has been observed in relatively affluent nations and also in impoverished nations. Moreover, the effect is stronger in measures of fluid intelligence—such as the Raven's Matrices—so it seems to reflect a genuine change in how quickly and flexibly people can think, and not just a worldwide increase in how much information people have.

There's disagreement about the causes of the Flynn effect (Daley et al., 2003; Dickens & Flynn, 2001; Flynn, 2009; Fox & Mitchum, 2013; Greenfield, 2009; Nisbett et al., 2012a; Pietschnig & Voracek, 2015), and it's likely that several factors contribute. Regardless of the explanation, though, the Flynn effect cannot be explained genetically. The human genome does change, but not at a speed commensurate with this effect. Therefore, this worldwide improvement becomes part of the evidence documenting that intelligence can indeed be improved by suitable environmental conditions.

The Interaction among Genetic Factors, Environment, and IQ

Unmistakably, genetic factors matter for IQ, and so do environmental factors. But how do we put these pieces together? The key here is that these influences interact in crucial ways, and one way to see this interaction is to consider the impact of poverty.

We've already noted that poverty interferes with intellectual development (Hackman & Farah, 2009; Lubinski, 2004; Raizada & Kishiyama, 2010), and if you live in poverty, that's a fact about your environment. But this environmental influence interacts with genetic influences. (See Turkheimer, Haley, Waldron, D'Onofrio, & Gottesman, 2003; also Bates, Lewis, & Weiss, 2013; Tucker-Drob, Rhemtulla, Harden, Turkheimer, & Fask, 2011.) Specifically, we've already noted that identical twins tend to have similar IQ scores, and this observation provides powerful evidence that genetic factors play a role. The picture is different, though, if we focus on impoverished families. In these families, the IQ resemblance for identical twins is markedly reduced—indicating that in this setting, genetic factors matter much less for shaping a person's intelligence.

The full explanation of this result is complex. Part of the explanation, though, hinges on the fact that genetic mechanisms enable someone to make full use of the "environmental inputs that support intellectual growth" (Bates et al., 2013, p. 2111). If there is a rich fabric of these inputs, the genetic mechanisms enable the person to gain from them and flourish. But if these inputs are absent, the genetic mechanisms have nothing to work with—so they produce little growth. In other words, the machinery that could promote growth is present, but with little input to work on, the machinery can't do its job. (For further discussion of how environmental factors interact with genes, see Davis, Hayworth, & Plomin, 2009; Taylor, Roehrig, Hensler, Connor, & Schatschneider, 2010; Tucker-Drob & Bates, 2016; Vinkhuyzen, van der Sluis, & Posthuma, 2011.)

The Complexity of Cereal Boxes

When calculators became widely available, some people lamented: "The next generation will have no reason to learn the rules of arithmetic; they'll just punch buttons on their calculators. As a result, the next generation will be less skilled in mathematics!" As GPS devices (in our cars, on our phones) became more widespread, some people lamented: "The next generation will never learn to navigate; they'll just follow the instructions on the screen. The next generation will therefore be less skilled in spatial reasoning!"

Concerns like these suggest that humans will gradually become stupider and stupider. Over the years, it is feared, we'll rely more and more on our electronic devices, and so we'll do less for ourselves, with the result that we'll lose skill after skill. In the end, we'll be totally dependent on (and perhaps at the mercy of) our gadgets.

These fears, however, are probably unfounded. It's true that the forward march of technology can eliminate the need for many activities, so that fewer people will retain the skill needed for those activities. As a result, when the batteries die in your GPS, you may have trouble getting where you need to be. Even so, it's okay if people shed some skills. (Think about the fact that in the modern world, few people know how to shoe a horse; it's a skill we no longer need.) More broadly, though, how deep is the concern here? Will our gadgets really make us stupid?

Evidence points toward the opposite claim. As the chapter describes, IQ scores are *rising* around the world—at the rate of roughly 3 points every decade. This improvement, termed the "Flynn effect," probably has multiple sources. In impoverished countries, for example, the explanation probably lies in a pattern of gradually improving nutrition and health care. These crucial changes make it possible for people to reach their biological potential. We need a different explanation, though, for the Flynn effect observed in wealthier countries (including Belgium, Norway, or Great Britain). Here, the key may be the *informational complexity* of the modern world.

Our ancient ancestors had fewer tools (no calculators, no GPS, no Internet access), but they also had less information to keep track of. As a result, they had no need to develop skill in interpreting complex data patterns, weighing dozens of facts against one another, or deciphering subtle messages. In the modern world, however, we do need these skills—whether we're trying to read a difficult academic text, hearing a nuanced political argument, or just trying to follow the plot of a complicated novel. Indeed, consider the information richness you might find on the back of a cereal box—information that includes a catalogue of ingredients; a listing of how well the cereal does (or doesn't) fill various dietary requirements (did you ingest the recommended amount of riboflavin today?); various recipes (e.g., all the things you can make from Rice Krispies); and perhaps a game you might play while eating your Fruitios.

Can we prove that it's this information richness that's driving the Flynn effect, by making us all acquire the skills needed to handle and interpret this flood of input? The answer is no. Even so, this does seem a plausible account of the Flynn effect, and the effect itself is undeniable. And, of course, if facts supporting or challenging this claim become available, you won't have to memorize them—you'll be able to find them easily with a Google search.

Comparisons between Groups

Most research on intelligence has focused on the differences from one person to the next. There has also been discussion, though, about differences between *groups*, with much of the debate centering on a comparison between American Whites and American Blacks. (There's also research comparing other groups, including the Asian and Latinx segments of the American population, and also research comparing the IQ scores of *men* and *women*. There's no question, though, that most of the research—and the heated debate—has focused on the racial differences.)

Studies indicate that the average intelligence score of American (and European) Whites is higher than the average score of African Americans. (See Dickens & Flynn, 2006; Jencks & Phillips, 1998; Jensen, 1985; Loehlin, Lindzey, & Spuhler, 1975; Reynolds, Chastain, Kaufman, & McLean, 1987; Rushton & Jensen, 2005; Rushton, 2012.) It's crucial to bear in mind, though, that this is a point about *averages*, and there is, in fact, a huge amount of overlap between the full set of scores for American Whites and American Blacks. Nonetheless, there's a detectable difference between the averages, leading us to ask what's going on here.

Part of the answer is economic, because Blacks and Whites in the United States often do not have the same opportunities or access to the same resources. On average, African Americans have lower incomes than Whites and live in less affluent neighborhoods. A higher proportion of Blacks than Whites are exposed to poor nutrition and poor health care, and as we've mentioned, these environmental factors have a substantial impact on IQ. On this basis, some of the difference between Blacks and Whites isn't a race difference at all; instead, it is an economic status difference (Neisser et al., 1996; Nisbett et al., 2012a; also see Jencks & Phillips, 1998).

In addition, let's emphasize that American Blacks are often treated differently from Whites by the people they encounter. They also grow up with different role models than Whites, and they typically make different assumptions about what life paths will be open to them. Do these facts matter for intelligence scores? Consider studies of **stereotype threat**, a term that describes the negative impact that social stereotypes, once activated, can have on task performance. Concretely, imagine an African American taking an intelligence test. She might become anxious because she knows this is a test on which members of her group are expected to do poorly. This anxiety might be compounded by the thought that her poor performance, if it occurs, will only serve to confirm others' prejudices. These feelings, in turn, could erode her performance by making it more difficult for her to pay attention and do her best work on the test. Moreover, given the thought that poor performance is a distinct possibility, she might simply decide not to expend enormous effort—if she's likely to do poorly, why struggle against the tide?

Evidence for effects like these comes from various studies, including some in which two groups of African Americans take exactly the same test. One group is told at the start that the test is designed to assess their intelligence;

HUMAN DIVERSITY

It is important to emphasize that the comparisons between groups — including the comparison between American Blacks and American Whites — are between the *averages* for each group. This point is crucial, because the scores of European American test takers vary enormously, as do the scores of African American test takers. In fact, the variation within each group is much, much larger than any between-group variations researchers have detected. As a related point, the overlap between the scores of American Blacks and American Whites is much more impressive than the relatively small difference between the averages. These points carry an important message: We learn little about any individual's abilities simply by knowing his or her group membership, and it would be wrong (and in most settings, illegal) to use group membership as a basis for making decisions about that individual.

the other group is led to believe that the test is simply composed of challenges and is not designed to assess them in any way. The first group, for which the instructions will likely trigger stereotype threat, does markedly worse than the second group. (See Steele, 2010; Steele & Aronson, 1995; also Autin & Croziet, 2012; Spencer, Logel, & Davies, 2016; Walton & Spencer, 2009.)

These results are important for many reasons, including the fact that they draw our attention back to the question of what intelligence is—or, more broadly, what it is that "intellectual tasks" require. One requirement, of course, is a set of cognitive skills and capacities (e.g., mental speed or executive control). A different requirement, however, is the proper attitude toward testing—and a bad attitude (e.g., anxiety about failing, fear of confirming others' negative expectations) can undermine performance. These attitudes, in turn, are influenced by social pressures and prejudice, and through this mechanism these external forces can powerfully shape each person's achievements—and can, in particular, contribute to the differences between IQ scores for Whites and Blacks.

What, therefore, is our path forward? As we have seen, intelligence is a predictor of many life outcomes—in the academic world, in the workplace, and beyond. These points add to the (already enormous) urgency of making sure that everyone receives adequate nutrition and health care, as well as appropriate educational opportunities—because we know these factors play an important role in shaping intellectual development. Research also suggests that we may be able to improve intelligence directly—perhaps with targeted training of executive function or with careful instruction to help people develop crystallized intelligence. (See Au et al., 2015; Nisbett, 2009; Shipstead, Redick, & Engle, 2012.) But, in addition, this discussion of stereotype threat suggests that we can also move forward by shifting people's expectations, because these too have a powerful influence on intellectual performance. The shift in expectations won't be easy, because these (often racist) expectations are held—and reinforced—by many teachers, parents, and even young children; the expectations are also built into many social institutions. Nonetheless, given what we know about the linkage between intelligence and success in the workplace, or between intelligence and health, efforts on all of these fronts must be a high priority for all of us.

TEST YOURSELF

16. What evidence makes it clear that *genetic factors* influence someone's level of intelligence? What evidence makes it clear that *environmental factors* influence someone's level of intelligence?
17. What is stereotype threat, and how does it influence performance on an intelligence test?

COGNITIVE PSYCHOLOGY AND EDUCATION

the goals of "education"

The evidence is clear that IQ tests measure something important. People with high scores on the test do better in a host of other domains—they do better in school; they're more successful in the workplace; they're healthier; they're less likely to end up with certain undesirable outcomes (including drug addiction, incarceration, and unwanted pregnancy); and so on. These results demand that we ask: What can we do to *improve* the capacities measured by the IQ test?

For a start, we know that one aspect of intelligence is *crystallized intelligence*—a person's accumulation of knowledge and skills. Part of the goal in education, therefore, should be an increase in knowledge and skill, and of course psychology can help us in reaching that goal. (See, e.g., Chapters 6, 7 and 8!)

A different aspect of intelligence is *fluid intelligence*—the ability to deal with new and unusual problems, and there is reason to believe that fluid intelligence is linked to a person's executive control—the person's ability to control his or her own thoughts. It's therefore encouraging that several research teams have suggested we can improve someone's executive functioning through various forms of training, whether we're training children (e.g., Rueda, Rothbart, McCandliss, Saccomanno, & Posner, 2005) or adults (e.g., Teper, Segal, & Inzlicht, 2013).

We should mention that the evidence is less encouraging for some of the commercially offered "brain-training" programs. Research evidence suggests that these programs do improve performance on the tasks *included within the program itself.* However, there's little indication that this training helps people with other tasks—and, therefore, little reason to believe that these programs can deliver what they promise (Simons et al., 2016).

More broadly, the chapter reminds us that someone's *attitudes* and *beliefs*—including students' expectations for themselves—have a powerful impact on intellectual performance. Concretely, performance in intellectual pursuits is often undermined by expectations of failure and fears that your poor showing will only confirm people's worst beliefs about you. Guided by these fears, you're likely to become anxious, which by itself can undermine your performance. You're also likely to interpret early frustrations or slow progress as "proof" that the problems you're working on are beyond your abilities. This interpretation can lead you to abandon your efforts or to try less hard whenever you encounter early obstacles.

Perhaps, then, we can improve performance by addressing these beliefs. In one study, women did less well on a math test if they came into the test believing that differences between men and women in math abilities are rooted in genetics and, therefore (they thought), unchangeable (Dar-Nimrod & Heine, 2006). Women performed better if they came into the test with the (correct!) belief that the gender difference is largely rooted in environmental factors and, no matter what the source of the difference may be, is certainly changeable.

In another study, middle-school students were asked to write a few sentences, at various points during the school year, about things they valued—such as athletic ability, being good at art, or creativity (Cohen, Garcia, Apfel, & Master, 2006; Cohen, Garcia, Purdie-Vaughns, Apfel, & Brzustoski, 2009). This simple exercise apparently reminded students that academic achievement—although important—didn't define who they were, and this was enough to provide a sense of perspective that diminished the students' anxieties and improved their academic performance. These (and other) studies suggest that it's possible to shift students' attitudes toward achievement and testing and thereby undercut the harmful effects of stereotype threat.

In addition, Stanovich's research on rationality reminds us that people need to have a set of intellectual habits that allow them to *use* whatever intelligence they have. Education should therefore seek to foster these habits—including a willingness to look at both sides of an issue; a willingness to set aside your beliefs if the facts don't fit with your view; and an ability to assess which of your beliefs are well supported by evidence (so that you can rely on those beliefs) and which ones are more tentative (so that you should be cautious in relying on them). Stanovich argues that many people—including some of our elected officials—may have high IQ scores but nonetheless lack these habits. As a result, they may be likely to draw conclusions that are entirely out of step with factual evidence and end up taking actions that are harmful to themselves and others. Plainly, therefore, we would be well served by an education system that highlights and encourages these crucial habits of rationality.

Finally, let's acknowledge the broader set of valuable human capacities. Intelligence and rationality are enormously important, and not having these attributes can profoundly limit someone's progress through life. But there are other capacities that we should value and nurture—such as the capacity to produce art, the capacity to understand ourselves, or the capacity to understand, work with, and help others. In fact, let's take this a step further. Many years ago, in a 1947 essay entitled "The Purpose of Education," Martin Luther King Jr. acknowledged that "education must enable one to sift and weigh evidence, to discern the true from the false, the real from the unreal, and the facts from the fiction." But he also expressed a concern that education can sometimes produce someone who is "gifted with reason, but with no morals." Dr. King argued, therefore, for a moral component in education, so that "complete education gives one not only power of concentration, but worthy objectives upon which to concentrate."

Overall, then, this chapter has showcased the importance of intelligence, and that discussion demands a high priority on educational steps that can enhance people's intelligence. There is no question that a *lack* of intelligence or rationality is the source of many problems in the world. Even so, education needs to have other goals as well, with the broad aim of improving our students, ourselves, and our world.

For more on this topic:

Cohen, G. L., Garcia, J., Apfel, N., & Master, A. (2006). Reducing the racial achievement gap: A social-psychological intervention. *Science, 313*, 1307–1310.

Cohen, G. L., Garcia, J., Purdie-Vaughns, V., Apfel, N., & Brzustoski, P. (2009). Recursive processes in self-affirmation: Intervening to close the minority achievement gap. *Science, 324*, 400–403.

Dar-Nimrod, I., & Heine, S. (2006). Exposure to scientific theories affects women's math performance. *Science, 314*, 435.

Stanovich, K. E. (2009). *What intelligence tests miss: The psychology of rational thought.* New Haven, CT: Yale University Press.

chapter review

SUMMARY

- Problem solving is often likened to a process of search in which you seek a path leading from a starting point to the goal. In many problems, though, there are too many paths to allow examination of each, and this is why problem-solving heuristics are crucial. Heuristics applicable to a wide range of problems include hill climbing and means-end analysis.

- Visual images and diagrams also aid problem solving, and so do analogies to earlier-solved problems. Nonetheless, analogies seem to be underused by many problem solvers, possibly because problem solvers search their memory with an emphasis on a problem's superficial features rather than its underlying dynamic. Analogy use can be promoted, therefore, by instructions or contexts that encourage people to focus on a problem's deeper structure.

- Experts in an area generally pay more attention to a problem's underlying structure than to its surface form, an approach that helps the experts to find and use analogies. Focusing on the problem's underlying structure also helps the experts to break the problem into subproblems.

- The likelihood of solving a problem is enormously influenced by how the person perceives or defines the problem. The problem definition can include unnoticed assumptions about the form the solution must take, assumptions about the use or function of elements contained within the problem, and assumptions about what types of procedures one should try in solving the problem. These various forms of problem-solving sets are usually helpful, because they guide the problem solver away from pointless lines of attack on the problem. But the problem-solving set can also be an obstacle—if, for example, the solution requires a change in the set. As a result, problem-solving sets in the form of functional fixedness can be significant obstacles to problem solution.

- Investigators who are interested in creativity have often relied on detailed case studies of famous creative individuals. These case studies have identified certain shared traits that seem to be "prerequisites" for great creativity. The case studies also suggest a need for a sociocultural approach to creativity.

- Some scholars suggest that creative problem solving proceeds through four stages: preparation, incubation, illumination, and verification. However, other researchers are skeptical about these four stages, and careful studies of creativity have provided little evidence to suggest that creativity involves special or exotic processes. For example, incubation is often mentioned as a form of unconscious problem solving, but some studies indicate that the benefits of incubation, when they occur, can be understood in simpler terms: recovery from fatigue or the forgetting of unfruitful earlier approaches. In the same way, the moment of illumination seems to indicate only that the problem solver has located a new approach to a problem; in many cases, this new approach ultimately leads to a dead end.

- In light of these data, many authors have suggested that creativity may simply be the extraordinary product that results from an assembly of ordinary elements—elements that include cognitive processes (memory search through spreading activation, heuristics, etc.) and also emotional and personality characteristics that foster the processes and circumstances needed for creativity.

- Data show that the commonly used measures of intelligence are reliable and valid. The reliability is evident in the fact that a person's IQ score is likely to be roughly the same if tested in childhood and then tested again decades later. The validity is indicated by correlations often observed between IQ scores and performance in tasks that seem to require intelligence. These correlations are well below 1.00, but this simply reminds us that other factors also matter for performance in most domains.

● Most intelligence tests involve numerous sub-tests, but people who do well on one portion of the test tend to do well across the board. This sort of evidence persuades researchers that there is such a thing as intelligence-in-general—usually referred to as *g*. However, we can also distinguish various forms of more specialized intelligence; therefore, performance on many tasks depends both on a person's level of *g* and his or her profile of more specific strengths and weaknesses. This pattern is often summarized in hierarchical models of intelligence.

● We need to distinguish between fluid and crystallized intelligence. Fluid intelligence involves the ability to deal with new and unusual problems. Crystallized intelligence involves acquired knowledge and skills.

● General intelligence, or *g*, is sometimes understood in terms of mental speed, on the idea that people whom we consider smart are literally faster in their intellectual functioning. A different proposal centers on the notion of *working-memory capacity* and *executive control,* with the suggestion that people who are intelligent are literally better able to monitor and direct their own thought processes.

● IQ scores don't assess all of a person's mental capacities. Researchers have also emphasized the importance of practical intelligence, rationality, and emotional intelligence. The theory of multiple intelligences goes further, proposing eight different types of intelligence.

● Genetic differences are part of the reason why people differ in intelligence. This is evident in the fact that people who resemble each other closely in their genetic profile (e.g., identical twins) also tend to resemble each other closely in their IQ scores; this remains true even if the twins were separated at birth and raised separately. It's also true, however, that environmental factors influence intelligence. This is reflected in the fact that various aspects of poverty can undermine intelligence and various forms of enrichment in the environment can improve it. The impact of environment is also evident in the worldwide improvement in IQ scores known as the Flynn effect.

● Crucially, we must understand the interaction between genetic and environmental forces in determining a person's IQ. In simple terms, we can think of the genes as specifying someone's potential, but how that potential will unfold is significantly shaped by the person's environment.

● There has been debate about differences in the average IQ scores of American Blacks and American Whites. The differences can be understood partly in terms of the lower levels of nutrition, medical care, and education that are available for many American Blacks as opposed to Whites. In addition, a large role is played by stereotype threat—a term referring to the negative impact that social stereotypes, once activated, can have on task performance.

KEY TERMS

TEST YOURSELF AGAIN

1. What does it mean to say that a problem-solving heuristic allows you to trim the size of the problem space?

2. What is means-end analysis?

3. Why do people seem to under-use analogies in solving problems?

4. What are some of the advantages that expert problem solvers have, compared to those who are not experts?

5. Why are problem-solving sets often a problem? But why are problem-solving sets also useful?

6. What is functional fixedness?

7. Define each of the stages proposed by Wallas—preparation, incubation, illumination, and verification.

8. What does research tell us about whether incubation truly helps problem solving?

9. What does research tell us is really going on in the "Aha!" moment of illumination?

10. What does it mean to assess a measurement's reliability and its validity?

11. What evidence tells us that IQ tests do have predictive validity?

12. What's the evidence that something like *g*—or intelligence-in-general—exists?

13. What's the difference between fluid intelligence and crystallized intelligence?

14. What hypotheses have been proposed for the processes or characteristics that give someone a lot of *g*?

15. What types of intelligence have been proposed that are separate from the capacities measured by the IQ test?

16. What evidence makes it clear that *genetic factors* influence someone's level of intelligence? What evidence makes it clear that *environmental factors* influence someone's level of intelligence?

17. What is stereotype threat, and how does it influence performance on an intelligence test?

THINK ABOUT IT

1. Men and women don't differ, on average, in their overall IQ scores. However, men seem to have an advantage in some tasks requiring spatial reasoning, and women seem to have an advantage in some tasks involving verbal reasoning. Can these differences be explained through the mechanism of stereotype threat? What other factors might play a role in producing these differences?

B eBOOK DEMONSTRATIONS & ESSAYS

Go to http://digital.wwnorton.com/cognition7 for the online demonstrations and essays relevant to this chapter. These can be found in the ebook.

Online Demonstrations

- Demonstration 13.1: Analogies
- Demonstration 13.2: Additional Incubation Exercises
- Demonstration 13.3: Verbalization and Problem Solving
- Demonstration 13.4: Additional Remote Associates Exercises
- Demonstration 13.5: IQ Testing

Online Applying Cognitive Psychology and the Law Essays

- Cognitive Psychology and the Law: Problem Solving in the Courts
- Cognitive Psychology and the Law: Intelligence and the Legal System

ZAPS COGNITION LABS

Go to http://digital.wwnorton.com/cognition7 to experience interactive online psychology labs relevant to this chapter.

The solutions to the puzzles on **p. 519** are: *reading between the lines, split-second timing, search high and low, hole in one, Jack in the Box,* and *double or nothing.*

The solutions to the puzzles on **p. 520** are: *spin (spinoff, topspin, tailspin), heart (heartache, sweetheart, heartburn), glasses (dark glasses, shot glasses, sunglasses), pit (armpit, coal pit, peach pit), boat (tugboat, gravy boat, showboat).*

chapter 14 | Conscious Thought, Unconscious Thought

what if...

This is a chapter about *consciousness*—what it is and what it's for. We can learn a great deal about this topic, though, by considering the opposite: the processes in our minds that we're *not* conscious of. For example, consider the achievement of *seeing* something, out in plain view in front of your eyes.

Imagine that your friend René puts a red rose on the table in front of you and asks, "What color is this?" You'd likely be puzzled by this question, but you could still answer, "It's red, obviously." Now, imagine that René asks, "How do you know?" Again, this seems an odd question, but a bit impatiently you'd probably say, "Because I can see it." René, however, is still not satisfied and asks, "But how do you know you can see it?" This question is even odder. After all, how could you *not* know what you're seeing?

This exercise reminds us of the commonsense point that "seeing" involves some sort of "visual awareness." Think about the sentence "Linda was looking right at the moose, but somehow she didn't see it." The sentence seems to indicate that Linda wasn't aware of the moose's presence, and that's why the sentence offers a contrast between "looking" and "seeing."

But what if these commonsense claims are mistaken? Consider patient D.B. He developed a tumor in his occipital cortex and underwent surgery to remove the tumor and, with it, a significant amount of brain tissue. As a result, D.B. became partially blind and was unable to see anything in the left half of the world in front of him. Careful testing, though, revealed a surprising pattern. In one study, D.B. sat in front of a computer screen while a target on the screen's left side moved in some trials and stayed still in others. D.B. insisted he couldn't see the target at all, but when forced to guess, he generally guessed correctly whether the target was moving. Likewise, if asked to reach toward an object off to his left, he insisted he couldn't—but when forced to reach, he generally moved his hand toward the proper location. Later, when researchers showed the results of these studies to D.B., he was bewildered by his own performance and had no idea how his guessing could have been so accurate.

Patient G.Y. showed a similar pattern. He was involved in a traffic accident when he was 8 years old and (like D.B.) suffered damage to the occipital cortex. As a result, G.Y. was blind—he insisted he couldn't see, and he failed to react to visual inputs. Yet, in one study G.Y. was asked to move his arm in a way that matched the motion of a moving target (a point of light). G.Y.'s performance was quite accurate even though he said he couldn't see the target at all. He claimed he only had an "impression" of motion and that he was "aware there was an object moving." But it's hard to interpret these remarks, because G.Y. insisted he had no idea what the moving object looked like.

To describe patients like these, Weiskrantz and Warrington coined the term "blind sight" (see, e.g., Weiskrantz, 1986, 1997). Blind-sight patients are, by any conventional definition, truly blind, but even so they're generally able to "guess" the color of targets that (they insist) they cannot see; they can "guess" the shape of a form (*X* or *O*, square or circle); they can also "guess" the orientation of lines. Some of these patients can even "guess" the emotional expression of faces that (apparently) they cannot see at all.

Patients with blind sight force us to distinguish between "seeing" and "having visual awareness"—because they apparently can do one but not the other. This separation raises questions about just what "seeing" is and why some aspects of seeing can go forward without consciousness. In addition, what might these observations tell us about consciousness itself? If consciousness isn't needed for visual perception, then when is it needed?

The Study of Consciousness

The field of psychology emerged as a separate discipline, distinct from philosophy and biology, in the late 1800s, and in those early years of our field, the topic of consciousness was a central concern. In Wilhelm Wundt's laboratory in Germany, researchers sought to understand the "elements" of consciousness; William James, in America, sought to understand the "stream" of consciousness.

The young field of psychology, however, soon rejected this focus on consciousness, arguing that this research was subjective and unscientific. By the early 20th century, therefore, the topic of consciousness was largely gone from mainstream psychological research (although theorizing about consciousness, without much experimentation, continued). In the last few decades, however, researchers have made enormous advances in their understanding of what consciousness is, how it functions, and how the brain makes consciousness possible. In fact, these advances have been woven into the material we've already covered, and so this chapter can do two things at once: describe what's known about consciousness, but also review where we've been for the last thirteen chapters.

Of course, questions about consciousness are extraordinarily difficult, because we're asking about a phenomenon that's invisible to anyone other than the experiencer. Indeed, in Chapter 1 we discussed concerns about *introspection* as a research tool, and consciousness researchers take those concerns seriously. Nonetheless, we now know a lot about consciousness—and so we've made considerable progress in exploring one of the mind's greatest mysteries.

Let's acknowledge at the start, though, that there's still much about consciousness that we don't understand; in fact, there's still disagreement about how consciousness should be defined. We'll return to this conceptual issue later in the chapter. For now, we'll proceed with this rough definition: Consciousness is a state of awareness of sensations or ideas, such that you can reflect on those sensations and ideas, know what it "feels like" to experience these sensations and ideas, and can, in many cases, report to others that you're aware of the sensations and ideas. As we'll see, this broad definition has certain problems, but it will serve us well enough as an initial guide for discussion.

The Cognitive Unconscious

Activities like thinking, remembering, and categorizing all feel quick and effortless. You instantly recognize the words on this page; you easily remember where you were this morning; you have no trouble deciding to have Cheddar on your sandwich, not Swiss. As we've seen throughout this book, however, these (and other) intellectual activities are possible only because of an elaborate "support structure"—processes and mechanisms working "behind the scenes." Describing this behind-the-scenes action has been one of the main concerns of this text.

Psychologists refer to this behind-the-scenes activity as the **cognitive unconscious**—the broad set of mental activities that you're not aware of but that make possible your ordinary interactions with the world. The processes that unfold in the cognitive unconscious are sophisticated and powerful, and as we'll see, it's actually quite helpful that a lot of mental work can take place without conscious supervision. At the same time, we also need to discuss the ways in which the absence of supervision can, in some cases, be a problem for you.

Unconscious Processes, Conscious Products

For many purposes, it's useful to distinguish the *products* created within your mind (beliefs you've formed, conclusions you've reached) from the *processes* that led to these products. This distinction isn't always clear-cut, and in some cases we can quibble about whether a particular mental step counts as "product" or "process." (See, for early discussion, Miller, 1962; Neisser, 1967; Nisbett & Wilson, 1977; Smith & Miller, 1978; White, 1988.) Even so, this distinction allows an important rule of thumb—namely, that you're generally aware of your mental products but unaware of your mental processes.

For example, we saw in Chapter 8 that your memories of the past seamlessly combine genuine recall with some amount of after-the-fact reconstruction. For example, when you "remember" your restaurant dinner last month, you're probably weaving together elements that were actually recorded into memory at the time of the dinner, along with other elements that are just inferences or assumptions. In that earlier chapter, we argued that this weaving together is a good thing, because it enables you to fill in bits that you've forgotten or bits that you didn't notice in the first place. But this weaving together also creates a risk of error: If the dinner you're trying to recall was somehow unusual, then assumptions based on the more typical pattern may be misleading.

Let's be clear, though, about what's conscious here and what's not. Your recollection of the dinner is a mental *product* and is surely something you're aware of. As a result, you can reflect on the dinner if you wish and can describe it if someone asks you. You're unaware, though, of the *process* that brought you this knowledge, so you have no way of telling which bits are supplied by memory retrieval and which bits rest on inference or assumption. And, of course, if you can't determine which bits are which, there's no way for you to reject the inferences or to avoid the (entirely unnoticed) assumptions. That's why memory errors are often undetectable: Since the process that brings you a "memory" is unconscious, you can't distinguish genuine recall from (potentially misguided) assumption.

Here's a different example. In Chapter 4, we considered a case in which research participants were briefly shown the stimulus "CORN"; we also considered a case in which participants were shown "CQRN." Despite the different stimuli, both groups perceived the input as "CORN"—a correct perception for the first group, but an error for the second.

For reasons we described in that chapter, though, people usually can't tell whether they're in the first group or the second, so they won't be able to tell whether they're perceiving correctly or *mis*-perceiving. Both groups are aware of the product created by their minds, so both groups have the conscious experience of "seeing" the word "CORN." But they're unaware of the processes and, specifically, are clueless about whether the stimulus was actually perceived or merely inferred. These processes unfold in (what we're now calling) the cognitive unconscious and, as such, are entirely hidden from view.

Unconscious Reasoning

The role of the cognitive unconscious is also evident in other settings, and here we meet another layer of complexity—because in many cases participants seem to be engaging in a process of unconscious *reasoning*.

In Chapter 7, we discussed a study in which participants convinced themselves that several fictitious names were actually the names of famous people. In this procedure, participants were apparently aware of the fact that some of the names they were reading were distinctive; their conscious experience told them that these names somehow "stood out" from other names on the list. But to make sense of the data from this study, we need to take a further step and argue that thoughts roughly like these were going through the participants' minds: "That name rings a bell, and I'm not sure why. But the experimenter is asking me about famous names, and there are other famous names on this list in front of me. So I guess that this one must also be the name of some famous person." This surely sounds like something we want to count as "thinking," but the evidence suggests that it's thinking of which the participants were entirely unaware—thinking that took place in their cognitive unconscious.

Similarly, imagine that someone is an eyewitness to a crime. The police might show this person a lineup, and let's say that the witness chooses Number Two as the robber. In Chapter 8, we explored what happens if the witness now gets *feedback* about this identification—if the police say something like, "Good; the person you've chosen is our suspect." In one study, witnesses who received no feedback said that their confidence in their lineup selection was (on average) 47%; witnesses who got the feedback, though, expressed much greater confidence: 71%. This leap in confidence makes no sense, because there's no way for the feedback to have "strengthened" the witnesses' memory or to have influenced their selection. (Bear in mind that the feedback arrived only after the witnesses had made the selection.) So why did the feedback elevate confidence? It seems that the witnesses must have been thinking something like, "The police say I got the right answer, so I guess I can set aside my doubts." Of course, witnesses aren't aware of making this adjustment—and so the thought process here is again unconscious.

But the effects of feedback don't stop there. Witnesses who receive this sort of feedback also end up "remembering" that they got a closer, longer,

FIGURE 14.1 THE (MANY) EFFECTS OF FEEDBACK

Participants in this study viewed a (videotaped) crime and then attempted to pick the perpetrator's picture out of a lineup. Later, participants received either confirming feedback for their choice ("Good, you identified the actual suspect"), disconfirming feedback ("Actually, the suspect was . . ."), or no feedback. Then, participants were asked further questions about the video. (Confidence was assessed on a 0 to 100 scale, so the numbers shown on the y-axis correspond to the actual responses from the research participants. The other questions were answered with a 0 to 10 scale.) Crucially, the feedback arrived well after participants had viewed the crime and after they'd made their ID selection. Therefore, the feedback couldn't possibly have changed the original event ("How good a view did you get?" or "How well did you see his face?"), nor could it have changed the experience of making the identification ("How easy was it for you to choose?"). Nonetheless, the feedback altered participants' memory for these earlier events. Those who had received confirming feedback now recalled that they'd gotten a better view of the crime, even though all participants got the same view! They also recalled that their ID had been fast and easy, even though their IDs had been no faster than anyone else's.   (AFTER WELLS, OLSON, & CHARMAN, 2003)

clearer view of the perpetrator, that the lighting was good, and so on (see **Figure 14.1**). Here, the witnesses seem to be thinking something like, "I chose the right person, so I guess I must have gotten a good view after all." Once more, however, these aren't conscious thoughts, and in this case the witnesses are being misled by some after-the-fact reconstruction.

Interpretation and Inference

In some settings, unconscious thinking can be even more sophisticated. In one early experiment (Nisbett & Schachter, 1966), participants were asked to undergo a series of electric shocks, with each shock being slightly more severe than the one before. The question of interest was how far into the series the participants would go. What was the maximum shock they would accept?

Before beginning the series of shocks, some of the participants were given a pill that, they were told, would diminish the pain but would also have several side effects: It would cause trembling in the hands, butterflies in the stomach, irregular breathing, and the like. Actually, none of this was true. The pill was a placebo and had no analgesic properties, nor did it produce any of these side effects. Even so, taking this inert pill was remarkably effective: Participants who took the pill were willing to accept four times as much amperage as control participants.

Why was the placebo so effective? Participants in the *control group* noticed that their hands were shaking, that their stomachs were upset, and so on. (These are, of course, common manifestations of fear—including the fearful anticipation of electric shock.) The participants then used these self-observations as evidence in judging their own states, drawing on what (in Chapter 12) we called "somatic markers." It's as if participants said to themselves, "Oh, look, I'm trembling! I guess I must be scared. Therefore, these shocks must really be bothering me." This led them to terminate the shock series relatively early. Placebo participants, in contrast, attributed the same physical symptoms to the pill. "Oh, look, I'm trembling! That's just what the experimenter said the pill would do. So I guess I can stop worrying about the trembling. Let me look for some other indication of whether the shock is bothering me." As a consequence, these participants were less influenced by their own physical symptoms. In essence, they overruled the evidence of their own anxiety and misread their own internal state. (For related studies, see Nisbett & Wilson, 1977; Wilson, 2002; Wilson & Dunn, 2004.)

Let's emphasize, though, that participants' reasoning about the pill was entirely unconscious. In fact, the participants were asked, after the procedure, why they had accepted so much shock, and in responding they never mentioned the pill. When asked directly, "During the experiment, did you think about the pill at all?" participants said things like, "No, I was too worried about the shock to think of anything else."

Apparently, then, the placebo participants detected their own symptoms and made an inference about the source of the symptoms—attributing them to the pill and not to the shock. Then, guided by this attribution, they were willing to continue with the experiment, accepting shocks at a higher amperage. Of course, we know that the participants were misattributing their symptoms and drawing false conclusions, but that takes nothing away from what they were doing intellectually—and unconsciously.

Mistaken Introspections

It does seem useful, then, to distinguish between the (unconscious) processes involved in thought and the (conscious) products that result from these processes. As we've said, this distinction isn't always clear-cut but it does support a useful rule of thumb about what you're aware of in your mental life and what you're not. In other words, you arrive at a conclusion, but the steps leading to the conclusion are hidden from view. You reach a decision, but again, you're unable to introspect about the processes leading to that decision. (For more on the types of thinking that can go on without consciousness, see Dijksterhuis & Strick, 2016.)

Sometimes, however, the processes of thought do seem to be conscious, and you feel like you can voice the reasons for your decision or the basis for your conclusion, if anyone asks. This surely sounds like a situation in which your thoughts *are* conscious. Remarkably, though, this sense of knowing your own thoughts may, in many cases, be an illusion.

We've just discussed one example of this pattern. In the Nisbett and Schachter (1966) study, participants firmly denied that their willingness to accept shock was influenced by the pill they'd taken. Instead, they offered other explanations that had nothing to do with the pill. It seems, then, that participants had some beliefs about why they had acted as they did, but their beliefs were *wrong*—systematically ruling out a factor (the pill) that actually was having an enormous impact.

Related examples are easy to find. Participants in one study read a brief excerpt from a novel and were asked to describe what emotional impact the excerpt had on them and also *why* the excerpt had the impact it did: Which sentences or which images, within the excerpt, led to the emotional "kick"? The participants were impressively consistent in their judgments, with 86% pointing to a particular passage, describing the messiness of a baby's crib, as crucial for the excerpt's emotional tone. These judgments, however, were simply wrong. Another group of participants read the same excerpt, but without the bit about the crib. These participants reacted to the overall excerpt in exactly the same way as the earlier group. Apparently, the bit about the crib wasn't crucial at all. (See Nisbett & Wilson, 1977; for other, more recent data, see Bargh, 2005; Custers & Aarts, 2010.)

In studies like these, participants think they know why they acted or reacted as they did, but they're mistaken. Their self-reports are offered with full confidence, and in many cases the participants insist that they carefully thought about their actions, so that the various causes and influences were, it seems, out in plain view. Nonetheless, from our perspective as researchers, we can see that these introspective reports are wrong—ignoring factors we know to be crucial, highlighting factors we know to be irrelevant.

After-the-Fact Reconstructions

How could these introspections get so far off track? The answer starts with a fact that we've already showcased—namely, that the processes of thought are often unconscious. People seeking to introspect, therefore, have no way to

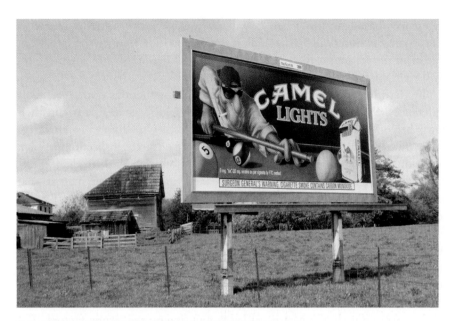

DO WE KNOW WHY WE DO WHAT WE DO?

For years, there has been debate over whether the government should regulate (and limit) cigarette advertising, based on the idea that we don't want to lure people into this unhealthy habit. In response, the tobacco industry has sometimes offered survey data, asking people: "Why did you start smoking?" The industry notes that in these surveys, the respondents typically don't attribute their start to the ads; therefore, the industry claims, the ads do no harm; therefore, the ads shouldn't be regulated. Let's be clear, though, that this argument assumes that people know why they do what they do, and this assumption is often mistaken.

inspect these processes, and so, if they're going to explain their own behavior, they need some other source of information. Often, that other source is likely to be an *after-the-fact reconstruction*. Roughly put, people reason in this fashion: "Why did I act that way? I have no direct information, but maybe I can draw on my broad knowledge about why, in general, people might act in certain ways in this situation. From that base, I can make some plausible inferences about why I acted as I did." So, for example: "I know that, in general, passages about babies or passages about squalor can be emotionally moving; I bet that's what moved me in reading this passage."

These after-the-fact reconstructions will often be correct, because people's beliefs about why they act as they do are generally sensible: "Why am I angry at Gail? She just insulted me, and I know that, in general, people tend to get angry when they've been insulted. I bet, therefore, that I'm angry because she insulted me." In cases such as this, an inference based on generic knowledge is likely to be accurate.

In other settings, however, these reconstructions can be totally wrong (as in the experiments we've mentioned). They'll go off track, for example, if someone's beliefs about a specific setting happen to be mistaken; in that case, inferences based on those beliefs will obviously be problematic. Likewise, the reconstructions will go off track if the person didn't notice some relevant factor in the setting; here, too, inferences not taking that factor into account will yield mistaken interpretations.

But let's be clear that these after-the-fact reconstructions don't "feel like" inferences. When research participants (or people in general) explain their own behaviors, they're usually convinced that they're simply *remembering* their own mental processes based on some sort of direct inspection of what went on in their own minds. These reconstructions, in other words, feel like genuine "introspections." The evidence we've reviewed, however, suggests that these subjective feelings are mistaken—and so, ironically, this is one more case in which people are conscious of the product and not the process. They're aware of the conclusion ("I acted as I did because . . .") but not aware of the process that led them to the conclusion. Hence, they continue to believe (falsely) that the conclusion rests on an introspection, when it actually rests on an after-the-fact reconstruction. Hand in hand with this, they continue to believe confidently that they know themselves, even though, in reality, their self-perception is (in these cases, at least) focusing on the wrong factors. (For more on this process of "self-interpretation," see Cooney & Gazzaniga, 2003.)

Unconscious Guides to Conscious Thinking

Many people find these claims to be troubling. We would all like to believe that we know ourselves reasonably well. We would all like to believe that we typically know why we've acted as we have or why we believe what we do. The research we're considering here, though, challenges these ideas. Often, we don't know where our beliefs, emotions, or actions came from. We don't know which of our "memories" are based on actual recall and which ones are inferences. We don't know which of our "perceptions" are mistaken. And even when we insist that we do know why we acted in a certain way and are sure we remember the reasoning that led to our actions, we can be wrong.

Sometimes, though, you surely are aware of your own thoughts. Sometimes you make decisions based on a clear, well-articulated "inner dialogue" with yourself. Sometimes you make discoveries based on a visual image that you carefully and consciously scrutinized. Even here, though, there's a role for the cognitive unconscious, because even here a support structure is needed—one that exists at what philosophers have called the "fringe" or the "horizon" of your conscious thoughts (Husserl, 1931; James, 1890).

Evidence for this unnoticed fringe comes from a variety of cases in which your thoughts are influenced by an "unseen hand." For example, in our description of problem solving (Chapter 13), we emphasized the role of a problem-solving *set*—unnoticed assumptions and definitions that guide your search for the problem's solution. Even when the problem solving is conscious and deliberate, even when you "think out loud" about the steps of the problem solution, you're guided by a set. We argued in the earlier chapter that for the most part this is a good thing, because the set keeps you focused,

CONSCIOUSNESS IS GUIDED BY UNCONSCIOUS FRAMEWORKS

Language understanding provides another example in which conscious experience is guided by unconscious processes. It's striking, for example, that you often fail to detect the ambiguity you encounter—such as the two ways to interpret "Out of Order." You choose one interpretation ("needs repair") so rapidly that you're generally unaware that another interpretation ("in the wrong position in the series") is even possible.

protecting you from distracting and unproductive lines of thought. But the set can sometimes be an obstacle to problem solving, and the fact that the set is unconscious makes it all the more difficult to overcome the obstacle: A problem solver cannot easily pause and reflect on the set, so she cannot alter the problematic beliefs or abandon the misleading assumptions.

Similarly, in our discussion of decision making (Chapter 12), we emphasized the importance of a decision's *frame*. You might be completely focused on the decision and fully aware of your options. Nonetheless, you'll be influenced by the (unnoticed) framing of the decision—the way the options are described and the way the question is posed. You don't think about the framing itself, but it unmistakably colors your thoughts about the decision and plays a large role in determining which option you'll choose.

In these ways, an unnoticed framework can guide your deliberate, conscious thinking—about problems, decisions, and more. In each case, this framework protects you from uncertainty and ambiguity, but it also governs the content and the sequence of your thoughts.

Disruptions of Consciousness

Further evidence for unconscious processes comes from patients who have suffered brain damage. Consider the discussion of Korsakoff's syndrome in Chapter 7. Patients suffering from this syndrome seem to have no conscious memory of events they've witnessed or things they've done. If asked directly about these events, the patients insist they have no recollection. If asked to

TEST YOURSELF

1. Give an example in which people are conscious of the "products" created within the mind but not conscious of the "processes" that led to these products.
2. What evidence suggests that unconscious processes can involve sophisticated reasoning?
3. What does it mean to say that sometimes "introspections" are actually just after-the-fact reconstructions?

perform tasks that require recollection—like navigating to the store, based on a memory of the store's location—the patients fail.

Even so, it's false to claim that these patients have "no memories," because on tests of *implicit* memory the amnesic patients seem quite normal. They do seem to "remember" if we probe their memories indirectly—not asking them explicitly what they recall, but instead looking for evidence that their current behavior is shaped by specific prior experiences. In these indirect tests, the patients are influenced by memories they don't know they have—and so, apparently, some aspects of remembering and some influences of experience can go forward even in the absence of a conscious memory. This is a pattern that Jacoby & Witherspoon (1982) have referred to as "memory without awareness."

Blind Sight

Parallel claims can be made for *perception*. As we said at the chapter's start, the phenomenon of **blind sight** is sometimes observed in patients who have suffered damage to the visual cortex. For all practical purposes, these patients are blind. If asked what they see, they insist they see nothing. They don't react to flashes of bright light. They hesitate to walk down a corridor, convinced they'll collide with obstacles in their path. Tests reveal, however, that these patients can respond with reasonable accuracy to questions about their visual environment. (See de Gelder, 2010; Rees, Kreiman, & Koch, 2002; Weiskrantz, 1986, 1997.) For example, they can answer questions about the shape and movement of visual targets, the orientation of lines, and even the emotional expression (sad vs. happy vs. afraid) on faces. If an experimenter requires them to reach toward an object, the patients tend to reach in the right direction and with a hand position (e.g., fingers pinched together or wide open) that's appropriate for the shape and size of the target. In all cases, though, the patients insist they can't see the targets, and they can offer no explanation for why their "guesses" are consistently accurate. Apparently, these patients are not aware of seeing but, even so, can in some ways "see."

How is this possible? Part of the answer lies in the fact that there may be "islands" of intact tissue within the brain area that's been damaged in these patients. (See Fendrich, Wessinger, & Gazzaniga, 1992; Gazzaniga, Fendrich, & Wessinger, 1994; Radoeva, Prasad, Brainard, & Aguirre, 2008.) In other patients, the explanation rests on the fact that there are several neural pathways carrying information from the eyeballs to the brain. Damage to one of these pathways is the reason that these patients seem (on many measures) to be blind. However, information flow is still possible along some of the other pathways—including a pathway through the superior colliculus in the midbrain (Leh, Johansen-Berg, & Ptito, 2006; Tamietto et al., 2010)—and this is what enables these patients to use visual information that they cannot consciously see. One way or the other, though, it's clear that we need to distinguish between "perception" and "conscious perception," because unmistakably it is possible to perceive in the absence of consciousness. (For more data, also showing a sharp distinction between a patient's conscious perception of

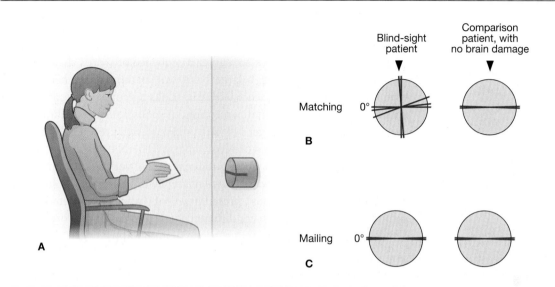

FIGURE 14.2 CONSCIOUS SEEING, UNCONSCIOUS SEEING

In this study, (Panel A) participants held a card and, in one condition, were asked to hold the card at an angle that matched the orientation of the slot in front of them. In another condition, they were asked to imagine that they were "mailing" the card, placing it into a "mail slot." In the matching task, the blind-sight patient made many errors (Panel B). In the "mailing" task, in contrast, the blind-sight patient performed perfectly, consistently matching the card's orientation to the orientation of the slot. It seems, then, that the patient is (consciously) blind, but able to see and to use the information she sees in guiding her own actions.

(AFTER GOODALE, MILNER, JACOBSON, & CAREY, 1991)

the world and her ability to gather and use visual information, see Goodale & Milner, 2004; Logie & Della Salla, 2005; and also **Figure 14.2.**)

Subliminal Perception

In the late 1950s, a market researcher named James Vicary allegedly inserted the words "Eat Popcorn" into a single frame of a movie. When the movie was shown in the theater, reports tell us, the brief exposure of this message wasn't enough for viewers to perceive the message consciously. Even so, the viewers were influenced by the message, and popcorn sales increased by more than 50%.

It turns out, though, that reports of this "Eat Popcorn" experiment were a hoax; no experiment was ever done (e.g., Rogers, 1992). More recent (and non-fraudulent) research, however, makes it clear that people actually can perceive and be influenced by visual inputs they didn't consciously perceive—a pattern referred to as **subliminal perception**. In one line of work, researchers showed participants trios of words (van Gaal et al., 2014; but also see Rabagliati, Robertson, & Carmel, 2018). The first two words were presented very rapidly, and both were followed by a mask that guaranteed that the words weren't consciously perceived. Then a third word was presented—at a longer exposure, with no mask, so that participants were aware of this third word.

The key measure in this study was a brain wave called the "N400." We mentioned this wave in Chapter 10, and there we noted that a larger N400 is observed when participants encounter a sequence of words that violates their expectations. For example, a large N400 will be observed when participants hear the last word in a sequence like, "He drinks his coffee with cream and dog."

In the study of subliminal perception, the conscious presentation of words like "war" produced a larger N400 if this word was preceded by a *subliminal* presentation of a positive word like "happy." The N400 was larger still if the first (and also subliminal) word in the series was "very"—so that the trio was an absurd sequence of "very happy war." In this setting, the (unconscious) prime made the (conscious) presentation of "war" unexpected, leading to the larger N400. Results were different, though, if the first word in the series was "not." Here, the unconscious prime of "not happy" made the (conscious) presentation of "war" less surprising, resulting in a smaller N400.

The results reversed if the second word in this trio was a negative word like "sad." Thus, the subliminal prime "very sad" led to a smaller N400 in response to "war." The subliminal prime "not sad" led to a larger N400 in response to negative words like "war."

It seems, then, that the subliminal words were detected and influencing subsequent perception—creating a context that in some conditions made the word "war" more surprising, and in other conditions less so. The important finding, though, is that participants had somehow combined the successive words, with the result that the phrases "very happy" and "not happy" had opposite effects (and likewise for "very sad" and "not sad"). Apparently, subliminal perception can involve more than the reading of single words; people also seem able (at least in a limited way) to integrate subliminal inputs in a linguistically appropriate fashion.

TEST YOURSELF

4. What is blind sight, and what does it imply about the need for consciousness in perception?
5. What is subliminal perception, and what does it tell us about the need for consciousness in understanding complex stimuli?

Consciousness and Executive Control

Where does all of this discussion leave us? Clearly, a huge range of activities, including complex activities, can be accomplished unconsciously. You can see, you can remember, you can interpret, you can infer—all without any awareness of these activities (and for still another example, see Mudrik, Faivre, & Koch, 2014). So why do you need consciousness at all? What function does it serve? And related to this, what things *can't* you do unconsciously?

The Limits of Unconscious Performance

In tackling these questions, let's start with the fact that your unconscious steps seem, in each of the cases we've discussed, quite sensible. If, for example, the police tell you that the guy you selected from a lineup is indeed their suspect,

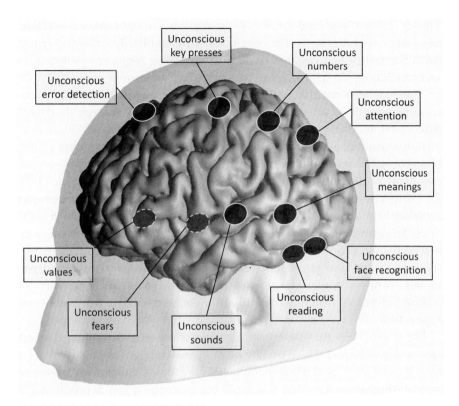

UNCONSCIOUS ACTIVATION

The text describes an experiment that documents unconscious detection of words. Similar experiments have documented other unconscious operations, and this figure (after Dehaene, 2014) summarizes some of the brain areas that we now know are capable of sophisticated processing in the absence of conscious awareness.

this suggests that you did, in fact, get a good look at him during the crime. (Otherwise, how were you able to recognize him?) It's not crazy, therefore, that you'd "adjust" your memory for what you saw, because you now know that your view must have been decent. Likewise, imagine that you're making judgments about how famous various people are, and you're looking at a list that includes some unmistakably famous names. If, in this setting, one of the other names seems somehow familiar, it again seems entirely sensible that you'd (unconsciously) infer that this name, too, belongs to someone famous.

Over and over, therefore, your unconscious judgments and inferences tend to be fast, efficient, and *reasonable*. In other words, your unconscious judgments and inferences are well tuned to, and appropriately guided by, cues in the situation. This pattern is obviously a good thing, because it means that your unconscious processing won't be foolish. But the pattern also provides an important clue about the nature of—and possible limitations on—unconscious processing.

Here's a proposal. Unconscious processing can be complex and sophisticated, but it's strongly guided either by the situation you're in or by prior habit.

Therefore, when you (unconsciously) draw a conclusion or make a selection, these steps are likely to be the ones favored by familiarity or by the setting itself. Similarly, when you unconsciously make some response—whether it's an overt action, like reaching for an object that you cannot consciously see, or a mental response, like noting the meaning of a word you didn't consciously perceive—you're likely to make a familiar response, one that's well practiced in that situation.

If this proposal is right, then unconscious processing will, to a large extent, be out of your control—governed by habit or by the setting, not by your current plans or desires. And, in fact, this is correct. For example, think about the inferences you rely on to fill gaps in what you remember. These inferences are often helpful, but we've discussed how they can lead to errors—in some cases, large and consequential errors. Knowing these facts about memory, however, is no protection at all. Just as you cannot choose to avoid a perceptual illusion, you also cannot choose to avoid memory error, and you cannot "turn off" your inferences even when you want to. The process of making inferences is automatic and effortless, and it's also irresistible (see **Figure 14.3**).

In the same way, the inferences and assumptions that are built into object recognition (Chapter 4) are usually helpful, enabling you to identify objects even if your view is brief or incomplete. Sometimes, though, you want to shut off these inferences, but you can't. For example, if you're proofreading

---

FIGURE 14.3   OUT OF CONTROL

A Müller–Lyer illusion   **B** Poggendorff illusion   **C** Ponzo illusion

The inferences you make in perception and memory are automatic and unconscious—and so they aren't something you can "turn off" when you want to. As a result, any errors produced by these inferences are like the perceptual illusions that shape your reality whether you like it or not. In Panel A, the two horizontals are the same length. In Panel B, the black segments are perfectly aligned, so if you could remove the yellow bars you'd see perfectly straight black lines. In Panel C, the two yellow horizontals are the same length. Knowing these facts, however, doesn't protect you from the illusions. (These illusions are named, by the way, in honor of the people who created them.)

something you've written, you want to be alert to what's actually on the page and not be fooled by your ideas about what *should* be there. Plainly, though, proofreading is hard—and you unconsciously "correct" what's on the page whether you want to or not, with the result that you often fail to see the misspelling or the missng letter. (Also see **Figure 14.4**.)

Similarly, the largely uncontrolled nature of routine makes it easy for you to become a victim of habit, relying on customary patterns even when you hope to avoid them. This is evident, for example, in **action slips**—cases in which you do something different from what you intend. In most cases, these slips involve doing what's *normal* in a situation, rather than what you want to do on that occasion. For example, you're in the car, driving to the store. You intend to turn left at the corner, but, distracted for a moment, you turn right, taking the route that you usually take on your way to school (Norman, 1981; Reason, 1990; also see Langer, 1989). This observation is just as we'd expect if routine is forceful, automatic, and uncontrolled.

A Role for Control

The idea, then, is that unconscious processes—in perception, memory, and reasoning—serve as a sophisticated and highly useful set of "mental reflexes." These "reflexes" are guided by the circumstances and therefore are generally appropriate for those circumstances. But at the same time, the "reflexes," because they are guided by the circumstances, are generally inflexible. (For a related view, see Kahneman, 2011; Stanovich, 2009, 2012. For an alternative view, see Hassin, 2013.)

In many regards, though, it's *helpful* not to have control. Since unconscious processes can operate without "supervision," you can run many of

---

FIGURE 14.4   COUNT THE F'S

FINISHED FILES ARE THE RESULT
OF YEARS OF SCIENTIFIC STUDY
COMBINED WITH THE EXPERIENCE
OF YEARS.

In ordinary reading, you skip over many of the letters on the page and rely on inferences to "fill in" what you've skipped. This process is automatic and essentially uncontrollable—and so it's hard to avoid the skipping even when you want to. Count the appearances here of the letter *F*. For this task, you want to read in a letter-by-letter fashion, but this turns out to be difficult. How many *F*'s are there? Did you find all six?

these processes at the same time—thereby increasing the speed and efficiency of your mental life. In addition, since you're not supervising these unconscious processes, you're free to devote your attention to other, more pressing matters.

But how do these often-complex processes manage to run without supervision? Part of the answer is biological, and the sequence of events for some unconscious processing (e.g., the steps needed for perception) is likely built into the essential structure of the nervous system. Therefore, no supervision, no attention, was ever required for these steps.

For other sorts of unconscious processing, the answer is different, and it's an answer we first met in Chapter 5. There, we argued that when learning a new task you need to monitor each step so that you'll know when it's time to start the next step. Then, you need to *choose* what the next step will be and get it started. This combination of monitoring, choosing, and launching does give you close control over how things proceed, but it can also make the performance quite demanding.

After some practice, however, things are different. The steps needed for the task are still there, but you don't think about them one by one. That's because you've stored in memory a complete routine that specifies what all the steps should be and when each step should be initiated. All you need to do is launch the overall routine, and from that point forward you let the familiar sequence unfold. Thus, with no need for monitoring or decisions, you can do the task without paying close attention to it.

The Prerequisites for Control

In Chapter 5, we described these changes, made possible by practice, in terms of *executive control*, and that idea is still important here. Unconscious actions (whether rooted in biology or created through practice) go forward without executive control. When you need to direct your own mental processes, though—to rise above habit or to avoid responding to prominent cues in your surrounding—you do need executive control. (For related claims, see Lapate, Rokers, Li, & Davidson, 2014. For some complications, see Cohen, Cavanagh, Chun, & Nakayama, 2012.) But what does executive control involve?

In order to perform its function, executive control needs, first of all, a means of launching desired actions and overriding unwanted actions. In other words, the executive needs an "output" side—things it can do, actions it can initiate. Second, the executive needs some way of representing its goals and subgoals so that they can serve as guides to action; as a related point, the executive needs some way of representing its plan or "agenda" (Duncan et al., 2008; Duncan, Schramm, Thompson, & Dumonthell, 2012). Third, on the "input" side, the executive needs to know what's going on in the mind: What bits of information are coming in? How can these bits be integrated with one another? Is there any conflict among the various elements of the arriving information, or conflict between the information and the current goals? Fourth, it also seems plausible that the executive needs to know how easily and how smoothly current processes are unfolding. If the processes are proceeding without difficulties, there's no need to make adjustments; but if the processes are stymied, the executive would probably seek an alternative path toward the goal.

As it turns out, these claims about the prerequisites for control fit well with the traits of conscious experience and also with current claims about the biological basis for consciousness. Before we turn to those claims, though, let's consider a slightly different perspective on issues of mental control.

Metacognition

Some years back, developmental psychologist John Flavell noted that as children grow up they need to develop (what Flavell called) **metacognitive skills**—skills in *monitoring* and *controlling* their own mental processes (e.g., Flavell, 1979). Metacognition matters for many domains but is especially important for memory, and so researchers often focus on **metamemory**—people's knowledge about, awareness of, and control over their own memory.

Metacognition (and metamemory in particular) is crucial for adults as well. Imagine that you're studying for an exam. As you look over your notes, you might decide that some facts will be easy to remember, so you'll devote little study time to them. Other facts will be more challenging, so you'll give them a lot of time. Then, while studying, you'll need to make further decisions: "Okay, I've got this bit under control; I can look at something else now" versus "I'm still struggling with this; I guess I should give it more time." In all these ways, you're making metamemory judgments—forecasts for your own learning and assessments of your learning so far. Metamemory also includes your *beliefs* about memory—for example, your belief that mnemonics can be helpful or that "deep processing" is an effective way to memorize (see Chapter 6). Another aspect of metamemory is your ability to *control* your own studying—so that you use your beliefs to guide your own behavior. (See Nelson & Narens, 1990; also Dunlosky & Bjork, 2008. For some indications, though, that students sometimes have *false beliefs about* and *inaccurate assessments of* their own memories, see Agarwal, Karpicke, Kang, Roediger, & McDermott, 2008.)

There's an obvious link between these claims about metacognition and our broader claims about executive control. In both cases, there's a need for self-monitoring; in both cases, there's a need for self-control and self-direction. In both cases, you're guided by a sense of goals—whether those goals are generated on the spot or derived from your long-standing beliefs about how your own memory functions.

Our emphasis here, however, will be on executive control, largely because it's the more inclusive process—concerned with all sorts of self-monitoring and self-control, not just the monitoring and control of, say, your own memory. Nonetheless, the notion of metacognition (and metamemory in particular) provides further illustration of the ways in which executive control matters for you and how important it is. But how are these points related to consciousness? Let's start with the relevant biology.

TEST YOURSELF

6. What sorts of actions can go forward without executive control? When is executive control needed?
7. What is metacognition?

The Cognitive Neuroscience of Consciousness

In the last decade or so, there has been an avalanche of research on the relationship between consciousness and brain function. Some of this research has focused on cases of brain damage, including the cases of amnesia or blind sight we mentioned earlier. Other research has scrutinized people with normal brains and has asked, roughly, what changes we observe in the brain when someone becomes conscious of a stimulus. (See Atkinson, Thomas, & Cleeremans, 2000; Baars & Franklin, 2003; Bogen, 1995; Chalmers, 1998; Crick & Koch, 1995; Dehaene & Naccache, 2001; Kim & Blake, 2005; Rees et al., 2002.) In other words, what are the **neural correlates of consciousness** (or, as one author puts it, the *neural signatures* of consciousness—Dehaene, 2014)? As we'll see, consideration of these correlates will lead us directly back to the questions we've just been pondering.

The Many Brain Areas Needed for Consciousness

To explore the neural correlates of consciousness, researchers rely on the recording techniques we described in Chapter 2. Some studies use neuroimaging (PET or fMRI) to assess activity at specific brain locations. Other studies use EEG to track the brain's electrical activity. With all of these methods, researchers can ask how the pattern of brain activity changes when someone shifts attention from one idea to another. Researchers can also track the changes that occur in brain activity when someone first becomes aware of a stimulus that's been in front of her eyes all along.

Research in this arena makes it clear that many different brain areas are crucial for consciousness. In other words, there is no group of neurons or some place in the brain that's the "consciousness center." There is no brain site that functions like a light bulb that "turns on" when you're conscious and then changes brightness when your mental state changes.

It's helpful, though, to distinguish two broad categories of brain sites, corresponding to two aspects of consciousness (see **Figure 14.5**). First, some

FIGURE 14.5   TWO SEPARATE ASPECTS OF CONSCIOUSNESS

At any given moment, a radio might be receiving a particular station either dimly or with a clear signal. Likewise, at any given moment the radio might be receiving a rock station, a jazz station, or the news. These two dimensions—the clarity of the signal and the station choice—correspond roughly to the two aspects of consciousness described in the text.

brain sites are crucial for your level of alertness or sensitivity, independent of what you're currently sensitive *to*. The difference here is (roughly) the difference that ranges from being sleepy and dimly aware of a stimulus (or an idea or a memory), at one extreme, and being fully awake, highly alert, and totally focused on a stimulus, at the other extreme. This aspect of consciousness is compromised when someone suffers damage to certain sites in either the thalamus or the *reticular activating system* in the brain stem—a system that controls the overall arousal level of the forebrain and also helps control the cycling between sleep and wakefulness (e.g., Koch, 2008).

Second, a different (and broader) set of brain sites matters for the *content* of consciousness. This content can, of course, vary widely. Sometimes you're thinking about your immediate environment; sometimes you're thinking about past events. Sometimes you're focused on a current task; sometimes you're dreaming about the future. These various contents for consciousness rely on different brain areas—and so cortical structures in the visual system are especially active when you're consciously aware of sights in front of your eyes (or aware of a visual image that you've created); cortical structures in the forebrain are essential when you're thinking about a stimulus that's no longer present in your environment; and so on.

The broad distinction between the *degree of awareness* and the *content of consciousness* is helpful, therefore, when we consider the diversity of brain areas involved in consciousness. (Although, for complications, see Auksztulewicz, Spitzer, & Blankerburg, 2012; Bayne, Hohwy, & Owen, 2016a, 2016b; Fazekas & Overgaard, 2016.) This distinction is also useful in thinking about *variations* in consciousness, as suggested by **Figure 14.6** (after Laureys, 2005; also Koch, 2008). In dreaming, for example, you're conscious of a richly detailed scene, with its various sights and sounds and events, and so there's

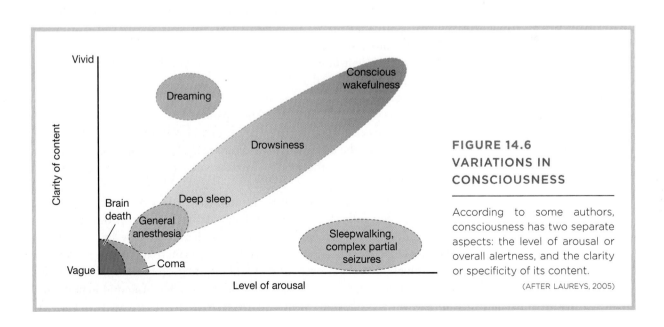

FIGURE 14.6 VARIATIONS IN CONSCIOUSNESS

According to some authors, consciousness has two separate aspects: the level of arousal or overall alertness, and the clarity or specificity of its content.

(AFTER LAUREYS, 2005)

a well-defined content, but your sensitivity to the environment is low. In contrast, in the mental state associated with sleepwalking, you're sensitive to certain aspects of the world so that you can, for example, navigate through the environment, but you seem to have no particular thoughts in mind, so the content of your consciousness isn't well defined.

The Neuronal Workspace

What is it in the brain that makes consciousness possible at all? Researchers have offered a variety of proposals, and there is no consensus. (See, for a sampling of views, Lamme & Roelfsema, 2000; Lau & Rosenthal, 2011; Tononi, Boly, Massimini, & Koch, 2016.) Many investigators, though, endorse one version or another of the **neuronal workspace hypothesis**. In broad outline, here is the proposal. As we discussed in Chapter 2, different areas within the brain seem highly specialized in their function. The brain areas that make vision possible, for example, are separate from those that support hearing. Even within vision, the various aspects of perception each depend on their own brain sites, with one area specialized for the perception of color, another for the perception of movement, another for the perception of faces, and so on.

We've already said, though, that these various brain sites need somehow to communicate with one another, so that the elements can be assembled into an integrated package. After all, you don't perceive *round + red + moving*; you instead perceive *falling apple*. You don't perceive *rectangular + white + still*; you instead perceive *book page*. In earlier chapters, we referred to this as the "binding problem"—the task of linking together the different aspects of experience in order to create a coherent whole.

We've also said that attention plays a key role in solving the binding problem. For example, a moving stimulus in front of your eyes will trigger a response in one brain area; a red stimulus will trigger a response in another area. In the *absence* of attention, these two neural responses will be independent of each other. However, if you're paying attention to a single stimulus that is red and moving, the neurons in these two systems fire in synchrony. (See Chapter 3; also see Kolb & Whishaw, 2008; Salazar, Dotson, Bressler, & Gray, 2012; Thompson & Varela, 2001.) When neurons fire in this coordinated way, the brain seems to register the activity as a linkage among the different processing areas. As a result, these attributes are bound together, so that you end up correctly perceiving the stimulus as a unified whole.

This synchronization requires communication, so that neurons in one brain area can influence (and be influenced by) neurons in other, perhaps distant, brain areas. This communication is made possible by "workspace neurons" that literally connect one area of the brain to another. Let's emphasize, though, that the process of carrying information back and forth via the workspace neurons is selective, so that not every bit of neural activity gets linked to every other bit. Instead, various mechanisms create a *competition* among different brain processes, and the "winner" (typically, the most active process) is communicated to other brain areas, while other information is not.

Which elements will "win" in this competition? Again, attention is crucial: When you pay attention to a stimulus, this involves (among other neural steps) activity in the prefrontal cortex that can *sustain* and *amplify* the activity in other neural systems (Dehaene, 2014, Maia & Cleeremans, 2005), and this will shape how the competition plays out. By increasing activity in one area or another, attention ensures that this area wins the competition—and thus ensures that information from this area is broadcast to other brain sites.

Notice, then, that the information flow from each brain area to all the others is *limited*; this point is guaranteed by the competition. At the same time, the information flow is *controllable,* by virtue of what you choose to pay attention to.

With this backdrop, we're ready for our hypothesis. The integrated activity, made possible by the workspace neurons, provides the biological basis for consciousness. The workspace neurons themselves don't carry the *content* of consciousness; the content—the sense of seeing something red, the sense of seeing something moving—is represented in the same neurons, the same processing modules, that analyzed the perceptual information in the first place. But what the workspace neurons do is glue these bits together, creating a unified experience and promoting the exchange of information from one module to the next. (For specific versions of this hypothesis, see Baars, 2005; Baars & Franklin, 2003; Cooney & Gazzaniga, 2003; Crick & Koch, 2003; Dehaene, 2014; Dehaene & Changeux, 2011; Dehaene & Naccache, 2001; Engel & Singer, 2001; Maia & Cleeremans, 2005; Roser & Gazzaniga, 2004. For alternatives, see Lamme & Roelfsema, 2000; Lau & Rosenthal, 2011; Morsella & Bargh, 2011; Morsella, Krieger, & Bargh, 2010; Tononi et al., 2016.)

The Function of the Neuronal Workspace

Let's pause to outline the proposal that's before us. Any idea—whether it's an idea about a stimulus in front of your eyes or an idea drawn from memory—is represented in the brain by means of a widespread pattern of activity, with different parts of the brain each representing just one of the idea's elements. You become *aware of* that idea, though, when these various elements are linked to one another in a single overarching representation made possible by the workspace.

What does this linkage do for you? And how is all this related to our earlier comments about executive control or metacognition? Let's start with some basic facts about conscious experience. It's important, first, that your experience feels unitary and coherent. As we've noted in other contexts, you're not aware of orange and also aware of movement, and of roundness, and of closeness. Instead, you're aware of a single experience in which the basketball is flying toward you. This integrated coherence is just what the workspace allows: one representation, constructed from

Mind Wandering

Discussions of consciousness invariably invite questions about *altered states of consciousness.* How should we understand someone's experience when the person is under the influence of some drug or in the midst of a religious experience? But let's note that there is an altered state that requires neither medication nor meditation; it's the state of mind wandering (Smallwood & Schooler, 2006, 2015).

Virtually everyone has experienced mind wandering. You're sitting at your desk, trying to read, and you suddenly realize that for the last few minutes you've been pointing your eyes at the text but thinking about something altogether different—your plans for the weekend, perhaps, or hopes for a romantic encounter this evening. In these episodes, your thoughts seem largely "unguided"—with each thought passively triggering the next. It does seem right, therefore, to say that your thoughts are "wandering" and not directed with any particular goal.

When you're mind wandering, you're surely aware of the content of your thoughts (the weekend plans or the encounter). Typically, though, there's a period during which you're not aware that your thoughts were wandering. Of course, at some point you do realize that your thoughts have moved away from your immediate task and—perhaps with some frustration—you re-focus on the text you're trying to read or the lecture you're trying to follow. But a moment earlier, you had wandered "off task" without realizing it.

Some researchers estimate that people spend at least 25% of their waking hours with their thoughts wandering in this fashion. These estimates come from various measures. In an "experience sampling" procedure, researchers interrupt people periodically and ask: "What are you thinking about *right now*?" In other procedures, researchers can document slips and errors in an assigned task when someone's thoughts have wandered away from the task. In still other studies, researchers can document changes in brain activity when someone's thoughts are wandering. (For an overview of these studies, see Smallwood & Schooler, 2006, 2015.)

Mind wandering can be consequential and, for example, may cause as many automobile accidents as driving while intoxicated. On the positive side, though, there's some suggestion that mind wandering can, at the least, help people to escape boredom and can, more ambitiously, enhance creativity.

People's thoughts wander in all sorts of directions. A great deal of mind wandering, though, involves "mental time travel," with people often thinking about real or possible future events. Mind wandering is also sometimes (although less often) focused on past events, and this past-focus seems especially likely among people who are unhappy.

In light of the costs of mind wandering, though—when driving, listening to an important lecture, or even talking with a friend—is there anything you can do to keep yourself "on task"? Active engagement with the task seems to help. For example, periodic memory tests interwoven into an online lecture helped to keep students engaged with the material (Szpunar, Khan, & Schacter, 2013). More broadly, training in mindfulness —whether a two-week program or just a brief breathing exercise—also turns out to reduce mind wandering (Smallwood & Schooler, 2015). Whether you *want* to avoid mind wandering, though, surely depends on the circumstances, and researchers are just beginning to explore possible benefits of this form of altered consciousness.

the coordinated activity of many processing components (Roser & Gazzaniga, 2004).

Likewise, we emphasized in Chapter 5 that conscious experience is *selective*. In other words, you're conscious of only a narrow slice of the objects and events in your world, so that you might focus on the rose's color but fail to notice its thorns, or a driver might be so absorbed in a phone call that he misses his exit. Moreover, you can typically *choose* what you're going to focus on (so that you might, when picking up the rose, decide to pay attention to those thorns). These observations, too, are easily accommodated by the workspace model: The information carried by the workspace neurons is, we've said, governed by a competition (and so is limited) and also shaped by how you focus attention. In this way, the properties of the workspace readily map onto the properties of your experience.

Let's also note that attention both amplifies *and sustains* neural activity. As a result, the workspace, supported by attention, enables you to maintain mental representations in an active state for an extended period. In other words, the workspace makes it possible for you to continue thinking about a stimulus or an idea even after the trigger for that idea has been removed. This point enables us to link the workspace proposal to claims about working memory (Chapter 6) and to the brain areas associated with working memory's function—specifically, the prefrontal cortex, or PFC (Goldman-Rakic, 1987). (For other evidence linking the PFC to conscious awareness, see McIntosh, Rajah, & Lobaugh, 1999; Miller & Cohen, 2001.) This connection seems appropriate, since working memory is the memory that holds materials you're currently *working on*, which presumably means materials currently within your conscious awareness. (For complications, though, in the linkage between consciousness and working memory, see Soto & Silvanto, 2014.)

The Neuronal Workspace and Executive Control

What is the connection between the neuronal workspace and executive control? Bear in mind that the workspace enables you to integrate what's going on in one neural system with what's going on in others. This integration allows you to reflect on relationships among various inputs or ideas; it also allows you to produce new combinations of ideas and new combinations of operations. Thus, the neural mechanisms underlying consciousness are just the right sort to help you to produce novel thoughts in which you can rise above habit or routine. In this way, the workspace provides a plausible neural basis for executive functioning and, with this, enables you to escape the *limits* that seem to characterize unconscious processing.

The workspace also provides another function. As we've noted, unconscious processes are generally inflexible—and so, for example, if there's a conflict between habit and current goals, this has little influence on the process. In contrast, conscious thought *is* guided by a sense of your goals, and it can launch exactly the behavior that will lead to those goals.

How does the workspace support this sensitivity to current goals? By linking the various processing modules, the workspace makes it possible to compare what's going on in one module with what's going on elsewhere in the brain, and this activity allows you to detect conflict—if, for example, two simultaneous stimuli are triggering incompatible responses, or if a stimulus is triggering a response incompatible with your goals. This detection, in turn, enables you to shift processing in one system (again, by adjusting how you pay attention) in light of what's going on in other systems.

In fact, this capacity to detect conflict may itself be supported by brain mechanisms specialized for just this function. One area that is crucial for this conflict detection is the **anterior cingulate cortex (ACC)**, a structure linked to (and slightly behind) the frontal cortex and also connected to structures (including the amygdala, nucleus accumbens, and hypothalamus) that play pivotal roles in emotion, motivation, and feelings of reward (Botvinick, Cohen, & Carter, 2004; van Veen & Carter, 2006). (For more on the link between the ACC and conscious awareness, see Dehaene et al., 2003; Mayr, 2004.)

The neuronal workspace idea also helps us with another puzzle—a shift in consciousness that every one of us experiences every day: the difference between being *awake* and being *asleep*. When you're asleep (and not dreaming), you're not conscious of the passing of time, not conscious of any ongoing stream of thought, and not conscious of many events taking place in your vicinity. This is not, however, because the brain is inactive during sleep; activity in the sleeping brain is, in fact, quite intense. What, then, is the difference between the sleeping brain and the "awake brain"? Evidence suggests that when you're asleep (and not dreaming), communication breaks down among different parts of the cortex, so that the brain's various activities aren't coordinated with one another. The obvious suggestion, then, is that this communication (mediated by the neuronal workspace) is crucial for consciousness, so it makes sense that sleeping people, having temporarily lost this communication, aren't conscious of their state or their circumstances (Massimini et al., 2005). (For a similar account of the loss of consciousness during surgical anesthesia, see Alkire, Hudetz, & Tononi, 2008. For more on other "states" of consciousness, see Gleitman, Gross, & Reisberg, 2011; also see **Figure 14.7**.)

The Role of Phenomenal Experience

In several ways, therefore, we can draw parallels between the functioning of the neuronal workspace and the traits and capacities of consciousness. We can also link our claims about the workspace to the needs of executive control. The workspace, for example, allows comparisons among the various processing streams, and these comparisons enable the executive to monitor mental processes—to ensure that there are no conflicts, and to choose

TEST YOURSELF

8. Cognitive neuroscientists often distinguish "degree of awareness" from the "content of consciousness." What do these two terms mean?

9. What is the neuronal workspace hypothesis? What is the function of the neuronal workspace?

There are many states in which a person suffers an interruption of consciousness. Researchers have therefore asked: What brain sites are compromised in these various states? As can be seen, wide tracts of the brain are involved, including prefrontal tissue (F), parietal tissue (P), and other regions as well.

processes that will move you toward your goals. The workspace also supports the sustained neural activity that enables the executive to keep its goals and plans in view, as you work on some endeavor. The mechanisms involved in the workspace can also amplify certain types of activity, and this allows the executive to take control of mental events—ramping up desired activities and allowing distractions to languish.

Qualia

These suggestions, though, leave a substantial puzzle untouched. In fact, some authors argue that the workspace proposal dodges what philosophers have called the "hard problem" of consciousness (e.g., Chalmers, 1996, 1998). Specifically, some authors claim that we need to distinguish between "access consciousness" and "phenomenal consciousness." (See, e.g., Block, 1997, 2005; Block et al., 2014; Bronfman, Brezis, Jacobson, & Usher, 2014; Kouider, de Gardelle, Sackur & Dupoux, 2010; Paller & Suzuki, 2014. But also see Cohen & Dennett, 2011; Lau & Rosenthal, 2011.) Access consciousness can be defined as someone's sensitivity to certain types of information (and thus the person's *access* to that information). Discussions of consciousness (like our discussion so far in this chapter) generally emphasize the function of this access—that is, what you can do if you have this access, and what you can't do *without* this access.

Phenomenal consciousness, in contrast, isn't about the use or function of information. Instead, this sort of consciousness centers on what it actually *feels like* to have certain experiences—that is, the subjective experience that distinguishes a conscious being from a "zombie" (or robot or computer) that might have access to the same information, but with no "inner experience."

Philosophers use the term **qualia** to refer to these subjective experiences. ("Qualia" is the plural form; the singular is "quale," pronounced KWAH-lee.) As an example, imagine meeting some unfortunate soul who has never tasted chocolate. You could offer this person a detailed and vivid description of what chocolate tastes like. You could compare chocolate's flavor to various other flavors. You might even provide a full account of chocolate's impact on the nervous system (which receptors on the tongue are activated, etc.). What you couldn't do, however, is convey the subjective first-person experience of just what chocolate tastes like. In other words, you could provide this person with lots of information, but not the *quale* of chocolate taste.

There are many questions to ask about qualia. Philosophers have wondered, for example, whether any one of us can truly understand the qualia experienced by other people—a question, in essence, about whether you experience the world in the same way I do (see **Figure 14.8**). Neuroscientists, in contrast, might ask how the nervous system produces qualia: How does biological tissue give rise to subjective states? But a cognitive psychologist might ask: How do qualia matter in shaping mental processes?

Processing Fluency

In truth, we know relatively little about how people are influenced by the subjective experience of consciousness. We've argued in this chapter that the *information content* of consciousness is crucial, but does it matter how this content "feels" from a first-person perspective?

Research provides some hints about these issues—but these are just *hints*, and claims here must be somewhat speculative. Surely, though, this is no surprise: Qualia are, by their nature, undetectable by anyone other than the person who experiences them, so they are obviously difficult to study. It is also possible that some qualia matter deeply in shaping a person's thoughts and actions, while others don't; as a result, research in this arena has to pursue leads wherever we can find them.

Consider, as an illustration, the experience of *processing fluency*. In Chapter 7, we discussed the fact that the steps of perception sometimes proceed swiftly and with little effort but at other times proceed more slowly and with a lot of effort. The same is true for the steps of remembering, or

FIGURE 14.8   THE INVERTED SPECTRUM

Does each of us experience the world in the same way? Philosophers some-times cast this question in terms of the "inverted spectrum" problem. Imag-ine that your nervous system is somehow "wired differently" from mine. When you perceive red, the color you're experiencing is the color I call "violet." When you perceive blue, the color you're experiencing is the color I call "yellow." Of course, you and I have both learned to call the color of stoplights "red," even though we have very different experiences when look-ing at a stoplight. We've both learned that mixing yellow and red paints creates orange, even though we have different experiences of this "orange." How, then, would we ever find out if your color experience differs from mine?

deciding, or any other mental process. In other words, overall, mental pro-cessing is sometimes more fluent and sometimes less so, and people seem sensitive to this degree of fluency: They know when their steps have gone easily, and when not.

We've discussed the fact, though, that people don't detect the fluency *as* fluency. They don't have the experience of "Boy, that object sure was easy to perceive." Instead, people simply have a broad sense that their processing was, on this occasion, somehow special—and then they try to figure out *why* the processing was special. So they might decide that the input is one they've met recently (and so the fluency leads to a subjective sense of *familiarity*). Or they might conclude that the name they're considering belongs to someone famous. And so on.

Fluency effects can be demonstrated in many arenas. For example, the confidence expressed in a particular memory is influenced by the fluency of retrieval, apparently based on reasoning along the lines of "That memory came to mind easily; I guess it must be a strong memory and therefore an *accurate* one, so I can be confident that the memory is right." This reasoning is often sensible — but it can be misleading. For example, if you retrieve a memory over and over, the retrieval becomes more fluent because of this "practice," quite independent of how firmly established the memory was at the start. As a result, repeated retrieval increases memory confidence — whether the memory is accurate or not (see Chapter 8).

Likewise, in Chapter 12, we discussed the *availability heuristic* — the strategy of judging how frequent something is in the world by relying on how easily you can think of relevant examples. For example, are you in general an assertive person? People seem to answer this question by trying to think of events in the past in which they've been assertive, and if the examples come easily to mind, they decide that, yes, they are frequently assertive (Schwarz et al., 1991). So here, too, fluency of retrieval guides your thoughts. (For more on the broad impact of fluency, see Besken, 2016; Besken & Mulligan, 2014; Birch, Brosseau-Liard, Haddock, & Ghrear, 2017; Dohle & Montoya, 2017; Griffin, Gonzalez, Koehler, & Gilovich, 2012; Kounios & Beeman, 2015; Lanska, Olds, & Westerman, 2013; Olds & Westerman, 2012; Oppenheimer & Alter, 2014; Oppenheimer & Frank, 2007; Westerman, Lanska, & Olds, 2015.)

Fluency is certainly different from the more commonly discussed examples of qualia: the raw experience of tasting chocolate, or the experience of itch, or red. Even so, you do notice and react to your own fluency — so this does seem to be an element of your mental life that you're conscious of. And just as with other qualia, you can experience your own fluency but no one else can, and you can't experience anyone else's fluency. It's also important that we can describe the subjective experience of fluency only in rough terms — talking about someone "resonating" to an input or suggesting that a visual stimulus somehow "rings a bell." To go beyond these descriptions, we need to rely on the fact that each of us knows what fluency feels like, because we've all experienced fluent processing and we've all experienced processing that's not fluent. Each of these points is a trait of qualia, so research on fluency may provide important insights about how and when people are influenced by this entirely personal, entirely subjective, aspect of conscious experience.

Consciousness as Justification for Action

Other evidence hints at a different role for the actual experience of consciousness — a role in promoting, and perhaps allowing, *spontaneous* and *intentional* behavior (Dehaene & Naccache, 2001). To understand this point, consider the blind-sight patients. We've emphasized the fact that these patients are sensitive to visual information, and this tells us something important: Apparently, some aspects of vision can go forward with no conscious awareness and no conscious supervision. But it's also striking that these patients insist that they are blind, and their behaviors are consistent with this self-assessment: They're fearful of walking across a room (lest they bump into something), they fail to react to many stimuli, and so on.

Note the puzzle here. If, as it seems, these patients can see (at least to some extent), why don't they *use* the information that they gain by vision—for example, to guide their reaching or to navigate across the room? The evidence suggests that these patients see enough so that they reach correctly when they do reach. Why, then, don't they reach out on their own? Why do they reach (in the right direction, with the right hand shape) only when the experimenter insists that they try? Is it possible that perceptual information has to be *conscious* before a person puts that information to use? (For further discussion, see Dennett, 1992; Goodale & Milner, 2004; Weiskrantz, 1997.)

Similar questions can be asked about people who suffer from amnesia. We've emphasized how much amnesic patients do remember, when properly tested (i.e., with tests of implicit memory). But it's also important that people with amnesia don't use this (implicitly) remembered information. For example, amnesic patients will insist that they don't know the route to the hospital cafeteria, so they won't go to the cafeteria on their own. However, if we demand that they *guess* which way to turn to get to the cafeteria, they typically guess correctly. Once again, therefore, we might ask: Why don't the amnesic patients spontaneously use their (implicit) memories? Why do they reveal their knowledge only when we insist that they guess? Is it possible that remembered information has to be conscious before it is put to use?

Similar questions arise when we consider people with no brain damage—such as ordinary college students. Participants in one study were shown a list of words and then, later, were tested in either of two ways (Graf, Mandler, & Haden, 1982). Some were explicitly asked to recall the earlier list and were given word stems as cues: "What word on the prior list began 'CLE'?" Other participants were tested indirectly: "Tell me the first word that comes to mind beginning 'CLE.'"

The results show rather poor memory in the explicit test but much better performance in the implicit test. This observation echoes many findings we have reviewed. You often have implicit memories for episodes you've explicitly forgotten. But note that there's something peculiar in this result. In the explicit test, participants could, in principle, have proceeded this way: "I don't recall any words from the list beginning with 'CLE.' Maybe I'll just guess. Let's see: What words come to mind that begin with 'CLE'?" In this way, participants could use their implicit memory to supplement what they remember explicitly. If they did this, the performance difference between the two conditions would be erased; performance on the explicit test would be just as good as performance on the implicit test. Given the results, however, participants are obviously not using this strategy. For some reason, participants in this situation seem unable or unwilling to use their implicit memories to guide explicit responding.

What is going on in all of these cases? Here is one plausible answer. In many situations, you need to take action based on remembered or perceived information. In some settings, the action is overt (walking across the room or making a verbal response); at other times, the action is mental (reaching a decision or drawing a conclusion). In all cases, though, it seems not enough merely to have access to the relevant information. You also seem to need some justification, some reason, to take the information seriously.

To make this point concrete, imagine that you're trying to remember a specific event, and some misty thoughts about that event come to mind. You vaguely recall that friends were present; you have a dim idea that food was served. You might hesitate to voice these thoughts, though, because you're not convinced that these thoughts are *memories*. (Maybe they're chance associations or dreams you once had.) As a result, you'll report your memory only if you're satisfied that you are, in fact, remembering. In other words, in order to report on your recollection, you need more than the remembered information. You also need some reason to believe the remembered information is credible.

How do you decide whether to trust your recollection? The answer, perhaps, is conscious experience. In other words, perhaps you'll take action based on some information only if the information "feels right"—that is, if it has the right qualia. If the experience has these qualities, this convinces you that the presented information is more than a chance association, and so you take the information seriously. However, if the conscious presentation is impoverished (as it seems to be in blind sight or in amnesia), you may not trust the information provided by your own eyes or your own memory, so you're paralyzed into inactivity. (For related discussion, see Johnson, 1988; Johnson, Hashtroudi, & Lindsay, 1993.)

In fact, these points can be linked to our earlier claims about the neuronal workspace. Bear in mind that the workspace allows an integration from multiple brain areas, and it's plausible that this integration is essential when you're trying to decide whether to take a memory (or a perception) seriously. The integration enables you to see, among other points, that the information provided by vision is confirmed by touch, that the information gained from your senses is consistent with your other beliefs, and so on. This convergence of cues may play a key role in persuading you that the perception or memory is real, not just a passing thought.

In Shakespeare's play, Macbeth asks himself whether the dagger he sees is real or a hallucination—"a dagger of the mind, a false creation proceeding from a heat-oppressed brain" (act 2, scene 1). He tries to decide by checking the visual information against other cues, asking whether the dagger is "sensible to feeling as to sight." The idea we're discussing here is similar: The confluence of inputs provided by the neuronal workspace helps provide the richness—and, plausibly, the conscious experience itself—that you use in deciding whether your ideas and perceptions and memories are "false creations" or, instead, are true to reality. And it's only after you decide that they're real that you use them as a basis for action.

TEST YOURSELF

10. What are qualia?
11. What evidence suggests that people are influenced by the quale of processing fluency?

A DAGGER OF THE MIND?

In act 2, scene 1, Macbeth asks himself whether he sees a real dagger or "a dagger of the mind, a false creation . . . [of] a heat-oppressed brain." He tries to decide by checking the visual information against other cues. The proposal we're considering is that this is a common pattern—in which you check the credibility of your own thoughts by considering the qualia associated with those thoughts.

Consciousness: What Is Left Unsaid

The cognitive unconscious is remarkably sophisticated—able to recognize objects in the world, to reason, to draw conclusions, to retrieve information from memory. As a result, you often have no direct information about why you decided what you did or acted as you did. We've seen throughout this book, however, that careful research can reveal these processes, leaving us with an understanding of these processes that is both theoretically rich and pragmatically useful.

The fact remains, though, that you *are* aware of some things in your mind, and as we've now seen, researchers have made progress in describing the function of this awareness and its biological underpinnings. There is, however, still a lot that we don't know about consciousness. Our remarks about qualia have been speculative, and debate continues about the completeness (or accuracy) of theorizing about the neuronal workspace. In this chapter, we've also held other issues to the side: Can we specify what it is that changes in conscious experience during meditation or when someone is taking drugs? And how should we think about an issue of consciousness that emerged in Chapter 11 in our discussion of visual imagery? There, we saw that individuals may *differ* in their conscious experience, with some people apparently enjoying rich, detailed visual images (so that their conscious experience often includes "mental pictures") but with other people insisting they have no mental imagery at all. This is a point in need of investigation—investigation that might illuminate the functional consequences of these differences and also their biological roots.

A different—and immensely difficult—puzzle centers on how the 3 pounds of the human brain make consciousness possible. The brain, after all, is a physical object with a certain mass, a certain temperature (a degree or two warmer than the rest of the body), and a certain volume (a bit less than a half gallon). It occupies a specific position in space. Our conscious thoughts and experiences, in contrast, aren't physical objects and have none of these properties. An idea, for example, doesn't have mass or a specific temperature; a feeling of sadness or fear has neither volume nor a location in space.

How, therefore, is it possible for a physical entity like the brain to give rise to nonphysical thoughts and feelings? Conversely, how can your thoughts and feelings *influence* your brain or your body? Imagine that you want to wave to a friend, and so you do. Your arm, of course, is a physical object with an identifiable mass. To move your arm, therefore, you need some physical force. But your initial idea ("I want to wave to Dan") isn't a physical thing with a mass or a position in space. How, then, could this (nonphysical) idea produce a (physical) force to move your arm?

The puzzles in play here stem from a quandary that philosophers refer to as the **mind-body problem**. The term refers to the fact that the mind (and the ideas, thoughts, and feelings it contains) is an entirely different sort of entity from the physical body, and yet the two, somehow, can influence each other. How can this be? The mind-body problem remains a mystery. In this chapter, we've discussed the *correlation* between brain states and conscious states, but we've left untouched the much harder question of how either of these states *causes* changes in the other.

Thus, we leave this chapter acknowledging that our discussion has only tackled part of the problem of consciousness and has left other parts untouched. In fact, it's possible that only some aspects of consciousness can be studied by means of scientific research, while other aspects require other forms of inquiry (e.g., philosophical analysis). Nonetheless, the data we've reviewed in this chapter, as well as the conclusions that flow from these data, provide powerful insights into the nature of consciousness, and these data will certainly inform future discussions of this profound and complex issue. This by itself—the mere fact that research can address these extraordinarily difficult issues—has to be a source of enormous satisfaction for investigators working on these intriguing problems.

COGNITIVE PSYCHOLOGY AND EDUCATION

mindfulness

As we have discussed in this chapter, you're able to accomplish a great deal through unconscious processing, and in many ways this is a good thing. With no attention paid to the low-level details of a task, and with no thought given to the exact processes needed for the task, you're able to focus attention on other priorities—on your broader goals or on the products (the ideas, memories, and beliefs) resulting from these unconscious, unnoticed processes.

The chapter makes it clear, though, that there's a cost associated with these benefits, because this state of affairs leaves you less able to control some of your own mental processes. The role of unconscious processes also guarantees that you end up being less well informed and less insightful about why you believe what you believe, perceive what you perceive, feel what you feel. As a result, with less control and less information about your own mental life, you end up more likely to rely on habit or routine, and more vulnerable to the pressures or cues built into the situations you encounter. You're also more likely to be influenced by chance associations and by the relatively primitive thought processes that in Chapter 12 we referred to as "Type 1 thinking."

It's not surprising, therefore, that some people urge us all to be more mindful of our actions and, in general, to seek a state of mindfulness. Sports coaches, piano teachers, writing instructors, and many others urge us to "pay attention" to what we're doing—on the sports field, at the piano, at the word processor—with the clear notion that by paying attention we'll be able to rise above old habits and adjust (and improve) our performance. In the same spirit, instructors sometimes complain about their students performing a task in a "mechanical" fashion or "on autopilot," with the broad

"PAY ATTENTION!"

Piano teachers, sports coaches, and many other instructors often urge their students to "pay attention." The idea here is that we often need to "rise above" our habits to improve performance.

suggestion that a thoughtful, more mindful performance would be better—more alert to the circumstances, better tuned to the situation. Likewise, commonsense wisdom urges us to "Look before you leap" or sometimes just to "Think!"—apparently based on the idea that some forethought or some thought during an action might help us to be more aware of, and therefore wiser about, what we're doing.

These various suggestions—all celebrating the advantages of mindfulness—fit well with the argument that unconscious processes tend to be inflexible and rigidly controlled by situational cues or prior patterns. But how should you use these suggestions? How should you try to be more mindful? You might start by asking yourself: "What is my usual practice in taking notes in class? What's my usual strategy when the time comes to prepare for an exam? What does the rhythm of my typical day look like?" In each case, you might pause to ask whether these practices and strategies developed for good reasons or simply arose out of habit. In each case, you might consider whether, on reflection, you might want to modify your practices to take advantage of suggestions you've read about in these chapters or found in other sources.

It's also worth mentioning that an emphasis on mindfulness is prominent in some forms of psychotherapy. In some types of therapy, people are encouraged to pause and pay attention to—and perhaps savor—their current state, with a nonjudgmental focus on their thoughts and feelings at just that moment. This notion of mindfulness is related to meditation practices in some forms of Buddhism, and the emphasis on mindfulness seems to have various benefits—helping people to reduce stress, to deal with some forms of mental illness, and more broadly to improve the quality of their lives.

In all of these ways, therefore, we can celebrate how much is accomplished through unconscious thought, but we should also acknowledge the potential benefits of sometimes shifting to conscious thought. Apparently, there are circumstances in which thoughtful, mindful reflection on your thoughts and behaviors may lead you to improvements in how you think, what you think, and how you feel and how you act.

chapter review

SUMMARY

- An enormous amount of cognitive processing happens "behind the scenes," in the cognitive unconscious. In many cases, you're conscious only of the products that result from your mental processes; the processes themselves are unconscious. This is reflected in the fact that you aren't conscious of searching through memory; you're aware only of the results produced by that search. Similarly, you cannot tell when you have truly perceived a word and when you have merely inferred the word's presence.

- Unconscious processing can be rather sophisticated. For example, implicit memory influences you without your being aware that you are remembering at all, and this influence is typically mediated by a complex process through which you attribute a feeling of fluency to a particular cause. Unconscious attributions can also shape how you interpret and react to your own bodily states.

- Even when your thinking is conscious, you're still influenced by unconscious guides that shape and direct your thought. This is evident in the effects of framing in decision making and in the effects of sets in guiding your problem-solving efforts.

- Still further evidence for unconscious achievements comes from the study of blind sight and amnesia. In both cases, patients seem to have knowledge (gained from perception or from memory) but no conscious awareness of that knowledge.

- The cognitive unconscious allows enormous efficiency, but at the cost of flexibility or control. Likewise, the cognitive unconscious keeps you from being distracted by the details of your mental processes, but in some cases there's a cost to your ignorance about how your mental processes unfolded and how you arrived at a particular memory or a particular perception. These trade-offs point the way toward the function of consciousness: Conscious thinking is less efficient but more controllable, and it is also better informed by information about process.

- The neuronal workspace hypothesis begins with the fact that most of the processing in the brain is carried out by separate, specialized modules. When you pay attention to a stimulus, however, the neurons in the various modules are linked by means of workspace neurons. This linkage amplifies and sustains the processing within individual modules, and it allows integration and comparison of the various modules. The integration, it is proposed, is what makes consciousness possible. The integration provides the basis for the unity in your experience; it also enables flexibility and the detection of conflict.

- Consciousness may give you a sense that you have adequate justification for taking an action. This may be why amnesic patients seem unable to take action based on what they (unconsciously) recall and why blind-sight patients seem unable to respond to what they (unconsciously) see.

- Several theorists have argued that we must distinguish types of conscious experience. The considerations in this chapter bear more directly on "access consciousness," which is a matter of how information is accessed and used within the mind. The chapter has had less to say about "phenomenal consciousness," which is concerned with the subjective experience of being conscious. Even so, research on mental *fluency* provides an intriguing hint both of how you are guided by qualia and how we can do research on the effects of qualia.

KEY TERMS

cognitive unconscious (p. 549)
blind sight (p. 558)
subliminal perception (p. 559)
action slips (p. 563)
metacognitive skills (p. 565)
metamemory (p. 565)

neural correlates of consciousness (p. 566)
neuronal workspace hypothesis (p. 568)
anterior cingulate cortex (ACC) (p. 572)
qualia (sing. quale) (p. 574)
mind-body problem (p. 580)

TEST YOURSELF AGAIN

1. Give an example in which people are conscious of the "products" created within the mind but not conscious of the "processes" that led to these products.

2. What evidence suggests that unconscious processes can involve sophisticated reasoning?

3. What does it mean to say that sometimes "introspections" are actually just after-the-fact reconstructions?

4. What is blind sight, and what does it imply about the need for consciousness in perception?

5. What is subliminal perception, and what does it tell us about the need for consciousness in understanding complex stimuli?

6. What sorts of actions can go forward without executive control? When is executive control needed?

7. What is metacognition?

8. Cognitive neuroscientists often distinguish "degree of awareness" from the "content of consciousness." What do these two terms mean?

9. What is the neuronal workspace hypothesis? What is the function of the neuronal workspace?

10. What are qualia?

11. What evidence suggests that people are influenced by the quale of processing fluency?

THINK ABOUT IT

1. In light of the evidence and arguments presented in this chapter, could a *computer* ever be conscious? Does a computer need something like "executive control"? (Think about the circumstances or achievements for which humans seem to need executive control; does that help with this question?) Would a computer ever need something like qualia?

e eBOOK DEMONSTRATIONS & ESSAYS

Go to http://digital.wwnorton.com/cognition7 for the online demonstrations and essays relevant to this chapter. These can be found in the ebook.

Online Demonstrations

- Demonstration 14.1: Practice and the Cognitive Unconscious
- Demonstration 14.2: The Quality of Consciousness

Online Applying Cognitive Psychology and the Law Essays

- Cognitive Psychology and the Law: Unconscious Thinking

ZAPS COGNITION LABS

Go to http://digital.wwnorton.com/cognition7 to experience interactive online psychology labs relevant to this chapter.

Appendix
Research Methods

R esearch in cognitive psychology yields results that are intriguing and useful. These results have value, however, only if they're based on sound methods and good science. If not, we may be offering practical suggestions that do more harm than good, and making theoretical claims that lead us away from the truth, not toward it.

It's therefore important to understand the methods that make our science possible. This understanding will enable you to see why our results are compelling and why we can, with confidence, draw the conclusions that we do. For this reason, this appendix contains a series of Research Methods "modules," each one highlighting a methodological issue or focusing on a research example.

Let's make a few quick points, though, about this presentation. First, these modules are no substitute for a full research methods course, a course of considerable value on its own. Even so, the methodological concepts covered here are crucial—not just for students who want to become scientists, but for anyone hoping to understand evidence (whether it's the evidence presented in this text, or the evidence you read about in the newspaper, or the evidence you hear in a conversation).

Second, each of the modules in this appendix is linked to a specific chapter. This linkage will allow you to read the modules (usually, one per chapter) in parallel with your reading of the text. I hope this configuration will help you see how these methodological points apply to concrete examples, which will, in turn, help you see why these points are so important. But, third, I don't want to distract those readers who want to focus exclusively on our field's content—and that's why these modules are in an appendix: easily available for readers who want them, but not a distraction for those who don't.

Chapter 1:   Testable Hypotheses
Chapter 2:   Control Groups
Chapter 3:   The Proper N

Chapter 1: The Science of the Mind

Testable Hypotheses

What is "science," and what is it about cognitive psychology that makes it count as a science? The key lies in the idea that science cannot be based just on someone's opinions about the world or on someone's (perhaps biased) interpretation of the facts. Instead, science needs to be based on the facts themselves, and that means the scientific community needs to check every one of its claims against the facts, to find out with certainty whether each claim is correct. If we learn that the evidence for a claim is weak or ambiguous, then we need to seek more evidence in order to achieve certainty. And, of course, if we learn that a claim does not fit with the facts, then we're obligated to set the claim aside, to make sure we only offer claims that we know are in line with reality.

Clearly, then, the notion of *testing* our claims, to make sure they match the facts, is essential for science, and this has a powerful implication for how we formulate our claims in the first place. Specifically, we need to make sure that all of our claims are formulated in a way that will allow the testing that is central to the scientific enterprise.

A scientist therefore begins by offering a *hypothesis*—a supposition about the facts that may or may not turn out to be true. Crucially, though, the hypothesis must be stated in a fashion that makes it **testable**. But how do we ensure testability? How do we ensure that it will be possible to confront our claims with the facts? Among other considerations, we need to make certain our claims never rely on ambiguous terms or vague phrasing; we also need to avoid escape clauses like "Maybe this will happen" or "Sometimes we'll observe X and sometimes we won't."

To see how this plays out, consider the claim "No matter what day of the year you pick, a famous psychologist was born on that day." To test this claim, you might hop onto the Internet and, with a bit of searching, assemble a long list of who was born on which day. Then let's imagine that as you look over this list, you realize that Daniel Reisberg is the most prominent psychologist born on December 19. Does this observation support the initial claim, because Reisberg is famous? (After all, thousands of students have read his books.) Or does it contradict the claim, because Reisberg isn't famous? (After all, most people have never heard of him.) Both of these positions seem plausible, and so your "test" of this claim about birthdays turns out to depend on opinion, not fact: If you hold the opinion that Reisberg is famous, then the evidence about the December 19 birthday confirms the claim; if you hold the opposite opinion, the same evidence doesn't confirm the claim. As a result, this claim is not testable—there's no way to say with certainty whether it fits with the facts or not.

Of course, we could make this claim testable if we could find a suitable definition of "famous." In that case, we could, with some certainty, decide whether Reisberg is famous or not, and then we could use this point to test our claim about birthdays. But until that is done, there is no way to test this claim in the fashion, not dependent on opinion, that science requires.

This example illustrates why a scientific hypothesis must be framed precisely—so that we can check the facts and then say with certainty whether the hypothesis is correct. But how do we check the facts? We'll explore this question in upcoming sections of this appendix.

Chapter 2: The Neural Basis for Cognition

Control Groups

In several passages in Chapter 2, we talk about this or that brain area as being activated during a particular activity—so that certain areas in the occipital lobe (for example) are especially active when someone is examining a visual stimulus, certain areas of the frontal lobe are especially active when someone is listening to a verbal input, and so on. We need to be clear, though, about what these claims really mean.

All cells in the brain are active all the time. When they receive some input, however, or when they are involved in a particular process, the brain cells *change* their activation level. Therefore, when we talk about, say, the occipital lobe's response to a visual input, we do not mean that the cells are active when an input arrives and dormant the rest of the time. Instead, we're saying that when a visual input arrives, the activity in the occipital lobe increases from its prior **baseline level**.

To measure these increases, we need a basis for comparison, and in fact this is a feature of virtually all scientific investigation: Usually, we can interpret a measurement or an observation only with reference to some appropriate baseline. This is true outside of science as well. Imagine that a TV ad boasts that 90% of the people who use Yippee toothpaste have no cavities when they see their dentists. Does this mean the toothpaste is effective? We'd need to ask how often people who use *other* toothpastes have cavity-free checkups. If that number is also 90%, then Yippee brings no benefits. If the number is 95%, then Yippee might actually be bad for your teeth.

In scientific research, our basis for comparison in evaluating data is typically provided by a **control condition**—a condition that enables us to see how things unfold in the absence of the experimental manipulation. If, therefore, we want to understand how the brain responds to visual inputs, we need to compare a condition with a visual input (the **experimental condition**) with a control condition lacking this input. The difference between the conditions is the **independent variable**—the factor that's varying and that differentiates the two conditions.

In our toothpaste example, the independent variable was the presence or absence of Yippee toothpaste. Let's be clear that there's just one thing that's varying in this comparison—whether Yippee is in use or not—and so there is just one independent variable. However, there are two options for this variable (with Yippee vs. without), so the one independent variable creates two conditions. (Technically, we'd say that this is one variable with two "levels.")

Likewise, if we are asking how visual stimulation changes brain activity, there is again just one factor that's varying: whether the stimulus is present or absent. But here, too, there are two options for this variable, so the single independent variable leaves us with two conditions. (In other, more complicated experiments, there might be three or more options for a variable—perhaps no visual input vs. dim input vs. bright input. Likewise, there might be more than one independent variable. We'll hold these complications to the side for now.)

The independent variable is sometimes called the "predictor variable," because our comparison is asking, in effect, whether we can use this variable to predict the experiment's outcome. (Does the use of Yippee toothpaste predict a greater chance of a good checkup? Is the presence of a visual input associated with greater brain activity, so that when the input is on the scene we can predict that the activity will increase?)

The variable we measure in our data collection is called the **dependent variable**, so that our study is asking, in essence, whether this variable depends on the predictor variable. In many cases, the dependent variable is straightforward (How many cavities did you have? What is the level of brain activity?), but sometimes it is not. We will return to this topic in a Research Methods module for Chapter 13.

We still need to ask, however, exactly how we should set up our study of brain activity, and how in particular we should set up the control condition. Imagine, as one possibility, that participants in our experimental condition are staring attentively at a computer screen, eagerly awaiting (and eventually seeing) a visual stimulus, while participants in our control condition are told merely to hang out, so that we can observe the functioning of their brains. If we found differences between these two conditions, we could draw no conclusions. That's because any differences we observe might be due to the presence of the visual stimulus in one condition and not the other, or they might be due to the fact that participants in one condition are attentive while those in the other condition are relaxed. With no way to choose between these options, we'd have no way to interpret the data.

Clearly, then, our control condition must be carefully designed so that it differs from the experimental condition in just one way (in our example, in the presence or absence of the visual stimulus). We want to make sure that the two conditions are essentially identical in all other regards. As part of this concern, we want to make sure that participants in the two conditions get similar instructions and have similar expectations for the experiment. Only then, with the independent variable being "isolated" in this fashion, will the contrast between the conditions be meaningful, enabling us to interpret the data and thus to properly test our hypothesis.

Chapter 3: Visual Perception

The Proper *N*

A researcher wonders: Who's better at crossword puzzles, men or women? To find out, the researcher recruits two friends, Jeff and Jane, and gives them each a puzzle to work on. Jane finishes 3 minutes sooner than Jeff, so the researcher concludes: Women are better.

It should be obvious, though, that this conclusion is silly. Among other problems, we've only considered two people, and perhaps Jane just happens to be extraordinarily skilled in puzzles (and not representative of women-in-general), or perhaps Jeff happens to be particularly inept. At the very least, we'd want more data before we draw any conclusions. In other words, we'd need an adequate number of research participants, and this number is usually referred to with the single (and capitalized) letter *N*.

But what is the proper *N* for a study? How many observations do we need? The answer depends (among other considerations) on how consistent the data are or, conversely, how *variable* the data are—that is, how much difference there is from one observation to the next. In the study of perception, for example, researchers often rely on a small *N,* and the reason is straightforward: Your eyes have two types of photoreceptors (rods and cones), just like everyone else's eyes. Your cones are concentrated in your eyeballs' foveas, just like everyone else's cones are. We could, therefore, just study your eyeballs and draw broad conclusions from our data.

In other cases, though, we do need more data. For example, some aspects of vision (e.g., deciding whether two shapes are "similar" or not) involve an element of judgment, and, of course, people differ in their judgments. Therefore, if we were studying, say, how people categorize visual forms, we'd need to study an adequate number of cases in order to accommodate this variation.

The *N* we'll need also depends on the **effect size**, or the size of the difference, we're trying to evaluate. Imagine that we're trying to confirm that elephants weigh more than fleas. Of course, elephants vary in their weight, and so do fleas, but this variation is tiny compared to the (massive) difference in the weights between these two creatures. Therefore, we could document this difference with a relatively small N. In contrast, imagine that we're asking which weighs more: fleas or mosquitoes. Now we're trying to assess a smaller difference, and it's a difference that could be obscured by the variation in weight from one flea to the next. To assess this small difference, then, we'll need a larger N.

What counts as a proper N therefore varies from case to case. It's common, though, for studies of visual perception to rely on just a half dozen research participants, while a study of memory accuracy might rely on 40 or 50, and a study of intelligence might rely on 100 participants or more.

But how exactly do we choose an N? Statisticians recommend that we perform what's called a "power calculation." This mathematical procedure starts with an estimate of the effect size we expect (or hope) to see in the data. Estimates of effect size reflect both how big a difference we expect to see between the conditions (will the experimental and control conditions differ by 1%? By 2%? By more?) and also how variable we expect the data to be. Once we have an estimate for effect size, a power calculation will tell us what N we'd need in order to have a specified probability of detecting an effect of that size.

Of course, we don't just want an adequately sized N. We also need to ensure that we've included the right observations in our data set. Specifically, we usually want a **representative sample**, but on this point, too, our methods must be chosen on a case-by-case basis. If we are studying some issue for which there is little variability, then it matters less who's in our **sample**. For example, the visual system of an American college student works the same way as it does in any other human, so a sample of college students *is* representative. In contrast, a sample of students might be inappropriate if we wanted to study how people in general make decisions or solve problems.

Researchers use several techniques to create a representative sample, but a crucial tool is the use of **random sampling**—a procedure in which every member of the **population** being studied has an equal chance of being picked for inclusion in the study. With random sampling (especially if the sample is large), the investigators hope to ensure that the diversity in the population is mirrored within their sample, so that the sample really can inform them about the properties of the overall population.

Chapter 4: Recognizing Objects

Dealing with Confounds

Imagine an experiment in which research participants are asked to recognize letter strings briefly presented on a computer screen—let's say for 30 milliseconds—followed by a mask. In the first 50 trials, the letter strings are random sequences (like "OKBO" or "PMLA"). In the next 50 trials, the letter strings are all common words ("BOOK," "LAMP," "TREE"). Let's say that the participants are able, on average, to identify 30% of the random sequences and 65% of the words. This is a large difference; what should we conclude from it?

In fact, we can conclude nothing from this (fictitious) experiment, because the procedure just described is flawed. The data tell us that participants did much better with the words, but why did this happen? One possibility is that words are, in fact, easier to recognize than nonwords. A different possibility, however, is that we are instead seeing an effect of *practice*: Maybe the participants did better with the word trials not because words are special, but simply because the words came later in the experiment, after the participants had gained some experience with the procedure. Conversely, perhaps the participants did worse with the nonwords not because they were hard to recognize, but because they were presented before any practice or warm-up.

To put this in technical terms, the experiment just described is **invalid**— that is, it does not measure what it is intended to measure (the difference between words and nonwords). The experiment is invalid because a **confound** is present—an extra variable that could have caused the observed data pattern. The confound in this particular case is the *sequence*, and the confound makes the data ambiguous: Maybe the words were better recognized because they're words, *or* maybe the words were better recognized simply because they came second. With no way in the data to choose between these interpretations, we cannot say which is the correct interpretation; hence, we can draw no conclusions from the experiment.

How should this experiment have been designed? One possibility is to **counterbalance** the sequence of trials: For half of the participants, we would show the words first, then the random letters; for the other half of the participants, we would use the reverse order—random letters, then words. This setup doesn't eliminate the effect of practice, but it ensures that practice has the same impact on both conditions. Specifically, with this setup, practice would favor one condition half the time and the other condition half the time. Thus, the contribution of practice would be the same for both conditions, so it could not be the cause of a *difference* between the conditions.

If this point isn't perfectly clear, consider an analogy. Imagine a championship football game between the Rockets and the Bulldogs. As it turns out, there's a strong wind blowing across the field, and the wind is coming from *behind* the Rockets. The wind helps the Rockets throw and kick the ball farther, giving them an unfair advantage. The referees have no way to eliminate the wind. What they can do, though, is have the teams take turns in which direction they're moving. For one quarter of the game, the Rockets have their backs to the wind; then, in the next quarter, the direction of play is reversed, so it's the Bulldogs who have their backs to the wind; and so on. (This is, of course, how football games operate.) That way, the wind doesn't favor one team over the other, and so, when the Rockets win, we can't say it was because of the wind; in other words, the wind could not have caused the difference between the teams' performance.

Returning to our word/nonword experiment, we know how it would turn out when properly designed: Words are, in fact, easier to recognize than random strings of letters. Our point here, though, lies in what it takes for the experiment to be "properly designed." In this and in all experiments, we need to remove confounds so that we can be sure what lies beneath the data pattern. Several techniques are available for dealing with confounds; we've mentioned just one of them (counterbalancing) here. The key, however, is to remove the confounds; only then can we legitimately draw conclusions from the experiment.

Chapter 5: Paying Attention

The Power of Random Assignment

Is it hazardous to talk on a cell phone while driving? Many people believe it is, and they point to evidence showing that people who use a cell phone while driving are more likely to be involved in accidents than people who do not use a cell phone while driving. This association—between increased accident risk and cell-phone use—stays in place even if we focus only on "hands-free" phones. The problem, it seems, is not that you take one hand off the steering wheel to hold the phone. Instead, the problem seems to be the phone conversation itself. But we need to ask: Is this evidence persuasive?

Actually, the accident statistics are ambiguous—open to more than one interpretation. Being alert to this sort of ambiguity is crucial for science, because if results can be interpreted in more than one way, then we can draw no conclusions from them. What is the ambiguity in this case? Perhaps talking on a cell phone while driving is, in fact, distracting and increases the likelihood of an accident. But, as an alternative, perhaps drivers who use cell phones while on the road are people who, from the start, are less cautious or more prone to take risks. This lack of caution is why these people talk on the phone while driving, and it's also the reason why they're more often involved in accidents. Thus, cell-phone use and accidents go together, but not because either one causes the other. Instead, both of these observations (cell-phone use and having accidents) are the by-products of a third factor: being a risk taker in the first place.

In technical terms, the concern here is called the **third-variable problem**—the possibility that two observations are correlated, not because either one is causing the other but because both are the result of some other (third) factor. The third-variable problem is one of the reasons why a *correlation* (e.g., the finding that cell-phone use and accidents are correlated) cannot, on its own, show *causation* (e.g., the idea that cell-phone use causes accidents).

How can we move forward in understanding the possible dangers involved in cell-phone use? The problem here comes from the fact that the people who drive while on the phone are a **self-selected group**. In other words, they decided for themselves whether they'd be in our "experimental group" (the cell-phone users) or our "control group" (people who don't use phones while they drive). Presumably, people make this choice for some reason—they have some tendency or attributes at the start that lead them to the behavior of using the phone while driving. And the problem, of course, is that it might be these initial attributes, not the cell-phone use itself, that caused the observed outcome—the increased accident rate.

If we really want to examine the effects of cell-phone use on driving, we need to make sure that our "phone group" and our "no-phone group" are equivalent to begin with, before cell phones enter the scene. If we then discover that cell-phone use is associated with more accidents, we'd know that the cell phones are indeed at fault, and not some preexisting difference between the groups.

Psychologists usually achieve this matching of groups by means of **random assignment**. In our example, rather than allowing research participants to sort themselves into a group of phone users and a group of nonusers, the experimenters would assign them to one group or the other on some random basis (perhaps a coin toss). This strategy wouldn't change the fact that some drivers are careful and others are not, or that some are more attentive than others. But our coin toss would ensure that careless drivers have an equal chance of ending up in the phone or no-phone group, and likewise for careful drivers or risky ones. As a result, our two groups would end up being matched to each other, not because all of our participants were alike but instead because each group would contain the same mix of different driver types.

Random assignment is one of the most important tools in a psychologist's research kit, ensuring that groups are matched before an experiment begins. That way, if the groups differ at the *end* of the experiment, we can be sure it's because of our experimental manipulation, and not because of some preexisting difference.

With all of this said, what about cell-phone use? The evidence suggests that talking on a cell phone while driving *is* dangerous, because of the distraction. The evidence comes from laboratory studies, because it would be unethical to require people to use phones while actually driving; this would put them in danger, so it is unacceptable as a research procedure. However, the studies use high-tech, realistic driving simulators, and the data are clear: Having phone conversations while driving increases the risk of accidents. Hence, there is an important message in these data—but it's not a message we can draw from the evidence mentioned at the start of this module (the greater accident frequency among cell-phone users). The properly designed studies, though, using random assignment, make it clear that the bumper stickers have it right when they advise us to "Hang up and drive."

Chapter 6: The Acquisition of Memories and the Working-Memory System

Replication

So far in this appendix, we've talked about some of the steps needed to make sure the results of an experiment are unambiguous. We've talked, for example, about the need for a precise hypothesis, so that there's no question about whether the results fit with the hypothesis. We've talked about the advantages of random assignment, to make certain that the results couldn't be the product of preexisting differences in our comparison groups. We've discussed the need to remove confounds, so that within the experiment there is no ambiguity about what caused the differences we observe.

Notice, though, that all of these points concern the interpretation of individual experiments. However, researchers rarely draw conclusions from individual experiments, no matter how well designed the experiment is. One reason is statistical: A successful **replication**—a reproduction of the result in a new experiment—provides assurance that the original result wasn't just a fluke or a weird accident. Another reason is methodological: If we can replicate a result with a new experimenter, new participants, and new stimuli, this tells us there was nothing peculiar about these factors in the first experiment. This is our guarantee that the result was produced by the factors that we deliberately varied in the experiment and was *not* the chance by-product of some unnoticed factor in the procedure or the context.

In addition, researchers generally don't repeat experiments exactly as they were run the first time. Instead, replications usually introduce new factors into the design, to ask how (or whether) the new factors alter the results. (In fact, many scientific journals are hesitant to publish straight replications, largely because space is limited in the journals; however, they routinely publish studies that include a replication as part of a larger design that also introduces some new variation in the procedure.)

This broad pattern of "replication + variation" enables researchers to refine their hypotheses and to test new hypotheses about a result. We gave one example of this approach in the text chapter: Specifically, if people are asked to recall as many words as they can from a list they just heard, the results show a characteristic U-shaped serial-position curve. This result is easily replicated, so we know it doesn't depend on the specific words that are used in the procedure, or the particular group of participants we recruit, or the time of day in which we run the experiment. This knowledge allows us to move forward, asking the next question: What produces this reliable pattern? One proposal, of course, is provided by the *modal model*, a theoretical account of memory's basic architecture. But is this model correct?

To address this question, researchers have varied a number of factors in the basic list-learning experiment—factors that should, if the hypothesis is correct, alter the results. One factor is speed of list presentation: According to our hypothesis, if we slow down the presentation, this should increase recall for all but the last few words on the list. A different factor is distraction right after the list's end: Our hypothesis predicts that this will decrease the *recency effect* but will have no other effects. These predictions both turn out to be right.

Notice, then, that our claims about the modal model rest on many results, not just on one. This is the typical pattern in any science. Single results are often open to more than one interpretation. Broad *patterns* of results, in contrast, usually allow just one interpretation—and that is what we want. Within the broad data pattern, some of the results show the replicability of the basic findings (e.g., the U-shaped data pattern). Other results provide tests of specific predictions derived from our model. In the end, though, it's the full fabric of results that tells us our explanation is correct, and it's this full fabric that tells us the explanation is powerful—able to explain a wide range of experimental data.

Chapter 7: Interconnections between Acquisition and Retrieval

Chronometric Studies

Our mental processes are usually quite fast, but even so, they do take a measurable amount of time, and by scrutinizing these times we can learn a great deal about the mind. This is why **chronometric studies** (or time-measuring studies) play a key role in cognitive psychology. In these studies, participants are asked a specific question in each trial, and we measure how long they need to respond; hence, our data take the form of **response times** (**RTs**). However, we need to be clear about what response-time data really tell us.

Let's take as an example a lexical-decision task. In each trial of this task, a sequence of letters is presented, and the participants must decide whether the sequence forms a word or not. If it does, the participants press one button; if not, then a different button. In this situation, the trials we're interested in are the ones in which the sequence does form a word; those trials tell us how rapidly the participants can "look up" the word in their "mental dictionary." Trials in which the letter sequences *aren't* words are not helpful for this question. Nonetheless, we need to include these nonword trials as **catch trials**. If we don't include them, then the correct answer would be "Yes, this sequence is a word" on every trial. Participants would quickly figure this out and would shift to a strategy of hitting the "yes" button every time without even looking at the stimulus. To avoid this problem, we include nonwords as catch trials to make sure that participants take the task seriously.

But let's focus on the trials that do involve words; those are the trials that provide our data. For these trials, we can, if we wish, think about the task as including several steps: On each trial, the participants first have to perceive the letters on the screen; then, they have to look up this letter sequence in memory. Then, when they locate the relevant information in storage, they must draw the conclusion that, yes, the sequence does form a word. Finally, they must make the physical movement of pressing the appropriate button to indicate their decision.

As it turns out, we're only interested in a part of this sequence—namely, the time needed to locate the word in memory. In other words, the *total* response time isn't useful for us, because it includes many elements that we really don't care about. How, then, can we isolate just that bit of the process that is of interest? The key, quite simply, is *subtraction*. Specifically, let's imagine a comparison between trials in which the target word has been primed and trials in which there has been no priming. Both types of trials include letter reading; both include a decision that, yes, the stimulus is a word; both include the physical movement of a button press. Therefore, if we find *differences* between these two types of trials, the differences cannot be the result of these elements, because these elements are the same in both types. Any differences, then, must be the result of the one stage that *is* different between the two types of trials—a memory look-up in the presence of priming, as opposed to a memory look-up without priming. By examining that difference, we can ask what the effect of priming is—and that, in general, is the key to chronometric studies. We are usually interested in the differences in response times between conditions, not the absolute times themselves; these differences enable us to isolate (and thus to measure) the processes we want to study.

Clearly, then, some craft is involved in the design of chronometric experiments. We must arrange for the proper comparisons so that we can isolate just the processes that we're interested in. But with the appropriate steps taken, chronometric studies can provide enormously useful information about memory, perception, imagery, and many other mental processes.

Double Dissociations

Chapter 7 describes a number of results indicating that implicit memories are different from explicit ones. For example, certain forms of brain damage affect explicit memory but leave implicit memory intact. Likewise, explicit memory is strongly influenced by the level of processing during encoding, whereas implicit memory may not be. And so on.

It turns out, though, that these various results are ambiguous, and as we've seen, ambiguity is a problem for science: If a result can be explained in more than one way, then we don't know which explanation is the right one and can draw no conclusions. Hence, many steps within science are aimed precisely at the *removal* of ambiguity.

What's the ambiguity with regard to implicit and explicit memory? On the one side, we can read the results as suggesting that implicit memory is fundamentally different from explicit memory—governed by its own principles and served by separate portions of the brain. But on the other side, perhaps implicit and explicit memory are not different types at all. Perhaps they are fundamentally the same, obeying the same rules and principles. In that case, the memories we call "explicit" might simply be a more fragile version of this single type of memory, and hence they're more easily influenced by external factors such as brain damage or level of processing.

The issue at stake here is whether the difference between the memory types is qualitative or quantitative, and it's important to get this straight. Claiming a *qualitative* difference is making a claim that the two are different "species" of memory. In that case, we will need different theories for implicit and explicit memory, and we'll confuse ourselves by classing the two types of memory together, seeking principles that apply to both. In contrast, claiming a *quantitative* difference is equivalent to saying that the two are fundamentally similar, differing only in some "adjustment" or "parameter." In this case, we'd be wasting our time if we search for separate governing principles, because the same principles apply to both.

How can we resolve this ambiguity? The key lies in realizing that the facts we've mentioned so far (the effects of brain damage or of level of processing) are all concerned with ways we can influence explicit memory with no effect on implicit. It's this "one-sidedness" that allows the possibility that the two forms of memory are basically the same, but with (what we're calling) explicit memory perhaps just a weaker, more fragile, variant of this memory. To demonstrate a qualitative difference, therefore, we also need the reverse result—cases in which we can influence implicit memory but not explicit. The moment we find such a result, we know that explicit memory is not just more easily influenced, more easily disrupted, than implicit memory—because sometimes, with some manipulations, it's implicit memory that's more easily influenced.

This overall pattern of evidence—with some factors influencing one sort of memory but not the other, and some factors doing the reverse—provides what is called a **double dissociation**. A double dissociation enables us to rule out the idea that one type of memory is just a weaker version of the other (because which is "weaker" and which is "stronger" flip-flops as we move from experiment to experiment). Instead, a double dissociation forces us to conclude that the two types are simply different from each other, each open to its own set of influences—and thus *qualitatively* different.

As it turns out, we do have a double dissociation for implicit and explicit memory. Certain factors (including forms of brain damage) influence explicit memory but not implicit. (Those factors provide a *dissociation*.) Other factors (and other forms of brain damage) influence implicit memory but not explicit (so that now we have a dissociation in the opposite direction, and hence a *double* dissociation).

With all these data in view, it's clear that neither type of memory is, in general, easier to influence than the other. Instead, the evidence tells us that each type of memory is indeed affected by its own set of factors. That tells us a lot about these forms of memory, but it also illustrates the power of a double dissociation.

Chapter 8: Remembering Complex Events

External Validity

How accurately do eyewitnesses to crimes remember what they have seen? To find out, many researchers have run "crime-simulation studies" in which they show their participants brief videos depicting a crime and then test the participants' memories for the video. But can we trust this research?

In these studies, we can set things up in just the way we like. We can design the video so that it allows the comparisons crucial for our hypotheses. We can take steps to remove confounds from the procedure and use random assignment to make sure our groups are matched at the experiment's start. Steps like these guarantee that our results will be unambiguous and informative.

But one thing about these studies is worrisome: The laboratory is in many ways an artificial setting, and it's possible that people behave differently in the lab than they do in other environments. In that case, the crime-simulation studies may lack **external validity**—that is, they may not reflect the real-world phenomena that ultimately we wish to understand. As a consequence, we cannot **generalize** the lab results to situations outside of the lab.

How do we decide whether a laboratory result is generalizable or not? This is an issue to be settled by research, not by argument. As one option, we can draw on the "replication + variation" strategy we discussed in the Research Methods module for Chapter 6. Specifically, we can see whether we get the same result with different participant groups, different stimuli, different instructions, and so on. If the result keeps emerging despite these changes in procedural detail, we can conclude that the result does not depend on these details in any way. This conclusion, in turn, would strengthen the claim that we can extrapolate from the results to new settings and new groups of people, including settings outside of the carefully designed research environment.

Another important strategy involves the effort toward making our controlled studies as realistic as possible—for example, using "live" (staged) crimes rather than videos depicting crimes, or conducting our studies in natural settings rather than in university laboratories. These steps, on their own, diminish the concern about external validity. In addition, these steps enable us to make some crucial comparisons: Does the effect we're interested in grow weaker and weaker as our studies become more and more realistic? If so, this is an argument *against* extrapolating the result to real-world settings. Or does the effect we're interested in hold steady, or perhaps even grow stronger, as our studies become more and more realistic? This pattern, when we observe it, is an argument *supporting* the extrapolation from our current data.

Yet another option is quite powerful but not always available. Sometimes we can collect data from field studies—for example, studies of actual witnesses to actual crimes—and then compare these new data to our controlled experiments. The field studies by themselves are often difficult to interpret. (We obviously can't arrange a crime to remove confounds from our comparisons, nor can we randomly assign witnesses to one condition or another. This means that the field studies by themselves often suffer from the ambiguities described in earlier modules in this appendix.) Nonetheless, we can ask whether the field data are as we would expect, based on the laboratory findings. If so, this increases our confidence that the lab findings must be taken seriously.

How do all of these efforts work out? Are our data, in the end, externally valid? There's no single answer here, because the pattern of the evidence varies, case by case. Some of our claims, based on lab findings, *can* be generalized to real-world settings—and so we can move forward with these claims. (We can, for example, offer these claims to the justice system, to help police and the courts evaluate eyewitness evidence—or, even better, to help them collect more reliable evidence.) For other claims, the external validity is less clear; in these cases, we sometimes need to change our research procedures (so that they will be valid), and we often need to figure out which circumstances outside of the lab *will* show the patterns we've seen in our research. Above all, though, let's emphasize that the broad issue here—and the question about external validity—needs to be taken seriously and has to be addressed through research. Only then do we know whether each of our claims, initially rooted in controlled studies, can be applied to the real-world phenomena we eventually want to explain.

Chapter 9: Concepts and Generic Knowledge

Converging Operations

How should we study conceptual knowledge? How can we find out what your concept of "dog" includes, or your concept of "ideal presidential candidate," or your concept of "worst date ever"? As you can see in Chapter 9, our research often begins with a simple task: We can show you various pictures and ask whether each is a dog or not. We can describe various dates and ask which comes closest to your worst-case scenario.

The problem, though, is that results from this task are ambiguous. It's possible that your judgments in this task reflect the pattern of your broad underlying knowledge, but it's also possible that your judgments merely reflect your approach *to this specific task*—a task in which we're explicitly asking you to use your concept to categorize new, unfamiliar cases. Perhaps, therefore, we'd get a different pattern if we give you some other task—for example, one that had you thinking about familiar cases, rather than cases we've made up. If so, then our first data set is providing only a partial portrait of your conceptual knowledge and might not tell us much about how you use this knowledge in other settings.

The issue here is once again ambiguity and the idea (which we've now met many times) that we can draw no conclusions if our results are ambiguous. To address this particular form of ambiguity, though, the path forward should be obvious: We can ask what happens if we give you a new concept task, perhaps one that involves familiar cases or one that doesn't explicitly require categorization. If the data pattern changes, we know that the first data set was shaped by the task itself. If the data pattern holds steady, we draw the opposite conclusion—namely, that we have succeeded in revealing the general character of your conceptual knowledge, a profile that would show up no matter how, on a particular occasion, you were using that knowledge.

This sort of issue arises throughout cognitive psychology. Of course, in some cases we do want to know how people perform a specific task—how they solve a particular type of problem or retrieve a certain type of information from memory. In many other cases, though, we're interested in people's underlying knowledge pattern, independent of how they've accessed the knowledge in a specific setting. Likewise, we're often interested in strategies that (we believe) are used in a wide variety of tasks, not just for the task we've set for our participants in a particular experiment.

These questions are especially prominent in the study of concepts. Here, we're trying to develop theories about conceptual knowledge itself, rather than theories about how this knowledge happens to be used on some special occasion or in some specialized context. It's crucial, therefore, that we test our claims with a diverse set of paradigms and a diverse set of stimuli. What we're hoping for, of course, is that we'll get similar patterns despite this variation in procedures. Technically speaking, we're hoping for **converging operations**—a variety of studies that all point toward (and so "converge on") the same theoretical claims.

Let's put all of this in concrete terms. We know that people rely on typicality when deciding whether newly encountered objects are in a specified category or not—whether a particular animal is a "dog" or a particular utensil is a "spoon." Is this simply the way people approach *this task*? If so, we might see a smaller role (or no role at all) for typicality in other tasks. Or is the typicality result a reflection of the basic nature of people's category knowledge? If so, we would expect a converging pattern of data—with evidence for typicality coming from a wide range of tasks.

As the chapter makes clear, the actual data lie somewhere between these two poles. People do rely on typicality in a range of tasks, and so the data from many tasks do converge on the idea that prototypes are a crucial part of conceptual knowledge. However, people do not rely on typicality in all tasks. And when they *do* rely on typicality, they need to supplement this knowledge with other knowledge. (We made this point in the chapter by arguing that judgments about typicality have to rely on an assessment of *resemblance*— usually, the resemblance between a candidate object and the category proto-type. Resemblance, in turn, depends on other knowledge—knowledge about which features matter for judging resemblance and which features can be ignored.)

It seems, therefore, that we do find convergence from a variety of tasks: a data pattern, across different procedures, consistently pointing toward a single conclusion (namely, the centrality of typicality). This is of enormous importance for us, but just as informative is the *limit* on the convergence. This limit tells us that typicality is important—but is not the whole story.

Putting these points into a larger context, the central message here is the importance of multiple experiments, and also *diverse* experiments, in test-ing our various claims. Indeed, we've mentioned in other modules that it's extremely rare in science that a claim rests on a single study, no matter how compelling that study is. Instead, science relies on a fabric of interwoven studies—drawing insights from the agreements and convergence across stud-ies, but also (as in this case) drawing insights from the disagreements.

Chapter 10: Language

The Broad Variety of Data Types

In most psychological research, we don't ask our research participants to reflect on, and tell us about, their mental processes. The reason (as we discussed in Chapter 1) is that introspection is an unreliable research tool, making investigators wary of the **self-report data** we gain from introspec-tion. However, sometimes we do care how people feel about, and talk about, the workings of their own minds. This was, for example, an issue for us in Chapter 8, where we discussed the assessments each of us makes about the status of our own memories when we decide how certain we are about this or that bit of recall. Self-assessment was also relevant for Chapter 7, where we discussed the ways people notice, and respond to, the *fluency* of their own mental processes.

Self-assessments also play an important role in language research—with participants often being asked to make **metalinguistic judgments**. In these cases, we are not asking people to *use* language as they ordinarily would, but instead we are asking them to *reflect on* and comment on language. Why are these judgments important? Let's start with the fact that for many purposes researchers do want to know what is said and not said in ordinary language use. However, data of this sort are limited in various ways, and so (for example) it's not clear what we should conclude if a word or phrase is *absent* from ordinary usage. If Henry never uses the word "boustrephedon," is it because he doesn't know the word or because he simply has no interest in talking about boustrephedon? If Lila never uses the word "unmicrowavable," is it because she regards the word as illegitimate or merely because she's in the habit of using some other term to convey this idea?

In addition, spontaneous speech is filled with performance errors. Sometimes you start a sentence with one idea in mind, but then you change your idea as you're speaking, perhaps realizing your words need clarification or even realizing you want to say something altogether different. Thus, you might end up saying, "He went my father went yesterday," even though you realize, as you are uttering these words, that this word sequence contains a grammatical error. On other occasions, you slip in your production and end up saying something different from what you had intended. You might say, "They were I mean weren't fine," even though you notice (and regret) the slip the moment you produce it.

These speech errors are of considerable importance if we are studying the ways in which speech is actually produced. However, these slips are a nuisance if we are trying to study the content of your linguistic knowledge. The reason is that in most cases you would agree that you had, in these utterances, made an error. In many cases, you know how to repair the error in order to produce a "correct" sentence. Clearly, therefore, your original performance, with its errors, doesn't reflect the full extent of your knowledge about how English sentences are constructed.

Because of considerations like these, we sometimes need to examine language *competence* rather than language *performance*, with "competence" being defined as the pattern of skills and knowledge that might be revealed under optimal circumstances. One way to reveal this competence is via metalinguistic judgments: People are asked to reflect on one structure or another (a particular word, phrase, or sentence) and to tell us whether they find the structure acceptable or not. Note that we are not asking people whether they find the structure to be clumsy, or pleasing to the ear, or useful. Instead, we are asking them whether the structure is something that one could say, if one wished. Thus, "There's the big blue house" seems fine, but "There's house blue big the" does not. Or, to return to an earlier example, you might slip and say, "He went my father went yesterday," but you certainly know there is something wrong with this sequence. It's often these "acceptability judgments" that reveal linguistic competence.

Let's emphasize that these judgments about language are not our only research tool. Indeed, Chapter 10 covers evidence drawn from a rich set of other measures and other procedures, and in some ways that's our point here: The study of language (like most areas) relies on a wide variety of data types. Within this pattern, though, metalinguistic judgments are an important source of evidence—and they are, in particular, of enormous value when we are trying to understand what's involved in language competence.

Chapter 11: Visual Knowledge

Expectations and Demand

In most research, we're trying to study how people behave under natural circumstances—how they behave when they're just being themselves. As a result, it is crucial that we take steps to minimize the **demand character** of the study.

As Chapter 11 describes, demand character refers to any cues in a procedure (including an experiment, a survey, or an interview) that might signal to participants how they "ought to" behave. In some cases, these cues can indicate to participants what results the researcher hopes for (i.e., results that would confirm the researcher's hypothesis), and this may encourage participants to make the hoped-for response, even if they were, on their own, inclined toward some other option. In other cases, a participant might choose to be defiant or rebellious, so that cues about the researcher's hypothesis might lead the participant to do the opposite of what the researcher wants. In still other cases, a procedure's demand character can somehow suggest that certain responses are more desirable than others—so that, for example, participants perceive some responses as indicating greater intelligence or greater sensitivity. It's then plausible that participants will choose these responses to avoid appearing stupid or insensitive.

What can we do to avoid all of these effects, so that we don't guide participants toward some particular response and, instead, observe them as they normally are? Researchers use several strategies. First, we do all we can to make sure that demand character never arises in the first place. Thus, we make sure that the procedure contains no signals about what the hypothesis is. Likewise, we do what we can to phrase our questions and cast the response options so that no response seems preferable to any others.

Second, it's often a good idea to direct participants' attention *away from* the study's main comparisons or, if the study is an experiment, away from the procedure's key manipulation. That way, the participants won't spend their efforts thinking about the crucial comparison, and this makes it more likely that they'll respond naturally and spontaneously to the variables we hope to understand. Likewise, by diverting attention away from the manipulation, we make it less likely that participants will try to guard against (or somehow tune) their response to the manipulation.

How do we divert the participants' attention in order to achieve these goals? Many procedures contain some sort of "cover story" about what the study is addressing. The cover story is designed, of course, to draw the participants' thinking away from the key aspects of the procedure. But, in addition, a good cover story encourages participants to take the study seriously and also makes it less likely that they'll spend their minutes, during the study, speculating about the procedure's true purpose.

Notice, by the way, that the cover story involves some amount of deception—and this raises an ethical issue: Is it okay to deceive participants? Researchers generally take the position that mild deception is acceptable, provided that there is good scientific reason for the deception and—crucially—that participants be fully "debriefed" at the end of the procedure. In the **debriefing**, the participants are told about the deception and why they were deceived. Participants are also told about the overall aims of the research—and so, in the end, get to learn something about research and research methods.

Finally, it's crucial that we make sure that participants in all conditions receive exactly the same treatment—so that they all have the same expectations about the study and the same motivations. For this purpose, many studies rely on a **double-blind procedure**, in which neither the participant nor the person administering the procedure knows what the study is about or whether a particular trial (or a particular test session) is in the experimental condition or the control condition. All of these steps ensure that the administrator won't be more encouraging or more forceful with one group in comparison with the other or in one condition rather than another. The steps also guarantee that all participants will have the same understanding and beliefs about the study.

With these various safeguards in place, can we be sure that participants' expectations, goals, and hypotheses play no role in shaping our data? Probably not, and this is one more reason why replications (with other participants and other procedures) are so important. Even so, we do what we can to minimize the contribution of these factors, making it far more likely that our results can be understood in the terms we intend.

Chapter 12: Judgment and Reasoning

Systematic Data Collection

As we saw in the chapter, in daily life you frequently rely on judgment *heuristics*—shortcuts that usually lead to the correct conclusion but that sometimes produce error. As a result, you sometimes draw inappropriate conclusions, but these errors are simply the price you pay for the heuristics' efficiency. To avoid the errors, you'd need to use reasoning strategies that would require much more time and effort than the heuristics do.

For scientists, though, efficiency is less of a priority; it's okay if we need months or even years to test a hypothesis. And, of course, accuracy is crucial for scientists: We want to make certain our claims are correct and our conclusions fully warranted. For these reasons, scientists need to step away from the reasoning strategies we all use in our daily lives and to rely instead on more laborious, but more accurate, forms of reasoning.

How exactly does scientific reasoning differ from ordinary day-to-day reasoning? The answer has many parts, but one part is directly relevant to points prominent in Chapter 12. In ordinary reasoning, people are heavily influenced by whatever data are easily available to them—the observations that they can think of first when they consider an issue, or the experiences that happen to be prominent in their memory when they try to think of cases pertinent to some question. This is an easy way to proceed, but it's risky, because the evidence that's easily available to someone may not be representative of the broader patterns in the world. Sometimes evidence is easily available simply because it's more memorable than other (perhaps more common) observations. Sometimes evidence is more available because the media have showcased it.

Yet another problem is that sometimes certain bits of evidence are more available because of the pattern known as **confirmation bias**. This term refers to the fact that when people search for evidence they often look only for evidence that might *support* their views; they do little to collect evidence that might challenge those views. This can lead to a lopsided collection of facts—and an inaccurate judgment.

Scientists avoid these problems by insisting on **systematic data collection**—either recording *all* the evidence or at least collecting evidence in a fashion carefully designed to be independent of the hypothesis being considered (hence, neither biased toward the hypothesis nor against it). Systematic data collection surely rules out consideration of **anecdotal evidence**—evidence that has been informally collected and reported—because an anecdote may represent a highly atypical case or may provide only one person's description of the data, with no way for us to know if the description is accurate or not. Anecdotal evidence is also easily swayed by confirmation bias: The anecdote describes just one observation, raising questions about how the observation was selected. The obvious concern is that the anecdotal case was noticed, remembered, and then reported merely because it fits well with prejudices the reporter had at the outset!

These points seem straightforward, but they have many implications, including implications for how we choose our participants (we can't just gather data from people likely to support our views) and for how we design our procedures. The requirement of systematic data collection also shapes how the data will be recorded. For example, we cannot rely on our memory for the data, because it's possible that we might remember just those cases that fit with our interpretation. Likewise, we cannot treat the facts we like differently from the facts we don't like, so that, perhaps, we're more alert to flaws in the observations that conflict with our hypotheses or less likely to report these observations to others.

Clearly, then, many elements are involved in systematic data collection. But all of these elements are crucial if we are to make certain that our hypotheses have been fully and fairly tested. In this regard, scientific conclusions are on a firmer footing than the judgments we offer as part of our daily experience.

The Community of Scientists

Our Research Methods modules have described many of the steps scientists take to ensure that their data are persuasive and their claims are correct. We need to add to our discussion, though, another important factor that keeps scientific claims on track—the fact that scientists don't work in isolation from one another. To see how this matters, consider the phenomenon of *confirmation bias*. This broad term refers to a number of different effects, all of which have the result of protecting our beliefs from serious challenge. Thus, for example, when we're evaluating beliefs, we tend to seek out information that might confirm the belief rather than information that might undermine it. Likewise, if we encounter information that is at all ambiguous, we are likely to interpret the information in a fashion that brings it into line with our beliefs. And so on.

Individual scientists do what they can to avoid this bias, but even so, scientists are, in the end, human and hence vulnerable to the same problems as everyone else—so it's no surprise that confirmation bias can be detected in scientific reasoning. Thus, when scientists encounter facts that fit with their preferred hypothesis, they tend to accept those facts as they are; when they encounter facts that don't fit, they scrutinize the facts with special care, seeking problems or flaws.

Some scholars, however, have argued that confirmation bias can be a *good thing* for scientists. After all, it takes effort to develop, test, and defend a scientific theory and, eventually, to persuade others to take that theory seriously. All of this effort requires motivation and commitment from the theory's advocates, and confirmation bias may help them to maintain this commitment: Thanks to this bias, the advocates remain certain that they're correct, and this certainty sustains their efforts in developing and promoting the theory. Perhaps it makes sense, therefore, that according to some studies the scientists who are most guilty of confirmation bias are often those who are considered by their peers to be most important and influential.

These points, however, do not diminish the serious problems that confirmation bias can create. How, therefore, do scientists manage to gain the advantages (in motivation) that confirmation bias creates, without suffering the negative consequences of this bias? Part of the answer lies in the fact that science depends on a *community* of scientists, and within this community there is almost always a diversity of views. As a result, the confirmation bias of one researcher can be counteracted by the corresponding bias of other researchers. To put it bluntly, I'll be gentle with the data favoring my view but harsh in scrutinizing the data favoring your claims. You'll be gentle with your data but harsh in scrutinizing mine. In the end, therefore, both your data and mine will receive careful examination—and that's precisely what we want.

To promote this scrutiny, scientists rely on a **peer-review process**. Before a new finding is taken seriously, it must be published in a scientific journal. And before any article can be published, it must be evaluated by the journal's editor (usually, a scientist with impressive credentials) and three or four experts in the field. (These are the "peers" who "review" the paper—hence, the term "peer review.") The reviewers are chosen by the editor to represent a variety of perspectives—including, if possible, a perspective likely to be critical of the paper's claims. If these reviewers find problems in the method or the interpretation of results, the article will not be published by the journal. Thus, any article can appear in print only if it has survived this evaluation—an essential form of quality control.

Then, once the paper is published, the finding is accessible to the broader scientific community and therefore open to scrutiny, criticism, and—if appropriate—attack. In addition, once the details of a study are available in print, other scientists can try to replicate the experiment to make sure that the result is reliable. These are significant long-term benefits from publication.

In short, we take a hypothesis seriously only after it has received the scrutiny of many scientists—both during the (pre-publication) formal process of peer review and in the months after the paper is published. These steps ensure that the hypothesis undergoes examination both by scientists who are inclined to protect the hypothesis and by others who are inclined to reject it. In this way, we can be certain that the hypothesis has been fully and persuasively tested, and thus the scientific community can gain from the commitment and motivation that are the good sides of confirmation bias, without suffering the problems associated with this bias.

Chapter 13: Problem Solving and Intelligence

Defining the Dependent Variable

In the Research Methods module for Chapter 1, we discussed the importance of testable hypotheses—that is, hypotheses framed in a way that makes it clear what evidence will confirm them and what evidence will not. Sometimes, though, it's not obvious how to phrase a hypothesis in testable terms. For example, in Chapter 13 we discuss research on creativity, and in this domain investigators often present hypotheses about the factors that might foster creativity or might undermine it. Thus, one hypothesis might be: "When working on a problem, an interruption (to allow incubation) promotes creativity." To test this hypothesis, we would have to specify what counts as an interruption (5 minutes of working on something else? An hour?). But then, we'd also need some way to measure creativity; otherwise, we couldn't tell if the interruption was beneficial or not.

For this hypothesis, creativity is the dependent variable—that is, the measurement that, according to our hypothesis, might "depend on" the factor being manipulated. The presence or absence of an interruption would be the independent variable—the factor that, according to our hypothesis, influences the dependent variable.

In many studies, it's easy to assess the dependent variable. For example, consider this hypothesis: "Context reinstatement improves memory accuracy." Here, the dependent variable is accuracy, and this is simple to check—for example, by counting up the number of correct answers on a memory test. In this way, we would easily know whether a result confirmed the hypothesis or not. Likewise, consider this hypothesis: "Implicit memories can speed up performance on a lexical-decision task." Here, the dependent variable is response time; again, it is simple to measure, allowing a straightforward test of the hypothesis.

The situation is different, though, for our hypothesis about interruptions and creativity. In this case, people might disagree about whether a particular problem solution (or poem, or painting, or argument) is creative. This will make it difficult to test our hypothesis.

Psychologists generally solve this problem by recruiting a panel of judges to assess the dependent variable. In our example, the judges would review each participant's response and evaluate how creative it was, perhaps on a scale from 1 to 5. By using a panel of judges rather than just one, we can check directly on whether different judges have different ideas about what creativity is. More specifically, we can calculate the **inter-rater reliability** among the judges—the degree to which they agree with one another in their assessments. If they disagree with one another, it would appear that the assessment of creativity really is a subjective matter and cannot be a basis for testing hypotheses. In that case, scientific research on this issue may not be possible. But if the judges do agree to a reasonable extent—if the inter-rater reliability is high—then we can be confident that their assessments are neither arbitrary nor idiosyncratic.

Let's be clear, though, that this is a measure of **reliability**—that is, a measure of how consistent our measurements are. As the text describes, reliability is separate from **validity**—that is, whether we've succeeded in measuring what we intended to measure. It's possible, for example, that all of our judges are reacting to, say, whether they find the responses humorous or not. If the judges all have similar senses of humor, they might agree with one another in this assessment (and so would have a high level of inter-rater reliability), but even so, they would be judging humor, not creativity (and so would not offer *valid* assessments). On this basis, measures of inter-rater reliability are an important step toward establishing our measure—but we still need other steps (perhaps what the chapter calls a **predictive validation**) before we're done.

Notice, in addition, that this way of proceeding doesn't require us to start out with a precise definition of creativity. Of course, a definition would be very useful because (among other benefits) it would enable us to give the judges on our panel relatively specific instructions. Even without a definition, though, we can just ask the judges to rely on their own sense of what's creative. This isn't ideal; we'd prefer to get beyond this intuitive notion. But having a systematic, non-idiosyncratic consensus measurement at least allows our research to get off the ground.

In the same way, consider this hypothesis: "College education improves the clarity of someone's writing." This hypothesis—and many others as well—again involves a complex dependent variable, and it might also require a panel of judges to obtain measurements we can take seriously. But by using these panels, we can measure things that seem at the outset to be unmeasurable, and in that way we appreciably broaden the range of hypotheses we can test.

Correlations

Often in psychology, data are analyzed in terms of **correlations**, and this is certainly true in the study of intelligence. We say that intelligence tests are reliable, for example, because measures of intelligence taken, say, when people are 6 years old are correlated with measures taken from the same people a dozen years later. (This is called **test-retest reliability**.) Likewise, we say that intelligence tests have validity because measures of intelligence are correlated with other performance measures (grades in school or some assessment of performance in the workplace; this is a predictive validation). Or, as one more example, we conclude that *g* (i.e., *general intelligence*) exists because we can observe correlations among the various parts of the IQ test— so that someone's score on a verbal test is correlated with her score on a spatial test. (This is—roughly—what a *factor analysis* evaluates.)

But what does any of this mean? What is a correlation? The calculation of a correlation begins with a list of *pairs:* someone's IQ score at, say, age 6 and then the same person's score at age 18; the *next person's* scores at age 6 and age 18; the same for the next person and the next after that. A correlation examines these pairs and asks, roughly, how well we can predict the second value within each pair once we know the first value. If we know your IQ score at age 6, how confident can we be in our prediction of your score a dozen years later?

Correlation values—usually abbreviated with the letter *r*—can fall between +1.0 (a so-called perfect correlation) and −1.0 (a perfect *inverse* correlation). Thus, the strongest possible correlation is *either* +1.0 *or* −1.0. The weakest possible correlation is zero—indicating no relationship. As some concrete examples, the correlation between your height, measured in inches, and your height, measured in centimeters, is +1.0 (because these two measurements are assessing the exact same thing). The correlation between your current distance from the North Pole and your current distance from the South Pole is −1.0 (because each mile you move closer to one pole necessarily takes you one mile away from the other pole). The correlation between your height and your IQ, in contrast, is zero: There's no indication that taller people differ in their intelligence from shorter people.

Most of the *r* values you'll encounter in psychology, though, are more moderate. For example, the chapter mentions a correlation of roughly *r* = +.50 between someone's IQ and his GPA in college; the correlation between someone's IQ score and the score of her (non-twin) brother or sister is about *r* = +.60. What do these values mean? The full answer is complicated, but here's an approximation.

Researchers routinely report *r* values, but the really useful statistic is r^2— that is, *r* × *r*. Bear in mind here that (as we've said) correlations are based on *pairs* of observations, and the r^2 value literally tells you how much of the overall variation in one measure within the pair can be predicted, based on the other measure in the pair. Thus, let's look at the correlation between IQ and school performance (measured in grade point average). The correlation is +.50, so r^2 is +.25. This means that 25% of the variation in GPA is predictable, if you know students' IQ scores. The remaining 75% of the variation, it seems, has to be explained in other terms.

One way of thinking about these points hinges on the "reduction of uncertainty." To understand this point, imagine that all we know about Kim is that she's a student at your school. If we had to guess Kim's GPA, our best option is just to guess the average for your school—since we have no basis for thinking Kim's above the average and no basis for thinking she's below it. But, of course, we'd have no reason to be confident in this estimate, so we'd probably want to hedge our bets, saying something like "her GPA is likely to be 3.1, plus-or-minus 1."

Now, let's imagine that we receive a new piece of information about Kim—that her IQ score is 118, well above the national average. In this setting, we'd probably estimate that her GPA will be above average as well (and so we'd predict a value greater than 3.1). Crucially, though, we'd also now be a bit more certain in our forecast, because we have more information to go on. Therefore, we might offer a more precise forecast—that is, with a smaller "plus-or-minus" bit. We might say, "her GPA is likely to be 3.5, plus-or-minus 0.4." We've therefore offered a new forecast *and* decreased our uncertainty (from +/– 1.0 to +/– 0.4). That's exactly what correlations allow us to do—first, to refine our predictions, and second, to decrease uncertainty; and the stronger the correlation, the more it reduces uncertainty. (By the way, if you have a math background, the notion here is that with stronger correlations the individual observations are more tightly clustered around the regression line. But more broadly, what's crucial here is the idea that correlations allow predictions and that stronger correlations allow more precise predictions.)

Let's once again note, though, that we usually find only modest correlations in psychology research. We've said, for example, that the correlation between IQ scores and academic performance is roughly +.50; using the r^2 value, this means that only 25% of the variation from student to student is predictable based on IQ, and the remaining 75% of the variation needs to be explained in other terms. Thus, knowing someone's IQ does decrease our uncertainty in forecasting what that person's academic performance will be—but the IQ score still leaves three quarters of the uncertainty in place. Or, put differently, the data are telling us that IQ is a major contributor to performance, but even so, a large amount of the observed variation—the differences between an A student and a B student, and so on—is influenced by *other* variables, separate from IQ. Some of these other variables, on their own, matter a lot (e.g., the amount of studying, or choice of strategy in studying, or, for that matter, whether the person has stayed healthy throughout the academic year, is getting enough sleep, and so on). Other variables contribute only a little to the overall pattern, but there are many, many of these variables, and so, in combination these various factors (some major, some minor) add to the 75% of the variation *not* accounted for by the IQ score. All of this is, again, a way of saying that IQ is a major factor in determining life outcomes, but a long list of other factors also play a role. As we noted in the chapter, IQ does measure something important, but your IQ score does not define your destiny.

Chapter 14: Conscious Thought, Unconscious Thought

Introspection

In Chapter 1, we discussed some of the limits on **introspection** as a research tool, and, in fact, our discussion throughout this book has rarely relied on introspective evidence. This is because, as one concern, introspection relies on what people *remember* about their own mental processes, and we cannot count on these memories being accurate. In addition, introspections are usually reported verbally: The person uses words to describe what happened in his or her own mind. But as we discussed in Chapter 11, some thoughts are nonverbal in content and may not be captured adequately by a verbal description.

As a further problem, your introspections, by definition, involve an "inspection" of your mental life, so this method necessarily rests on the assumption that your mental state is "visible" to you. (You can't inspect something that's invisible.) As Chapter 14 describes, however, a great deal of mental activity goes on outside of awareness and is therefore "invisible" to introspection. This provides yet another limit on introspection as a source of scientific evidence—because introspective data will necessarily be incomplete in what they tell us about mental processes.

Let's be careful, though, not to overstate these claims, because unmistakably, introspective reports sometimes do have value. For example, in the study of problem solving, researchers sometimes ask people simply to "think out loud" as a means of discovering what strategies the people use as they work on the problem. Likewise, in Chapter 11 we acknowledged the complexities attached to someone's introspective reports about the vividness of his or her own mental images, but we also argued that these vividness reports can be an important source of data about images. And in Chapter 7 we explored the nature of implicit memories; an important source of data there was people's introspective reports about whether a stimulus "felt familiar" or not.

How can we reconcile these uses of introspective data with the concerns we've raised about introspection? How can we argue that introspective data are of questionable value but then turn around and use introspective data? The answer lies in the simple fact that *some* thoughts *are* conscious, memorable, and easily verbalized; for thoughts like these, introspection can provide valuable data. The obvious challenge, therefore, lies in determining which thoughts are in this category—and so available for introspectively based self-report—and which thoughts are not.

How does this determination proceed? Let's say that "think out loud" data indicate that participants are relying on a certain strategy in solving problems. We then need to find *other* evidence that might confirm (or disconfirm) this introspection. We can ask, for example, whether people make the sorts of errors that we'd expect if they are, in fact, using the strategy suggested by the self-report. We can also ask whether people have trouble with problems that can't easily be solved via the strategy suggested by the self-report. In these ways, we can *check on* the introspections and thus find out if the self-reports provide useful evidence.

Likewise, in Chapter 11 we discussed some of the evidence indicating that self-reports of image vividness do have value. Specifically, we described evidence that reveals a relationship between these reports, on the one hand, and how well people do in certain imagery tasks, on the other hand. Other evidence indicates a link between these imagery self-reports and activation levels in the visual cortex. So here, too, we can document the value of the introspective evidence by checking the introspections against other types of data, including behavioral data and data from neuroscience.

The point, then, is that introspection is neither wholly worthless nor wonderfully reliable. Instead, introspection can provide fabulous clues about what's going on in someone's mind—but we then need to find other means of checking on those clues to determine whether they are misleading. But let's note that introspection is not unique in this regard. Any research tool must prove its worth—by means of data that in one fashion or another validate the results obtained with that tool. (Consider our discussion in Chapter 13 of the steps needed to assess the validity of intelligence tests.) In this way, we use our research methods to build our science, but we also use our science to check on and, where possible, refine our research methods.

Key Research Methods Concepts

In this appendix, we have covered many crucial concepts; you should by now be familiar with all of these:

anecdotal evidence	invalid experiment
baseline level	metalinguistic judgments
catch trials	N
chronometric studies	peer-review process
confirmation bias	population
confound	predictive validation
control condition	r
converging operations	r^2
correlations	random assignment
counterbalancing	random sampling
debriefing	reliability
demand character	replication
dependent variable	representative sample
double dissociation	response times (RTs)
double-blind procedure	sample (vs. population)
effect size	self-report data
experimental condition	self-selected group
external validity	systematic data collection
generalizability	test-retest reliability
independent variable	testable hypothesis
inter-rater reliability	third-variable problem
introspection	validity

Glossary

"7 plus-or-minus 2" A range often offered as an estimate of the number of items or units able to be contained in *working memory*.

acquisition The process of placing new information into *long-term memory*.

action potential A brief change in the electrical potential of an *axon*. The action potential is the physical basis of the signal sent from one end of a *neuron* to the other; it usually triggers a further (chemical) signal to other neurons.

action slip An error in which a person performs some behavior or makes some response that is different from the behavior or response intended.

activation level A measure of the current status for a *node* or *detector*. Activation level is increased if the node or detector receives the appropriate input from its associated nodes or detectors; activation level will be high if input has been received frequently or recently.

acuity The ability to see fine detail.

affective forecasting The process in which a person predicts how he or she will feel at some future point about an object or state of affairs. It turns out that people are surprisingly inaccurate in these predictions and, for example, understate their own capacity to adapt to changes.

agnosia A disturbance in a person's ability to identify familiar objects.

all-or-none law The principle stating that a *neuron* or *detector* either fires completely or does not fire at all; no intermediate responses are possible. (Graded responses are possible, however, by virtue of the fact that a neuron or detector can fire more or less frequently, and for a longer or shorter time.)

amnesia A disruption of memory, often due to brain damage.

amygdala (pl. amygdalae) An almond-shaped structure in the *limbic system* that plays a central role in emotion and in the evaluation of stimuli.

anomia A disorder, often arising from specific forms of brain damage, in which the person loses the ability to name certain objects.

anterior cingulate cortex (ACC) A brain structure known to play a crucial role in detecting and resolving conflicts among different brain systems.

anterograde amnesia An inability to remember experiences that occurred after the event that triggered the memory disruption. Often contrasted with *retrograde amnesia*.

aphasia A disruption to language capacities, often caused by brain damage. See also *fluent aphasia* and *nonfluent aphasia*.

apraxia A disturbance in the capacity to initiate or organize voluntary action, often caused by brain damage.

Area V1 The site on the *occipital lobe* where *axons* from the *lateral geniculate nucleus* first reach the cerebral *cortex*. This site is (for one neural pathway) the location at which information about the visual world first reaches the brain.

articulatory rehearsal loop One of the low-level assistants hypothesized as being part of the *working-memory system*. This loop draws on *subvocalized* (covert) speech, which serves to create a record in the *phonological buffer*. Materials in this buffer then fade, but they can be refreshed by another cycle of covert speech.

association cortex The traditional name for the portion of the human *cortex* outside the motor and sensory projection areas.

associations Functional connections that are hypothesized to link *nodes* within a mental network or *detectors* within a detector network; these associations are often hypothesized as the "carriers" of activation from one node or detector to the next.

associative links See *associations*.

attended channel A stimulus (or group of stimuli) that a person is trying to perceive. Ordinarily, information is understood or remembered from the attended channel. Often contrasted with *unattended channel*.

attribute substitution A commonly used strategy in which a person needs one type of information but relies instead on a more accessible form of information. This strategy works well if the more accessible form of information is well correlated with the desired information. An example is the case in which someone needs information about how frequent an event is in the world and relies instead on how easily he or she can think of examples of the event.

attribution The step of explaining a feeling or event, usually by identifying the factors (or an earlier event) that are the cause of the current feeling or event. This term is often elaborated with the more specific term "causal attribution."

autobiographical memory The aspect of memory that records the episodes and events in a person's life.

automatic tasks Tasks that are well practiced and that do not require flexibility; these tasks usually require little or no attention, and they can be carried out if the person is also busy with some other task. Usually contrasted with *controlled tasks*.

automaticity A state achieved by some tasks and some forms of processing, in which the task can be performed with little or no attention. In many cases, automatized actions can be combined with other activities without interference. Automatized actions are also often difficult to control, leading many psychologists to refer to them as "mental reflexes."

availability heuristic A particular form of *attribute substitution* in which the person needs to judge the frequency of a certain type of object or the likelihood of a certain type of event. For this purpose, the person is likely to assess the ease with which examples of the object or event come to mind; this "availability" of examples is then used as an index of frequency or likelihood.

axon The part of a *neuron* that typically transmits a signal away from the neuron's cell body and carries the signal to another location.

base-rate information Information about the broad likelihood of a particular type of event (also referred to as "prior probability"). Often contrasted with *diagnostic information*.

basic-level categorization A level of categorization hypothesized as the "natural" and most informative level, neither too specific nor too general. People tend to use basic-level terms (such as "chair," rather than the more general "furniture" or the more specific "armchair") in their ordinary conversation and in their reasoning.

behaviorist theory Broad principles concerned with how behavior changes in response to different configurations of stimuli (including stimuli that are often called "rewards" and "punishments"). In its early days, behaviorist theory sought to avoid mentalistic terms (terms that referred to representations or processes inside the mind).

belief bias A tendency, within logical reasoning, to endorse a conclusion if the conclusion happens to be something one believes is true anyhow. In displaying this tendency, people seem to ignore both the *premises* of the logical argument and logic itself, and they rely instead on their broader pattern of beliefs about what is true and what is not.

belief perseverance A tendency to continue endorsing some assertion or claim, even when the clearly available evidence completely undermines that claim.

bigram detectors Hypothetical units in a recognition system that respond, or fire, whenever a specific letter pair is in view.

binding problem The problem of reuniting the various elements of a scene, given that these elements are initially dealt with by different systems in the brain.

binocular disparity A *distance cue* based on the differences between the two eyes' views of the world. This difference becomes less pronounced the farther away an object is from the observer.

binocular rivalry A pattern that arises when the input to one eye cannot be integrated with the input to the other eye. In this circumstance, the person tends to be aware of only one eye's input at a time.

bipolar cells A type of *neuron* in the eye. Bipolar cells receive their input from the *photoreceptors* and transmit their output to the retinal *ganglion cells*.

blind sight A pattern resulting from brain damage, in which the person seems unable to see in part of his or her field of vision but can often correctly respond to visual inputs when required to do so by an experimenter.

bottom-up processing A sequence of events that is governed by the stimulus input itself. Often contrasted with *top-down processing*.

boundary extension A tendency for people to remember pictures as being less "zoomed in" (and therefore having wider boundaries) than they actually were.

brightness constancy The achievement of perceiving the constant brightness of objects despite changes in the light reaching the eye that result from variations in illumination.

Broca's area An area in the left *frontal lobe* of the brain; damage here typically causes *nonfluent aphasia*.

categorical perception The pattern in which speech sounds are heard "merely" as members of a category—the category of [z] sounds, the category of [p] sounds, and so on. Because of categorical perception, perceivers are highly sensitive to the acoustic contrasts that distinguish sounds in different categories; people are much less sensitive to the acoustic contrasts that distinguish sounds within a category.

categorical syllogisms A logical argument containing two *premises* and a conclusion, and concerned with the properties of, and relations between, categories. An example is "All trees are plants. All plants require nourishment. Therefore, all trees require nourishment." This is a valid syllogism, since the truth of the premises guarantees the truth of the conclusion.

cell body The area of a biological cell containing the nucleus and the metabolic machinery that sustains the cell.

center-surround cells A type of *neuron* in the visual system that has a "donut-shaped" *receptive field*. Stimulation in the center of the *receptive field* has one effect on the cell; stimulation in the surrounding ring has the opposite effect.

central fissure The separation dividing the *frontal lobes* on each side of the brain from the *parietal lobes*.

cerebellum The largest area of the *hindbrain*, crucial for the coordination of bodily movements and balance.

cerebral hemisphere One of the two hemispherical brain structures—one on the left side, one on the right—that constitute the major part of the *forebrain* in mammals.

change blindness A pattern in which perceivers either do not see or take a long time to see large-scale changes in a visual stimulus. This pattern reveals how little people perceive, even from stimuli in plain view, if they are not specifically attending to the target information.

chronometric studies Literally, "time-measuring" studies; generally, studies that measure the amount of time a task takes. Often used as a way of examining the task's components or as a way of examining which brain events are simultaneous with specific mental events.

chunks The hypothetical storage units in *working memory*; it is estimated that working memory can hold *7 plus-or-minus 2* chunks. However, an unspecified quantity of information can be contained within each chunk, because the content of each chunk depends on how the memorizer has organized the materials to be remembered.

clinical neuropsychology The study of brain function that uses, as its main data source, cases in which damage or illness has disrupted the working of some brain structure.

coarticulation A trait of speech production in which the way a sound is produced is altered slightly by the immediately preceding and immediately following sounds. Because of this "overlap" in speech production, the acoustic properties of each speech sound vary according to the context in which that sound occurs.

coding The system through which one type of information stands for, or represents, a different type of information. In the context of the nervous system, this term refers to the way in which activity in *neurons* manages to stand for, or represent, particular ideas or thoughts.

cognitive neuroscience The effort toward understanding humans' mental functioning through close study of the brain and nervous system.

cognitive unconscious The broad set of mental activities of which people are completely unaware but that make possible ordinary thinking, remembering, reasoning, and so on.

commissure One of the thick bundles of fibers along which information is sent back and forth between the two *cerebral hemispheres*.

computerized axial tomography (CT scans) A *neuroimaging technique* that uses X-rays to construct a precise three-dimensional image of the brain's anatomy.

concurrent articulation A requirement that a research participant speak or mime speech while doing some other task. In many cases, the person is required to say "Tah-Tah-Tah" over and

over, or "one, two, three, one, two, three." These procedures occupy the muscles and control mechanisms needed for speech, so they prevent the person from using these resources for *subvocalization*.

conditional statement A statement of the format "If X then Y," with the first part (the "if" clause, or antecedent) providing a condition under which the second part (the "then" clause, or consequent) is guaranteed to be true.

cones *Photoreceptors* that are able to discriminate hues and that have high *acuity*. Cones are concentrated in the *retina*'s *fovea* and become less frequent in the visual periphery. Often contrasted with *rods*.

confirmation bias A family of effects in which people seem more sensitive to evidence that confirms their beliefs than they are to evidence that challenges their beliefs. Thus, if people are given a choice about what sort of information they would like in order to evaluate their beliefs, they request information that's likely to confirm their beliefs. Likewise, if they're presented with both confirming and disconfirming evidence, they're more likely to pay attention to, be influenced by, and remember the confirming evidence, rather than the disconfirming.

conjunction error An error in perception in which a person correctly perceives what features are present but misperceives how the features are joined, so that (for example) a red circle and a green square might be

misperceived as a red square and a green circle.

connection weight The strength of a connection between two *nodes* in a network. The greater the connection weight, the more efficiently activation will flow from one node to the other.

connectionist networks Proposed systems of knowledge representation that rely on *distributed representations*, and that therefore require *parallel distributed processing* to operate on the elements of a representation.

consolidation The biological process through which new memories are "cemented in place," acquiring some degree of permanence through the creation of new (or altered) neural connections.

context reinstatement A procedure in which a person is led to the same mental and emotional state he or she was in during a previous event; context reinstatement can often promote accurate recollection of that event.

context-dependent learning A pattern of data in which materials learned in one setting are well remembered when the person returns to that setting, but are less well remembered in other settings.

contralateral control A pattern in which the left half of the brain controls the right half of the body, and the right half of the brain controls the left half of the body.

controlled tasks Tasks that are novel or that require flexibility in one's approach; these tasks usually require attention, so they cannot be carried out if the person is also busy with some other task. Usually contrasted with *automatic tasks*.

convergent thinking An ability to find ways in which seemingly distinct ideas might be interconnected. Often contrasted with *divergent thinking*.

convolutions The wrinkles visible in the cerebral *cortex* that allow the enormous surface area of the human brain to fit into the relatively small volume of the skull.

cornea The transparent tissue at the front of each eye that plays an important role in focusing the incoming light.

corpus callosum The largest of the *commissures* linking the left and right *cerebral hemispheres*.

correlations The tendency for two variables to change together. If one goes up as the other goes up, the correlation is positive; if one goes up as the other goes down, the correlation is negative. A value of +1.00 indicates a perfect positive correlation; a value of –1.00 indicates a perfect negative (or inverse) correlation; a value of 0 indicates that there is no relationship at all between the variables.

cortex The outermost surface of an organ in the body; psychologists are most commonly interested in the brain's cortex and, specifically, the cerebral cortex.

covariation A relationship between two variables such that the presence (or magnitude) of one variable can be predicted from the presence (or magnitude) of the other. Covariation can be positive or negative. If it is positive, then increases in one variable occur when increases in the other occur. If it is negative, then decreases in one variable occur when increases in the other occur.

crystallized intelligence A person's acquired knowledge, including his or her repertoire of verbal knowledge and cognitive skills. See also *fluid intelligence*.

decay theory of forgetting The hypothesis that with the passage of time, memories may fade or erode.

deduction A process through which a person starts with claims, or general assertions, and asks what further claims necessarily follow from these *premises*. Often contrasted with *induction*.

deep processing A mode of thinking in which a person pays attention to the meaning and implications of the material; deep processing typically leads to excellent memory retention. Often contrasted with *shallow processing*.

demand character Cues within an experiment that signal to the participant how he or she is "supposed to" respond.

dendrite The part of a *neuron* that usually detects the incoming signal.

descriptive rules Rules that simply describe the regularities in a pattern of observations, with no commentary on whether the pattern is "proper," "correct," or "desirable."

detector A *node* within a processing network that fires primarily in response to a specific target contained within the incoming perceptual information.

diagnostic information Information about a particular case; often contrasted with *base-rate information*.

dichotic listening A task in which research participants hear two simultaneous verbal messages—one presented via headphones to the left ear and a second one presented to the right ear. In typical experiments, participants are asked to pay attention to one of these inputs (the *attended channel*) and are urged to ignore the other (the *unattended channel*).

digit-span task A task often used for measuring *working memory*'s storage capacity. Research participants are read a series of digits (e.g., "8 3 4") and must immediately repeat them back. If they do this successfully, they are given a slightly longer list (e.g., "9 2 4 0"), and so forth. The length of the longest list a person can remember in this fashion is that person's digit span. Also see *operation span*.

direct memory testing A form of memory testing in which people are asked explicitly to remember some previous event. *Recall* and standard *recognition* testing are both forms of direct memory testing. Often contrasted with *indirect memory testing*.

distance cues Information available to the perceiver that allows the perceiver to judge how far off a target object is.

distributed representation A mode of representing ideas or contents in which there is no one *node* (or specific group of nodes) representing the content and no one place where the content is stored. Instead, the content is represented via a pattern of simultaneous activity across many nodes within a network. The same nodes will also participate in other patterns, so those nodes will also be part of other distributed representations. Often contrasted with *local representation*.

divergent thinking An ability to move one's thoughts in novel, unanticipated directions. Often contrasted with *convergent thinking*.

divided attention The skill of performing multiple tasks simultaneously.

DRM procedure A commonly used experimental procedure, named after its originators—Deese, Roediger, and McDermott—for eliciting and studying memory errors. In this procedure, a person sees or hears a list of words that are related to a single theme; however, the word that names the theme is not itself included. Nonetheless, people are very likely to remember later that the theme word was presented.

dual coding A theory that imageable materials, such as high-imagery words, will be doubly represented in memory: The word itself will be remembered, and so will the corresponding mental image.

dual-process model Any model of thinking that claims people have two distinct means of making judgments—one of which is fast, efficient, but prone to error, and one that is slower, more effortful, but also more accurate.

early selection hypothesis A proposal that *selective attention* operates at an early

stage of processing, so that the unattended inputs receive little analysis.

edge enhancement A process created by *lateral inhibition* in which the *neurons* in the visual system give exaggerated responses to edges of surfaces.

effect size A statistical measure of how large the difference is between two groups or between two conditions.

eidetic imagery A relatively rare capacity in which the person can retain long-lasting and detailed visual images of scenes that can be scrutinized as if they were still physically present.

electroencephalogram (EEG) A recording of voltage changes occurring at the scalp that reflect activity in the brain underneath.

emotional intelligence The ability to understand one's own and others' emotions and to control one's emotions appropriately.

encoding specificity The tendency, when memorizing, to place in memory both the materials to be learned and some amount of their context. As a result, these materials will be recognized as familiar, later on, only if the materials appear again in a similar context.

endogenous control of attention A mechanism through which a person chooses (often on the basis of some meaningful signal) where to focus attention.

event-related potentials Changes in an *electroencephalogram (EEG)* in the brief period just before, during, and after an explicitly defined event, usually measured by averaging

together many trials in which this event has occurred.

excitatory connection A link from one *node*, or one *detector*, to another, such that activation of one node activates the other. Often contrasted with *inhibitory connection*.

executive control The *mental resources* and processes that are used to set goals, choose task priorities, and avoid conflict among competing habits or responses.

exemplar-based reasoning Reasoning that draws on knowledge about specific category members, or exemplars, rather than drawing on more general information about the overall category.

exogenous control of attention A mechanism through which attention is automatically directed, essentially as a reflex response, to some "attention-grabbing" input.

explicit memory A memory revealed by *direct memory testing* and usually accompanied by the conviction that one is, in fact, remembering—that is, drawing on some sort of knowledge (perhaps knowledge about a specific prior episode, or perhaps more general knowledge). Often contrasted with *implicit memory*.

extralinguistic context The social and physical setting in which an utterance is encountered; usually, cues within this setting guide the interpretation of the utterance.

factor analysis A statistical method for studying the interrelations among various tests. The goal is to discover the extent to which the tests are influenced by the same factors.

familiarity In some circumstances, the subjective feeling that one has encountered a stimulus before; in other circumstances, the objective fact that one has indeed encountered a stimulus before and is now in some way influenced by that encounter, whether or not one recalls that encounter or feels that the stimulus is familiar.

family resemblance The idea that members of a category (e.g., all dogs, all games) resemble one another. In general, family resemblance relies on some number of *features* being shared by any group of category members, even though these features may not be shared by all members of the category. Therefore, the basis for family resemblance may shift from one subset of the category to another.

feature nets Systems for recognizing patterns that involve a network of *detectors*, with detectors for features as the initial layer in each system.

figure/ground organization The processing step in which the perceiver determines which aspects of the stimulus belong to the central object (or "figure") and which aspects belong to the background (or "ground").

filter A hypothetical mechanism that would block potential distractors from further processing.

fixation target A visual mark (e.g., a dot or a plus sign) at which research participants point their eyes, or fixate. Fixation targets help research participants to control their eye position.

flashbulb memory A memory of extraordinary clarity, typically for some highly emotional event, that is retained over many years. Despite their remarkable vividness, flashbulb memories sometimes are inaccurate.

fluent aphasia A disruption of language, caused by brain damage, in which afflicted individuals are able to produce speech but the speech is not meaningful, and the individuals are not able to understand what is said to them. Often contrasted with *nonfluent aphasia*.

fluid intelligence The ability to deal with new and unusual problems. See also *crystallized intelligence*.

Flynn effect A worldwide increase in IQ scores over the last several decades, occurring in both impoverished and developed nations, and proceeding at a rate of roughly 3 points per decade.

forebrain One of the three main structures (along with the *hindbrain* and the *midbrain*) of the brain; the forebrain plays a crucial role in supporting intellectual functioning.

four-card task See *selection task*.

fovea The center of the *retina* and the region on the eye in which *acuity* is best; when a person looks at an object, he or she is lining up that object with the fovea.

framing In the context of decision making, a term referring to how the options for a decision (or, in some cases, the decision itself) are described. Often, the framing determines whether the decision is cast in terms of gains or positive attributes (e.g., what you might gain from this or that option), or whether the decision is cast in terms of losses or negative attributes.

free recall A method used for testing what research participants remember; participants are given a broad cue ("What happened yesterday?" or "What words were on the list?") and then try to name the relevant items, in any order they choose. It is the flexibility in order that makes this recall "free."

frequency One of the central influences on a *detector*'s or *node*'s activation level. Frequency refers to whether the detector or node has been activated often in the past. Often contrasted with *recency*—whether the detector or node has been activated in the recent past. Note that this usage of "frequency" contrasts with the usage of "frequency" within the term "frequency estimate" (someone's assessment of how often an event has occurred in the past or how common an object is in the world).

frequency estimate An essential step in judgment, in which someone makes an assessment of how often he or she has experienced or encountered a particular object or event.

frontal lobe The lobe of the brain in each *cerebral hemisphere* that includes the prefrontal area and the *primary motor projection area*.

functional fixedness A tendency to be rigid in how one thinks about an object's function. This generally involves a strong tendency to think of an object only in terms of its *typical* function.

functional magnetic resonance imaging (fMRI scans) A *neuroimaging technique* that uses magnetic fields to construct a detailed three-dimensional representation of the activity levels in different areas of the brain at a particular moment in time.

fusiform face area (FFA) A brain area apparently specialized for the perception of faces.

ganglion cells A type of *neuron* in the eye. The ganglion cells receive their input from the *bipolar cells*, and then the *axons* of the ganglion cells gather together to form the *optic nerve*, carrying information back to the *lateral geniculate nucleus*.

garden-path sentence A *sentence* that initially leads the reader to one understanding of how the sentence's words are related but then requires a change in this understanding to comprehend the full sentence. Examples are "The old man ships" and "The horse raced past the barn fell."

general intelligence (*g*) A mental capacity that is hypothesized as contributing to the performance of virtually any intellectual task. The existence of *g* is documented by the statistical overlap, usually revealed through *factor analysis*, among diverse forms of mental testing.

generativity The trait that allows someone to combine and recombine basic units to create (or "generate") new and more-complex entities. Linguistic rules, for example,

are generative because they allow a person to combine and recombine a limited set of words to produce a vast number of *sentences*.

geons Basic shapes proposed as the building blocks of all complex three-dimensional forms. Geons take the form of cylinders, cones, blocks, and the like, and they are combined to form "geon assemblies." These are then combined to produce entire objects.

Gestalt principles A small number of rules that seem to govern how observers organize the visual input, grouping some elements together but perceiving other elements to be independent of one another.

glia A type of cell found (along with *neurons*) in the central nervous system. Glial cells have many functions, including the support of *neurons*, the repair of neural connections in case of damage, and a key role in guiding the initial development of neural connections. A specialized type of glia also provide electrical insulation for some neurons, allowing much faster transmission of neuronal signals.

goal neglect A pattern of behavior in which a person fails to keep his or her goal in mind, so that, for example, the person relies on habitual responses even if those responses will not move him or her toward the goal.

graded membership The idea that some members of a category are "better" members and therefore are more firmly in the category than other members.

heuristic A strategy that is reasonably efficient and works most of the time. In using a

heuristic, one is choosing to accept some risk of error in order to gain efficiency.

hill-climbing strategy A commonly used strategy in *problem solving*. If people use this strategy, then whenever their efforts toward solving a problem give them a choice, they will choose the option that carries them closer to the goal.

hindbrain One of the three main structures (along with the *forebrain* and the *midbrain*) of the brain; the hindbrain sits atop the spinal cord and includes several structures crucial for controlling key life functions.

hippocampus (pl. hippocampi) A structure in the *temporal lobe* that is involved in the creation of *long-term memories* and spatial memory.

holistic perception A process in which the ability to identify an object depends on the whole, or the entire configuration, rather than on an inventory of the object's parts. In holistic perception, the parts do play a role—but by virtue of creating the patterns that are critical for recognition.

hypothalamus A small structure at the base of the *forebrain* that plays a vital role in the control of motivated behaviors such as eating, drinking, and sexual activity.

ill-defined problem A problem for which the goal state is specified only in general terms and the operations available for reaching the goal state are not obvious at the start.

illumination The third in a series of stages often hypothesized as crucial for creativity. The first stage is *preparation*; the second, *incubation*. Illumination is the stage in which some new key insight or new idea suddenly comes to mind and is then (on this hypothesis) followed by *verification*.

illusion of truth An effect of *implicit memory* in which claims that are familiar end up seeming more plausible.

image files Visual information stored in *long-term memory*, specifying what a particular object or shape looks like. Information within the image file can then be used as a "recipe" or set of instructions for how to construct an active image of this object or shape.

image-scanning procedure An experimental procedure in which participants are instructed to form a specific mental image and then are asked to scan, with their "mind's eye," from one point in the image to another. By timing these scans, the experimenter can determine how long "travel" takes across a mental image.

implicit memory A memory revealed by *indirect memory testing* and usually manifested as a *priming* effect in which current performance is guided or facilitated by previous experiences. Implicit memories are often accompanied by no conscious realization that one is, in fact, being influenced by specific past experiences. Often contrasted with *explicit memory*.

inattentional blindness A pattern in which perceivers seem literally not to see stimuli right in front of their eyes; this pattern is caused by the participants focusing their attention on some other stimulus and not expecting the target to appear.

incidental learning Learning that takes place in the absence of any intention to learn and, correspondingly, in the absence of any expectation of a subsequent memory test. Often contrasted with *intentional learning*.

incubation The second in a series of stages that are often hypothesized as crucial for creativity. The first stage is *preparation*; the third, *illumination*; the fourth, *verification*. Incubation is hypothesized to involve events that occur when a person puts a problem out of his or her conscious thoughts but continues nonetheless to work on the problem unconsciously. Many current psychologists are skeptical about this process, and they propose alternative accounts for data that ostensibly document incubation.

indirect memory testing A form of memory testing in which research participants are not told that their memories are being tested. Instead, they're tested in such a way that previous experiences can influence current behavior. Examples of indirect tests include *word-stem completion*, the *lexical-decision task*, and *tachistoscopic* recognition. Often contrasted with *direct memory testing*.

induction A pattern of reasoning in which a person seeks to draw general claims from specific bits of evidence. Often contrasted with *deduction*.

inhibitory connection A link from one *node*, or one *detector*, to another, such that activation of one node decreases the *activation level* of the other. Often contrasted with *excitatory connection*.

inspection time The time a person needs to make a simple discrimination between two stimuli; used in some settings as a measure of mental speed, and then used as a way to test the claim that intelligent people literally have faster processing in their brains.

integrative agnosia A disorder caused by a specific form of damage to the *parietal lobe*; people with this disorder appear relatively normal in tasks requiring them to detect whether specific features are present in a display, but they are impaired in tasks requiring them to judge how the features are bound together to form complex objects.

intentional learning The acquisition of memories in a setting in which people know that their memory for the information will be tested later. Often contrasted with *incidental learning*.

interference theory The hypothesis that materials are lost from memory because of interference from other materials that are also in memory. Interference caused by materials learned prior to the learning episode is called "proactive interference"; interference caused by materials learned after the learning episode is called "retroactive interference."

interposition A *monocular distance cue* that relies on the fact that objects farther away are blocked from view by closer objects that happen to be in the viewer's line of sight.

introspection The process through which one "looks within," to observe and record the contents of one's own mental life.

intrusion error A memory error in which a person recalls elements that were not part of the original episode.

invalid syllogism A syllogism (such as a *categorical syllogism,* or a syllogism built on a *conditional statement*) in which the conclusion is not logically demanded by the *premises.*

inversion effect A pattern typically observed for faces in which the specific face is much more difficult to recognize if the face is presented upside-down; this effect is part of the evidence indicating that face recognition relies on processes different from those involved in other forms of recognition.

Korsakoff's syndrome A clinical syndrome characterized primarily by dense *anterograde amnesia.* Korsakoff's syndrome is caused by damage to specific brain regions, and it is often precipitated by a form of malnutrition that is common among long-term alcoholics.

late selection hypothesis A proposal that *selective attention* operates at a late stage of processing, so that the unattended inputs receive considerable analysis.

lateral fissure The separation dividing the *frontal lobes* on each side of the brain from the *temporal lobes.*

lateral geniculate nucleus (LGN) An important way station in the *thalamus* that is the first destination for visual information sent from the eyeball to the brain.

lateral inhibition A pattern in which cells, when stimulated, inhibit the activity of neighboring cells. In the visual system, lateral inhibition in the *optic nerve* creates *edge enhancement.*

lens The transparent tissue located near the front of each eye that (together with the *cornea*) plays an important role in focusing incoming light. Muscles control the degree of curvature of the lens, allowing the eye to form a sharp image on the *retina.*

lesion A specific area of tissue damage.

level of processing An assessment of how "deeply" newly learned materials are engaged; *shallow processing* involves thinking only about the material's superficial traits, whereas *deep processing* involves thinking about what the material means. Deep processing is typically associated with a greater probability of remembering the now-processed information.

lexical-decision task A test in which participants are shown strings of letters and must indicate, as quickly as possible, whether or not each string of letters is a word in English. It is proposed that people perform this task by "looking up" these strings in their "mental dictionary."

limbic system A set of brain structures including the *amygdala, hippocampus,* and parts of the *thalamus.* The limbic system is believed to be involved in the control of emotional behavior and motivation, and it also plays a key role in learning and memory.

limited-capacity system A group of processes in which *mental resources* are limited, so that extra resources supplied to one process must be balanced by a withdrawal of resources somewhere else—with the result that the total resources expended do not exceed the limit of what is available.

linear perspective A cue for distance based on the fact that parallel lines seem to converge as they get farther away from the viewer.

linguistic relativity The proposal that the language people speak shapes their thought, because the structure and vocabulary of their language create certain ways of thinking about the world.

local representation A mode of representation in which information is encoded in a small number of identifiable *nodes.* Local representations are sometimes spoken of as "one idea per node" or "one content per location." Often contrasted with *distributed representation.*

localization of function The research endeavor of determining what specific job is performed by a particular region of the brain.

long-term memory (LTM) The storage system in which we hold all of our knowledge and all of our memories. Long-term memory contains memories that are not currently activated; those that are activated are represented in *working memory.*

longitudinal fissure The separation dividing the brain's left *cerebral hemisphere* from the right.

M cells Specialized cells within the *optic nerve* that provide the input for the *magnocellular cells* in the *lateral geniculate nucleus*. Often contrasted with *P cells*.

Mach band A type of illusion in which one perceives a region to be slightly darker if it is adjacent to a bright region, and also perceives a region to be slightly brighter if it is adjacent to a dark region. This illusion, created by *lateral inhibition*, contributes to *edge enhancement*.

magnetic resonance imaging (MRI scans) A *neuroimaging technique* that uses magnetic fields (created by radio waves) to construct a detailed three-dimensional representation of brain tissue. Like *CT scans*, MRI scans reveal the brain's anatomy, but they are much more precise than CT scans.

magnocellular cells Cells in the *lateral geniculate nucleus* specialized for the perception of motion and depth. Often contrasted with *parvocellular cells*.

maintenance rehearsal A rote, mechanical process in which items are continually cycled through *working memory*, merely by being repeated over and over. Often contrasted with *relational (or elaborative) rehearsal*.

manner of production The way in which a speaker momentarily obstructs the flow of air out of the lungs to produce a speech sound. For example, the airflow can be fully stopped for a moment, as in the [t] or [b] sound; or the air can continue to flow, as in the pronunciation of [f] or [v].

mapping The process of figuring out how aspects of one situation or argument correspond to aspects of some other situation or argument; this process is crucial for a problem solver's ability to find and use analogies.

mask A visual presentation that is used to interrupt the processing of another visual stimulus.

means-end analysis A strategy used in *problem solving* in which the person is guided, step by step, by a comparison of the difference between the current state and the goal state, and by a consideration of the operations available for reducing that difference.

memory rehearsal Any mental activity that has the effect of maintaining information in *working memory*. Two types of rehearsal are often distinguished: *maintenance rehearsal* and *relational (or elaborative) rehearsal*.

mental resources Some process or capacity needed for performance, but in limited supply.

mental-rotation task An experimental procedure in which participants have to determine whether a shape differs from a target only in its position (rotated or not, mirror-image or not) or whether the shape has a form different from the shapes of the targets.

metacognitive skills Skills that allow people to monitor and control their own mental processes.

metamemory People's knowledge about, awareness of, and control over their own memory.

midbrain One of the three main structures (along with the *forebrain* and the *hindbrain*) of the brain; the midbrain plays an important role in coordinating movements, and it contains structures that serve as "relay" stations for information arriving from the sensory organs.

mind-body problem The difficulty in understanding how the mind (a nonphysical entity) and the body (a physical entity) can influence each other, so that physical events can cause mental events, and mental events can cause physical ones.

misinformation effect An effect in which reports about an earlier event are influenced by misinformation that the person received after experiencing the event. In the extreme, misinformation can be used to create false memories concerning an entire event that actually never occurred.

mnemonic strategies Techniques designed to improve memory accuracy and to make learning easier; in general, mnemonic strategies seek to help memory by imposing an organization on the materials to be learned.

modal model A nickname for a specific conception of the "architecture" of memory. In this model, *working memory* serves both as the storage site for material now being contemplated and as the "loading dock" for *long-term memory*. Information can reach working memory through the processes of perception, or it can be drawn from long-term memory. Once in working memory, material can be further processed or can simply be recycled for subsequent use. This model prompted a large quantity of valuable research, but it has now largely been set aside, with modern theorizing offering a very different conception of working memory.

monocular distance cues Features of the visual stimulus that indicate distance even if the stimulus is viewed with only one eye.

morpheme The smallest language unit that carries meaning. Psycholinguists distinguish content (or "free") morphemes (the primary carriers of meaning) from function (or "bound") morphemes (which specify the relations among words).

motion parallax A *distance cue* based on the fact that as an observer moves, the retinal images of nearby objects move more rapidly than do the retinal images of objects farther away.

myelin sheath The layer of tissue, formed by specialized *glial* cells, that provides insulation around the *axons* of many *neurons*. There are, however, gaps in this insulation, and the neuronal signal essentially has to "jump" from one gap to the next, dramatically increasing the speed of neurotransmission.

N The conventional abbreviation for the total number of participants in a study or, in some circumstances, the total number of participants in a particular condition.

Necker cube One of the classic *reversible (or ambiguous) figures*; the figure is a two-dimensional drawing that can be perceived as a cube viewed from above or as a cube viewed from below.

neglect syndrome See *unilateral neglect syndrome*.

neural correlates of consciousness Events in the nervous system that occur at the same time as, and may be the biological basis of, a specific mental event or state.

neural synchrony A pattern of firing by *neurons* in which neurons in one brain area fire at the same time as neurons in another area; the brain seems to use this pattern as an indication that the neurons in different areas are firing in response to the same stimulus.

neuroimaging techniques Non-invasive methods for examining either the structure or the activation pattern within a living brain.

neuron An individual cell within the nervous system.

neuronal workspace hypothesis A specific claim about how the brain makes conscious experience possible; the proposal is that "workspace neurons" link together the activity of various specialized brain areas, and this linkage makes possible integration and comparison of different types of information.

neurotransmitter One of the chemicals released by *neurons* to stimulate adjacent neurons. See also *synapse*.

node An individual unit within an associative network. In a scheme using *local representations*, nodes represent single ideas or concepts. In a scheme using *distributed representations*, ideas or concepts are represented by a pattern of activation across a wide number of nodes; the same nodes may also participate in other patterns and therefore in other representations.

nonfluent aphasia A disruption of language, caused by brain damage, in which a person loses the ability to speak or write with any fluency. Often contrasted with *fluent aphasia*.

object recognition The steps or processes through which people identify the objects they encounter in the world around them.

occipital lobe The rearmost lobe in each *cerebral hemisphere*, and the one that includes the primary visual projection area.

operation span A measure of *working memory*'s capacity. This measure turns out to be predictive of performance in many other tasks, presumably because these tasks all rely on working memory. This measure is also the modern replacement for the (less useful) measure obtained from the *digit-span task*.

optic flow The pattern of change in the retinal image in which the image grows larger as the viewer approaches an object and shrinks as the viewer retreats from it.

optic nerve The bundle of nerve fibers, formed from the *retina*'s *ganglion cells*, that carries information from the eyeball to the brain.

overregularization error An error in which a person perceives or remembers a word or event as being closer to the "norm" than it really is. For example, misspelled words are read as though they were spelled correctly; atypical events are misremembered in a way that brings them closer to more-typical events; words with an irregular past tense (such as "ran") are replaced with a regular past tense ("runned").

P cells Specialized cells within the *optic nerve* that provide the input for the *parvocellular cells* in the *lateral geniculate nucleus*. Often contrasted with *M cells*.

parallel distributed processing (PDP) A system of handling information in which many steps happen at once (i.e., in parallel) and in which various aspects of the problem or task are represented only in a distributed way.

parallel processing A system in which many steps are going on at the same time. Usually contrasted with *serial processing*.

parietal lobe The lobe in each *cerebral hemisphere* that lies between the *occipital* and *frontal lobes* and that includes some of the *primary sensory projection areas*, as well as circuits that are crucial for the control of attention.

parse To divide an input into its appropriate elements—for example, dividing the stream of incoming speech into its constituent words—or a sequence of words into its constituent phrases. In some settings, parsing also includes the additional step of determining each element's role within the sequence.

parvocellular cells Cells in the *lateral geniculate nucleus* that are specialized for the perception of patterns. Often contrasted with *magnocellular cells*.

peg-word systems A type of *mnemonic strategy* using words or locations as "pegs" on which to "hang" the materials to be remembered.

percepts Internal representations of the world that result from perceiving; percepts are organized depictions.

perceptual constancy The achievement of perceiving the constant properties of objects in the world (e.g., their size, shape, and color) despite changes in the sensory information we receive that are caused by changes in our viewing circumstances.

perseveration error A pattern of responding in which a person produces the same response over and over, even though the person knows that the task requires a change in response. This pattern is often observed in patients with brain damage in the *frontal lobe*.

phoneme A unit of sound that distinguishes one word (or one *morpheme*) from another. For example, the words "peg" and "beg" differ in their initial phoneme—[p] in one case, [b] in the other. Some contrasts in sound, however, do not involve phonemes; these contrasts might indicate the speaker's emphasis, or might involve a regional accent, but do not change the identity of the words being spoken. (These contrasts are sometimes said to be "subphonemic.")

phonemic-restoration effect A pattern in which people "hear" *phonemes* that actually are not presented but that are highly likely in that context. For example, if one is presented with the word "legislature" but with the [s] sound replaced by a cough, one is likely to hear the [s] sound anyhow.

phonological buffer A passive storage system used for holding a representation (essentially an "internal echo") of recently heard or self-produced sounds.

photoreceptors Cells on the *retina* that are sensitive to light and that fire (i.e., send a signal to adjacent cells) when they are stimulated by light.

phrase-structure rule A constraint that governs what elements must be contained within a phrase and, in many languages, what the sequence of those elements must be.

pictorial cues Patterns that can be represented on a flat surface to create the sense of a three-dimensional object or scene.

place of articulation The position at which a speaker momentarily obstructs the flow of air out of the lungs to produce a speech sound. For example, the place of articulation for the [b] sound is the lips; the place of articulation for the [d] sound is where the tongue briefly touches the roof of the mouth.

population The entire group about which an investigator wants to draw conclusions.

positron emission tomography (PET scans) A *neuroimaging technique* that determines how much glucose (the brain's fuel) is being used by specific areas of the brain at a particular moment in time.

postsynaptic membrane The cell membrane of the *neuron* "receiving" information across the *synapse*. Often contrasted with *presynaptic membrane*.

practical intelligence The ability to solve everyday problems through skilled reasoning that relies on tacit knowledge acquired through experience.

pragmatics A term referring to knowledge of how language is ordinarily used—for example, knowledge that tells most English speakers that "Can you pass me the salt?" is actually a request for the salt, not an inquiry about someone's arm strength.

predictive validity An assessment of whether a test measures what it is intended to measure, based on whether the test scores correlate with (i.e., can predict) some other relevant criterion.

prefrontal cortex The outer surface (*cortex*) of the frontmost part of the brain (i.e., the frontmost part of the *frontal lobe*). The prefrontal cortex has many functions but is crucial for the planning of complex or novel behaviors, so this brain area is often mentioned as one of the main sites underlying the brain's executive functions.

premises The assertions used as the starting point for a logical argument. The premises may or may not be true; logic is concerned instead only with whether a conclusion follows from the premises.

preparation In problem solving, the first in a series of stages often hypothesized as crucial for creativity. The second stage is *incubation*; the third, *illumination*; the fourth, *verification*. Preparation is the stage in which one begins effortful work on the problem, often with little progress.

prescriptive rules Rules describing how things are supposed to be instead of how they are. Often called "normative rules" and contrasted with *descriptive rules*.

presynaptic membrane The cell membrane of the *neuron* "sending" information across the *synapse*. Often contrasted with *postsynaptic membrane*.

primacy effect An often-observed advantage in remembering the early-presented materials within a sequence of materials. This advantage is generally attributed to the fact that a person can focus his or her full attention on these items because, at the beginning of a sequence, the person is not trying to divide attention between these items and other items in the series. Often contrasted with *recency effect*.

primary motor projection areas The strip of tissue, located at the rear of the *frontal lobe*, that is the departure point for nerve cells that send their signals to lower portions of the brain and spinal cord, and that ultimately result in muscle movement.

primary sensory projection areas The main points of arrival in the *cortex* for information arriving from the eyes, ears, and other sense organs.

priming A process through which one input or cue prepares a person for an upcoming input or cue.

problem solving A process in which a person begins with a goal and seeks some steps that will lead toward that goal.

problem space The set of all states that can be reached in solving a problem, as the problem solver moves, by means of the problem's operations, from the problem's initial state toward its goal state.

problem-solving set The starting assumptions that a person uses when trying to solve a new problem. These assumptions are often helpful, because they guide the person away from pointless strategies. But these assumptions can sometimes steer the person away from worthwhile strategies, in which case they can be an obstacle to problem solving.

processing fluency The speed or ease of processing involved in recognizing or thinking about a stimulus or idea; usually understood as a reflection of the speed or ease with which activation moves through a *processing pathway*.

processing pathway The sequence of *nodes* and connections between nodes through which activation flows when recognizing or thinking about a stimulus or idea. The speed or ease of activation flow is referred to as *processing fluency*.

production task An experimental procedure used in studying concepts, in which the participant is asked to name as many examples (e.g., as many fruits) as possible.

proposition The smallest unit of knowledge that can be either true or false. Propositions are often expressed via simple *sentences*, but this is merely a convenience; other modes of representation are available.

prosody The pattern of pauses and pitch changes that characterize speech production. Prosody can be used (among other functions) to emphasize elements of a spoken *sentence*, to highlight the sentence's intended structure, or to signal the difference between a question and an assertion.

prosopagnosia A syndrome in which individuals lose their ability to recognize faces and to make other fine-grained discriminations within a highly familiar category, even though their other visual abilities seem relatively intact.

prototype theory The claim that mental categories are represented by means of a single "best example," or prototype, identifying the "center" of the category. In this view, decisions about category membership, and inferences about the category, are made with reference to this best example. Often, the prototype is an average of the examples of that category that the person has actually encountered.

qualia (sing. quale) The subjective conscious experiences, or "raw feels," of awareness. Examples include the pain of a headache and the exact flavor of chocolate.

r The numerical value used in assessing a *correlation*, varying from −1.00 (a perfect inverse correlation) to +1.00 (a perfect correlation).

r^2 The numerical value calculated by multiplying *r* by itself (that is, by squaring *r*). This value tells you how much of the overall variation in one measure can be predicted, based on some second (predictor) measure. Equivalently, this value tells you how much your uncertainty about the first measure is reduced if you also have access to a second measure that predicts the first. If the second measure provides no basis for prediction, then r^2 is zero. If the second measure perfectly predicts the target value, then r^2 is 1.0.

random sampling A procedure in which every member of the *population* being studied has an equal chance of being picked for inclusion in the data collection.

rating task A task in which research participants must evaluate some item or category with reference to some dimension, usually expressing their response in terms of some number. For example, they might be asked to evaluate birds for how *typical* they are within the category "birds," using a "1" response to indicate "very typical" and a "7" response to indicate "very atypical."

reason-based choice A proposal for how people make decisions. The central idea is that people make a choice when—and only when—they detect what they believe to be a persuasive reason for making that choice.

recall The task of memory *retrieval* in which the remember must come up with the desired materials, sometimes in response to a cue that names the context in which these materials were earlier encountered (e.g., "Name the pictures you saw earlier"), and sometimes in response to a cue that broadly identifies the sought-after information (e.g., "Name a fruit" or "What is the capital of California?"). Often contrasted with *recognition*.

recency One of the central influences on a *detector*'s or *node*'s activation level. Recency refers to whether the detector or node has been activated in the recent past. Often contrasted with *frequency*— whether the detector or node has been activated often in the past. Note that this usage of "recency" contrasts with the usage of "recency" within the term "recency effect" (a memory advantage for some types of material).

recency effect The tendency to remember materials that occur late in a series. If the series was just presented, the recency effect can be attributed to the fact that the late-arriving items are still in *working memory* (because nothing else has arrived after these items to bump them out of working memory).

receptive field The portion of the visual field to which a cell within the visual system responds. If the appropriately shaped stimulus appears in the appropriate position, the cell's firing rate will change. The firing rate will not change if the stimulus is of the wrong form or is in the wrong position.

recognition The task of memory *retrieval* in which the items to be remembered are presented and the person must decide whether or not the item was encountered in some earlier circumstance. For example, one might be asked, "Have you ever seen this person before?" or "Is this the poster you saw in the office yesterday?" Often contrasted with *recall*.

recognition by components (RBC) model A model of *object recognition*. In this model, a crucial role is played by *geons*, the (hypothesized) basic building blocks out of which all the objects we recognize are constructed.

relational (or elaborative) rehearsal A form of mental processing in which one thinks about the relations, or connections, among ideas. The connections created (or strengthened) in this way will later guide memory search.

reliability The degree of consistency with which a test measures a trait or attribute. See also *test-retest reliability*.

"remember/know" distinction A distinction between two experiences a person can have in recalling a past event. If you "remember" having encountered a stimulus before, then you usually can offer information about that encounter, including when, where, and how it occurred. If you merely "know" that you encountered a stimulus before, then you're likely to have a sense of *familiarity* with the stimulus but may have no idea when or where it was last encountered.

repetition priming A pattern of *priming* that occurs simply because a stimulus is presented a second time; processing is more efficient on the second presentation.

representative sample A *sample* drawn from a *population* in such a way that the properties of the sample are likely to reflect the properties of the population at large.

representativeness heuristic A strategy that is often used in making judgments about categories. This strategy is broadly equivalent to making the assumption that, in general, the instances of a category will resemble the *prototype* for that category and, likewise, that the prototype resembles each instance.

response threshold The quantity of information or activation needed to trigger a response in a *node* or *detector*, or, in a neuroscience context, a response from a *neuron*.

response time (RT) The amount of time (usually measured in milliseconds) needed for a person to respond to a particular event (such as a question or a cue to press a specific button).

retention interval The amount of time that passes between the initial learning of some material and the subsequent memory *retrieval* of that material.

retina The light-sensitive tissue that lines the back of the eyeball.

retrieval The process of locating information in memory and activating that information for use.

retrieval failure A mechanism that probably contributes to a great deal of forgetting. Retrieval failure occurs when a memory is, in fact, in long-term storage but the person is unable to locate that memory when trying to retrieve it.

retrieval path A connection (or series of connections) that can lead to a sought-after memory in long-term storage.

retrograde amnesia An inability to remember experiences that occurred before the event that triggered the memory disruption. Often contrasted with *anterograde amnesia*.

reversible (or ambiguous) figures Drawings that can be readily perceived in more than one way. Classic examples include the vase/profiles, the duck/rabbit, and the *Necker cube*.

risk aversion A tendency toward avoiding risk. People tend to be risk averse when contemplating gains, choosing instead to hold tight to what they already have. Often contrasted with *risk seeking*.

risk seeking A tendency toward seeking out risk. People tend to be risk seeking when contemplating losses, presumably because they're willing to gamble in hopes of avoiding (or diminishing) their losses. Often contrasted with *risk aversion*.

rods *Photoreceptors* that are sensitive to very low light levels but that are unable to discriminate hues and that have relatively poor *acuity*. Often contrasted with *cones*.

sample The subset of the *population* that an investigator studies to learn about the population at large.

savant syndrome A pattern of traits in a disabled person such that the person has some remarkable talent that contrasts with his or her very low level of *general intelligence*.

schema (pl. schemata) Knowledge describing what is typical or frequent in a particular situation. For example, a "kitchen schema" would stipulate that a stove and refrigerator are likely to be present, whereas a coffeemaker may be or may not be present, and a piano is not likely to be present.

selection task An experimental procedure, commonly used to study reasoning, in which a person is presented with four cards with certain information on either side of the card. The person is also given a rule that may describe the cards, and the person's task is to decide which cards must be turned over to find out if the rule describes the cards or not. Also called the *four-card task*.

selective attention The skill through which a person focuses on one input or one task while ignoring other stimuli that are also on the scene.

self-report data A form of evidence in which the person is asked directly about his or her own thoughts or experiences.

self-schema The set of interwoven beliefs and memories that constitute one's knowledge about oneself.

semantic bootstrapping An important process in language learning in which a person (usually a child) uses knowledge of semantic relationships as a basis for figuring out the *syntax* of the language.

semantic priming A process in which activation of an idea in memory causes activation to spread to other ideas related to the first in meaning.

sensory memory A form of memory that holds on to just-seen or just-heard input in a "raw" sensory form.

sentence A sequence of words that conforms to the rules of *syntax* (and so has the right constituents in the right sequence).

sentence verification task An experimental procedure used for studying memory in which participants are given simple *sentences* (e.g., "Cats are animals") and must respond as quickly as possible whether the sentence is true or false.

serial position A data pattern summarizing the relationship between some performance measure (often, likelihood of *recall*) and the order in which the test materials were presented (i.e., where the materials were located within the series). In memory studies, the serial-position curve tends to be U-shaped, with people being best able to recall the first-presented items (the *primacy effect*) and also the last-presented items (the *recency effect*).

serial processing A system in which only one step happens at a time (and so the steps occur in a series). Usually contrasted with *parallel processing*.

shadowing A task in which research participants repeat back a verbal input, word for word, as they hear it.

shallow processing A mode of thinking about material in which one pays attention only to appearances and other superficial aspects of the material; shallow processing typically leads to poor memory retention. Often contrasted with *deep processing*.

shape constancy The achievement of perceiving the constant shape of objects despite changes in the shape of the retinal image that result from variations in viewing angle.

short-term memory An older term for what is now called *working memory*.

single-cell recording A technique for recording the moment-by-moment *activation level* of an individual *neuron* within a healthy, normally functioning brain.

size constancy The achievement of perceiving the constant size of objects despite changes in the size of the retinal image that result from variations in viewing distance.

somatic markers States of the body used in decision making. For example, a tight stomach and an accelerated heart rate when a person is thinking about a particular option can signal to the person that the option has risk associated with it.

source confusion A memory error in which one misremembers where a bit of information was learned or where a particular stimulus was last encountered.

source memory A form of memory that enables a person to recollect the episode in which learning took place or the time and place in which a particular stimulus was encountered.

spatial attention The mechanism through which a person allocates processing resources to particular positions in space, so that he or she more efficiently processes any inputs from that region in space.

specific-language impairment (SLI) A disorder in which individuals seem to have normal intelligence but experience problems in learning the rules of language.

speech segmentation The process through which a stream of speech is "sliced" into its constituent words and, within words, into the constituent *phonemes*.

spreading activation A process through which activation travels from one *node* to another, via *associative links*. As each node becomes activated, it serves as a source for further activation, spreading onward through the network.

stereotype threat A mechanism through which a person's performance is influenced by the perception that his or her score will confirm stereotypes about his or her group.

storage The state in which a memory, once acquired, remains until it is retrieved. Many people understand storage to be a "dormant" process, so that the memory remains unchanged while it is in storage. Modern theories, however, describe a more dynamic form of storage, in which older memories are integrated with (and sometimes replaced by) newer knowledge.

Stroop interference A classic demonstration of *automaticity* in which research participants are asked to name the color of ink used to print a word, and the word itself is the name of a different color. For example, participants might see the word "yellow" printed in blue ink and be required to say "blue." Considerable interference is observed in this task, with participants apparently being unable to ignore the word's content even though it is irrelevant to their task.

subcortical structures Identified pieces of the brain that are underneath the *cortex*, and therefore hidden from view in drawings of an intact brain. These structures include the *thalamus*, the *hypothalamus*, and the various components of the *limbic system*.

subliminal perception A pattern in which people perceive and are in some ways influenced by inputs they did not consciously notice.

subthreshold activation Activation levels below *response threshold*. Subthreshold activation, by definition, will not trigger a response; nonetheless, this activation is important because it can accumulate, leading eventually to an *activation level* that exceeds the *response threshold*.

subvocalization Covert speech in which one goes through the motions of speaking, or perhaps forms a detailed motor plan for speech movements, but without making any sound.

summation The addition of two or more separate inputs so that the effect of the combined inputs is greater than the effect of any one input by itself.

synapse The area that includes the *presynaptic membrane* of one *neuron*, the *postsynaptic membrane* of another neuron, and the tiny gap between them. The presynaptic membrane releases a small amount of *neurotransmitter* that drifts across the gap and stimulates the postsynaptic membrane.

syntax Rules governing the sequences and combinations of words in the formation of phrases and *sentences*.

tachistoscope A device that allows the presentation of stimuli for precisely controlled amounts of time, including very brief presentations.

temporal lobe The lobe of the *cortex* lying inward and down from the temples. The temporal lobe in each *cerebral hemisphere* includes the primary auditory projection area, *Wernicke's area*, and, subcortically, the *amygdala* and *hippocampus*.

test-retest reliability An assessment of whether a test is consistent in what it measures from one occasion to another, determined by asking whether the test's results on one occasion are correlated with results from the same test (or a close variant on it) given at a later time.

thalamus A part of the lower portion of the *forebrain* that serves as a major relay and integration center for sensory information.

theory of multiple intelligences A proposal put forward by Howard Gardner that there are many forms of intelligence, including linguistic, spatial, musical, bodily-kinesthetic, and personal.

threshold The activity level at which a cell or *detector* responds, or fires.

top-down processing A sequence of events that is heavily shaped by the knowledge and expectations that the person brings to the situation. Often contrasted with *bottom-up processing*.

TOT phenomenon An often-observed effect in which people are unable to remember a particular word, even though they are certain that the word (typically identified via its definition) is in their vocabulary. People in this state often can remember the starting letter for the word and its number of syllables, and they insist that the word is on the "tip of their tongue" (therefore, the "TOT" label).

transcendental method A type of theorizing proposed by the philosopher Immanuel Kant. To use this method, an investigator first observes the effects or consequences of a process and then asks: What must the process have been to bring about these effects?

transcranial magnetic stimulation (TMS) A technique in which a series of strong magnetic pulses at a specific location on the scalp causes temporary disruption in the brain region directly underneath this scalp area.

tree structure A style of depiction often used to indicate hierarchical relationships, such as the relationships (specified by *phrase-structure rules*) among the words in a phrase or *sentence*.

Type 1 thinking A commonly used name for judgment and reasoning strategies that are fast and effortless, but prone to error.

Type 2 thinking A commonly used name for judgment and reasoning strategies that are slower and require more effort than *Type 1 thinking*.

typicality The degree to which a particular case (an object, situation, or event) is typical for its kind.

unattended channel A stimulus (or group of stimuli) that a person is not trying to perceive. Ordinarily, little information is understood or remembered from the unattended channel. Often contrasted with *attended channel*.

unconscious inference The hypothesized steps that perceivers follow in order to take one aspect of the visual scene (e.g., viewing distance) into account in judging another aspect (e.g., size).

unilateral neglect syndrome A pattern of symptoms in which affected individuals ignore all inputs coming from one side of space. Individuals with this syndrome put only one of their arms into their jackets, eat food from only half of their plates, read only half of words (e.g., they might read "blouse" as "use"), and so on.

utility maximization The proposal that people make decisions by selecting the option that has the greatest utility.

valid syllogism A syllogism for which the conclusion follows from the *premise*, in accord with the rules of logic.

validity The extent to which a method or procedure measures what it is supposed to measure. Validity is assessed in a variety of ways, including through *predictive validity*.

verification One of the four steps that are commonly hypothesized as part of creative *problem solving*; in this step, the problem solver confirms that a new idea really does lead to a problem solution, and then he or she works out the details. (The other steps are *preparation, incubation,* and *illumination*.)

viewpoint-dependent recognition A process in which the ease or success of recognition depends on the perceiver's particular viewing angle or distance with regard to the target object.

viewpoint-independent recognition A process in which the ease or success of recognition does *not* depend on the perceiver's particular viewing angle or distance with regard to the target object.

visual features The elements of a visual pattern—vertical lines, curves, diagonals, and so on—that, together, form the overall pattern.

visual search task An often-used laboratory task in which research participants are asked to search for a specific target (e.g., a shape, or a shape of a certain color) within a field of other stimuli; usually, the researcher is interested in how quickly the participants can locate the target.

visuospatial buffer One of the low-level assistants used as part of the *working-memory system*. This buffer plays an important role in storing visual or spatial representations, including visual images.

voicing One of the properties that distinguishes different categories of speech sounds. A sound is considered "voiced" if the vocal folds are vibrating while the sound is produced. If the vocal folds start vibrating sometime after the sound begins (i.e., with a long voice-onset time), the sound is considered "unvoiced."

well-formedness A measure of the degree to which a string of symbols (usually letters) conforms to the usual patterns (for letters: the rules of spelling); for example, the nonword "FIKE" is well formed, but "IEFK" is not.

Wernicke's area An area in the *temporal lobe* of the brain, where the temporal and *parietal lobes* meet; damage here typically causes *fluent aphasia*.

what **system** The system of visual circuits and pathways leading from the visual *cortex* to the *temporal lobe* and especially involved in object recognition. Often contrasted with the *where system*.

where **system** The system of visual circuits and pathways leading from the visual *cortex* to the *parietal lobe* and especially involved in the spatial localization of objects and in the coordination of movements. Often contrasted with the *what system*.

word-stem completion A task in which research participants are given the beginning of a word (e.g., "TOM") and must provide a word that starts with the letters provided. In some versions of the task, only one solution is possible, so performance is measured by counting the number of words completed. In other versions of the task, several solutions are possible for each stem, and performance is assessed by determining which responses fulfill some other criterion.

word-superiority effect (**WSE**) The data pattern in which research participants are more accurate and more efficient in recognizing letters if the letters appear within a word (or a word-like letter string) than they are in recognizing letters appearing in isolation.

working memory The storage system in which information is held while that information is being worked on. All indications are that working memory is a system, not a single entity, and that information is held here via active processes, not via some sort of passive storage. Formerly called *short-term memory*.

working-memory capacity (**WMC**) A measure of *working memory* derived from *operation span* tasks. Although termed a "memory capacity," this measure can perhaps best be understood as a measure of a person's ability to store some materials while simultaneously working with other materials.

working-memory system A system of mental resources used for holding information in an easily accessible form. The central executive is at the heart of this system, and the executive then relies on a number of low-level assistants, including the *visuospatial buffer* and the *articulatory rehearsal loop*.

References

Ackerman, P. L., Beier, M. E., & Boyle, M. O. (2002). Individual differences in working memory within a nomological network of cognitive and perceptual speed abilities. *Journal of Experimental Psychology: General, 131,* 567–589.

Ackermann, S., & Rasch, B. (2014). Differential effects of non-REM and REM sleep on memory consolidation. *Current Neurology and Neuroscience Reports, 14,* 430.

Agarwal, P., Karpicke, J., Kang, S., Roediger, H., & McDermott, K. (2008). Examining the testing effect with open- and closed-book tests. *Applied Cognitive Psychology, 22,* 861–876.

Aggleton, J. P., & Brown, M. W. (2006). Interleaving brain systems for episodic and recognition memory. *Trends in Cognitive Sciences, 10,* 455–463.

Akers, K. G., Martinez-Canabal, A., Restivo, L., Yiu, A. P., De Cristofaro, A., Hsiang, H. L., Wheeler, A. L., Guskjolen, A., Niibori, Y., Shoji, H., Ohira, K., Richards, B. A., Miyakawa, T., Josselyn, S. A., & Frankland, P. W. (2014, May 9). Hippocampal neurogenesis regulates forgetting during adulthood and infancy. *Science, 344*(6184), 598–602.

Albers, A. M., Kok, P., Toni, I., Dijkerman, H. C., & de Lange, F. P. (2013). Shared representations for working memory and mental imagery in early visual cortex. *Current Biology, 23,* 1427–1431.

Alexander, K. W., Quas, J. A., Goodman, G. S., Ghetti, S., Edelstein, R. S., Redlich, A. D., et al. (2005). Traumatic impact predicts long-term memory for documented child sexual abuse. *Psychological Science, 16,* 33–40.

Alkire, M., Hudetz, A., & Tononi, G. (2008). Consciousness and anesthesia. *Science, 322,* 876–880.

Allen, A. L., & Strand, N. K. (2015). Cognitive enhancement and beyond: Recommendations from the Bioethics Commission. *Trends in Cognitive Sciences, 19,* 549–555.

Allport, A. (1989). Visual attention. In M. Posner (Ed.), *Foundations of cognitive science* (pp. 631–682). Cambridge, MA: MIT Press.

Allport, D., Antonis, B., & Reynolds, P. (1972). On the division of attention: A disproof of the single channel hypothesis. *Quarterly Journal of Experimental Psychology, 24,* 225–235.

Almor, A., & Sloman, S. A. (2000). Reasoning versus text processing in the Wason selection task: A non-deontic perspective on perspective effects. *Memory & Cognition, 28,* 1060–1070.

Altmann, E. M., & Schunn, C. D. (2012). Decay versus interference: A new look at an old interaction. *Psychological Science, 23,* 1435–1437.

Alvarez, M. J., Miller, M. K., & Bornstein, B. H. (2016). "It will be your duty . . .": The psychology of criminal jury instructions. In M. K. Miller & B. H. Bornstein (Eds.), *Advances in psychology and law* (Vol. 1, pp. 119–158). New York, NY: Springer.

Amer, T., Ngo, K. W. J., & Hasher, L. (2016). Cultural differences in visual attention: Implications for distractor processing. *British Journal of Psychology, 108,* 244–258.

Amishav, R., & Kimchi, R. (2010). Perceptual integrality of componential and configural information in faces. *Psychonomic Bulletin & Review, 17,* 743–748.

Anderson, J. R. (1976). *Language, memory, and thought.* Hillsdale, NJ: Erlbaum.

Anderson, J. R. (1980). *Cognitive psychology and its implications.* San Francisco, CA: Freeman.

Anderson, J. R. (1993). Problem solving and learning. *American Psychologist, 48,* 35–44.

Anderson, J. R., & Bower, G. H. (1973). *Human associative memory.* Washington, DC: Winston.

Anderson, M. C., & Bell, T. (2001). Forgetting our facts: The role of inhibitory processes in the loss of propositional knowledge. *Journal of Experimental Psychology: General, 130,* 544–570.

Anderson, R., & Helstrup, T. (1993). Visual discovery in mind and on paper. *Memory & Cognition, 21,* 283–293.

Andor, J. (2011). Reflections on speech act theory: An interview with John R. Searle. *International Journal of Pragmatics, 3,* 113–134.

Ariely, D. (2009). *Predictably irrational.* New York, NY: Harper.

Arkes, H. (1991). Costs and benefits of judgment errors: Implications for debiasing. *Psychological Bulletin, 110,* 486–498.

Armstrong, S. L., Gleitman, L. R., & Gleitman, H. (1983). What some concepts might not be. *Cognition, 13,* 263–308.

Arneson, J. J., Sackett, P. R., & Beatty, A. S. (2011). Ability-performance relationships in education and employment settings: Critical tests of the more-is-better and the good-enough hypotheses. *Psychological Science, 22,* 1336–1342.

Aron, A. (2008). Progress in executive-function research. *Current Directions in Psychological Science, 17,* 124–129.

Arrigo, J. M., & Pezdek, K. (1997). Lessons from the study of psychogenic amnesia. *Current Directions in Psychological Science, 6,* 148–152.

Ash, I. K., & Wiley, J. (2006). The nature of restructuring in insight: An individual-differences approach. *Psychonomic Bulletin & Review, 13,* 66–73.

Ashbridge, E., Walsh, V., & Cowey, A. (1997). Temporal aspects of visual search studied by transcranial magnetic stimulation. *Neuropsychologia, 35,* 1121–1131.

Ashby, F. G., & Rosedahl, L. (2017). A neural interpretation of exemplar theory. *Psychological Review, 124,* 472–482.

Asher, E. J. (1935). The inadequacy of current intelligence tests for testing Kentucky Mountain children. *Journal of Genetic Psychology, 46,* 480–486.

Aslin, R. N., Saffran, J. R., & Newport, E. L. (1998). Computation of conditional probability statistics by 8-month-old infants. *Psychological Science, 9,* 321–324.

Atkinson, A. P., Thomas, M. S. C., & Cleeremans, A. (2000). Consciousness: Mapping the theoretical landscape. *Trends in Cognitive Sciences, 4,* 372–382.

Atkinson, R. C., & Shiffrin, R. M. (1968). Human memory: A proposed system and its control processes. In K. W. S. Spence &. J. T. Spence (Eds.), *The psychology of learning and motivation* (pp. 89–105). New York, NY: Academic Press.

Atran, S. (1990). *Cognitive foundations of natural history.* New York, NY: Cambridge University Press.

Au, J., Sheehan, E., Tsai, N., Duncan, G. J., Buschkuehl, M., & Jaeggi, S. M. (2015). Improving fluid intelligence with training on working memory: A meta-analysis. *Psychonomic Bulletin & Review, 22,* 366–377.

Auksztulewicz, R., Spitzer, B., & Blankenburg, F. (2012). Recurrent neural processing and somatosensory awareness. *Journal of Neuroscience, 32,* 799–805.

Autin, F., & Croziet, J. C. (2012). Improving working memory efficiency by reframing metacognitive interpretation of task difficulty. *Journal of Experimental Psychology: General, 141,* 610–618.

Awh, E., & Pashler, H. (2000). Evidence for split attentional foci. *Journal of Experimental Psychology: Human Perception and Performance, 26,* 834–846.

Azevedo, F. A., Carvalho, L. R., Grinberg, L. T., Farfel, J. M., Ferretti, R. E., Leite, R. E., Jacob Filho, W., Lent, R., & Herculano-Houzel, S. (2009). Equal numbers of neuronal and nonneuronal cells make the human brain an isometrically scaled-up primate brain. *Journal of Comparative Neurology, 513,* 532–541.

Baars, B. J. (2005). Global workspace theory of consciousness: Toward a cognitive neuroscience of human experience. *Progress in Brain Research, 150,* 45–53.

Baars, B. J., & Franklin, S. (2003). How conscious experience and working memory interact. *Trends in Cognitive Sciences, 7,* 166–172.

Bacharowski, J.-A. (1999). Vocal expression and perception of emotion. *Current Directions in Psychological Science, 8,* 53–57.

Baddeley, A. (2000). The episodic buffer: A new component of working memory? *Trends in Cognitive Sciences, 4,* 417–423.

Baddeley, A. (2012). Working memory: Theories, models, and controversies. *Annual Review of Psychology, 63,* 1–29.

Baddeley, A., Eysenck, M., & Anderson, M. C. (2009). *Memory.* New York, NY: Psychology Press.

Baddeley, A., & Wilson, B. A. (2002). Prose recall and amnesia: Implications for the structure of working memory. *Neuropsychologia, 40,* 1737–1743.

Baddeley, A. D. (1986). *Working memory.* Oxford, England: Clarendon.

Baddeley, A. D. (1992). Is working memory working? The fifteenth Bartlett lecture. *Quarterly Journal of Experimental Psychology, 44A,* 1–31.

Baddeley, A. D. (2012). Working memory: Theories, models, and controversies. *Annual Review of Psychology, 63,* 1–12.

Baddeley, A. D., Aggleton, J. P., & Conway, M. A. (Eds.). (2002). *Episodic memory: New directions in research.* New York, NY: Oxford University Press.

Baddeley, A. D., & Hitch, G. (1974). Working memory. In G. Bower (Ed.), *Recent advances in learning and motivation* (pp. 47–90). New York, NY: Academic Press.

Baddeley, A. D., & Hitch, G. (1977). Recency re-examined. In S. Dornic (Ed.), *Attention and performance VI* (pp. 646–667). Hillsdale, NJ: Erlbaum.

Baguley, C. M., McKimmie, B. M., & Masser, B. M. (2017). Deconstructing the simplification of jury instructions: How simplifying the features of complexity affects jurors' application of instructions. *Law & Human Behavior, 41,* 284–304.

Bahrick, H. (1984). Semantic memory content in permastore: 50 years of memory for Spanish learned in school. *Journal of Experimental Psychology: General, 113,* 1–29.

Bahrick, H., Bahrick, P. O., & Wittlinger, R. P. (1975). Fifty years of memory for names and faces: A cross-sectional approach. *Journal of Experimental Psychology: General, 104,* 54–75.

Bahrick, H., & Hall, L. (1991). Lifetime maintenance of high school mathematics content. *Journal of Experimental Psychology: General, 120,* 20–33.

Bahrick, H., Hall, L. K., & Berger, S. A. (1996). Accuracy and distortion in memory for high school grades. *Psychological Science, 7,* 265–271.

Baird, B., Smallwood, J., Mrazek, M. D., Kam, J. W. Y., Franklin, M. S., & Schooler, J. W. (2012). Inspired by distraction: Mind wandering facilitates creative incubation. *Psychological Science, 23,* 1117–1122.

Balch, W., Bowman, K., & Mohler, L. (1992). Music-dependent memory in immediate and delayed word recall. *Memory & Cognition, 20,* 21–28.

Bang, M., Medin, D., & Atran, S. (2007). Cultural mosaics and mental models of nature. *Proceedings of the National Academy of Sciences, 104,* 13868–13874.

Barclay, J., Bransford, J., Franks, J., McCarrell, N., & Nitsch, K. (1974). Comprehension and semantic flexibility. *Journal of Verbal Learning & Verbal Behavior, 13,* 471–481.

Bargh, J. B. (2005). Toward demystifying the nonconscious control of social behavior. In R. Hasslin, J. Uleman, & J. A. Bargh (Eds.), *The new unconscious* (pp. 37–58). New York, NY: Oxford University Press.

Barkley, R. A., Murphy, K. R., & Fischer, M. (2008). *ADHD in adults: What the science says.* New York, NY: Guilford.

Baron, J. (1988). *Thinking and reasoning.* Cambridge, England: Cambridge University Press.

Baron, J., Scott, S., Fincher, K., & Metz, S. E. (2015). Why does the Cognitive Reflection Test (sometimes) predict utilitarian moral judgments (among other things)? *Journal of Applied Research in Memory and Cognition, 4,* 265–284.

Barsalou, L. (1983). Ad hoc categories. *Memory and Cognition, 11,* 211–227.

Barsalou, L. (1985). Ideals, central tendency, and frequency of instantiation. *Journal of Experimental Psychology: Learning, Memory, & Cognition, 11,* 629–654.

Barsalou, L. (1988). The content and organization of autobiographical memories. In U. Neisser & E. Winograd (Eds.), *Remembering reconsidered* (pp. 193–243). Cambridge, England: Cambridge University Press.

Barsalou, L., & Sewell, D. R. (1985). Contrasting the representation of scripts and categories. *Journal of Memory and Language, 24,* 646–665.

Barsalou, L. W. (2008). Grounded cognition. *Annual Review of Psychology, 59,* 617–645.

Barsalou, L. W. (2016). On staying grounded and avoiding Quixotic dead ends. *Psychonomic Bulletin & Review, 23,* 1122–1142.

Bartlett, F. C. (1932). *Remembering: A study in experimental and social psychology.* Cambridge, England: Cambridge University Press.

Bartolomeo, P., Bachoud-Levi, A-C., De Gelder, B., Denes, G., Barba, G. D., Brugieres, P., et al. (1998). Multiple-domain dissociation between impaired visual perception and preserved mental imagery in a patient with bilateral extrastriate lesions. *Neuropsychologia, 36*(3), 239–249.

Bassok, M. (1996). Using content to interpret structure: Effects on analogical transfer. *Current Directions in Psychological Science, 5,* 54–57.

Bassok, M., & Novick, L. R. (2012). Problem solving. In K. J. Holyoak & R. G. Morrison (Eds.), *The Oxford handbook of thinking and reasoning* (pp. 413–432). New York, NY: Oxford University Press.

Bates, T. C., Lewis, G. J., & Weiss, A. (2013). Childhood socioeconomic status amplifies genetic effects on adult intelligence. *Psychological Science, 24,* 2111–2116.

Bates, T. C., & Shieles, A. (2003). Crystallized intelligence as a product of speed and drive for experience: The relationship of inspection time and openness to *g* and *Gc. Intelligence, 31,* 275–287.

Bauer, P. J. (2007). *Remembering the times of our lives: Memory in infancy and beyond.* Mahwah, NJ: Erlbaum.

Bayne, T., Hohwy, J., & Owen, A. M. (2016a). Are there levels of consciousness? *Trends in Cognitive Sciences, 20,* 405–413.

Bayne, T., Hohwy, J., & Owen, A. M. (2016b). Response to Fazekas and Overgaard: Degrees and levels. *Trends in Cognitive Sciences, 20,* 716–717.

Beach, C. M. (1991). The interpretation of prosodic patterns at points of syntactic structural ambiguity: Evidence for cue trading relations. *Journal of Memory and Language, 30,* 644–663.

Beaty, R. E., Silvia, P. J., Nusbaum, E. C., Jauk, E., & Benedek, M. (2014). The roles of associative and executive processes in creative cognition. *Memory & Cognition, 42,* 1186–1197.

Bechara, A., Damasio, H., & Damasio, A. R. (2003). Role of the amygdala in decision-making. *Annals of the New York Academy of Sciences, 985,* 356–369.

Bechara, A., Tranel, D., Damasio, H., Adolphs, R., Rockland, C., & Damasio, A. (1995). Double dissociation of conditioning and declarative knowledge relative to the amygdala and hippocampus in humans. *Science, 269,* 1115–1118.

Becker-Blease, K., & Freyd, J. J. (2017). Additional questions about the applicability of "false memory" research. *Applied Cognitive Psychology, 31,* 34–36.

Becklen, R., & Cervone, D. (1983). Selective looking and the noticing of unexpected events. *Memory & Cognition, 11,* 601–608.

Bédard, J., & Chi, M. (1992). Expertise. *Current Directions in Psychological Science, 1,* 135–139.

Begg, I., Anas, A., & Farinacci, S. (1992). Dissociation of processes in belief: Source recollection, statement familiarity, and the illusion of truth. *Journal of Experimental Psychology: General, 121,* 446–458.

Begg, I., Armour, V., & Kerr, T. (1985). On believing what we remember. *Canadian Journal of Behavioral Science, 17,* 199–214.

Behrmann, M. (2000). The mind's eye mapped onto the brain's matter. *Current Directions in Psychological Science, 9,* 50–54.

Behrmann, M., & Avidan, G. (2005). Congenital prosopagnosia: Face-blind from birth. *Trends in Cognitive Sciences, 9,* 180–187.

Behrmann, M., Peterson, M. A., Moscovitch, M., & Suzuki, S. (2006). Independent representation of parts and relations between them: Evidence from integrative agnosia. *Journal of Experimental Psychology: Human Perception and Performance, 32,* 1169–1184.

Behrmann, M., & Tipper, S. (1999). Attention accesses multiple reference frames: Evidence from visual neglect. *Journal of Experimental Psychology: Human Perception and Performance, 25,* 83–101.

Bekerian, D. A., & Baddeley, A. D. (1980). Saturation advertising and the repetition effect. *Journal of Verbal Learning & Verbal Behavior, 19,* 17–25.

Belli, R. B. (Ed.). (2012). *True and false recovered memories: Toward a reconciliation of the debate.* New York, NY: Springer.

Benjamin, L. (2008). *A history of psychology.* New York, NY: Wiley-Blackwell.

Berger, S. A., Hall, L. K., & Bahrick, H. P. (1999). Stabilizing access to marginal and submarginal knowledge. *Journal of Experimental Psychology: Applied, 5,* 438–447.

Berko, J. (1958). The child's learning of English morphology. *Word, 14,* 150–177.

Besken, M. (2016). Picture-perfect is not perfect for metamemory: Testing the perceptual fluency hypothesis with degraded images. *Journal of Experimental Psychology: Learning, Memory & Cognition, 42,* 1417–1433.

Besken, M., & Mulligan, N. W. (2014). Perceptual fluency, auditory generation, and metamemory: Analyzing the perceptual fluency hypothesis in the auditory modality. *Journal of Experimental Psychology: Learning, Memory, & Cognition, 40*(2), 429–440.

Besner, D., Risko, E. F., Stolz, J. A., White, D., Reynolds, M., O'Malley, S., & Robidoux, S. (2016). Varieties of attention: Their roles in word recognition. *Current Directions in Psychological Science, 25,* 162–168.

Bever, T. (1970). The cognitive basis for linguistic structures. In J. R. Hayes (Ed.), *Cognition and the development of language* (pp. 279–362). New York, NY: Wiley.

Bialystok, E., Craik, F., Green, D., & Gollan, T. (2009). Bilingual minds. *Psychological Science in the Public Interest, 10,* 89–129.

Bialystok, E., & Grundy, J. G. (2018). Science does not disengage. *Cognition, 170,* 330–333.

Biederman, I. (1987). Recognition by components: A theory of human image understanding. *Psychological Review, 94,* 115–147.

Biederman, I. (1990). Higher-level vision. In D. Osherson, S. Kosslyn, & J. Hollerbach (Eds.), *An invitation to cognitive science: Visual cognition and action* (Vol. 2, pp. 41–72). Cambridge, MA: MIT Press.

Biederman, I., & Shiffrar, M. M. (1987). Sexing day-old chicks: A case study and expert systems analysis of a difficult perceptual learning task. *Journal of Experimental Psychology: Learning, Memory & Cognition, 13,* 640–645.

Bindemann, M., Brown, C., Koyas, T., & Russ, A. (2012). Individual differences in face identification postdict eyewitness accuracy. *Journal of Applied Research in Memory & Cognition, 1,* 96–103.

Binder, J. R. (2016). In defense of abstract conceptual representations. *Psychonomic Bulletin & Review, 23,* 1096–1108.

Birch, S. A. J., Brosseau-Liard, P. E., Haddock, T., & Ghrear, S. E. (2017). A "curse of knowledge" in the absence of knowledge? People misattribute fluency when judging how common knowledge is among their peers. *Cognition, 166,* 447–458.

Bishop, D., & Norbury, C. F. (2008). Speech and language disorders. In M. Rutter, D. Bishop, D. Pine, S. Scott, J. Stevenson, E. Taylor, & A. Thapar (Eds.). *Rutter's child and adolescent psychiatry* (pp. 782–801). Oxford, England: Blackwell.

Bisiach, E., & Luzzatti, C. (1978). Unilateral neglect of representational space. *Cortex, 14,* 129–133.

Bisiach, E., Luzzatti, C., & Perani, D. (1979). Unilateral neglect, representational schema, and consciousness. *Brain, 102,* 609–618.

Blake, A. B., Nazarian, M., & Castel, A. D. (2015). The Apple of the mind's eye: Everyday attention, metamemory, and reconstructive memory for the Apple logo. *Quarterly Journal of Experimental Psychology, 68,* 858–865.

Bleckley, M. K., Foster, J. L., & Engle, R. W. (2015). Working memory capacity accounts for the ability to switch between object-based and location-based allocation of visual attention. *Memory & Cognition, 43,* 479–488.

Blinkhorn, S. (2005). A gender bender. *Nature, 438,* 31–32.

Block, N. (1997). Biology vs. computation in the study of consciousness. *Behavioral and Brain Sciences*, *20*, 1.

Block, N. (2005). Two neural correlates of consciousness. *Trends in Cognitive Sciences*, *9*, 46–52.

Block, N., Carmel, D., Fleming, S. M., Kentridge, R. W., Koch, C., Lamme, V. A. F., Lau, H., & Rosenthal, D. (2014). Consciousness science: Real progress and lingering misconceptions. *Trends in Cognitive Sciences*, *18*, 556–557.

Blount, G. (1986). Dangerousness of patients with Capgras Syndrome. *Nebraska Medical Journal*, *71*, 207.

Bobak, A. K., Hancock, P. J. B., & Bate, S. (2015). Super-recognisers in action: Evidence from face-matching and face memory tasks. *Applied Cognitive Psychology*, *30*, 81–91.

Bobrow, S., & Bower, G. H. (1969). Comprehension and recall of sentences. *Journal of Experimental Psychology*, *80*, 455–461.

Boduroglu, A., Shah, P., & Nisbett, R. E. (2010). Cultural differences in allocation of attention in visual information processing. *Journal of Cross-Cultural Psychology*, *40*, 349–360.

Bogen, J. E. (1995). On the neurophysiology of consciousness: I. An overview. *Consciousness & Cognition: An International Journal*, *4*, 52–62.

Boole, G. (1854). *An investigation of the laws of thought, on which are founded the mathematical theories of logic and probabilities*. London, England: Maberly.

Boone, A. P., & Hegarty, M. (2017). Sex differences in mental rotation tasks: Not just in the mental rotation process! *Journal of Experimental Psychology: Learning, Memory & Cognition*, *43*, 1005–1019.

Borges, J. L. (1964). *Labyrinths*. New York, NY: New Directions.

Borghi, A. M., Binkofski, F., Castelfranchi, C., Cimatti, F., Scorolli, C., & Tummolini, L. (2017). The challenge of abstract concepts. *Psychological Bulletin*, *143*, 263–292.

Bornstein, B. (1963). Prosopagnosia. In L. Halpern (Ed.), *Problems of dynamic neurology* (pp. 283–318). Jerusalem, Israel: Hadassah Medical Organization.

Bornstein, B., Sroka, H., & Munitz, H. (1969). Prosopagnosia with animal face agnosia. *Cortex*, *5*, 164–169.

Boroditsky, L. (2001). Does language shape thought? Mandarin and English speakers' conceptions of time. *Cognitive Psychology*, *43*, 1–22.

Boroditsky, L. (2011, February). How language shapes thought. *Scientific American*, 63–65.

Borst, G., Thompson, W., & Kosslyn, S. (2011). Understanding the dorsal and ventral systems of the human cerebral cortex. *American Psychologist*, *66*, 624–632.

Bottini, R., Bucur, M., & Crepaldi, D. (2016). The nature of semantic priming by subliminal spatial words: Embodied or disembodied? *Journal of Experimental Psychology: General*, *145*, 1160–1176.

Botvinick, M. M., Cohen, J. D., & Carter, C. S. (2004). Conflict monitoring and anterior cingulate cortex: An update. *Trends in Cognitive Sciences*, *8*, 539–546.

Bouchard, T. J., Jr., Lykken, D. T., McGue, M., Segal, N. L., & Tellegen, A. (1990). Sources of human psychological differences: The Minnesota study of twins reared apart. *Science*, *250*, 223–250.

Bourke, P. A., & Duncan, J. (2005). Effect of template complexity on visual search and dual-task performance. *Psychological Science*, *16*, 208–213.

Bowden, E., Jung-Beeman, M., Fleck, J., & Kounios, J. (2005). New approaches to demystifying insight. *Trends in Cognitive Sciences*, *9*, 322–328.

Bower, G. H. (1970). Analysis of a mnemonic device. *American Scientist*, *58*, 496–510.

Bower, G. H. (1972). Mental imagery and associative learning. In L. W. Gregg (Ed.), *Cognition in learning and memory* (pp. 51–88). New York, NY: Wiley.

Bower, G. H., Karlin, M. B., & Dueck, A. (1975). Comprehension and memory for pictures. *Memory & Cognition*, *3*, 216–220.

Bower, G. H., & Reitman, J. S. (1972). Mnemonic elaboration in multilist learning. *Journal of Verbal Learning and Verbal Behavior*, *11*, 478–485.

Bower, G. H., & Winzenz, D. (1970). Comparison of associative learning strategies. *Psychonomic Science*, *20*, 119–120.

Bower, J. M., & Parsons, L. M. (2003, August). Rethinking the "lesser brain." *Scientific American*, *289*, 50–57.

Bowles, B., Crupi, C., Mirsattari, S. M., Pigott, S. E., Parrent, A. G., Pruessner, J. C., Yonelinas, A., & Köhler, S. (2007). Impaired familiarity with preserved recollection after anterior temporal-lobe resection that spares the hippocampus. *Proceedings of the National Academy of Sciences*, *104*, 16382–16387.

Brackett, M. A., & Mayer, J. D. (2003). Convergent, discriminant, and incremental validity of competing measures of emotional intelligence. *Personality and Social Psychology Bulletin*, *29*, 1147–1158.

Bradfield Douglas, A., & Pavletic, A. (2012). Eyewitness confidence malleability. In B. L. Cutler (Ed.), *Conviction of the innocent: Lessons from psychological research* (pp. 149–165). Washington, DC: American Psychological Association.

Bransford, J. (1979). *Human cognition: Learning, understanding and remembering*. Belmont, CA: Wadsworth.

Bransford, J., & Franks, J. J. (1971). The abstraction of linguistic ideas. *Cognitive Psychology*, *2*, 331–350.

Bransford, J., & Johnson, M. K. (1972). Contextual prerequisites for understanding: Some investigations of comprehension and recall. *Journal of Verbal Learning and Verbal Behavior*, *11*, 717–726.

Bransford, J. D., Brown, A. L., & Cocking, R. R. (Eds.) (1999). *How people learn: Brain, mind, experience and school.* Washington, DC: National Academy Press.

Brase, G. (2008). Frequency interpretation of ambiguous statistical information facilitates Bayesian reasoning. *Psychonomic Bulletin & Review, 15,* 284–289.

Brewer, J., Zhao, Z., Desmond, J., Glover, G., & Gabrieli, J. (1998). Making memories: Brain activity that predicts how well visual experience will be remembered. *Science, 281,* 1185–1187.

Brewer, W., & Treyens, J. C. (1981). Role of schemata in memory for places. *Cognitive Psychology, 13,* 207–230.

Brewin, C. R., & Andrews, B. (2014). Why it is scientifically respectable to believe in repression: A response to Patihis, Ho, Tingen, Lilienfeld, and Loftus. *Psychological Science, 25,* 1964–1966.

Brewin, C. R., & Andrews, B. (2017). Creating memories for false autobiographical events in childhood: A systematic review. *Applied Cognitive Psychology, 31*(1), 2–23.

Brigham, J., & Cairns, D. L. (1988). The effect of mugshot inspections on eyewitness identification accuracy. *Journal of Applied Social Psychology, 18,* 1394–1410.

Broadbent, D. E. (1958). *Perception and communication.* London, England: Pergamon.

Bronfman, Z. Z., Brezis, N., Jacobson, H., & Usher, M. (2014). We see more than we can report: "Cost free" color phenomenality outside focal attention. *Psychological Science, 25,* 1394–1403.

Brown, A. S. (1991). A review of the tip-of-the-tongue experience. *Psychological Bulletin, 109,* 204–223.

Brown, A. S. (2002). Consolidation theory and retrograde amnesia in humans. *Psychonomic Bulletin & Review, 9,* 403–425.

Brown, A. S., & Halliday, H. E. (1990, November). *Multiple-choice tests: Pondering incorrect alternatives can be hazardous to your knowledge.* Paper presented at the meeting of the Psychonomic Society, New Orleans, LA.

Brown, A. S., & Marsh, E. (2008). Evoking false beliefs about autobiographical experience. *Psychonomic Bulletin & Review, 15,* 186–190.

Brown, A. S., & Murphy, D. R. (1989). Cryptomnesia: Delineating inadvertent plagiarism. *Journal of Experimental Psychology: Learning, Memory & Cognition, 15,* 432–442.

Brown, E., Deffenbacher, K., & Sturgill, W. (1977). Memory for faces and the circumstances of encounter. *Journal of Applied Psychology, 62,* 311–318.

Brown, J., Reynolds, J., & Braver, T. (2007). A computational model of fractionated conflict-control mechanisms in task-switching. *Cognitive Psychology, 55,* 37–85.

Brown, P. C., Roediger, H. L., & McDaniel, M. A. (2014). *Make it stick: The science of successful learning.* New York, NY: Belknap Press.

Brown, R., & Kulik, J. (1977). Flashbulb memories. *Cognition, 5,* 73–99.

Brown, R., & McNeill, D. (1966). The "tip of the tongue" phenomenon. *Journal of Verbal Learning and Verbal Behavior, 5,* 325–337.

Brown, T. (2005). *Attention deficit disorder: The unfocused mind in children and adults.* New Haven, CT: Yale University Press.

Bruce, V., & Young, A. W. (1986). Understanding face recognition. *British Journal of Psychology, 77,* 305–327.

Bruck, M., & Ceci, S. J. (2009). Developmental science in the courtroom. In S. Lilienfeld and J. Skeem (Eds.), *Psychological science in the courtroom: Controversies and consensus.* New York, NY: Guilford.

Bruck, M., Ceci, S. J., & Francoeur, E. (1999). The accuracy of mothers' memories for conversations with their preschool children. *Journal of Experimental Psychology, 5,* 89–106.

Bruner, J. S. (1973). *Beyond the information given.* New York, NY: Norton.

Bruyer, R. (2011). Configural face processing: A meta-analytic survey. *Perception, 40,* 1478–1490.

Buchanan, T. W. (2007). Retrieval of emotional memories. *Psychological Bulletin, 133,* 761–779.

Buchanan, T. W., & Adolphs, R. (2004). The neuroanatomy of emotional memory in humans. In D. Reisberg & P. Hertel (Eds.), *Memory and emotion* (pp. 42–75). New York, NY: Oxford University Press.

Bukach, C., Gauthier, I., & Tarr, M. J. (2006). Beyond faces and modularity: The power of an expertise framework. *Trends in Cognitive Sciences, 10,* 159–166.

Bullock, T. H., Bennett, M. V., Johnston, D., Josephson, R., Marder, E., & Fields, R. D. (2005). The neuron doctrine, redux. *Science, 310,* 791–793.

Bundesen, C., Kyllingsbaek, S., & Larsen, A. (2003). Independent encoding of colors and shapes from two stimuli. *Psychonomic Bulletin & Review, 10,* 474–479.

Burgess, G. C., Braver, T. S., Conway, A. R. A., & Gray, J. R. (2011). Neural mechanisms of interference control underlie the relationship between fluid intelligence and working memory span. *Journal of Experimental Psychology: General, 140,* 674–692.

Burton, A. M., Jenkins, R., & Schweinberg, S. R. (2011). Mental representations of familiar faces. *British Journal of Psychology, 102,* 943–958.

Burton, A. M., Schweinberger, S. R., Jenkins, R., & Kaufmann, J. M. (2015). Arguments against a configural processing account of familiar face recognition. *Perspectives on Psychological Science, 10,* 482–496.

Burton, A. M., Young, A., Bruce, V., Johnston, R., & Ellis, A. (1991). Understanding covert recognition. *Cognition, 39,* 129–166.

Burzzone, P. (2008). Religious aspects of organ transplantation. *Transplantation Proceedings, 40,* 1064–1067.

Buschman, T. J., & Miller, E. K. (2007). Top-down and bottom-up control of attention in the prefrontal and posterior parietal cortices. *Science, 315,* 1860.

Busey, T. A., Tunnicliff, J., Loftus, G. R., & Loftus, E. F. (2000). Accounts of the confidence-accuracy relation in recognition memory. *Memory & Cognition, 7,* 26–48.

Busigny, T., Graf, M., Mayer, E., & Rossion, B. (2010). Acquired prosopagnosia as a face-specific disorder: Ruling out the general visual similarity account. *Neuropsychologia, 48,* 2051–2067.

Butler, A. C., Rice, H. J., Wooldridge, C. L., & Rubin, D. C. (2016). Visual imagery in autobiographical memory: The role of repeated retrieval in shifting perspective. *Consciousness and Cognition, 42,* 237–253.

Butler, K., Arrington, C., & Weywadt, C. (2011). Working memory capacity modulates task performance but has little influence on task choice. *Memory & Cognition, 39,* 708–724.

Buzsáki, G., & Draguhn, A. (2004). Neuronal oscillations in cortical networks. *Science, 304,* 1926–1929.

Cabeza, R., & Moscovitch, M. (2012). Memory systems, processing modes, and components: Functional neuroimaging evidence. *Perspective on Psychological Science, 8,* 49–55.

Cabeza, R., & Nyberg, L. (2000). Imaging cognition II: An empirical review of 275 PET and fMRI studies. *Journal of Cognitive Neuroscience, 12,* 1–47.

Cabeza, R., & St. Jacques, P. (2007). Functional neuroimaging of autobiographical memory. *Trends in Cognitive Sciences, 11,* 219–227.

Calvo, A., & Bialystok, E. (2013). Independent effects of bilingualism and socioeconomic status on language ability and executive functioning. *Cognition, 130,* 278–288.

Campbell, R., Coleman, M., Walker, J., Benson, P. J., Wallace, S., Michelotti, J., & Baron-Cohen, S. (1999). When does the inner-face advantage in familiar face recognition arise and why? *Visual Cognition, 6,* 197–216.

Cann, A., & Ross, D. A. (1989). Olfactory stimuli as context cues in human memory. *American Journal of Psychology, 102,* 91–102.

Capgras, J., & Reboul-Lachaux, J. (1923). L'illusion des "sosies" dans un déliré systématisé chronique. *Bulletine de Société Clinique de Medicine Mentale, 11,* 6–16.

Cappiello, M., & Zhang, W. (2016). A dual-trace model for visual sensory memory. *Journal of Experimental Psychology: Human Perception & Performance, 42,* 1903–1922.

Caramazza, A., & Shelton, J. (1998). Domain-specific knowledge systems in the brain: The animate-inanimate distinction. *Journal of Cognitive Neuroscience, 10,* 1–34.

Carli, L. L. (1999). Cognitive reconstruction, hindsight, and reactions to victims and perpetrators. *Personality & Social Psychology Bulletin, 25,* 966–978.

Carlson, C. A., Young, D. F., Weatherford, D. R., Carlson, M. A., Bednarz, J. E., & Jones, A. R. (2016). The influence of perpetrator exposure time and weapon presence/timing on eyewitness confidence and accuracy. *Applied Cognitive Psychology, 30,* 898–910.

Carmichael, L. C., Hogan, H. P., & Walters, A. A. (1932). An experimental study of the effect of language on the reproduction of visually perceived form. *Journal of Experimental Psychology, 15,* 73–86.

Carmon, Z., & Ariely, D. (2000). Focusing on the foregone. *Journal of Consumer Research, 27,* 360–370.

Carpenter, A. C., & Schacter, D. L. (2017). Flexible retrieval: When true inferences produce false memories. *Journal of Experimental Psychology: Learning, Memory & Cognition, 43,* 335–349.

Carpenter, P., & Eisenberg, P. (1978). Mental rotation and the frame of reference in blind and sighted individuals. *Perception & Psychophysics, 23,* 117–124.

Carpenter, P. A., et al. (1999). Graded functional activation in the visuospatial system and the amount of task demand. *Journal of Cognitive Neuroscience, 11,* 14.

Carpenter, S., Pashler, H., & Cepeda, N. (2009). Using tests to enhance 8th grade students' retention of U.S. history facts. *Applied Cognitive Psychology, 23,* 760–771.

Carrasco, M., Ling, S., & Read, S. (2004). Attention alters appearance. *Nature Neuroscience, 7,* 308–313.

Carrasco, M., Penpeci-Talgar, C., & Eckstein, M. (2000). Spatial covert attention increases contrast sensitivity across the CSF: Support for signal enhancement. *Vision Research, 40,* 1203–1215.

Carreiras, M., Armstrong, B. C., Perea, M., & Frost, R. (2014). The what, when, where, and how of visual word recognition. *Trends in Cognitive Sciences, 18,* 90–98.

Carroll, J. B. (1993). *Human cognitive abilities: A survey of factor-analytic studies.* New York, NY: Cambridge University Press.

Carroll, J. B. (2005). The three-stratum theory of cognitive abilities. In D. P. Flanagan & P. L. Harrison (Eds.), *Contemporary intellectual assessment: Theories, tests, and issues* (2nd ed., pp. 69–76). New York, NY: Guilford.

Castel, A. D., Vendetti, M., & Holyoak, K. J. (2012). Fire drill: Inattentional blindness and amnesia for the location of fire extinguishers. *Attention, Perception and Psychophysics, 74,* 1391–1396.

Castelhano, M. S., & Henderson, J. M. (2008). Stable individual differences across images in human saccadic eye movement. *Canadian Journal of Experimental Psychology, 62,* 1–14.

Catrambone, R., Craig, D., & Nersessian, N. (2006). The role of perceptually represented structure in analogical problem solving. *Memory & Cognition, 34,* 1126–1132.

Cattell, J. M. (1885). Über die Zeit der Erkennung and Benennung von Schriftzeichen, Bildern and Farben. *Philosophische Studien, 2*, 635–650.

Cave, R. (2013). Spatial attention. In D. Reisberg (Ed.), *The Oxford handbook of cognitive psychology* (pp. 117–130). New York, NY: Oxford University Press.

Chabris, C., & Simons, D. (2010). *The invisible gorilla: How our intuitions deceive us.* New York, NY: Crown Archetype.

Chalmers, D. (1996). *The conscious mind.* New York, NY: Oxford University Press.

Chalmers, D. (1998). What is a neural correlate of consciousness? In T. Metzinger (Ed.), *Neural correlates of consciousness: Empirical and conceptual issues* (pp. 17–39). Cambridge, MA: MIT Press.

Chambers, D., & Reisberg, D. (1985). Can mental images be ambiguous? *Journal of Experimental Psychology: Human Perception and Performance, 11*, 317–328.

Chan, J., Paletz, S. B., & Schunn, C. D. (2012). Analogy as a strategy for supporting complex problem solving under uncertainty. *Memory & Cognition, 40*, 1352–1365.

Chao, L., Weisberg, J., & Martin, A. (2002). Experience-dependent modulation of category related cortical activity. *Cerebral Cortex, 12*, 545–551.

Chapman, J., & Chapman, L. J. (1959). Atmosphere effect re-examined. *Journal of Experimental Psychology, 58*, 220–226.

Charman, S. D., Wells, G. L., & Joy, S. W. (2011). The dud effect: Adding highly dissimilar fillers increases confidence in lineup identifications. *Law & Human Behavior, 35*, 479–500.

Charniak, E. (1972). *Toward a model of children's story comprehension.* Unpublished doctoral dissertation, Massachusetts Institute of Technology, Cambridge, MA.

Chase, W., & Ericsson, K. A. (1982). Skill and working memory. In G. H. Bower (Ed.), *The psychology of learning and motivation* (pp. 1–58). New York, NY: Academic Press.

Chase, W., & Simon, H. (1973). Perception in chess. *Cognitive Psychology, 4*, 55–81.

Chen, J.-Y. (2007). Do Chinese and English speakers think about time differently? Failure of replicating Boroditsky (2001). *Cognition, 104*, 427–436.

Chen, Z., & Cave, K. R. (2006). Reinstating object-based attention under positional certainty: The importance of subjective parsing. *Perception and Psychophysics, 68*, 992–1003.

Cheng, P., Holyoak, K. J., Nisbett, R. E., & Oliver, L. M. (1986). Pragmatic versus syntactic approaches to training deductive reasoning. *Cognitive Psychology, 18*, 293–328.

Cherry, E. C. (1953). Some experiments on the recognition of speech with one and with two ears. *Journal of the Acoustical Society of America, 25*, 975–979.

Chi, M. (1976). Short-term memory limitations in children: Capacity or processing deficits? *Memory & Cognition, 4*, 559–572.

Chi, M., Feltovich, P., & Glaser, R. (1981). Categorization and representation of physics problems by experts and novices. *Cognitive Science, 5*, 121–152.

Chincotta, D., & Underwood, G. (1997). Digit span and articulatory suppression: A cross-linguistic comparison. *European Journal of Cognitive Psychology, 9*, 89–96.

Choi, H.-Y., Kensinger, E. A., & Rajaram, S. (2017). Mnemonic transmission, social contagion, and emergence of collective memory. *Journal of Experimental Psychology: General, 146*, 1247–1265.

Chomsky, N. (1959). Review of B. F. Skinner, Verbal Behavior. *Language, 32*, 26–58.

Chomsky, N., & Halle, M. (1968). *The sound pattern of English.* New York, NY: Harper & Row.

Chow, M., & Conway, A. R. A. (2015). The scope and control of attention: Sources of variance in working memory capacity. *Memory & Cognition, 43*, 325–339.

Christen, F., & Bjork, R. A. (1976). *On updating the loci in the method of loci.* Paper presented at the meeting of the Psychonomic Society, St. Louis, MO.

Christensen, B. T., & Schunn, C. D. (2005). Spontaneous access and analogical incubation effects. *Creativity Research Journal, 17*, 207–220.

Christiaansen, R., Sweeney, J., & Ochalek, K. (1983). Influencing eyewitness descriptions. *Law and Human Behavior, 7*, 59–65.

Christophel, T. B., Klink, P. C., Spitzer, B., Roelfsema, P. R., & Haynes, J.-D. (2017). The distributed nature of working memory. *Trends in Cognitive Sciences, 21*, 111–124.

Chrobak, Q. M., & Zaragoza, M. S. (2008). Inventing stories: Forcing witnesses to fabricate entire fictitious events leads to freely reported false memories. *Psychonomics Bulletin and Review, 15*, 1190–1195.

Chrobak, Q. M., & Zaragoza, M. S. (2013). In A. Ridley, F. Gabbert, & D. J. La Rooy (Eds.), *Suggestibility in legal contexts: Psychological research and forensic implications* (pp. 21–44). New York, NY: Wiley.

Chrysikou, E. G., Csasanto, D., & Thompson-Schill, S. L. (2017). Motor experience influences object knowledge. *Journal of Experimental Psychology: General, 146*, 395–408.

Chuderski, A., & Jastrzębski, J. (2018). Much ado about aha! Insight problem solving is strongly related to working memory capacity and reasoning ability. *Journal of Experimental Psychology: General, 147*, 257–281.

Chun, W. Y., & Kruglanski, A. W. (2006). The role of task demands and processing resources in the use of base-rate and individuating information. *Journal of Personality and Social Psychology, 91*, 205–217.

Claparède, E. (1951). Reconnaissance et moitié. In D. Rapaport (Ed.), *Organization and pathology of thought* (pp. 58–75). New York, NY: Columbia University Press. (Original work published in 1911.)

Clark, H. H. (1996). *Using language.* Cambridge, England: Cambridge University Press.

Clark, I. A., & Maguire, E. A. (2016). Remembering preservation in hippocampal amnesia. *Annual Review of Psychology, 67,* 51–82.

Cochran, K. J., Greenspan, R. L., Bogart, D. F., & Loftus, E. F. (2016). Memory blindness: Altered memory reports lead to distortion in eyewitness memory. *Memory & Cognition, 44,* 717–726.

Cohen, G. L., Garcia, J., Apfel, N., & Master, A. (2006). Reducing the racial achievement gap: A social-psychological intervention. *Science, 313,* 1307–1310.

Cohen, G. L., Garcia, J., Purdie-Vaughns, V., Apfel, N., & Brzustoski, P. (2009). Recursive processes in self-affirmation: Intervening to close the minority achievement gap. *Science, 324,* 400–403.

Cohen, M., & Dennett, D. (2011). Consciousness cannot be separated from function. *Trends in Cognitive Sciences, 15,* 358–364.

Cohen, M. R. (2012). When attention wanders. *Science, 338,* 58–59.

Cohen, N. J., & Squire, L. R. (1980). Preserved learning and retention of pattern analyzing skill in amnesics: Dissociation of knowing how and knowing that. *Science, 210,* 207–210.

Coley, J. D., Medin, D. L., & Atran, S. (1997). Does rank have its privilege? Inductive inferences within folkbiological taxonomies. *Cognition, 64,* 73–112.

Collins, A. M., & Quillian, M. R. (1969). Retrieval time from semantic memory. *Journal of Verbal Learning and Verbal Behavior, 8,* 240–247.

Conrad, C. (1972). Cognitive economy in semantic memory. *Journal of Experimental Psychology, 92,* 149–154.

Conway, A. R., Cowan, N., & Bunting, M. F. (2001). The cocktail party phenomenon revisited: The importance of working memory capacity. *Psychonomic Bulletin & Review, 8,* 331–335.

Conway, M., Anderson, S., Larsen, S., Donnelly, C., McDaniel, M., McClelland, A. G. R., et al. (1994). The formation of flashbulb memories. *Memory & Cognition, 22,* 326–343.

Conway, M., Cohen, G., & Stanhope, N. (1991). On the very long-term retention of knowledge acquired through formal education: Twelve years of cognitive psychology. *Journal of Experimental Psychology: General, 120,* 395–409.

Conway, M., Cohen, G., & Stanhope, N. (1992). Why is it that university grades do not predict very long term retention? *Journal of Experimental Psychology: General, 121,* 382–384.

Conway, M., & Haque, S. (1999). Overshadowing the reminiscence bump: Memories of a struggle for independence. *Journal of Adult Development, 6,* 35–43.

Conway, M., & Holmes, A. (2004). Psychosocial stages and the accessibility of autobiographical memories across the life cycle. *Journal of Personality, 72,* 461–480.

Conway, M., & Pleydell-Pearce, C. W. (2000). The construction of autobiographical memories in the self-memory system. *Psychological Review, 107,* 261–288.

Conway, M., & Ross, M. (1984). Getting what you want by revising what you had. *Journal of Personality and Social Psychology, 39,* 406–415.

Conway, M. A., Wang, Q., Hanyu, K., & Haque, S. (2005). A cross-cultural investigation of autobiographical memory. *Journal of Cross-Cultural Psychology, 36,* 739–749.

Cooney, J. W., & Gazzaniga, M. S. (2003). Neurological disorders and the structure of human consciousness. *Trends in Cognitive Sciences, 7,* 161–165.

Cooper, L., & Shepard, R. N. (1973). Chronometric studies of the rotation of mental images. In W. G. Chase (Ed.), *Visual information processing* (pp. 75–176). New York, NY: Academic Press.

Corbetta, M., & Shulman, G. L. (2002). Control of goal-directed and stimulus-driven attention in the brain. *Nature Reviews Neuroscience, 3*(3), 201–215.

Corbetta, M., & Shulman, G. L. (2011). Spatial neglect and attention networks. *Annual Review of Neuroscience, 34,* 569–599.

Coricelli, G., Dolan, R., & Sirigu, A. (2007). Brain, emotion and decision making: The paradigmatic example of regret. *Trends in Cognitive Sciences, 11,* 258–265.

Corkin, S. (2013). *Permanent present tense: The unforgettable life of the amnesic patient, H. M.* New York, NY: Basic Books.

Corter, J., & Gluck, M. (1992). Explaining basic categories: Feature predictability and information. *Psychological Bulletin, 111,* 291–303.

Cosmides, L., & Tooby, J. (1996). Are humans good intuitive statisticians after all? Rethinking some conclusions from the literature on judgment. *Cognition, 58,* 1–73.

Costa, A., Hernández, M., Costa-Faidella, J., & Sebastián-Galés, N. (2009). On the bilingual advantage in conflict processing: Now you see it, now you don't. *Cognition, 113,* 135–149.

Courtney, S. M., Petit, L., Maisog, J. M., Ungerleider, L. G., & Haxby, J. V. (1998). An area specialized for spatial working memory in human frontal cortex. *Science, 279,* 1347–1351.

Cowan, R., & Carney, D. (2006). Calendrical savants: Exceptionality and practice. *Cognition, 100,* B1–B9.

Coyle, T., Pillow, D., Snyder, A., & Kochunov, P. (2011). Processing speed mediates the development of general intelligence (g) in adolescence. *Psychological Science, 22,* 1265–1269.

Craik, F. I. M., & Lockhart, R. S. (1972). Levels of processing: A framework for memory research. *Journal of Verbal Learning and Verbal Behavior, 11,* 671–684.

Craik, F. I. M., & Tulving, E. (1975). Depth of processing and the retention of words in episodic memory. *Journal of Experimental Psychology: General, 104,* 269–294.

Craik, F. I. M., & Watkins, M. J. (1973). The role of rehearsal in short-term memory. *Journal of Verbal Learning and Verbal Behavior, 12,* 599–607.

Crick, F., & Koch, C. (1990). Towards a neurobiological theory of consciousness. *Seminars in the Neurosciences, 2,* 263–275.

Crick, F., & Koch, C. (1995). Are we aware of neural activity in primary visual cortex? *Nature, 375,* 121–123.

Crick, F., & Koch, C. (2003). A framework for consciousness. *Nature Neuroscience, 6,* 119–126.

Crombag, H. F. M., Wagenaar, W. A., & van Koppen, P. J. (1996). Crashing memories and the problem of "source monitoring." *Applied Cognitive Psychology, 10,* 95–104.

Csibra, G., Davis, G., Spratling, M. W., & Johnson, M. H. (2000). Gamma oscillations and object processing in the infant brain. *Science, 290,* 1582–1585.

Cui, X., Jeter, C. B., Yang, D., Montague, P. R., & Eagleman, D. M. (2007). Vividness of mental imagery: Individual variability can be measured objectively. *Vision Research, 47,* 474–478.

Cummins, D. (1992). Role of analogical reasoning in induction of problem categories. *Journal of Experimental Psychology: Learning, Memory, & Cognition, 18,* 1103–1124.

Cummins, D. (2004). The evolution of reasoning. In J. P. Leighton & R. J. Sternberg (Eds.), *The nature of reasoning* (pp. 339–374). New York, NY: Cambridge University Press.

Cummins, D., & Allen, C. (Eds.). (1998). *The evolution of mind.* New York, NY: Oxford University Press.

Cunningham, C. A., & Egeth, H. E. (2016). Taming the white bear: Initial costs and eventual benefits of distractor inhibition. *Psychological Science, 27,* 476–485.

Custers, R., & Aarts, H. (2010). The unconscious will: How the pursuit of goals operates outside of conscious awareness. *Science, 329,* 47–50.

Daftary-Kapur, T., Penrod, S. D., O'Connor, M., & Wallace, B. (2014). Examining pretrial publicity in a shadow jury paradigm: Issues of slant, quantity, persistence and generalizability. *Law and Human Behavior, 38,* 462–477.

Dalenberg, C. J., Brand, B. L., Gleaves, D. H., Dorahy, M. J., Loewenstein, R. J., Cardeña, E., Frewen, P. A., Carlson, E. B., & Spiegel, D. (2012, March 12). Evaluation of the evidence for the trauma and fantasy models of dissociation. *Psychological Bulletin, 138,* 550–588.

Daley, T. C., Whaley, S. E., Sigman, M. D., Espinosa, M. P., & Neumann, C. (2003). IQ on the rise: The Flynn effect in rural Kenyan children. *Psychological Science, 14,* 215–219.

Dalton, P., & Fraenkel, N. (2012). Gorillas we have missed: Sustained inattentional deafness for dynamic events. *Cognition, 124,* 367–372.

Damasio, A. (1994). *Descartes' error: Emotion, reason, and the human brain.* London, England: Penguin.

Damasio, A. R. (1985). Disorders of complex visual processing. In M.-M. Mesulam (Ed.), *Principles of behavioral neurology.* Philadelphia, PA: Davis.

Damasio, A. R., Damasio, H., & Van Hoesen, G. W. (1982). Prosopagnosia: Anatomic basis and behavioral mechanisms. *Neurology, 32,* 331–341.

Damasio, A. R., Tranel, D., & Damasio, H. (1989). Disorders of visual recognition. In H. Goodglass & A. R. Damasio (Eds.), *Handbook of neuropsychology* (Vol. 2, pp. 317–332). New York, NY: Elsevier.

Damasio, A. R., Tranel, D., & Damasio, H. (1990). Face agnosia and the neural substrates of memory. *Annual Review of Neuroscience, 13,* 89–109.

Damasio, H., Grabowski, T., Tranel, D., Hichwa, R. D., & Damasio, A. R. (1996). A neural basis for lexical retrieval. *Nature, 380,* 499–505.

Daneman, M., & Hannon, B. (2001). Using working memory theory to investigate the construct validity of multiple-choice reading comprehension tests such as the SAT. *Journal of Experimental Psychology: General, 130,* 208–223.

Daniel, T. A., & Katz, J. S. (2017). Primacy and recency effects for taste. *Journal of Experimental Psychology: Learning, Memory & Cognition,* Advance online publication.

Daniloff, R., & Hammarberg, R. (1973). On defining coarticulation. *Journal of Phonetics, 1,* 185–194.

Danthiir, V., Roberts, R. D., Schulze, R., & Wilhelm, O. (2005). Mental speed: On frameworks, paradigms, and a platform for the future. In O. Wilhelm & R. W. Engle (Eds.), *Handbook of understanding and measuring intelligence* (pp. 27–46). Thousand Oaks, CA: Sage.

Dar-Nimrod, I., & Heine, S. (2006). Exposure to scientific theories affects women's math performance. *Science, 314,* 435.

Davachi, L., & Dobbins, I. (2008). Declarative memory. *Current Directions in Psychological Science, 17,* 112–118.

Davachi, L., Mitchell, J., & Wagner, A. (2003). Multiple routes to memory: Distinct medial temporal lobe processes build item and source memories. *Proceedings of the National Academy of Science, 100,* 2157–2162.

Davis, D., & Friedman, R. D. (2007). Memory for conversation: The orphan child of witness memory research. In R. C. L. Lindsay, D. F. Ross, J. D. Read, & M. P. Toglia (Eds.), *The handbook of eyewitness psychology: Vol. 2. Memory for people* (pp. 3–52). Mahwah, NJ: Erlbaum.

Davis, D., Loftus, E., Vanous, S., & Cucciare, M. (2008). "Unconscious transference" can be an instance of "change blindness." *Applied Cognitive Psychology, 22,* 605–623.

Davis, J. P., Lander, K., Evans, R., & Jansari, A. (2016). Investigating predictors of superior face recognition ability in police super-recognizers. *Applied Cognitive Psychology, 30*, 827–840.

Davis, O. S. P., Haworth, C. M. A., & Plomin, R. (2009). Dramatic increase in heritability of cognitive development from early to middle childhood: An 8-year longitudinal study of 8,700 pairs of twins. *Psychological Science, 20*, 1301–1308.

de Bruin, A., Treccani, B., & Della Salla, S. (2015). Cognitive advantage in bilingualism: An example of publication bias? *Psychological Science, 26*, 99–107.

de Gelder, B. (2010, May). Uncanny sight in the blind. *Scientific American*, 60–64.

de Groot, A. (1965). *Thought and choice in chess*. The Hague, Netherlands: Mouton.

de Groot, A. (1966). Perception and memory versus thought: Some old ideas and recent findings. In B. Kleinmuntz (Ed.), *Problem solving* (pp. 19–50). New York, NY: Wiley.

de Haan, E., & Cowey, A. (2011). On the usefulness of "what" and "where" pathways in vision. *Trends in Cognitive Sciences, 15*, 460–466.

De Neys, W. (2006). Dual processing in reasoning: Two systems but one reasoner. *Psychological Science, 17*, 428–433.

De Renzi, E., Faglioni, P., Grossi, D., & Nichelli, P. (1991). Apperceptive and associative forms of prosopagnosia. *Cortex, 27*, 213–221.

Deary, I. J. (2012). Intelligence. *Annual Review of Psychology, 63*, 453–482.

Deary, I. J. (2014). The stability of intelligence from childhood to old age. *Current Directions in Psychological Science, 23*, 239–245.

Deary, I. J., & Derr, G. (2005). Reaction time explains IQ's association with death. *Psychological Science, 16*, 64–69.

Deary, I. J., Pattie, A., & Starr, J. M. (2013). The stability of intelligence from age 11 to age 90: The Lothian birth cohort of 1921. *Psychological Science, 24*, 2361–2368.

Deary, I. J., Weiss, A., & Batty, G. D. (2010). Intelligence and personality as predictors of illness and death: How researchers in differential psychology and chronic disease epidemiology are collaborating to understand and address health inequalities. *Psychological Science in the Public Interest, 11*, 53–79.

Deese, J. (1957). Serial organization in the recall of disconnected items. *Psychological Reports, 3*, 577–582.

Deese, J., & Kaufman, R. A. (1957). Serial effects in recall of unorganized and sequentially organized verbal material. *Journal of Experimental Psychology, 54*, 180–187.

Deffenbacher, K., Bornstein, B., Penrod, S., & McCorty, E. (2004). A meta-analytic review of the effects of high stress on eyewitness memory. *Law and Human Behavior, 28*, 687–706.

Deffenbacher, K. A., Bornstein, B., & Penrod, S. (2006). Mugshot exposure effects: Retroactive interference, mugshot commitment, source confusion, and unconscious transference. *Law and Human Behavior, 30*, 287–307.

DeGutis, J., Wilmer, J., Mercado, R., & Cohan, S. (2013). Using regression to measure holistic face processing reveals a strong link with face recognition ability. *Cognition, 126*, 87–100.

deHaan, R. L. (2011). Teaching creative science thinking. *Science, 334*, 1499–1500.

Dehaene, S. (2014). *Consciousness and the brain: Deciphering how the brain codes our thoughts*. New York, NY: Penguin Books.

Dehaene, S., Artiges, E., Naccache, L., Martelli, C., Viard, A., Schurhoff, F., et al. (2003). Conscious and subliminal conflicts in normal subjects and patients with schizophrenia: The role of the anterior cingulate. *Proceedings of the National Academy of Sciences, USA, 100*, 13722–13727.

Dehaene S., & Changeux, J. (2011). Experimental and theoretical approaches to conscious processing. *Neuron, 70*, 200–227.

Dehaene, S., & Naccache, L. (2001). Toward a cognitive neuroscience of consciousness: Basic evidence and a workspace framework. *Cognition, 79*, 1–37.

Dehaene, S., Sergent, C., & Changeux, J. (2003). A neuronal network model linking subjective reports and objective physiological data during conscious perception. *Proceedings of the National Academy of Science, USA, 100*, 8520–8525.

Demonet, J. F., Wise, R. A., & Frackowiak, R. S. J. (1993). Language functions explored in normal subjects by positron emission tomography: A critical review. *Human Brain Mapping, 1*, 39–47.

Dempster, F. N. (1981). Memory span: Sources of individual and developmental differences. *Psychological Bulletin, 89*, 63–100.

Dennett, D. (1992). *Consciousness explained*. Boston, MA: Little, Brown.

Dennison, S. M., & Thomson, D. M. (2002). Identifying stalking: The relevance of intent in commonsense reasoning. *Law & Human Behavior, 26*, 543–561.

DePaulo, B., Lindsay, J., Malone, B., Muhlenbruck, L., Charlton, K., & Cooper, H. (2003). Cues to deception. *Psychological Bulletin, 129*, 74–118.

Devine, D. (2012). *Jury decision making: The state of the science*. New York, NY: New York University Press.

Dewar, M., Cowan, N., & Della Salla, S. (2010). Forgetting due to retroactive interference in amnesia. In S. Della Sala (Ed.), *Forgetting* (pp. 185–209). New York, NY: Taylor & Francis.

Diamond, A., & Lee, K. (2011). Interventions shown to aid executive function development in children from 4 to 12 years old. *Science, 333*, 959–964.

Diamond, R., & Carey, S. (1986). Why faces are and are not special: An effect of expertise. *Journal of Experimental Psychology: General, 115*, 107–117.

Diana, R., Yonelinas, A., & Ranganath, C. (2007). Imaging recollection and familiarity in the medial temporal lobe: A three-component model. *Trends in Cognitive Sciences, 11*, 379–386.

Dickens, W. T., & Flynn, J. R. (2006). Black Americans reduce the racial IQ gap: Evidence from standardization samples. *Psychological Science, 17*, 913–920.

Dickson, R., Pillemer, D., & Bruehl, E. (2011). The reminiscence bump for salient personal memories: Is a cultural life script required? *Memory & Cognition, 39*, 977–991.

Diemand-Yauman, C., Oppenheimer, D. M., & Vaughan, E. B. (2011). Fortune favors the **bold** (and the *italicized*): Effects of disfluency on educational outcomes. *Cognition, 118*, 111–115.

Dijksterhuis, A., & Strick, M. (2016). A case for thinking without consciousness. *Perspectives on Psychological Science, 11*, 117–132.

Dittrich, L. (2016, August 7). The untold story of the fight over the brain of "H.M."—the patient who revolutionized the science of memory. *The New York Times Magazine.*

Dobbins, I. G., Foley, H., Wagner, A. D., & Schacter, D. L. (2002). Executive control during episodic retrieval: Multiple prefrontal processes subserve source memory. *Neuron, 35*, 989–996.

Dodds, R. A., Ward, T. B., & Smith, S. M. (2007). A review of the experimental literature on incubation in problem solving and creativity. In M. Runco (Ed.), *Creative research handbook* (3rd ed.). Cresskill, NJ: Hampton.

Dodds, R. A., Ward, T. B., & Smith, S. M. (2012). A review of experimental literature on incubation in problem solving and creativity. In M. A. Runco (Ed.), *Creativity research handbook* (Vol. 3). Cresskill, NJ: Hampton Press.

Dohle, S., & Montoya, A. K. (2017). The dark side of fluency: Fluent names increase drug dosing. *Journal of Experimental Psychology: Applied, 23*, 231–239.

Donnelly, C. M., & McDaniel, M. A. (1993). Use of analogy in learning scientific concepts. *Journal of Experimental Psychology: Learning, Memory, & Cognition, 19*, 975–986.

Doré, B. P., Meksin, R., Mather, M., Hirst, W., & Ochsner, K. N. (2016). Highly accurate prediction of emotions surrounding the attacks of September 11, 2001. *Journal of Experimental Psychology: General, 145*, 788–795.

Dorek, K., Brooks, L., Weaver, B., & Norman, G. (2012). Influence of familiar features on diagnosis: Instantiated features in an applied setting. *Journal of Experimental Psychology: Applied, 18*, 109–125.

Douglas, A., Neuschatz, J., Imrich, J., & Wilkinson, M. (2010). Does post identification feedback affect evaluations of eyewitness testimony and identification procedures? *Law & Human Behavior, 34*, 282–294.

Dove, G. (2016). Three symbol ungrounding problems: Abstract concepts and the future of embodied cognition. *Psychonomic Bulletin & Review, 23*, 1109–1121.

Drew, T., Võ, M. H., & Wolfe, J. M. (2013). The invisible gorilla strikes again: Sustained inattentional blindness in expert observers. *Psychological Science, 24*, 1848–1853.

Drews, F. A., Pasupathi, M., & Strayer, D. L. (2008). Passenger and cell phone conversations in simulated driving. *Journal of Experimental Psychology: Applied, 14*, 392–400.

Dror, I. E., & Charlton, D. (2006). Why experts make errors. *Journal of Forensic Identification, 56*, 600–616.

Duchaine, B. C., & Nakayama, K. (2006). Developmental prosopagnosia: A window to content-specific face processing. *Current Opinion in Neurobiology, 16*, 166–173.

Duncan, J. (1994). Attention, intelligence, and the frontal lobes. In M. Gazzaniga (Ed.), *The cognitive neurosciences*. Cambridge, MA: MIT Press.

Duncan, J., Parr, A., Woolgar, A., Thompson, R., Bright, P., Cox, S., Bishop, S., & Nimmo-Smith, I. (2008). Goal neglect and Spearman's g: Competing parts of a complex task. *Journal of Experimental Psychology: General, 137*, 131–148.

Duncan, J., Schramm, M., Thompson, R., & Dumontheil, I. (2012). Task rules, working memory, and fluid intelligence. *Psychonomic Bulletin and Review, 19*, 864–870.

Duncker, K. (1945). *On problem-solving* (Psychological Monographs: General and Applied, Vol. 58, No. 5 [whole no. 270]). Washington, DC: American Psychological Association.

Dunlosky, J., & Bjork, R. A. (Eds.) (2008). *Handbook of metamemory and memory*. New York, NY: Psychology Press.

Dunn, B., Galton, H., Morgan, R., Evans, D., Oliver, C., Meyer, M., et al. (2010). Listening to your heart: How interoception shapes emotion experience and intuitive decision making. *Psychological Science, 21*, 1835–1844.

Dunning, D., & Parpal, M. (1989). Mental addition versus subtraction in counterfactual reasoning. *Journal of Personality and Social Psychology, 57*, 5–15.

Durgin, F. H. (2000). The reverse Stroop effect. *Psychonomic Bulletin & Review, 7*, 121–125.

Duyme, M., Dumaret, A. C., & Tomkiewicz, S. (1999). How can we boost IQs of "dull children"? A late adoption study. *Proceedings of the National Academy of Sciences, 96*, 8790–8794.

Dysart, J. E., Lawson, V. Z., & Rainey, A. (2012). Blind lineup administration as a prophylactic against the postidentification feedback effect. *Law & Human Behavior, 36*, 312–319.

Easterbrook, J. A. (1959). The effect of emotion on cue utilization and the organization of behavior. *Psychological Review, 66*, 183–201.

Eberhard, K. M., Spivey-Knowlton, M. J., Sedivy, J. C., & Tanenhaus, M. K. (1995). Eye movements as a window into real-time spoken language comprehension in natural contexts. *Journal of Psycholinguistic Research, 24,* 409–436.

Eberhardt, J. L., Dasgupta, N., & Banaszynski, T. L. (2003). Believing is seeing: The effects of racial labels and implicit beliefs on face perception. *Personality and Social Psychology Bulletin, 29,* 363–66.

Ecker, U., Lewandowsky, S., Chang, E. P., & Pillai, R. (2014). The effects of subtle misinformation in news headlines. *Journal of Experimental Psychology: Applied, 20,* 323–335.

Eddy, D. M. (1982). Probabilistic reasoning in clinical medicine: Problems and opportunities. In D. Kahneman, P. Slovic, & A. Tversky (Eds.), *Judgment under uncertainty: Heuristics and biases* (pp. 249–267). Cambridge, England: Cambridge University Press.

Edelson, M., Sharon, T., Dolan, R., & Dudai, Y. (2011). Following the crowd: Brain substrates of long-term memory conformity. *Science, 333,* 108–111.

Edelstyn, N. M. J., & Oyebode, F. (1999). A review of the phenomenology and cognitive neuropsychological origins of the Capgras Syndrome. *International Journal of Geriatric Psychiatry, 14,* 48–59.

Eich, J. E. (1980). The cue-dependent nature of state dependent retrieval. *Memory & Cognition, 8,* 157–173.

Eichenbaum, H. (2017). Memory: Organization and control. *Annual Review of Psychology, 68,* 19–45.

Eldridge, L. L., Knowlton, B. J., Furmanski, C. S., Bookheimer, S. Y., & Engel, S. A. (2000). Remembering episodes: A selective role for the hippocampus during retrieval. *Nature Neuroscience, 3,* 1149–1152.

Elliott, M. A., & Müller, H. J. (2000). Evidence for 40-Hz oscillatory short-term visual memory revealed by human reaction-time measurements. *Journal of Experimental Psychology: Learning, Memory, & Cognition, 26,* 7093–7718.

Ellis, H. D., & De Pauw, K. W. (1994). The cognitive neuropsychiatric origins of the Capgras delusion. In A. S. David & J. C. Cutting (Eds.), *The neuropsychology of schizophrenia* (pp. 317–335). Hillsdale, NJ: Erlbaum.

Ellis, H. D., & Lewis, M. B. (2001). Capgras delusion: A window on face recognition. *Trends in Cognitive Sciences, 5,* 149–156.

Ellis, H. D., & Young, A. (1990). Accounting for delusional misidentifications. *British Journal of Psychiatry, 157,* 239–248.

Elstein, A., Holzman, G., Ravitch, M., Metheny, W., Holmes, M., Hoppe, R., et al. (1986). Comparison of physicians' decisions regarding estrogen replacement therapy for menopausal women and decisions derived from a decision analytic model. *American Journal of Medicine, 80,* 246–258.

Engel, A. K., & Singer, W. (2001). Temporal binding and the neural correlates of sensory awareness. *Trends in Cognitive Sciences, 5,* 16–25.

Engel de Abreu, P. M. J., Cruz-Santos, A., Tourinho, C. J., Martion, R., & Bialystok, E. (2012). Bilingualism enriches the poor: Enhanced cognitive control in low-income minority children. *Psychological Science, 23,* 1364–1371.

Engle, R. W., & Kane, M. J. (2004). Executive attention, working memory capacity, and a two-factor theory of cognitive control. In B. Ross (Ed.), *The psychology of learning and motivation (Vol. 44,* pp. 145–199). New York, NY: Elsevier.

Enz, K. F., & Talarico, J. M. (2015). Forks in the road: Memories of turning points and transitions. *Applied Cognitive Psychology, 30,* 188–195.

Ericsson, K. A. (2003). Exceptional memorizers: Made, not born. *Trends in Cognitive Sciences, 7,* 233–235.

Ericsson, K. A., & Towne, T. J. (2012). Experts and their superior performance. In D. Reisberg (Ed.), *The Oxford handbook of cognitive psychology.* New York, NY: Oxford University Press.

Estes, Z. (2003). Domain differences in the structure of artifactual and natural categories. *Memory & Cognition, 31,* 199–214.

Evans, J. S. B. T. (1989). *Bias in human reasoning.* Hillsdale, NJ: Erlbaum.

Evans, J. S. B. T. (2006). The heuristic-analytic theory of reasoning: Extension and evaluation. *Psychonomics Bulletin & Review, 13,* 378–395.

Evans, J. S. B. T. (2012a). Dual-process theories of deductive reasoning: Facts and fallacies. In K. J. Holyoak & R. G. Morrison (Eds.), *The Oxford handbook of thinking and reasoning* (pp. 115–133). New York, NY: Oxford University Press.

Evans, J. S. B. T. (2012b). Reasoning. In D. Reisberg (Ed.), *The Oxford handbook of cognitive psychology.* New York, NY: Oxford University Press.

Evans, J. S. B. T., Newstead, S. E., & Byrne, R. M. J. (1993). *Human reasoning: The psychology of deduction.* London, England: Erlbaum.

Evans, K., Birdwell, R., & Wolfe, J. M. (2013). If you don't find it often, you often don't find it: Why some cancers are missed in breast cancer screening. *PLOS One, 8,* e64366.

Eysenck, M. W. (1982). *Attention and arousal: Cognition and performance.* Berlin, Germany: Springer.

Farah, M. J. (1985). Psychophysical evidence for a shared representational medium for mental images and percepts. *Journal of Experimental Psychology: General, 114,* 91–103.

Farah, M. J. (1990). *Visual agnosia: Disorders of object recognition and what they tell us about normal vision.* Cambridge, MA: MIT Press.

Farah, M. J., Hammond, K. M., Levine, D. N., & Calvanio, R. (1988). Visual and spatial mental imagery: Dissociable systems of representation. *Cognitive Psychology, 20,* 439–462.

Farah, M. J., & Smith, A. (1983). Perceptual interference and facilitation with auditory imagery. *Perception & Psychophysics*, *33*, 475–478.

Farah, M. J., Soso, M., & Dasheiff, R. (1992). Visual angle of the mind's eye before and after unilateral occipital lobectomy. *Journal of Experimental Psychology: Human Perception and Performance*, *18*, 241–246.

Farmer, G. D., Warren, P. A., & Hahn, U. (2017). Who "believes" in the Gambler's Fallacy and why? *Journal of Experimental Psychology: General*, *146*, 63–76.

Fawcett, J. M., Peace, K. A., & Greve, A. (2016). Looking down the barrel of a gun: What do we know about the weapon focus effect? *Journal of Applied Research in Memory and Cognition*, *5*, 257–263.

Fazekas, P., & Overgaard, M. (2016). Multidimensional models of degrees and levels of consciousness. *Trends in Cognitive Sciences*, *20*, 715–716.

Feldman, H., Goldin-Meadow, S., & Gleitman, L. (1978). Beyond Herodotus: The creation of language by linguistically deprived deaf children. In A. Lock (Ed.), *Action, gesture and symbol: The emergence of language* (pp. 351–414). New York, NY: Academic Press.

Fendrich, R., Wessinger, C. M., & Gazzaniga, M. S. (1992). Residual vision in a scotoma: Implications for blindsight. *Science*, *258*, 1489–1491.

Fenske, M. J., Raymond, J. E., Kessler, K., Westoby, N., & Tipper, S. P. (2005). Attentional inhibition has social-emotional consequences for unfamiliar faces. *Psychological Science*, *16*, 753–758.

Ferreira, M. B., Garcia-Marques, L., Sherman, S. J., & Sherman, J. W. (2006). Automatic and controlled components of judgment and decision making. *Journal of Personality & Social Psychology*, *91*, 797–813.

Fiedler, K., Walther, E., Armbruster, T., Fay, D., & Naumann, U. (1996). Do you really know what you have seen? Intrusion errors and presuppositions effects on constructive memory. *Journal of Experimental Social Psychology*, *2*, 484–511.

Finke, R., & Kosslyn, S. M. (1980). Mental imagery acuity in the peripheral visual field. *Journal of Experimental Psychology: Human Perception and Performance*, *6*, 126–139.

Finke, R., & Pinker, S. (1982). Spontaneous imagery scanning in mental extrapolation. *Journal of Experimental Psychology: Learning, Memory, & Cognition*, *8*, 142–147.

Finucane, M. L., Alhakami, A., Slovic, P., & Johnson, S. M. (2000). The affect heuristic in judgments of risks and benefits. *Journal of Behavioral Decision Making*, *13*, 1–17.

Fischhoff, B., Slovic, P., & Lichtenstein, S. (1978). Fault trees: Sensitivity of estimated failure probabilities to problem representation. *Journal of Experimental Psychology: Human Perception & Performance*, *4*, 330–344.

Fisher, R., & Schreiber, N. (2007). Interview protocols to improve eyewitness memory. In M. P. Toglia et al. (Eds.), *Handbook of eyewitness psychology*. Mahwah, NJ: Erlbaum.

Fisher, R. P., & Geiselman, R. E. (1992) *Memory-enhancing techniques in investigative interviewing: The cognitive interview*. Springfield, IL: C. C. Thomas.

Fisher, R. P., Milne, R., & Bull, R. (2011). Interviewing cooperative witnesses. *Current Directions in Psychological Science*, *20*, 16–19.

Fitousi, D. (2013). Mutual information, perceptual independence, and holistic face perception. *Attention, Perception, & Psychophysics*, *75*, 983–1000.

Flanagan, D. P., McGrew, K. S., & Ortiz, S. (2000). *The Wechsler Intelligence Scales and Gf-Gc Theory: A contemporary approach to interpretation*. Boston, MA: Allyn & Bacon.

Flavell, J. H. (1979). Metacognition and cognitive monitoring. A new area of cognitive-development inquiry. *American Psychologist*, *34*(10), 906–911.

Fleck, J. I., Beeman, M., & Kounios, J. (2012) Insight. In D. Reisberg (Ed.), *The Oxford handbook of cognitive psychology*. New York, NY: Oxford University Press.

Fleck, J. I., & Weisberg, R. W. (2004). The use of verbal protocols as data: An analysis of insight in the candle problem. *Memory & Cognition*, *32*, 990–1006.

Flusberg, S. J., & McClelland, J. L. (2017). Connectionism and the emergence of mind. In S. E. F. Chipman (Ed.), *The Oxford Handbook of Cognitive Science* (pp. 69–89). New York, NY: Oxford University Press.

Flynn, J. R. (1984). The mean IQ of Americans: Massive gains 1932 to 1978. *Psychological Bulletin*, *95*, 29–51.

Flynn, J. R. (1987). Massive IQ gains in 14 nations: What IQ tests really measure. *Psychological Bulletin*, *101*, 171–191.

Flynn, J. R. (1999). Searching for justice: The discovery of IQ gains over time. *American Psychologist*, *54*, 5–20.

Flynn, J. R. (2009). Requiem for nutrition as a cause of IQ gains: Raven's gains in Britain 1938–2008. *Economics & Human Biology*, *7*, 18–27.

Fong, G., Krantz, D., & Nisbett, R. (1986). The effects of statistical training on thinking about everyday problems. *Cognitive Psychology*, *18*, 253–292.

Fong, G., & Nisbett, R. (1991). Immediate and delayed transfer of training effects in statistical reasoning. *Journal of Experimental Psychology: General*, *120*, 34–45.

Fox, C. R. (2006). The availability heuristic in the classroom: How soliciting more criticism can boost your course ratings. *Judgment and Decision Making*, *1*, 86–90.

Fox, M. C., & Mitchum, A. L. (2013). A knowledge-based theory of rising scores on "cultural-free" tests. *Journal of Experimental Psychology: General*, *142*, 979–1000.

Franconeri, S. L. (2013). The nature and status of visual resources. In D. Reisberg (Ed.), *The Oxford handbook of cognitive psychology* (pp. 147–162). New York, NY: Oxford University Press.

Franconeri, S. L., Alvarez, G. A., & Cavanagh, P. (2013). Flexible cognitive resources: Competitive content maps for attention & memory. *Trends in Cognitive Sciences, 17*, 134–141.

Frederick, S. (2005). Cognitive reflection and decision making. *Journal of Economic Perspectives, 19*, 25–42.

Fredrickson, B. L. (2000). Extracting meaning from past affective experiences: The importance of peaks, ends, and specific emotions. *Cognition & Emotion, 14*(4), 577–606.

Frenda, S. J., Nichols, R. M., & Loftus, E. F. (2011). Current issues and advances in misinformation research. *Current Directions in Psychological Science, 20*, 20–23.

Freyd, J. J. (1996). *Betrayal trauma: The logic of forgetting childhood abuse.* Cambridge, MA: Harvard University Press.

Freyd, J. J. (1998). Science in the memory debate. *Ethics & Behavior, 8*, 101–113.

Friedman, A. (1979). Framing pictures: The role of knowledge in automatized encoding and memory for gist. *Journal of Experimental Psychology: General, 108*, 316–355.

Friedman, A., & Brown, N. R. (2000a). Reasoning about geography. *Journal of Experimental Psychology: General, 129*, 193–219.

Friedman, A., & Brown, N. R. (2000b). Updating geographical knowledge: Principles of coherence and inertia. *Journal of Experimental Psychology: Learning, Memory, & Cognition, 26*, 900–914.

Fries, P., Reynolds, J. H., Rorie, A. E., & Desimone, R. (2001). Modulation of oscillatory neural synchronization by selective visual attention. *Science, 291*, 1560–1563.

Frings, C., & Wühr, P. (2014). Top-down deactivation of interference from irrelevant spatial or verbal stimulus features. *Attention, Perception, & Psychophysics, 76*, 2360–2374.

Fukuda, K., Vogel, E., Mayr, U., & Awh, E. (2011). Quantity, not quality: The relationship between fluid intelligence and working memory capacity. *Psychonomic Bulletin & Review, 17*, 673–679.

Gabbert, F., & Hope, L. (2013). Suggestibility and memory conformity. In A. Ridley, F. Gabbert, & D. J. La Rooy (Eds.), *Suggestibility in legal contexts: Psychological research and forensic implications* (pp. 63–83). New York, NY: Wiley.

Gable, P. A., & Harmon-Jones, E. (2008). Approach-motivated positive affect reduces breadth of attention. *Psychological Science, 19*, 476–482.

Gainotti, G., & Marra, C. (2011). Differential contributions of right and left temporo-occipital and anterior temporal lesions to face recognition disorders. *Frontiers in Human Neuroscience, 5*, 55.

Gallistel, C. R. (2017). The coding question. *Trends in Cognitive Sciences, 21*, 498–508.

Gallo, D. A. (2010). False memories and fantastic beliefs: 15 years of the DRM illusion. *Memory & Cognition, 38*, 833–848.

Gallo, D. A., Roberts, M. J., & Seamon, J. G. (1997). Remembering words not presented in lists: Can we avoid creating false memories? *Psychonomic Bulletin & Review, 4*, 271–276.

Gallo, V., & Chitajullu, R. (2001). Unwrapping glial cells from the synapse: What lies inside? *Science, 292*, 872–873.

Galton, F. (1883). *Inquiries into human faculty.* London, England: Dent.

Gardiner, J. M. (1988). Functional aspects of recollective experience. *Memory & Cognition, 16*, 309–313.

Gardner, H. (1974). *The shattered mind: The person after brain damage.* New York, NY: Vintage.

Gardner, H. (1983). *Frames of mind: The theory of multiple intelligences.* New York, NY: Basic Books.

Gardner, H. (2006). *Multiple intelligences: New horizons in theory and practice.* New York, NY: Basic Books.

Garrett, B. (2011). *Convicting the innocent: Where criminal prosecutions go wrong.* Cambridge, MA: Harvard University Press.

Garrison, T. M., & Williams, C. C. (2013). Impact of relevance and distraction on driving performance and visual attention in a simulated driving environment. *Applied Cognitive Psychology, 27*, 396–405.

Garry, M., Manning, C. G., Loftus, E. F., & Sherman, S. J. (1996). Imagination inflation: Imagining a childhood event inflates confidence that it occurred. *Psychonomic Bulletin & Review, 3*, 208–214.

Gaspar, J. G., Street, W. N., Windsor, M. B., Carbonari, R., Kaczmarski, H., Kramer, A. F., & Mathewson, K. E. (2014). Providing views of the driving scene to drivers' conversation partners mitigates cell phone-related distraction. *Psychological Science, 25*, 2136–2146.

Gathercole, S. E., & Pickering, S. J. (2000). Assessment of working memory in six- and seven-year-old children. *Journal of Educational Psychology, 92*, 377–390.

Gauthier, I. L., Skudlarski, P., Gore, J. C., & Anderson, A. W. (2000). Expertise for cars and birds recruits brain areas involved in face recognition. *Nature Neuroscience, 3*, 191–197.

Gazzaniga, M. S., Fendrich, R., & Wessinger, C. M. (1994). Blindsight reconsidered. *Current Directions in Psychological Science, 3*, 93–96.

Gazzaniga, M. S., Ivry, R. B., & Mangun, G. R. (2014). *Cognitive neuroscience: The biology of the mind* (4th ed.). New York, NY: Norton.

Gelman, S., & Wellman, H. (1991). Insides and essences: Early understandings of the non-obvious. *Cognition, 38*, 213–244.

Gentner, D., & Smith, L. A. (2012). Analogical learning and reasoning. In D. Reisberg (Ed.), *The Oxford handbook of cognitive psychology.* New York, NY: Oxford University Press.

Georgopoulos, A. P. (1990). Neurophysiology of reaching. In M. Jeannerod (Ed.), *Attention and performance XIII: Motor representation and control* (pp. 227–263). Hillsdale, NJ: Erlbaum.

Georgopoulos, A. P. (1995). Motor cortex and cognitive processing. In M. S. Gazzaniga (Ed.) *The cognitive neurosciences* (pp. 507–517). Cambridge, MA: MIT Press.

Geraerts, E., Lindsay, D. S., Merckelbach, H., Jelicic, M., Raymaekers, L., Arnold, M. M., et al. (2009). Cognitive mechanisms underlying recovered-memory experiences of childhood sexual abuse. *Psychological Science, 20,* 92–99.

Gerlach, C., Law, I., & Paulson, O. B. (2002). When action turns into words. Activation of motor-based knowledge during categorization of manipulable objects. *Journal of Cognitive Neuroscience, 14,* 1230–1239.

German, T., & Barrett, H. C. (2005). Functional fixedness in a technologically sparse culture. *Psychological Science, 16,* 1–5.

Gernsbacher, M. A., & Kaschak, M. P. (2013). Text comprehension. In D. Reisberg (Ed.), *The Oxford handbook of cognitive psychology* (pp. 462–474). New York, NY: Oxford University Press.

Geschwind, N. (1970). The organization of language and the brain. *Science, 170,* 940–944.

Gibson, E. (2006). The interaction of top-down and bottom-up statistics in the resolution of syntactic category ambiguity. *Journal of Memory & Language, 54,* 363–388.

Gibson, E., Bishop, C., Schiff, W., & Smith, J. (1964). Comparison of meaningfulness and pronounceability as grouping principles in the perception and retention of verbal material. *Journal of Experimental Psychology, 67,* 173–182.

Gibson, J. J. (1950). *The perception of the visual world.* Boston, MA: Houghton Mifflin.

Gibson, J. J. (1966). *The senses considered as perceptual systems.* Boston, MA: Houghton Mifflin.

Gibson, J. J. (1979). *The ecological approach to visual perception.* Boston, MA: Houghton Mifflin.

Gick, M., & Holyoak, K. J. (1980). Analogical problem solving. *Cognitive Psychology, 12,* 306–355.

Giesbrecht, T., Lynn, S. J., Lilienfeld, S., & Merckelbach, H. (2008). Cognitive processes in dissociation: An analysis of core theoretical assumptions. *Psychological Bulletin, 134,* 617–647.

Gigerenzer, G. (1991). From tools to theories: A heuristic of discovery in cognitive psychology. *Psychological Review, 98,* 254–267.

Gigerenzer, G., & Gaissmaier, W. (2011). Heuristic decision making. *Annual Review of Psychology, 62,* 451–482.

Gigerenzer, G., Gaissmaier, W., Kurz-Milcke, E., Schwartz, L. M., & Woloshin, S. (2008). Helping doctors and patients make sense of health statistics. *Psychological Science in the Public Interest, 8,* 53–96.

Gigerenzer, G., Hell, W., & Blank, H. (1988). Presentation and content: The use of base rates as a continuous variable. *Journal of Experimental Psychology: Human Perception and Performance, 14,* 513–525.

Gigerenzer, G., & Hoffrage, U. (1995). How to improve Bayesian reasoning without instruction: Frequency formats. *Psychological Review, 102,* 684–704.

Gigerenzer, G., & Hug, K. (1992). Domain-specific reasoning: Social contracts, cheating and perspective change. *Cognition, 43,* 127–172.

Gilbert, D. T. (2006). *Stumbling on happiness.* New York, NY: Random House.

Gilbert, D. T., & Ebert, J. E. J. (2002). Decisions and revisions: The affective forecasting of changeable outcomes. *Journal of Personality and Social Psychology, 82,* 503–514.

Gilbert, S. J., & Shallice, T. (2002). Task switching: A PDP model. *Cognitive Psychology, 44,* 297–337.

Gilhooly, K. J., Georgiou, G. J., Garrison, J., Reston, J. D., & Sirota, M. (2012). Don't wait to incubate: Immediate versus delayed incubation in divergent thinking. *Memory & Cognition, 40,* 966–975.

Gilovich, T. (1983). Biased evaluation and persistence in gambling. *Journal of Personality & Social Psychology, 44,* 1110–1126.

Gilovich, T. (1991). *How we know what isn't so.* New York, NY: Free Press.

Gilovich, T., & Douglas, C. (1986). Biased evaluations of randomly determined gambling outcomes. *Journal of Experimental Social Psychology, 22,* 228–241.

Girotto, V. (2004). Task understanding. In J. P. Leighton & R. J. Sternberg (Eds.), *The nature of reasoning* (pp. 103–128). New York, NY: Cambridge University Press.

Giudice, N. A., Betty, M. R., & Loomis, J. M. (2011). Functional equivalence of spatial images from touch and vision: Evidence from spatial updating in blind and sighted individuals. *Journal of Experimental Psychology: Learning Memory, & Cognition, 37,* 621–634.

Giuditta, A. (2014). Sleep memory processing: The sequential hypothesis. *Frontiers in Systems Neuroscience, 8,* 219.

Glanzer, M., & Cunitz, A. R. (1966). Two storage mechanisms in free recall. *Journal of Verbal Learning and Verbal Behavior, 5,* 351–360.

Glass, A., & Sinha, N. (2013). Multiple-choice questioning is an efficient instructional methodology that may be widely implemented in academic courses to improve exam performance. *Current Directions in Psychological Science, 22,* 471–477.

Gleitman, H. (1963). Place-learning. *Scientific American, 209,* 116–122.

Gleitman, H., Gross, J., & Reisberg, D. (2011). *Psychology* (8th ed.). New York, NY: Norton.

Gleitman, L., & Papafragou, A. (2012). Relations between language and thought. In D. Reisberg (Ed.), *The Oxford handbook of cognitive psychology.* New York, NY: Oxford University Press.

Glisky, E. L., Polster, M. R., & Routhieaux, B. C. (1995). Double dissociation between item and source memory. *Neuropsychology, 9,* 229–235.

Godden, D. R., & Baddeley, A. D. (1975). Context-dependent memory in two natural environments: On land and underwater. *British Journal of Psychology*, 66, 325–332.

Godfrey, R. D., & Clark, S. E. (2010). Repeated eyewitness identification procedures: Memory, decision making, and probative value. *Law and Human Behavior*, 34, 241–258.

Goebel, R., Khorram-Sefat, D., Muckli, L., Hacker, H., & Singer, W. (1998). The constructive nature of vision: Direct evidence from functional magnetic resonance imaging studies of apparent motion and motion imagery. *European Journal of Neuroscience*, 10, 1563–1573.

Gold, P.-E., Cahill, L., & Wenk, G. L. (2002). Ginkgo biloba: A cognitive enhancer? *Psychological Science in the Public Interest*, 3, 2–11.

Goldenberg, G., Müllbacher, W., & Nowak, A. (1995). Imagery without perception—A case study of anosognosia for cortical blindness. *Neuropsychologia*, 33, 1373–1382.

Goldenberg, J., Mazursky, D., & Solomon, S. (1999). Creative sparks. *Science*, 285, 1495–1496.

Goldin-Meadow, S. (2003). *The resilience of language: What gesture creation in deaf children can tell us about how all children learn language*. New York, NY: Psychology Press.

Goldin-Meadow, S. (2017). What the hands can tell us about language emergence. *Psychonomic Bulletin & Review*, 24(1), 213–218.

Goldinger, S. D., Papesh, M. H., Barnhart, A. S., Hansen, W. A., & Hout, M. C. (2016). The poverty of embodied cognition. *Psychonomic Bulletin & Review*, 23, 959–978.

Goldman-Rakic, P. S. (1987). Development of cortical circuitry and cognitive function. *Child Development*, 58, 601–622.

Goldman-Rakic, P. S. (1998). The prefrontal landscape: Implications of functional architecture for understanding human mentation and the central executive. In A. C. Roberts & T. W. Robbins (Eds.), *The prefrontal cortex: Executive and cognitive functions* (pp. 87–102). New York, NY: Oxford University Press.

Goldsmith, S. F., & Morton, J. B. (2018). Time to disengage from the bilingual advantage hypothesis. *Cognition*, 170, 328–329.

Goldstein, N. E. S., Messenheimer, S., Riggs Romaine, C. L., & Zelle, H. (2012). Potential impact of juvenile suspects' linguistic abilities on Miranda understanding and appreciation. In P. Tiersman & L. Solan (Eds.), *Oxford handbook on linguistics and law* (pp. 299–311). New York, NY: Oxford University Press.

Goldstone, R. L, & Son, J. Y. (2012). Similarity. In K. J. Holyoak & R. G. Morrison (Eds.), *The Oxford handbook of thinking and reasoning* (pp. 155–176). New York, NY: Oxford University Press.

Gonthier, C., & Thomassin, N. (2015). Strategy use fully mediates the relationship between working memory capacity and performance on Raven's matrices. *Journal of Experimental Psychology: General*, 144, 916–924.

Goodale, M. A. (1995). The cortical organization of visual perception and visuomotor control. In S. M. Kosslyn & D. Osherson (Eds.), *Visual cognition: An invitation to cognitive science* (2nd ed., pp. 167–213). Cambridge, MA: MIT Press.

Goodale, M. A., & Milner, A. D. (2004). *Sight unseen*. New York, NY: Oxford University Press.

Goodale, M. A., Milner, A. D., Jacobson, L. S., & Carey, D. P. (1991). A neurological dissociation between perceiving objects and grasping them. *Nature*, 349, 154–156.

Goodman, G. S., Ghetti, S., Quas, J. A., Edelstein, R. S., Alexander, K. W., Redlich, A. D., et al. (2003). A prospective study of memory for child sexual abuse: New findings relevant to the repressed-memory controversy. *Psychological Science*, 14, 113–118.

Goodman, N. (1972). Seven strictures on similarity. In N. Goodman (Ed.), *Problems and projects* (pp. 437–446). New York, NY: Bobbs-Merrill.

Gordon, H. (1923). Mental and scholastic tests among retarded children. *Educational pamphlet, no. 44*. London, England: Board of Education.

Gordon, R. D. (2006). Selective attention during scene perception: Evidence from negative priming. *Memory & Cognition*, 34, 1484–1494.

Gottfredson, L. S. (1997). Why *g* matters: The complexity of everyday life. *Intelligence*, 24, 79–132.

Gottfredson, L. S. (2003). Dissecting practical intelligence theory: Its claims and evidence. *Intelligence*, 31, 343–397.

Gottfredson, L. S. (2004). Intelligence: Is it the epidemiologists' elusive "fundamental cause" of social class inequalities in health? *Journal of Personality and Social Psychology*, 86, 174–199.

Grady, R. H., Butler, B. J., & Loftus, E. F. (2016). What should happen after an officer-involved shooting? Memory concerns in police reporting procedures. *Journal of Applied Research in Memory and Cognition*, 5, 246–251.

Graesser, A. C., & Forsyth, C. M. (2013). Discourse comprehension. In D. Reisberg (Ed.), *The Oxford handbook of cognitive psychology* (pp. 475–491). New York, NY: Oxford University Press.

Graesser, A. C., Millis, K. K., & Zwaan, R. A. (1997). Discourse comprehension. *Annual Review of Psychology*, 48, 163–189.

Graf, P., Mandler, G., & Haden, P. E. (1982). Simulating amnesic symptoms in normals. *Science*, 218, 1243–1244.

Graf, P., & Schacter, D. L. (1985). Implicit and explicit memory for new associations in normal and amnesic subjects. *Journal of Experimental Psychology: Learning, Memory, & Cognition*, 11, 501–518.

Grainger, J., Rey, A., & Dufau, S. (2008). Letter perception: From pixels to pandemonium. *Trends in Cognitive Sciences, 12,* 381–387.

Grainger, J., & Whitney, C. (2004). Does the huamn mnid raed wrods as a wlohe? *Trends in Cognitive Sciences, 8,* 58–59.

Grant, H. M., Bredahl, L. C., Clay, J., Ferrie, J., Groves, J. E., McDorman, T. A., et al. (1998). Context-dependent memory for meaningful material: Information for students. *Applied Cognitive Psychology, 12,* 617–623.

Gray, J. R., Chabris, C. F., & Braver, T. S. (2003). Neural mechanisms of general fluid intelligence. *Nature Neuroscience, 6,* 316–322.

Greenberg, D. L., & Knowlton, B. J. (2014). The role of visual imagery in autobiographical memory. *Memory & Cognition, 42,* 922–934.

Greenfield, P. M. (2009). Technology and informal education: What is taught, what is learned. *Science, 323,* 69–71.

Gregg, M. K., & Samuel, A. G. (2008). Change deafness and the organizational properties of sounds. *Journal of Experimental Psychology: Human Perception & Performance, 34,* 974–991.

Grewal, D., & Salovey, P. (2005). Feeling smart: The science of emotional intelligence. *American Scientist, 93,* 330–339.

Grice, P. (1989). *Studies in the way of words.* Cambridge, MA: Harvard University Press.

Griffin, D. W., Gonzalez, R., Koehler, D. J., & Gilovich, T. (2012). Judgmental heuristics: A historical overview. In K. J. Holyoak & R. G. Morrison (Eds.), *The Oxford handbook of thinking and reasoning* (pp. 322–345). New York, NY: Oxford University Press.

Griggs, R., & Cox, J. R. (1982). The elusive thematic-materials effect in Wason's selection task. *British Journal of Psychology, 73,* 407–420.

Grigorenko, E. L., Jarvin, I., & Sternberg, R. J. (2002). School-based tests of the triarchic theory of intelligence. *Contemporary Educational Psychology, 27,* 167–208.

Grill-Spector, K., Knouf, N., & Kanwisher, N. (2004). The fusiform face area subserves face perception, not generic within-category identification. *Nature Neuroscience, 7,* 555–562.

Grodner, D., & Gibson, E. (2005). Consequences of the serial nature of linguistic input. *Cognitive Science, 29,* 261–291.

Gruber, H. E. (1981). *Darwin on man: A psychological study of scientific creativity* (2nd ed.). Chicago, IL: University of Chicago Press.

Guilford, J. (1967). *The nature of human intelligence.* New York, NY: Scribner.

Guilford, J. (1979). Some incubated thoughts on incubation. *Journal of Creative Behavior, 13,* 1–8.

Haber, R. N. (1969). Eidetic images. *Scientific American, 220,* 36–44.

Haber, R. N., & Haber, L. (1988). The characteristics of eidetic imagery. In D. Fein & L. Obler (Eds.), *The exceptional brain* (pp. 218–241). New York, NY: Guilford.

Hackman, D., & Farah, M. (2009). Socioeconomic status and the developing brain. *Trends in Cognitive Sciences, 13,* 65–73.

Hahn, B., Ross, T. J., & Stein, E. A. (2006). Neuroanatomical dissociation between bottom-up and top-down processes of visuospatial selective attention. *NeuroImage, 32,* 842–853.

Hahn, U., Prat-Sala, M., Pothos, E. M., & Brumby, D. P. (2010) Exemplar similarity and rule application. *Cognition, 114,* 1–18.

Halamish, V., & Bjork, R. (2011). When does testing enhance retention? A distribution-based interpretation of retrieval as a memory modifier. *Journal of Experimental Psychology: Learning, Memory, & Cognition, 37,* 801–812.

Halberstadt, J., & Rhodes, G. (2003). It's not just average faces that are attractive: Computer-manipulated averageness makes birds, fish, and automobiles attractive. *Psychonomic Bulletin & Review, 10,* 149–156.

Hale, R. G., Brown, J. M., & McDunn, B. A. (2016). Increasing task demand by obstructing recognition increases boundary extension. *Psychonomic Bulletin & Review, 23,* 1497–1503.

Halle, M. (1990). Phonology. In D. Osherson & H. Lasnik (Eds.), *Language: An invitation to cognitive science* (pp. 43–68). Cambridge, MA: MIT Press.

Halpern, D. (1984). *Thought and knowledge: An introduction to critical thinking.* Hillsdale, NJ: Erlbaum.

Hamann, S. (2001). Cognitive and neural mechanisms of emotional memory. *Trends in Cognitive Sciences, 5,* 394–400.

Hamill, R., Wilson, T. D., & Nisbett, R. E. (1980). Insensitivity to sample bias: Generalizing from atypical cases. *Journal of Personality and Social Psychology, 39,* 578–589.

Hampshire, A., Duncan, J., & Owen, A. M. (2007). Selective tuning of the blood oxygenation level-dependent response during simple target detection dissociates human frontoparietal subregions. *Journal of Neuroscience, 27(23),* 6219–6223.

Hanako, Y., & Smith, L. B. (2005). Linguistic cues enhance the learning of perceptual cues. *Psychological Science, 16,* 90–95.

Handel, S. (1989). *Listening: An introduction to the perception of auditory events.* Cambridge, MA: MIT Press.

Hardt, O., Einarsson, E., & Nader, K. (2010). A bridge over troubled water: Reconsolidation as a link between cognitive and neuroscientific memory research traditions. *Annual Review of Psychology, 61,* 141–168.

Hardt, O., Nader, K., & Nadel, L. (2013). Decay happens: The role of active forgetting in memory. *Trends in Cognitive Sciences, 17,* 111–120.

Harinck, F., Van Dijk, E., Van Beest, I., & Mersmann, P. (2007). When gains loom larger than losses: Reversed loss aversion for small amounts of money. *Psychological Science, 18,* 1099–1105.

Harley, T. A., & Bown, H. E. (1998). What causes a tip-of-the-tongue state? Evidence for lexical neighbourhood effects in speech production. *British Journal of Psychology, 89*(1), 151–174.

Harmon-Jones, E., Gable, P. A., & Price, T. F. (2013). Does negative affect always narrow and positive affect always broaden the mind? *Current Directions in Psychological Science, 22,* 301–307.

Harrison, T. L., Shipstead, Z., & Engle, R. W. (2015). Why is working memory capacity related to matrix reasoning tasks? *Memory & Cognition, 43,* 389–396.

Hartmann. P., Ramseier, A., Gudat, F., Mihatsch, M. J., Polasek, W., & Geisenhoff, C. (1994). Normal weight of the brain in adults in relation to age, sex, body height and weight. *Der Pathologe, 15,* 165–170.

Harvey, L. O., Jr., & Leibowitz, H. (1967). Effects of exposure duration, cue reduction, and temporary monocularity on size matching at short distances. *Journal of the Optical Society of America, 57,* 249–253.

Harwood, D. G., Barker, W. W., Ownby, R. L., & Duara, R. (1999). Prevalence and correlates of Capgras syndrome in Alzheimer's disease. *International Journal of Geriatric Psychiatry, 14,* 415–420.

Hasel, L. E., & Kassin, S. M. (2009). On the presumption of evidentiary independence: Can confessions corrupt eyewitness identifications? *Psychological Science, 20,* 122–126.

Hass, R. W. (2017). Tracking the dynamics of divergent thinking via semantic distance: Analytic methods and theoretical implications. *Memory & Cognition, 45,* 233–244.

Hassin, R. R. (2013). Yes it can: On the functional abilities of the human unconscious. *Perspectives on Psychological Science, 8,* 195–207.

Hayne, H. (2004). Infant memory development: Implications for childhood amnesia. *Developmental Review, 24,* 33–73.

Hayward, W., & Williams, P. (2000). Viewpoint dependence and object discriminability. *Psychological Science, 11,* 7–12.

Hayward, W. G. (2012). Whatever happened to object-centered representations? *Perception, 41,* 1153–1162.

Hayward, W. G., Crookes, K., Chu, M. H., Favelle, S. K., & Rhodes, G. (2016). Holistic processing of face configurations and components. *Journal of Experimental Psychology: Human Perception & Performance, 42,* 1482–1489.

Healy, A. F., Jones, M., Lalchandani, L. A., & Tack, L. A. (2017). Timing of quizzes during learning: Effects on motivation and retention. *Journal of Experimental Psychology: Applied, 23,* 128–137.

Heckman, J. J. (2006). Skill formation and the economics of investing in disadvantaged children. *Science, 312,* 1900–1902.

Hegarty, M. (2004). Mechanical reasoning by mental simulation. *Trends in Cognitive Sciences, 8,* 280–285.

Hegarty, M., & Stull, A. T. (2012). Visuospatial thinking. In K. J. Holyoak & R. G. Morrison (Eds.), *The Oxford handbook of thinking and reasoning* (pp. 606–630). New York, NY: Oxford University Press.

Heil, M., Rösler, F., & Hennighausen, E. (1993). Imagery-perception interaction depends on the shape of the image: A reply to Farah. *Journal of Experimental Psychology: Human Perception and Performance, 19,* 1313–1319.

Heine, S. J. (2015). *Cultural psychology* (3rd ed.). New York, NY: Norton.

Heit, E. (2000). Properties of inductive reasoning. *Psychonomic Bulletin & Review, 7,* 569–592.

Heit, E., & Bott, L. (2000). Knowledge selection in category learning. In D. L. Medin (Ed.), *The psychology of learning and motivation: Advances in research and theory* (Vol. 39, pp. 163–199). San Diego, CA: Academic Press.

Heit, E., & Feeney, A. (2005). Relations between premise similarity and inductive strength. *Psychonomic Bulletin & Review, 12,* 340–344.

Hélie, S., & Sun, R. (2010). Incubation, insight, and creative problem solving: A unified theory and a connectionist model. *Psychological Review, 117,* 994–1024.

Heller, M. A., & Gentaz, E. (2014). *Psychology of touch and blindness.* New York, NY: Taylor & Francis.

Helmholtz, H. (1909). *Wissenschaftliche Abhandlungen, II* (pp. 764–843). Leipzig, Germany: Barth.

Helmuth, L. (2001). Boosting brain activity from the outside in. *Science, 292,* 1284–1286.

Henderson, J. M. (2013). Eye movements. In D. Reisberg (Ed.), *The Oxford handbook of cognitive psychology* (pp. 69–82). New York, NY: Oxford University Press.

Henderson, J. M., & Hollingworth, A. (2003). Global transsaccadic change blindness during scene perception. *Psychological Science, 14,* 493–497.

Hennessey, B., & Amabile, A. (2010). Creativity. *Annual Review of Psychology, 61,* 569–598.

Herlitz, A., & Rehnman, J. (2014). Sex differences in episodic memory. *Current Directions in Psychological Science, 17,* 52–56.

Hermer-Vazquez, L., Spelke, E. S., & Katsnelson, A. S. (1999). Sources of flexibility in human cognition: Dual-task studies of space and language. *Cognitive Psychology, 39,* 3–36.

Hernández, M., Costa, A., & Humphreys, G. (2012). Escaping caption: Bilingualism modulates distraction from working memory. *Cognition, 122,* 37–50.

Hertwig, R., Herzog, S. M., Schooler, L. J., & Reimer, T. (2008). Fluency heuristic: A model of how the mind exploits a by-product of information retrieval.

Journal of Experimental Psychology: Learning, Memory, & Cognition, 34, 1191–1206.

Hertwig, R., & Ortmann, A. (2003). Economists' and psychologists' experimental practices: How they differ, why they differ, and how they could converge. In I. Brocas & J. D. Carrillo (Eds.), *The psychology of economic decisions: Rationality and well-being* (Vol. 1, pp. 253–272). New York, NY: Oxford University Press.

Hicks, J. L., & Marsh, R. L. (1999). Remember-Know judgments can depend on how memory is tested. *Psychonomic Bulletin & Review, 6,* 117–122.

Higbee, K. L. (1977). *Your memory: How it works and how to improve it.* Englewood Cliffs, NJ: Prentice-Hall.

Hilchey, M., & Klein, R. (2011). Are there bilingual advantages on nonlinguistic interference tasks? Implications for the plasticity of executive control processes. *Psychonomic Bulletin & Review, 18,* 625–658.

Hill, A. L. (1978). Savants: Mentally retarded individuals with specific skills. In N. R. Ellis (Ed.), *International review of research in mental retardation* (Vol. 9). New York: Academic Press.

Hillyard, S. A., Vogel, E. K., & Luck, S. J. (1998). Sensory gain control (amplification) as a mechanism of selective attention: Electrophysiological and neuroimaging evidence. *Philosophical Transactions of the Royal Society: Biological Sciences, 353,* 1257–1270.

Hilton, D. J. (2003). Psychology and the financial markets: Applications to understanding and remedying irrational decision-making. In I. Brocas & J. D. Carrillo (Eds.), *The psychology of economic decisions: Rationality and well-being* (Vol. 1, pp. 273–297). New York, NY: Oxford University Press.

Hilts, P. J. (1995). *Memory's ghost: The strange tale of Mr. M and the nature of memory.* New York, NY: Simon & Schuster.

Hirst, W., Coman, A., & Stone, C. B. (2012). Memory and jury deliberation: The benefits and costs of collective remembering. In L. Nadel & W. P. Sinnott-Armstrong (Eds.), *Memory and law* (pp. 161–184). New York, NY: Oxford University Press.

Hirst, W., Phelps, E., Buckner, R., Budson, A., Cuc, A., et al. (2009). Long-term memory for the terrorist attack of September 11: Flashbulb memories, event memories, and the factors that influence their retention. *Journal of Experimental Psychology: General, 138,* 161–176.

Hirst, W., & Phelps, E. A. (2016). Flashbulb memories. *Current Directions in Psychological Science, 25,* 36–41.

Hirst, W., Spelke, E., Reaves, C., Caharack, G., & Neisser, U. (1980). Dividing attention without alternation or automaticity. *Journal of Experimental Psychology: General, 109,* 98–117.

Hodges, J. R., & Graham, K. S. (2001). Episodic memory: Insights from semantic dementia.

In A. D. Baddeley, J. P. Aggleton, & M. A. Conway (Eds.), *Episodic memory: New directions in research* (pp. 132–152). New York, NY: Oxford University Press.

Holmberg, D., & Homes, J. G. (1994). Reconstruction of relationship memories: A mental models approach. In N. Schwarz & S. Sudman (Eds.), *Autobiographical memory and the validity of retrospective reports* (pp. 267–288). New York, NY: Springer.

Holtgraves, T. M. (2002). *Language as social action: Social psychology and language use.* New York, NY: Psychology Press.

Holway, A. F., & Boring, E. G. (1947). Determinants of apparent visual size with distance variant. *American Journal of Psychology, 54,* 21–37.

Holyoak, K. (2012). Analogy and relational reasoning. In K. J. Holyoak & R. G. Morrison (Eds.), *The Oxford handbook of thinking and reasoning* (pp. 234–259). New York, NY: Oxford University Press.

Hon, N., Epstein, R. A., Owen, A. M., & Duncan, J. (2006). Frontoparietal activity with minimal decision and control. *Journal of Neuroscience, 26*(38), 9805–9809.

Hope, L., Gabbert, F., & Fraser, J. (2013). Postincident conferring by law enforcement officers: Determining the impact of team discussions on statement content, accuracy, and officer beliefs. *Law & Human Behavior, 37,* 117–127.

Hope, L., Lewinski, H., Dixon, J., Blocksidge, D., & Gabbert, F. (2012). Witnesses in action: The effect of physical exertion on recall and recognition. *Psychological Science, 23,* 386–390.

Horn, J. L. (1985). Remodeling old models of intelligence. In B. B. Wolman (Ed.), *Handbook of intelligence: Theories, measurements, and applications* (pp. 267–300). New York: Wiley.

Horn, J. L., & Blankson, N. (2005). Foundations for better understanding of cognitive abilities. In D. Flanagan & P. Harrison (Eds.), *Contemporary intellectual assessment: Theories, tests, and issues* (2nd ed., pp. 41–68). New York: Guilford.

Horn, J. L., & Noll, J. (1994). A system for understanding cognitive capabilities: A theory and the evidence on which it is based. In D. K. Detterman (Ed.), *Current topics in human intelligence* (Vol. 4, *Theories of intelligence*). Norwood, NJ: Ablex.

Hornby, P. (1974). Surface structure and presupposition. *Journal of Verbal Learning and Verbal Behavior, 13,* 530–538.

Horrey, W. J., Lesch, M. F., & Garabet, A. (2008). Assessing the awareness of performance decrements in distracted drivers. *Accident Analysis & Prevention, 40,* 675–682.

Horry, R., Cheong, W., & Brewer, N. (2015). The other-race effect in perception and recognition: Insights from the complete composite task. *Journal of Experimental Psychology: Human Perception & Performance, 41,* 508–524.

Hoschedidt, S. M., Dongaonkar, B., Payne, J., & Nadel, L. (2012). Emotion, stress and memory. In D. Reisberg (Ed.), *The Oxford handbook of cognitive psychology*. New York, NY: Oxford University Press.

Howe, M. L. (2011). The adaptive nature of memory and its illusions. *Current Directions in Psychological Science, 20*, 312–315.

Howe, M. L., Courage M. L., and Rooksby, M. (2009). The genesis and development of autobiographical memory. In M. L. Courage & N. Cowan (Eds.), *The development of memory in infancy and childhood* (pp. 177–196). Hove, England: Psychology Press.

Hsee, C. K., & Hastie, R. (2005). Decision and experience: Why don't we choose what makes us happy? *Trends in Cognitive Sciences, 10*, 31–37.

Hsee, C. K., Hastie, R., & Chen, J. (2008). Hedonomics: Bridging decision research with happiness research. *Perspectives on Psychological Science, 3*, 224–243.

Hubel, D. (1963, November). The visual cortex of the brain. *Scientific American, 209*, 54–62.

Hubel, D., & Wiesel, T. (1959). Receptive fields of single neurones in the cat's visual cortex. *Journal of Physiology, 148*, 574–591.

Hubel, D., & Wiesel, T. (1968). Receptive fields and functional architecture of monkey striate cortex. *Journal of Physiology, 195*, 215–243.

Huey, E. D., Krueger, F., & Grafman, J. (2006). Representations in the human prefrontal cortex. *Current Directions in Psychological Science, 5*, 167–171.

Hummel, J. E. (2013). Object recognition. In D. Reisberg (Ed.), *The Oxford handbook of cognitive psychology* (pp. 32–45). New York, NY: Oxford University Press.

Hummel, J. E., & Biederman, I. (1992). Dynamic binding in a neural network for shape recognition. *Psychological Review, 99*, 480–517.

Humphreys, G., & Riddoch, J. (2014). *A case study in visual agnosia: To see but not to see.* New York, NY: Psychology Press.

Hung, J., Driver, J., & Walsh, V. (2005). Visual selection and posterior parietal cortex: Effects of repetitive transcranial magnetic stimulation on partial report analyzed by Bundesen's theory of visual attention. *Journal of Neuroscience, 25*(42), 9602–9612.

Hunt, E. (1995). *Will we be smart enough? A cognitive analysis of the coming workforce.* New York, NY: Russell Sage Foundation.

Hunt, R., & Ellis, H. D. (1974). Recognition memory and degree of semantic contextual change. *Journal of Experimental Psychology, 103*, 1153–1159.

Huntley, J., & Costanzo, M. (2003). Sexual harassment stories: Testing a story-mediated model of juror decision-making in civil litigation. *Law and Human Behavior, 27*, 29–51.

Huntsinger, J. R. (2012). Does positive affect broaden and negative affect narrow attentional scope? A new answer to an old question. *Journal of Experimental Psychology: General, 141*, 595–600.

Huntsinger, J. R. (2013). Does emotion directly tune the scope of attention? *Current Directions in Psychological Science, 22*, 265–270.

Husain, M., & Mehta, M. A. (2011). Cognitive enhancement by drugs in health and disease. *Trends in Cognitive Sciences, 15*, 28–36.

Husserl, E. (1931). *Ideas.* New York, NY: Collier.

Hutchison, K. A. (2003). Is semantic priming due to association strength or feature overlap? A microanalytic review. *Psychonomic Bulletin & Review, 10*, 785–813.

Hyde, T. S., & Jenkins, J. J. (1969). Differential effects of incidental tasks on the organization of recall of a list of highly associated words. *Journal of Experimental Psychology, 82*, 472–481.

Hyde, T. S., & Jenkins, J. J. (1973). Recall for words as a function of semantic, graphic, and syntactic orienting tasks. *Journal of Verbal Learning and Verbal Behavior, 12*, 471–480.

Hyman, I., Boss, M., Wise, B., McKenzie, K., & Caggiano, J. (2010). Did you see the unicycling clown? Inattentional blindness while walking and talking on a cell phone. *Applied Cognitive Psychology, 24*, 597–607.

Hyman, I. E., Jr. (2000). Creating false autobiographical memories: Why people believe their memory errors. In E. Winograd, R. Fivush, & W. Hirst (Eds.), *Ecological approaches to cognition: Essays in honor of Ulric Neisser.* Hillsdale, NJ: Erlbaum.

Hyman, I. E., Jr., Husband, T. H., & Billings, F. J. (1995). False memories of childhood experiences. *Applied Cognitive Psychology, 9*, 181–197.

Intons-Peterson, M. J. (1983). Imagery paradigms: How vulnerable are they to experimenters' expectations? *Journal of Experimental Psychology: Human Perception & Performance, 9*, 394–412.

Intons-Peterson, M. J. (1999). Comments and caveats about "scanning visual mental images." *Cahiers de Psychologie Cognitive, 18*, 534–540.

Intons-Peterson, M. J., & White, A. (1981). Experimenter naiveté and imaginal judgments. *Journal of Experimental Psychology: Human Perception and Performance, 7*, 833–843.

Intraub, H., & Bodamer, J. (1993). Boundary extension: Fundamental aspect of pictorial representation or encoding artifact? *Journal of Experimental Psychology: Learning, Memory, & Cognition, 19*, 1387–1397.

Intraub, H., & Dickinson, C. A. (2008). False memory 1/20th of a second later. *Psychological Science, 19*, 1007–1014.

Intraub, H., Gottesman, C. V., & Bills, A. J. (1998). Effects of perceiving and imagining scenes on memory for pictures. *Journal of Experimental Psychology: Learning, Memory, & Cognition, 24*, 1–16.

Intraub, H., Hoffman, J. E., Wetherhold, C. J., & Stoehs, S.-A. (2006). More than meets the eye: The effect of planned fixations on scene representation. *Perception and Psychophysics, 68*, 759–769.

Intraub, H., & Richardson, M. (1989). Wide-angle memories of close-up scenes. *Journal of Experimental Psychology: Learning, Memory, & Cognition, 15,* 179–187.

Isha, A., & Sagi, D. (1995). Common mechanisms of visual imagery and perception. *Science, 268,* 1772–1774.

Jackendoff, R. (1972). *Semantic interpretation in generative grammar.* Cambridge, MA: MIT Press.

Jacoby, L., & Hollingshead, A. (1990). Reading student essays may be hazardous to your spelling: Effects of reading incorrectly and correctly spelled words. *Canadian Journal of Psychology, 44,* 345–358.

Jacoby, L. L. (1978). On interpreting the effects of repetition: Solving a problem versus remembering a solution. *Journal of Verbal Learning and Verbal Behavior, 17,* 649–667.

Jacoby, L. L., & Dallas, M. (1981). On the relationship between autobiographical memory and perceptual learning. *Journal of Experimental Psychology: General, 3,* 306–340.

Jacoby, L. L., Jones, T. C., & Dolan, P. O. (1998). Two effects of repetition: Support for a dual process model of know judgments and exclusion errors. *Psychonomic Bulletin & Review, 5,* 705–709.

Jacoby, L. L., Kelley, C. M., Brown, J., & Jasechko, J. (1989). Becoming famous overnight: Limits on the ability to avoid unconscious influences of the past. *Journal of Personality and Social Psychology, 56,* 326–338.

Jacoby, L. L., Lindsay, D. S., & Hessels, S. (2003). Item-specific control of automatic processes: Stroop process dissociations. *Psychonomic Bulletin & Review, 10,* 638–644.

Jacoby, L. L., & Whitehouse, K. (1989). An illusion of memory: False recognition influenced by unconscious perception. *Journal of Experimental Psychology: General, 118,* 126–135.

Jacoby, L. L., & Witherspoon, D. (1982). Remembering without awareness. *Canadian Journal of Psychology, 36,* 300–324.

Jaeger, C. B., Levin, D. T., & Porter, E. (2017). Justice is (change) blind: Applying research on metacognition in legal settings. *Psychology, Public Policy, & Law, 23,* 259–279.

James, L. E., & Burke, D. M. (2000). Phonological priming effects on word retrieval and tip-of-the-tongue experiences in young and older adults. *Journal of Experimental Psychology: Learning, Memory, & Cognition, 26,* 1378–1391.

James, W. (1890). *The principles of psychology* (Vol. 2). New York, NY: Dover.

January, D., & Kako, E. (2007). Re-evaluating evidence for linguistic relativity: Reply to Boroditsky (2001). *Cognition, 104,* 417–426.

Jeffries, R., Polson, P., Razran, L., & Atwood, M. (1977). A process model for missionaries-cannibals and other river-crossing problems. *Cognitive Psychology, 9,* 412–440.

Jencks, C., & Phillips, M. (Eds). (1998). *The Black-White test score gap.* Washington, DC: Brookings Institution.

Jenkins, R., Lavie, N., & Driver, J. (2005). Recognition memory for distractor faces depends on attentional load at exposure. *Psychological Bulletin & Review, 12,* 314–320.

Jennings, D. L., Amabile, T. M., & Ross, L. (1982). Informal covariation assessment: Data-based versus theory-based judgments. In D. Kahneman, P. Slovic, & A. Tversky (Eds.), *Judgments under uncertainty: Heuristics and biases* (pp. 211–230). Cambridge, England: Cambridge University Press.

Jensen, A. R. (1985). The nature of the black-white difference on various psychometric tests: Spearman's hypothesis. *Behavioral and Brain Sciences, 8,* 193–263.

Jewsbury, P. A., Bowden, S. C., & Strauss, M. E. (2016). Integrating the switching, inhibition, and updating model of executive function with the Cattell-Horn-Carroll model. *Journal of Experimental Psychology: General, 145,* 220–245.

Joels, M., Fernandez, G., & Roosendaal, B. (2011). Stress and emotional memory: A matter of timing. *Trends in Cognitive Sciences, 15,* 280–288.

Johnson, E., & Goldstein, D. G. (2003). Do defaults save lives? *Science, 302,* 1338–1339.

Johnson, H., & Seifert, C. (1994). Sources of the continued influence effect: When misinformation affects later inferences. *Journal of Experimental Psychology: Learning, Memory, & Cognition, 20,* 1420–1436.

Johnson, M. K. (1988). Reality monitoring: An experimental phenomenological approach. *Journal of Experimental Psychology: General, 117,* 390–394.

Johnson, M. K., Hashtroudi, S., & Lindsay, S. (1993). Source monitoring. *Psychological Bulletin, 114,* 3–28.

Johnson, S. K., & Anderson, M. C. (2004). The role of inhibitory control in forgetting semantic knowledge. *Psychological Science, 15,* 448–453.

Johnson, W., Carothers, A., & Deary, I. J. (2008). Sex differences in variability in general intelligence. *Perspectives on Psychological Science, 3,* 518–531.

Johnson, W., Nijenhuis, J., & Bouchard, T. (2007). Replication of the hierarchical visual-perceptual-image rotation model in de Wolff and Buiten's (1963) battery of 46 tests of mental ability. *Intelligence, 35,* 69–81.

Johnson, W., Segal, N. L., & Bouchard, T. J., Jr. (2008). Heritability of fluctuating asymmetry in a human twin sample: The effect of trait aggregation. *American Journal of Human Biology, 20,* 651–658.

Johnson-Laird, P. N. (1988). A computational analysis of consciousness. In A. Marcel & E. Bisiach (Eds.), *Consciousness in contemporary science* (pp. 357–368). Oxford, England: Oxford University Press.

Johnston, J., & McClelland, J. (1973). Visual factors in word perception. *Perception & Psychophysics, 14*, 365–370.

Jones, J. L., Esber, G. R., McDannald, M. A., Gruber, A. J., Hernandez, A., Mirenzi, A., & Schoenbaum, G. (2012). Orbitofrontal cortex supports behavior and learning using inferred but not cached values. *Science, 338*, 953–956.

Jones, T. C., & Bartlett, J. C. (2009). When false recognition is out of control: The case of facial conjunctions. *Memory & Cognition, 37*, 143–157.

Jonides, J., Kahn, R., & Rozin, P. (1975). Imagery instructions improve memory in blind subjects. *Bulletin of the Psychonomic Society, 5*, 424–426.

Jung, R., & Haier, R. (2007). The parieto-frontal integration theory (P-FIT) of intelligence: Converging neuroimaging evidence. *Behavioral and Brain Sciences, 30*, 135–154.

Just, M., Carpenter, P. A., & Hemphill, D. D. (1996). Constraints on processing capacity: Architectural or implementational? In D. Steier & T. Mitchell (Eds.), *Mind matters: A tribute to Allen Newell* (pp. 141–178). Mahwah, NJ: Erlbaum.

Just, M. A., & Buchweitz, A. (2017). What brain imaging reveals about the nature of multitasking. In S. E. F. Chipman (Ed.), *The Oxford handbook of cognitive science* (pp. 265–279). New York, NY: Oxford University Press.

Kahneman, D. (1973). *Attention and effort.* Englewood Cliffs, NJ: Prentice-Hall.

Kahneman, D. (2003). A perspective on judgment and choice: Mapping bounded rationality. *American Psychologist, 58*, 697–720.

Kahneman, D. (2011). *Thinking, fast and slow.* New York, NY: Farrar, Straus and Giroux.

Kahneman, D., & Klein, G. (2009). Conditions for intuitive expertise: A failure to disagree. *American Psychologist, 64*, 515–526.

Kahneman, D., Knetsch, J. L., & Thaler, R. H. (1990). Experimental tests of the endowment effect and the Coase Theorem. *Journal of Political Economy, 98*, 1325–1348.

Kahneman, D., & Tversky, A. (1973). On the psychology of prediction. *Psychological Review, 80*, 237–251.

Kahney, H. (1986). *Problem solving: A cognitive approach.* Milton Keynes, England: Open University Press.

Kanaya, T., Scullin, M. H., & Ceci, S. (2003). The Flynn effect and U.S. policies: The impact of rising IQ scores on American society via mental retardation diagnoses. *American Psychologist, 58*, 778–790.

Kane, M. J., Conway, A., Hambrick, D., & Engle, R. (2007). Variation in working memory capacity as variation in executive attention and control. In A. Conway, K. Jarrold, M. Kane, A. Miyake, & J. Towse (Eds.), *Variation in working memory* (pp. 21–46). New York, NY: Oxford University Press.

Kane, M. J., & Engle, R. W. (2003). Working-memory capacity and the control of attention: The contributions of goal neglect, response competition, and task set to Stroop interference. *Journal of Experimental Psychology: General, 132*, 47–70.

Kanerva, K., & Kalakoski, V. (2016). The predictive utility of a working memory span task depends on processing demand and the cognitive task. *Applied Cognitive Psychology, 30*, 681–690.

Kanwisher, N. (2006). What's in a face? *Science, 311*, 617–618.

Kanwisher, N., McDermott, J., & Chun, M. M. (1997). The fusiform face area: A module in human extrastriate cortex specialized for face perception. *Journal of Neuroscience, 17*, 4302–4311.

Kanwisher, N., & Yovel, G. (2006). The fusiform face area: A cortical region specialized for the perception of faces. *Philosophical Transactions of the Royal Society of London B, 361*, 2109–2128.

Kaplan, A. S., & Murphy, G. L. (2000). Category learning with minimal prior knowledge. *Journal of Experimental Psychology: Learning, Memory, & Cognition, 26*, 829–846.

Kaplan, R. L., Van Damme, I., & Levine, L. J. (2012). Motivation matters: Differing effects of pre-goal and post-goal emotions on attention and memory. *Frontiers in Psychology, 3*, 404.

Karpicke, J., & Blunt, J. (2011). Retrieval practice produces more learning than elaborative studying with concept mapping. *Science, 331*, 772–775.

Karpicke, J. D. (2012). Retrieval-based learning: Active retrieval promotes meaningful learning. *Current Directions in Psychological Science, 21*, 157–163.

Kassin, S., Bogart, D., & Kerner, J. (2012). Confessions that corrupt: Evidence from the DNA exoneration cases. *Psychological Science, 23*, 1–5.

Kassin, S. M., Drizin, S. A., Grisso, T., Gudjonsson, G. H., Leo, R. A., & Redlich, A. D. (2010). Police-induced confessions, risk factors, and recommendations: Looking ahead. *Law and Human Behavior, 34*, 49–52.

Kassin, S. M., Dror, I. E., & Kukucka, J. (2013). The forensic confirmation bias: Problems, perspectives, and proposed solutions. *Journal of Applied Research in Memory and Cognition, 2*, 42–52.

Kassin, S. M., & McNall, K. (1991). Police interrogations and confessions. *Law and Human Behavior, 15*, 231–251.

Kastner, S., Schneider, K., & Wunderlich, K. (2006). Beyond a relay nucleus: Neuroimaging views on the human LGN. *Progress in Brain Research, 155*, 125–143.

Katona, G. (1940). *Organizing and memorizing.* New York, NY: Columbia University Press.

Kaufman, J. C., Kaufman, S. B., & Plucker, J. (2012). Contemporary theories of intelligence. In D. Reisberg (Ed.), *The Oxford handbook of cognitive psychology.* New York, NY: Oxford University Press.

Kay, K. N., Naselaris, T., Prenger, R. J., & Gallant, J. L. (2008). Identifying natural images from human brain activity. *Nature, 452*, 352–355.

Kay, P., & Regier, T. (2007). Color naming universals: The case of Berinmo. *Cognition, 102,* 289–298.

Keefe, P. R. (August, 2016). Total recall: The detectives who never forget a face. *The New Yorker.*

Keil, F. C. (1986). The acquisition of natural-kind and artifact terms. In W. Demopoulos & A. Marras (Eds.), *Language, learning, and concept acquisition* (pp. 133–153). Norwood, NJ: Ablex.

Keil, F. C. (1989). *Concepts, kinds, and cognitive development.* Cambridge, MA: MIT Press.

Keil, F. C. (2003). Folkscience: Coarse interpretations of a complex reality. *Trends in Cognitive Sciences, 7,* 368–373.

Kellenbach, M. L., Brett, M., & Patterson, K. (2003). Actions speak louder than functions: The importance of manipulability and action in tool representation. *Journal of Cognitive Neuroscience, 15,* 30–46.

Kelley, W. M., Macrae, C. N, Wyland, C. L., Cagalar, S., Inatai, S., & Heatherton, T. F. (2002). Finding the self? An event-related fMRI study. *Journal of Cognitive Neuroscience, 14,* 785–794.

Kensinger, E. (2007). Negative emotion enhances memory accuracy. *Current Directions in Psychological Science, 16,* 213–218.

Keogh, R., & Pearson, J. (2011). Mental imagery and visual working memory. *PLoS ONE, 6,* e29221.

Kermer, D., Driver-Linn, E., Wilson, T., & Gilbert, D. (2006). Loss aversion is an effective forecasting error. *Psychological Science, 17,* 649–653.

Kerr, N. H. (1983). The role of vision in "visual imagery" experiments: Evidence from the congenitally blind. *Journal of Experimental Psychology: General, 112,* 265–277.

Kerr, N. H., & Domhoff, G. W. (2004). Do the blind literally "see" in their dreams? A critique of a recent claim that they do. *Dreaming, 14,* 230–233.

Kershaw, T. C., & Ohlsson, S. (2004). Multiple causes of difficulty in insight: The case of the nine-dot problem. *Journal of Experimental Psychology: Learning, Memory, & Cognition, 30,* 3–13.

Kersten, A. W., & Earles, J. L. (2017). Feelings of familiarity and false memory for specific associations resulting from mugshot exposure. *Memory & Cognition, 45,* 93–104.

Keys, D., & Schwartz, B. (2007). "Leaky" rationality: How research on behavioral decision making challenges normative standards of rationality. *Perspectives on Psychological Science, 2,* 162–180.

Khlemani, S., & Johnson-Laird, P. N. (2012). Theories of the syllogism: A meta-analysis. *Psychological Bulletin, 138,* 427–457.

Kieras, D. E. (2017). A summary of the EPIC cognitive architecture. In S. E. F. Chipman (Ed.), *The Oxford handbook of cognitive science* (pp. 27–48). New York, NY: Oxford University Press.

Kihlstrom, J. F. (2006). Trauma and memory revisited. In B. Uttl, N. Ohta, & A. Siegenthaler (Eds.), *Memory and emotion: Interdisciplinary perspectives* (pp. 259–291). Malden, MA: Blackwell.

Kim, C.-Y., & Blake, R. (2005). Psychophysical magic: Rendering the visible "invisible." *Trends in Cognitive Sciences, 9,* 381–388.

Kim, N. S., & Ahn, W.-K. (2002). Clinical psychologists' theory-based representations of mental disorders predict their diagnostic reasoning and memory. *Journal of Experimental Psychology: General, 131,* 451–476.

Kimberg, D. Y., D'Esposito, M., & Farah, M. J. (1998). Cognitive functions in the prefrontal cortex in working memory and executive control. *Current Directions in Psychological Science, 6,* 185–192.

King, R. N., & Koehler, D. J. (2000). Illusory correlations in graphological inference. *Journal of Experimental Psychology: Applied, 6,* 336–348.

Klahr, D., & Simon, H. A. (2001). What have psychologists (and others) discovered about the process of scientific discovery? *Current Directions in Psychological Science, 10,* 75–79.

Klauer, K. C., & Zhao, Z. (2004). Double dissociations in visual and spatial short-term memory. *Journal of Experimental Psychology: General, 133,* 355–381.

Klayman, J., & Brown, K. (1993). Debias the environment instead of the judge: An alternative approach to reducing error in diagnostic (and other) judgment. *Cognition, 49,* 97–122.

Klein, R. (2013). *Seeing what others don't: The remarkable ways we gain insights.* New York, NY: PublicAffairs.

Knowlton, B., & Foerde, K. (2008). Neural representations of nondeclarative memories. *Current Directions in Psychological Science, 17,* 107–111.

Kocab, K., & Sporer, S. L. (2016). The weapon focus effect for person identifications and descriptions: A meta-analysis. In M. K. Miller & B. H. Bornstein (Eds.), *Advances in psychology and law* (Vol. 1, pp. 71–118). New York, NY: Springer.

Koch, C. (2008). The neuroscience of consciousness. In L. R. Squire, F. E. Bloom, N. C. Spiter, S. du Lac, A. Ghosh, & D. Berg (Eds.), *Fundamental neuroscience* (3rd ed., pp. 1223–1236). Burlington, MA: Academic Press.

Koehler, D. J. (2016). Can journalistic "false balance" distort public perception of consensus in expert opinion? *Journal of Experimental Psychology: Applied, 22,* 24–38.

Koehler, D. J., Brenner, L., & Griffin, D. W. (2002). The calibration of expert judgment: Heuristics and biases beyond the laboratory. In T. Gilovich, D. Griffin, & D. Kahneman (Eds.), *Heuristics and biases: The psychology of intuitive judgment* (pp. 686–715). New York, NY: Cambridge University Press.

Kolb, B., & Whishaw, I. Q. (2008). *Fundamentals of human neuropsychology.* New York, NY: Worth.

Kopelman, M. D., & Kapur, N. (2001). The loss of episodic memories in retrograde amnesia: Single-case and group studies. In A. D. Baddeley, J. P. Aggleton, & M. A. Conway (Eds.), *Episodic memory: New directions in research* (pp. 110–131). New York, NY: Oxford University Press.

Koppel, J., & Rubin, D. C. (2016). Recent advances in understanding the reminiscence bump: The importance of cues in guiding recall from autobiographical memory. *Current Directions in Psychological Science*, *25*, 135–140.

Kosslyn, S. M. (1976). Can imagery be distinguished from other forms of internal representation? Evidence from studies of information retrieval times. *Memory & Cognition, 4*, 291–297.

Kosslyn, S. M. (1980). *Image and mind*. Cambridge, MA: Harvard University Press.

Kosslyn, S. M. (1983). *Ghosts in the mind's machine*. New York, NY: Norton.

Kosslyn, S. M. (1994). *Image and brain: The resolution of the imagery debate*. Cambridge, MA: MIT Press.

Kosslyn, S. M., Ball, T. M., & Reiser, B. J. (1978). Visual images preserve metric spatial information: Evidence from studies of image scanning. *Journal of Experimental Psychology: Human Perception and Performance, 4*, 1–20.

Kosslyn, S. M., Pascual-Leone, A., Felician, O., Camposano, S., Keenan, J. P., Thompson, W. L., et al. (1999). The role of area 17 in visual imagery: Convergent evidence from PET and rTMS. *Science, 284*, 167–170.

Kosslyn, S. M., & Thompson, W. L. (1999). Shared mechanisms in visual imagery and visual perception: Insights from cognitive neuroscience. In M. S. Gazzaniga (Ed.), *The new cognitive neurosciences* (pp. 975–986). Cambridge, MA: MIT Press.

Kosslyn, S. M., & Thompson, W. L. (2003). When is early visual cortex activated during mental imagery? *Psychological Bulletin, 129*, 723–746.

Kouider, S., de Gardelle, V., Sackur, J., & Dupoux, E. (2010). How rich is consciousness? The partial awareness hypothesis. *Trends in Cognitive Sciences, 14*, 301–307.

Kounios, J., & Beeman, M. (2014). The cognitive neuroscience of insight. *Annual Review of Psychology, 65*, 71–93.

Kounios, J., & Beeman, M. (2015). *The Eureka factor*: Aha *moments, creative insight, and the brain*. New York, NY: Random House.

Kovelman, I., Shalinsky, M. H., Berens, M. S., & Petitto, L. (2008). Shining new light on the brain's "bilingual signature": A functional Near Infrared Spectroscopy investigation of semantic processing. *Neuroimage, 39*, 1457–1471.

Kozhevnikov, M., Kosslyn, S., & Shephard, J. (2005). Spatial versus object visualizers: A new characterization of visual cognitive style. *Memory & Cognition, 33*, 710–726.

Kraus, N., & Slater, J. (2016). Beyond words: How humans communicate through sound. *Annual Review of Psychology, 67*, 83–103.

Krauzlis, R. J., Bollimunta, A., Arcizet, F., & Wang, L. (2014). Attention as an effect not a cause. *Trends in Cognitive Sciences, 18*, 457–464.

Kroll, J. F., Bobb, S. C., & Hoshino, N. (2014). Two languages in mind: Bilingualism as a tool to investigate language, cognition, and the brain. *Current Directions in Psychological Science, 23*, 159–163.

Kroll, J. F., & Potter, M. C. (1984). Recognizing words, pictures, and concepts: A comparison of lexical, object, and reality decisions. *Journal of Verbal Learning and Verbal Behavior, 23*, 39–66.

Kubricht, J. R., Lu, H., & Holyoak, K. J. (2017). Individual differences in spontaneous analogical transfer. *Memory & Cognition, 45*, 576–588.

Kunar, M., Carter, R., Cohen, M., & Horowitz, T. (2008). Telephone conversation impairs sustained visual attention via a central bottleneck. *Psychonomic Bulletin & Review, 15*, 1135–1140.

Kuncel, N. R., Hezlett, S. A., & Ones, D. S. (2004). Academic performance, career potential, creativity, and job performance: Can one construct predict them all? *Journal of Personality and Social Psychology, 86*, 148–161.

Küpper, C. S., Benoid, R. G., Dalgleish, T., & Anderson, M. C. (2014). Direct suppression as a mechanism for controlling unpleasant memories in daily life. *Journal of Experimental Psychology: General, 143*, 1443–1449.

Kurtz, K., & Loewenstein, J. (2007). Converging on a new role for analogy in problem solving and retrieval: When two problems are better than one. *Memory & Cognition, 35*, 334–341.

LaBar, K. (2007). Beyond fear: Emotional memory mechanisms in the human brain. *Current Directions in Psychological Science, 16*, 173–177.

LaBar, K., & Cabeza, R. (2006). Cognitive neuroscience of emotional memory. *Nature Reviews Neuroscience, 7*, 54–64.

Labov, B. (2007). Transmission and diffusion. *Language, 83*, 344–387.

Labuschagne, E. M., & Besner, D. (2015). Automaticity revisited: When print doesn't activate semantics. *Frontiers in Psychology, 6*, 117.

Laeng, B., & Suluvedt, U. (2014). The eye pupil adjusts to imaginary light. *Psychological Science, 25*, 188–197.

Lai, C. S., Fisher, S. E., Hurst, J. A., Vargha-Khadem, F., & Monaco, A. P. (2001). A forkhead-domain gene is mutated in a severe speech and language disorder. *Nature, 413*, 519–522.

Lakoff, G. (1987). Cognitive models and prototype theory. In U. Neisser (Ed.), *Concepts and conceptual development* (pp. 63–100). Cambridge, England: Cambridge University Press.

Lamb, M. E., Orbach, Y., Sternberg, K. J., Hershkowitz, I., & Horowitz, D. (2000). Accuracy of investigators' verbatim notes of their forensic interviews with alleged child abuse victims. *Law and Human Behavior, 24*, 699–708.

Lamble, D., Kauranen, T., Laakso, M., & Summala, H. (1999). Cognitive load and detection thresholds in car following situations: Safety implications for using mobile (cellular) telephones while driving. *Accident Analysis & Prevention, 31,* 617–623.

Lamme V. A. F., & Roelfsema, P. R. (2000). The distinct modes of vision offered by feedforward and recurrent processing. *Trends in Neuroscience, 23,* 571–579.

Lampinen, J. M., Erickson, W. B., Moore, K. N., & Hittson, A. (2014). Effects of distance on face recognition: Implications for eyewitness identification. *Psychonomic Bulletin & Review, 21,* 1489–1494.

Lane, S. M., & Schooler, J. W. (2004). Skimming the surface: Verbal overshadowing of analogical retrieval. *Psychological Science, 15,* 715–719.

Laney, C. (2012). The sources of memory errors. In D. Reisberg (Ed.), *The Oxford handbook of cognitive psychology.* New York, NY: Oxford University Press.

Laney, C., & Loftus, E. F. (2010). False memory. In J. Brown & E. Campbell (Eds.), *The Cambridge handbook of forensic psychology* (pp. 187–194). Cambridge, England: Cambridge University Press.

Lange, N. D., Thomas, R. P., Dana, J., & Dawes, R. M. (2011). Contextual biases in the interpretation of auditory evidence. *Law & Human Behavior, 35,* 178–187.

Langer, E. (1989). *Mindfulness.* Reading, MA: Addison-Wesley.

Lanska, M., Olds, J. M., & Westerman, D. L. (2013). Fluency effects in recognition memory: Are perceptual fluency and conceptual fluency interchangeable? *Journal of Experimental Psychology: Learning, Memory, & Cognition, 40,* 1–11.

Lapate, R. C., Rokers, B., Li, T., & Davidson, R. J. (2014). Nonconscious emotional activation colors first impressions: A regulatory role for conscious awareness. *Psychological Science, 25,* 349–357.

Lau, H., & Rosenthal, D. (2011). Empirical support for higher-order theories of conscious awareness. *Trends in Cognitive Sciences, 15,* 365–373.

Laureys, S. (2005). The neural correlate of (un)awareness: Lessons from the vegetative state. *Trends in Cognitive Sciences, 9,* 556–559.

Lavie, N. (2001). Capacity limits in selective attention: Behavioral evidence and implications for neural activity. In J. Braun, C. Koch, & J. L. Davis (Eds.), *Visual attention and cortical circuits* (pp. 49–68). Cambridge, MA: MIT Press.

Lavie, N. (2005). Distracted and confused? Selective attention under load. *Trends in Cognitive Sciences, 9,* 75–82.

Lavie, N., Lin, Z., Zokaei, N., & Thoma, V. (2009). The role of perceptual load in object recognition. *Journal of Experimental Psychology: Human Perception & Performance, 35,* 1346–1358.

Layard, R. (2010). Measuring subjective well being. *Science, 327,* 534–535.

LeBoeuf, R. A., & Shafir, E. (2012). Decision making. In K. J. Holyoak & R. G. Morrison (Eds.), *The Oxford handbook of thinking and reasoning* (pp. 301–321). New York, NY: Oxford University Press.

Leh, S. E., Johansen-Berg, H., & Ptito, A. (2006). Unconscious vision: New insights into the neuronal correlate of blindsight using diffusion tractography. *Brain, 129,* 1822–1832.

Lehman, D. R., Lempert, R. O., & Nisbett, R. E. (1988). The effects of graduate training on reasoning: Formal discipline and thinking about everyday-life events. *American Psychologist, 43*(6), 431–442.

Lehman, D. R., & Nisbett, R. (1990). A longitudinal study of the effects of undergraduate education on reasoning. *Developmental Psychology, 26,* 952–960.

Leshinskaya, A., & Caramazza, A. (2016). For a cognitive neuroscience of concepts: Moving beyond the grounding issue. *Psychonomic Bulletin & Review, 23,* 991–1001.

Levin, D., Takarae, Y., Miner, A., & Keil, F. (2001). Efficient visual search by category: Specifying the features that mark the difference between artifacts and animals in preattentive vision. *Perception and Psychophysics, 63,* 676–697.

Levin, D. T., & Simons, D. J. (1997). Failure to detect changes to attended objects in motion pictures. *Psychonomic Bulletin and Review, 4,* 501–506.

Levin, I., & Gaeth, G. (1988). How consumers are affected by the framing of attribute information before and after consuming the product. *Journal of Consumer Research, 15,* 374–378.

Levin, I., Schnittjer, S., & Thee, S. (1988). Information framing effects in social and personal decisions. *Journal of Experimental Social Psychology, 24,* 520–529.

Levine, L. J. (1997). Reconstructing memory for emotions. *Journal of Experimental Psychology: General, 126,* 165–177.

Levine, L. J., & Edelstein, R. S. (2009). Emotion and memory narrowing: A review and goal relevance approach. *Cognition and Emotion, 23,* 833–875.

Levy, B. J., Kuhl, B. A., & Wagner, A. D. (2010). The functional neuroimaging of forgetting. In S. Della Sala (Ed.), *Forgetting* (pp. 135–163). New York, NY: Taylor & Francis.

Levy, J., & Pashler, H. (2008). Task prioritisation in multitasking during driving: Opportunity to abort a concurrent task does not insulate braking responses from dual-task slowing. *Applied Cognitive Psychology, 22,* 507–525.

Li, P., Abarbanell, L., Gleitman, L., & Papafragou, A. (2011). Spatial reasoning in Tenejapan Mayans. *Cognition, 120,* 33–53.

Li, P., & Gleitman, L. R. (2002). Turning the tables: Language and spatial reasoning. *Cognition, 83,* 265–294.

Liberman, A. (1970). The grammars of speech and language. *Cognitive Psychology, 1,* 301–323.

Liberman, A., Harris, K., Hoffman, H., & Griffith, B. (1957). The discrimination of speech sounds within and across phoneme boundaries. *Journal of Experimental Psychology, 54,* 358–368.

Lichtenstein, S., Slovic, P., Fischhoff, B., Layman, M., & Combs, B. (1978). Judged frequency of lethal events. *Journal of Experimental Psychology: Human Learning and Memory, 4,* 551–578.

Liesefeld, H. R., & Zimmer, H. D. (2013). Think spatial: The representation in mental rotation is nonvisual. *Journal of Experimental Psychology: Learning, Memory, & Cognition, 39,* 167–182.

Light, L. L., & Carter-Sobell, L. (1970). Effects of changed semantic context on recognition memory. *Journal of Verbal Learning and Verbal Behavior, 9,* 1–11.

Lindsay, D. S., Hagen, L., Read, J. D., Wade, K. A., & Garry, M. (2004). True photographs and false memories. *Psychological Science, 15,* 149–154.

Lindsay, D. S., & Hyman, I. E. (2017). Commentary on Brewin and Andrews. *Applied Cognitive Psychology, 31,* 37–39.

Lindsay, R. C. L., Semmler, C., Weber, N., Brewer, N., & Lindsay, M. R. (2008). How variations in distance affect eyewitness reports and identification accuracy. *Law and Human Behavior, 32,* 526–535.

Lisker, L., & Abramson, A. (1970). *The voicing dimension: Some experiments in comparative phonetics.* Paper presented at the Proceedings of the Sixth International Congress of Phonetic Sciences, Prague.

Lockhart, R. S., Craik, F. I. M., & Jacoby, L. (1976). Depth of processing, recall, and recognition. In J. Brown (Ed.), *Recall and recognition* (pp. 75–102). New York, NY: Wiley.

Loehlin, J. C., Lindzey, G., & Spuhler, J. N. (1975). *Race difference in intelligence.* San Francisco, CA: Freeman.

Loewenstein, G., & Schkade, D. (1999). Wouldn't it be nice? Predicting future feelings. In D. Kahneman, E. Diener, & N. Schwarz (Eds.), *Well-being: The foundations of hedonic psychology* (pp. 85–105). New York, NY: Russell Sage Foundation.

Loewenstein, G., Weber, E. U., Hsee, C. K., & Welch, N. (2001). Risk as feelings. *Psychological Bulletin, 127,* 267–286.

Loftus, E. F. (2003). Make-believe memories. *American Psychologist, 58,* 867–873.

Loftus, E. F. (2004). Memories of things unseen. *Current Directions in Psychological Science, 13,* 145–147.

Loftus, E. F. (2017). Eavesdropping on memory. *Annual Review of Psychology, 68,* 1–18.

Loftus, E. F., & Palmer, J. C. (1974). Reconstruction of automobile destruction: An example of the interaction between language and memory. *Journal of Verbal Learning and Verbal Behavior, 13,* 585–589.

Loftus, G. R., & Harley, E. M. (2005). Why is it easier to identify someone close than far away? *Psychonomic Bulletin and Review, 12,* 43–65.

Logie, R. H. (2012). Disorders of attention. In D. Reisberg (Ed.), *The Oxford handbook of cognitive psychology.* New York, NY: Oxford University Press.

Logie, R. H., & Cowan, N. (2015). Perspectives on working memory: Introduction to the special issue. *Memory & Cognition, 43,* 315–324.

Logie, R. H., & Della Salla, S. (2005). Disorders of visuospatial working memory. In P. Shah & A. Miyake (Eds.), *The Cambridge handbook of visuospatial thinking* (pp. 81–120). New York, NY: Cambridge University Press.

Lopes, P. N., Salovey, P., Côté, S., & Beers, M. (2005). Emotion regulation ability and the quality of social interaction. *Emotion, 5,* 113–118.

Lubinski, D. (2004). Introduction to the special section on cognitive abilities: 100 years after Spearman's (1904) "'General intelligence,' objectively determined and measured." *Journal of Personality and Social Psychology, 86,* 96–111.

Lucas, M. (2000). Semantic priming without association: A meta-analytic review. *Psychonomic Bulletin & Review, 7,* 618–630.

Luminet, O., & Curci, A. (Eds.). (2009). *Flashbulb memories: New issues and new perspectives.* New York, NY: Psychology Press.

Luria, A. R. (1966). *Higher cortical functions in man.* New York, NY: Basic Books.

Luria, A. R. (1968). *The mind of a mnemonist: A little book about a vast memory.* New York, NY: Basic Books.

Lynn, S., Neuschatz, J., Fite, R., & Rhue, J. (2001). Hypnosis and memory: Implications for the courtroom and psychotherapy. In M. Eisen & G. Goodman (Eds.), *Memory, suggestion, and the forensic interview.* New York, NY: Guilford Press.

MacDonald, J., & Lavie, N. (2008). Load induced blindness. *Journal of Experimental Psychology: Human Perception & Performance, 34,* 1078–1091.

MacDonald, M., Pearlmutter, N., & Seidenberg, M. (1994). The lexical nature of syntactic ambiguity. *Psychological Review, 101,* 676–703.

MacGregor, J. N., Ormerod, T. C., & Chronicle, E. P. (2001). Information processing and insight: A process model of performance on the 9-dot and related problems. *Journal of Experimental Psychology: Learning, Memory, & Cognition, 27,* 176–201.

Mack, A. (2003). Inattentional blindness: Looking without seeing. *Current Directions in Psychological Science, 12,* 180–184.

Mack, A., & Rock, I. (1998). *Inattentional blindness.* Cambridge, MA: MIT Press.

MacLean, C. L., Stinson, V., Kelloway, E. K., & Fisher, R. P. (2011). Improving workplace incident investigations by enhancing memory recall. *International Journal of Workplace Health Management, 4,* 257–273.

Mahon, B., & Caramazza, A. (2009). Concepts and categories: A cognitive neuropsychological perspective. *Annual Review of Psychology, 60,* 27–51.

Mahon, B., & Hickok, G. (2016). Arguments about the nature of concepts: Symbols, embodiment, and beyond. *Psychonomic Bulletin & Review, 23,* 941–958.

Maia, T. V., & Cleeremans, A. (2005). Consciousness: Converging insights from connectionist modeling and neuroscience. *Trends in Cognitive Sciences, 9,* 397–404.

Majid, A., Bowerman, M., Kita, S., Haun, D. B. M., & Levinson, S. (2004). Can language restructure cognition? The case for space. *Trends in Cognitive Sciences, 8,* 108–114.

Malone, J. C. (2009). *Psychology: Pythagoras to present.* Cambridge, MA: MIT Press.

Malt, B. C., & Smith, E. E. (1984). Correlated properties in natural categories. *Journal of Verbal Learning and Verbal Behavior, 23,* 250–269.

Mandler, G. (2011). *A history of modern experimental psychology.* Cambridge, MA: MIT Press.

Mandler, J. M., & Ritchey, G. H. (1977). Long-term memory for pictures. *Journal of Experimental Psychology: Human Learning and Memory, 3,* 386–396.

Marcus, G. B. (1986). Stability and change in political attitudes: Observe, recall, and "explain." *Political Behavior, 8,* 21–44.

Marcus, G. F. (2001). *The algebraic mind: Integrating connectionism and cognitive science (learning, development, and conceptual change).* Cambridge, MA: MIT Press.

Marcus, G. F., Pinker, S., Ullman, M., Hollander, M., Rosen, T., & Xu, F. (1992). *Overregularization in language acquisition* (Monographs of the Society for Research in Child Development, Vol. 57, No. 4 [serial no. 228]). Chicago, IL: University of Chicago Press.

Marcus, G. F., Vijayan, S., Rao, S. B., & Vishton, P. M. (1999). Rule learning by seven-month-old infants. *Science, 283,* 77–80.

Markman, A. B., & Gentner, D. (2001). Thinking. *Annual Review of Psychology, 52,* 223–247.

Markman, A. B., & Rein, J. R. (2013). The nature of mental concepts. In D. Reisberg (Ed.), *The Oxford handbook of cognitive psychology* (pp. 321–329). New York, NY: Oxford University Press.

Marmor, G. S., & Zabeck, L. A. (1976). Mental rotation by the blind: Does mental rotation depend on visual imagery? *Journal of Experimental Psychology: Human Perception and Performance, 2,* 515–521.

Marsh, R. L., Ward, T. B., & Landau, J. D. (1999). The inadvertent use of prior knowledge in a generative cognitive task. *Memory & Cognition, 27,* 94–105.

Marslen-Wilson, W. D., & Teuber, H. L. (1975). Memory for remote events in anterograde amnesia: Recognition of public figures from news photographs. *Neuropsychologia, 13,* 353–364.

Martin, R. C. (2003). Language processing: Functional organization and neuroanatomical basis. *Annual Review of Psychology, 54,* 55–89.

Masicampo, E., & Baumeister, R. (2008). Toward a physiology of dual-process reasoning and judgment: Lemonade, willpower, and expensive rule-based analysis. *Psychological Science, 19,* 255–260.

Massimini, M., Ferrarelli, F., Huber, R., Esser, S., Singh, H., & Tononi, G. (2005). Breakdown of cortical effective connectivity during sleep. *Science, 309,* 2228–2232.

Masuda, T., Ellsworth, P. C., Mesquita, B., Leu, J., Tanida, S., & van de Veerdonk, E. (2008). Placing the face in context: Cultural differences in the perception of facial emotion. *Journal of Personality and Social Psychology, 94,* 365–381.

Masuda, T., & Nisbett, R. E. (2006). Culture and change blindness. *Cognitive Science, 30,* 1–19.

Mattys, S. (2012). Speech perception. In D. Reisberg, (Ed.), *The Oxford handbook of cognitive psychology.* New York, NY: Oxford University Press.

Mayer, J. D., Roberts, R. D., & Barsade, S. G. (2008). Human abilities: Emotional intelligence. *Annual Review of Psychology, 59,* 507–536.

Mayer, R. E. (2012). Problem solving. In D. Reisberg (Ed.), *The Oxford handbook of cognitive psychology.* New York, NY: Oxford University Press.

Mayr, U. (2004). Conflict, consciousness, and control. *Trends in Cognitive Sciences, 8,* 145–148.

Mazzoni, G., Loftus, E. F., & Kirsch, I. (2001). Changing beliefs about implausible autobiographical events. *Journal of Experimental Psychology: Applied, 7,* 51–59.

Mazzoni, G., & Lynn, S. (2007). Using hypnosis in eyewitness memory. In D. Ross, M. Toglia, R. Lindsay, & D. Read (Eds.), *Handbook of eyewitness memory* (Vol. 1, *Memory for events*). Mahwah, NJ: Erlbaum.

Mazzoni, G., & Memon, A. (2003). Imagination can create false autobiographical memories. *Psychological Science, 14,* 186–188.

McAdams, C., & Reid, R. (2005). Attention modulates the responses of simple cells in the monkey visual cortex. *Journal of Neuroscience, 25,* 11022–11033.

McAlonan, K., Cavanaugh, J., & Wurtz, R. H. (2008). Guarding the gateway to cortex with attention in visual thalamus. *Nature, 456,* 391–394.

McCabe, J. A., Redick, T. S., & Engle, R. W. (2016). Brain-training pessimism, but applied memory optimism. *Psychological Science in the Public Interest, 17,* 187–191.

McCaffrey, T. (2012). Innovation relies on the obscure: A key to overcoming the classic problem of functional fixedness. *Psychological Science, 23,* 215–218.

McClelland, J. L., & Rumelhart, D. E. (1981). An interactive model of context effects in letter perception. Part 1: An account of basic findings. *Psychological Review, 88,* 375–407.

McDaniel, M., Anderson, J., Derbish, M., & Morrisette, N. (2007). Testing the testing effect in the classroom. *European Journal of Cognitive Psychology, 19,* 494–513.

McDaniel, M. A., Maier, S. F., & Einstein, G. O. (2002). "Brain-specific" nutrients: A memory cure? *Psychological Science in the Public Interest, 3*, 12–38.

McDermott, K. B., Agarwal, P. K., D'Antonio, L., Roediger, H. L., & McDaniel, M. A. (2014). Both multiple-choice and short-answer quizzes enhance later exam performance in middle and high school classes. *Journal of Experimental Psychology: Applied, 20*, 3–21.

McDermott, K. B., & Roediger, H. (1994). Effects of imagery on perceptual implicit memory tests. *Journal of Experimental Psychology: Learning, Memory, & Cognition, 20*, 1379–1390.

McDermott, K. B., & Roediger, H. (1998). False recognition of associates can be resistant to an explicit warning to subjects and an immediate recognition probe. *Journal of Memory & Language, 39*, 508–520.

McDunn, B. A., Siddiqui, A. P., & Brown, J. M. (2014). Seeking the boundary of boundary extension. *Psychonomic Bulletin & Review, 21*, 370–375.

McFarland, C., & Buehler, R. (2012). Negative moods and the motivated remembering of past selves: The role of implicit theories of personal stability. *Journal of Personality and Social Psychology, 102*, 242–263.

McGaugh, J. L. (2015). Consolidating memories. *Annual Review of Psychology, 66*, 1–24.

McGaugh, J. L., & LePort, A. (2014, February). Remembrance of all things past. *Scientific American*, 41–45.

McGrew, K. (2009). CHC theory and the human cognitive abilities project: Standing on the shoulders of the giants of psychometric intelligence research. *Intelligence, 37*, 1–10.

McGue, M., Bouchard, T. J., Jr., Iacono, W. G., & Lykken, D. T. (1993). Behavioral genetics of cognitive ability: A life span perspective. In R. Plomin & G. E. McClearn (Eds.), *Nature, nurture and psychology* (pp. 59–76). Washington, DC: American Psychological Association.

McGugin, R. W., Gatenby, J. C., Gore, J. C., & Gauthier, I. (2012). High-resolution imaging of expertise reveals reliable object selectivity in the fusiform face area related to perceptual performance. *Proceedings of the National Academy of Sciences, 109*, 17063–17068.

McGurk, H., & MacDonald, J. (1976). Hearing lips and seeing voices. *Nature, 264*, 746–748.

McIntosh, A. R., Rajah, M. N., & Lobaugh, N. J. (1999). Interactions of prefrontal cortex in relation to awareness in sensory learning. *Science, 284*, 1531–1533.

McKelvie, S. (1995). The VVIQ as a psychometric test of individual differences in visual imagery vividness: A critical quantitative review and plea for direction. *Journal of Mental Imagery, 19*(3&4), 1–106.

McKone, E., Kanwisher, N., & Duchaine, B. C. (2007). Can generic expertise explain special processing for faces? *Trends in Cognitive Sciences, 11*, 8–15.

McNally, R. (2017). False memories in the laboratory and in life. Commentary on Brewin & Andrews (2017) *Applied Cognitive Psychology, 31*, 40–41.

McNally, R. J. (2003). Recovering memories of trauma: A view from the laboratory. *Current Directions in Psychological Science, 12*, 32–35.

McNally, R. J., Lasko, N., Clancy, S. A., Macklin, M. L., Pitman, R. K., & Orr, S. P. (2004). Psychophysiological responding during script-driven imagery in people reporting abduction by space aliens. *Psychological Science, 15*, 493–497.

McRae, K., & Jones, M. (2012). Semantic memory. In D. Reisberg (Ed.), *The Oxford handbook of cognitive psychology*. New York, NY: Oxford University Press.

Meadows, J. C. (1974). Disturbed perception of colours associated with localized cerebral lesions. *Brain, 97*, 615–632.

Medeiros-Ward, N., Watson, J. M., & Strayer, D. L. (2015). On supertaskers and the neural basis of efficient multitasking. *Psychonomic Bulletin & Review, 22*, 876–883.

Medin, D. L. (1989). Concepts and conceptual structure. *American Psychologist, 44*, 1469–1481.

Medin, D. L., Coley, J. D., Storms, G., & Hayes, B. K. (2003). A relevance theory of induction. *Psychonomic Bulletin & Review, 10*, 517–532.

Medin, D. L., Goldstone, R., & Gentner, D. (1993). Respects for similarity. *Psychological Review, 100*, 254–278.

Medin, D. L., & Ortony, A. (1989). Psychological essentialism. In S. Vosniadou & A. Ortony (Eds.), *Similarity and analogical reasoning* (pp. 179–195). New York, NY: Cambridge University Press.

Medin, D. L., Schwartz, H., Blok, S. V., & Birnbaum, L. A. (1999). The semantic side of decision making. *Psychonomic Bulletin & Review, 6*, 562–569.

Mednick, S. (1962). The associative basis of the creative process. *Psychological Review, 69*, 220–232.

Mednick, S., & Mednick, M. (1967). *Examiner's manual, Remote Associates Test*. Boston, MA: Houghton Mifflin.

Meijer, E. H., Selle, N. K., Elber, L., & Ben-Shakhar, G. (2014). Memory detection with the Concealed Information Test: A meta-analysis of skin conductance, respiration, heart rate, and P300 data. *Psychophysiology, 51*, 879–904.

Meissner, C. A., & Brigham, J. C. (2001). Thirty years of investigating the own-race bias in memory for faces: A meta-analytic review. *Psychology, Public Policy, and Law, 7*, 3–35.

Mella, N., Fagot, D., Lecerf, T., & de Ribaupierre, A. (2015). Working memory and intraindividual variability in processing speed. *Memory & Cognition, 43*, 349–356.

Memon, A., Meissner, C. A., & Fraser, J. (2010). The cognitive interview: A meta-analytic review and study space analysis of the past 25 years. *Psychology, Public Policy, and Law, 16*(4), 340–372.

Mervis, C. B., Catlin, J., & Rosch, E. (1976). Relationships among goodness-of-example, category norms and word frequency. *Bulletin of the Psychonomic Society, 7,* 268–284.

Metcalfe, J. (1986). Premonitions of insight predict impending error. *Journal of Experimental Psychology: Learning, Memory, & Cognition, 12,* 623–634.

Metcalfe, J., & Weibe, D. (1987). Intuition in insight and noninsight problem solving. *Memory & Cognition, 15,* 238–246.

Meyer, D. E., & Schvaneveldt, R. W. (1971). Facilitation in recognizing pairs of words: Evidence of a dependence between retrieval operations. *Journal of Experimental Psychology, 90,* 227–234.

Meyer, D. E., Schvaneveldt, R. W., & Ruddy, M. G. (1974). Functions of graphemic and phonemic codes in visual word recognition. *Memory & Cognition, 2,* 309–321.

Michel, C., Rossion, B., Han, J., Chung, C.-S., & Caldara, R. (2006). Holistic processing is finely tuned for faces of one's own race. *Psychological Science, 17,* 608–615.

Milivojevic, B. (2012). Object recognition can be viewpoint dependent or invariant: It's just a matter of time and task. *Frontiers in Computational Neuroscience, 6,* 27.

Mill, J. S. (1874). *A system of logic* (8th ed.). New York, NY: Harper.

Miller, D. I., & Halpern, D. F. (2013). The new science of cognitive sex differences. *Trends in Cognitive Sciences, 18*(1), 37–45.

Miller, E. K., & Cohen, J. D. (2001). An integrative theory of prefrontal cortex function. *Annual Review of Neuroscience, 24,* 167–202.

Miller, G. A. (1951). *Language and communication.* New York, NY: McGraw-Hill.

Miller, G. A. (1956). The magical number seven plus or minus two: Some limits on our capacity for processing information. *Psychological Review, 63,* 81–97.

Miller, G. A. (1962). *Psychology: The science of mental life.* New York, NY: Harper & Row.

Miller, G. A., Bruner, J. S., & Postman, L. (1954). Familiarity of letter sequences and tachistoscopic identification. *Journal of General Psychology, 50,* 129–139.

Miller, G. A., Galanter, E., & Pribram, K. (1960). *Plans and the structure of behavior.* New York, NY: Holt, Rinehart and Winston.

Miller, L. K. (1999). The Savant Syndrome: Intellectual impairment and exceptional skill. *Psychological Bulletin, 125,* 31–46.

Miller, M. B., van Horn, J. D., Wolford, G. L., Handy, T. C., Valsangkar-Smyth, M., Inati, S., et al. (2002). Extensive individual differences in brain activations associated with episodic retrieval are reliable over time. *Journal of Cognitive Neuroscience, 14,* 1200–1214.

Miller, R. R. & Springer, A. D. (1973). Amnesia, consolidation, and retrieval. *Psychological Review, 80,* 69–89.

Milner, B. (1966). Amnesia following operation on the temporal lobes. In C. W. M. Whitty & O. L. Zangwill (Eds.), *Amnesia* (pp. 109–133). London, England: Butterworths.

Milner, B. (1970). Memory and the medial temporal regions of the brain. In K. H. Pribram & D. E. Broadbent (Eds.), *Biology of memory* (pp. 29–48). New York, NY: Academic Press.

Mitroff, S. R., & Biggs, A. T. (2014). The ultra-rare-item effect: Visual search for exceedingly rare items is highly susceptible to error. *Psychological Science, 25,* 284–289.

Miyake, A., & Friedman, N. (2012). The nature and organization of individual differences in executive functions: Four general conclusions. *Current Directions in Psychological Science, 21,* 8–14.

Miyashita, Y. (1995). How the brain creates imagery: Projection to primary visual cortex. *Science, 268,* 1719–1720.

Molden, D. C., & Higgins, E. T. (2012). Motivated thinking. In K. J. Holyoak & R. G. Morrison (Eds.), *The Oxford handbook of thinking and reasoning* (pp. 390–412). New York, NY: Oxford University Press.

Montaldi, D., Spencer, T. J., Roberts, N., & Mayes, A. R. (2006). The neural system that mediates familiarity memory. *Hippocampus, 16,* 504–520.

Montoy, R. M., Horton, R. S., Vevea, J. L., Citkowicz, M., & Lauber, E. A. (2017). A re-examination of the mere exposure effect: The influence of repeated exposure on recognition, familiarity, and liking. *Psychological Bulletin, 143,* 459–498.

Moons, W. G., Mackie, D. M., & Garcia-Marques, T. (2009). The impact of repetition-induced familiarity on agreement with weak and strong arguments. *Journal of Personality & Social Psychology, 96,* 32–44.

Moore, C. M., & Egeth, H. (1997). Perception without attention: Evidence of grouping under conditions of inattention. *Journal of Experimental Psychology: Human Perception and Performance, 23,* 339–352.

Moore, T., & Zirnsak, M. (2017). Neural mechanisms of selective visual attention. *Annual Review of Psychology, 68,* 47–52.

Moors, A. (2016). Automaticity: Componential, causal, and mechanistic explanations. *Annual Review of Psychology, 67,* 263–287.

Moors, A., & De Houwer, J. (2006). Automaticity: A theoretical and conceptual analysis. *Psychological Bulletin, 132,* 297–326.

Morawetz, C., Holz, P., Baudewig, J., Treue S., & Dechent, P. (2007). Split of attentional resources in human visual cortex. *Visual Neuroscience, 24,* 817–826.

Moray, N. (1959). Attention in dichotic listening: Affective cues and the influence of instructions. *Quarterly Journal of Experimental Psychology, 11,* 56–60.

Morewedge, C. K., & Giblin, C. E. (2015). Explanations of the endowment effect: An integrative review. *Trends in Cognitive Sciences, 19*, 339–348.

Morgan, C., Hazlett, G., Doran, A., Garrett, S., Hoyt, G., Thomas, P., Baronoski, M., & Southwick, S. (2004). Accuracy of eyewitness memory for persons encountered during exposure to highly intense stress. *International Journal of Law and Psychiatry, 27*, 264–279.

Morgan, C., Southwick, S., Steffan, G., Hazlett, G., & Loftus, E. F. (2013). Misinformation can influence memory for recently experienced, highly stressful events. *International Journal of Law and Psychiatry, 36*, 11–17.

Morrison, C., & Conway, M. (2010). First words and first memories. *Cognition, 116*, 23–32.

Morsella, E., & Bargh, J. (2011). Unconscious action tendencies: Sources of "unintegrated" action. In J. Cacioppo & J. Decety (Eds.), *The handbook of social neuroscience* (pp. 335–347). New York, NY: Oxford University Press.

Morsella, E., Krieger, S., & Bargh, J. (2010). Minimal neuroanatomy for a conscious brain: Homing in on the networks constituting consciousness. *Neural Networks, 23*, 14–15.

Moscovitch, M. (1982). Multiple dissociations of function in amnesia. In L. S. Cermak (Ed.), *Human memory and amnesia* (pp. 337–370). Hillsdale, NJ: Erlbaum.

Moseley, P., Smailes, D., Ellison, A., & Fernyhough, C. (2016). The effect of auditory verbal imagery on signal detection in hallucination-prone individuals. *Cognition, 146*, 202–216.

Most, S. B., Simons, D. J., Scholl, B. J., Jimenez, R., Clifford, E., & Chabris, C. F. (2001). How not to be seen: The contribution of similarity and selective ignoring to sustained inattentional blindness. *Psychological Science, 12*, 9–17.

Mudrik, L., Faivre, N., & Koch, C. (2014). Information integration without awareness. *Trends in Cognitive Sciences, 18*, 488–496.

Mulligan, N. W., & Besken, M. (2013). Implicit memory. In D. Reisberg (Ed.), *The Oxford handbook of cognitive psychology* (pp. 220–231). New York, NY: Oxford University Press.

Mumford, M., & Antes, A. (2007). Debates about the "general" picture: Cognition and creative achievement. *Creativity Research Journal, 19*, 367–374.

Murdock, B. B., Jr. (1962). The serial position effect of free recall. *Journal of Experimental Psychology, 64*, 482–488.

Murphy, G., & Greene, C. M. (2016). Perceptual load induces inattentional blindness in drivers. *Applied Cognitive Psychology, 30*, 479–483.

Murphy, G., & Greene, C. M. (2017). The elephant in the road: Auditory perceptual load affects driver perception and awareness. *Applied Cognitive Psychology, 31*, 258–263.

Murphy, G., Groeger, J. A., & Greene, C. M. (2016). Twenty years of load theory—Where are we now, and where should we go next? *Psychonomic Bulletin & Review, 23*, 1316–1340.

Murphy, G. L. (2003). *The big book of concepts.* Cambridge, MA: MIT Press.

Murphy, G. L. (2016). Is there an exemplar theory of concepts? *Psychonomic Bulletin & Review, 23*, 1035–1042.

Murphy, G. L., & Medin, D. L. (1985). The role of theories in conceptual coherence. *Psychological Review, 92*, 289–316.

Murphy, G. L., & Ross, B. H. (2005). The two faces of typicality in category-based induction. *Cognition, 95*, 175–200.

Murphy, J., Gray, K. L. H., & Cook, R. (2017). The composite face illusion. *Psychonomic Bulletin & Review, 24*, 245–261.

Murphy, S., & Dalton, P. (2016). Out of touch? Visual load induces inattentional numbness. *Journal of Experimental Psychology: Human Perception & Performance, 42*, 761–765.

Murphy, S. T. (2001). Feeling without thinking: Affective primacy and the nonconscious processing of emotion. In J. A. Bargh & D. K. Apsley (Eds.), *Unraveling the complexities of social life: A festschrift in honor of Robert B. Zajonc* (pp. 39–53). Washington, DC: American Psychological Association.

Murray, C., Pattie, A., Starr, J. M., & Deary, I. J. (2012). Does cognitive ability predict mortality in the ninth decade? The Lothian birth cohort 1921. *Intelligence, 40*, 490–498.

Nadel, L., & Moscovitch, M. (2001). The hippocampal complex and long-term memory revisited. *Trends in Cognitive Sciences, 5*, 228–230.

Naqvi, N., Shiv, B., & Bechara, A. (2006). The role of emotion in decision making. *Current Directions in Psychological Science, 15*, 260–264.

Nash, R. A., Wade, K. A., Garry, M., Loftus, E. F., & Ost, J. (2017). Misrepresentations and flawed logic about the prevalence of false memories. *Applied Cognitive Psychology, 31*, 31–33.

National Research Council (2014). *Identifying the culprit: Assessing eyewitness identification.* Washington, DC: National Academies Press.

National Research Council, Committee to Review the Scientific Evidence on the Polygraph, Division of Behavioral and Social Sciences and Education. (2003). *The polygraph and lie detection.* Washington, DC: National Academies Press.

Neisser, U. (1967). *Cognitive psychology.* New York, NY: Appleton-Century-Crofts.

Neisser, U., & Becklen, R. (1975). Selective looking: Attending to visually specified events. *Cognitive Psychology, 7*, 480–494.

Neisser, U., Boodoo, G., Bouchard, T. J., Jr., Boykin, A. W., Brody, N., Ceci, S. J., et al. (1996). Intelligence: Knowns and unknowns. *American Psychologist, 51*(2), 77–101.

Neisser, U., & Harsch, N. (1992). Phantom flashbulbs: False recollections of hearing the news about *Challenger*. In E. Winograd & U. Neisser (Eds.), *Affect and accuracy in recall: Studies of "flashbulb" memories* (pp. 9–31). Cambridge, England: Cambridge University Press.

Neisser, U., Winograd, E., & Weldon, M. S. (1991, November). *Remembering the earthquake: "What I experienced" vs. "How I heard the news."* Paper presented at the meeting of the Psychonomic Society, San Francisco, CA.

Nelson, T. O., & Narens, L. (1990). Metamemory: A theoretical framework and new findings. *Psychology of Learning and Motivation, 26*, 125–173.

Nettelbeck, T. (2003). Inspection time and g. In H. Nyborg (Ed.), *The scientific study of general intelligence: A tribute to Arthur Jensen* (pp. 77–92). New York, NY: Elsevier.

Newcombe, F., Ratcliff, G., & Damasio, H. (1987). Dissociable visual and spatial impairments following right posterior cerebral lesions: Clinical, neuropsychological and anatomical evidence. *Neuropsychologia, 25*, 149–161.

Newell, A., & Simon, H. (1972). *Human problem solving.* Englewood Cliffs, NJ: Prentice-Hall.

Newell, A., & Simon, H. A. (1959). Report on a general problem-solving program. *Proceedings of the International Conference on Information Processing* (pp. 256–264).

Nickerson, R. S., & Adams, M. J. (1979). Long-term memory for a common object. *Cognitive Psychology, 11*, 287–307.

Nisbett, R. E. (Ed.). (1993). *Rules for reasoning.* Hillsdale, NJ: Erlbaum.

Nisbett, R. E. (2003). *The geography of thought.* New York, NY: Free Press.

Nisbett, R. E. (2009). *Intelligence and how to get it.* New York, NY: Norton.

Nisbett, R. E., Aronson, J., Blair, C., Dickens, W., Flynn, J., Halpern, D. F., & Turkheimer, E. (2012a). Group differences in IQ are best understood as environmental in origin. *American Psychologist, 67*, 503–504.

Nisbett, R. E., Aronson, J., Blair, C., Dickens, W., Flynn, J., Halpern, D. F., & Turkheimer, E. (2012b). Intelligence: New findings and theoretical developments. *American Psychologist, 67*, 130–159.

Nisbett, R. E., Krantz, D. H., Jepson, C., & Kunda, Z. (1983). The use of statistical heuristics in everyday inductive reasoning. *Psychological Review, 90*, 339–363.

Nisbett, R. E., Peng, K., Choi, I., & Norenzayan, A. (2001). Culture and systems of thought: Holistic vs. analytic cognition. *Psychological Review, 108*, 291–310.

Nisbett, R. E., & Ross, L. (1980). *Human inference: Strategies and shortcomings of social judgment.* Englewood Cliffs, NJ: Prentice-Hall.

Nisbett, R. E., & Schachter, S. (1966). Cognitive manipulation of pain. *Journal of Experimental Social Psychology, 2*, 277–236.

Nisbett, R. E., & Wilson, T. (1977). Telling more than we can know: Verbal reports on mental processes. *Psychological Review, 84*, 231–259.

Nørby, S. (2015). Why forget? On the adaptive value of memory loss. *Perspectives on Psychological Science, 10*, 551–578.

Norman, D. (1981). Categorization of action slips. *Psychological Review, 88*, 1–15.

Norman, D., & Shallice, T. (1986). Attention to action: Willed and automatic control of behavior. In R. Davidson, G. Schwartz, & D. Shapiro (Eds.), *Consciousness and self-regulation* (pp. 1–18). New York, NY: Plenum.

Northup, T., & Mulligan, N. (2013). Conceptual implicit memory in advertising research. *Applied Cognitive Psychology, 27*, 127–136.

Northup, T., & Mulligan, N. (2014). Online advertisements and conceptual implicit memory: Advances in theory and methodology. *Applied Cognitive Psychology, 28*, 66–78.

Noveck, I., & Reboul, A. (2008). Experimental pragmatics: A Gricean turn in the study of language. *Trends in Cognitive Sciences, 12*, 425–431.

Noveck, J., & Sperber, D. (2005). *Experimental pragmatics.* New York, NY: Oxford University Press.

Novick, L., & Holyoak, K. (1991). Mathematical problem solving by analogy. *Journal of Experimental Psychology: Learning, Memory, & Cognition, 17*, 398–415.

Nyberg, L., Habib, R., McIntosh, A. R., & Tulving, E. (2000). Reactivation of encoding-related brain activity during memory retrieval. *Proceedings of the National Academy of Sciences, 97*, 11120–11124.

O'Connor, D., Fukui, M., Pinsk, M., & Kastner, S. (2002). Attention modulates responses in the human lateral geniculate nucleus. *Nature Neuroscience, 5*, 1203–1209.

O'Connor, M., Walbridge, M., Sandson, T., & Alexander, M. (1996). A neuropsychological analysis of Capgras syndrome. *Neuropsychiatry, Neuropsychology, and Behavioral Neurology, 9*, 265–271.

O'Craven, K. M., & Kanwisher, N. (2000). Mental imagery of faces and places activates corresponding stimulus-specific brain regions. *Journal of Cognitive Neuroscience, 12*, 1013–1023.

O'Kane, G., Kensinger, E. A., & Corkin, S. (2004). Evidence for semantic learning in profound amnesia: An investigation with patient H.M. *Hippocampus, 14*(4), 417–425.

Oaksford, M., & Hall, S. (2016). On the source of human irrationality. *Trends in Cognitive Sciences, 20*, 336–344.

Oberauer, K., & Hein, L. (2012). Attention to information in working memory. *Current Directions in Psychological Science, 21*, 164–169.

Obrecht, N., Chapman, G., & Gelman, R. (2009). An encounter frequency account of how experience affects likelihood estimation. *Memory & Cognition*, *37*, 632–643.

Ochsner, K. N., & Schacter, D. L. (2000). A social cognitive neuroscience approach to emotion and memory. In J. C. Borod (Ed.), *The neuropsychology of emotion* (pp. 163–193). New York, NY: Oxford University Press.

Oldfield, R. (1963). Individual vocabulary and semantic currency: A preliminary study. *British Journal of Social and Clinical Psychology*, *2*, 122–130.

Olds, J. M., & Westerman, D. L. (2012). Can fluency be interpreted as novelty: Retraining the interpretation of fluency in recognition memory. *Journal of Experimental Psychology: Learning, Memory & Cognition*, *38*, 653–664.

Oliphant, G. W. (1983). Repetition and recency effects in word recognition. *Australian Journal of Psychology*, *35*, 393–403.

Öllinger, M., Jones, G., Faber, A. H., & Knoblich, G. (2013). Cognitive mechanisms of insight: The role of heuristics and representational change in solving the eight-coin problem. *Journal of Experimental Psychology: Learning, Memory, & Cognition*, *39*, 931–939.

Oppenheimer, D. (2006). Consequences of erudite vernacular utilized irrespective of necessity: Problems with using long words needlessly. *Applied Cognitive Psychology*, *20*, 139–156.

Oppenheimer, D. M. (2004). Spontaneous discounting of availability in frequency judgment tasks. *Psychological Science*, *15*, 100–105.

Oppenheimer, D. M. (2008). The secret life of fluency. *Trends in Cognitive Sciences*, *12*, 237–241.

Oppenheimer, D. M., & Alter A. L. (2014). The search for moderators in disfluency research. *Applied Cognitive Psychology*, *28*, 502–504.

Oppenheimer, D. M., & Frank, M. C. (2007). A rose in any other font wouldn't smell as sweet: Fluency effects in categorization. *Cognition*, *106*, 1178–1194.

Ost, J. (2013). Recovered memories and suggestibility for entire events. In A. Ridley, F. Gabbert, & D. J. La Rooy (Eds.), *Suggestibility in legal contexts: Psychological research and forensic implications* (pp. 107–128). New York, NY: Wiley.

Ost, J., Vrij, A., Costall, A., & Bull, R. (2002). Crashing memories and reality monitoring: Distinguishing between perceptions, imaginations and "false memories." *Applied Cognitive Psychology*, *16*, 125–134.

Otgaar, H., Merckelbach, H., Jelicic, M., & Smeets, T. (2017). The potential for false memories is bigger than what Brewin and Andrews suggest. *Applied Cognitive Psychology*, *31*, 24–25.

Overton, D. (1985). Contextual stimulus effects of drugs and internal states. In P. D. Balsam & A. Tomie (Eds.), *Context and learning* (pp. 357–384). Hillsdale, NJ: Erlbaum.

Owens, J., Bower, G. H., & Black, J. B. (1979). The "soap opera" effect in story recall. *Memory & Cognition*, *7*, 185–191.

Özgen, E. (2004). Language, learning, and color perception. *Current Directions in Psychological Science*, *13*, 95–98.

Özgen, E., & Davies, I. R. L. (2002). Acquisition of categorical color perception: A perceptual learning approach to the linguistic relativity hypothesis. *Journal of Experimental Psychology: General*, *131*, 477–493.

Pachur, T., Hertwig, R., & Steinmann, F. (2012). How do people judge risks: Availability heuristic, affect heuristic, or both? *Journal of Experimental Psychology: Applied*, *18*, 314–330.

Paivio, A. (1969). Mental imagery in associative learning and memory. *Psychological Review*, *76*, 241–263.

Paivio, A. (1971). *Imagery and verbal processes.* New York, NY: Holt, Rinehart & Winston.

Paivio, A., & Okovita, H. W. (1971). Word imagery modalities and associative learning in blind and sighted subjects. *Journal of Verbal Learning and Verbal Behavior*, *10*, 506–510.

Paivio, A., Smythe, P. C., & Yuille, J. C. (1968). Imagery versus meaningfulness of nouns in paired-associate learning. *Canadian Journal of Psychology*, *22*, 427–441.

Paivio, A., Yuille, J. C., & Madigan, S. (1968). Concreteness, imagery, and meaningfulness values for 925 nouns. [Monograph supplement]. *Journal of Experimental Psychology*, *76*(1), Pt. 2. Washington, DC: American Psychological Association.

Paller, K. A., & Suzuki, S. (2014). Response to Block et al.: First-person perspectives are both necessary and troublesome for consciousness science. *Trends in Cognitive Sciences*, *18*, 557–558.

Palmer, S., Schreiber, C., & Fox, C. (1991, November). *Remembering the earthquake: "Flashbulb" memory for experienced vs. reported events.* Paper presented at the meeting of the Psychonomic Society, San Francisco, CA.

Pansky, A., & Koriat, A. (2004). The basic-level convergence effect in memory distortions. *Psychological Science*, *15*, 52–59.

Papafragou, A., Li, P., Choi, Y., & Han, C-h. (2007). Evidentiality in language and cognition. *Cognition*, *103*, 253–299.

Parker, E. S., Cahill, L., & McGaugh, J. L. (2006, February). A case of unusual autobiographical remembering. *Neurocase*, *12*(1): 35–49.

Parkhurst, D., Law, K., & Niebur, E. (2002). Modeling the role of salience in the allocation of overt visual attention. *Vision Research*, *42*, 107–123.

Parkin, A. J. (1984). Levels of processing, context, and facilitation of pronunciation. *Acta Psychologia*, *55*, 19–29.

Pashler, H., Rohrer, D., Cepeda, N., & Carpenter, S. (2007). Enhancing learning and retarding forgetting: Choices and consequences. *Psychonomic Bulletin & Review, 14*, 187–193.

Paterson, H. M., & Kemp, R. I. (2006). Comparing methods of encountering post-event information: The power of co-witness suggestion. *Applied Cognitive Psychology, 20*, 1083–1099.

Patihis, L., Lilienfeld, S. O., Ho, L., & Loftus, E. F. (2014). Unconscious repressed memory is scientifically questionable. *Psychological Science, 25*, 197–198.

Patihis, L., & Loftus, E. F. (2015). Crashing memories 2.0: False memories for an upsetting childhood event. *Applied Cognitive Psychology, 30*, 41–50.

Patrick, J., & Ahmed, Afia. (2014). Facilitating representation change in insight problems through training. *Journal of Experimental Psychology: Learning, Memory & Cognition, 40*, 532–543.

Patrick, J., Ahmed, A., Smy, V., Seeby, H., & Sambrooks, K. (2015). A cognitive procedure for representation change in verbal insight problems. *Journal of Experimental Psychology: Learning, Memory & Cognition, 41*, 746–759.

Payne, L., & Sekuler, R. (2014). The importance of ignoring: Alpha oscillations protect selectivity. *Current Directions in Psychological Science, 23*, 171–177.

Payton, A. (2009). The impact of genetic research on our understanding of normal cognitive aging: 1995 to 2009. *Neuropsychology Review, 19*, 451–477.

Paz-Alonso, P., & Goodman, G. (2008). Trauma and memory: Effects of post-event misinformation, retrieval order, and retention interval. *Memory, 16*, 58–75.

Peace, K. A., & Porter, S. (2004). A longitudinal investigation of the reliability of memories for trauma and other emotional experiences. *Applied Cognitive Psychology, 18*, 143–159.

Pearson, J. (2014). New directions in mental-imagery research: The binocular-rivalry technique and decoding fMRI patterns. *Current Directions in Psychological Science, 23*, 178–183.

Pearson, J., Clifford, C. W. G., & Tong, F. (2008). The functional impact of mental imagery on conscious perception. *Current Biology, 18*, 982–986.

Pearson, J., Naselaris, T., Holmes, E. A., & Kosslyn, S. M. (2015). Mental imagery: Functional mechanisms and clinical applications. *Trends in Cognitive Sciences, 19*, 590–602.

Pearson, J., Rademaker, R. L., & Tong, F. (2011). Evaluating the mind's eye: The metacognition of visual imagery. *Psychological Science, 22*, 1535–1542.

Pederson, E., Danziger, E., Wilkins, D., Levinson, S., Kita, S., & Senft, G. (1998). Semantic typology and spatial conceptualization. *Language, 74*, 557–589.

Pedrone, R., Hummel, J. E., & Holyoak, K. J. (2001). The use of diagrams in analogical problem solving. *Memory & Cognition, 29*, 214–221.

Peissig, J., & Tarr, M. J. (2007). Visual object recognition: Do we know more now than we did 20 years ago? *Annual Review of Psychology, 58*, 75–96.

Pelham, S., & Abrams, L. (2014). Cognitive advantages and disadvantages in early and late bilinguals. *Journal of Experimental Psychology: Learning, Memory, & Cognition, 40*(2), 313–325.

Pennycook, G., Cheyne, J. A., Koehler, D. J., & Fugelsang, J. A. (2016). Is the cognitive reflection test a measure of both reflection and intuition? *Behavior Research Methods, 48*, 341–348.

Pennycook, G., Trippas, D., Handley, S. J., & Thompson, V. A. (2014). Base rates: Both neglected and intuitive. *Journal of Experimental Psychology: Learning, Memory, & Cognition, 40*, 544–554.

Peru, A., & Avesani, R. (2008). To know what it is for, but not how it is: Semantic dissociations in a case of visual agnosia. *Neurocase, 14*, 249–263.

Peterson, M., Kihlstrom, J. F., Rose, P., & Glisky, M. (1992). Mental images can be ambiguous: Construals and reference-frame reversals. *Memory & Cognition, 20*, 107–123.

Pezdek, K., & Blandon-Gitlin, I. (2017). It is just harder to construct memories for false autobiographical events. *Applied Cognitive Psychology, 31*, 42–44.

Pezdek, K., Blandon-Gitlin, I., & Gabbay, P. (2006). Imagination and memory: Does imagining implausible events lead to false autobiographical memories? *Psychonomic Bulletin & Review, 13*, 764–769.

Phillips, J. A., Noppeney, U., Humphreys, G. W., & Price, C. J. (2002). Can segregation within the semantic system account for category-specific deficits? *Brain, 125*, 2067–2080.

Piaget, J. (1952). *The origins of intelligence in children.* New York, NY: International Universities Press.

Pietschnig, J., & Voracek, M. (2015). One century of global IQ gains: A formal meta-analysis of the Flynn Effect (1909–2013). *Perspective on Psychological Science, 10*, 282–306.

Pillemer, D. B. (1984). Flashbulb memories of the assassination attempt on President Reagan. *Cognition, 16*, 63–80.

Pinker, S. (1987). The bootstrapping problem in language acquisition. In B. MacWhinney (Ed.), *Mechanisms of language acquisition* (pp. 339–441). Hillsdale, NJ: Erlbaum.

Pinker, S. (1994). *The language instinct: How the mind creates language.* New York, NY: Harper Perennial.

Pittham, J., & Scherer, K. R. (1993). Vocal expressions and communication of emotion. In M. Lewis & J. M. Haviland (Eds.), *Handbook of emotions* (pp. 185–197). New York, NY: Guilford Press.

Plomin, R., Fulker, D. W., Corley, R., & DeFries, J. C. (1997). Nature, nurture, and cognitive development from 1 to 16 years: A parent-offspring adoption study. *Psychological Science, 8,* 442–447.

Plomin, R., Haworth, C., Meaburn, E., Price, T. S., et al. (2013). Common DNA markers can account for more than half of the genetic influence on cognitive abilities. *Psychological Science, 24,* 562–568.

Plomin, R., & Spinath, F. M. (2004). Intelligence: Genetics, genes, and genomics. *Journal of Personality and Social Psychology, 86,* 112–129.

Pollack, I., & Pickett, J. M. (1964). Intelligibility of excerpts from fluent speech: Auditory vs. structural context. *Journal of Verbal Learning & Verbal Behavior, 3,* 79–84.

Popper, K. (1934). *The logic of scientific discovery.* London, England: Routledge.

Porter, S., & Peace, K. A. (2007). The scars of memory: A prospective, longitudinal investigation of the consistency of traumatic and positive emotional memories in adulthood. *Psychological Science, 18*(5), 435–441.

Posner, M., & Rothbart, M. (2007). Research on attention networks as a model for the integration of psychological science. *Annual Review of Psychology, 58,* 1–23.

Posner, M., & Snyder, C. (1975). Facilitation and inhibition in the processing of signals. In P. Rabbitt & S. Dornic (Eds.), *Attention and performance V* (pp. 669–682). New York, NY: Academic Press.

Posner, M., Snyder, C., & Davidson, B. (1980). Attention and the detection of signals. *Journal of Experimental Psychology: General, 109,* 160–174.

Postman, L., & Phillips, L. W. (1965). Short-term temporal changes in free recall. *Quarterly Journal of Experimental Psychology, 17,* 132–138.

Powers, P. A., Andriks, J. L., & Loftus, E. F. (1979). Eyewitness accounts of females and males. *Journal of Applied Psychology, 64,* 339–347.

Prebble, S. C., Addis, D. R., & Tippett, L. J. (2013). Autobiographical memory and sense of self. *Psychological Bulletin, 139,* 815–840.

Preston, J., & Wegner, D. M. (2007). The Eureka error: Inadvertent plagiarism by misattributions of effort. *Journal of Personality and Social Psychology, 92,* 575–584.

Pretz, J. (2008). Intuition versus analysis: Strategy and experience in complex everyday problem solving. *Memory & Cognition, 36,* 554–566.

Protzko, J., Aronson, J., & Blair, C. (2013). How to make a young child smarter: Evidence from the Database of Raising Intelligence. *Perspective on Psychological Science, 8,* 25–40.

Pulvermüller, F. (2013). How neurons make meaning: Brain mechanisms for embodied and abstract-symbolic semantics. *Trends in Cognitive Sciences, 17,* 458–470.

Putnam, A. L., Nestojko, J. F., & Roediger, H. L. (2016). Improving student learning: Two strategies to make it stick. In J. C. Horvath, J. Lodge, & J. A. C. Hattie (Eds.), *From the laboratory to the classroom: Translating the science of learning for teachers* (pp. 94–121). Oxford, United Kingdom: Routledge.

Putnam, A. L., Sungkhasettee, V. W., & Roediger, H. L. (2016). Optimizing learning in college: Tips from cognitive psychology. *Perspectives on Psychological Science, 11,* 652–660.

Pyc, M. A., & Rawson, K. A., (2012). Why is test-restudy practice beneficial for memory? An evaluation of the mediator shift hypothesis. *Journal of Experimental Psychology: Learning, Memory & Cognition, 38,* 737–746.

Pylyshyn, Z. (1981). The imagery debate: Analogue media versus tacit knowledge. In N. Block (Ed.), *Imagery* (pp. 151–206). Cambridge, MA: MIT Press.

Quinlan, P. T. (2003). Visual feature integration theory: Past, present and future. *Psychological Bulletin, 129,* 643–673.

Quiroga, R. Q., Reddy, L., Kreiman, G., Koch, C., & Fried, I. (2005). Invariant visual representation by single neurons in the human brain. *Nature, 435,* 1102–1107.

Rabagliati, H., Robertson, A., & Carmel, D. (2018). The importance of awareness for understanding language. *Journal of Experimental Psychology: General, 147,* 190–208.

Radel, R., Davaranche, K., Fournier, M., & Dietrich, A. (2015). The role of (dis)inhibition in creativity: Decreased inhibition improves idea generation. *Cognition, 134,* 110–120.

Radoeva, P. D., Prasad, S., Brainard, D. H., & Aguirre, G. K. (2008). Neural activity within area V1 reflects unconscious visual performance in a case of blindsight. *Journal of Cognitive Neuroscience, 20*(11), 1927–1939.

Raghubir, P., & Menon, G. (2005). When and why is ease of retrieval informative? *Memory & Cognition, 33,* 821–832.

Raizada, R., & Kishiyama, M. (2010). Effects of socioeconomic status on brain development. *Frontiers in Human Neuroscience, 5,* 1–18.

Rakover, S. (2013). Explaining the face-inversion effect: The face-scheme incompatibility (FSI) model. *Psychonomic Bulletin & Review, 20,* 665–692.

Ramachandran, V. S., & Blakeslee, S. (1998). *Phantoms in the brain.* New York, NY: Morrow.

Ramsden, S., Richardson, F., Josse, G., Thomas, M., Ellis, C., Shakeshaft, C., Seghier, M., & Price, C. (2011). Verbal and nonverbal intelligence changes in the teenage brain. *Nature, 479,* 113–116.

Randhawa, G., Brocklehurst, A., Pateman, R., & Kinsella, S. (2010). "Opting-in or opting out?"—The views of the UK's faith leaders in relation to organ donation. *Health Policy, 96,* 36–44.

Ranganath, C., & Blumenfeld, R. S. (2005). Doubts about double dissociations between short- and long-term memory. *Trends in Cognitive Sciences, 9,* 374–380.

Ranganath, C., Yonelinas, A. P., Cohen, M. X., Dy, C. J., Tom, S., & D'Esposito, M. (2003). Dissociable correlates for familiarity and recollection within the medial temporal lobes. *Neuropsychologia, 42,* 2–13.

Rao, G. A., Larkin, E. C., & Derr, R. F. (1986). Biologic effects of chronic ethanol consumption related to a deficient intake of carbohydrates. *Alcohol and Alcoholism, 21,* 369–373.

Rasch, B., & Born, J. (2013). About sleep's role in memory. *Physiological Reviews, 93,* 681–766.

Rathbone, C. J., Moulin, C. J. A., & Conway, M. A. (2008). Self-centered memories: The reminiscence bump and the self. *Memory & Cognition, 36,* 1403–1414.

Rathbone, C. J., O'Connor, A. R., & Moulin, C. J. A. (2017). The tracks of my years: Personal significance contributes to the reminiscence bump. *Memory & Cognition, 45,* 137–150.

Raven, J., & Raven, J. (Eds.). (2008). *Uses and abuses of intelligence: Studies advancing Spearman and Raven's quest for non-arbitrary metrics.* Unionville, NY: Royal Fireworks Tests.

Ravenzwaaij, D. V., Brown, S., & Wagenmakers, E.-J. (2011). An integrated perspective on the relation between response speed and intelligence. *Cognition, 119,* 381–393.

Rayner, K., & Pollatsek, A. (2011). Basic processes in reading. In D. Reisberg (Ed.), *Handbook of cognitive psychology.* New York, NY: Oxford University Press.

Rayner, K., Schotter, E. R., Masson, M. E. J., Potter, M. C., & Treiman, R. (2016). So much to read, so little time: How do we read, and can speed reading help? *Psychological Science in the Public Interest, 17,* 4–34.

Reason, J. T. (1990). *Human error.* Cambridge, England: Cambridge University Press.

Redelmeier, D., & Shafir, E. (1995). Medical decision making in situations that offer multiple alternatives. *Journal of the American Medical Association, 273*(4), 302–305.

Redelmeier, D., & Tversky, A. (1996). On the belief that arthritis pain is related to the weather. *Proceedings of the National Academic of Sciences, USA, 93,* 2895–2896.

Redick, T. S., Shipstead, Z., Harrison, T. L., Hicks, K. L., Fried, D. E., Hambrich, D. Z., Kane, M. J., & Engle, R. W. (2013). No evidence of intelligence improvement after working memory training: A randomized, placebo-controlled study. *Journal of Experimental Psychology: General, 142,* 359–379.

Redick, T. S., Shipstead, Z., Meier, M. E., Montroy, J. J., Hicks, K. L., Unsworth, N., Kane, M. J., Hambrick, D. Z., & Engle, R. W. (2016). Cognitive predictors of a common multitasking ability: Contributions from working memory, attention control, and fluid intelligence. *Journal of Experimental Psychology: General, 145,* 1473–1492.

Reed, S. (1993). Imagery and discovery. In B. Roskos-Ewoldsen, M. J. Intons-Peterson, & R. Anderson (Eds.), *Imagery, creativity, and discovery: A*

cognitive perspective (pp. 287–312). New York, NY: North-Holland.

Reed, S. K. (2017). Problem solving. In S. E. F. Chipman (Ed.), *The Oxford handbook of cognitive science* (pp. 231–247). New York, NY: Oxford University Press.

Rees, G., Kreiman, G., & Koch, C. (2002). Neural correlates of consciousness in humans. *Nature Reviews Neuroscience, 3,* 261–270.

Rehder, B., & Hastie, R. (2004). Category coherence and category-based property induction. *Cognition, 91,* 113–153.

Rehder, B., & Ross, B. H. (2001). Abstract coherent categories. *Journal of Experimental Psychology: Learning, Memory, & Cognition, 27,* 1261–1275.

Reicher, G. M. (1969). Perceptual recognition as a function of meaningfulness of stimulus material. *Journal of Experimental Psychology, 81,* 275–280.

Reilly, J., Peele, J. E., Garcia, A., & Crutch, S. J. (2016). Linking somatic and symbolic representation in semantic memory: The dynamic multilevel reactivation framework. *Psychonomic Bulletin & Review, 23,* 1002–1014.

Reisberg, D. (1996). The non-ambiguity of mental images. In C. Cornold, R. H. Logie, M. Brandimonte, G. Kaufmann, & D. Reisberg (Eds.), *Stretching the imagination: Representation and transformation in mental imagery* (pp. 119–171). New York, NY: Oxford University Press.

Reisberg, D. (2014). *The science of perception and memory: A pragmatic guide for the justice system.* New York, NY: Oxford University Press.

Reisberg, D., & Heuer, F. (2004). Memory for emotional events. In D. Reisberg & P. Hertel (Eds.), *Memory and emotion* (pp. 3–41). New York, NY: Oxford University Press.

Reisberg, D., Pearson, D. G., & Kosslyn, S. M. (2003). Intuitions and introspections about imagery: The role of imagery experience in shaping an investigator's theoretical views. *Applied Cognitive Psychology, 17,* 147–160.

Rensink, R. A. (2002). Change detection. *Annual Review of Psychology, 53,* 245–277.

Rensink, R. A. (2012). Perception and attention. In D. Reisberg (Ed.), *Handbook of cognitive psychology.* New York, NY: Oxford University Press.

Rensink, R. A., O'Regan, J. K., & Clark, J. J. (1997). To see or not to see: The need for attention to perceive changes in scenes. *Psychological Science, 8,* 368–373.

Repovš, G., & Baddeley, A. (2006). The multicomponent model of working memory: Explorations in experimental cognitive psychology. *Neuroscience, 139,* 5–21.

Repp. B. (1992). Perceptual restoration of a "missing" speech sound: Auditory induction or illusion? *Perception & Psychophysics, 51,* 14–32.

Reynolds, C. R., Chastain, R. L., Kaufman, A. S., & McLean, J. E. (1987). Demographic characteristics and IQ among adults: Analysis of the WAIS-R standardization sample as a function of the stratification variables. *Journal of School Psychology, 25*(4), 323–342.

Reynolds, J. H., Pasternak, T., & Desimone, R. (2000). Attention increases sensitivity of V4 neurons. *Neuron, 26,* 703–714.

Rezlescu, C., Susilo, T., Wilmer, J. B., & Caramazza, A. (2017). The inversion, part-whole, and composite effects reflect distinct perceptual mechanisms with varied relationships to face recognition. *Journal of Experimental Psychology: Human Perception & Performance, 43,* 1961–1973.

Rhodes, G. (2012). Face recognition. In D. Reisberg (Ed.), *Handbook of cognitive psychology.* New York, NY: Oxford University Press.

Rhodes, G., Brake, S., & Atkinson, A. (1993). What's lost in inverted faces? *Cognition, 47,* 25–57.

Rhodes, M. G., & Anastasi, J. S. (2012). The own-age bias in face recognition: A meta-analytic and theoretical review. *Psychological Bulletin, 138,* 146–174.

Riccio, D. C., Millin, P. M., & Gisquet-Verrier, P. (2003). Retrograde amnesia: Forgetting back. *Current Directions in Psychological Science, 12,* 41–44.

Rich, P. R., & Zaragoza, M. S. (2016). The continued influence of implied and explicitly stated misinformation in news reports. *Journal of Experimental Psychology: Learning, Memory & Cognition, 42,* 62–74.

Richard, A. M., Lee, H., & Vecera, S. P. (2008). Attentional spreading in object-based attention. *Journal of Experimental Psychology: Human Perception & Performance, 34,* 842–853.

Richler, J. J., Cheung, O. S., & Gauthier, I. (2011). Holistic processing predicts face recognition. *Psychological Science, 2,* 464–471.

Richler, J. J., & Gauthier, I. (2014). A meta-analysis and review of holistic face processing. *Psychological Bulletin, 140,* 1281–1302.

Riesenhuber, M., & Poggio, T. (1999). Hierarchical models of object recognition in cortex. *Nature Neuroscience, 2,* 1019–1025.

Riesenhuber, M., & Poggio, T. (2002). Neural mechanisms of object recognition. *Current Opinion in Neurobiology, 12,* 162–168.

Rinck, M. (1999). Memory for everyday objects: Where are the digits on numerical keypads? *Applied Cognitive Psychology, 13,* 329–350.

Rips, L. (1975). Inductive judgements about natural categories. *Journal of Verbal Learning and Verbal Behavior, 14,* 665–681.

Rips, L. (1990). Reasoning. *Annual Review of Psychology, 41,* 321–353.

Rips, L. J., Smith, E. E., & Medin, D. L. (2012). Concepts and categories: Memory, meaning, and metaphysics. In K. J. Holyoak & R. G. Morrison (Eds.), *The Oxford handbook of thinking and reasoning* (pp. 177–209). New York, NY: Oxford University Press.

Ritchie, J. M. (1985). The aliphatic alcohols. In A. G. Gilman, L. S. Goodman, T. W. Rall, & F. Murad (Eds.), *The pharmacological basis of therapeutics* (pp. 372–386). New York, NY: Macmillan.

Rizzi, T., & Posthuma, D. (2012). Genes and intelligence. In D. Reisberg (Ed.), *The Oxford handbook of cognitive psychology.* New York, NY: Oxford University Press.

Roberson, D., Davies, I., & Davidoff, J. (2000). Color categories are not universal: Replications and new evidence from a stone-age culture. *Journal of Experimental Psychology: General, 129,* 369–398.

Robertson, L., Treisman, A., Friedman-Hill, S., & Grabowecky, M. (1997). The interaction of spatial and object pathways: Evidence from Balint's syndrome. *Journal of Cognitive Neuroscience, 9,* 295–317.

Roediger, H. L. (1980). The effectiveness of four mnemonics in ordering recall. *Journal of Experimental Psychology: Human Learning and Memory, 6,* 558–567.

Roediger, H. L., & Abel, M. (2015). Collective memory: A new arena of cognitive study. *Trends in Cognitive Sciences, 19,* 349–361.

Roediger, H. L., & McDermott, K. (1995). Creating false memories: Remembering words not presented in lists. *Journal of Experimental Psychology: Learning, Memory, & Cognition, 21,* 803–814.

Roediger, H. L., & McDermott, K. (2000). Tricks of memory. *Current Directions in Psychological Science, 9,* 123–127.

Rogers, R., Hazelwood, L. L., Sewell, K. W., Harrison, K. S., & Shuman, D. W. (2008). The language of Miranda warnings in American jurisdictions: A replication and vocabulary analysis. *Law & Human Behavior, 32,* 124–136.

Rogers, R., Rogstad, J. E., Gillard, N. D., Drogin, E. Y., Blackwood, H. L., & Shuman, D. W. (2010). "Everyone knows their Miranda rights": Implicit assumptions and countervailing evidence. *Psychology, Public Policy, & Law, 16,* 300–318.

Rogers, S. (1992). How a publicity blitz created the myth of subliminal advertising. *Public Relations Quarterly, 37,* 12–17.

Rogers, T. T., & Patterson, K. (2007). Object categorization: Reversals and explanations of the basic-level advantage. *Journal of Experimental Psychology: General, 136,* 451–469.

Rosch, E. (1973). On the internal structure of perceptual and semantic categories. In T. E. Moore (Ed.), *Cognitive development and the acquisition of language* (pp. 111–144). New York, NY: Academic Press.

Rosch, E. (1975). Cognitive representations of semantic categories. *Journal of Experimental Psychology: General, 104,* 192–233.

Rosch, E. (1978). Principles of categorization. In E. Rosch & B. B. Lloyd (Eds.), *Cognition and categorization* (pp. 27–48). Hillsdale, NJ: Erlbaum.

Rosch, E., & Mervis, C. B. (1975). Family resemblances: Studies in the internal structure of categories. *Cognitive Psychology, 7,* 573–605.

Rosch, E., Mervis, C. B., Gray, W., Johnson, D., & Boyes-Braem, P. (1976). Basic objects in natural categories. *Cognitive Psychology, 3,* 382–439.

Rosenfeld, J. P., Ben-Shakhar, G., & Ganis, G. (2012). Detection of concealed stored memories with psychophysiological and neuroimaging methods. In L. Nadel & W. P. Sinnott-Armstrong (Eds.), *Memory and law* (pp. 263–305). New York, NY: Oxford University Press.

Roser, M., & Gazzaniga, M. S. (2004). Automatic brains—Interpretive minds. *Current Directions in Psychological Science, 13,* 56–59.

Ross, J., & Lawrence, K. A. (1968). Some observations on memory artifice. *Psychonomic Science, 13,* 107–108.

Ross, L., & Anderson, C. (1982). Shortcomings in the attribution process: On the origins and maintenance of erroneous social assessments. In D. Kahneman, P. Slovic, & A. Tversky (Eds.), *Judgment under uncertainty: Heuristics and biases* (pp. 129–152). New York, NY: Cambridge University Press.

Ross, L., Lepper, M., & Hubbard, M. (1975). Perseverance in self perception and social perception: Biased attributional processes in the debriefing paradigm. *Journal of Personality and Social Psychology, 32,* 880–892.

Ross, M., & Wilson, A. E. (2003). Autobiographical memory and conceptions of self: Getting better all the time. *Current Directions in Psychological Science, 12,* 66–69.

Rouder, J. N., & Ratcliff, R. (2006). Comparing exemplar- and rule-based theories of categorization. *Current Directions in Psychological Science, 5,* 9–13.

Rowland, C. A. (2014). The effect of testing versus restudy on retention: A meta-analytic review of the testing effect. *Psychological Bulletin, 140,* 1432–1463.

Rubin, D. C. (1997). *Memory in oral traditions: The cognitive psychology of epic, ballads, and counting-out rhymes.* New York, NY: Oxford University Press.

Rubin, D. C., & Greenberg, D. L. (1998). Visual memory-deficit amnesia: A distinct amnesic presentation and etiology. *Proceedings of the National Academy of Sciences, 95,* 5413–5416.

Rubin, D. C., & Kontis, T. S. (1983). A schema for common cents. *Memory & Cognition, 11,* 335–341.

Rubin, D. C., & Kozin, M. (1984). Vivid memories. *Cognition, 16,* 81–95.

Rubin, D. C., & Talarico, J. (2007). Flashbulb memories are special after all; in phenomology, not accuracy. *Applied Cognitive Psychology, 21,* 557–558.

Rubin, D. C., & Umanath, S. (2015). Event memory: An evidence-based replacement for episodic memory. *Psychological Review, 122,* 1–23.

Rubin, E. (1915). *Synoplevede figuren.* Copenhagen, Denmark: Gyldendalske.

Rubin, E. (1921). *Visuell wahrgenommene figuren.* Copenhagen, Denmark: Gyldendalske.

Rueckl, J. G., & Oden, G. C. (1986). The integration of contextual and featural information during word identification. *Journal of Memory and Language, 25,* 445–460.

Rueda, M. R., Rothbart, M. K., McCandliss, B. D., Saccomanno, L., & Posner, M. I. (2005). Training, maturation, and genetic influences on the development of executive attention. *Proceedings of the National Academy of Sciences, 102,* 14931–14936.

Rugg, M. D., & Curran, T. (2007). Event-related potentials and recognition memory. *Trends in Cognitive Sciences, 11,* 251–257.

Rugg, M. D., & Yonelinas, A. P. (2003). Human recognition memory: A cognitive neuroscience perspective. *Trends in Cognitive Sciences, 7,* 313–319.

Rumelhart, D. E., & Siple, P. (1974). Process of recognizing tachistoscopically presented words. *Psychological Review, 81,* 99–118.

Rundus, D. (1971). Analysis of rehearsal processes in free recall. *Journal of Experimental Psychology, 89,* 63–77.

Rushton, J. P. (2012). No narrowing in mean Black-White IQ differences—Predicted by heritable *g*. *American Psychologist, 67,* 500–501.

Rushton, J. P., & Jensen, A. R. (2005). Thirty years of research on race differences in cognitive ability. *Psychology, Public Policy, and Law, 11,* 235–294.

Russell, R., Duchaine, B., & Nakayama, K. (2009). Super-recognizers: People with extraordinary face recognition ability. *Psychonomic Bulletin and Review, 16,* 252–257.

Ruthruff, E., Johnston, J. C., & Remington, R. W. (2009). How strategic is the central bottleneck: Can it be overcome by trying harder? *Journal of Experimental Psychology: Human Perception & Performance, 35,* 1368–1384.

Ruva, C. L., & Guenther, C. C. (2015). From the shadows into the light: How pretrial publicity and deliberation affect mock jurors' decisions, impressions, and memory. *Law & Human Behavior, 39,* 294–310.

Saalmann, Y., Pigarev, I., & Vidyasagar, T. (2007). Neural mechanisms of visual attention: How top-down feedback highlights relevant locations. *Science, 316,* 1612–1615.

Sackett, P., Borneman, M., & Connelly, B. (2008). High-stakes testing in higher education and employment: Appraising the evidence for validity and fairness. *American Psychologist, 63,* 215–227.

Sacks, O. (1985). *The man who mistook his wife for a hat and other clinical tales.* New York, NY: Harper & Row.

Sadeh, T., Ozubko, J. D., Winocur, G., & Moscovitch, M. (2016). Forgetting patterns differentiate between two forms of memory representation. *Psychological Science, 27,* 810–820.

Saffran, J. R. (2003). Statistical language learning: Mechanisms and constraints. *Current Directions in Psychological Science, 12,* 110–114.

Saj, A., Fuhrman, O., Vuilleumier, P., & Boroditsky, L. (2014). Patients with left spatial neglect also neglect the "left side" of time. *Psychological Science, 25,* 207–214.

Sala, G., & Gobet, F. (2017). Experts' memory superiority for domain-specific random material generalizes across fields of expertise: A meta-analysis. *Memory & Cognition, 45,* 183–193.

Salazar, R. F., Dotson, N. M., Bressler, S. L., & Gray, C. M. (2012). Content-specific fronto-parietal synchronization during visual working memory. *Science, 338,* 1097–1100.

Salthouse, T., & Pink, J. (2008). Why is working memory related to fluid intelligence? *Psychonomic Bulletin & Review, 15,* 364–371.

Salthouse, T. A. (2004). What and when of cognitive aging. *Current Directions in Psychological Science, 13,* 140–144.

Salthouse, T. A. (2012). Consequences of age-related cognitive declines. *Annual Review of Psychology, 63,* 201–226.

Salvucci, D. D. (2017). ACT-R and beyond. In S. E. F. Chipman (Ed.), *The Oxford handbook of cognitive science* (pp. 15–26). New York, NY: Oxford University Press.

Samuel, A. G. (1987). Lexical uniqueness effects on phonemic restoration. *Journal of Memory and Language, 26,* 36–56.

Samuel, A. G. (1991). A further examination of attentional effects in the phonemic restoration illusion. *Quarterly Journal of Experimental Psychology: Human Experimental Psychology, 43,* 679–699.

Sanbonmatsu, D. M. Strayer, D. L., Biondi, F., Behrends, A. A., & Moore, S. M. (2016). Cell-phone use diminishes self-awareness of impaired driving. *Psychonomic Bulletin & Review, 23,* 617–623.

Sanbonmatsu, D. M., Strayer, D. L., Medeiros-Ward, N., & Watson, J. M. (2013). Who multi-tasks and why? Multi-tasking ability, perceived multi-tasking ability, impulsivity, and sensation thinking. *PloS ONE, 8,* e54402.

Savage-Rumbaugh, E. S., & Fields, W. (2000). Linguistic, cultural and cognitive capacities of bonobos (*Pan paniscus*). *Culture & Psychology, 6,* 131–153.

Savage-Rumbaugh, S., & Lewin, R. (1994). *Kanzi, the ape at the brink of the human mind.* New York, NY: Wiley.

Savova, V., Roy, D., Schmidt, L., & Tenenbaum, J. (2007). *Discovering syntactic hierarchies.* Proceedings of the Twenty-Ninth Annual Conference of the Cognitive Science Society, Nashville, TN.

Sawyer, R. K. (2006). *Explaining creativity: The science of human innovation.* New York, NY: Oxford University Press.

Schab, F. (1990). Odors and the remembrance of things past. *Journal of Experimental Psychology: Learning, Memory, & Cognition, 16,* 648–655.

Schacter, D. (1996). *Searching for memory: The brain, the mind, and the past.* New York, NY: Basic Books.

Schacter, D., Guerin, S., & St. Jacques, P. (2011). Memory distortion: An adaptive perspective. *Trends in Cognitive Sciences, 15,* 467–474.

Schacter, D., & Tulving, E. (1982). Amnesia and memory research. In L. S. Cermak (Ed.), *Human memory and amnesia* (pp. 1–32). Hillsdale, NJ: Erlbaum.

Schacter, D., Tulving, E., & Wang, P. (1981). *Source amnesia: New methods and illustrative data.* Paper presented at the meeting of the International Neuropsychological Society, Atlanta, GA.

Schenk, T., Ellison, A., Rice, N., & Milner, A. D. (2005). The role of V5/MT+ in the control of catching movements: An rTMS study. *Neuropsychologia, 43,* 189–198.

Schlegel, A., Kohler, P. J., Fogelson, S. V., Alexander, P., Konuthula, D., & Tse, P. U. (2013). Network structure and dynamics of the mental workspace. *Proceeds of the National Academy of Sciences, USA, 110,* 16277–16282.

Schmidt, F. L., & Hunter, E. (1998). The validity and utility of selection methods in personnel psychology: Practical and theoretical implications of 85 years of research findings. *Psychological Bulletin, 124,* 262–274.

Schmidt, F. L., & Hunter, E. (2004). General mental ability in the world of work: Occupational attainment and job performance. *Journal of Personality and Social Psychology, 86,* 162–173.

Schmidt, S. R. (2012). *Extraordinary memories for exceptional events.* New York, NY: Taylor & Francis.

Schnuerch, R., Kreiz, C., Gibbons, H., & Memmert, D. (2016). Not quite so blind: Semantic processing despite inattentional blindness. *Journal of Experimental Psychology: Human Perception & Performance, 42,* 459–463.

Schraw, G., Dunkle, M., & Bendixen, L. (1995). Cognitive processes in well-defined and ill-defined problem solving. *Applied Cognitive Psychology, 9,* 523–538.

Schubert, A.-L., Hagemann, D., & Frischkom, G. (2017). Is general intelligence little more than the speed of higher-order processing? *Journal of Experimental Psychology: General, 146,* 1498–1512.

Schulz-Hardt, S., Frey, D., Lüthgens, C., & Moscovici, S. (2000). Biased information search in group decision making. *Journal of Personality and Social Psychology, 78,* 655–669.

Schwartz, B. (2003). *The paradox of choice.* New York, NY: Ecco.

Schwartz, B. L., & Metcalfe, J. (2011). Tip-of-the-tongue (TOT) states: Retrieval, behavior, and experience. *Memory & Cognition, 39,* 737–749.

Schwarz, N. (1998). Accessible content and accessibility experiences: The interplay of declarative and experiential information in judgments. *Personality and Social Psychology Review, 2,* 87–99.

Schwarz, N., Bless, H., Strack, F., Klumpp. G., Rittenauer-Schatka, H., & Simons, A. (1991). Ease of retrieval as information: Another look at the availability heuristic. *Journal of Personality & Social Psychology, 61,* 195–202.

Schwitzgebel, E., & Cushman, F. (2015). Philosophers' biased judgments persist despite training, expertise, and reflection. *Cognition, 141,* 127–137.

Scoboria, A., & Mazzoni, G. (2017). Invited commentary on Brewin and Andrews (2017). *Applied Cognitive Psychology, 31,* 28–30.

Scoboria, A., Mazzoni, G., Kirsch, I., & Jimenez, S. (2006). The effects of prevalence and script information on plausibility, belief, and memory of autobiographical events. *Applied Cognitive Psychology, 20,* 1049–1064.

Sedivy, J. C., Tanenhaus, M. K., Chambers, C. G., & Carlson, G. N. (1999). Achieving incremental semantic interpretation through contextual representation. *Cognition, 71,* 109–147.

Seegmiller, J. K., Watson, J. M., & Strayer, D. L. (2011). Individual differences in susceptibility to inattentional blindness. *Journal of Experimental Psychology: Learning, Memory, & Cognition, 37,* 785–791.

Segal, S., & Fusella, V. (1970). Influence of imaged pictures and sounds in detection of visual and auditory signals. *Journal of Experimental Psychology, 83,* 458–474.

Segal, S., & Fusella, V. (1971). Effect of images in six sense modalities on detection of visual signal from noise. *Psychonomic Science, 24,* 55–56.

Selfridge, O. (1955). *Pattern recognition and modern computers.* Proceedings of the Western Joint Computer Conference, Los Angeles, CA.

Selfridge, O. (1959). Pandemonium: A paradigm for learning. In D. Blake & A. Uttley (Eds.), *The mechanisation of thought processes: Proceedings of a symposium held at the National Physics Laboratory* (pp. 511–529). London, England: H. M. Stationery Office.

Seli, P., Smallwood, J., Cheyne, J. A., & Smilek, D. (2015). On the relation of mind wandering and ADHD symptomatology. *Psychonomic Bulletin & Review, 22,* 629–636.

Seltzer, B., & Benson, D. F. (1974). The temporal pattern of retrograde amnesia in Korsakoff's Disease. *Neurology, 24,* 527–530.

Semmler, C., & Brewer, N. (2006). Postidentification feedback effects on face recognition confidence: Evidence for metacognitive influences. *Applied Cognitive Psychology, 20,* 895–916.

Senghas, A., Román, D., & Mavillapalli, S. (2006). *Simply unique.* London: Leonard Cheshire International.

Servos, P., & Goodale, M. A. (1995). Preserved visual imagery in visual form agnosia. *Neuropsychologia, 33,* 1383–1394.

Sevdalis, N., & Harvey, N. (2007). Biased forecasting of postdecisional affect. *Psychological Science, 18,* 678–681.

Shafir, E. (1993). Choosing versus rejecting: Why some options are both better and worse than others. *Memory & Cognition, 21,* 546–556.

Shafir, E., & LeBoeuf, R. A. (2002). Rationality. *Annual Review of Psychology, 53,* 491–517.

Shafir, E., Simonson, I., & Tversky, A. (1993). Reason-based choice. *Cognition, 49,* 11–36.

Shaklee, H., & Mims, M. (1982). Sources of error in judging event covariations. *Journal of Experimental Psychology: Learning, Memory, & Cognition, 8,* 208–224.

Sharman, S. J., & Barnier, A. J. (2008). Imagining nice and nasty events in the distant or recent past: Recent positive events show the most imagination inflation. *Acta Psychologica, 129,* 228–233.

Shaw, J., & Porter, S. (2015). Constructing rich false memories of committing crime. *Psychological Science, 26,* 291–301.

Shepard, R. N., & Cooper, L. A. (1982). *Mental images and their transformations.* Cambridge, MA: MIT Press.

Shepard, R. N., & Metzler, J. (1971). Mental rotation of three-dimensional objects. *Science, 171,* 701–703.

Sheppard, L. D. (2008). Intelligence and speed information-processing: A review of 50 years of research. *Personality and Individual Differences, 44,* 535–551.

Shidlovski, D., Schul, Y., & Mayo, R. (2014). If I imagine it, then it happened: The implicit truth value of imaginary representations. *Cognition, 133,* 517–529.

Shields, G. S., Sazma, M. A., McCullough, A. M., & Yonelinas, A. P. (2017). The effects of acute stress on episodic memory: A meta-analysis and integrative review. *Psychological Bulletin, 143,* 636–675.

Shiffrin, R. M., & Schneider, W. (1977). Controlled and automatic human information processing: II. Perceptual learning, automatic attending, and a general theory. *Psychological Review, 84,* 127–190.

Shilowich, B. E., & Biederman, I. (2016). An estimate of the prevalence of developmental phonagnosia. *Brain and Language, 159,* 84–91.

Shin, H., & Kominski, R. (2010). *Language use in the United States, 2007.* Washington, DC: U.S. Dept. of Commerce Economics and Statistics Administration, U.S. Census Bureau.

Shipstead, Z., Harrison, T. L., & Engle, R. W. (2015). Working memory capacity and the scope and control of attention. *Attention, Perception & Psychophysics, 77,* 1863–1880.

Shipstead, Z., Redick, T. S., & Engle, R. W. (2012). Is working memory training effective? *Psychological Bulletin, 138,* 628–654.

Shore, D. I., & Klein, R. M. (2000). The effects of scene inversion on change blindness. *Journal of General Psychology, 127,* 27–43.

Sieroff, E., Pollatsek, A., & Posner, M. I. (1988). Recognition of visual letter strings following injury to the posterior visual spatial attention system. *Cognitive Neuropsychology, 5,* 427–450.

Silbersweig, D. A., Stern, E., Frith, C., Cahill, C., Holmes, A., Grootoonk, S., et al. (1995). A functional neuro-anatomy of hallucinations in schizophrenia. *Nature, 378,* 176–179.

Simons, D. J., & Ambinder, M. S. (2005). Change blindness: Theory and consequences. *Current Directions in Psychological Science, 14,* 44–48.

Simons, D. J., Boot, W. R., Charness, N., Gathercole, S. E., Chabris, C. F., Hambrick, D. Z., & Stine-Morrow, E. A. L. (2016). Do "brain-training" programs work? *Psychological Science in the Public Interest, 17,* 103–173.

Simons, D. J., & Chabris, C. F. (1999). Gorillas in our midst: Sustained inattentional blindness for dynamic events. *Perception, 28,* 1059–1074.

Simons, D. J., & Rensink, R. A. (2005). Change blindness: Past, present, and future. *Trends in Cognitive Sciences, 9,* 1–20.

Simonton, D. K. (2003). Scientific creativity as constrained stochastic behavior: The integration of product, person, and process perspectives. *Psychological Bulletin, 129,* 475–494.

Simonton, D. K. (2009). Creativity as a Darwinian phenomenon: The blind-variation and selective-retention model. In M. Krausz, D. Dutton, & K. Bardsley (Eds.), *The idea of creativity* (2nd ed., pp. 63–81). Leiden, Netherlands: Brill.

Simonton, D. K. (2011). Creativity and discovery as blind variation: Campbell's (1960) BVSR model after the half-century mark. *Review of General Psychology, 15,* 158–174.

Simonton, D. K., & Damian, R. D. (2012). Creativity. In D. Reisberg (Ed.), *The Oxford handbook of cognitive psychology.* New York, NY: Oxford University Press.

Sio, U. N., Kotovsky, K., & Cagan, J. (2017). Interrupted: The roles of distributed effort and incubation in preventing fixation and generating problem solutions. *Memory & Cognition, 45,* 553–565.

Skinner, B. F. (1957). *Verbal Behavior.* New York, NY: Copley Group.

Skotko, B. G., Kensinger, E. A., Locascio, J. J., Einstein, G., Rubin, D. C., Tupler, L. A., et al. (2004). Puzzling thoughts for H.M.: Can new semantic information be anchored to old semantic memories? *Neuropsychology, 18*(4), 756–769.

Skotko, B. G., Rubin, D., & Tupler, L. (2008). H.M.'s personal crossword puzzles. *Memory, 16,* 89–96.

Slamecka, N. J., & Graf, P. (1978). The generation effect: Delineation of a phenomenon. *Journal of Experimental Psychology: Human Learning and Memory, 4,* 592–604.

Slobin, D. (1966). Grammatical transformations and sentence comprehension in childhood and adulthood. *Journal of Verbal Learning and Verbal Behavior, 5,* 219–227.

Slovic, P., Finucane, M., Peters, E., & MacGregor, D. G. (2002). The affect heuristic. In T. Gilovich, D. Griffin, & D. Kahneman (Eds.), *Heuristics and biases* (pp. 397–420). New York, NY: Cambridge University Press.

Slovic, P., & Peters, E. (2010). Risk perception and affect. *Current Directions in Psychological Science, 15,* 322–325.

Smalarz, L., & Wells, G. L. (2014). Confirming feedback following a mistaken identification impairs memory for the culprit. *Law & Human Behavior, 38,* 283–292.

Smallwood, J., & Schooler, J. W. (2006). The restless mind. *Psychological Bulletin, 132,* 946–958.

Smallwood, J., & Schooler, J. W. (2015). The science of mind wandering: Empirically navigating the stream of consciousness. *Annual Review of Psychology, 66,* 487–518.

Smeets, T., Jelicic, M., Peters, M. J. V., Candel, I., Horselenberg, R., & Merckelbach, H. (2006). "Of course I remember seeing that film"—How ambiguous questions generate crashing memories. *Applied Cognitive Psychology, 20,* 779–789.

Smith, E. E., Rips, L. J., & Shoben, E. J. (1974). Structure and process in semantic memory: A featural model for semantic decisions. *Psychological Review, 81,* 214–241.

Smith, E. R., & Miller, F. (1978). Limits on perception of cognitive processes: A reply to Nisbett & Wilson. *Psychological Review, 85,* 355–362.

Smith, J. D., Zakrzewski, A. C., Johnson, J. M., & Valleau, J. C. (2016). Ecology, fitness, evolution: New perspectives on categorization. *Current Directions in Psychological Science, 25,* 266–274.

Smith, K. A., Huber, D. E., & Vul, E. (2013). Multiply constrained semantic search in the Remote Associates Test. *Cognition, 128,* 64–75.

Smith, S. M. (1979). Remembering in and out of context. *Journal of Experimental Psychology: Human Learning and Memory, 5,* 460–471.

Smith, S. M. (1985). Background music and context-dependent memory. *American Journal of Psychology, 6,* 591–603.

Smith, S. M., & Blankenship, S. E. (1989). Incubation effects. *Bulletin of the Psychonomic Society, 27,* 311–314.

Smith, S. M., & Blankenship, S. E. (1991). Incubation and the persistence of fixation in problem solving. *American Journal of Psychology, 104,* 61–87.

Smith, S. M., Glenberg, A., & Bjork, R. A. (1978). Environmental context and human memory. *Memory & Cognition, 6,* 342–353.

Smith, S. M., & Vela, E. (2001). Environmental context-dependent memory: A review and meta-analysis. *Psychonomic Bulletin & Review, 8,* 203–220.

Smith, S. M., & Ward, T. B. (2012). Cognition and the creation of ideas. In K. J. Holyoak & R. G. Morrison (Eds.), *The Oxford handbook of thinking and reasoning* (pp. 456–474). New York, NY: Oxford University Press.

Snow, R. E. (1994). Abilities in academic tasks. In R. J. Sternberg & R. K. Wagner (Eds.), *Mind in context: Interactionist perspectives on human intelligence* (pp. 3–37). Cambridge, England: Cambridge University Press.

Snow, R. E. (1996). Aptitude development and education. *Psychology, Public Policy, and Law, 2,* 536–560.

Soto, D., & Silvanto, J. (2014). Reappraising the relationship between working memory and conscious awareness. *Trends in Cognitive Sciences, 18,* 520–525.

Spearman, C. (1904). "General intelligence," objectively determined and measured. *American Journal of Psychology, 15,* 201–293.

Spearman, C. (1927). *The abilities of man.* New York, NY: Macmillan.

Speekenbrink, M., & Shanks, D. (2012). Decision making. In D. Reisberg (Ed.), *The Oxford handbook of cognitive psychology.* New York, NY: Oxford University Press.

Spelke, E., Hirst, W., & Neisser, U. (1976). Skills of divided attention. *Cognition, 4,* 215–230.

Spellman, B. A., Holyoak, K. J., & Morrison, R. G. (2001). Analogical priming via semantic relations. *Memory & Cognition, 29,* 383–393.

Spencer, S. J., Logel, C., & Davies, P. G. (2016). Stereotype threat. *Annual Review of Psychology, 67,* 415–437.

Sperling, G. (1960). The information available in brief visual presentations. *Psychological Monographs, 74,* 1–29.

Spiegel, D. (1995). Hypnosis and suggestion. In D. L. Schacter, J. T. Coyle, G. D. Fischbach, M.-M. Mesulam, & L. E. Sullivan (Eds.), *Memory distortion: How minds, brains and societies reconstruct the past* (pp. 129–149). Cambridge, MA: Harvard University Press.

Sporer, S. (1988). Long-term improvement of facial recognition through visual rehearsal. In M. Gruneberg, P. Morris, & R. Sykes (Eds.), *Practical aspects of memory: Current research and issues* (pp. 182–188). New York, NY: Wiley.

Squire, L., & McKee, R. (1993). Declarative and nondeclarative memory in opposition: When prior events influence amnesic patients more than normal subjects. *Memory & Cognition, 21,* 424–430.

Stangor, C., & McMillan, D. (1992). Memory for expectancy-congruent and expectancy-incongruent information: A review of the social and social developmental literatures. *Psychological Bulletin, 111,* 42–61.

Stanovich, K. E. (2009). *What intelligence tests miss: The psychology of rational thought.* New Haven, CT: Yale University Press.

Stanovich, K. E. (2012). On the distinction between rationality and intelligence: Implications for understanding individual differences in reasoning. In K. J. Holyoak & R. G. Morrison (Eds.), *The Oxford handbook of thinking and reasoning* (pp. 433–455). New York, NY: Oxford University Press.

Stanovich, K. E., & West, R. F. (2000). Individual differences in reasoning: Implications for the rationality debate. *Behavioral and Brain Sciences, 23,* 645–665.

Stanovich, K. E., West, R. F., & Toplak, M. E. (2016). *The Rationality Quotient: Toward a test of rational thinking.* Cambridge, MA: MIT Press.

Stapel, D., & Semin, G. (2007). The magic spell of language: Linguistic categories and their perceptual consequences. *Journal of Personality and Social Psychology, 93,* 23–33.

Stark, L.-J., Perfect, T., & Newstead, S. (2008). The effects of repeated idea elaboration on unconscious plagiarism. *Memory & Cognition, 36,* 65–73.

Steblay, N. M. (1992). A meta-analytic review of the weapon focus effect. *Law and Human Behavior, 16,* 413–424.

Steele, C. (2010). *Whistling Vivaldi: And other clues to how stereotypes affect us.* New York, NY: Norton.

Steele, C. M., & Aronson, J. (1995). Stereotype threat and the intellectual test performance of African Americans. *Journal of Personality and Social Psychology, 69*(5), 797–811.

Stein, T., Reeder, R. R., & Peelen, M. V. (2016). Privileged access to awareness for faces and objects of expertise. *Journal of Experimental Psychology: Human Perception & Performance, 42,* 788–798.

Steiner, K. L., Thomsen, D. K., & Pillemer, D. B. (2017). Life story chapters, specific memories, and conceptions of the self. *Applied Cognitive Psychology, 31,* 478–487.

Sternberg, R. J., & Grigorenko, E. L. (2004). Successful intelligence in the classroom. *Theory into Practice, 43,* 274–280.

Sternberg, R. J., Kaufman, J. C., & Grigorenko, E. L. (2008). *Applied intelligence.* New York, NY: Cambridge University Press.

Stevens, A., & Coupe, P. (1978). Distortions in judged spatial relations. *Cognitive Psychology, 10,* 422–437.

Storm, B., Angello, G., & Bjork, E. (2011). Thinking can cause forgetting: Memory dynamics in creative problem solving. *Journal of Experimental Psychology: Learning, Memory, & Cognition, 37,* 1287–1293.

Storm, B. C., & Patel, T. N. (2014). Forgetting as a consequence and enabler of creative thinking. *Journal of Experimental Psychology: Learning, Memory & Cognition, 40,* 1594–1609.

Stothart, C., Mitchum, A., & Yehnert, C. (2015). The attentional cost of receiving a cell phone notification. *Journal of Experimental Psychology: Human Perception & Performance, 41,* 893–897.

Stough, C., & Pase, M. P. (2015). Improving cognition in the elderly with nutritional supplements. *Current Directions in Psychological Sciences, 24,* 177–183.

Strayer, D. L., & Drews, F. A. (2007). Cell phone–induced driver distraction. *Current Directions in Psychological Science, 16,* 128–131.

Strayer, D. L., Drews, F. A., & Johnston, W. A. (2003). Cell phone–induced failures of visual attention during simulated driving. *Journal of Experimental Psychology: Applied, 9,* 23–32.

Strayer, D. L., & Johnston, W. A. (2001). Driven to distraction: Dual-task studies of simulated driving and conversing on a cellular phone. *Psychological Science, 12,* 462–466.

Strenze, T. (2007). Intelligence and socioeconomic success: A meta-analytic review of longitudinal research. *Intelligence, 35,* 401–426.

Stromeyer, C. (1982). *An adult eidetiker.* In U. Neisser (Ed.), *Memory observed* (pp. 399–404). New York, NY: Freeman.

Stroop, J. R. (1935). Studies of interference in serial verbal reaction. *Journal of Experimental Psychology, 18,* 643–662.

Stuss, D. T., & Alexander, M. P. (2007). Is there a dys-executive syndrome? *Philosophical Transactions of the Royal Society of London, Series B, Biological Sciences, 362,* 901–915.

Stuss, D. T., & Levine, B. (2002). Adult clinical neuro-psychology: Lessons from studies of the frontal lobes. *Annual Review of Psychology, 53,* 401–433.

Sulin, R. A., & Dooling, D. J. (1974). Intrusion of a thematic idea in retention of prose. *Journal of Experimental Psychology, 103,* 255–262.

Sunstein, C. R. (2016). The Council of Psychological Advisers. *Annual Review of Psychology, 67,* 713–737.

Svartik, J. (1966). *On voice in the English verb.* The Hague, Netherlands: Mouton.

Swanson, J., Posner, M. I., Cantwell, D., Wigal, S., Crinella, F., Filipek, P., Emerson, J., Tucker, D., & Nalcioglu, O. (2000). Attention Deficit/Hyperactivity Disorder: Symptom domain, cognitive processes and neural networks. In R. Parasuraman (Ed.), *The attentive brain* (pp. 445–460). Cambridge, MA: MIT Press.

Swire, B., Ecker, U. K. H., & Lewandowsky, S. (2017). The role of familiarity in correcting inaccurate information. *Journal of Experimental Psychology: Learning, Memory & Cognition, 43,* 1948–1961.

Symons, C. S., & Johnson, B. T. (1997). The self-reference effect in memory: A meta-analysis. *Psychological Bulletin, 121,* 371–394.

Szpunar, K. K., Khan, N. Y., & Schachter, D. L. (2013). Interpolated memory tests reduce mind wandering and improve learning of online lectures. *Proceedings of the National Academy of Sciences, USA, 110*(63), 13–17.

Tabachnick, B., & Brotsky, S. (1976). Free recall and complexity of pictorial stimuli. *Memory & Cognition, 4,* 466–470.

Talarico, J. M., & Rubin, D. C. (2003). Confidence, not consistency, characterizes flashbulb memories. *Psychological Science, 14,* 455–461.

Talmi, D. (2013). Enhanced emotional memory: Cognitive and neural mechanisms. *Current Directions in Psychological Science, 22,* 430–436.

Talmi, D., Grady, C. L., Goshen-Gottstein, Y., & Moscovitch, M. (2005). Neuroimaging the serial position curve: A test of single-store versus dual-store models. *Psychological Science, 16,* 716–723.

Tamietto, M., et al. (2010). Collicular vision guides nonconscious behavior. *Journal of Cognitive Neuroscience, 22,* 888–902.

Tanenhaus, M. K., & Spivey-Knowlton, M. J. (1996). Eye-tracking. *Language & Cognitive Processes, 11,* 583–588.

Tanenhaus, M. K., & Trueswell, J. C. (2006). Eye movements and spoken language comprehension. In M. J. Traxler & M. A. Gernsbacher (Eds.), *Handbook of psycholinguistics* (2nd ed.). Amsterdam, Netherlands: Elsevier.

Tardif, J., Fiset, D., Zhang, Y., Estéphan, A., Cai, Q., Luo, C., Sun, D., Gosselin, F., & Blais, C. (2017). Culture shapes spatial frequency tuning for face identification. *Journal of Experimental Psychology: Human Perception & Performance, 43,* 294–306.

Tarr, M. (1995). Rotating objects to recognize them: A case study on the role of viewpoint dependency in the recognition of three-dimensional objects. *Psychonomic Bulletin & Review, 2,* 55–82.

Tarr, M. (1999). News on views: Pandemonium revisited. *Nature Neuroscience, 2,* 932–935.

Tarr, M., & Bülthoff, H. (1998). Image-based object recognition in man, monkey and machine. *Cognition, 67,* 1–208.

Taylor, J., Roehrig, A., Hensler, B., Connor, C., & Schatschneider, C. (2010). Teacher quality moderates the genetic effects on early reading. *Science, 328,* 512–514.

Teper, R., Segal, Z., & Inzlicht, M. (2013). How mindfulness enhances emotion regulation through improvements in executive control. *Current Directions in Psychological Science, 6,* 449–454.

Terr, L. C. (1991). Acute responses to external events and posttraumatic stress disorders. In M. Lewis (Ed.), *Child and adolescent psychiatry: A comprehensive textbook* (pp. 755–763). Baltimore, MD: Williams & Wilkins.

Terr, L. C. (1994). *Unchained memories: The stories of traumatic memories, lost and found.* New York, NY: Basic Books.

Thaler, R., & Sunstein, C. (2009). *Nudge: Improving decisions about health, wealth, and happiness.* New York, NY: Penguin.

Thaler, R. H. (2009, September 26). Opting in vs. opting out. *The New York Times.*

Thioux, M., Stark, D. E., Klaiman, C., & Shultz, R. T. (2006). The day of the week when you were born in 700 ms: Calendar computation in an autistic savant. *Journal of Experimental Psychology: Human Perception and Performance, 32,* 1155–1168.

Thirion, B., Duchesnay, E., Hubbard, E., Dubois, J., Poline, J.-B., Lebihan, D., & Dehaene, S. (2006). Inverse retinotopy: Inferring the visual content of images from brain activation patterns. *Neuroimage, 33,* 1104–1116.

Thomas, A. K., & Loftus, E. F. (2002). Creating bizarre false memories through imagination. *Memory & Cognition, 30,* 423–431.

Thomas, J. (1974). An analysis of behavior in the Hobbits-Orcs problem. *Cognitive Psychology, 6,* 257–269.

Thompson, E., & Varela, F. J. (2001). Radical embodiment: Neural dynamics and consciousness. *Trends in Cognitive Sciences, 5,* 418–425.

Thompson, P. (1980). Margaret Thatcher: A new illusion. *Perception, 9,* 483–484.

Thompson, W. L., & Kosslyn, S. M. (2000). Neural systems activated during visual mental imagery: A review and meta-analyses. In J. Mazziotta & A. Toga (Eds.), *Brain mapping II: The applications* (pp. 535–560). New York, NY: Academic Press.

Thompson, W. L., Kosslyn, S. M., Hoffman, M. S., & Van der Kooij, K. (2008). Inspecting visual mental images: Can people "see" implicit properties as easily in imagery and perception? *Memory & Cognition, 36,* 1024–1032.

Thompson, W. L., Slotnick, S., Burrage, M., & Kosslyn, S. (2009). Two forms of spatial imagery: Neuroimaging evidence. *Psychological Science, 20,* 1245–1253.

Thomsen, D. K., & Berntsen, D. (2009). The long-term impact of emotionally stressful events on memory characteristics and life story. *Applied Cognitive Psychology, 23,* 579–598.

Tinti, C., Schmidt, S., Sotgiu, I., Testa, S., & Curci, A. (2009). The role of importance/consequentiality appraisal in flashbulb memory formation: The case of the death of Pope John Paul II. *Applied Cognitive Psychology, 23,* 236–253.

Tinti, C., Schmidt, S., Testa, S., & Levine, L. J. (2014). Distinct processes shape flashbulb and event memories. *Memory and Cognition, 42,* 539–551.

Tolman, E. C. (1948). Cognitive maps in rats and men. *Psychological Review, 55,* 189–208.

Tong, F., Nakayama, K., Vaughan, J. T., & Kanwisher, N. (1998). Binocular rivalry and visual awareness in human extrastriate cortex. *Neuron, 21,* 753–759.

Tononi, G., Boly, M., Massimini, M., & Koch, C. (2016). Integrated information theory: From consciousness to its physical substrate. *Nature Reviews Neuroscience, 17,* 450–461.

Tononi, G., & Cirelli, C. (2013). New hypothesis explains why we sleep. *Scientific American, 309*(2).

Trahan, L. H., Stuebing, K. K., Fletcher, J. M., & Hiscock, M. (2014). The Flynn effect: A meta-analysis. *Psychological Bulletin, 140,* 1332–1360.

Travers, E., Rolison, J. J., & Feeney, A. (2016). The time course of conflict on the Cognitive Reflection Test. *Cognition, 150,* 109–118.

Tree, J. J., Horry, R., Riley, H., & Wilmer, J. B. (2017). Are portrait artists superior face recognizers? Limited impact of adult experience on face recognition ability. *Journal of Experimental Psychology: Human Perception & Performance, 43,* 667–676.

Treffert, D. A. (2014, August). Accidental genius. *Scientific American,* 52–57.

Treisman, A. (1964). Verbal cues, language, and meaning in selective attention. *American Journal of Psychology, 77,* 206–219.

Treisman, A., & Gelade, G. (1980). A feature-integration theory of attention. *Cognitive Psychology, 12,* 97–136.

Treisman, A., Sykes, M., & Gelade, G. (1977). Selective attention and stimulus integration. In S. Dornic (Ed.), *Attention and performance VI* (pp. 333–361). Hillsdale, NJ: Erlbaum.

Trippas, D., Thompson, V. A., & Handley, S. J. (2017). When fast logic meets slow belief: Evidence for a parallel-processing model of belief bias. *Memory & Cognition, 45,* 539–552.

Trippas, D., Verde, M. F., & Handley, S. J. (2014). Using forced choice to test belief bias in syllogistic reasoning. *Cognition, 133,* 586–600.

Trueswell, J. C., Tanenhaus, M.K., & Garnsey, S. M. (1994). Semantic influences on parsing: Use of thematic role information in syntactic ambiguity resolution. *Journal of Memory and Language, 33,* 285–318.

Tsai, C., & Thomas, M. (2011). When does feeling of fluency matter? How abstract and concrete thinking influence fluency effects. *Psychological Science, 22,* 348–354.

Tsushima, Y., Sasaki, Y., & Watanabe, T. (2006). Greater disruption due to failure of inhibitory control on an ambiguous distractor. *Science, 314,* 1786–1788.

Tucker-Drob, E. M., & Bates, T. C. (2016). Large cross-national differences in gene x socioeconomic status interaction on intelligence. *Psychological Science, 27,* 138–149.

Tucker-Drob, E. M., Rhemtulla, M., Harden, K. P., Turkheimer, E., & Fask, D. (2011). Emergence of a gene x socioeconomic status interaction on infant mental ability between 10 months and 2 years. *Psychological Science, 22,* 125–133.

Tuffiash, M., Roring, R., & Ericsson, K. A. (2007). Expert performance in SCRABBLE: Implications for the study of the structure and acquisition of complex skills. *Journal of Experimental Psychology: Applied, 13*, 124–134.

Tulving, E. (1983). *Elements of episodic memory.* Oxford, England: Oxford University Press.

Tulving, E. (1993). What is episodic memory? *Current Directions in Psychological Science, 2*, 67–70.

Tulving, E. (2002). Episodic memory: From mind to brain. *Annual Review of Psychology, 53*, 1–25.

Tulving, E., & Gold, C. (1963). Stimulus information and contextual information as determinants of tachistoscopic recognition of words. *Journal of Experimental Psychology, 92*, 319–327.

Tulving, E., Mandler, G., & Baumal, R. (1964). Interaction of two sources of information in tachistoscopic word recognition. *Canadian Journal of Psychology, 18*, 62–71.

Turkheimer, E., Haley, A., Waldron, M., D'Onofrio, B., & Gottesman, I. I. (2003). Socioeconomic status modifies heritability of IQ in young children. *Psychological Science, 14*, 623–628.

Tversky, A., & Kahneman, D. (1973). Availability: A heuristic for judging frequency and probability. *Cognitive Psychology, 5*, 207–232.

Tversky, A., & Kahneman, D. (1974). Judgments under uncertainty: Heuristics and biases. *Science, 185*, 1124–1131.

Tversky, A., & Kahneman, D. (1982). Evidential impact of base rates. In D. Kahneman, P. Slovic, & A. Tversky (Eds.), *Judgment under uncertainty: Heuristics and biases* (pp. 153–160). New York, NY: Cambridge University Press.

Tversky, A., & Kahneman, D. (1987). Rational choice and the framing of decisions. In R. Hogarth & M. Reder (Eds.), *Rational choice: The contrast between economics and psychology* (pp. 67–94). Chicago, IL: University of Chicago Press.

Tweney, R. D., Doherty, M. E., & Mynatt, C. R. (1981). *On scientific thinking.* New York, NY: Columbia University Press.

Ullman, S. (2007). Object recognition and segmentation by a fragment-based hierarchy. *Trends in Cognitive Sciences, 11*, 58–64.

Ungerleider, L. G., & Haxby, J. V. (1994). "What" and "where" in the human brain. *Current Opinions in Neurobiology, 4*, 157–165.

Ungerleider, L. G., & Mishkin, M. (1982). Two cortical visual systems. In D. J. Ingle, M. A. Goodale, & R. J. W. Mansfield (Eds.), *Analysis of visual behavior* (pp. 549–586). Cambridge, MA: MIT Press.

Unkelbach, C. (2007). Reversing the truth effect: Learning the interpretation of processing fluency in judgments of truth. *Journal of Experimental Psychology: Learning, Memory, & Cognition, 33*, 219–230.

Unsworth, N., & Engle, R. (2007). The nature of individual differences in working memory capacity: Active maintenance in primary memory and controlled search in secondary memory. *Psychological Review, 114*, 104–132.

Valentine, T. (1988). Upside-down faces: A review of the effects of inversion upon face recognition. *British Journal of Psychology, 79*, 471–491.

Valentine, T., Davis, J. P., Memon, A., & Roberts, A. (2012). Live showups and their influence on a subsequent video line-up. *Applied Cognitive Psychology, 26*, 1–23.

Valentine, T., & Mesout, J. (2008). Eyewitness identification under stress in the London Dungeon. *Applied Cognitive Psychology, 23*, 151–161.

Van der Lely, H. K. J. (2005). Domain-specific cognitive systems: Insight from grammatical-SLI. *Trends in Cognitive Sciences, 9*, 53–59.

Van der Lely, H. K. J., & Pinker, S. (2014). The biological basis for language: Insight from developmental grammatical impairments. *Trends in Cognitive Sciences*, 586–595.

Van Essen, D. C., & DeYoe, E. A. (1995). Concurrent processing in the primate visual cortex. In M. S. Gazzaniga (Ed.), *The cognitive neurosciences* (pp. 383–400). Cambridge, MA: MIT Press.

van Gaal, S., Naccache, L., Meuwese, J. D. I., van Loon, A. M., Leighton, A. H., Cohen, L., & Dehaene, S. (2014). Can the meaning of multiple words be integrated unconsciously? *Philosophical Transactions of the Royal Society B*, 20130212.

Van Steenburgh, J. J., Fleck, J. I., Beeman, M., & Kounios, J. (2012). Insight. In K. J. Holyoak & R. G. Morrison (Eds.), *The Oxford handbook of thinking and reasoning* (pp. 475–491). New York, NY: Oxford University Press.

Van Veen, V., & Carter, C. S. (2006). Conflict and cognitive control in the brain. *Current Directions in Psychological Science, 15*, 237–240.

Vandierendonck, A., Liefooghe, B., & Verbruggen, F. (2010). Task switching: Interplay of reconfiguration and interference control. *Psychological Bulletin, 136*, 601–626.

Vanduffel, W., Tootell, R. B. H., & Orban, G. G. (2000). Attention-dependent suppression of metabolic activity in the early stages of the macaque visual system. *Cerebral Cortex, 10*, 109–126.

Vanpaemel, W., & Storms, G. (2008). In search of abstraction: The varying abstraction model of categorization, *Psychonomic Bulletin & Review, 15*, 732–749.

Vargha-Khadem, F., Gadian, D. G., Copp. A., & Mishkin, M. (2005). FOXP2 and the neuroanatomy of speech and language. *Nature Reviews Neuroscience, 32*, 131–138.

Vartanian, O., Martindale, C., & Matthews, J. (2009). Divergent thinking ability is related to faster relatedness judgments. *Psychology of Aesthetics, Creativity, and the Arts, 3*, 99–103.

Vergauwe, E., Barrouillet, P., & Camos, V. (2010). Do mental processes share a domain-general resource? *Psychological Science, 21*, 384–390.

Vernon, P. A. (Ed.). (1987). *Speed of information processing and intelligence*. Canada: Ablex.

Verstijnen, I. M., Hennessey, J. M., van Leeuwen, C., Hamel, R., & Goldschmidt, G. (1998). Sketching and creative discovery. *Design Studies, 19*, 519–546.

Verstijnen, I. M., van Leeuwen, C., Goldschmidt, G., Hamel, R., & Hennessey, J. M. (1998). Creative discovery in imagery and perception: Combining is relatively easy, restructuring takes a sketch. *Acta Psychologica, 99*, 177–200.

Vinkhuyzen, A. A., van der Sluis, S., & Posthuma, D. (2011). Life events moderate variation in cognitive ability (g) in adults. *Molecular Psychiatry, 16*(1), 4–6.

Visser, B., Ashton, M., & Vernon, P. (2006). Beyond "g": Putting multiple intelligences theory to the test. *Intelligence, 34*, 487–502.

Vitevitch, M. S. (2003). Change deafness: The inability to detect changes between two voices. *Journal of Experimental Psychology: Human Perception and Performance, 29*, 333–342.

Võ, M. L.-H., & Henderson, J. M. (2009) Does gravity matter? Effects of semantic and syntactic inconsistencies on the allocation of attention during scene perception. *Journal of Vision, 9*(3), 1–15.

Von Bastian, C. C., Souza, A. S., & Gade, M. (2016). No evidence for bilingual cognitive advantages: A test of four hypotheses. *Journal of Experimental Psychology: General, 145*, 246–258.

von Neumann, J., & Morgenstern, O. (1947). *Theory of games and economic behavior*. Princeton, NJ: Princeton University Press.

Vredeveldt, A., Knol, J. W., & van Kopen, P. J. (2017). Observing offenders: Incident reports by surveillance detectives, uniformed police, and civilians. *Legal and Criminological Psychology, 22*, 150–163.

Vul, E., & Pashler, H. (2007). Incubation benefits only after people have been misdirected. *Memory & Cognition, 35*, 701–710.

Vuong, Q. C., & Tarr, M. (2004). Rotation direction affects object recognition. *Vision Research, 44*, 1717–1730.

Wade, K. A., Garry, M., & Pezdek, K. (2017). Deconstructing rich false memories of committing crime: Commentary on Shaw & Porter (2015). *Psychological Science*, Advance online publication.

Wade, K. A., Garry, M., Read, J. D., & Lindsay, D. S. (2002). A picture is worth a thousand lies: Using false photographs to create false childhood memories. *Psychononic Bulletin & Review, 9*, 597–603.

Wagemans, J., Elder, J. H., Kubovy, M., Palmer, S. E., Peterson, M. A., Singh, M., & von der Heydt, R. (2012). A century of Gestalt psychology in visual perception: I. Perceptual grouping and figure-ground organization. *Psychological Bulletin, 138*, 1172–1217.

Wagemans, J., Feldman, J., Gephstein, S., Kimchi, R., Pomerantz, J. R., Van der Helm, P., & Van Leeuwen, C. (2012). A century of Gestalt psychology in visual perception: II. Conceptual and theoretical foundations. *Psychological Bulletin, 138*, 1218–1252.

Wagner, A. D., Koutstaal, W., & Schacter, D. L. (1999). When encoding yields remembering: Insights from event-related neuroimaging. *Philosophical Transactions of the Royal Society of London, Biology, 354*, 1307–1324.

Wagner, A. D., Schacter, D. L., Rotte, M., Koutstaal, W., Maril, A., Dale, A., et al. (1998). Building memories: Remembering and forgetting of verbal experiences as predicted by brain activity. *Science, 281*, 1188–1191.

Wagner, A. D., Shannon, B., Kahn, I., & Buckner, R. (2005). Parietal lobe contributions to episodic memory retrieval. *Trends in Cognitive Sciences, 9*, 445–453.

Wagner, R. K. (2000). Practical intelligence. In R. J. Sternberg (Ed.), *Handbook of human intelligence* (pp. 380–395). New York, NY: Cambridge University Press.

Wai, J., Putallaz, M., & Makel, M. C. (2012). Studying intellectual outliers: Are there sex differences, and are the smart getting smarter? *Current Directions in Psychological Science, 21*, 382–390.

Wallas, G. (1926). *The art of thought*. New York, NY: Harcourt, Brace.

Wallis, G. (2013). Toward a unified model of face and object recognition in the human visual system. *Frontiers in Psychology, 4*.

Wallis, G., & Bülthoff, H. (1999). Learning to recognize objects. *Trends in Cognitive Sciences, 3*, 22–31.

Walton, G., & Spencer, S. (2009). Latent ability: Grades and test scores systematically underestimate the intellectual ability of negatively stereotyped students. *Psychological Science, 20*, 1132–1139.

Wan, L., Crookes, K., Dawel, A., Pidcock, M., Hall, A., & McKone, E. (2017). Face-blind for other-race faces: Individual differences in other-race recognition impairments. *Journal of Experimental Psychology: General, 146*, 102–122.

Wan, L., Crookes, K., Reynolds, K. J., Irons, J. L., & McKone, E. (2015). A cultural setting where the other-race effect on face recognition has no social-motivational component and derives entirely from lifetime perceptual experiences. *Cognition, 144*, 91–115.

Wang, R., Li, J., Fang, H., Tian, M., & Liu, J. (2012). Individual differences in holistic processing predict face recognition ability. *Psychological Science, 23*, 169–177.

Wang, S. H., & Morris, R. G. (2010). Hippocampal-neocortical interactions in memory formation, consolidation, and reconsolidation. *Annual Review of Psychology, 61*, 49–79.

Wanke, M., & Hansen, J. (2015) Relative processing fluency. *Current Directions in Psychological Science, 24*, 195–199.

Wantz, A., Borst, G., Mast, F. W., & Lobmaier, J. S. (2015). Colors in mind: A novel paradigm to investigate pure color imagery. *Journal of Experimental Psychology: Learning, Memory & Cognition, 41,* 1152–1161.

Warrington, E. K., & McCarthy, R. (1983). Category specific access dysphasia. *Brain, 106,* 859–878.

Warrington, E. K., & McCarthy, R. (1987). Categories of knowledge: Further fractionations and an attempted integration. *Brain, 110,* 1273–1296.

Warrington, E. K., & Shallice, T. (1984). Category specific semantic impairments. *Brain, 107,* 829–854.

Wason, P. (1966). Reasoning. In B. Foss (Ed.), *New horizons in psychology* (pp. 135–151). Middlesex, England: Penguin.

Wason, P. (1968). Reasoning about a rule. *Quarterly Journal of Experimental Psychology, 20,* 273–281.

Watkins, M., Wilson, S., Kotz, K., Carbone, M., & Babula, T. (2006). Factor structure of the Wechsler Intelligence Scale for Children—Fourth edition among referred students. *Educational and Psychological Measurement, 66,* 975–983.

Watkins, M. J. (1977). The intricacy of memory span. *Memory & Cognition, 5,* 529–534.

Wattenmaker, W. D., Dewey, G. I., Murphy, T. D., & Medin, D. L. (1986). Linear separability and concept learning: Context, relational properties, and concept naturalness. *Cognitive Psychology, 18,* 158–194.

Waugh, N. C., & Norman, D. A. (1965). Primary memory. *Psychological Review, 72,* 89–104.

Wearing, D. (2011). *Forever today: A memoir of love and amnesia.* New York, NY: Doubleday.

Weaver, C. (1993). Do you need a "flash" to form a flashbulb memory? *Journal of Experimental Psychology: General, 122,* 39–46.

Weber, E., & Johnson, E. (2009). Mindful judgment and decision making. *Annual Review of Psychology, 60,* 53–85.

Wechsler, D. (2003). *Wechsler Intelligence Scale for Children—Fourth edition.* San Antonio, TX: Psychological Corporation.

Weiner, K. S., & Grill-Spector, K. (2013). The improbable simplicity of the fusiform face area. *Trends in Cognitive Sciences, 16,* 251–254.

Weisberg, R., & Alba, J. (1981). An examination of the alleged role of "fixation" in the solution of several "insight" problems. *Journal of Experimental Psychology: General, 110,* 169–192.

Weisberg, R. W. (1986). *Creativity: Genius and other myths.* New York, NY: Freeman.

Weisberg, R. W. (2006). *Creativity: Understanding innovation in problem solving, science, invention and the arts.* New York, NY: Wiley.

Weiskrantz, L. (1986). *Blindsight: A case study and implications.* New York, NY: Oxford University Press.

Weiskrantz, L. (1997). *Consciousness lost and found.* New York, NY: Oxford University Press.

Wells, G. L., & Bradfield, A. L. (1998). "Good, you identified the suspect": Feedback to eyewitnesses distorts their reports of the witnessed experience. *Journal of Applied Psychology, 83,* 360–376.

Wells, G. L., Olson, E. A., & Charman, S. D. (2002). The confidence of eyewitnesses in their identifications from lineups. *Current Directions in Psychological Science, 11,* 151–154.

Wells, G. L., Olson, E. A., & Charman, S. D. (2003). Distorted retrospective eyewitness reports as functions of feedback and delay. *Journal of Experimental Psychology: Applied, 9,* 42–51.

Wells, G. L., & Quinlivan, D. S. (2009). Suggestive eyewitness identification procedures and the Supreme Court's reliability test in light of eyewitness science: 30 years later. *Law and Human Behavior, 33,* 1–24.

Westerman, D. L., Lanska, M., & Olds, J. M. (2015). The effect of processing fluency on impressions of familiarity and liking. *Journal of Experimental Psychology: Learning, Memory & Cognition, 41,* 426–438.

Westmacott, R., & Moscovitch, M. (2003). The contribution of autobiographical significance to semantic memory. *Memory & Cognition, 31,* 761–774.

Wharton, C., Holyoak, K., Downing, P., & Lange, T. (1994). Below the surface: Analogical similarity and retrieval competition in reminding. *Cognitive Psychology, 26,* 64–101.

Wheeler, D. (1970). Processes in word recognition. *Cognitive Psychology, 1,* 59–85.

Wheeler, M. E., Petersen, S. E, & Buckner, R. L. (2000). Memory's echo: Vivid remembering reactivates sensory-specific cortex. *Proceedings of the National Academy of Sciences, USA, 97,* 11125–11129.

White, J. (2008). Illusory intelligences? *Journal of Philosophy of Education, 42,* 611–630.

White, P. (1988). Knowing more than we can tell: "Introspective access" and causal report accuracy 10 years later. *British Journal of Psychology, 79,* 13–45.

Whitney, C. (2001). How the brain encodes the order of letters in a printed word: The SERIOL model and selective literature review. *Psychonomic Bulletin & Review, 8,* 221–243.

Whittlesea, B. W. A. (2002). False memory and the discrepancy-attribution hypothesis: The prototype-familiarity illusion. *Journal of Experimental Psychology: General, 131,* 96–115.

Whittlesea, B. W. A., Jacoby, L., & Girard, K. (1990). Illusions of immediate memory: Evidence of an attributional basis for feelings of familiarity and perceptual quality. *Journal of Memory and Language, 29,* 716–732.

Whorf, B. L. (1956). *Language, thought, and reality.* Cambridge, England: Technology Press.

Willemsen, M., Böckenholt, U., & Johnson, E. (2011). Choice by value encoding and value construction: Processes of loss aversion. *Journal of Experimental Psychology: General, 140,* 303–324.

Williams, L. M., Liddell, B. J., Kemp, A. H., Bryant, R. A., Meares, R. A., Peduto, A. S., & Gordon, E. (2006). Amygdala-prefrontal dissociation of subliminal and supraliminal fear. *Human Brain Mapping, 27*(8), 652–661.

Wilmer, J. B. (2017). Individual differences in face recognition: A decade of discovery. *Current Directions in Psychological Science, 26*, 225–230.

Wilson, K., & French, C. C. (2006). The relationship between susceptibility to false memories, dissociativity, and paranormal belief and experience. *Personality and Individual Differences, 41*, 1493–1502.

Wilson, T. D. (2002). *Strangers to ourselves: Discovering the adaptive unconscious.* Cambridge, MA: Harvard University Press.

Wilson, T. D., & Brekke, N. (1994). Mental contamination and mental correction: Unwanted influences on judgments and evaluations. *Psychological Bulletin, 116*, 117–142.

Wilson, T. D., & Dunn, E. W. (2004). Self-knowledge: Its limits, value, and potential for improvement. *Annual Review of Psychology, 55*, 493–518.

Wilson, T. D., Wheatley, T., Meyers, J. M., Gilbert, D., & Axsom, D. (2000). Focalism: A source of durability bias in affective forecasting. *Journal of Personality and Social Psychology, 78*, 821–836.

Winawer, J., Witthoft, N., Frank, M. C., Wu, L., Wade, A. R., & Boroditsky, L. (2007). Russian blues reveal effects of language on color discrimination. *Proceedings of the National Academy of Sciences, 104*, 7780–7785.

Winkielman, P., & Schwarz, N. (2001). How pleasant was your childhood? Beliefs about memory shape inferences from experienced difficulty of recall. *Psychological Science, 12*, 176–179.

Winograd, E., & Neisser, U. (Eds.). (1993). *Affect and accuracy in recall: Studies of "flashbulb" memories.* New York, NY: Cambridge University Press.

Wiseman, S., & Neisser, U. (1974). Perceptual organization as a determinant of visual recognition memory. *American Journal of Psychology, 87*, 675–681.

Wittgenstein, L. (1953). *Philosophical investigations* (G. E. M. Anscombe, Trans.). Oxford, England: Blackwell.

Wixted, J. (2004). The psychology and neuroscience of forgetting. *Annual Review of Psychology, 55*, 235–269.

Witxted, J. D., & Wells, G. L. (2017). The relationship between eyewitness confidence and identification accuracy: A new synthesis. *Psychological Science in the Public Interest, 18*, 10–65.

Wixted, J. T., Mickes, L., Clark, S. E., Gronlund, S. D., & Roediger, H. L., III (2015). Initial eyewitness confidence reliably predicts eyewitness identification accuracy. *American Psychologist, 70*, 515–526.

Wolfe, J. M. (1999). Inattentional amnesia. In V. Coltheart (Ed.), *Fleeting memories* (pp. 71–94). Cambridge, MA: MIT Press.

Wollen, K. A., Weber, A., & Lowry, D. (1972). Bizarreness versus interaction of mental images as determinants of learning. *Cognitive Psychology, 3*, 518–523.

Womelsdorf, T., Schoffelen, J.-M., Oostenveld, R., Singer, W., Desimone, R., Engel, A., & Fries, P. (2007). Modulation of neuronal interactions through neuronal synchronization. *Science, 316*, 1609–1612.

Wood, N., & Cowan, N. (1995). The cocktail party phenomenon revisited: How frequent are attention shifts to one's name in an irrelevant auditory channel? *Journal of Experimental Psychology: Learning, Memory, & Cognition, 21*, 255–260.

Wright, D., & Skagerberg, E. (2007). Postidentification feedback affects real eyewitnesses. *Psychological Science, 18*, 172–177.

Wright, D. B., & Carlucci, M. E. (2011). The response order effect: People believe the first person who remembers an event. *Psychonomics Bulletin & Review, 18*, 805–812.

Wright, R. D., & Ward, L. M. (2008). *Orienting of attention.* New York, NY: Oxford University Press.

Wyatt, N., & Machado, L. (2013). Distractor inhibition: Principles of operation during selective attention. *Journal of Experimental Psychology: Human Perception & Performance, 39*, 245–256.

Xu, F., & Garcia, V. (2008). Intuitive statistics by 8-month-old infants. *Proceedings of the National Academy of Sciences, 105*, 5012–5015.

Yantis, S. (2008). The neural basis of selective attention: Cortical sources and targets of attentional modulation. *Current Directions in Psychological Science, 17*, 86–90.

Yarbus, A. L. (1967). *Eye movements and vision.* New York, NY: Plenum Press. (Translated from Russian by Basil Haigh. Original Russian edition published in Moscow, 1965.)

Yates, F. A. (1966). *The art of memory.* London, England: Routledge and Kegan Paul.

Yee, E., & Thompson-Schill, S. L. (2016). Putting concepts into context. *Psychonomic Bulletin & Review, 23*, 1015–1027.

Yeni-Komshian, G. (1993). Speech perception. In J. B. Gleason & N. B. Ratner (Eds.), *Psycholinguistics* (pp. 90–133). New York, NY: Harcourt Brace Jovanovich.

Yin, R. (1969). Looking at upside-down faces. *Journal of Experimental Psychology, 81*, 141–145.

Yonelinas, A., & Jacoby, L. (2012). The process-dissociation approach two decades later: Convergence, boundary conditions, and new direction. *Memory & Cognition, 40*, 663–680.

Yonelinas, A. P., & Ritchey, M. (2015). The slow forgetting of emotional episodic memories: An emotional binding account. *Trends in Cognitive Sciences, 19*, 259–267.

Young, A. W., & Burton, A. M. (2017). Recognizing faces. *Current Directions in Psychological Science, 26*, 212–217.

Young, A. W., Hellawell, D., & Hay, D. C. (1987). Configurational information in face perception. *Perception, 16*, 747–759.

Zabelina, D., Saporta, A., & Beeman, M. (2016). Flexible or leaky attention in creative people: Distinct patterns of attention for different types of creative thinking. *Memory & Cognition, 44*, 488–498.

Zaragoza, M. S., Payment, K. E., Ackil, J. K., Drivdahl, S. B., & Beck, M. (2001). Interviewing witnesses: Forced confabulation and confirmatory feedback increases false memories. *Psychological Science, 12*, 473–477.

Zechmeister, E. B., Chronis, A. M., Cull, W. L., D'Anna, C. A., & Healy, N. A. (1995). Growth of a functionally important lexicon. *Journal of Reading Behavior, 27*(2), 201–212.

Zeki, S. (1991). Cerebral akinetopsia (visual motion blindness): A review. *Brain, 114*, 811–824.

Zelazo, P. D. (2006). The dimensional change card sort (DCCS): A method of assessing executive function in children. *Nature Protocols, 1*, 297–301.

Zeman, A., Dewar, M., & Della Sala, S. (2015). Lives without imagery—Congenital aphantasia. *Cortex, 73*, 378–380.

Zeman, A., Dewar, M., & Della Sala, S. (2016). Reflections on aphantasia. *Cortex, 74*, 336–337.

Zhao, M., Bülthoff, H. H., & Bülthoff, I. (2016). Beyond faces and expertise: Facelike holistic processing of nonface objects in the absence of expertise. *Psychological Science, 27*, 213–222.

Zhou, B., & Kross, A. (2016). Data trimming procedure can eliminate bilingual cognitive advantage. *Psychonomic Bulletin & Review, 23*, 1221–1230.

Zihl, J., von Cramon, D., & Mai, N. (1983). Selective disturbance of movement vision after bilateral brain damage. *Brain, 106*, 313–340.

Zihl, J., von Cramon, D., Mai, N., & Schmid, C. (1991). Disturbance of movement vision after bilateral posterior brain damage. Further evidence and follow up observations. *Brain, 114*, 2235–2252.

Zillmer, E. A., Spiers, M. V., & Culbertson, W. C. (2008). *Principles of neuropsychology*. Belmont, CA: Wadsworth.

Zimler, J., & Keenan, J. M. (1983). Imagery in the congenitally blind: How visual are visual images? *Journal of Experimental Psychology: Learning, Memory, & Cognition, 9*, 269–282.

Zimmer, C. (2010). The brain. *Discover*, 28–29.

Zimmer, C. (2015, June 22). Picture this? Some just can't. *The New York Times*, p. D3. http://www.nytimes.com/2015/06/23/science/aphantasia-minds-eye-blind.html?emc=eta1&_r=0

Zwaan, R. A. (2016). Situation models, mental simulations, and abstract concepts in discourse comprehension. *Psychonomic Bulletin & Review, 23*, 1028–1034.

Credits

Photographs

FRONT MATTER

Page ix top: Steve Prezant/Corbis via Getty Images; **p. ix bottom:** David De Lossy/Getty Images; **p. x top:** Digital Vision/Getty Images; **p. x bottom:** Gozooma/ Gallery Stock; **p. xi:** Sean Justice/Getty Images.

CHAPTER 1

Page 2: Steve Prezant/Corbis via Getty Images; **p. 4:** Brooks Kraft/Corbis via Getty Images; **p. 5:** Image Source/SuperStock; **p. 6:** J. Carlee Adams/Bullshotz Photography; **p. 7:** Dr. Jacopo Annese, The Brain Observatory; **p. 9:** The Drs. Nicholas and Dorothy Cummings Center for the History of Psychology, The University of Akron; **p. 11:** Ferdinand Hamburger Archives, Sheridan Libraries, Johns Hopkins University; **p. 13:** Billion Photos/Shutterstock; **p. 14:** Lebrecht Music and Arts; **p. 15:** Emory University Photo/ Video; **p. 16:** University of Cambridge Psychology; **p. 20:** Stefan Hard/*The Times Argus* via AP Photo.

CHAPTER 2

Page 24: Cary Wolinksy/Aurora Photos; **p. 27:** SPL/Science Source; **p. 28:** Dr. Fred Hossler/Visuals Unlimited, Inc.; **p. 29:** Agren, T., et al. (2012). "Disruption of reconsolidation erases a fear memory trace in the human amygdala," *Science*, Vol. 337, No. 6101, pp. 1550-1552. ©2012, American Association for the Advancement of Science. **p. 32 left:** Warren Anatomical Museum in the Francis A. Countway Library of Medicine; **p. 32 center:** Damasio, H., Grabowski, T., Frank, R., Galaburda, A.M., & Damasio, A.R. (1994), "The return of Phineas Gage," *Science*, 264; courtesy Hanna Damasio; **p. 32 right:** Warren Anatomical Museum in the Francis A. Countway Library of Medicine Gift of Jack and Beverly Wilgus; **p. 39:** Dr. M. Phelps and Dr. J. Mazziotta et al./Neurology/Science Source; **p. 40 left:** James Cavallini/Science Source; **p. 40 center:** Geoff Tompkinson/Science Source; **p. 40 right:** Camazine S./Science Source/Getty Images; **p. 42:** © Jack Liu; **p. 43 left and right:** Reprinted from Tong, F., Kakayma, K., Vaughen, J.T., and Kanwisher, N. "Binocular rivalry and visual awareness in human estra striate cortex," *Neuron* 21, 735–759, ©1998 with permission from Elsevier; **p. 45:** Kosslyn, et al. "Visual Images Preserve Metric Spatial Information: Evidence from Studies of Image Scanning," *Journal of Experimental Psychology: Human Perception and Performance* 1978, Vol. 4, No. 1, 47–60; **p. 48:** © The Trustees of The Natural History Museum, London; **p. 51 left:** SPL/Science Source; **p. 51 center:** Overseas/ CNRI/Science Source; **p. 51 right:** Guigoz/Dr. A Privat/ Petit Format/Science Source; **p. 58 top:** B. Christopher/ Alamy Stock Photo; **p. 58 bottom:** Prisma/Superstock.

CHAPTER 3

Page 62: David De Lossy/Getty Images; **p. 66:** Omikron/Science Source; **p. 71:** AP/Wide World Photos; **p. 82:** sirius1/Shutterstock; **p. 83:** Photograph by Jeffrey Grosscup; **p. 91:** Shepard, Roger N.; Levitin, Daniel J., "Cognitive psychology and music," (2002). *Foundations of Cognitive Psychology*: (pp. 503–514). Cambridge, MA, US: MIT Press, xvi, 862 pp.; **p. 96 left:**

Brand X Pictures/Getty Images; **p. 96 right**: Luciopix/Alamy; **p. 97 left**: REX/Shutterstock; **p. 97 right**: Solent News/REX/Shutterstock; **p. 98**: ScienceCartoonsPlus.com; **p. 101**: Adam Lacy/CSM/REX/Shutterstock.

CHAPTER 4

Page 106: Powerofforever/Getty Images; **p. 108**: James, T.W., et al.; Ventral occipital lesions impair object recognition but not object-directed grasping: An fMRI study, *Brain* 2003; 126 (11): 2463–2475, doi: 10.1093/brain/awg248. Reproduced by permission of Oxford University Press on behalf of the Guarantors of Brain. vl.4; **p. 109**: P. Servos, M.A. Goodale and G.K. Humphrey (March 1993). "The drawing of objects by a visual form agnosic: Contribution of surface properties and memorial representations," *Neuropsychologia*, Vol. 31, No. 3, pp. 251–259. ©1993 Published by Elsevier Ltd.; **p. 111**: Russell Glenister/Corbis; **p. 132**: R. Quian Quiroga, L. Reddy, G. Kreiman, C. Koch and I. Fried, "Invariants visual representation by single neurons in the human brain," *Nature,* June 23, 2005. 435:23 1102–1107. doi: 10.1038/nature03687, ©2005 Nature Publishing Group; **p. 135**: Thompson, Peter, *Perception* Vol. 9, pp. 483–484, ©1980 by SAGE Publication, Ltd. Reprinted by Permission of SAGE Publication, Ltd.; **p. 137**: Nancy Kanwisher and Galit Yovel, "The fusiform face area: a cortical region specialized for the perception of faces," *Phil. Trans R. Soc. B* (2006) 361, 2109–2128 doi: 10.1098/rstb.2006.1934. Permission conveyed through Copyright Clearance Center, Inc.; **p. 139**: Hugh Jackman: Sydney Alford/Alamy Stock Photo; Justin Timberlake: WFPA/Alamy Stock Photo; **p. 142**: M. Bar, K.S. Kassam, A.S. Ghuman, J. Boshyan, A.M. Schmid, A.M. Dale, M.S. Hamalainen, K. Markinkovic, D.L. Schacter, B.R. Rosen, and E. Halgren, "Top-down facilitation of visual recognition," *Proceedings of the National Academy of Sciences* Jan. 10, 2006, Vol. 103, no. 2. pp. 449–454. © (2006) National Academy of Sciences, U.S.A; **p. 143**: Fuse/Thinkstock/Getty Images.

CHAPTER 5

Page 148: Paul Bradbury/Getty Images; **p. 151**: Courtesy of Daniel J. Simons and Christopher Chabris. Simons, D. J., & Chabris, C. F. (1999). "Gorillas in our midst: Sustained inattentional blindness for dynamic events," *Perception*, 28, 1059–1074; **p. 152**: Javier Pierini/Getty Images; **p. 154**: iStockphoto; **p. 155 top**: Galina Barskaya/Dreamstime.com; **p. 155 bottom**:

Titania1980/Dreamstime.com; **p. 156**: Daniel T. Levin, Daniel J. Simons, "Failure to Detect Changes to Attended Objects in Motion Pictures," *Psychonomic Bulletin and Review*, 1997, 4(4), 501–506. Fig.1; **p. 166**: Rykoff Collection/Corbis via Getty Images; **p. 169**: from figure 5, "The neural mechanisms of top-down attentional control," J. B. Hopfinger, M. H. Buonocore & G. R. Mangun (2000), *Nature Neuroscience*, Vol. 3, pp. 284–291, doi:10.1038/72999; **p. 170 inset**: Unexpected, 1884–88 (oil on canvas), Repin, Ilya Efimovich (1844–1930)/Tretyakov Gallery, Moscow, Russia/Bridgeman Images; **p. 170**: adapted from figure 109, p. 174 and republished with permission of Springer Science and Bus Media B V, from *Eye Movement and Vision* by Alfred L. Yarbus. Trans Plenum Press New York 1967; permission conveyed through Copyright Clearance Center, Inc.; **p. 171**: Isopix/REX/Shutterstock; **p. 173**: Gilles Mingasson/Getty Images; **p. 174**: Kimberg, D.Y., D'Esposito, M., and M.J. Farah. "Cognitive Functions in the Prefrontal Cortex-Working Memory and Executive Control," *Current Directions in Psychological Science*, Volume 6(6), p.186, 1997; **p. 178**: Gaius Julius Caesar (100–44 BC.) was a Roman military and political leader. Statue. Louvre Museum. Paris. Francia/Tarker/Bridgeman Images; **p. 181**: AP Photo/Marshall Gorby, *Springfield News-Sun.*

CHAPTER 6

Page 194: Digital Vision/Getty Images; **p. 196 top**: Ros Drinkwater/Alamy; **p. 196 bottom**: Jiri Rezac/Polaris; **p. 205**: Talmi et al. "Neuroimaging the serial position curve," *Psychological Science*, 2005 Sept.; 16 (9): 716–23; **p. 211**: courtesy Dr. John Jonides; **p. 215**: Alberto Pomares/Getty Images; **p. 222 left**: Imagic Chicago/Alamy; **p. 222 right**: Stuart Black/Alamy; **p. 224**: Mnesmosyne, 1881 (oil on canvas), Rossetti, Dante Gabriel Charles (1828–82)/Delaware Art Museum, Wilmington, USA/Samuel and Mary R. Bancroft Memorial/Bridgeman Images; **p. 230**: Wiseman, S., & Neisser, U. (1974), "Perceptual organization as a determinant of visual recognition memory," *American Journal of Psychology*, 87(4), 675–681; **p. 233**: Blend Images/Getty Images.

CHAPTER 7

Page 238: Tim Macpherson/Cultura/Getty Images; **p. 240**: Photo by Project Neuron, University of Illinois at Urbana-Champaign; **p. 245**: Wheeler et al. (2000), "Memory's echo: Vivid remembering reactivates sensory-specific cortex," *Proceedings of the National Academy of Sciences*, September 26, 2000, vol. 97, no. 20, 11125–11129. Copyright (2000) National Academy of Sciences, U.S.A.; **p. 253 left:** Tony DiMaio/SilverHub/REX/Shutterstock; **p. 253 center left:** Rob Latour/Variety/REX/Shutterstock; **p. 253 center:** Brian To/REX/Shutterstock; **p. 253 center right:** Dave Allocca/StarPix/REX/Shutterstock; **p. 253 right:** Chelsea Lauren/Deadline/REX/Shutterstock; **p. 254:** Ranganath, et al. "Dissociable correlates of recollection and familiarity within the medial temporal lobes," *Neuropsychologia,* © 2003 Elsevier Ltd. All rights reserved; **p. 259:** Courtesy of Daniel Reisberg; **p. 263:** Junko Kimura/Getty Images; **p. 268:** The Canadian Press/Helen Branswell; **p. 269:** Corkin et al., "H.M.'s medial temporal lobe lesion: Findings from magnetic resonance imaging," *The Journal of Neuroscience* 17: 3964–3979, Copyright © 1997 Society of Neuroscience; **p. 273:** Hero Images Inc./Alamy Stock Photo.

CHAPTER 8

Page 278: Ryan McVay/Getty Images; **p. 282:** Photograph from "Role of schemata in memory for places," by W. F. Brewer and J. C. Treyens, *Cognitive Psychology,* 13 (1981): 207–230; **p. 288:** Kevin Sullivan/*The Orange County Register* via AP; **p. 292:** Wade, K. A., Garry, M., Read, J. D., Lindsay, D. S., "A picture is worth a thousand lies: Using false photographs to create false childhood memories," *Psychonomic Bulletin & Review* 9, no. 3 (2002): 597–603; **p. 293:** Lindsay, D. S., et al., "True photographs and false memories," *Psychological Science* 15 (2004): 149–154; **p. 294:** Barney Wayne/Keystone/Getty Images; **p. 301:** Orne, M. T., "The nature of hypnosis: Artifact and essence," *Journal of Abnormal and Social Psychology* (1959): 277–299; **p. 305:** Kelley et al., "Finding the self? An event-related fMRI study," *Journal of Cognitive Neuroscience,* 14 (2002): 785–794, Copyright © 2002, Massachusetts Institute of Technology; **p. 309 left:** David Levenson/Getty Images; **p. 309 center:** Sean Adair/Reuters/Newscom; **p. 309 right:** AP Photo/Joel Ryan; **p. 318:** Will & Deni McIntyre/Corbis via Getty Images.

CHAPTER 9

Page 324: Gozooma/Gallery Stock; **p. 328:** Tierfotoagentur/Alamy; **p. 330:** German Shepherd: GK Hart/Vikki Hart/Getty Images; Chihuahua, Maltese, Poodle, Collie, and Great Dane: Eric Isselée/Dreamstime.com; Komondor: REX/Shutterstock; Bedlington Terrior: Vanessa Grossemy/Alamy Stock Images; **p. 333:** Adrian Lewart/Dreamstime.com;

p. 334 top: Rick & Nora Bowers/Alamy; **p. 334 bottom left:** Avalon/Photoshot License/Alamy Stock Photo; **p. 334 bottom right:** Hiroya Minakuchi/Minden Pictures/Getty Images; **p. 336:** Mick Tsikas/Epa/REX/Shutterstock; **p. 339:** Look and Learn/Bridgeman Art Library; **p. 341:** ScienceCartoonsPlus.com; **p. 343:** age fotostock/Superstock; **p. 345:** Courtesy of Robert Malseed; **p. 347:** courtesy of the author; **p. 360 left and right:** Courtesy National Gallery of Art, Washington.

CHAPTER 10

Page 364: Photosindia/AgeFotostock; **p. 371:** © By permission of Leigh Rubin and Creators Syndicate, Inc.: **p. 373:** Savushkin/Getty Images; **p. 379:** Lebrecht Music & Arts; **p. 380:** Lucasfilm/Fox/Kobal/REX/Shutterstock; **p. 381:** Hulton-Deutsch Collection/Corbis via Getty Images; **p. 384 :** ScienceCartoonsPlus.com; **p. 393:** Dronkers, N.F., et al.; Paul Broca's historic cases: High resolution MR imaging of the brains of Leborgne and Lelong, *Brain* 2007; 130 (5): 1432–1441, doi: 10.1093/brain/awm042. Reproduced by permission of Oxford University Press on behalf of the Guarantors of Brain. vl.4 **p. 395:** Vikki Martin/Alamy Stock Photo; **p. 397:** Stu Porter/Alamy; **p. 398 left:** Rolls Press/Popperfoto/Getty Images; **p. 398 right:** Hulton Archive/Getty Images; **p. 399:** ColsTravel/Alamy; **p. 404:** Wavebreak Media Ltd/Alamy Stock Photo.

CHAPTER 11

Page 410: © Friderike Heuer; **p. 418:** Claus Fritzmann/dieKleinert/Alamy Stock Photo; **p. 421:** Adapted by Marcel Just from Carpenter, P. A., Just, M. A, Keller, T. A., et al. (1999), "Graded functional activation in the visuospatial system and the amount of task demand," *Journal of Cognitive Neuroscience,* 11 (1), p.14. (doi: 10.1162/089892999563210), ©1999 Massachusetts Institute of Technology; **p. 422:** Comstock/Getty Images; **p. 425:** O'Craven, K. M., & Kanwisher, N. (2000), "Mental imagery of faces and places activates corresponding stimulus-specific brain regions," *Journal of Cognitive Neuroscience* 12:6 pp. 1013–1023, © 2000 Massachusetts Institute of Technology https://doi.org/10.1162/08989290051137549; **p 427:** Stefano Amantini/Atlantide Phototravel/Corbis via Getty Images; **p. 429:** Thompson, W. L., Slotnick, S., Burrage, M., & Kosslyn, S. (2009), "Two forms of spatial imagery: Neuroimaging evidence," *Psychological Science,* 20, 1245–1253; **p. 433:** Cui, X., Jeter, C. B., Yang, D., Montague, P. R., & Eagleman, D. M. (2007), "Vividness of mental imagery: individual variability can be measured objectively," *Vision Research*, 47(4), 474–478; **p. 435:** Tenniel, John (1820–1914)/Private Collection/The Bridgeman Art Library; **p. 437:** © National Portrait Gallery, London; **p. 438:** Kellydt/Dreamstime.com; **p. 446:** Intraub, H., and Richardson, M., "Boundary extension in picture memory," *Journal of Experimental Psychology*, 15, 179–87. Reprinted by permission; **p. 449:** Phanie/Alamy.

CHAPTER 12

Page 454: Sean Justice/Getty Images; **p. 457:** Paul Wicks/Wikimedia Commons; **p. 461:** Fuse/Corbis: **p. 467:** De Neys, W., and Goel, V. (©2011). "Heuristics and biases in the brain: Dual neural pathways for decision making," in O. Vartanian and D. R. Mandel (Eds.), *Neuroscience of Decision Making*. Hove, UK: Psychology Press. Reproduced by permission of Taylor and Francis Group, LLC, a division of Informa PLC; **p. 472:** Sidney Harris/Cartoonstock.com; **p. 476:** ScienceCartoonsPlus.com; **p. 485:** Marc Arts/Shutterstock; **p. 490:** © Mark Parisi/www.offthemark.com.

CHAPTER 13

Page 498: Lucidio Studio, Inc./Getty Images; **p. 513:** Sam Gross/The New Yorker Collection/www.cartoonbank.com; **p. 517:** from Kounios and Beeman (2009), "The Aha! Moment: The Cognitive Neuroscience of Insight" *Current Directions in Psychological Science* 18:4 pp. 210–216, https://doi.org/10.1111/j.1467-8721.2009.01638.x; **p. 523 Part B:** Sample item similar to those in the Wechsler Adult Intelligence Scale, Fourth Edition (WAIS-IV). Copyright © 2008 NCS Pearson, Inc. Reproduced with permission. All rights reserved; **Part C:** Sample item similar to those in the Raven's Progressive Matrices (Standard Parallel, Sets A–E). Copyright © 1998 NCS Pearson, Inc. Reproduced with permission. All rights reserved. "Wechsler Adult Intelligence Scale", "WAIS', and "Raven's Progressive Matrices" are trademarks, in the US and/or other countries, of Pearson Education, Inc. or its affiliates(s); **p. 529:** From Jung, R. E. and Haier, R. J., "The Parieto-Frontal Integration Theory (P-FIT) of intelligence: Converging neuroimaging evidence," *Behavioral and Brain Sciences* (2007) 30, 135–187. Courtesy Brain and Behavioral Associates, PC; **p. 531:** John Alex Maguire/REX/Shutterstock; **p. 532:** Tom Dymond/Thames/REX/Shutterstock; **p. 538:** Rawpixel/Shutterstock; **p. 541:** Mark Scott/Getty Images.

CHAPTER 14

Page 546: Sarah Wilmer/Gallery Stock; **p. 555:** Joel W. Rogers/Corbis via Getty Images; **p. 557:** © John Caldwell; **p. 561:** "Figure 13" by Stanislas Dehaene; from *CONSCIOUSNESS AND THE BRAIN: DECIPHERING HOW THE BRAIN CODES OUR THOUGHTS* copyright © 2014 by Stanislas Dehaene. Used by permission of Viking Books, an imprint of Penguin Publishing Group, a division of Penguin Random House LLC. All rights reserved; **p. 566:** Angela Waye/Alamy Stock Photo; **p. 573:** Naotsugu Tsuchiya and Ralph Adolphs, "Emotion and consciousness," from *Trends in Cognitive Sciences* Vol. 11 No. 4. DOI: 10.1016/j.tics.2007.01.005. ©2007 Elsevier Ltd. All rights reserved; **p. 579:** John Springer Collection/Corbis via Getty Images; **p. 581:** Inmagine Asia/Corbis.

Figures

Figure 4.3 (p. 110): Figure 3 from Selfridge, O. G., "Pattern Recognition and Modern Computers." *AFIPS '55 (Western) Proceedings of the March 1–3, 1955, western joint computer conference.* Copyright © 1955 by the Association for Computing Machinery, Inc. doi:10.1145/1455292.1455310. Reprinted by permission; **Figure 4.11 (p. 128):** Figure 3 from James L. McClelland and David E. Rumelhart, "An interactive model of context effects in letter perception," *Psychological Review* 88(5): 375–407, September 1981. Copyright © 1981 by the American Psychological Association. Reprinted with permission; **Figure 5.6A (p. 159):** Figure 6.7A from *Principles of Cognitive Neuroscience*, 2nd Ed. by Purves, Cabeza, Huettel, LaBar, Platt, and Woldorff. © 2012 by Sinauer Associates, Inc. Used by permission of Oxford University Press; **Figure 5.6B (p. 159):** Figure 6.7B from *Principles of Cognitive Neuroscience*, 2nd Ed. by Purves, Cabeza, Huettel, LaBar, Platt, and Woldorff. Originally published as Figure 1, Hillyard et. al. "Electric signs of selective attention in the human brain," *Science* 182, p. 178. © 1973 AAAS. Reprinted with permission from AAAS. 10.1126/science.182.4108.177; **Figure 6.6 (p. 208):** Figure 7 from Cabeza, R., & Nyberg, L., "Imaging cognition II: An empirical review of 275 PET and fMRI studies." *Journal of Cognitive Neuroscience*, 12(1), pp. 1–47. Copyright © 2000 by the Massachusetts Institute of Technology. Reprinted by permission of MIT Press Journals. http://www.mitpressjournals.org; **Figure 8.12 (p. 314):** Figure 1 from Martin A. Conway, Gillian

Author Index

Gobet, F., 508
Godden, D. R., 242, *243*
Goebel, R., 424
Gold, C., 140
Gold, P. E., 57
Goldenberg, G., 428
Goldenberg, J., 521
Goldinger, S. D., 350
Goldin-Meadow, S., 395
Goldman-Rakic, P. S., 182, 571
Goldschmidt, G., 437, 449, 504
Goldsmith, S. F., 403
Goldstein, D. G., 485
Goldstone, R. L., 342
Gollan, T., 403
Gonthier, C., 530
Gonzalez, R., 265, 576
Goodale, M. A., 77, 428, *559*, 559, *577*
Goodman, G., 310, 316
Goodman, N., 342
Gordon, H., 534
Gordon, R. D., 303
Gore, J. C., 136
Goshen-Gottstein, Y., 204, *205*
Gottesman, C. V., 445
Gottesman, I. I., 535
Gottfredson, L. S., 524, 530
Grabowecky, M., 80, 112
Grabowski, T., *349*
Grady, C. L., 204, *205*
Graesser, A. C., 391, 392
Graf, M., 134
Graf, P., 219, 255, 271, *577*
Grafman, J., 183
Graham, K. S., 304
Grainger, J., 120
Grant, H. M., 243
Gray, J. R., 209, 530
Gray, K. L. H., 138
Gray, W., 329
Green, D., 403
Greenberg, D. L., 433
Greene, C. M., 181
Greenfield, P. M., 535
Greenspan, R. L., 291
Gregg, M. K., 156
Grewal, D., 531
Grice, P., 392
Griffin, D. W., 265, 465, 466, 576
Griffith, B., 375

Griggs, R., 479
Grigorenko, E. L., 530
Grill-Spector, K., 136
Grodner, D., 385
Groeger, J. A., 181
Gronlund, S. D., 296
Gross, J., 572
Grossi, D., 134
Gruber, H. E., 520
Grundy, J. C., 403
Gudat, F., 31
Guerin, S., 303
Guilford, J., 520, *521*

Haber, L., 434
Haber, R. N., 434, *435*
Habib, R., 282
Hacker, H., 424
Hackman, D., 535
Haddock, T., 576
Haden, P. E., 255, 577
Hagemann, D., 529
Hagen, L., 293
Hagoort, P., *389*
Hahn, B., 163
Hahn, U., 462, 506
Haier, R., *529*
Halamish, V., 302, 318
Halberstadt, J., *334*
Hale, R. G., 445
Haley, A., *535*
Hall, L., 305, 313, 317
Hall, S., 468
Halle, M., 370, 375
Halliday, H. E., 257
Halpern, D., 509
Hamann, S., 310
Hamarberg, R., 372
Hambrick, D., 181
Hamel, R., 437, 449, 504
Hamill, R., 463
Hammond, K. M., 428
Hampshire, A., 169
Han, C-h., 402
Han, J., 140
Hanako, Y., 402
Hancock, P. J. B., 134
Handel, S., 375
Handley, S. J., 465, 478
Hannon, B., 209
Hansen, J., 262
Hansen, W. A., 350
Hanyu, K., 315
Haque, S., 315

Harden, K. P., 535
Hardt, O., 299, 306
Harinck, F., 483
Harley, T. A., 299
Harmon-Jones, E., 307, 308
Harris, K., 375
Harrison, T. L., 181, 210, 530
Harsch, N., 296, 308
Hartmann, P., 31
Harvey, L. O., Jr., 88
Harvey, N., 490
Harwood, D. G., 25
Hasher, L., 172
Hashtroudi, S., 578
Hass, R. W., 520
Hassin, R. R., 563
Hastie, R., 347, 348, 490
Hattie, J. A. C., 319
Haun, D. B. M., 400
Haxby, J. V., 77, 183
Hay, D. C., 138
Hayes, B. K., 347
Hayne, H., 315
Hayward, W. G., 131, 132, 137
Hayworth, C. M. A., 535
Hazlett, G., 316
Healy, A. F., 302
Healy, N. A., 377
Hecht, P., 181
Heckman, J. J., 534
Hegarty, M., 420, 428, 430
Heil, M., 424
Hein, L., 206
Heine, S., 172, 539, 541
Heit, E., 346, 347
Hélie, S., 518
Hell, W., 468
Hellawell, D., 138
Heller, M. A., 428
Helmholtz, H. von, 88–89, *89*, 90, 95
Helmuth, L., 42, 426
Helstrup, T., 504
Hemphill, D. D., 181
Henderson, J. M., 167, 171, 287, 445
Hennessey, B., 514, 515
Hennessey, J. M., 437, 449, 504
Hennighausen, E., 424
Hensler, B., 535

Herlitz, A., 220
Hermer-Vazquez, L., 402
Hernández, M., 403
Hertwig, R., 265, 466, 487
Herzog, S. M., 265
Hessels, S., 152
Heuer, F., 306, 307
Hezlett, S. A., 524
Hichwa, R. D., *349*
Hickok, G., 348, 350
Hicks, J. L., 253
Higbee, K. L., 226
Higgins, E. T., 306
Hilchey, M., 403
Hill, A. L., 532
Hillyard, S. A., 158
Hilton, D. J., 466
Hilts, P. J., 7
Hirst, W., 187, 296, 308, 309, 489
Hiscock, M., 535
Hitch, G., 201, 203, 210, 299–300, *300*
Ho, L., 312
Hodges, J. R., 304
Hoffman, H., 375
Hoffman, J. E., 445
Hoffman, M. S., 437
Hoffrage, U., 468
Hogan, H. P., 440, *441*
Hohwy, J., 567
Holden, C., 525t
Hollingshead, A., 274
Hollingworth, A., 445
Holmberg, D., 305
Holmes, A., 306
Holmes, E. A., 424
Holtgraves, T. M., 392
Holway, A. F., 88
Holyoak, K. J., 140, *215*, 479, 505, 506, *506*
Holz, P., 169
Homes, J. G., 305
Hon, N., 169
Hope, L., 309, 310, 311
Horn, J. L., 527, 528
Hornby, P., 386
Horowitz, T., 180
Horry, R., 134, 138
Horton, R. S., 261
Horvath, J. C., 319
Hoschedidt, S. M., 306
Hoshino, N., 403
Hout, M. C., 350
Howe, M. L., 303, 315

Michel, C., 140
Mickes, L., 296
Mihatsch, M. M., 31
Milivojevic, B., 132
Mill, J. S., 477
Miller, E. K., 80, 169, 181, 571
Miller, F., 550
Miller, G. A., 17, 116, 206, 372, 378, 550
Miller, L. K., 532
Miller, M. B., *307*
Miller, R. R., 221
Millin, P. M., 268
Millis, K. K., 392
Milner, A. D., 64, 77, *559, 559, 577*
Milner, B., 195, 269
Mims, M., 464
Miner, A., 340
Mishkin, M., 77
Mitchell, J., 253
Mitchum, A., 180, 535
Mitroff, S. R., 171
Miyake, A., 181
Miyashita, Y., 424
Mohler, L., 243
Molden, D. C., 306
Monaco, A. P., 395
Montague, P. R., 432
Montaldi, D., 253
Montoy, R. M., 261
Montoya, A. K., 576
Moons, W. G., 257
Moore, C. M., 157
Moore, S. M., 180
Moore, T., 158, 163, 167
Moors, A., 185, 186
Morawetz, C., 169
Moray, N., 152
Morewedge, C. K., *485*
Morgan, C., 311, 316
Morgenstern, O., 480
Morris, R. G., 306
Morrisette, N., 302
Morrison, C., 315
Morrison, R. G., 140
Morsella, E., 569
Morton, J. B., 403
Moscovici, S., 472
Moscovitch, M., 112, 204, *205*, 256, 271, 299, 304
Moseley, P., 423
Most, S. B., 156

Moulin, C. J. A., 315
Muckli, L., 424
Mudrik, L., 560
Müllbacher, W., 428
Müller, H. J., 79
Mulligan, N., 256, 258, 265, *576*
Mumford, M., 515
Munitz, H., 136
Murdock, B. B., Jr., 201
Murphy, D. R., 260
Murphy, G., 181
Murphy, G. L., 333, 336, 342, 344, 346
Murphy, J., 138
Murphy, K. R., 168, 168t
Murphy, S., 154
Murphy, S. T., 261
Murphy, T. D., 346
Murray, C., 524
Mynatt, C. R., 464

Naccache, L., 566, 569, 576
Nadel, L., 299, 306
Nader, K., 299, 306
Nakayama, K., 133, 134, 137, 564
Naqvi, N., 487
Narens, L., 565
Nasar, J., 181
Naselaris, T., 424, 425
Nash, R. A., 294
Naumann, U., 257
Nazarian, M., 216
Nee, D. E., *211*
Neisser, U., *15,* 151, 176, 187, 230, *230,* 296, 308, 309, 537, 550
Nelson, T. O., 565
Nersessian, N., 507
Nestojko, J. F., 319
Nettelbeck, T., 529
Neumann, C., 535
Neuschatz, J., 297, 301
Newcombe, F., 77
Newell, A., 17, 500, *503*
Newport, E. L., 396
Newstead, S., 274
Ngo, K. W. J., 172
Nichelli, P., 134
Nichols, R. M., 291
Nickerson, R. S., 216
Niebur, E., 170

Nijenhuis, J., 526
Nisbett, R. E., 172, 462, 463, 464, 466, 468, 469, *469,* 470, 476, 479, 493, 534, 535, 537, 539, 550, 553, 554
Nitsch, K., 244
Noll, J., 528
Noppeney, U., 348
Norbury, C. F., 395
Nørby, S., 303
Norenzayan, A., 172
Norman, D., 181, 198, 563
Norman, G., 360
Northup, T., 258
Noveck, I., 392
Noveck, J., 392
Novick, L. R., 500, 507, 517
Nowak, A., 428
Nusbaum, E. C., 520
Nyberg, L., *208,* 268, 282, 394

Oaksford, M., 468
Oberauer, K., 206
Obrecht, N., 460
Ochalek, K., 291
Ochsner, K. N., 305, 489
O'Connor, A. R., 315
O'Connor, D., 158
O'Connor, M., 27
O'Craven, K. M., 424
Oden, G. C., 140
Ohlsson, S., 513
O'Kane, G., 269
Okovita, H. W., 428
Old, J. M., 265, 576
Oldfield, R., 377
Oliphant, G. W., 255
Oliver, L. M., 479
Öllinger, M., 513
Olson, E. A., 297, *552*
Ones, D. S., 524
Oppenheimer, D. M., 117, 265, 406, 466, 576
Orban, G. G., 158
O'Regan, J. K., 155
Ormerod, T. C., 513
Ortiz, S., 526
Ortmann, A., 466
Ortony, A., 345
Ost, J., 281, 294, 312

Otgaar, H., 294
Overgaard, M., 567
Overton, D., 242
Owen, A. M., 169, 567
Owens, J., 284, *284*
Ownby, R. L., 25
Oyebode, F., 27
Özgen, E., 400, 402
Ozubko, J. D., 299

Pachur, T., 487
Paivio, A., 428, 442, 443, 444
Paletz, S. B., 505
Paller, K. A., 573
Palmer, J. C., 289, *289*
Palmer, S., 309
Pansky, A., 333
Papafragou, A., 402
Papesh, M. H., 350
Parker, E. S., 279
Parkhurst, D., 170
Parkin, A. J., 218
Parpal, M., 484
Parsons, L. M., 33
Pase, M. P., 57
Pashler, H., 169, 180, 302, 318, 518
Pasternak, T., 158
Pasupathi, M., 180
Patel, T. N., 518
Pateman, R., 485
Patihis, L., 281, 312
Patrick, J., 517
Patterson, K., 333
Pattie, A., 524
Paulson, O. B., 348
Pavletic, A., 297
Payment, K. E., 290
Payne, J., 306
Payne, L., 152
Payton, A., 534
Paz-Alonso, P., 310, 316
Peace, K. A., 310
Pearlmutter, N., 387
Pearson, D. G., 433
Pearson, J., 424, 425, 432, 434, 440
Pederson, E., 400
Pedrone, R., 507
Peele, J. E., 350
Peeler, M. V., 136
Peissig, J., 132
Pelham, S., 403

Subject Index

(Note: Italicized page numbers indicate figures; notes and tables are denoted with "n" and "t" next to the page numbers.)

prosopagnosia and, 133
  unilateral neglect syndrome and, 149
  visual imagery and, 426, 428–430
brain lesions, 38, 42, 43, 48, 77, *108*
brain stem, *33*
brightness constancy, 87, 90
Broca, Paul, 32
Broca's area, *393, 393*
Buddhist meditation, 187, 582
Bushmen of Africa, 370

calendar calculators, 531–532
Cambridge Face Memory Test, 134
candle problem, *510,* 510–511
Capgras syndrome, 25–31, 44, 48, 58, 78, 252
  explaining, 26–31
  learning from, 30–31
  neural basis for, 27–30
  symptoms of, 25
Carroll, Lewis, 379, *379*
Carson, Rachel, 521
catch trials, A-11
categorical perception, *373,* 373–375, *374*
categorical syllogisms, *477, 477*
categorization, 328–333
  basic-level, 332–333, *333,* 361
  event, 348
  exemplars and (*see* exemplars)
  goal-derived, 348
  importance of, 346, *347*
  privileged, 331, 332–333, 337
  prototypes and (*see* prototypes)
  relational, 348
  via resemblance, 328–329, 337–343, *341, 343*
  subordinate labeling, *333*
  typicality differences from, 337–343, *339*
category homogeneity, 461–462, 463
causation *vs.* correlation, A-8
cell body, 49, *50*
cell phone use
  driving and, 179–180, *180, 183–185,* A-8–9
  pedestrian danger and, *181*
center-surround cells, 72, *72*
central executive, 210–211, 212, 214
  See also executive control
central fissure (brain), *28, 34*
cerebellum, *28,* 33, *33*

cerebral cortex, 36, 44–48
  association areas, 44, 48
  defined, 34
  motor areas, 44–46, 348–350
  sensory areas, 44, 46–48, 348–350
cerebral hemisphere, 34
chance, role for, 468
change blindness, *155,* 155–156, *156,* 172
children
  bilingual, 403
  categorization by, 339–340
  false memories in, 291
  language acquisition and use in, 394–397, 407
  "wolf," *398,* 398–399
choice
  cost of too many, 486
  paradox of, 491
  reason-based, 485–486
chronometric studies, 415–422, 450
  defined, 415
  research methods, A-11–12
chunks, 206–207
cingulate cortex, *35*
classical conditioning, 266
clinical neuropsychology, 18, 37–38
closure, *84*
coarticulation, 372
Cochrane, Kent (K. C.;amnesia patient), *268*
cocktail party effect, *152*
coding, 54–55
  dual, 444, 450
  verbal, 440–442, *441*
  See also encoding; visual coding
cognition
  animal, 13n
  defined, 3
  embodied or grounded, 350
  food supplements and, 55–57
  meta-, 565, 569
cognitive capacity limits, 190
  in early and late selection, 156–158
  executive control and, 182
  extent of, 186–187
  priming and, 164
  review, 176–177
  spatial attention and, 165
cognitive interviews, 301–302
cognitive maps, 15, 16
cognitive neuroscience
  of consciousness, 566–572
  defined, 18
  See also brain

cognitive psychology
  applying, 19–20
  defined, 3, 7
  education and (*see* education)
  research in, 17–19
  scope of, 3–8
Cognitive Psychology (Neisser), *15*
Cognitive Reflection Test (CRT), *470,* 470–471
cognitive revolution, 8–17
  behaviorism and (*see* behaviorism)
  computers and, 16–17
  defined, 8
  European roots of, 16
  intellectual foundations of, 13–15
  introspection limits and, 8–10
  key ideas of, 8
cognitive unconscious, 549–557, 583
  conscious products of, 550–551
  defined, 549–550
  guides to conscious thinking in, 556–557, *557*
  limits of performance, 560–563
  mistaken introspection and, 554–556, *555*
  processes in, 550–551
  reasoning in, 551–553
collectivist cultures, 171
color blindness, 78, 78n, 428
color perception, 66, 78, 400, *401,* 402
column-row image, *439*
commissures, 36
complexity
  informational, 536
  of similarity, 341–343
  of speech perception, 370–375
composite effect, 138, *139*
computerized axial tomography (CT), 38, 42
computers
  cognitive revolution and, 16–17
  memory of, 197
  speech of, *374*
concepts, 324–363
  abstract, 350
  the brain and, 348–350, *349*
  definitions and, 327–328, *328*
  different profiles for, 347–348
  learning new, 358–360, *360*
  research methods, A-15–16
  as theories, 343–349
  understanding, 326–329
  See also categorization; knowledge networks; prototypes; resemblance; typicality

conceptual mental maps, *442*
concurrent articulation, 212, *213*
conditional statements, 478
cones, *65, 66, 66–68,* 76
confirmation and disconfirmation, 471–476
confirmation bias, 471–473, *474,* 492, 494, A-20, A-21, A-22
  defined, *464,* 472
  forms taken by, *473*
  logic *vs.,* 476
confounds, A-6–8
confusion
  recovery from, 121–122
  source, 258–259, *259*
conjunction errors, 80
connection weights, 357–358
connectionist networks, 354
connections
  creativity and, *520*
  excitatory, 128
  inhibitory, 127–129
  memory and, 221–224, *222,* 231, *233,* 282–284, *285*
consciousness, 546–585
  access, 573–574, *583*
  cognitive neuroscience of, 566–572
  content of, *567, 574*
  defined, *549*
  disruptions of, *557–560*
  executive control and, *560–565*
  "hard problem" of, *573*
  phenomenal (*see* phenomenal experience)
  research methods, A-25–27
  study of, 548–549
  two separate aspects of, *566, 566–568*
  the unconscious and (*see* cognitive unconscious)
  the unsaid in, *579–580*
  variations in, *567, 567–568*
consolidation, 306, 310
constancy, 87–92, 103
  brightness, 87, 90
  illusions and, 90–92, *91, 92*
  perceptual, 87
  shape, 87, *87,* 90, 91
  size, 87, *88,* 88–90, *89,* 92
  unconscious inference and, 88–90
context
  benefits of larger, 140–142
  extralinguistic, 388–390, *390*
  object recognition and, 110, *110,* 111, 140–142

word recognition and, 114, 115, 123, 125
context reinstatement, 244, 251, 302, A-22
context-dependent learning, *242,* 242–244, *243,* 275
contralateral control, 46
contrast effect, 92
control condition, A-4
control groups, *553,* A-3–5
convergent thinking, 520
converging operations, A-15–16
convolutions (brain), 34
cornea, *65, 65*
corpus callosum, 36
correlations, 42, A-8, A-23–25
cortex
  cerebral (*see* cerebral cortex)
  cingulate, *35*
  defined, 34
  occipital, 36, 38, 48, 75, 76–77
  orbitofrontal, *455, 457,* 487
  parietal, 75
  prefrontal, 29–30, 51, 182, 571
  temporal, 36, 75
  visual, *169*
count the F's exercise, *563*
counterbalance, A-7, A-8
covariation, 463–465, 494
  base-rate information and, 464–465
  defined, 463
  illusions of, 464
cover stories (in research), A-18–19
co-witness contamination, 309
creativity, 514–521, 542, A-22–23
  Big-C, 514
  brain lateralization and, 36
  case studies of, 514–515
  connections and, *520*
  illumination stage, 515–517
  incubation stage, 515, 517–518, *519*
  nature of, *519–521*
  preparation stage, 515
  verification stage, 515
criminal justice system. *See* legal system
cross-race face perception, 138
CRT (Cognitive Reflection Test), *470,* 470–471
cryptoplagiarism, 260
crystallized intelligence, 527–528, *528, 539,* 543
CT scans. *See* computerized axial tomography

culture
  attention and, 171–172
  memory and, 220
Curie, Marie, 514

D. B. (blindsight patient), 547
D. F. (agnosia patient), 107, *108, 109*
Darwin, Charles, 391, 413, 514, 519–520, *521*
data
  broad variety of types, A-16–18
  systematic collection of, A-19–20
deafness
  inattentional, 154
  language acquisition and, 394–395
  working memory and, 213–214
debriefing, A-19
decay theory of forgetting, 299, 300
decision making, 480–491
  amygdala and, 30
  cost of too many options in, *486*
  costs and benefits in, 480
  emotion and, 18–19, 30, 455–456, 487–490, *488, 495*
  framing in (*see* framing)
  opt-in *vs.* opt-out, 484–485
  utility maximization and, 480, 485–486
deduction, 471
deep processing, *219,* 219–220, *222, 223,* 223–224, 235
definitions, 327–328, *328*
delta rhythm, 40
demand character, 420–422, A-18–19
dendrites, 49–50, *50, 52*
dependent variables, A-4, A-22–23
depictions, 415, 418, 437
depth perception, 92–99, 103
  binocular cues, 93, *93, 96, 96,* 97, 98
  illusions and, 91
  monocular cues, 93–95, 99
  through motion, 95–98
  redundancy and, 98–99
descriptions, 415, 418, 437
descriptive rules, 380–381
desirable difficulty, 117
detectors
  bigram, 120, *120, 121,* 122, 123, 128
  feature, 122, 130
  inhibitory connections among, 127–129

eye movements, *170,* 170–171, 172
eyes
 cones, *65, 66,* 66–68, 76
 cornea, *65, 65*
 "educated," 99–101, *101*
 fovea, 47, 67–68
 lens, *65, 65*
 retina, *65, 65,* 67–68, 76
 rods, *65, 65*–66, *66,* 67, 76
 structure and functioning of, *65*
 See also visual system
eyewitnesses, 19, 99–100, 134,
  154, 258–259, 288, 551–552,
  A-13–14

face recognition, 133–140
 Capgras syndrome and, 26
 holistic, 137–140
 inversion effect and, 134–136,
  135
 special nature of, 133–137
factor analysis, *526,* A-24
false memories, 289–294, 304
 autobiographical, 312, 316
 encouraged through "evidence,"
  292, *292*–293, *293*
 false confessions and, 293–294
 misinformation effect and,
  291–292, 320
 planting, *289,* 289–291
familiarity
 Capgras syndrome and, 26, 30,
  31, 44, 252
 illusion of, *264, 265*
 nature of, *264,* 264–265
 source memory and, 251–254,
  253, 254, 256–257, 261,
  263, 265, 447
 treacherous, *273,* 273–274
 word recognition and, 113
family resemblance, 328–329, *329,*
  361
 See also resemblance
feature detectors, 122, 130
feature nets, 116–132, 140, 145
 ambiguous inputs and, 122–123
 decendants of, 127–132
 defined, 118
 design of, *118,* 118–119
 distributed knowledge and,
  125–126
 efficiency *vs.* accuracy in, 126–127
 McClelland and Rumelhart
  model, 127–129, *128*

recognition by components model,
  129–131, 132
 recognition errors and, 123–125
 recovery from confusion and,
  121–122
 well-formedness and, 119–120
 word recognition and, 116–127
features
 form perception and, *85,* 85–87, *86*
 object recognition and, 111–112,
  112
feedback
 belief perseverance and, 474–476
 eyewitness accounts and, 551–552
 memory errors and, 296–297,
  297, 551–552, *552*
FFA. *See* fusiform face area
field studies, A-14
figure/ground organization, 82
filters, 152
fixation target, 153–154
flashbulb memories, 308–310, *309,* 316
flashcards, 317–318
fluent aphasia, 394
fluid intelligence, 527–528, *528,*
  539, 543
Flynn effect, 534–535, *536,* 543
fMRI. *See* functional magnetic
  resonance imaging
fonts, 117
food supplements, 55–57
forebrain, 32, 34
forgetting, 297–302
 causes of, 298–301
 curve, *298*
 decay theory of, 299, 300
 incubation benefit from, *519*
 undoing, 301–302
form perception, 80–87
 Gestalt principles, *83,* 83–85,
  84, 103
 organization and features in, *85,*
  85–87, *86*
fornix, *35*
four-card task, *478,* 478–480, *479,* 495
fovea, 47, 67–68
FOXP2 gene, 397
framing, 480–484, 486, 490, 557
 defined, 482
 in monetary choices, *482*
 negative frame, *481*
 of outcomes, 480–483
 positive frame, *481*
 of questions and evidence,
  483–484, *484*

free morphemes, 367
free recall procedures, 200, *201*
frequency, 113, *113,* 119, 140
frequency estimates, 458
frontal lobes, 28, 29–30, 34, 38
functional fixedness, *510,* 510–511,
  511
functional imaging, 38
functional magnetic resonance
  imaging (fMRI)
 applications of, 29, 38–39
 Capgras syndrome and, 29–30
 combined with other techniques,
  42
 conceptual thinking tracked with,
  348
 consciousness tracked with, 566
 illustrated, *27, 43, 45*
 learning tracked with, 217–218
 memory tracked with, 204, 253
 visual imagery tracked with, 426,
  428, 432
"Funes the Memorious" (Borges),
  325
fusiform face area (FFA), 42, *43,*
  136, *137, 425*

g. See general intelligence
G. Y. (blindsight patient), 547–548
Gage, Phineas, 31–32, *32,* 182, 185
gamblers, 473–474
gambler's fallacy, 462, 494
gamma rhythm, 40
ganglion cells, *65,* 68
garden-path sentences, *384,*
  384–385, 386–387, 391, 407
 defined, 385
 extralinguistic context and,
  388–390
gender
 the brain and, 31
 IQ test scores and, 537, 540
 memory and, 220
general and fortress problem, *505,*
  506, 506
general intelligence *(g),* 525–526,
  527, *527,* 528–530, 543, A-24
generalizability, 315–316, A-13
generativity of language, 378, 397
genetics and intelligence, *533,*
  533–534, 535, 543
geon assemblies, 130–131
geons, *130,* 130–131, 137
Gestalt principles, *83,* 83–85, *84,* 103

Gestalt psychology, 16, 21, 80–81, 80n, 83–85
Gifford, Gabby, 365
Ginkgo biloba, 56, *56,* 57
glia, 31, 49, 52
goal neglect, *182,* 182–183
goal-derived categories, 348
good continuation, *84*
graded membership, 330–331, 374
grounded cognition, 350

H. M. (amnesia patient), 6–7, *7,* 18, 35, 195, 239, 268–269, *269*
happiness research, 490–491
Harrison, George, 260
"Hearing Lips and Seeing Voices" (McGurk & McDonald), 376
heuristics, 467, 502
  defined, 459
  problem-solving, 502–503
  See also availability heuristic; representativeness heuristic
highly superior autobiographical recall (HSAM), 279
hill-climbing strategy, 502, 504
hindbrain, 32–33
hippocampus, 34–35, *35,* 36, 38, *271,* 271–272, 306
Hobbits and Orcs problem, *501,* 501–502
holistic perception, 137–140
home sign, 395
HSAM (highly superior autobiographical recall), 279
hyperthymesia, 279
hypnosis, 301, *301*
hypothalamus, 34, *35*
hypotheses, testable, 14, 18, A-2–3, A-22–23

iconic memory, 198, *199*
identical twins. *See* monozygotic twins
ill-defined problems, 509–510
illumination (creativity stage), 515–517
illusion of familiarity, *264,* 265
illusion of truth, 257–258
illusions, 70, 90–92, *91, 92, 562*
  of covariation, 464
  Müller-Lyer, *157, 562*
  Poggendorff, *562*
  Ponzo, *562*
  3-D, *96,* 96–97, *97*

image files, 440
image-scanning procedure, *416,* 416–417, *417*
implicit memory, 254–267, 275, 577–578, 583, A-22, A-26
  attributing to wrong source, 258–259, *259*
  cryptoplagiarism and, 260
  defined, 255–256
  explicit memory and, 270–272, A-12–13
  false fame effect and, 256–257
  illusion of truth and, 257–258
  as memory without awareness, 255–256, 261, 558
  subcategories of, 266, *266*
  theoretical treatments of, 261–265
inattentional blindness, *153,* 153–154, *154,* 158, 171, 181, 190
inattentional deafness, 154
inattentional numbness, 154
incidental learning, 218–221
incubation (creativity stage), 515, 517–518, *519*
independent variables, A-4, A-5, A-22
indirect memory testing, 256, 272
individualistic cultures, 171
induction, 471, *472,* 494
inference to best explanation, 14
inferences
  based on theories, 346–347
  speed-reading and, 143–144
  unconscious, 88–90, 553, *562,* 562–563
informational complexity, 536
information-processing view of memory, *199*
inhibitory connections, 127–129
inner ear, 211, *211,* 212, 213
inner hand, 214
inner voice, 211, *211,* 213, 214
inputs
  ambiguous, 122–123
  attended, 158
  unattended, 152, 157, 159, 160, 190
insight problems, 515–516, *516*
inspection time, 529
integrative agnosia, 112

intelligence, 499, 522–541, 542–543
  bodily-kinesthetic, 531, 532
  building blocks of, 528–530
  crystallized, 527–528, *528, 539,* 543
  defining, 522
  emotional, 531, 532
  environmental factors in, 533, *534,* 534–535, 543
  fluid, 527–528, *528, 539,* 543
  general, 525–526, 527, *527,* 528–530, 543, A-24
  genetic factors in, *533,* 533–534, 535, 543
  hierarchical model of, 526–527
  interpersonal, 531
  intrapersonal, 531
  across the lifespan, 528, *528*
  linguistic, 531
  logical-mathematical, 531
  multiple, 531–532
  musical, 531, 532
  naturalistic, 531
  practical, 530
  rationality measures, 530
  research methods, A-22–25
  roots of, 533–539
  spatial, 531
  specialized, 525–526
  talent distinguished from, 532, *532*
  technology impact on, 536
  testing (*see* IQ tests)
intentional learning, 218–221
interference theory, 299–301, *300*
interpersonal intelligence, 531
interpolated activity, 203, *203*
interposition, 94, *94*
inter-rater reliability, A-23
intrapersonal intelligence, 531
introspection, 13, 14, 549
  behaviorism on, 11
  defined, 9
  limits of, 8–10
  mistaken, 554–556, *555*
  research methods, A-25–27
  about visual images, 413–415
intrusion errors, 283–284
intuition, triggers for skilled, 468
Inuit people, *399*
invalid experiments, A-7
invalid syllogisms, 477
inversion effect, 134–136, *135*
inverted spectrum problem, *575*
"invisible gorilla" video, 151, *151*

IQ tests, 522–526, 542–543,
A-23–25
highway deaths related to score,
525t
improving capacities measured by,
539–541
intelligence beyond, 530–532
items on, 523
race and performance on,
537–539, 538, 543
reliability of (see reliability)
rising scores in, 536
validity of (see validity)

"Jabberwocky" (Carroll), 379, 379
judgment, 456–471
attribute substitution and,
457–458, 459t, 465, 494
covariation and, 463–465
dual-process models and,
466–471, 467, 494
heuristics in (see heuristics)
research methods, A-19–22
Julius Caesar, 178

K. C. (amnesia patient), 268
Kamala (wild child), 398–399
Kant, Immanuel, 13–14, 14
Kanzi (bonobo), 397–398
Khoisan, 370
King, Martin Luther, Jr., 541
knowledge, 323–452
cognitive psychology as the study
of, 3, 7
distributed, 125–126
diversity of, 447–448
See also background knowledge;
concepts; language;
schemata; visual knowledge
knowledge networks, 350–358, 361
connection weights and, 357–358
distributed processing and, 354–357
knowledge retrieval in, 350–352,
351, 353
propositional, 353–354, 355
Korsakoff's syndrome, 239–240,
269–271, 272, 448, 557–558

L. H. (brain-damaged patient),
428–430
L. M. (akinetopsia patient), 63–64
labiodental sounds, 369

language, 364–409
animal, 397, 397–398
bilingualism, 403, 408
biological roots of, 392–399
generativity of, 378, 397
linguistic relativity hypothesis,
400–402
organization of, 366–368, 367
phonology (see phonology)
pragmatics and, 391–392
process of learning, 395–397
research methods, A-16–18
sentence parsing (see sentence
parsing)
syntax (see syntax)
thought and, 399, 399–403, 401,
407
writing, 404–406
late selection hypothesis, 157,
157–158
lateral fissure (brain), 28, 34
lateral geniculate nucleus (LGN), 68,
74, 76, 129, 158
lateral inhibition, 68–70, 69, 92
lateralization (brain), 36
leading questions, 289, 289
learning
brain activity during, 217, 217–218
connection weight settings and,
357–358
context-dependent, 242, 242–244,
243, 275
incidental, 218–221
intentional, 218–221
language, 395–397
massed, 233
memory retrieval and, 241–244
optimal, 272–273
perceptual, 266
spaced, 233
study techniques, 232–233
synapses in, 54
left-branching sentences, 404
legal system, 19–20
"educated eyes," 99–101, 101
eyewitnesses (see eyewitnesses)
photo lineups, 258–259
lens, 65, 65
lesions. See brain lesions
letter combinations, 119–120
letter detectors, 122, 123, 129
level of processing, 219–221
lexical-decision task, 248–250, 250,
255, 256, 262, 275, A-11–12,
A-22

LGN. See lateral geniculate nucleus
light and vision, 64–65, 65, 66, 67, 68
limbic system, 34, 35
limited-capacity system, 164
See also cognitive capacity limits
linear perspective, 95, 98
linguistic intelligence, 531
linguistic relativity, 400–402
lip-reading, 376
listening, dichotic, 150–152
local representations, 126, 354
localization of function (brain), 44
logic, 476, 476–480
four-card task, 478, 478–480,
479, 495
syllogisms in, 476–478
logical-mathematical intelligence, 531
longitudinal fissure (brain), 34
long-term memory (LTM), 198
brain regions supporting, 205
defined, 199
encoding and, 216–218
improving retention, 317–318
need for engagement and,
214–221
visual (see long-term visual
memory)
working memory compared with,
200–204, 205, 205, 235
long-term visual memory, 439–448
image information in, 439–440
imagery helpful in, 442–447
for pictures, 444–447, 446
verbal coding of materials in,
440–442, 441
LTM. See long-term memory

M cells, 76, 76n
Mach bands, 70, 70
magnetic resonance imaging (MRI),
27, 27, 38, 40, 42
magnocellular cells, 76
maintenance rehearsal, 215–216,
218, 231, 235
mamillary body, 35
"man who" argument, 462, 463,
466, 494
manner of production, 368, 370
mapping, 506
mask, 113
massed learning, 233
maxims, 392
McClelland and Rumelhart model,
127–129, 128

Müller-Lyer illusion, *157, 562*
multiple intelligences, 531–532
multitasking. *See* divided attention
musical intelligence, 531, 532
myelin sheath, *50, 52*

N, A-5–6
name-matching task, 313, *313*
natural kinds, 347–348
naturalistic intelligence, *531*
Necker cube, 81, *81,* 83, 436, *436*
negative frame, *481*
neglect syndrome. *See* unilateral
    neglect syndrome
networks
    connectionist, 354
    knowledge (*see* knowledge
        networks)
    memory, 246–250
    propositional, 353–354, *355*
neural correlates of consciousness, 566
neural synchrony, 79–80
neuroimaging techniques, 19, 566
    Capgras syndrome and, 26–30
    combining, 42–43
    data from, 38–39
    See also specific techniques
neuronal workspace, 568–573, 579,
    583
    defined, 568
    executive control and, 571–573
    function of, *569–571*
neurons, 39–40, 246–247
    coding and (*see* coding)
    defined, 39
    from different areas, *49*
    feature nets compared with, 119,
        129
    firing of, 52–54, 71, 247
    object recognition and, 131–132
    regions of, 49–50, *50*
    single-cell recording and, 71, 103
neuropsychology. *See* clinical
    neuropsychology
neurotransmitters, 39, 52, *53, 54*
N400 brain wave, *388, 389,* 560
nine-dot problem, *512,* 512–514
nodes
    activation of, 246–248, *248,* 249,
        250, 261, 283, 350–352, 354,
        357
    defined, 246
    knowledge networks and,
        350–352, 353–354, 357

nonfluent aphasia, 393–394
nonredundancy principle, 352

object models, 131
object recognition, 106–147, 247,
    562–563
    bottom-up influences on, 111,
        118
    early considerations, 110–112
    features and, 111–112, *112*
    research methods, A-6–8
    top-down influences on, 111,
        140–142, *142*
    viewpoint-dependent, 131–132,
        132
    viewpoint-independent, 131, 132,
        133
    See also face recognition; feature
        nets; word recognition
object-based attention, 173–176,
    175, 177
occipital cortex, 36, 38, 48, 75,
    76–77
occipital face area (OFA), *137*
occipital lobes, *28,* 34, 46, 47, 68,
    76–77
ocular dominance, 97
O'Keeffe, Georgia, 521
operation span, 207–210, *209,*
    212
optic flow, 95–98
optic nerve, *65,* 68
opt-in *vs.* opt-out decisions,
    484–485
orbitofrontal cortex, 455, *457,*
    487
organization
    form perception and, *85,* 85–87,
        86
    of language, 366–368, *367*
    memory and, 224–230
orientation-specific visual fields, *73*
orienting system, 167–168
orthography, 377
outcomes, framing of, 480–483
outgroup homogeneity effect,
    356
overregularization errors, 396

P cells, 76, 76n
paradox of choice, 491
parahippocampal place area (PPA),
    43, 425

parallel distributed processing
    (PDP), 357
parallel processing, 74–78, *75, 77,*
    86, 103
parietal cortex, 75
parietal lobes, *28,* 34, 46, 47, 48,
    149
parsing. *See* sentence parsing
parvocellular cells, 76
passive-voice sentences, 386, 388,
    404
peer editing, *404,* 405
peer-review process, A-21–22
peg-word systems, 226, 233
perception
    blind sight and, *558–559*
    cognitive capacity limits and,
        176–177
    depth (*see* depth perception)
    form (*see* form perception)
    holistic, 137–140
    speech (*see* speech perception)
    subliminal, *559–560*
    unconscious, *157*
    visual (*see* visual perception)
Perception and Communication
    (Broadbent), 17
percepts, 437
perceptual constancy, 87
perceptual learning, *266*
perfect correlation, A-24
perfect inverse correlation, A-24
perseveration error, 182
PET scans. *See* positron emission
    tomography
PFC. *See* prefrontal cortex
P-fit model, *529*
phenomenal experience, 572–578,
    583
    as justification for action,
        576–578
    processing fluency and,
        574–576
    qualia and, 573–574, 576, 578,
        579, 579
phobias and visual imagery, 434
phonemes, 407
    combining, 375–377
    defined, 367
    in linguistic hierarchy, 367, *367*
    number of in English, 370
phonemic restoration effect,
    372–373
phonological buffer, 211
phonological representation, 377

phonology, 368–377
  phoneme combining, 375–377
  speech perception (*see* speech perception)
  speech production, 368–370, *369*
photo lineups, 258–259, *259*
photoreceptors, 64–68
phrases, 367, *367*, 378
phrase-structure rules, 380–382, 407
  ambiguous, *383*
  defined, 380
  descriptive, 380–381
  function of, 381–382
  organization aids, *382*
  prescriptive, 380–381, *381*
  tree structure illustrating, 380, *380*
physical attributes, 152
Picasso, Pablo, 514, 520, 521
pictorial cues, 94, 96, 97
pictures
  the brain while looking at, *45*
  memory for, 444–447, *446*
  problem solving and, 503–504
  See also mental pictures
place of articulation, 369, 370
placebo effect, 553
plagiarism, 260
Poggendorff illusion, *562*
pons, *33*
Ponzo illusion, *562*
population, A-6
positive frame, *481*
positron emission tomography (PET), 27, 38, *39*, 42, 566
postsynaptic membrane, 52
poverty and intelligence, 534, 535
power calculation, A-6
PPA. *See* parahippocampal place area
practical intelligence, 530
practice, 183–186, 187, A-7
  automaticity and, 185–186, 190
  resource demand and, 185
pragmatics, 391–392
predictive validity, 524, 525, A-23, A-24
predictor variables. *See* independent variables
prefrontal cortex (PFC), 29–30, 51, 182, 571
premises, 477
preparation (creativity stage), 515
prescriptive rules, 380–381, *381*

presynaptic membrane, 52
primacy effect, *201*, 214
  defined, 200
  explaining, 202
  memory for pictures and, 447
  testing claims about, 202–204
primary motor projection areas, 46, 47
primary projection areas, 46, 47
primary sensory projection areas, 46
priming, 114, 120, 122, 123, 124, 125, 126, 129, 140, 141
  attention and, 176–177, 184, 190
  biological mechanisms for, *163*
  cryptoplagiarism and, 260
  as implicit memory subcategory, 266, *266*
  repetition, *113*, 114, 119, 145, 160, 161t, 249, 255
  selection via, 158–164, 161t, *162*
  semantic, 248–250, *250*
  spatial attention and, 169
  two types of, 160–163, *163*
problem solving, 500–521
  analogies and, 504–507, *505, 506*, 542
  creativity and (*see* creativity)
  defined, 500
  defining the problem in, 509–514, 542
  experience and, 504–509
  expert, 507, *508*, 542
  general methods for, 500–504
  heuristics for, 502–503
  pictures and diagrams in, 503–504
  research methods, A-22–25
  as search, 500–502
  subgoals in, 507–509, 510
  unconscious guides to, 556–557
problem space, *501*, 501–502
problem-solving set, 512–514, 542, 556–557
procedural memory, 266
processing fluency, 261–264, *263*, 574–576
processing pathway, 261–262
production task, 331
proper *N*, A-5–6
propositional networks, 353–354, *355*
prosody, 390–391, 397, 405
prosopagnosia, 133, 136

prototypes, 329–333, 334, 339, 352, 358, 359, 361
  defined, 329
  exemplars and, 335–337, *336*
  explanatory theories and, 344, 345
  graded membership and, 330–331
  resemblance and, 341, 342
  stereotypes distinguished from, 356
  testing the notion of, 331–332
proximity, 84, *84*
"Purpose of Education, The" (King), 541

qualia, 573–574, 576, 578, 579, *579*
questions
  framing of, 483–484, *484*
  leading, 289, *289*

r, A-24
  See also correlations
r^2, A-24, A-25
race
  face recognition and, 138
  IQ scores and, 537–539, *538*, 543
Ramu (wild child), *398*
random assignment, A-8–9
random chance, 468
random sampling, A-6
rating tasks, 331–332
rationality measures, 530
Raven's Progressive Matrices Test, *522, 523*, 535
RBC model. *See* recognition by components model
reading span, 208–209
reason-based choice, 485–486
reasoning, 471–491
  confirmation and disconfirmation in, 471–476
  decision making and (*see* decision making)
  logic in (*see* logic)
  research methods, A-19–22
  about syllogisms, 476–478
  unconscious, 551–553
recall, 251
recency, 114, 119, 140
recency effect, *201*, A-10
  defined, 200–201
  explaining, 201
  interpolated activity and, 203, *203*
  memory for pictures and, 447
  testing claims about, 202–204

receptive fields, 71–74, *72, 73*
recognition, 251
    See also face recognition;
        object recognition; word
        recognition
recognition by components (RBC)
    model, 129–131, 132
recognition errors, 123–125, *124*
"recovered" memories, 311–312
reduction of uncertainty, A-24–25
redundancy, 98–99
regret, *490*
rehearsal, memory. *See* memory
    rehearsal
relational categories, 348
relational (elaborative) rehearsal,
    215–216, 235
reliability, 522–525
    defined, 522, A-23
    inter-rater, A-23
    test-retest, 524, A-23
Remembering (Bartlett), 16
remember/know distinction, 252–253
reminiscence bump, 315, *315*
Remote Associates Test, 520
repetition priming, *113,* 114, 119,
    145, 160, 161t, 249, *255*
replication, A-9–11
representative samples, A-6
representativeness heuristic, 459,
    461–463, 465, 466, 494
    defined, 458
    reasoning from one case to a
        population, 462–463
repression, 311–312
research methods, A-1–28
    chronometric studies, A-11–12
    community of scientists, A-20–22
    confounds, A-6–8
    control groups, A-3–5
    converging operations, A-15–16
    correlations, A-23–25
    data collection, systematic, A-19–20
    data types, broad variety of, A-16–18
    dependent variable, defining,
        A-22–23
    double dissociation, A-12–13
    expectations and demand,
        A-18–19
    external validity, A-13–14
    hypotheses, testable, A-2–3
    introspection, A-25–27
    proper *N,* A-5–6
    random assignment, A-8–9
    replication, A-9–11

resemblance, 328–329, *329, 359,*
    361
    complexity of similarity in,
        341–343
    difficulties of categorizing via,
        337–343, *341, 343*
    representativeness heuristic and,
        458, 459, 465
resources
    competition, 184
    demand, 185, 187
    generality of, 179–181, 187
    specificity of, 178–179, *179,* 187
response threshold, 118, 246
response time (RT), 18, 160–162,
    165, A-11–12, A-22
retention interval, *298,* 298–299,
    300, 313, 314, 315
reticular activating system, 567
retina, *65, 65,* 67–68, 76
retrieval failure, 299, 302, 312
retrieval paths, 224, 241, 251, 275,
    283, 288, 303
retrograde amnesia, *267, 267*
reversible (ambiguous) figures,
    81–82, *82, 83*
right-branching sentences, 404
risk aversion, 483
risk seeking, 483
Ritalin, 188–189
rods, *65,* 65–66, *66,* 67, 76
RT. *See* response time

salt-passing behavior, 12–13, *13*
same-race face perception, 138
sample (*vs.* population), A-6
sample size, *469,* 470
savant syndrome, 531–532
    See also autistic savants
schemata, 16, *16,* 303
    defined, 286
    evidence for, 286–288
    long-term visual memory and,
        445, 446–447
    self-, 304–305
schizophrenia, 30
scientists, community of, A-20–22
selection task. *See* four-card task
selective attention, 150–164, 183,
    187
    change blindness in, *155,*
        155–156, *156*
    costs and benefits of, 163–164
    defined, 150

    dichotic listening and, 150–152
    inattentional blindness in, *153,*
        153–154, *154,* 158
    inhibiting distractors in,
        152–153
    via priming, 158–164, 161t, *162*
self-reference effect, 304, *305,* 320
self-report data, 413–414, A-16–18
self-schema, 304–305
self-selected group, A-8
semantic bootstrapping, 397
semantic memory, 266, *266,*
    267–268, *268*
semantic priming, 248–250, *250*
semantic processing, *388*
semantic representation, 377
sensory areas (cerebral cortex), 44,
    46–48, 348–350
sensory homunculus, *48*
sensory memory, 198–199
sentence parsing, 382–391, 407
    background knowledge as a guide
        to, 386–388
    brain activity and, *388, 389*
    defined, 383
    extralinguistic context and,
        388–390, *390*
    prosody and, 390–391
    syntax as a guide to, 385–386
sentence verification task, 331, 351,
    353
sentences, 378–379
    active-voice, 386, 388, 400, 404
    defined, 367
    garden-path (*see* garden-path
        sentences)
    interpreting complex, *387*
    left-branching, 404
    in linguistic hierarchy, 367, *367*
    number of possible, 378
    passive-voice, 386, 388, 404
    right-branching, 404
serial processing, 76
serial-position effect, 201, *204,* A-10
"7 plus-or-minus 2" items, 206
sexual assault and alcohol use, 51
shadowing, 151, 152, 178, 179
shallow processing, *219,* 219–220,
    235
shape constancy, 87, *87,* 90, 91
Shereshevsky, Solomon, 325, 326
short-term memory, 198, 214
    See also working memory
sign language, 213–214, 394–395,
    395

similarity
  complexity of, 341–343
  Gestalt principle, 84, *84*
simplicity, *84*
single-cell recording, 71, 103, *132*
size constancy, 87, *88,* 88–90, *89,* 92
skin conductance response (SCR),
    271, *271*
sleep, 306, 572
somatic markers, 487, 553
somatosensory area, 46, 47, *47*
sound-alike errors, 212
source confusion, 258–259, *259*
source memory
  defined, 251
  familiarity and, 251–254, *253,*
    254, 256–257, 261, 263,
    265, 447
space alien abduction "memories,"
    294, 295
spaced learning, 233
spatial attention, 164–176, *165*
  defined, 165
  object-based attention compared
      with, 173–176, *175,* 177
  spotlight beam metaphor, *166,*
      166–173, 190
spatial imagery, 426–430, *429,* 432,
    433, 438, 450
spatial intelligence, 531
spatial position, 79, 441–442
specialized intelligence, 525–526
specific-language impairment (SLI),
    395
speech
  actual pattern of, *370*
  production of, 368–370, *369*
speech perception, 407
  aids to, 372–373
  categorical, *373,* 373–375, *374*
  complexity of, 370–375
speech segmentation, *370, 371,*
    371–372
speed-reading, 142–144, *143*
spinal cord, *33*
split-brain patients, 36, *37*
spreading activation, 246–247, *250*
  creativity and, 518
  defined, 247
  knowledge networks and,
      350–352, 354, 357
stereoscope, *96, 96*
stereotype threat, 537, 538, 540,
    543
stereotypes, 356, 464

stimuli
  behaviorism on, 11, 12, 13
  face recognition and, 134
  form perception and, 83
  implicit memory and, 261, 262,
      263, 264–265
  object recognition and, 110–111,
      111
  priming and, 160–163, *162,* 176–177
  selective attention and, 153, 158–163
  spatial attention and, 165, 166, 169
  word recognition and, 113, 115,
      127
stress and memory, 310–311
Stroop interference, 185–186, *186*
structural imaging, 38
study techniques, 232–233
subcortical structures (brain), 34–35, *35*
subgoals, 507–509, 510
subliminal perception, 559–560
subthreshold activation, 246, 248, *250*
subvocalization, 211, 212
suicide-note task, 474
summation, 246
superior temporal sulcus, *137*
syllogisms, 476–478
synapses, 52–54, *53*
synaptic gap, 52
synaptic vesicles, *53*
syntactic processing, *388*
syntax, 378–382, 407
  animal language corresponding to,
      397, 398
  defined, 379
  as a guide to parsing, 385–386
  in "Jabberwocky," 379, *379*
  phrase-structure rules (*see*
      phrase-structure rules)
  in Yoda's dialect, *380*
systematic data collection, A-19–20

tachistoscope, 113, 114, 145
technology and intelligence, 536
temporal cortex, 36, 75
temporal lobes, 28, *28,* 34, 36, 46, 77
testing effect, 302, 318
test-retest reliability, *524,* A-23
texture gradients, *95, 95,* 98
thalamus, 34, *35*
theories
  concepts as, 343–349
  explanatory, 344–346, *345*
  inferences based on, 346–347
thinking, 453–585

convergent, *520*
divergent, *520–521, 521*
language and, *399,* 399–403, *401,*
    407
Type 1, 466–468, 494, 581
Type 2, 466–468, 471, 494
See also cognitive unconscious;
    consciousness; intelligence;
    judgment; problem solving;
    reasoning
thinking outside the box, *512,*
    512–514, *513*
third-variable problem, A-8
3-D illusion, *96,* 96–97, *97*
threshold (postsynaptic cell), 52
Titchener, Edward Bradford, 8–9
TMS. *See* transcranial magnetic
    stimulation
top-down processing
  in object recognition, 111,
      140–142, *142*
  in speech perception, 372, 373
TOT phenomenon, 299
transcendental method, 13–14
transcranial magnetic stimulation
    (TMS), 42–43, 112, 426
"transplant" errors, 283
traumatic memories, 310–311, 316
tree structure, 380, *380*
tumor problem, *505,* 505–506, *506*
twin studies (of intelligence), 533,
    533, 534, 543
two-alternative, forced-choice
    procedure, 114, *115*
two-string problem, *511*
Type 1 thinking, 466–468, *467,* 494,
    581
Type 2 thinking, 466–468, *467,* 471,
    494
typicality, *329,* 329–333, 361
  attractiveness and, *334*
  categorization differences from,
      337–343, *339*
  defined, 337
  ratings, 332t, 338t

ultra-rare item effect, 171, *171*
unattended channel, 150, 151, 152
unattended input, 152, 157, 159,
    160, 190
uncertainty, reduction of, A-24–25
unconscious inference, 88–90, 553,
    562, 562–563
unconscious perception, *157*